Preface

AutoCAD is the world's leading design CAD software and has recently become the CAD program choice in our colleges and universities. It is important for technologists and engineers to acquire facility with AutoCAD and to be able to create CAD drawings easily and quickly.

AutoCAD with Lab Applications is designed to introduce technology and engineering students to AutoCAD software. With step-by-step explanations of all the commands, thorough examples, and practical exercises, the book leads the student from a beginner's level to more-advanced 3D applications.

AutoCAD with Lab Applications features an assortment of design formats and is therefore useful for mainstream technology programs, specific engineering programs, and part-time upgrade courses. The book is designed to be used as a course outline, with exercises to be completed at the end of each chapter, and final tests and projects at the end of each unit. While there are some manuals available that explain the system of AutoCAD commands, the instructor will normally prepare exercises for the class to complete. This can be time consuming and demanding, as each exercise should be tested and its level of difficulty assessed before being assigned to the class. *AutoCAD with Lab Applications* helps the instructor by providing practical, class-tested examples.

Instructors using *AutoCAD with Lab Applications* will find exercises covering a wide range of technological and engineering disciplines — architectural, civil, mechanical, and electrical. These exercises are the result of the author's extensive experience in developing CAD courses. For students who have had some exposure to other CAD programs, there are special exercises called Challengers. The Challenger exercises can help maintain the interest of students who are slightly more advanced or who need a greater challenge.

The book is organized into three units. The first 12 chapters are introductory in level. The next 12 chapters focus on customizing and interfacing. The last 12 cover 3D applications. The chapters within a unit build upon each other, allowing for a consistent learning curve. Each chapter opens with a list of chapter objectives and at the end of each chapter there are projects that test the mastery of these objectives. The general objectives of the three units are outlined below:

OBJECTIVES OF UNIT 1
INTRODUCTION

Upon completion of the first 12 chapters, the student should be able to produce the following introductory-level drawings in AutoCAD.

1. Lines, arcs, circles, plines, ellipses, points, solid figures
2. Layers that illustrate seven or more colours and differing line fonts
3. Text in different fonts and qualities
4. Blocks of data; symbols, titles etc.
5. Dimensioning and related notation
6. Hatching
7. Scaled drawings

The student should also be able to explain the procedures for downloading this information onto output peripherals for 2D plotting.

OBJECTIVES FOR UNIT 2
CUSTOMIZING AND INTERFACING

Upon completion of the second 12 chapters, the student should be able to create and modify non-graphic data in drawings and customize the user interface for practical applications. The student will be able to produce:

1. Attributes and download them to Lotus or a text editor
2. Slides and script files
3. DXFIN and DXFOUT plus parametric programming
4. Graphics and text transfers
5. Macros and user defined tablets
6. XREFerences and external data interfaces
7. Area and volume calculations
8. Variable changes in the data base

The student should be able to customize and manage an AutoCAD system, plus prepare files for use in other software programs.

OBJECTIVES FOR UNIT 3
3D DIMENSIONS

Upon completion of the final set of chapters, the student should be able to produce three-dimensional models and drawings in AutoCAD. The student will be able to produce:

1. Models on any plane
2. Models with 3DFACES
3. Models with Surfaces
4. Dimensioning and related notation for 3D objects
5. Three-dimension model merging
6. Viewing of the model in perspective
7. Models created with AME

The student will also be able to edit any portion of the model and to surface many existing geometry.

This book covers the three most recent releases of AutoCAD. Releases 10 and 11 are presented in the main text and new features introduced by release 12 are highlighted in the margins for quick reference. This format was chosen for many reasons. Instructors may be teaching AutoCAD in two differently equipped labs. Where the versions of AutoCAD differ, this format allows the instructor the ability to quickly reference the information relevant to the current teaching environment. As well, for instructors and students using the Student Edition of AutoCAD, it allows for quick recognition of the possible differences between the commands available in the Student Edition and the version of AutoCAD installed in the lab.

INSTRUCTOR'S RESOURCE PACKAGE

For instructors adopting *AutoCAD with Lab Applications*, the publisher will provide, free of charge, the Instructor's Resource Package. The package contains the Instructor's Manual and disks containing AutoCAD files for the discipline-specific exercises at the end of the chapters. The Instructor's Manual provides the answers to the final tests at the end of each unit. The disks aid the instructor in marking the student's work on the exercises. The Instructor's Resource Package can be requested from your local Addison-Wesley sales representative upon adoption of the book.

AUTOCAD®
WITH LAB APPLICATIONS

RELEASES 10, 11, AND 12

S. R. Kyles

Addison-Wesley Pubishers
Don Mills, Ontario • Reading, Massachusetts
Menlo Park, California • New York • Wokingham, England
Amsterdam • Bonn • Sydney • Tokyo • Madrid • San Juan

PUBLISHER: Ron Doleman
COORDINATING EDITOR: Katherine Goodes
COPY EDITOR: David McCorquodale
DESIGNER: Anthony Leung
PRINTER: Bryant Press Ltd.

Canadian Cataloguing in Publication Data

Kyles, S.R. (Shannon R.)
AutoCAD with Lab Applications: release 10, 11, and 12

Includes index.
ISBN 0-201-60247-4

1. AutoCAD (Computer file). 2. Engineering design - Computer programs. 3. Computer graphics. I. Title.

T385.K95 1993   620'.0042'02855369   C93-093159-9

ISBN 0-201-60247-4

Printed and bound in Canada.

A B C D E F - BRY - 97 96 95 94 93

TRADEMARKS

Acknowledgments

The exercises in this book went through many years of student testing at Mohawk College. I would like to thank all my students for working with my notes as they went through the transition between notes and the stage you currently see. I would like to thank Dave Goede of Goede and Associates for his continuing assistance with details of the AutoCAD applications, Dave Bradford of Autodesk Inc. for his support and help in obtaining information, Peter Mann of Mohawk College for his encouragement and inspiration, Peter Rudyk of DOFASCO for his expertise in providing technical support in the mechanical area, and Graham Roebuck and Susan Hardy for their help in layout and initial conception. In an effort to provide interesting examples at current industry standards, several illustrations have been generously supplied by Sylvia Smith of UMA Engineering Limited in Edmonton, Alberta, Jim Ellis at Micro-Rel in Arizona, Dave Umbach at Tarsons, Brenckerhoff, Gore and Storrie Incorporated, Lloyd Muth at Mohawk College in Hamilton, Ontario, and Andy Slupeki from Dundas, Ontario. My publisher put the manuscript through several intensive rounds of reviewing. To each of these reviewers, I express my deepest thanks:

Wally Baumback	Southern Alberta Institute of Technology
Richard T. Burton	University of Saskatchewan
Bill Hill	Computer OnSight Services
Jag Mohan	Sheridan College
Paul Morrison	British Columbia Institute of Technology
Evelyn W. Richards	University of New Brunswick
Ron Sandalack	Northern Alberta Institute of Technology
Edward R. Syme	Georgian College
Roger Winn	University College of Cape Breton

In addition, I would like to offer my thanks to Katherine Goodes, coordinating editor and Ventura guru, for all of her assistance during the production phase. Last, but not least, I'd like to thank Nick Nowitski, formerly of Loyalist College, for his assistance in proofing the final draft.

It is the responsibility of the author and publisher to correct any problems that users might find within the book. We encourage you to send all of your concerns to the publisher at the following address:

Ron Doleman
Addison-Wesley Publishers Limited
26 Prince Andrew Place
Don Mills, Ontario M4C 2T8

S.R. Kyles
January 4, 1993

To the Student

AutoCAD with Lab Applications is designed to teach you the AutoCAD software programme in a simple, easy-to-follow manner. To become more comfortable with this textbook, please take a minute or two to familiarize yourself with the conventions and terminology used.

AutoCAD commands may either be typed on the keyboard or selected from the screen, pull-down or template menus. In this book, they will be presented as if they were typed on the keyboard (unless otherwise specified). The responses that you must type on the keyboard are shown in bold text.

Command: **TRACE** ↵

Once your response has been typed, you must either press the space bar or the return (enter) key to have the computer accept the response. Pressing the return or enter key is indicated by the return symbol (↵).

The responses controlled by other input such as picking or selecting are in italic.

Command: **TRACE** ↵

From point: *(pick 3)*

To point: *(pick 5)*

Purchasing a System

If you are considering the purchase of an AutoCAD system, there are some points regarding AutoCAD and hardware that you should be aware of. Any authorized AutoCAD dealer will be able to give you advice on which hardware configuration best suits your purposes, but some basics requirements are the processor, RAM, hard drive, floppy disk drives, graphics card, and the mouse or digitizing tablet.

The Processor

All your calculations take place in the CPU or Central Processing Unit and one of the most important features of the CPU is the processor. The newest processor on the market is the 80586 or simply the 586. It is considered to be better and faster than the 486, which is considered to be better and faster than the 386. In processors, the higher number indicates more calculating speed and a more recent release. For Releases 10, 11 and 12, a 386 is adequate as long as there is a math co-processor also installed. The math co-processor is not needed on the 486 or 586.

The processor number is often quoted with a clock speed that indicates its speed. The clock speed on each of the above mentioned chips ranges from 25 megahertz to 50 megahertz or higher. The higher number indicates more speed. Before purchasing a computer, check with the instructor about new hardware, whether there have been problems with any new releases, or whether the system has been well tested. It's not necessary to purchase the latest equipment, often a well-tested hardware configuration is preferrable.

RAM

The RAM or Random Access Memory, often called internal memory, is the area of memory where the AutoCAD software is run. If you are planning to create 3D models with surfacing or do intricate interfacing, you will need a minimum of 8 megabytes of RAM.

Hard Drive
Most files are stored on the hard drive. When using Release 12 and all of its extensions, 25 megabytes of memory is used. Many drawing files are one megabyte or more in size. Therefore, no less than 120 meg of memory is suggested for a personal computer, and you may have to add to that amount.

Floppy Disk Drives
In an ideal world, everyone would have floppy disks of the same size and volume, but in the 90s, this is not the case. What you are looking for in floppy disk drives is maximum flexibility. It is best to purchase two floppy drives, one 3½" and one 5¼".

Graphics Card
There are many good graphics cards on the market. Buy the best one you can afford. Remember, AutoCAD's Release 12 supports 256 colours and, for rendering, this is just the beginning. If you are on a budget, the minimum requirement is a VGA card.

The Digitizer Versus The Mouse
This is a personal decision and there is no correct choice. You should choose the one that best suits your purpose. It would be worthwhile to call a few industries that are in your discipline to see what they are using. If there are a lot of macros or customized routines used in your field, the digitizer tablet may be the best choice. Many people, however, find the mouse more convenient and easier on the arm. Be sure to test the equipment, either at a store or a local college or university, to see which one you like the best. It is not possible to use AutoCAD efficiently without either a mouse or a digitizer tablet. When purchasing either piece of hardware, be sure you also have a compatible driver file (.DRV).

S.R. Kyles
January 4, 1993

TABLE OF CONTENTS

Unit One *Introduction*

Chapter 6 – Working with Layers

Chapter 7 – Dimensioning

Chapter 8 – TEXT and DTEXT

Chapter 9 – Creating Hatches

Chapter 10 – BLOCKS

Chapter 11 – Setting Up Drawings and Plotting

Chapter 12 – Final Tests and Projects

Unit Two *Customizing and Interfacing*

Chapter 13 – Defining Attributes

Chapter 14 – Editing Attributes and Data Ectracts

Chapter 15 – MEASURE, DIVIDE, and INQUIRY Commands

Chapter 16 – Scripts and Slide Shows

Chapter 17 – Exchanging Graphics and Text Files

Chapter 18 – Drawing Interchange Format (DXF)

Chapter 19 – Macros

Chapter 20 – Customizing Menus

Chapter 21 – Creating Icon Menus

Chapter 22 – Customizing Prototype Drawings

Chapter 23 – Advanced Blocking and XREFs

Chapter 24 – Final Tests and Projects

Unit 3 *3D Dimensions*

Chapter 25 – Generating 3D Models

Chapter 26 – Extruding 2D Shapes into 3D Shapes

Chapter 27 – User Coordinate Space

Chapter 28 – 3DFACE and Point Filters

Chapter 29 – Dynamic Viewing

Chapter 30 – Creating 3D Drawings

Chapter 31 – Surfacing

Chapter 32 – 3D Shapes

Chapter 33 – Merging 3D Models

Chapter 34 – Creating 3D Modelling Using AME

Chapter 35 – Regions and Calculations on AME Models

Chapter 36 – Dimensioning 3D Parts

Chapter 37 – Final Tests and Projects

Appendices

INTRODUCTORY GEOMETRY AND SETTING UP

Upon completion of this chapter, the student should be able to:

1. Sign on to AutoCAD
2. Change the limits, snap, and grid of a screen
3. Use coordinate entry methods
4. Create a simple piece of geometry using LINE, ARC, CIRCLE, and FILLET

Welcome to the world of AutoCAD. If you are familiar with computers, begin by reading the section, Drawing Editor. If you are new to the computer environment, refer to the Preface in the front of this book for information on the various computer components and how they work, before reading further.

INTRODUCTION TO FLOPPY DISKS

It is wise to keep your information stored on a floppy disk if the computer you are using may be accessed by others. If you are sharing the computer, read the following; if not, skip to the next heading, Drawing Editor.

In order to access AutoCAD in a learning environment, you may need a floppy disk in drive A. A floppy disk must first be formatted using one of the format commands, such as FORMAT A:, while the C:\ prompt is present. Your instructor will know how the system is set up. Usually,

If the floppy disk has already been formatted and has information on it, do not reformat unless you want to erase all the information stored on the disk.

FORMAT A: on a 360K drive will format a 360K disk,

FORMAT A: on a 1.2MB drive will format a 1.2MB disk,

FORMAT A:/f:360 on a 1.2MB drive will format a 360K disk,

FORMAT A: on a 1.44MB drive will format a 1.44MB disk,

FORMAT A:/f:720 on a 1.44MB drive will format a 720K disk.

If you are using a B: drive, replace the A: in the FORMAT command with B:.

Make a note of the correct FORMAT command of your computer here: ___________________________

DRAWING EDITOR

Once the floppy disk is formatted and the system has been turned on, enter the AutoCAD Drawing Editor by using the sign-on code (ACAD or ACAD11).

ACAD is usually your sign-on code. If there are two or more versions of AutoCAD running on the network, check the notation on the main menu for specific package information, i.e., ACAD11 may mean AutoCAD Release 11, ACAD10 may mean AutoCAD Release 10, ACAD386 may mean AutoCAD 386.

Enter the sign-on code here:_______________

The sign-on code will retrieve the AutoCAD menu.

AutoCAD
Copyright (c) 1982-90 Autodesk Inc
Release 11 (10/22/90) 386 DOS Extender
Serial Number 000-00000000
Licensed to: Addison-Wesley
Obtained From: Autodesk Inc

0. Exit AutoCAD
1. Begin a NEW file
2. Edit an EXISTING file
3. Plot a file
4. Print plot a file

5. Configure AutoCAD
6. File Utilities
7. Compile shape/font description file
8. Convert old drawing file
9. Recover damaged drawing

Release 12 Notes:

There is no main menu in Release 12. Once you have entered the sign-on code, you will immediately be in a new file in the Drawing Editor.

Press the space bar or the return key after typing your response for the computer to accept what you have typed. ↵ represents the Return or Enter key.

`Enter Selection:`*(pick a number) (pick 1)* ↵

`Enter name of drawing:`**`A:first`** ↵

If the hard drive is being used to store your files, the A: will not be needed. After retrieving a drawing, the Drawing Editor will be activated.

The Drawing Editor divides the screen into four sections.

System Response Area: Three text lines at the bottom of the screen indicate the status of the commands and the system. Watch this area carefully to avoid frustration; it indicates the command being used. Command: is the system prompt. It indicates that a new command can be entered. If this prompt is not on the screen, it means there is another command in progress. Use the Control-C key combination to get back to the Command: prompt.

Graphics Display Area: This is the working space where a file or model is displayed.

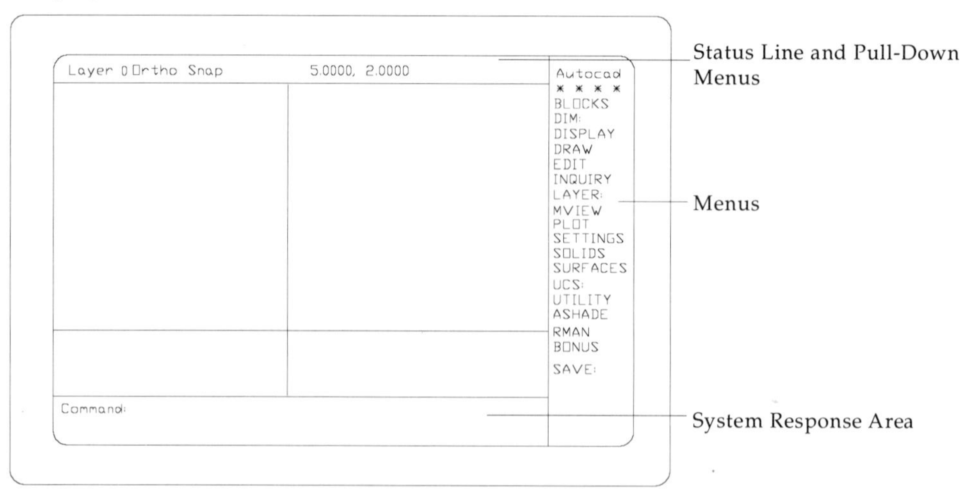

Figure 1-1. The Drawing Editor screen

Status Line: Located at the top of the screen the status line displays the position of the cursor, the settings of modes or options, and, on versions of AutoCAD after Release 9, the pull-down menu selection bar.

Screen Menu: Located at the right of the screen, this allows access to the screen menus.

Once in the Drawing Editor, information can be entered with the keyboard, puck, mouse, or digitizer.

Function Keys

To become familiar with the system, start with the keyboard toggle switches. Move the mouse around the screen and locate the keyboard function keys.

Now press F6.	*Notice how the numbers on the status line change as you move the mouse. These are the X- and Y-coordinate values.*
Now press F9.	*Notice how the numbers snap to even values and observe the word Snap in the status line.*
Now press F7.	*Observe a grid on the screen.*

Many systems provide toggle switches by means of function keys. These allow the user to turn on a specific function simply by pressing the key. These function switches are:

SNAP	ORTHO	COORDS	GRID	FLIP SCREEN
F9	F8	F6	F7	F1

Pointing Devices

Pointing devices are used to pick the position of objects, to access commands on the on-screen menus, the pull-down menus located under the status line, or to use the Tablet menu on the digitizer board.

There are many different kinds of pointing devices or mice on the market. Some have two or three buttons, and others have as many as 20.

On all mice there will be a point or command indicator or pick button. On the Logitech mouse, this button is usually yellow. On a two- or three-button mouse, this button is usually on the left side of the device.

Release 12 Notes:

The Shift- and Control-key combinations allow you to invoke more commands with the digitizer buttons. See Chapter 20 for programming.

The pick button is used to indicate the required command to be accessed either from the on-screen menu or from the digitizer tablet.

Another button functions the same as the Enter or Return key on the keyboard to signal the end of a command.

Other buttons can mean cancel (Ctrl-C), OSNAP, or various other commands.

The mouse is intended to work in conjunction with the keyboard for the entry of commands.

Before entering a command, be sure the Command: prompt is displayed.

To return to the Command: prompt, use Ctrl-C.

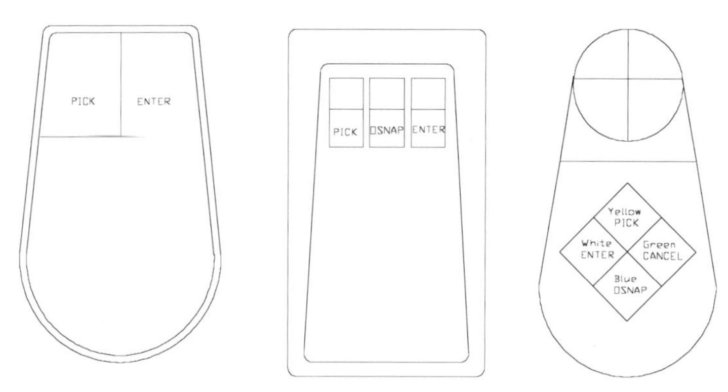

Figure 1-2. Examples of mice

SETTING UP THE SCREEN

Once in the Drawing Editor, AutoCAD establishes a default working environment. This includes Limits set to 12 by 9 inches, Grid set at one dot per inch, and Snap set to one-unit increments. These values will probably change for each design created. When you are ready to output drawings, you can then determine the scale and paper size.

While working in AutoCAD, a file is created that contains graphic data. This file is usually referred to as a model because the object being created on-screen represents an object to be built, created, or changed in some way. A drawing can be created from this file by transferring the image to paper.

The AutoCAD system utilizes many different menus to help create a model. The Draw menu contain commands that create objects or entities such as LINE, ARC, CIRCLE, etc. The Settings menu allows the screen to be set up for maximum use of the commands. The Edit menu contains the commands needed to change or modify objects, and the Display menu contains all the information needed to view a model.

All the menus noted above are found under either the screen menu or the pull-down menus. Use the pointing device to pick the desired menu choice, then pick the points on the screen where the object is to be drawn.

All models in AutoCAD should be entered at a scale of 1 = 1. To allow the screen to accept the length of lines and arcs required, the LIMITS command must be changed.

LIMITS *sets the basic size of the model.*

Now that the overall size is set, it must be viewed.

ZOOM All *allows the chosen size to be viewed. Be sure the limits and zoom are correct by pressing F6 and moving the cursor around. The coordinates should change.*

Finally, there are tools that will help create the model.

SNAP *sets an increment for the cursor to move by.*

GRID *sets a visual aid to help place objects. The grid is often set to twice the snap value.*

Here are some examples of limits that you may set:

- = *the position of the origin*

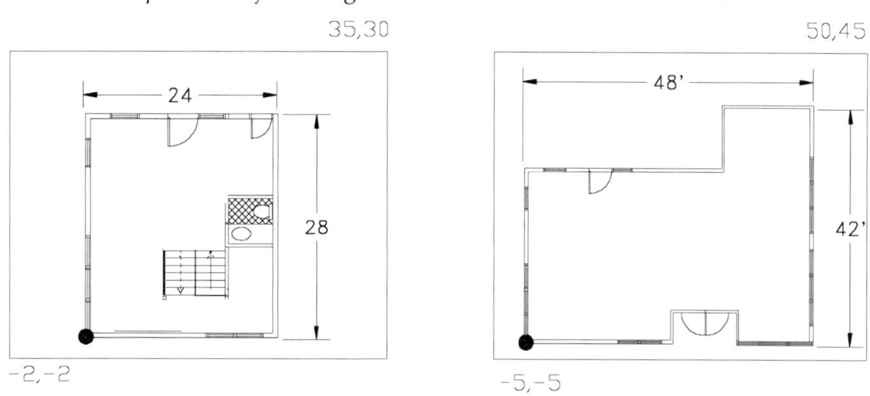

Figure 1-3a. Limits set in architectural applications

In architectural applications, dimensions are either interior or exterior. The origin is often at the bottom left.

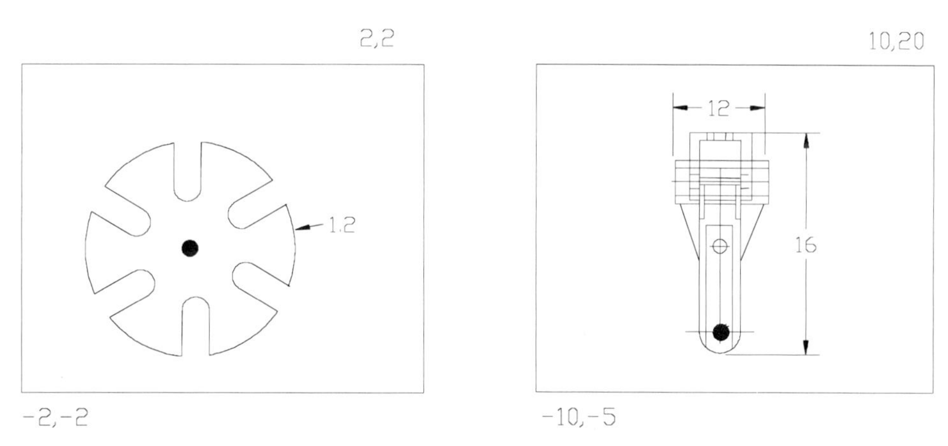

Figure 1-3b. Limits set in mechanical applications

In mechanical applications, the parts are often symmetrical, so the origin is found on the part for easy measuring.

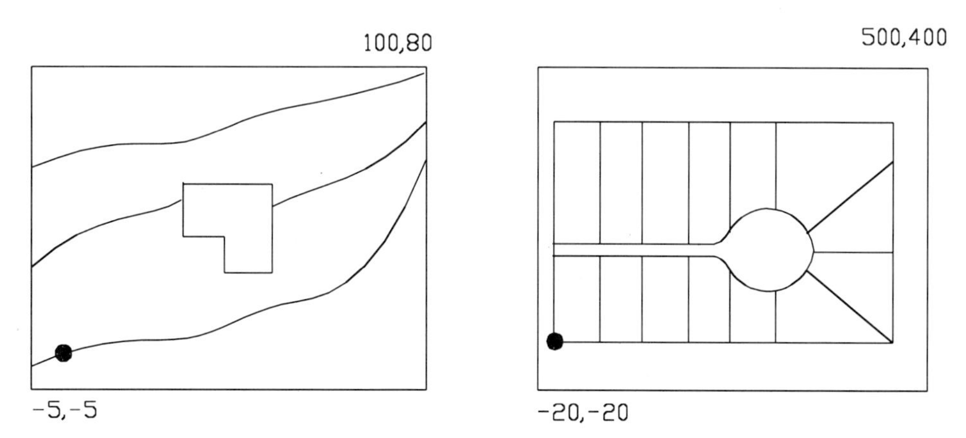

Figure 1-3c. Limits set in civil applications

In civil or surveying, large sizes are needed for lots. The origin 0,0 is usually on the bottom left.

Selecting Work Area Size

To select a work area size, use the following commands:

Example A1: *A house measuring 40′ x 36′*

```
Command:LIMITS
Lower left corner <0.0000,0.0000>:-5,-5
Upper right corner <12.0000,9.0000>:45,40
Command:ZOOM
All/Center/Dynamic/Extents/Left/Previous/Vmax/Window/<scale>:ALL
Command:SNAP
On/Off/value/Aspect/Rotate/Style/<1.0000>:1
Command:GRID
On/Off/value/Aspect/<1.0000>:5
```

These settings will provide plenty of viewing space on either side of the drawing and allow the units to be entered by decimal point. The smallest integer picked will be one unit. This can be changed at any time.

Example M1: *A template measuring 220″ x 160″*

```
Command:LIMITS
Lower left corner <0.0000,0.0000>:-5,-40
Upper right corner <12.0000,9.0000>:240,180
Command:ZOOM
All/Center/Dynamic/Extents/Left/Previous/Vmax/Window/<scale>:ALL
Command:SNAP
On/Off/value/Aspect/Rotate/Style/<1.0000>:5
Command:GRID
On/Off/value/Aspect/Rotate/Style/<1.0000>:10
```

These settings will provide plenty of viewing space on either side of the model and allow a minimum 5-unit integer entry.

Example C1: *An intersection measuring 15m by 12m*

```
Command:LIMITS
Lower left corner <0.0000,0.0000>:-5,-5
Upper right corner <12.0000,9.0000>:20,15
Command:ZOOM
All/Center/Dynamic/Extents/Left/Previous/Vmax/Window/<scale>:ALL
Command:SNAP
On/Off/value/Aspect/Rotate/Style/<1.0000>:.5
Command:GRID
On/Off/value/Aspect/<1.0000>:10
```

Again, these settings provide plenty of viewing space and allow a minimum 0.5-unit integer entry.

LIMITS *sets a flexible general size for the drawing.*

AutoCAD is a design system as opposed to a drafting system; thus it is advisable to create each item at a 1 = 1 scale. When you decide to make a drawing from the design, you can scale it to fit the paper size. Setting the limits does not limit the model; it merely allows you to set an approximate size for the screen. Should the design change, the limits can be changed at any time. If square limits are set, e.g., 10 x 10, only part of the screen will be used because the screen's *X* value is larger than the *Y*.

Choosing the Origin

The next major concern is choosing the position for the origin. This should be the most easily accessible point. If a large percentage of the dimensions on a model stem from one point, then this should be the origin. The coordinates displayed on the status line help you find your position relative to the origin. The placement of the origin is important to establish a base for all measurements.

ENTRY OF POINTS

Many of the commands used in AutoCAD need a reference point. In order to create a line, you need to know where it might start and where it might end. To create a line, for example, in the main menu pick DRAW, in the Draw menu pick LINE.

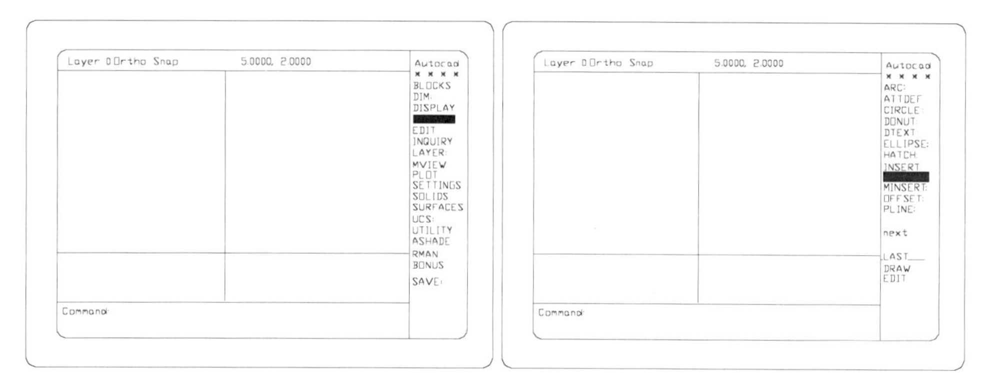

Figure 1-4. Creating a line

All parts of geometry are entered by means of points. Lines have two points; circles have a centre point and a point determining the radius; arcs have a centre point, a radius point, a starting point and an endpoint.

There are three ways of entering points:

- entering points by coordinates: absolute values, incremental values, or polar values
- picking points on the screen, with or without the SNAP command
- entering points relative to existing geometry

In this chapter, the first two methods of point entry will be discussed.

Coordinate Entry

Coordinates of an item, the *X*, *Y*, and *Z* values, can be entered either relative to the origin, the absolute value, or relative to the last entered point, the incremental value.

The origin of the model does not change, but the objects can move relative to the origin. To enter the absolute value of an item, type in the *X* value, then the *Y* value, separated by a comma.

```
Command:LINE
from point:0,0
```

```
to point:4,0
```

To enter an incremental or relative value, place an @ symbol (Shift-2) before the number.

```
to point:@4,0
```

Example: *Absolute and Incremental Entry*

Absolute	**Incremental**
Command:**LINE**	Command:**LINE**
from point:**0,0**	from point:**5,5**
to point:**4,0**	to point:**@4,0**
to point:**4,4**	to point:**@0,4**
to point:**0,4**	to point:**@-4,0**
to point:**0,0**	to point:**@0,-4**
to point:↵	to point:↵

The first example will create a four-unit square starting at 0,0. The second will create a four-unit square starting at 5,5.

5,5

0,0

To draw a line from point 5,6 to point 8.37,6 use either of the following:

Absolute	**Incremental**
Command:**LINE**	Command:**LINE**
from point:**5,6**	from point:**5,6**
to point:**8.37,6**	to point:**@3.37,0**

The choice of method is determined by what is known. If it is known that the final point is going to be 8.37,6, use the absolute value. If it is known that the line is going to be 3.37 units in positive X from the first point, then enter the coordinates incrementally.

Example: *Absolute and Incremental Coordinate Entry*

Absolute	**Incremental**
Command:**LINE**	Command:**LINE**
from point:**0,0**	from point:**7,5**
to point:**2,0**	to point:**@2,0**
to point:**2,3**	to point:**@0,3**
to point:**4,3**	to point:**@2,0**
to point:**4,2**	to point:**@0,-1**
to point:**6,2**	to point:**@2,0**
to point:**6,4**	to point:**@0,2**
to point:**0,4**	to point:**@-6,0**
to point:**0,0**	to point:**@0,-4**
to point:↵	to point:↵

The objects should look like the example on the opposite page, one starting at 0,0 and the other starting at 7,5.

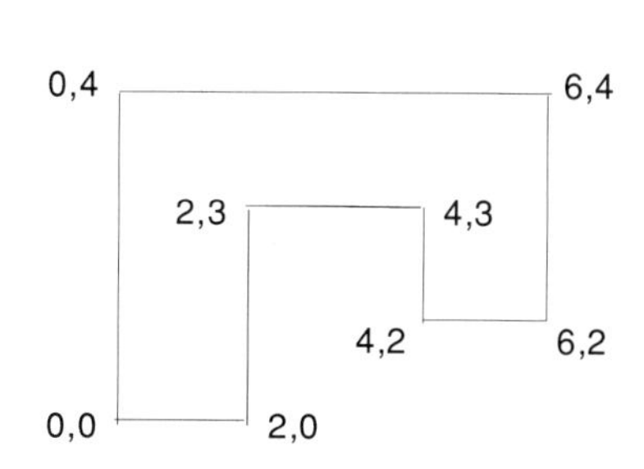

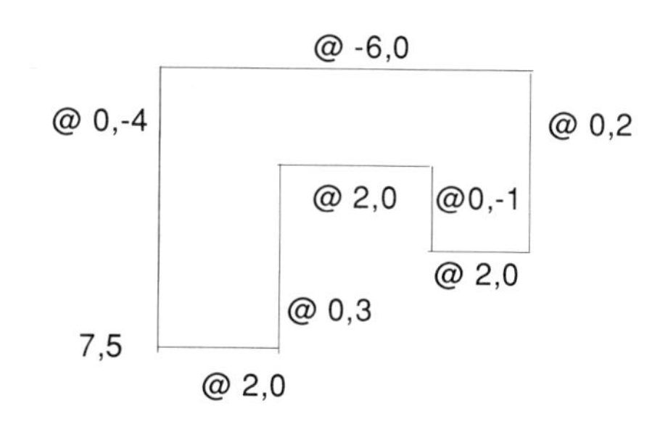

When entering the coordinates of points from the keyboard, *never* use an incremental integer as a first entry. Use @ only when entering relative to the last point entered. If you use @ at the beginning of a command string, the point will be at the specified distance from *the last point you entered.* Chances are that you do not know the location of the last point.

```
Command:LINE
From point:@3,4
```

This command starts a line at 3 units in positive *X* and 4 units in positive *Y* from the last point entered. Where was the last point entered?

```
Command:LINE
From point:3,4
To point:@2,0
```

This command draws a line from *X*3, *Y*4 — relative to the origin — to a position 2 units in positive *X* and 0 units in positive *Y*. This can also be expressed as delta *Y* = 0. Delta in this case means in the direction of.

Polar Coordinates

Polar coordinates allow an item to be entered relative to the last item at an angle. To draw a line at a specific angle, use the following:

```
Command:LINE
from point:3,4
to point:@4<45
```

Where:

@ = relative to the last point
4 = the length of the line
< = angle
45 = the angle at which the line will be drawn

Example: *Polar Coordinate Entry*

```
Command:LINE
from point:6,0
to point:@2<0
to point:@3<90
to point:@2<0
to point:@1<270
to point:@2<0
to point:@2<90
to point:@6<180
to point:@4<270
```

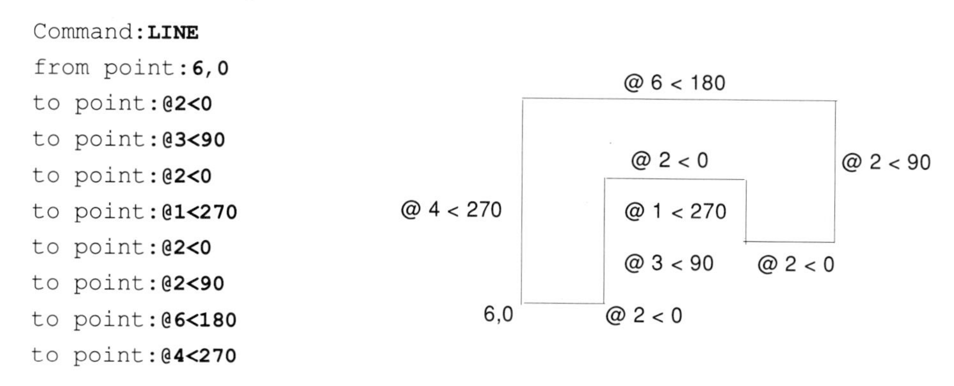

Polar coordinates are best suited for designs where angles are more prevalent. In the next example, use a polar coordinate, @3<250, to create a line at an angle of 70 degrees from the baseline.

The command to create this line is:

```
Command:LINE
From point: (pick 1)
To point:@3<250
```

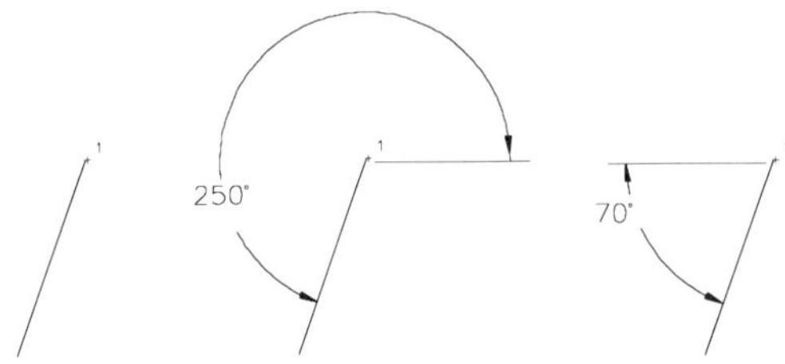

Figure 1-5. Creating a line at an angle

The line is three units in length at a 70-degree angle from the horizontal line, or 250 degrees counter-clockwise using polar coordinates.

Point Entry Using Digitizing

The "pick" button on the mouse will enter a point every time it is pressed while in a geometry command. Digitizing or picking points becomes much easier and much more accurate when using the Snap function.

By using Snap, lines, arcs, or circles can be drawn at preset integers. If the Snap is set to 0.25, all entries will be to the nearest 0.25 interval as shown below:

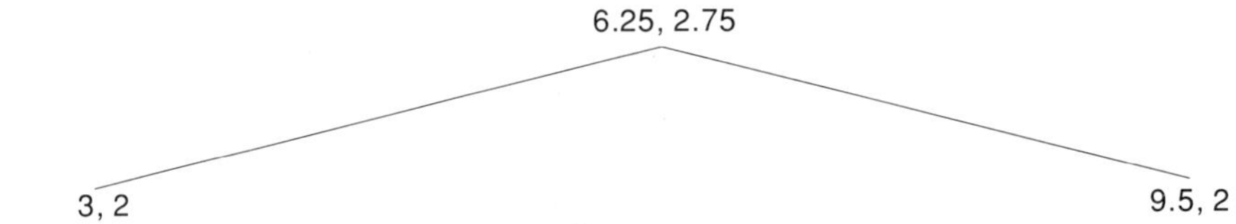

Figure 1-6. Lines drawn at preset integers

If the Snap is set to 1, all the points that are digitized or picked on the screen will be accurate to one-unit integers. You cannot be accurate without using Snap when picking points on the screen.

Do not make the mistake of thinking the grid will help you place items on the screen. The grid is for visual reference only.

With the Ortho option (F8), lines can only be drawn vertically or horizontally. Be sure the Snap is set at 0.25 and enter the following:

Figure 1-7. Lines drawn using the Ortho option

Notice the cursor only moves vertically and horizontally. By pressing F8, diagonal lines can be drawn again.

The Grid function (F7) allows a visual display of distance.

The coordinates or position on the screen can be seen on the status line if the Coords function (F6) is enabled.

CAD PRIMITIVES

A CAD primitive is any simple object command such as LINE, ARC, or CIRCLE. These are found under the Draw menu.

Lines

The LINE command is as easy to use as the above examples indicate. Simply indicate with either a "pick" on the screen or a coordinate keyboard entry the points between which the line will be drawn.

```
Command:LINE
From point: (pick 1)
To point:@3<250
To point: (pick 2)
To point:↵
```

Release 12 Notes:

A new command called RECTANGLE allows you to create a closed triangle in only two picks.

```
Command:RECTANGLE
First point: (pick 1)
Second point: (pick2)
```

When you are drawing lines, you are creating objects that are described to the system by two points: a start point and an endpoint. Any number of points can be entered in the LINE command; each point will be joined to the last entered point creating a separate line. If five or six lines are entered in a single command, any single line out of the entered set can be erased.

LINE options:

C *will create a line from the last point in a string of lines to the first point.*

U *will undo the last entered point.*

Circles

A circle is also described as an object with two points; a centre and a radius.

The CIRCLE command will prompt for the information needed to complete the circle. The command is:

```
Command:CIRCLE
3P/2P/TTR/<Center point>: (pick 1)
Diameter/<Radius>: (pick 2) (move cursor or drag, then pick)
```

Where:

3P = a circle fit through three points

2P = a circle fit through two points

TTR = a circle that is tangent to the objects indicated with a specified radius

<Center point>: = the default circle, which is described by a centre point and a radius, in that order

Diameter <Radius>: = the default circle specified by a radius or a diameter

Drag = the drag mode, the circle will expand and contract following the movement of the cursor

Typing CIRCLE will achieve the above. If CIRCLE is picked from either the screen menu or the pull-down menu, the system will prompt for one of the options listed above. All the options for creating circles are shown in Figure 1-8.

Arcs

Arcs are created in much the same way as circles, by using options to control how the arc is entered. An arc is described by three of four possible points: a centre, a radius, a starting point, and an endpoint. The command is:

```
Command:ARC
Center/<Start point>: (pick 1)
Center/End/<Secondpoint>: (pick 2)
Endpoint: (pick 3)
```

Where:
Center = the option to pick a centre point

<Start point>: = the default first point to create an arc stretched through three points

End = the option to pick the endpoint

<Second point>: = the default for a three-point arc

Endpoint = the end of a three-point arc

There are many variations on the ARC command illustrated in Figure 1-9.

Fillet

The FILLET command will be explained more fully later, but for now, pick FILLET, then pick R for Radius, enter the radius required, and pick the two items that need filleting. See Figure 1-8.

EXERCISES

Using AutoCAD as a design tool offers three advantages over a drawing created manually on paper:

- the item never needs to be drawn twice
- a high degree of accuracy is attained, if done correctly
- the data can be used for non-graphic information

To take advantage of these benefits, all objects must be designed at full scale. In Chapter 3, there will be a discussion on how to change the units on a model, but for now full units will be used.

When doing the exercises, use the LINE, ARC, CIRCLE, and FILLET commands. Dimensions are not needed.

Do all the exercises if you have time.

Figure 1-8

CIRCLES
DRAW MENU

CEN RAD

If you know the centre and the radius.

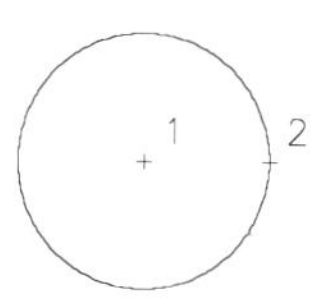

Command:CIRCLE 3P/2P/TTR/<Center point>: *(pick 1)*

Diameter<Radius>:**DRAG** *(pick 2)*

CEN DIA

If you know the centre and the diameter.

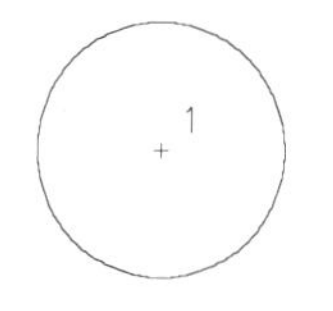

Command:CIRCLE 3P/2P/TTR/<Center point>: *(pick 1)*

Radius <Diameter>: *(pick 2)*

2 POINT

If you can fit the circle within two points.

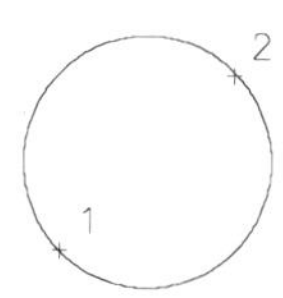

Command:CIRCLE 3P/2P/TTR/<Center>:**2P**

first point on diameter: *(pick 1)*

Second point on diameter:**DRAG** *(pick 2)*

3 POINT

If you can fit the circle within three points.

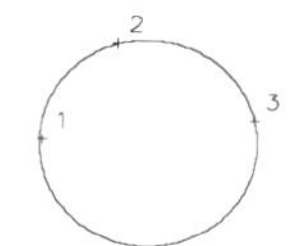

Command:CIRCLE 3P/2P/TTR/<Center point>:**3P**

First point: *(pick 1)*

Second point: *(pick 2)*

Third point:**DRAG** *(pick 3)*

TTR
(Tangent, Tangent, Radius)

If you know the radius, and the circle is tangent to two items.

Command:CIRCLE 3P/2P/TTR/<Center point>:**TTR**

Radius <Diameter>: *(pick 2)*

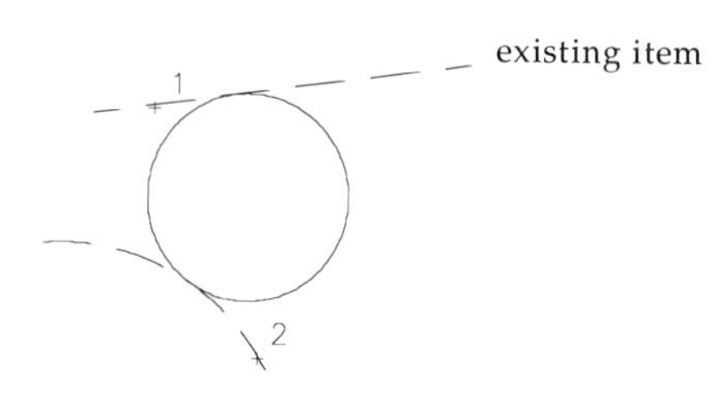

FILLET
EDIT MENU

Command:FILLET Polyline/Radius/<Select two objects>:

Enter fillet radius <3.0000>:**1**

Command:FILLET Polyline/Radius/<Select two objects>: *(pick 1 2)*

(pick the two items that you want filleted)

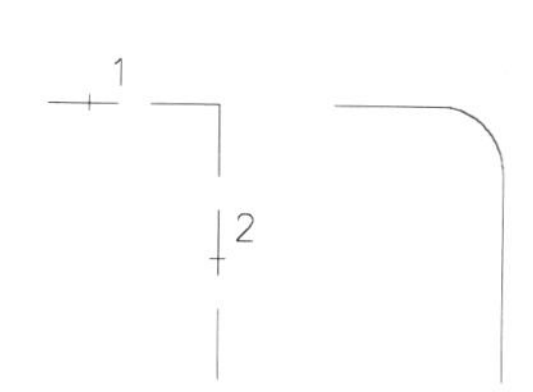

Figure 1-9

ARC
DRAW MENU

3 point

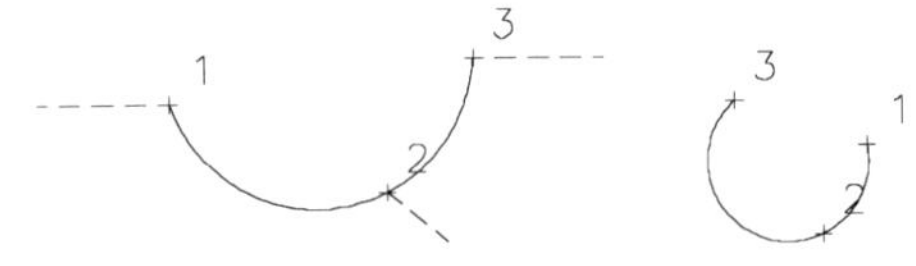

Command:ARC Center/<Start point>: *(pick 1)*

Center/End/<Second point>: *(pick 2)*

Endpoint:**DRAG** *(pick 3)*

S,C,E Start, Center, End

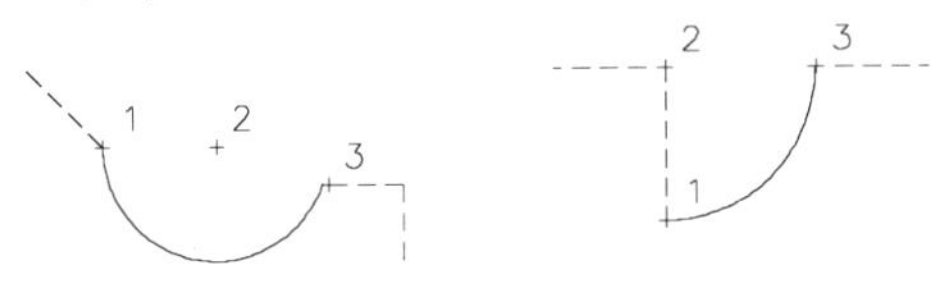

Command:ARC Center/<Start point>: *(pick 1)*

Center/<Start point>:**DRAG** *(pick 2)*

Angle/Length of Chord/<Endpoint>: *(pick 3)*

S,C,A Start, Center, End

Command:ARC Center/<Start point>: *(pick 1)*

Center/End/<Second point>:C Center: *(pick 2)*

A included angle:**90** *(-135 second example)*

S,C,L Start, Center, Length of Chord

Command:ARC Center/<Start point>: *(pick 1)*

Center/Endpoint/<Second point>:C Center: *(pick 2)*

Length of chord:**DRAG** *(pick 3)*

S,E,A Start, End, Angle

Command:ARC Center/<Start point>: *(pick 1)*

Endpoint: *(pick 2)*

A included angle: *(pick 3)*

S,E,R Start, End, Radius

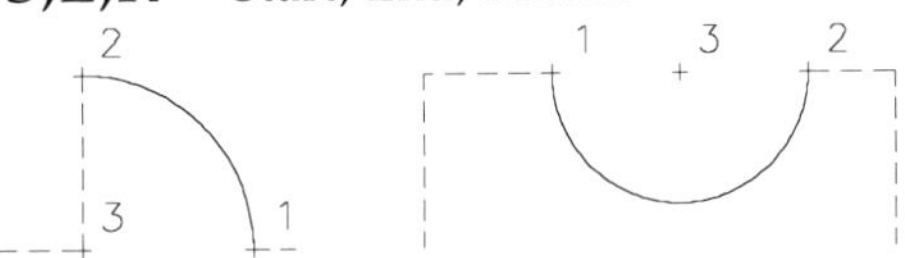

Command:ARC Center/<Start point>: *(pick 1)*

Endpoint: *(pick 2)*

Angle/Direction/Radius/<CCenter point>:**R**

Radius:**Drag** *(pick 3)*

S,E,D Start, End, Direction

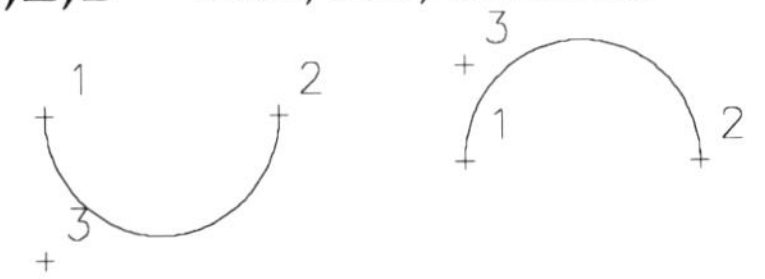

Command:ARC Center/<Start point>: *(pick 1)*

Endpoint: *(pick 2)*

Direction from start point: *(pick 3)*

C,S,E Center, Start, End

Command:ARC Center/<Start point>:**C** *(pick 1)*

Start point: *(pick 2)*

Angle/Length of Chord/<Endpoint>:**DRAG** *(pick 3)*

C,S,A Center, Start, Angle

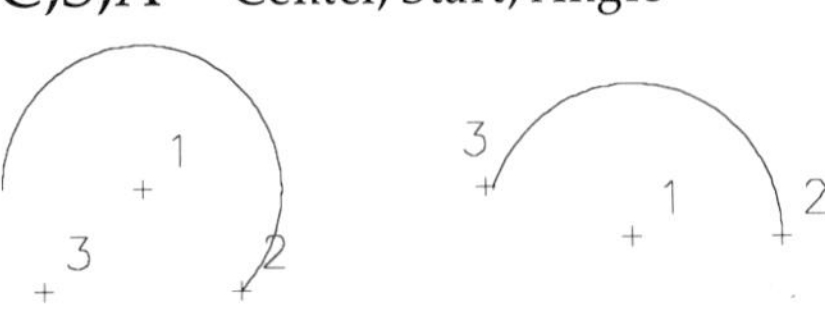

Command:ARC Center/<Start point>: *(pick 1)*

Start point: *(pick 2)*

A included angle: *(pick 3)*

C,S,L Center, Start, Length of Chord

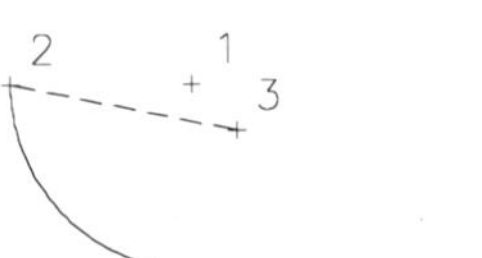

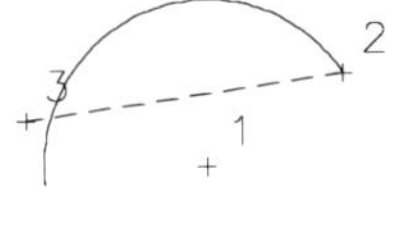

Command:ARC Center/<Start point>:**C** *(pick 1)*

Start point: *(pick 2)*

Length of chord:**DRAG** *(pick 3)*

Exercise A1

SETTINGS MENU

Command:**LIMITS**

Bottom-left corner <0.0000,0.0000>:**-2,-2**

Upper-right corner <12.0000,9.0000>:**30,25**

DISPLAY MENU

Command:**ZOOM**

All/Center/Dynamic/Extents/Left/Previous/Vmax/Window:**All**

SETTINGS MENU

Command:**SNAP**

On/Off/value/Aspect/Rotate/Style/<1.0000>:**1**

Command:**GRID**

On/Off/value<0.0000>:**3**

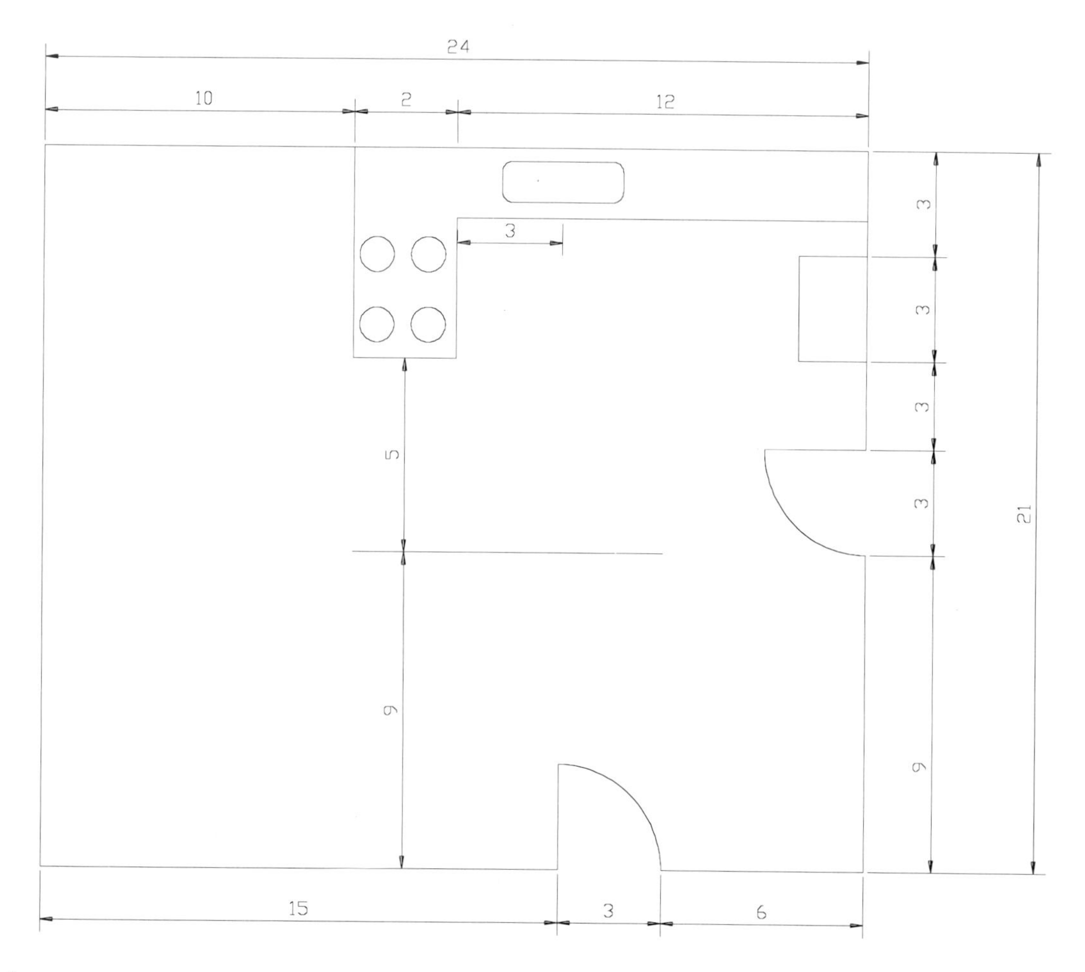

If the space bar is pressed without entering a command, the system will offer the Help files. If you do not want the Help files, use the cancel button on the mouse or Ctrl-C to cancel, then press F1 to bring the screen back to the graphics mode.

Do not enter the dimensions. Create only the geometry.

Hints on A1

Use the following commands to complete the drawing.

Be sure the Command: prompt is present before starting a new command. If it is not, use Ctrl-C or the Cancel button.

ARC, LINE, and CIRCLE are under the Draw menu. FILLET is under the Edit menu.

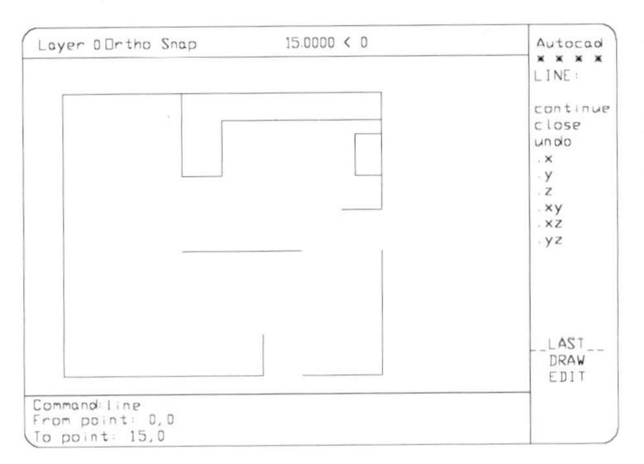

Lines

With your Snap on draw the lines. Use only LINE, not X, Y, etc.

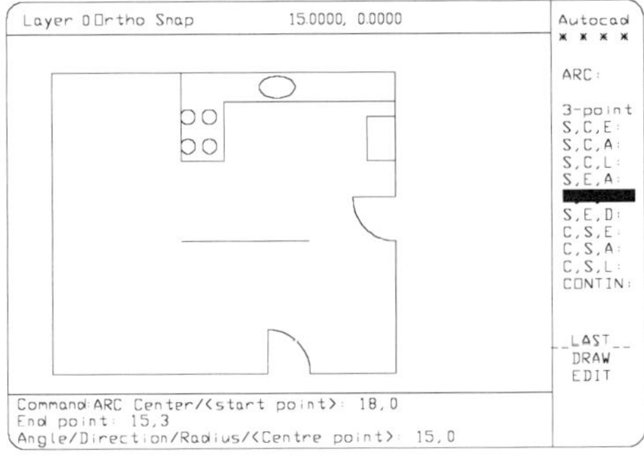

Arcs

Use Start, End, Radius for arcs. Remember, only counter-clockwise.

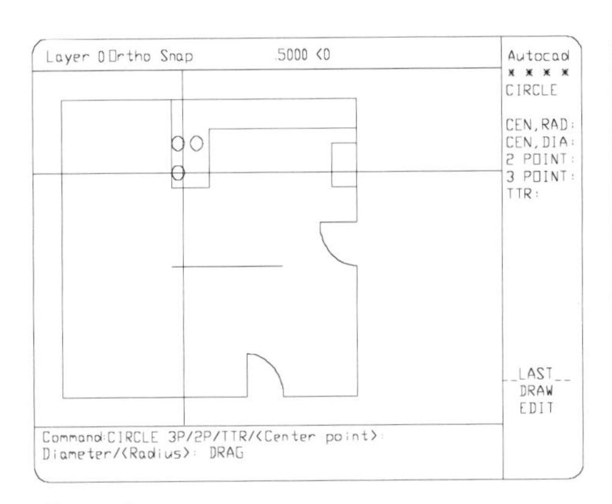

Circles

Use CEN *(centre)* RAD *(radius)* for circles. Drag the radius over, use Snap.

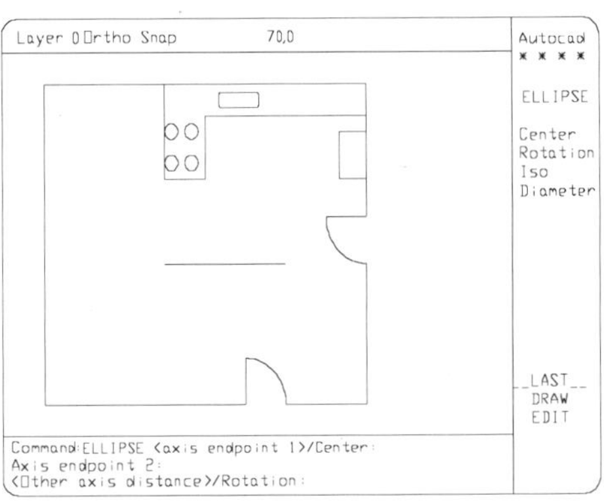

Fillets

Fillets are under the Edit menu. Change the Radius.

When you are finished, type END. This will save your work on the floppy disk and exit you from the Drawing Editor.

Exercise M1

SETTINGS MENU

Command:**LIMITS**

Bottom-left corner <0.0000,0.0000>:**-10,-40**

Upper-right corner <12.0000,9.0000>:**220,110**

DISPLAY MENU

Command:**ZOOM**

All/Center/Dynamic/Extents/Left/Previous/Vmax/Window:**All**

SETTINGS MENU

Command:**SNAP**

On/Off/value/Aspect/Rotate/Style/<1.0000>:**5**

Command:**GRID**

On/Off/value<1.0000>:**10**

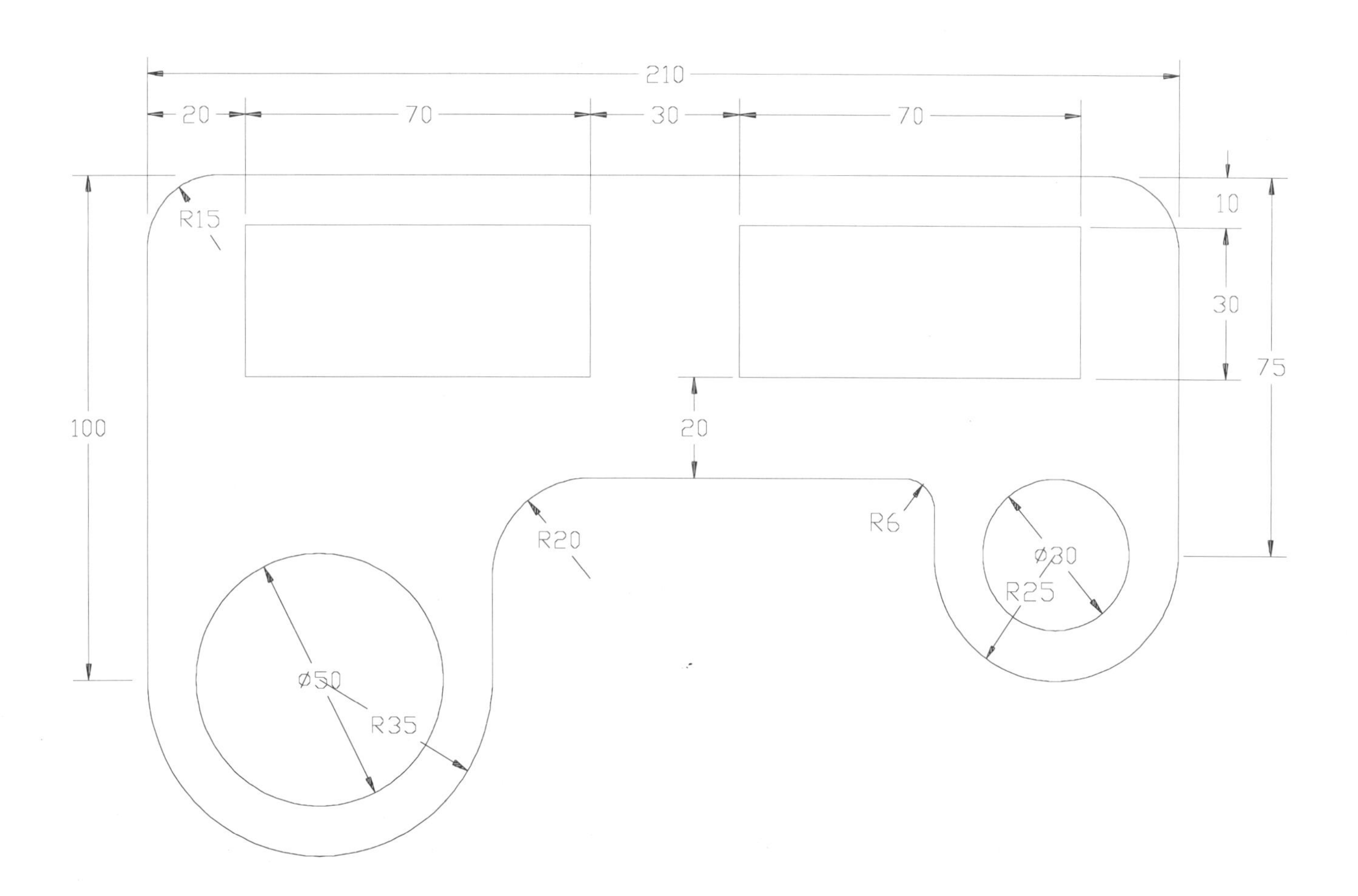

If the space bar is pressed without entering a command, the system will offer the Help files. If you do not want the Help files, use the cancel button on the mouse or Ctrl-C to cancel, then press F1 to bring the screen back to the graphics mode.

Create the geometry only. No dimensions are needed yet.

Hints for M1

Use the following commands to complete the exercise.

Be sure the Command: prompt is present before starting a new command. If it is not, use Ctrl-C or the Cancel button.

ARC, LINE, and CIRCLE are under the Draw menu. FILLET is under the Edit menu.

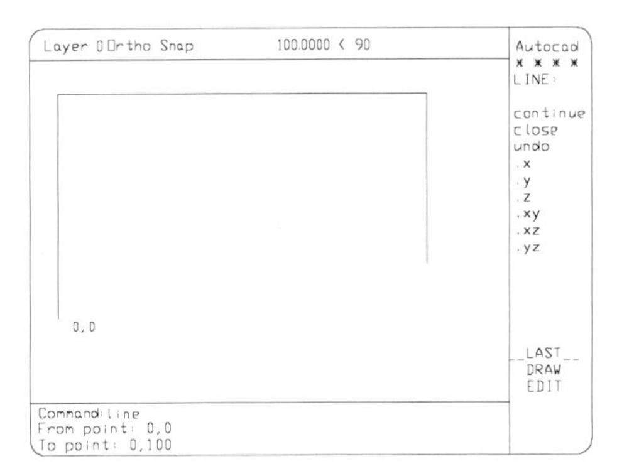

Lines

With your Snap on, draw the lines. Watch the top line for position.

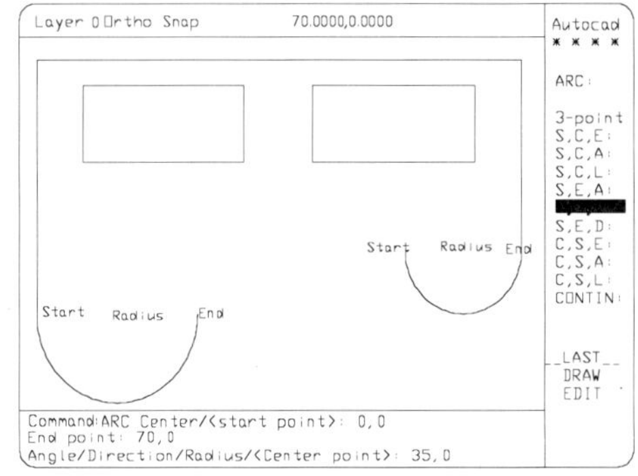

Arcs

Use Start, End, Radius for arcs. Remember to go counter-clockwise.

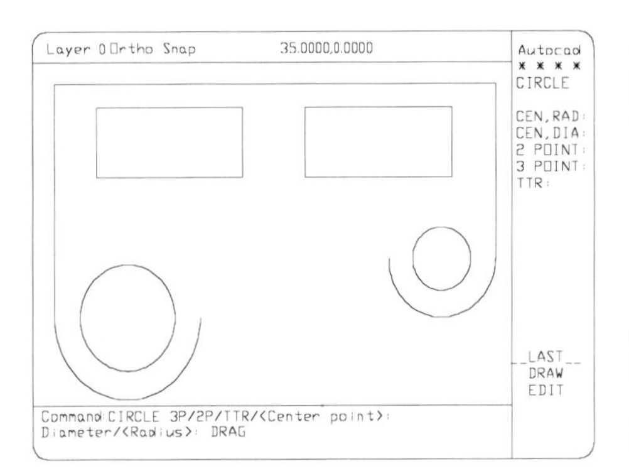

Circles

Use CEN *(centre)* RADius for the circles. DRAG means drag out the radius.

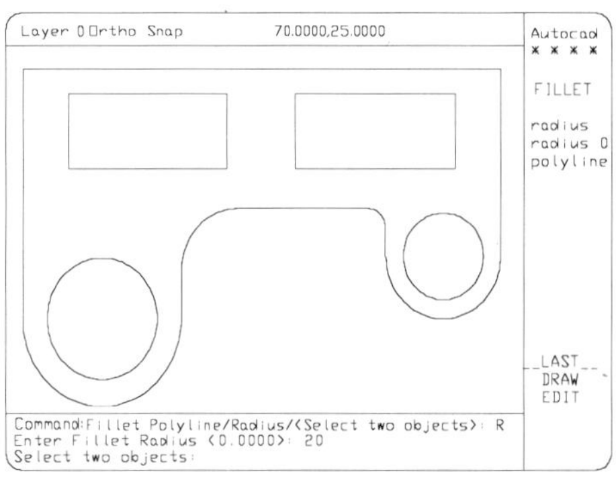

Fillets

Fillets are under the Edit menu. Change the Radius.

When you are finished, type END. This will save your work on the floppy disk and exit you from the Drawing Editor.

Exercise C1

SETTINGS MENU

```
Command:LIMITS
Bottom-left corner <0.0000,0.0000>:-5,-5
Upper-right corner <12.0000,9.0000>:35,25
```

DISPLAY MENU

```
Command:ZOOM
All/Center/Dynamic/Extents/Left/Previous/Vmax/Window:All
```

SETTINGS MENU

```
Command:SNAP
On/Off/value/Aspect/Rotate/Style/<1.0000>:1
Command:GRID
On/Off/value<1.0000>:5
```

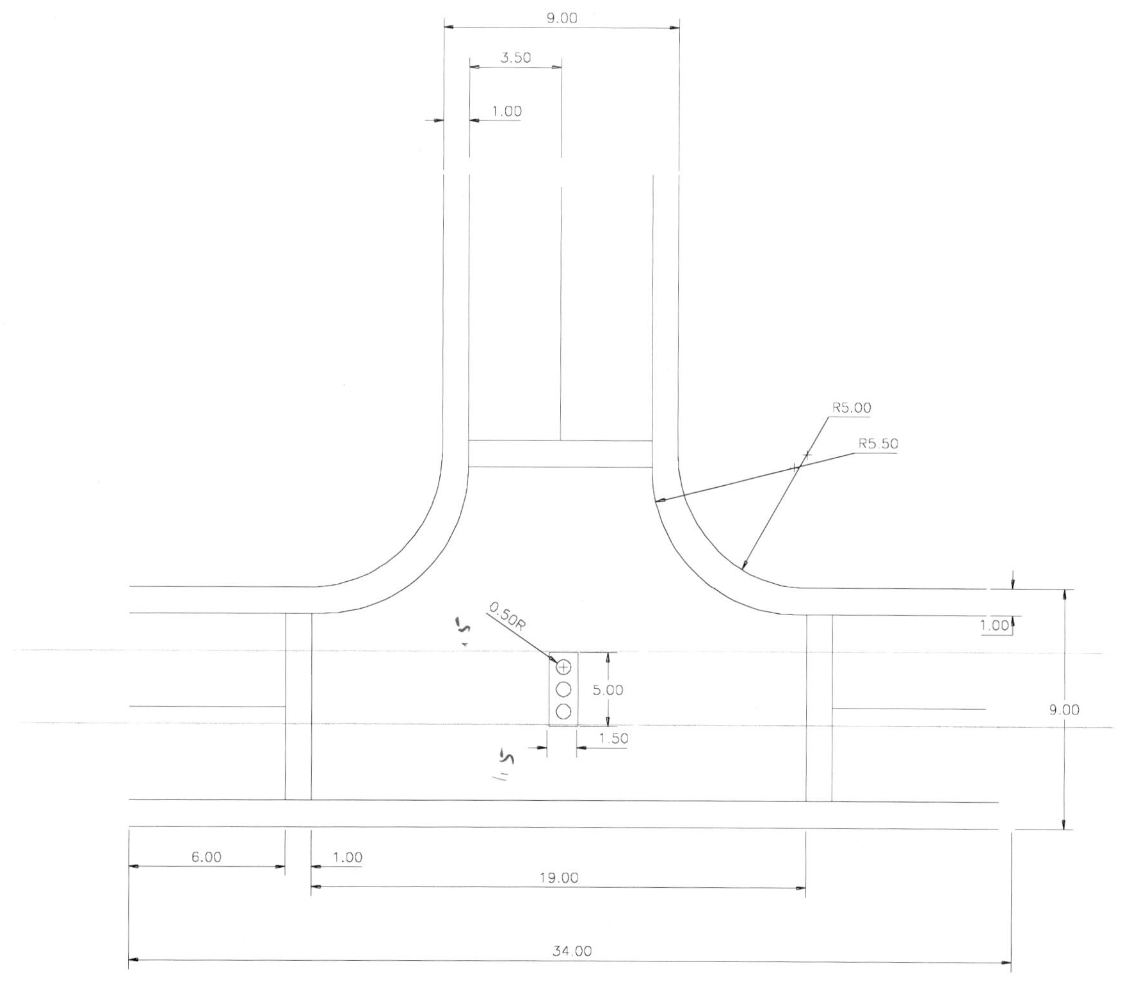

If the space bar is pressed without entering a command, the system will offer the Help files. If you don't want the Help files, use the cancel button on the mouse or Ctrl-C to cancel, then press F1 to bring the screen back to the graphics mode.

Create the geometry only. Do not enter the dimensions.

Hints for C1

Use the following commands to complete the exercise.

Be sure to have a Command: prompt before starting a new command. If it is not present, use Ctrl-C or the Cancel button.

ARC, LINE, and CIRCLE are under the Draw menu. FILLET is under the Edit menu.

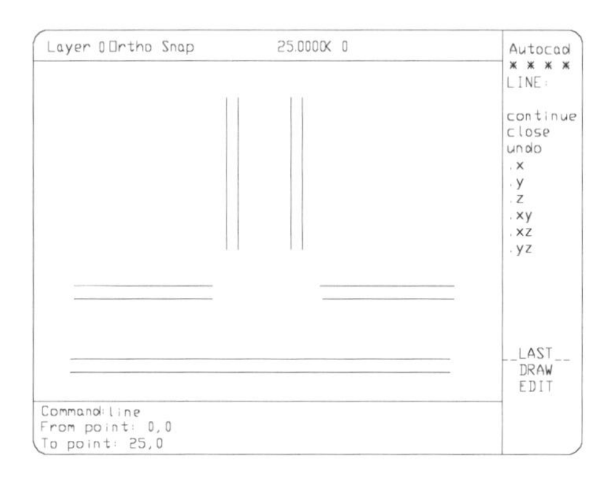

Lines

With your Snap on, draw the lines.

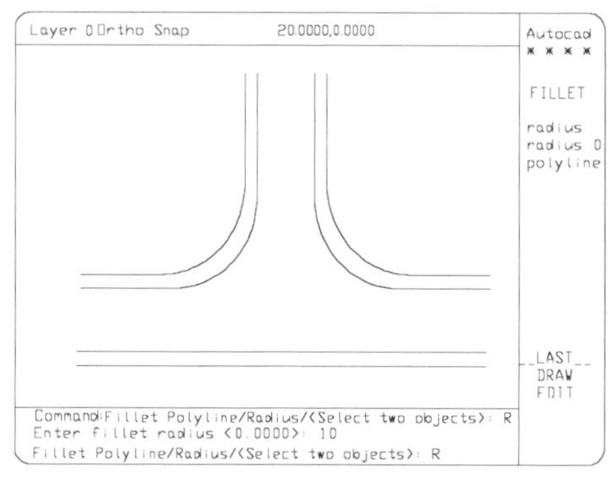

Fillets

Fillets are under the Edit menu. Change the radius.

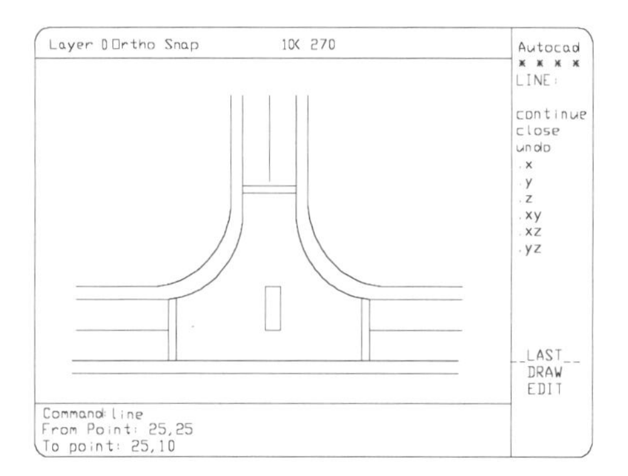

Lines

Change the Snap for more accuracy.

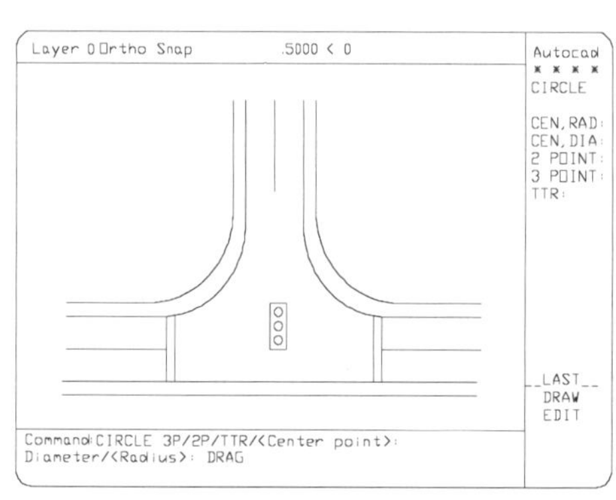

Circles

Use CEN *(centre)* RAD *(radius)* for circles. Use Drag to change the radius.

When you are finished, type END. This will save your work on the floppy disk and exit you from the Drawing Editor.

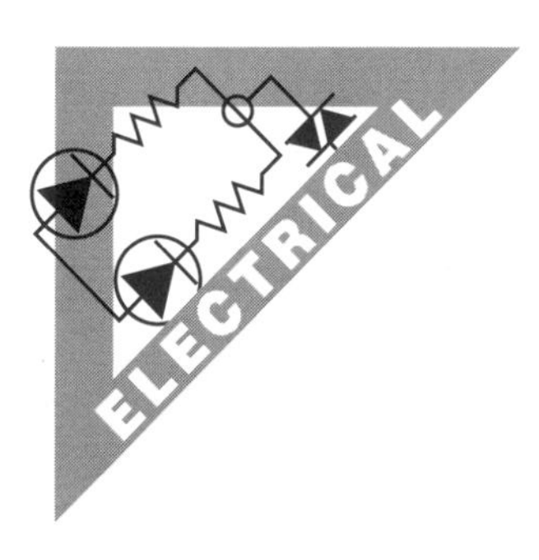

Exercise E1

SETTINGS MENU

```
Command:LIMITS
Bottom-left corner <0.0000,0.0000:-1,-1
Upper-right corner <12.0000,9.0000:↵
```

DISPLAY MENU

```
Command:ZOOM
All/Center/Dynamic/Extents/Left/Previous/Vmax/Window:All
```

SETTINGS MENU

```
Command:SNAP
On/Off/value/Aspect/Rotate/Style/<1.0000>:.5
Command:GRID
On/Off/value<1.0000>:1
```

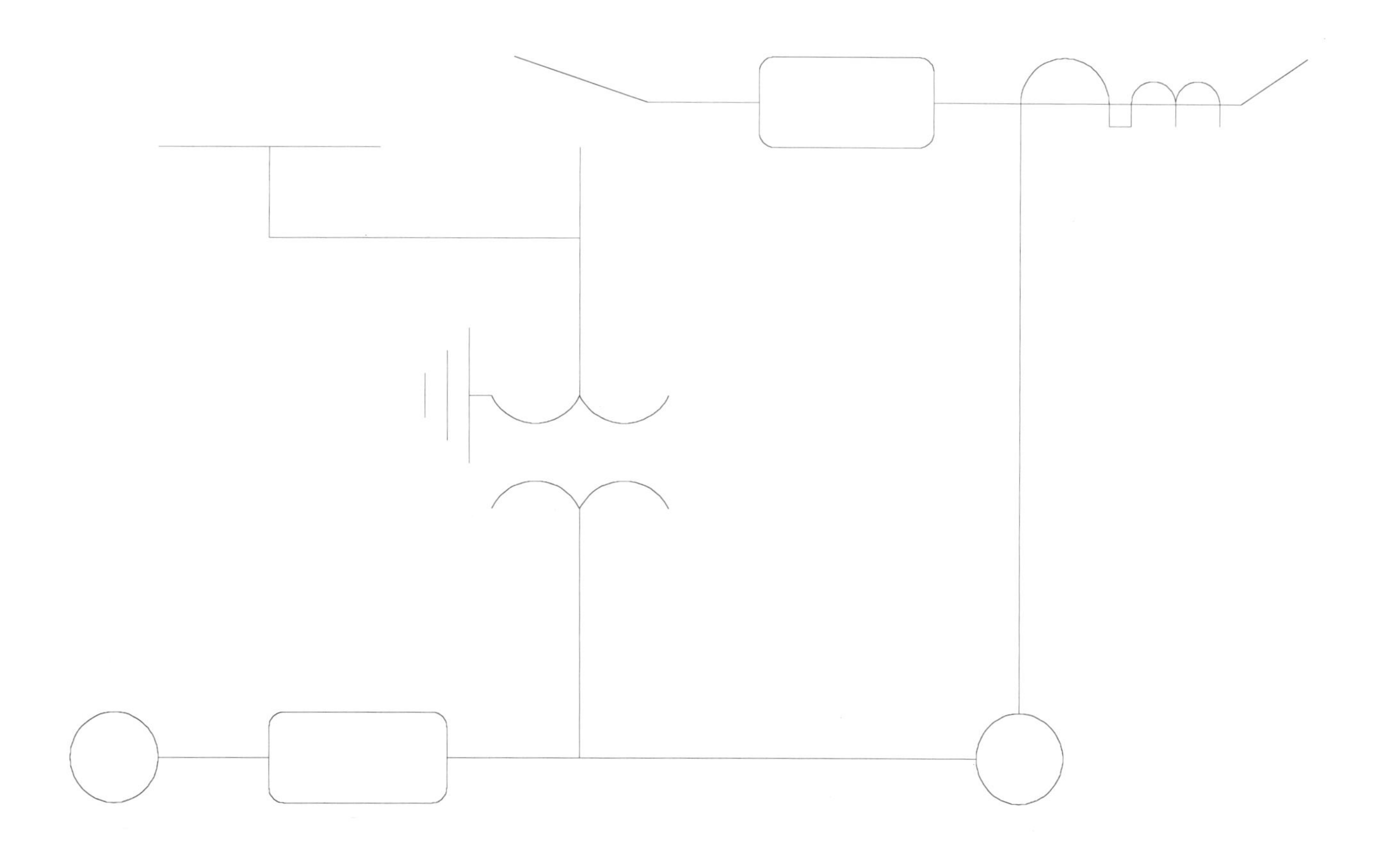

If the space bar is pressed without entering a command, the system will offer the Help files. If you do not want the Help files, use the cancel button on the mouse or Ctrl-C to cancel, then press F1 to bring the screen back to the graphics mode.

Create only the geometry. Do not enter the dimensions.

Hints for E1

Use the following commands to complete the exercise.

Be sure the Command: prompt is present before starting a new command. If it is not, use Ctrl-C or the Cancel button.

ARC, LINE, and CIRCLE are under the Draw menu. FILLET is under the Edit menu.

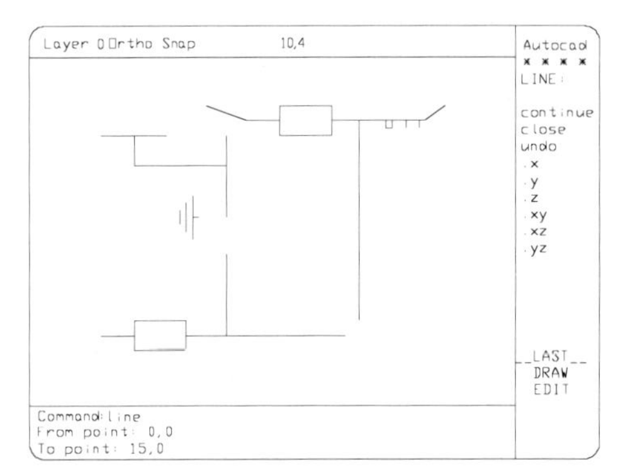

Lines

With your Snap on, draw the lines. Use only LINE, not X, Y, etc.

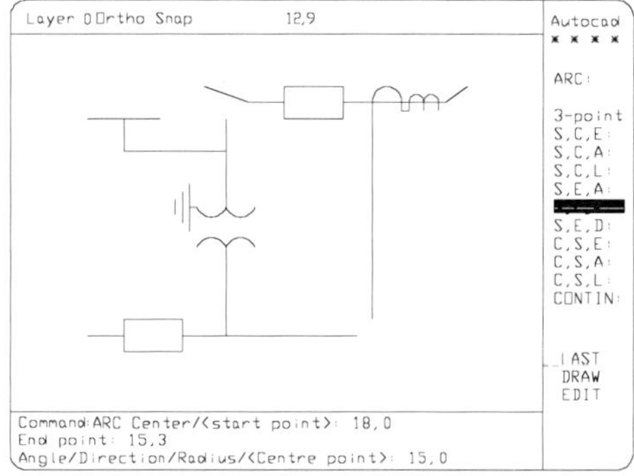

Arcs

Use Start, End, Radius for arcs. Remember, only counter-clockwise.

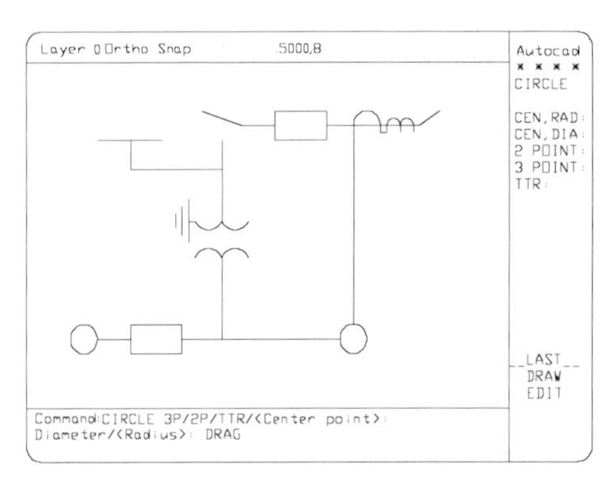

Circles

Use CEN *(centre)* RAD*(radius)* for circles. Drag the radius over, using Snap.

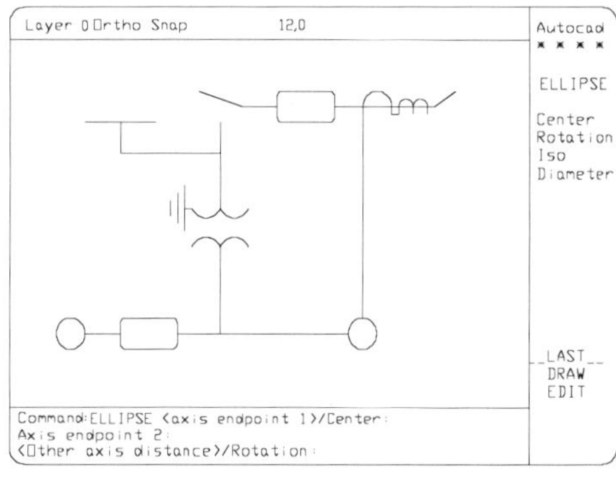

Fillets

Fillets are under the Edit menu. Change the radius.

When you are finished, type END. This will save your work on the floppy disk and exit you from the Drawing Editor.

The Challenger

This exercise is quite difficult and is meant to offer a challenge for advanced students.

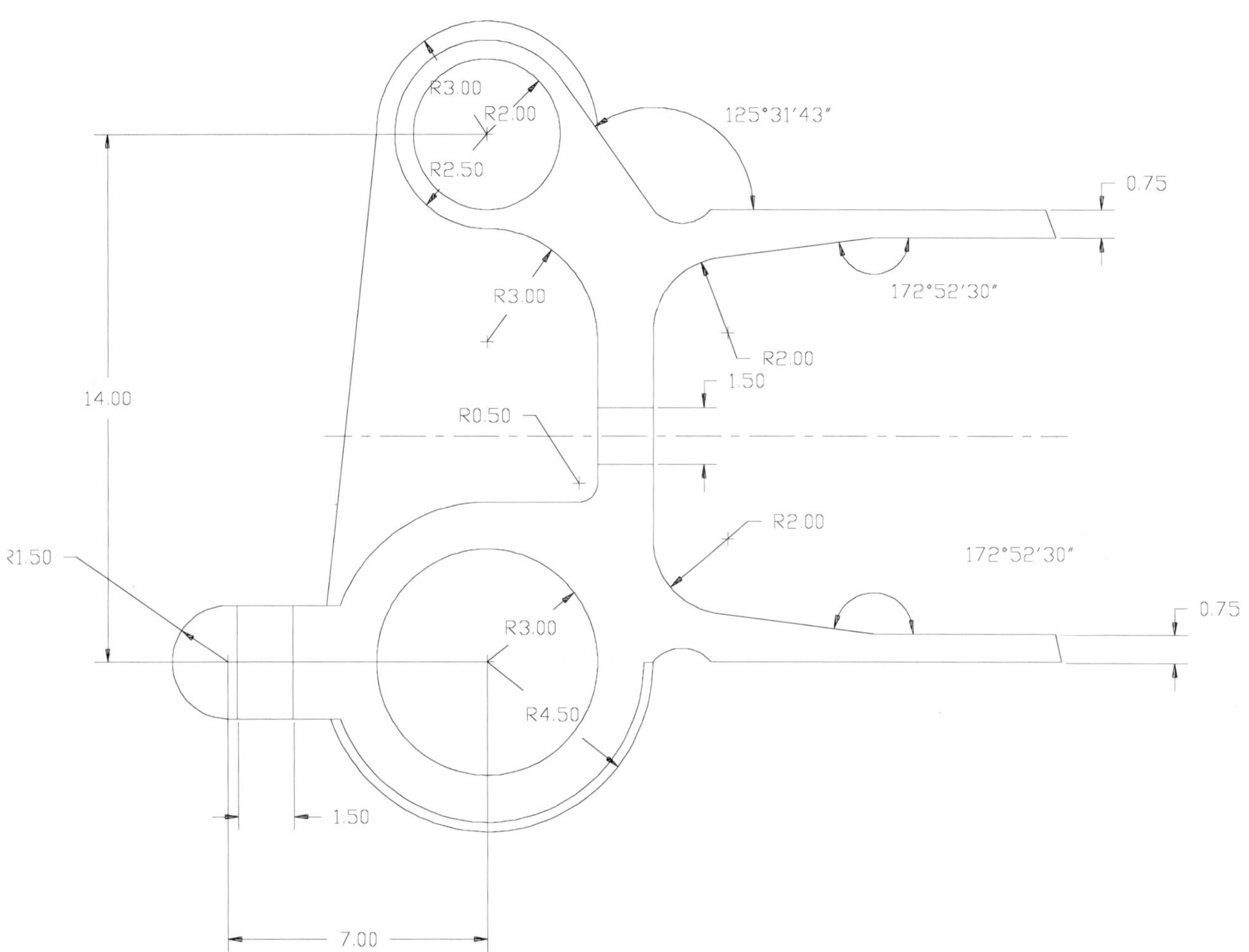

HELP FILES AND DISPLAY COMMANDS

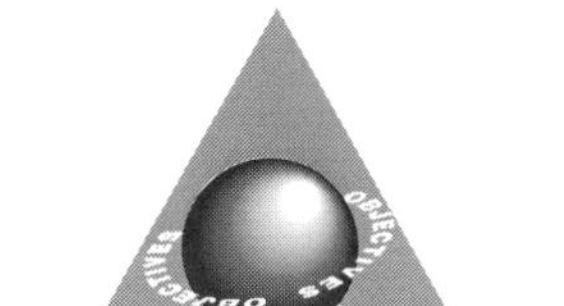

Upon completion of this chapter, the student should be able to:

1. Retrieve on-line documentation or Help files
2. Use the commands GRID and SNAP effectively
3. Use the commands ZOOM and PAN effectively
4. Use Osnap within a command and as a setting
5. Use ERASE to delete objects
6. Effectively save current models

START-UP REVIEW

There are two ways of starting files: one generates a drawing of an item, the other generates a design of an item which can be used for a drawing, an assembly, a symbol library, a manufactured part, or for generating information for engineering analysis. The first method creates a computer "paper" using Setup (MVSETUP or a similar customized "paper" environment). The second method considers the screen as a base for a model or 3D item. For now, assume you are designing something rather than only producing a drawing.

LIMITS — *defines the general size of the model.*

ZOOM ALL — *produces a view of the entire working area. To make sure it has changed, press* F6 *and move the cursor around.*

SNAP — *sets an increment to which the cursor will move.*

GRID — *sets a visual pattern to aid the placement of objects.*

Limits can be turned off if you prefer to work with no set working area. The Snap setting can be used without setting the limits.

HELP FILES

Release 12 Notes

Type HELP. Select Index, then hold the select button in the select square to advance the list of Help files.

Once you have learned how to sign on to the system and to select menus, you then need to learn how each command works. Theoretically, from this point on, you can learn the system operation from on-screen documentation available under the Help files. The Help files do not always tell you what you need to know in the way that you want to hear it, but they were developed in a logical, straightforward manner.

Help files have two main functions. First they serve as an index of all of the system commands. If you know a certain command exists that will change the magnification of the data on the screen, but you cannot remember the command, you can use the following:

```
Command:HELP
```

```
Command name (return for list):↵
```

This will display a listing of the various commands available on the system. By reading the various command names, you should be able to identify a command that is similar in meaning to the one you are after. If you are feeling adventurous and are curious about the system, press **?** and take a chance on a command.

The second function of the Help files permits you to quickly retrieve information about a specific command. If you have tried a command three times, and it is not working, chances are you do not understand the system prompts. Most problems in getting commands to work stem from an attempt to enter information on one level while the system is prompting for something else.

Release 12 Notes

The dialogue box allows you to either type in the command or choose the command from the index.

The system responds to a command by displaying a series of prompts. In the following example, the second line is the prompt, and it offers the options for the first point of the arc: either a point to start a three-point arc, or C for the centre point.

```
Command:ARC
Center <Start point>:
```

Trying to enter a radius at this point will not work. If you do not understand a prompt, check the Help files for more information. These files are accessible at any time and will explain some of the less obvious items in the command prompts.

The HELP command will display the following information about the options of the ARC command:

```
Command:HELP
Command name (return for list):ARC

The ARC command draws an arc (circle segment) as specified by
any of the following methods:

• three points on the arc
• start point, center, end point
• start point, center, including angle
• start point, center, length of chord
• start point, end point, radius
• start point, end point, including angle
• start point, end point, starting direction
• continuation of previous line or arc

3-point format ARC Center/<start point>: (point)
Center/End/<second point>: (point)
End point: (point)

Options:
 A = included angle D = starting Direction L = length of chord
 C = Center point   E = End point           R = Radius
To continue previous line or arc, reply to first prompt with
RETURN

See also: Section 4.4 of Reference Manual.
```

The Help message lists all the options and single-keystroke option codes used by the ARC command when ARC is selected. It also states the prompt combinations available and gives an example of the easiest arc, the 3-point.

In any prompt, the information offered in angle brackets is the default. This is the option the command will automatically select unless a new one is entered. In the case of the ARC command, it expects the first entry to be a start point.

In the first two or three weeks of classes, students often press the keyboard space bar before entering any command. If you do this immediately after signing on, the system will enter the Help function. Also, when trying to pick the AutoCAD prompt on the top of the side menu, you may pick HELP by mistake. In any case, you may find yourself in the Help files without knowingly asking for them. This can be disconcerting because the screen toggles from blue to black as it flips from graphics to alphanumeric format.

To get out of the Help files, press either the cancel button on the pointing device and then F1, or Ctrl-C and then F1, and the screen will revert to the Graphics mode.

When trying new commands, if you use the Help files as a guide, you should have no problem entering the appropriate responses to the system command option prompts.

Help files are also useful once you have learned AutoCAD; when you switch to a system using another release version, the command structure may differ from that to which you are accustomed.

SNAP and GRID

The SNAP command sets a spacing for your point entries. The GRID command places dots on the screen. The Snap (F9) and Grid (F7) functions act as toggle keys but are modified through the command system. Type GRID or SNAP, then type the desired spacing length. The grid aspect ratio (*X* versus *Y*) will be 1:1 unless changed with the Aspect option.

As we have seen, the SNAP command allows for the positioning of points on the screen at preset regular integers. It also allows a rotated or isometric drawing to be entered.

```
Command:SNAP
On/Off/value/Aspect/Rotate/Style:R
Base point <0' - 0.00",0'-0.00">:↵ (return to accept the default)
Rotation Angle <0.00>:45 (will rotate at 45 degrees)
```

Where:
On = the snap is activated or on

Off = the snap is deactivated or turned off

value = the spacing of the snap entered by number

Aspect = the option of changing the X value in relation to the Y value

Rotate = the option of rotating the snap for drawing at a given angle

Style = the option of changing the style from Standard to Isometric, thus allowing isometric drawing

The grid size will follow the snap size unless changed by the GRID command.

The GRID command sets a visual aid for drawing.

```
Command:GRID
On/Off/value(x)/Aspect:A
Value of X for square grid:1
Aspect of Y for rectangular grid:2
```

Where:

The grid and snap values can be changed at any time during the creation of a drawing.

On = the grid has been activated or turned on

Off = the grid has been deactivated or turned off

value = the spacing between grid dots

Aspect = the option of changing the relative X and Y values.

DISPLAY

The Display menu offers commands that will change the display of the model relative to the screen. Commands from the Display menu will not change the coordinates or position of the model or database; it will only change the view.

At this stage, you should learn the following commands from the Display menu:

PAN	*moves the model across the screen without changing the zoom or magnification factor.*
REDRAW	*updates the view, and clears blips and erase marks.*
REGEN	*recomputes the file.*
ZOOM	*magnifies a section of the screen.*

Zoom

The following list describes the ZOOM command options. You can type ZOOM and the modifiers or use the side menu to pick the ZOOM command. You can also use the pull-down menu; however, the choices for the ZOOM command on the pull-down menu are limited.

```
Command:ZOOM
All/Center/Dynamic/Extents/Left/Previous/Vmax/Window/(X/VP):
```

Release 12 Notes

XP in scale is used for size relative to paper space.

Where:

A = All. Expands or shrinks the model to fit onto the screen relative to the limits or the largest area of the drawing.

C = Center. Centres the model on the screen.

D = Dynamic. Creates a dynamic display of the item for zooming.

E = Extents. Expands or shrinks the model to fit the screen relative to the largest area of the model.

P = Previous. Returns display to the previous zoom factor.

V = View maximum. Zooms the object as far out as possible without causing a Regen (not in Release 10).

W = Window. Describes, by two diagonal points, a rectangle around the area to view.

X = a percentage of the existing view size. For example, .8x will display an image at 80% of its current size, .5x will display an image at half the current size, and 2x will display an image at twice the current size.

PAN

As you can see below, the PAN command moves the model across the screen, while ZOOM magnifies the model within the screen. The concepts and terminology are similar to those of a camera. You use a zoom lens to increase or decrease the size of an object to be photographed, and you use the lens in a sweeping motion to pan the viewing area.

To view an area not currently in view while maintaining the same magnification factor, use PAN to translate the data across the screen. Since PAN does not often require a screen regeneration, a lot of time will be saved.

Past a certain point, in either Pan or Zoom, a screen regeneration is required. This can take quite a lot of time depending on the amount of information in the database. The following commands will suffice to get started:

- **ZOOM Window** will let you select a portion of the current view.
- **ZOOM All** will expand the model to either the set limits or the furthest object.
- **ZOOM .5x** will display the model at half its current size.
- **PAN** will move the model across the screen without changing the magnification factor.

Release 12 Notes

Window is automatically loaded with the ZOOM command.

```
Command:ZOOM
All/Center/Dynamic/Extents/Left/Previous/Vmax/Window:W
```

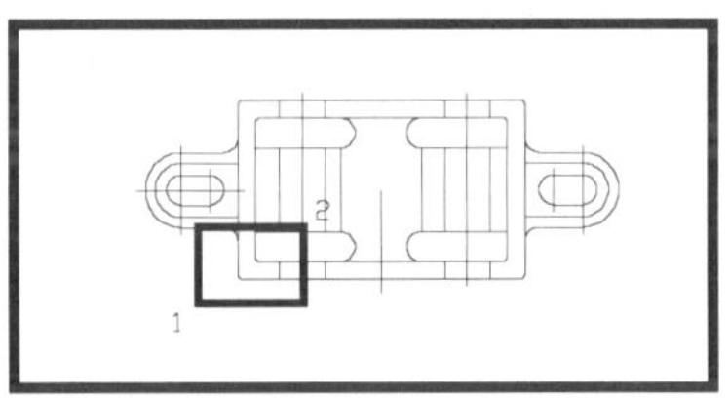

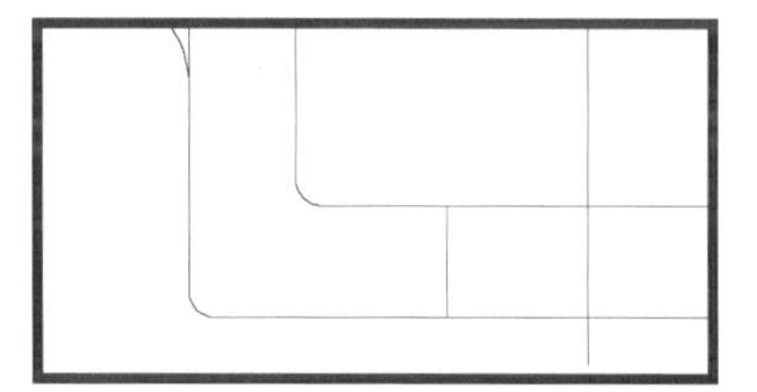

Figure 2-1. ZOOM with Window

```
Command:ZOOM
All/Center/Dynamic/Extents/Left/Previous/Vmax/Window:A
```

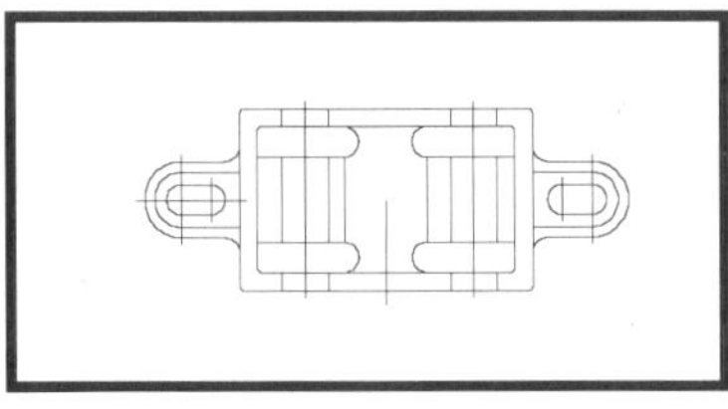
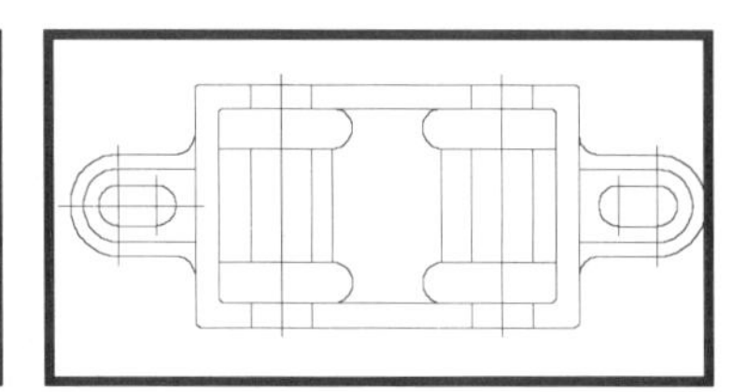

Figure 2-2. ZOOM All

```
Command:ZOOM
All/Center/Dynamic/Extents/Left/Previous/Vmax/Window:.5X
```

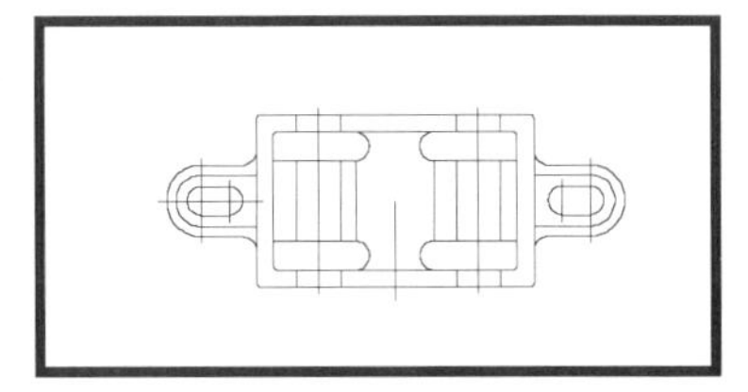
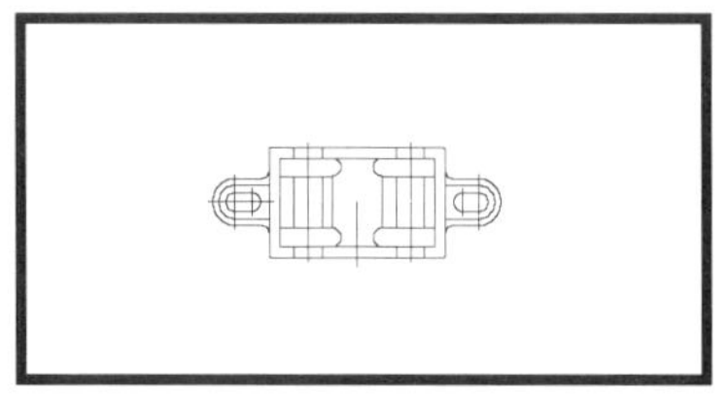

Figure 2-3. ZOOM at half the current size

```
Command:PAN
First point: (pick 1)
Other point: (pick 2)
```

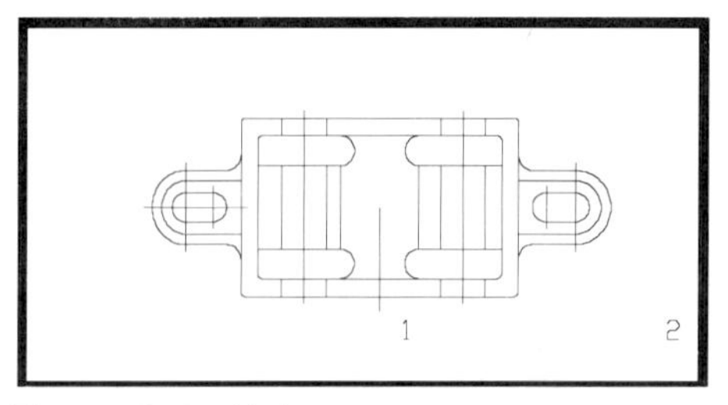

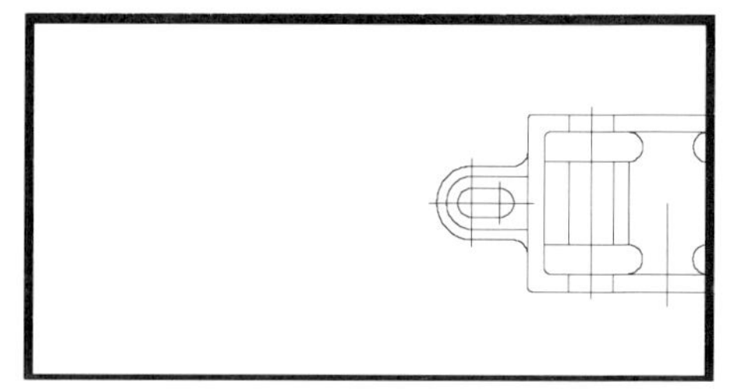

Figure 2-4. Using PAN

Once you are comfortable with these options, experiment with the others.

REGEN AND REDRAW

While the data is always available, to save space in RAM, it is not always completely generated. Thus, sometimes ZOOM or PAN results in a screen regeneration.

The REDRAW command cleans up the display and redraws information that may be absent due to erasing or changing the position of objects. It simply refreshes the screen from the available generated data. While you are creating a model, the screen will fill up with a series of small figures, called blips, which look like tiny crosses. These indicate points that have been digitized or picked on the screen. To clean up the screen, use the REDRAW command, or, if the grid is properly set, press F7 twice (Grid on, Grid off), and this will clean up the screen as well.

The REGEN command regenerates all of the design data and will therefore take much longer than a Redraw. This command is most often used in the introductory design stage to update arc and circle displays to make the objects look more rounded. When an arc or circle is displayed with a ZOOM Window command, it may appear as an octagon, or at least as a series of connected straight-line segments rather than rounded. To improve the image of the circle, use Regen. This will update the display of an arc or circle relative to the current magnification factor and display a much superior image.

In Figure 2-5, the blips have been removed by entering the command REDRAW, or, if the grid is visible, by pressing F7 twice.

BEFORE AFTER

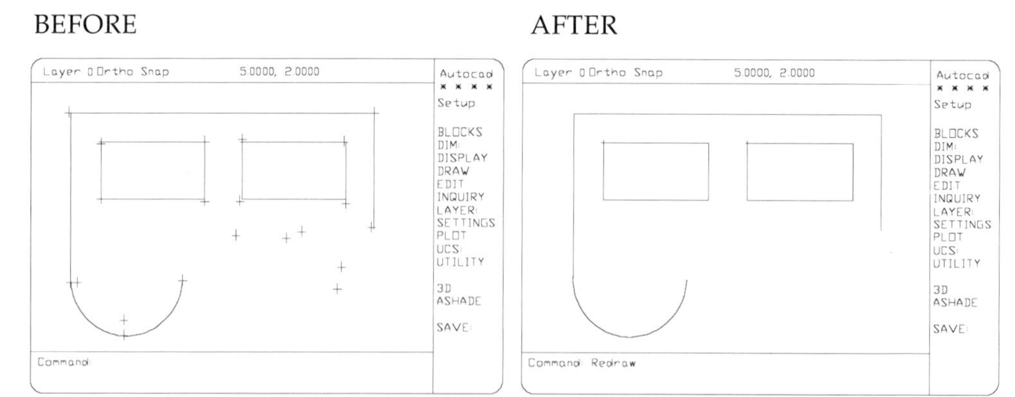

Figure 2-5. Using F7 twice to perform a redraw

POINT ENTRY REVIEW

In most CAD systems, there are three basic ways to enter points:

- Picking a point on the screen
- Coordinate entry
- Entity selection

Picking
When you pick or digitize a point on the screen, the object will be placed at the exact point you indicate. The SNAP command can be used to place a point within a preset integer margin of accuracy. The GRID and ORTHO commands also help improve the accuracy of point entry.

Coordinate Entry
Absolute, relative, or incremental, and polar coordinates can be entered in any order.

Object Selection
The Object Snap (Osnap) mode allows exact points on already existing objects to be selected with absolute accuracy regardless of grid and snap settings.

OSNAP: OBJECT SNAP

While creating a design, it may be necessary to adjust the snap many times to allow access to points with greater accuracy. When creating irregular geometry or geometry with many arcs and circles, this can become tedious; you would be continually changing the Snap to join objects and create circles at particular start and centre points. Osnap is extremely useful in these circumstances because it allows you to access existing objects in order to create new objects.

An Osnap can be seen as the object qualifier in a command string. For example, place the line from the centre of this circle tangent to a given line. Break that line from the intersection of the two objects; copy that list of objects from the endpoint of the first item to the midpoint of the second.

If you use guesswork to position and connect objects, a ZOOM Window may be required to check the accuracy of the drawing.

For many reasons, the lines, arcs, circles, etc. you enter must be absolutely accurate. Using OSNAP will help you enter the geometry properly the first time and save hours of editing later.

Example: *Centre and Endpoint*

CEN — *identifies the centre of an arc or circle.*

Only items with a defined radius can have a centre point.

END — *identifies the closest endpoint.*

All lines are made up of two endpoints. Circles have one endpoint, and arcs have two.

```
Command:LINE
start point:END (pick 1)
second point:CEN (pick 2)
```

In Figure 2-6, the line drawn starts at the closest end of the first object selected to the centre of the second object selected.

Figure 2-6. Picking objects with Object Snaps

When picking arcs and circles, pick the object itself, not the spot where you think the centre might be; the system will calculate that for you.

Example: *Midpoint and Perpendicular*

MID *identifies the midpoint of a selected item.*

This option is for objects that have no defined radii, such as lines and plines.

PER *forms a perpendicular to an identified object.*

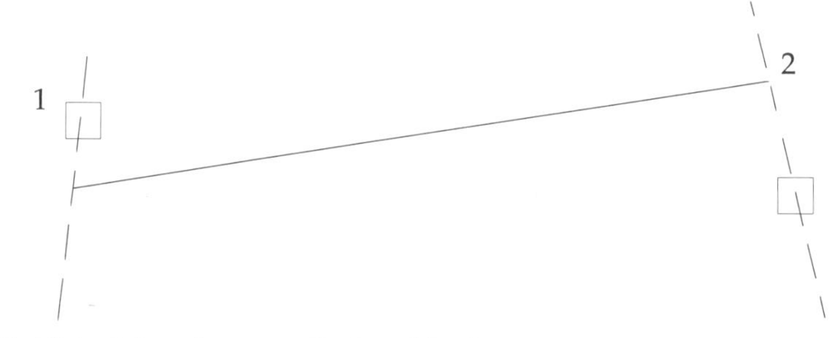

Figure 2-7. Midpoint and perpendicular object snaps

```
Command:LINE
from point:MID (pick 1)
to point:PER (pick 2)
```

In Figure 2-7, the first pick indicates the midpoint of the object, in this case, a line; the second pick indicates a perpendicular to the other line so that the second point of the line will be at 90 degrees to the second the object identified.

Example *Tangent*

TAN *creates a tangent to the identified object from the last object.*

This creates a line, arc, or circle tangent to a circle or arc.

Figure 2-8. Tangent object snap

```
Command:LINE
from point:TAN (pick 1)
to point:TAN (pick 2)
```

The system will calculate the tangent; all you do is indicate on which side of the object the tangent should be placed.

Using Osnap in Editing

Osnap is particularly useful in editing because objects can be edited very precisely. Osnaps can define the exact points required any time a point entry is prompted.

INT *identifies the intersection of two items.*

This option is used to define the intersection of any two objects: arcs, lines, circles, etc. The objects must be identified in the area of the intersection, preferably where the objects intersect.

```
Command:BREAK
Select Object: (pick 1)
Enter second point (or F for first point):F
Enter first point:INT (pick 2)
Enter second point:INT (pick 3)
```

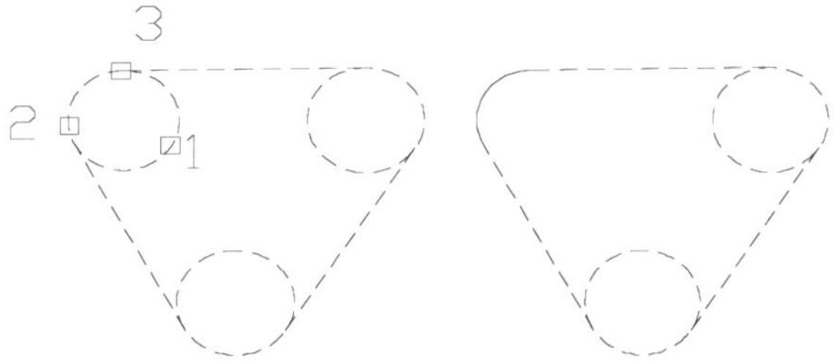

Figure 2-9. BREAK using object snaps

In Figure 2-9, the first pick indicates a particular object (the arc) and should be placed where the system cannot mistake it for any other object.

The second pick indicates the first point at which the item will be broken.

The third, measured counter-clockwise around the arc from pick 2, is the final break point.

Once you have mastered these Osnaps, try some others.

OBJECT SNAP MODE

When a particular Osnap option is selected outside of a command, the system understands that that Osnap option will apply to every subsequent object selected.

```
Command:OSNAP
Object snap modes:END
```

This informs the system that you want to pick up only endpoints.

While in the Object Snap mode, the cursor will display a "target" box in the middle of the cross-hairs.

Cursor symbol with Osnap off | Cursor symbol with Osnap on

Figure 2-10. The cursor showing Osnap

Release 12 Notes

Osnaps are located under the Assist menu in Release 12.

Osnap is found under [****] on the screen menu, the Tools pull-down menu in Release 10, or the Assist pull-down menu in Release 11. It could also be one of the buttons on the pointing device.

Always use Osnap for precision accuracy. Use APERTURE to change the size of the box.

TYPING VS. DIGITIZING

Commands may be typed in rather than picked from menus; but they must be spelled correctly. Any on-screen commands followed by a colon can be typed in.

Menus, however, cannot be accessed by typing in the menu titles: note that menu selections are not followed by colons. If you type Edit by mistake, the screen display will change to alphanumeric format because you have entered Edlin, the DOS editor. Just press Enter to return to the graphics screen.

Osnaps are indicated with the first three letters of an option. This means that, to access an Osnap, you can type, for example, END or CEN instead of locating and picking the option on the pull-down menu. Sometimes, depending on how the system is set up, an E for endpoint or a C for Center will also work.

Speeding Up Your Entries

The space bar on the keyboard and the Enter key on the pointing device, when used with a Command: prompt, will retrieve the last command entered. Effective use of this technique can greatly enhance the speed of entering lines, etc.

ERASE

The ERASE command will delete objects from a file. There are several options to help you choose items.

```
Command:ERASE
Select Objects:
```
(use either Window, Crossing, or individual items)

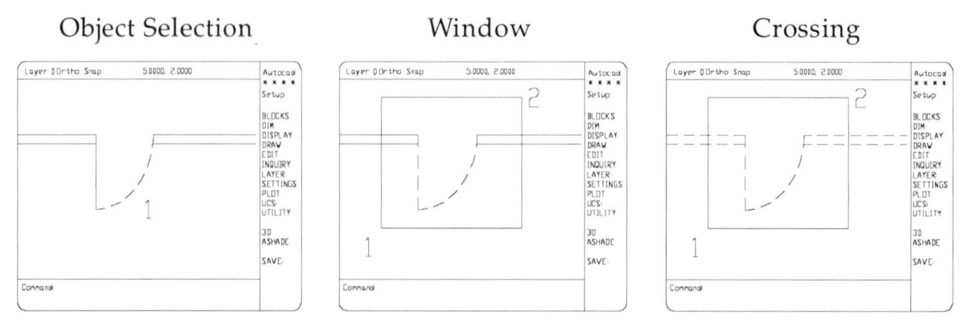

Figure 2-11. Object selection with ERASE.

In the first illustration of Figure 2-11, the user has indicated only the door swing; therefore, this is the only object to be erased. In the second, all objects totally contained in the Window illustrated by the two picks will be erased. In the third, all objects that are either entirely or partially enclosed in the crossing rectangle will be erased. Press Enter to delete the objects.

Other options are Last, which will identify the last object entered, and Remove, which will be explained in detail later.

If you have just erased an object or group of objects and then realized they should not have been erased, you can use the OOPS command to retrieve the erased items as long as you have not initiated another command immediately after using ERASE.

Command:**ERASE**

Select Objects: *(pick 1, 2)*

Select Objects:↵

Command:**OOPS** *(all erased objects will reappear)*

EXITING

While working with AutoCAD, the system is generating a temporary file on the drive that you are accessing. To verify this, use a DOS directory list command to view the filename. (Depending on your lab use, the system manager has set up the system so that one, none, or many of these DOS commands will work.)

Command:**DIR A**: *(a: indicates the floppy disk in Drive A.)*

or

Command:**SH**

Dos Command:**DIR A**:

or

Command:**SHELL**

Dos Command:**DIR A**:

The screen will display a list of files contained on the floppy disk in Drive A; the AutoCAD temporary file filename will appear similar to the following:

```
AC$EF     .$A        0      10-10-92   12:34.00
```

Where:
AC$EF = the name of the temporary file

.$A = the extension of the temporary file

0 = none of the space is yet officially recorded

10-10-92 = the date

12:34.00 = the time

If you use END to exit and save a new file, the system will convert this temporary file into a drawing file and exit from AutoCAD. The file will be saved, and the floppy disk, if you are using one, will have enough storage space to hold the file of the model.

If you use QUIT, the drawing will not be recorded, the temporary file will be erased, and you will successfully exit from AutoCAD.

If you use SAVE to save a new file, an entirely new file will be written onto the disk. If you are using the hard drive, there should be ample room for files. If you are using a floppy disk, there may be problems with the floppy not having enough remaining storage space. The temporary file is taking up room on the disk as well. If there is plenty of storage space on the disk, use SAVE; if not, use END. When saving a new file, SAVE will create a file that takes up less room than a file created by the END command, but SAVE creates an entirely new file, whereas END simply makes the .$A file permanent.

SAVE *creates new file or updates existing file.*

END *creates new file or updates existing file and exits AutoCAD*

QUIT *exits AutoCAD without saving.*

When working in an environment where the computer is accessible to others, there is always the possibility that someone, for whatever reason, will quit your file if you leave it unattended. It is also possible that a severe storm or power surge could cut off the electricity temporarily, thereby erasing your on-screen data. If you perform a SAVE every half-hour or hour, this reduces the amount of work accidentally lost.

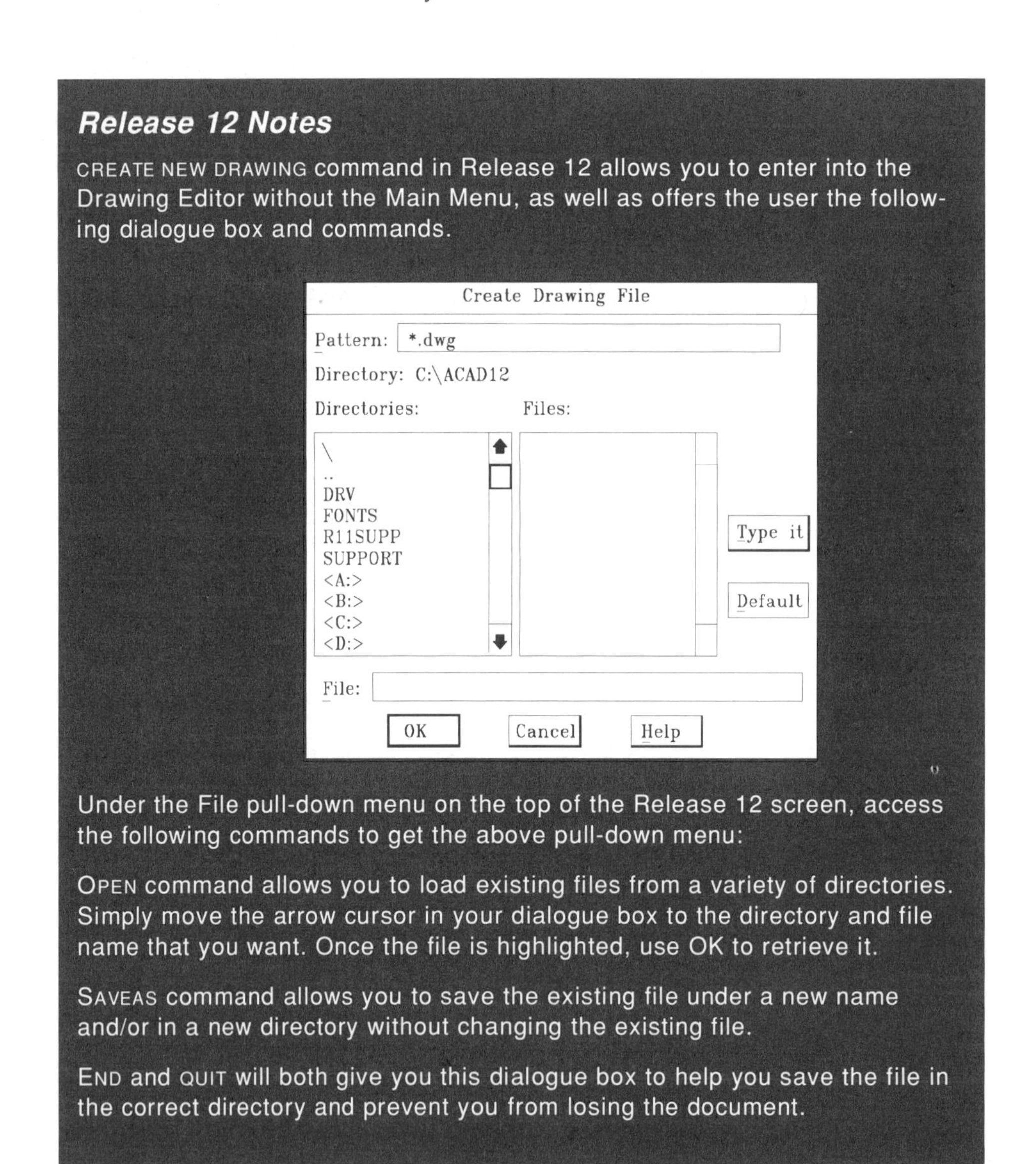

Release 12 Notes

CREATE NEW DRAWING command in Release 12 allows you to enter into the Drawing Editor without the Main Menu, as well as offers the user the following dialogue box and commands.

Under the File pull-down menu on the top of the Release 12 screen, access the following commands to get the above pull-down menu:

OPEN command allows you to load existing files from a variety of directories. Simply move the arrow cursor in your dialogue box to the directory and file name that you want. Once the file is highlighted, use OK to retrieve it.

SAVEAS command allows you to save the existing file under a new name and/or in a new directory without changing the existing file.

END and QUIT will both give you this dialogue box to help you save the file in the correct directory and prevent you from losing the document.

Exercise A2

For this exercise, set up a file as follows:

```
LIMITS -5,-5
       70,55
SNAP   1
GRID   5
ZOOM   All
```

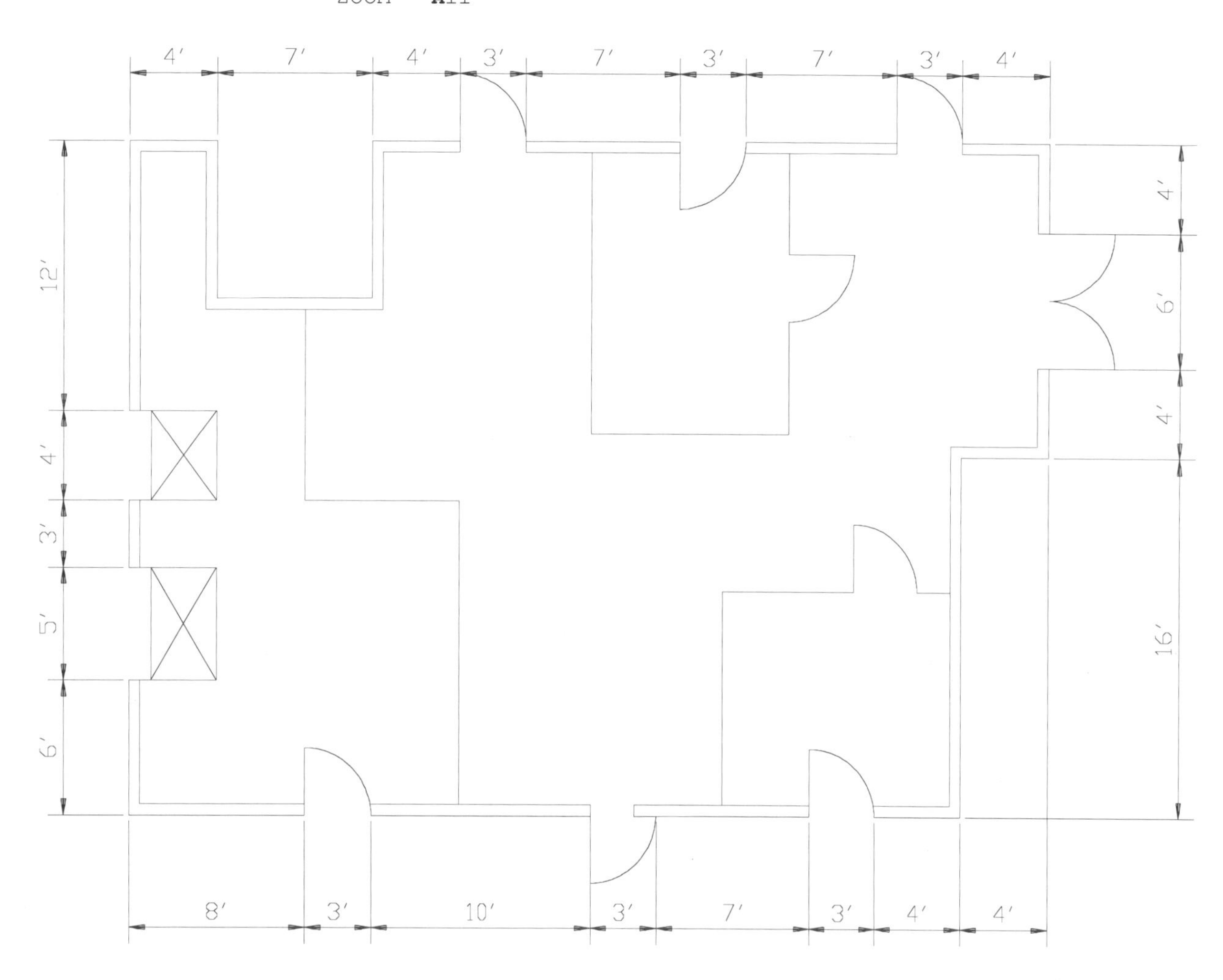

Use LINE for the outline of the building. Once the outside walls are complete, change the Snap to .5 and enter the interior walls at a width of 6 inches or .5 units. Use the space bar to speed up your entries. You will find it is quicker to enter the walls and leave spaces for the door openings than to enter the walls and later break them.

Use ARC Start, End, Radius for the doors. Remember that all arcs are measured counter-clockwise.

Use ZOOM to get a good look at what are doing. Then pan the drawing lines to complete an adjacent section.

Do not dimension the layout. Work on M2 if you finish early.

MECHANICAL

Exercise M2

Set up a file as follows:

```
LIMITS -3,-3
       12,9
SNAP    .25
GRID    1
ZOOM    All
```

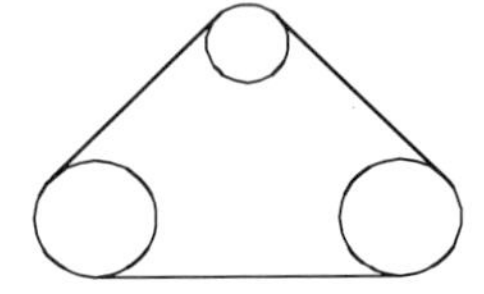

Draw the circles.
Draw the lines using TAN
Break the circles using INT

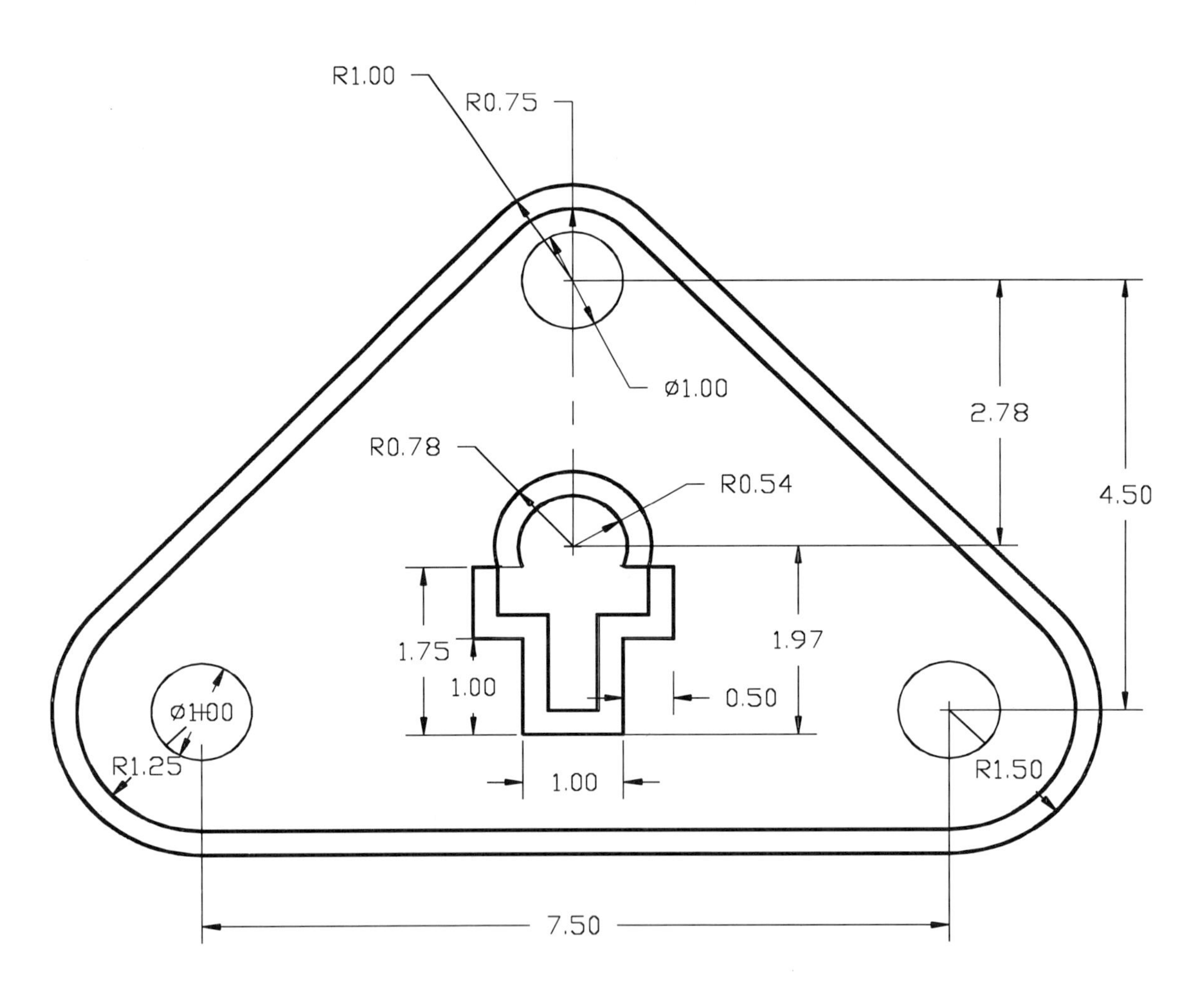

Use Osnap END (endpoint) for the arcs in the centre. See the notes on INT (intersection) to break the circles (page 33).

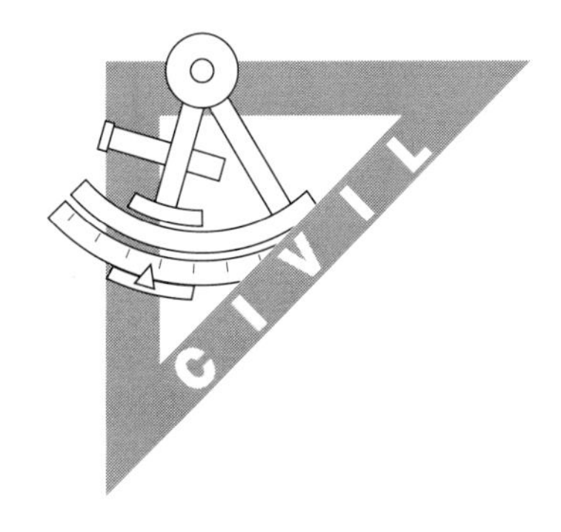

Exercise C2

Set up a file as follows:

```
LIMITS  -5,-5
        60,40
SNAP    1
GRID    5
ZOOM    All
```

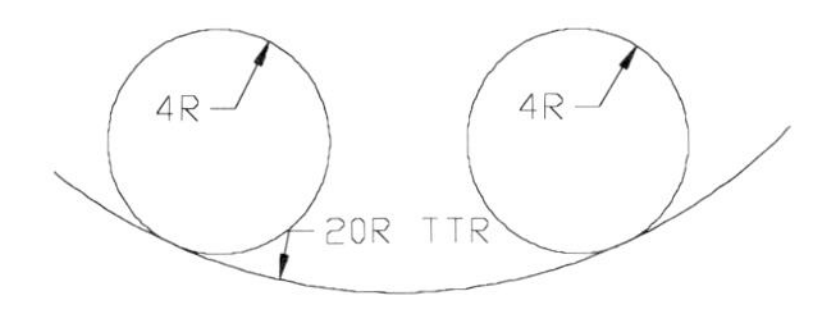

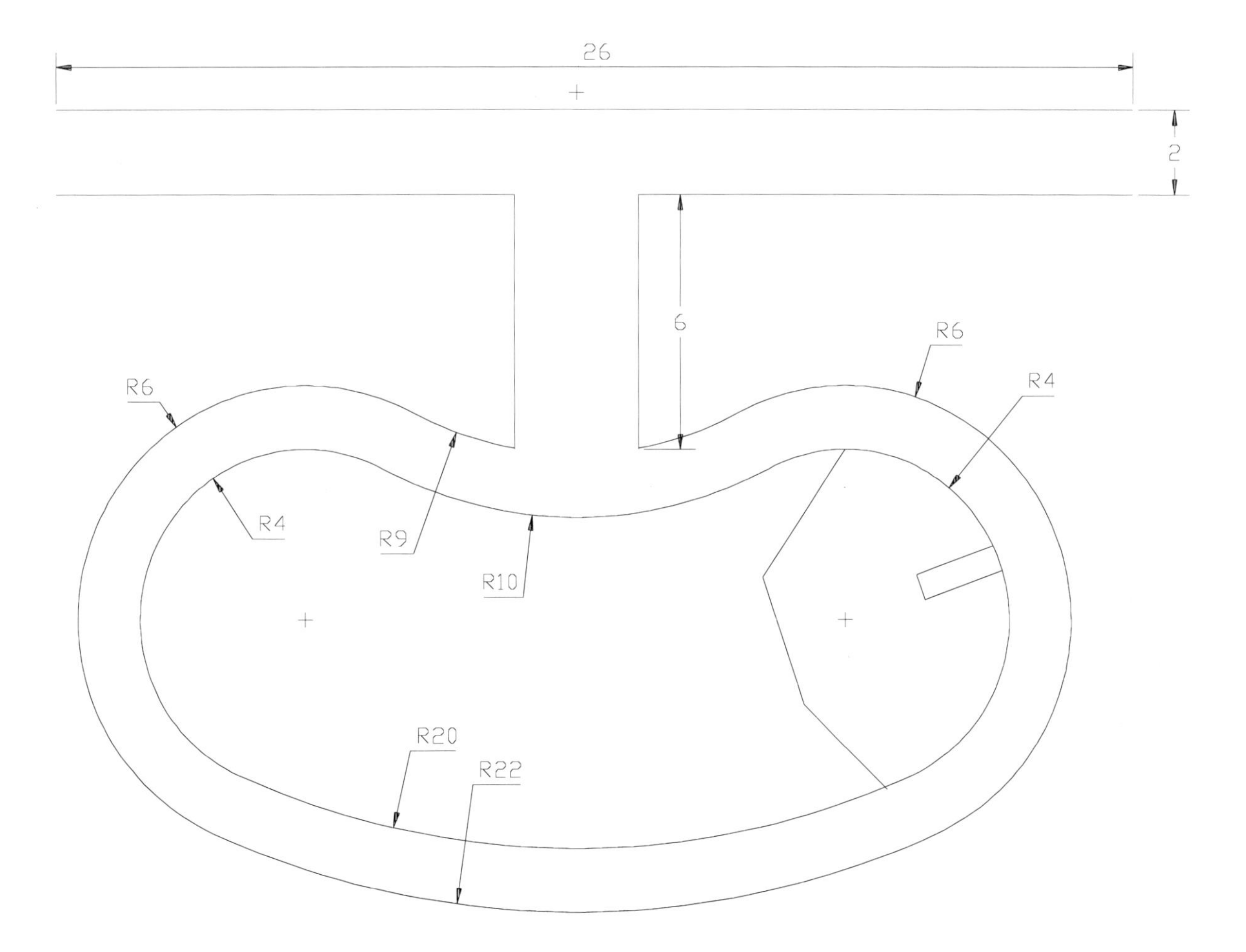

Use Osnap to enter objects correctly in this swimming pool design.

Place two circles at 4R then two circles at 6R. You will need CIRCLE Tangent, Tangent, Radius (TTR) to connect them, INT for the Break sections, and Near to place the diving board.

Use ZOOM to get a good look at what you are doing.

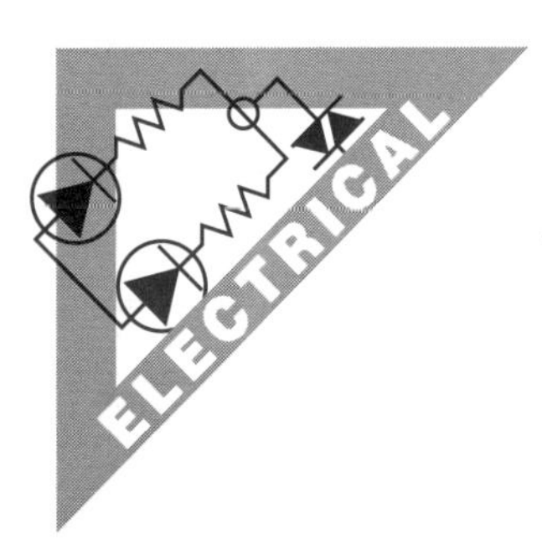

Exercise E2

For this exercise, set up a file as follows:

```
LIMITS   -5,-5
         45,30
SNAP     1
GRID     5
ZOOM     All
```

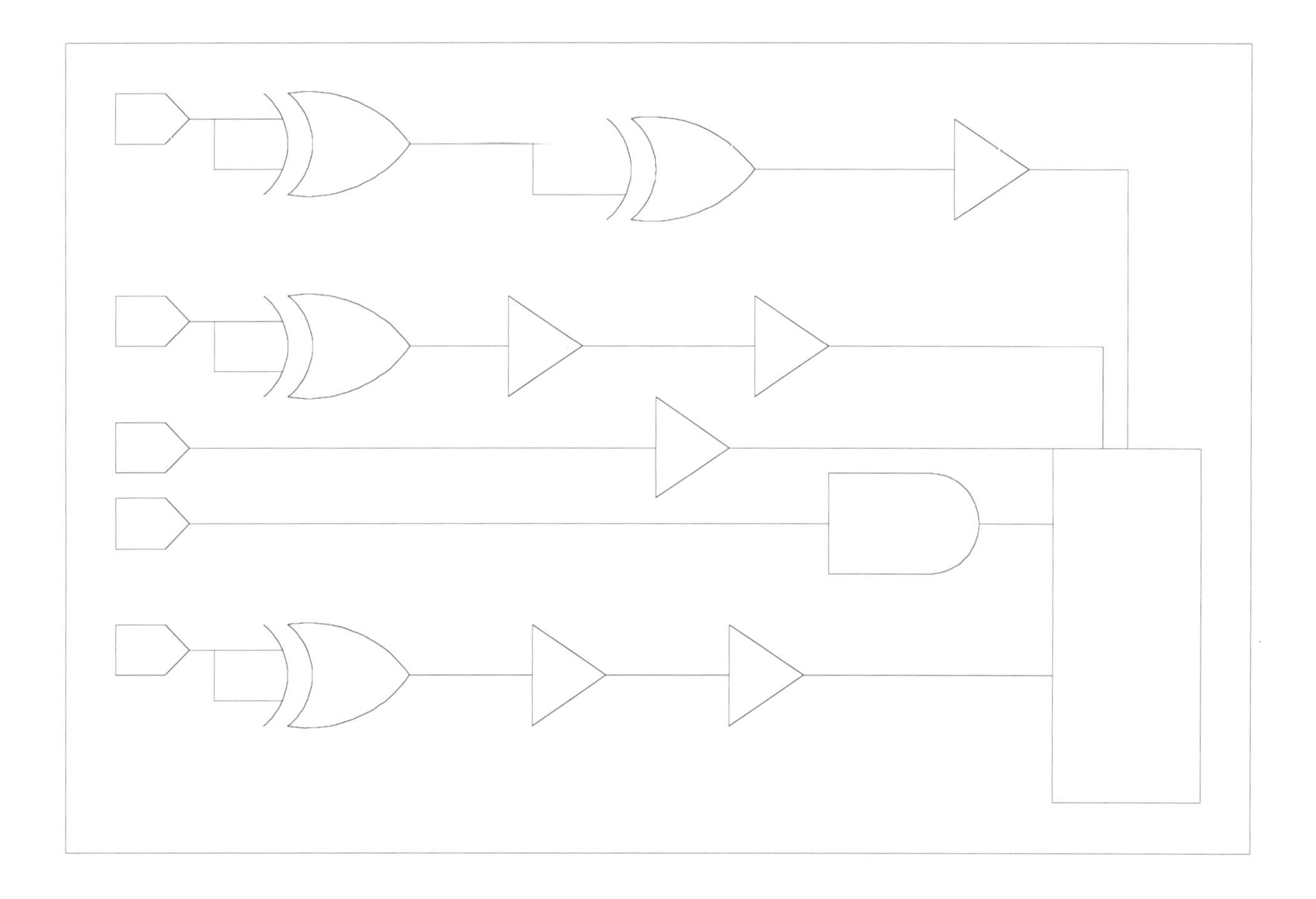

Use LINE for the outline of the schematic. Then change the Snap to .5 and enter the lines. Use the space bar to speed up the entries. Place the arcs overlapping the lines and use BREAK to create a good corner.

Use ZOOM to get a good look at what you are doing; then pan the drawing over to complete an adjacent section.

Do not dimension the layout. Work on M2 if you finish early.

Challenger 2

This is an excellent Osnap exercise.

Use LINE, ARC, CIRCLE, FILLET, OFFSET (Chapter 4), and BREAK to create this model. The origin should be the centre of the small circle.

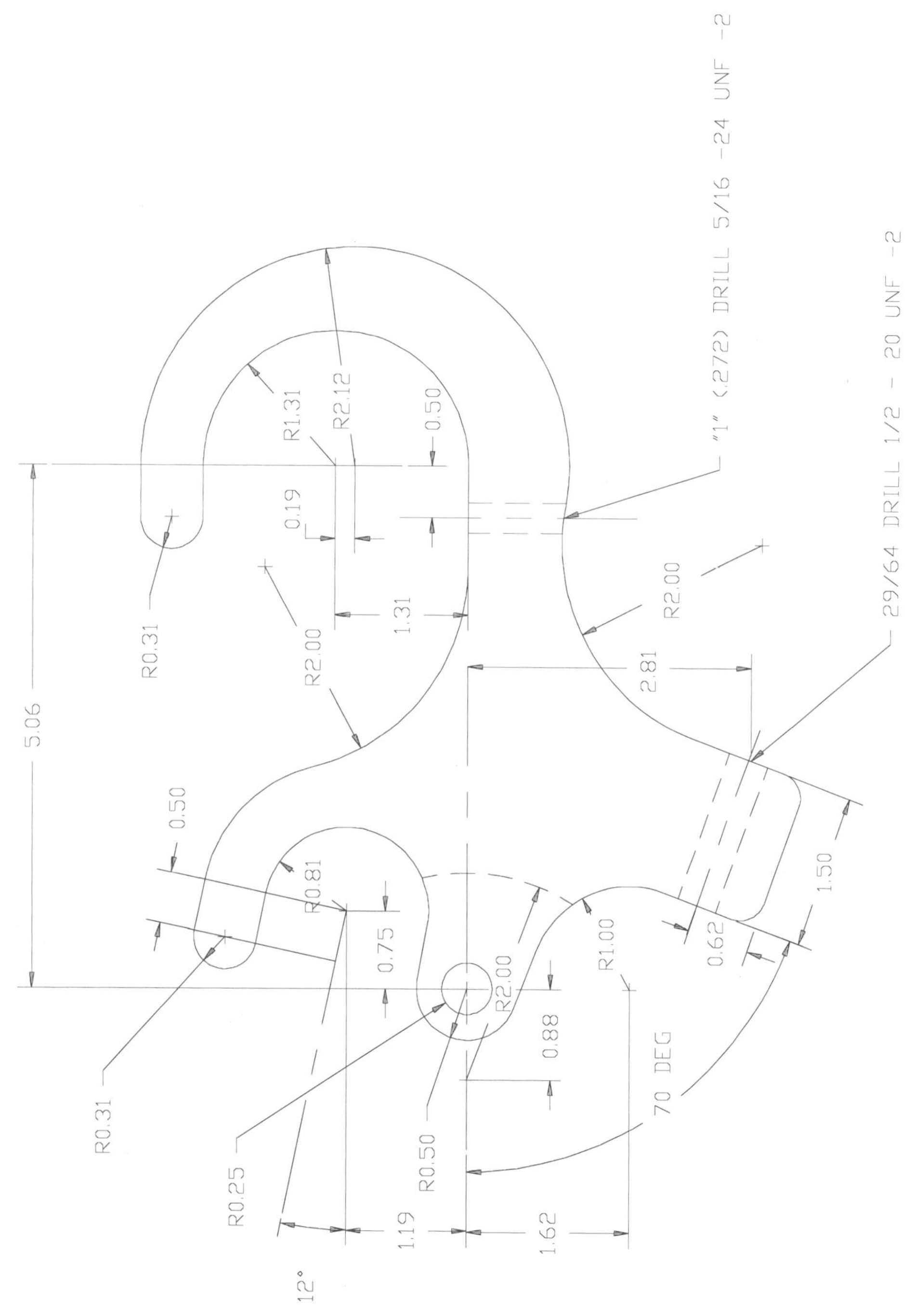

UNITS AND ENTITY COMMANDS WITH WIDTH

Upon completion of this chapter, the student should be able to:

1. Create a TRACE
2. Create a polyline (pline) with acceptable corners and widths
3. Edit a pline using PEDIT to change the width and curve factors
4. Create a SOLID
5. Create a DONUT with a specific width
6. Change the drawing units

TRACE

The TRACE command was introduced into AutoCAD in the earlier releases — Releases 1 and 2 — to make thick lines for borders, logos, and objects.

Traces are drawn in the same way as lines, from point to point; the difference is that a width must be specified, and the corners will be bevelled or mitred. The TRACE command prompt is similar to that of LINE, with a From point: and a To point: prompt. The first prompt is for the trace width.

```
Command:TRACE
Trace width <0'-0.05">:.1
From Point:5,.5
To Point:11,.5
```

The trace line segment will show up one pick behind because it is calculating the mitre to the next edge. If you want to keep this mitre, draw in an extra segment to have the mitre calculated, then erase it as in the following examples.

```
Command:TRACE
Trace width<0.5>:.2
From point: (pick 1)
To point: (pick 2)
To point: (pick 3)
To point: (pick 4)
To point: (pick 5)
To point: (pick 6) ↵
```

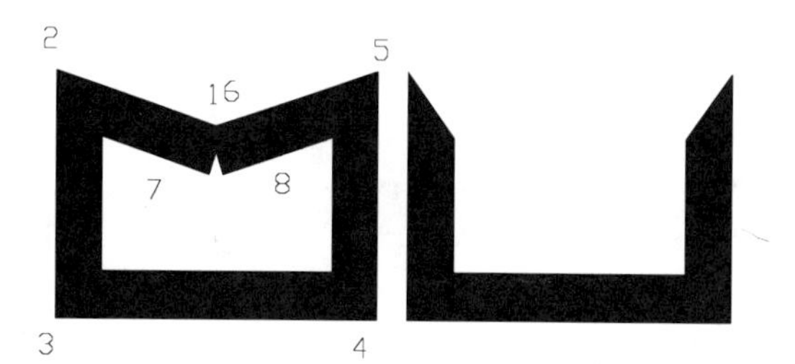


```
Command:ERASE
Select objects: (pick 7,8)
```

```
Command: TRACE
Trace width: .2
From point: (pick 1)
To point: (pick 2)
To point: (pick 3)
To point: (pick 4)
To point: ↵

Command: ERASE
select objects: (pick 5, 6)
```

The advantage of using TRACE is that it allows you to create a mitred or bevelled edge.

Each segment of the trace is a separate entity once it is placed, and thus the segments adjacent to the mitred edges can be erased to provide a final mitred edge.

The disadvantage of TRACE is that it cannot be edited. To create thick lines that can be edited, use PLINE.

PLINE or PolyLINE

Pline is a single-drawing entity that includes line and curve sections that may vary in thickness. The individual segments are connected at vertices; the direction, tangency, and line width are stored at each vertex. The PLINE command will create boxes as single entities as well as curved segments of varying thickness.

Figure 3-1. Polylines

Both of the objects of Figure 3-1 were created using PLINE. The arrow and the curve are one object only.

In addition to the capability of having thickened lines, PLINE offers Spline and Fit curve functions that can create contour lines on plot plans or surveys.

In an engineering environment, PLINE is also used to create splines and to fit curves through points for making polynomial surfaces. This is explained later in this chapter, under PEDIT.

The following describes the PLINE command.

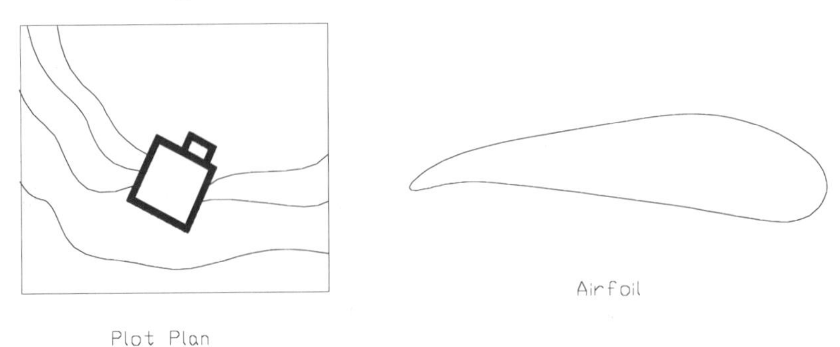

Figure 3-2. Polylines using PEDIT with Spline option

```
Command:PLINE
From point:
The current line-width is 0.1000
Arc/Close/Halfwidth/Length/Undo/Width/<Endpoint of line>:
```

Where:
Arc = a change from line entry to arc entry.

Close = a closed pline; the first point will be joined to the last entered point in the pline to make a closed object. More than two points are needed to have a closed pline.

Halfwidth = a specified halfwidth on either side of the pline vector.

Length = the length of the pline.

Undo = an undo of the last point entered.

Width = a specified width of the line or arc segments on either side of the pline vector.

The first PLINE command prompt is to enter a point at which the Pline will start.

```
Command:PLINE
From Point: (pick a point)
```

You *must* enter the first point, then you can choose one of the options (e.g., Width, Arc, etc.).

The next command default is to enter the second point, <Endpoint of line>. Therefore, if you pick a second point, this assumes a straight segment or a line. If you continue picking points, the object created will look like a series of lines, but it will be a pline and thus a single object that can be edited using PEDIT.

The Arc options are:

```
Command:PLINE
From point: (pick a point)
The current pline width is 0.1000
Arc/Close/Halfwidth/Length/Undo/Width/<Endpoint of line>:A
Angle/Center/Close/Direction/Halfwidth/Line/Radius/Second
pt/Undo/Width/<Endpoint of Arc>:
```

The command default is to create a two-point arc. (The options above are available on Release 11. There are fewer options available on Release 10.)

To change the width of a pline, enter the first point, then specify width by entering the letter W or picking Width from the side menu. The system will prompt you for both the beginning and end widths. If these are the same, press the Return key for the second entry.

```
Command:PLINE
From point:2,2
The current pline is 4.00 units
Arc/Close/Halfwidth/Length/Undo/Width/<Endpoint of Line>:W
Start width<4.00>:.25
End width<0.25>:↵
Arc/Close/Halfwidth/Length/Undo/Width/<Endpoint of Line>:6,2
```

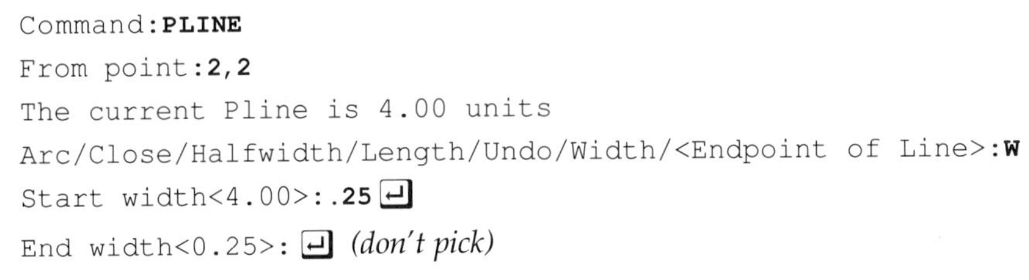

Figure 3-3. PLINE with constant width

You can continue drawing with this line at the current thickness or change it at any time.

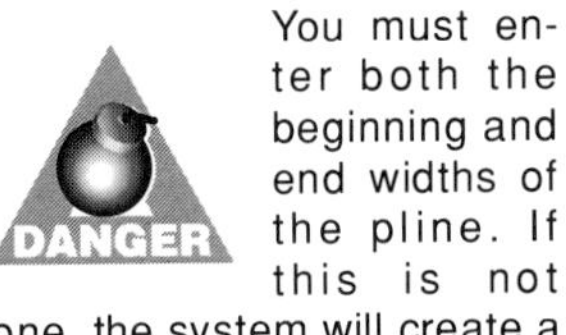

You must enter both the beginning and end widths of the pline. If this is not done, the system will create a triangle. When prompted for the second point, if you pick a point in space, the PLINE command assumes that the distance between the first and second points entered is the ending width.

To achieve a perfect corner on a box or rectangle, use the Close option. This will attach the first point to the last entered point and create a clean, bevelled corner.

```
Command:PLINE
From point:2,2
The current Pline is 4.00 units
Arc/Close/Halfwidth/Length/Undo/Width/<Endpoint of Line>:W
Start width<4.00>:.25 ↵
End width<0.25>: ↵ (don't pick)
```

Do not pick! If you pick, you will create an object similar to that of Figure 3-4.

```
Arc/Close/Halfwidth/Length/Undo/Width/<Endpoint ofLine>:6,2 ↵
```

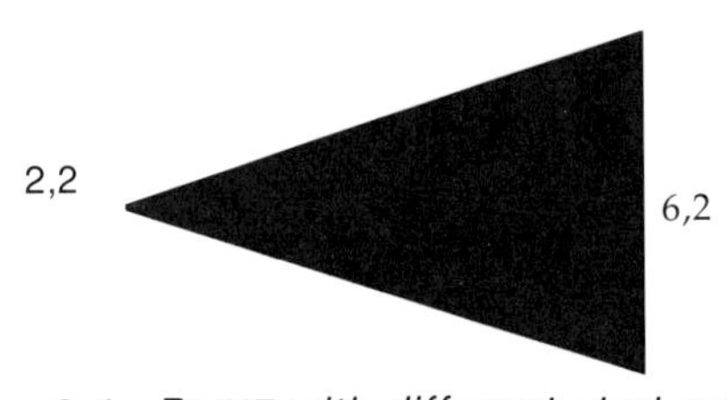

Figure 3-4. PLINE with different start and end width

The second pick was assumed to be the width of the endpoint of your pline, measured from the first entered point.

Using PLINE Effectively

There are a few tricks with PLINE that will make the entered plines perfect. First, let us look at creating good corners.

Remember, the points entered for a pline are considered to be vertices. This means the pline is to be calculated as a series of contiguous points or points entered with a specific sequence in mind.

When creating lines, you are creating pairs of points through which the lines will be entered.

The Close option of LINE creates a line from the last point entered to the first point entered.

```
Command:LINE
From point:0,0
To point:4,0
To point:4,3
To point:0,3
To point:Close
```

This command sequence creates four lines, one from 0,0 to 4,0, the second from 4,0 to 4,3, the third from 4,3 to 0,3, and the last from 0,3 to 0,0. If the same points are used to describe a pline with a width of 0.5 units, one object is created that is fit through the same points but has a width of 0.5 units. As the pline changes direction, the end of each pline is calculated relative to the points or vertices used to create it. If a thickened pline is created with just two points, the ends of the pline are calculated perpendicular to the pline vector. If three points are used to create a pline, the end of the pline that attaches to a segment going in another direction is calculated to create a sharp corner.

Figure 3-5. Creating plines with a constant width

As shown in Figure 3-5, the ends of the plines are perpendicular to the direction of the pline itself.

When entering plines, do not pick a point twice in the same spot; this will create a corner that has two perpendicular ends as shown in Figure 3-6. To get the corners to close properly, only one pick per corner is needed.

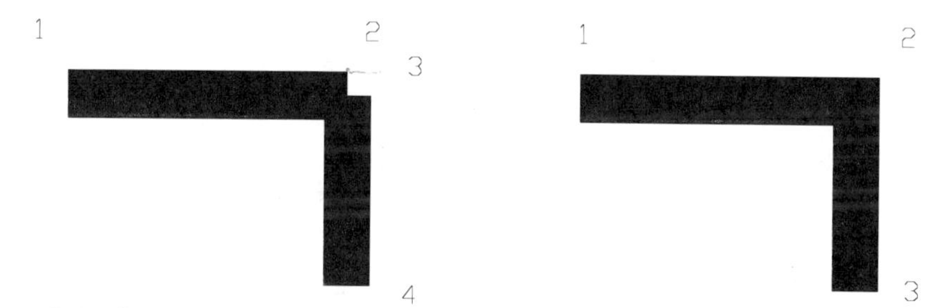

Figure 3-6. Creating plines with corners

If a drawing is becoming too dark or is taking a long time to regenerate after ZOOM commands, you may want to use the FILL command. This allows the lines to show the edges of your pline, but the pline will not be filled in.

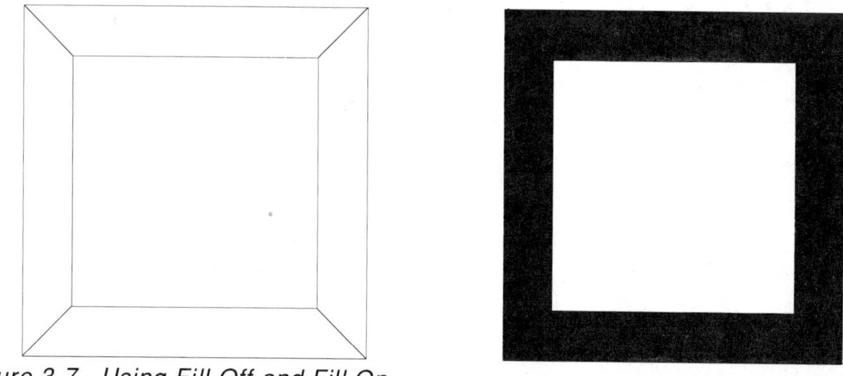

Figure 3-7. Using Fill Off and Fill On

Figure 3-7 demonstrates how the Fill option can change the appearance of a pline. On the left, the Fill is off; on the right, the Fill is on.

The PLINE command can create line and arc segments that become one object. Plines are used very effectively in conjunction with commands such as AREA (see Chapter 15), MEASURE, and DIVIDE.

If PLINE is used to describe a wall or road section, MEASURE can be used to mark off station points or services without regard to vertices.

When PLINE is used to create sidewalks, boundaries, or details that have line and arc segments, these plines can be divided into sidewalk sections, bricks, seating arrangements, etcetra, with the DIVIDE command.

PEDIT

One of the great advantages of PLINE is that, once the pline is entered, it can be modified using PEDIT (Polyline Edit).

In the introductory stages, this command sequence is used most often to change the width of a pline. In Figure 3-8, a border is edited from 0.5 units to 0.25 units.

New width for all segments: **.25**

The PEDIT command changes the width of all the segments of the identified pline.

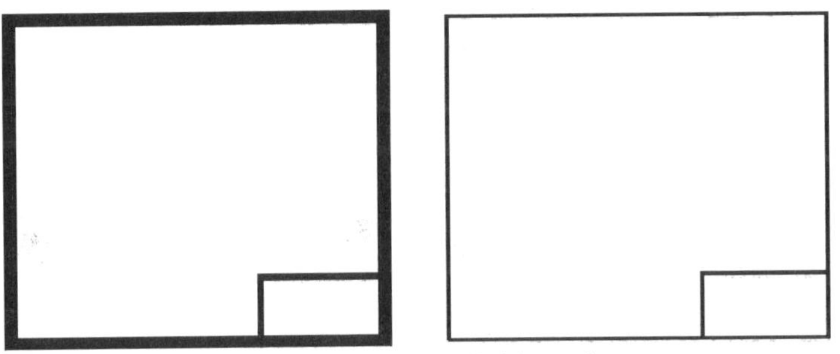

Figure 3-8. Using PEDIT with the Width option

> ***Release 12 Notes***
>
> PEDIT options include: Open, which opens a closed polyline; Fit, which replaces Fit Curve; and Type gen, which generates a continuous linetype.
>
> When Ltype gen is turned on, the linetype of the polyline is continuous, regardless of the placement of the vertices. When Ltype gen is turned off, the linetype is displayed with a dash at each vertex.

More segments can be added to the pline by using the Join option. This will add lines or arcs to a pline which can then be edited for width.

Below, the arc and the two lines identified by picks 2, 3, and 4 are added to the pline identified with the first pick by the command option Join.

```
Command:PEDIT
Select polyline: (pick 1)
Close/Join/Width/Edit vertex/Fit
curve/Spline curve/Decurve/Undo/
eXit<X>:J
Select object: (pick 2)
Select object: (pick 3)
Select object: (pick 4)
Select objects:↵
Close/Join/Width/Edit vertex/Fit
curve/Spline curve/Decurve/Undo/
eXit<X>:↵
```

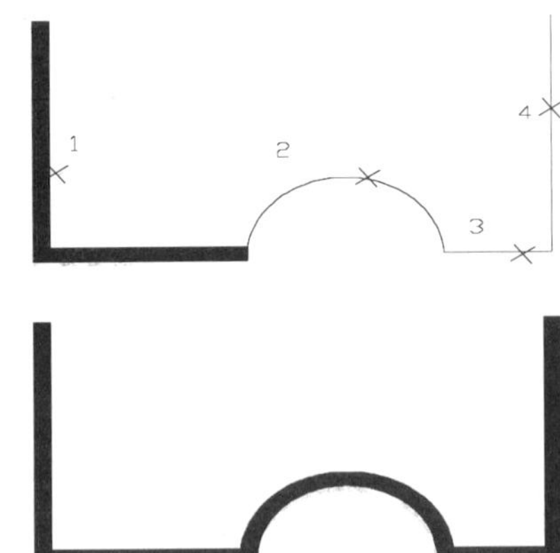

Finally, for those interested in designing airplanes, windsurf boards, or boat keels, or for those needing to create contour lines and other items for surveying, etc., a pline can be modified to become a spline or fit a curve through a series of points.

The Spline Curve option of PEDIT will make the pline according to a series of points. Make sure you use the Close option when entering the pline to get a continuous spline.

Release 12 Notes

New continuous polyline linetypes through PEDIT facilitate contour mapping and other Spline and Fit curve applications.

The Fit curve option of PEDIT will create continuous curves through a series of points.

The object of Figure 3-9 is an "airfoil" shape. The pline is closed and was drawn without a width.

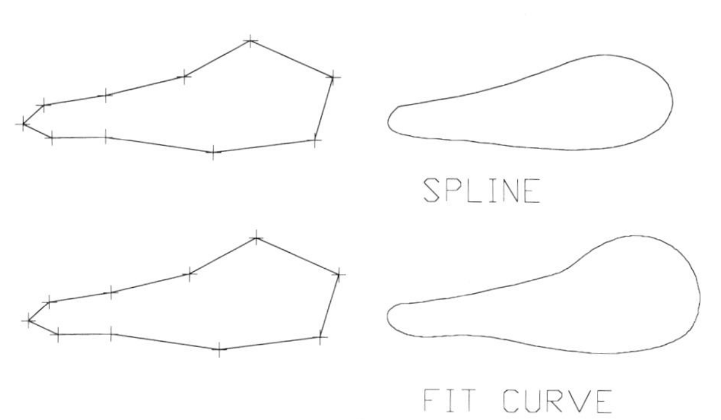

Figure 3-9. Using Spline and Fit curve

In the first example, the Spline option was used to create a smooth curve using the points as a guide. The curve has a continuous sweep through all of the points.

In the second example, the Fit curve option was used, and the resulting curve is much more "choppy" because Fit curve will fit the pline through each of the points in the pline.

The Spline option, on the other hand, uses the points as a guide but has a degree of continuity through each of the adjacent points.

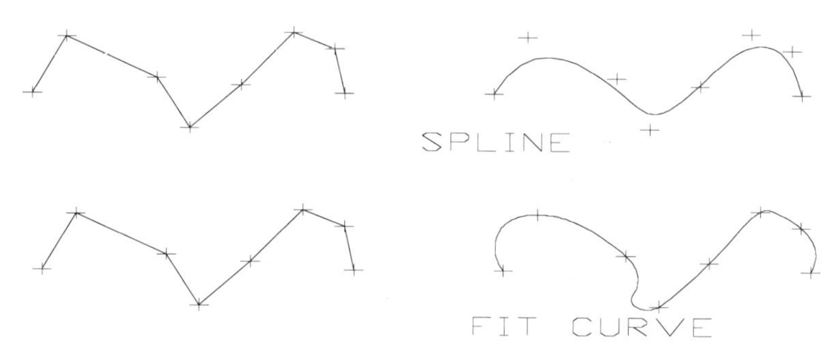

Figure 3-10. Fitting curves through points

In Figure 3-10, a simple pline with points illustrating the vertices further demonstrates the difference between the Spline and the Fit curve options.

The mathematical calculations used to create these curves are outside the limits of this chapter and are not really necessary for an introductory understanding of the two commands.

Further information on the PEDIT command is offered in the Surfacing chapters of this book, and there are 25 pages of very useful information in David Cohn's excellent reference book, *Complete AutoCAD*, also published by Addison-Wesley Publishers.

All the line segments of plines are defined by vertices, which can be edited for width and position. Although one could spend several labs examining the PLINE command in detail, the two pages of exercises on plines will show you how to use them more competently.

Release 12 Notes

When Ltype gen is turned on, the linetype of the polyline is continuous regardless of the placement of the vertices. When Ltype gen is turned off, the linetype is displayed with a dash at each vertex.

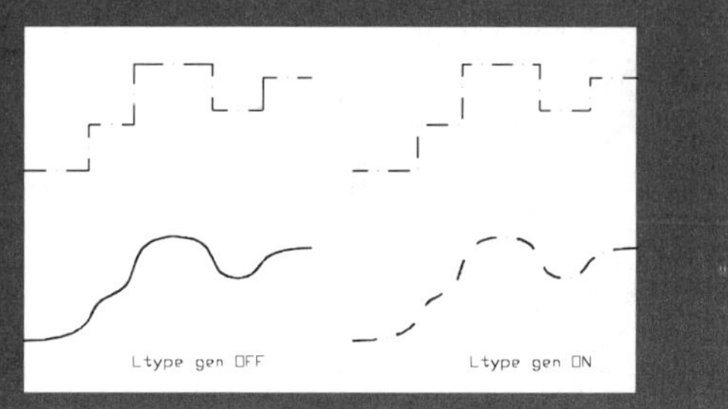

SOLID and DONUT

The SOLID command creates a polygon filled with the currently selected colour. The Fill ON option will fill in the solid with each screen regeneration, while the Fill OFF option will display only an outline for quicker redraws.

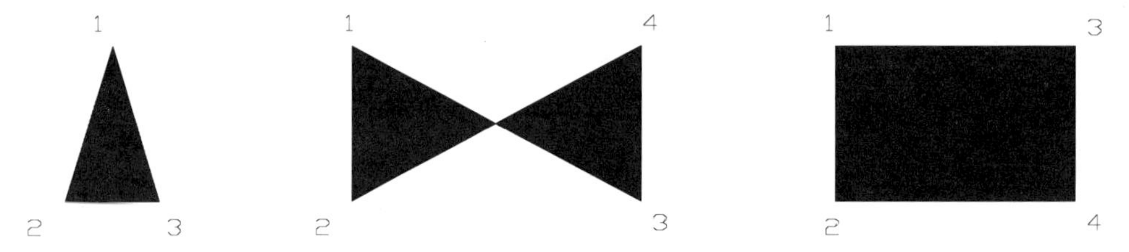

Figure 3-11. Using the SOLID command

The order in which points are entered is very important. Figure 3-11 provides some examples:

If you continue to digitize after the fourth entry, the system will continue to add to the original entity until you terminate with ↵.

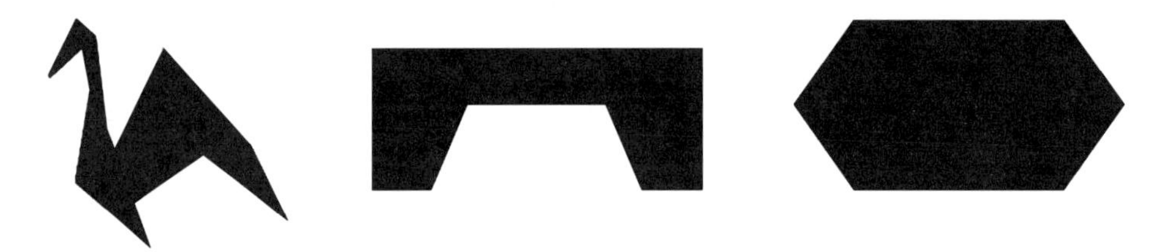

Figure 3-12. Solids with multiple points

The DONUT command is used to create a solid or thicker circle. The inside diameter is used to determine the hole of the donut. Use an inside diameter of zero to create a solid circle; use a larger diameter to create a ring. Once DONUT is active, a donut will be drawn every time you digitize until you press ↵.

The HATCH command can be useful when you are trying to fill an irregular shape. The problem with HATCH, however, is that every given space is filled with a series of vectors. This can take up a lot of room on the disk. Try creating an irregular shape with PLINE, and then change the width to fill in the given space.

UNITS

Now that you are familiar with signing on, creating objects, and using LIMITS, GRID, SNAP, and ZOOM commands, we will look at the various types of measurement units offered by AutoCAD.

The UNITS command is part of the Settings menu. As AutoCAD is considered to be an "open architecture" program, the units of measure can be changed to suit your purpose. The basic command prompt takes you through a series of prompts in order to select the method of measurement you need.

```
Command:UNITS
Report formats:
1. Scientific      1.55E+01
2. Decimal         15.50
3. Engineering     1-3.58"
4. Architectural   1'-3 1/2"
5. Fractional      15' 1/2"
```

With the exception of the engineering and architectural formats, these formats can be used with any basic unit of measurement. For example, decimal mode is perfect for metric units and may also be used for imperial units. The scientific, decimal, and fractional modes simply equate one drawing unit to one displayed unit. The engineering and architectural modes assume that one drawing unit equals one inch.

```
Enter choice, 1 to 5:
```

Once the type of unit you want to use is selected, you are then prompted for the precision. After selecting one of the first three options, you will be prompted as follows:

```
Number of digits to the right of the decimal point (0 to 8):
```

If you selected the architectural or fractional option, the following prompt will appear:

```
Denominator of smallest fraction to display
(1, 2, 4, 8, 16, 32, or 64):
```

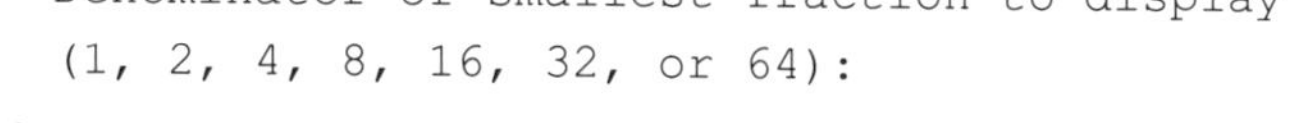

The number chosen here will only reflect the number that is displayed.

The value you want to use must be entered or press Enter to accept the default.

The UNITS command does not function like the SNAP command and, therefore, will not help you to enter data more precisely.

The following sections will deal with the special requirements of each area.

ARCHITECTURAL

When using architectural or imperial measurements, the most important thing to understand is that each numerical entry is accepted as an inch. Once architectural units is selected and numbers are being entered, the ' and " signs must be used to differentiate between feet (') and inches (").

```
Command:LINE
From point:2,3
To point:@4,0
```

The above command is drawing a 4-inch line, not a 4-foot line.

Also important is the understanding that, while the display uses the notation 4'-2", the dash (-) is not needed when entering, and both decimal and fractional entries are accepted.

```
Command:LINE
From point:3'4",0
To point:@1'6",0
```

If architectural units are used to create, for example, a residential layout, an accuracy of less than one inch is not needed, and, probably, not less than six inches. Therefore, setting the precision to 16 (one-sixteenth of an inch) will make it much more difficult to read the coordinates and will offer little advantage. When was the last time you saw a house built to one sixteenth of an inch?

All the angles will be measured in decimal degrees in a counter-clockwise direction. If you want to change this option, use the following:

```
Systems of angle measure:
1. Decimal degrees                       45.0000
2. Degrees/minutes/seconds               45deg0'0"
3. Grads                                 50.0000g
4. Radians                               0.7854r
5. Surveyor's units                      N45d0'0"E
Enter choice, 1 to 5:
```

Usually the default is picked for the angle measure. The next few options are mainly for surveyors, so just keep accepting the defaults until the Command: prompt is reached, then press F1 to toggle back to the graphics screen. Do not worry about the paper size until you are ready to plot.

MECHANICAL

Since decimals are recognized in the daily lives of most people, the default unit is the decimal unit.

When drawing with decimal units, these can represent either imperial or metric units. The actual plotted size is determined in the PLOT command.

The system accepts the units ultimately as inches, so there will be a need to scale the drawing to fit a paper or another output peripheral when that stage is reached. The SCALE command can be used to change the size of a model for drawing purposes or use the Scale option of the PLOT command. Examples of linear scales, etc. are found in Chapter 11.

SCIENTIFIC

In scientific notation, the E is the exponent and is shown with a plus sign. The quantity of 4.1325E+6 is read as 4132500.

This notation is used when the magnitude of the numbers is very large, such as in astronomy or physics, and reduces the need for a large number of trailing zeros.

ENGINEERING

Often, in engineering, there is a need to express feet and inches without fractions. With this option, you can do exactly that.

```
3'4 3/4" = 3' 4.75"
```

In fact, with engineering units, the inch symbol is not required. Therefore, you are able to place objects in inches and have good precision as well.

```
Command:LINE
From point:4'3.5,2'3.5
To point:@4.4,0
```

FRACTIONAL

With fractional units, the information is entered as a fraction with a slash, but a dash must be added with the slash.

```
Command:LINE
From point:1-1/2,2-3/4
To point:@3/4,0
```

Next, with all the above options, choose the required precision.

SURVEYING

There is a special method of expressing angles for surveying applications. The surveyor's "compass rose" is much the same as a ship's compass — divided into four parts with the top being North, the left being West, etc. Angles are expressed in 90-degree quadrants.

The quadrant between North and East, for example, starts at 0 degrees due East and progresses 90 degrees to due North. To express 25 decimal degrees using AutoCAD's default origin for angles, enter N25d0'0"E.

When entering this measurement, do not use spaces.

Measuring Angles

AutoCAD's default setting for angles is zero degrees at due East. You may change this zero-degree reference point to due North, West, or South. These are the only four positions offered by the UNITS command. If you want to orient the zero reference at an angle other than those specified, change the User Coordinate System (UCS) as explained in Chapter 27.

CLOCKWISE OR COUNTER-CLOCKWISE

These two angle rotations can be applied to all angles. The rotation always starts at the zero reference point.

UNTRANSLATED ANGLES

If the UNITS command is set to a non-decimal angular mode (radians, for example), an angle can be preceded by a <<< to enter a measurement counter-clockwise from three o'clock.

If an angle measurement direction or origin has been changed, enter < < before an angle measurement to have the angle measured counter-clockwise from three o'clock.

USING UNITS EFFECTIVELY

Remember, the UNITS command does not operate like the SNAP command. The status line will indicate the position relative to the units that were specified, but points will not be entered exactly at the position specified without setting the Snap.

The units can either be changed when beginning a model or when entering all or part of a model. If you have drawn, for example, a floor layout at 1 = 1 decimal units, you can switch to architectural units and then scale the entire model by 12. See Chapter 13 for plotting scales.

Release 12 Notes

This dynamic display dialogue box (DDUNITS) shows units, angles, and direction settings.

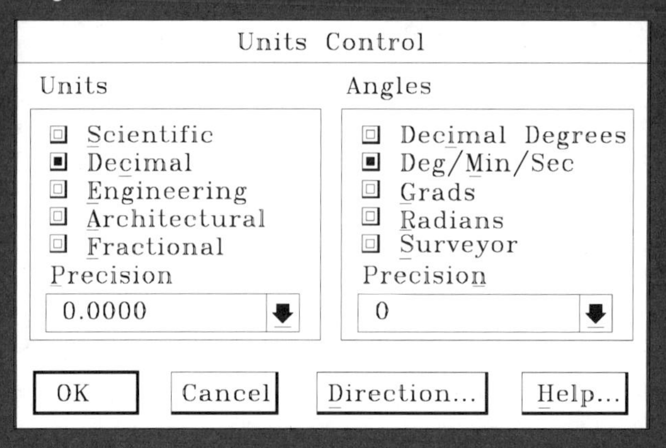

By using the Direction option, you access this secondary dialogue box from which you can choose the directions.

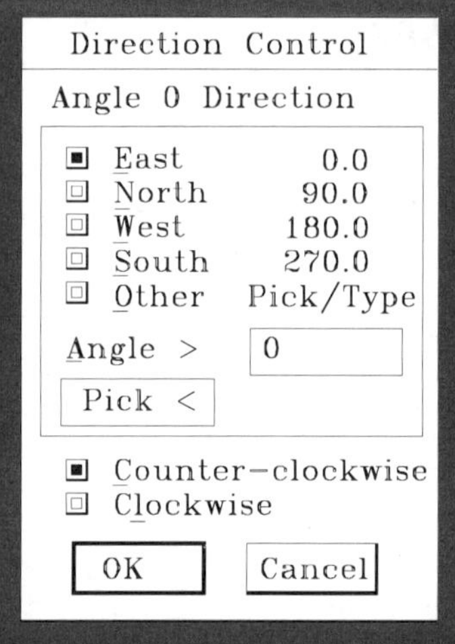

The Help option will outline the various options for angles and directions.

Practice 3A

Use DONUT to create buoys or markers for a sailing regatta.

Now use PLINE to illustrate the course for the sailors.

Use PEDIT to fit a spline through the course.

Now use PEDIT with the Edit vertex option to create arrows showing the direction of the course. You may have to Undo the spline to get this to work.

Options are:

Edit vertex

in Pedit.

Then:

Next vertex

Previous vertex

Break

Insert

Move point

Regen

Straighten

Tangent

Width

e**X**it

in the Edit vertex submenu.

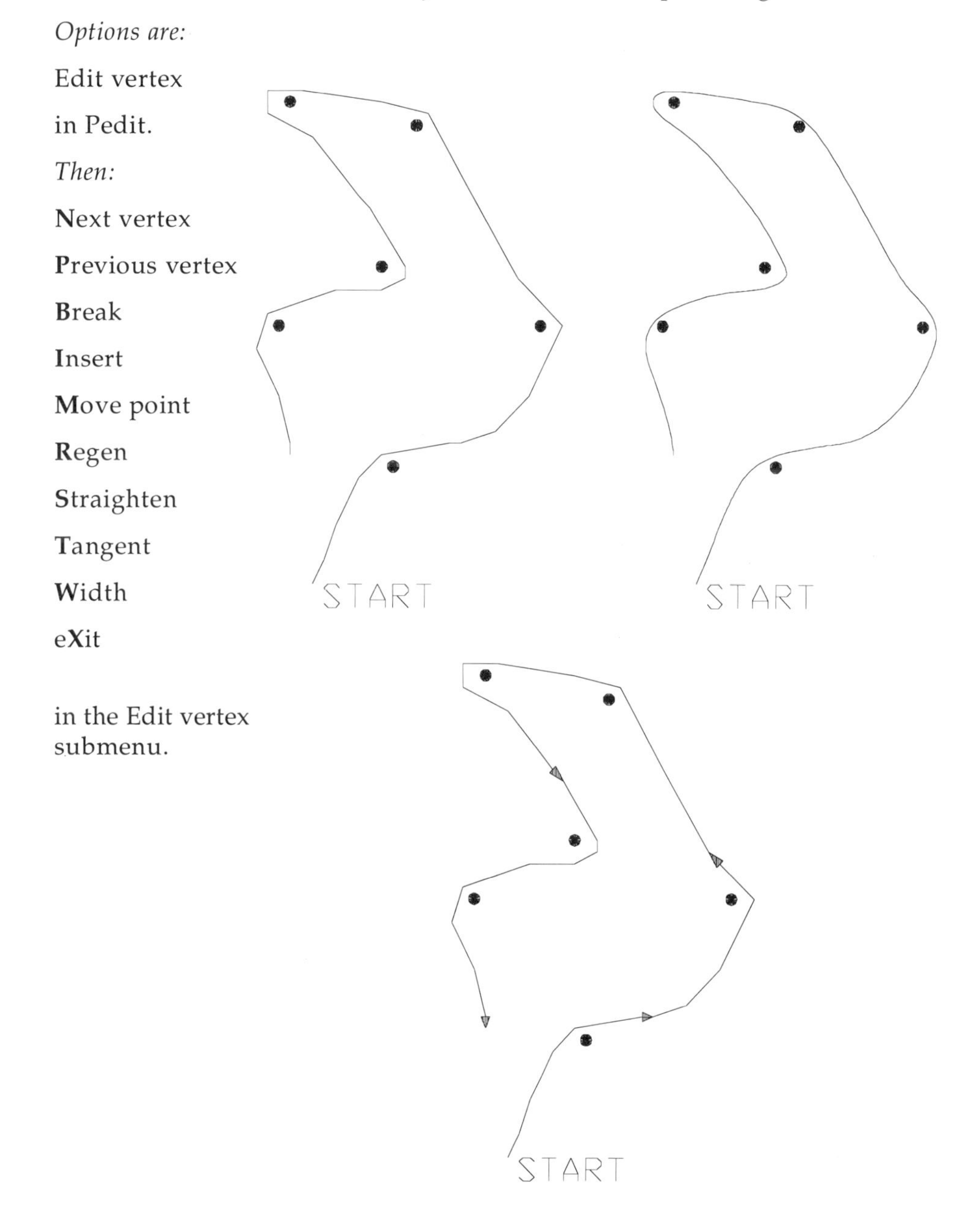

The colour can be changed under the Settings menu to produce a different colour for the buoys

Practice 3B

Using a windsurf board and sail, illustrate the flow of the wind past either side of the sail as it generates thrust. The wind will hit the sail and separate to pass on either side. It is accelerated on the leeward side by the curve of the sail.

Use PLINE and PEDIT to create the board and the sail. Change the colour under the Settings menu to cyan to illustrate the various directions of the wind and its behaviour when passing the sail.

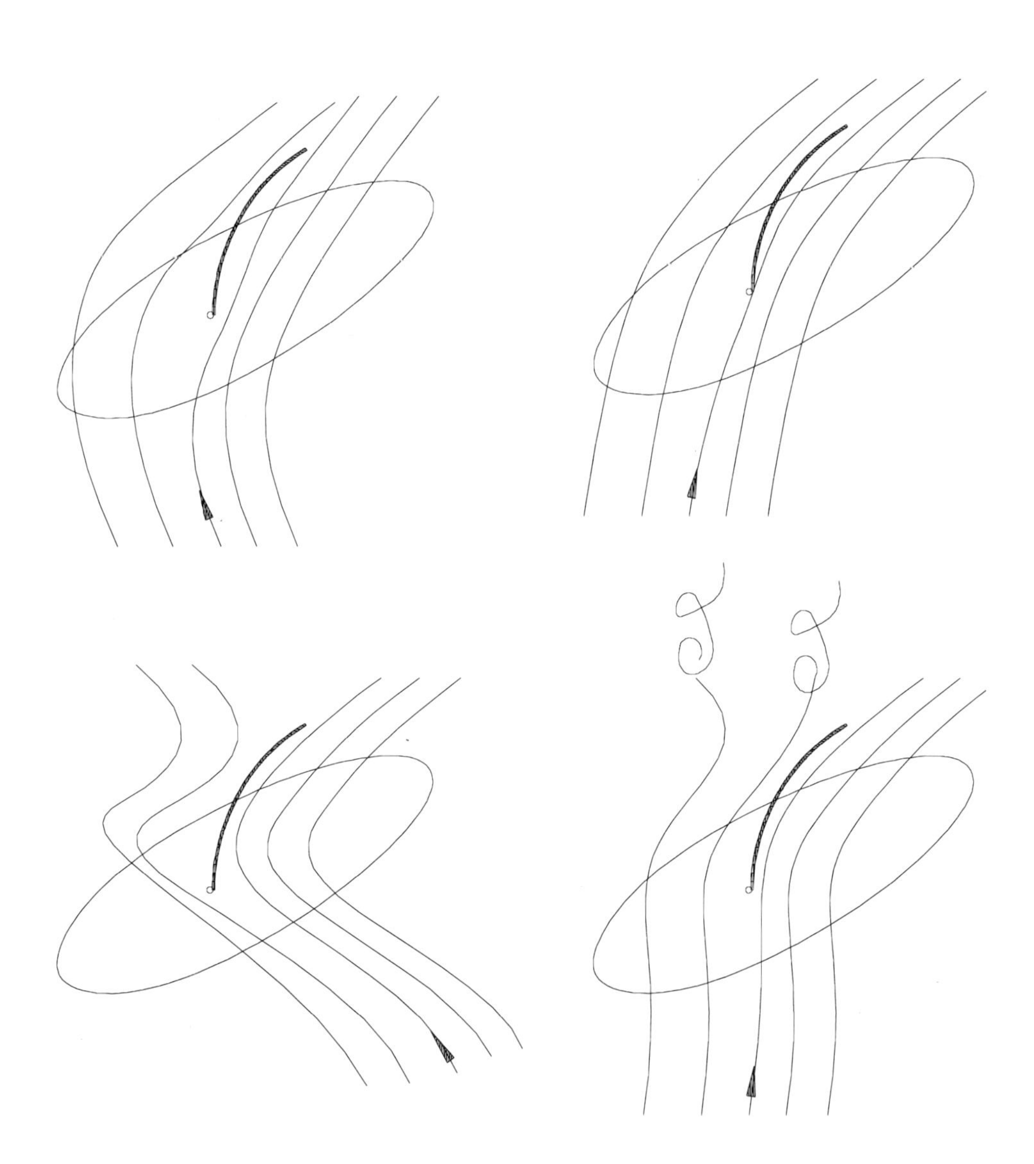

Exercise A3

UNITS	**Architectural**
Smallest denominator	**1**
LIMITS	**-5′,-5′**
	50′,40′
GRID	**3′**
SNAP	**1′**

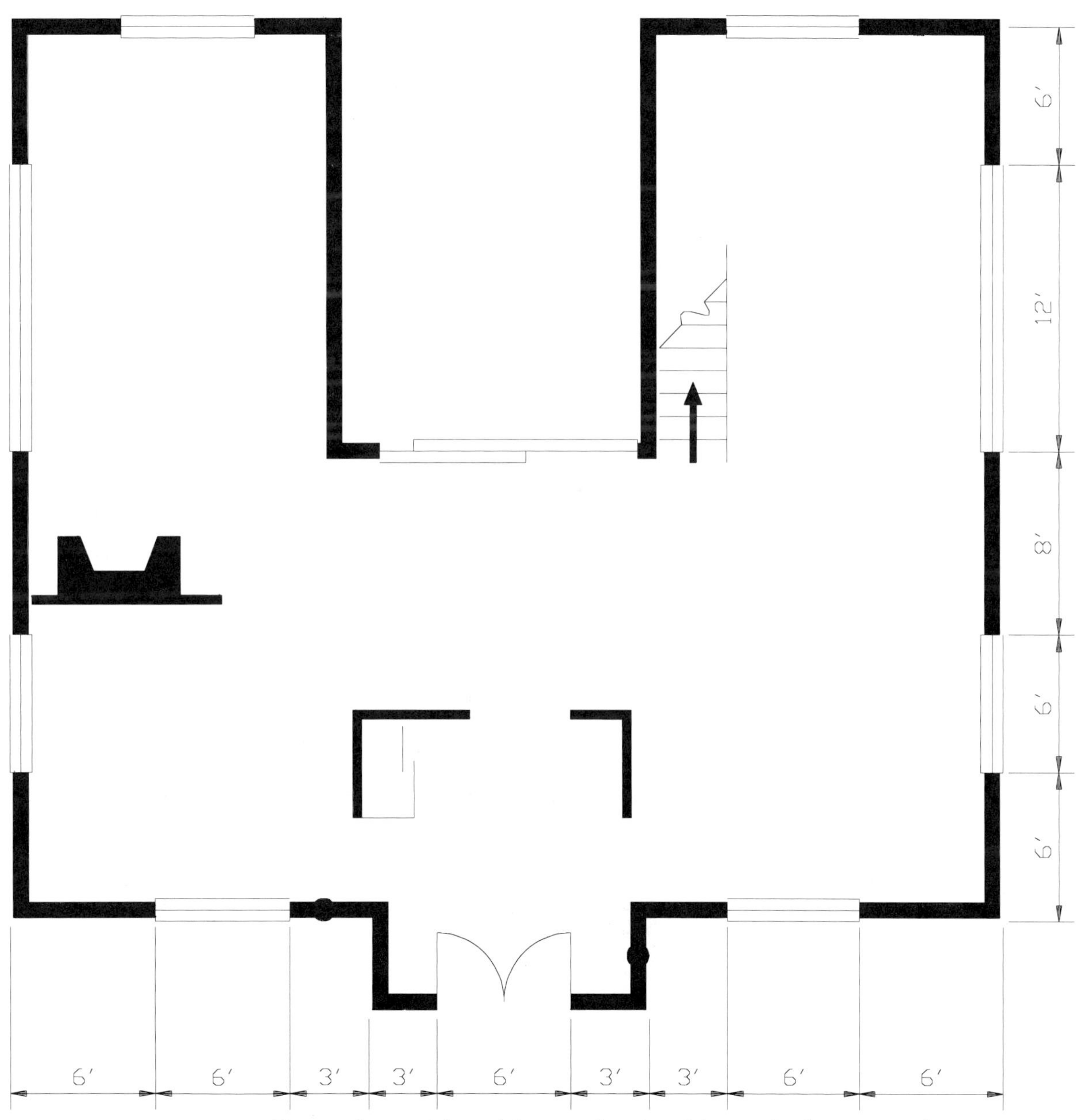

Remember, with architectural units, 1 is one inch, not one foot.

Use PLINE to create the walls for this presentation drawing. The arrow and break on the stairs are also plines. Use LINE to finish the windows and doors and SOLID to fill in the fireplace. Try to create the fireplace using only one SOLID command. Add exterior hedges with DONUT if you finish early.

Exercise M3

UNITS	**Fraction**
Smallest denominator	**1/4**
LIMITS	**0,0**
	12,9
GRID	**1**
SNAP	**1/2**

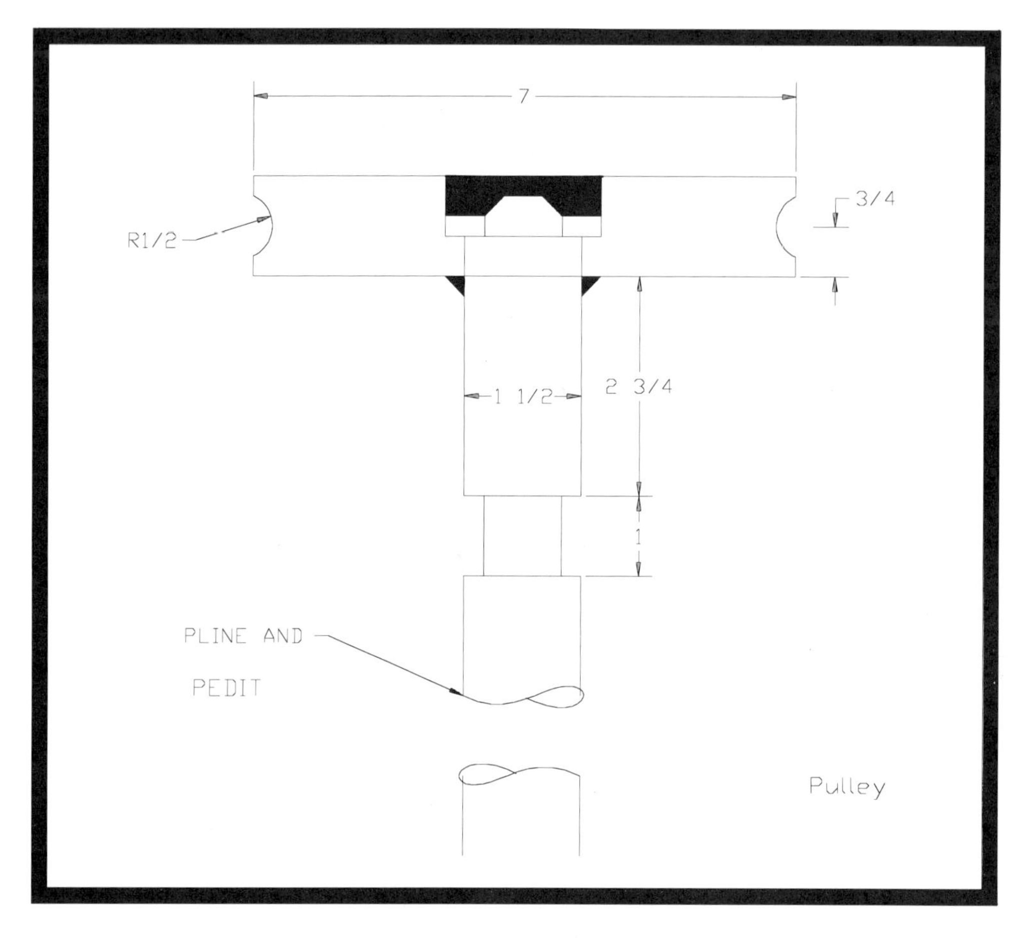

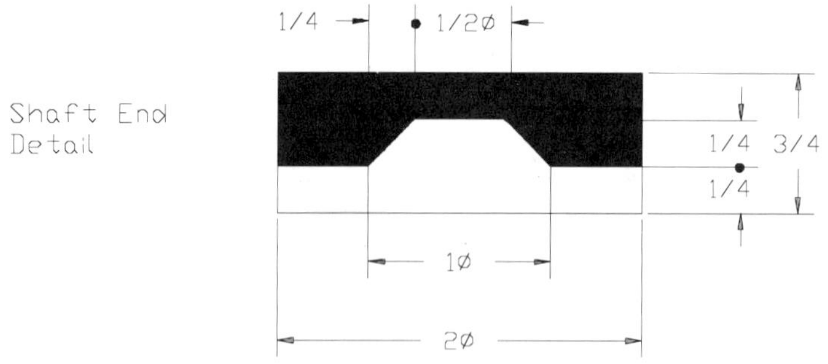

Change the units to fractional and the smallest denominator to 4.

In this Lifting Screw Assembly, use SOLID for the filled-in areas and PLINE for the break as shown. PEDIT should be used for the ends of the cylinders. Put a thick pline around the drawing just for practice.

Exercise C3

UNITS	**Decimal**
Decimal Places	**2**
System of angle measurement	**Surveyors**
Fractional places for angles	**2**
LIMITS	**0,0**
	250,200
GRID	**10**
SNAP	**5**

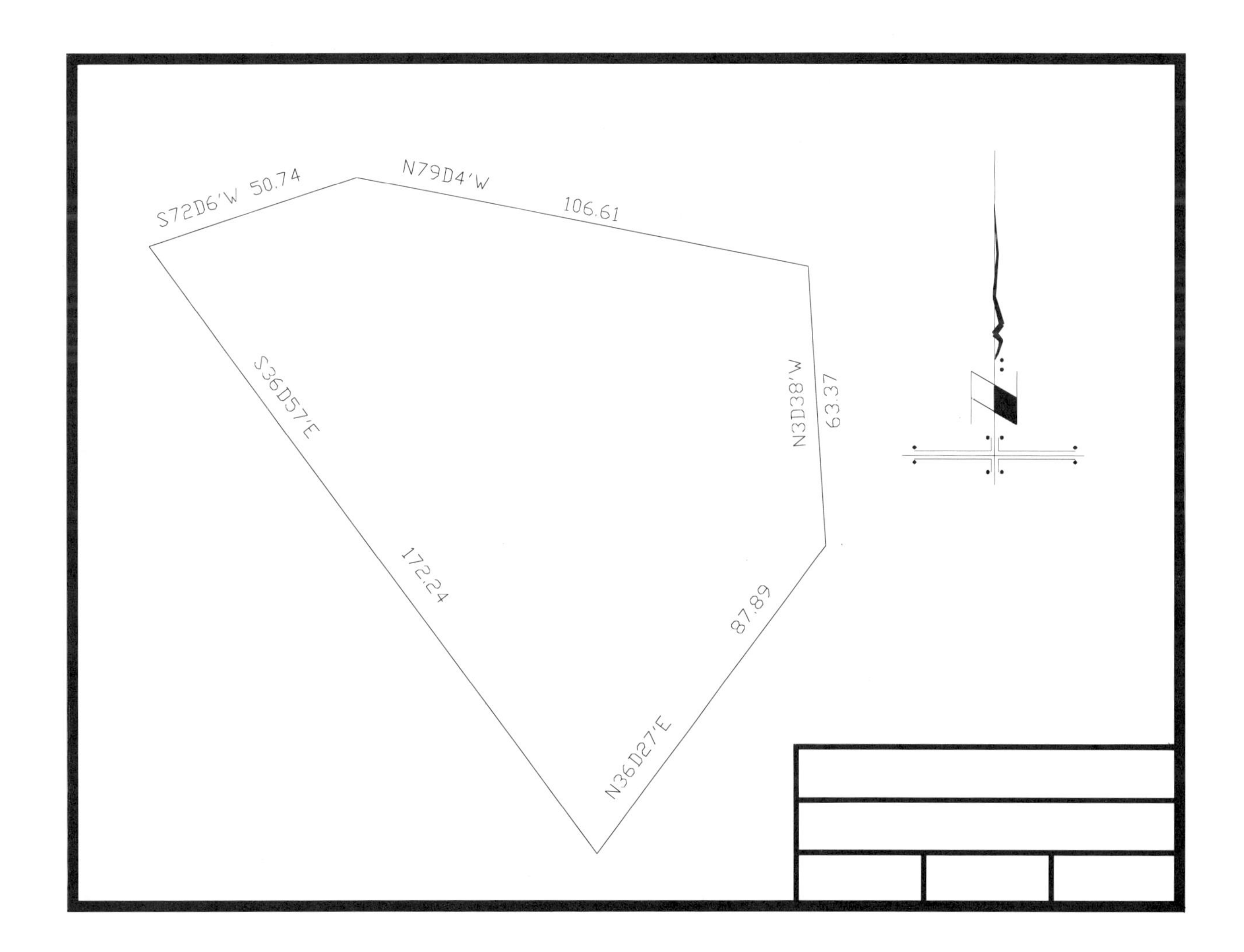

Draw the outline of the property by entering the dimensions of the property as in the drawing. Then add the title block with Pline set at a width of 2. Then draw the area for the lettering with the Pline set at 1.

Zoom in to the area where you are going to place your north arrow, and set the Snap to .50.

Use PLINE for the curves at the top of the arrow and PEDIT to make them curve properly.

ELECTRICAL

Exercise E3

UNITS	**Decimal**
Smallest denominator	**1**
LIMITS	**-5,-5**
	50,40
GRID	**5**
SNAP	**1**

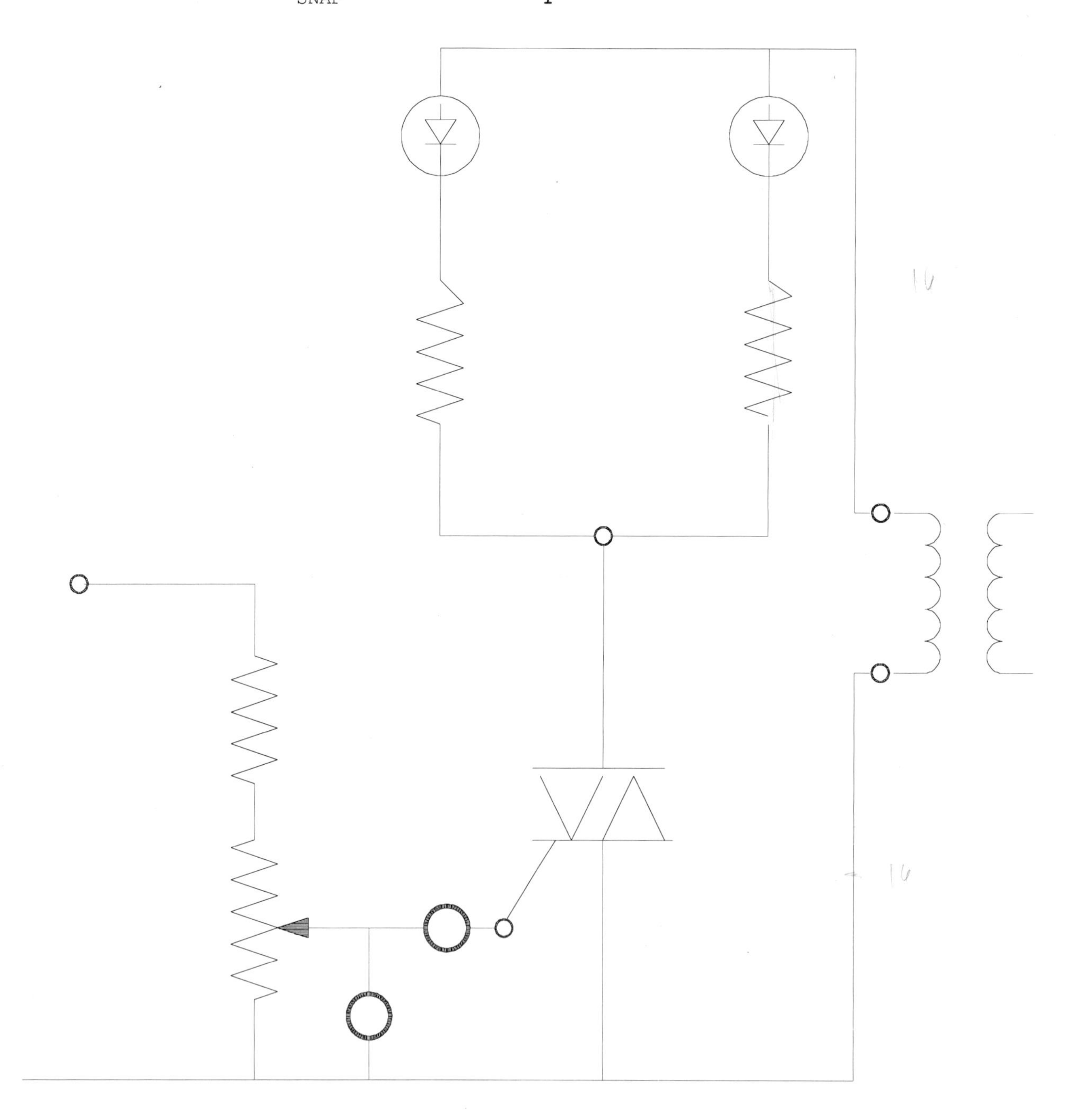

Use PLINE to create the schematic. The arrow is also a pline. Use the Arc option of PLINE for the sections within the schematic lines. Use DONUT for the smaller complete circles.

Challenger 3

This illustration details the design of the spire of a Victorian mansion.

You can use whatever units you feel would be appropriate to reproduce it.

This exercise is very good for your hand-eye coordination — autophysical responses — and helps you to become familiar with PLINE and SOLID.

DONUT was also used to create the smaller circles on the top half of the spire.

Variations on the theme are acceptable.

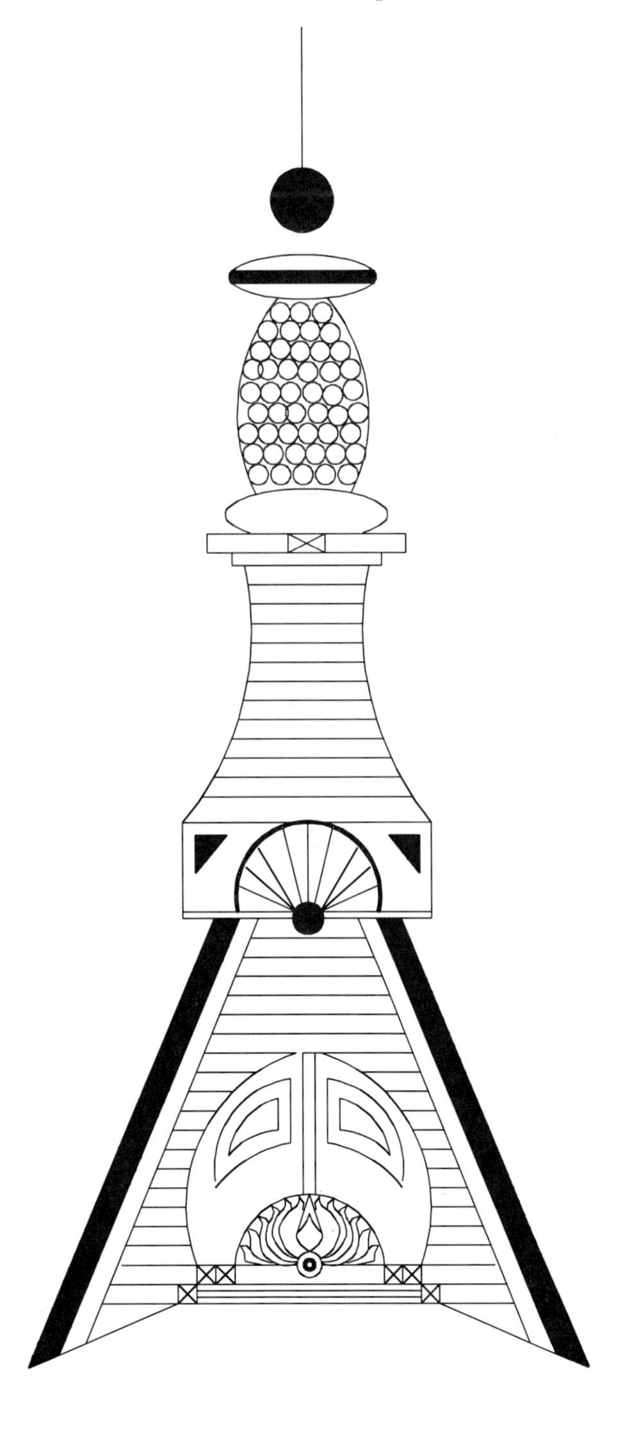

OBJECT SELECTION AND EDITING

Upon completion of this chapter, the student should be able to:

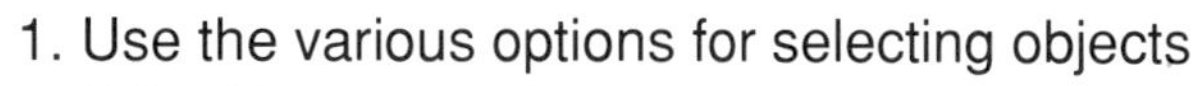

1. Use the various options for selecting objects
2. Edit objects with the MOVE command
3. Edit objects with the COPY command
4. Edit objects with the MIRROR command
5. Use FILLET Rad 0
6. ROTATE objects

Many people find they are able to "draw" items on paper much more quickly than they can do so on the screen. However, in any CAD package, you edit much more than you create. Edit commands greatly increase one's design flexibility and offer a definite advantage over hand-drawn designs.

The process of editing points is particularly important because you have a definite position in mind when editing an item, and if it is not done right the first time, the process will have to be repeated until you finally get the correct location. Using OSNAP will help to reference objects relative to other items. Use it as often as possible.

SELECTING OBJECTS Part One

In virtually every EDIT command, you will be prompted to select objects. This makes sense because the EDIT command will change the position or the parameters of objects, and thus the system needs to know which items you want to change.

Objects are generally selected in one of four ways:

- digitizing the desired item
- indicating a group of items with the Window option
- indicating the last entered item using the Last option
- indicating items with the Crossing option

> ***Release 12 Notes***
> Entity selection on large drawings in Release 12 is dramatically improved.

The object selection default is to have every item picked one by one. This is convenient when you want to break or erase a single item, but is not convenient when a series of objects must be moved or rotated.

The system will also keep prompting you to select objects once the initial selection has been made; so objects can be added or subtracted from the list of items that have already been selected.

To continue with the EDIT command after selecting objects, press ⏎.

Figure 4-1 demonstrates two methods of selecting objects.

`Command:`**`ERASE`**
`Select objects:` *(pick 1)*

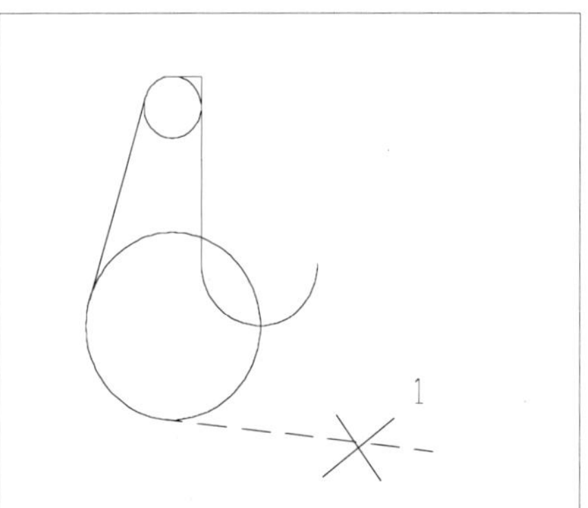

`Command:`**`COPY`**
`Select objects:`**`L`** *(Last)*

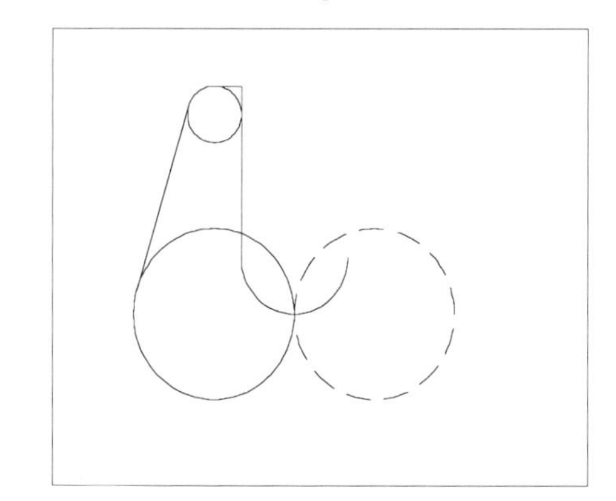

Figure 4-1. Using digitizing and Last

The ERASE command deletes the line selected by pick 1. Then, assuming the larger circle was the last object entered, it will be the object chosen to be copied when the Last option is selected.

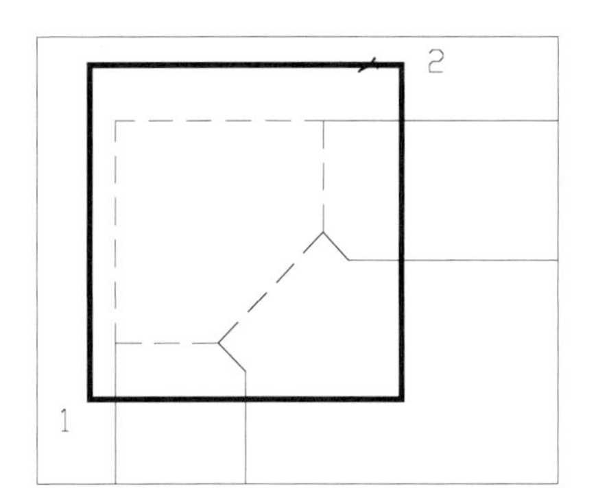

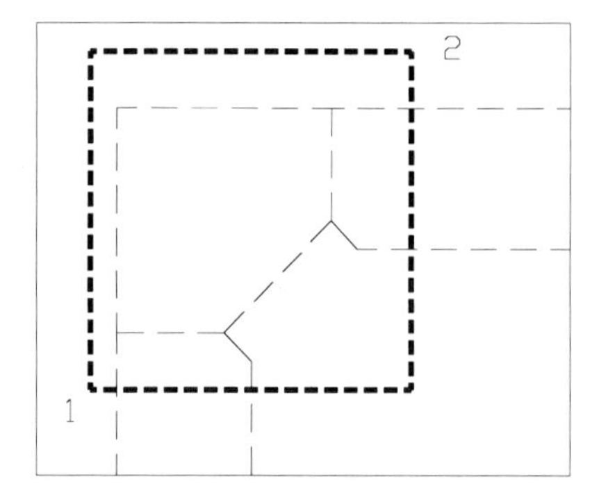

Figure 4-2. Using Window and Crossing

`Command:COPY`
`Select Objects:`**`W`** *(Window) (pick 1, 2)*

`Command:`**`COPY`**
`Select Objects:`**`C`** *(Crossing) (pick 1, 2)*

The first COPY command of Figure 4-2 selects all the objects that are fully contained within the window, while the second COPY command selects on the right picks up any object that crosses the boundary of the crossing rectangle.

Release 12 Notes

Select options (under Objects) includes Fence, which allows you to indicate objects with a single line, and CPolygon or WPolygon, which allow you to indicate objects with closed polygons.

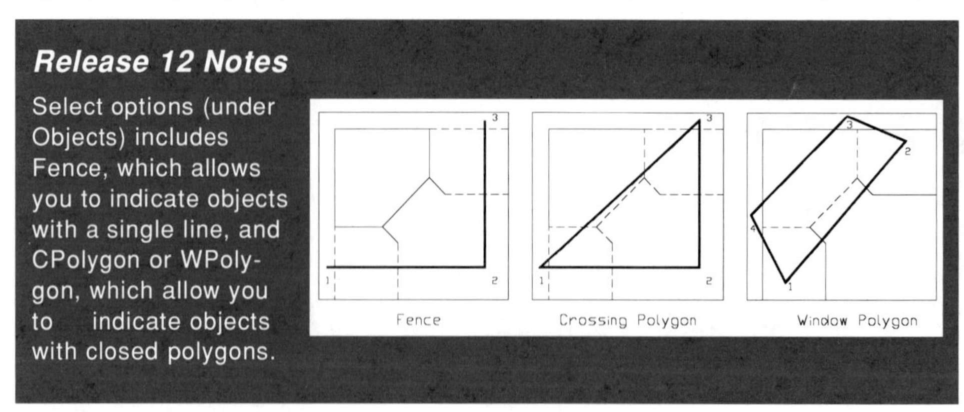

COPY

The COPY command takes an item or group of items and places a copy at another location or at multiple locations.

```
Command:COPY
Select objects:W (Window) (pick 1, 2)
<Base point> or Multiple:END (pick 3)
Displacement:END (pick 4)
```

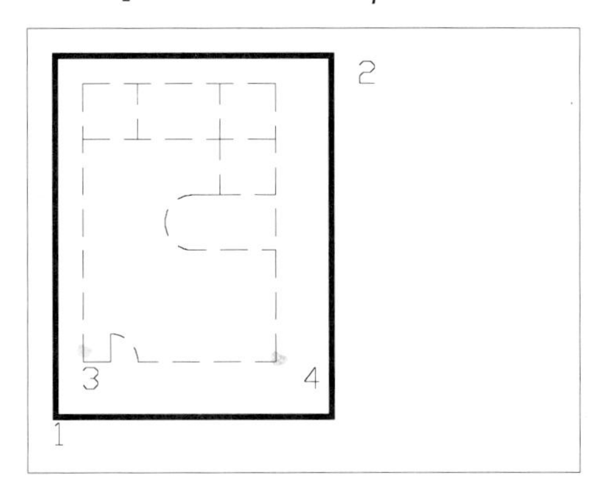

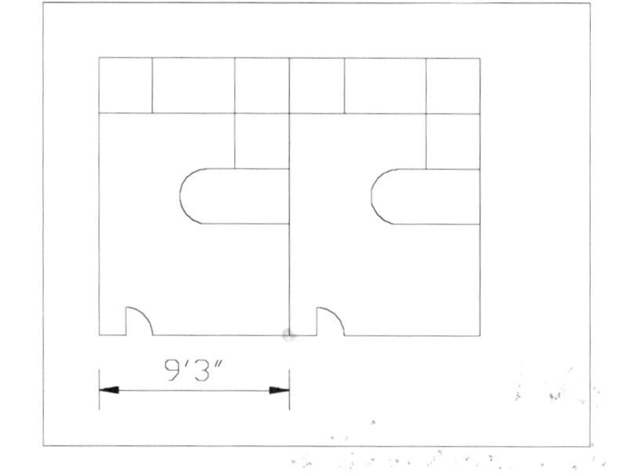

Figure 4-3. Using the COPY *command*

In the example of Figure 4-3, if you knew the exact location of the displacement in relation to the base point, an incremental value could be used. For example:

```
Displacement:@ 9'3",0
```

The COPY command can be used to place multiple copies of objects at random spacing. Once the objects have been selected, the command prompts for either the base point or the Multiple option.

```
<Base point> or Multiple:M
```

If you choose the multiple option, the system will place a copy of the selection set at each displacement point. All displacements are relative to the first base point, so be sure to pick the base point well.

In Figure 4.4, the eight lines are picked up using the Window option, then the endpoint of the bottom left corner is chosen as the base point. This point is referenced each time the object is to be placed.

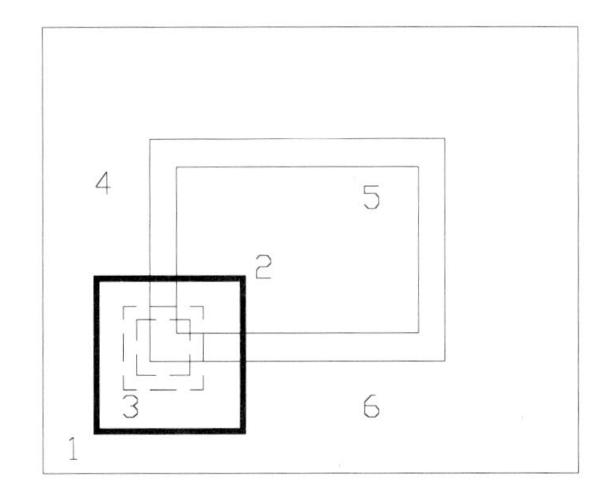

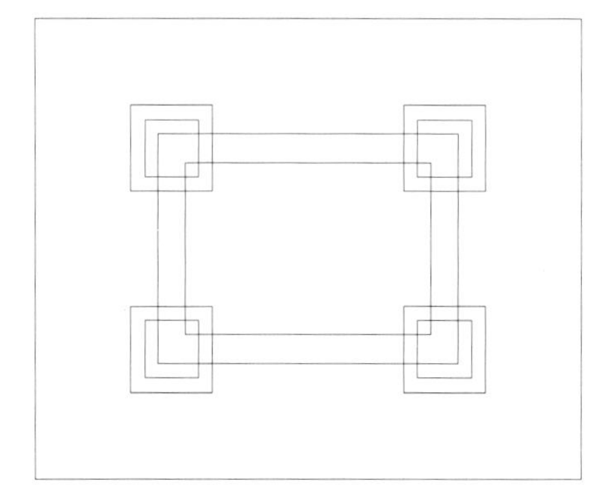

Figure 4-4. COPY *with the Multiple option*

MOVE

The MOVE command moves an object or series of objects from one point to another, relative to the origin.

What is the difference between the PAN command and the MOVE command?

PAN takes an image and translates it across the screen. It is a DISPLAY command. After the PAN command is finished, the parameters or the coordinates of each object will be the same: even though they appear to have moved, they have only moved relative to the screen. MOVE actually moves the items from one point to another; the coordinates of the objects will change.

> **Release 12 Notes**
>
> When accessing the Edit commands by any method, the screen will automatically update to reflect the currently running command.

```
Command:MOVE
Select Objects:W (Window) (pick 1, 2)
Base point: (pick 3) (from where)
Displacement: (pick 4) (to where)
```

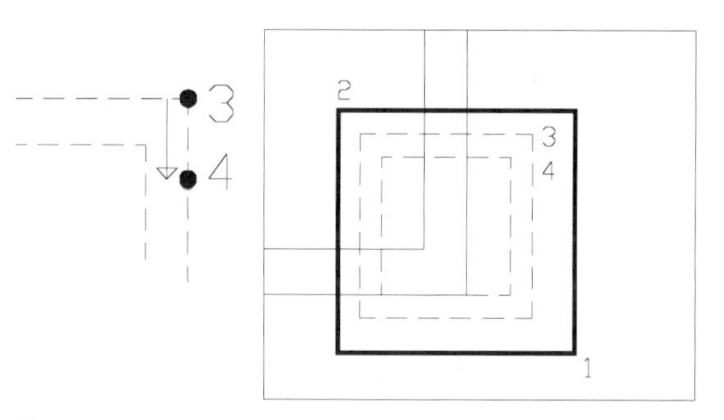

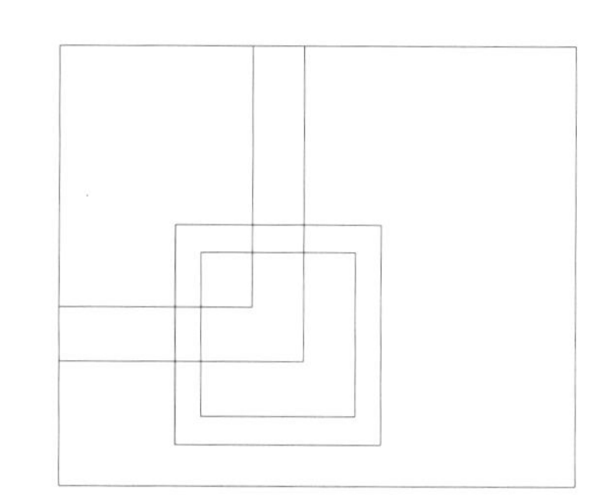

Figure 4-5. Using the MOVE command

In Figure 4-5, pick 3 determines the part of the object that will be used as the reference point, which will be repositioned at the point described by pick 4.

```
Command:MOVE
Select Objects: (pick 1)
Base Point:0,0
Displacement:@-2,0
```

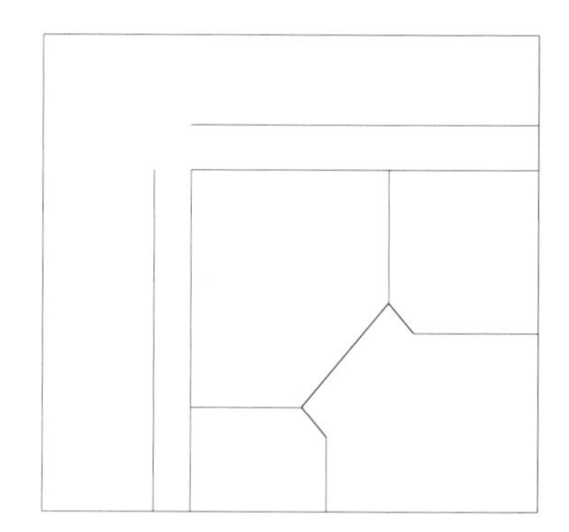

Figure 4-6. Using MOVE with an increment

In the example of Figure 4-6, the selection of the base point was irrelevant. This point could have been picked up anywhere on the screen. The second point, @-2,0, describes a point two units in negative X from the current position. By entering an incremental value for the displacement, the system moved the object according to a certain vector because values were entered rather than points picked on the screen. Both, however, achieve the same result of describing the movement.

How would you move a selected group of objects from their current position to 0,0?

The objects are identified by a Window. The base point is identified by a pick. Since the exact endpoint of that object must be at 0,0, use END (endpoint). The displacement is given as an absolute value.

```
Command:MOVE
Select Objects:W (Window) (pick 1, 2)
Base point:END (pick 3)
Displacement:0,0
```

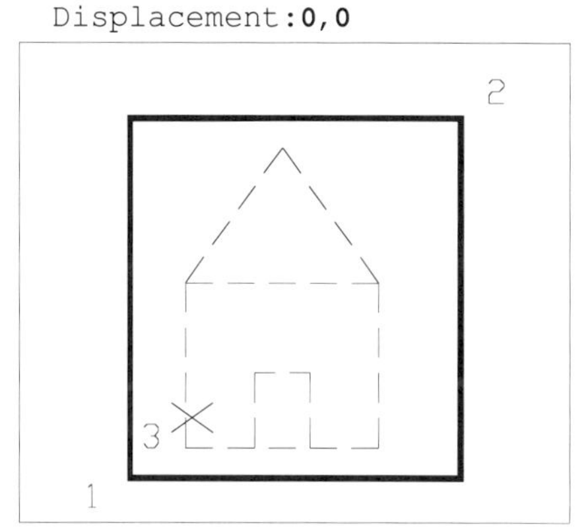

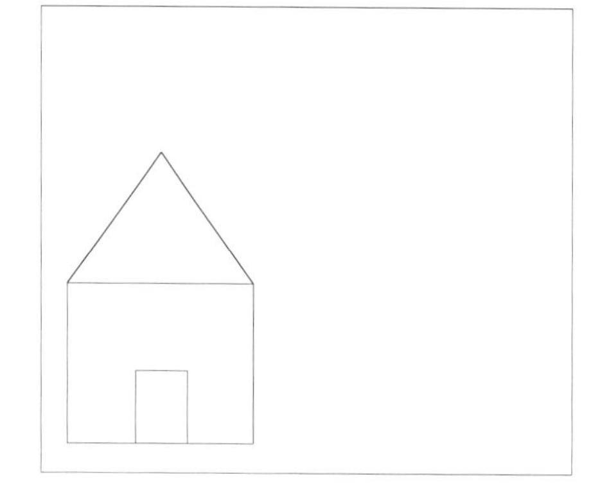

Figure 4-7. Moving objects to 0,0

The system was told to move that group of objects totally contained in the window from the endpoint indicated by pick 3 to 0,0.

Questions related to MOVE and COPY

What happens when you move or copy something to the wrong place?

The U command negates the previous command. Almost any type of command can be undone. Using U ⏎ will undo any number of commands back to the beginning of the current editing session. ERASE can be used in conjunction with Last to erase the last drawing entity, but only the last one, while U can be used on multiple entries.

UNDO is similar to U, but UNDO offers more control and is more dangerous. UNDO will prompt for the number of commands to be undone and undo them in a single operation.

Instead of changing over to ERASE, use U ⏎ to undo the command you have just entered. It will erase the last objects entered by undoing the COPY or MOVE command.

What happens when you move or copy a group of objects and they disappear?

Use U ⏎ to retrieve the data or ZOOM A to view the spot to which it was moved or copied.

MIRROR

The MIRROR command creates a mirror image of an item or group of items through a specified mirroring plane.

In Figure 4-8, the object is mirrored through a mirroring-plane object inserted at the halfway point of the desired new object. The mirror line was deleted and horizontal lines were added after the mirror was completed.

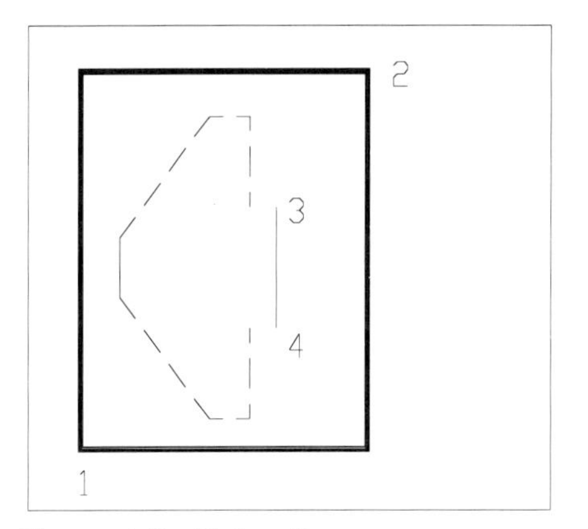

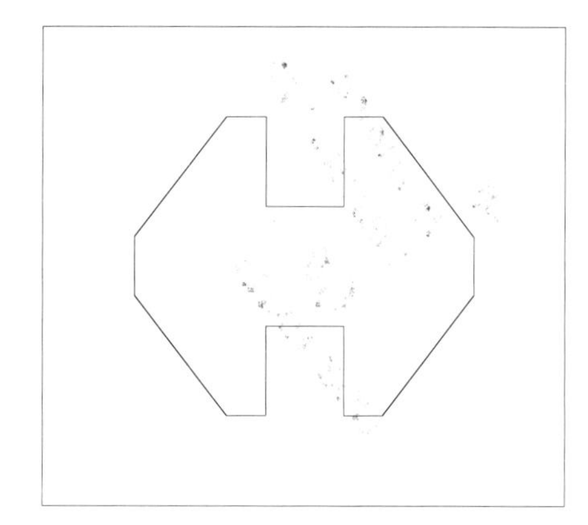

Figure 4-8. Using the MIRROR command

```
Command:MIRROR
Select Objects:W (Window) (pick 1, 2)
First point of mirroring plane:END (pick 3)
Second point of mirroring plane:END (pick 4)
```

If there are existing objects that can be used to describe the mirroring plane, use them.

In Figure 4-9, the mirroring plane is calculated from the center of the circle, in the centre at the bottom. With ORTHO on, the mirroring plane would be easier to identify.

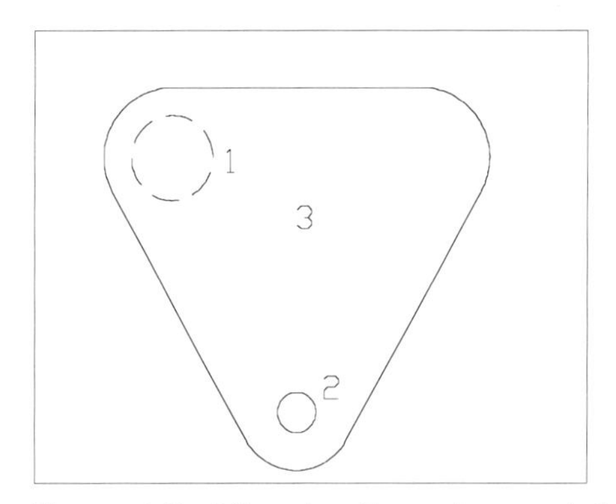

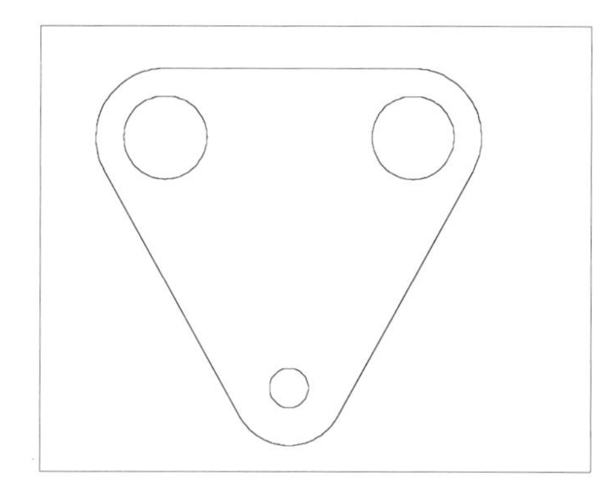

Figure 4-9. Mirroring through an existing item

```
Command:MIRROR
Select Objects: (pick 1)
First point of mirroring plane:CEN (centre) (pick 2)
Second point of mirroring plane: (pick 3) (use Ortho)
```

If no object is accessible as a mirroring-plane base point, one can calculate the distance using the coordinates and pick them on the screen. The mirroring plane can be indicated by picking points or by entering values as demonstrated in Figure 4-10.

When MIRROR prompts for a point, any kind of point may be entered.

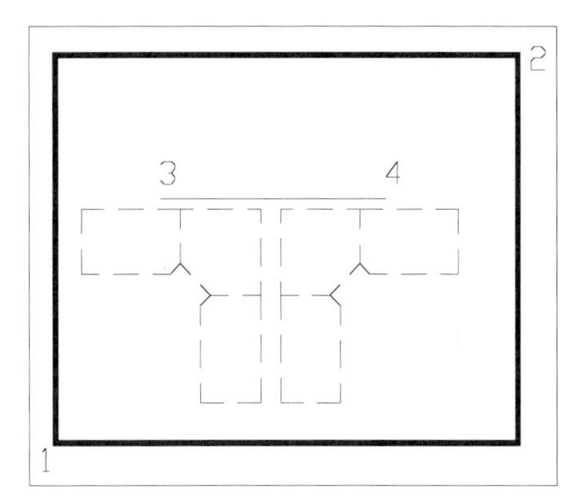

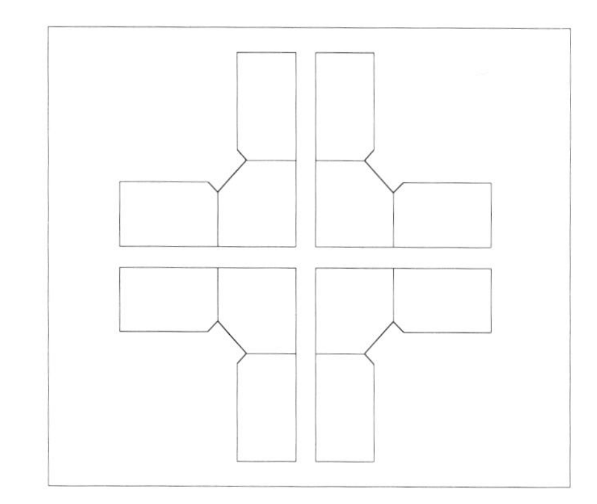

Figure 4-10. Mirroring using an incremental coordinate

```
Command:MIRROR
Select objects:W (pick 1, 2)
First point of mirroring plane:5,6.3
Second point of mirroring plane:@3,0
```

ROTATE

The ROTATE command rotates an object or series of objects around a specified base point.

Using the command sequence of Figure 4-11, the objects are rotated 45 degrees around a point in the middle of the object itself. To view the rotation of the object, move the cursor in a circle around the base point.

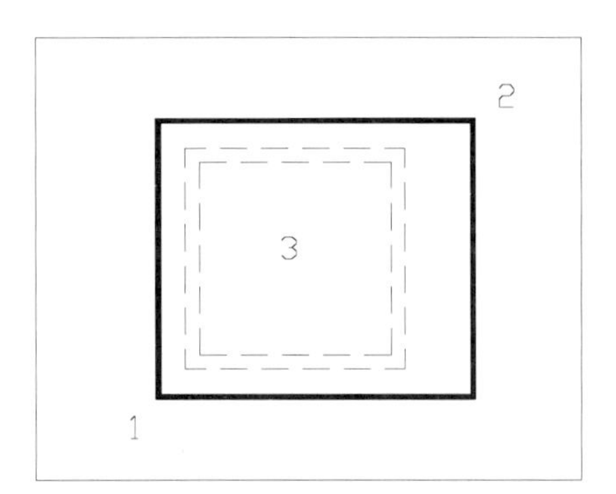

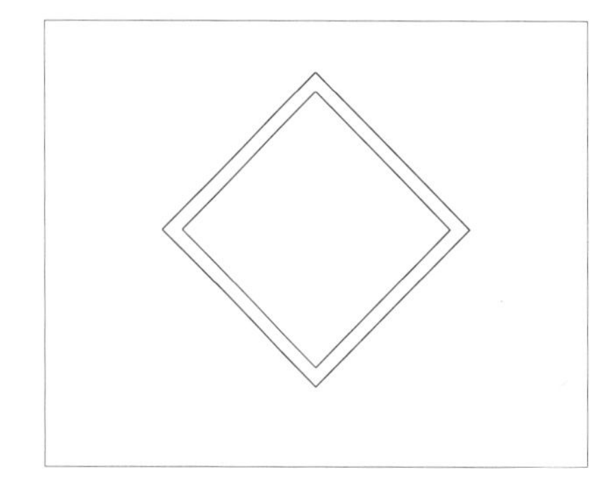

Figure 4-11. Rotating objects

```
Command:ROTATE
Select objects:W (pick 1, 2)
Base point: (pick 3) (use SNAP for accuracy)
<Rotation angle>\reference:45
```

In Figure 4-12, the objects were first copied from the position on the front wall, then rotated relative to the base point at the ENDpoint of the window so it fits perfectly into the space provided.

```
Command:ROTATE
Select objects:W (pick 1, 2)
Base point:END (pick 3)
<Rotation angle>\reference: (pick 4) (use ORTHO for accuracy).
```

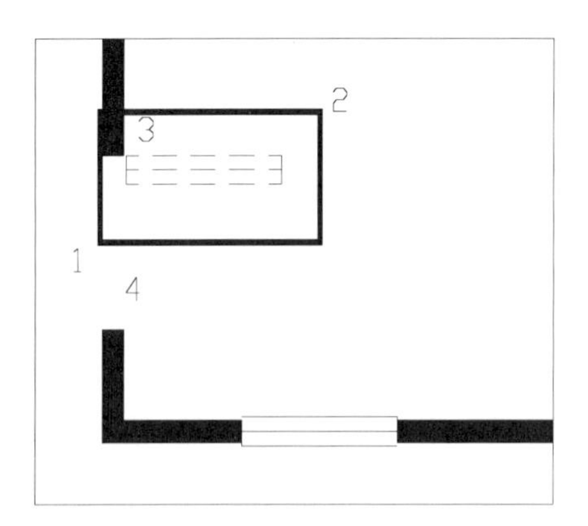

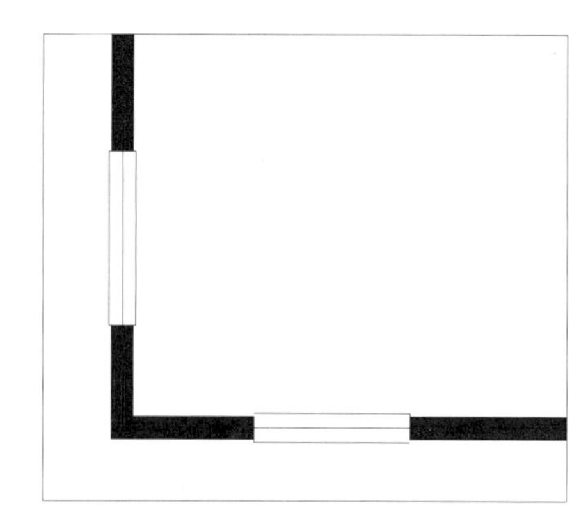

Figure 4-12. Rotating around an existing point

In Figure 4-13, the objects are copied first, then rotated around a point identified as the middle of the object.

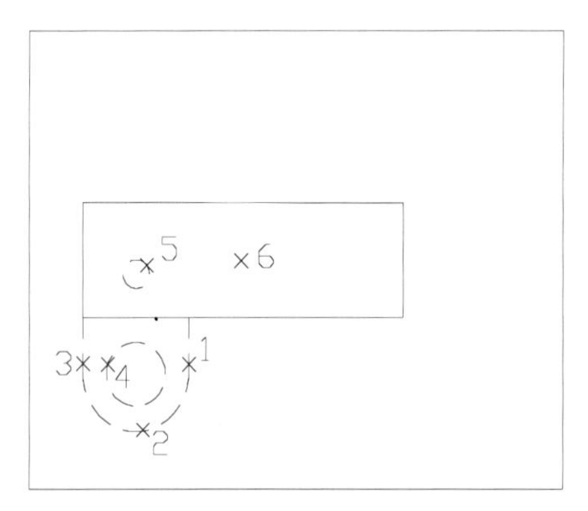

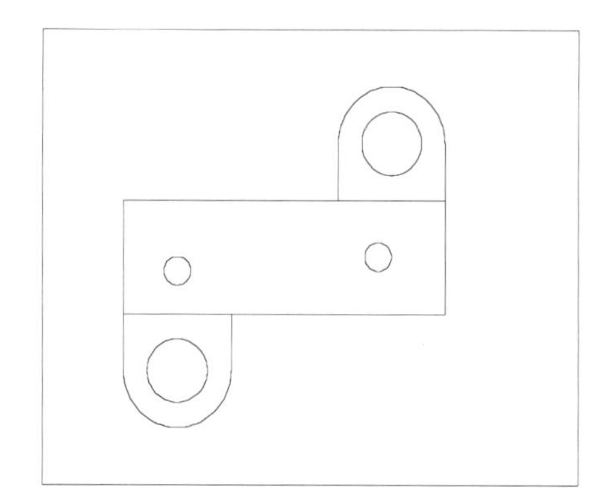

Figure 4-13. Rotating copied objects

```
Command:COPY
Select objects:W (pick 1, 2)
<Base point>\Multiple:0,0
Second point:↵
```

This makes a duplicate copy of the arc, two circles, and two lines at the same spot.

```
Command:ROTATE
Select objects: (pick 1, 2, 3, 4, 5)
Base point: (pick 6)
<Rotation angle>\reference:180
```

Pick the items individually, otherwise both the original and the copy will be rotated.

EDITING

What can go wrong with editing? Most editing commands have a similar format. The system will prompt you for the information it needs to complete the task. Try to cooperate with the system and give it the information when it prompts for it. For example, if the system is prompting to Select objects: during a COPY command, do not try to tell it where the objects are being copied to.

Do not try to enforce your will on the system. It will not work.

If the system is prompting for the items you would like to move, do not tell it where to move them to. The prompts will always be:

- what?
- how much or how many?
- where or around what?

As long as you answer the questions, you will be all right.

Getting Out of a Bad Edit

AutoCAD generates a hidden file of all the commands used while you are editing information. If you enter DIR A:, a listing of your files including a temporary file with the extension .$A will be retrieved. The .$A stores the commands that have been entered to create the model or drawing.

All the commands are stored in the order that they were performed. Use U ↵ to undo a command that did not work. To override an UNDO, use REDO. This command must directly follow the UNDO command. For example, to undo the last five entries, use UNDO 5.

It is a good idea to save the model with either END or SAVE before doing extensive editing. Then if you undo more than you expected, you can quit the file and reload the unchanged file.

Getting Good Results the First Time

Always use SNAP, OSNAP, or actual coordinates to pick base points. If a reference object is needed to complete an editing command (for example, a line in the MIRROR command), insert it, reference it with OSNAP, then get rid of it. Remember, there is no point inserting a reference point accurately, then not referencing it.

Your ability to complete the editing commands is directly related to your communication skills. Always read the bottom of the screen and use the Help menu if you do not understand a prompt.

Release 12 Notes

The Grip facility has been added to help you edit information without having to access OSNAP as frequently. A grip is a square that appears at a specific position on the entity that you are editing. The following is an illustration of the location of some common grips.

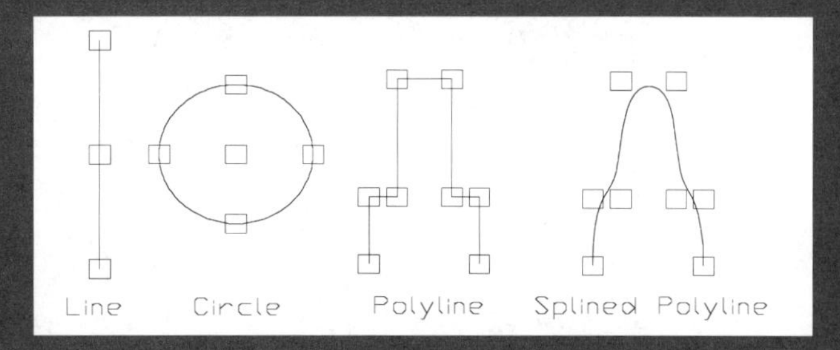

The grips can be used on five editing commands – MIRROR, ROTATE, SCALE, STRETCH. Instead of choosing the comand first, just pick a window of objects or select an object that needs editing. Once selected, simply move cursor and pick the area of the grip you would like to move. No OSNAP is necessary. As long as the cursor is within the grip, the exact end, midpoint, or centre of the object will be chosen.

Release 12 Notes (cont'd)

Example: Grips

Create a series of six lines.

Command: *(pick 1)* Other corner: *(pick 2)* *(select the entire set simply by picking around the objects)*
The grips will appear in blue on the set of objects that you have chosen.

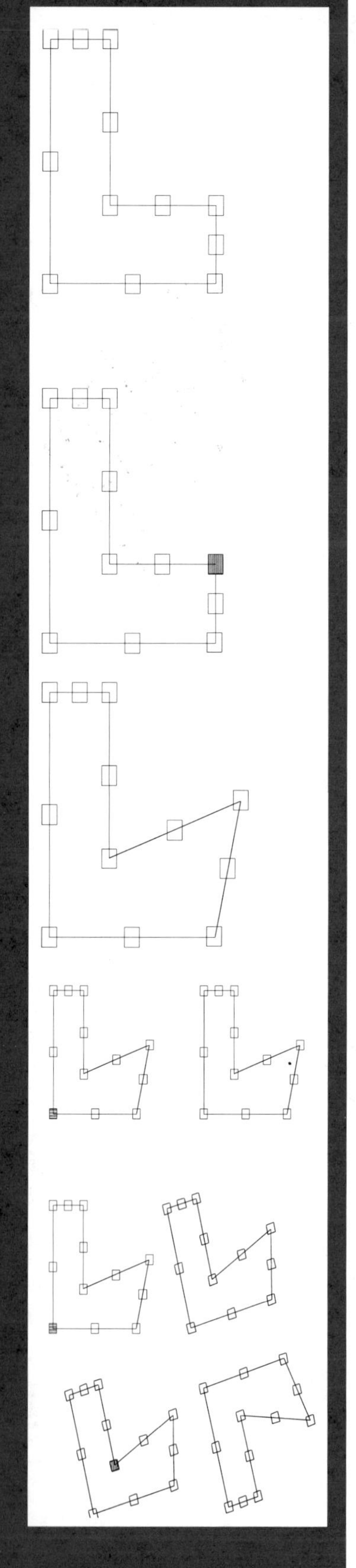

Command: *(pick 3) (pick the right corner of the object)*
The base grip will be identified with a solid colour, probably red.

Command: **STRETCH**
<Stretch to point>/Base/Copy/Undo/eXit:
(pick a point away from the original base point and that corner will stretch)
If you to stretch two points, hold the shift key down while selecting the base grip points.

Command: *(pick 5) (pick another base grip point, then choose Move from the screen menu to move the selection set)*
<Move point>/Base point/Copy/Undo/eXit:

Command: *(pick 7) (choose another base grip point, then choose Scale from the screen menu to scale the objects)*
<Scale factor>/Base point/Copy/Undo/Reference/eXit: **.5**

Command: *(pick 8) (choose another base grip and then choose Rotate from the screen menu)*
<Rotation angle>/ Base point/ Copy/Undo/Reference/eXit: **25**
Notice that the original selection set is taken each time.

Command: *(pick 9) (choose another base grip and then choose Mirror from the screen menu)*
<Second point>/Base point/Copy/Undo/eXit:
When using grips, the dialogue box DDGRIPS will help to define the colours and size of the grips.

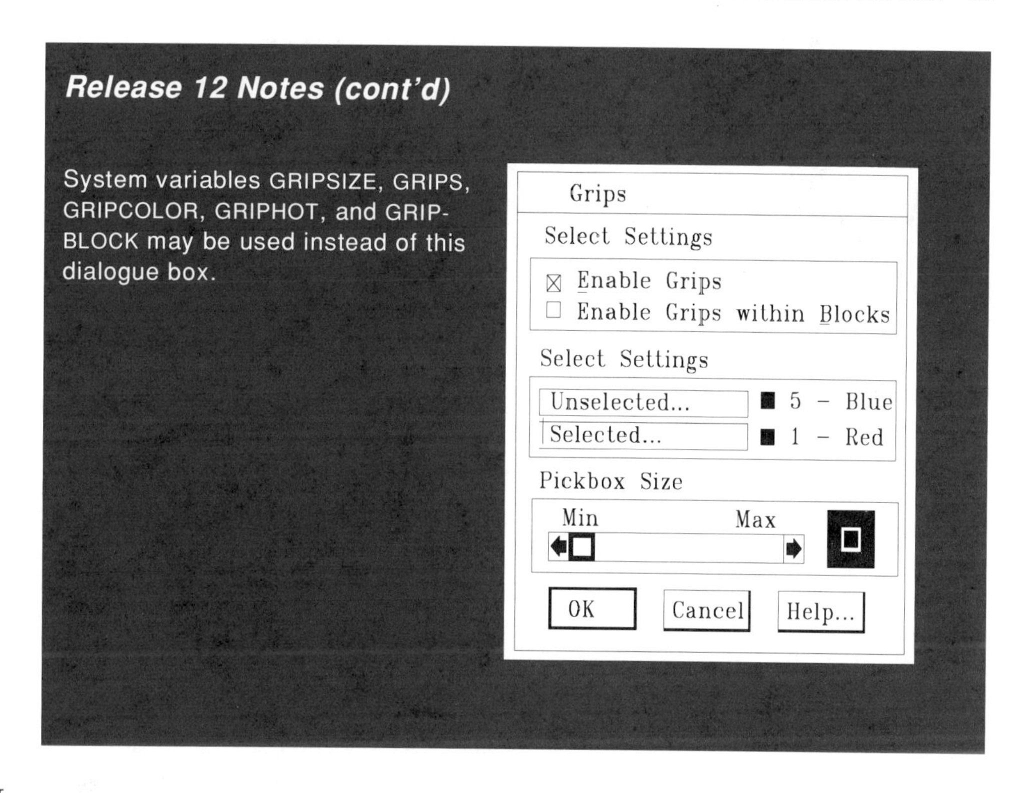

SYSTEM MANAGEMENT

By this time you should have several files. Many DOS functions are necessary to help manage disk storage and to avoid disk problems. A number of standard procedures must also be followed to avoid messing up the disk.

Saving the Floppy Disk from Clusters

When the floppy disk is in drive A and you are working on an AutoCAD drawing, *do not remove the floppy until you have exited from AutoCAD.*

If you do, bad clusters will be created that could destroy the files. A cluster is a portion of the .$A or temporary file that has been created while using AutoCAD. If you do not exit properly, the .$A file becomes lost on the disk — the address is gone — and these bad clusters remain until they are identified and deleted.

Once you have exited from AutoCAD, make copies of your files.

Checking for .CHK files and RAM Problems

To check the disk for bad clusters, use CHKDSK A:/F

This DOS command will locate bad files or clusters that have been created by removing the floppy disk before exiting AutoCAD, and will put them into identifiable files which can then be deleted.

The CHKDSK readout will also indicate how much RAM is in the computer and how much is usable.

In a lab situation, many people have access to the computers. If someone has re-addressed the RAM for another software program, there could be trouble signing on to AutoCAD. Use CHKDSK A:/F before starting AutoCAD to avoid problems.

The CHKDSK A:/F readout should look similar to the following:

Release 12 Notes

File management is much simpler in Release 12. Use the File pull-down menu to take a current file into another directory (SAVEAS) or to view the files on the disk.

```
C:> 1213952  bytes in total disk space (a 1.2MB floppy disk)
     480256  bytes in 23 user files
     733696  bytes available on disk
        512  bytes in each allocation unit
       2371  total allocation units on disk
       1433  available allocation units on disk

     655360  bytes memory  RAM
     558224  bytes free
```

If bad sectors are found, copy the files over to another floppy and reformat the first floppy. Usually bad sectors occur when a floppy disk has been formatted incorrectly. If there is still a message saying BAD SECTORS after you have formatted correctly, destroy the disk with the bad sectors and use another floppy disk.

The third line of the readout indicates the amount of storage space available on the floppy disk. If there is less than 100,000 bytes available, use another disk.

The last two lines of the readout refer to the RAM available on the computer. About 100,000 bytes of RAM will be used for DOS (Disk Operating System) and the network, if there is one. If there are less that 400,000 bytes, it will be impossible to start an AutoCAD file (in Release 10, 11, or 12); so check to be sure there is enough RAM if you are having trouble signing on.

Note: the CHKDSK readout does not show expanded memory. Try the MEM command to obtain an actual RAM count. See the Preface at the beginning of this book for further information on RAM.

Floppies

Regular double-sided, double-density floppy disks contain 360,000 bytes of storage space. Double-sided, high-density floppy disks contain 1.2MB of storage space. The disks with larger memory will not only store more files, but will cut down on possible loss of data or crashes caused by trying to save a model to a disk with insufficient memory. AutoCAD is programmed to help you in every way possible, but if you do not have enough space on the disk to save the model, it may be lost.

Most users can tell sad stories of their first major computer crash disaster that resulted in the loss of files that were not backed up properly. Take the necessary precautions and keep copies of your work on backup disks. This will save you a lot of grief.

Locating Your Files

To find out the number, size, and name of the files, use DIR A:. This DOS command will also display the number of bytes of memory there is left on the floppy disk.

Do not start a new file with less than 50,000 bytes of memory on the disk.

Identifying Files

When you list files with DIR A:, the filenames end with a three-letter extension; for example, A:NAME.DWG.

Where:
A: = the drive

NAME = the name of the file

.DWG = the extension describing the type of file

Common file extensions include:
.BAK = a backup file for the drawing

.CHK = check file or a file containing bad clusters

.DWG = a drawing file

.$A = a temporary file

Erasing Files

To erase files from the disk, use:

```
C:\ERASE A:NAME.CHK   or
C:\DEL A:NAME.CHK
```

Where:
A: = the drive

NAME = the name of the file

.CHK = the extension or type of file

Copying Files

To make a duplicate copy of a floppy disk, use DISKCOPY A: B:.

This will copy all the files from the disk in drive A to the diskette in drive B. If the computer has only one disk drive, you will be prompted to first put the source disk into drive A, then the target or destination disk into drive A.

When you use the DISKCOPY command, be sure that both disks are the same size, i.e., both are either 360K or 1.2MB. You cannot interchange them.

DISKCOPY A: B: will format the disk in drive B, i.e., all existing files on the Drive B disk will be erased.

COPY A:NAME.DWG B:NAME.DWG will copy the drawing file NAME.DWG onto another disk.

COPY A:NAME.BAK A:NAME1.DWG will copy the backup file NAME.BAK to a drawing file called NAME1.DWG on the same disk.

If you are planning to use a computer or to be a system manager or use several computer programs, it is a good idea to take a DOS course.

Computer Viruses

At this point, also be aware of the possibility of the system becoming infected with a virus. The most popular virus cleaner is McAfee Associates' Virus Scan and Cleaner. If this program is available on the hard drive or network, use it before saving any files. The command to scan a disk is:

C:**SCAN** *(if the virus scan is on the main path)*

or

C:**CD\VIRSCAN**

VIRSCAN:**SCAN** *(if the virus scan is under the VIRSCAN directory)*

If the virus scan program cannot be accessed by either of these commands, ask the instructor or the lab monitor how to access it.

Release 12 Notes

There are many improvements in Release 12's Operating System usage. Since there is no main menu, you are automatically placed in a drawing file when entering AutoCAD. You may also specify a drawing file name from the system prompt.

C:\ACAD>:**ACAD FLRPLAN**

If there is no file named FLRPLAN, AutoCAD will create a new drawing with the specified name.

In addition, the Save, Saveas, and Qsave options of the File pull-down menu can help you save time making backup files. AutoCAD changes the previous copy of the drawing from a .DWG file type to a .BAK file type. The previous .BAK file is deleted and the current file becomes the .DWG file.

To automatically have your work saved at a specific interval, use the SAVETIME system variable. This will save the current drawing as a .DWG file type and the current .DWG to a .BAK file type.

Several system variables with release 12 will make file management easier. SAVEFILE is a read-only variable that gives the name of the automatic saved file.

SAVENAME is a read-only variable that give the user defined file name. The RENAME command allows you to rename named objects from the command line. The format is:

Command: **RENAME**

Block/Dimstyle/LAyer/LType/Style/Ucs/VIew/VPort:

You will be prompted for the old name, then the new name.

Practice 4

Use COPY, ROTATE, and MIRROR to complete the drawing.

Create the arrows with PLINE.

Use common measures for road and sidewalk widths.

Once completed, ZOOM .1x to get a much smaller look at the drawing, then copy this corner two or three times to create a modern city or suburban area.

Use TRIM and EXTEND to join the streets. Add some winding streets with PLINE and PEDIT.

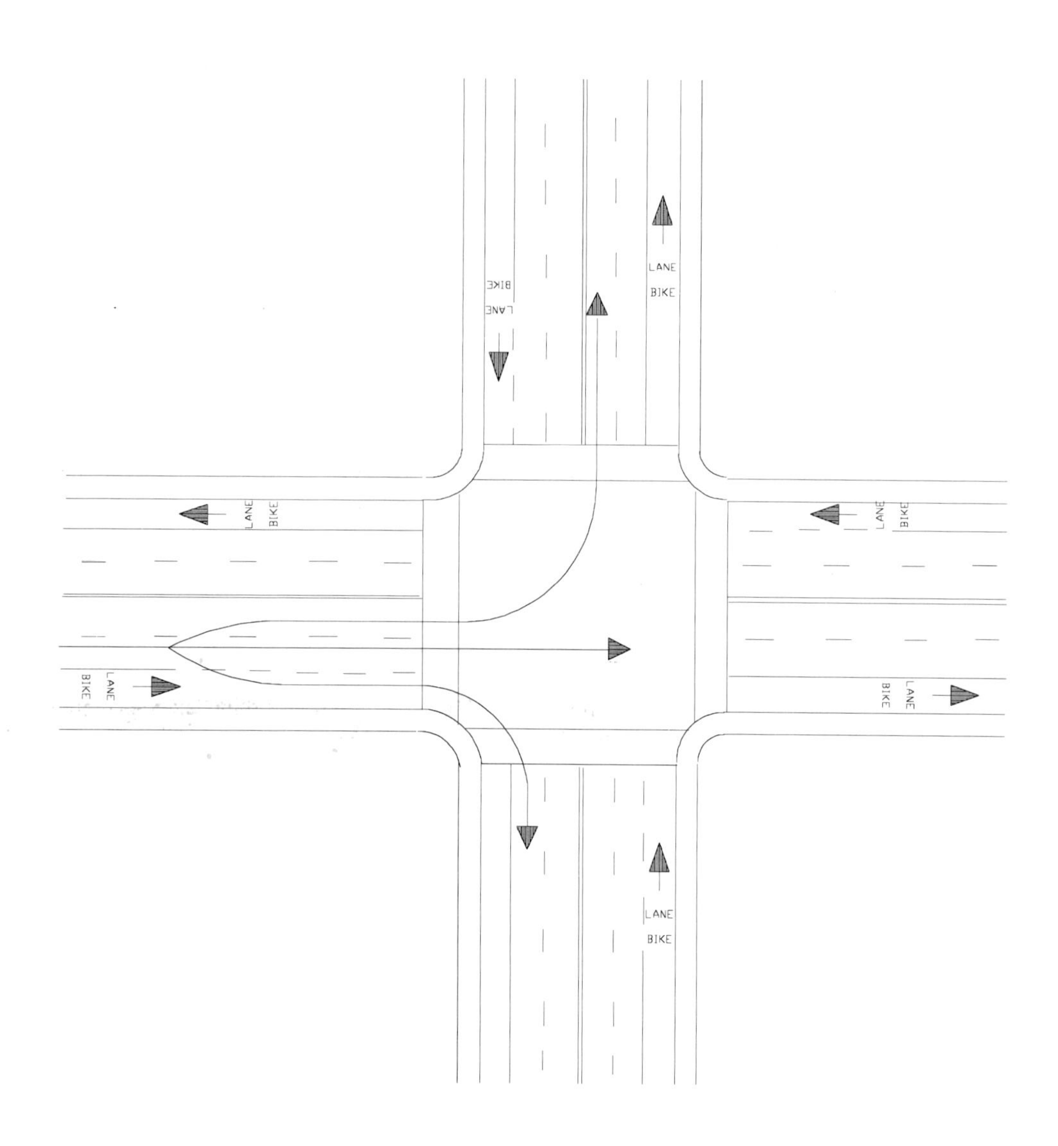

Exercise A4

View from the side to gain maximum use of the screen.

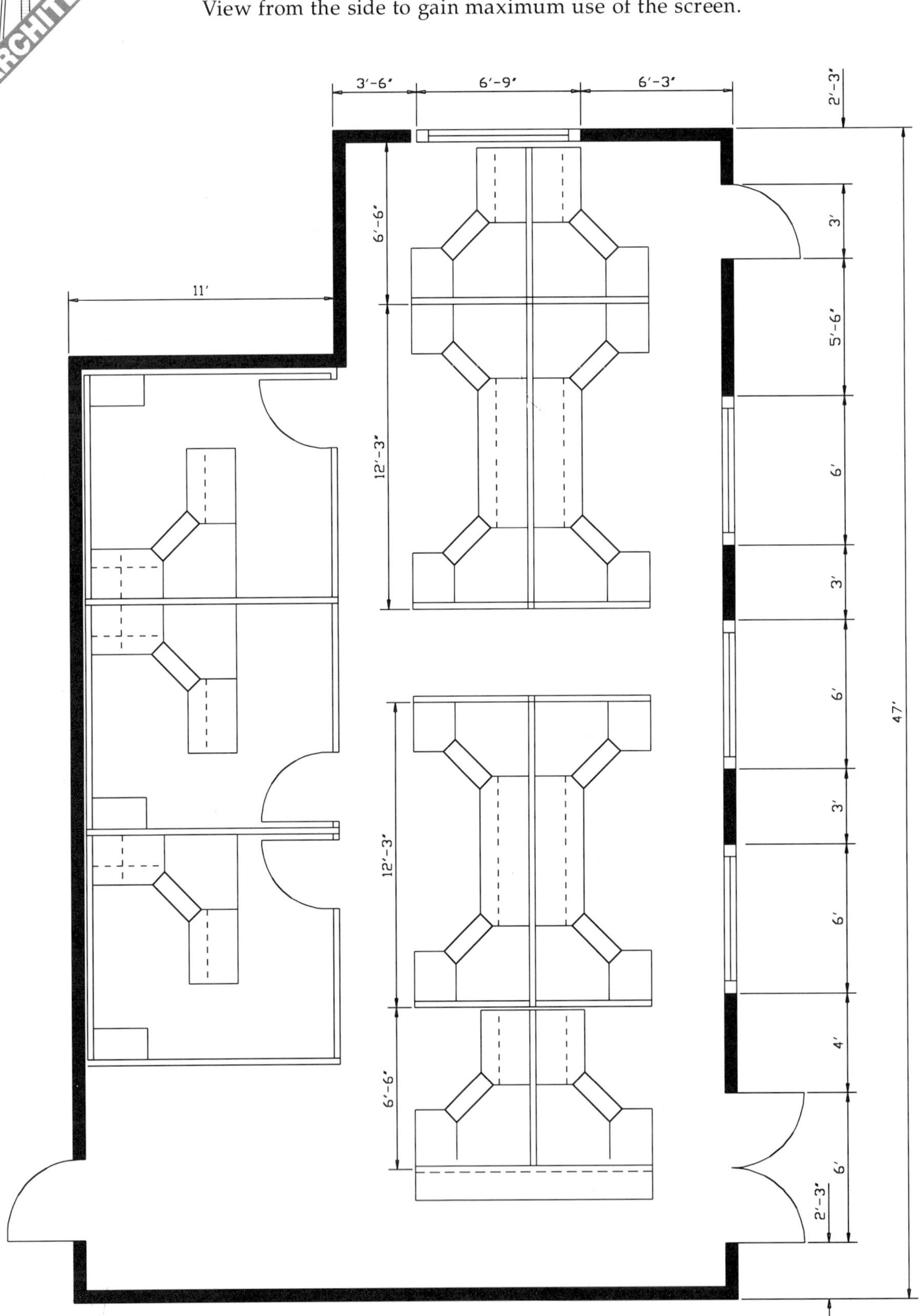

Hintson A4

In this example, either use decimal units with .25 as 3 inches, or change to architectural units with a Snap value of 3.

Remember, any number entered without a foot (') or inch (") symbol will be accepted as inches.

The drawing is of modular furniture. Create the offices by using lines. The panels separating the offices are 3 inches thick. Be sure to leave enough space for them.

Use ROTATE, COPY, and MOVE to create the offices exactly as you see them.

PLINE can be used to make the exterior walls easier to see.

Do not dimension.

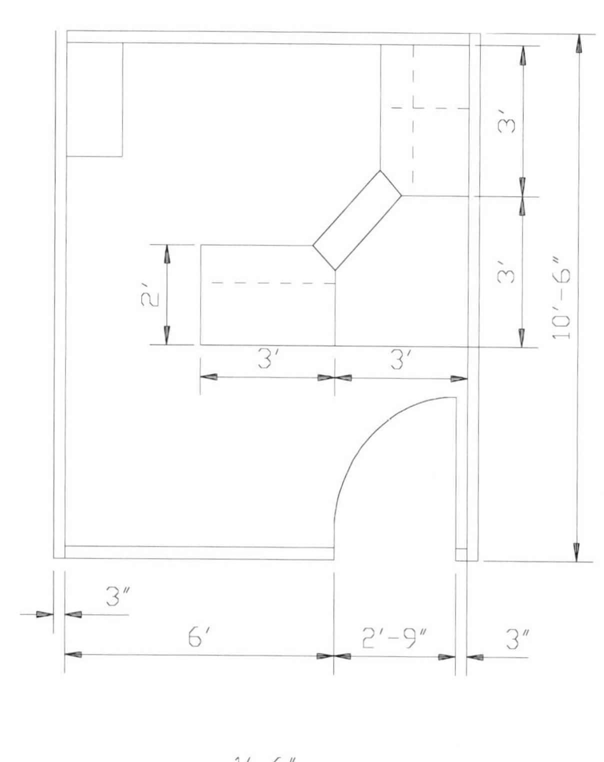

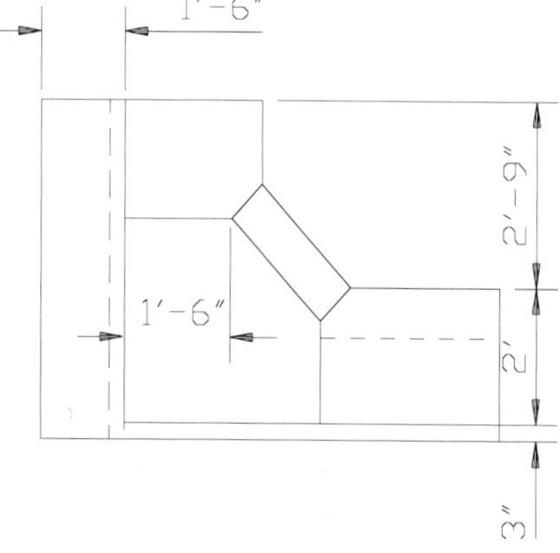

When finished with this drawing, save it so you can edit it later with STRETCH, and dimension it as shown in Chapter 7.

Exercise M4

Create the geometry below using COPY, MIRROR, MOVE, and ROTATE.

Centre lines are not needed. They are only shown to show where the parts go.

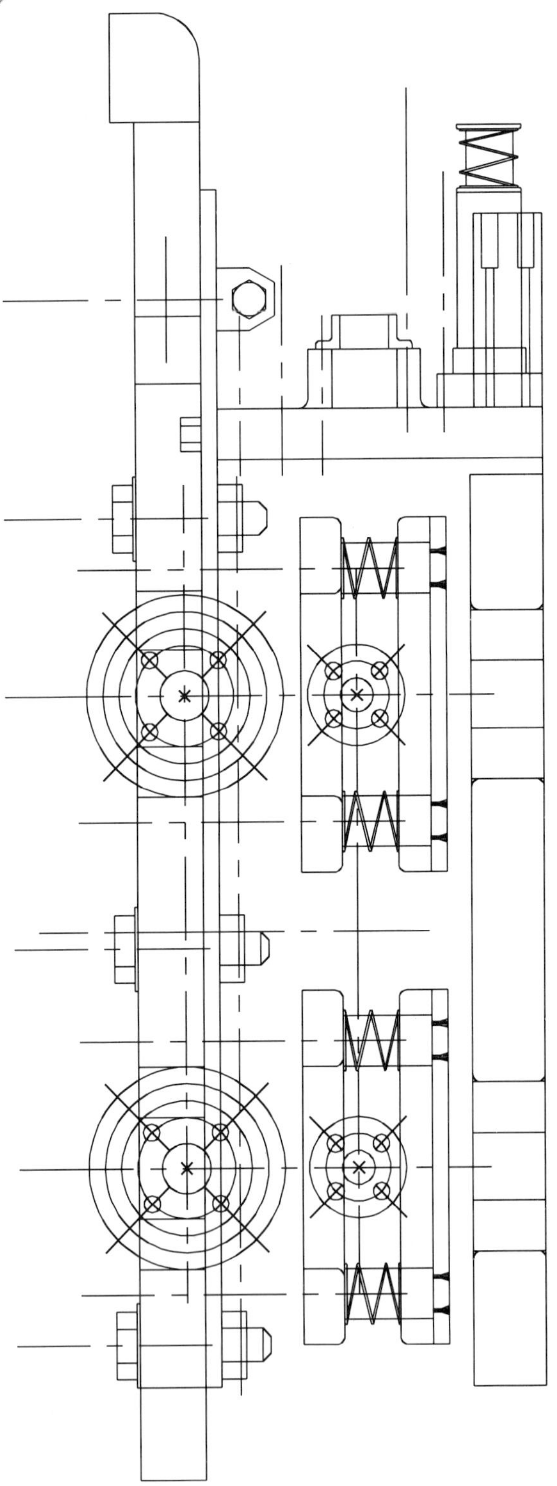

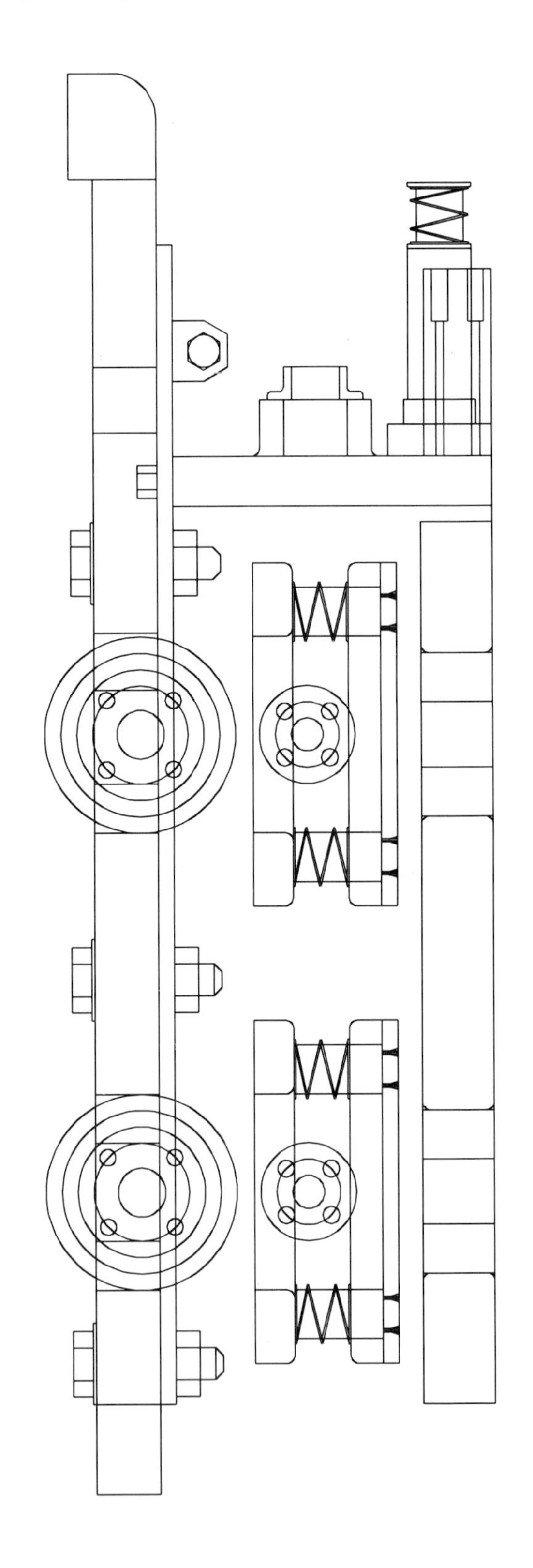

Hints on M4

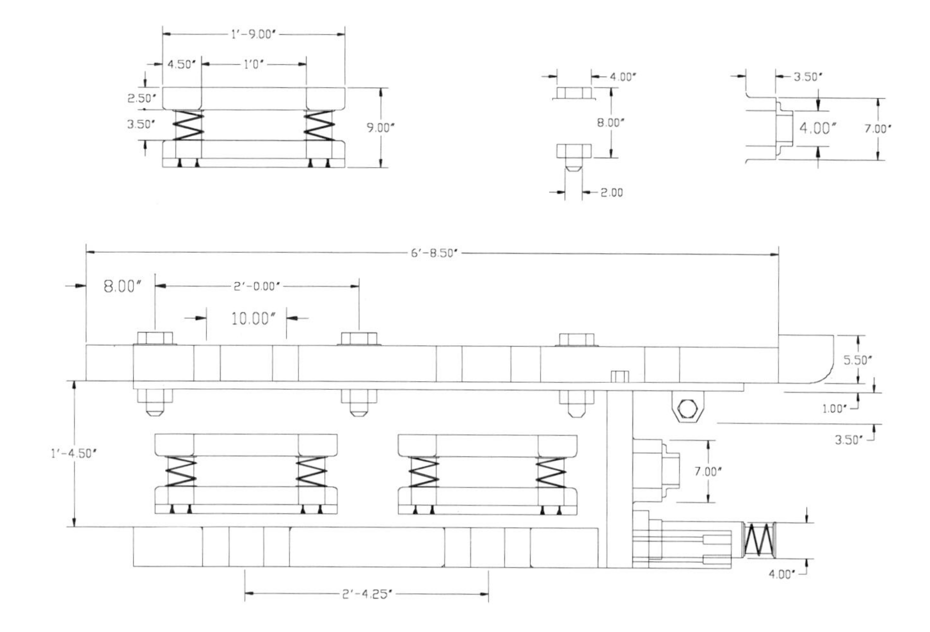

Create the two modules below using the dimensions at the bottom. Make one and copy it.

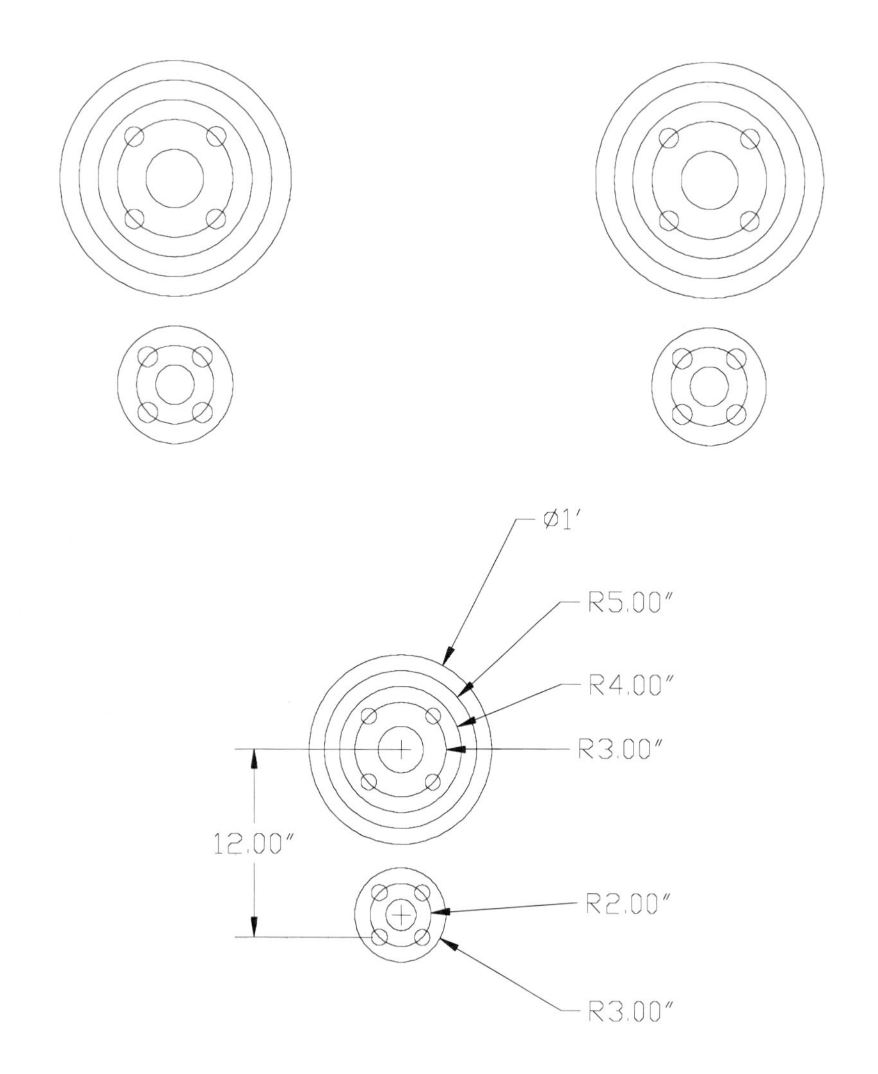

Exercise C4

Mapping and surveying are often used in conjunction with services. Use COPY, ROTATE, and MOVE to create this transformer rack.

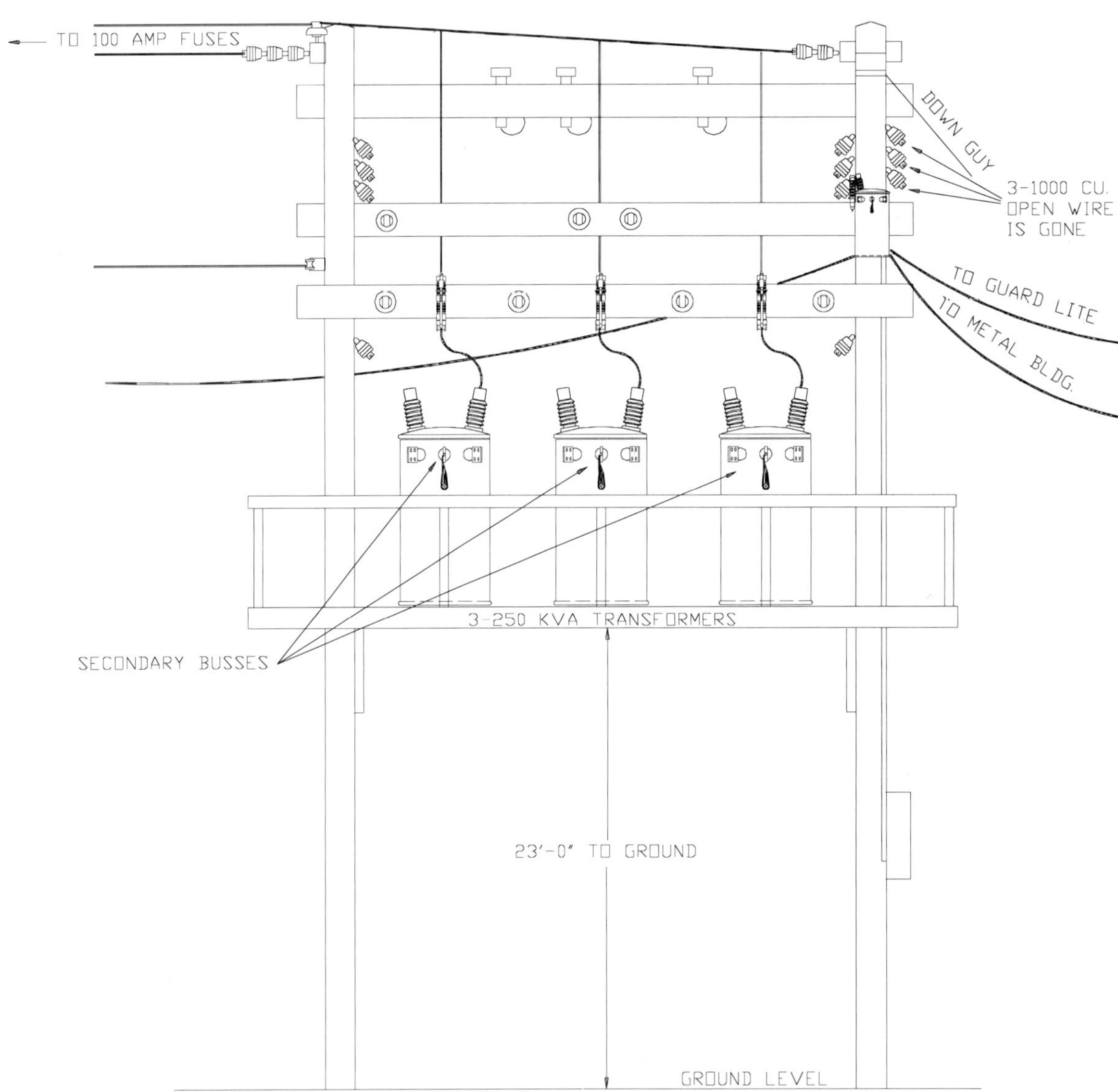

The individual parts are actually quite simple to draw. Once drawn, they can be copied and rotated to fit the illustration. See the next page for overall measurements.

Hints on C4

Use the overall dimensions above to create the individual items, then place them using MOVE, COPY, MIRROR, and ROTATE.

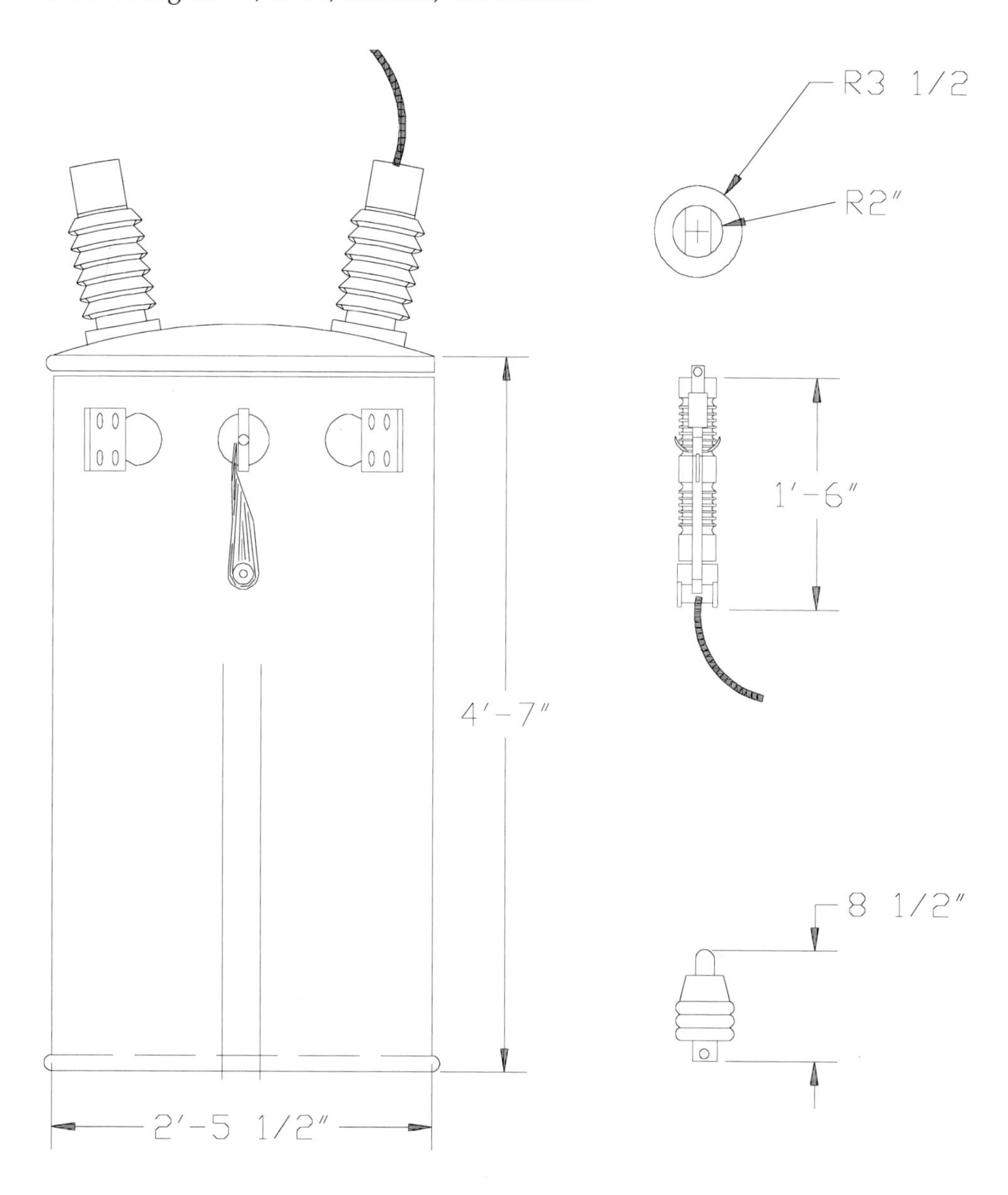

(Drawing compliments of Johnny Barton.)

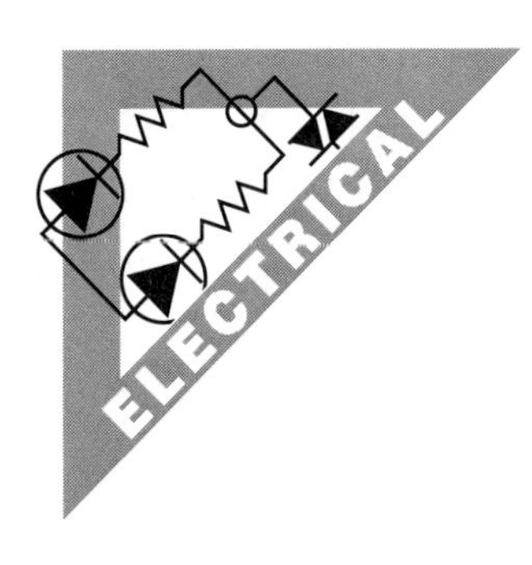

Exercise E4

Create the geometry using COPY, MOVE, MIRROR and ROTATE.

Use OSNAP to access the endpoints of objects and the midpoints of objects.

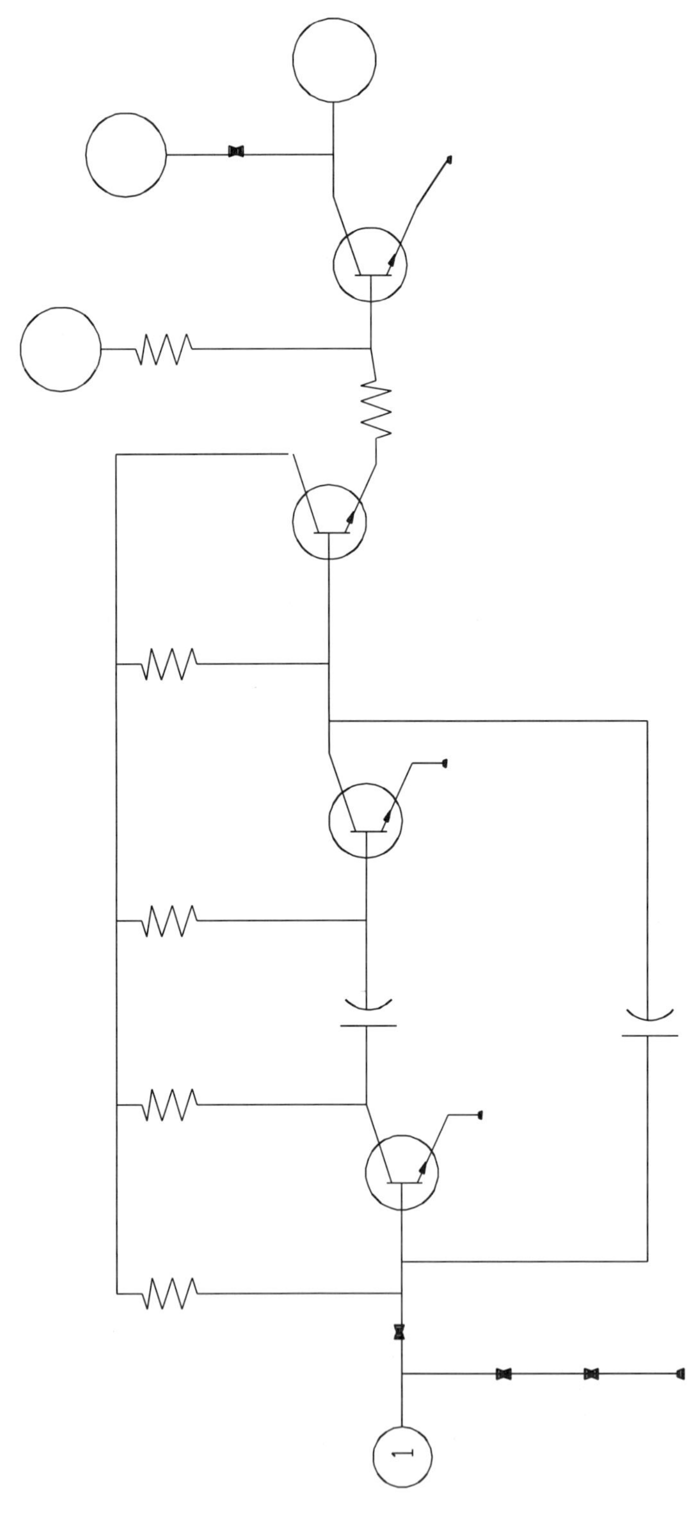

CHALLENGER

Challenger 4

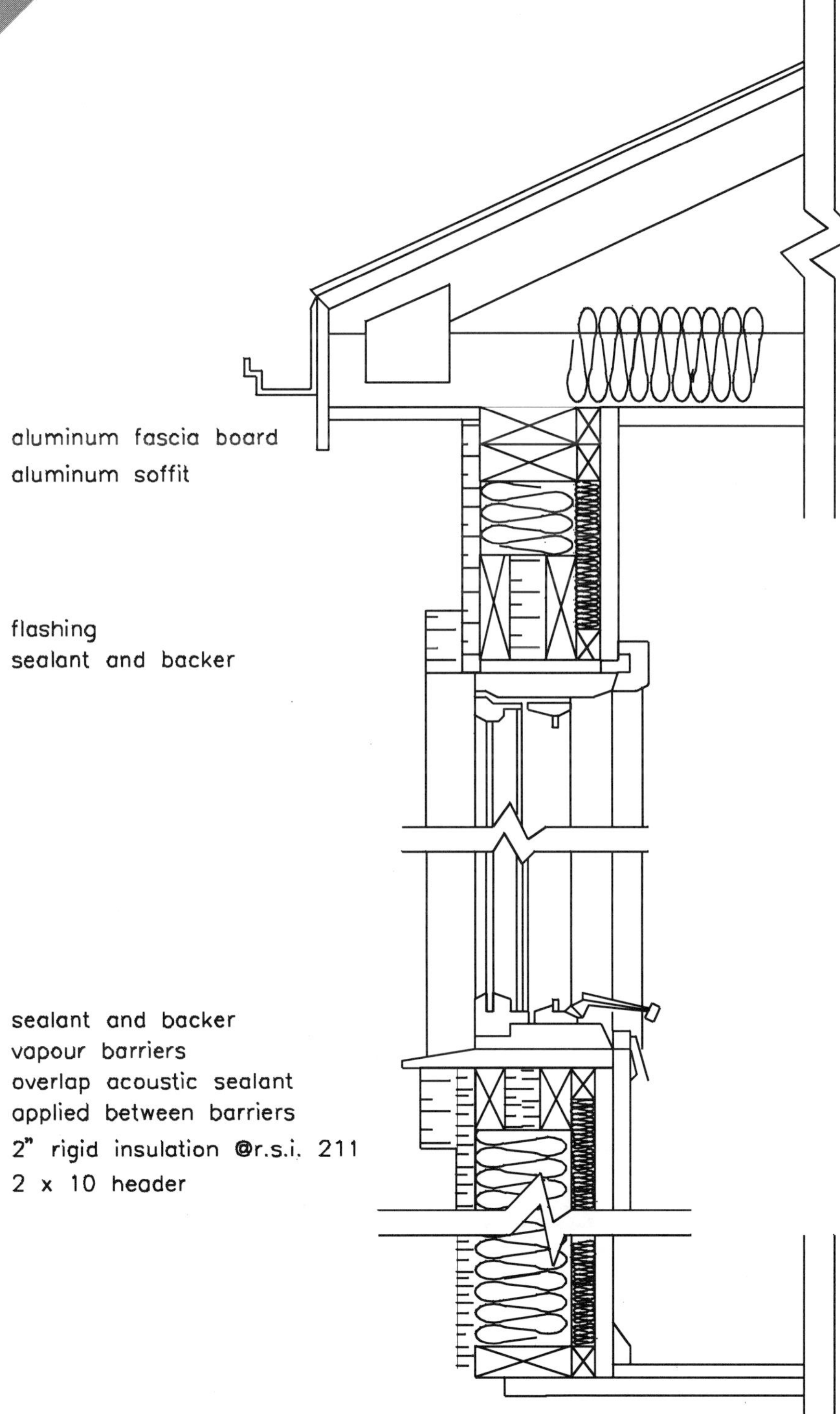
treated cardboard
insulation stop
20 inches batt
insulation @ r.s. 17.04
2 x 8 trusses
24 inches on centre
aluminum fascia board
aluminum soffit
gypsum board ceiling
2–2 x 8 top plates
1 x 1 strapping
2– 2 x 6 lintel
flashing
sealant and backer
wood trim
clad window frame
2– 2 x 4
1/2 " floor
1/2" plywood subfloor
sealant and backer
vapour barriers
overlap acoustic sealant
applied between barriers
2" rigid insulation @r.s.i. 211
2 x 10 header

ADVANCED EDITING

Upon completion of this chapter, the student should be able to:

1. Edit objects using the STRETCH command
2. Edit objects using the TRIM command
3. Extend objects to a selected boundary
4. Create objects using the OFFSET command
5. Array objects in both Polar and Rectangular arrays

REMOVE

Now that we have practised indicating or selecting objects using Window and Crossing, what happens if we have selected objects using these options, but have included objects that we do not need? What we do then is remove them.

The Remove option changes the Select objects: prompt to a Remove objects: prompt. This allows objects to be removed from the selection set. Items *not* to be included in the editing command are then selected by individually picking them or by using Window or Crossing. If there are more items to be added to the list of those being edited, selecting Add will return the prompt to Select objects:.

This kind of activity is similar to a shopping experience. A person may say, "I want to take that bunch of items over there (Window) but not the red one (Remove), and (Add) that whole table full of stuff there (Crossing), except for the long one (Remove)." What the person is doing is identifying a list or series of items that will be affected by the exchange.

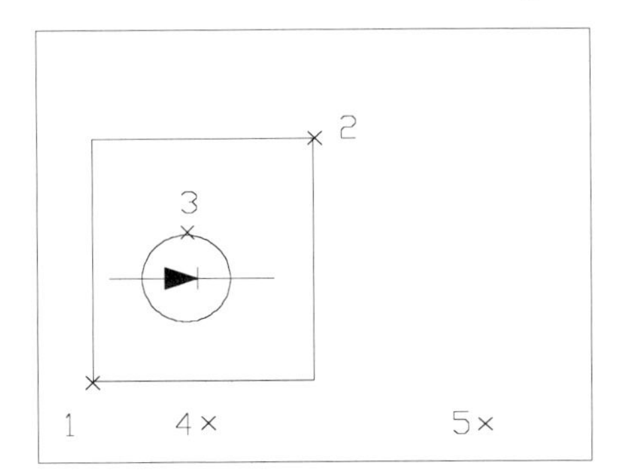

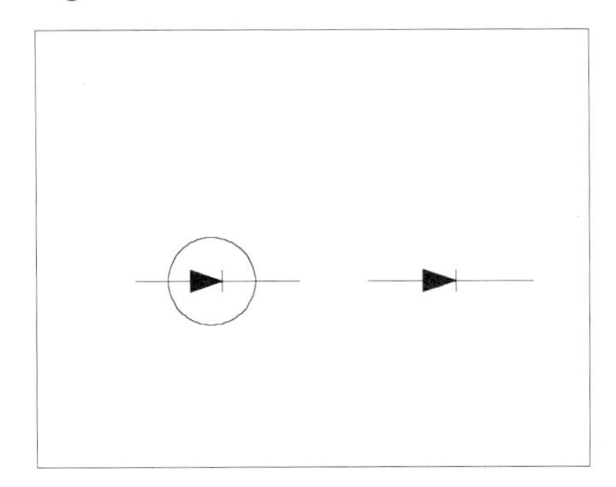

Figure 5-1. Remove option

In Figure 5-1, the geometry being edited is identified with Window. The lines and pline are to be copied to the right, but the original object is to remain in its current position. It is much easier to choose the whole set with Window and Remove the circle than to pick each object individually.

Command:**COPY**

Select objects:**W** *(pick 1, 2)*

Select objects:**R**

Remove objects: *(pick 3)*

Remove objects:⏎

Base point: *(pick 4)*

Displacement: *(pick 5)*

STRETCH

Crossing - "C" when using Stretch command

The STRETCH command is easy to understand when one can see that all objects are defined by a series of points: a line has a beginning point and an endpoint, and a circle has a centre point and a radius. The STRETCH command simply changes or redefines one of the points. To stretch a line, simply identify which point is to be moved, and the line will be redrawn relative to the new endpoint, while the other point will remain at its original position.

Figure 5-2. Demonstration of the STRETCH command

Command:**STRETCH**

Select objects:**C** *(pick 1, 2)*

Select objects:⏎

Base point:**4,1**

New point:**@3,0** *(stretch object three units in positive X direction)*

All objects chosen by the Crossing are highlighted.

Only the right side of the object is affected by the command above because only the right-side point was selected with the Crossing option. The line is reconstructed at 7,1, thus making it longer.

1, 1 7, 1

Figure 5-3. The STRETCH command

The line can also be made shorter or diagonal by changing the position of the new point.

Base point:**7,1**	Base point: **7,1**
New point:**@-4,0**	New point:**@-4,3**

1,1 3,1 3,4 1,1

Figure 5-4. Using STETCH with incremental entries

In Figure 5-4, the left-side point has not changed, the item has been stretched by identifying the right-side point and moving it in relation to the left-side point.

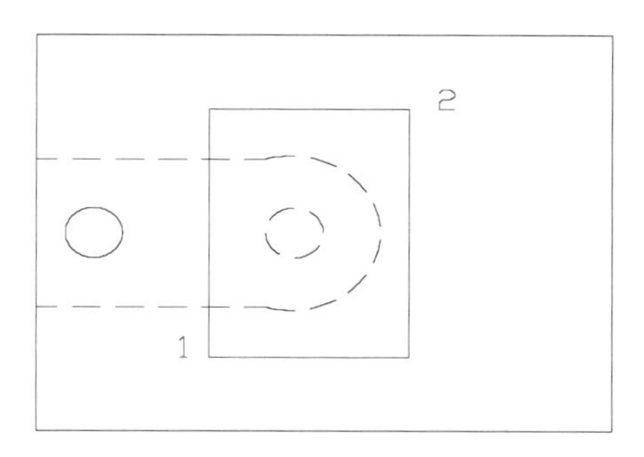

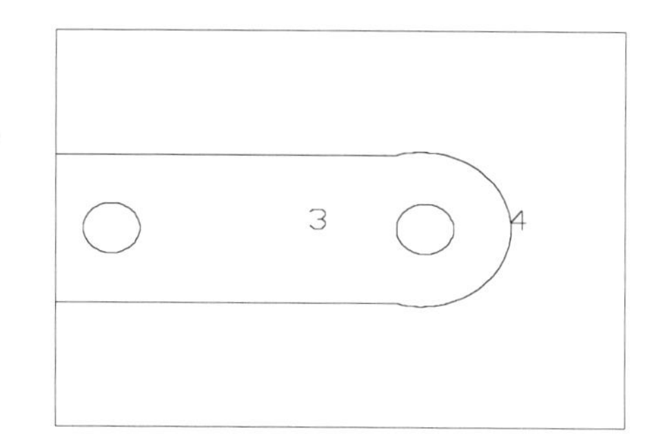

Figure 5-5. Using STRETCH

In Figure 5-5, the STRETCH Crossing causes the circle to move as an entire object and not turn into an ellipse. The points on the circle are selected as a pair. One side of an arc can be selected, however, and stretched out to make an arc with a different radius.

Objects identified by the Crossing option will be highlighted.

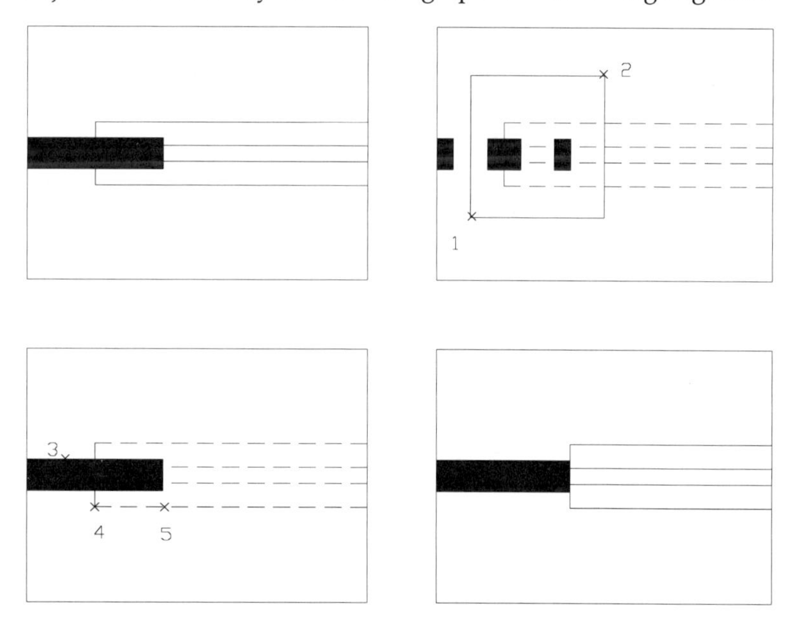

Figure 5-6. Using STRETCH *with Remove*

`Command:`**`STRETCH`**

`Select objects:`**`C`** *(pick 1, 2) (selects all the objects)*

`Select objects:`**`R`** *(indicates items are to be removed)*

`Remove objects:` *(pick 3) (indicates that pline is not to be stretched)*

`Remove objects:`↵ *(indicates no more items on the list)*

`Base point:` *(pick 4)*

`New point:` *(pick 5) (this can also be an incremental entry)*

The objects identified will be "loaded on the cursor" and will move along with the cursor while identifying the new point.

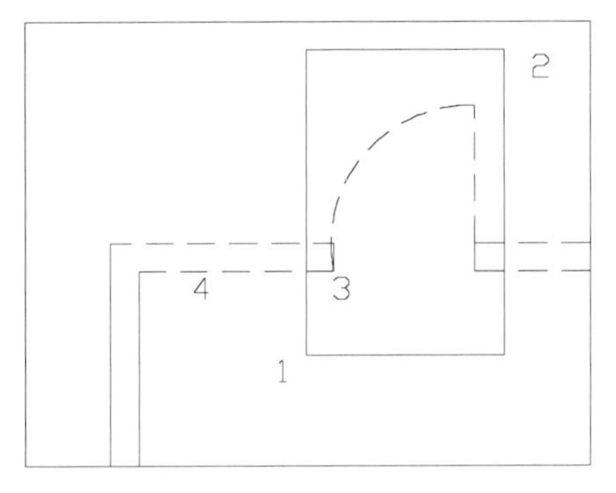

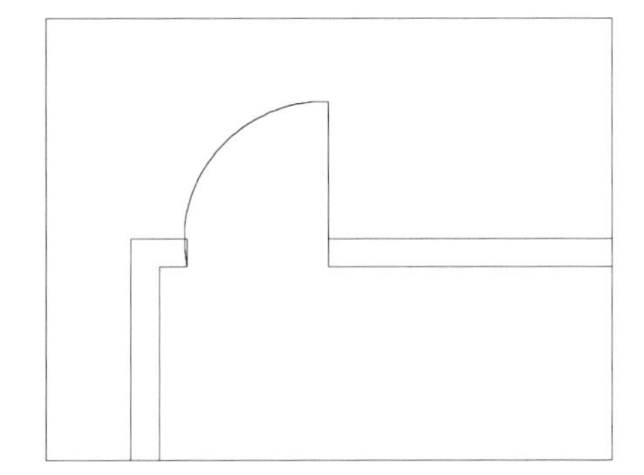

Figure 5-7. STRETCH with Ortho

In Figure 5-7, notice that the door opening retains its width when the wall on either side is selected and stretched. Ortho was used to ensure that the walls remained straight.

It is advisable to use STRETCH or EXTEND when making an object fit into a larger space than was originally intended. Never create another line or arc to add onto an existing one.

TRIM

The TRIM command is used to cut off an object or a series of objects as they intersect a boundary or cutting edge. The cutting edge or boundary must already exist on the drawing before TRIM can be used to cut other objects. Again, with editing commands, always read what is required in the command string before identifying objects.

In Figure 5-8, the cutting edge is clearly the diagonal line. It is highlighted when chosen.

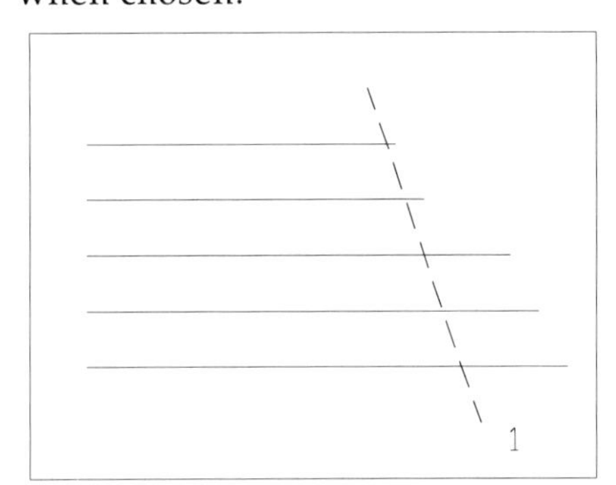

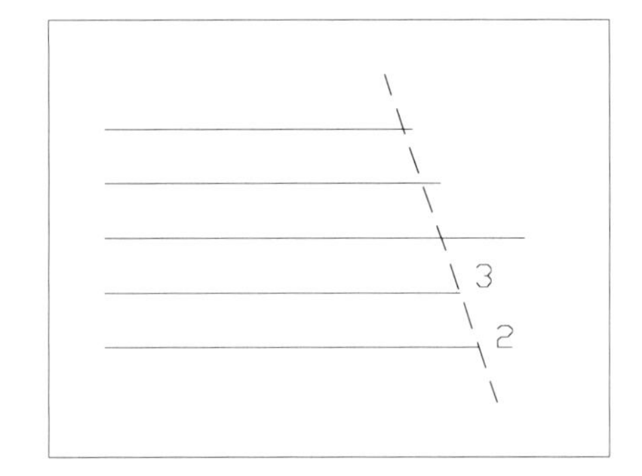

Figure 5-8. Using TRIM

The objects to be trimmed are the horizontal lines. Any number of objects can be trimmed in one command.

```
Command: TRIM
Select cutting edges: (pick 1)
Select objects:↵ (no more cutting edges are needed)
object to trim/Undo: (pick 2)
object to trim/Undo: (pick 3)
object to trim/Undo:↵
```

The first pick indicates the trim boundary, and the following picks are those items which will be trimmed to this boundary. Any number of objects can be trimmed.

The objects are trimmed to the closest cutting edge. The endpoint chosen on the object to be trimmed is the actual end trimmed.

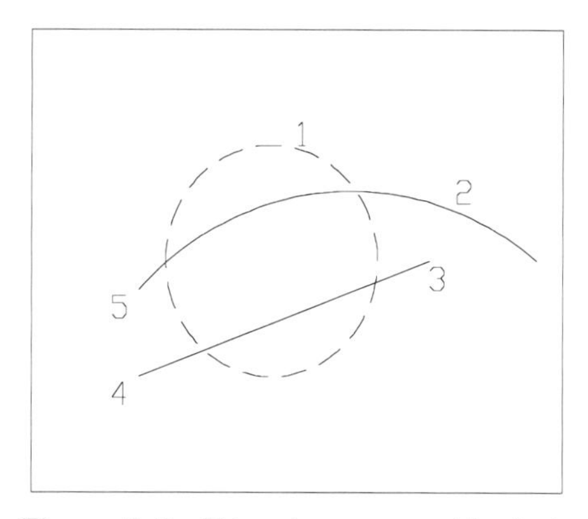

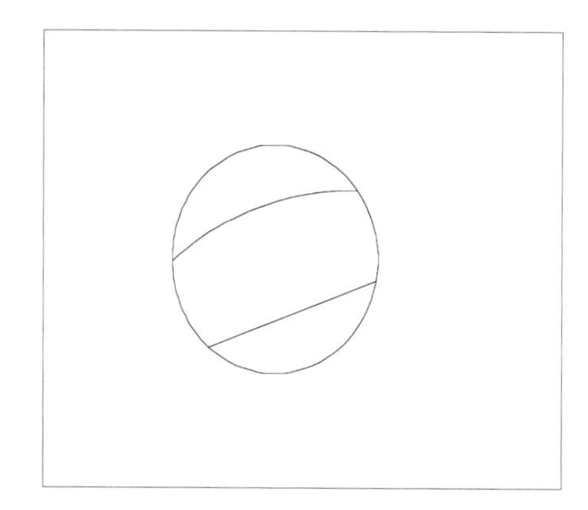

Figure 5-9. Trimming many objects to one boundary

```
Command:TRIM
Select cutting edges:
Select objects: (pick 1)
Select objects:↵
Select object to Trim: (pick 2,3,4,5)
```

The objects will be trimmed as you pick them.

To retain the lines on the outside of the circle of Figure 5-9 and remove only the portion of the lines within the circle, use Break.

You can also use Window to select the cutting edges.

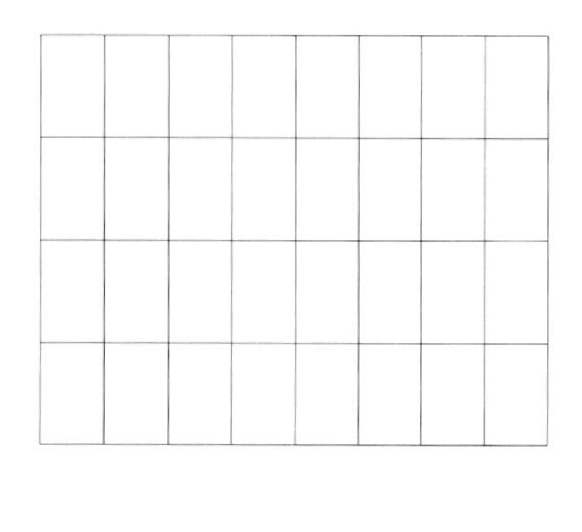

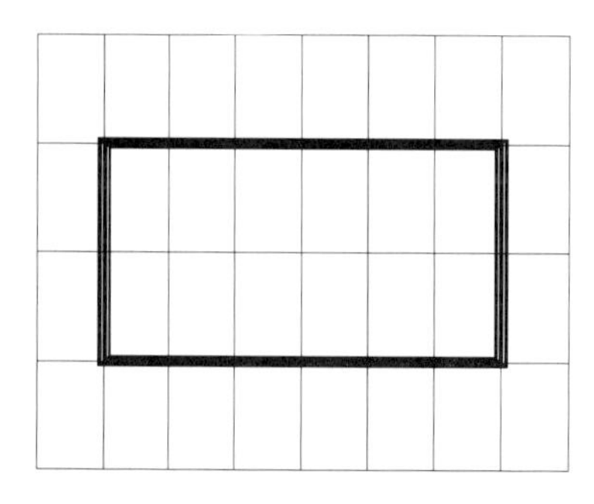

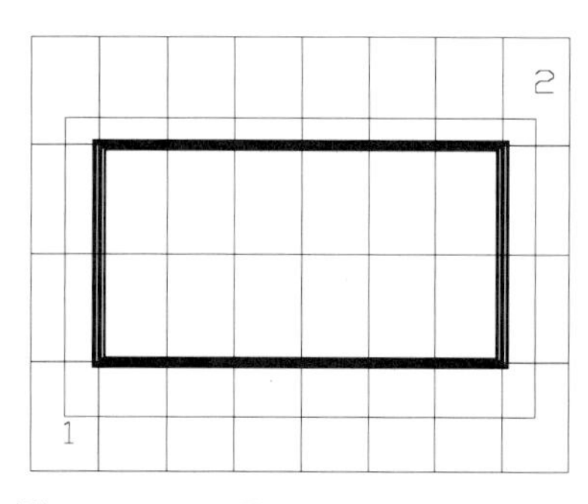

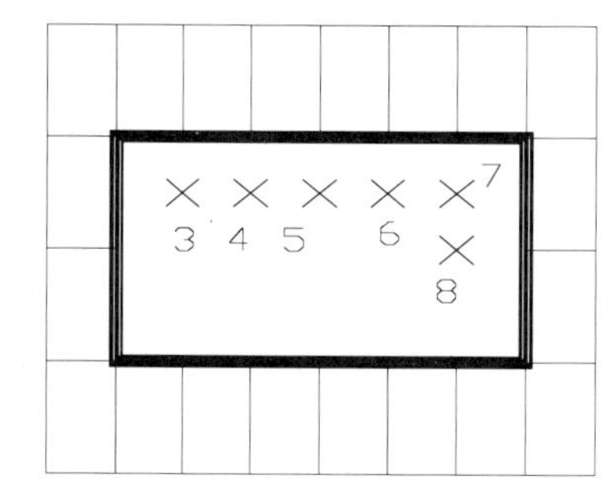

Figure 5-10. TRIM with a pline or Window

In Figure 5-10, the user wants to break out the portion of the geometry within the pline.

Using BREAK would be tedious, so it is best to create a pline where the objects are to be edited.

Then, by choosing the closed pline with a window, the cutting edge is identified.

```
Command:TRIM
Select cutting edges:
Select objects:W (pick 1, 2)
Select objects:↵
object to trim/Undo: (pick 3, 4, 5, 6, 7, 8)
```

Multiple objects can also be chosen as the cutting edge. In Figure 5-11, all of the objects are considered cutting edges.

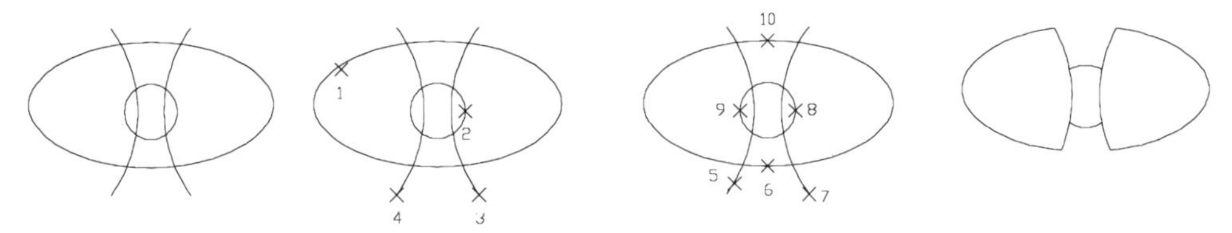

Figure 5-11. TRIM with multiple cutting edges

Picks 1, 2, 3, and 4 are the cutting edges. Creating the desired object is simple. Much can be learned about TRIM by performing this example.

EXTEND

The EXTEND command also uses a boundary or boundaries, but uses the boundary as the item to which objects are extended.

In Figure 5-12, the boundary is clearly the diagonal line. Once picked, it will be highlighted.

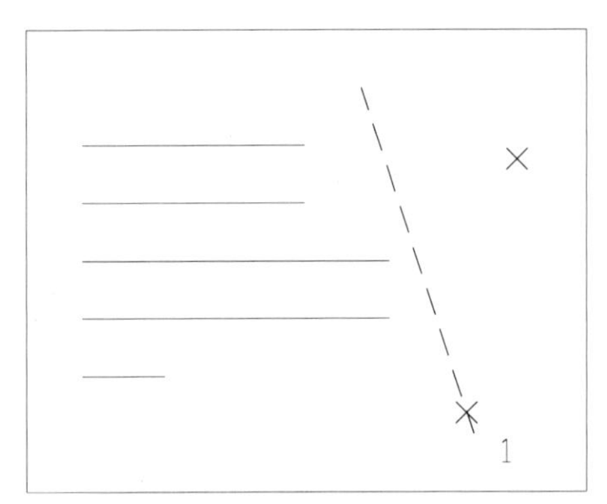

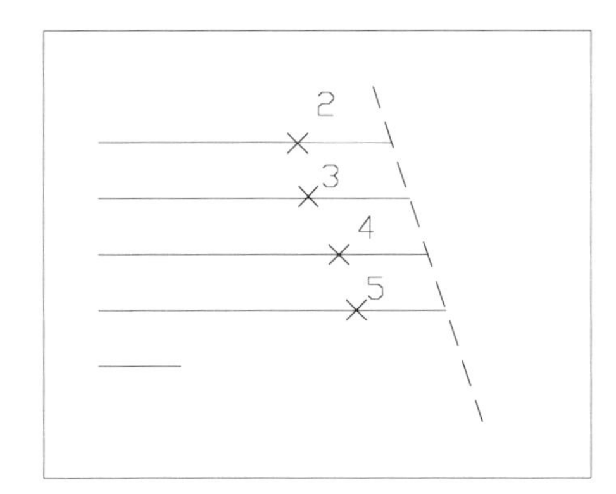

Figure 5-12. The EXTEND command

```
Command:EXTEND
Select boundary edges:
Select objects: (pick 1)
Select objects:↵
Select object to extend/Undo: (pick 2)
Select object to extend/Undo: (pick 3, etc)
```

The Undo option will undo the previous pick while still in the command.

In Figure 5-13, the lines are extended to the closest boundary selected. More than one boundary can be chosen for objects to extend to, and the closest endpoint will always be extended to the boundary chosen.

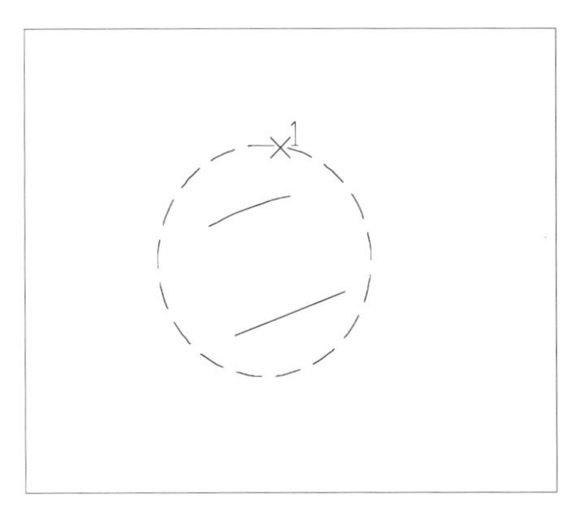

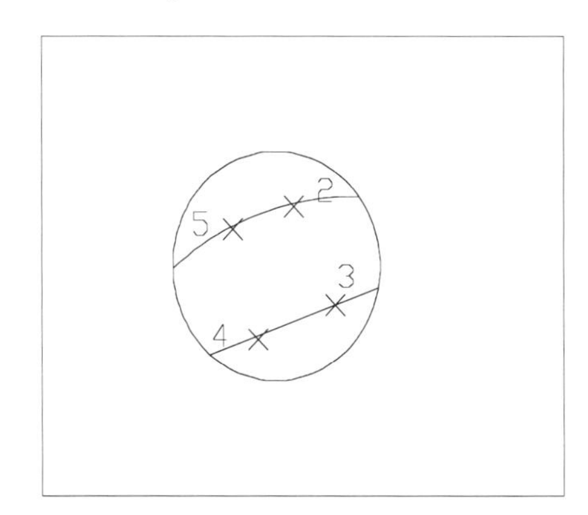

Figure 5-13. Extending many objects to one boundary

```
Command:EXTEND
Select boundary edges:
Select objects: (pick 1)
Select objects:↵
Select object to extend/Undo: (pick 2,3,4,5)
```

What can go wrong with TRIM and EXTEND

If AutoCAD responds with:

`No edges selected`, then you have chosen an object that cannot be referenced as a boundary or cutting edge. Often, a pline is not a valid edge and will be rejected.

`Cannot extend this entity`, then the object chosen cannot be extended. If a complete circle is chosen, it cannot be extended.

`Entity does not intersect an edge`, then the object does not line up with the edge selected. Try using FILLET Radius 0.

OFFSET

OFFSET is perhaps the most often used editing command on the system. Once there are a few objects on a model, much of the other data relative to it can be offset. In relation to lines, the OFFSET command draws a parallel line at a given distance. This can be tremendously useful when creating architectural or primarily linear drawings.

The command first requires the offset distance. This is the distance by which all the objects will be offset. Then an item must be chosen to be offset, then a side on which it will be offset. The OFFSET command, like many editing commands, works only in the X-Y plane.

```
Command:OFFSET
Offset distance or Through <last distance>:8
Select object to offset: (pick 1)
Side to offset?: (pick 2)
Select object to offset: (pick 3)
Side to offset?: (pick 4, etc)
```

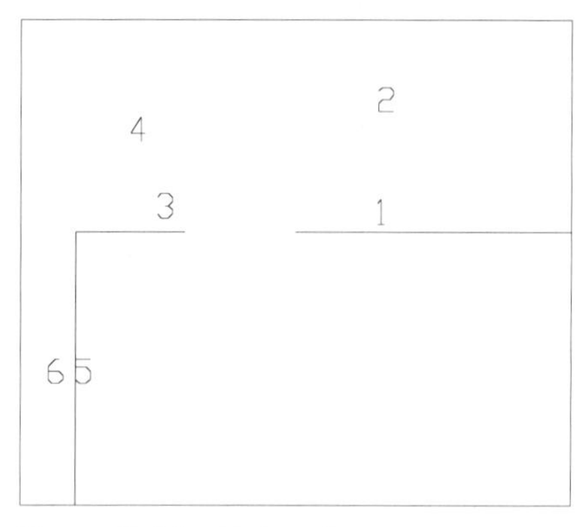

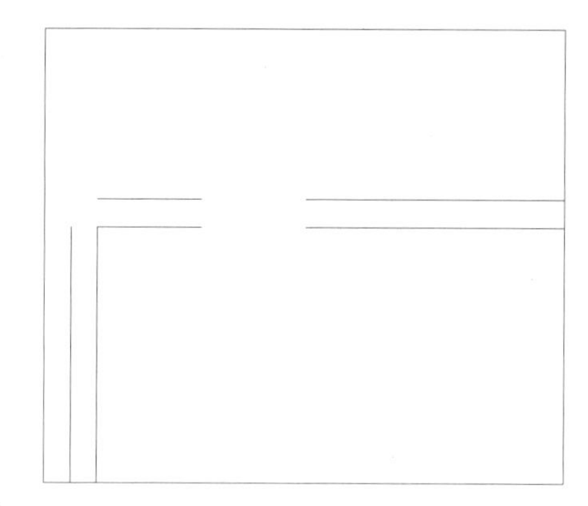

Figure 5-14. Using the OFFSET command

The prompts for the objects to offset and the side to offset will continue in a paired sequence until the Enter key is pressed. After the walls are created, the corners are cleaned up with FILLET Rad 0. Pick the corners that are either overlapping or not intersecting. The FILLET command will create 90-degree edges.

OFFSET functions much like COPY for the line commands, except it is offsetting the objects relative to the distance chosen. A line, after it is offset, will have the same length as the original line, but it will be "away from," or parallel to, the first line at a specified distance.

Offsetting a circle or an arc will result in the second object having the same centre, but the radius will be larger or smaller by the offset distance. The centre point does not change, only the size of the circle or arc changes.

Similarly, with plines that are fit into curves or splines, the resulting object is fit through the same series of points at an offset distance.

Arcs, circles, and lines can all be offset.

The first pick is the object to be offset, the second is the direction.

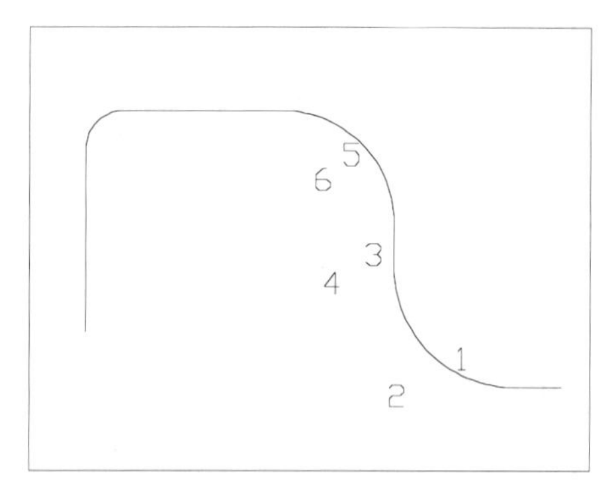

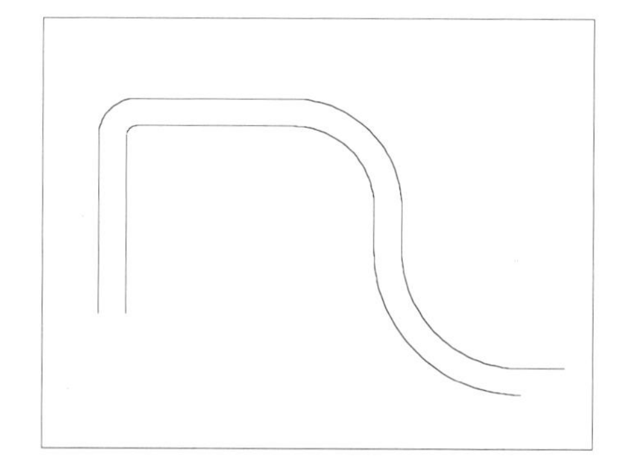

Figure 5-15. Offsetting arcs and lines

```
Command:OFFSET
Offset distance or Through <last distance>:8
Select object to offset: (pick 1)
Side to offset?: (pick 2)
Select object to offset: (pick 3, etc)
```

Plines can also be offset. This becomes very useful for making moulds and designs for parts that are irregular in shape.

The inside offset spline of Figure 5-16 will be defined by the same number of vertices, but the distance between the vertices will be different.

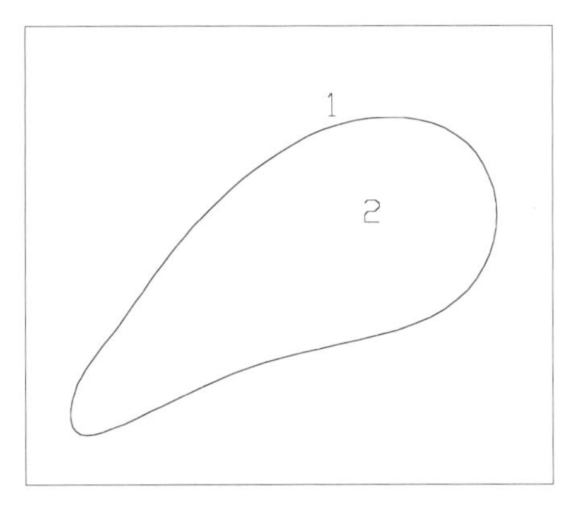

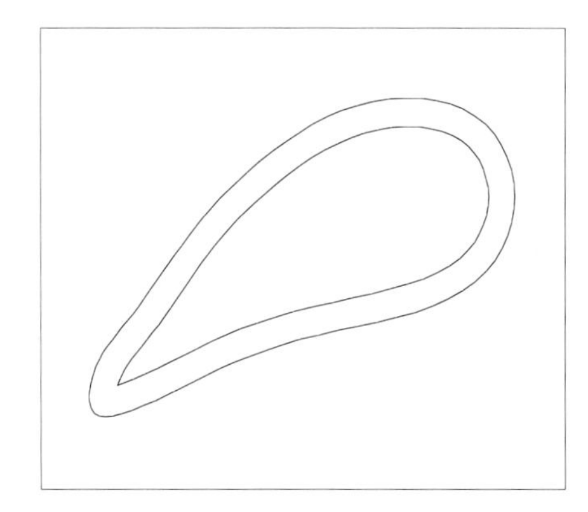

Figure 5-16. Offsetting plines

```
Command:OFFSET
Offset distance or Through <last distance>:8
Select object to offset: (pick 1)
Side to offset?: (pick 2)
```

The Through option in OFFSET is used to specify a point through which the offset can be calculated, as opposed to having a specified distance.

OFFSET allows for a totally different attitude in designing a part and is extremely useful in designing parts where distances are not in regular integers, and therefore not easily accessible by SNAP and GRID. Practise the examples given to become more familiar with OFFSET.

ARRAY (POLAR)

The ARRAY command creates circular (polar) or rectangular patterns of selected objects by copying them along or around an identified point. The command prompts first for the objects that are to be arrayed. It then prompts for the type of array — polar or rectangular. Finally, it asks to specify how many and how far.

In a polar array, the object (the smaller circle) is arrayed around the larger circle at equal distances.

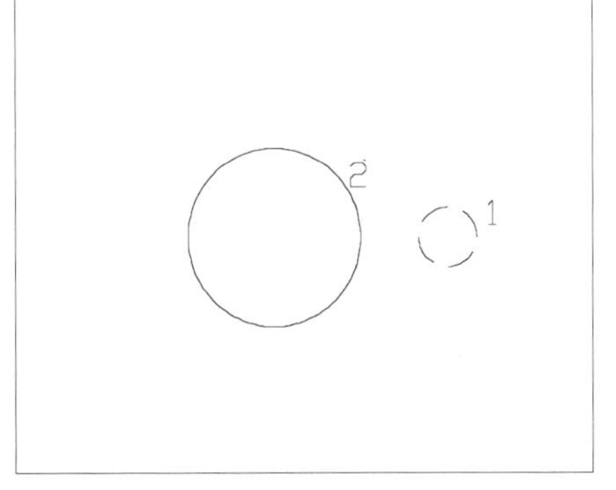

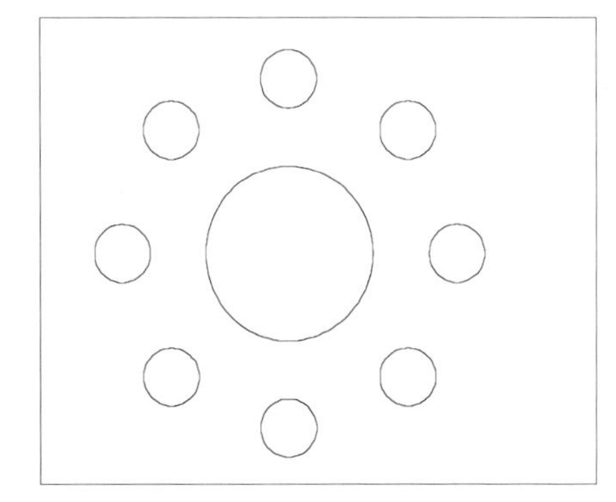

Figure 5-17. The ARRAY command with Polar option

```
Command:ARRAY
Select objects: (pick 1)
Select objects:↵ (indicates that no more are needed)
```

```
Rectangular/Polar array (R/P):P
Center point of array:CEN (pick 2)
Number of items:8
Angle to fill (+=CCW,-=CW)<360>:↵ (accepts default of 360)
Rotate objects as they are copied? <y>:↵ (accepts default)
```

With a polar array, the incremental distance can be specified rather than the total distance. The distance needed between the items must be known. Respond with a 0 when prompted for the angle to fill, and the command will then prompt for the incremental angle.

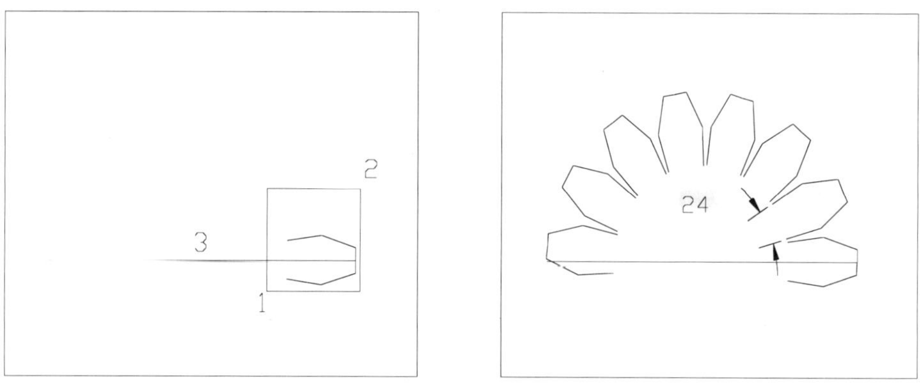

Figure 5-18. ARRAY with an incremental angle

```
Command:ARRAY
Select objects:W (pick 1, 2)
Select objects:↵ (indicates no more objects are needed)
Rectangular/Polar array (R/P):P
Center point of array:MID (pick 3)
Number of items:8
Angle to fill (+=CCW,-=CW)<360>:0 (indicates incremental angle)
Angle between items (+=CCW, -=CW):24
Rotate objects as they are copied? <y>:↵ (accepts default)
```

ARRAY (RECTANGULAR)

In the diagram of Figure 5-19, the objects are arrayed along the X axis or in columns.

Note: the distance between the columns is the width of the item itself.

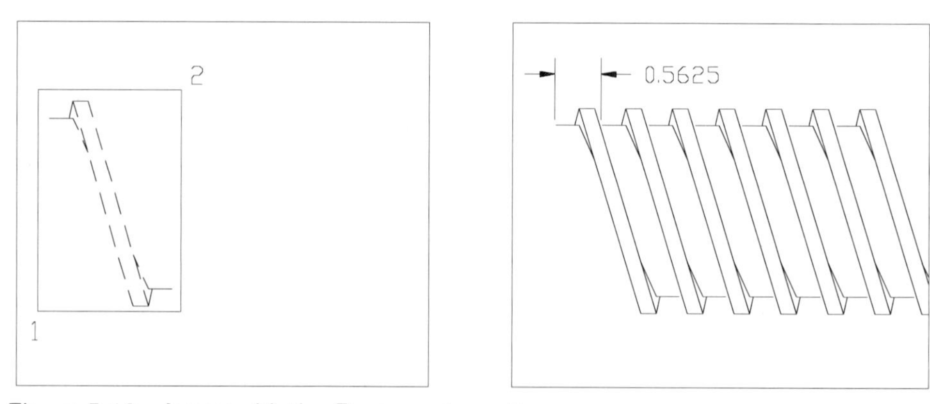

Figure 5-19. ARRAY with the Rectangular option

Command:**ARRAY**

Select objects:**W** *(pick 1, 2)*

Select objects:↵ *(indicates no more objects are needed)*

Rectangular/Polar array (R/P):**R**

Number of rows <1>:↵ *(accepts the default of 1)*

Number of columns <1>:**7**

Distance between the columns:**.5625**

When producing layouts that contain many objects in both the X-and the Y-direction, specify the number of rows and columns.

If there is a chair that is 24 inches wide and an aisle of 18 inches is needed between it and the next chair, the spacing would be the width of the chair plus the width of the aisle (24 + 18 = 3′6").

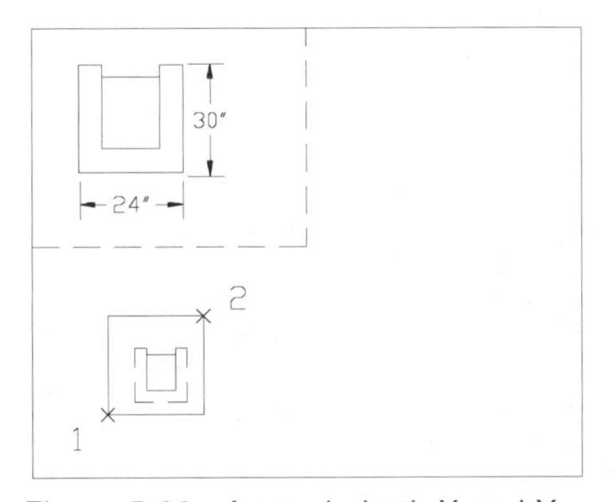

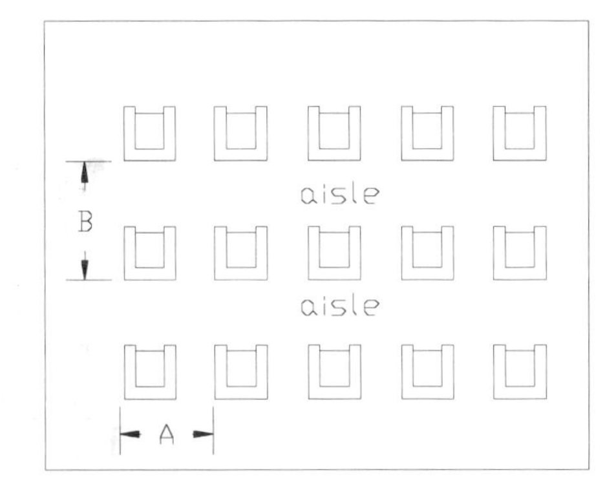

Figure 5-20. ARRAY in both X and Y

Command:**ARRAY**

Select objects:**W** *(pick 1, 2)*

Select objects:↵ *(indicates no more objects are needed)*

Rectangular/Polar array (R/P):**R**

Number of rows:**3**

Number of columns:**5**

Distance between the rows:**48** *(distance B)*

Distance between the columns:**42** *(distance A)*

A negative distance will place the array in a negative direction, to the left and down, from the existing point.

COMMAND STRING LOGIC

In aiming for success with editing commands, there is only one thing that needs to be remembered: *answer the system prompts that are being asked.*

It is no good trying to enforce your will on the system. First, it will not work, and second, it will only make you angry. All of the editing commands have more or less the same format. The system needs to know certain things in order to complete a command.

Take a look at these editing commands:

Command: **ARRAY** Command: **BREAK** Command: **COPY**

Command: **MOVE** Command: **ROTATE** Command: **STRETCH**

Select objects: is always the first prompt. Objects may be selected with single object picking, Crossing, Window, Remove, or Add.

The next prompt is how many and how far.

With ERASE, the prompt is Select objects: to be erased.

With EXTEND, OFFSET, and TRIM, the prompt asks for the information in a completely different order.

First, the prompt is for the distance either by numeric value or through selecting a boundary; then, the prompt asks for the list of items affected by the boundary. This change in format is for your convenience and makes the command much easier to use.

Most students have trouble with the Select objects prompt. Once you have selected the objects required, you must indicate to the system that there are no further items to be included by pressing the Enter or Return key. If you do not, the system will assume that you want to continue picking objects to be affected by the commands.

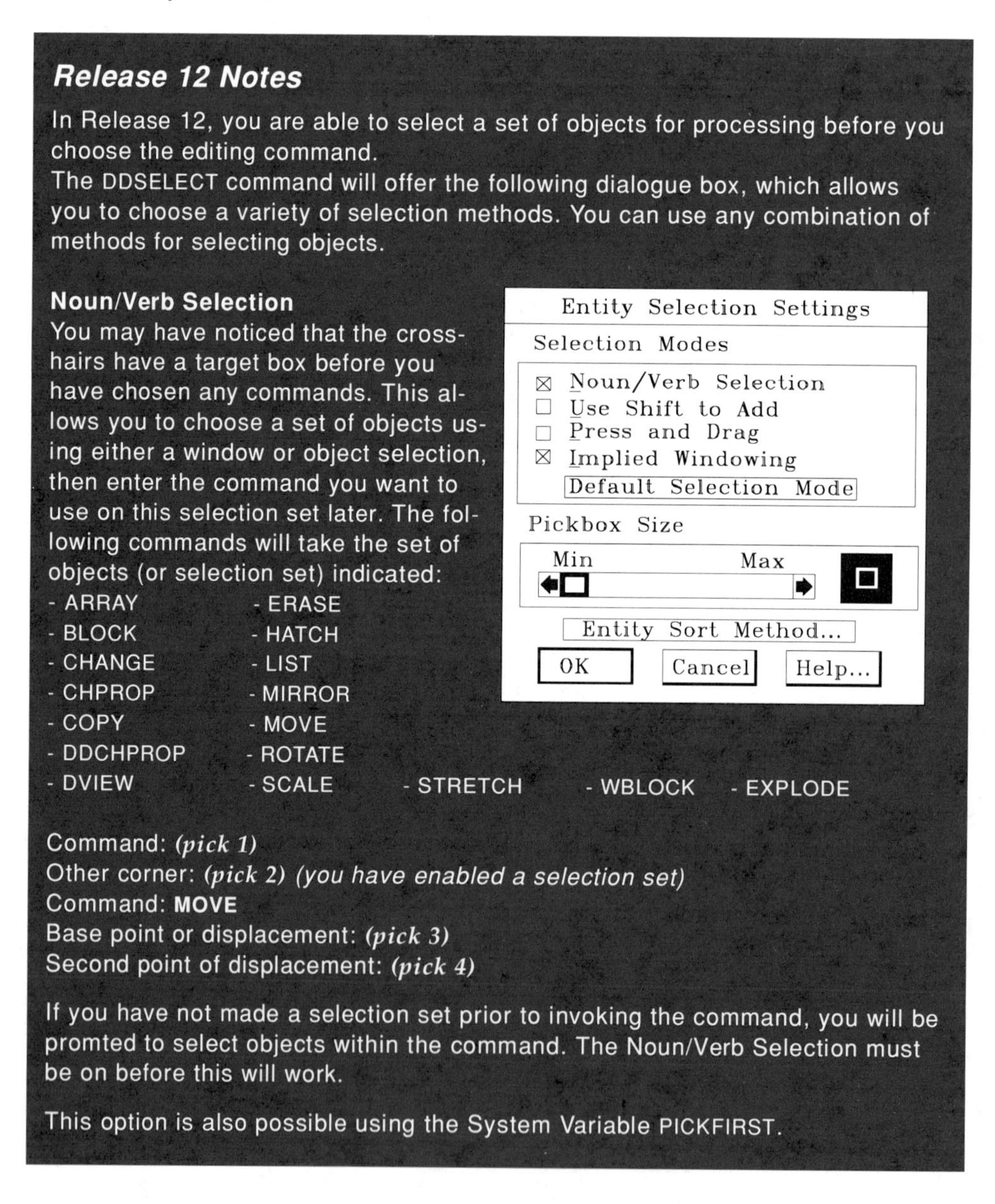

Release 12 Notes

In Release 12, you are able to select a set of objects for processing before you choose the editing command.
The DDSELECT command will offer the following dialogue box, which allows you to choose a variety of selection methods. You can use any combination of methods for selecting objects.

Noun/Verb Selection
You may have noticed that the cross-hairs have a target box before you have chosen any commands. This allows you to choose a set of objects using either a window or object selection, then enter the command you want to use on this selection set later. The following commands will take the set of objects (or selection set) indicated:

- ARRAY
- BLOCK
- CHANGE
- CHPROP
- COPY
- DDCHPROP
- DVIEW
- ERASE
- HATCH
- LIST
- MIRROR
- MOVE
- ROTATE
- SCALE
- STRETCH
- WBLOCK
- EXPLODE

Command: *(pick 1)*
Other corner: *(pick 2) (you have enabled a selection set)*
Command: **MOVE**
Base point or displacement: *(pick 3)*
Second point of displacement: *(pick 4)*

If you have not made a selection set prior to invoking the command, you will be promted to select objects within the command. The Noun/Verb Selection must be on before this will work.

This option is also possible using the System Variable PICKFIRST.

Release 12 Notes (cont'd)

Use Shift to Add
This option allows you to add entities to an existing selection set. Without this option on, only the last item picked will be highlighted. Hold the Shift key down while picking the items and they will all be added to the selection set.

This option is also available using the System Variable PICKADD.

Press and Drag
This check box allows you to draw a selection window with one pick of the pointing device. Simply hold down the pick button and drag the cursor across the screen. When you release the button, the diagonal corner of the window is created.

This option is also available using the System Variable PICKDRAG.

Implied Windowing
This option allows you, when the Select objects: prompt appears, to select a set of objects using a window. You do not need to enter Window or W. If you draw the selection window from left to right, you select a crossing of entities, or entities within and crossing the selection area.

This option is also available using the System Variable PICKAUTO.

Practice Exercises

Over the next few pages, you will find a series of examples that will help you improve your skills. Practising is the only way to help improve your AutoCAD skills.

PRACTICE 5A

Use the editing commands as much as possible to create these drawings.

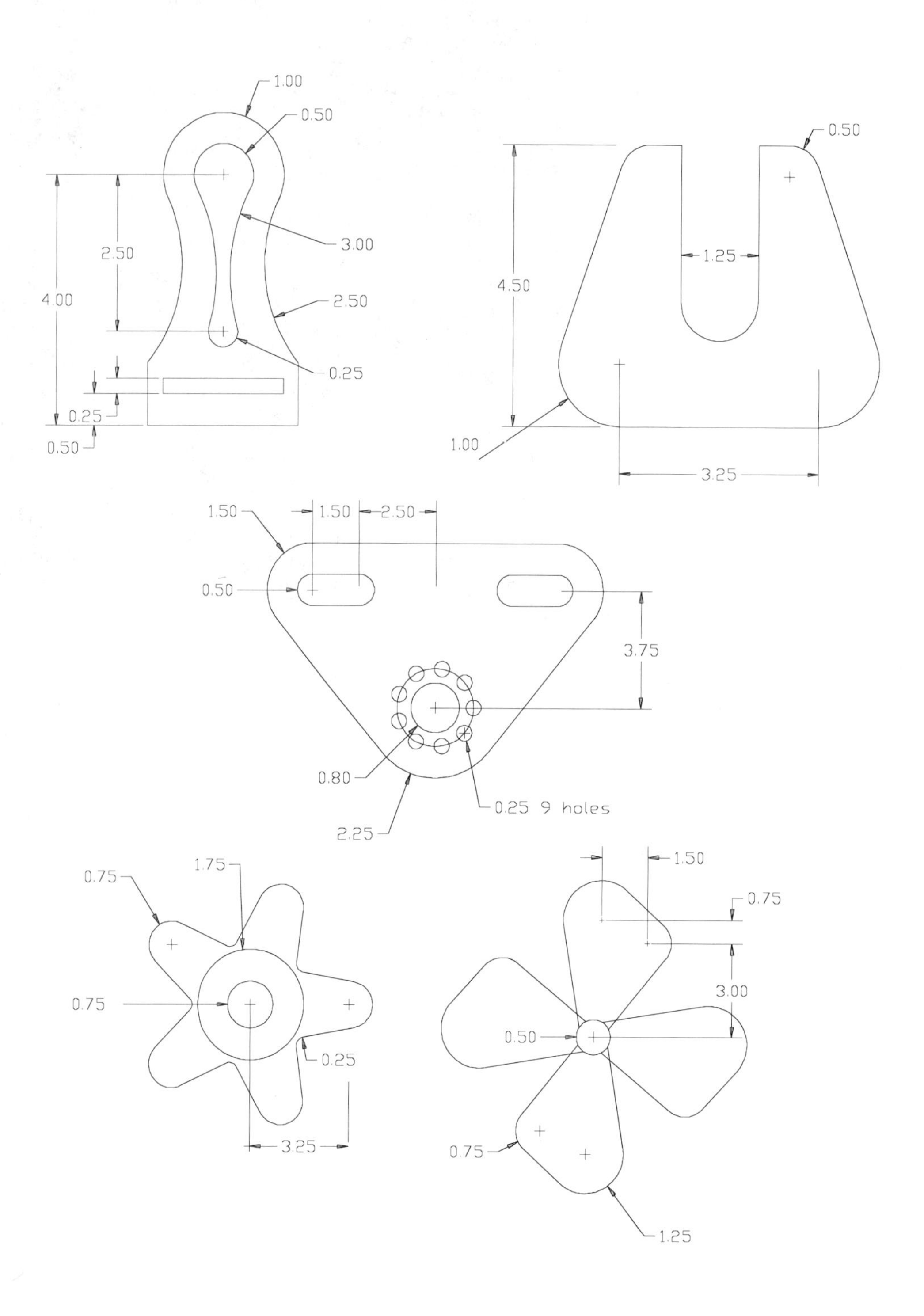

PRACTICE 5B

In the digital display, use SOLID to create the display numerals and DONUT, CIRCLE, LINE, and FILLET to finish the geometry.

Use ARRAY and FILLET Rad 0 to speed up the process.

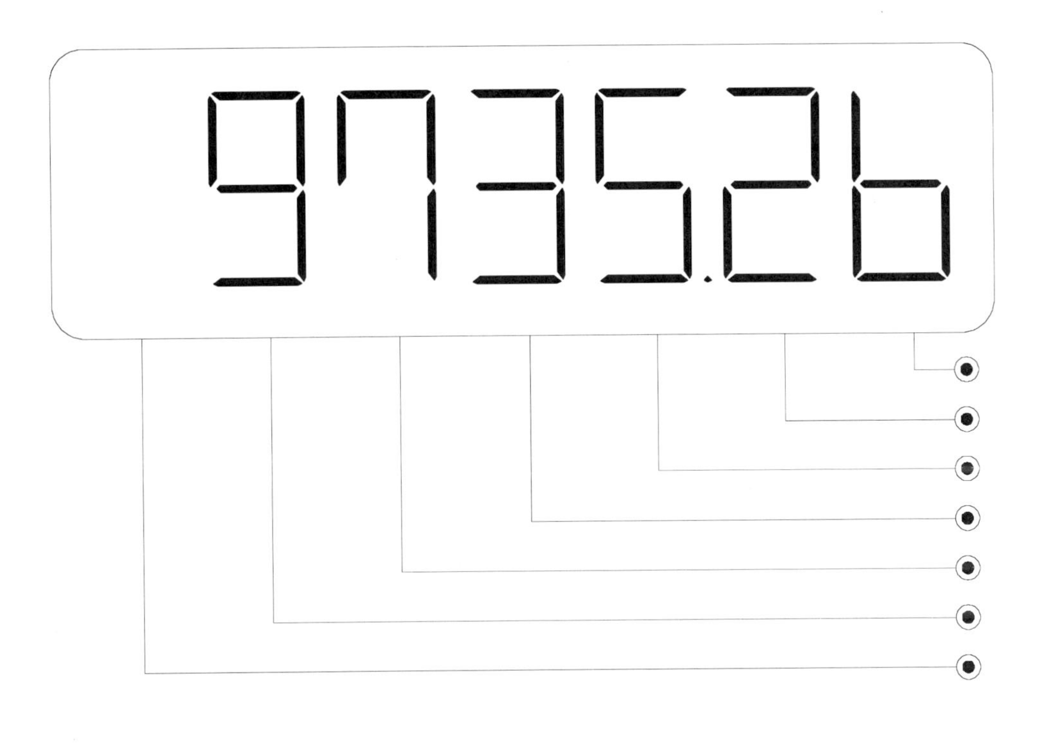

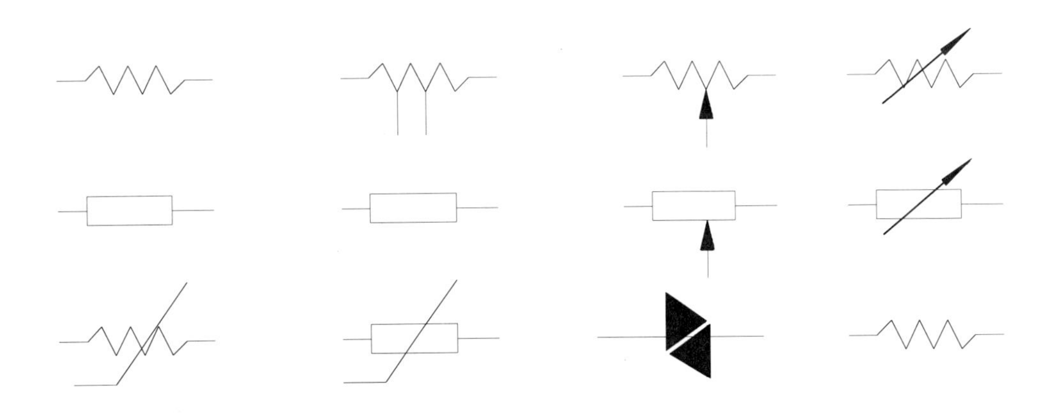

Use the edit commands to create these symbols as well. Be sure to have the snap on to achieve straight lines.

PRACTICE 5C

Use Copy and Mirror to create the steps. Consult the graphic standards or local Building Code if you are not sure of the measurements.

PRACTICE 5D

Use COPY, MIRROR, ARRAY, and ROTATE to create this South Elevation.

This is much easier to do by using different colours. Set the colour in the SETTINGS command.

When this is completed, work on a pattern for the roofing.

Use PLINE and PEDIT to landscape the front of the house or create a chimney or weather vane.

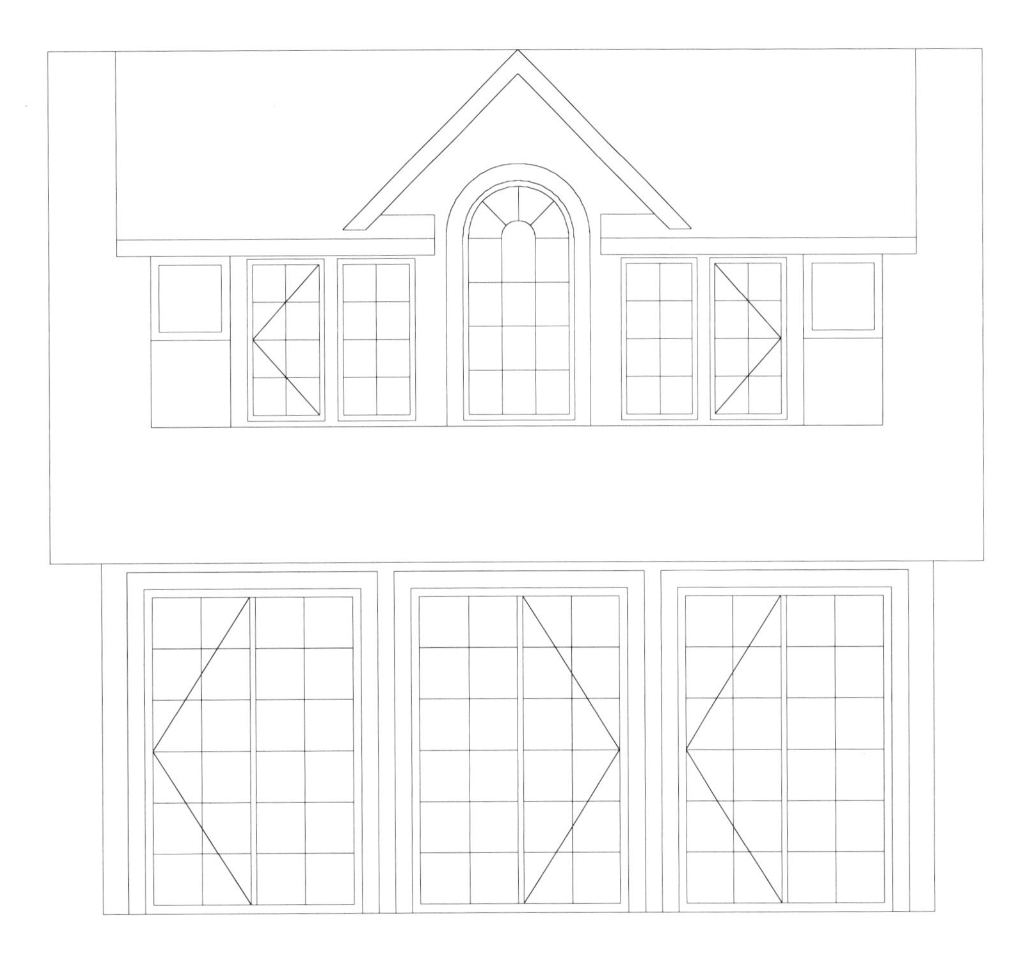

Exercise A5

First, create the outline of this presentation drawing using PLINE. If you are working in architectural units, use 8 inches. If you are working in decimal units, use .70.

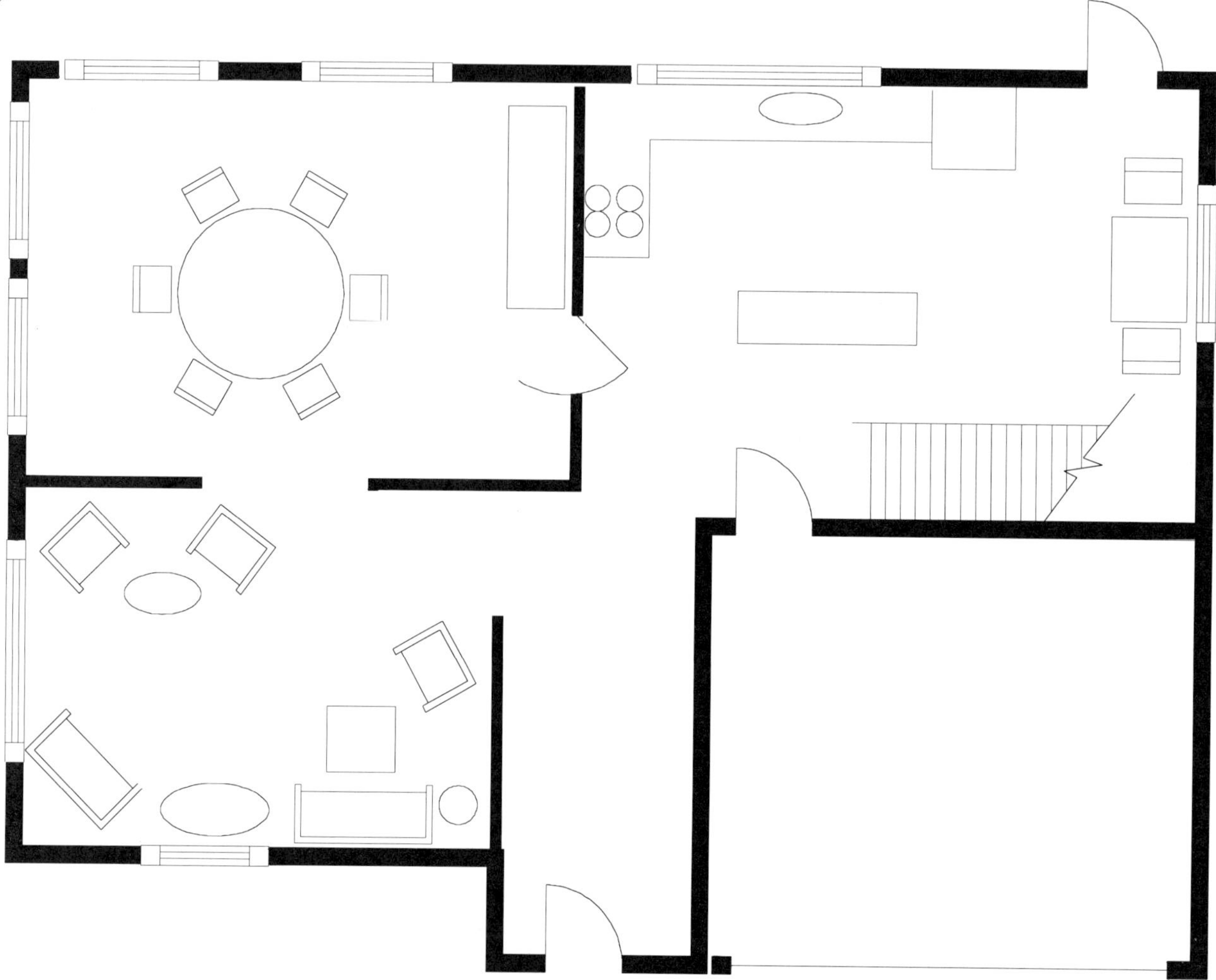

This will achieve an 8-inch wall.

Then draw in the windows. Draw one, then copy and rotate the others into place. Try to make the openings for the windows of various sizes so that the STRETCH command can be used to make the window fit the opening.

Do not hesitate to use the STRETCH command. Your instructor should be able to help you with this during lab time as it is twice as difficult to blunder through on your own. STRETCH is very useful on sofas and counters.

Hints on A5

Once the outline and the windows are complete, enter the interior walls. Be sure to change the pline to a width of 5 inches or .45.

Now make a diningroom table and a designer chair, and array the chair around the table to get a full diningroom set.

You can also use ARRAY to create a staircase. Again, avoid drawing the lines one by one or even copying the lines using Multiple; you already know how to do that. Use ARRAY with columns.

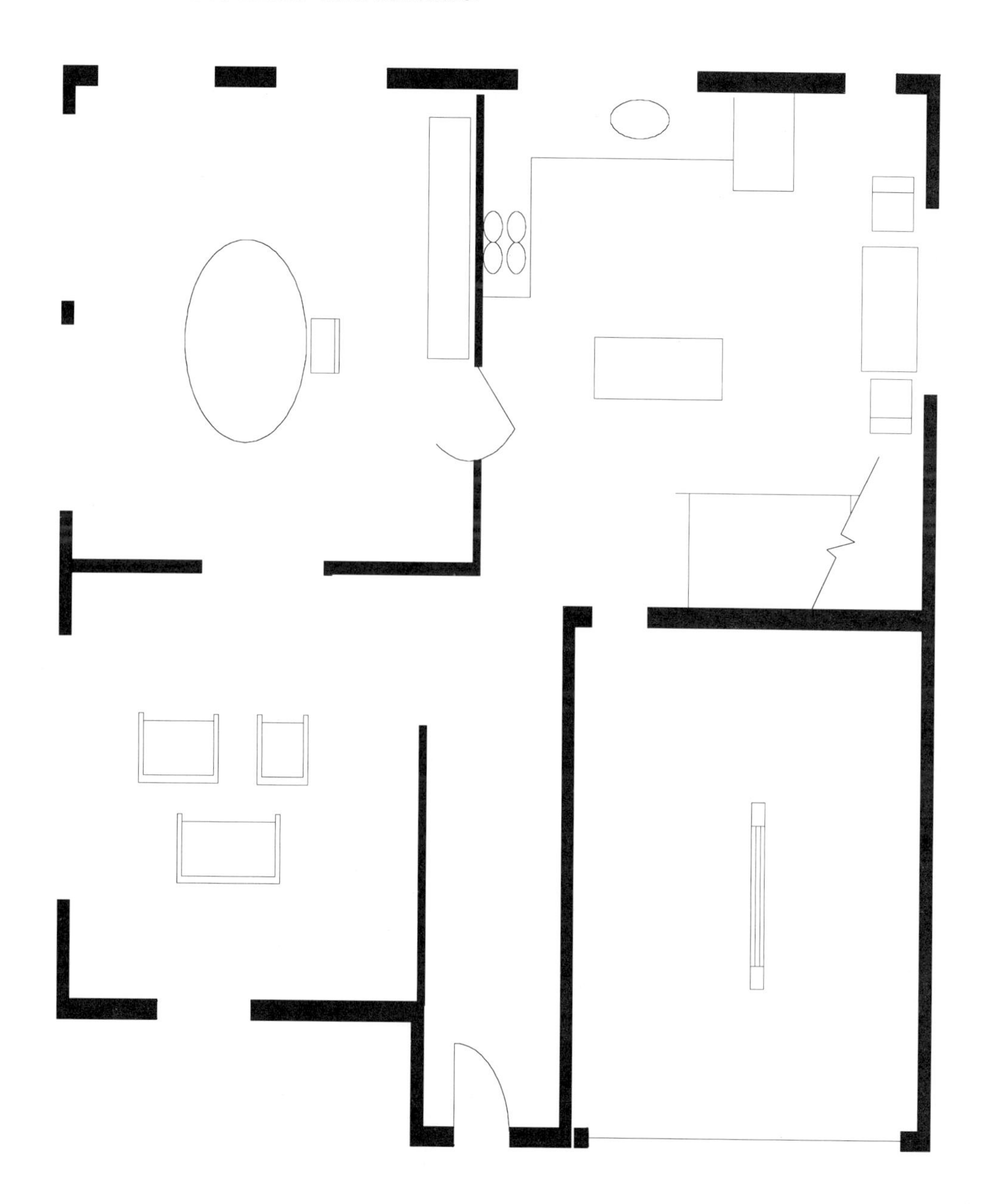

Now draw a chair, make two copies, and stretch the copies to make a three-seater couch and a two-seater love seat. Now copy these around, rotate them for maximum comfort, and draw in a couple of coffee tables.

Once the kitchen is drawn, try using SOLID and DONUT with ARRAY to create oriental rugs. LINE with ARRAY will make a nice kitchen tile pattern.

Exercise M5

Use the commands on the following page to make this model.

Once you are finished, press SAVE or END so you can add dimensions in a future exercise.

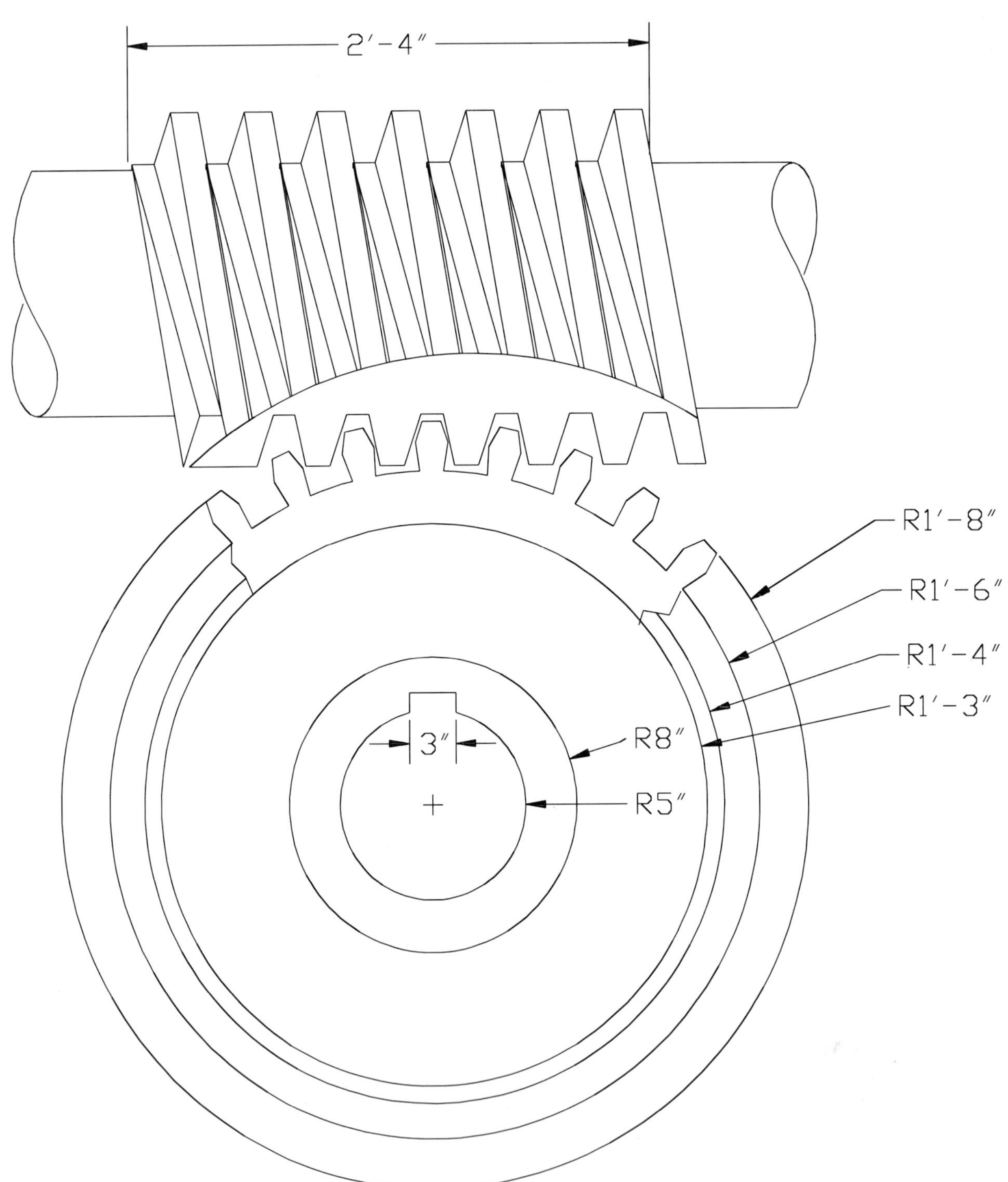

HINTS on M5

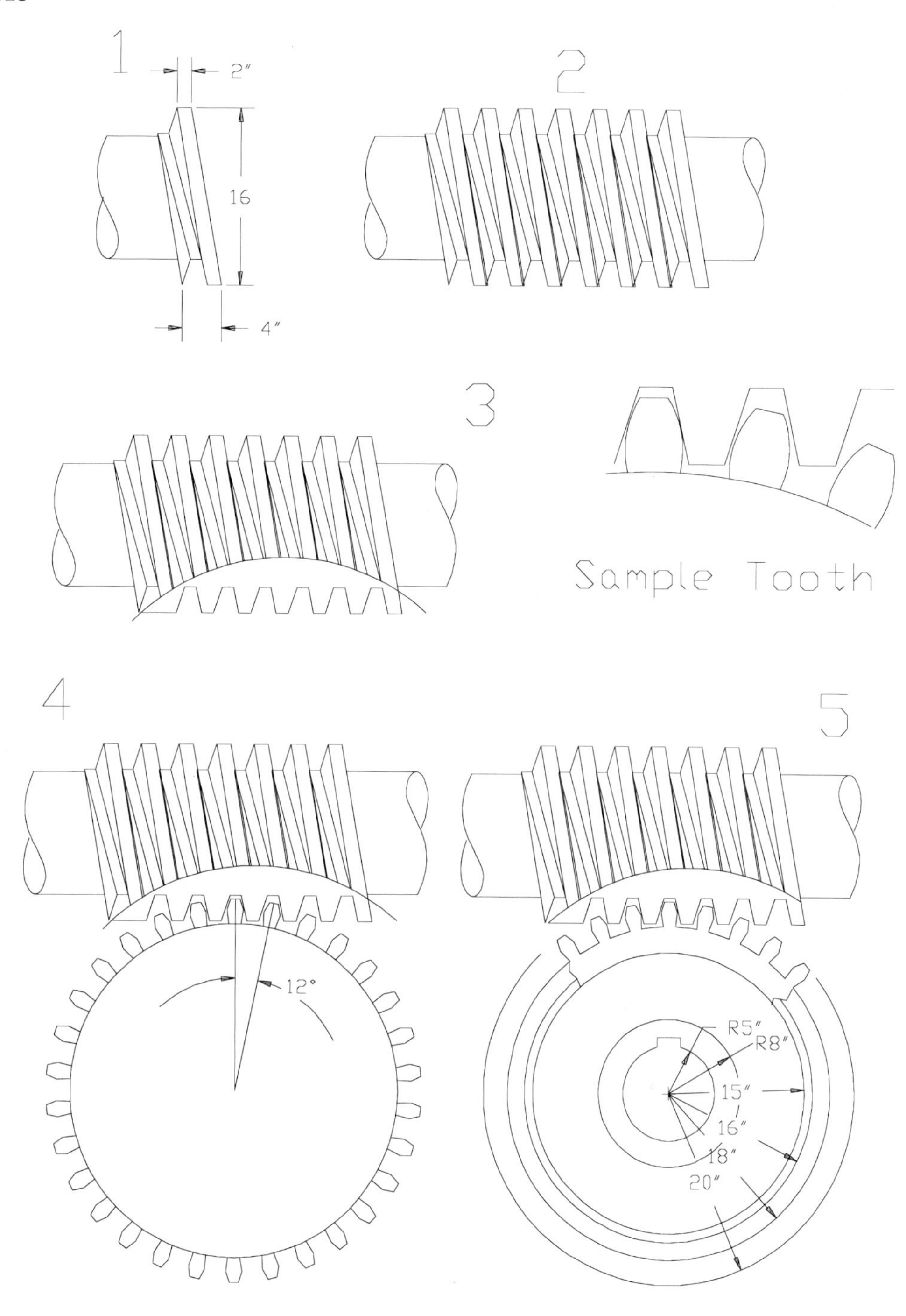

Draw the part as shown.

Array the part over seven columns, four units apart.

Draw in an arc, then use this arc to trim the lines.

Draw one tooth. Draw the circle that it will be revolved around. Array thetooth around the centre of the circle.

Clean up the lines and add the circles.

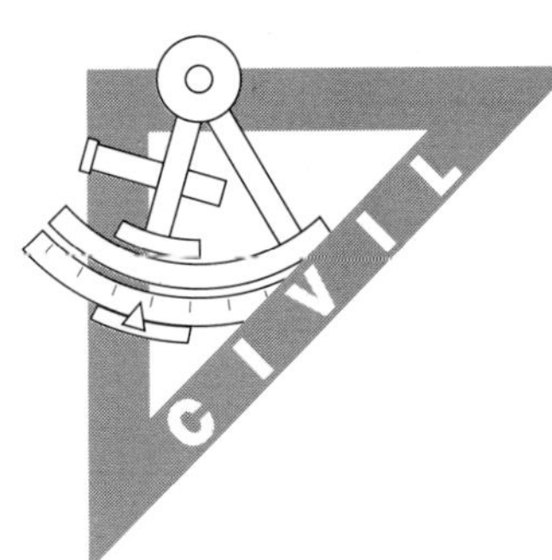
CIVIL

Exercise C5

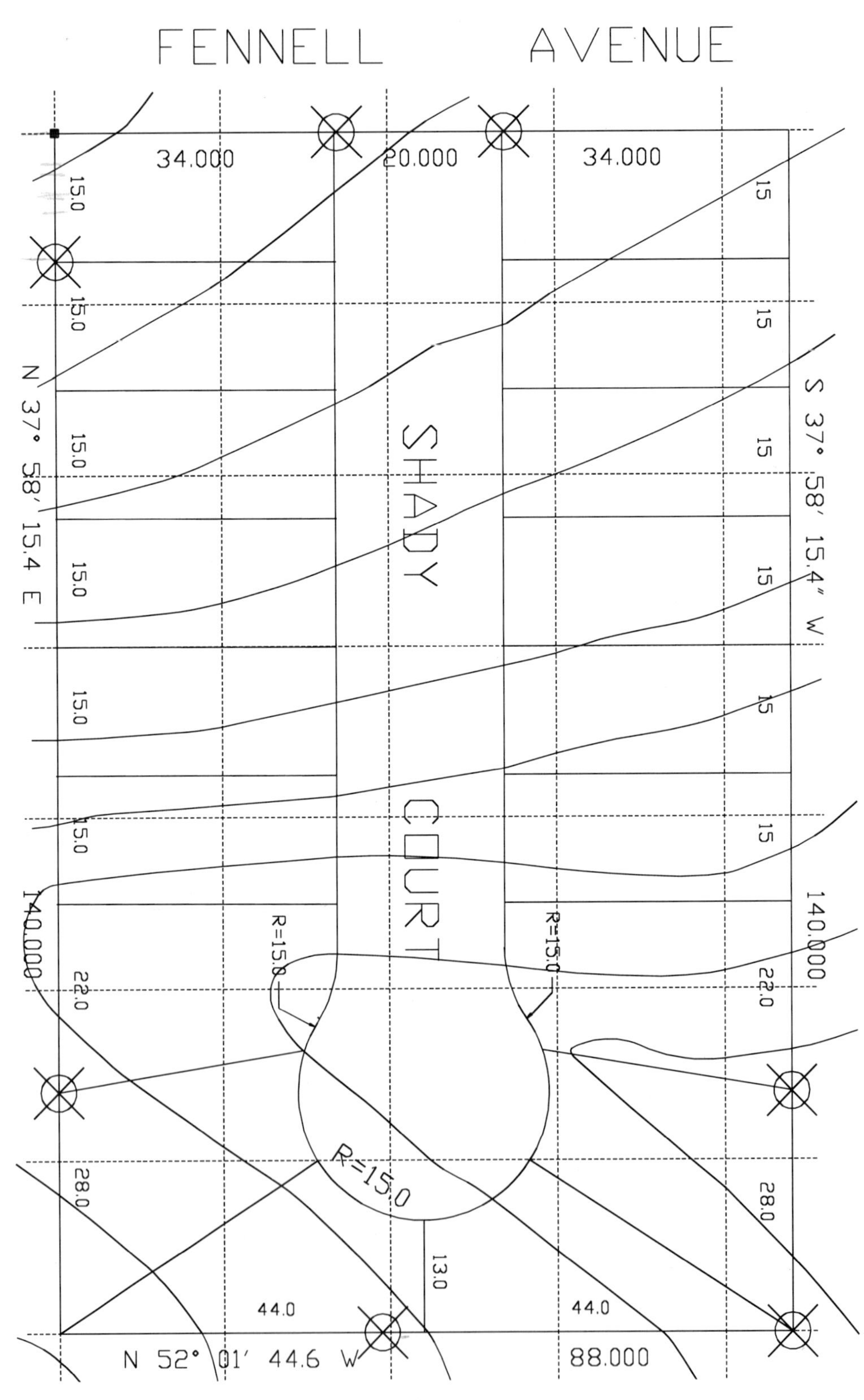
FENNELL AVENUE
34.000
20.000
34.000
15.0
15.0
15.0
15.0
15.0
15.0
15
15
15
15
15
15
N 37° 58′ 15.4 E
S 37° 58′ 15.4″ W
SHADY COURT
R=15.0
R=15.0
140.000
140.000
22.0
22.0
R=15.0
28.0
28.0
13.0
44.0
44.0
N 52° 01′ 44.6 W
88.000

Hints on C5

First create the geometry for this court. Change the units to surveying units.

Use OFFSET as much as possible. Do not forget the OSNAP commands.

Change the colour under the Settings menu to red, then add a grid to the overall design. Use OFFSET to create the grid.

To generate the contours, use PLINE with PEDIT and the Spline function. You can also experiment with the OFFSET command on a spline in this case. Once it is in, it can be trimmed to the proper size.

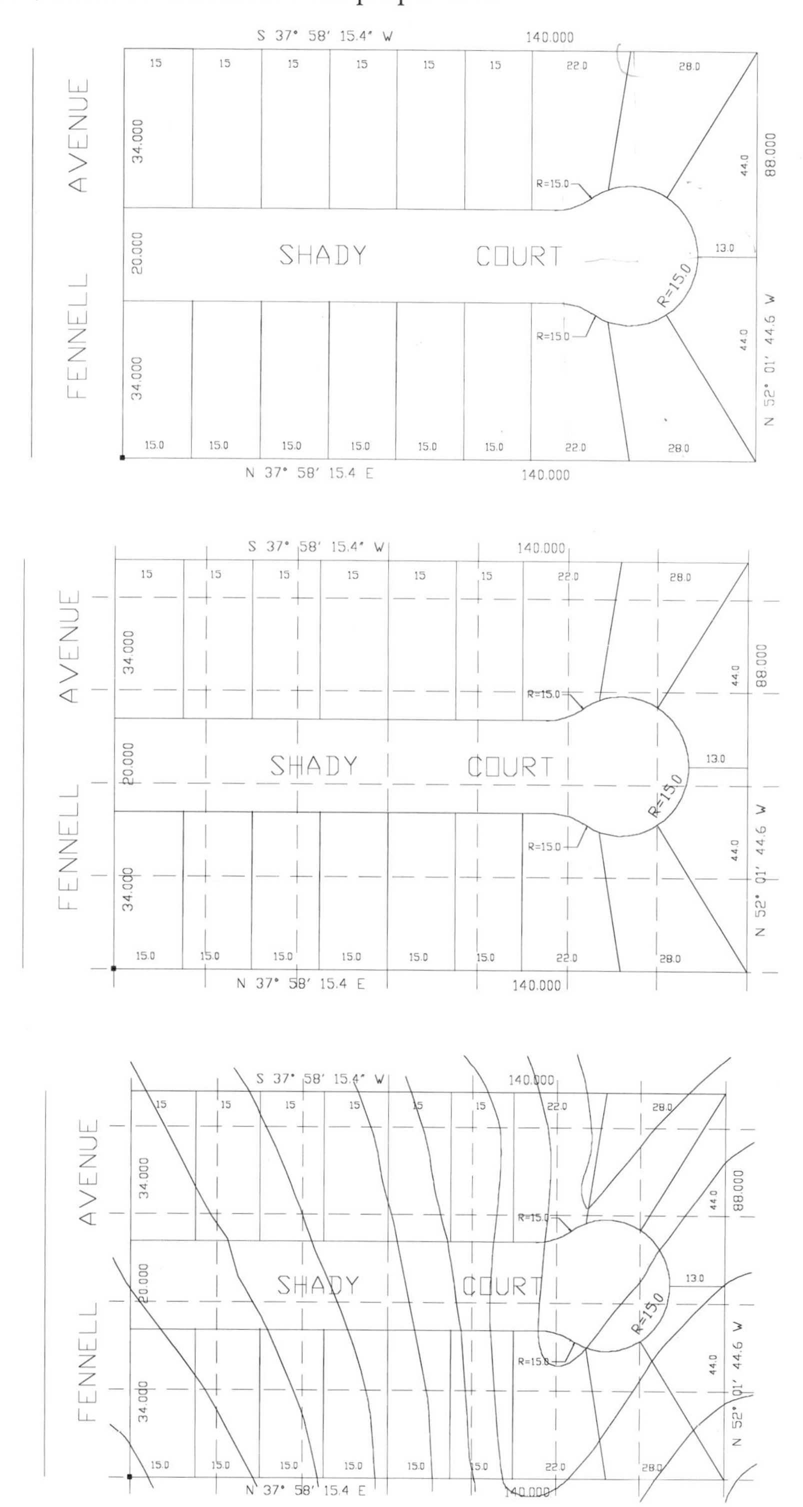

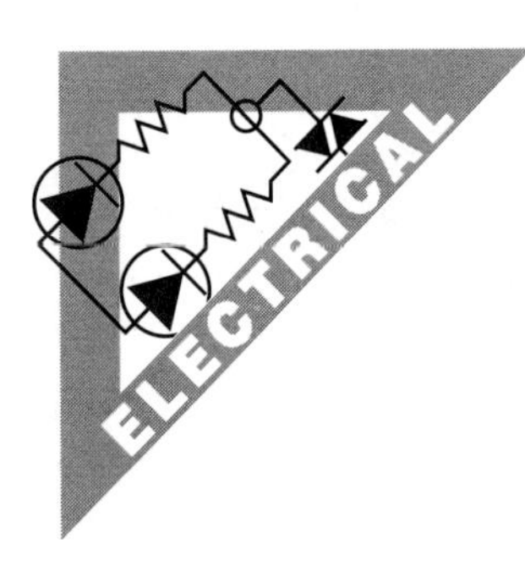

Exercise E5

Create a symbol, copy it, then use the editing commands to edit the copied symbols in order to create them more efficiently. Use the SCALE command to change the relative size of the pline when entering it as an arrow.

Once completed, use the symbols to create a logical schematic.

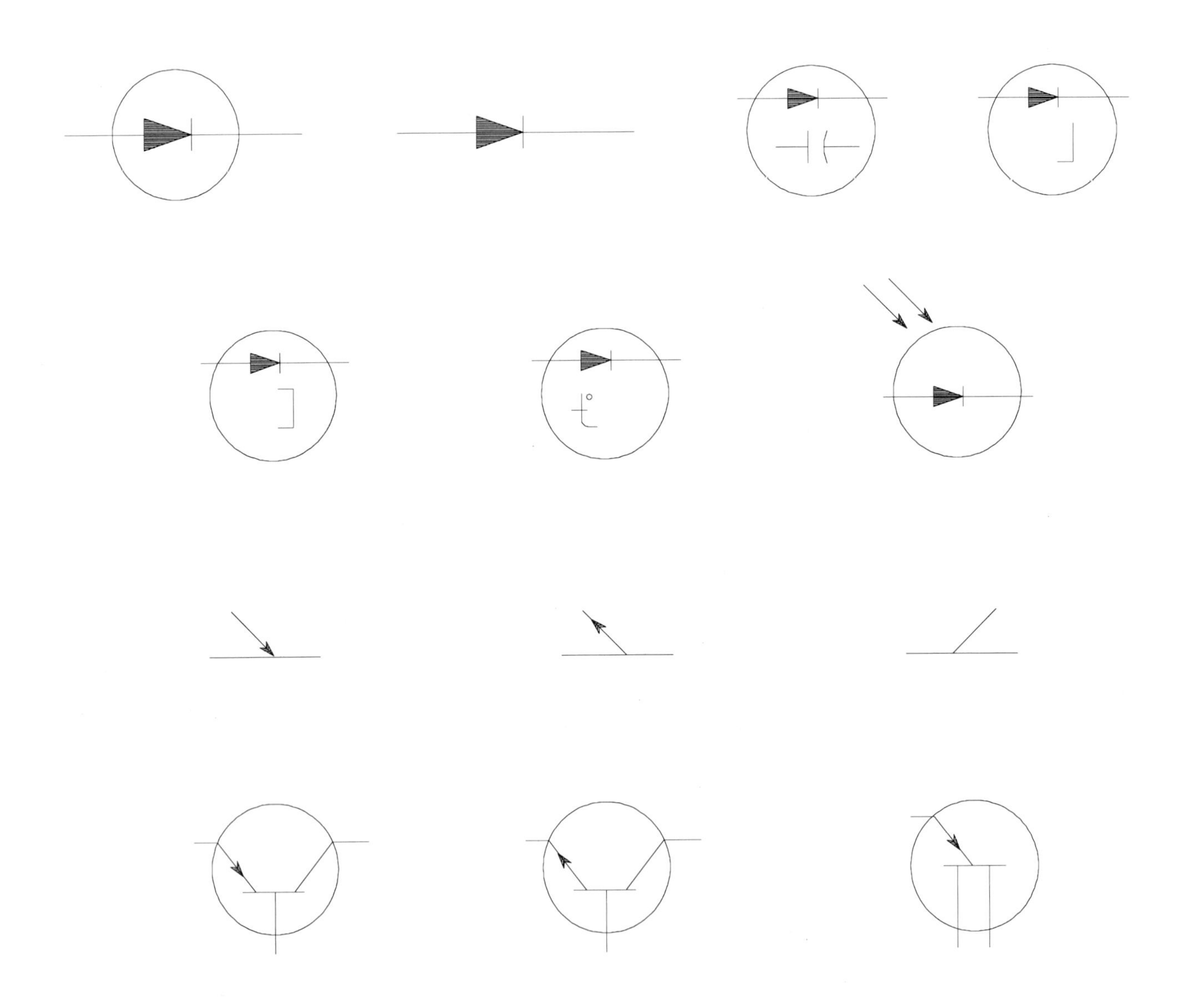

Challenger 5

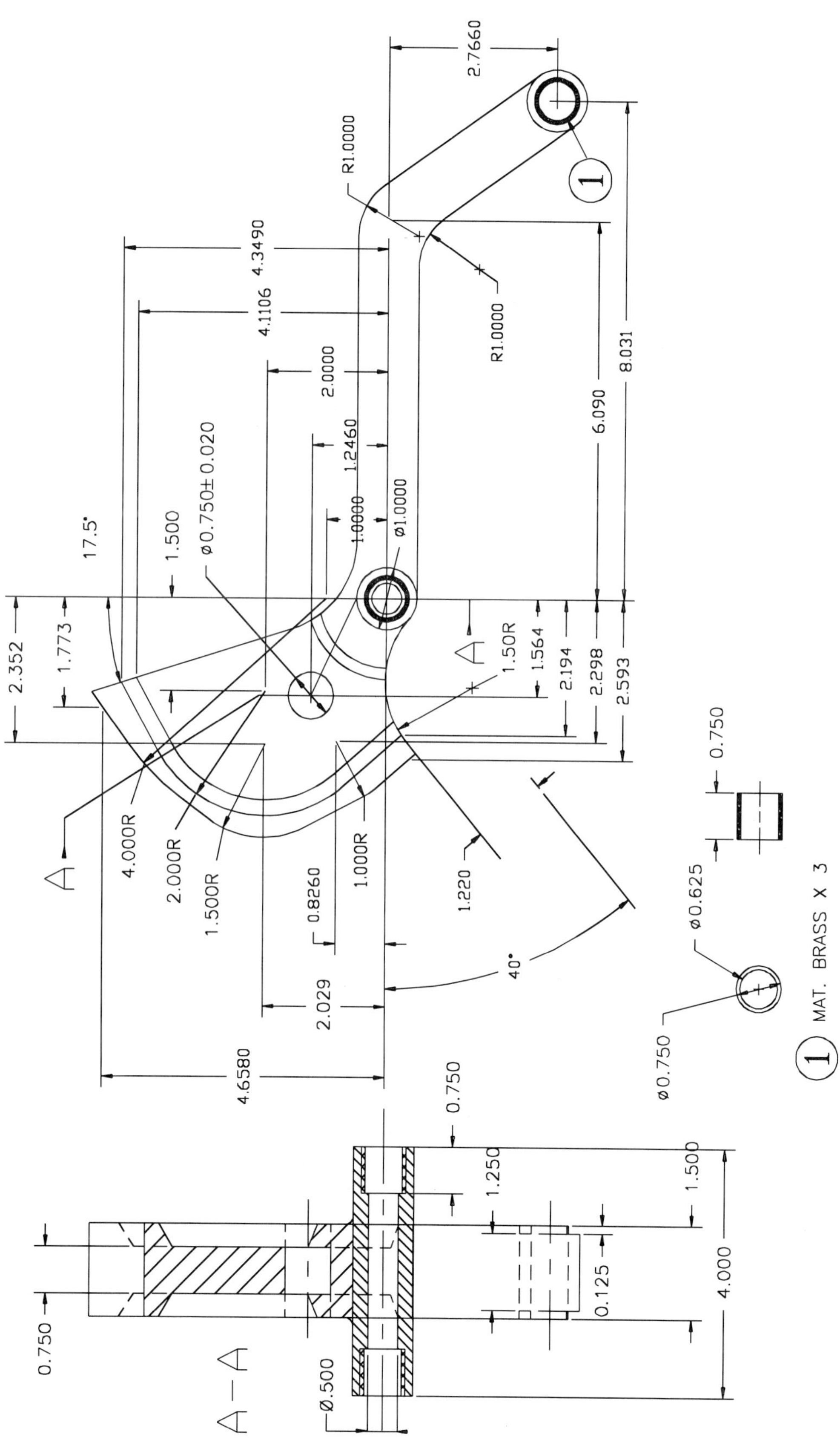

WORKING WITH LAYERS

Upon completion of this chapter, the student should be able to:

1. Set up LAYERs and create geometry on them
2. Set colours to layers
3. Set up and use LINETYPE
4. Use CHANGE and CHPROP with layers
5. Use Freeze/Thaw and LAYER ON/OFF

LAYER

The LAYER command allows you to control the drawing by means of visible entities. In a sense, it is like a set of transparencies or acetate overlays that may contain different colours and linestyles that are either visible or invisible. Layering is a powerful organizational tool and should be used on all drawings.

For example, when creating architectural drawings, there are always drawings of the same structure showing the different levels, electrical and mechanical services, furnishing layouts, etc. In mechanical drawings, there are often many details and sections of a part that must be illustrated with more accuracy. In mapmaking and surveying, the services are often on a different sheet from the physical contours of an area.

In AutoCAD, different colours and linetypes can be associated with different layers and can be either displayed or undisplayed, active or inactive, accessible or inaccessible to help you complete your database. The number of layers you can use is unlimited.

The format of the LAYER command is as follows:

```
LAYER ?/Make/Set/New/On/Off/Color/LType/Freeze/Thaw:
```

Where:

? lists the layer names, colours, linetypes, and status.

MAKE creates a new layer and makes it the current layer.

SET makes a layer active or current. You can work on only one layer at a time.

NEW creates new layers that are not current.

ON indicates the layers that are displayed or visible.

OFF indicates the layers that are not displayed. They are still part of the file, but they are turned off temporarily.

COLOR assigns colours to specified layers.
1 RED 2 YELLOW 3 GREEN 4 CYAN 5 BLUE 6 MAGENTA 7 WHITE

LTYPE assigns a linetype to a specified layer.

FREEZE makes a layer inaccessible. This saves time during regens and redraws because the information is not active.

THAW turns off Freeze.

The LAYER command is accessed by typing LAYER or selecting the LAYER command from the side menu. An easier way to access and change the layers is to access the DDLMODE. This is found in the pull-down menu under Settings. Just pick Layer Control (Modify Layer in Release 10) to access a dialogue box that will offer you all the information you wish to change or set.

SETTINGS PULL-DOWN MENU

In order to get to the layer dialogue box, select the Settings pull-down menu. To do this, bring the cursor to the very top of the screen. Once you have passed the top of the graphics area, the status line will change to a menu selection area. Pick the Settings option and then Layer Control DDLMODE on the pull-down menu, and you will get the dialogue box of Figure 6-2.

Release 12 Notes

An updated dialogue box allows for Locking and Unlocking of layers. See page 122.

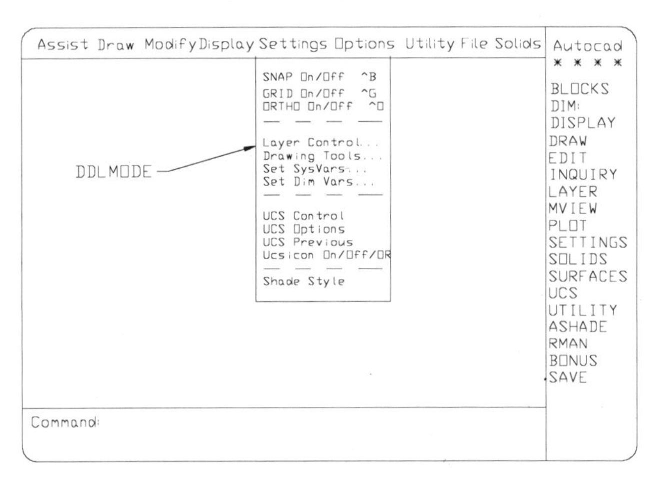

Figure 6-1. Settings menu

To create a new layer, you must pick the New Layer box.

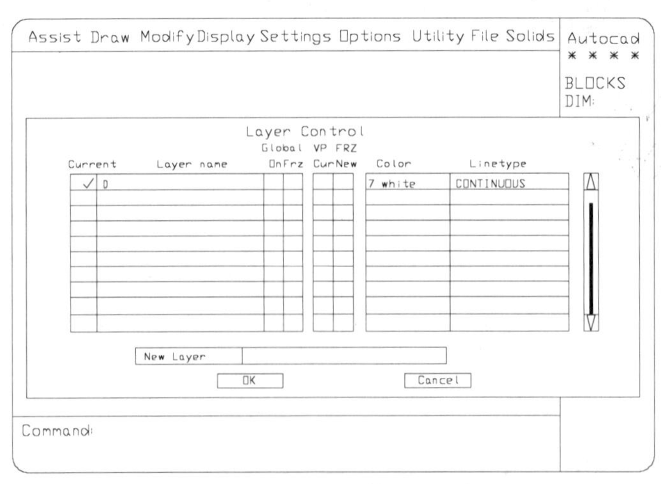

Figure 6-2. DDLMODE or Layer dialogue box

The dialogue box of Figure 6-2 will provide an overview of the layers in use, and allow you to set up a layer. There is only enough room for 10 layers in the display box provided, but you may enter as many as you like and the screen will scroll down. To make a layer current, change the position of the check mark that is under Current to correspond with the desired layer.

To change the colour or linetype of a layer, pick the corresponding area, and a new submenu will appear.

NAMING A NEW LAYER

Use the cursor to pick the box beside the New Layer box. The box will turn black. Now type the name of the new layer.

When typing layer names, keep the following rules in mind:

1. Use no spaces in the names. To indicate the layer for a side bracket, for example, use SIDE-BR.

2. The system will not accept slash (/) or period (.) characters.

3. You may enter as many as 255 characters for a layer name, but you will be able to read only eight letters on the Status line, so try to limit the entry to eight characters.

Once you have entered the layer name, press the Enter or Return key and the layer name will be displayed on the next available layer line. You *must* enter a new name using this procedure; it will not be accepted if typed directly on the list.

If you type the name incorrectly, place the cursor over the new name. The area will turn black, and you can correct the spelling. Also, if you have created a layer you do not need, you can change its name by the same method.

If you have created a layer that will never be used, delete it with Purge. (See page 191.)

CHANGING LAYER COLOUR

Create a layer using the New Layer box. Change the colour by moving the cursor to the area that displays 7 white on the same line as the new layer name. As the cursor arrow moves over the colour box, it will turn black to show that this is the area now indicated. Pick that area and the screen will change, providing a new colour overlay submenu as shown in Figure 6-3.

Notice that the 0 layer is still current and all the layers are on.

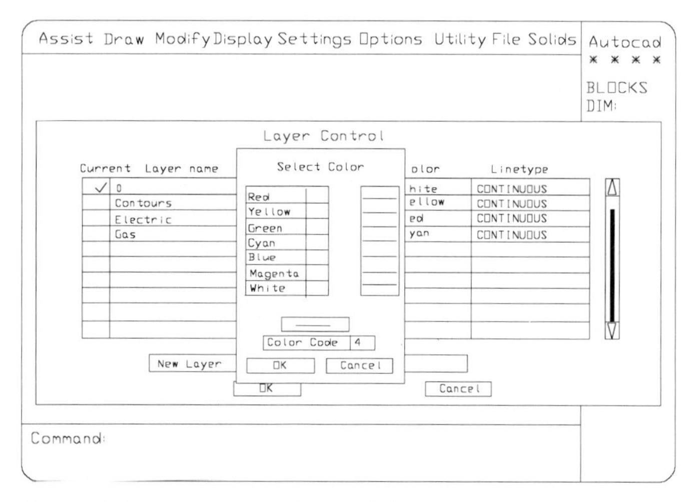

Figure 6-3. Colour overlay with Layers

When you are changing colours, the submenu or overlay will offer seven different colours. Pick the box in the check-mark column beside the colour you wish to choose. Notice that each colour has a number as well as a name. (All computers use the same number code for the first seven colours.) Once you have done this, the colour code box will display the number which corresponds to that colour, and the colour will show up in the area provided.

Try adding four new layers and assign them different colours. Your dialogue box should look like that of Figure 6-4.

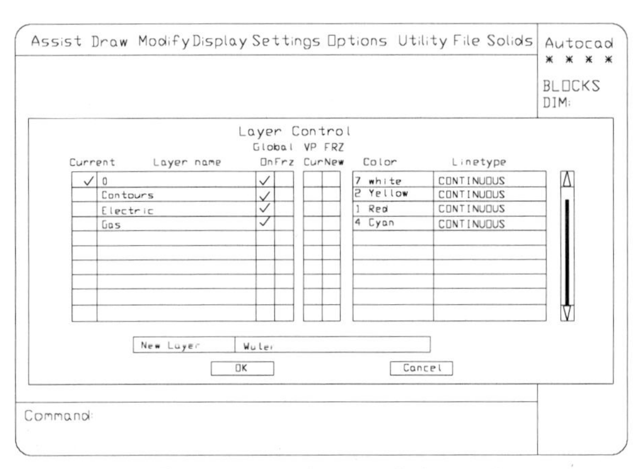

Figure 6-4. DDLMODE or Layer dialogue box

You will notice that there are only seven colours listed. If you have an enhanced EGA or VGA card in your computer, you can select from 15 or more colours. Place the cursor arrow over the Color Code number area and enter a number greater than 7 to view more colours. If you want to see all the available colours, exit the dialogue box, pick COLOR, and then Chroma. This will provide a slide of the available colours. Use Redraw to return to your file.

Once you have chosen the colour you want, you select it by picking OK. You will then return to the Layer Control menu.

Making a Layer Current

In the illustration of Figure 6-4, we have created four new layers, but layer 0 is still current. In order to work on a layer, put a check-mark in the Current column on the same line as the layer you want to work on. Now you can pick OK to accept the layer colour and setting. The screen will return to the graphics area, and the name of that layer will replace the 0 in the Status line beside the word Layer. While working on a model, you can easily check to see what layer is in use by reading the Status line. All of your work from this point on will be on the layer you have created. To change to another layer, go back to the dialogue box and make it current.

LOADING LINETYPES

In addition to different colours, you can also use different linetypes on different layers. The linetypes are not loaded with the basic AutoCAD drawing and are thus not available under the listing of linetypes in the dialogue box. To use different linetypes, they must be loaded into the file.

Under the Settings menu on the right (not the pull-down menus), select the command LINETYPE. Enter **?** to obtain a list of the available linetypes:

```
Command:LINETYPE
?/Create/Load/Set:?
```

```
border     __ __ . __ __ . __ __ . __ __ .
border2    __ __ . __ __ . __ __ . __ __ .
borderX2   __ __ . __ __ . __ __ . __ __ .
center     ___ _ ___ _ ___ _ ___ _ ___ _ ___
center2    ___ _ ___ _ ___ _ ___ _ ___ _ ___
centerx2   ____ _ ____ _ ____ _ ____ _ ____
dashdot    __ . __ . __ . __ .
dashdot2   _._._._._._._._._._._._._._._
dashdotx2  ___.___.___.___.___.___.___.___._
dashed     __ __ __ __ __ __ __ __ __ __ __ __
dashed2    _ _ _ _ _ _ _ _ _ _ _ _ _ _ _ _ _
dashedx2   ___ ___ ___ ___ ___ ___ ___ ___ ___
divide     -..-..-..-..-..
divide2    -..-..-..-..-..
dividex2   ___ .. ___ .. ___ .. ___ .. ___
dot        . . . . . . . . . . . . . . . . . .
dot2       ..................................
dotx2      .  .  .  .  .  .  .  .  .  .  .  .
hidden     - - - - - - - - - - - - - - - - -
hidden2    - - - - - - - - - - - - - - - - -
hiddenx2   __ __ __ __ __ __ __ __ __ __ __ __
phantom    _____ _ _ _____ _ _ _____ _ _ _____ _ _
phantom2   _____ _ _ _____ _ _ _____ _ _ _____ _ _
phantomx2  ______ _ _ ______ _ _ ______ _ _ ___
?/Create/Load/Set:
```

Continuous is the default linetype.

```
continuous ________________________
```

The linetypes above are those listed under the default ACAD linetype listing. Many companies have their own linetypes listed under their own filenames; that is why you will be prompted to confirm that the lines are taken from the ACAD file list.

Once you have invoked the linetype command and seen a list of the default linetypes, the command string will come back offering several options.

```
Command:LINETYPE
?/Create/Load/Set:
```

Where:
Set = a setting of that linetype, only that type of line can be used.

Load = a load of that linetype onto the system. Once loaded, you can use it whenever you want or attach it to a layer.

Create = the ability to create new linetype patterns.

To load a linetype, pick **L** for Load.

```
Command:LINETYPE
Set/Load/Create/?:L
File to search ACAD:↵ (accepts the default file listing)
```

This indicates that you want to select a linetype from the list of ACAD patterns. The file it is referring to is the AutoCAD default file for linetype patterns. To load a linetype from the ACAD default file, use ↵.

```
Command:LINETYPE
Set/Load/Create/?:L
File to search ACAD:↵
Linetype name:HIDDEN
File to load ACAD:↵

Linetype HIDDEN has been loaded

Set/Load/Create/?:
```

Be careful to type the linetype exactly as it is spelled in the listing; otherwise, it will not load. For Canadians, the spelling of Centre is the most common stumbling block. Be sure to use the American spelling — Center.

Once the linetype is loaded, you can go back to the Layer Control dialogue box, DDLMODE under the Settings pull-down menu, and choose a linetype in the same way that you chose a colour.

To load all the available linetypes, use the DOS wildcard option *.

```
Command:LINETYPE
Set/Load/Create/?:L
File to search <ACAD>:↵
Linetype name:*
File to load <ACAD>:↵
```

All linetypes will be loaded.

What Can Go Wrong with LAYER, COLOR, and LINETYPE

When working with linetype and colour, keep in mind that both can be changed independent of Layer. *You can set to a particular linetype and colour, and this will override any setting made under the Layer format.*

Both Linetype and Color can be set under the Settings menu on the right side of the screen. This means that if Color, for example, is set to red, all of the geometry will show up as red even if the current layer is blue. Similarly, if the Linetype is set to hidden, all the lines will be hidden lines, even if the current layer asks for centre lines.

The Linetype and Color settings must be set to Bylayer to access the different linetypes and colours associated with each layer.

CHANGING LTSCALE

When a layer linetype is changed, all the lines, circles, arcs, etc. that had been created on that layer will update to the current linetype, and all future geometry added will use this linetype. If the linetype is the hidden type, all entities on that layer will be displayed in hidden lines, unless they are overridden by the LINETYPE command.

Depending on the size of an object, the linetype may not show up as hidden. If this is the case, either the objects you thought were on that layer are not, in fact, on that layer, or the scale of the drawing is too large or too small for the actual linetype to show up.

All scales are set to be viewed on a 12" x 9" screen. This means that a hidden line, for example, will show up with three long dashes for every actual inch of line. If a screen is showing a line 200 units in length, this means there are 600 actual segments to that line. Obviously, you cannot see 600 segments of a line on a screen that is 14 inches wide, so the line will appear to be a continuous line. What you must do is change the scale of the screen display.

Again, under the Settings menu on the right side of the screen, pick LTSCALE.

```
Command:LTSCALE
New scale factor:13
```

To determine the Ltscale of the screen, take the furthest point in X and divide by 15. If you have set up the screen but have not as yet entered any points or geometry, take the furthest limit in positive X and divide by 15. If the limits are 200,160, then the Ltscale will be 200/15, or approximately 13. If the limits are 3, then the Ltscale will be 3/15, or .02.

If you used Setup to create your layout, the Ltscale will be automatic (not available in Release 11 and up).

CHPROP and CHANGE with LAYERS

If the geometry is not appearing in the colour or linetype that you expected, use CHPROP (change properties) under the Edit menu.

```
Command:CHPROP
Select objects:W 1, 2 (pick the whole screen)
Select objects:↵
Change what property (Color/LAyer/LType/Thickness):C
New Color <current>:BYLAYER
Change what property (Color/LAyer/LType/Thickness):LT
New linetype <current>:BYLAYER
Change what property (Color/Layer/LType/Thickness):↵
```

If everything changes to the correct colour and linetype, check to see that both COLOR and LINETYPE are set to Bylayer as well.

If the objects still do not show the colour or linetype you expected, they are probably in the wrong layer. Again, use CHPROP.

```
Command:CHPROP
Select objects:W (pick 1, 2) (pick the objects to change)
Select objects:↵
Change what property (Color/LAyer/LType/Thickness):LA
New Layer <current>:hidden (for example)
Change what property (Color/LAyer/LType/Thickness):↵
```

The CHANGE command can also be used to change the properties of objects.

Command:**CHANGE**

Select objects: *(pick 1)*

Properties/<Change point>:**P**

Change what property (Color/LAycr/LType/Thickness):**LA**

New Layer <current>:**hidden** *(for example)*

Change what property (Color/LAyer/LType/Thickness):↵

If things are still not as you want them, try REGEN. If it is still not what you expect, there is something wrong with the entity itself. Use LIST under the Inquiry menu to show the properties and position of the object or objects that are not reacting to the above commands. Often, the objects are not on the layer that you thought they were on.

Command:**LIST**

Select objects: *(pick 1) (pick the object)*

The screen will now display information on the object, including the layer of the object selected and whether there is a colour or linetype overriding those set on that layer.

Command:**LIST**

Select objects: *(pick 1)*

```
          CIRCLE     Layer:Electric
                     Space:Model space
         center point, X=  4.0000  Y= 3.0000   Z=  0.0000
         radius      3.000
  circumference      18.8496
           area      28.2743
          color      cyan
```
(this overrides the layer)

In a perfect world, you would probably always use the dialogue box; but for many reasons, sometimes the dialogue boxes do not work. This could be a hardware problem, usually associated with the graphics card, or it could be because you are using an older version of AutoCAD which does not have pull-down menus. It is also possible that the digitizer has become disabled when the screen changes.

In any case, if the dialogue box cannot be accessed, use the following:

Command:**LAYER**

?/Make/Set/New/On/Off/Color/LType/Freeze/Thaw:**N**

New layer name(s):**Electric**

?/Make/Set/New/On/Off/Color/LType/Freeze/Thaw:**C**

Color:**1**

Layer name:**Graphic**

?/Make/Set/New/On/Off/Color/LType/Freeze/Thaw:**L**

Linetype:**Dashed**

Layer name:**Graphic**

None of the Layer options will take effect until the command is exited.

The default layer is 0 (zero). You have just created an additional layer that is red for electrical details in dashed lines.

To view the list of layers, use the ? option. AutoCAD then prompts for the layers you want listed. The wildcard * can be used to list all the layers or to search for specific layers if the list occupies more than one screen display.

```
Command:LAYER
?/Set/New/On/Off/Color/LType/Freeze/Thaw:?
Layer name(s) for listing <*>:↵
```

Layer name	State	Color	Linetype
0	on	white	continuous
electric	on	red	dashed
plumbing	off	blue	hidden

If there are a large number of layers, the * can be used in the same way that it is in DOS. For example, *DOORS will list all the layers that end with DOORS — INTDOORS, EXTDOORS, 1DOORS, etc.

The symbol ? can be used with listing to represent a single character. For example, ?DOORS will list 1DOORS, but not INTDOORS or EXTDOORS.

The trick to successfully creating layers outside of the dialogue box is to answer the questions that the system is asking you. If you list the layers and find layers you did not create — for example, SET, NEW, MAKE — you have not answered the prompts correctly but rather have tried to force the system to accept a new request when it did not have sufficient information to complete the first request. Understand that you must enter information in the same sequence as the system prompts.

If you have created layers with names such as MAKE and NEW, you have entered another option when the system was prompting for a name. If the layer dialogue box is not working, you can purge these layers by exiting and restarting AutoCAD (see page 191).

FREEZE/THAW AND ON/OFF IN LAYERS

Turning off a layer will make that specific layer invisible. To turn it off, use Off in the LAYER command or use the dialogue box to remove the check-mark beside a specific layer under the On column. Use On or a check-mark to view it again.

Freezing a layer will tell AutoCAD to ignore any entities on the specified layer when regenerating the drawing. When a drawing gets quite large, this option is used to save time in regenerating items that will not be viewed. Freeze is also used with the HIDE command in Dview so that any objects that obscure the view of an object you are working with will not be displayed on screen.

Frozen layers must be thawed before they can be viewed or plotted.

Release 12 Notes

The Layer Control Dialogue Box has been completely revamped to include three new functions.

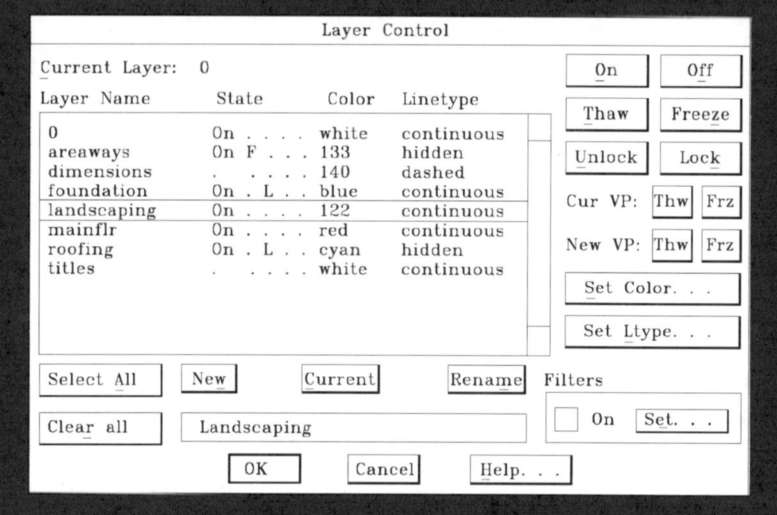

The Layer Name Edit Box is used to create new names and edit existing names. The cursor must be on the word New to be able to enter a new name. It must be on Rename to change the currently selected name.

Unlock or Lock is a very useful option. It allows the user to add entities to an existing layer without allowing changes in any existing information. Once a layer is locked, it can be visible, but no edit commands can be used on entities in that layer. If the locked layer is current, new information can be added to that layer. With both frozen and off options, the layer can't be edited, but it also can't be seen. This allows visibility without vulnerability.

The Filters area allows you to filter or manage your layers more easily. For example, using the Set Layer Filters dialogue box, which is accessed through Set..., you can get a listing of all the layers that have hidden lines, or all the layers that are red, or all the layers that are frozen. This can be really useful if you are using multiple layers.

DDLMODES is accessed under the pull-down menu Settings, or by typing it in.

LAYER MANAGEMENT

While you are creating a model in AutoCAD, keep in mind that other people may want to work with your file at some point, and, in order to do so, your layers should be named in a logical, straightforward manner. Since AutoCAD is the most popular CAD software package in North America, it is likely that you will be swapping files with other users in your field at some point. It is necessary, therefore, to have a logical layer format.

Many industries have developed layering standards that specify that certain objects are to occupy certain layers. When you start working for a company, be sure you know the company's layering standards, and ask if there are any standards outside the company that you should be aware of.

Most communities have an AutoCAD user group in their general area. If you contact this group, you can find out the names of the companies in that area that are using AutoCAD and perhaps get an idea of the local layering standards in your field.

As you become more involved with CAD, your files will become more complex, and you will amass a large volume of files. If you have different layering standards on each file, you will have a very difficult time accessing the specific data you want.

In the exercises, if you do not use the layer names suggested, at least make sure your names are logical.

Freezing unused layers will save a great deal of time when working with larger models. Layers that have been frozen will not display when they are first thawed; they must be regenerated first.

If you are making a layer current, make sure as well that the layer is on and not frozen. It is possible to have a layer current when it is also off or frozen, and you will be creating objects on the invisible layer without seeing what you are creating. If you have drawn objects that are not showing up, check to see that your layer is turned on.

Once you start dimensioning, you will notice that you have a layer called DEFPOINTS that is automatically turned off. This layer contains the definition points for the dimensions. You should create another layer for the actual dimensions themselves.

Only in Releases 11 and 12 can the 0 layer and the DEFPOINTS layer (if dimensions are present) be renamed or deleted from a file.

Exercise A6

```
LIMITS  0',0'
        60',45'
GRID    4'
SNAP    various
```

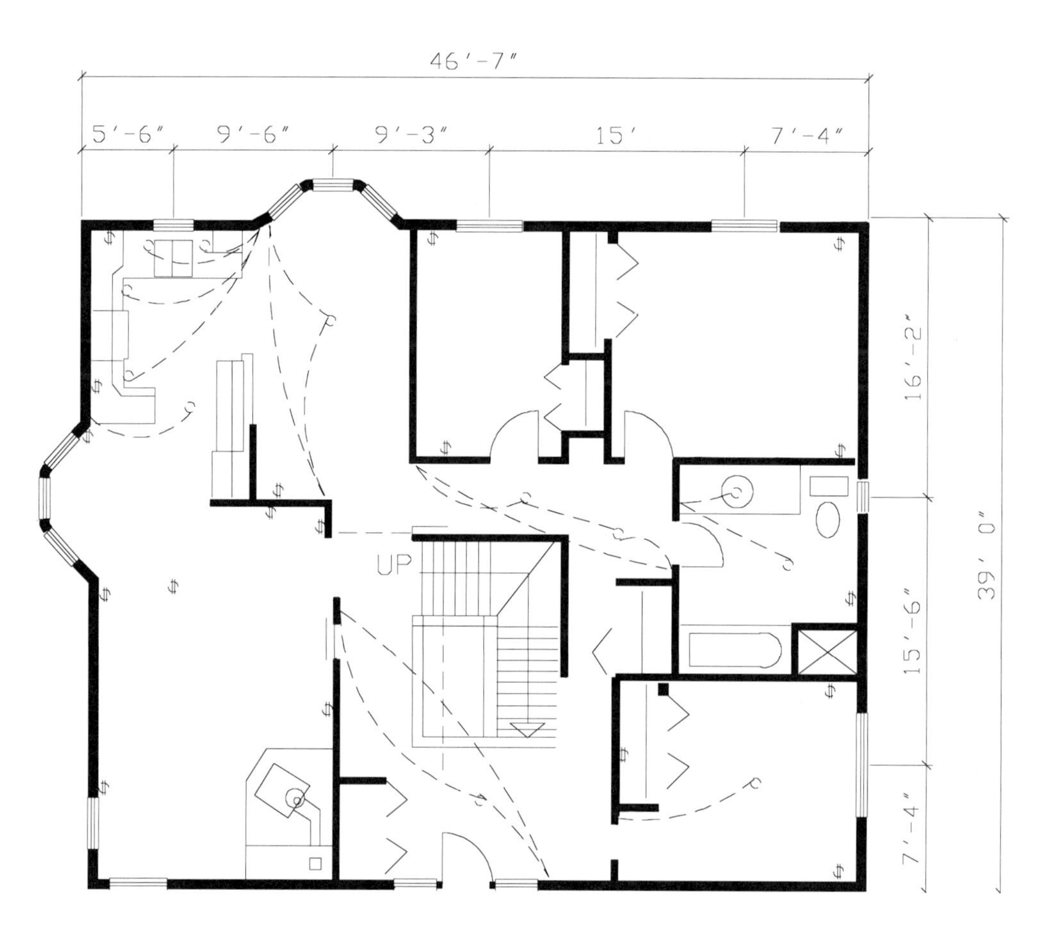

This exercise will not only reinforce what you learned in the last session, but will give you practice on layers.

Use editing commands as often as possible, resist the temptation to always use the commands you are sure of.

Suggested Layer Schedule:

Name	Color	Linetype
Windows	Cyan	Continuous
Walls	White	Continuous
Electric	Yellow	Hidden
Doors	Red	Continuous
Fixtures	Green	Dashdot

Exercise M6

```
LIMITS  12,9
GRID    .5
SNAP    various
```

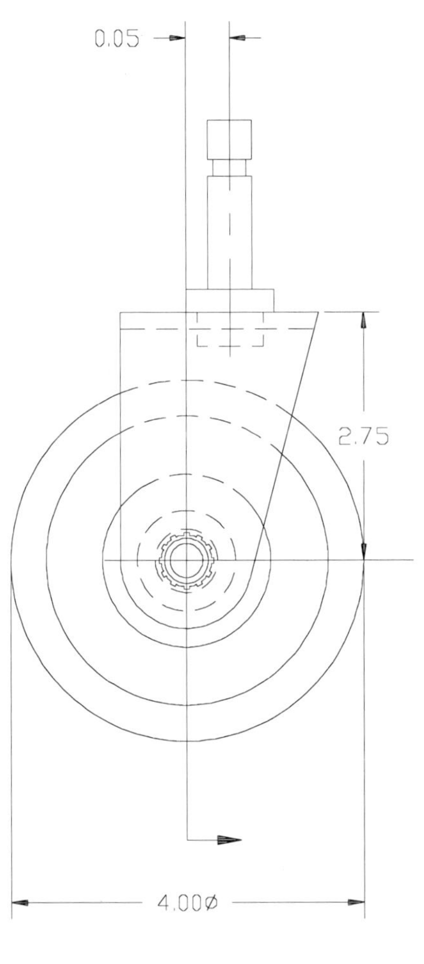

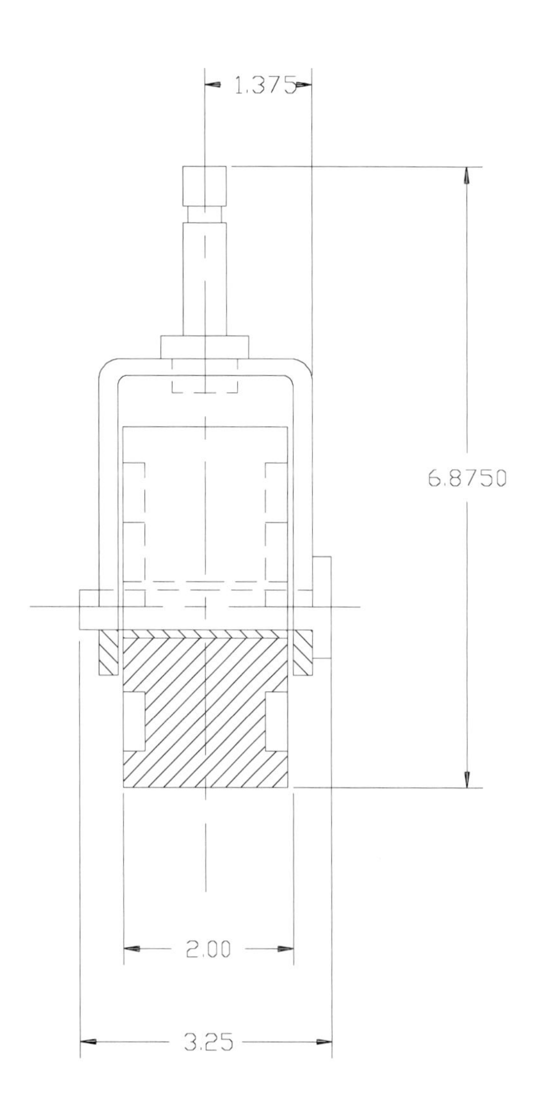

Make different layers for each linetype and use different colours. The hatching is included as a visual aid only, do not add it at this point unless you are using LINE and ARRAY instead of HATCH.

Suggested Layer Schedule:

Name	**Color**	**Linetype**
0	White	Continuous
One	Red	Continuous
Center	Blue	Center
Hidden	12	Hidden

Exercise C6

```
LIMITS  60,40
GRID    5
SNAP    .5
```

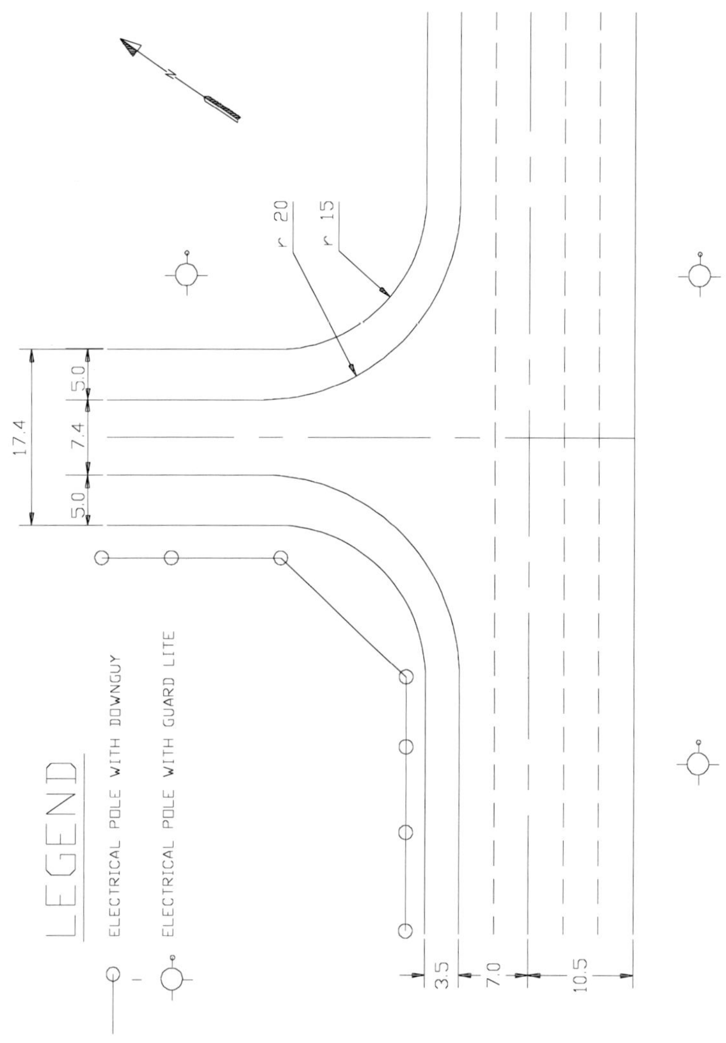

Make different layers for each linetype. Use as many colours and editing commands as you can.

Suggested Layer Schedule:

Name	**Color**	**Linetype**
0	White	Continuous
One	Red	Continuous
Center	Blue	Center
Hidden	12	Hidden

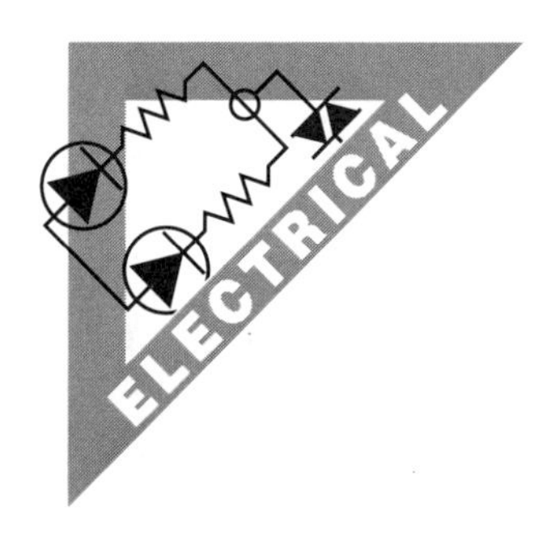

Exercise E6

This circuit diagram was created with LINE, CIRCLE, and PLINE. The text was placed by simply using TEXT.

See Chapter 9 for details on entering text. The default is to have the text justified on the bottom left of the character. Once in the command, pick the size of lettering and the rotation angle, then enter the text.

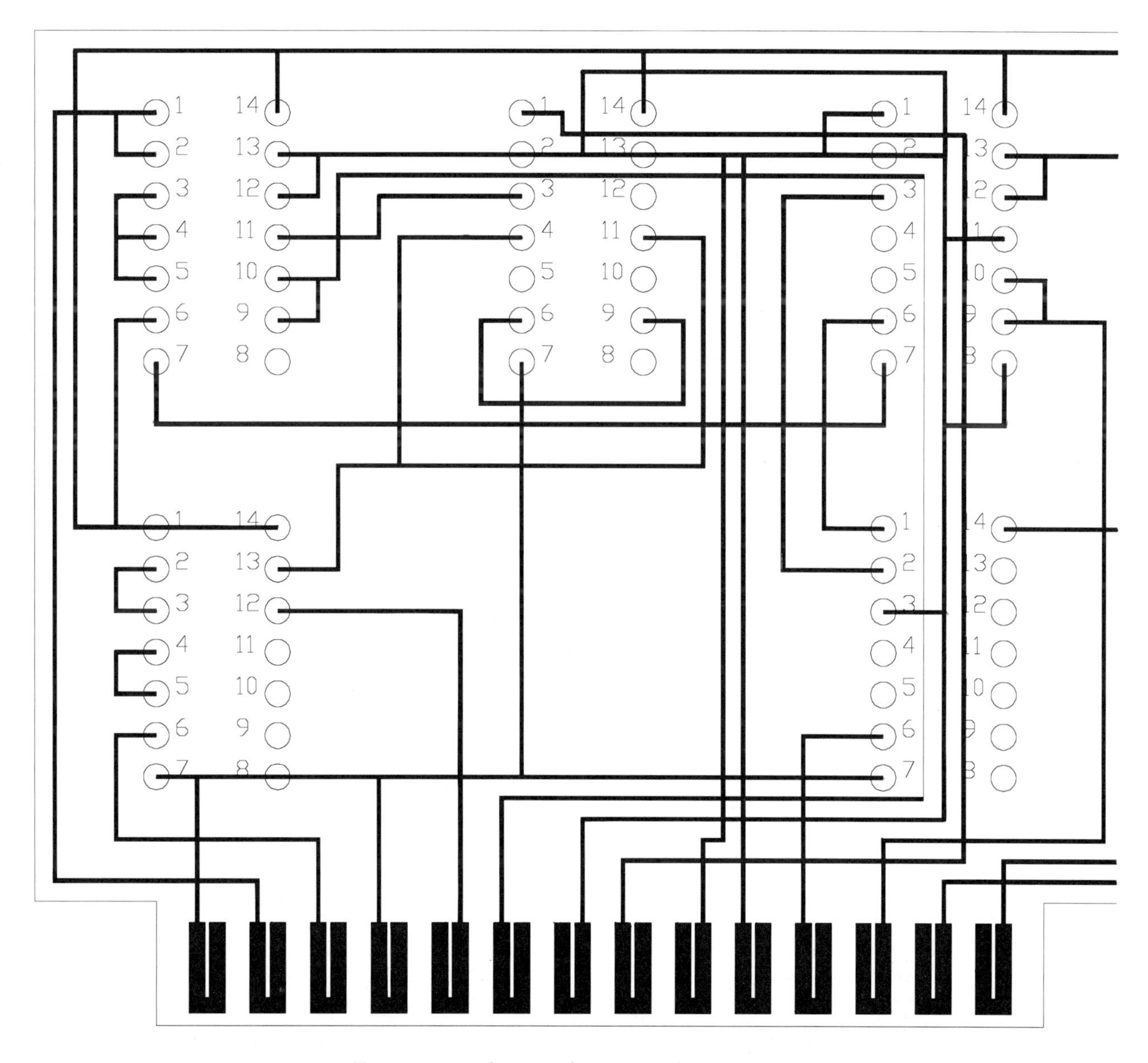

HINT: To position the numbers exactly, create one number, then use COPY with Multiple and SNAP to place the character in even rows. Use the CHANGE command to change the actual number once it has been placed.

Challenger 6

This is an illustration of what you can do with patterns. There are many good computer-aided manufacturing programs for knitting and other fabric applications, and much research is currently being done on cutting using lasers.

Creating this pattern seems at first quite simple, but it will be a challenge to attain proportions that are pleasing to the eye.

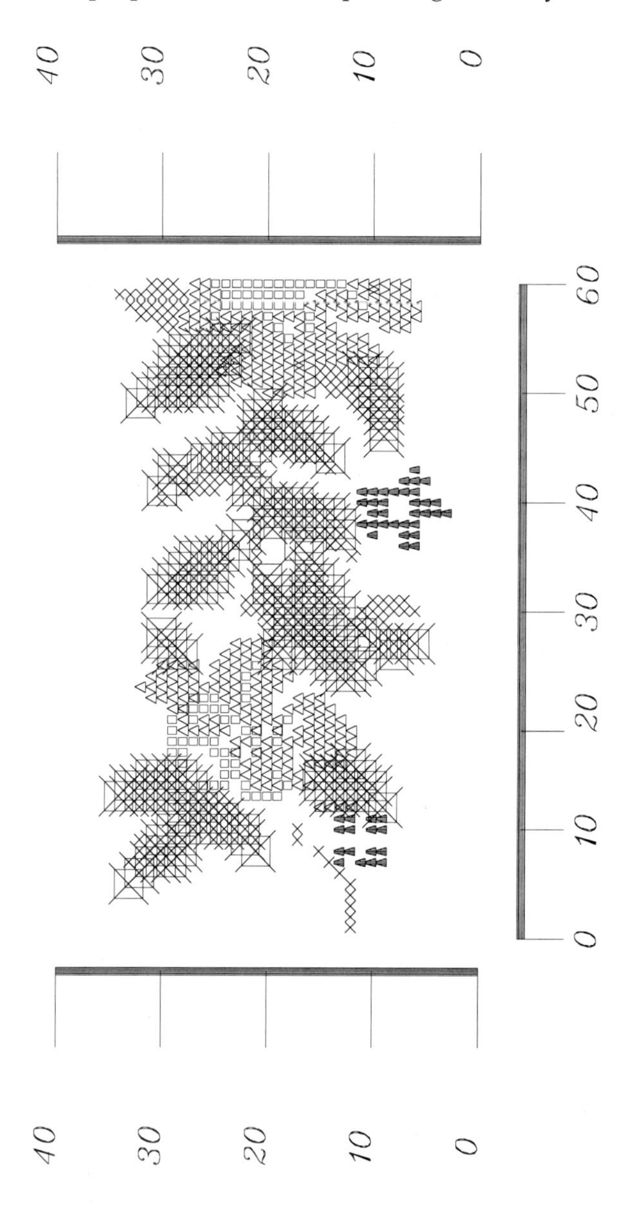

This kind of patterning can also be used in architectural applications, particularly in renovations.

Challenger 6 (Mirrored)

Once entered, the pattern from the previous page can of course be mirrored and copied as on this page.

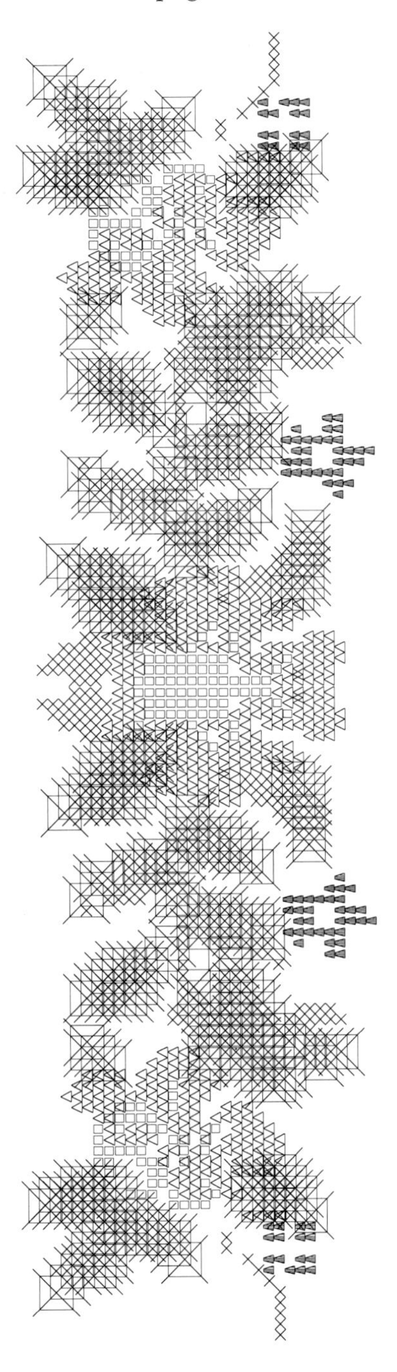

Be careful when doing this exercise, because it will take up a lot of room on your disk.

DIMENSIONING

Upon completion of this chapter, the student should be able to:

1. Add dimensions in linear, radial, or angular fashion
2. Using DIMVARS to adjust the dimension variables to fit the object being dimensioned
3. Edit dimensions with DIMASO on
4. UPDate dimensions when DIMVARS or UNITS have been changed

With any CAD system, the information concerning the parameters of the part or the model is part of the actual database. In other words, when you create the lines, circles, arcs, etc., you should be creating them perfectly every time.

There are many reasons for creating a CAD database, only one of which is to generate accurate and attractive drawings. You can also use the database for the following:

- Computer-Aided Manufacturing or CAM,
- analysis programs such as Finite Element Analysis, Stress Analysis, Load Analysis, etc.,
- calculating stock for ordering and estimating purposes and Bills of Materials,
- creating a model base for further model building,
- generating three-dimensional information for downloading 3D plotters or stereolithography equipment
- sales and marketing of products and services.

In each of these cases and the many other applications for which CAD will eventually be used, it is imperative that data is entered correctly. If you get into the habit of entering information in a sloppy or slapdash manner, it will catch up with you later when you try to dimension or hatch the data. In addition, all of the analysis information will be incorrect.

One of the greatest problems with CAD is that people sometimes know how to use the CAD system and can apply it to an application, but they do not know much about the application. The system printouts may seem reasonable to a person who has little experience, but could cost the company a lot of time and money, and, of course, probably cost the operator his or her job if the data is not entered correctly.

While creating the data, keep asking yourself, Does this size seem reasonable or can this object be built or manufactured? When dimensioning, these questions are particularly important, because the dimensions are, after all, the actual sizes of each component, and these will be used by whoever will be creating the finished product. It is a sad fact of life, but office personnel are often viewed with a certain scepticism by shop personnel because the former are seen to make a limited effort to make their drawings practical. This is liable to be the case on a drafting table and can be even more of a hazard on a CAD system as the operator becomes more dependent on the computing power of the CAD system for calculations. Keep in mind your long-term credibility before you produce a drawing that does not make sense.

GETTING READY TO DIMENSION

AutoCAD was originally a system just for making drawings, and thus the SETUP command was invented. If you have Release 10 or 9, you can use SETUP to instantly adjust the dimensioning parameters for the final drawing. In Release 11, the SETUP facility can be found under the Bonus menu. For most cases, however, particularly when using the PAPERSPACE facility, it is more useful to understand how to adjust the dimensions to fit the object or part being dimensioned, and then fit it onto paper later.

Units

Before you start to dimension a model, check the units to make sure they are appropriate. The system defaults to inches. If you have been using decimal units and assume each unit to be a foot, or a metre, or a light year, now is the time to use SCALE to adjust the size of the drawing to fit the final paper format.

Decimal

If you have not changed the default, you will have four decimal places of accuracy on the on-screen status line. This is the degree of accuracy that will show up on your dimensions. In many cases, you need only two decimal places; in other cases, you will need six or seven. If you want to change the unit display, pick the UNITS command (Settings menu) and change the second option to whatever size you need.

Architectural

If you assumed that each unit is one foot and used decimal units rather than architectural units, use the following command to convert feet to inches:

```
Command:SCALE
Select objects:W (pick 1, 2, etc.)  (pick everything)
Select objects:↵ (indicates no more objects are required)
Base point:0,0
<Scale factor>/Reference:12
```

This takes the information that is in inches and converts it to feet by making it 12 times larger.

The information may disappear from the screen because it is too large to be viewed in the space provided. Use ZOOM All to restore it. Once you have used ZOOM All, the objects leave no room for dimensions, so use ZOOM .7X to make the information smaller on the screen (see page 29).

Now select UNITS from the Settings menu and choose architectural units (choice number 4).

The second choice is the smallest denominator. If you are using fractions, your coordinate display will be in the fraction chosen, thus, if you choose 16, the accuracy will be one sixteenth of an inch. If you are detailing, this is appropriate. If you are creating a layout for a building, you will of course change this to 1 or one inch because buildings are not made to a tolerance of one sixteenth of an inch.

The display for each unit choice is as follows:

Scientific	1.55E+01
Decimal	15.50
Engineering	1'-3.50"
Architectural	1'-3 1/2"
Fractional	15 1/2

Pick the type of unit that you require and make sure that you have a reasonable smallest denominator.

Pick the other appropriate units that you require or press ↵ to accept the defaults. You will eventually return to the Command: prompt; then you can press F1 to return to the graphics screen.

Save the model before dimensioning and make sure you have enough space left on your disk for more data. If you have been using a 360K disk, your disk may be almost full. If this is the case, get a new one and copy the item you want to dimension onto the new disk (see page 75 for details).

Before you start dimensioning, it is also a good idea to set up a new layer for your dimensions, because you may want to freeze them or turn them off in the future.

Dimensioning Components

Dimensioning on any CAD system will depend on one thing, the integrity of the data. All of the dimensions will be taken from the model itself. Garbage in - garbage out. The size reflected on the dimensioned part will be the size at which it was entered.

> **Release 12 Notes**
>
> The dimension is created in highlighted format at the Dimension line location prompt. You can position the dimension by dragging then using a pick to finalize the position and add the dimension text.

What you are doing with dimensioning is using the system to place the dimensions, thus utilizing the conventions of your discipline. You should not have to know what the dimensions are; that should be part of the existing data.

Extension lines or witness lines extend from the object to show the entities measured.

Dimension lines, with the text and arrows, hold the dimension.

The text or dimension itself will be within or above the dimension line.

The point at which you start your dimension is the reference point or defpoint. There should be a gap between this point and the start of the extension line, and the extension line should continue beyond the intersection with the dimension line to create an overshoot.

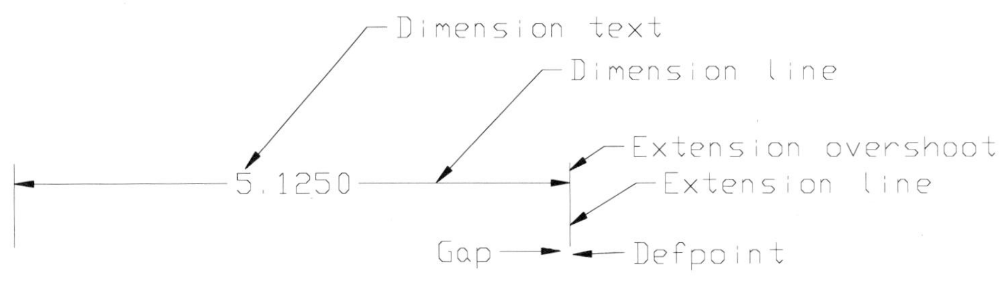

Figure 7-1. Dimension components

ARROW BLOCKS

AutoCAD's dimension lines default to the outside of the dimension text itself. Sometimes it is preferable to have an arrowhead that has a smaller dimension line extension. If a block of an arrowhead is made, it can be placed at will. The text can be inserted within the necessary space after the block is inserted (see Chapter 10).

Dimensioning Mode

When you select DIM: from the side menu, you enter the Dimensioning mode, Draw commands, the edit commands, and many of the display commands are no longer accessible. What you are doing is accessing the data for dimensioning purposes only. You can change the size of a part on the screen by the Display pull-down menu, but you can do nothing else.

Once you are in the DIM: mode, a new set of commands controls the dimensioning features of AutoCAD. In addition, the Command: prompt will change to DIM:.

In essence, anything you can do with dimensioning by hand you can also do with the DIM: commands in the AutoCAD system. All the tools are there, but you may find that it takes a while to find exactly what you are after.

In this book we will concentrate on producing a few sample drawings. You may require a reference text for all the dimension variables and styles. Again, David Cohn's reference text *Complete AutoCAD* has as complete an explanation of the DIMension VARiables as I have seen. He offers over 100 pages of explanations of the dimension variables, complete with illustrations. Only a few of the DIM VARS are explained in this chapter, since that is all you will need to get started. Use the Help files for more information if a reference text is not available.

Once you have set up the screen with a reasonable zoom factor, and your units are correct, you can create a dimension layer and go on to the Dimension mode. The screen will look like Figure 7-2.

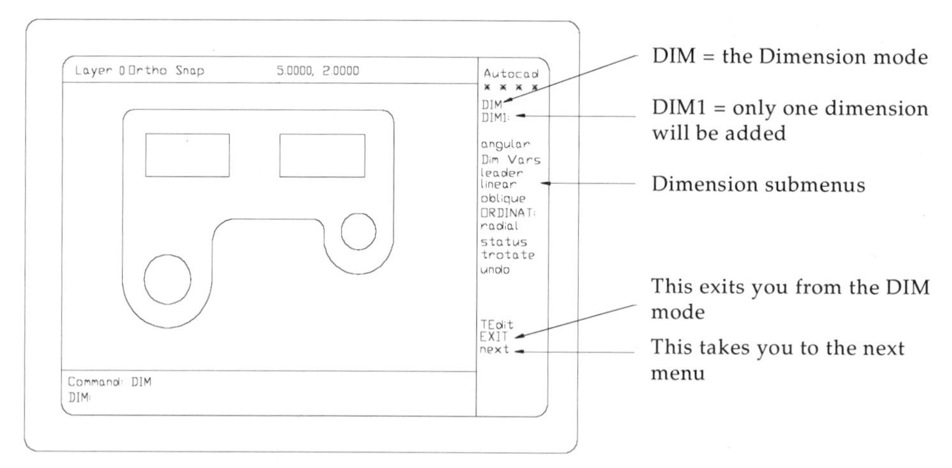

Figure 7-2. The Dimension mode

Where:

DIM: = the dimensioning mode

DIM1: = only one dimension

ANGLE = angular dimensions selector

DIM VARS = Dimension Variables

LEADER = a notation with an arrow and leader line

LINEAR = linear dimensions selector

OBLIQUE = tilted extension lines on linear dimensions

ORDINATE = ordinate dimensions

RADIAL = radial dimensions selector

STATUS = the default values of the DIM VARS

TROTATE = the ability to rotate the text on specific dimensions

UNDO = the ability to erase the last dimension

TEDIT = text edit without EXPLODE

EXIT = exit from the Dimensioning mode

NEXT = next menu for more choices

Many of the options provided have submenus of commands to choose from.

GETTING STARTED

To begin your dimensioning, make sure that you have the units set and you are in the Dimensioning mode.

DIM takes you from the root menu into a different mode. Remember that you cannot move, copy, edit or create geometry. With the DIM: prompt, you are allowed only to create dimensions. An EXIT or CANCEL will return you to the Main menu.

As an introduction to dimensioning, we will outline some of the basic dimension commands, then you can try some of the example chapter. If you need more information on dimensioning, see Chapter 36, Dimensioning 3D Parts. The basic commands are as follows:

LINEAR — *creates a dimension between two entities in a straight line. You must specify vertical, horizontal, aligned, or rotated. Make sure that you specify the correct one.*

ANGULAR — *creates an angular dimension through two lines indicating the angle between the lines. Points can also be used.*

RADIAL — *dimensions the radius or diameter of circles and arcs.*

LEADER — *allows you to slip in an arrowhead and a leader line for notations regarding the drawing. It is also useful for "fudging" a dimension when you just cannot seem to get a dimension to go where you want it.*

Essentially, these are all the commands you will need to get started.

In the example Figure 7-3 on the following page, we are creating a horizontal dimension.

As we create the dimension, if we have Coords on (F6), the coordinates displayed on the status line can be used as a guide to determine the correct length of the extension line.

```
Command:DIM
DIM:LINEAR
DIM:HORIZONTAL
```

`First extension line or RETURN to select:`**END** *(pick 1)*

`Second extension:`**END** *(pick 2)*

`Dimension line location:` *(pick 3)*

`Dimension text <210>:`↵ *(Return to accept the default)*

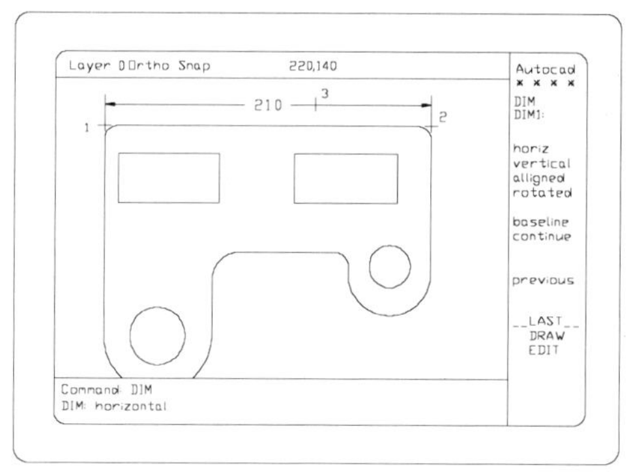

Figure 7-3. Horizontal DIM

The horizontal command calculates the distance between the two endpoints of the two objects that were picked. Osnap is essential.

The same command can work like this:

`DIM:`**HORIZONTAL**

`First extension line or RETURN to select:`↵

`Select line arc or circle:` *(pick 1) (pick the line you want dimensioned)*

`Dimension line location:` *(pick 2)*

`Dimension text <190>:`↵ *(return to accept the default)*

Any text can now be added.

In this case, the system will read the length of the item you select, because of the filleted corners, the first method may be what you want.

Before you will get this type of command to work, however, there is a dimension variable you will have to change.

You will note that the overall width or X value of the part is 210 units. As with LINETYPE, the default for screen display is 11 x 8 1/2 ". If you put the dimensions on without changing their scale, they will show up quite small.

To calculate the DIMSCALE or the size of the dimensions relative to the object being dimensioned, take the largest value in the X direction and divide by 12. This will give you a DIMSCALE that will make the dimensions visible. In this case, the X value is 210, we divide that by 12, then under the Dim Vars option, we change the DIMSCALE to 16.

For further information on how to calculate scales, see Chapter 11.

Once you have changed the DIMSCALE on this sample part, the command is quite simple. Remember to read the prompts.

`DIM:`**HORIZONTAL**

`First extension line or RETURN to select:` *(pick 1)*

`Second extension:` *(pick 2)*

`Dimension line location:` *(pick 3)*

`Dimension text <210>:`↵ *(return to accept the default)*

First you enter the Dimensioning mode by selecting DIM:. Then pick LINEAR, then HORIZONTAL.

Surprisingly, many students at one point during the lab pick horizontal when they mean vertical, and vertical when they mean horizontal. If your linear dimension does not work, check to see that you have the correct option.

Once this is done, pick the first extension line. Make sure the snap is on so that the reading is consistent, or use OSNAP. You will automatically get an overshoot distance, so pick the object itself or the place from which the extension line is to start.

Next pick the second extension line start point. Finally, indicate where the dimension line is to actually start. Note that the arrowhead, the dimension lettering, the gap, and the overshoot distance all become scaled with the DIMSCALE command.

All parts of the dimension, arrowhead, etc. are changed with DIMSCALE.

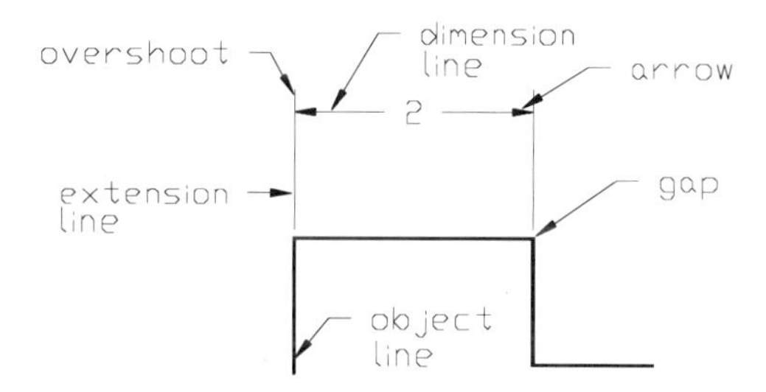

Figure 7-4. Using DIMSCALE to change the dimension scale

If you start to change each aspect of the dimension separately, you may run into trouble remembering which ones you have changed and what the default values are. DIMSCALE is the easiest way to change sizes.

DIM VARS

It has just been demonstrated how a horizontal dimension is added to a sample part. As long as everything that needs to be done corresponds to the default values, there will be no problem dimensioning. If there is trouble, however, with a few of the dimensions, you may want to change some of the Dim Vars.

Release 12 Notes

Under the Settings pull-down menu is a dialogue box (DDIM) accessed through Dimension Style. This will allow you to change the style of the dimension without using the DIM VARS.

To find out what the default values are, choose STATUS in the DIM: menu. A two- or three-screen listing of the various dimension variables will be displayed. It is not important to remember all these dimension variables, and only a total savage would ever make up a memory test of them. Use this as a resource only. Know where this list is and practise changing five or six Dim Vars to see how they work. Listed on the following page are some of the most often used variables to help you become familiar with the concept.

In changing the Dim Vars, note that every variable is either a toggle switch or a scale. (It is either On/Off or becomes larger or smaller.)

Once the dimension variable is changed, it will remain changed until it is changed again.

Once the Dim Vars are set, practise dimensioning, making sure that DIMASO (associative dimensioning mode) is on. This will allow the dimensions to be edited once they are in. Once finished, experiment with UPDATE.

The following list provides the usual defaults used by some of the common Dim Vars. For a full listing, see STATUS under the Dim: menu.

DIMSCALE	*1.0 overall scale factor. Assumes that the part is either 8–24 inches long or that it has been sized-blocked to fit the paper (See Chapter 10)*
DIMASZ	*0.18 arrow size*
DIMBLK	*(None.) holds the name of the block to be inserted in lieu of an arrow or tick, etc.*
DIMCEN	*0.09 centre-mark size*
DIMEXO	*0.0625 extension line offset. Specifies the offset from the area you specify.*
DIMDLE	*0.0 dimension line extension. Used in conjunction with ticks only.*
DIMDLI	*0.38 dimension line increment for continuation or baseline commands*
DIMEXE	*0.18 extension line extension beyond dimension line*
DIMTP	*0.0 plus tolerance*
DIMTM	*0.0 minus tolerance*
DIMRND	*0.00 rounds off a dimension to the size indicated*
DIMTXT	*0.1800 text height. Not the same as the regular text height.*
DIMTSZ	*0.0 tick size*
DIMTOL	*Off add +/- to dimension text*
DIMTIH	*On horizontal text inside extensions*
DIMTOH	*On horizontal text outside extensions*
DIMSE1	*Off suppresses first extension line.*
DIMSE2	*Off suppresses second extension line.*
DIMTAD	*Off puts text above the dimension line.*

Contained in this chapter are example pages for each of the various types of dimensions and a discussion on some common changes to the system defaults or Dim Vars.

As AutoCAD is set up to service a variety of industries, there are certain parameters that are applicable to mechanical and architectural drawings that are not applicable to municipal and surveying drawings. The defaults are usually set for mechanical drawings, and, if an application is not mechanical, many defaults may have to be changed before dimensioning.

It is very useful to learn how to change defaults rather than only accepting a customized file already set up with the changes made. Learning to change defaults will help you become familiar with the system prompts, default operation, and the communication necessary to change these defaults.

Dimensions Without Lines

When a notation of distance between two items is needed, but not the dimension lines, extension lines, or arrowheads, the Dim Vars must be set as follows:

DIMASZ to 0 — to eliminate arrowheads

DIMSE1 to ON — to suppress first extension line

DIMSE2 to ON — to suppress second extension line

In the first dimension of Figure 7-5, all the defaults are used except DIMTAD, which is turned ON.

In the second (from left), DIMASZ is set to 0.

In the third, both DIMSE1 and DIMSE2 are OFF.

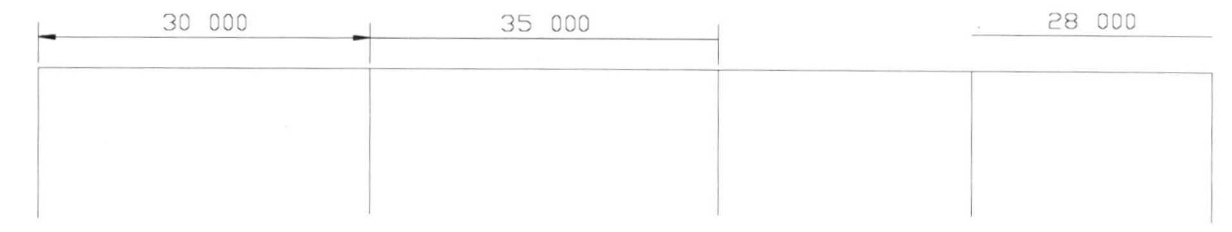

Figure 7-5.

The text will appear on top of the dimension line if DIMTAD is set on. Once the dimensioning has been completed, the dimension lines can be deleted. There is no way of suppressing the dimension lines so far in AutoCAD, except by writing a LISP routine.

Alternate Unit Dimensioning (DIMALT)

The most common method of alternate unit dimensioning is using metric versus imperial. By setting DIMALT on, the value indicated is measured in the units specified and in the alternate units set by DIMALTF (alternate units scale factor). The default is 25.4, the number of millimetres in an inch. DIMALTD determines the number of decimal places of accuracy in the alternate dimension.

Special Text Characters

When the DIM command prompts to either accept the default dimension or text, you can enter any text string. You can enter degree symbols, etc. in the text string when prompted for text by using:

%%d	*draws a degree symbol*
%%nnn	*draws special character represented by code number nnn*
%%c	*draws a circle diameter dimension symbol*
%%p	*draws a plus/minus symbol*
%%u	*toggles underlining on or off*
%%o	*toggles overscoring on or off*

The characters on this page are often needed in the drafting world but are not found on regular keyboards. Just type in the special characters as they appear above, and you will get the desired effect.

Example: *Special Characters*

Type this: `%%UNOTE:%%U THE OBJECT SHOULD BE 60%%C`

`AND SHOULD APPEAR %%P 0.05%%D FROM THE ENDPOINT`

You will get:

<u>NOTE:</u> THE OBJECT SHOULD BE 60⌀ AND SHOULD APPEAR ± 0.05° FROM THE ENDPOINT

In Release 10 and earlier releases, the special characters will work in the TEXT command but will not work in the DTEXT command.

ROTATING DIMENSION TEXT

AutoCAD is set to ANSI (American National Standards Institute) specifications for dimensioning and specifies "unidirectional" dimensioning, or horizontal dimensioning, where possible.

DIMTIH *aligns the text to the dimension line if the text is drawn within the extension lines.*

DIMTOH *aligns the text to the dimension lines if it is drawn outside of the extension lines.*

TROTATE *changes the orientation of one or more existing dimensions as long as they are associative (DIMASO).*

The three examples of Figure 7-6 illustrate the use of some common dimensioning variables.

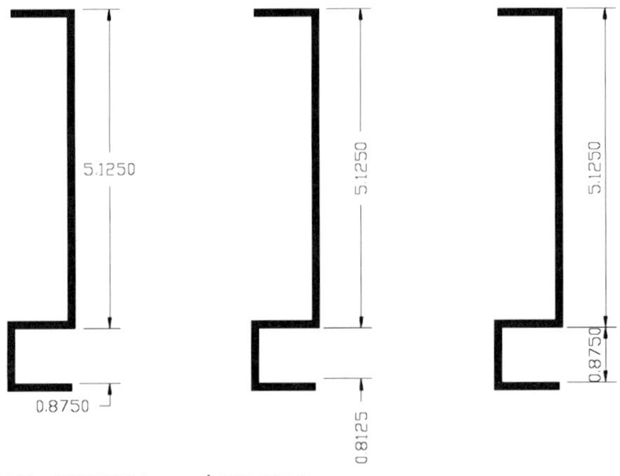

Figure 7-6. DIMTIH, DIMTOH, and DIMTAD

In the first, all defaults are used. In the second, DIMTOH and DIMTIH are off. In the third, DIMTAD is on.

The dimension lines are set up relative to the extension line origins. If the line is horizontal, the text will be horizontal.

If vertical is chosen, the text will be horizontal or vertical depending on the DIMTIH and DIMTOH. DIMTAD places the text above the dimension.

The examples of Figure 7-7 illustrate how text rotates with an object.

If ALIGNED is chosen, the extension lines begin at the point picked, and the extension lines maintain a constant length. The text may or may not be rotated, depending on DIMTIH and DIMTOH.

If ROTATED is chosen, the dimension line is rotated at a distance relative to the horizontal, and the extension lines will be adjusted to fit.

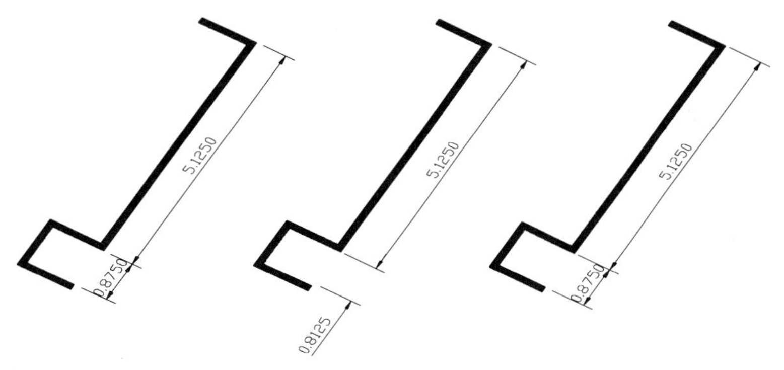

Figure 7-7. Text follows dimension line in Rotated linear dimensions

TROTATE allows the rotation of the text to change once it is entered. With TROTATE, only the text is rotated; none of the extension or dimension lines change.

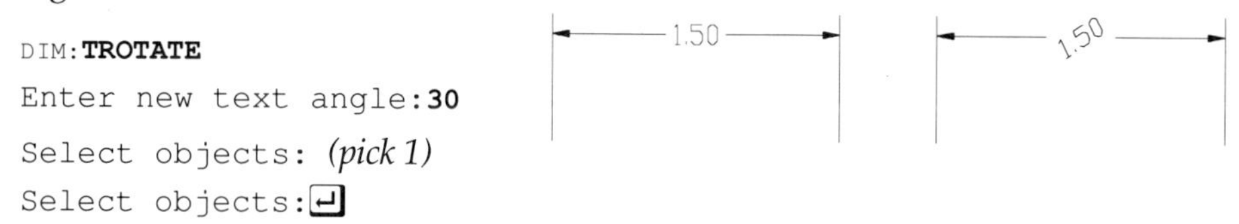


```
DIM:TROTATE
Enter new text angle:30
Select objects: (pick 1)
Select objects:↵
```

NEWTEXT can be used to update the dimension text once it is entered.

Utility Commands

STYLE

The dimension text is drawn using the current text style. The text style can be changed by using the style dimensioning utility command. This will be explained further in the next chapter.

```
DIM:STYLE
New Text style <current>: new name, italic,
                          leroy, (etc.)
```

UNDO

erases the annotations produced by the most recent dimensioning command.

EXIT

brings the system back to the Command: prompt.

EDITING DIMENSIONS

Using dimensioning commands can be frustrating, simply because there are so many variables, and it takes some time to get used to them. AutoCAD's dimensioning can do almost anything, but, at first, it takes some time to learn how to do it.

Explode

If you need to get a drawing done quickly and you are having trouble with a particular dimension, put the dimension in as best as you can and return to the Command: prompt. Then use editing commands (MOVE, STRETCH, ROTATE, etc.) to position it. EXPLODE will break apart the various elements of the dimension — the lines, the text, and the arrows — into individual objects for editing.

Associative Dimensioning (DIMASO)

Release 12 Notes

You can use the selection grips to simplify the editing process. Create a simple triangle and dimension all three sides. Exit the DIM mode and use selection grips to stretch the longer side of the triangle. The dimension will automatically update if ASODIM is on.

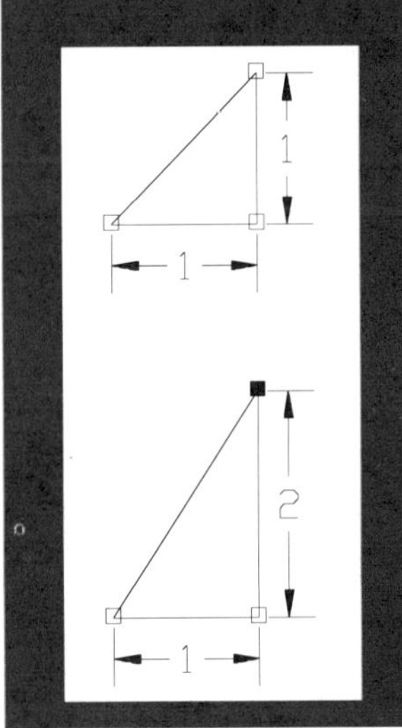

DIMASO will create associative dimensions on a drawing. This means that if all the dimensions are in the wrong scale, or the wrong units, or the arrowheads should be ticks, etc., the dimensions can be edited singly or in groups with the aid of Window and Crossing all at once rather than erasing them and putting them back in. UPDate will update the dimensions to the new variable.

When creating dimensions, the dimension itself is being entered relative to a definition point or defpoint. When the first dimension has been created, a layer called defpoints is added automatically to the layer listing. If the associative dimension mode or DIMASO is on, the defining point of the dimension will be automatically tied to the object that it annotates. Thus, any change in the scale or position of the object will be automatically updated on the dimension.

With DIMASO on, any changes that are made in the DimVars can be updated in the dimensions by typing UPD for Update.

Many of the edit commands can be used in conjunction with DIMASO to edit dimension. Edit commands that are affected by DIMASO are ARRAY, EXTEND, MIRROR, ROTATE, SCALE, STRETCH, and TRIM.

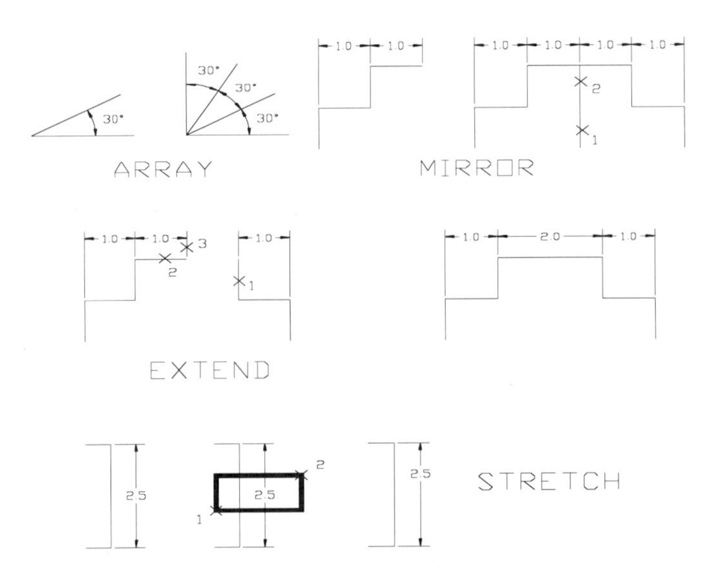

Figure 7-8. Editing Dimensions with DIMASO

In the array illustration of Figure 7-8, the angular dimension was arrayed using a polar array around the intersection of the two lines. The dimensions were rotated as they were copied.

The four lines with dimensions were mirrored through the centre line. Once mirrored, there are two lines in the centre, one unit in length, that need to be replaced with one line of two units.

The two lines plus the dimension are erased, then the line *and* the dimension are extended to the line boundary indicated by pick 1. Finally, the dimension text in the final example is stretched to a different position. Experiment with DIMASO editing to see how useful and flexible it is.

DIMENSIONING COMMANDS

LINEAR DIMENSIONS

The most common form of dimensioning is linear. The Linear subcommand provides six options: horizontal, vertical, aligned, rotated, baseline, and continue.

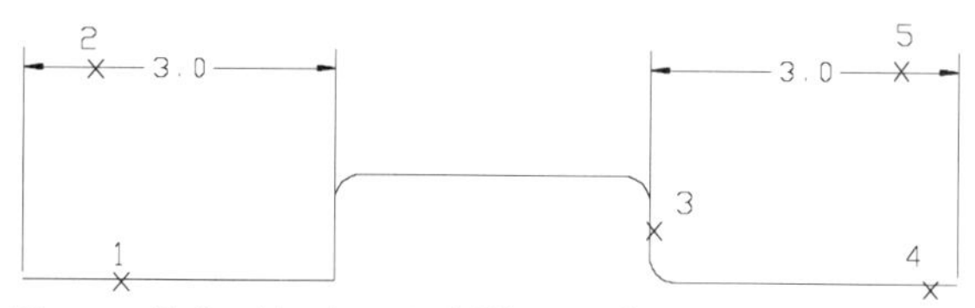

Figure 7-9. Horizontal Dimension

> **Release 12 Notes**
>
> Most dimensioning commands are on the main dimension menu, not in submenus.

Horizontal

DIM:**HORIZONTAL**

First extension line or RETURN to select:↵

Select line arc or circle: *(pick 1)*

Dimension line location: *(pick 2)*

Dimension text <9.0000>:↵ *(Accept the default. Any text can now be added.)*

DIM:**HORIZONTAL**

First extension line or RETURN to select: *(pick 3)*

Second extension line: *(pick 4)*

Dimension line location: *(pick 5)*

Dimension text <3.0000>:↵ *(Accept the default. Any text can now be added.)*

When using linear dimensions, be sure to use OSNAP to pick the exact point on each object.

Continue

After you have placed the first dimension, use CONTINUE to place all other dimensions in the string. This will ensure that the dimension line is lined up and that you are not duplicating the extension line in each dimension.

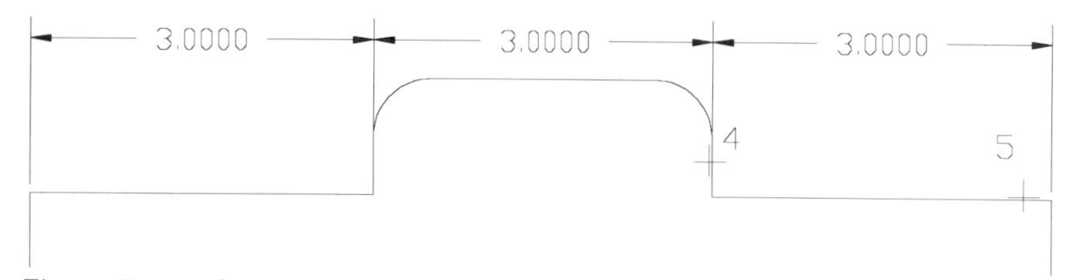

Figure 7-10. Continue Dimension

DIM:**CONTINUE**

Second extension line: *(pick 4)*

Dimension text <3.000>:↵

DIM:**CONTINUE**

Second extension line: *(pick 5)*

Dimension text <3.000>:↵

Vertical

Vertical dimensions are just as easy and use the same command structure.

DIM:**VERTICAL**

First extension line or RETURN to select:**END** *(pick 1)*

```
Second extension line:END (pick 2)
Dimension line location: (pick 3)
Dimension text<2.0>:↵ (Type a value or accept the default)
DIM:CONTINUE
Second extension line: (pick 4)
Dimension text <2.0>:1.5

DIM:CONTINUE
Second extension line: (pick 5)
Dimension text <3.0000>:3.00
```

DIMTIH can be used to rotate the text so that it lines up with the dimension line.

If you type in the text as shown, it will not update using UPD if changes are needed later. Change the units instead of entering the numbers as shown.

Aligned

The dimensions can be aligned to the points you choose or to the object you choose.

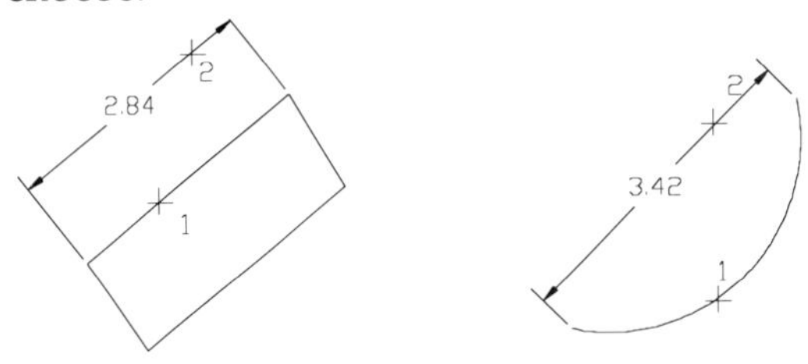

Figure 7-11. Aligned Dimension

```
DIM:ALIGNED
First extension line or RETURN to select:↵
Select line arc or circle: (pick 1)
Dimension line location: (pick 2)
Dimension text <2.84>:↵ (accept the default)
```

The dimension will align itself to the object chosen. In the case of the arc, the dimension is lined up with the two endpoints of the arc.

Baseline

```
Command:DIM
Dim:HORIZ
First extension line origin or RETURN to select: (pick 1)
Second extension line origin: (pick 2)
Dimension line location: (pick 3)
Dimension text <1.9879>:
Dim:BASELINE
Second extension line origin: (pick 4)
Dimension text <4.1288>:
Dim:BASELINE
Second extension line origin: (pick 5)
```

Rotated

Rotated dimensions can make a drawing look tidier.

```
DIM:ROTATED
Dimension line angle <0>:30
First extension line or RETURN to select: ↵
Select line arc or circle: (pick 1)
Dimension line location: (pick 2)
Dimension text <3.31>:↵ (accept the default)
```

Angular Dimensions

Angular dimensions are used to dimension the angle between two lines. In AutoCAD Release 11, the ANGULAR dimensioning subcommand can also measure the angle subtended by an arc, the angle around a portion of a circle, and the angle formed by three points.

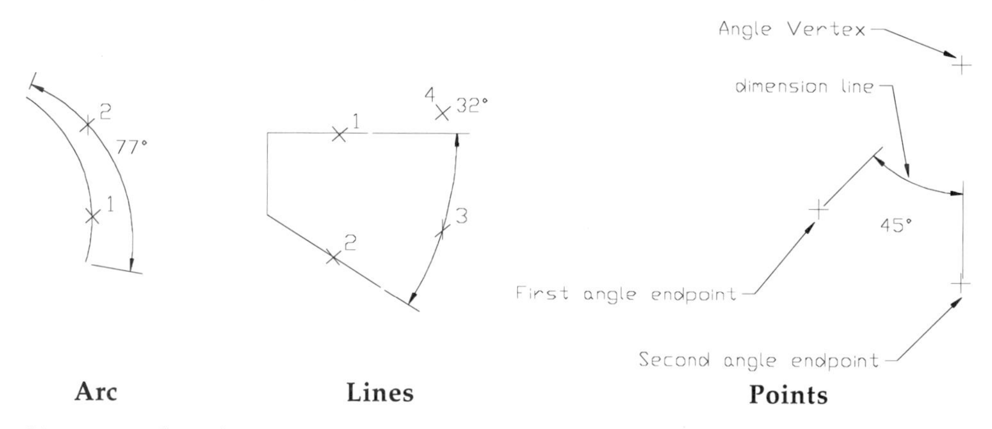

Arc **Lines** **Points**

You can select the arc as in the Arc illustration.

```
DIM:ANGULAR
Select arc, circle line or RETURN: (pick 1)
Dimension line arc location: (pick 2)
Dimension text <77>:↵
```

You can choose the lines that make up the angle as in the Lines illustration or you can choose points as in the points example with the following command sequence.

```
DIM:ANGULAR
Select arc, circle line or RETURN:↵
Angle Vertex: (as shown)
First angle endpoint: (as shown)
Second angle endpoint: (as shown)
Enter dimension line arc location: (as shown)
Dimension text <45>:↵
Enter text location: (as shown)
```

Angles are measured counter-clockwise around the object. Extension lines will be added to objects where the lines are not long enough to contain the dimension, and also to point dimensions.

When typing the command, the ANGULAR subcommand can be abbreviated to ANG.

Radial Dimensions

The RADIAL subcommand of DIM: provides three dimensioning options: Diameter, Radius, and Center.

DIAMETER

Once the circle or arc to be dimensioned is selected, the diameter subcommand measures, draws, and annotates it. Figure 7-12 illustrates three different and acceptable diameter dimensions.

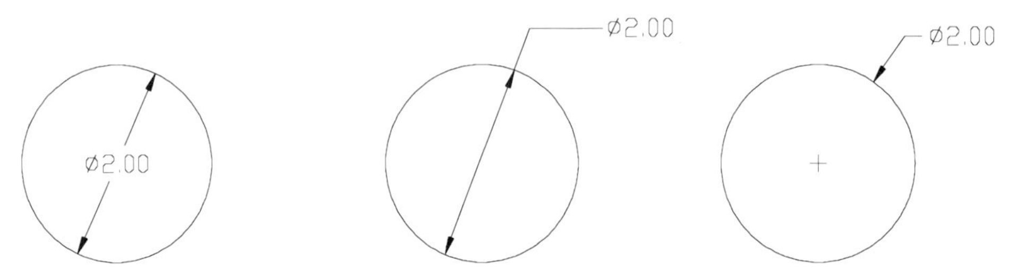

Figure 7-12. Diameter Dimension

DIMTIX = **on**	DIMTIX = **off**	DIMTIX = **off**
DIMTOFL = **either**	DIMTOFL = **on**	DIMTOFL = **off**

DIM:**DIAMETER**

Select arc or circle: *(pick 1)*

Dimension text <2>:↵ *(accept the default)*

If there is not enough room for the dimension text inside the circle, you will see the following prompt:

Text does not fit in. Enter leader length for text: *(pick 2)*

The position of the text relative to the circle is dictated by where you pick the object. If there is sufficient space, then the dimension will be fully contained within the circle.

If you need to change the size of the circle once it is already dimensioned, use SCALE to change *both* the size of the circle and the attached dimension. Use Window to select the items to scale.

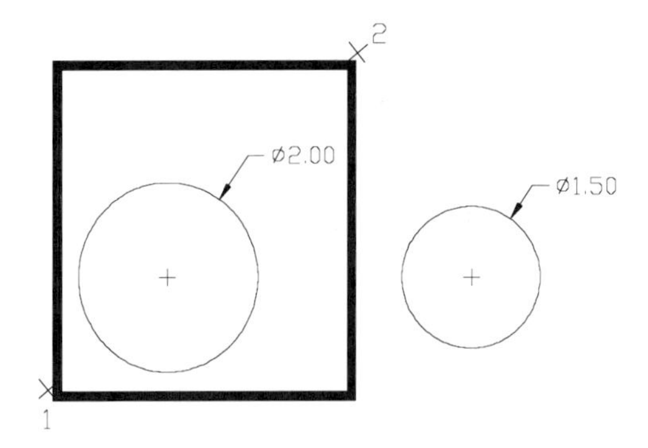

Figure 7-13. Scaling the existing dimensions

If the dimension is not working and you are pressed for time to complete the drawing, use LIST to reaffirm the exact dimension, then use LEADER to place the arrow and the leader line as shown in Figure 7-13. Remember to use %%c for the diameter symbol when typing in the diameter, i.e., Text: %%c2.00.

Radius

As with the diameter subcommand, the radius option measures and places the radius text once a circle or arc has been selected.

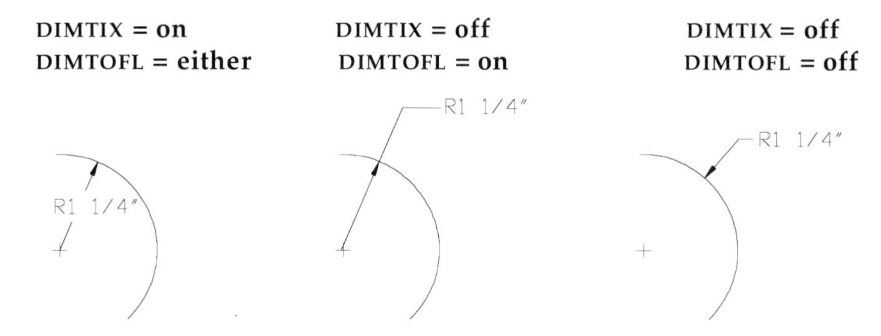

Figure 7-14. Radius dimension

```
DIM:RADIUS
Select arc or circle: (pick 1)
Dimension text <1.21>:↵
Text does not fit. Enter leader length for text: (pick 2)
```

Again you will be prompted for the text location if it will not fit into the space provided. LEADER can also be used if you are desperate.

As shown below, any type of unit can be used; these are architectural. The dimension variable DIMRND can also be changed to have the dimension rounded off to a certain integer.

```
DIM:DIMRND
New value:.125
```

R1 1/8"

DIMRND only rounds off numbers, the UNITS command controls the number of decimal places and the type of unit.

EXERCISES

On the next four pages are nine dimensioning examples. Since technologists will be expected to dimension more than just one type of product, it is a good idea to try many of the examples shown. For example, Exercise A7 has a fire rating assembly in the mechanical format and a floor plan in the architectural format. You are well advised to study the difference in format.

You can start by editing Exercise 1 from Chapter 1 and dimensioning that. Once completed, try another from your disk, or go on to the examples shown.

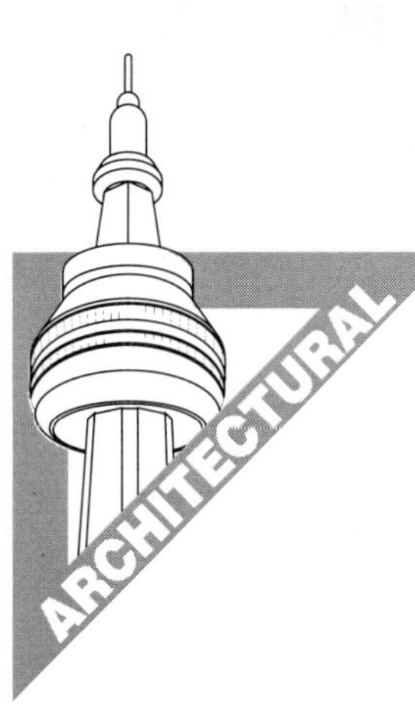

Exercise A7

Dimension a floor plan from a previous chapter, then draw this roof assembly for a fire rating illustration and dimension it.

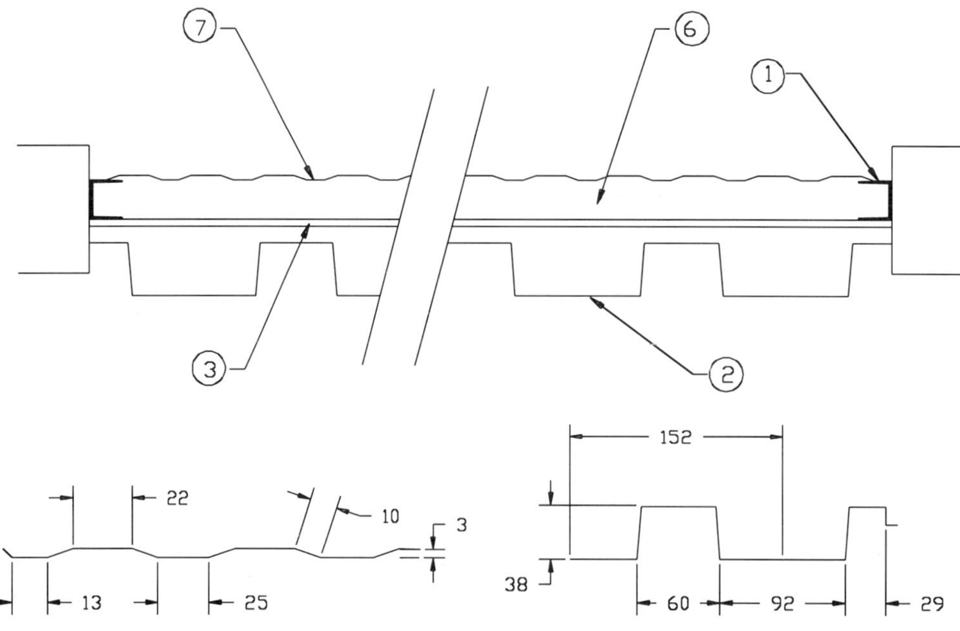

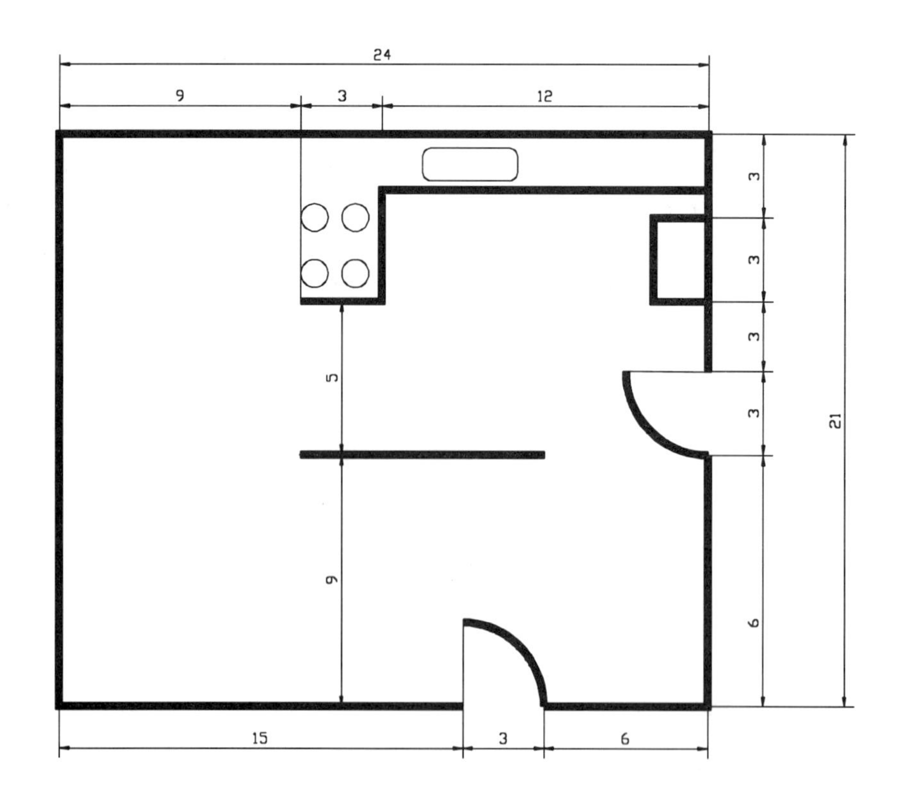

Exercise M7

Use Edit an Existing Drawing on the Main menu to access the first exercise you did and add the dimensions as shown on a new layer. Once that is completed, draw and dimension the rocker arm shown. If you finish early, start on the fire rating assembly of Exercise A7.

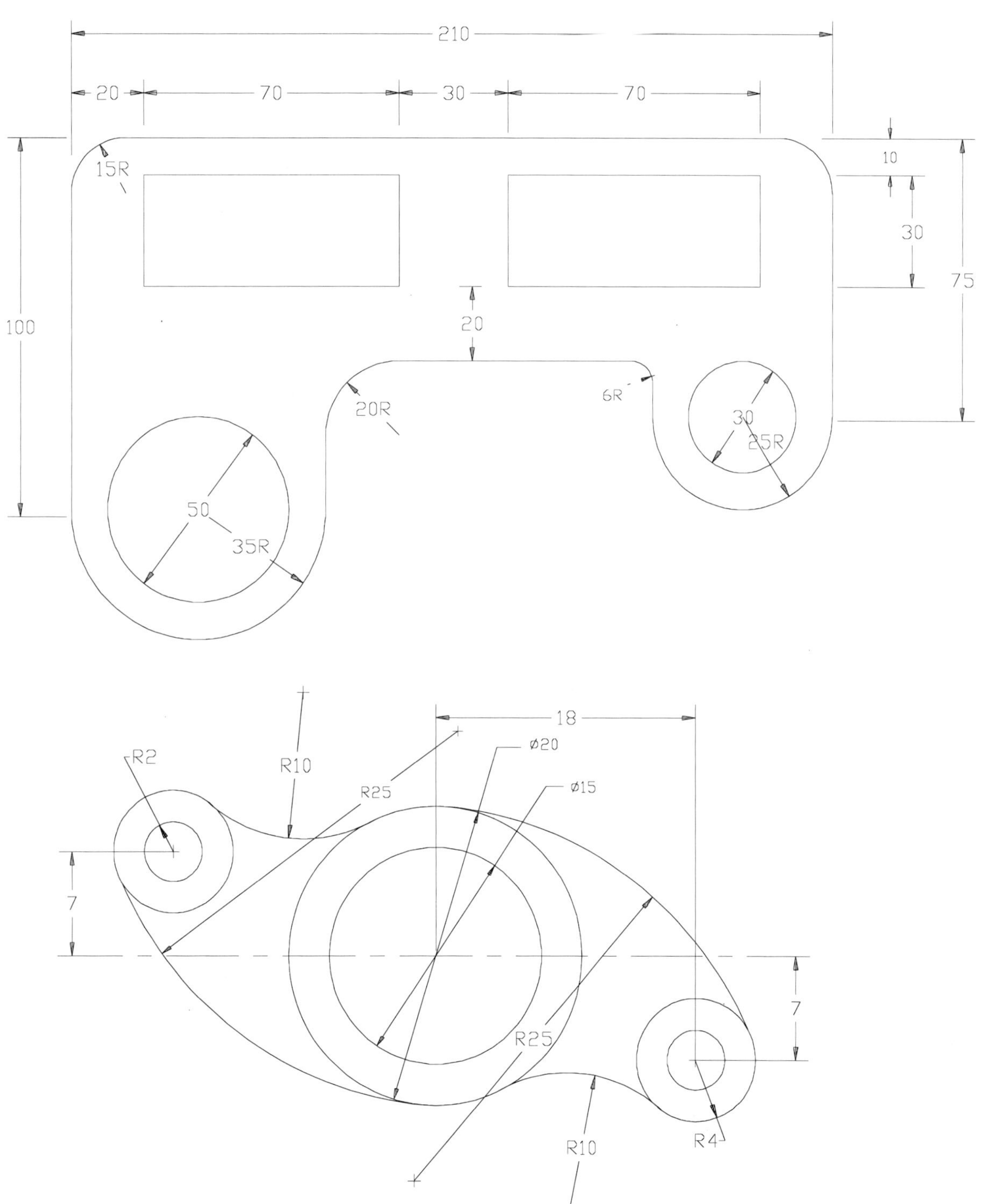

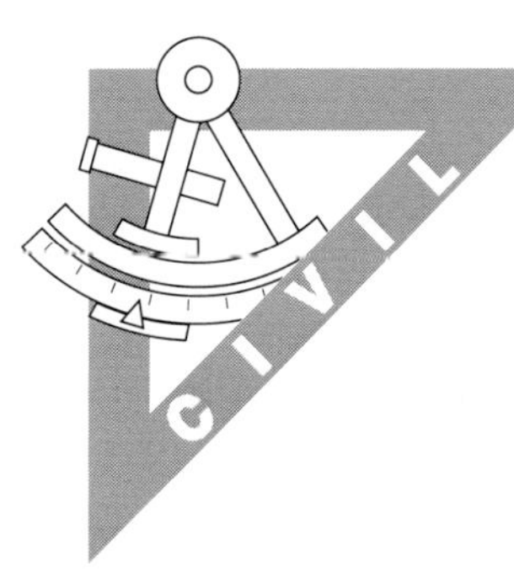

Exercise C7

Use Edit an Existing Drawing on the Main menu to access two of your earlier exercises, one with arrowheads and one without. If you finish early, start on the fire rating assembly of Exercise A7.

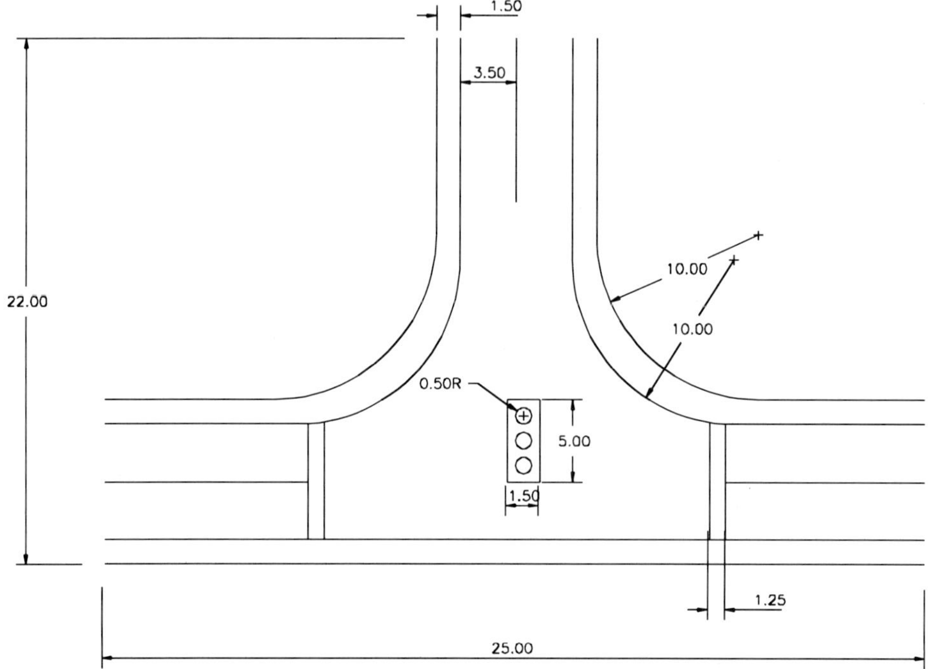

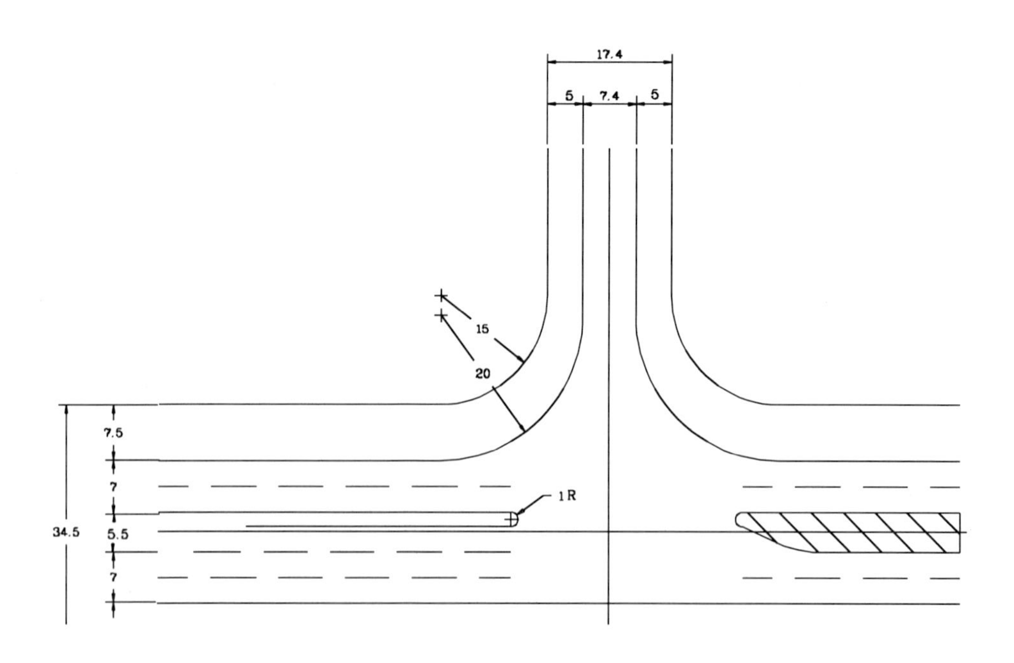

Challenger 7

Be sure to use different layers.

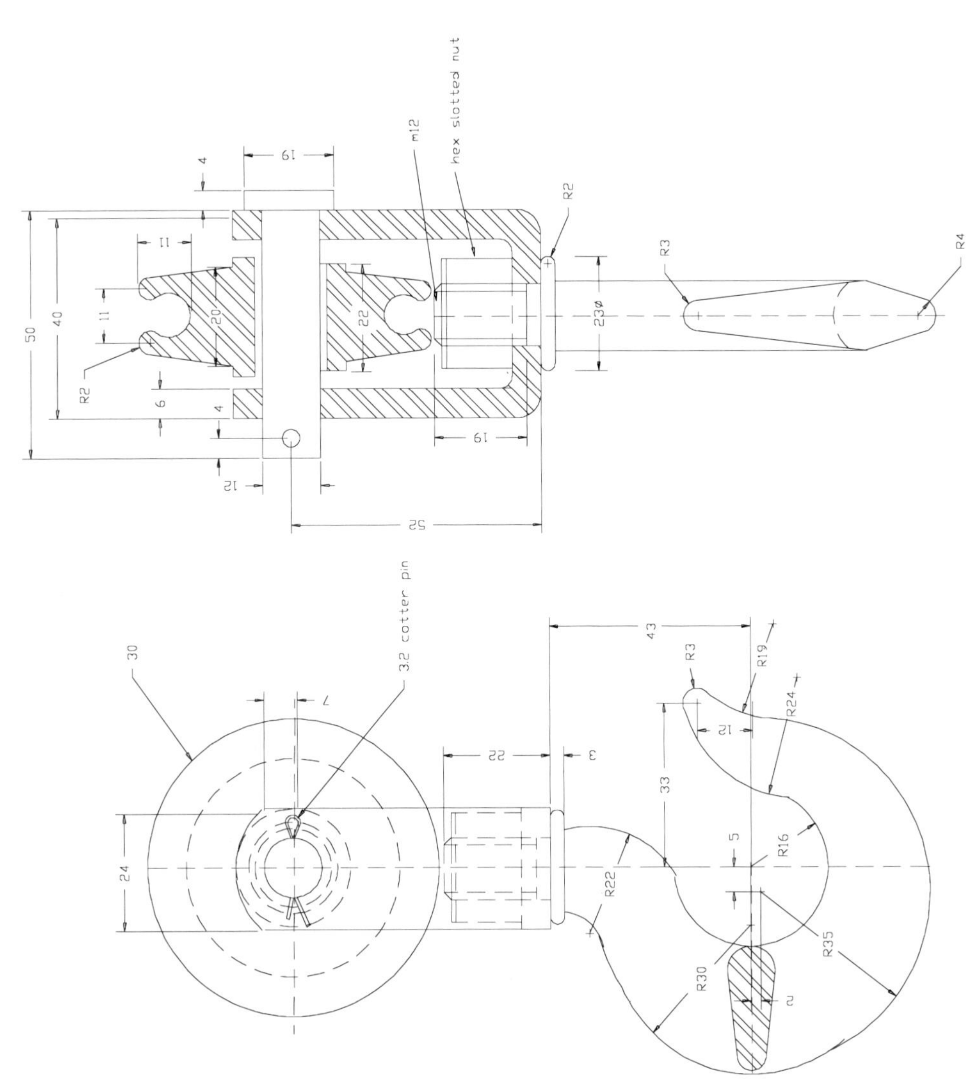

TEXT

Upon completion of this chapter, the student should be able to:

1. Place text in any size or at any rotation angle on a drawing
2. Access and use the option menu for fonts
3. Modify an existing text string
4. Set up an isometric text
5. Enter text in dimensioning commands

TEXT AND DTEXT

The commands TEXT and DTEXT will place strings of characters on a drawing. When entering text, AutoCAD will prompt for a height for each character, a rotation angle for the string, and a point at which to place the text string on the model or drawing. The TEXT command is as follows:

```
Command:TEXT
Justify/Style/<start point>:J
Align/Center/Fit/Middle/Right/TL/TC/TR/ML/MC/MR/BL/BC/BR:
```

Release 12 Notes

Under the Draw pull-down menu, choose Text. The options will be Dynamic, which will invoke the DTEXT command; Import Text, which will load the ASCTEXT lisp program (see Chapter 16); and Set Style, which is the same as the Options-Fonts menu in Release 11, offering you a list of possible styles. In Release 12, there are 16 new styles added to the old style. Choose the one you want from the scroll bar.

Where:
Justify = the placement of the text

Style = the style of the letters. The styles must be loaded in AutoCAD to be accessible.

Align = an alignment by the endpoints of the baseline. The aspect ratio (x versus y) will correspond to the preset distance.

Center = the centre point of the baseline. This option will fit the text through the centre point indicated.

Fit = an adjustment of width only of the characters that are to be fit or stretched between the indicated points.

Middle = a placement of the text around the point; i.e., the top and bottom of the text are centred as well as the sides.

Right = an alignment with the right side of the text.

The examples on the right demonstrate the standard justifications.

The default is left justification at the baseline of the text string.

DEFAULT CENTERED
ALIGNED MIDDLE
FIT F I T RIGHT

These are options available in Release 10; in Releases 11 and 12 there are more.

The justification options are as follows:

TL = Top Left
TC = Top Centre
TR = Top Right
ML = Middle Left
MC = Middle Centre
MR = Middle Right
BL = Bottom Left
BC = Bottom Centre
BR = Bottom Right

Top Left	Middle Left	Bottom Left
Top Center	Middle Center	Bottom Center
Top Right	Middle Right	Bottom Right

Once you have chosen a point to place the text, the command will prompt for the height of the letters, the rotation angle, and the text or string of characters itself.

```
Command: TEXT
Justify/Style/<start point>: (pick 1)
Height <.2000>: .5
Rotation angle <0>: ↵ (accept the default)
Text: Front Elevation ↵
```

1 Front Elevation

In this example, the default or bottom-left corner was chosen, so the other options for placement were not offered. If Justify had been chosen, the following prompt would have appeared. (Note: in Release 10, only one line of options is offered.)

```
Align/Center/Fit/Middle/Right/TL/TC/TR/ML/MC/MR/BL/BC/BR:
```

Adding Multi-line Text

A new text string will line up with the previously entered text string if there are no changes in the base point or justification options in the TEXT command. Once you have finished your first line of text, press ↵ to exit the command, then ↵ again to bring back the TEXT command. One more ↵ will accept the default position, and the text will line up with the previous entry. If Center is chosen, all the text will be centred (B); if no option is chosen, all text strings will be left justified (A). The last string of text entered will be highlighted to show where the next line will line up.

If you do not want the text to line up with the last string entered, simply identify a new start point. The DTEXT command, outlined on the page opposite allows multi-line text in one command.

While entering text, the character height required can be chosen by typing in the number that indicates the height or by picking the height on the screen.

Once the text has been entered, it is accepted as one item and can be edited using any of the edit commands such as COPY, MOVE, ERASE, ROTATE, and ARRAY.

DTEXT

When using the TEXT command, the text string will only appear at the bottom of the screen in the command prompt area. The DTEXT or Dynamic Text command allows the text to be displayed on the screen as you enter it. Many people find this a more useful format. DTEXT always displays text as left-justified on the screen (default) regardless of the format chosen. The justification will be corrected when the command is finished.

As in the command ZOOM Dynamic, there are those who will argue that the D in DTEXT stands for Difficult instead of Dynamic, because, once entered, it is more difficult to get out. The DTEXT command automatically offers you a second string for text. To exit from the command, just use ↵.

```
Command:DTEXT
Justify/Style/<start point>:J
Align/Center/Fit/Middle/Right/TL/TC/TR/ML/MC/MR/BL/BC/BR:M
Middle point: (pick 1)
Height <.5000>:.25
Rotation angle <0>:↵ (Accept the default)
Text:front elevation ↵
Text:↵ (exit from DTEXT)
```

The cursor can also be repositioned to start a string of text in another area of the screen at any point within the command by simply choosing another point. This allows text of a similar height to be positioned at various places on the drawing with one DTEXT command. The pull-down menus are disabled throughout this command.

When using special character fonts with the DTEXT command, the special characters will be displayed as you type them; i.e., %%uFront Elevation%%u. The entry will be updated to the desired text once the command is finished.

If the Cancel button or ^C is issued within the DTEXT command, all the strings of text entered in that command will be lost. Always use ↵ to exit from the DTEXT command.

TEXT FONTS

Text fonts are the style or design of the letters and numbers. The AutoCAD text fonts are based on accepted text face design. The AutoCAD text fonts are illustrated below.

Fast Fonts:

TXT	To enter text use TEXT or DTEXT . ABC 123
MONOTXT	To enter text use TEXT or DTEXT . ABC 123

Roman Characters:

ROMANS simplex	To enter text use TEXT or DTEXT . ABC 123
ROMAND duplex	To enter text use TEXT or DTEXT . ABC 123
ROMANC complex	To enter text use TEXT or DTEXT . ABC 123
ROMANT triplex	To enter text use TEXT or DTEXT . ABC 123

Script Characters:

SCRIPTS simplex	To enter text use TEXT or DTEXT . ABC 123
SCRIPTC complex	To enter text use TEXT or DTEXT . ABC 123

Italic Characters:

ITALICC complex	*To enter text use TEXT or DTEXT . ABC 123*
ITALICT triplex	*To enter text use TEXT or DTEXT . ABC 123*

Greek Characters:

GREEKS simplex	Το εντερ τεξτ υσε ΤΕΞΤ ορ ΔΤΕΞΤ . ΑΒΧ 123
GREEKC complex	Το εντερ τεξτ υσε ΤΕΞΤ ορ ΔΤΕΞΤ . ΑΒΧ 123

Gothic Characters:

GOTHICE English	To enter text use TEXT or DTEXT . ABC 123
GOTHICG German	To enter text use TEXT or DTEXT . ABC 123
GOTHICI Italian	To enter text use TEXT or DTEXT . ABC 123

Cyrillic Characters:

CYRILLIC	Уо днудс удчу фтд УДЧУ ос ГУДЧУ . АБВ 123
CYRILTLC	To enter text use TEXT or DTEXT . ABC 123

Symbol Fonts:

SYASTRO astronomical
SYMAP mapping
SYMATH mathematics
SYMETEO meterological
SYMUSIC music

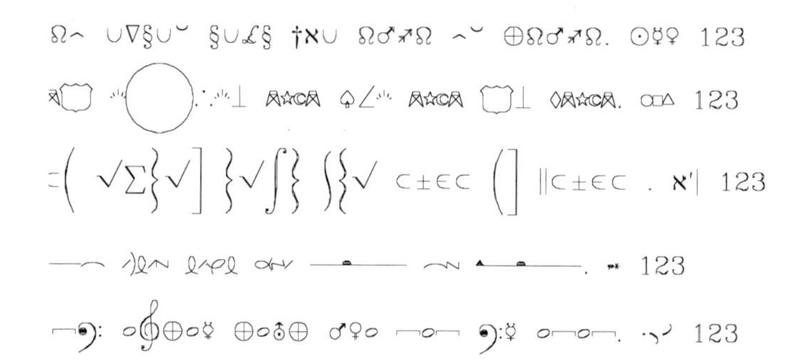

Accessing Fonts

To set the text style, select the Options menu on the top line and pick Dtext Options. On the next page of the menu pick Text Font. The dialogue box of Figure 8-1 will appear from which you can pick a style. There are three pages of selections.

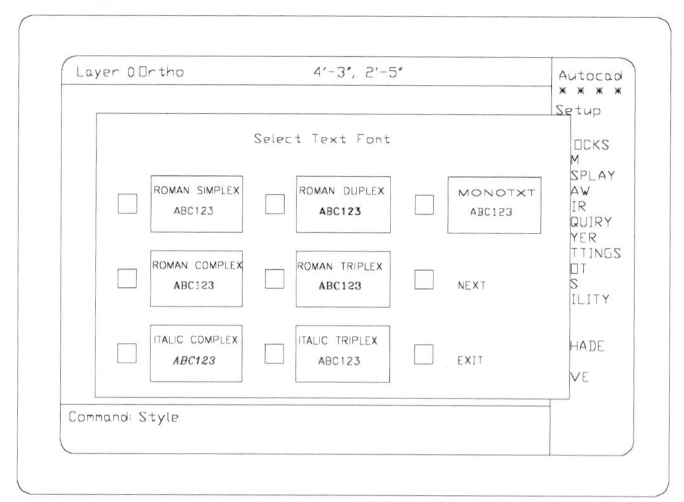

Figure 8-1. Accessing fonts

Release 12 Notes

Choose the text fonts through the Draw menu. Choose Text then Options - Fonts for the Icon menu.

Pick the font that you want to use. Once you have chosen the font style, you will be asked the following questions.

Command:**STYLE**

Text Style name <Monotxt>:**Romans** *(Monotxt is the default.)*

Font File:**Romans** *(You are loading the Roman simplex style.)*

Height <0.00>:↵

Width <1.00>:↵

Obliquing factor <0>:↵

Backward <N>:↵

Upside Down <N>:↵

Vertical <N>:↵

The obliquing angle is the angle of the text characters themselves, i.e., the slant.

Here are some examples of how the text will look.

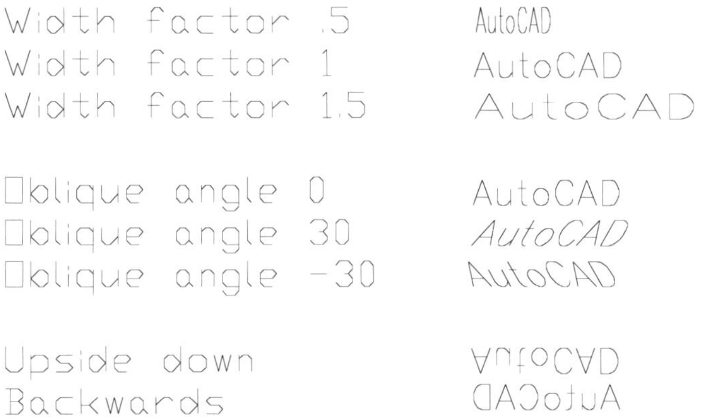

Width factor .5 AutoCAD
Width factor 1 AutoCAD
Width factor 1.5 AutoCAD

Oblique angle 0 AutoCAD
Oblique angle 30 AutoCAD
Oblique angle -30 AutoCAD

Upside down AutoCAD
Backwards AutoCAD

Figure 8-2. Examples of text options

Note that the options Height and Width are in fact the aspect ratio or relative X-Y value of the text. If you change the height of the text here, you forfeit the flexibility of changing it in the TEXT command.While you are learning AutoCAD, *never change the height of the text in the STYLE command,* because there are many instances where this will cause great inconvenience, such as with dimensions and annotations.

The Vertical option places text vertically. To rotate the text, change the rotation angle in the TEXT command; do not change Vertical in the STYLE command.

USING TEXT FONTS

Now that you have been working with AutoCAD for some weeks, you should be becoming aware that the number of lines on a drawing is directly related to the amount of disk space that the file occupies. Take a look at your floppy disk files with the DOS command DIR A:, and you will see that the Chapter 7 file is much larger than the Chapter 1 file.

AutoCAD's text fonts are made up of a series of small line segments. Each style uses a different number of line segments. The more complicated the style, the more line segments there will be, and the more disk space the text will take up. While the Gothic letters are attractive, they take up a lot of space and are not really appropriate for many jobs. Before choosing a font, try to determine which one is best suited to the job to avoid overloading the disk.

Monotext	**Roman Simplex**	**English Gothic**
7 Line Segments	19 Line Segments	70 Line Segments

Figure 8-3. Font line segment examples

In the illustrations of Figure 8-3, you can see that the Gothic letter has 10 times the number of lines as the Monotext. This may be appropriate for a title, but not for a notation or a dimension.

Additional text fonts can be purchased through third-party programmers, or you can develop them yourself if you have the time.

A text font will be active until it is replaced with a different one. The font will be active, whether you file the model or not, until it is manually changed.

Since text takes up memory space, to save time during regenerations, it is a good idea to have a separate layer for text and to turn it off or FREEZE it when you do not need to see it.

QTEXT

If regenerations and redraws are very slow, but you do not want to turn the layer for text off because you need to position objects in reference to the text, try QTEXT.

This option will replace a text string with a rectangle the approximate size of the text. This will save a lot of time during editing commands, zooms, and regenerations. The text is not made up of characters, but of vectors, and thus occupies a lot of memory. By placing a simple rectangle in the same spot as the text, only four lines need to be regenerated per text string.

Remember to turn QTEXT off before plotting; otherwise only the rectangles will plot.

EDITING TEXT AND DTEXT

The text string is considered an object and can therefore be moved, copied, placed on different layers, and created in different colours. The text string itself can also be changed as well as the height, the rotation angle, and the style of the characters by using CHANGE.

Example: *Changing Text*

```
Command:CHANGE
Select objects: (pick 1)
Select objects:↵
Properties/<change point>:↵
Enter TEXT insertion point:↵
Text style:STANDARD (Illustration 1)
New style or RETURN for no change:Romans
New height <5.0000>:10 (Illustration 2)
New rotation angle <0>:30 (Illustration 3)
New text <AutoCLAD>:AutoCAD ↵ (Illustration 4)
```

This command provides the options to change all of the variables in the TEXT command as shown in the illustrations of Figure 8-4.

Figure 8-4. Changing variables in the TEXT command

SPECIAL CHARACTER FONTS

As mentioned in the previous chapter, special fonts are available in AutoCAD as follows.

%%u	underscore	%%o	overscore
%%d	degree symbol	%%p	plus–minus tolerance symbol
%%c	diameter symbol	%%nnn	ASCII character

MAKING ISOMETRIC LETTERING

As mentioned earlier, SNAP sets a spacing for point entries, and GRID places a dot grid on the screen.

SNAP allows points or positions on the screen to be indicated at preset regular integers. SNAP also allows a rotated or isometric drawing to be entered.

```
Command:SNAP
On/Off/value/Aspect/Rotate/Style:S ↵
Standard/Isometric <Standard>:I ↵
Vertical spacing <0.4>: ↵ (will provide an isometric grid and snap)
```

The grid size will follow the snap size unless changed by the GRID command.

The GRID and SNAP can be changed at any time during a drawing. This is particularly important in creating text because text is often close to, but not on, an existing item or line.

To create isometric lettering, change the SNAP to Isometric. Then change the obliquing angle in the STYLE or FONT command to either 30 or -30. This will adjust the slant. Then enter letters using Fit.

Isometric Text Exercise

Use your own initials to fill in the spaces of the cube.

STEP 1:
Change the SNAP style to Isometric and draw a cube.

STEP 2:
Pick a font from the pull-down menu (Roman, Standard, or Monotext are the best for this purpose) and change the obliquing angle to 30. This is calculated by measuring the angle from the horizontal. Use Fit to place the text.

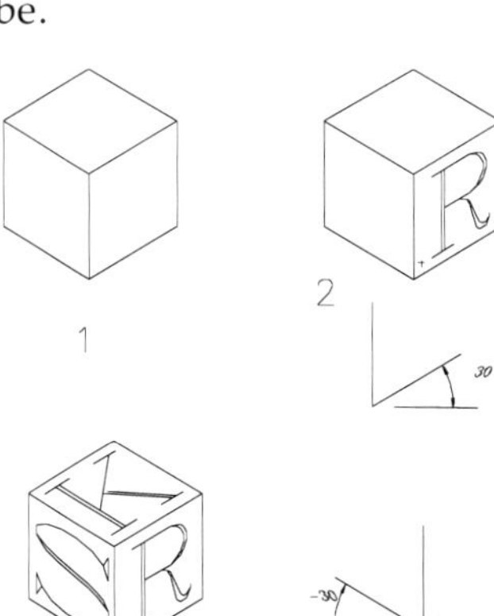

STEP 3:
Pick the same font and change the obliquing angle to -30. Use Fit to place the text. Use your own judgement to create the last letter.

USING LEADER TO CREATE NOTATIONS

The LEADER command in the DIM: menu allows for the creation of text with a leader line or series of leader lines and an arrowhead. The command is as shown below:

```
Command:DIM:
DIM:LEADER
Leader start point: (pick 1)
To point: (pick 2)
To point: (pick 3)
To point:↵
Dimension text<>:24%%c %%p0.02 ↵
```

You can enter as many points on the leader line as are necessary.

All special text characters can be used in this dimension as well.

The arrowhead size is set by DIMSCALE or DIMASZ.

To enter a leader line without related text, enter a single blank space when prompted for the dimension text. This can be done with all dimension entries.

As in the LINE command, U can be used to undo the previous point entry without exiting the command.

Entering Two Lines of Text

If there are two strings of text associated with the leader line, the easiest way to enter the second string is to copy the first line directly below itself using ORTHO, then change the text of the second string. This will ensure that both text strings are the same size and character font. There are also Lisp routines available that offer this facility.

Entering Vertical Fractions

As of the writing of this text, there are no vertical fractions available in AutoCAD's basic character font offerings. There are third-party programs that offer text fonts that contain vertical fractions. If you use a limited number of different fractions, you can use the TEXT command to create them, then save them as blocks to be inserted when needed. (See Chapter 10.)

Practice Exercises

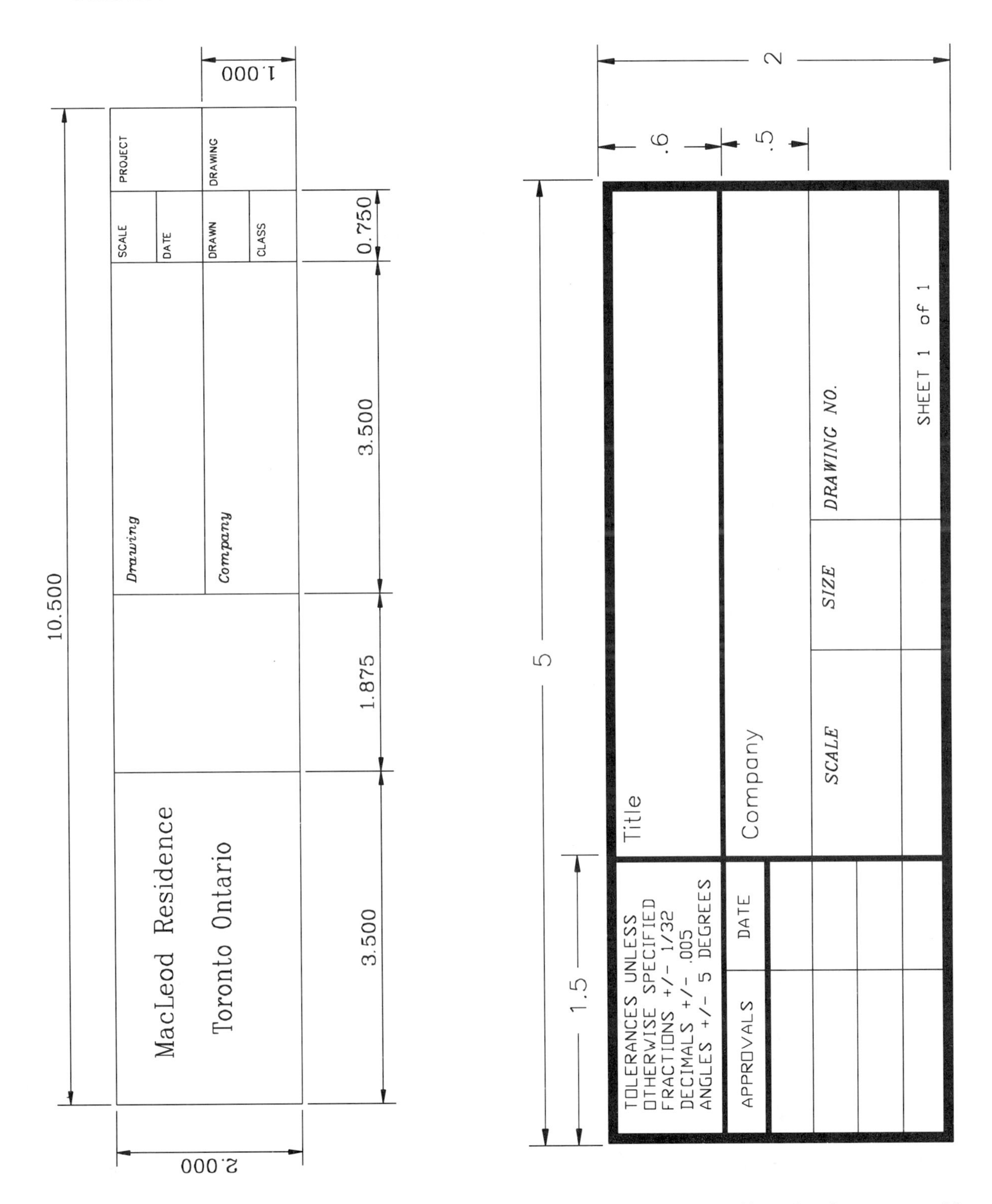

Use a pline to make the outer edges. Be sure to use Close for the corners. Use at least three different styles of letters to enter the information.

Do not forget to change the snap to line up the lettering.

If you prefer another style of title block, that is fine, as long as it is acceptable to your department.

Exercise A8

Draw the title block and the text within it first, then draw the stair detail and add the leader lines. The detail should be quite simple to create with edit commands.

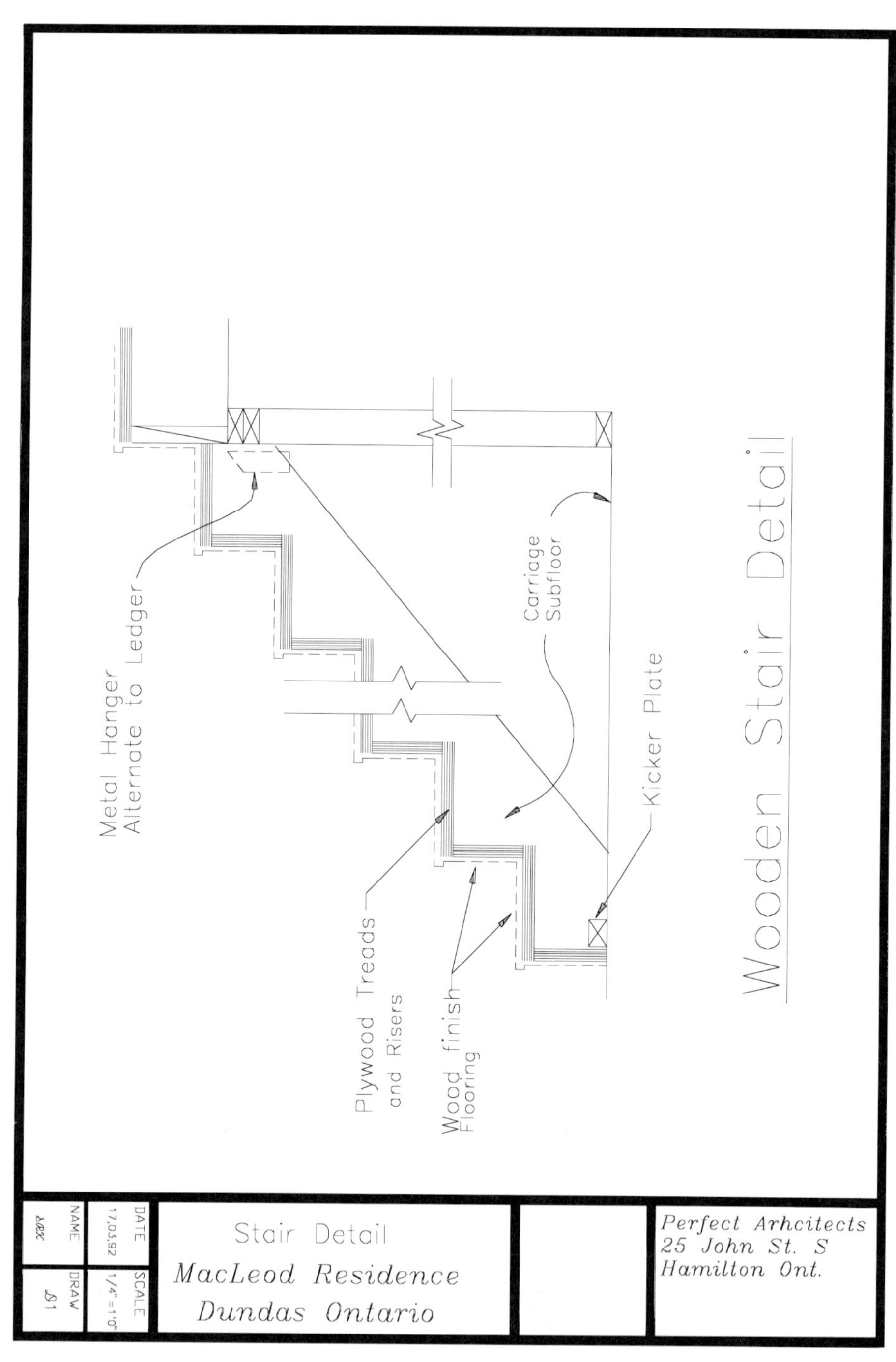

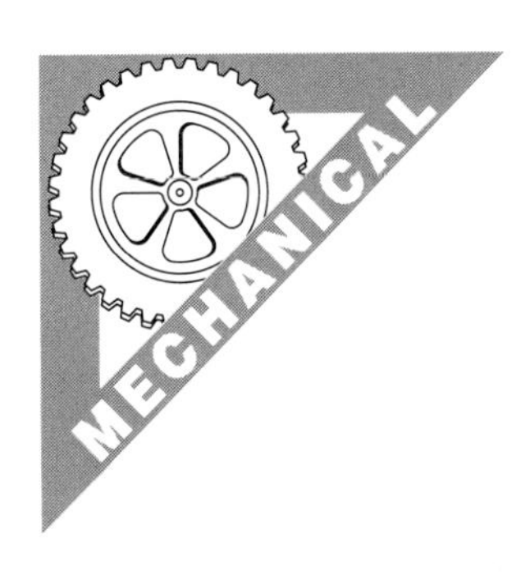

Exercise M8

Draw in the title block first and then add the text. Once this is completed, start the drawing and add the notations. Change the snap to get the isometric in easily.

(Many thanks to UMA for this drawing.)

TYPE–A

MOTOR SIDE RAILS

PART

REVISIONS

The making of any portion of this drawing or any portion thereof by any means is expressly prohibited unless authorized in writing

Job

Drwn

Date

Scale

App

Company

DWG No.

Exercise C8

Draw in the title block first, then add the notations.

(Many thanks to Johnny Barton for this drawing.)

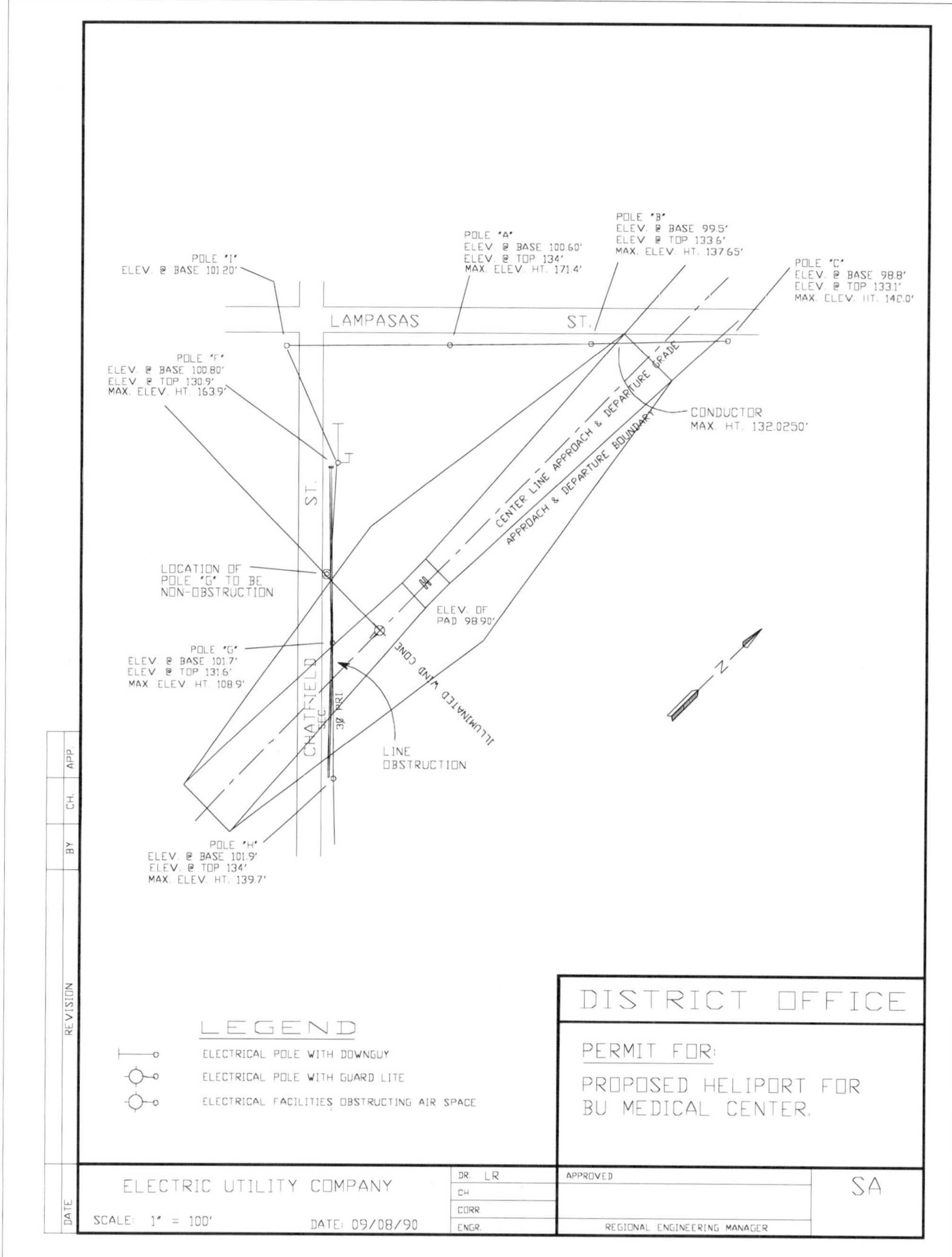

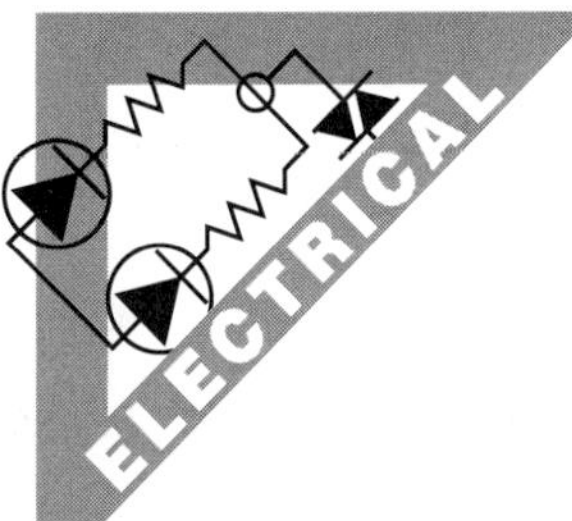

Exercise E8

Draw the title block in first and then add the text. Once this is completed, start the drawing and add the notations.

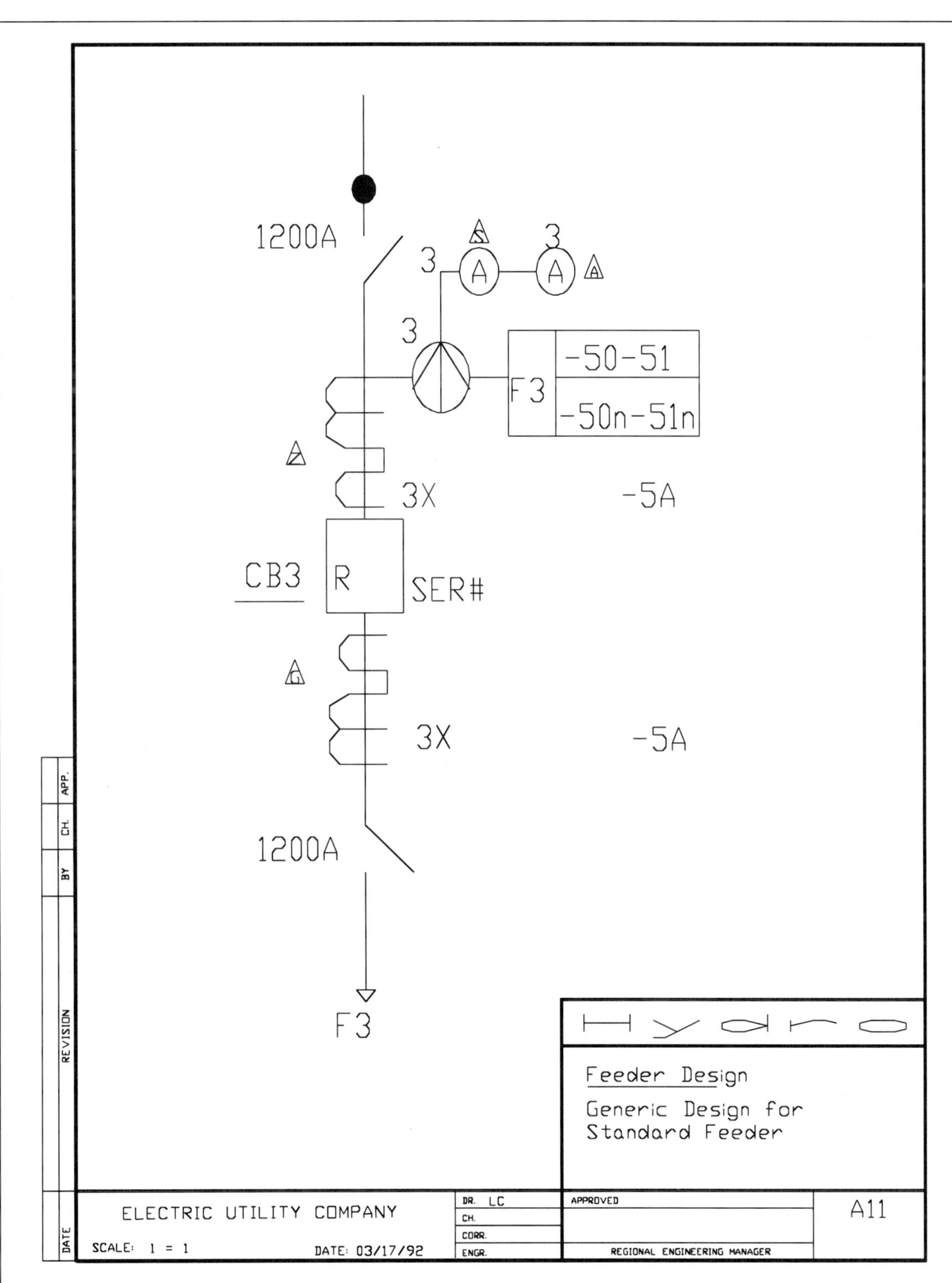

Challenger 8

This is a good example of a heating and cooling pump schematic. The same part is displayed on page XXX in 3D format.

(Many thanks to UMA for this drawing.)

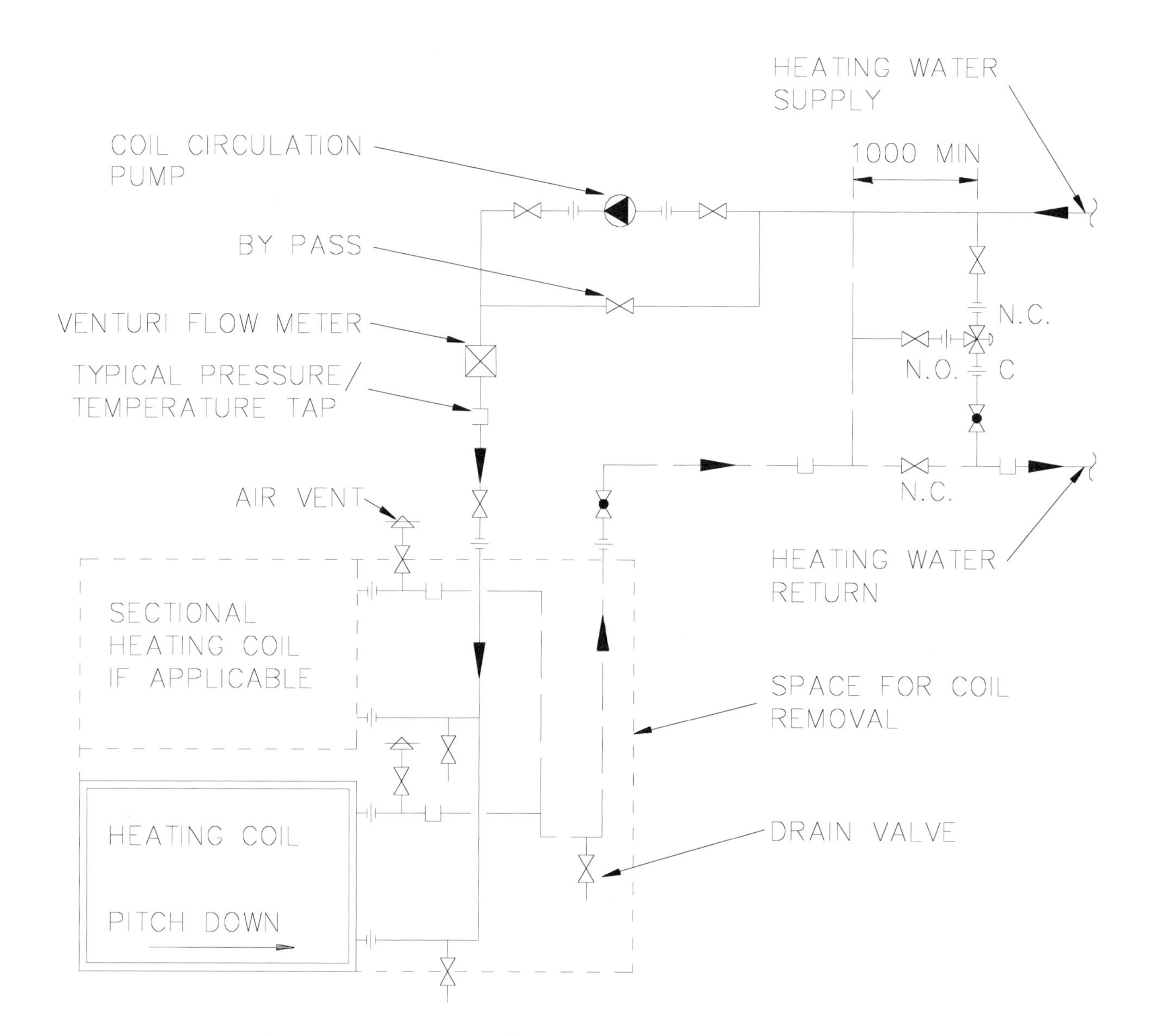

Challenger 8 (continued)

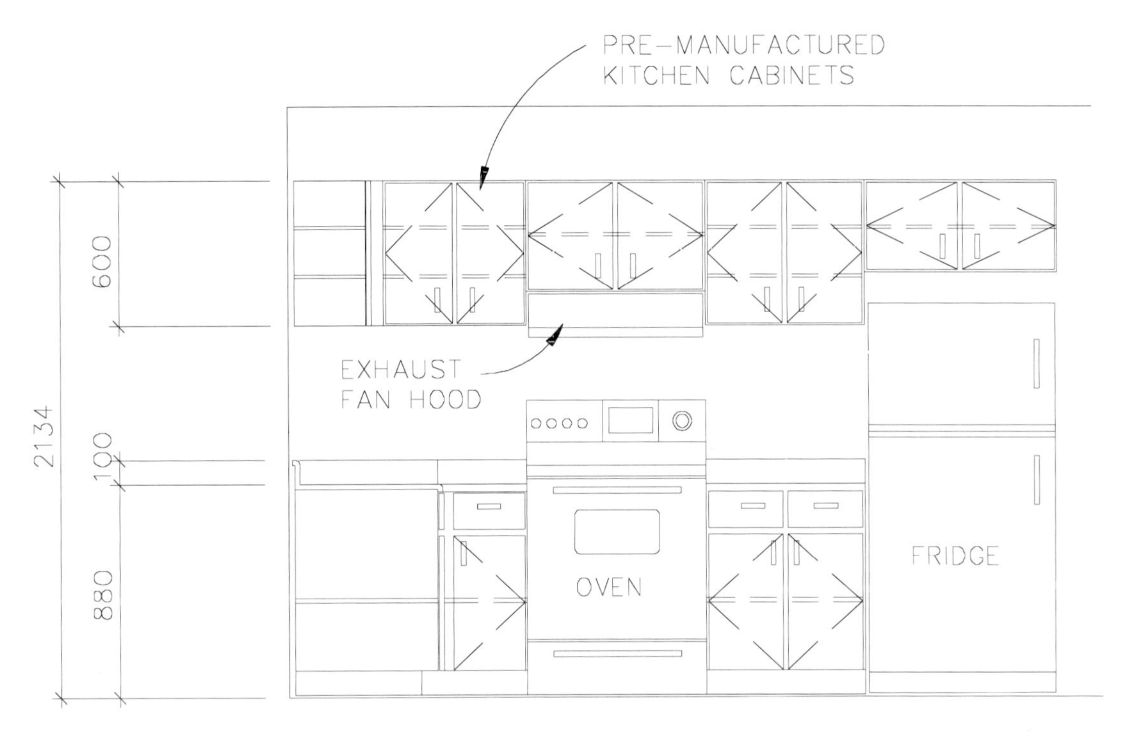

(Many thanks to UMA for these details)

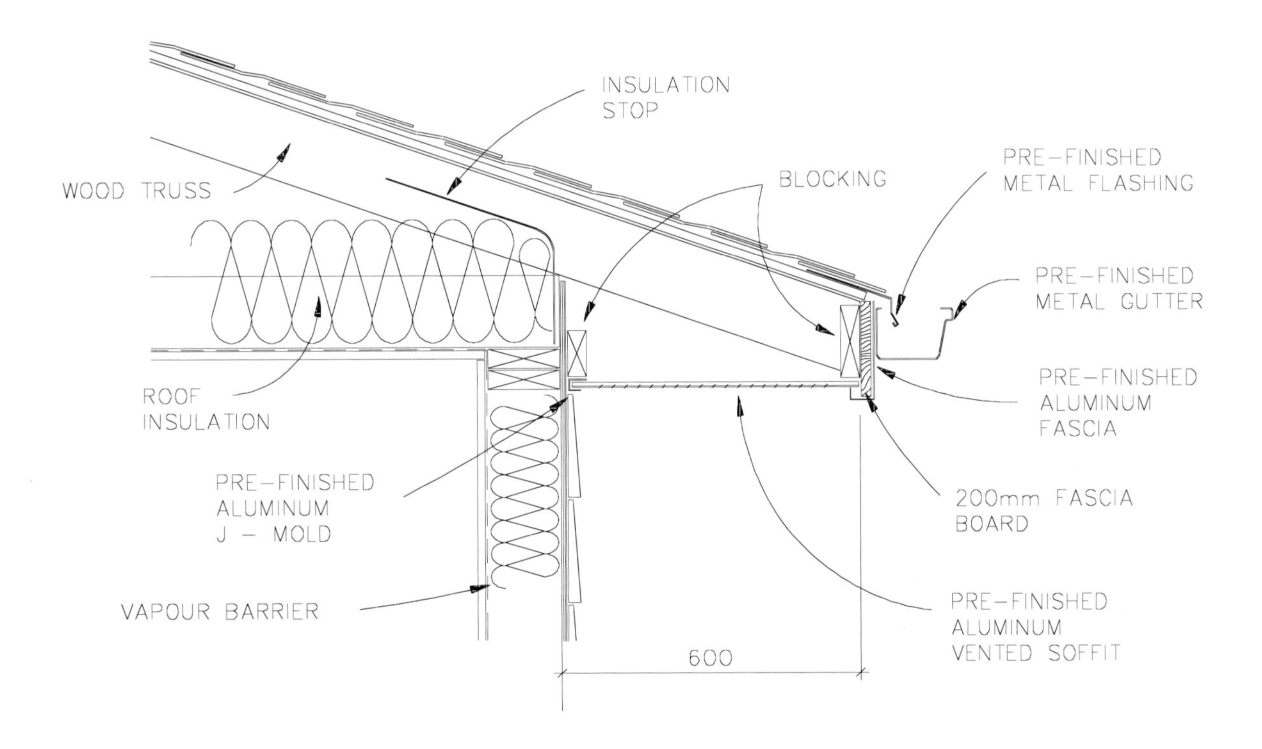

CREATING HATCHES

Upon completion of this chapter, the student should be able to:

1. Access the pull-down menu for hatching
2. Use HATCH within the model
3. Place user-defined hatching on the model
4. Use the SKETCH command

HATCH COMMAND

The HATCH command creates hatching within a specified boundary within a model. You can either choose one of the existing hatch patterns from the pull-down menu, or create a series of straight, parallel lines to form your own hatch pattern by selecting the User option.

To start, a boundary must be created to create the hatch. The geometry must be perfect: the corners must all meet, there must be no overlapping items, and the items must end at the edge of the boundary and not extend further through the model.

Release 12 Notes

The hatch patterns are found under the Draw menu.

Once you have defined your boundary, you can choose a hatch pattern from the AutoCAD hatch library. In Release 10, the hatch patterns are part of the HATCH command in the pull-down menu under DRAW.

In Release 11, the hatch patterns are under the Options pull-down menu and the submenu hatch pattern. Pick a hatch pattern from those listed. In the pull-down menu, the patterns are displayed as in Figure 9-1.

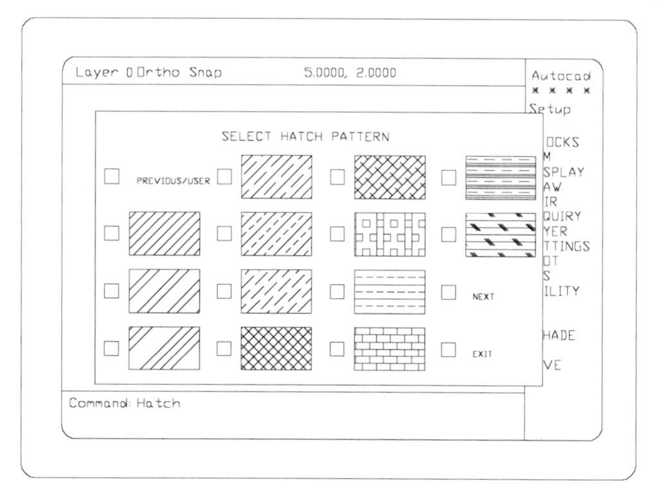

Figure 9-1. Hatch patterns

The HATCH command will also display a listing of the hatch patterns when a ? is entered at the first prompt.

The HATCH command displays the names of the patterns, and the hatch pattern option displays the patterns themselves. A page of hatch patterns and associated names can be found on page 176 at the end of this chapter.

With the hatch pull-down menu, a hatch pattern can be chosen from the choices given by picking the small box. After the hatch pattern is loaded, the HATCH command will return.

HATCH will prompt for three hatch parameters: the size, the rotation angle, and the items that are to be hatched.

HATCH SCALE

```
Command:HATCH
Pattern (? OR NAME/u,STYLE) ansi31:GRASS
Scale factor <1.0000>:
```

If you do not adjust your scale factor, AutoCAD will attempt to create the hatch at the default scale. There is a good chance you will run out of floppy disk space and be forced to exit from the file. Save your file before hatching, just in case.

The HATCH command default scale factor is 1. This scale is determined by the size of the final drawing, not the size of the object being hatched. The hatch patterns offered by AutoCAD conform to ANSI specifications; the scale is relative to the "lines-per-inch" standard dictated by ANSI. For example, the ANSI31 pattern generates three lines per inch at 1 to 1. Thus, the pattern for each hatch is accurate if used at a scale of 1 = 1. If the object will fit on an 11" x 8 ½" sheet at a scale of 1 = 1, then the scale will be correct. If you have changed the limits and the model is larger than 11 units in X, you *must* change the scale factor. The scale factor for screen display of the hatch should be the maximum X value divided by 12, the same as the scale factor for LTSCALE. For example, limits at 0,0 and 24,18 would be a scale factor of 2.

Other scale sizes are listed below. Remember, if you are using architectural units or feet and inches, each unit is an inch, not a foot.

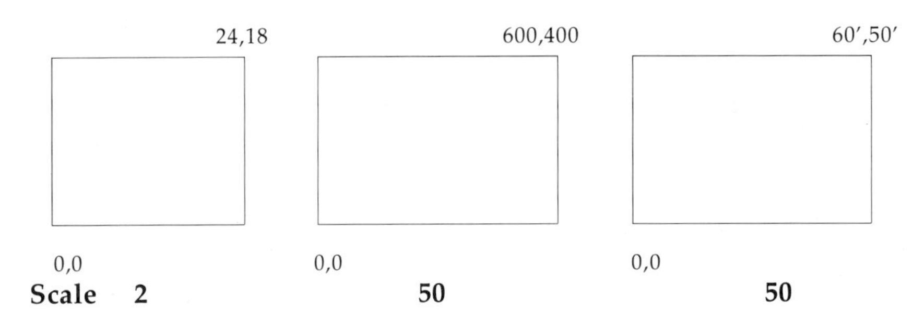

If you do not change the scale factor, there will be far too many patterns to view, and the lines from the patterns will quickly fill up space on your disk. If you have not changed the scale factor and the pattern is much too small, then you can expect a system crash or to be forced to exit your file. AutoCAD will make an attempt to save everything on your file up to the point where the hatch started; but there is no guarantee.

It is a good practice, when learning, to create a small test pattern on the screen about 1 inch by 1 inch relative to the real size or actual vectored inches of the screen, i.e., not relative to the limits, but to the screen. You can tell by the test pattern if the scale is appropriate. If, on the other hand, the test area is totally filled in or remains blank, the scale needs to be changed.

Usually, people add hatches to models because they are going to be placing the model onto a drawing. If the scale of a hatch must be changed, keep in mind the final size of the drawing as well as the size of the model relative to the screen. In Chapter 11, there is a long discussion on scale with regard to the size of the hatch and linetype scales and the size of the drawing. Before producing the final drawings, check this chapter to see that the hatch is accurate.

When doing the hatch exercises, concentrate on getting HATCH to work and on trying out the various hatch patterns and styles. Once you are comfortable with the command, then you can start thinking of the final product and how it will look on a drawing.

ROTATION ANGLE

When a hatch is picked from the pull-down menu, the rotation angle will be exactly as shown. For example, the first hatch pattern below is ANSI31 and is displayed at an angle of 45 degrees. To pick this pattern as it appears on the screen, do not change the rotation angle; leave it at zero, because that is the angle of the pattern itself.

SELECT HATCH PATTERN

PREVIOUS/USER

Some hatches are created at a 90-degree angle, whereas others are meant to be at 45 degrees. To make a pattern perpendicular to the one shown on the menu, use a 90-degree rotation.

When using user-defined hatch patterns, the rotation angle is calculated at a horizontal, rotating counter-clockwise.

SELECTING OBJECTS TO HATCH

For many students, this is where the difficulties begin, because before Release 12 the objects had to form a perfect boundary.

Objects can be selected in any of the expected ways — Window, Crossing, or individually selecting each object. The problem that many students encounter is that, when entering the geometry, the lines and circles, etc. are sometimes not entered accurately. SNAP and OSNAP are not always used effectively, and consequently the lines are crooked, do not have tidy intersections with adjacent items, etc., and thus do not provide an adequate boundary for hatching. Poor entry of objects will lead to other problems as well.

If you are drawing a series of objects at a certain scale, and then you need to make more objects at a smaller scale, do not turn the snap off, just change it.

When you discover that an object is not quite long enough, and it does not quite intersect where it should, *do not put in another line or object;* extend the first one or use FILLET Radius 0 to clean up the corners.

To create an enclosed boundary, use EXTEND or FILLET Rad 0.

If you have what appears to be four objects on the screen, there should be only four objects on the screen. If you list the objects using Window, the listing should identify four objects. If there are more than four objects, you will have trouble. Do not try to enter a hatch until the geometry is cleaned up.

Command:**LIST**

Select objects: *(pick 1)*

Select objects: *(pick 2)*

Window contains 10 objects:⏎

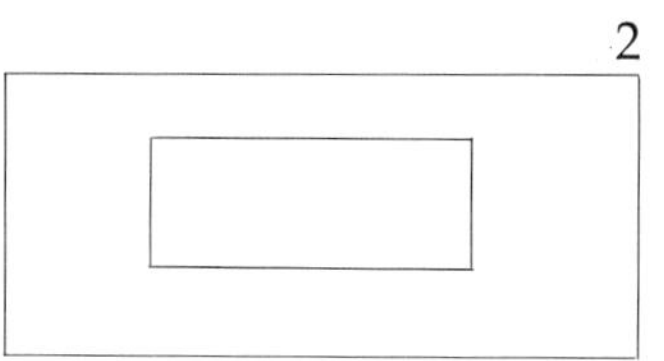

If you see four objects and the LIST command counts ten objects, do not continue until your data is cleaned up. Erase unwanted objects before continuing.

HATCH STYLE

Once the data is correct, Window the objects to be hatched, and the hatch pattern you have chosen will fill the boundary starting from the outer boundary. If there are closed boundaries within the outer boundary, the default is to have the hatch show up on alternating boundaries. To change this default, choose the Hatch Style option under the Options pull-down menu. (Release 11 and onward only.)

Example: *Hatch style examples*

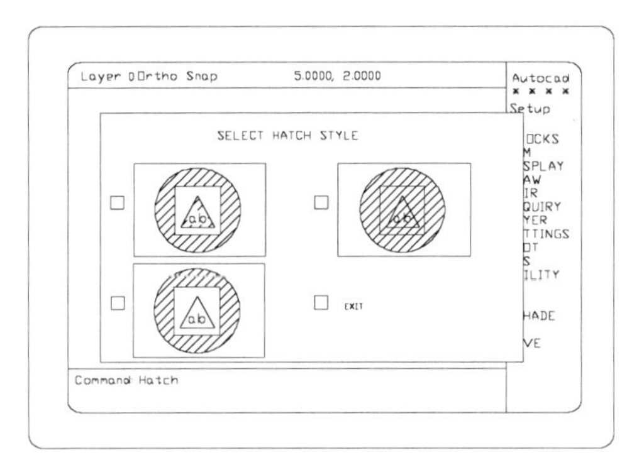

Figure 9-2. Selecting hatch parameters

Try the simple exercises of Figure 9-3 to get the feeling of HATCH before you try the day's exercise. Open a new file, do not change the limits, just turn on snap and draw these simple objects. Then use HATCH with Window to fill in the hatched areas.

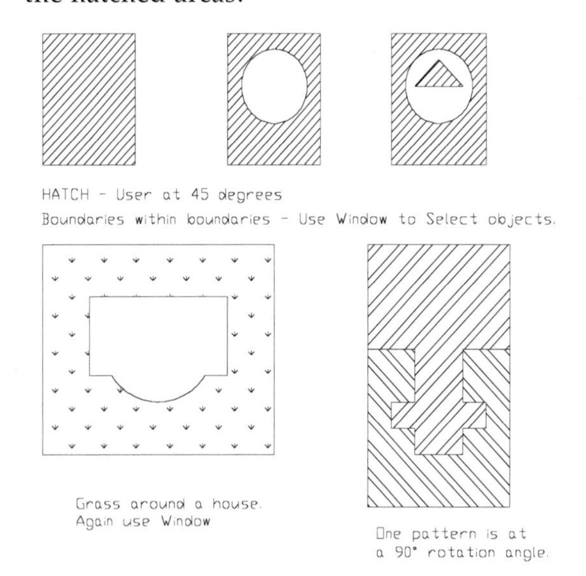

Figure 9-3. Hatch example patterns

Filling a boundary with a hatch is similar to filling a form with concrete, or filling a mould with plastic, or filling a pan with cake batter. The hatch will spill out if there are holes in the mould or form.

HATCH BOUNDARIES

HATCH will not be able to determine the boundary if the objects extend beyond where the hatch is needed. If a line or arc extends beyond the boundary, the hatch will be generated to fill the object's full length. The examples of Figure 9-4 illustrate some common problems and how to avoid them.

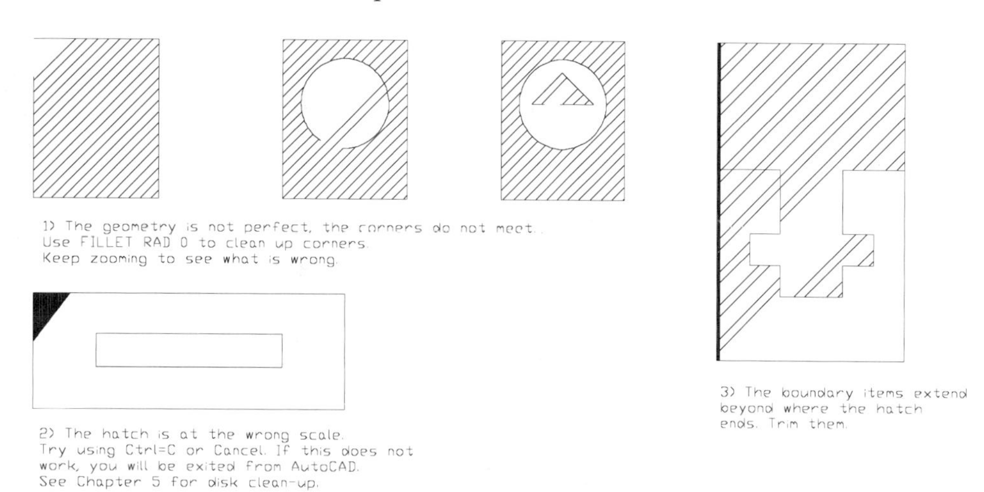

1) The geometry is not perfect, the corners do not meet.
Use FILLET RAD 0 to clean up corners.
Keep zooming to see what is wrong.
2) The hatch is at the wrong scale.
Try using Ctrl=C or Cancel. If this does not
work, you will be exited from AutoCAD.
See Chapter 5 for disk clean-up.
3) The boundary items extend
beyond where the hatch
ends. Trim them.

Figure 9-4. Examples of improper hatch boundaries

Many of the above problems can be avoided by always using SNAP or OSNAP and by testing the hatch scale.

It is a good idea to put the hatch boundaries on a separate layer. By doing this, you can turn off all the layers you do not need to access for the hatch boundary. This makes it easier to identify the boundary for hatching purposes, and makes it easier to change the boundary if the hatch does not work.

There are several ways to speed up clean-up routines and avoid needless frustration. Of course, the best idea is to create the objects properly to start with. Try LIST and MOVE to help clean up the geometry.

In the first example below, the boundary looks complete, and, if it has been entered properly, the hatch will look like the object beside the clear boundary.

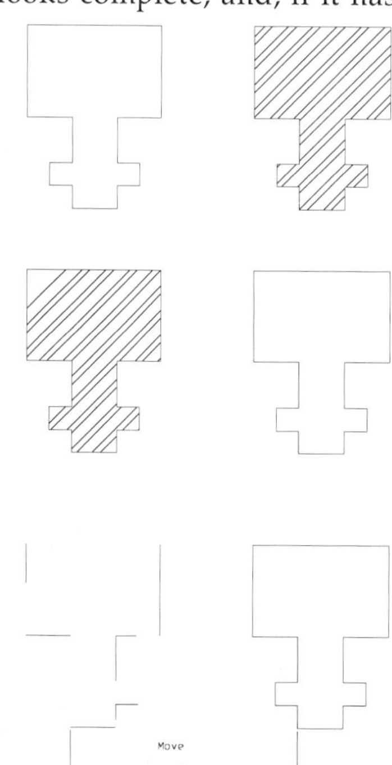

If a hatch is not working, use the LIST command, under the Inquiry menu on the right to list the objects that make up the boundary by Window to obtain the number of boundary objects.

If there are many more items listed than you can count, you have duplicate objects that are causing the hatch to mess up.

Use MOVE to pick up the items one by one that you wish to make up your boundary. Do not use Window or you will pick up unwanted items. Now, making sure SNAP is on, move the items out of the way.

Redraw the screen to view duplicate items.

Erase the duplicates and clean up the geometry. Now, with SNAP on, move the boundary back to where it was and try again.

Keep your geometry perfect, and you will not have any problems with HATCH.

While creating hatch patterns on models, you should be aware of the standards for hatch patterns for your discipline and keep these in mind when generating both the scale and the rotation angle of a hatch.

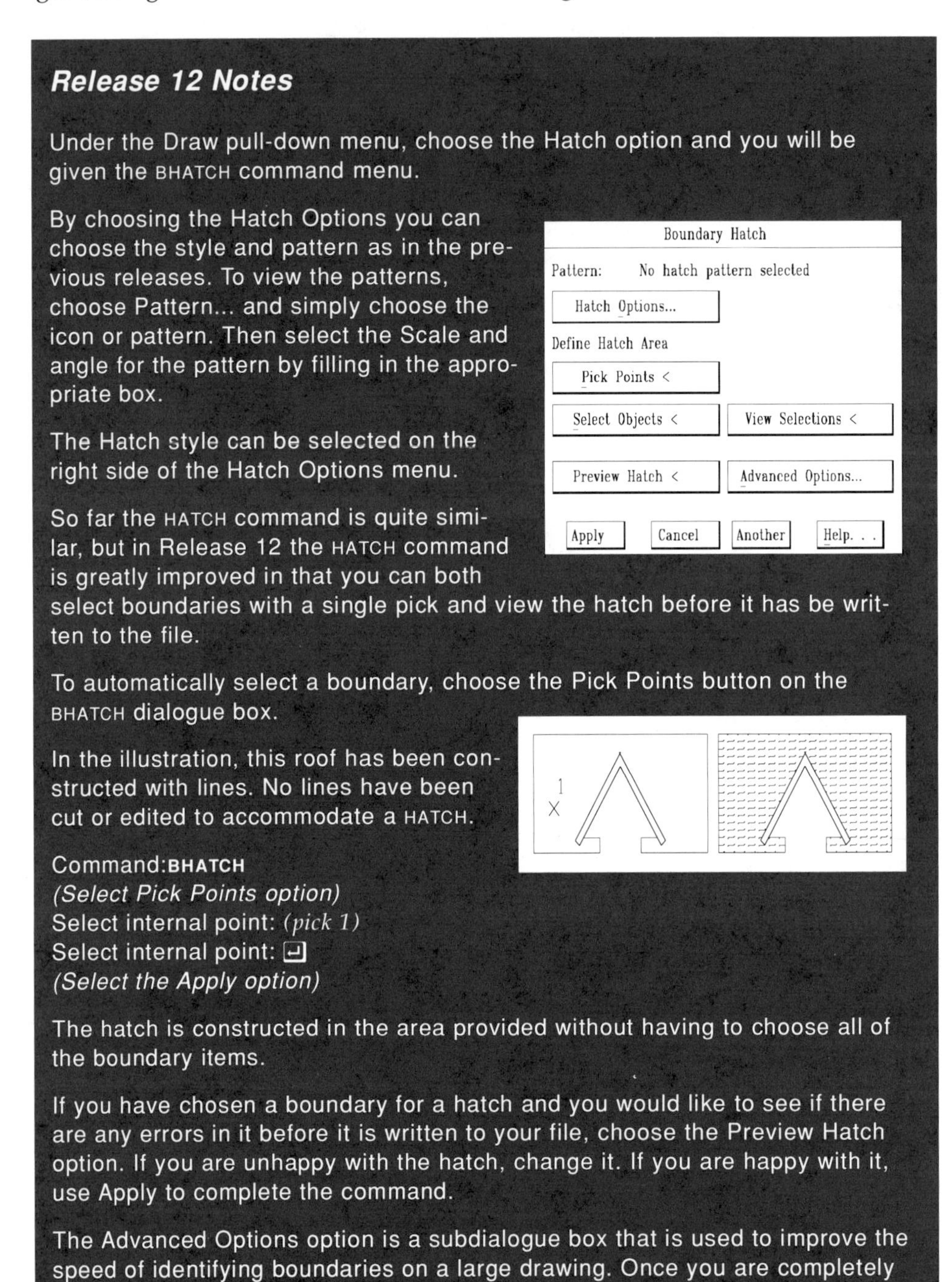

Release 12 Notes

Under the Draw pull-down menu, choose the Hatch option and you will be given the BHATCH command menu.

By choosing the Hatch Options you can choose the style and pattern as in the previous releases. To view the patterns, choose Pattern... and simply choose the icon or pattern. Then select the Scale and angle for the pattern by filling in the appropriate box.

The Hatch style can be selected on the right side of the Hatch Options menu.

So far the HATCH command is quite similar, but in Release 12 the HATCH command is greatly improved in that you can both select boundaries with a single pick and view the hatch before it has be written to the file.

To automatically select a boundary, choose the Pick Points button on the BHATCH dialogue box.

In the illustration, this roof has been constructed with lines. No lines have been cut or edited to accommodate a HATCH.

Command:**BHATCH**
(Select Pick Points option)
Select internal point: *(pick 1)*
Select internal point: ↵
(Select the Apply option)

The hatch is constructed in the area provided without having to choose all of the boundary items.

If you have chosen a boundary for a hatch and you would like to see if there are any errors in it before it is written to your file, choose the Preview Hatch option. If you are unhappy with the hatch, change it. If you are happy with it, use Apply to complete the command.

The Advanced Options option is a subdialogue box that is used to improve the speed of identifying boundaries on a large drawing. Once you are completely familiar with how the BHATCH command works, experiment with Ray Casting

HATCH AND LAYERS

The boundary should be on a separate layer so that you can pick it easily for creating the hatch. The hatch should be on a separate layer so that you can freeze it to save time on regenerations and redraws. It is also useful to turn it off when you are working in 3D.

SKETCH

The SKETCH command is included in this chapter because, like HATCH, it is often used to make final notations on drawings before they are plotted. In addition, the HATCH command has a tendency to take up a lot of room on a disk, and the SKETCH command, because it can contain many vectors, can also take up more room than expected on a disk.

SKETCH provides freehand designs for undefined areas on a drawing. The motion of the mouse or digitizer determines the position of the sketch segments; the accuracy of the sketch segments is determined within the command.

The SKETCH command will prompt for the increment, or distance between segments; for smoother curves, use smaller increments. The command is as follows:

```
Command:SKETCH
Record increment:.1
Sketch, Pen eXit Quit Record Erase Connect:P
Sketch:
```

Where:
Pen = the pen being lowered. The system prompts to "put your pen down"; whatever move you make with your cursor will be recorded.

eXit = the end of the command. **X** will exit the SKETCH command, retaining all segments created up to that point.

Quit = a cancellation of the segments created in the command. **Q** will leave SKETCH without saving the segments.

Record = a save of all the lines drawn so far. **R** will produce a permanent record of the segments without exiting the command.

Erase = an erasing of some of the line segments drawn. **E** will allow lines to be erased up to a certain point; it acts as a "backspace" over segments created.

Connect = a continuation of a previous sketch. **C** allows a sketch to be picked up again at the last entered endpoint after it has been ended.

Segments are not recorded on the disk until the Record option is used. Because each segment is added as a separate object of geometry, SKETCH can take up a lot of room on a disk. The computer will offer a series of warning beeps to let you know that you are moving too quickly or that the disk is full. Raise your pen and record your lines to date before continuing.

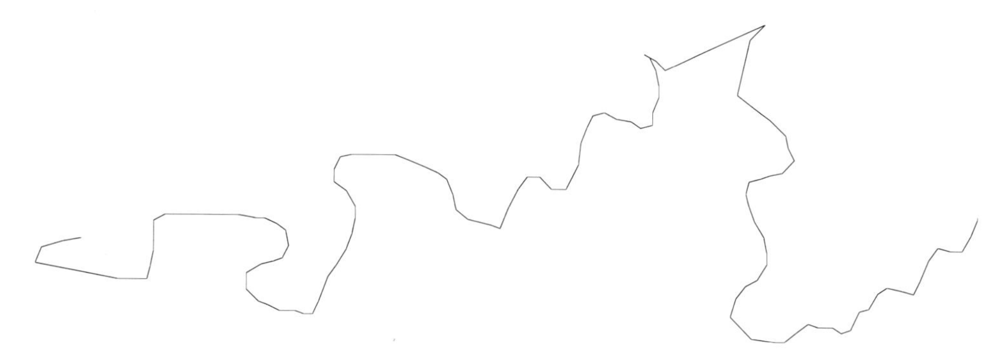

Figure 9-5. The SKETCH command

Hatch Patterns

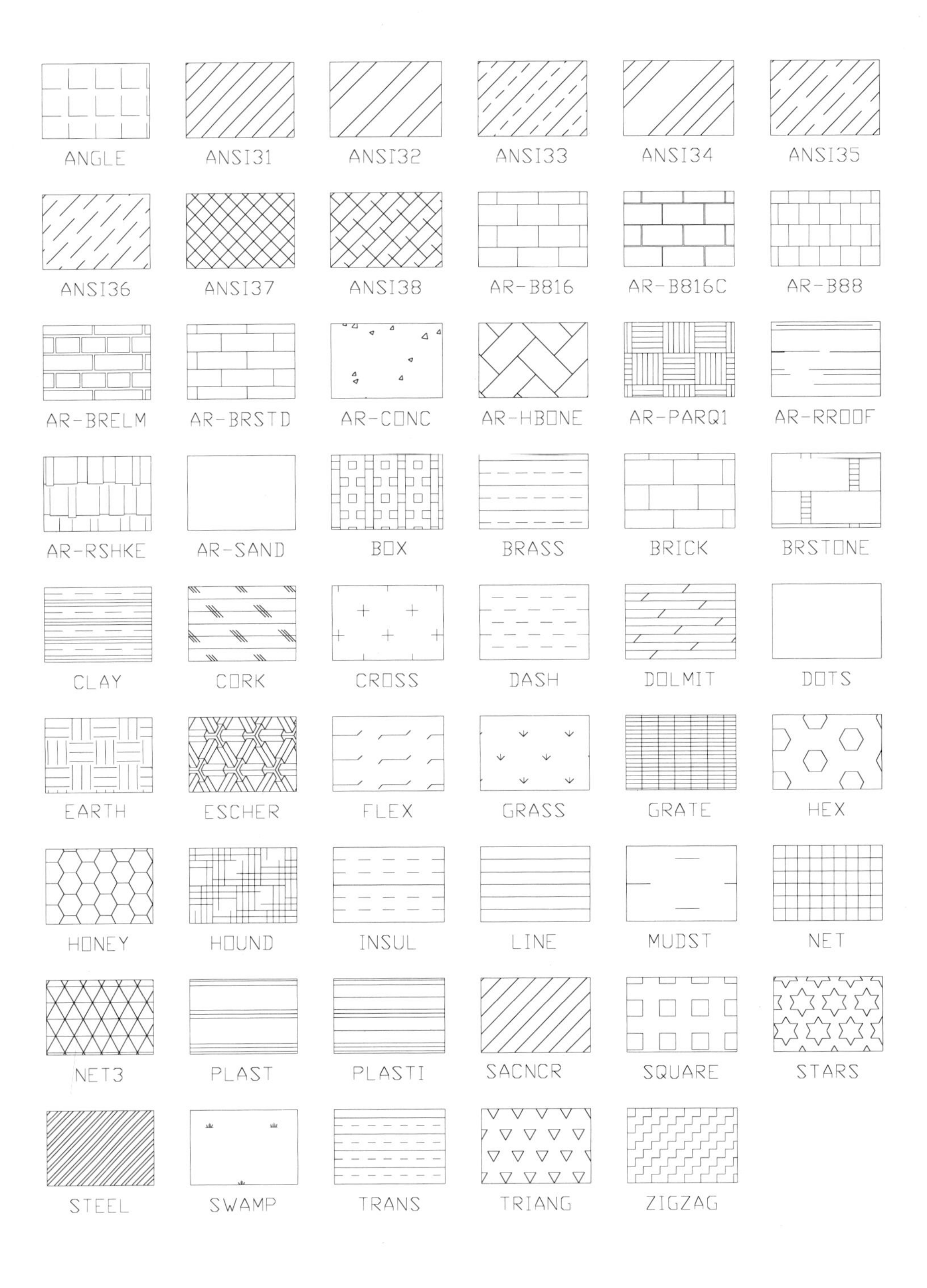

Exercise A9

```
LIMITS  20',15'
SNAP    6"
GRID    1'
ZOOM    All
```

Use LAYERS to make each separate outline as in A9 Hints.

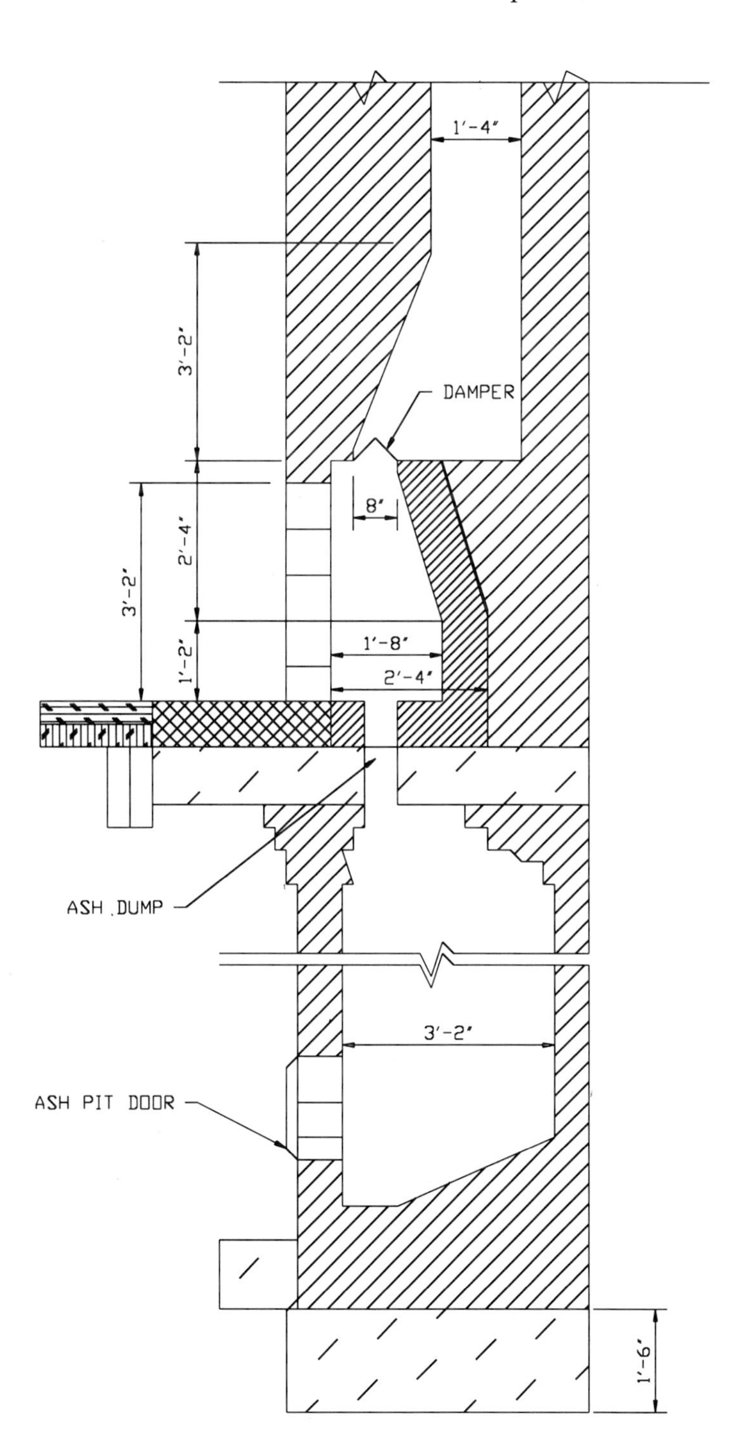

Hints on A9

Create each separate area on a different layer.

When you are ready to hatch a section, turn off the layers you do not need for the boundary of each hatch pattern.

If you are using architectural units, make sure you change the hatch scale factor to at least 12.

Once all the layers are completely hatched, turn them all back on.

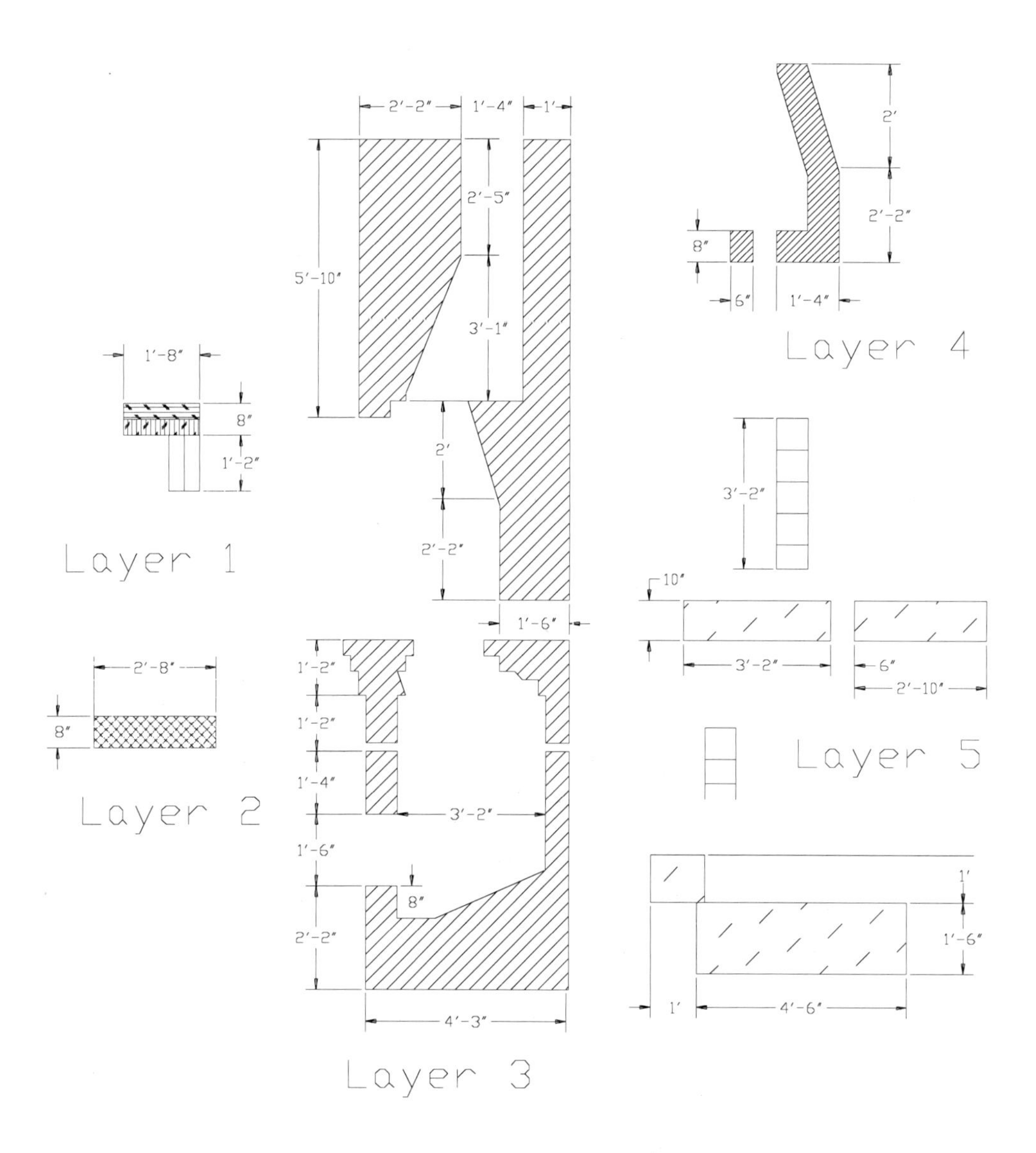

Exercise M9

```
LIMITS  5,7
GRID     .5
SNAP     .25
ZOOM    All
```

Complete the drawing as in M8 Hints, keeping the outlines for each part on a separate layer. Then turn LAYERS off to hatch.

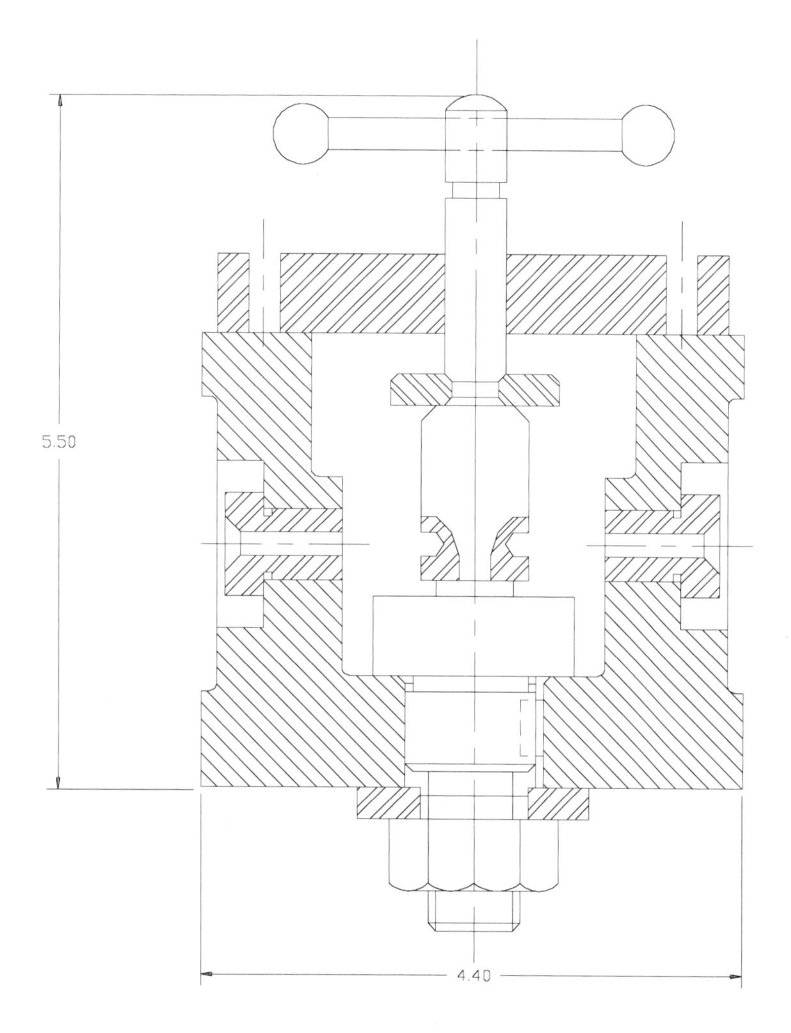

Create the drawing as in Hints on M9 on the next page.

Hints on M9

Draw the boundaries on separate layers.

Once the boundaries are in, turn off the layers you do not need for the boundary of each hatch pattern.

Make sure the boundary geometry is complete and perfect. Then use HATCH to fill in the hatch patterns.

You will need to rotate one hatch by 90 degrees.

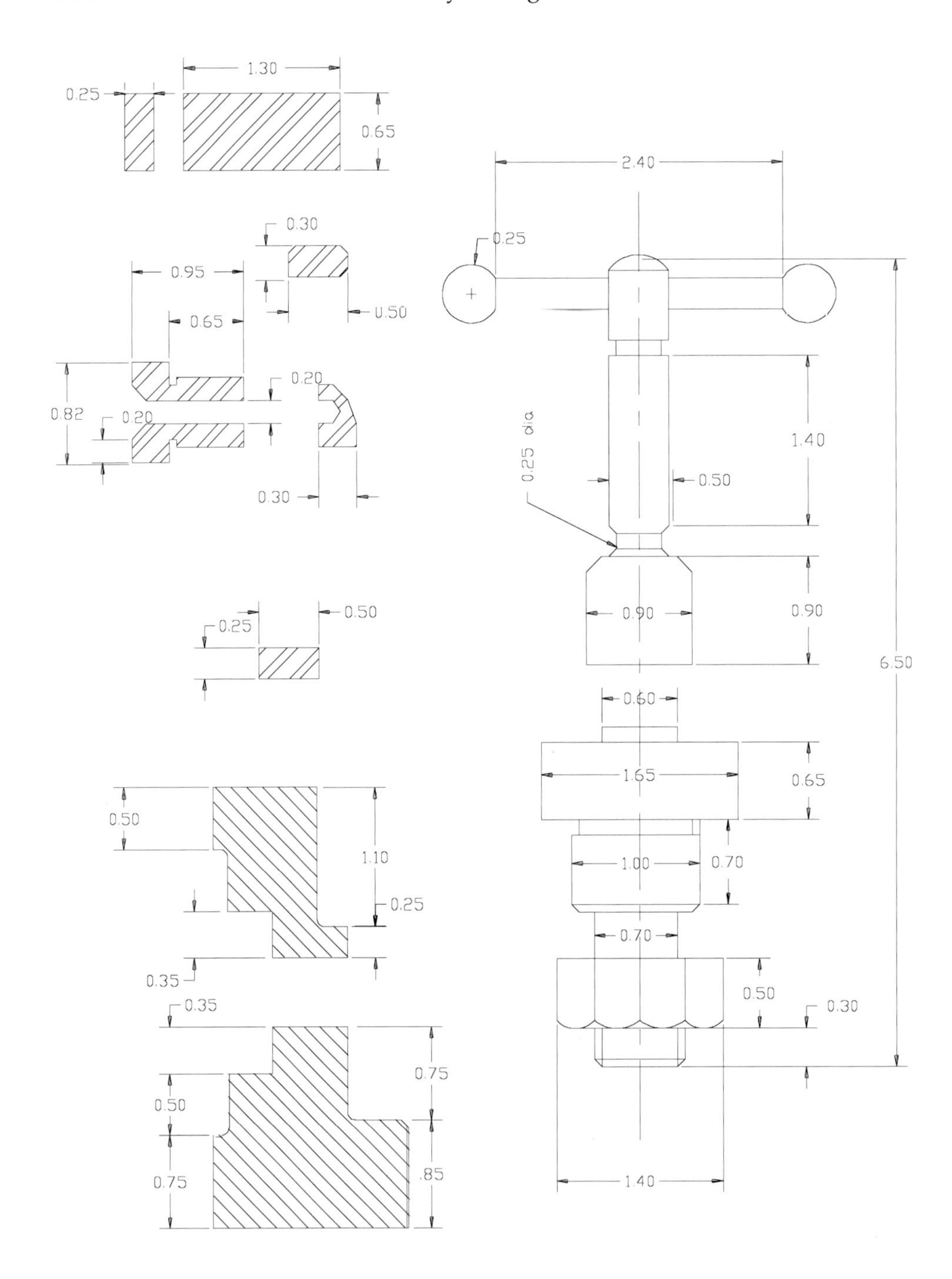

Exercise C9

LIMITS	**300,250**
GRID	**10**
SNAP	**5**
ZOOM	**A**ll

Cavity wall at corner parapet.

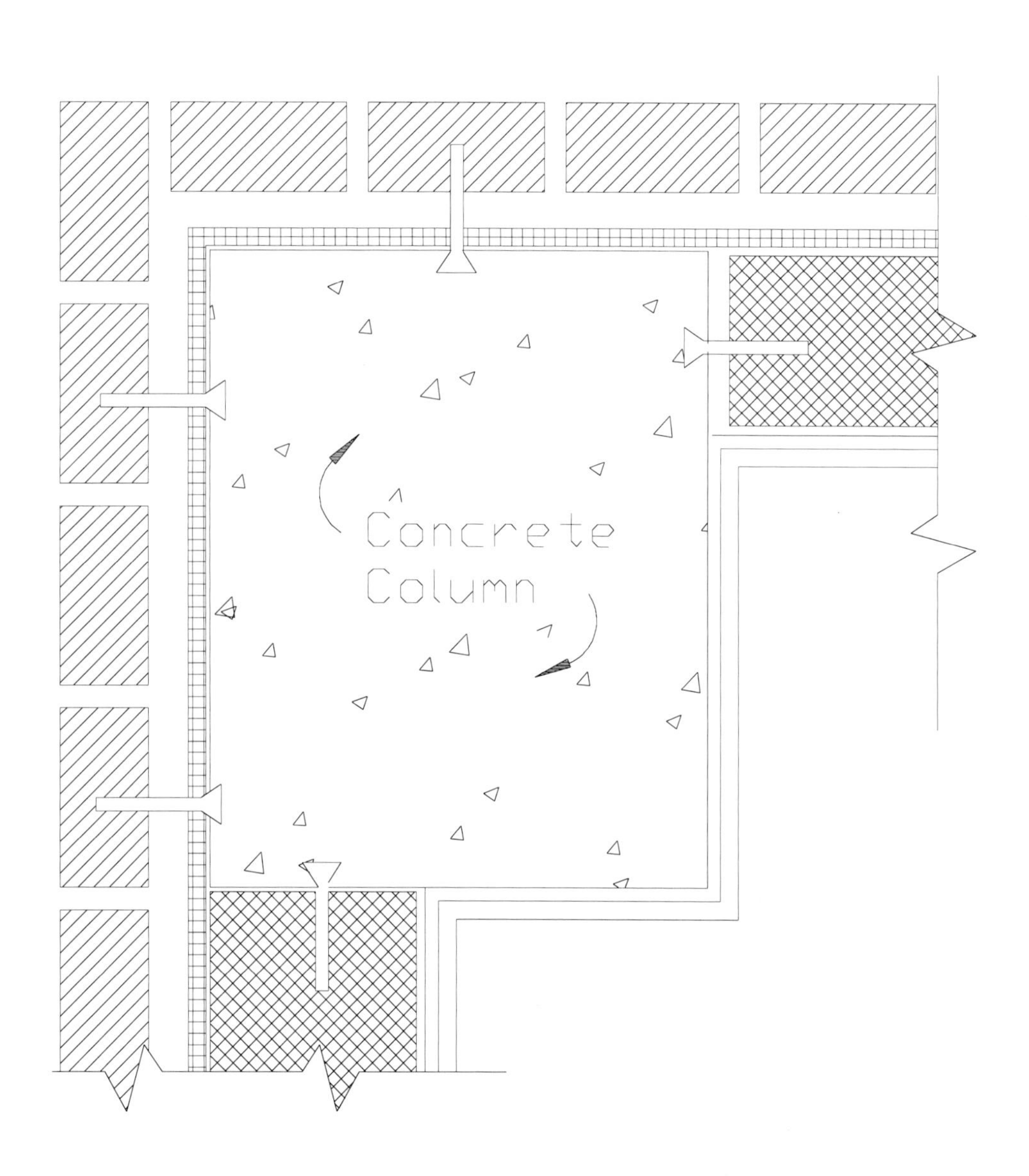

Hints on C9

Turn off the layer of sections you are not using when creating hatches. Remember, you will have to change the hatch scale factor because the limits are large.

Keep the text within the boundary when hatching, and it will be accepted as a separate enclosed boundary. If you are finished early, add a layer for the mortar, the pins, and the notations.

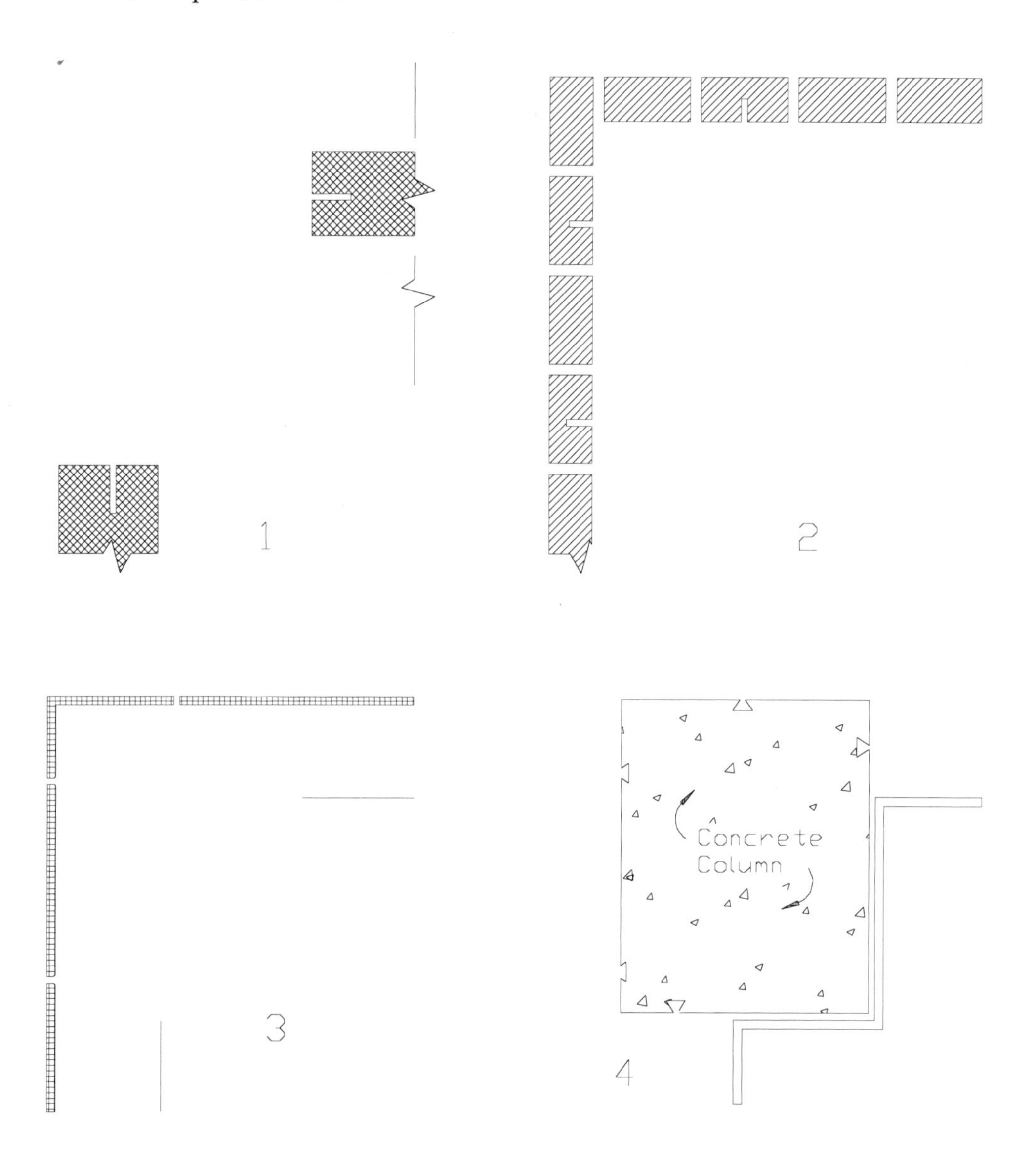

Challenger 9

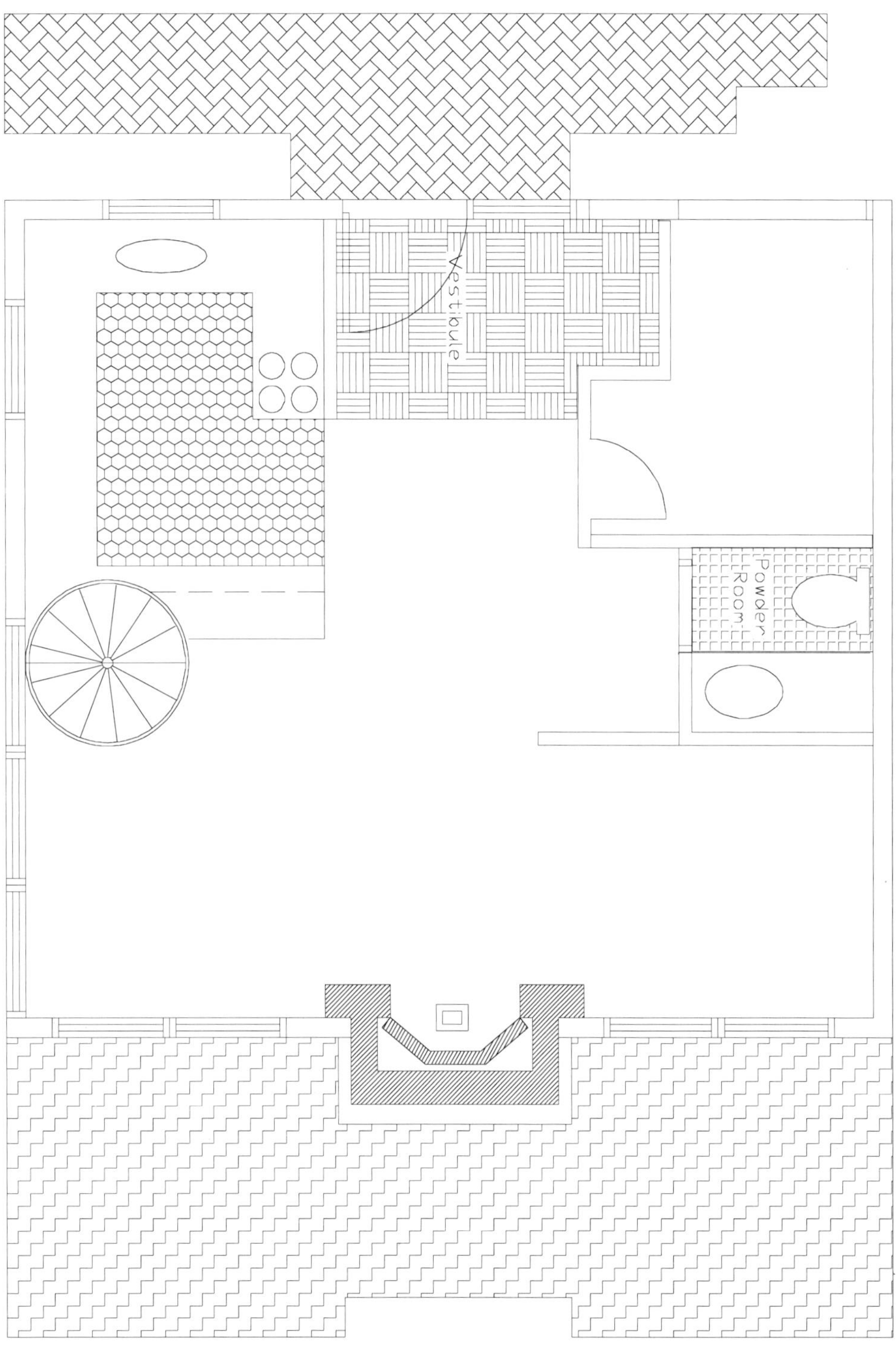

BLOCKS

Upon completion of this chapter, the student should be able to:

1. Create a BLOCK
2. Create a WBLOCK
3. INSERT both BLOCKs and WBLOCKs
4. EXPLODE BLOCKs and WBLOCKs
5. Understand how COLOR, LAYERs, and other data are affected by the BLOCKs

BLOCKS

The theory is that CAD should make the production of parts and drawings much more efficient. Blocks are an important aspect of productivity improvement because blocks allow the designer to create a library of parts used repeatedly on drawings and designs, and thus avoid creating the same objects over and over again. In addition, by using blocks on large projects, you can speed up your response time by keeping portions of the drawing not currently needed on a different file and merging them when needed.

While designing with AutoCAD, think of your design as a model rather than a drawing. As you are creating the layout for a house or an assembly of parts, many of the parts you need may already be available in your database; so simply locate them and add them on, like using building blocks.

If you were designing custom houses using AutoCAD, most of the major vendors of windows, doors, etc. would have supplied you with a database of their products so that you could fit a window or door exactly where you want it, and you would be sure that it would fit.

In a manufacturing environment, models of standard-size bolts, plugs, etc. used by your company would be on a central database, and you would simply insert them on the model wherever required.

In City Hall, models of all the road signs, traffic lights, and major service components are available on the central database and can be inserted on the design model of new surveys or renovations of old surveys.

Examples of blocks commonly used strictly for production of drawings are logos, drawing borders, title blocks, and drawing symbols. These blocks are inserted on the models before they are printed, and contain the standard company information.

> ***Release 12 Notes***
>
> A dialogue box (DDINSERT) offers the same options as the INSERT command in a pull-down format.

Blocks, when inserted, are treated as individual entities and manipulated much more rapidly than a group of entities. Blocks can be edited with MOVE, COPY, SCALE, ROTATE, and other editing commands. They can consist of many layers, colours, linetypes, and text forms.

BLOCK/ WBLOCK (Write BLOCK)

Blocks exist within the drawing and cannot be accessed except within the base drawing. A block is an identified list, group, or set of entities saved in a separate portion of the existing file and inserted when needed. Because it is both identified and used exclusively within one file, it is referred to as an internal block. For example, you might use a block in designing a large building with a specific chair used in many different rooms, on many different floors. The block of the chair is in the file, and the chair can be inserted anywhere.

If the chair were to be copied onto another part of the file, it would need to be identified by selecting the objects off the screen by means of a Window, Crossing, etc. However, with a block, the set of objects is identified by the name of the block.

Wblocks are separate files. They are stored separately on a disk and have the extension .DWG.

Any file on a disk can be inserted as a wblock *onto a drawing.*

Any existing file can be used as a wblock. If you want to take a portion of a file and use it on another file, you can create a wblock of that portion.

Because wblocks exist outside of a current file, they are referred to as external blocks.

Once a block or wblock has been inserted into the file, it is referred to as a block instance. In other words, this is a copy of the original file. The original file still exists, but a copy of it has been used in the drawing, just as a rubber stamp creates a stamp impression.

There can be only one definition of a block under each specific name. If you change or update the original block, the new block instances will be the new block; the old block instances will remain the same. If the drawing file for the wblock has been changed or updated, however, the original wblock will be inserted. The original wblock is in memory and must be updated to the new drawing file in order to be updated. For more information on this, see Chapter 23.

> **Release 12 Notes**
>
> Searching for wblocks is much easier with the file management facilities under the File pull-down menus.
>
> Mirrored blocks can now be exploded.

The commands used with blocks are:

BLOCK	*creates an internal block.*
INSERT	*inserts either a block or a wblock.*
WBLOCK	*creates an external block.*

All of the above are found under the Blocks menu.

To create a block, use:

Command:**BLOCK** *(creates an internal block)*

Block name(or ?):**name** *(the name can be up to 31 characters)*

Insertion base point:**0,0** *(pick or type in)*

Select objects: *(indicate the objects to be included in the block using Window, Crossing, etc.)*

To create a wblock from an existing block, use:

Command:**WBLOCK** *(write block onto the disk)*

File name:**a:logo**

Block name (or ?):**Logo** *(this must be the name of an existing block)*

To create a wblock from existing geometry, use:

```
Command:WBLOCK (write block onto a disk)
File name:a:title
Block name (or ?):↵ (you do not have a block to use)
Insertion base point:0,0
Select objects: (indicate the objects to be included in the wblock, using Window, Crossing, etc.)
```

The insertion base point you choose will be the handle or reference point for placing the block. It is much the same as the base point chosen in the COPY or MOVE command. This is the point at which the new block will be placed, so choose it wisely; remember OSNAP.

In Figure 10-1, the insertion base points indicate the logical spot to reference existing geometry: the window can be placed squarely on a wall and rotated; the lot can be placed next to another lot; the diode symbol can be placed on the schematic; and the drill hole can be positioned accurately with regard to the measurement of the part.

Once the objects to be included in the block or wblock have been selected, they will be highlighted on the screen. When you press ↵ or Enter to accept these

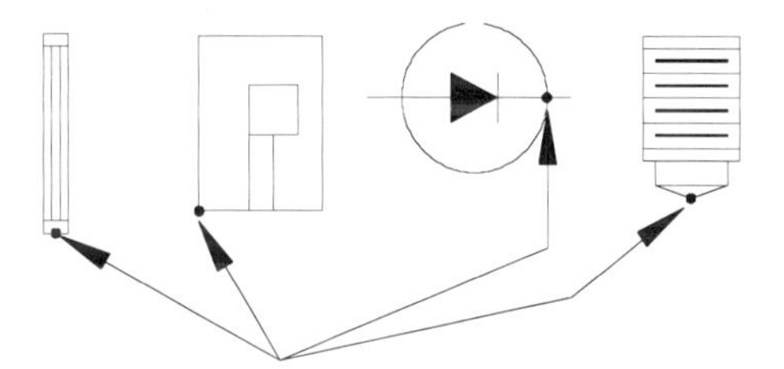

Figure 10-1. Insertion base point

objects, *the objects will disappear*. Now the identified objects are a block entity, and you can insert them wherever you want.

```
Command:INSERT (inserts either a block or a wblock)
Block name (OR ?):name
Insertion point: (pick 1) (enter any kind of point)
X scale factor<1>/Corner/XYZ:↵
Y scale factor (default = X):↵
Rotation angle:↵ (this will be counter-clockwise)
```

Scale Factor or Aspect Ratio

The X scale factor defaults to 1. Any number smaller than 1 will make the block smaller than its original size; any larger number will make it larger than the original. If you want a mirror image of the block, you can use a negative X and/or negative Y value. A positive X and a negative Y will mirror the block about a horizontal line. A negative X and a positive Y will mirror the block along a vertical line. A negative X and a negative Y will produce the same result as a rotation angle of 180 degrees.

The Y scale factor defaults to X. If you want the objects to be stretched out, change the Y value.

While inserting blocks, you can move the cursor to the spot on the screen to insert the block at the correct size instead of entering an X value. This is the same effect as DRAG in the CIRCLE command. By moving horizontally, you are stretching the X value; by moving vertically, you are stretching the Y value.

By changing the block's values of X and Y as they are inserted, you are changing the aspect ratio. Many of the editing commands (such as SCALE) are disabled when the aspect ratio has been modified.

INSERT is also used to bring wblocks or drawing files into the current file.

The diagram of Figure 10-2 consists of two files inserted onto the base file to create a file to be plotted. The ttle block was drawn to match the size of the

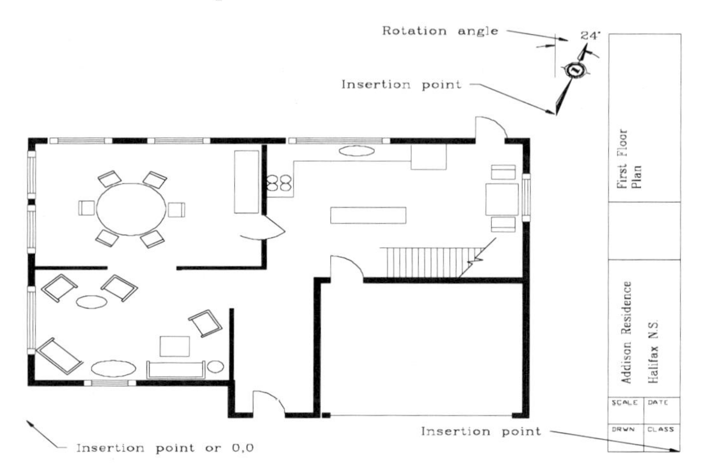

Figure 10-2. Inserting files at different scales

paper to be used. The floor plan was drawn at a scale of 1 = 1; since it is the largest and most important file, it will remain at 1 = 1. The drawing is to be plotted at a scale of 1⁄4" = 1'0", so the title block is inserted at a scale of 48 (4 x 12). The arrow was inserted also at a scale of 48 the rotation angle would be the angle of North. The entire drawing would be plotted at a scale of 1⁄48 or .02083. Once plotted, if there are any changes or corrections to be made, they can be made on the original drawing.

In Release 11, the Paper Space option will make the process of compiling drawings much simpler. This method of creating a final drawing is used for compiling different files that are not necessarily part of a single file.

EDITING BLOCKS AND WBLOCKS

Once a block has been placed in a file, it is edited as a single entity. An entity select pick will load the whole block. If one object on the block is picked, the whole block will be selected.

There are two methods of editing individual entities in a block. First, if you are loading a block or wblock and you know you want to change portions of it, enter a * before the block name. This inserts the block as separate entities and allows each item to be edited.

```
Command:INSERT (inserts either a block or a wblock)
Block name (OR ?):*title
Insertion point:0,0
X scale factor <1>/Corner/XYZ:↵
Y scale factor (default = X):↵
Rotation angle:↵
```

This will load the title block as a series of polylines, lines, and text entities as opposed to a single block entity.

The second method of editing block entities is to EXPLODE the block once it is placed. If you have already loaded a block and want to change it, use EXPLODE to separate the block into individual items or entities.

For example:

```
Command:INSERT (inserts either a block or a wblock)
Block name (OR ?):title
Insertion point:0,0
X scale factor <1>/Corner/XYZ:↵
Y scale factor (default = X):↵
Rotation angle:↵

Command:EXPLODE
Select block reference, polyline, dimension, or mesh: (pick 1)
```

Once you have inserted the block called TITLE, use EXPLODE from the Edit menu to reduce the objects to their original individual entities.

Remember, if you change the aspect ratio of the block, certain editing commands will not work.

COLOR AND LAYER

You will have noticed that the default layer is 0 and that this layer cannot be either renamed or deleted. This is because layer 0 is very important with regard to blocks. Layer 0 is referred to as the universal layer. Once you have created a number of blocks or wblocks, file management becomes more difficult because you must remember what size the blocks are as well as the directory they are in and the layer they are on.

If items are created on a layer other than 0 in a wblock, these new layers will be added to the list of layers in the current file once the wblock file is inserted.

All blocks created on layer 0 will be automatically placed on the current layer and will assume the current layer colour and linetype when the block is inserted. These are not necessarily bylayer. If the Color or Linetype setting is not Bylayer, colour and linetype of the block will conform to those of the current setting, which overrides the layer setting. To check the current settings, use STATUS.

If you want a particular wblock to always occupy a specific layer and to maintain its linetype and colour, assign these explicitly; do not leave the wblock on layer 0.

BYBLOCK

If the colour and linetype are defined by BYBLOCK in the original file, the colours and linetypes can be changed once the file is inserted. If you want the colour and linetype of the wblock to always assume those of the layer on which it is inserted, use BYLAYER as the setting for the colour and linetype.

Once a block has been inserted, the objects will retain the original layers if they are not layer 0. Neither CHANGE nor CHPROP can be used to alter the layer of a portion of a block. In order to change the layers on the block entities, you must explode the block.

Naming Blocks, Wblocks, and Layers

From the previous discussion you can see that if five wblocks are inserted into a file, and each one has five separate and unique layer names, you will have a file with 25 different layer names. This can be a problem and a terrific waste of time. When designing, try to use standard layer names to avoid problems. Also, remember to use the LIST command to locate the layer something is on.

When naming blocks and wblocks, students are often tempted to use names of friends, enemies, rock groups, or just two or three letters. You may have the impression that you will remember the names and their significance later. You will not.

Try to name the blocks and files in a complete and logical manner. You should be able to identify your files by looking at the directory listing using the DOS command DIR A:. If you are asked to insert the project you completed in Chapter 6, and you insert three files before you obtain the correct one, you have a problem. Keep in mind that it will be difficult for your instructor to consider you capable and intelligent if you cannot even locate your own files. An employer may be even less tolerant.

Using the date on the directory listing display to locate files is useful, but every time you retrieve a file then END or SAVE it, the date will change.

When working on large projects that have several different files and several different layers, it is a good idea to keep a project designation sheet containing the names of all of the files needed, the date they were last updated, the names of all layers, and what is contained on those layers. This will save you a lot of time later in trying to figure out the files you are dealing with.

ACCESSING FILES FOR INSERTING

If all your files are on different floppy disks, you must copy them all to one floppy to insert them. If you have two or three files on different disks, END the current file, exit from AutoCAD, copy the files to a clean new disk, and then insert the disk.

You may be allowed to access other people's files to complete the day's exercises. Do not remove someone's disk while they are still in AutoCAD. You will damage that disk and seriously compromise your popularity.

Remember not to remove your floppy disks while you are in the AutoCAD Drawing Editor. If you do, you will be creating bad clusters on your disk which will eventually cause a crash.

MINSERT (Multiple Insert)

MINSERT is a combination of the INSERT command and the ARRAY command. It inserts the block as a rectangular array. The result is a series of blocks spaced at a preset distance. These cannot be exploded, and you cannot use *MINSERT (* before INSERT allows blocks to be entered as separate entities).

```
Command:MINSERT
Block name or ?:LOT
Insert point: (pick 1)
X scale factor <1>/Corner/XYZ:↵
Y scale factor (default = X):↵
Rotation angle:↵ (this will be counter-clockwise)
Number of rows (—) <1>:↵
Number of columns ( III ):5
Distance between the columns ( III ):1.25
```

The distance between the columns in the illustration of Figure 10-3 is the full distance of the object itself, thus allowing the objects to sit beside each other and not overlap.

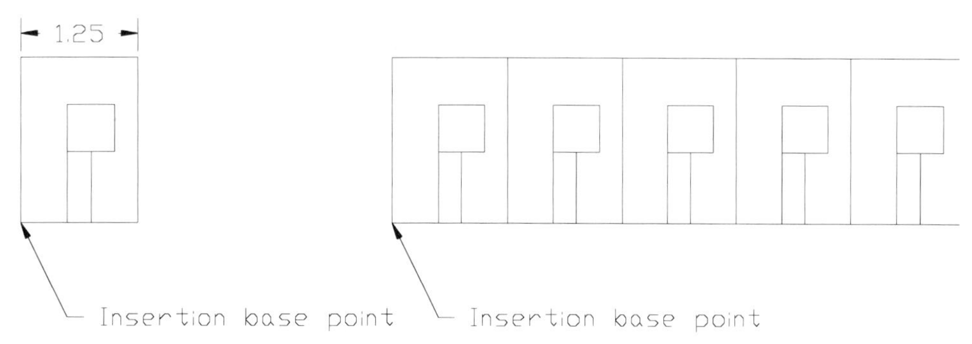

Figure 10-3. Multiple insert

PURGING

Each time a block or wblock is inserted into a file, a copy of it is placed in the drawing memory or default area. To clean up file, you must purge the blocks.

The PURGE command will erase all unused blocks, layers, text styles, linetypes, etc. that are on a file. Any blocks, layers, etc. that have been brought into the file but never used can be erased. This command is used only upon entry to a file. It erases the information from the file defaults and settings.

When a wblock is inserted, then erased, the copy of the wblock remains in memory in case it is needed again. If the original file is changed, and the user wants to insert the wblock again, the original file can be purged in order to accept the new file.

Use the PURGE command, then END, then retrieve the file again to insert the updated wblock.

```
Command:PURGE
Purge unused Blocks/LAyers/LTypes/SHapes/STyles/All:A
Purge block DOOR30 ? <n>:n
Purge block WINDOW48 <n>:y
Purge block SINK24 <n>:y
```

Another way to insert an updated block is to use FILENAME=. This will indicate that the file has been updated, and the base file will search for the updated file. A message will be displayed stating that the block has been redefined.

```
Command:INSERT
Block name (OR ?):title=title1
Insertion point:0,0
X scale factor <1>/Corner/XYZ:↵
Y scale factor (default = X):↵
Rotation angle:↵
```

This command sequence will insert the new copy of the file called TITLE.

BLOCK FILE REFERENCES

A file is laid out into many different areas as shown below.

FILE

Current Settings	Geometry	Display	Drawing	Other
Radius .255	Line	Vie	Dimensi	Surfaces
Limits 12 x 9	Arcs	Viewports	Notes	Shading
Pline W .25	Circles		Leaders	Slides
Layers lines	Plines		Centers	
hatch	Ellipse		Titles	
dim	Hatch			
hidden	Text			
Blocks title				
detail				
north				
Linetypes				
hidden				
center				

The block information is part of the information that is loaded with the file before a model is started. There are many reasons for using blocks; many other features of blocks are discussed in Chapter 23. Please refer to this chapter for advanced lessons on the use of blocks.

BLOCK TIPS

Objects must be visible to be included in a block, but they can be on many layers. If you are trying to block information from only one layer, turn the other layers off for easy selecting.

When in doubt, use 0,0 as the insertion point. If all of the files are created at a 1 = 1 scale, then the data will always fit.

If you have inserted the wrong block, undo it and the block reference on the file will be deleted as well.

Exercise A10

Blocks are not easy to work with, and it is suggested that you do all three of the following exercises.

STEP 1
Draw the first house. Block it. Insert it at different scales and aspect ratios. Using the same block, create some row housing with MINSERT.

STEP 2
INSERT a floor plan from the exercises of Chapter 5 or Chapter 7.

STEP 3
Create an empty new file. Insert your Chapter 8 title block. Insert a floor plan from a previous exercise. Finally, add a north arrow.

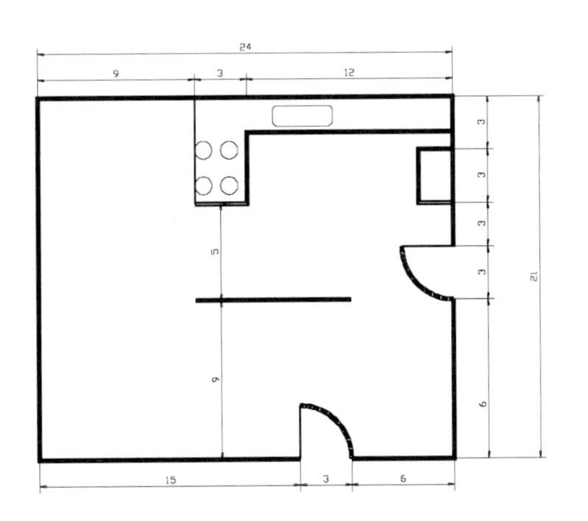

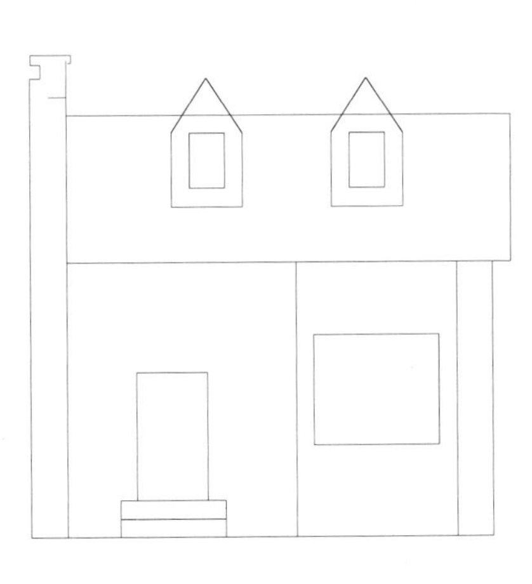

Exercise M10

STEP 1
Create the blocks for this layout, then create the house and insert them as needed. If you are finished early, add a title block.

STEP 2
Do Exercise C10 to practise MINSERT.

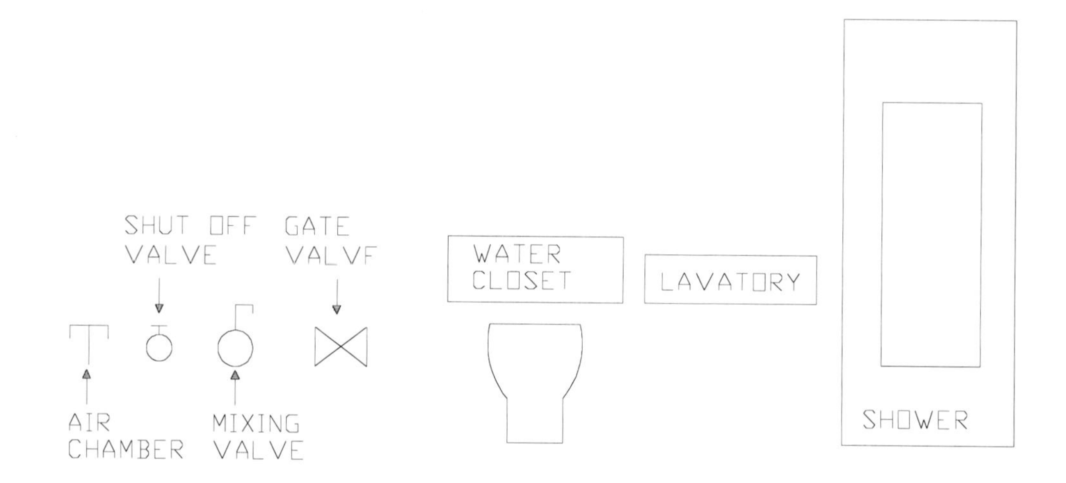

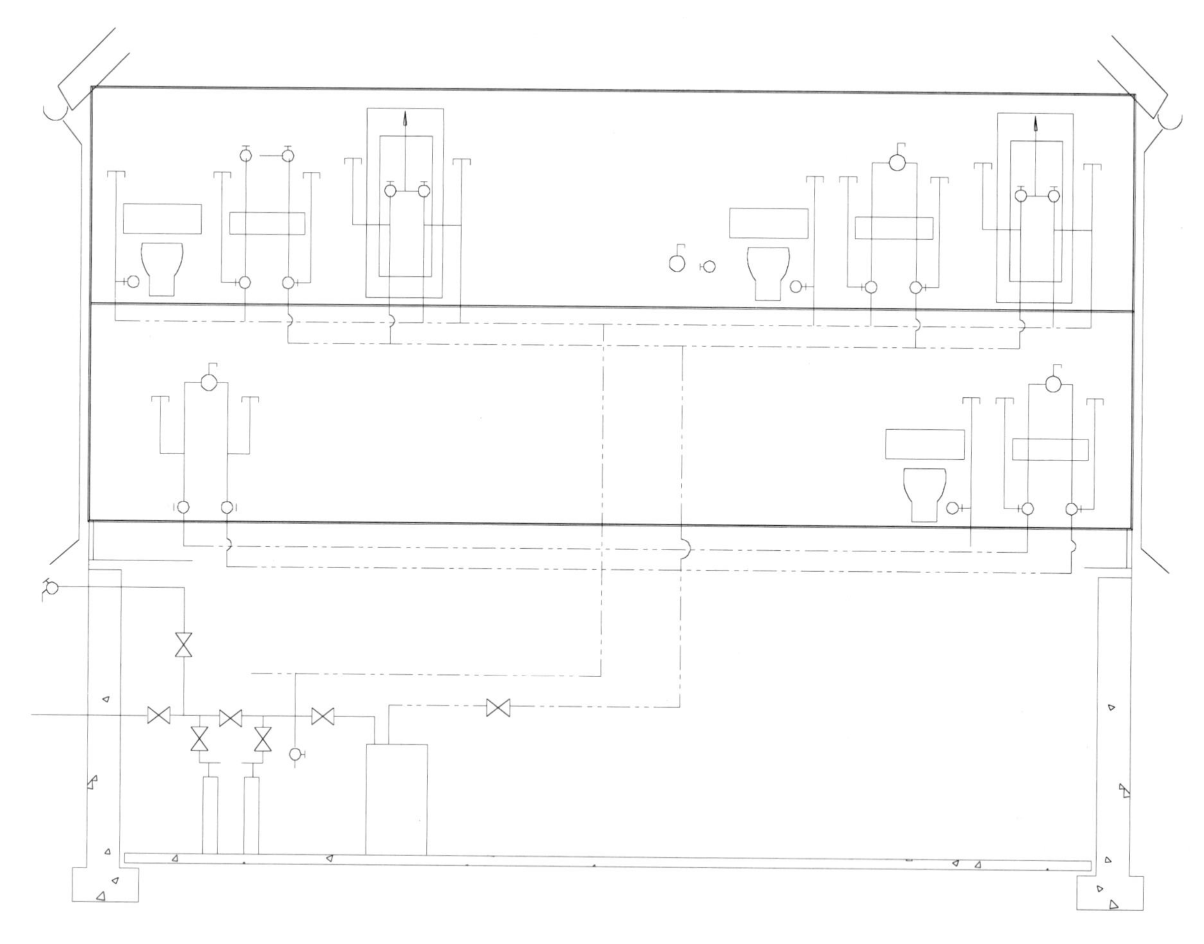

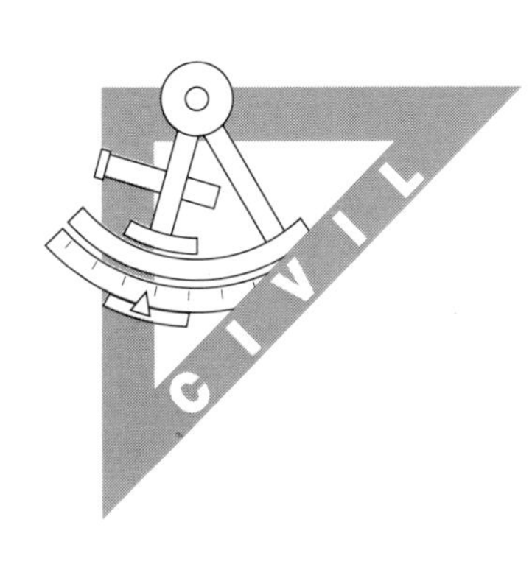

Exercise C10

Blocks are not easy to work with, and it is suggested that you do both of the following exercises.

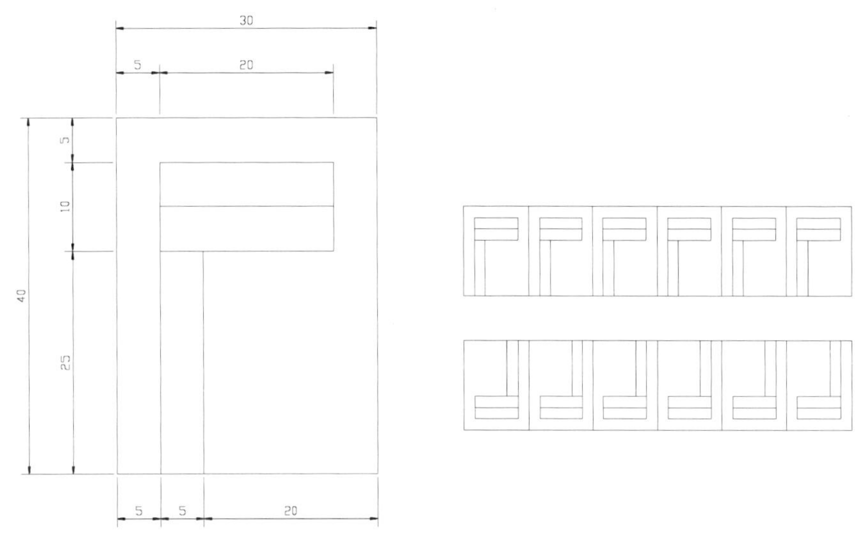

STEP 1

Draw the lot at the size suggested. Block it. Insert it at the left-hand side of the page as in the example. Now MINSERT the first row of houses at a scale of (X value of) .25. Note that the distance between the columns will be 1/4 the width of the property. Now MINSERT the bottom row at a rotation angle of 180.

STEP 2

Create an empty new file. Insert the Chapter 8 title block. Insert a part from Chapter 4 and a north arrow from Chapter 3, making sure they all fit on the drawing.

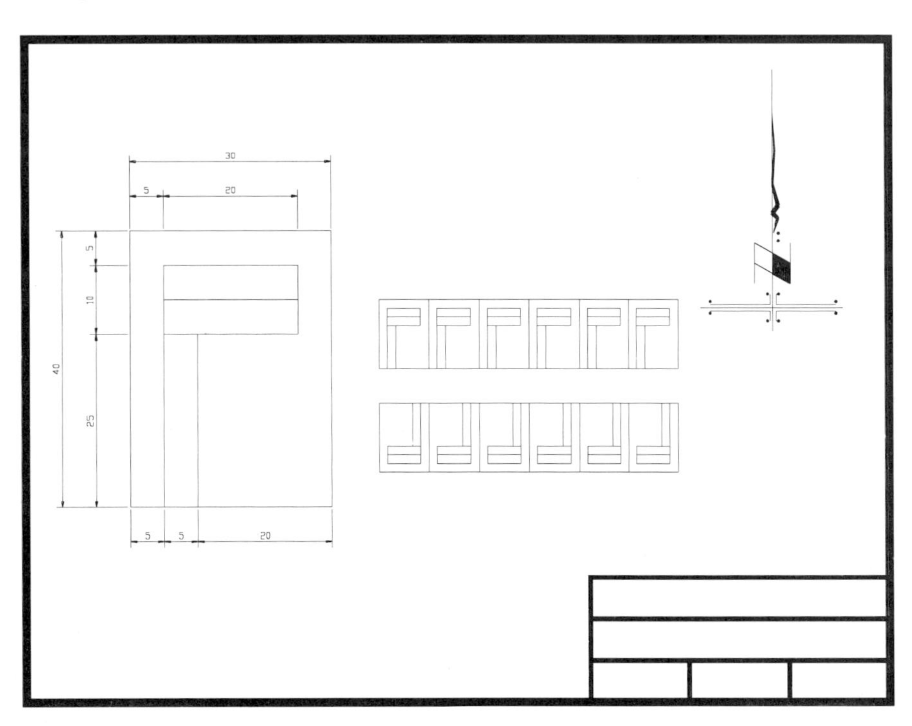

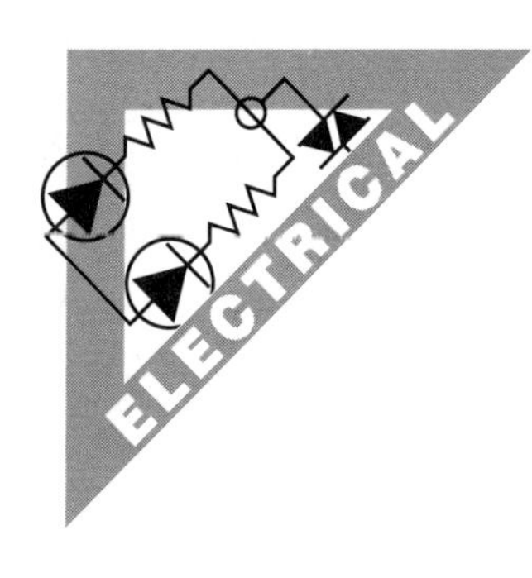

Exercise E10

STEP 1

Create the blocks needed to make this computer logic diagram. Then insert the blocks and add the lines to create the layout. If you have time, add a title block.

STEP 2

Do exercise C10 to practise MINSERT.

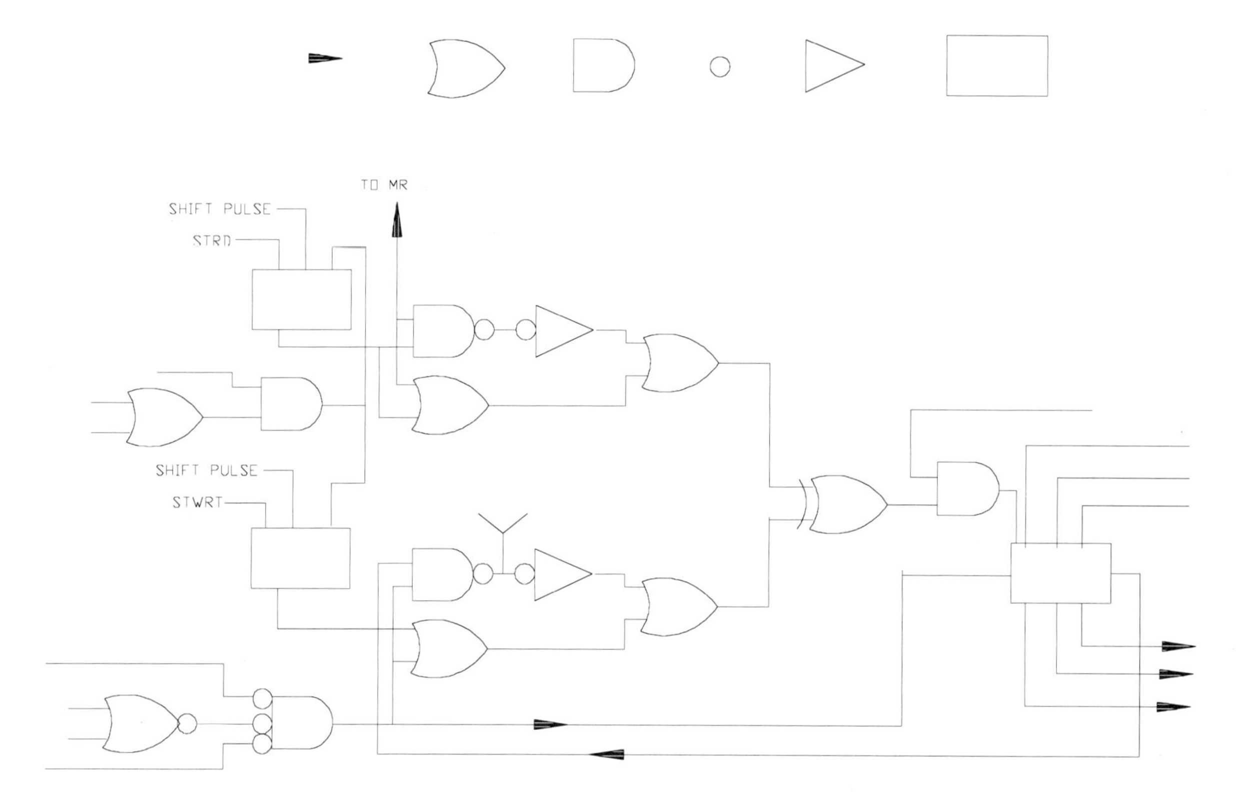

Challenger 10

Create each view of this part separately and then insert them onto the same title block.

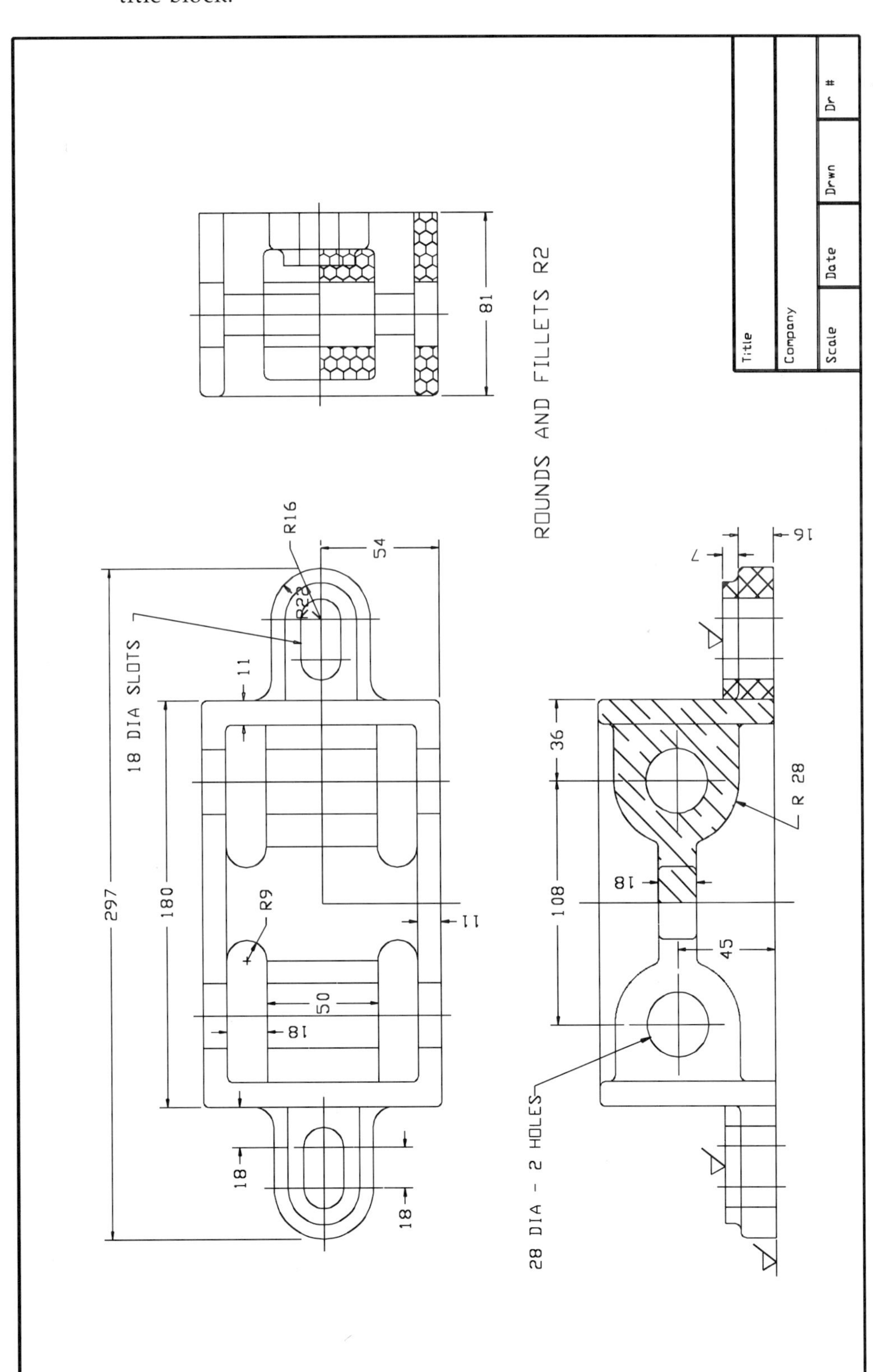

SETTING UP DRAWINGS AND PLOTTING

Upon completion of this chapter, the student should be able to:

1. Create a title block to fit a standard-paper drawing size and insert three views of an object at different scale factors
2. Set TEXT, HATCH, and LINETYPE sizes for any drawing
3. Create a prototype drawing for future use
4. PLOT a drawing

SET UP AND SCALE FOR 2D DRAWINGS

When Computer-Aided Design was first introduced to the general populace as a design tool in 1981, the systems available were very large, very expensive, and not entirely user friendly. At that time, there were basically two types of students: the first was the confident and far-thinking individual who recognized the potential of the technology and embraced it with an open heart and an equally open mind, regardless of the seeming inaccessibility of the software; the second was a tragic hero, paralysed with fear and convinced that an in-depth understanding of CAD signalled madness and instant death. The programmers at AutoDESK, being loving, caring souls, thus started programming software for the second group in an effort to ease them into the future.

AutoCAD was originally intended as the "low-end" CAD program, the one that was easy to use and relatively inexpensive to buy. Once people got used to it, they could progress to the "real systems" that could cut metal and perform analysis. The user was given every opportunity to be coddled into the program, and the first step in doing this was the SETUP program. This program allowed the user to set up an environment that made him think that he was using paper. The program prompted the user for the intended size of paper, the intended scale, the intended units, and every other detail of a paper drawing. In essence, all the program really did was set up a scaled overlay so that all of the scales — DIMSCALE, LTSCALE, HATCH, UNITS, etc. — were already set by the program. While this made some students comfortable and provided a good working environment for many, it also limited the flexibility of the data and, in many cases, also limited the understanding of the student. I have met many students in advanced classes who, having been taught to use SETUP, have no comprehension of the data as a model. In some cases, a student perfectly capable of drawing and editing within SETUP is immediately disabled if the SETUP is not available due to overlay or LISP problems.

Now that AutoCAD has become a program capable of cutting metal and performing analysis, and students are getting used to computers, the SETUP program is no longer necessary and is therefore not included in the main menu of software releases after Release 11. (MVSETUP is still available and is discussed in Chapter 30.) The concepts used by the larger systems — model space and paper space — are taking over, leaving no room for the SETUP environment. Chapters 25 to 36 will explain further how to use model space and paper space to the best advantage. Right now, what we want to do is get three views of a related part onto one border and title block.

For the past 10 chapters, we have been working on AutoCAD models as individual sets of data. The geometry is being entered relative to the origin (0,0). The data, once entered to perfection, can then be used for a variety of purposes including:

- computer-aided manufacturing (CAM)
- analysis
- a block used in other models
- downloading to a computer graphics program for marketing purposes
- downloading to a stereolithography system
- estimating and costing
- a prototype
- downloading as a drawing for communication to others

If the model is initially scaled to fit a paper, many of the above applications are complicated. With the model scaled at 1 = 1, all we need to do is extract from the model the views that we want to see on a drawing and then scale them appropriately.

There are two ways of creating a scaled plot. The first is to draw the model at 1 = 1, then insert the title block at an appropriate scale factor, and plot the file at a specific scale.

For example: A layout for a house is 30′ x 40′ and drawn in real units at a scale of 1 = 1. You want to have this plotted at ¼" = 1′0". As you can see in Chart 1 (page 202), ¼" = 1′0" is the same as 1⁄48.

The title block is set up for a 24 x 36 sheet. In order to have this visible at the correct scale on the layout, the title block can be inserted at a scale of 48. Then, when plotting the model, scale the view and the model at 1⁄48.

This is by far the best method of plotting and scaling because it allows you to maintain the model at a scale factor of 1 = 1. For all the information that requires scaling, such as DIMSCALE, HATCH, LINETYPE, TEXT, etc., 48 can be used for each individual unit.

In Figure 11-1, however, there are several different scale factors, and at least one of the views will need to be scaled to fit the first view.

When plotting many different scale factors, and also to save time in testing your plots, a second method is to create blocks of the views and files you want and insert them at the accepted scale factor onto a title block or accepted drawing sheet. This also saves time in generating multiple plots because the plots can always be done at a scale of 1 = 1. In Chapter 30 we will see how paper space takes this a step further.

In the drawing of Figure 11-1, two separate files were inserted onto a drawing sheet that measures 36" x 24".

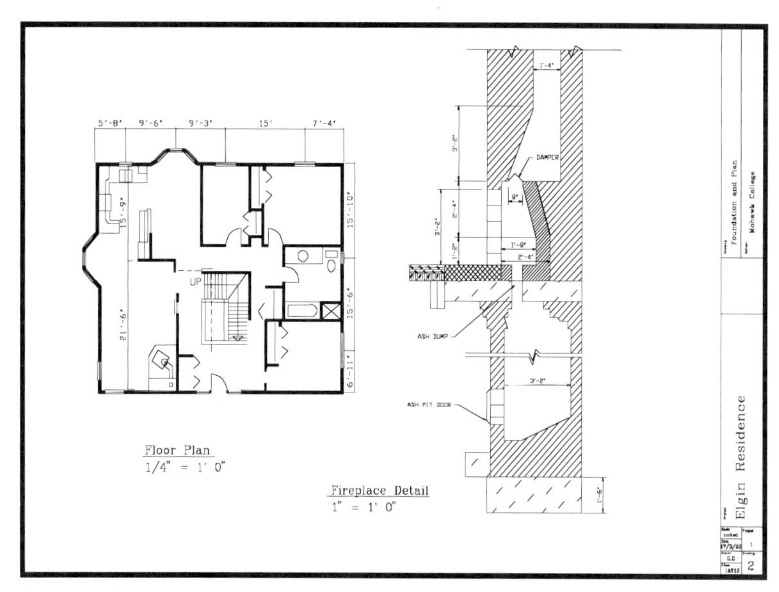

Figure 11-1. Scale factors

The three separate stored files include:

- a title block at 36" x 24"
- a fireplace detail at 20 feet vertically
- a floor plan 35′ x 30′

The title block was inserted, then the other two files were inserted at the specified scale factor. In this case, the floor plan was inserted at ¼" = 1′0", and the fireplace, being a detail, was inserted at a scale factor of 1" = 1′0".

This method of creating drawings is useful for many reasons. Often, you have details that can be used on various drawings. If the details are merged with each file, this would take up a lot of room on your disk. But they are kept as separate files and simply merged when a drawing is to be plotted, this will save both time and space. The drawing can be compiled with many views, plotted, and then erased. If the drawing is to be plotted many times, a plot file (.PLT) can be generated for this purpose. In either single drawings or multiple drawings, the parts can all be merged in the final drawing stage at the scale factor particular to each drawing. If all drawings are done at a scale of 1 = 1, there is no problem inserting them. In Chapter 16 you will learn how to view files in slide format to make this process even easier.

DETERMINING DRAWING SCALE

After you have retrieved the title block on a new file, you will next determine the scale of the views. This involves finding the ratio between the size of the part, usually 1, and the scale at which you want to view it.

Taking the example of ¼" = 1′0", the ratio is actually 1⁄48. We can see this also as .25 = 12 or as .0208333 = 1 (1 divided by 48 equals .0208333). The scale you would use to insert the file into the title block is thus .0208333.

```
Command: INSERT
Block name (OR ?):floorpl
Insertion point: (pick 1) (sets the 0,0 of the file)
X scale factor <1>/Corner/XYZ:.0208333
Y scale factor (default = X):↵
Rotation angle:↵
```

This command sequence will insert the floor plan into the title block at a scale of 1/4" = 1'0". After Release 11, 1/48 can also be used.

```
X scale factor <1>/Corner/XYZ:1/48
```

Chart 1 details the various typical scale factors that can be used to scale blocks for insertion into the title block or to scale a drawing in the PLOT command.

CHART 1

SCALE FACTOR		DECIMAL VALUE	FRACTION
Architectural or Imperial			
3" = 1'0"	3 = 12	.25	1/4
1" = 1'0"	1 = 12	.0833333	1/12
1/2" = 1'0"	.5 = 12	.0416666	1/24
1/4" = 1'0"	.25= 12	.0208333	1/48
3/16" = 1'0"	.1875 = 12	.0156246	1/64
1/8" = 1'0"	.125 = 12	.0104166	1/96
1/16" = 1'0"	.0625 = 12	.0052083	1/192
Mechanical			
3/4" = 1"	.75 = 1	.75	
1/2" = 1"	.50 = 1	.5	
1/4" = 1"	.25 = 1	.25	
Metric			
1:10		.1	
1:50		.02	
1:100		.01	
1:1000		.001	

The scale from Chart 1 will help you scale the model correctly; now the dimensions, text, hatch, and linetype must be scaled to fit the drawing.

SCALING DIMENSIONS AND ANNOTATIONS

You will have noticed that when creating text and dimensions, you often had to change the scale factors to see them correctly on the screen. This is even more difficult when they are merged with a group of other files or views in a drawing at various scale factors.

If you remember your introductory drafting classes, the ANSI standard for the text in dimensions is 1/8" or 3mm. This is also the default for the dimension text in AutoCAD. This will need to be changed, however, if you are entering the part or view at a scale different than 1 = 1. You want the part to be scaled, but you still want the dimension text to show up at 1/8". If you were to create the text on the fireplace detail at 1/8", you would never be able to read it on either the screen or the drawing.

What you need to do, then, is to determine the text size needed for each particular scale at which you will be inserting the view or file. Remember, by changing the DIMSCALE and then using the UPD command in the DIM mode, you can automatically change dimensions if they are not the correct size for the scale factor you want to plot.

The first step is to determine the scale factor at which you want to plot the view, and then change the DIMSCALE and other notations to fit.

If, for example, you want to make sure the text on the above floor plan is at 1/8" on the final drawing, you would need to find the relationship between 1/8" on the paper and the size of the text on the floor plan, so that when it is inserted at 1/48, it will be displayed at 1/8". If 1/4" on the paper is equivalent to 12 inches on the model, then 1/8" or half of that value will be 6 inches on the model. So, if you create the notations and dimensions at 6 inches when creating the part, the final drawing at 1/4" = 1'0" will have 1/8" text.

If you want to take a portion of the same floor plan and blow it up to 1/2" = 1'0" to show some extra detailing, you can still have your final dimension text displayed at 1/8" if you change the size on the model to 3 inches. If 1/2" on paper will equal 12 inches on the model, then 1/8" or a quarter of that value will be 3 inches on the model.

Text, dimensions, and related notations should be scaled to attain the appropriate size on the paper. Chart 2 shows at what sizes to scale dimensions to obtain the proper size on the final drawing. Find the size you want the plotted text to be and the scale you intend to use, then set the model text size and DIMSCALE accordingly. Again, remember that you can change existing dimensions with UPD as long as DIMASO is on (see Chapter 7).

CHART 2

PLOTTED TEXT SIZE	SCALE	MODEL TEXT SIZE	DIMSCALE
Architectural or Imperial			
1/8"	1/16" = 1'0"	24"	192
(0.18 units)	1/8" = 1'0"	12"	96
	3/16" = 1'0"	8"	64
	1/4" = 1'0"	6"	48
	1/2" = 1'0"	3"	24
	1" = 1'0"	1.5"	12
1/4"	1/16" = 1'0"	48"	
	1/8" = 1'0"	24"	
	3/16" = 1'0"	16"	
	1/4" = 1'0"	12"	
	1/2" = 1'0"	6"	
	1" = 1'0"	3"	
3/16"	1/16" = 1'0"	36"	
	1/8" = 1'0"	18"	
	3/16" = 1'0"	12"	

CHART 2 (cont'd)

PLOTTED TEXT SIZE	SCALE	MODEL TEXT SIZE	DIMSCALE
Architectural or Imperial			
3⁄16"	1⁄4" = 1′0"	8"	
	1⁄2" = 1′0"	4.5"	
	1" = 1′0"	2.25"	
Mechanical			
.25"	1:2	.5"	
	1:10	25.0"	
	2:1	.125"	
.125"	1:2	25"	2
	1:10	12.50"	10
	2:1.06	25"	.5
.1875"	1:2	.3875"	
	1:10	18.75"	
	2:1	.09375"	
Metric			
3mm	1:10	30	
	1:100	300	
	1:500	1500	

For dimensions on a drawing that will be 1/4"=1′0" change the DIMSCALE to:

```
DIM:DIMSCALE
Current Value <1.000>:48
```

LTSCALE AND HATCH SCALE

While working with views to be placed on a drawing, other commands to consider are HATCH and LINETYPE. In creating these drawing aids for display on a screen, we determined that the scale for these functions should be the furthest value of X on the screen divided by 12. This provided a working area that was visible on the screen and easy enough to work with without risking the possibility of crashing the disk.

To place views onto a sheet of paper with the linetype and hatch sizes at the proper paper format, use the same setting as that used for 1⁄4" text. If the view is to be inserted at 1⁄16" scale, use 48. If it is to be inserted at a 1⁄4" scale, use 12, etc. This will ensure that the hatch and lines are visible.

SETTING UP A PROTOTYPE DRAWING

Now you have learned almost everything necessary for creating a two-dimensional image on a screen. Now that you have been introduced to the technology, it is time to start thinking of using it in a logical manner.

Every time you retrieve a file, you must, at one time or another, set the following commands to the correct parameters:

- LIMITS
- GRID
- SNAP
- UNITS
- LAYERS
- LTSCALE
- LINETYPES
- TEXT fonts
- DIM VARS
- PLOT variables

Before changing these parameters, review the AutoCAD default settings.

- UNITS Decimal, 4 digits to the right of the decimal
- LIMITS 12 X 9
- SNAP OFF, set to 1
- GRID OFF, set to snap
- LAYER 0
- LTSCALE visible at 12 x 9
- LINETYPE continuous
- DIMSCALE visible at 12 x 9

The defaults are set for mechanical engineering and are fine for getting started. You should, however, know what parameters are most useful to you and be able to set them.

Setting Up Your Own Prototype

Start with a new file and set the parameters according to the following considerations.

UNITS
Choose the type of units you use most often. Make sure you change not only the discipline, but the degrees of accuracy as well. For example, if you are creating floor plans for houses, you may want architectural units, and you will not need to be more accurate than 1/2 inch; if you are designing surveys and town planning, you will need to change the system of angle measurement; if you are designing moulds for contact lenses, you will need much more accuracy than four decimal places.

LIMITS
Once you have determined which units to use, decide on the typical size of object that you design. For example, if you are designing mid-price houses, the floor plans will range from 30′ x 40′ to 50′ x 60′; if you are planning new developments for 10–15 lots, you will want an average LIMITS size for 15

normal lots; if you are designing parts for the automotive job shop industries, use the average mould size. Remember, LIMITS can be changed or simply turned off at any time. All you are trying to do here is save yourself the trouble of changing the limits each time a file is started.

SNAP

Change the SNAP size to the average size you will use. For example, if the door and window suppliers all have products that are 24, 30, 36, and 42 inches wide, chances are you will not need a SNAP accuracy anything less than 3 inches; if your local by-laws dictate the size of lots in five-unit increments, then that is what the SNAP should be. If you usually allow tolerancing of more or less 0.0125, then maybe that would be the most suitable default setting. Again, these can be changed.

GRID

A good rule of thumb is to have the GRID twice the size of the SNAP, so you will have two snap points for every visible grid point.

LAYER

This area is particularly important when trying to plan for ease in future designs. Many hours have been spent trying to make one person's layers accessible to others wishing to use a particular file. Try to find out what the accepted layer settings are for your industry and use those.

Once you start working with a particular company, that company will most likely have a set series of layer names and colours to use. If you are planning to create AutoCAD drawings on your own, make your files compatible with those of your client. If you are just starting off in the AutoCAD market, you will gain credibility by trying to organize standard layering protocols with your clients. You will probably find a local AutoCAD user's group that has people interested in your discipline. Find out what they use. Concentrate on the colours and linetypes that are associated with each layer as well.

If you are simply concerned with passing the course and getting a decent mark, try to choose layer names that are logical and communicate immediately to the user what portion of the drawing you want to illustrate. You will be surprised at how little you remember of your files once you have been away from them for a few weeks.

LTSCALE

Set your LTSCALE to match the size of plot or view you usually use. This can always be changed, but it is nice to have your hidden lines show up the first time you use them.

LINETYPE

The linetypes take up extra room on a file, as do the text fonts, and that is why they are not loaded with the basic AutoCAD file. If you will never in your life use a dot line, then do not load it. Certainly load all those linetypes you are likely to use, but, generally speaking, most people need only the hidden and centre. Load these so that they are ready, and remember that the others are always there should you need them.

TEXT FONT

As with linetypes, there are only a few you will ever use. Set them up ready for use and forget about the rest until you need them.

DIM VARS

These may take a few minutes to set up if you are doing dimensioning for applications other than mechanical engineering. Use the Status option to show what is available and change the parameters to those you need.

DIMSCALE is the obvious first choice if you have changed LIMITS and UNITS. If you are using architectural and surveying units, you will also want to change DIMTOH, DIMTIH, and DIMTAD. You may use more ticks than arrows. If so, change that option, etc.

USING THE PROTOTYPE

You may have spent 20 minutes to an hour setting the parameters for your own prototype file. This is now your personal start model and will save you that amount of time every time you start a new model. Now you can save the model, calling it START2D or PROTO or PROTO1.

You can use this prototype in one of two ways:

1. Instead of using option 1 on the Main menu, use option 2, Edit an existing file, to begin a new drawing. Be careful when saving the model, however, as you do not want to END and have the empty prototype file filled with geometry.

2. Start a new drawing with the prototype parameters by using the following:

```
Enter selection:1 (begin a new drawing)
Enter name of drawing:NAME=PROTO
```

This will load a new file identical to PROTO named NAME.

If you are starting work with a firm that has been using AutoCAD for a while, ask the name of the prototype file to use, and they may get the impression that you know what you are doing. If they do not have one, make one.

Scale Examples

Create a file to plot two views at different scale factors. If you have been working on a final term project, practise on getting the files into the title block for plotting, particularly if you are responsible for a plot generated on open-access time. If you are not working on a final project, use views from the term. For example:

ARCHITECTURE The title block from Chapter 8, the floor plan from Chapter 6, and the fireplace detail from Chapter 9.

MECHANICAL The title block from Chapter 8 and the gear from Chapter 5 with a detail at half the original size.

SURVEYING OR CIVIL The title block from Chapter 8, the cul de sac from Chapter 5, and a corner detail.

Follow these steps:

Remember not to remove your floppy disk from the Drawing Editor of AutoCAD. See Chapter 5 for details. If you are swapping floppies to get all the files you need, exit AutoCAD first.

1. Decide on the final size of the drawing and the different scales for each view.
2. Enter each file and make sure the text and dimension sizes will be correct for the final drawing using Chart 2 as a reference. Use UPD and DIMSCALE, etc. to get the correct sizes. Save each file as it is changed.
3. Make sure that hatch and linetype information is entered correctly.
4. Start a new file and insert the title block and the two views (three if you have time) onto the title block.
5. Add additional text such as view titles and scales and fill in the title block.
6. Save this file for plotting in the next chapter.

Making Full Use of the Hardware

If you are trying to create a drawing on a 360K drive, you will have many problems because of the insufficient space on the floppy. If you are creating a drawing on a larger format disk, 1.2MB or 2.4MB or larger, you may still run into insufficient memory problems if the drawing has a large hatch or a lot of text.

While you are creating an AutoCAD file, a temporary file is being created in the directory on the disk that the file is being created on. The temporary file is the same size as the drawing file, if not larger. Therefore, on a 1.2MB disk, the largest file you will be able to access is about 450,000K; the extra space is needed for the temporary file to be written.

To avoid this situation, assuming that the hard drive is C; at the Main menu use the following:

```
Enter selection:1 (begin a new drawing)
Enter name of drawing:DWGNAME=A:DWGNAME
```

A:DWGNAME becomes the prototype drawing. AutoCAD and DOS will think you are running from the hard drive. The temporary files and swap files are placed on the current drive, or drive C.

When exiting, make sure the drawing is saved on drive A if you are concerned that the drawing could be lost or stolen if left on drive C.

Reconfiguring for Extra Space

If you are working on extremely large files — in 3D this is particularly important — you can have temporary files and swap files located in a reserved directory of the hard drive to speed up regens and shading, etc. Use CFIG-PHAR.EXE to place swap files on reserved directory.

Use a batch file that will delete the contents of these directories when AutoCAD is started.

PLOTTERS AND OUTPUT PERIPHERALS

Before we discuss how to plot the drawing or data, it is a good idea to outline some of the common plotters to see what they are and how they are used.

Output peripherals are devices that convert the data from the computer memory to a format that the device can interpret. Two broad categories of peripheral devices are monitors and plotters. Plotters, in the broadest definition, allow the viewing of the data by producing a reproduction of the data in hardcopy format, or, in other words, a drawing.

Ctrl-Q sets the Printer Echo mode on and all your commands will be printed. Use Ctrl-Q to also turn off the echo.

There are many types of plotters and printers available, and prices are on the decline as capabilities advance. Some common plotters and printers include dot matrix printers, pen plotters, electrostatic plotters, and laser printers.

Also, at the high end of plotters is 3D plotting, which includes mills, lathes, and stereolithography, which manufactures a plastic prototype with the use of photopolymers and laser technology.

Dot Matrix Printers

Dot matrix printers form each character out of a pattern of ink dots. The dots are printed by a print head containing an array of seven or nine hammers that strike against a ribbon. Inside the printer, a ROM chip stores the pattern of ink dots associated with each character. The printer receives the ASCII character code for a letter, and the ROM chip tells the print head which hammers are to strike the ribbon. A belt driven by a motor moves the print head back and forth as the paper is wound forward.

Dot matrixes are used in both printers and plotters, allowing reasonable graphics up to a C-size drawing and letter quality printing. The result is an adequate drawing at a reasonable cost.

When plotting on a dot matrix, the drawing is usually not to scale. It is important to make sure that the storage or memory on the printer is sufficient for graphics. Dot matrix printers are useful for many reasons, but they are particularly desirable in a classroom situation because the only components that need regular adjustment are the paper and the ribbon.

Dot matrix printers are usually used to create quick prints of drawings or check plots. The printout is not to scale, but it gives an idea of what the model looks like.

Pen Plotters

The most well-known vendors of plotters are Calcomp, Hewlett Packard, Houston Instruments, Roland, Versatec, and Ioline. The criteria used to judge or evaluate these types of plotters are:

Resolution The measure of the smallest dimension the plotter can legibly draw. Typical values are in the 0.001" range.

Repeatability The measure of the maximum distance the plotter would be out if it were to draw the same object twice in the same place. Typical values are 0.002"– 0.005".

Speed Usually the diagonal speed of the pen, measured in inches per second. Typically 14–18" can be expected.

Buffer Size The built-in memory in the plotter, so that when graphics data is sent to the plotter, the computer can be freed up to do other things. The graphics data is sent by processed vectors. Typical buffer sizes are from 0MB to 8MB. This is perhaps the most important quality to consider; in many plotters, the plots will simply not work if the drawing is too large for the buffer. Some plotters are capable of splitting the file and plotting it in sections, but this takes a long time.

Number of Pens The size of the carousel and the number of pens it will hold. Typically 2–8 pens can be expected.

Paper Size The largest size that can be plotted, usually an A–D size on larger plotters and a B on smaller plotters.

Accuracy The measure of the difference of the length of the line that is being sent to the plotter and the length of the line actually drawn. This value is usually quoted as a percentage, typically 0.1%.

Price Can range from $2,000 to $30,000 depending on size, performance, and number of pens. Other features to look for are continuous-feed paper, single-sheet feeders, and control panels.

If your system cannot multitask, the PC's CPU can be tied up for the time that the drawing is being plotted. A black box can be used as a buffer to store the drawing data until the plotter process it, thus freeing the terminal for further work.

Pens

There are several types of pens available on the market, ranging in price from less than $1.00 to $75.00. Felt tip and ball point are the two most popular types of pens. Regardless of the type of pen you are using, it needs to be capped when the drawing is completed, and, in many cases, should be stored in a horizontal position. If you are planning to do a lot of plots, it is suggested that you purchase your own pens to provide consistency in your plots.

If you have a local pen dealer or sales representative, they are often only too glad to address the class regarding the various types of pens available for the plotter you are using. A good rep should cover all issues related to width of pen, pen quality versus paper quality, colour, cleaning, and general maintenance of pens. If you do not have this resource available, be advised that all of these properties are important and should be considered when organizing your plot.

Paper

The paper is held on the plotter by a series of small wheels. The size of the paper is often read by the plotter itself; thus, there is a certain portion of the paper that is held in place while the paper is being read. The size of paper used to create an A-size plot will need to be slightly larger than an A-size drafting paper. Before you start a plot, make sure you have plotter paper large enough to hold the drawing and to allow for the mechanics of the plotter.

The quality of the paper is also important. Make sure that the pens are appropriate for the type of paper you are using. Pens are also available for mylar and vellum: these are usually not the same pens used in normal plots. If you are testing a plot before using good paper, certainly try it out for size on a sheet of paper, but *never plot on blueprint paper*, because one plot alone can effectively demolish a pen.

Electrostatic Plotters

This type of plotter is capable of producing "photographic images" and is excellent for drawings as well as presentation graphics. Also known as a Xerographic printer, it forms an optical image on specially treated paper. The dark areas are charged and the light areas are uncharged; the ink adheres to the charged areas. The paper is heated causing the ink to dry and adhere to the paper.

These plotters are not usually found in a classroom, but if this is the type of final product you are after, you can take your floppy disk to a graphics store and have an electrostatic plot produced there. Some large computer stores may also provide this service.

Laser Printers

The laser printer is the second step of the electrostatic printer. It creates an image by charging the paper with electrostatic energy using a laser beam, but the paper does not have to be specially treated.

Fast and silent, this is the popular choice in low-cost printers. The final product is also usually impressive. Difficulties may be encountered, however, in making the plotter compatible with the existing system. When buying a laser printer for your home, make sure the store will take it back if it is not compatible. The size of the buffer is also very important, again, when dealing with graphics.

Like the dot matrix printer, the laser printer does not produce drawings to scale unless they are on an 8 ½ x 11" sheet; but the final product is very good and easily reproduced.

Stereolithography

While plotting is usually considered to produce a paper copy of data, there are also small mills and lathes that can produce an image through use of plotter-type files.

One of the newest and most expensive means of obtaining a visual image of data is stereolithography or three-dimensional printing.

The stereolithography system makes parts without tooling, machining, or cutting of any kind. It provides a 3D image of the data by changing the property of liquid plastic (photopolymers) that solidifies in the presence of ultraviolet radiation provided by laser beams. The laser "draws" the object in slices, as tiny as 200 slices to the inch, with cross-sections through the part from the bottom to the top. The laser ultraviolet energy converts the liquid to a solid, slice by slice, until the part is produced.

The advantage of this system is most clearly apparent in the mechanical engineering area, because the part can be inspected immediately after design. With this technology, no tooling needs to be generated, and the part can be produced virtually within a week of completion of the design.

This photopolymer part can then be moulded if appropriate. The process is very similar to CNC, in that a certain amount of post-processing is required before the part can be downloaded, but it is included here because it is referred to as 3D plotting.

All major CAD companies can generate the interface to stereolithography. The final product is absolutely astounding.

PLOTTING AN AUTOCAD FILE

Plotting can be done either from the Main menu or from the Drawing Editor.

```
Main Menu
 0. Exit AutoCAD
 1. Begin a NEW drawing
 2. Edit an existing drawing
 3. Plot a drawing
 4. Printer Plot a drawing
 5. Configure AutoCAD
 6. File Utilities
 7. Compile shape/font description file
 8. Convert old drawing file
 9. Recover damaged selection

 Enter Selection:
```

If you choose:

2 – you will retrieve an existing file. After you have made sure the data is centred on the screen, you can either print or plot using Display, Window, View, Extents, or Limits. The file will regenerate once again after the plot is finished. If you are in a hurry, this is a terrible waste of time.

3 – you will access a file, but you will not see it on the screen. You will be generating a plot. Again, you can choose any of the plotting options as above. The difference is that, if you have saved the file properly, you will save the time for the two regenerations of the previous option.

4 – you will access a file as in option 3, but this time you will create a plot.

Plotting a File onto a Pen Plotter

To Get Ready:

- Move the plotter away from any wall or surface that could obstruct the free movement of the paper and turn the plotter on.
- Switch ports if necessary. (In a classroom environment, there are often two or three stations linked up to each plotter. In some situations, there is only one plotter and only two or three stations have access to it. Find out where the link is and make sure you have switched the port to address the plotter from the station you are on.)
- Check the pens for the correct colour, width, and quality. Taking the pen out of the carousel and drawing a few lines is a sufficient test.
- Load the paper: secure the grippers on the side of the paper making sure that it can move without obstacles.

Example: HP plotter #7580B

Load the paper so that both sides hang equally from the centre, press the CHART HOLD button to secure the grippers, then press REMOTE for the plotter to read the paper size.

Loading the paper in the plotter is not often as simple as it seems. If there are two or three steps that you have to remember, write them down on paper in concise, logical format, and tape this information to the plotter, the side of the desk next to the plotter, or somewhere else so you can refer to it next time you need it. You may think that the steps are so obvious that, once told, you will remember them in three weeks. You will not.

PLOT COMMAND

If you are plotting from the Main menu, enter **3** for Plot a drawing. You will be prompted for the name of the drawing as in option 2, Edit an existing drawing. Then enter the name of the drawing and the area you want plotted.

If you are plotting from an on-screen file or the Drawing Editor, enter PLOT. In Release 11, the PLOT command performs the same as in earlier releases if you are in paper space or in one viewport. If you have multiple viewports and are in model space, the PLOT command will select only the objects in the current viewport.

The first step is to identify the area of the drawing to plot.

```
Command:PLOT
What to plot — Display,Extents,Limits,View or Window <D>:
```

The default <D> in this case means that the last person using the PLOT command plotted the Display. Make your choice:

Display Selects everything on screen – in paper space from all viewports, in model space from only the current viewport.

Extents Selects all portions of the drawing that contain entities. By using ZOOM Extent before plotting, you will be able to check for geometry floating outside the limits that will be plotted using this option.

Limits Selects only that portion of the file contained in the limits.

Window Allows you to select a rectangular portion of the file, a detail, or the whole view. It can only be used if you are in the Drawing Editor.

View Selects a stored view of the data. Like Window, it can be all or a portion of the file. In order to plot a view, you must have saved a view prior to using the PLOT command. This option is particularly useful when you are plotting from the Main menu because you can be sure what you will get. The VIEW command is explained further in Chapter 26. Essentially, the command will prompt for the name of the view and a Window containing the information you want named.

Once the portion of data to plot has been selected, the PLOT default parameters will be displayed. The defaults are determined by the last person using the command. The display will look like this:

```
Plot will NOT be written to a selected file
Sizes are in inches: (American system)
Plot origin at 0.00,0.00
Plotting area is ________ _________
Plot is NOT rotated 90 degrees
Pen width is 0.010
Area fill will not be adjusted for pen width
Hidden lines will NOT be removed
Plot will be scaled to fit available area.

Do you want to change anything?    <N>
```

To change any default settings, press Y, and you will be given the following options:

```
Entity         Pen    Line   Pen    Entity      Pen  Line  Pen
Color          No.    Type   Speed  Color       No.  Type  Speed
1 (red)        1       0      36     9           3    0     36
2 (yellow)     2       0      36     10          4    0     36
3 (green)      3       0      36     11          5    0     36
4 (cyan)       4       0      36     12          6    0     36
5 (blue)       5       0      36     13          1    0     36
6 (magenta)    6       0      36     14          2    0     36
7 (white)      1       0      36     15          3    0     36
8 (white)      2       0      36
Line Types     0 = continuous line
               1 = ....................
               2 = — — — — —
               3 = —- —- —- —-

Do you want to change any of the above parameters ?  <n>:Y
Enter values, blank = next value, Cn = color n, S = Show
current values, X = eXit.
```

If you want to change the pens or the linetypes, you can do it now. You will notice that usually there are no cyan or magenta pens, and the pen colours you have are not the same as the on-screen colours. Your colours will be determined by the colour of the layers you have on-screen.

In order to have the on-screen reds match the on-paper reds, put the red pen in carousel 1. If you have a purple pen and want purple lines where the magenta lines are, put the purple pen in carousel 6, etc. Once done, return the carousel to the plotter. If you want all the lines to be black and you have only one black pen, make all the pen assignments read 1 and put the black pen in carousel 1.

Thick lines can also be created by placing a thicker pen in one carousel and having the layer for the thicker lines assigned to that carousel number.

When you have completed the required changes, press **X** for eXit.

```
Write the plot to a file ?<N>
Size units (Inches or Millimeters)<I>:
Plot origin in Inches <0.00, 0.00>:
Standard Values for plotting size
A      10.50  8.00
MAX    15.64  9.96
Enter size or Width, Height (in inches)<A>:
Rotate plot 0/90/180/270 <0>:
Pen width <0.010>:
Adjust area fill boundaries for pen width ?<N>:
Remove Hidden lines?<N>:
```

The following information describes the parameters for the size and origin of the plot.

`Write the plot to a file ? <N>:` This will create a .PLT file of the currently configured driver. If you want to convert graphics to word processing format, enter Yes. If you want a drawing enter No.

`Size units (Inches or Millimeters) <I>:` This will inform the plotter of the units to use, either metric or imperial.

`Plot origin in inches <0,0>:` The plot origin is always assumed to be the bottom-left corner of the paper. If you want to relocate the origin of the plot to another portion of the paper, reset this parameter. This is usually done to place a title block onto an existing drawing or to place a missing view onto an otherwise completed drawing. In fact, some skill is needed here, so it is suggested you try placing the view or plot onto a test sheet before placing it on the final paper, particularly if there are drawings existing on the paper that could be destroyed. You cannot specify a negative plot origin.

`Standard values for Plotting size <A>:` This will be set up during the software installation to agree with the available sizes of your plotter. In other words, you will not be offered the size for a very large sheet of paper if your plotter cannot handle it. The standard sizes should agree with the national standards, and there will be an option for a larger or custom size for your plot. Simply choose the letter designation in response to the plotting-size prompt.

`Rotate Plot 0/90/180/270 <0>:` This option is used for addressing printers and plotters. The default on a plotter is to have the drawing's X value perpendicular to the bar of the plotter, and the Y value parallel to the plotting bed, or as the drawing usually looks on screen. For printers, however, the X value of the drawing is the 8 ½ value of the paper, and the Y value is the 11 value of the paper. Therefore, you will probably *not* want to change this on a pen plotter, but probably will want to change this for a printout. The rotation chosen will become the default for the next plot. The final screen display before printing will tell you the size of your plotting area and will give you the option of checking the plot rotation.

`Pen Width <0.10>:` This option is available to control the density of polylines, solids, and donuts. You can adjust the width of the pen to create a denser fill, which takes more time to plot, or a less dense fill, which takes less time to plot.

`Adjust area fill boundaries for pen width?<N>:` Again, for plotting solids and polylines, you can set the fill accuracy to half the pen width specified. This is usually not necessary.

`Remove hidden lines?<N>:` If you are plotting a 3D view, this will allow you to take out the hidden lines in the same way that HIDE will take out the hidden lines. The difference is that, during the PLOT command, this takes about four times as long to do.

`Specify scale by entering:`
`Plotted Inches = Drawing Units or Fit or ?<F>:`**`1=1`** The drawing may be plotted at several different scales. If you have a drawing that can be plotted at 1 = 1, then use this, and you will get a perfect plot. If you have not scaled the drawing and you want it to fit the entire paper, use Fit.

Once all the variables have been changed, the paper size will be displayed.

```
Effective plotting area:  33.66 wide
                          23.00 high
```

This means that the X distance of the paper, as read by the plotter, is 33.66 inches, and the Y value is 23.00 inches.

```
Position paper in plotter
Press ↵ to continue
```

You can now put the paper in the printer, if you have not already done so, and start to plot.

When the plot is complete, press ↵ to continue. This will return you to either the Main menu or the file you were working with. Use VIEW and then CHART UNLOAD to remove the plot from the plotter (HP 7580B).

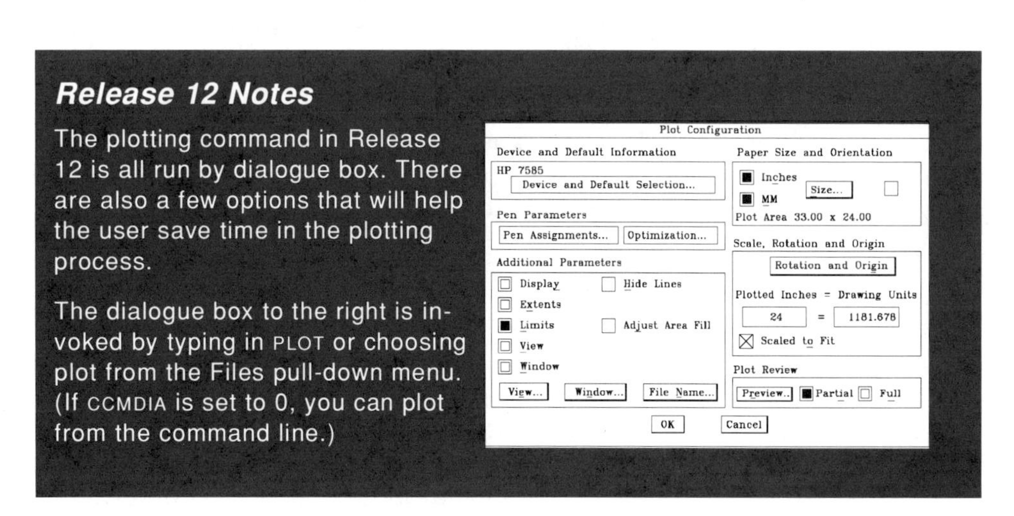

Release 12 Notes

The plotting command in Release 12 is all run by dialogue box. There are also a few options that will help the user save time in the plotting process.

The dialogue box to the right is invoked by typing in PLOT or choosing plot from the Files pull-down menu. (If CCMDIA is set to 0, you can plot from the command line.)

Release 12 Notes (cont'd)

All the options available with the plot command are found in this menu. You must access the various submenus to perform functions such as Window and File name. The advantage is that the parameters of the window picked are verified and the filenames of all plots in the directory are visible within the submenus of the plot command. As in the other pull-down menus, enhanced command transparency allows for many functions to be performed and available through a single command structure.

The real advantage of the new plot format, however, is its ability to preview the position of the plot on the paper, using the Preview option, before plotting.

PRINTING A DRAWING

Most of the same parameters apply to the print (PRPLOT) command. The printer operates by sending horizontal lines of graphics output across the page, thus the references to pen width and area fill are not necessary.

The command to create a print is PRPLOT and is found under the same menu as the PLOT command. Both of these commands can also be found under the File pull-down menu.

In 3D printing, the view in the current viewport is the one that will be chosen.

Since many people usually access the same plotters and printers, make sure the default values are those which you need; the default values of the last plot are retained.

Trouble-shooting

Be sure you have a backup copy of the file before you plot it, in case you get an error message. You must have as much memory space left on the disk as that occupied by the file you wish to plot. You cannot plot a file from a floppy disk that occupies more than ⅓ of the disk memory space.

Ideally, you should plot from a hard drive when possible, but, because of the limits of many classrooms, this is not always possible.

If your paper is regular size, e.g., B size, and cannot be adjusted to plotters, plot to a scale of .9 = 1. The gripper rollers will occupy a certain area of the paper.

Technical difficulties

Plotter maintenance is mandatory. Pens will dry out if not recapped between plots. Cap them and put them away. In addition, the pens will run out of ink and, if felt tipped, will wear down.

When making plots, remember that continuous lines improve plot speed. There is no point in having a hidden line if the LTSCALE is too small for it to be read. If the plot is taking a very long time, you may have forgotten to change the LTSCALE.

Practise at least one plot before your final project is due. Plots seldom work perfectly the first time.

When a project is due, consider the number of available plotters and the number of students who are going to need to access those plotters. Now consider the percentage of those students who are naïve enough to think they will have no problem plotting their projects, like everyone else, the day they are due. Plan your plotting time accordingly.

Exercises A11, M11, C11

STEP 1
Compile a drawing using a title block and at least two views from previous weeks. Make sure that the two views placed onto the drawing format have two different scale factors.

Check to see that the size of the text on the title block is the same as the text size on the inserted views. Make sure that both inserted views have dimensioning and that the dimension text on each individual view is the same. Use the charts provided to make sure that all text, dimensions, hatch, and linetypes are of a correct size.

Once compiled, plot the drawing.

STEP 2
Plot the final project, hand it in early, and go relax.

STEP 3
Once you are comfortable with plotting, try plotting a drawing title block or logo on an existing drawing by changing the origin of the plot.

FINAL TEST AND PROJECTS

FINAL TEST REVIEW

If you have been completing the exercises from the past 11 chapters, then you have demonstrated an ability to use AutoCAD. It is also important that you understand what you are doing to communicate this knowledge to other people and to apply it to other software systems that may be used in conjunction with AutoCAD.

The next few pages offer 99 questions on the first 11 chapters of this book. Your instructor may give you these or similar questions as a final exam. If you are not required to write a final exam, these questions are nonetheless useful to answer so that you have some idea of how much you understand.

RESEARCH PAPERS

Unless you spend 8–10 hours a day working with CAD, it will be virtually impossible for you to keep up-to-date on everything that is happening in the CAD field. There is no way a printed book can keep current because the CAD world is expanding daily.

Students can keep up-to-date by reading periodicals such as *CADalyst*, *Cadence*, *IEEE Computer Graphics*, *Computer Graphics World*, *Byte*, and *PCworld*.

Research Paper Topics

The following research topics are offered as topics that relate to CAD. If a research paper is required, the following areas of discussion should be considered: the most current news on the topic, where it can be seen or found, how it relates to AutoCAD, and where more information can be gathered.

- Graphics cards
- The importance of RAM in CAD
- Multitasking
- Windows
- Stereolithography
- GIS
- CAM
- Memory allocation
- Customization
- Screens
- Scanning
- Shading

FINAL TEST

INTRODUCTION TO AUTOCAD

Please circle the response that is the *most* correct. You will have 55 minutes for this exam.

1. Who makes the AutoCAD software?
   a) AutoCAD
   b) AutoDESK
   c) AutoSHADE

2. What do you call the section of the screen that tells you if ORTHO is on, what your coordinates are, etc.?
   a) response area
   b) status line
   c) pull-down menus

3. What function key do you use to see your position with relation to the origin?
   a) F7
   b) F8
   c) F6

4. What function sets your point picks to a preset integer?
   a) GRID
   b) SNAP
   c) LIMITS

5. How would you draw a line of 3 units in length at 45 degrees?
   a) @3<45
   b) @3>45
   c) @45<3

6. What do you call the process of entering coordinates relative to each other?
   a) integral
   b) polar
   c) incremental

7. What does F7 do?
   a) Tablet on/off
   b) SNAP on/off
   c) GRID on/off

8. What does the C stand for in the CIRCLE command?
   a) Center
   b) Close
   c) Clip

9. What does the C stand for in the ZOOM command?
   a) Clip
   b) Centre
   c) Cut

10. What does the R stand for in the ERASE command?
    a) Replace
    b) Remove
    c) Restore

11. How do you cancel a command?
    a) QUIT
    b) ESC
    c) CTRL-C

12. How do you change the screen format to alphanumeric?
    a) F1
    b) HELP
    c) LIST
    d) all of the above

13. How do you edit a polyline?
    a) CHANGE
    b) PEDIT
    c) EDIT

14. How do you get a fully solid circle?
    a) SOLID
    b) FILLET Rad 0
    c) DONUT

15. Can you change the grid size once the drawing has started?
    a) yes
    b) no
    c) sometimes

16. Can you use the cursor to pick the points for the bottom-left and top-right of your limits?
    a) yes
    b) no

17. Can you turn the limits off?
    a) yes
    b) no
    c) sometimes

18. Does a ZOOM ALL affect the size of your limits?
    a) yes
    b) no
    c) sometimes

19. What does U ↵ do?
    a) erases the last line
    b) edits the last erase
    c) undoes the last command

20. What can you use to reference particular portions of or positions on existing objects?
    a) a different aperture size
    b) OSNAP
    c) LISP routines
    d) all of the above

21. What does the L option stand for in the Select Objects: prompt?
    a) LINE
    b) Last
    c) Lost

22. What command places multiple copies of objects in patterns that are either polar or rectangular?
    a) ROTATE
    b) ARRAY
    c) TWIST

23. What does the F stand for in BREAK?
    a) First point
    b) Freeze
    c) Find

24. How do you make many copies of an item at random placing?
    a) COPY Multiple
    b) ARRAY
    c) ROTATE

25. EXTEND helps you to elongate items to reach what?
    a) a boundary
    b) a cutting line
    c) a corner

26. What do you need to create an OFFSET?
    a) an object, a distance, and a side to offset
    b) an object, a cutting line, and an edge
    c) an object, a centre point, and an edge

27. What command allows you to break off and delete any overhangings beyond a cutting edge that you specify?
    a) TRIM
    b) BREAK
    c) EXTEND

28. How do you check what an editing command requires of you?
    a) read the manual
    b) read the HELP files
    c) read the prompts

29. Under what circumstances does the cursor turn into a box?
    a) when the zoom factor is too low
    b) when an item selection is needed
    c) when a prompt is missing

30. Can you use incremental values (@3,4) in the MOVE command?
    a) yes
    b) no

31. What two commands may automatically do a REGEN on a file?
    a) ZOOM and PAN
    b) DISPLAY and EDIT
    c) MOVE and BREAK

32. What do the angle brackets (< >) in a command string indicate?
    a) a default value
    b) a preset integer
    c) the suggested size

33. How can you get out of the HELP files?
    a) QUIT
    b) CTRL-C F1
    c) END

34. How can you get out of the OSNAP mode?
    a) OSNAP END
    b) OSNAP OFF

35. What does the DOS command SHELL allow you to do?
    a) exit AutoCAD into DOS
    b) exit DOS into AutoCAD
    c) end the file

36. What does .$A stand for?
    a) a temporary file
    b) a backup file
    c) an erased file
    d) all of the above

37. Can you change the width of a pline once it has been entered?
    a) yes
    b) no
    c) sometimes

38. Must your mirroring line in the MIRROR command always be part of the object?
    a) yes
    b) no
    c) sometimes

39. What happens if you enter UNDO 5?
    a) the last five erases will be undone
    b) the last five commands will be undone
    c) the last five lines will be undone

40. How do you check your disk for bad clusters?
    a) CHKCST A:/4
    b) CHKDSK A:/f
    c) FORMAT A:/4

41. In the FILE A:AC$EF.$A, what does the A: stand for?
    a) the drive
    b) the directory
    c) the extension

42. In DOS, what command do you use to get a listing of your files on the A drive?
    a) DIR A:
    b) LIST A:
    c) UTILITY A:

43. In DOS, how would you copy a drawing file on the A drive to a drawing file on the B drive?
    a) COPY A:NAME.BAK B:NAME.DWG
    b) COPY A:NAME.DWG B:NAME.DWG
    c) COPY B:NAME.DWG A:NAME.DWG

44. How would you erase a drawing file from your disk?
    a) ERASE a:*.DWG
    b) ERASE a:NAME.DWG
    c) ERASE A:*.*
    d) none of the above

45. Why is it important not to remove your disk from the drive while you are in AutoCAD?
    a) you may lose the address of the temporary file
    b) you may insert the wrong diskette later
    c) the RAM will not be able to retrieve the file

46. Why is DISKCOPY an incorrect command when you have a 360K floppy in the A drive and a 1.2MB floppy in the B drive?
    a) because the files will be stretched to fit the larger format
    b) because the DISKCOPY command reformats the target disk
    c) because you cannot use two different sizes of floppy diskettes

47. Is the system you are currently using on a network?
    a) yes
    b) no
    c) sometimes

48. When using the STRETCH command, what is the system automatically set to if you pick the command from the screen menu?
    a) Crossing
    b) Window
    c) Last
    d) none of the above

49. If you stretch a circle, does it turn into an ellipse?
    a) yes
    b) no
    c) only with ORTHO on

50. If you change the rotation of the grid and Snap, does the Ortho rotate as well?
    a) yes
    b) no

51. How would you determine the layer of an object?
    a) Undo
    b) LIST
    c) CHPROP

52. Why must you press ↵ once you have selected all of the objects you need?
    a) to signal the end of the object selection
    b) to exit OSNAP
    c) to reset the cursor

53. If you have selected a Window full of objects for editing, but one item was picked up that you do not want to edit, how would you release it from the list?
    a) Release
    b) Remove
    c) Undo

54. If you have an item in one layer, but you want it to be on another layer, how can you alter it?
    a) CHPROP
    b) LIST
    c) DDLMODES
    d) any of the above

55. Do you need to use ? in the LAYER command if you are using DDLMODE?
    a) yes
    b) no
    c) sometimes

56. How do you change the spelling of a layer name once entered?
    a) type over the original in DDLMODE
    b) PURGE and re-enter
    c) turn the layer off, then re-enter
    d) all of the above

57. Can you delete a layer once it is created?
    a) not if there are objects in it
    b) if it is empty, you can PURGE it
    c) not while it is current
    d) all of the above

58. Of what use is OK within the layer format?
    a) to exit DDLMODE
    b) to unfreeze layers
    c) to change colours

59. What wildcard can you use to load all the linetypes?
    a) CTRL-F1
    b) *
    c) ?

60. If you have a set linetype, will this override your current layer linetype?
    a) yes
    b) no
    c) sometimes

61. What is the default setting for the COLOR command?
    a) Black
    b) White
    c) Red

62. Is the number of colours displayed a software or hardware question?
    a) hardware
    b) software

63. How do you change the size of the dashes in your hidden line display?
    a) LINETYPE
    b) LTSCALE
    c) DIM VAR

64. When you select the DIM: option on the side menu, what happens to the screen?
    a) the screen switches to alphanumeric
    b) the prompt changes
    c) the lines change

65. To what discipline are the default settings of the dimensioning commands set?
    a) Mechanical
    b) Architectural
    c) Civil

66. If you want to change any of the dimensioning default settings, what do you need to access?
    a) SET VAR
    b) DIM VAR
    c) UNITS

67. How do you use different text fonts in the dimension text area?
    a) set the new font before creating the dimensions
    b) set a new font then use UPD
    c) either of the above

68. What command do you use to make an image appear at 70% of its current size for purposes of dimensioning?
    a) SCALE .7
    b) ZOOM .7X
    c) ZOOM 70

69. What do you use if you only want to add one dimension?
    a) DIM1
    b) DIM CTRL-C
    c) 1DIM

70. What command do you use if you have changed the unit display and want to have your existing dimensions revised according to the current setting?
    a) DIMALT
    b) DIMUNIT
    c) UPD

71. Why does text already entered become highlighted when the command TEXT is re-entered?
    a) in case you want to replace it
    b) to show you where to place the next paragraph
    c) to show you the text default positioning

72. What is the purpose of QTEXT?
    a) QTEXT allows you to enter the text more quickly
    b) QTEXT allows for quicker regens
    c) QTEXT allows you to read the text as it is being entered

73. Can you pick the height with your cursor when entering text, or do you need to use a numeric entry?
    a) a numeric entry is needed
    b) both cursor and numeric entries are allowed
    c) only a numeric entry is allowed

74. When will the TEXT command not offer you a height option?
    a) when you have changed the aspect ratio in Style
    b) when you have used your cursor to pick the first height
    c) when you are using QTEXT

75. What command do you use to change the type of letters to use?
    a) Load with TEXT
    b) Style or Font options
    c) DTEXT

76. What does an obliquing angle do?
    a) sets the angle of a string of text
    b) sets the angle of a character
    c) makes lines oblique

77. What command would you use (besides ERASE) to alter the spelling within a text string?
    a) CHPROP
    b) UPD
    c) CHANGE
    d) all of the above

78. Name two ways of repositioning text once entered.
    a) MOVE and CHANGE
    b) MOVE and COPY
    c) COPY and CHPROP

79. Which of these lettering styles takes up the most room on the disk?
    a) Gothic English
    b) Roman Simplex
    c) Monotxt

80. How do you change the aspect ratio of your lettering?
    a) DIMALT
    b) CHANGE
    c) change the height in the Style option

81. What is the most important factor to consider when entering a hatch?
    a) scale
    b) angle
    c) size

82. Which standard are the hatch patterns derived from?
    a) ASCII
    b) ANSI
    c) CSA

83. How can you get a screen display of the available hatch patterns?
    a) use the pull-down menus
    b) type HATCHSTYLE
    c) both of the above

84. How can you get a listing of the hatch names?
    a) use HATCHSTYLE
    b) use HATCH?
    c) use the pull-down menus

85. If you are using a user-defined hatch pattern, what will it be made up of?
    a) lines
    b) lines and points
    c) lines and circles

86. What does the hatch need to fit into?
    a) an existing entity
    b) an open polygon
    c) a closed boundary

87. What must you do if you have been silly enough to crash your disk by not putting a hatch in properly?
    a) use CHKDSK to see if there are any lost clusters
    b) reformat your disk
    c) erase the backup

88. Once your hatches are in, how can you get them off the screen so REDRAW will not take so long?
    a) BLOCK them
    b) turn the hatch layer off
    c) Freeze the hatch layer

89. If you move the boundary of the hatch, does the hatch go with it?
    a) no
    b) yes

90. Can you stretch a hatch?
    a) no
    b) yes

91. What is an internal block?
    a) a block that is part of an existing file
    b) a block that exists on a floppy disk as a .DWG file
    c) a block that is contained within another block

92. What symbol can you use to have a wblock placed on a file as separate entities?
    a) ^
    b) *
    c) #

93. How do you insert a wblock?
    a) WBLOCK
    b) BLOCK
    c) INSERT

94. How do you modify an entity on the block once it has been entered?
    a) CHANGE the entity
    b) EDIT the entity
    c) EXPLODE the block

95. With what command do you erase wblocks from your file that are not part of the file but only part of the memory?
    a) DBLIST
    b) ERASE in DOS
    c) PURGE

96. Under what condition can you not SCALE a wblock instance?
    a) if the aspect ratio is changed
    b) if the entities have been changed
    c) if the object was inserted with MINSERT
    d) both a) and c)

97. What happens to the LTSCALE of your wblock instance when it is inserted onto another drawing?
    a) it takes the LTSCALE of the original drawing
    b) it takes the LTSCALE of the current drawing

98. How can you get object lines on a plot thicker than dimension lines without using pline?
    a) change the pens so that one is thicker
    b) change the DIMLIN and UPD
    c) change the LTSCALE

99. How do you change the units of a model currently in architectural units to mechanical units?
    a) change the UNITS
    b) change the DIMALT
    c) change the drawing size

FINAL PROJECT

A final project is important to the student for the following reasons:

- Thinking your way through a two-hour exercise is very different from thinking your way through a 12-hour project.
- It will give you some experience in file management. *Back up your files every hour*. If you do not remember how to do this, refer to Chapter 4. If you lose your files, it is your fault.
- It will provide you with material to demonstrate your capabilities during a job interview.
- There are many commands you have tried in one or two capacities. This project will give you an opportunity to try other variations of known commands.

These projects may be started at Chapters 7 or 8 and are to be submitted in the final week of the term, depending on open access time.

The projects will be marked on the following criteria:

LINES must be straight, no spaces, no overlaps
CIRCLES AND ARCS must join properly to objects
PLINES must have good corners and be consistent
LAYERS at least three with different colours
TEXT at least three types of fonts
HATCHES must have no glitches
DIMENSIONS must be realistic, accurate, legible, and conform to your own discipline

These projects will give you an idea of the size of the project that can be expected to be completed within 12 hours. If you would prefer to do a project that is more relevant to your own course of study or that reflects a project that you are working on, that should be acceptable also.

The final project, to be suitable both for assessment by an instructor and for a job search portfolio, should contain all of the elements in the first 11 chapters.

While completing your project, consider project management as well. Address the following questions before you start, and you will find the completion of the project much easier.

1. What kinds of layers will be needed and will the same layers be useful on other views?
2. How many wblocks will be needed and where will they be stored?
3. What will be the final drawing size and how many different drawing scales will be needed?
4. How many colours will be needed?

Architectural Final

ELEVATION

Create at least one elevation and two floor plans of a residence.

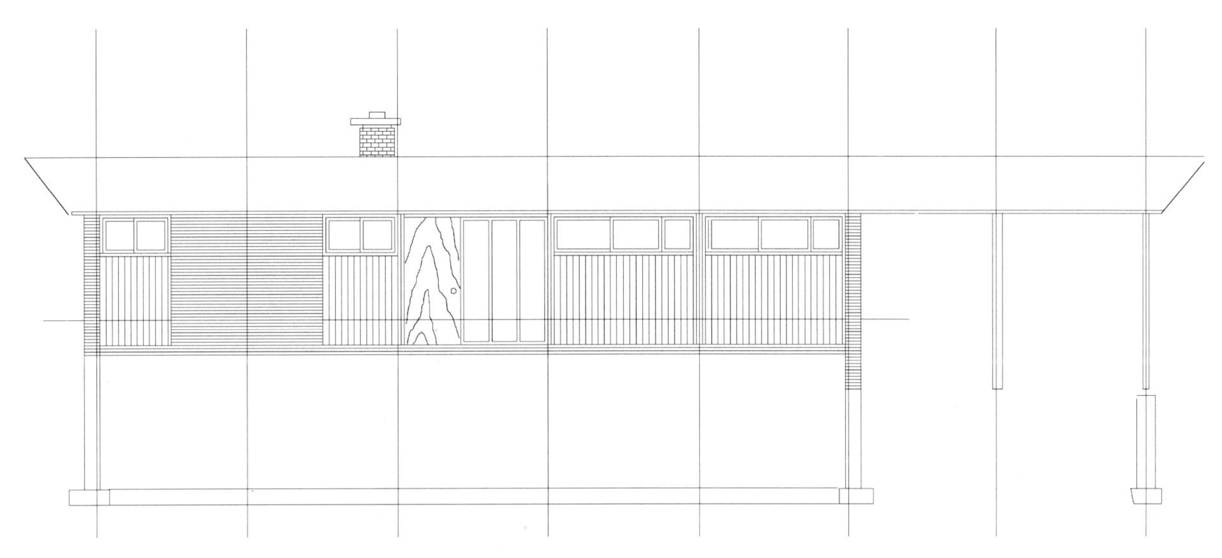

Place all three views plus a North arrow on an acceptable title. Be sure you have:

- Underlined view titles
- Scales
- Title block filled in

Architectural Final (continued)

FLOOR PLANS

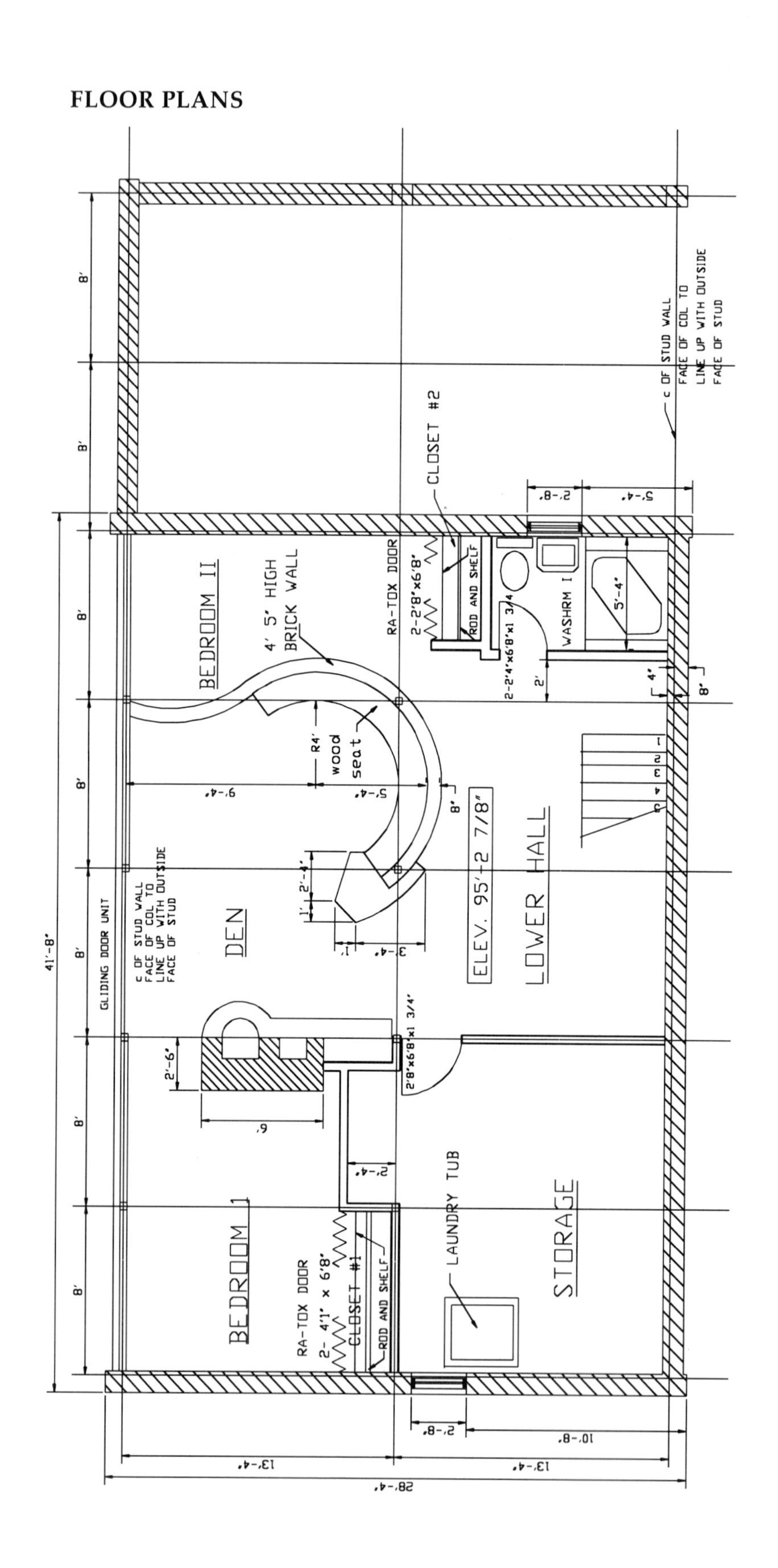

Architectural Final (continued)

FLOOR PLAN – UPPER GRADE

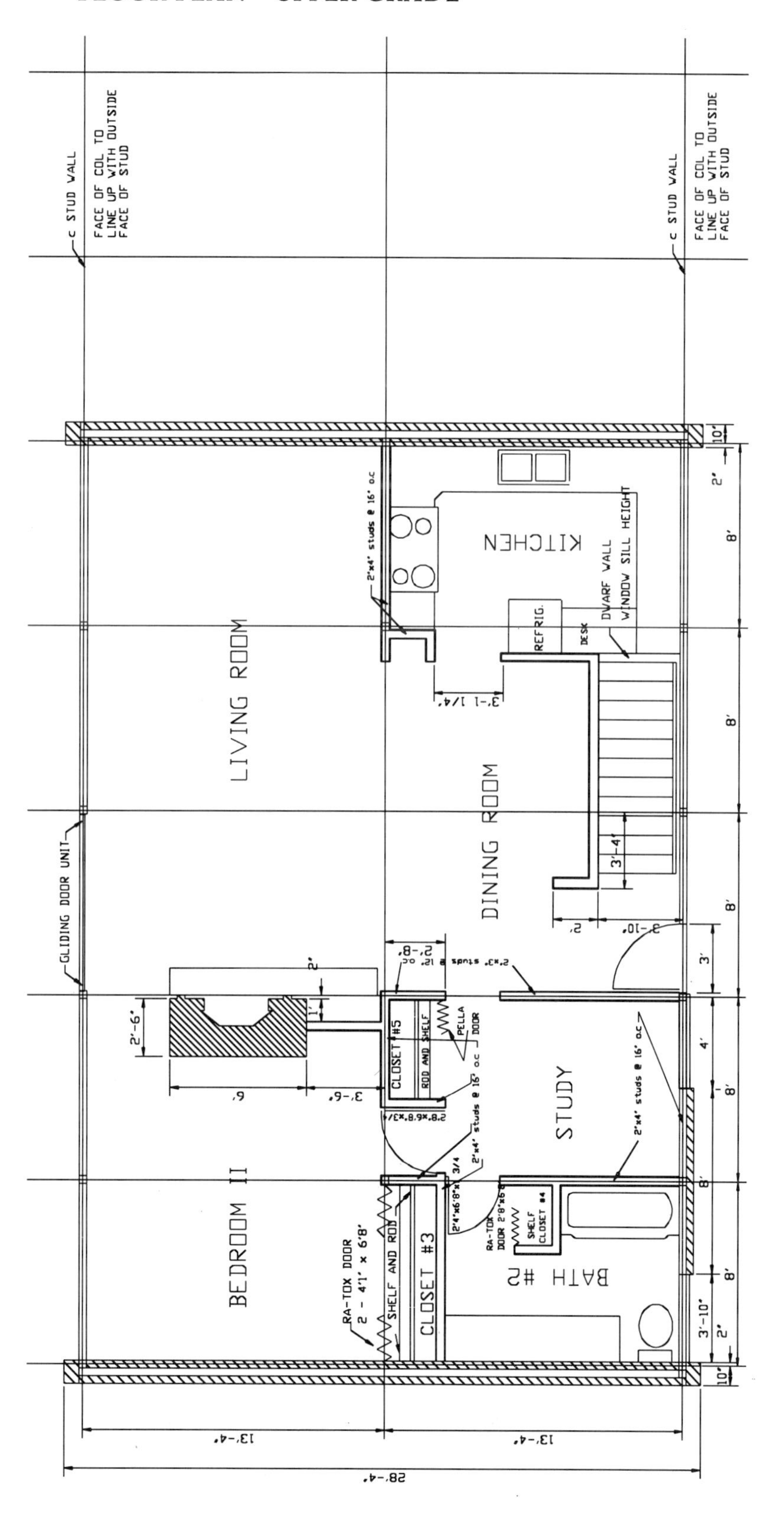

Mechanical Final

Create this model or one of similar difficulty.

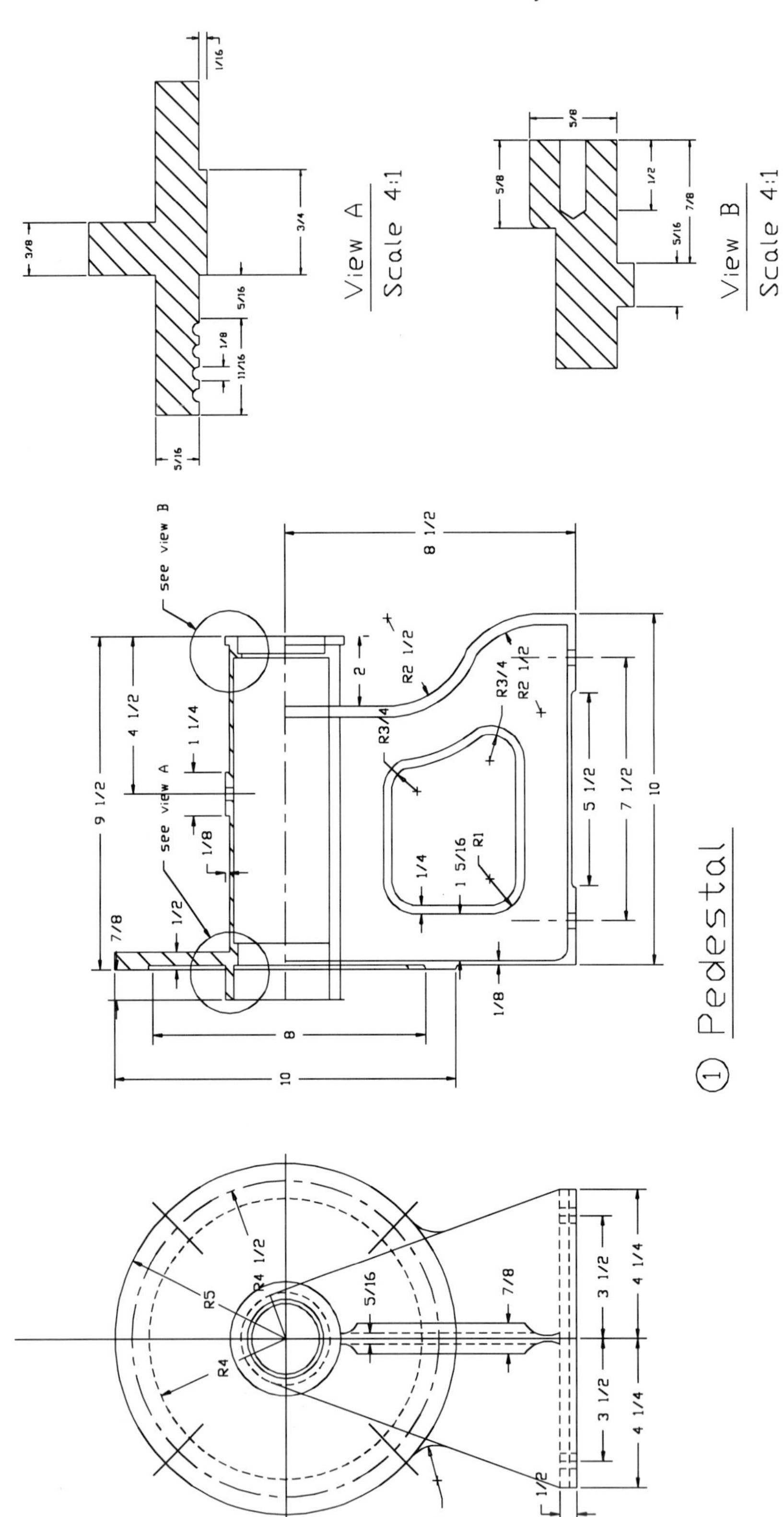

Mechanical Final (continued)

Create each view as a separate file, then INSERT them once fully dimensioned onto the final drawing.

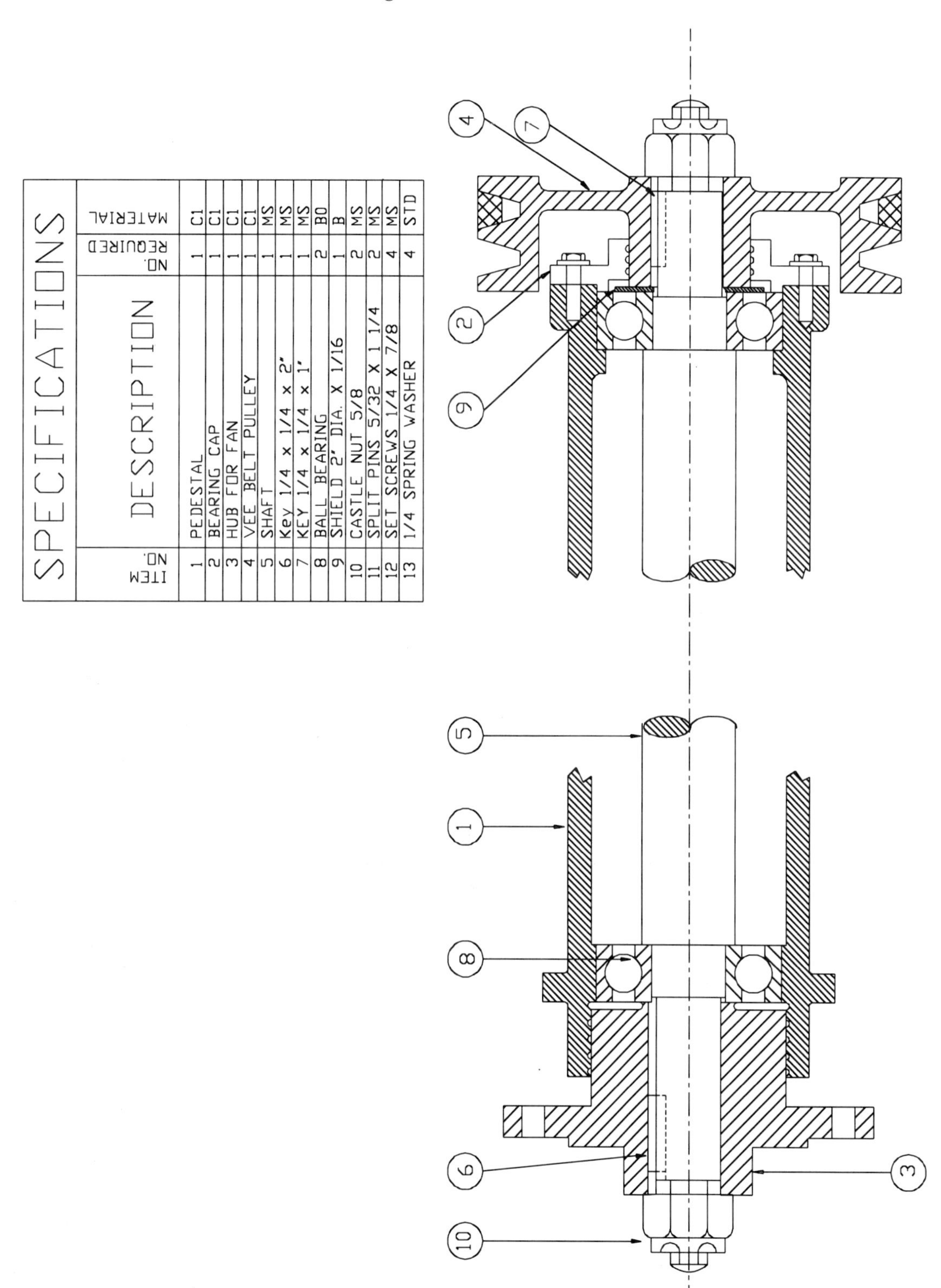

SPECIFICATIONS

ITEM NO.	DESCRIPTION	NO. REQUIRED	MATERIAL
1	PEDESTAL	1	CI
2	BEARING CAP	1	CI
3	HUB FOR FAN	1	CI
4	VEE BELT PULLEY	1	CI
5	SHAFT	1	MS
6	Key 1/4 x 1/4 x 2"	1	MS
7	KEY 1/4 x 1/4 x 1"	1	MS
8	BALL BEARING	2	BO
9	SHIELD 2" DIA. X 1/16	1	B
10	CASTLE NUT 5/8	2	MS
11	SPLIT PINS 5/32 X 1 1/4	2	MS
12	SET SCREWS 1/4 X 7/8	4	MS
13	1/4 SPRING WASHER	4	STD

Mechanical Final (continued)

PEDESTAL AND BEARING DETAILS FOR FANDRIVE

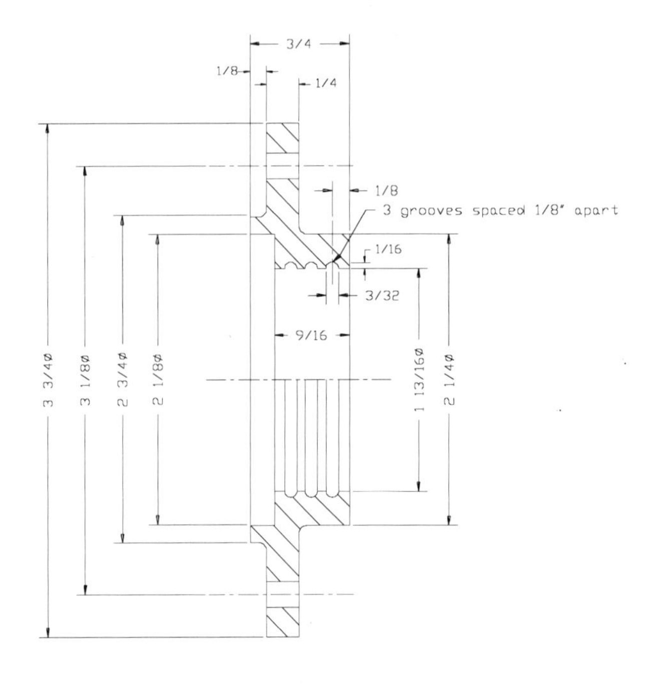

Bearing Cap Detail

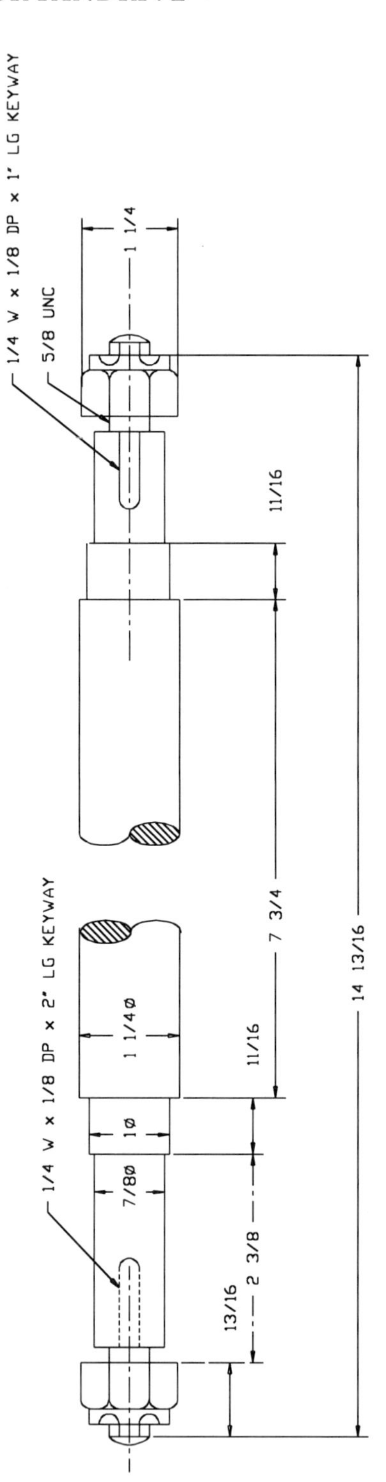

Be sure each separate part is dimensioned so that the final dimensions will be the same scale on the final drawing.

When inserting the titles and title blocks, be sure the text sizes will be the same.

While this is not necessarily a high technology part, it demonstrates every aspect of the AutoCAD commands that are described in the first 11 chapters.

Civil Final

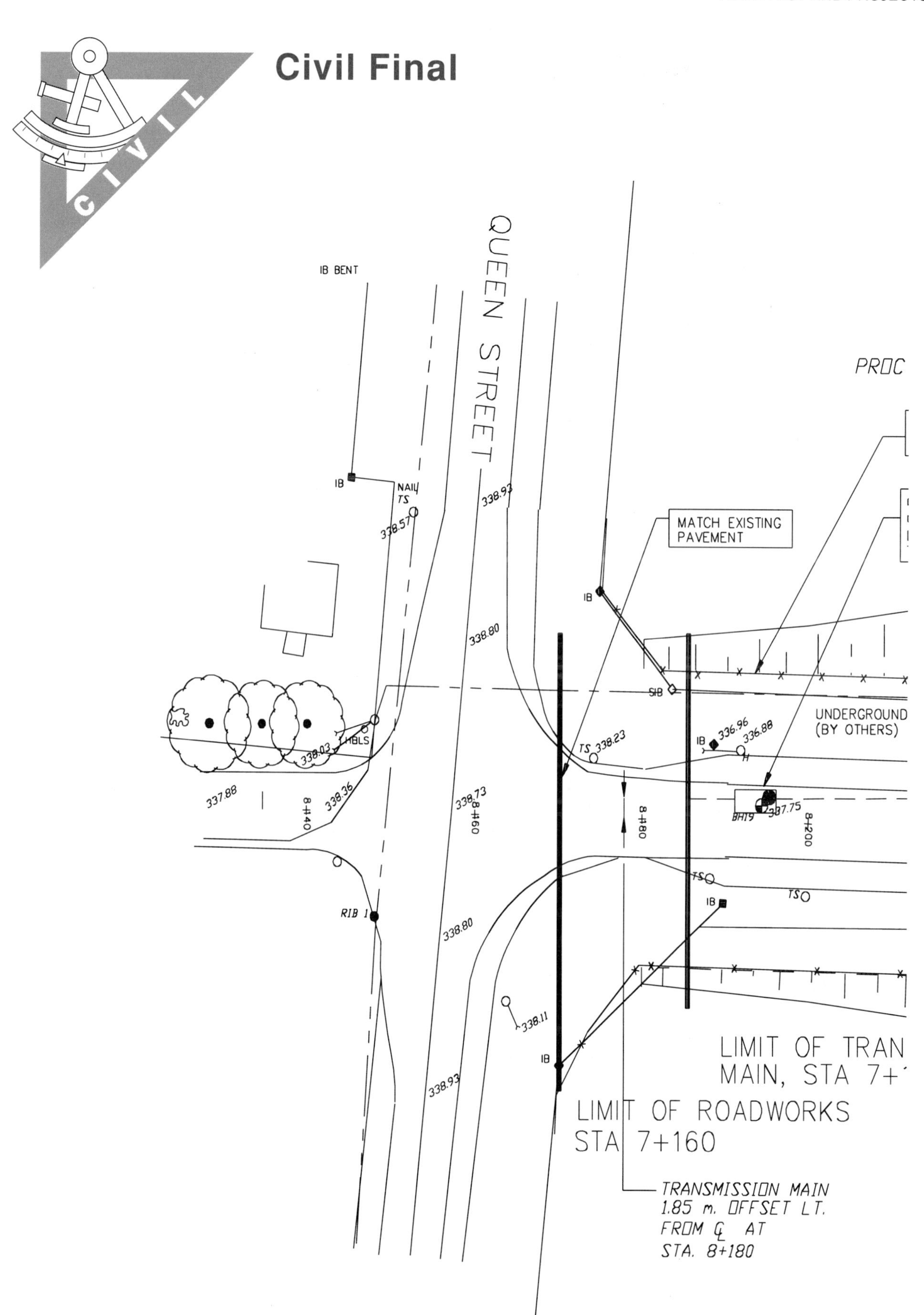
CIVIL
QUEEN STREET
IB BENT
IB
NAIL
TS
338.57
338.93
MATCH EXISTING
PAVEMENT
PROC
IB
338.80
SIB
UNDERGROUND
(BY OTHERS)
IB
336.96
336.88
TS 338.23
338.03
HBLS
337.88
338.36
8+140
338.73
8+160
8+180
BH19
337.75
8+200
TS
TS
IB
RIB 1
338.80
338.11
IB
338.93
LIMIT OF TRAN
MAIN, STA 7+
LIMIT OF ROADWORKS
STA 7+160
TRANSMISSION MAIN
1.85 m. OFFSET LT.
FROM ℄ AT
STA. 8+180

Civil Final (continued)

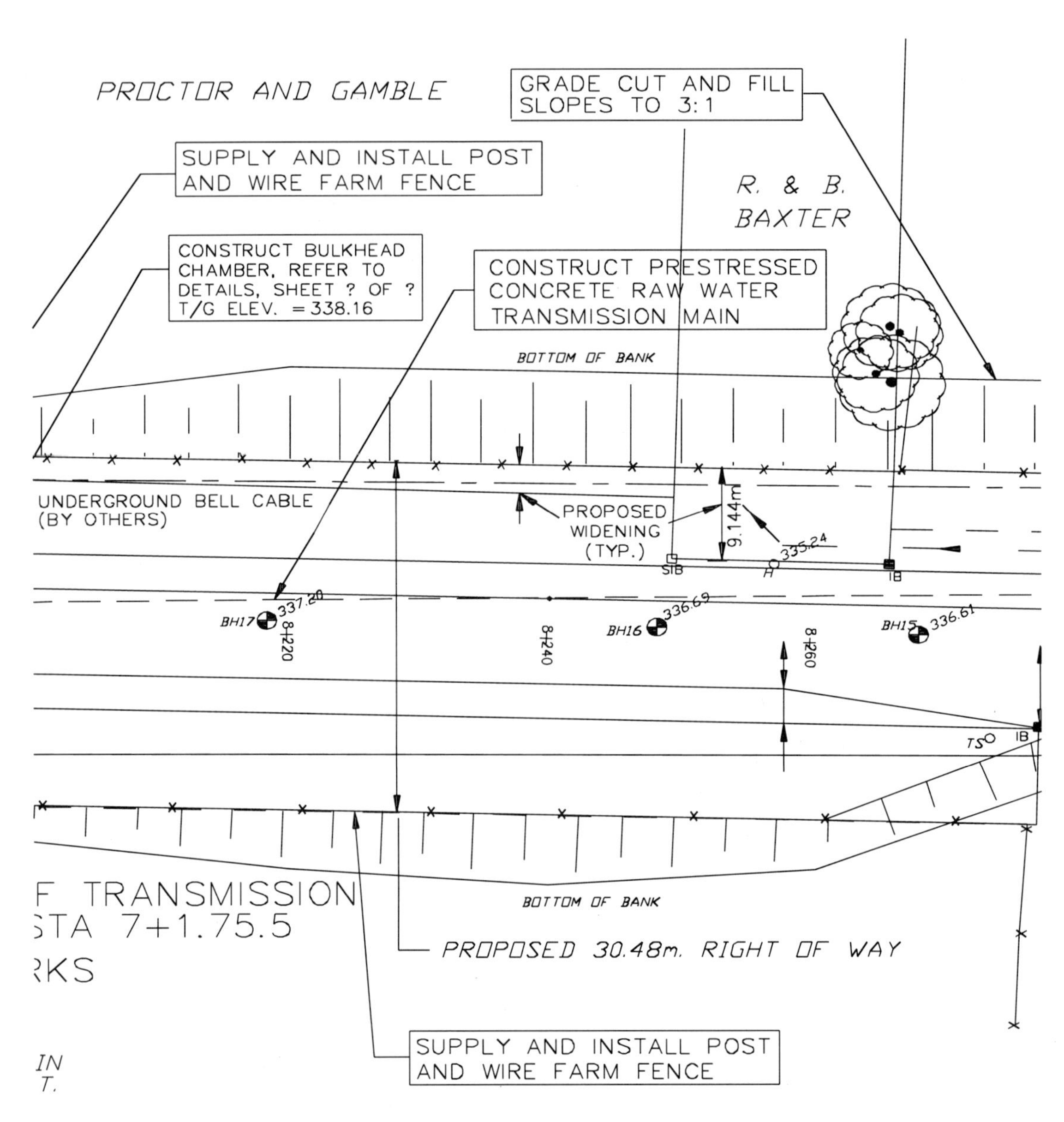
PROCTOR AND GAMBLE
GRADE CUT AND FILL SLOPES TO 3:1
SUPPLY AND INSTALL POST AND WIRE FARM FENCE
R. & B. BAXTER
CONSTRUCT BULKHEAD CHAMBER, REFER TO DETAILS, SHEET ? OF ? T/G ELEV. =338.16
CONSTRUCT PRESTRESSED CONCRETE RAW WATER TRANSMISSION MAIN
BOTTOM OF BANK
UNDERGROUND BELL CABLE (BY OTHERS)
PROPOSED WIDENING (TYP.)
9.144m
335.24
SIB
H
IB
BH17
337.20
8+220
8+240
BH16
336.69
8+260
BH15
336.61
TS
IB
BOTTOM OF BANK
F TRANSMISSION
STA 7+1.75.5
RKS
PROPOSED 30.48m. RIGHT OF WAY
SUPPLY AND INSTALL POST AND WIRE FARM FENCE
IN
T.
R. MACLEOD

Electrical Final

Create this or a similar schematic.

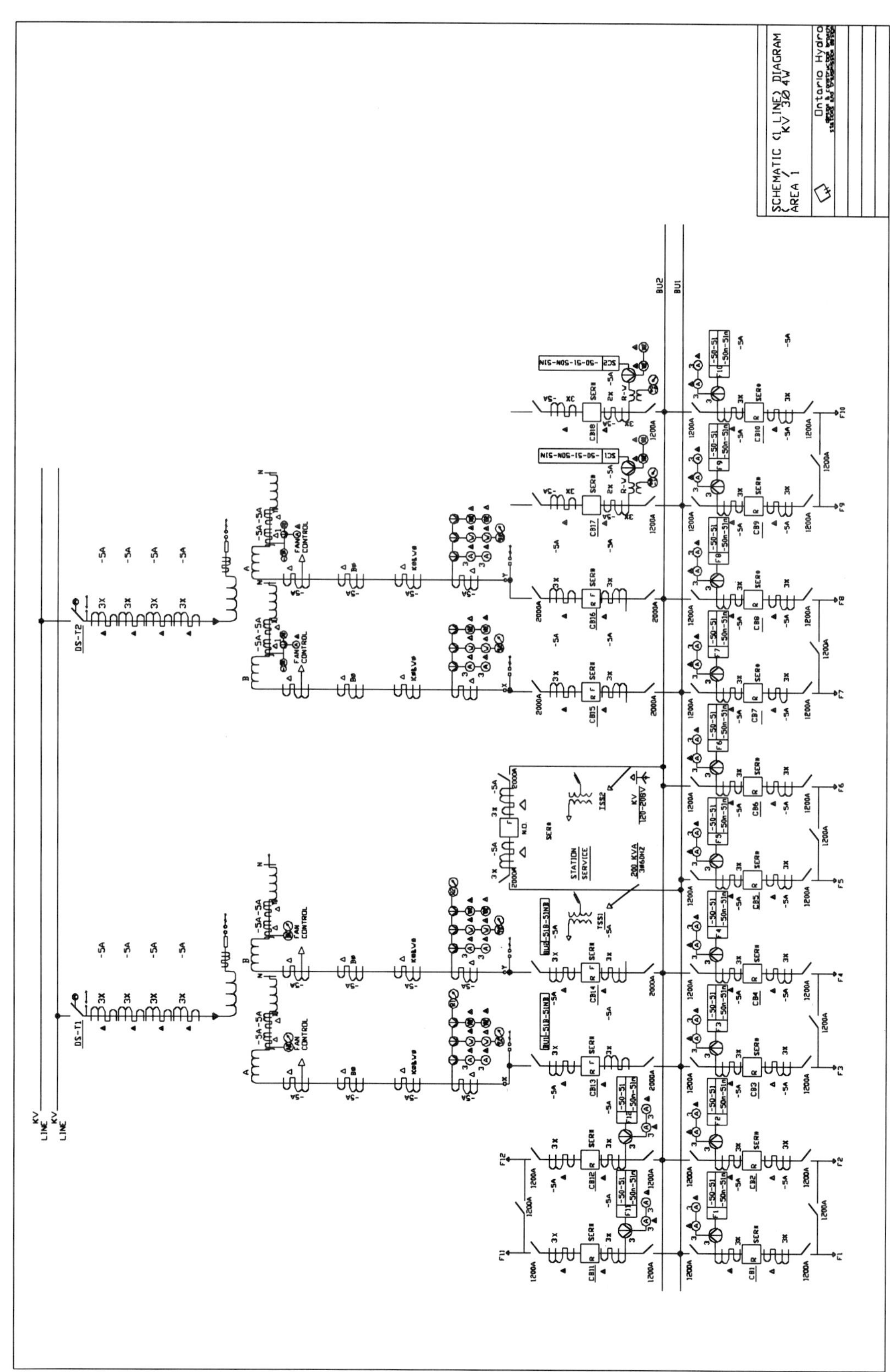

DEFINING ATTRIBUTES

Upon completion of this chapter, the student should be able to:

1. Define a series of attributes
2. Block the attributes
3. Insert the attributes onto a drawing
4. Use the attribute dialogue box (ATTDIA)
5. Edit the attribute definitions (ATTDEF)

NON-GRAPHIC INTELLIGENCE

The AutoCAD system allows you to create geometry for a variety of purposes, including production, creating drawings, and developing data for sales and marketing. In addition, AutoCAD and many other programs allow for the generation of non-graphic information that can be accessed in the form of bills of materials, schedules, and other data that is cross-referenced on the drawing. This data is not necessarily displayed on the drawing, but is filed with the drawing. This non-graphic intelligence is called an attribute. Some typical examples are:

Parts
You can create attributes to access part numbers and create a Bill of Materials.

Houses
You can create attributes for the colour and size of rooms or related data; they can later be downloaded onto estimating or specifications sheets.

Surveys
You can create attributes for lot and house numbers, services, and other necessary data.

Offices
You can create attributes for office layouts so that each piece of office equipment and workstation configuration is assigned to a specific individual.

Attributes can also be used to generate templates for fill-in-the-blank situations such as on drawing notations and title blocks.

In the last chapter, we learned how to block information and add it to the drawing currently in use. For example, you can add a title block from your database to the current drawing. If the title block has associated attributes, you will be prompted during the INSERT command to fill in the blanks of the title block — name, date, etc. — while inserting it.

When you define an attribute, you are creating a program to prompt the user for data. You decide what the user must enter by creating the prompts for the entry of data.

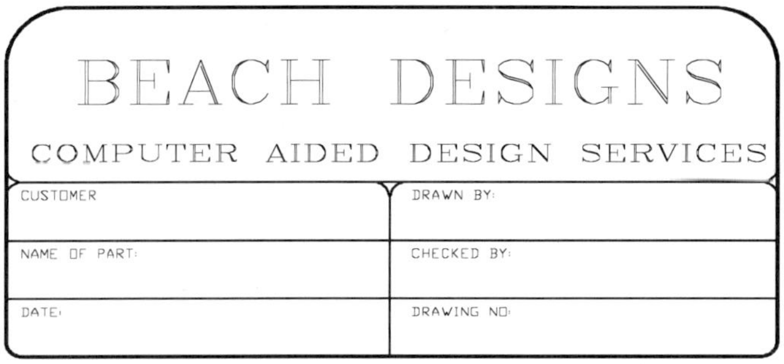

BEACH DESIGNS
COMPUTER AIDED DESIGN SERVICES
CUSTOMER
DRAWN BY:
NAME OF PART:
CHECKED BY:
DATE:
DRAWING NO:

Figure 13-1. A block without attributes

In the example of Figure 13-1, the title block and headings for the title block are created using the PLINE and TEXT commands. This title block can be used over and over again because this information does not change.

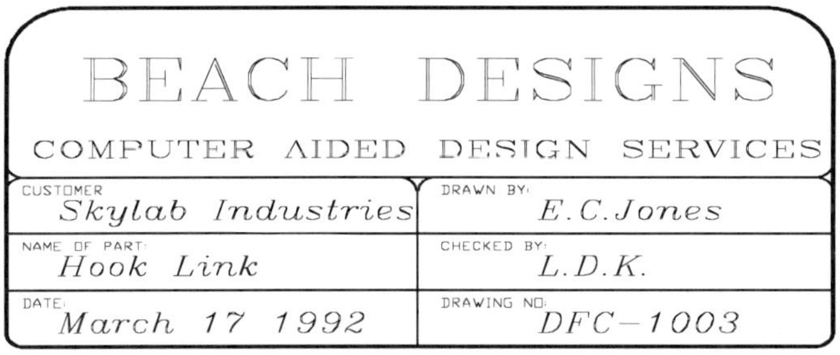

BEACH DESIGNS
COMPUTER AIDED DESIGN SERVICES
CUSTOMER
Skylab Industries
DRAWN BY:
E.C.Jones
NAME OF PART:
Hook Link
CHECKED BY:
L.D.K.
DATE:
March 17 1992
DRAWING NO:
DFC-1003

Figure 13-2. A block with attributes

In the example of Figure 13-2, the information concerning one drawing in particular has been added using attributes. The INSERT command is used to insert the title block, and once the size and rotation have been determined, it prompts for all the necessary information.

All the sizes for the inserted text are determined at the time the attribute is defined and blocked, as is the placement of the text and the lettering font. All the user needs to do is add the missing information for the customer, name of part, date, name of designer, etc.

If you had just inserted this title block, the INSERT command would look like this:

```
Command:INSERT
Block name (or ?):Titleblock
Insertion point:0,0
X scale factor <1>/ Corner/XYZ:↵
Y scale factor (default = X):↵
Rotation angle <0>:↵
Customer <Skylab Industries>:↵
Name of Part <>:Hook Link
Date Month/dd/yy<>:March 17 1992
Drawn by <E.C.Jones>:↵
Checked by:L.D.K.
Drawing no. DFC-####<>:DFC-1003
```

All the prompts — customer, name of part, etc. — were created by the designer who defined the attribute. The defaults in the angle brackets (<>) were also created by the same designer. Some responses offer default values, which are accepted by using ↵, others have no default because they would never be the same. In the case of the drawing designer, this is E.C. Jones's title block, so he may accept the default by using ↵, but any other designer would have to use his or her own name.

In some cases, the prompt also contains information concerning the format of the output; for example, the date **Month dd yy**. In the case of the date, you know that the accepted format is to have the month written out, then the day, then the year. Again, all the prompt information is determined by the designer.

The title block example demonstrates how attributes are used to speed up the entry of data onto a standard part or into a standard format. Later in this chapter, we will see how attributes can also be used to list information relative to specific portions of a drawing. First, we will take a look at how to create attributes.

CREATING ATTRIBUTES

Attributes are always associated with blocks. To create an attributed block, first create the geometry for the final block, if there is any, then add the attributes.

ATTDEF is the command used to create the attribute definition. It enters the data you want to be associated with each block, thus making it an attributed block. You can add attributes to existing blocks by using ATTDEF and then reblocking the block.

Once the attributed block is inserted, it acts as a complete and separate object with both the attribute text and any graphics. If this block is erased, all of the attribute information is erased as well.

ATTDEF *defines how the attributes will be stored.*

ATTDISP *controls the display of items.*

Prior to creating an attributed block, it is a good idea to think through the information you are likely to need. How much is needed and where? A bit of forethought can save you hours of editing. Decide on the final product and work back from there.

For example, if you are making a title block, this is simply a fill-in-the-blank application. You need to decide the format of the user responses, the size of the lettering, the lettering style, and the point at which text will be inserted. Make sure you have left enough room for all the characters likely to be added to this block.

In the example below, the user is creating a chair with attributes describing the supplier, the colour, the style number, and the price. The following command will create an attribute definition that will prompt the user for the name of the supplier.

Example: *ATTDEF*

Command:**ATTDEF**

Attribute modes – Invisible-N, Constant-N, Verify-N, Preset-N

Enter (ICVP) to change, RETURN when done:↵

Attribute tag:**Supplier** *(summarizes the attribute)*

Attribute prompt:**Supplier Name** *(If there is anything else that needs to be added to the prompt, such as location, do so at this point. If you do not add a prompt, the tag will be the default prompt.)*

`Default attribute value:`**`Krug Furniture, Kitchener`** *(This offers the user the default of this one particular company. If the user is working with one firm in particular, then it is a good idea to have a default. If not, then none is needed.)*

`Justify/Style/<Start point>:`**`J`** *(as in the TEXT command)*

`Align/Center/Fit/Middle/Right/TL/TC/TR/ML/MC/MR/BL/BC/BR:`**`M`**

`Middle point:` *(pick a point)*

`Height <5.0000>:`**`2`** *(This sets the size of lettering. Make sure this is both logical and readable.)*

`Rotation angle:`↵

The attribute has now been added at the spot designated by picking a point. Notice that what you now see is the tag. You can create more attributes, which will be added to this one to create the attributed block.

Attribute Modes

The first option in the command is the mode. These can be set as follows to make attributed block insertion easier:

Invisible
Hides data associated with a block that does not need to be seen; for example, on a desk layout you may want to have the name of the current occupant for reference; but if providing specs for a decorator, this is not necessary.

Constant
Makes an attribute uneditable; for example, the president's desk is always the president's desk; but the president may change.

Verify
Allows you to take a final look at what you have entered prior to having it added to the drawing.

Preset
Is used when creating attributes that will always have the same value. This lets you insert a block that has an attribute or a set of attributes automatically attached to it. No user response is needed because the attribute never changes. An example of this would be a part that would always have the same order number. The number would be inserted with the attribute, but the user would not be prompted for any change.

Attribute Display

The modes are useful while creating blocks and can increase your efficiency while entering data. Once in, however, you may want to change the display. If this is the case, use ATTDISP. ATTDISP overrides the above modes.

```
Command:ATTDISP
Normal/On/Off<current value>:
```

Where:
On = all attributes visible

Off = all attributes invisible

Normal = normal visibility set individually

BLOCKING ATTRIBUTES

Once the attributes are defined, block the information in the order you want the prompts to appear by picking each attribute. You can use a Window, but this will not always be easy to use, depending on where the Window starts.

The attributes are now ready to use. Remember that the attributed block will disappear once it is blocked. Insert the attributed block and check that you have specified the proper size of lettering and that prompts are clear. A good way of checking it is to have a fellow student insert the block and fill in the details of the attributes without your help. If he or she has any problem understanding the prompts, go back and edit them.

Attributes can be used with both the BLOCK and the WBLOCK commands.

EDITING ATTRIBUTE DEFINITIONS

If you have created an attributed block and notice any errors in the definition, you can change the ATTDEF and then reblock it. This will not change the *value* of the attribute, but will change the *definition* of the attribute.

First explode the block. Once inserted, the block will contain the values for each attribute in that particular instance or application. When you explode it, it will revert back to the tag format.

Block with Tags

BEACH DESIGNS
COMPUTER AIDED DESIGN SERVICES
CUSTOMER Customer
DRAWN BY: Drawn
NAME OF PART: Part
CHECKED BY Checked
DATE: Date
DRAWING NO: Drw#

Inserted Block

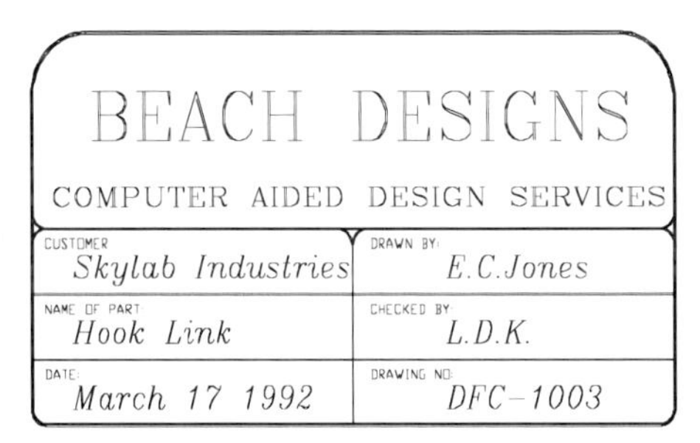

Figure 13-3. A title block with attributes and block instances

The illustrations in Figure 13-3 demonstrate the difference between a block with attribute tags and the inserted block with the instance values.

If you use EXPLODE, you can return the attributed block to the attribute definitions, and only the tags will be shown. The CHANGE command can now be used to update the attribute definitions. CHANGE will prompt for changes in the properties — layer, colour, etc. — and then cycle through the same sequence as that of text changes, finally offering the tag, prompt, default, and other strictly attribute-related data to change. Once changed, the attribute can be reblocked and reinserted.

In the attributes for the window on the right, the word SUPPLIER has been misspelled. Use CHANGE to correct it.

```
Command:CHANGE
Select objects: (pick 1)
Select objects:↵
Properties/<change point>:↵
Enter text insertion point:↵
Text Style:STANDARD
New style or RETURN for no change:↵
New height<0.20000>:↵
New rotation angle <0>:↵
New tag <SUPPLIER>:SUPPLIER ↵
```

Product
Suppkier
Colour
Price

Product
Supplier
Colour
Price

```
New prompt <Enter supplier>:↵
New default value <0>:↵
```

If you prefer to use dialogue boxes, use DDEDIT for the same process.

```
Command:DDEDIT
<Select a TEXT or ATTDEF object>/Undo: (pick ATTDEF)
```

This will display three input boxes to change the tag, prompt, or default value within the dialogue box.

To edit the text in any of these boxes, move the cursor arrow into the input box so the box is highlighted in the same way you would change the layer names.

This display is only possible if your graphics display supports the Advanced User Interface; it is not available prior to Release 11.

As with other dialogue boxes, no more than 255 characters are allowed per line. Only 48 characters can be displayed in the box at any one time.

Other editing commands such as MOVE, COPY, and ROTATE can also be used with attributes to place them where needed within the block. Layer, colour, and linetype can also be changed.

ATTRIBUTE DIALOGUE BOX

The attribute dialogue box is similar to the pull-down menus used by the HATCH and LAYER commands. It will automatically display a list of all the attribute data you have entered as soon as the INSERT command has been activated. The attribute dialogue box will allow you to change the data on-screen. The command is as follows:

```
Command:ATTDIA
New value for ATTDIA <0>:1
```

SETVAR is needed to access the ATTDIA variable prior to Release 11.

With the ATTDIA at 0, the box does not display. With the ATTDIA set to 1, the box will display.

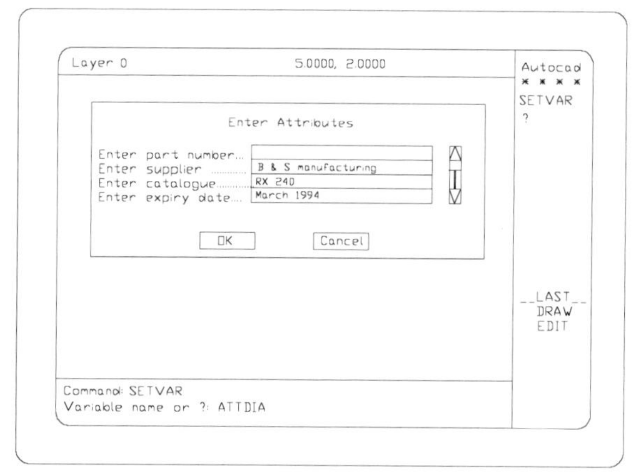

Figure 13-4. ATTDIA set to 1

The information within the box, see Figure 13-4, is the default value. Indicate the defaults you want to change by using the cursor arrow to highlight them. Then type in the new value and press OK to have the attribute display on the screen where placed.

Using ATTDIA is advantageous if there are a number of attributes that need to be coordinated.

Example: *Attribute Definitions*

We will create an office layout using modular furniture. We will begin by deciding what information we need to order the furniture when the design is finished. On a typical purchase order, you would require the following:

- Supplier
- Part description
- Part number
- Fabric colour
- Base colour
- Finish or other details
- Cost

We do not need to know the quantity required, because we will determine that when the design is finished. In case there are any details we have forgotten, we can add the attribute Finish.

Figure 13-5 shows the four components that will make up the new office: two types of desks and two types of chairs.

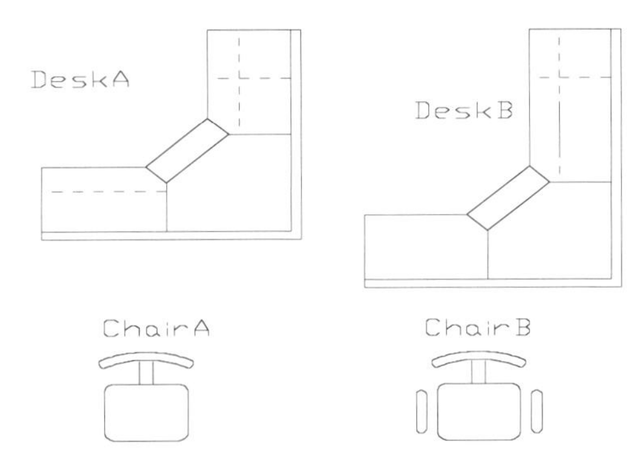

Figure 13-5. Attributed office components

STEP 1
Create two different chairs and two different desks.

STEP 2
Create a set of attributes containing prompts for:
Supplier
Part Description

- Part Number
- Fabric Colour
- Base Colour
- Finish
- Cost

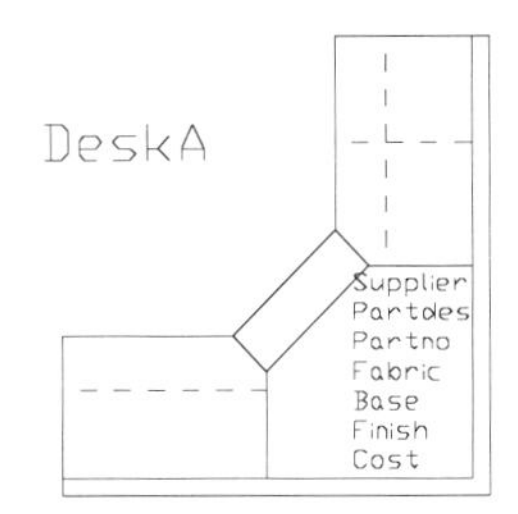

STEP 3
Once the first set of attributes is created, the attributes can either be re-created for each different type of furniture, or they can be copied over to each different type of furniture and the attributes can be changed to reflect the type of furniture to be blocked with the attributes.

In the illustration at the bottom of the previous page, you can see that both the chair and the desk have the same attribute tags, but the defaults for colour, supplier, and finishes would be different.

STEP 4
Create four separate blocks for the four separate types of furniture. Include both the geometry and the attribute definitions in the block.

STEP 5
Design the room and add the components that make up the furnishings.

Some of the attribute values will remain the same for each object. The supplier, for example, probably will not change, so it would be logical to have the supplier attribute preset in the attribute mode setting. The attributes could also be made invisible during the design of the room so that the text for each component will not clutter the drawing. This could be done either with the Preset mode or by using ATTDISP.

In this case, the attributed blocks are connected to the geometry. If you were designing a series of rooms, the attributes for the room finishes would not be related to any geometry.

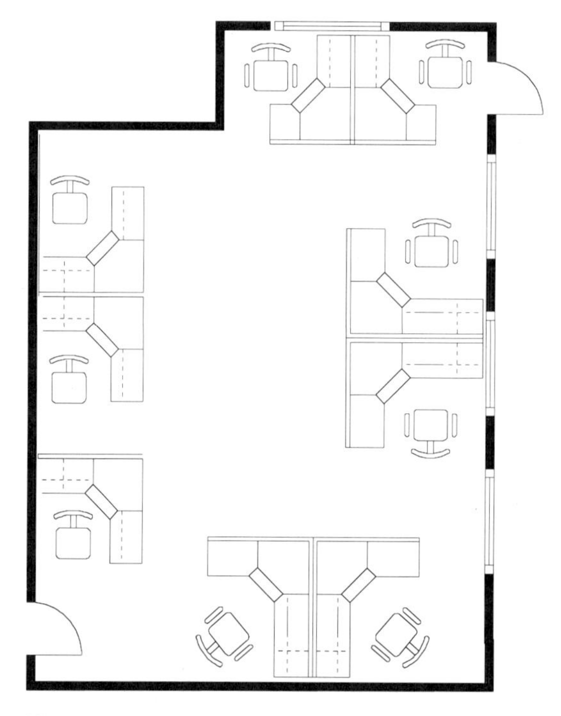

Figure 13-6. Adding blocked components to room

In the next chapter, we will look at how the attributes can be extracted to be placed on a purchase order.

Exercise A13

STEP 1
Retrieve your title block from Chapter 8 or generate a new one. Be sure to put in the headings — scale, date, class — with text.

Project		Drawing	Scale	Project
Project		Drawing info	Scale	Pro
			Date Date	
		School	Drawn Drawn	Drawing
		School	Class Class	DR#

STEP 2
Use ATTDEF to define attributes that will change with each use or instance of the attributed block. Make sure the size of lettering you choose is appropriate.

STEP 3
Block the title block including text, lines, and attribute definitions when they are completed.

STEP 4
Insert the attributed block and fill in the blanks to make a reasonable title block.

STEP 5
If any of the attributes do not work, explode the block and change the attribute definitions.

Project		Drawing	Scale	Project
Elgin Residence		Foundation and Plan	1" = 1'0"	1
			Date 17/3/92	
		School	Drawn G.G	Drawing
		Mohawk College	Class 1AT12	2

STEP 6
Create one block containing the indicated attributes. No geometry is needed with this block. Draw a simple floor plan, insert the block, and change the finishes for each room.

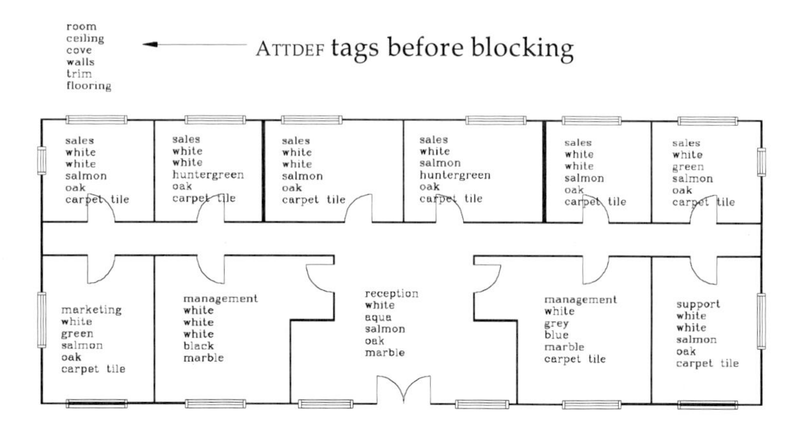

In the next session we will place these attributes on a spreadsheet for specifications.

Exercise M13

STEP 1
Retrieve your title block from Chapter 8 or generate a new one. Be sure to put in the headings — scale, date, class — with text.

TOLERANCES UNLESS OTHERWISE SPECIFIED FRACTIONS +/- 1/32 DECIMALS +/- .005 ANGLES +/- .5 DEGREES		Title *Title*		
APPROVALS	DATE	Company *Company*		
		SCALE	SIZE	DRAWING NO
		Scale	*Size*	*DRW#*
				Numbering

STEP 2
Use ATTDEF to define attributes that will change with each use or instance of the attributed block. Make sure the size of lettering you choose is appropriate.

STEP 3
Block the text, lines, and attribute definitions when they are completed.

STEP 4
Insert the attributed block and fill in the blanks to make a reasonable title block.

TOLERANCES UNLESS OTHERWISE SPECIFIED FRACTIONS +/- 1/32 DECIMALS +/- .005 ANGLES +/- .5 DEGREES		Title *Crane Hook*		
APPROVALS	DATE	Company *Miller Inc*		
		SCALE	SIZE	DRAWING NO
		1=1	*A4*	*ch-48*
				Sheet 1 of 1

STEP 5
If any of the attributes do not work, explode the block and change the attribute definitions.

STEP 6
In the following, we will be making an assembly drawing for an oiler tray. Create one wire support rod. Add the part, part number, etc. as attributes. Once completed, block it. Then insert it six times on the drawing where needed.

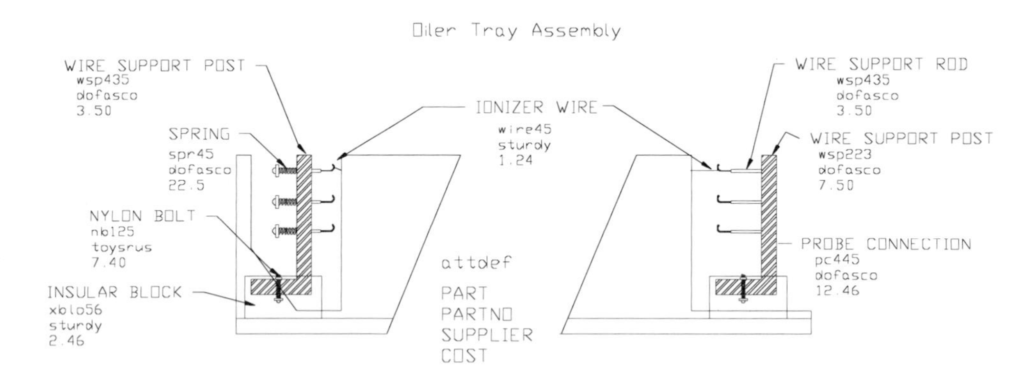

Do the same for each separate part. Create the geometry, add the attributes, block them, then insert as many times as needed. In the next chapter, we will use the attributes to create a bill of materials.

Exercise C13

STEP 1
Retrieve your title block from Chapter 8 or generate a new one. Be sure to put in the headings — scale, date, class — with text.

Part REVISIONS
The making of any copy of this drawing or any portion thereof by any means is expressly prohibited unless authorised in writing.
Job DWN DRWN
Job Date DATE
Scale Scale
App. App.
Company DWG No.
Company DRW#

STEP 2
Use ATTDEF to define attributes that will change with each use or instance of the attributed block. Make sure the size of lettering you choose is appropriate for many different titles: not too small to read nor too large to fit into the space provided.

STEP 3
Block the text, lines, and attribute definitions when they are completed.

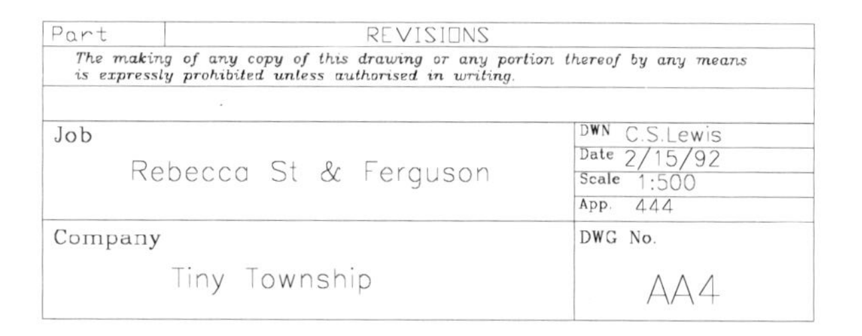

STEP 4
Insert the attributed block and fill in the blanks to make a title block.

STEP 5
If any of the attributes do not work, explode the block and change the attribute definitions.

STEP 6
Draw a simple survey. Create attributes for the desired services and particulars as illustrated below. Block the attributes. Then insert the block into each lot indicating the different lot numbers and services for each lot.

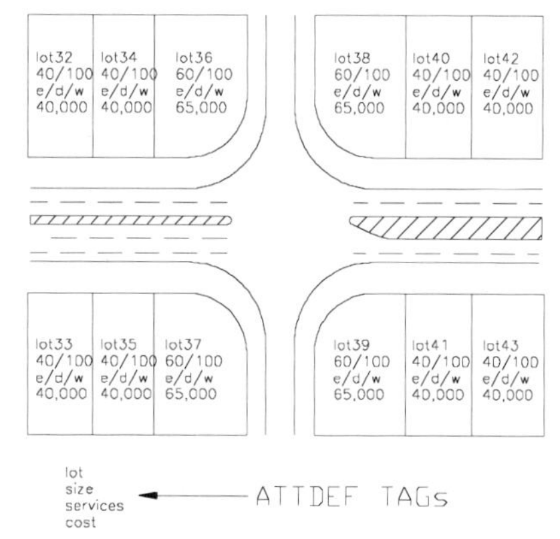

In the next chapter we will make a list of these attributes on a spreadsheet.

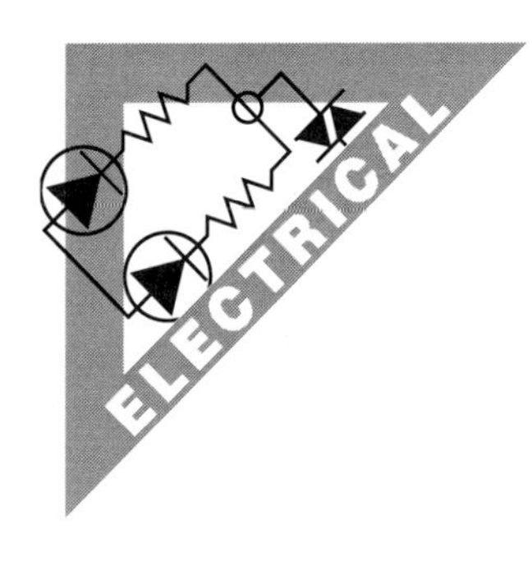

Exercise E13

STEP 1

Retrieve the title block from Chapter 8 or generate a new one. Be sure to put in the headings — scale, date, and class — with text.

Project		Drawing	Scale	Project
Project		Drawing info	Scale	Pro
			Date	
		School	Drawn	Drawing
		School	Class	DR#

STEP 2

Use ATTDEF to define attributes that will change with each use or instance of the attributed block. Be sure the size of lettering you choose is appropriate.

STEP 3

Block the title block including text, lines, and attribute definitions when they are completed.

STEP 4

Insert the attributed block and fill in the blanks to make a reasonable title block.

Project		Drawing	Scale	Project
Elgin Residence		Foundation and Plan	1" = 1'0"	1
			Date 17/3/92	
		School	Drawn G.G	Drawing
		Mohawk College	Class 1AT12	2

STEP 5

If any of the attributes do not work, explode the block and change the attribute definitions.

STEP 6

Create four wiring devices with attributes containing colour, price, and finish. Insert the blocks with attributes where necessary.

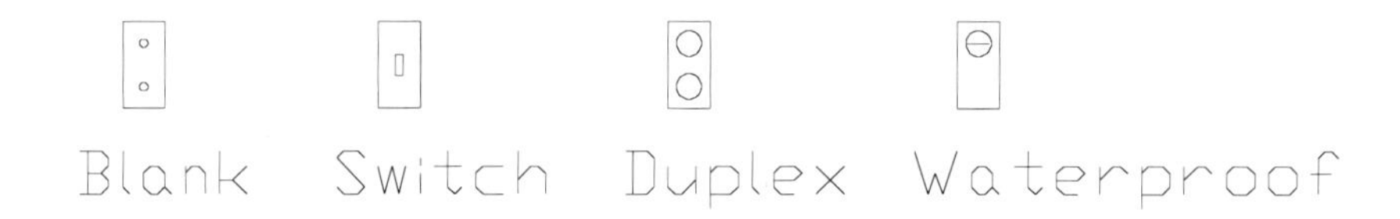

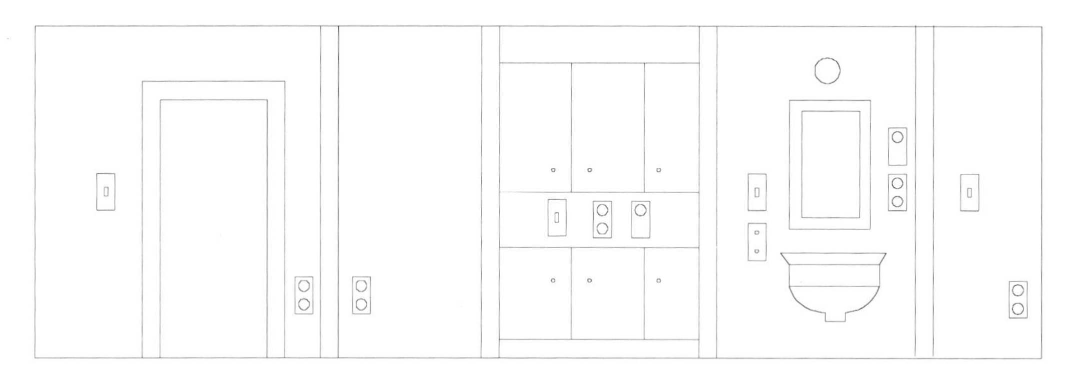

In the next chapter, the attributes will be placed on a spreadsheet for specifications.

Challenger 13

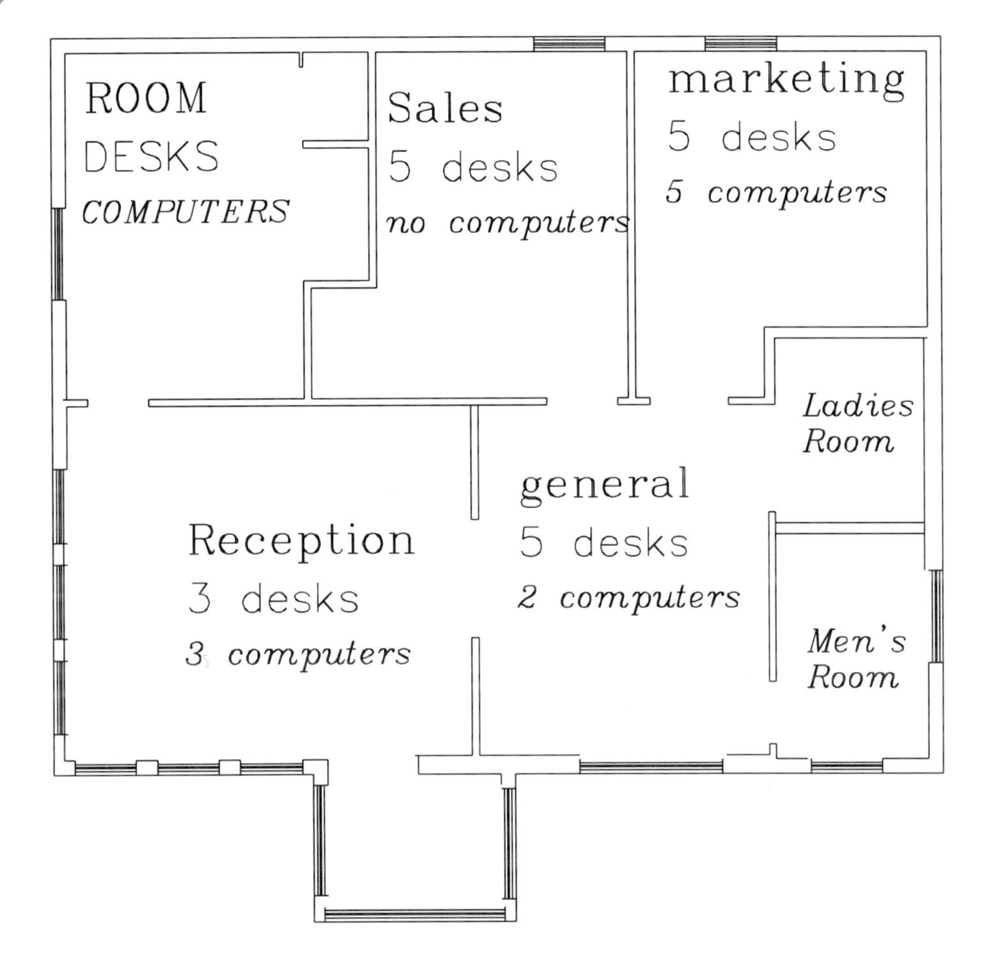
ROOM
DESKS
COMPUTERS
Sales
5 desks
no computers
marketing
5 desks
5 computers
Ladies Room
general
5 desks
2 computers
Reception
3 desks
3 computers
Men's Room

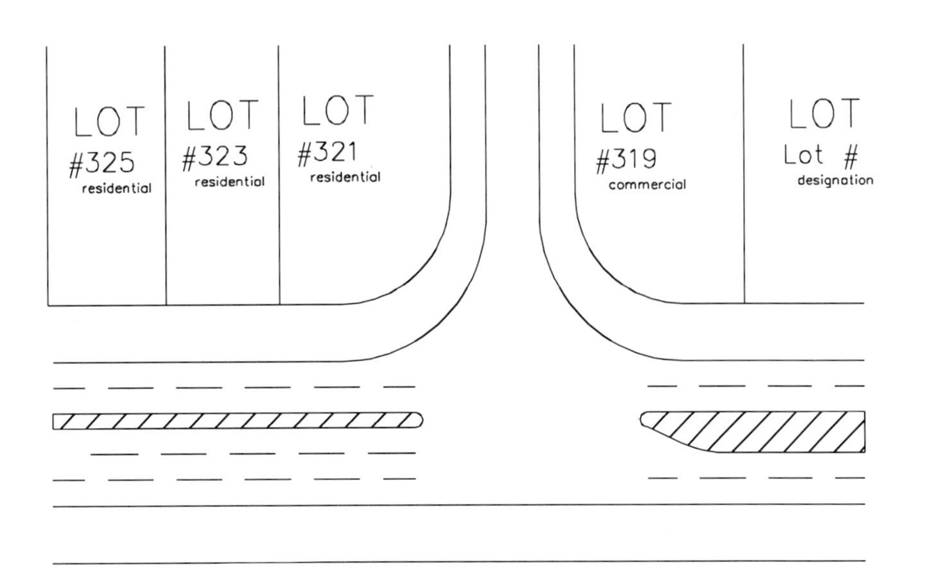
LOT
#325
residential
LOT
#323
residential
LOT
#321
residential
LOT
#319
commercial
LOT
Lot #
designation

EDITING ATTRIBUTES AND DATA EXTRACTS

Upon completion of this chapter, the student should be able to:

1. Perform a single edit on an attribute
2. Perform a global edit on many attributes
3. Extract the data from the AutoCAD drawing into a word processing or Lotus format

ATTRIBUTE EDITING

Once the attribute is in the drawing, the information it contains can be edited by using ATTEDIT. This changes the attribute instance or that particular application of the attribute, not the attribute definition itself as CHANGE does.

When you are editing attributes one by one, you can change any of the values (orientation, text height, location, or string value), but when you perform a global edit, only the string value changes. A global edit is an edit that changes all of the attributes, like doing a UPD on a Window of dimensions. A string value is the text actually created by the attributed block instance; a string of text is simply a line of characters.

The command is as follows:

```
Command:ATTEDIT
Edit attributes one by one? <Y>:
```

A positive response (Y) will identify and edit each attribute one by one. A negative response (N) will edit all of the attributes at once; this is called a global edit. Again, only the text string changes in a global edit.

AutoCAD then allows you to filter the attributes for editing.

```
Block name specification <*>:
Attribute tag specification <*>:
Attribute value specification <*>:
```

Release 12 Notes

ATTribute EXTract in Release 12 can be found under the Utility pull-down menu.

The * is a wildcard symbol and indicates that all the items will be changed. You can accept the default * and change all the blocks, tags, and values. If you want to change just one type of attribute or one tag, e.g., room size, specify this so you will not spend time circling through all the information you do not intend to change.

Finally, you are asked to select which attributes to change. A Window may be used to define these. When all the attributes have been chosen and you have pressed the Return key, an X will appear on the attribute you are editing. Then you will be prompted for the following possible changes:

VAL	*attribute value (the text string)*
POS	*text position*
Hgt	*text height*
ANG	*text angle*
Style	*text style*
Lay	*layer*
Color	*colour*
Next	*next*

The response to this command is similar to that of CHANGE. Be sure you are answering the question and you will be fine.

Figure 14-1 shows attributed blocks with the tags:

- office
- colour
- coats *(number of coats of paint)*
- size *(square feet)*

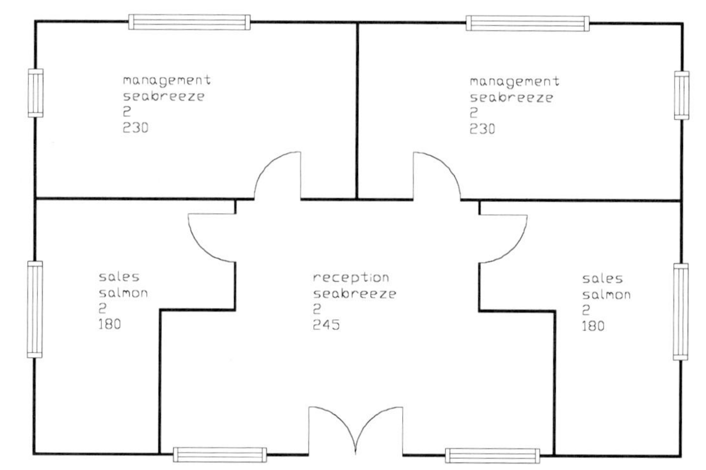

Figure 14-1. Using tags

In this example, the sales offices are to be painted salmon while the other offices are seabreeze. We want to change the colour of the sales office to dove grey and the other paint colour to cranberry.

```
Command:ATTEDIT
Edit attributes one by one? <y>:
Drawing must be regenerated afterwards.
Block name specification <*>:paint
Attribute tag specification <*>:colour
Attribute value specification <*>:↵
Select attributes:W First corner: (pick 1) Other corner: (pick 2)
5 attributes selected.
Value/Position/Height/Angle/Style/Layer/Color/Next <N>:V
Change or Replace:R
```

```
New string:Dove Grey
Value/Position/Height/Angle/Style/Layer/Color/Next <N>:N
Value/Position/Height/Angle/Style/Layer/Color/Next <N>:V
```
(etc.)

This will highlight the string values one by one and offer the user the possibility of changing each one.

Example: *ATTEDIT for Global Edit*

If you had a situation where there were many attributed block instances that needed to be changed, making the changes one by one would take a lot of time. The ATTEDIT command allows you to do a global edit or change all the string values associated with either a tag or a specific value.

Before ATTEDIT **After** ATTEDIT

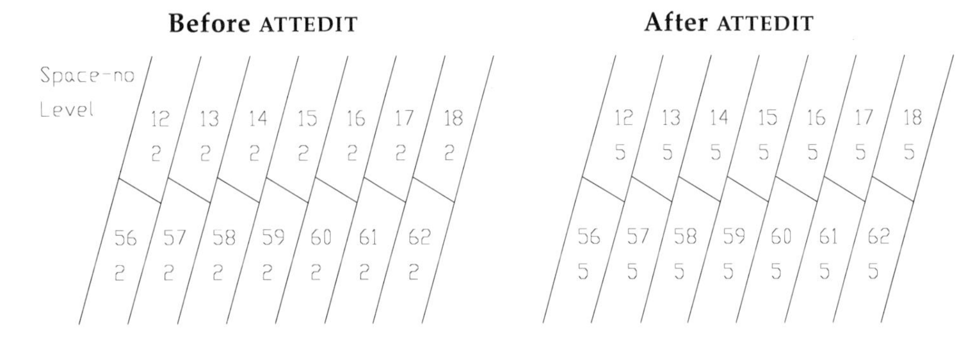

STEP 1
Draw a series of parallel lines as in the parking lot illustration on the left. Create an attribute to define a space number and a level. Insert the attribute left making a series of different space numbers.

STEP 2
Copy the parking lot over to the right. All the attributed block instances will be copied as well as the geometry.

STEP 3
The second parking lot will be on level 5. The space number information will remain the same but the level will change.

Use ATTEDIT to quickly change all the level specifications.

```
Command:ATTEDIT
Edit attributes one by one? <y>:N

Global edit of attribute values.
Edit only attributes visible on screen? <Y>:

Block name specification <*>:park
Attribute tag specification <*>:level
Attribute value specification <*>:2
Select attributes:W  First corner: (pick 1) Other corner: (pick 2)
14 attributes selected.
String to change:2
New string:5
```

Notice that the prompts change when you pick certain options. In this example, it is a global edit, so *all* attributes will be changed at once. Since the attributes will not be highlighted, the system asks if the invisible attributes will be changed as well.

You can use the block name, the tag name, and the string value to limit the number of attributes that will be edited.

Be careful to choose a string justification that will allow editing of the text, because the text string will be repositioned when the number of characters changes.

DDATTE

For those who enjoy working with dialogue boxes, there is a dialogue box for individual changes in an attributed block instance.

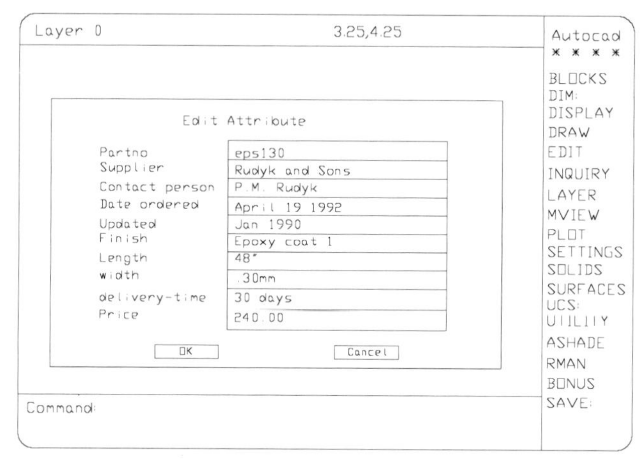

Figure 14-2. Dialogue box

The dialogue box in Figure 14-2 allows interactive editing of all the attributes on an attribute block instance.

Use the arrow cursor to indicate the text string that needs to be changed, then simply type in the new value.

Up to 15 attributes can be displayed at one time; if there are more, the dialogue box will scroll.

`Command:`**`DDATTE`**

`Select block:` *(pick the block)*

The command is completed and the values are saved by moving the arrow cursor to OK then pressing the pick button.

ATTREDEF LISP Program

ATTREDEF, a LISP routine available with most AutoCAD releases, redefines a block and updates the attributes associated with any previous insertions of that block. First a new attributed block is defined, then you indicate the name of the block that this will replace. The new attributes are added to the old attributes and given the new default value(s). Any existing attributes will retain their original value. Old attributes not included in the new block will be erased.

`Command:`**`ATTREDEF`**

`Name of block you wish to redefine:` *(enter name of block to be replaced)*

`Select new block.....`

`Select objects:` *(pick the objects)*

`Insertion base point of new block:` *(pick a point)*

This can be an extremely useful command if you have two or three changes to an attribute that are not easily done with the ATTEDIT command. For example, if you have just changed suppliers and there is an extra location and salesperson to add to your attributed blocks, it will be easier to create the new block and update the old one using ATTREDEF than to simply change the supplier and have to add on new attributes for the additional information.

DATA EXTRACTION

Now that the data is entered correctly, you can have it printed out onto a spreadsheet or materials list by using the command ATTEXT. This operation does not change the drawing in any way, but formats the attribute data for either dBASE, Lotus 1-2-3, or your favourite word processor. There are three main formats for data extraction.

- CDF = Comma Delimited Format
- SDF = Standard Delimited Format
- DXF = Data eXtract File

CDF — Comma Delimited Format

This takes each attributed block and extracts the attributes into a record where each attribute is separated by a comma.

```
Command:ATTEXT
CDF, SDF, or DXF attribute extract? <C>:
Template file <default>: (enter template filename)
Extract file name <drawing name>: (enter name)
```

Using the attributed blocks from the previous floor layout example, the extract file would look like this. The first item is the office, the second is the colour, the third is the number of coats of paint, and the fourth is the square footage. This information can be used as a listing in WordPerfect or for calculation and estimating in Lotus 1-2-3.

```
management, seabreeze, 2, 230
management, seabreeze, 2, 230
sales, salmon, 2, 180
sales, salmon, 2, 180
reception, seabreeze, 2, 245
```

SDF — Standard Data Format

Again, this will provide one line for each occurrence of each block. In this format, there are no commas, the template file must specify the length of field for each extract, and any data that exceeds this limit is truncated.

```
Command:ATTEXT
CDF, SDF, or DXF attribute extract? <C>:SDF
Template file <default>: (enter template filename)
Extract file name <drawing name>: (enter name)
```

Note the difference in the format for this file as opposed to the CDF file. Note also that the area where the office and the actual colour appear must be large enough to contain all the letters.

```
management      seabreeze     2     230
management      seabreeze     2     230
sales           salmon        2     180
sales           salmon        2     180
reception       seabreeze     2     245
```

Both the CDF and the SDF files must be made with a template file.

DXF — Drawing Interchange Format

This format is used by many third-party programmers for drawing enhancements, analysis programs, and related programs. The DXF format is also used for exchange of engineering data, geological data, and nesting routines as well as the extraction of purely spatial information. The extract file will contain all the information in the block such as insertion point, rotation angle, and X, Y, Z values.

This ATTEXT option creates a file with a .DXX extension. DXF files are covered more thoroughly in Chapter 18.

Extracting Data to a WordPerfect File

Any ASCII-based file can be used to create a template. The most popular text editors that accept this data are MS-DOS Editor, the DOS program Edlin, WordPerfect's DOS-text file option, the WordPerfect Library Program Editor, WordStar in non-document mode, PC Write, Microsoft Word in text-only format, and Norton's Editor, Sidekick. All of these will produce the standard ASCII file format required.

See Appendix F for text editing formats.

The following example is for an SDF extract to a WordPerfect file. This is a very simple example; other data such as coordinates, layer, scale factor, etc. can also be extracted, but are not needed in this case. We will simply extract the data associated with the attributes or the string value as shown above. This data is identified by the tag.

A knowledge of WordPerfect is a distinct advantage here, although any other word-processing package that accepts ASCII text is fine. A Lotus 1-2-3 or similar package is also fine.

Example: *Data Extract to WordPerfect*

Using the office layout as an example:

STEP 1
Retrieve or generate an AutoCAD file that contains attributes and make note of the tags of your attributes. If you have forgotten what they are, use LIST. Note the name of the tag exactly (no spelling errors are allowed), then exit the file.

STEP 2
Start a WordPerfect file by entering WP or WP51, or use Edlin or MS-DOS Editor to create the template. See Appendix F if you are not familiar with WordPerfect.

We will be making a template file that will contain all of the attribute data. Each line of the template represents one field to be listed in the extract file. The field will look like this:

```
OFFICE C010000
```

Where:
OFFICE = the tag

C = character field type

010 = 10 characters in the office name

000 = the number of decimal places (none of course are needed)

Create the template file by entering the appropriate tags and the appropriate code for the number of characters. If you have numerical input, e.g., square feet, it would be entered as:

```
SIZE N010002
```

Where:
SIZE = the tag

N = number field type

010 = 10 digits in the number

002 = the number of decimal places — two

Release 12 Notes

DDATTEXT dialogue box will help with data extracts.

Your file might look like this:

```
OFFICE C010000
COLOUR C015000
COATS N008001
SIZE N008001
```

Each entry has a maximum number of characters, depending on the length of the tag name needed for each particular field. You must use a C if there is anything other than a numeric value for the entry. If the entry contains both numbers and letters, use C.

STEP 3
The template must now be saved as an ASCII or DOS file. AutoCAD does not read WordPerfect or any other processing package directly, therefore you must translate it into a format that it can understand — an ASCII file.

Save the WordPerfect file as an ASCII file (DOS file) by using the following:

- press Ctrl-F5 to create text output
- press 1 for DOS Text
- press 1 for Save
- enter Name the file a:template.txt

In **A:template.txt:**

A: = the name of the drive

Template = the name of the file, and can be changed

.txt = the filename extension, and cannot be changed

That will save the file in ASCII format. Now exit WordPerfect by using the following:

- press F7

- enter N (do not save the file in WordPerfect format unless you give it a different name)
- enter Y (exit WordPerfect)

STEP 4

Retrieve the AutoCAD file. Purge all unused blocks by using the PURGE command. Then enter ATTEXT.

ATTEXT (ATT[*ribute*] EXT[*raction*]) is used to extract the data from the AutoCAD file directly into the WordPerfect format. It uses the template file A:Template.TXT and the attribute data to merge the files.

```
Command:ATTEXT
CDF, SDF, or DXF attribute extract ? (or entities) <C>:SDF
Template file <default>:TEMPLATE
Extract file name <default>:A:PAINTSCH
5 records in extract file.
```

AutoCAD will tell you how many extracts you have. Now exit the AutoCAD file and retrieve the new WordPerfect file to see the listing.

The extract filename will default to the drawing name and enter a .TXT extension. When entering the template filename, you do not need to add the .TXT extension.

WHAT CAN GO WRONG

1. If a "Field overflow" error message displays after the ATTEXT command, this means there are not enough spaces for characters in the template file. To remedy this situation, you must return to the template file and allow for more characters in the field. For example, if you have allowed for eight characters in the Office tag,

```
OFFICE C008000
```

the string value "management" will be truncated, and there will be a field overflow because the string contains 10 letters.

2. When you are entering your template file, enter a hard return on the last line of text, but do not enter another hard return after the final entry.

```
OFFICE C010000[HR]
COLOUR C015000[HR]
COATS N008001[HR]
SIZE N008001[HR]
```

Prior to Release 11 this may cause your extract to be unrecorded.

There should be only one space between the tag and the SDF format. You may get a rejection prompt if there is more than one space.

Flow Chart for Created Attribute Extracts

The new file being created has the extension .TXT. Be sure you do not have the same name for the template and the extract file, otherwise you will lose one of the files. There is no prompt to tell you that you are overwriting the first file.

You can start by creating the drawing and the attributes and then create the template file, or you can start by creating the template file, as long as both the template and the attributed block instances are created when you use ATTEXT.

If you *start* by creating a template file, you can decide what information you need and then create the attributes to provide this information.

```
Create template      Create            Use ATTEXT to
a:template.txt       attributes        extract data

Create               Create template   Use ATTEXT to
attributes           a:template.txt    extract data
```

Extracting Data to a Lotus 1-2-3 file

Example: *Data Extract to Lotus 1-2-3*

STEP 1
Create or retrieve a file with attributes and note the attribute tags.

STEP 2
Enter either DOS, EDLIN or another ASCII text editor and create your template file.

```
TAG C010000
TAG C010000    etc.
```

While writing this file, keep in mind that the numbers that are 2nd, 3rd and 4th in the code stand for the size of the field that you will be accessing in Lotus 1-2-3.

```
TAG C010000  = 10 characters in the field
```

STEP 3
Return to AutoCAD and use ATTEXT to extract the attributes.

STEP 4
Enter Lotus 1-2-3. Use /**F**ile **I**mport to bring the file into Lotus 1-2-3. This option will import any standard ASCII file.

The data will be brought into Lotus 1-2-3 as a text file. You must use /Data Parse to convert the column of long labels into several columns of labels or numbers. This will break up the long labels into individual cell entries that 1-2-3 can use to perform regular 1-2-3 tasks such as numeric analysis (adding and subtracting for starters) and graphing.

The first settings sheet will list the location of the input column and the output range. Place the cell pointer in the top cell of the column you want to parse, then use **F**ormat-Line **C**reate to help you divide the large block of data into several columns. You can make one or more format lines using this option. The data will then be in cell format and ready to perform calculations.

Exercise A14

STEP 1
Finish the office and attributes started last week.

STEP 2
Once the first set of offices is complete, copy the office and attributes to a different portion of the screen.

STEP 3
Use ATTEDIT to change the wall colours, the flooring, and the trim with a more expensive set of materials.

STEP 4
End your file and create a WP template file to list the various components of this flooring. (A Lotus 1-2-3 file can also be generated using the same tag and template information. On the Lotus 1-2-3 file, generate the equations to automatically calculate the cost.)

STEP 5
Generate two extract files of this data from the two drawings. Use the SDF format, and make sure that both have no field overflows or truncated data. Add headings for all the columns.

STEP 6
Calculate the total cost for the flooring and submit as two estimates.

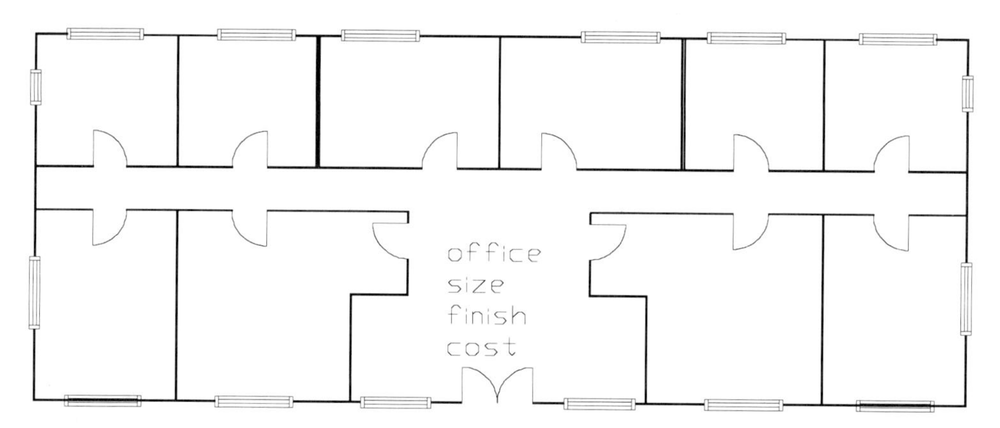

Colour Schedule 1 for ABC Offices

Ceiling	Coves	Walls	Trim	Flooring

Exercise M14

STEP 1
Finish your assembly of parts from last week. Use the following tags:

PART	*part name*
PARTNO	*part number*
SUPPLIER	*company that supplies the parts*
COST	*cost per unit*

STEP 2
Once completed, copy the entire drawing to a different portion of the screen.

STEP 3
Use ATTEDIT to change the suppliers and costs for the various parts.

STEP 4
End the file and create a WP template file to list the various components of this part. (A Lotus 1-2-3 file can also be generated using the same tag and template information. On the Lotus 1-2-3 file, generate the equations to automatically calculate the cost.)

STEP 5
Generate two extract files of this data from the two drawings. Use the SDF format, and make sure that both have no field overflows or truncated data. Add headings for all the columns of information and list the final estimate at the bottom.

STEP 6
Calculate the total cost for the flooring and submit as two estimates.

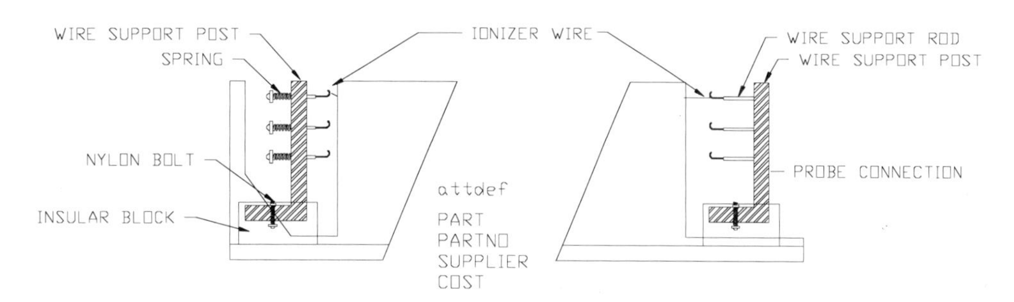

Estimate 1 for Oiler Tray Assembly

Part	Part Number	Supplier	Cost

Exercise C14

STEP 1
Finish your drawing of the 12 lots from last week. Be sure that your tags contain the following information.

LOT	*lot name*
ZONING	*zone — residential or commercial*
SERVICES	*services needed for each lot*
COST	*cost per lot*

STEP 2
Once completed, copy the drawing to a different portion of the screen.

STEP 3
Use ATTEDIT to change the services provided for these lots and the cost of the lots.

STEP 4
End the file and create a WP template file to list the various components of this survey. (A Lotus 1-2-3 file can also be generated using the same tag and template information. On the Lotus 1-2-3 file, generate the equations to automatically calculate the cost.)

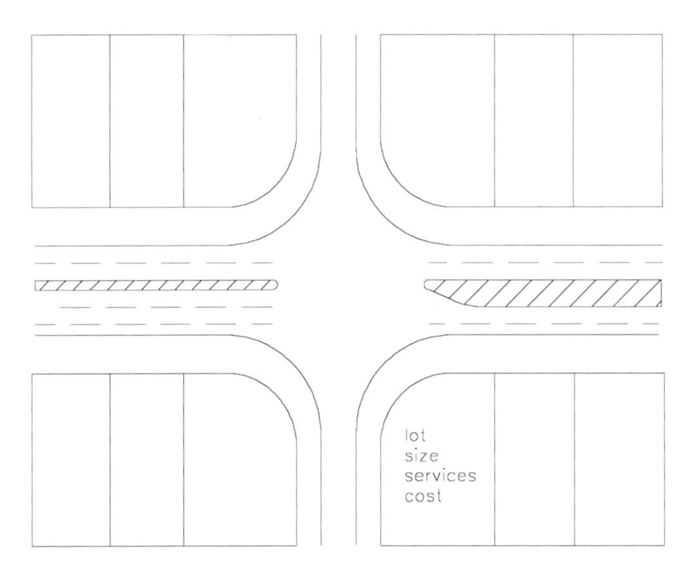

STEP 5
Generate two extract files of this data from the two drawings. Use the SDF format, and make sure that both have no field overflows or truncated data. Add headings for all the columns of information, and list the final estimate at the bottom.

STEP 6
Calculate the total cost for the surveys and submit as two estimates.

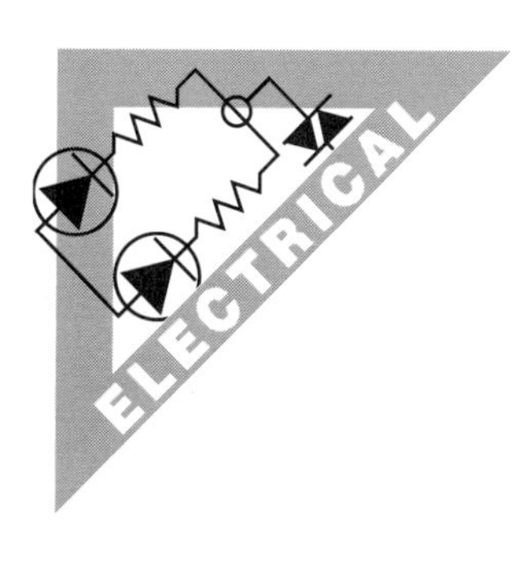

Exercise E14

STEP 1
Finish the residence and attributes started last week.

STEP 2
Once the first floor is complete, copy the layout and attributes to a different portion of the screen.

STEP 3
Use ATTEDIT to change the fixture colours and the trim with a more expensive set of materials (brass/gold plate).

STEP 4
End your file and create a WP template file to list the various components of this layout. (A Lotus 1-2-3 file can also be generated using the same tag and template information. On the Lotus 1-2-3 file, generate the equations to automatically calculate the cost.)

STEP 5
Generate two extract files of this data from the two drawings. Use the SDF format, and make sure that both estimates have no field overflows or truncated data. Add headings for all of the columns of colours.

STEP 6
Calculate the total cost for the wiring devices in both the less expensive and the more expensive formats. Submit as two estimates.

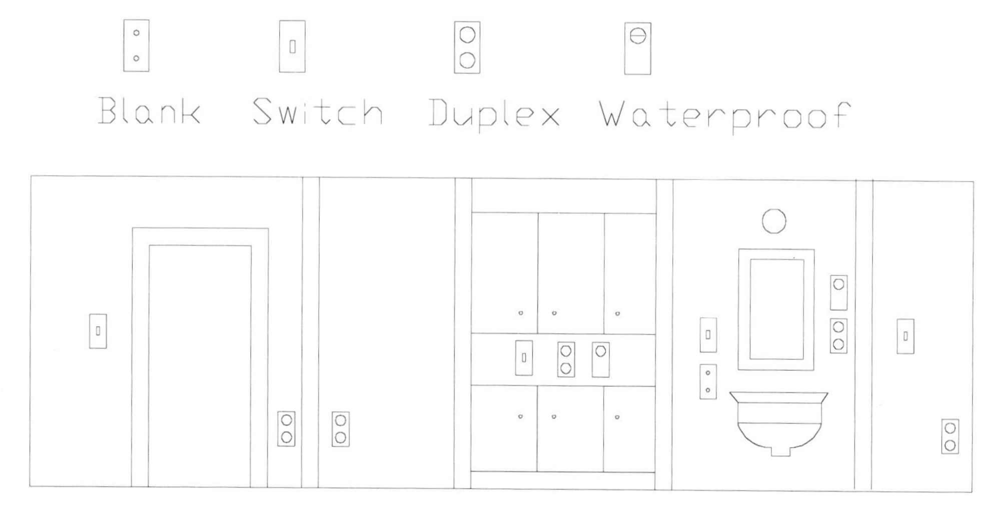

Electrical Schedule for House 1 and 2

Receptacles	Colour	Finish	Price
Duplex	brass	glossy	$1.75

Challenger 14

Using a current "Office System" line, create a layout for the desired amount of pods, and provide a full estimate of the cost and the materials to be ordered.

You will need to produce

- one layout (plan view) for the pods and electrical access,
- one Customer Quote including List of Materials to be ordered and cost to customer including GST and PST, delivery and installation.
- and one Confidential Quote including the cost to the client, the cost to the salesman, and the profit.

The above should include

1) Cost to the firm is list -50, -03.
2) To this add shipping and freight costs ($75.00 per pod).
3) Profit, the company wants to make 20% on goods ordered.
4) To this add installation fees:

   two people per day at $80.00 per day each

   two people can assemble four pods in one day

The layout will be submitted in AutoCAD. The costing will be taken from attributes of the information provided.

The client would like to have:

three management pods at 9′ x 12′
- 81 inch panels plus glazed overpanels

eight sales pods at 6′ x 5′
- 66 inches minimum height

All of these are to be in the office provided.

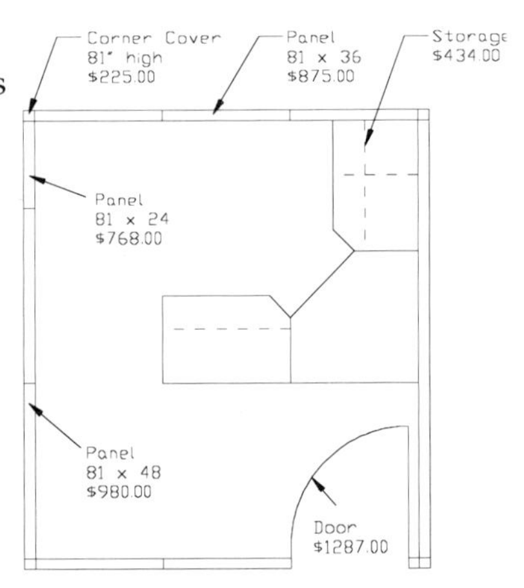

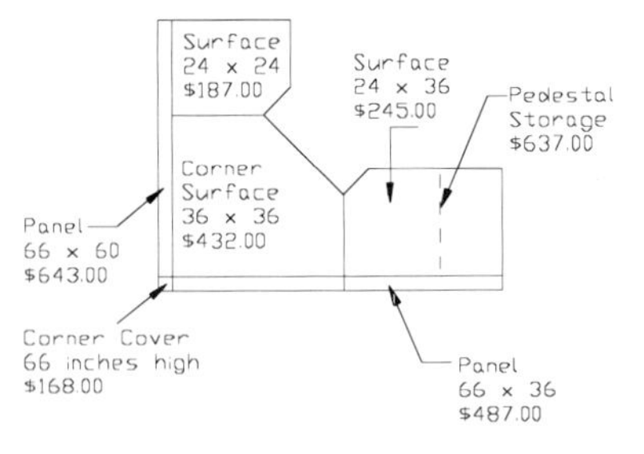

MEASURE, DIVIDE, AND INQUIRY COMMANDS

Upon completion of this chapter, the student should be able to:

1. Change the PDMODE and PDSIZE
2. Use DIVIDE and MEASURE to place multiple objects where desired within a model
3. Check the parameters and properties of objects within the model
4. Check the overall size of the model
5. Calculate an area of a model
6. Use the time management facility

POINT DISPLAY OR PDMODE OPTIONS

When an object is divided or measured, points are used to show the divisions. The point entities are usually displayed as a single pixel regardless of the zoom factor. In order to make the points more visible and to have different styles of points, Point Display Mode or PDMODE can be used.

0 1 2 3 4

32 33 34 35 36

64 65 66 67 68

96 97 98 99 100

Figure 15-1. AutoCAD's point styles

Figure 15-1 illustrates AutoCAD's available point styles. These are found under the Options pull-down menu, under Point Type (in Release 10, simply type in Points).

You must then either use the Options menu to change the point style or type in PDMODE and the number that corresponds to the point display you want. (In Release 10 and earlier, use SETVAR.)

```
Command:PDMODE
Point number:34
```

Release 12 Notes

In Release 12, choose the Settings menu, then Point Display for an Icon menu of point styles. Choose the style you want by picking the exact icon, then change the screen size or the Absolute Unit size if desired.

This command will set the style of the point. The points will then be added in at the points that are determined by either the DIVIDE or the MEASURE command.

PDSIZE

The size of the point display can be altered by changing PDSIZE.

```
Command:PDSIZE
New value for PDSIZE <0.0000>:2
Command:REGEN
```

If you enter a positive number for the PDSIZE, this will represent the actual size, in drawing units, of the point. An adjustment in the zoom factor will result in an adjustment of the point size.

If you enter a negative number, this number is taken as a relative percentage of the screen size, and a difference in the zoom factor will make no difference in the size of the point display. A larger negative value will result in a larger point.

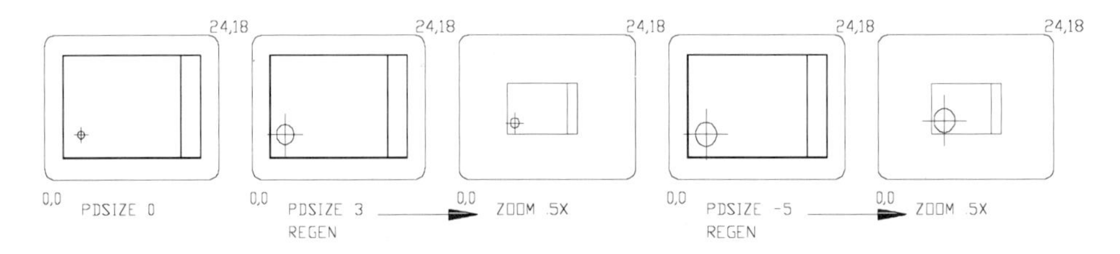

Figure 15-2. The zoom factor

To make the new point display size visible, a REGEN will be necessary. In releases prior to 11, SETVAR is needed to change PDSIZE.

Points, either created by MEASURE and DIVIDE or entered using the POINT command, can be accessed with OSNAP NODE. This is particularly important when entering blocks at specific points, or, in 3D, when finding centres for fillets, etc.

USING DIVIDE AND MEASURE

DIVIDE or MEASURE is used to cut an object or space that needs to be cut into equal pieces or portions.

DIVIDE will visually divide any linear element — arc, circle, line, pline — into a specified number of equal parts.

MEASURE will visually measure a linear element — arc, circle, line, pline — into segments of a specified length.

DIVIDE

DIVIDE can be used to divide a window into several equally spaced measures to place a mullion, or to divide an irregular shape into equal linear portions, or to divide a specific area of land into equal portions along a specific line. DIVIDE does not divide areas, but creates linear divisions that can be extended. The user is prompted to specify an object to be divided, and either a point or a block will be placed at equally spaced intervals. The illustrations in Figure 15-3 demonstrate the use of DIVIDE.

Command:**DIVIDE**

Select object to divide: *(pick the object)*

<Number of segments>/Block:**6**

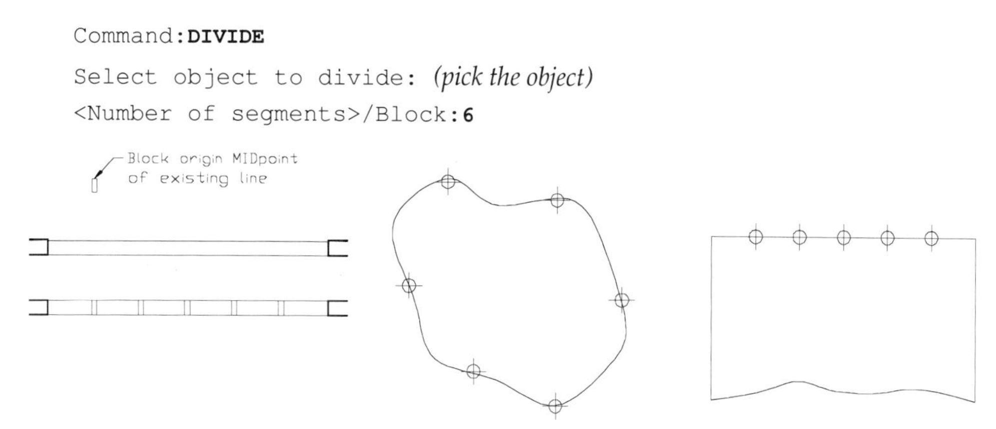

Figure 15-3. Using DIVIDE

The selected object is not altered in any way, but there are markers at regular intervals. In the first example, the window has been divided into six equal portions using a stored block as the division marker. In the second, an irregular shape is divided using points, and, in the third, the same point is used to illustrate the placement of markers along a lakefront property.

The point display of the last two examples is 34.

Example: *DIVIDE Using a Block*

In the next example, we will use a block to divide a window into equally spaced sections. Both a window and a block called Mullion will be needed.

In the diagram on the right we have a window and a block called Mullion, which is the shape of a mullion. Note the position of the insertion point on the block.

The command will place this block at regular intervals along the window.

Command:**DIVIDE**

Select object to divide: *(pick the object)*

<Number of segments>/Block:**B**

Block name to insert:**Mullion**

Align block with object? <Y>:↵

Number of segments:**6**

The block must already exist to be able to insert it into the divided object at the division points. Any attributes associated with the block will not be added.

Once the points are added to the file or model, they become objects themselves. You may wish to create a separate layer for the points. If the points are not needed, use ERASE Previous to remove them.

MEASURE

The MEASURE command is very similar to the DIVIDE command in that it divides a specified object into a series of equal portions. The difference is that the equal portions are given a specific length, and thus there may be an unequal portion of the object left over when the command is finished.

Again, the MEASURE command works on lines, arcs, circles, and plines, and the markers can be either points or blocks.

While picking either DIVIDE or MEASURE, you can only pick an object by selecting it individually; Window, Crossing, and Last do not work. After you have selected the object, AutoCAD will prompt for the segment length and then add the markers to the selected object.

Example: MEASURE

In Figure 15-4, use point display #4 and change the length to 18 metres with PDSIZE 18. Then use MEASURE to divide a road illustrated by a pline (a), into equally spaced lots (b). The pline representing the road will be needed.

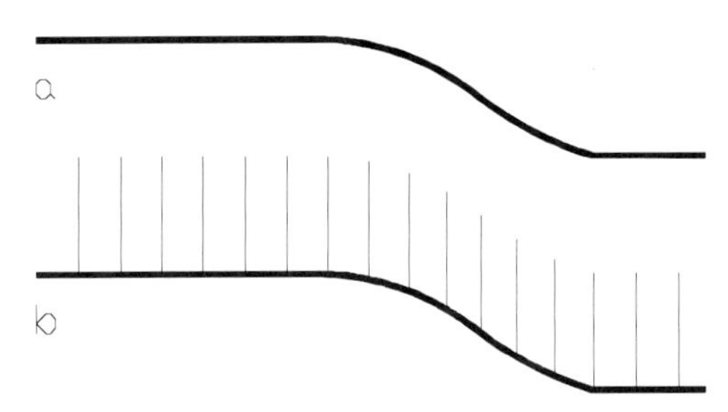

Figure 15-4. Using MEASURE

To change the point style, pick the Point Style option under the Options pull-down menu. Then pick Point Size under the same menu.

```
Command:PDMODE
Select new point mode <1>:4
Command:PDSIZE
Enter new point size <1.000>:18
```

In the illustration, we have used MEASURE to insert the lots.

```
Command:MEASURE
Select object to measure: (pick 1)
&lt;Segment length&gt;/Block:15
```

We now have a road that is divided into equal portions of 15-metre lengths with a depth of 18 metres each. Notice that the road is created with pline and thus has line and arc segments.

Example: *MEASURE Using Blocks*

In this example, we will place a block of a toilet along an existing wall. Both a line representing a 19-foot wall and a block that represents a toilet will be needed.

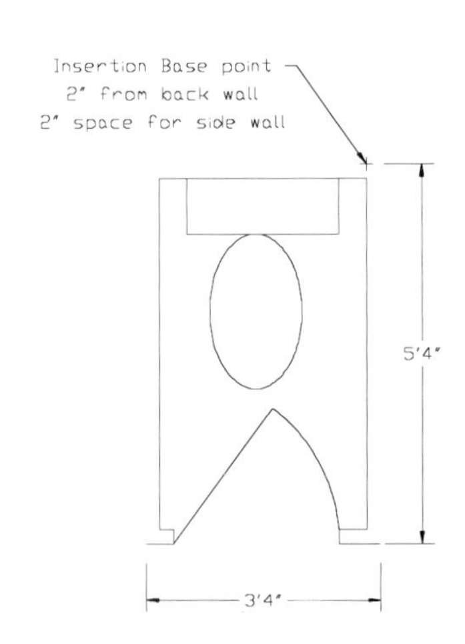

Create a toilet enclosed in an interior space of 3′ x 5′.

Now BLOCK the toilet making sure that the insertion base point leaves enough space for a 2-inch wall on the back and on the sides.

```
Command:BLOCK
Block name:Toilet
Insertion base point: (pick)
Select objects:Window
```

Now use MEASURE to place the toilet along a 19-foot wall.

```
Command:MEASURE
Select object to measure: (pick 1)
(pick the left side of the 19-foot wall)
&lt;Segment length&gt;/Block:B
Block name to insert:toilet
Align block with object <Y>:↵
Segment length:3'4"
```

When creating a block to be used in a MEASURE command, be sure no items overlap.

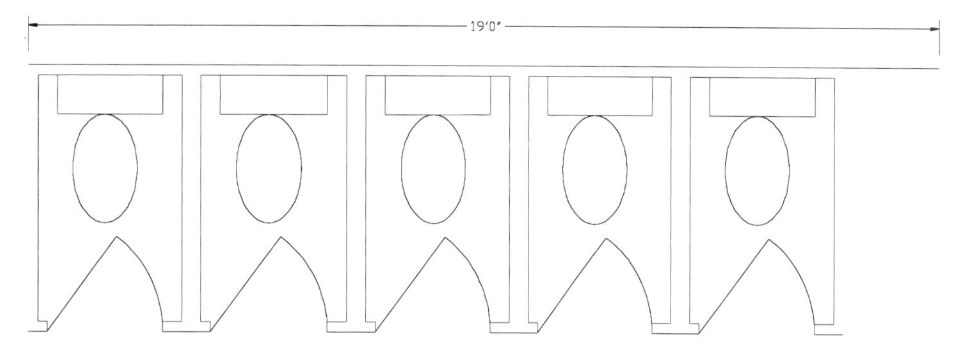

Figure 15-5. Ensure no overlapping

If you use points in either the DIVIDE or MEASURE commands, you will have to change the PDMODE to be able to see the displayed points. Once placed, these points become objects in the file and will be affected by all the editing commands, such as ERASE, MOVE, COPY, etc. If you do not change the PDMODE, these may be difficult to see.

When using releases after 10, the MEASURE and DIVIDE commands will ignore the current elevation setting and the current UCS and place the points or blocks on the elevation of the object selected.

When using DIVIDE and MEASURE with blocks, keep in mind that subsequent changes in the blocks may affect existing blocks. Sometimes ARRAY is preferable.

INQUIRY COMMANDS

AutoCAD's inquiry commands allow you to find out the parameters and properties of existing items and to perform utility functions within the AutoCAD Drawing Editor. HELP was covered in Chapter 2, so we will first look at the inquiry-oriented functions, and then we will look at the utility functions.

Under INQUIRY we find:

AREA *computes the area of a closed polygon.*

DBLIST *lists all the information on all the entities in a given drawing.*

DIST *computes the distance between two points.*

HELP *offers an explanation of a given command or a list of all the commands.*

ID *identifies a point.*

LIST *lists the position and properties of a specific object or group of objects.*

STATUS *displays the parameters of the file itself.*

TIME *displays the time and the means to set or change it.*

The two commands LIST and DBLIST display a list of the parameters and properties of objects either as specifically identified with LIST or as in the drawing as a whole with DBLIST.

LIST

We looked at LIST briefly in the first section of the book to help identify objects that had already been entered to establish the layer, colour, and linetype properties of those objects. In addition to these properties, LIST is an extremely useful command for the following exercises:

- cleaning up objects before hatching and editing
- determining the angle of an existing line
- determining the radius of a specified circle
- determining text fonts and sizes
- finding out if existing items were placed incorrectly or without the use of SNAP

In 3D, LIST can be used to find out the current Z depth and extrusion length of an object as well as the properties listed above. LIST can also be used to show the number of objects within a specified window to check that the objects follow good CAD practice. In the following example, we will see how LIST can also be used to tell us if the dimension for an object is real or "fudged."

In the illustration on the right, there are two associative dimensions listed. To the eye, they look to be the same. They are identified by being highlighted in the Dot linetype.

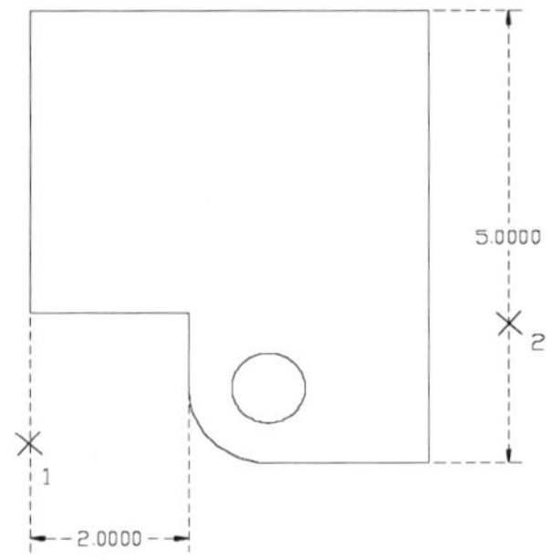

Note the difference in the screen display after the LIST command has been used.

5.0000
2
1
2.0000

```
Command:LIST
Select objects: (pick 1, 2)
DIMENSION Layer:DIM
type:horizontal
1st extension defining point:   X= 2.0000 Y= 4.5000 Z= 0.0000
2nd extension defining point:   X= 4.0000 Y= 3.5000 Z= 0.0000
dimension line defining point:  X= 4.0000 Y= 2.5000 Z= 0.0000
default text position:          X= 3.875  Y= 2.5000 Z= 0.0000
default text:
dimension style:*UNNAMED
DIMENSION Layer:DIM
type:vertical
1st extension defining point:   X= 6.0000 Y= 8.5000 Z= 0.0000
2nd extension defining point:   X= 6.0000 Y= 3.0000 Z= 0.0000
```

```
dimension line defining point:  X= 6.5000 Y= 2.5000 Z= 0.0000
default text position:          X= 6.500  Y= 5.7500 Z= 0.0000
dimension text modifier: 5.0000
dimension style: *UNNAMED
```

You can see that the first dimension has been entered properly, and the text for the dimension is the default text. In the second dimension, however, the dimension text has been modified to read 5.0000. If you subtract the second extension defining point from the first in the Y value, you will notice that the actual distance should read 5.5000, but the dimension text has been altered before it was entered.

In addition to checking your own work to ensure it is entered correctly and that no items overlap, you can check that the dimensions associated with the drawing you have on file are correct and not altered in any way.

Another great advantage of LIST is to determine if there are overlapping lines when making hatches and dimensions. Use LIST, then Crossing, to see the number of overlapping objects.

DBLIST

The DBLIST command is useful for obtaining a listing of the entire file or database. You will probably use this more for debugging than finding entities within the file. If the printer echo is on (Ctrl-Q), you will get a printout of all the items in your file.

The DBLIST command takes a long time to display all the information in a file and can use up a lot of paper needlessly; so, before using it, make sure this is indeed the command you want. You can stop the display at any time by using Ctrl-C.

DIST

The distance command (DIST) will display the actual distance between two points. Remember that, when dealing with points in AutoCAD or any other CAD package, you can specify the points in three ways:

- points associated with objects and identified with OSNAP, such as END(*point*), MID(*point*), etc.
- points in space identified by picking on the screen, with or without the use of SNAP
- points entered by coordinates

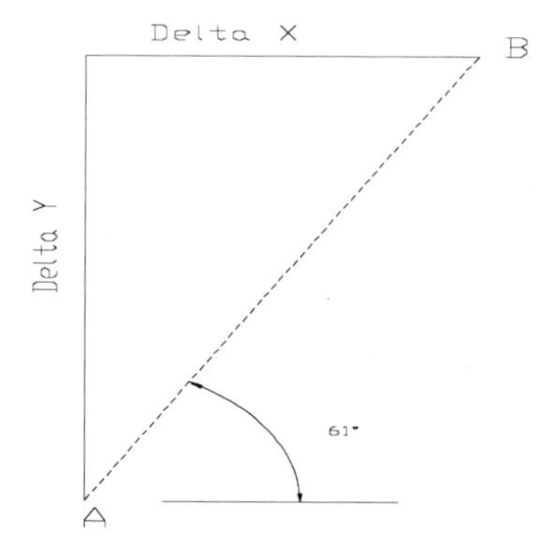

Figure 15-6. Calculating distance

When calculating a distance, you can identify the points by any combination of the above methods. First enter the DIST command, then respond with the two points that identify the distance you want to know. Be sure to specify the exact points you want with either OSNAP or a coordinate entry. As with the other commands, you will be offered the information relative to the current units specified.

Note that the display contains not only the distance, but the angle from the X-Y plane, and the length and the height of the object.

```
Command:DIST
First point: (pick point A)
Second point: (pick point B)
Distance= 10.2956, Angle in X-Y Plane= 61, Angle from X-Y
Plane=0
Delta X = 5.0000  Delta Y = 9.0000    Delta Z = 0.0000
```

ID

The ID command is similar to the LIST command in that it gives an exact position. The difference is that it gives an exact position of a point rather than an object. This command is used in three-dimensional modelling more frequently than in two-dimensional modelling to determine the Z depth of items. In 2D, this can be useful to determine the exact position you are looking at on a zoomed screen or to simply get your bearings. Keep in mind when picking a point in space that SNAP will provide a more readable display.

The location of the point will be relative to the origin or 0,0,0 of the model. If a point in space is chosen, the Z depth will be the current elevation; if an object is chosen with OSNAP, the actual Z depth of the object will be used.

There are basically two ways of using ID. The first is to find the parameters of a point on the screen.

```
Command:ID
Select point: (pick 1)
X = 34.6375      Y = 24.8758     Z = 0.0000
```

This will give the coordinates of a point in space in the units you are using.

The second method is to locate a point by typing in the coordinates.

```
Command:ID
Select point:23,4,0
```

If BLIPMODE is on, you will get a blip on the screen at the exact location of the point entered. The blip will disappear with the next REDRAW.

STATUS

As you become proficient with AutoCAD, you will find the STATUS command more and more useful because it displays a listing of all the statistics of a file.

If you are using a 386 version of AutoCAD, the STATUS command will also display information on the virtual memory and the partition on the hard drive where your temporary file or .$A file is being stored. If you run out of space in this partition (in a classroom this is often the A drive), the program will terminate after saving your file.

In a regular DOS version, STATUS will show the amount of free RAM, free disk space, and I/O page space. The following is a typical display:

```
Command:STATUS
842 entities in A:HOUSING
Model space limits are  X:   -5.0000      Y:  -5.0000
                        X:   60.0000      Y:  45.0000
Model space uses        X:   -2.0000      Y:  -1.5000
                        X:   46.5000      Y:  41.0000
Display shows           X:   12.3453      Y:   6.9846
                        X:   13.6937      Y:   7.9375
Insertion base is       X:    0.0000      Y:   0.0000
                        Z:    0.0000
Snap resolution is      X:    0.5000      Y:   0.5000
Grid spacing is         X:    1.0000      Y:   1.0000

Current space:          Model space
Current layer:          dims
Current color:          1 (red)
Current linetype:       Bylayer — continuous
Axis off Fill on Grid off Ortho on Qtext off Snap off Tablet off
Object snap modes:   Endpoint

Free disk:  21958656 bytes
Virtual memory allocated to program: 2120K
Amount of program in physical memory/Total (virtual) program
size: 100%
Total conventional memory: 368K   Total extended memory: 6528K
Swap file size: 388K bytes
Page faults: 24   Swap writes: 0  Swap reclaims: 12
```

TIME

The TIME command under the Inquiry menu is useful for setting the current time. The time and date, of course, are added to all models when they are saved to help you manage and maintain your files. An internal battery in the computer usually maintains the current time within the operating system of the computer.

The TIME command offers the current time plus other valuable time-related information concerning your current file as well as the opportunity to set a secondary elapsed-time timer.

```
Command:TIME
Current time:           17 Mar 1992 at 19:03:30.456
Drawing created:        02 Mar 1992 at 09:03:45.834
Drawing last updated:   16 Mar 1992 at 15:45:34.592
Time in drawing editor: 2 days 02:45:78.394
Elapsed timer:          0 days 04:23:34.968
Timer on
Display/On/Off/Reset:
```

The timers set by the above command are part of the SETVAR command and can be viewed there. While you can change the secondary timer in this command, the other variables can only be viewed and can be reset only with the following SETVAR commands:

DATE	*current date and time*
TDCREATE	*date and time the current drawing was created*
TDINDWIG	*total editing time*
TDUPDATE	*date and time of the last update and save*
TDUSRTIMER	*elapsed time that the user has been working*

AREA

Since the AREA command can be used in many ways and will be used extensively in the exercises, we have left it until the last to discuss. In short, AutoCAD offers built-in area computational abilities that also display the perimeter of the object calculated. This is useful for calculations of plines and irregular shapes.

Example: *AREA Using an Entity*

This example illustrates a pline that has been fit with a spline curve; the area and perimeter are to be calculated. Here, an entity is chosen for the AREA option.

```
Command:AREA
<First point>/Entity/Add/Subtract:E
Select circle or polyline: (pick 1)
Area = 16.1434   Perimeter = 19.6824
```

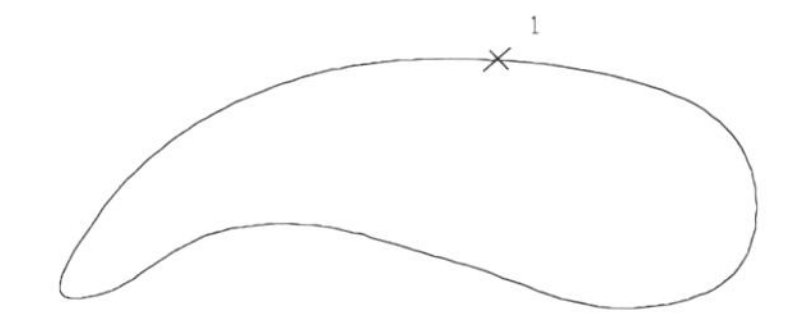

Example: *AREA Using Lines*

When calculating a series of straight lines, the Point option is used as in the following command sequence.

If the points are not exactly on a snap integer, change the SNAP or make the object into a pline.

```
Command:AREA
<First point>/Entity/Add /Subtract: (pick 1)
Next point: (pick 2)
Next point: (pick 3)
Next point: (pick 4)
Next point: (pick 5)
Next point: (pick 6)
Next point:↵
Area = 67.5000   Perimeter = 31.1131
```

AREA can be extremely useful to calculate a floor area or other areas for estimating. Portions of the total space can be subtracted as well. This will help you calculate such things as floor area for tiling. The Subtract and Add options are explained in the following example.

Example: *Area with Multiple Objects*

Calculate the net floor area of a bathroom.

Calculate the total floor area of the bathroom of the example diagram on the next page (top diagram, 8′5" x 5′5"). Then subtract the spaces occupied by the tub, the sink, and the toilet.

Command:**OSNAP**
Object snap modes:**END**

Command:**AREA**
<First point>/Entity/Add /Subtract:**A**
First point: *(pick 1)*
Next point: *(pick 2)*
Next point: *(pick 3)*
Next point: *(pick 4)*
Next point:↵
Area = 6534 square inches
(45.38 square feet)
Perimeter = 27′ 6"
Total area 6534 square inches
(45.38 square feet)

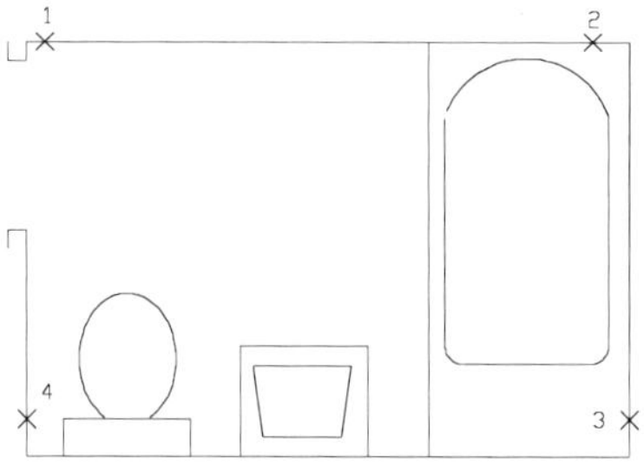

<First point>/Entity/Subtract:**S**
(SUBTRACT mode)<First point>/Entity/
Add: *(pick 5)*
Next point: *(pick 6)*
Next point: *(pick 7)*
Next point: *(pick 8)*
Next point:↵
Area = 2178 square inches
(15.13 square feet)
Perimeter = 16′ 6"
Total area 4356 square inches
(30.25 square feet)

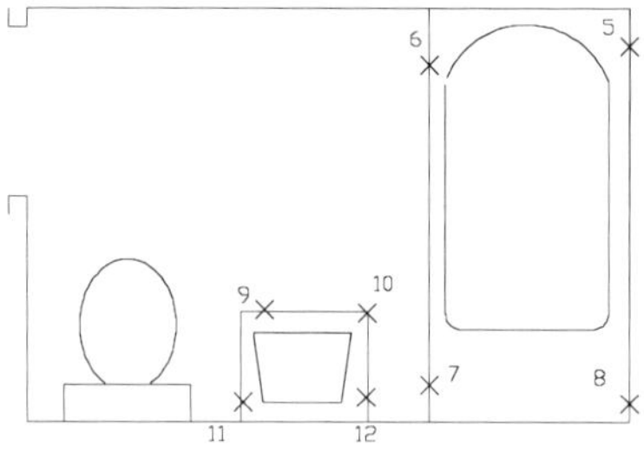

(SUBTRACT mode)<First point>/Entity/
Add: *(pick 9)*
Next point: *(pick 10)*
Next point: *(pick 11)*
Next point: *(pick 12)*
Next point:↵
Area = 378 square inches (2.63 square feet) Perimeter = 6′ 6"
Total area 3978 square inches (27.63 square feet)

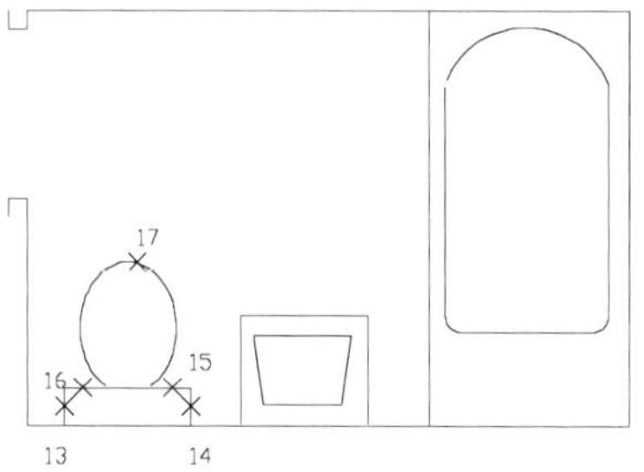

(SUBTRACT mode)<First point>/Entity/Add: *(pick 13)*
(SUBTRACT mode) Next point: *(pick 14)*
(SUBTRACT mode) Next point: *(pick 15)*
(SUBTRACT mode) Next point: *(pick 16)*
(SUBTRACT mode) Next point:↵
Area = 126 square inches (0.88 square feet) Perimeter = 4′ 6"
Total area 3852 square inches (26.75 square feet)

(SUBTRACT mode)<First point>/Entity/Add:**E**
Select circle or polyline: *(pick 17)*
Area = 260 square inches (1.81 square feet) Length = 4′ 2"
Total area 3592 square inches (24.94 square feet)
(SUBTRACT mode) Select circle or polyline:↵

As you can see from the example above, points and entities can be used together. With the Subtract mode, subsequent area calculations are subtracted from the accumulated area. Use Add to enter the first area, then Subtract for the subsequent areas. With the Add mode, subsequent areas will be added to the accumulated area.

The area calculations are made by entities such as circles and plines or by straight-line segments. The lines must be placed exactly on a snap integer or be accompanied by an osnap to be accurate, or you must use PEDIT to make the various segments of an outline into one object that can be picked with Entity, or create a pline on a different layer that echoes exactly the outline of the area you wish to calculate. If a pline is not closed, AutoCAD will assume a straight line between the first and the last points of the selected pline, but will not include this distance in the length of the pline.

In three-dimensional calculations, all the points used for calculation must be on the same plane. The UCS can be changed to allow for this. The extrusion direction of entities must also be parallel with the current UCS.

AREA and PERIMETER are also system variables and can be viewed but not changed. Use the SETVAR command to access the system variable. If you calculated an area, but neglected to jot it down, type AREA as the variable name and the last calculated area will be displayed.

To find the length of a circle, arc, or pline, use the LIST command.

Be sure to change the units to the desired values before entering the AREA command, otherwise the readings may be inaccurate.

Exercise A15

STEP 1

Draw a ladies' bathroom for an assembly occupancy with the dimensions of 36 feet on the west and east walls and 18 feet along the north and south. At the south entrance add a set of double doors and a vestibule, as shown.

STEP 2
Create a toilet block using the specifications on page 272 and, using MEASURE, place eight along the east wall.

STEP 3
Create a bank for lights along the west wall from the north down. Make the bank 29′ x 1′.

STEP 4
Load point display 34, and, using DIVIDE, place seven lights through the centre of this bank.

STEP 5
Create a counter two feet deep and place a sink under each light.

STEP 6
Use the AREA command to calculate the total floor area that needs to be tiled. (Subtract the toilets and sinks from the total area.)

STEP 7
Use LIST to find the length of the swing of the door.

Use DIST to find the total length of the row of toilets.

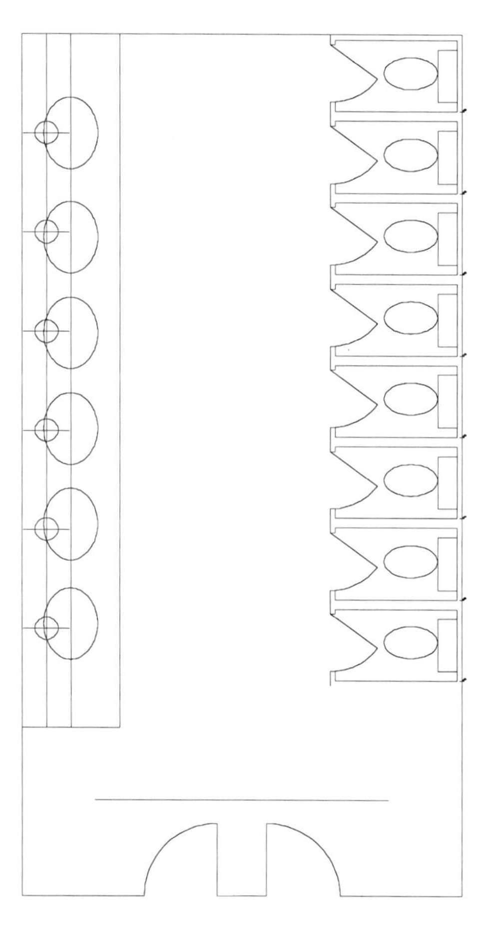

If the southwest corner of the room is at 0,0, what is the exact point at the centre of the first sink?

What is the total area taken up by the toilet stalls?

How much space is left in your partition or RAM?

When you are finished, note the time and the elapsed time needed to complete this project.

MECHANICAL

Exercise M15

STEP 1

Draw the outlines for the sprocket below. If the SNAP is set at .25, it will be quite simple.

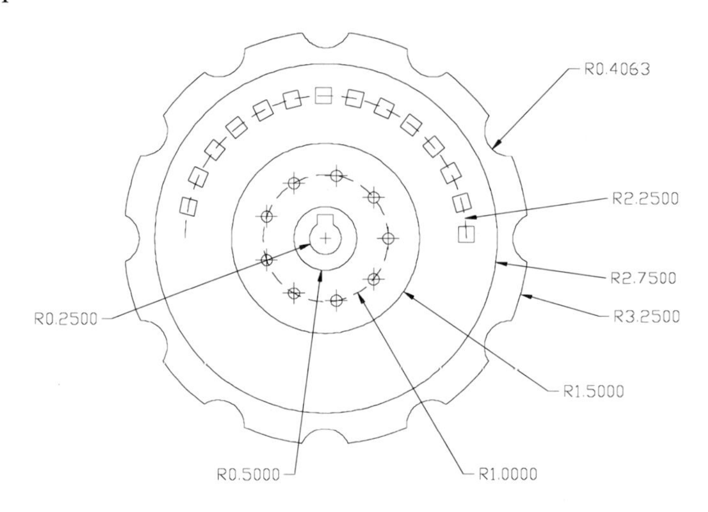

STEP 2

Change the point display to 34 and use DIVIDE to place nine points to indicate the tap holes on the one-unit radius centre line.

STEP 3

Create a block of a square .25 units x .25 units. Use MEASURE to place this block at a distance of 0.5 units along the 2.25 radius arc.

STEP 4

Use the AREA command to calculate the total area of the sprocket making sure to subtract the keyway.

STEP 5

Use LIST to find the length of arc along the perimeter of the sprocket.

Use DIST to find the minimum distance between one square and another on the sprocket.

If the centre of the sprocket is at 0,0, what is the exact location of the left side of the keyway opening?

What is the total area taken up by the squares?

How much space is left in your partition or RAM?

When you are finished, note the time and the elapsed time needed to complete this project.

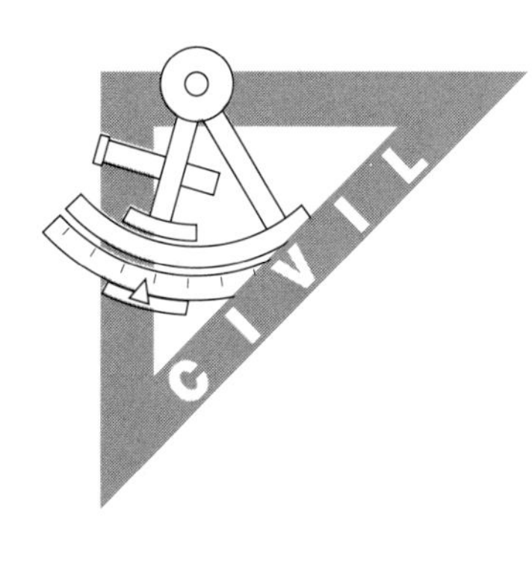

Exercise C15

STEP 1
Use PLINE to create a riverbank fit through the following points.

0,0

6.8,-.2

13.0,-.8

18.7,-1.6

24.3,-2.5

29.7,-3.4

35.2,-4.2

40.9,-4.8

47.0,-5.0

Once in, use PEDIT to create a spline through the pline points.

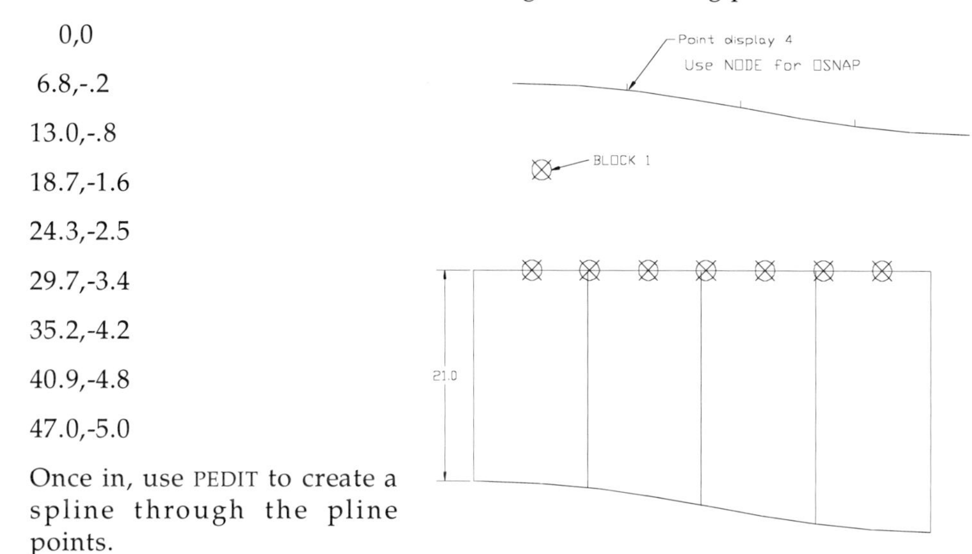

STEP 2
Create a light as shown in the illustration and BLOCK it under the name LIGHT.

STEP 3
Using DIVIDE, divide the riverbank into four equal sections. Use the OSNAP NODE to create lot lines between these sections and the road, 21 metres to the north of the river.

STEP 4
Use MEASURE to place the lights along the roadway at spaces of 7 metres each.

STEP 5
Use the AREA command to calculate the total area of each lot. Make sure you have the correct area, not an area with a straight line from the intersection of the lot line and the plines.

STEP 6
Use LIST to find the length of road along the northern edge of these four lots. Use DIST to find the total length in a straight line from the southwest end of the first lot to the southeast end of the last lot.

If the southwest corner of the lots is at 0,0, what is the exact point at the centre of the four lots?

What is the total area taken up by the lots?

How much space is left in your partition or RAM?

When you are finished, note the time and the elapsed time needed to complete this project.

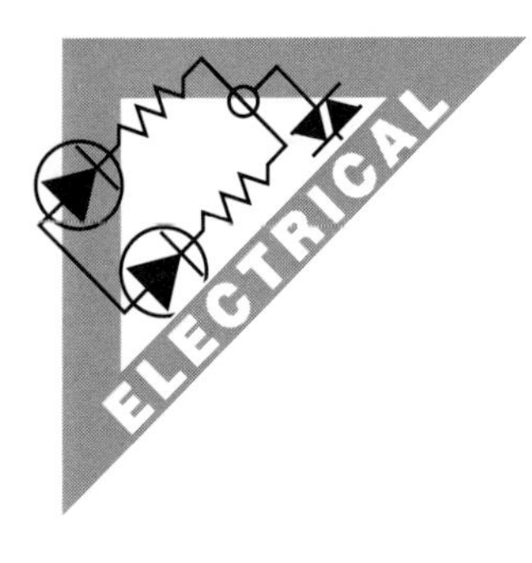

Exercise E15

STEP 1

Use DIVIDE and MEASURE to create this partial drawing of electrical connections in an oscilloscope. Use DIVIDE and MEASURE to place connections in both a circular and a linear fashion. In the linear example, the block was not rotated. In the circular, it was.

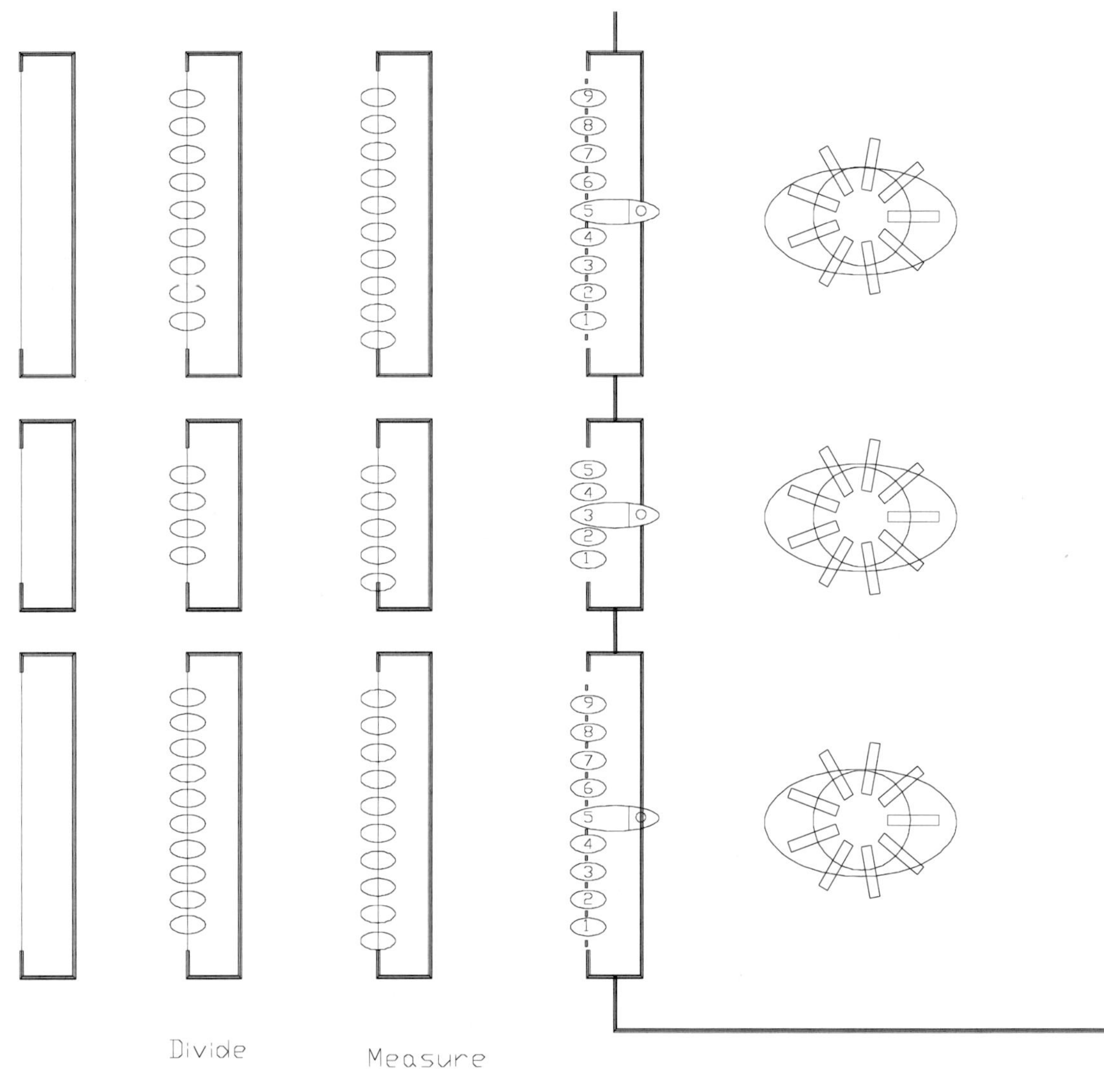

STEP 2

Use LIST to find the length of the connections.

Use DIST to find the height of the schematic.

How much is left in the partition or RAM?

When you are finished, note the time and the elapsed time needed to complete the project.

Challenger 15

STEP 1
Create a standard 2 x 6 stud for an exterior wall using 3dface.

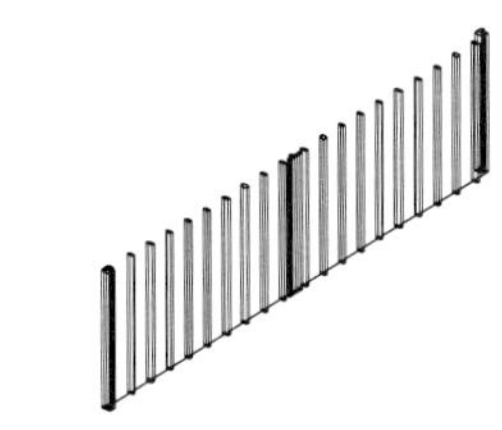

STEP 2
Block the stud. Create a line the length of a cottage wall. Use MEASURE to fit the studs onto the base line at a spacing of 16 inches on centre.

STEP 3
Create base plates and top plates, and add joists according to current code specifications.

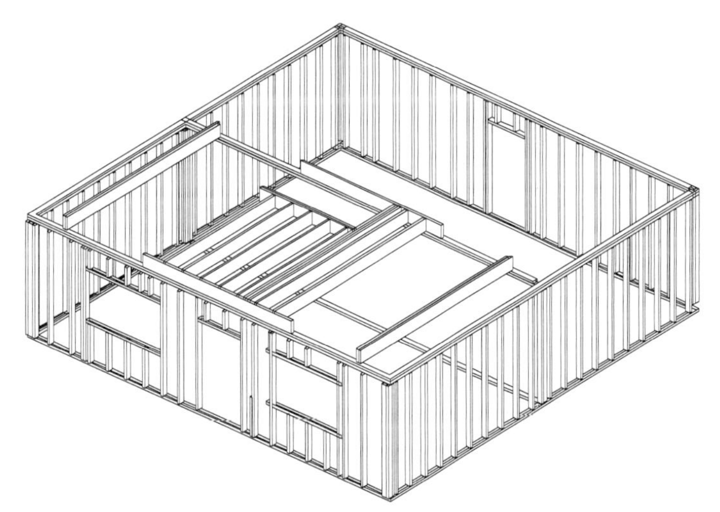

STEP 4
Add rafters using the same BLOCK and MEASURE sequence.

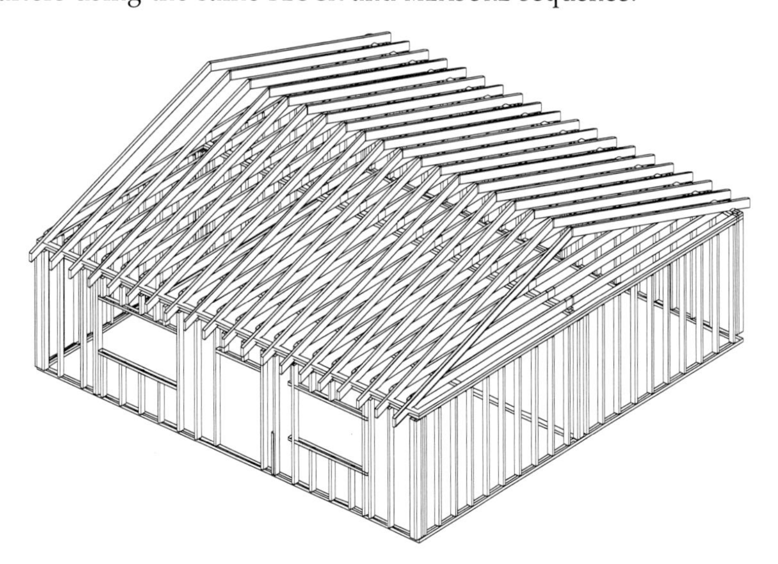

SCRIPTS AND SLIDE SHOWS

Upon completion of this chapter, the student should be able to:

1. Create slides from graphics data using MSLIDE
2. Access on-line slides using VSLIDE
3. Create SCRIPT files for viewing of the slides and other purposes

SLIDES

In order to understand slides and script files, it is important to understand what is happening when you are working on a CAD program. I regret to say that we cannot go any further without getting grotesquely technical. An understanding of the following material, however, will be a big help when you get into larger files and viewports.

The first step in creating a CAD model or drawing is the creation of a vector file by using the available commands — LINE, ARC, and CIRCLE. This is called a vector file because all the geometry is calculated by vectors; the system relates all entered data to a fixed origin, 0,0,0.

Once the geometry is on the screen, it can be edited because it is all referenced to 0,0,0. The various parts are moved in space relative to the origin. If you were clever enough to design a part using only the coordinates of the various objects of geometry, you would not need the screen to view the part at all. In the mechanical engineering field, people did manual parts programming and APT (Automatically Programmed Tool) programming for many years doing exactly that. In fact, for many parts, such as turbine blades and propeller blades comprised of calculated splines and bonded surfaces using specialized mathematical formulae, it is still common to have the designer concentrate largely on the coordinates, with or without the view file. Entering data without a view file is called parametric programming, because it relies on the parameters.

In our case, however, we need to see the information on the screen in order to visualize it, edit it, and, finally, dimension and plot it. The image must be displayed on the screen, and, thus, the screen must be able to somehow display the vectors.

Each screen is made up of a series of small, addressable spots called pixels. Each pixel can display a certain number of colours depending on the quality of the screen. The colours are a mixture of red, green, and blue (RGB) using the subtractive colour theory. When people refer to the resolution of a screen, they are referring to the number of pixels that are displayed horizontally and vertically. A 1024 x 1024 screen has 1024 horizontal pixels and 1024 vertical pixels.

Once the vector file is created, the next step is to have the vector file magnified to fit the user's purposes in one, two, or four viewports.

The final step is to have the image relayed to the screen starting from the top left of the screen and moving in rows down the screen, pixel by pixel. The same process occurs to display an image on a television screen, except it is not often a vector file. This part of the process is referred to as the pixel address format because the image is being addressed to the screen as a series of pixels.

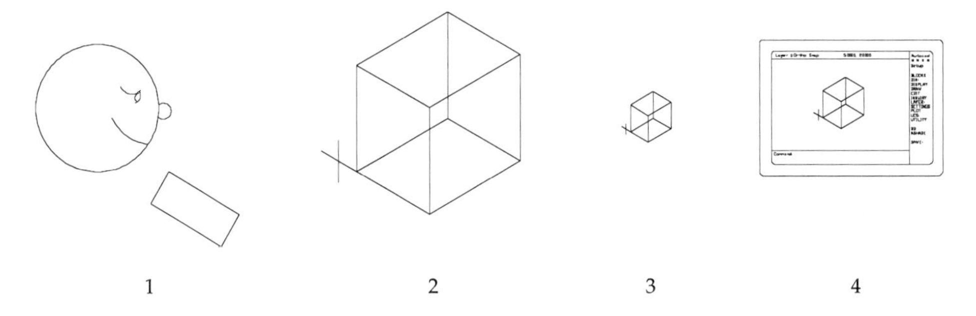

Figure 16-1. Steps to display a vector file

STEP 1 The user enters the commands to create the geometry.

STEP 2 The input data is made into a vector file.

STEP 3 The data is organized to fit the screen.

STEP 4 The image is relayed to the screen pixel by pixel.

Note also that the on-screen menus are addressed in the same manner, so a large part of the image space is taken up by non-image data. The menus can be taken off the screen if you want to leave more room for the image.

Up until now you have been using vector files to create and manipulate images. You may also have noticed that the size of the file you retrieve is directly related to the amount of time it takes to retrieve the file. This delay occurs because the vector files are large and take time to be manipulated and magnified to produce the screen image. In certain situations, you may not need to work on the CAD file, but only want to see it. Therefore, it is desirable to access just the pixel address file and not the other parts of the file. A slide does this by extracting the pixel address portion of the file for viewing.

Slides are useful for several applications:

- to provide a slide show of a particular product for clients
- to provide a slide show of your work for a prospective employer
- to have available on file an easily viewed set of images of your own blocks, line fonts, title blocks, etc.
- to have an instruction tool to tell a story or explain a concept

The slides you make on-screen are similar to photograph slides you could take of the screen using a camera to show with the aid of a projector.

MSLIDE

The procedure for making slides is very simple, but the concepts behind the command are sometimes difficult to grasp at first for those who have not worked extensively with computers.

STEP 1
The first thing you must do is create the graphics for the slide. This is done in the regular Drawing Editor using standard drawing and editing commands.

STEP 2
Once the drawing is complete, use ZOOM and PAN to centre the objects on the screen. The slide you will be making will take up the entire screen; it is not defined by a Window, so be sure you have the view of the object you want.

Now make a slide of this geometry using the command MSLIDE. You need only enter the name of the desired slide file, and AutoCAD will make a slide of the image on the screen.

```
Command:MSLIDE
Slide file <firerate>:firert1
```

This will create a slide file (FIRERT1.SLD) in the same directory as your drawing file (FIRERATE.DWG). If you want to specify a drive and directory, use the following.

```
Command:MSLIDE
Slide file <firerate>:D:\slides\firert1
```

Where:
<firerate> = the name of the file you are in

D: = the directory

slides\\ = the slides subdirectory

firert1 = the name of the slide

You can simply enter the name of the slide if you are not concerned with the directory or the subdirectory. If you are working on drive A, your slide will be saved on that drive.

Try checking the directory (DIR A:); you should have a file with the extension .SLD; this is your slide file. The extension is added automatically with each MSLIDE command.

The slide is now ready to access and can be accessed at any time by invoking the command VSLIDE.

VSLIDE

There are a few sample slides available with your AutoCAD program. If you make a directory listing in the AutoCAD main directory, you should see at least the following:

- COLORWH.SLD
- CHROMA.SLD
- POINTS.SLD

These slides are available for users to see the available point designs for SETVAR PDMODE or point display mode and to view the colours available on your own screen.

To view any of the slides, simply use VSLIDE and the name as in the following:

```
Command:VSLIDE
Slide file <default>:chroma
```

The AutoCAD slide CHROMA will be retrieved over the top of your current drawing. You have not lost your drawing; a simple REDRAW will bring it back.

Just as in the INSERT command, you need to specify the directory or drive if it is not the one currently being used. If you are using Release 10 or above and you have multiple viewports, the slide will be displayed in the current viewport.

The icon menus you have been accessing since AutoCAD Release 9 — hatch, font, etc. — are based on MSLIDE files. We will use slides again in Chapter 21 to create icon menus.

Slides, REGENS, and REDRAWS

A REDRAW will refresh the screen with the image displayed before the slide was invoked. This should take much less time than a REGEN because only the pixel address or bit map file is being refreshed. It would be a good idea at this point to look at the size of files to get a better understanding of the REGEN command with relation to the REDRAW command. Look at the slide files using DIR A:. Note the size of the slide files (.SLD) relative to the size of the drawing files (.DWG).

Turning back to the illustration on page 284, you can see the difference in the .SLD files and the .DWG files.

- .SLD files are step 4 only
- .DWG files are steps 2, 3, and 4
- A REDRAW is step 4 only
- A REGEN is steps 2, 3, and 4

Now you can see why it takes so much longer to do a REGEN than a REDRAW.

Slide Libraries

Managing slides in a specific slide library is an efficient way to avoid cluttering a disk. The library will have an extension of .SLB and will contain all your slides either for slideshows or for icon menus. (The creation of slide libraries will be explained in more detail in Chapter 21.)

To access or view a slide from a specific library, use the following:

```
Command:VSLIDE
Slide file <default>:(library name) (slide name)
```

The sample slides available in AutoCAD are from the ACAD.SLB file.

SCRIPT

A script is a simple text file that contains AutoCAD commands. The script can be run from either inside or outside of the Drawing Editor from the operating system prompt. Script files are used to automate or preprogram a process such as viewing slides, running plots, or configuring a menu. First the script file is written, then, when invoked, each line of the file is read and executed as if it had been typed in at the command prompt. The script file essentially records the keystrokes needed to perform a certain function.

As with the template file for ATTEXT, any ASCII-based file can be used to create a script file. The most popular text editors that accept this data are MS-DOS Editor, the DOS program Edlin, WordPerfect's DOS-text file option, the WordPerfect Library Program Editor, WordStar in non-document mode, PC Write, Microsoft Word in text-only format, and Norton's Editor, Sidekick. All of these will produce the required ASCII file format. See Appendix F for text editing formats.

To create a script file you need to know both the command and the responses exactly. Each keystroke is important. For example, a script file to centre a drawing and generate a plot might look like this:

ZOOM	*ZOOM command*
All	*All [ZOOM ALL]*
ZOOM	*ZOOM command*
.95x	*centres the view, a little smaller than the total screen area*
PLOT	*PLOT command*
D	*plot display*
N	*want to change anything?*
	blank line is a return to start plotting

In creating a script file for the slide show, you will be preprogramming a series of VSLIDE commands that will allow the user to view a series of slides without touching the keyboard. This is a popular technique at trade shows, etc.; it displays many drawing files, one by one, while the station is unattended. The commands needed to perform the slide show are as follows:

VSLIDE **name**	*will view a slide*
DELAY **1000**	*will delay 1 second for viewing (2000 = 2 seconds, etc.)*
VSLIDE ***name**	*will preload a slide for viewing*
VSLIDE	*will display a preloaded slide*
RSCRIPT	*will repeat the entire program, ^C will stop it*

A CTRL-C will stop the script file. A backspace will temporarily halt it. Use RESUME to continue if the script file has been halted.

On page 292 are images for a test slide show. It is not terribly serious in nature and should take less than one hour to generate if you want to try it. The following is the script file for producing the sequence. Again, for those not familiar with text files, the example at the end of this chapter should show you the easiest way to create it.

VSLIDE **A:BUBBLE1**	*views slide BUBBLE1*
DELAY **1000**	*delays for 1 second*
VSLIDE **A:BUBBLE2**	*views slide BUBBLE2*
VSLIDE ***A:BUBBLE3**	*preloads BUBBLE3*
DELAY **1000**	*delays view of BUBBLE2*
VSLIDE	*views immediately BUBBLE3*
VSLIDE ***A:BUBBLE4**	*preloads BUBBLE4*

DELAY 1000	*delays view of BUBBLE3*
VSLIDE	*views slide BUBBLE4*
VSLIDE *A:BUBBLE5	*preloads BUBBLE5*
DELAY 1000	*delays view of BUBBLE4*
SLIDE	*views slide BUBBLE5*
VSLIDE *A:BUBBLE6	*preloads BUBBLE6*
DELAY 1000	*delays view of BUBBLE5*
SLIDE	*views slide BUBBLE6*
RSCRIPT	*repeats the script*

The command to load the slides is VSLIDE; no extension is needed.

Example: *Scripts and Slides*

This splatter file of a young girl blowing a bubble is very simple and should take less than an hour. It also takes up a very small amount of space, so can be useful in testing out slides and scripts without using up too much of your time and disk space. If this is too violent for your liking, try another cartoon sequence, making sure there is a distinct difference between each slide. (Colour 14 for grape bubble.)

Create the first view using arcs. Copy the view and make minor adjustments.

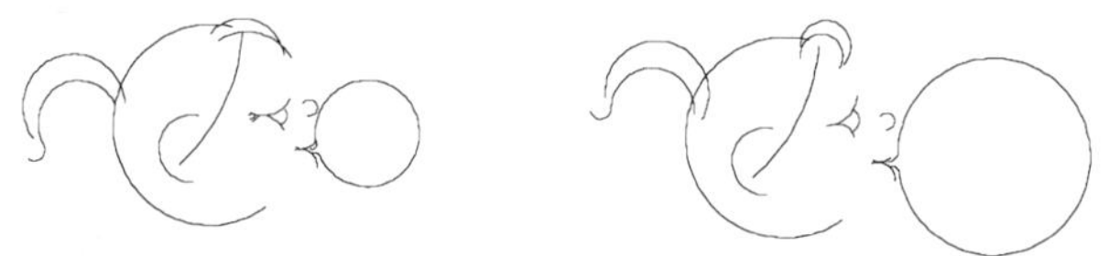

Copy both of the existing views, and create a sequence of events.

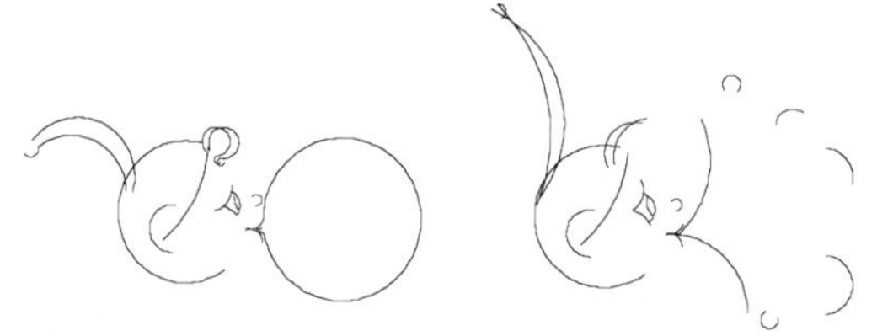

Now use ZOOM Window to bring each view separately onto the screen and use MSLIDE to create a slide. Be careful to number them in sequence. Now create a script file in Edlin as outlined above to generate your own moving picture. (See Appendix C for Edlin commands.) Use SCRIPT to make it run.

Example: *Scripts for Beginning a Drawing*

There are many ways to customize your AutoCAD environment to make it more suitable for completing projects. In many offices, only one standard drawing size is created. If this is the case, then a prototype drawing is all you need. If, on the other hand, there are several different sizes of drawings, then you can create script files that will accommodate these various sizes and set-ups for your model or drawing.

For example, if you are working on a part that is 18 x 14, you may find a script file called A2.SCR useful. It might look like this:

UNITS	*units command*
2	*decimal linear units*
2	*two decimal places*
1	*decimal angular units*
	Space to accept angle default
n	*measure angles counter-clockwise*
LIMITS	*LIMITS command*
-1,-1	*Lower limit*
20,16	*Upper limit*
ZOOM	*ZOOM command*
A	*All*
GRID	*GRID command*
2	*Two-unit spacing for grid*
SNAP	*SNAP command*
.5	*5-unit SNAP spacing*

This script file can be accessed as soon as you enter the Drawing Editor. It will give you all the sizes you need to start the project.

A script file can easily take the place of a prototype drawing file if you find this method more suitable to your AutoCAD environment.

The script file can be very useful for creating standardized plots with similar layer/colour and layer/linetype adjustments.

Release 12 notes

AutoCAD displays a standard dialogue box entitled "Create Slide File" in release 12. If you include a filename and include the file type, it must be .sld. Slides are made of the image found in the selected viewport. With a shaded image black lines may be seen interspersed among the lines of the shaded image. Use a full screen image rather than a smaller viewport, and set to the highest resolution available to avoid this.

Exercise A16

STEP 1

Take six attributed wblock files (create them quickly if you do not have six on file), place them on a file, and create a slide using MSLIDE for each individual block. Make up at least six blocks.

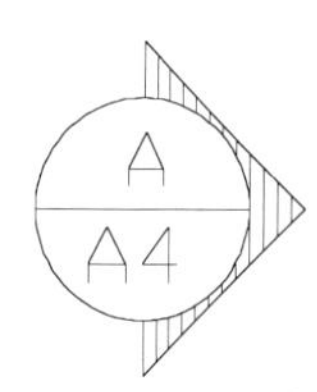

Attributed block
Building Section
BLOCK NAME: ATTBS

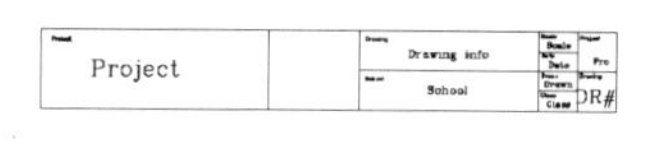

Attributed block
Horizontal Title Block
BLOCK NAME: ATTHT

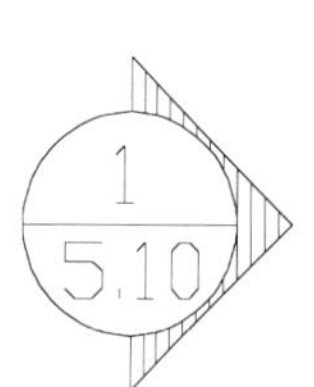

Attributed block
Wall Section
BLOCK NAME: ATTWS

Block
North Arrow
BLOCK NAME: ARROW

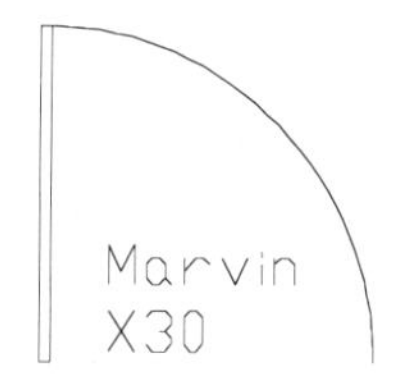

Attributed block
Door
BLOCK NAME: ATTDOOR

Attributed block
Window
BLOCK NAME: ATTWINDO

STEP 2

Now generate a script file using SCRIPT to view each of these attributed blocks as a reference. Other information you could add to this format is origin and scale of the blocks.

STEP 3

Create a slide show.

Exercise M16

STEP 1
Take six attributed wblock files (create them quickly if you do not have six on file), place them on a file, and create a slide using MSLIDE for each individual block. Make at least six blocks.

Attributed block
Section Arrow
BLOCK NAME: ATTSA

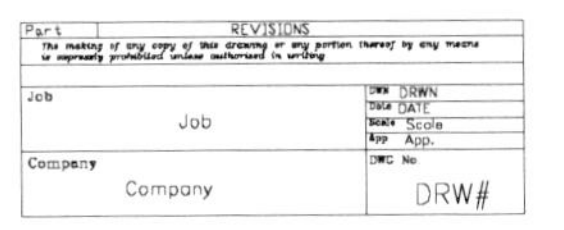

Attributed block
Horizontal Title Block
BLOCK NAME: ATTHT

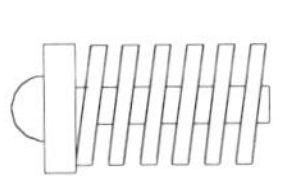

ACME
sp486

Attributed block
Spring set
BLOCK NAME: ATTSS

Attributed block
Bolt
BLOCK NAME: ATTBOLT

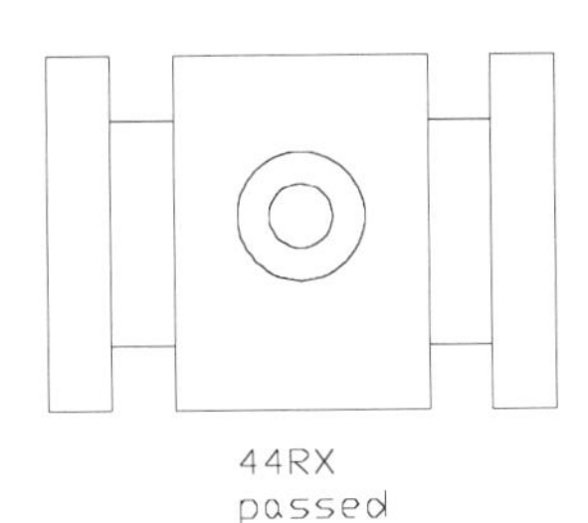

Attributed block
Centre Pin
BLOCK NAME: ATTPIN

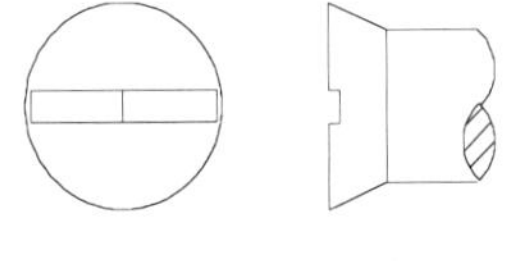

Slotted
.23xx

Attributed block
Slotted
BLOCK NAME: ATTSLOT

STEP 2
Now generate a script file using SCRIPT to view each of these attributed blocks as a reference. Other information you could add to this format is origin and scale of the blocks.

STEP 3
Create a slide show.

Exercise C16

STEP 1
Take six attributed wblock files (create them quickly if you do not have six on file), place them on a file, and create a slide using MSLIDE for each individual block. Make at least six blocks.

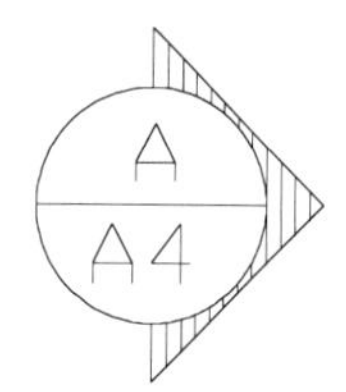

Attributed block
Road Section
BLOCK NAME: ATTRS

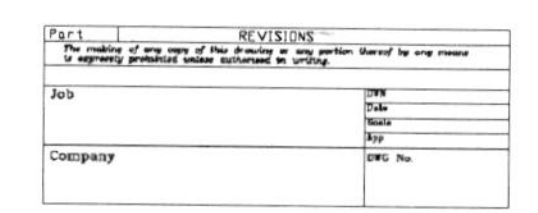

Attributed block
Horizontal Title Block
BLOCK NAME: ATTHT

Attributed block
Curb Cut Approach
BLOCK NAME: ATTCCA

Block
North Arrow
BLOCK NAME: ARROW

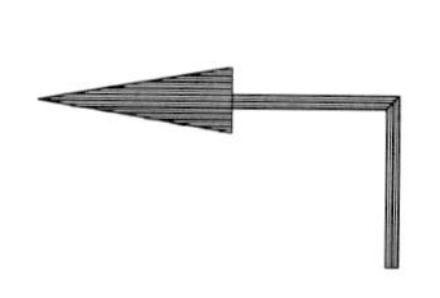

Attributed block
Turn Arrow
BLOCK NAME: ATTTARR

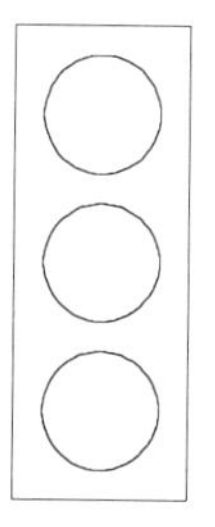

Attributed block
Stop Light
BLCOK NAME: ATTSTOP

STEP 2
Now generate a script file using SCRIPT to view each of these attributed blocks as a reference. Other information you could add to this format is origin and scale of the blocks.

STEP 3
Create a slide show.

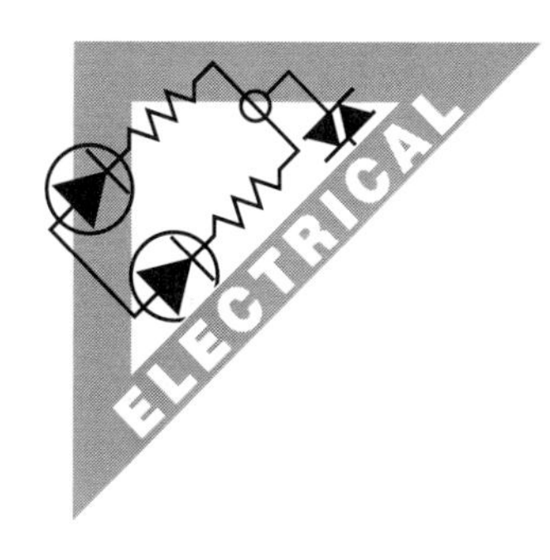

Exercise E16

STEP 1
Take six attributed wblock files (create them quickly if you do not have six on file), place them on a file, and create a slide using MSLIDE for each individual block. Make at least six blocks.

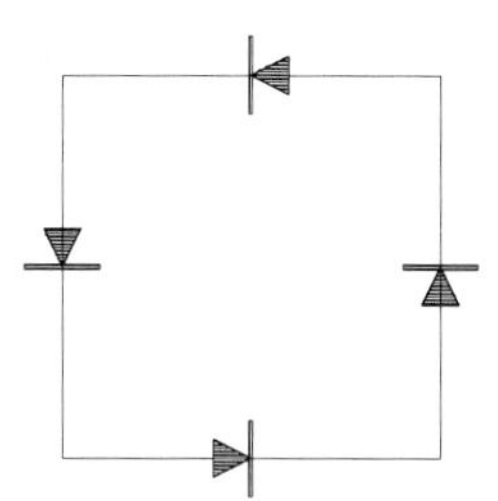

Attributed block
Rectifier
Full Wave Bridge
BLOCK NAME: FWB

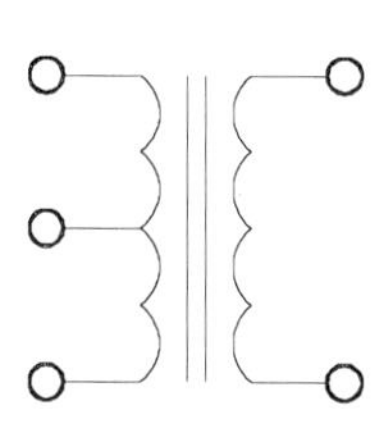

Attributed block
Transformer
Magnetic Core/Single
BLOCK NAME: MCST

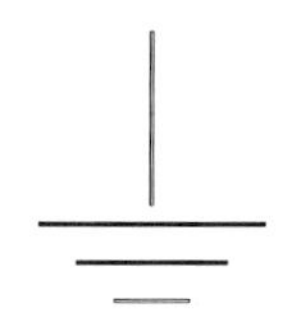

Attributed block
Connecting
Dots
BLOCK NAME: DOTS

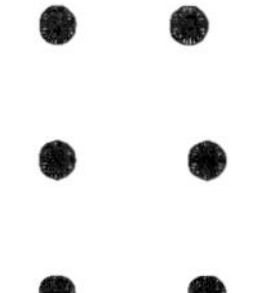

Attributed block
Connecting
Dots
BLOCK NAME: DOTS

Attributed block
Variable
Resistor
BLOCK NAME: VR

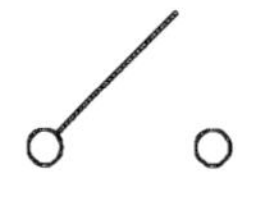

Attributed block
Switch
Single Pole
BLOCK NAME: SPSWITCH

STEP 2
Now generate a script file using SCRIPT to view each of these attributed blocks as a reference. Other information you could add to this format is origin and scale of the blocks.

STEP 3
Create a slide show.

Challenger 16

In this drawing of ventilation patterns, we can see how the first view illustrates an insulated house and the ventilation going into it. The second two houses are ventilation patterns through windows, etc.

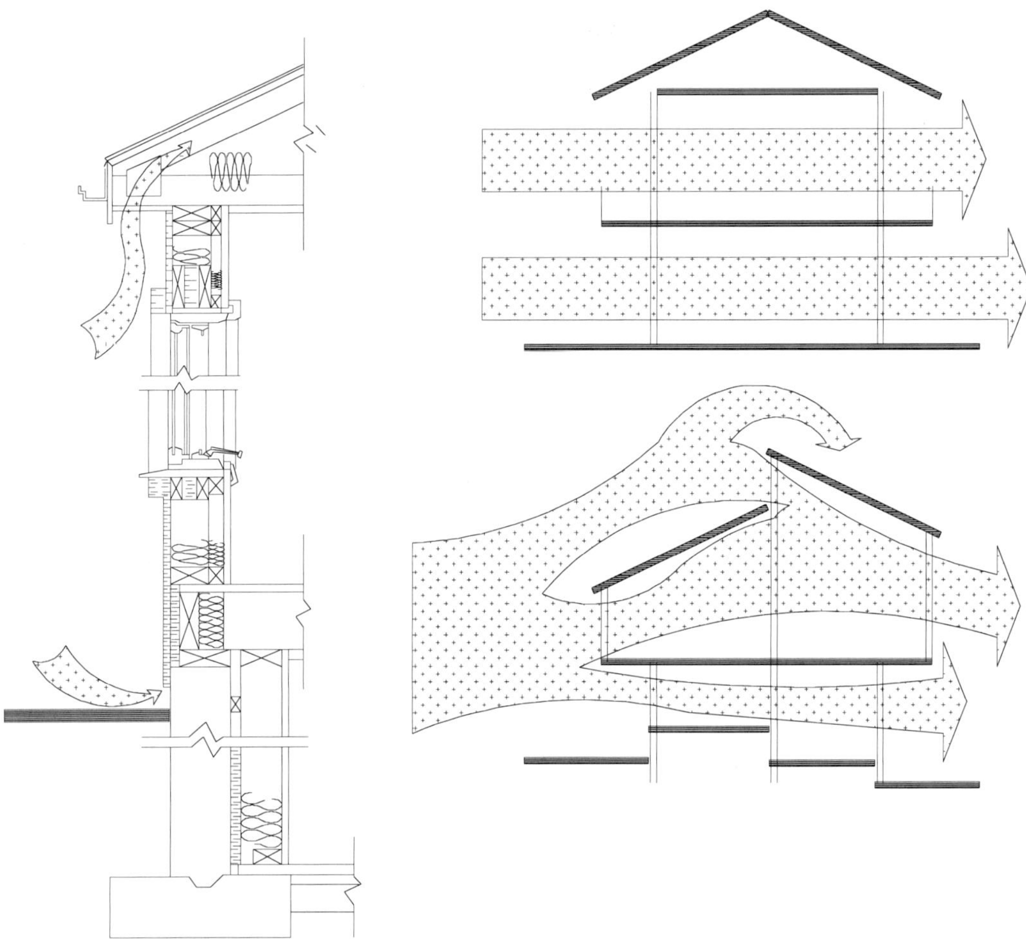

Using a condition that exists in your discipline, generate a group of views that develop a certain thought process or project and develop a slide show for presentation.

MECHANICAL – movements of a robotic arm

– drilling a piece of metal

– turning gears

ARCHITECTURAL – different framing techniques

– movement of a window

– renovation of a kitchen

CIVIL – traffic flow problems

– cut and fill before and after

— installation of services in an area

EXCHANGING GRAPHICS AND TEXT FILES

Upon completion of this chapter, the student should be able to:

1. Transfer a graphic from AutoCAD to WordPerfect
2. Transfer a WordPerfect document to AutoCAD

TRANSFERRING GRAPHICS

There are many reasons for transferring graphics to a word processing format; the most obvious is to allow the user to illustrate a note or letter to a colleague or for marketing purposes. The graphic can be in either two-dimensional or three-dimensional format and can be inserted into the word processor document at any size that will fit the sheet. The word processor we will be using for this example is WordPerfect, but any comparable word processor will perform in the same manner. Any WordPerfect release past 5.0 will have this capability.

Example: *Transferring AutoCAD Graphics to WordPerfect*

STEP 1
Generate the graphic in AutoCAD using any of the two-dimensional or three-dimensional formats. Text and dimensions may be added too, but be careful that the sizing will allow viewing on an 8 1/2" x 11" sheet. Generally, the space given for graphics is about 6" x 6". If your text is barely readable on the screen at 8 1/2 x 11, there is no chance you will see it on a WordPerfect sheet.

STEP 2
Generate a plot file (a:name.plt) for the graphics to be exported by using the PLOT command (to be discussed shortly).

> **Note:** Graphics must be generated in a Hewlett Packard plot-file format. Before a plot file is made, make sure your system is configured for a Hewlett Packard plotter. The HP.DRV file (plotter driver file) is standard on any AutoCAD release past Release 9. If you need to reconfigure a plotter, select task 5 from the AutoCAD main menu — Reconfigure AutoCAD — then choose option 5, Configure plotter. This will offer you a list of the various plotters supported by AutoCAD. If your system has been set up properly, all you need to do is choose the HP driver. Exit from the Reconfigure menu and save the changes.

Release 12 Notes
In the Plot dialogue box, be sure to pick the HP plotter from the available listing.

Use the PLOT command in AutoCAD to select the drawing or portion of a drawing to be exported. In the PLOT command, select Yes at the "Make a Plot File" prompt. This will generate a plot file but not send the drawing to the plotter. Also, make sure the plot is scaled to Fit; otherwise, your graphics will not be accepted properly. The plot file should look like this:

```
Command:PLOT
What to plot —Display,Extents,Limits,View or Window <D>:
*Plot will be written to a selected file
 Sizes are in inches:
 Plot origin at 0.00,0.00
 Plotting area is ________ _________
 Plot is NOT rotated 90 degrees
 Pen width is 0.010
 Area fill will not be adjusted for pen width
 Hidden lines will NOT be removed
*Plot will be scaled to fit available area.
```

If you see the message:

```
Plot will NOT be written to a select file
```

change that option in the command. Also, be sure the plot is scaled to fit.

The size of the plot, the units, the area fill, etc. at this point are not important, because you will be changing all these options when you import the file to WordPerfect. When the plot information is accepted, you will be requested to enter the name of the plot file.

```
Enter file name for plot <template>:a:test
```

You may enter any name for the plot file; the default will be the current drawing name. The plot file will have an extension of .PLT automatically appended to it. (DIR A: will display a listing of the files.)

Once your plot file is generated, END to save the .DWG file and exit AutoCAD.

STEP 3
Start WordPerfect. If you are not familiar with WordPerfect basic command structures, refer to Appendix F. The .PLT file is also referred to as an HPGL file and can be imported into other word processing packages as well by using figure boxes or other graphic devices. The methods are similar; we have chosen the WordPerfect format because it is the standard word processing package in most colleges.

You can insert the graphics file at any point in your WordPerfect file, as long as you have enough room to view it. If you want the graphic to be 6 inches in height, you must leave that amount of space on the sheet, or it simply will not work. The graphic, being identified as a User Box, will show up on the next page if you do not allow enough room for it. This can become confusing because the user box is shown on the reveal codes screen (ALT-F3) to be on one page, but the box itself may show up on the next page. If you keep in mind that you need to provide enough space on the page for the graphic, you should be fine.

When you are ready to import the graphic file (.PLT) into your text file, enter:

ALT-F9 - WordPerfect Graphics option
4 - user defined box
1 - create

You are now in the User Box menu and can enter the information needed to place the box where you want it.

Choose the options from the following list to place your graphics.

1.`Filename - `**`drive:filename.plt`** *(example, a:test.plt)*
2.`Contents - empty` *(will display GRAPHIC when full)*
3.`Caption - ` *(usually done in AutoCAD)*
4.`Anchor type - paragraph`
5.`Vertical position - 0` *(insert the graphic at the present cursor position)*
6.`Horizontal position - Right` *(options are left, right, centre, and full)*
7.`Size - 3.25" x 3.25"` *(You may take this up to 6.2 inches with no trouble. Note also that some systems take inches as a format and some take positions up to 75. Note your format before starting.)*
8.`Wrap text around box - yes` *(allows the text to wrap around the user box)*
9.`Edit`

The justification (5 & 6) as well as the size of the graphic may be adjusted to fit the page. The box size will automatically contain all the graphics in the plot file regardless of the paper size specified in the PLOT command of AutoCAD.

If the scale of your insert is critical — for example, you are entering a detail of an object that is 5" x 4" and it must be to scale — make sure the scale is exact in AutoCAD. Use the same box size as the part, and you should be close.

Once the graphic is accepted, you can view the page to see how it looks.

Enter the Print menu **SHIFT-F7**
Then choose **6** *(View Document)*

You can change the size of the document being viewed by selecting one of the numbers at the bottom of the screen display.

Press the space bar to exit.

Once the graphic is inserted into the document, you will notice the area on the screen where the graphic should appear. If you want to change the size of the graphic or edit it in any other way, use:

`ALT-F9`

`4` `- user box`

`2` `- edit`

You will be prompted for the user box number you want to edit. All user boxes are identified by number; make sure you are editing the correct box.

If you decide the graphic is entirely wrong and want to delete it, press ALT-F3, find the area on the screen referring to the user box, and use either the Backspace or Delete key to erase it.

ALT-F3 is reveal codes. To turn this function off, press **ALT-F3** again.

Other Options

The box in Figure 17-1 is justified on the right, has wrap-around text, and is 2 inches in width and 1.5 inches in height.

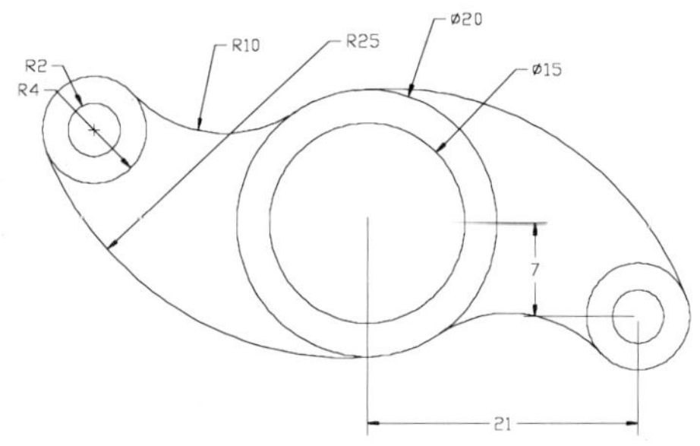

Figure 17-1. Graphic inserted

In the user box in Figure 17-2, the same .PLT file was used, but

- the size was changed (**7, 1**)
- the justification was set to left (**6, 1, 1**)
- a double border was added (**ALT-F9, 4, 4, 1, 3**)

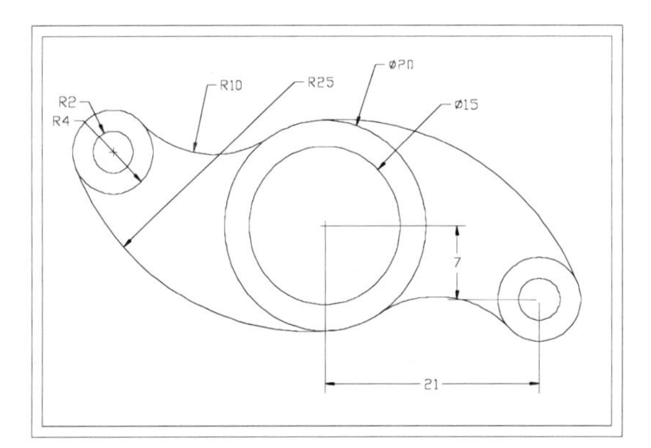

Figure 17-2. Graphic inserted with borders

Release 12 Notes

Under the File pull-down menu, by Import/Export, are options for PostScript in and out. This allows you to both import and export .EPS files directly. The PSOUT command is similar to a plot command: you are prompted for what area of the drawing you would like to export.

Command: **PSOUT**
What to export—Display, Extents, Limits, View, or Window :

In a 3D model, the exported EPS image is from the three-dimensional viewpoint most recently established in the current space (either model space or paper space). The View option takes the user's line-of-sight.

In Release 12 there is also the ability to add "postage stamp" images in the form of an EPSI format defined by Adobe or in a TIFF format that is more common in MS-DOS. These images are used in desktop publishing to preview the .EPS file. Once you have chosen the portion of the drawing that you would like exported you are given the following prompt:
Include a screen image preview in the file? (None/EPSI/TIFF) :

If you choose either EPSI or TIFF you will then be prompted for pixel resolution; the smallest size (128x128) is the most common.

Release 12 Notes (cont'd)

If you have chosen None or when you have completed the choice of export image format and resolution, you will be prompted for ww by hh of the current plotting area. You are then prompted for the units, scale, and output size.

In addition to direct EPS output, AutoCAD reads the PostScript files directly into AutoCAD as anonymous block images, PostScript Adobe Type 1 fonts into AutoCAD drawings. They can be used dynamically or compiled into conventional Shape/Font files for easy loading. These fonts when loaded can be used exactly as normal text fonts except that they will be displayed as outlines on screen; on paper they will fill as defined by the font definition.

For a regular PostScript file use the following:

Command: **PSIN**
PostScript file name:
Insertion point ,0,0):
Scale factor:

No extension is required, .EPS is assumed.

PSDRAG
The PSDRAG command allows the image to be fully displayed (1) or seen only as a bounding box (0) as it is dragged into position.

PSQUALITY
This controls the quality or resolution of the image.

PSFILL
This command allows you to fill closed polylines with a PostScript pattern.

EXTENSIONS AND OTHER GRAPHIC TRANSFERS

There are other software packages that accept AutoCAD graphic files but may not accept AutoCAD .PLT files. Here is a listing of some of the possible graphic extensions and how to access them.

.EPS — *Encapsulated Postscript. This can be configured as an output similar to an HPGL file in AutoSHADE.*

.GIF — *Graphics Image File. Much the same as an .SLD file. Simply rename the .SLD file to a .GIF file.*

.HPG (L) — *Hewlett Packard Graphics Language. Simply rename the .PLT file to an .HPG file, making sure that the HP driver (7475) is the plotter driver. This format is used in Ventura and other desktop publishing software.*

.TIF (F) — *Tagged Image File Format. Used extensively in AutoSHADE, this is a direct image output from AutoSHADE.*

.WPG — *WordPerfect Graphics. Use a .DXF file to convert to .WPG.* See Chapter 18.

The three basic graphic extract file types are .EPS, .HPG, and .TIF. Most graphic files will be one of the above formats. Knowing how to extract these from AutoCAD, you should be able to take one of these file formats and simply rename it to the graphics extension you need.

Third-party vendors also sell conversion products. *HiJaak* by Inset and *CAD-VERT* by Interface are examples.

What Can Go Wrong with Importing a Graphics Extract

Incompatible file format
If this is your response when trying to import the graphic into the word processor program, you have extracted an incorrect file type. Make sure the driver is the HP 7475 driver in the Configure option of AutoCAD's main menu.

Occasionally, when trying to create a .PLT file in AutoCAD, the file will not be written properly, and the response during the Calculating Vectors sequence of the PLOT command is a screen display of all the vectors. In this case, the .PLT file has not worked, usually because of the name you have used. Try using the default name or the drawing name, and this should work.

File not found
Make sure you have entered the .PLT extension, because the WordPerfect program will be looking for a .WPG file.

TRANSFERRING TEXT FILES

There are many reasons for transferring text files into AutoCAD, the most obvious being that most text editors are far superior in flexibility to the AutoCAD TEXT command. In addition, it seems a shame to have to retype information onto AutoCAD when the information already exists in WordPerfect, Norton Editor, WordStar, etc. Any ASCII text editor will do to create this type of text format.

In addition, if there are notations that are always added to drawings, this method will reduce the possibilities for error, particularly considering the typing skills illustrated by many AutoCAD students. Many text editors also have a Spellcheck utility that can prevent wear and tear on a client's or an instructor's good nature.

STEP 1
Create a document using your favourite word processor. WordPerfect will be the software package illustrated here. If you are not fully conversant with WordPerfect, see Appendix F.

STEP 2
Save the document in an ASCII format using the following:

```
Ctrl-F5
(DOS text)    1 (save)
              1
Document to be saved (DOS text):a:A17
```

Make a note of the name and any filename extensions. This is the same file exit procedure used by ATTEXT, but no .TXT is needed.

Exit WordPerfect, but do not save your document again under the same name in a WordPerfect format.

```
F7
Save document N
Exit WordPerfect Y
```

STEP 3

Retrieve the AutoCAD file that is to receive the text. Load the LISP program ASCTEXT exactly as shown here.

```
Command:(LOAD "ASCTEXT")
C:ASCTEXT

Command:ASCTEXT
File to read (including extension):A:A17
Start point or Center/Middle/Right: (pick 1)
Height <0.2000>:.1
Rotation Angle <0>:↵
Change Text Options? <n>:↵
```

The text will be loaded in strings. If there are any character editing changes required, use CHANGE.

The inserted text can be justified using any of the standard text justifications.

If you want to change some of the text options in the last option,

```
Change Text Options? <n>:Y
```

the following prompts will appear:

```
Distance between line/<Auto>: (enter a distance or ↵)
First line to read/<1>: (enter an integer or ↵)
Number of lines to read/<All>: (enter an integer or ↵)
Underscore each line?<N>:↵
Overscore each line?<N>:↵
Change text case? Upper/Lower/<N>:↵
Set up columns?<N>:↵
```

If you answer yes to the "Set up columns?" prompt, AutoCAD prompts for the distance between the columns and the number of lines per column.

```
Distance between columns: (enter a distance)
Number of lines per column: (enter an integer)
```

The ASCTEXT.LSP program should be a standard program on AutoCAD. If you are having trouble loading it, first check to see that you have spelled it correctly, then, if you are still unsuccessful, ask your system manager if the LISP routines have been added to another directory.

Exercise A17

In AutoCAD, create a detail drawing of a problem that has occurred at a particular site. Generate a plot file or HPGL file of this detail and exit AutoCAD.

In WordPerfect, generate a polite letter of complaint to the contractor outlining the problem in the illustration.

Example:

D. Adams
Trion Sewers and Pipes
485 Galaxy Road
Hammersmith

July 29 1993

Dear Sir,

There appears to be a problem with the foundation work you did for my firm in the latter part of last year at the location of Mr. Dirk Gently's Detective Agency. A mild amount of disruption has caused leakage in the basement. Where the weeping tile and the gravel meet, there is a distinct leakage. I am assuming that the exterior parging was not done properly, but as you can see, the weeping tile is also perhaps too high and thus doesn't catch all of the water going past. I have enclosed a diagram of the problem area and hope that the problem will be remedied within 30 days.

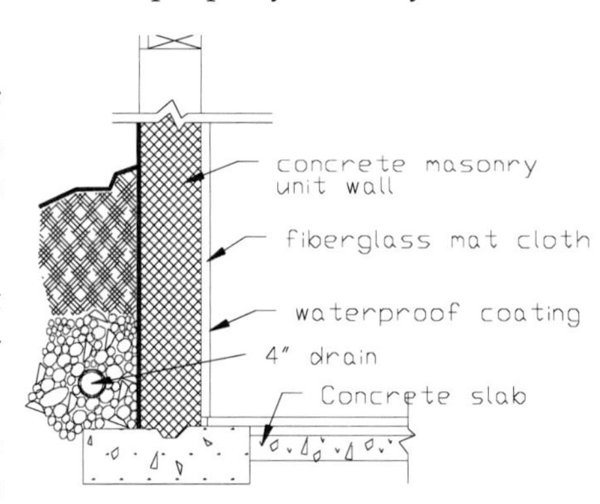

The water is seeping just at the point where the concrete slab meets the concrete masonry unit wall.

My client will be out of town for two weeks and would like the leakage stopped.

Thank you for your immediate attention to this matter.

Yours very truly,

George Trion
Trion General Contractors

Exercise A17 (continued)

Having created a word processor file that contains graphics, now we can try creating a graphic that contains word processor text.

Locate a portion of a detailed drawing that needs special notation, such as the section in Part 1.

In WordPerfect, develop a series of notes that could pertain to this drawing. Word this information so that it is usable for all drawings with this structure. Save these notations as an ASCII file.

In AutoCAD, retrieve the detail, insert a title block and import the available notes.

Notes:

1.. Exterior parging to be no less than 1/4" in thickness throughout.
2. No less than 8 inches of 3/4" screening to be applied above 4-inch tile.
3. 4-inch tile to be installed so that it drains to municipal sewer at a rate
   of 1/4" over 10 feet.
4. Place tile 2 inches below top of footing.

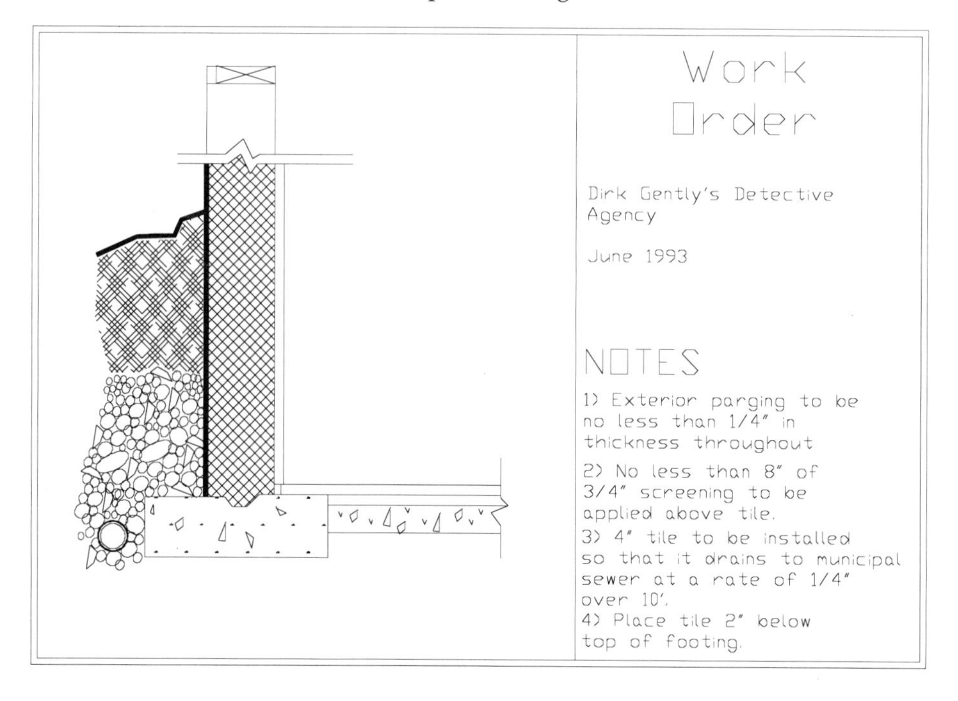

Exercise M17

In AutoCAD, create a detail drawing of a problem that has occurred on a particular part. Generate a plot file or HPGL file of this detail and exit AutoCAD.

In WordPerfect, generate a polite letter of complaint to the contractor outlining the problem in the illustration.

Example:

Martin Hopkins
ACDC Metals
Boston, Mass.

July 29 1993

Dear Mr. Hopkins,

The mould for the part that you sent June 30 1993 is perfect in the exterior, but the interior radii are not to tolerance. As you can see by the dimensions of the final moulded part, it is not to required specs.

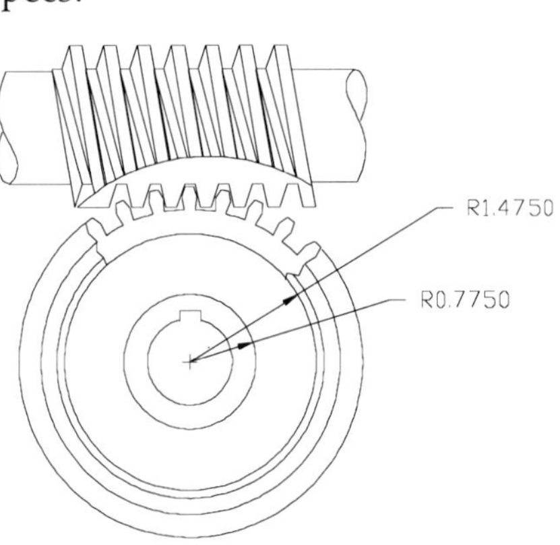

We are returning the die and hope that the interior will be corrected in a relatively short time. I will look forward to discussing this part with you in Phoenix next month at our annual meeting.

Thank you for your immediate attention to this matter.

Yours very truly,

Ted Hacker
Marriot Consulting

Exercise M17 (continued)

Having created a word processor file that contains graphics, now we can try creating a graphic that contains word processor text.

Locate a portion of a detailed drawing that needs special notation, such as the section in Part 1.

In WordPerfect, develop a series of notes that could pertain to this drawing. Put them in a logical format that could be applicable with slight changes to many drawings, then you will not have to retype it every time. Save these notations as an ASCII file.

In AutoCAD, retrieve the detail, insert a title block, and import the available notes.

Example:

NOTES

DRAFT ANGLE 60 DEG
1/8 X 45 DEG CHAMFER
FINISH ALL OVER
TOLERANCES APPLY AFTER PLATING

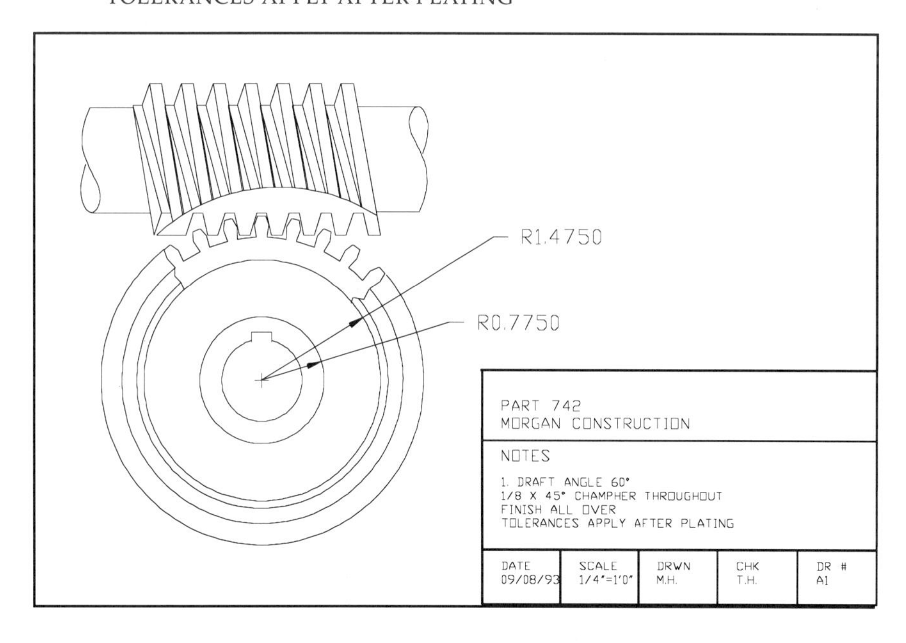

The format for notations on the title block can be cross-referenced readily and used repeatedly.

Exercise C17

In AutoCAD, create a detail drawing of a problem that has occurred at a particular site. Generate a plot file or HPGL file of this detail and exit AutoCAD.

In WordPerfect, generate a polite letter of complaint to the contractor outlining the problem in the illustration.

Example:

B. Moose
Rocky Roads and Curves
192 Main St.
Calgary, Alta.

July 29 1993

Dear Sir,

We have noted a problem with the grading in the section of the road you constructed in May of this year. The elevation on the south side is too high to allow proper drainage over the sidewalk. This has caused some inconvenience to local residents, who request that the site be lowered. I have enclosed a detail of the area mentioned and look forward to your correspondence concerning the possibility of renovating it.

We hope that the problem will be remedied within 30 days.

Note the elevation as marked.

Thank you for your immediate attention to this matter.

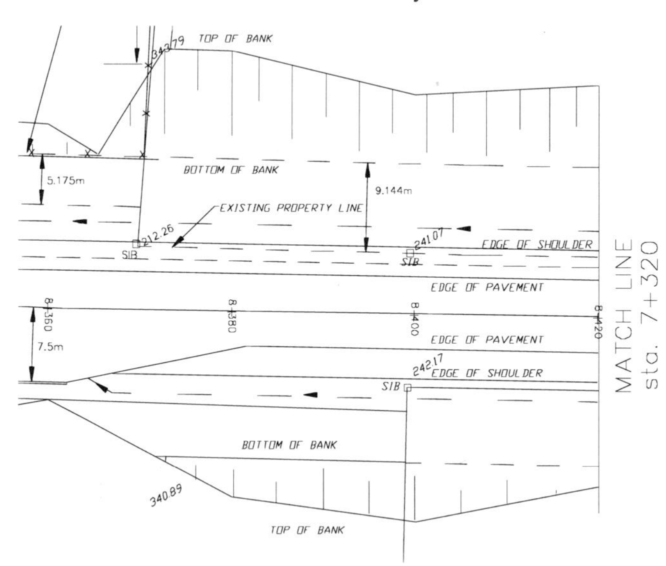

Yours very truly,

D.D. Mountie

Exercise C17 (continued)

Having created a word processor file that contains graphics, now we can try creating a graphic that contains word processor text.

Locate a portion of a detailed drawing that needs special notation, such as the section in Part 1.

In WordPerfect, develop a series of notes that could pertain to this drawing. Put them in a logical format that could be applicable with slight changes to many drawings, so you will not have to retype it every time. Save these notations as an ASCII file.

In AutoCAD, retrieve the detail, insert a title block, and import the available notes as in the illustrations for M17-Part 2 and A17-Part 2.

While inserting this information, note that to change anything in the AutoCAD format, the changes must be made line by line, whereas changes in the WordPerfect format are much more simple. Note the quality of text in the following disclosure.

The positions of poles, lines, conduits, watermains, sewers, and other underground and above ground utilities and structures are not necessarily shown on the contract drawings, and where shown, the accuracy of the position of such utilities and structures is not guaranteed. Before starting work, the Contractor shall inform Himself of the exact location of such utilities and structures and shall assume all liability for damage to them.

The position of pole lines, conduits,
watermains, sewers and other underground
and above ground utilities and structures
are not necessarily shown on the
contract drawings, and where shown, the
accuracy of the position of such utilities
and structures is not guaranteed.
Before starting work, the Contractor
shall inform Himself of the exact location
of all such utilities and structures, and
shall assume all liability for damage to them.

The text as shown in graphics format within the user box on the right is inserted as a unit from WordPerfect, but is accepted as individual lines of text thereafter. Any grammatical or spelling errors, any global changes, and any minor revisions must be searched out manually and corrected line by line.

If this information is kept in a WordPerfect file, simple changes can be quickly made. In the second example, note how easily changes to the text could occur.

notes

1. ALL PLAN BASES HAVE BEEN ROTATED 26°48'07" FROM PAGE NORTH IN THE CLOCKWISE DIRECTION.
2. BENCHMARK: TOPOGRAPHICAL SURVEY MONUMENT #660432, BRASS CAP IN 2' CONCRETE PIER – EAST SIDE OF QUEEN STREET EAST ON TOP OF BANK. 544+/– NORTH OF JANE ROAD CONTROL MONUMENT #001673709 (HORIZONTAL)

   ELEVATION = 352.465M.

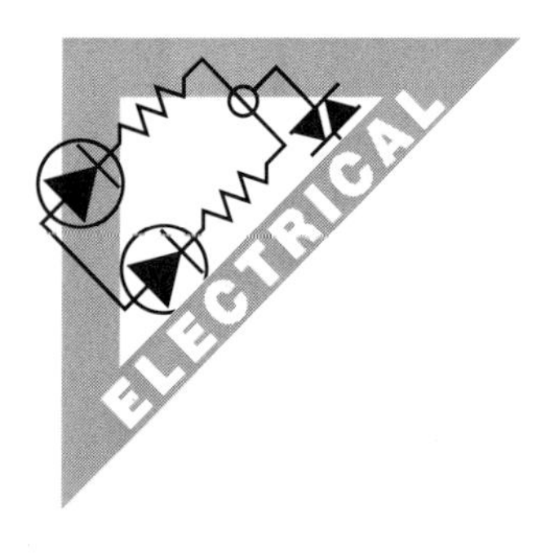

Exercise E17

In AutoCAD, create a detail drawing of a problem that has occurred in a particular receiver. Generate a plot file or .HPGL file of this detail and exit AutoCAD.

In WordPerfect, generate a polite letter of complaint to the contractor outlining the problem in the illustration.

Example:

D. Adams
Trion Sewers and Pipes
485 Galaxy Road
Hammersmith

July 29 1993

Dear Sir,

There appears to be a problem with the receiver that you sent to us last week.

We need a two-tube receiver, and you have sent us a simple one-tube receiver. We would like to return the receiver in question and have you send us the required receiver at your earliest possible convenience.

I am enclosing a schematic of the desired receiver, and I hope that you will be able to supply it immediately.

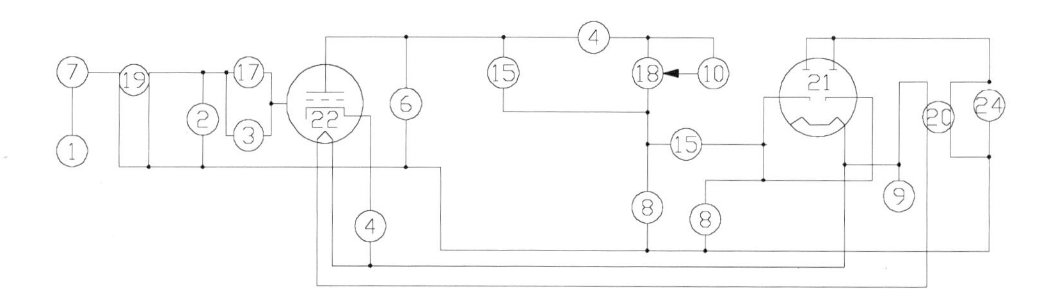

Thank you for your immediate attention to this matter.

Yours very truly,

George Trion
Trion General Contractors

Exercise E17 (continued)

Having created a word-processed file that contains graphics, now we can try creating a graphic that contains word-processed text.

Locate a portion of a detailed drawing that needs special notation, such as the section in Part 1.

In WordPerfect, develop a series of notes that could pertain to this drawing. Word this information so that it is usable for all drawings with this structure. Save these notations as an ASCII file.

In AutoCAD, retrieve the detail, insert a title block and import the available notes.

Parts List for a Two-tube Receiver

1 Antenna, Aerial	9 Lamp, Incandescent	17 Resistor
2 Capacitor, Variable	10 Receiver, Headset	18 Resistor
3 Capacity 250mmf	11 Rectifier	19 Transformer
4 Capacitor 1 mfd	12 Resistor, 1000	20 Transformer
5 Capacitor .002	13 Resistor 25000	21 Tube 6H6
6 Capacitor .02	14 Resistor 47000	22 Tube 6J5
7 Capacitor .005	15 Resistor 100000	23 Tube 6SJ7
8 Capacitor 20 mfd	16 Resistor 270000	24 110 V supply

Parts List for Two-Tube Receiver

1 Antenna, Aerial	9 Lamp, Incandescent	17 Resistor
2 Capacitor, Variable	10 Receiver, Headset	18 Resistor
3 Capacity 250mmf	11 Rectifier	19 Transformer
4 Capacitor 1 mfd	12 Resistor, 1000	20 Transformer
5 Capacitor .002	13 Resistor 25000	21 Tube 6H6
6 Capacitor .02	14 Resistor 47000	22 Tube 6J5
7 Capacitor .005	15 Resistor 100000	23 Tube 6SJ7
8 Capacitor 20 mfd	16 Resistor 270000	24 110 V supply

Challenger 17

Using the office layout from Chapter 14, create a three-dimensional image using Thickness and Elevation (Chapter 25). Then create a minimum of four plot files that can be inserted into a letter explaining to the client the advantages both of the system and of the layout that you have provided.

The letter might contain such views as those following:

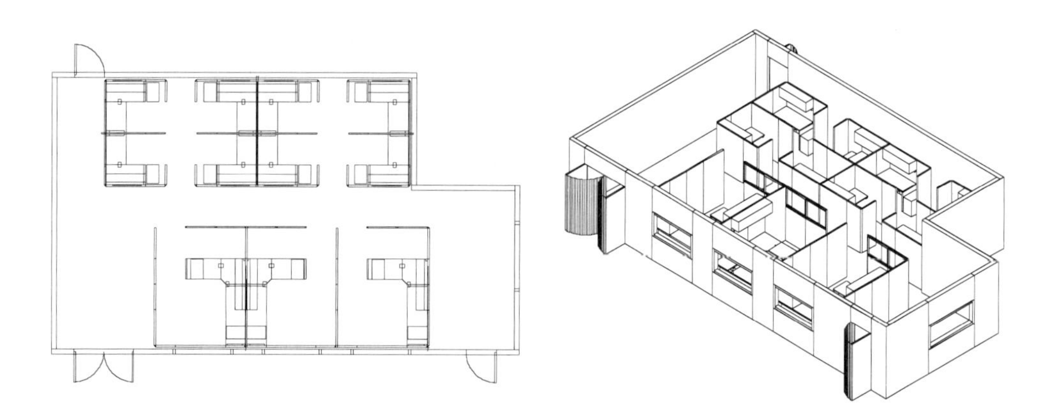

Details of the offices may also be added.

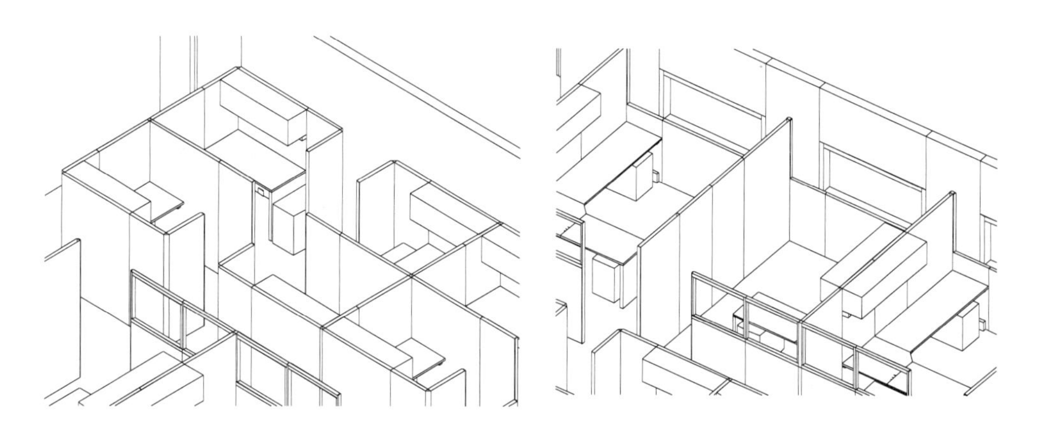

You can explain the advantages of the overhead storage areas and the difference in size between the sales offices and the management offices.

DRAWING INTERCHANGE FORMAT (DXF)

Upon completion of this chapter, the student will be able to:

1. Create DXF files in AutoCAD and insert them in other files or earlier AutoCAD releases
2. Insert a DXF file into a WordPerfect file
3. Edit a WordPerfect file, adding geometry parametrically, and then return it to AutoCAD
4. Recognize graphics files from AutoCAD in WordPerfect or similar character-based files

DXF FILES

DXF files are the ASCII-code or DOS-text files for the graphics or vector statements. These files are the clean files that can be transferred to other graphics packages and word processing, analysis, or accounting files.

DXF and Graphics Packages

DXFs or Drawing Interchange Format files are the easiest way to transfer files from AutoCAD to a similar or more specialized CAD program. AutoCAD is, if we can believe market share, the most accessible PC-based CAD program available. The DXF capability allows users to access the fairly inexpensive AutoCAD system for data entry and then have the graphics data entered into an expensive system — Intergraph, CALMA, CV, KATIA — thereby greatly reducing the cost per seat in a CAD lab. In addition, it makes the graphics data of AutoCAD available for third-party or specialized software program.

DXF and Text Editors

DXF files are also handy for editing large strings of text since word processor text editors are much more powerful than AutoCAD's vector format text editor.

The most popular text editors that accept this data (and the data generated through SDF and CDF files) are MS-DOS Editor, the DOS program Edlin, WordPerfect's DOS-text file option, the WordPerfect Library Program Editor, WordStar in non-document mode, PC Write, Microsoft Word in text-only format, and Norton's Editor, Sidekick. All of these software packages will produce a standard ASCII-format file.

As in Chapter 17, we will be using WordPerfect for demonstration purposes, but any of the editing packages noted above may be used. Should you wish to use a software package not listed, look up the ASCII options in the user manual to see if it can create on ASCII-format file.

In Chapter 17 we transferred the bit-map or pixel-address files into a word processor file, here we will transfer the vector files.

EXPORTING DXF FILES

As you are creating a drawing on the screen, a file is being generated that records all of your movements by means of numbers and letters, and later by 0s and 1s.

While you are in the AutoCAD Drawing Editor, you can export the file of the numbers and letters to your disk as an ASCII file. This file can then be read by any other CAD program that can read an ASCII format.

Example: *DXF Graphics Transfer*

Release 12 Notes

DXF in and out is located under the File pull-down menu.

Try this example:

- In AutoCAD, create a file called A:DXTEST. Change the limits, snap, and grid from the defaults to any other value, just so you can see that it has been changed. Enter at least one line, one arc, and one circle. Create a new layer called 1 with colour 1 (Red). Enter the text style Romanc, and then enter three lines of text.
- Save this file creating an A:DXTEST.DWG file on your disk or C drive if you are not using floppies.
- While still in the graphics editor, pick DXF/DXB from the Utilities menu. From this submenu, pick DXFOUT.

```
Command:DXFOUT
File name <a:DXTEST>:↵ (or enter desired name)
```

AutoCAD will automatically enter the extension DXF to the file. The default filename is the file you are currently using, so you have created DXTEST.DXF.

```
Enter decimal places of accuracy (0-16)/Entities/Binary <6>:4
```

This allows you to select the accuracy of the exported file. The output will be in the form of numbers; this tells the system how many decimal places to read.

If you pick E for entities, you can export a section or block of information from your file. Object selection options are under the DXF/DXB menu. The B option will write a binary file.

AutoCAD will now create the DXF file A:DXTEST.DXF. This DXF file can now be inserted into many other CAD and third-party programs.

IMPORTING DXF FILES

If you are fortunate enough to have a different CAD software package at your site, use this instead of AutoCAD. If you do not have another CAD package on site, import the file into AutoCAD. If you have an earlier release of AutoCAD (Release 9), try importing to it.

Example: *DXF Import*

Exit from the current file (it is not necessary to save it again), and continue as follows:

- Create a new file in AutoCAD called TEST1
- Go to the DXF/DXB menu and select DXFIN

```
Command:DXFIN
File name <test1>:A:DXTEST
```

This prompt asks for the name of the DXF file to import. Prior to Release 11, any extension would cancel the command; after Release 11, extensions are accepted. Here we do not need one.

AutoCAD will load the DXTEST file complete with the settings used. What is the difference between this and a block insert?

- When inserting a block, you are prompted to change the size or rotation of the block insert so it fits into the current file. With DXF imports, you are not prompted for this information because the imported file forms the complete file.
- With block inserts you are prompted for the location of the origin of the block; with DXFs you are not, because you are entering the entire file, not just a set of objects, thus 0,0,0 is the origin.
- All settings are included in the DXF file. Limits, grid, snap, all dimension variables, and all system variables will be included in the imported file.

Always use an empty drawing to import a DXF file, before any blocks, layers, linetypes, viewports, fonts, or geometry are entered. This way, you will get a complete DXF file. If the current drawing file is not empty, you will have added only the entities. If you enter a previously altered file, the prompt,

```
Not a new drawing — only entities section will be printed
```

will tell you that only the geometry data has been added. In fact, the data imported to a previously started file is much like a block; it contains no variables or settings. To make sure that your files are empty, use TEST= when starting.

This exercise was performed in AutoCAD to give you a feeling for how it works, but the intention of the command is to import the AutoCAD data to another CAD package. The process should be as easy as that outlined above.

DIALOGUE BOXES

As in the ATTEDIT command, if you are using Release 11 and the FILEDIA variable is set at 1, you will get the following dialogue boxes when using the DXFIN and DXFOUT commands.

DXFIN

The dialogue box in Figure 18-1 will allow you to scroll through the list and select a DXF file. You can choose the Type It option to add a filename to the list.

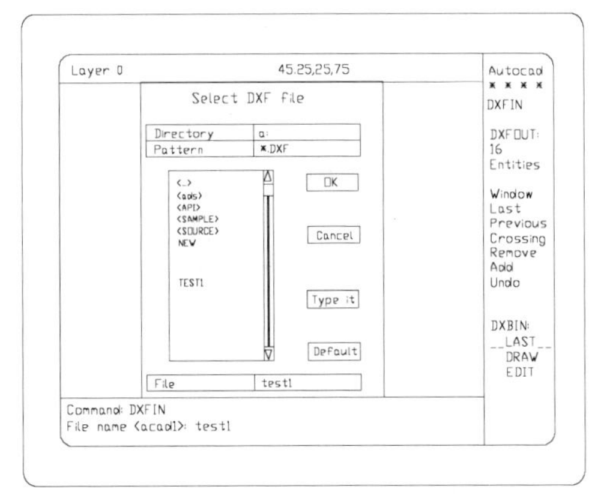

Figure 18-1. DXF dialogue box

DXFOUT

The DXFOUT dialogue box of Figure 18-2 displays a warning prompt so you do not overwrite existing files.

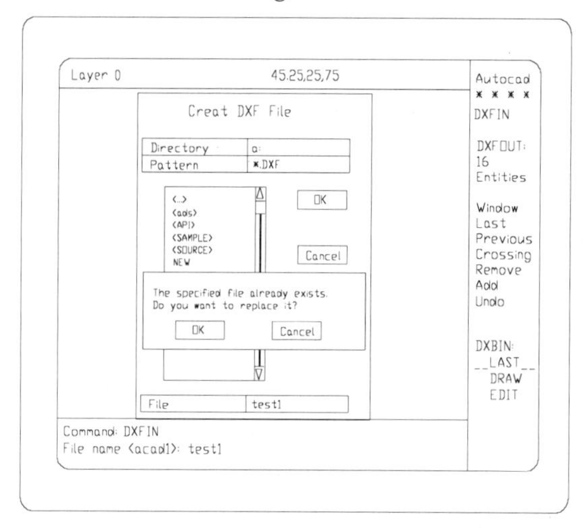

Figure 18-2. DXFOUT dialogue box

Both of these dialogue boxes are also available by typing in the tilde sign (~) when prompted for the filename if FILEDIA is not set at 1.

The FILEDIA option is under the settings Setvar menu. This feature is available only if you have the Advanced User Interface.

DXF FILES AND OTHER VERSIONS OF AUTOCAD

For many reasons, AutoCAD and almost all other CAD programs have files that are instantly upward compatible, but not always downward compatible. That is, if you have a file that was generated on AutoCAD Release 9, and you want to import it into Release 11, this is done without any problem; it is a transparent change. But if you want to import it back to Release 9, you will get a prompt saying the file was generated on an incompatible version of AutoCAD.

Since Autodesk is constantly upgrading its software, files created on newer versions contain information that is incompatible with older versions, thus the files cannot be automatically transferred.

The DXF commands will help you get around this problem, but it is not an easy task, because you must erase everything from the file that is obviously incompatible and then use DXFIN to import it to the lower release version.

Because of the great differences between Release 2 and Release 9, there may be a lot of problems importing files to a Release 2 or earlier software package. If you intend to import a file from Releases 9, 10, or 11 to Release 2, you must erase everything dealing with pull-down menus and 3D because they were not used in the Release 2 software.

Importing files from Release 10 back to Release 9 is fairly simple because there are few major changes; but taking files from Release 11 to Release 10 is much more difficult because of the addition of the AME software and the proliferation of extra dialogue boxes.

If you need to transfer many files from Release 11 to Release 10, there is a program called CHGREL by Rich Frank that can perform this function quite quickly and painlessly.

Other Uses of DXF

The DXF command can be useful in fixing up programs that have been damaged either by an internal error or a system crash. If you retrieve the file in text format, often you can recognize immediately where the problem is because the format is out of sync, and, once corrected, the file may again be readable in the graphics editor. Use DXFIN to import damaged files.

The process of cleaning up files is tedious and time consuming and requires an in-depth knowledge of DXF files, but it can be a lifesaver.

FILE LOCKING

File locking is a relatively new development of particular importance on networks. It allows the system manager to control access to files, thereby preventing two people from editing the same file at the same time. With file locking in place, only the first person to ask for a file is given access to it. Others receive a message that the file is currently in use.

With DXF files in Release 11 and upward, the file is immediately locked as soon as it is imported as a DXF file. If a file with the same filename is imported into the same directory, it will be given the extension .DXK for identification purposes. Files can also be locked using DXFOUT. See the *AutoCAD User's Manual* by Autodesk if you want to set this up.

LOOKING AT DXF FILES

The DXF file contains coded text information about a file. We need to be able to read at least some of the coding in order to manipulate it.

If you want to look at the format for a DXF file, exit AutoCAD and go to DOS. If your floppy disk is where you have this information, enter the following to obtain a listing of the DXTEST file in Edlin.

```
more <a:dxtest.dxf
```

Where:
A: is the drive or directory

dxtest is the name of the file

dxf is the filename extension

more < will display the file contents screen by screen

If the DOS command MORE does not work, use any DOS command for printing or displaying the contents of a DOS file. Often, in a classroom atmosphere, the DOS commands are changed to suit the system manager or another class. Any command that will allow you to read the file screen by screen is fine.

The DXF file data is arranged in a "binary" kind of format. The first number/letter/line indicates a code, the second indicates what the code refers to.

Code	Explanation
0	*the next line is the description, start of an entry*
SECTION	*this is the beginning of a section or file*
2	*what follows is the name of the section*
HEADER	*the section is the header or set-up of the file*
9	*what follows is the name of the software package*

Code	Explanation
$ACADVER	*this identifies the file as an AutoCAD file*
1	*what follows is the version of AutoCAD*
AC1006	*the version is Release 10.06*
9	*what follows is the insertion base point*
$INSBASE	*this indicates a base point*
10	*the next line is the X value entry*
0.0	*X value is 0,0*
20	*the next line is the Y value entry*
0.0	*Y value is 0.0*
30	*the next line is the Z value entry*
0.0	*Z value is 0.0*

Press ↵ to continue scrolling the file. ^C will exit the file.

The file you are viewing is a long list of text, integers, and real numbers which contain the variables that define the drawing, such as settings, the names of linetypes, text styles, layers, blocks, dimensioning and system variables, etc., and, finally, the list of objects contained in the file. Note that all the settings are first. How does this relate to the PURGE command?

The PURGE command must be the first command in the system because the first set of information in the file contains the layer, block, and linetype data, etc. If you want to delete anything from the file, it must be done in the portion of the file where the information exists, at the beginning.

DXF and Parametric Programming

DXF files can be used for parametric programming, i.e., creating the object strictly by entering its parameters. This is usually done by point entry and not by entering data with the aid of the graphics editor, the traditional CAD way. By using parametric programming, bonded surfaces or surfaces using spline data are much more readily entered, as are staircases or formula-related objects that need a variety of standard measurements, e.g., tread size, tread height, rise, etc.

In civil engineering and surveying, DXF files are often used to locate the positions of certain services and allow the user to change or edit this data and return it to the original file.

Parametric programming can also be done in AutoLISP or by many of the available third-party software programs.

The purpose of the following exercise is simply to introduce you to what DXF files are all about so you can see what is available once you have mastered the basics of AutoCAD.

EDITING DXF FILES

Once you have created a DXF file, it can be read in any graphics editor that accepts ASCII format. We will edit the file you have just created to see how flexible it is.

Example: *DXF File Editing*

STEP 1

Having created your DXF file in AutoCAD (DXTEST.DXF), enter WordPerfect (or your choice of text editor) and use Ctrl F5 to retrieve the file.

The format of the file will be updated to accept information in WordPerfect. The first several pages of text will be the default parameters, the origin, the linetypes loaded, etc. The geometry will be added at the end of the file.

STEP 2

Pass by the default parameters and find the position of the circle. This could be 8–10 pages from the beginning.

In WordPerfect, you can do this by using the arrow keys to move the cursor down the file. The Page Down key will advance the cursor more quickly. Be careful not to use the space bar.

When working with DXF files, be very careful not to use the space bar, the Enter key, or any other keys unless you need to. If you add a space or a hard return at the wrong place, you will get an error message when importing your file.

Once you have found the circle data, it should look like this:

Code	Explanation
CIRCLE	*indicates the entity type*
8	*indicates the next data is the layer number*
0	*the layer is 0*
10	*indicates that the next data is the X value*
10.0	*X is 10*
20	*indicates that the next data is the Y value*
7.0	*Y is 7*
30	*indicates that the next data is the Z value*
0.0	*Z is 0*
40	*indicates the radius*
1.0	*the radius is 1.0*
0	*indicates the end of the entry*

Change the size of the circle by changing the radius.

40	*indicates that the next value is the radius*
2.0	*the radius is now 2.0*

You have changed the circle in the existing file; now add to the existing file a series of lines to form a box.

The following is the format for a line entry. Figure out on which layer you want to see the lines, and then enter the line data by copying the LINE command and changing only the X-Y parameters. The line format should look like the codes and explanations on the next page.

Code	Explanation
LINE	*indicates that the next sequence will be a line*
8	*the next information will be the layer number*
1	*the layer is 1*
10	*indicates that the next data will be the first point in X*
6.85	*X is 6.85*
20	*indicates that the next data will be the first point in Y*
2.7	*Y is 2.7*
30	*indicates that the next data will be the first point in Z*
0.0	*Z is 0,0*
11	*indicates that the next data will be the end point in X*
8.21	*the X value is 8.21*
21	*indicates that the next data will be the end point in Y*
2.68	*the Y value is 2.68*
31	*indicates that the next data will be the end point in Z*
0.0	*the Z value is 0,0*
0	*signals the end of the line; remember that each line has only two points*

STEP 3

Now using the coding illustrated above, create a one-unit square.

LINE

8

1

10 *(The line starts at 1,1,0 and is on layer 1.)*

1.0

20

1.0

30

0.0

11 *(The line ends at 2,1,0.)*

2.0

21

1.0 *(Once this first line is added, add the other three lines.)*

31

0.0

0

LINE

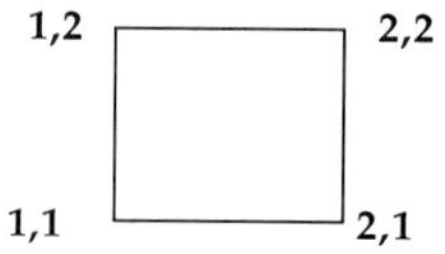

The easiest way to create another line is to copy and edit the existing line entry. Use Alt F4 and Ctrl F4.

If you are creating many lines of text in WordPerfect and making only minor changes, copy the information down and use TYPEOVER to change just those items that need changing.

Alt F4 will indicate a block of information. Use the arrow keys to identify the block of information you want to copy. Once the information you need is highlighted, use Ctrl F4 to copy the block of data.

Ctrl F4
block **1**
copy **2**

Use the arrow keys to select the final position of the block and use the Enter key to position it.

STEP 4
Once you have entered all four lines, save the new DXF file as a DOS text file (Ctrl F5).

DANGER When you exit WordPerfect, DO NOT SAVE the file as a WordPerfect file; this will overwrite the DOS file.

Select DOS file **1** and Save **1.** Give it a new name, DXTEST1.DXF. Do not forget to enter the extension.

F7- *exit* **Save File - N** **Exit WP - Y**

STEP 5

In AutoCAD, start a new file and import the new DXF file using DXFIN. Check to see that the box is in and the circle has changed. If you have difficulties importing, check the section Common Errors for corrections.

With the above exercise you have begun parametric programming, or programming using only the parameters and not the graphics data.

COMMON ERRORS IN DXF IMPORTS

The most common errors are (a) not remembering the correct name of your file and (b) adding spaces, returns, and other characters within the file. Here are some error messages and fixes.

Invalid filename
You have entered the wrong name.

Do not use the .DXF extension when importing with DXFIN; check your directory to make sure you have the correct name.

Error on Line 1
The file does not start on line 1 of the .DXF file. Return to WordPerfect, find your DXF file, and make sure the file starts on line 1. If the first line of the file is blank, delete the hard return to bring the first line of text back to line 1.

```
0        This must be line 1.
SECTION
```

Error on Line 847
You have added a space or a hard return where not wanted, or one of your new commands is incorrect. Return to your DXF file, find the line in question, and correct it. For beginners, often it is easier just to try the whole exercise again. Watch out for the space bar.

USING DXF TO CREATE GRAPHICS IN WORDPERFECT

We have just seen how DXF files can be used to perform parametric programming (alphanumeric data entry). You can also use DXF files to insert graphics in the same way you used the HPGL files in Chapter 17. It is always useful to have two ways of doing things, particularly in the area of high technology, where work in general has a particularly high mess-up factor.

To have a graphics file imported to WordPerfect, we must convert it to a format that WordPerfect can interpret. We have seen that plotting using an HPGL file will work, but if the HP driver is disabled, a DXF file can be used.

Example: *DXF Files as Graphics*

To produce graphics for a WordPerfect file, convert a DXF file to a WPG or WordPerfect graphics file.

STEP 1
Use AutoCAD to create a file, then use DXFOUT to create a DXF file.

```
Command:DXFOUT
File name <a:test>:↵ (accept TEST, or enter another name)
Enter decimal places of accuracy (0-16)/Entities/Binary <6>:4
```

End the file, thus saving the graphics data as .DWG as well.

STEP 2
In DOS, access the WordPerfect directory.

```
C:CD\WP51
```

STEP 3
Type GRAPHCNV to start the graphics conversion utility.

```
C:\WP51:GRAPHCNV
WordPerfect Graphics Conversion Utility
Version 1.1, (c) Copyright 1989, WordPerfect Corp. Orem UT.

For Help, type graphcnv/h at the DOS prompt.

Press F1 to cancel.

Enter name of file to convert:A:DXTEST.DXF

Enter name of output file:C:\WP51\DXTEST.WPG:A:DXTEST.WPG

Converting

A:DXTEST.DXF (.DXF) to A:DXTEST.WPG (.WPG) — ok

Press any key to continue
```

Now in WordPerfect, use Alt F9, 4 (User box), 1 (Create) to place the graphic in a user box.

READING DXF CODES

DXF CODE CHART

Group Code	Format on Next Line
0-9	*string value*
10-59	*floating point value*

Group Code	Format on Next Line
60-79	*integer value*
210-239	*floating point value*
999	*remarks (a comment within the file)*
1000-1100	*extended entity data*

Code	Explanation
0	*start of an entry*
SECTION	*entry is the beginning of a section*
2	*What follows is the name of the section.*
HEADER	*header of the file*

The next few pages contain AutoCAD set-up data — limits, grid, snap; loading blocks, text, and linetypes; etc. When you are changing data or performing parametric programming, look for the following section:

0	*start of an entry*
SECTION	*Entry is the beginning of a section of the file.*
2	*What follows is the beginning of a section.*
ENTITIES	*This is the beginning of the entities section.*
0	*start of an entry*
LINE	*The next few lines will be the layer, X,Y, and Z values for a two-point line.*
0	*start of an entry*
CIRCLE	*The next few lines will be the layer, X,Y, and Z value of the centre and the radius of a circle.*
8	*The next entry is the layer name.*
10	*The next entry is from-point-X coordinate.*
20	*The next entry is from-point-Y coordinate.*
30	*The next entry is from-point-Z coordinate.*
11	*The next entry is to-point-X coordinate.*
21	*The next entry is to-point-Y coordinate.*
31	*The next entry is to-point-Z coordinate.*
40	*The next entry is a radius.*
ENDSEC	*end of entities section*
0	*start of entry*
EOF	*end of file*

Exercise A18

PART A

STEP 1
In AutoCAD, generate a file that has two layers, seven lines, a circle, and an arc. Change the limits of the file, plus the snap and the grid. Also add some text so you can view it in the .DXF alphanumeric file.

STEP 2
Use DXFOUT to make a .DXF file. (Turn on FILEDIA if you are using Release 11 with Advanced User Interface.) Start another file in AutoCAD and import the first file using DXFIN. Once complete, take a look at it.

STEP 3
Exit the new file and enter WordPerfect (or your favourite word processor). Retrieve the .DXF file. At the appropriate area in the file, enter some geometry: two lines, one circle. Edit the text string.

STEP 4
Exit WordPerfect and save the file in DOS text format (use Ctrl F5).

STEP 5
Retrieve the new file in AutoCAD to make sure the changes are correct.

STEP 6
Using the original .DXF file, perform a graphics conversion on the model and insert it into a WordPerfect file as a .WPG file.

PART B

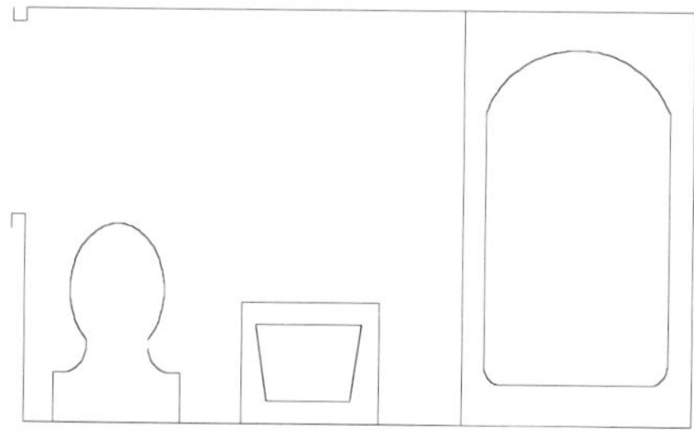

Standard Bath

Figure A

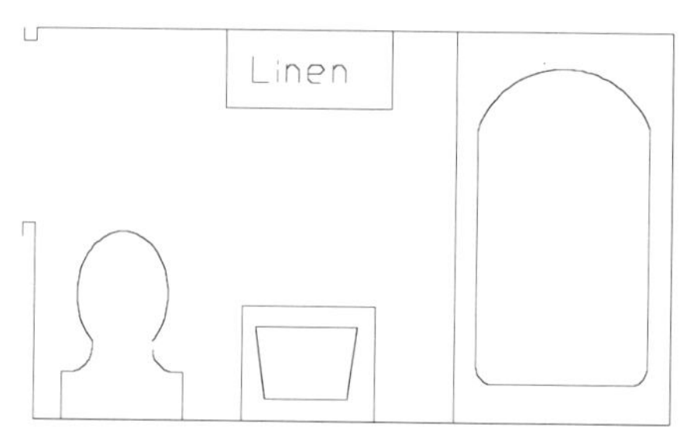

Standard Bath

Figure B

STEP 7
Create the standard bath layout in Figure A. Import it into another file using DXF commands. Check the limits once in the new file to make sure they changed along with the entry of the data. With the file still active, take note of where the new linen closet is and where you would start your text string for the word "linen." Now enter this information in WordPerfect to create Figure B.

STEP 8
Now insert it into a WordPerfect file as graphics.

Exercise M18

PART 1

STEP 1
In AutoCAD, generate a file that has two layers, seven lines, a circle, and an arc. Change the limits of the file, plus the snap and the grid. Also add some text so you can view it in the .DXF alphanumeric file.

STEP 2
Use DXFOUT to make a .DXF file. (Turn on FILEDIA if you are using Release 11 with Advanced User Interface.) Start another file in AutoCAD and import the first file using DXF. Once complete, take a look at it.

STEP 3
Exit the new file and enter WordPerfect (or your favourite word processor). Retrieve the .DXF file. At the appropriate area in the file, enter some geometry: two lines, one circle. Edit the text string.

STEP 4
Exit WordPerfect and save the file in DOS text format (use Ctrl F5).

STEP 5
Retrieve the new file in AutoCAD to make sure the changes are correct.

STEP 6
Using the original .DXF file, perform a graphics conversion on the model and insert it into a WordPerfect file as a .WPG file.

PART B

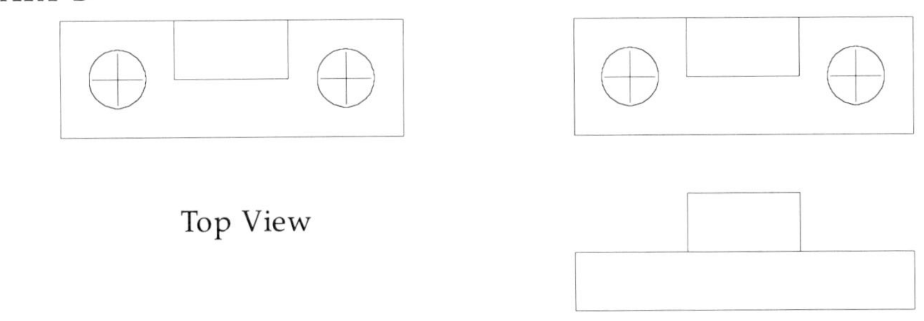

Top View

Top and Front View

STEP 7
Create the top view and label it. Now take it out of the first file using a .DXF format and retrieve it as a new file. While in the new file, take note of the positions of the new data and of the difference of position needed for the new text.

STEP 8
Exit the file and retrieve it in WordPerfect. Make the necessary changes and return to AutoCAD to see if you have done it correctly. Now take the edited file and retrieve it into WordPerfect as graphics.

Exercise C18

PART A

STEP 1
In AutoCAD, generate a file that has two layers, seven lines, a circle, and an arc. Change the limits of the file, plus the snap and the grid. Also add some text so you can view it in the .DXF alphanumeric file.

STEP 2
Use DXFOUT to make a .DXF file. (Turn on FILEDIA if you are using Release 11 with Advanced User Interface.) Start another file in AutoCAD and import the first file using DXF. Once complete, take a look at it.

STEP 3
Exit the new file and enter WordPerfect (or your favourite word processor). Retrieve the .DXF file. At the appropriate area in the file, enter some geometry: two lines, one circle. Edit the text string.

STEP 4
Exit WordPerfect and save the file in DOS text format (use Ctrl-F5).

STEP 5
Retrieve the new file in AutoCAD to make sure the changes are correct.

STEP 6
Using the original .DXF file, perform a graphics conversion on the model and insert it into a WordPerfect file as a .WPG file.

PART B

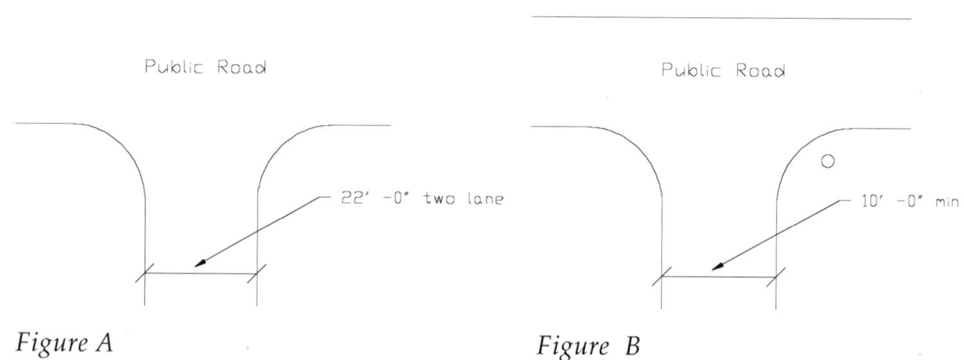

Figure A *Figure B*

STEP 7
Create the graphics of Figure A and export them using a .DXF format. Insert them into a new file using DXFIN and check to see that your limits, etc. have changed as well. While in the graphics file, make note of the positions of the text, etc. for entry later in WordPerfect. Then retrieve the .DXF file in WordPerfect and make the necessary changes to create Figure B. Import it into an AutoCAD file to make sure it is correct. Now import the .DXF file into WordPerfect as graphics.

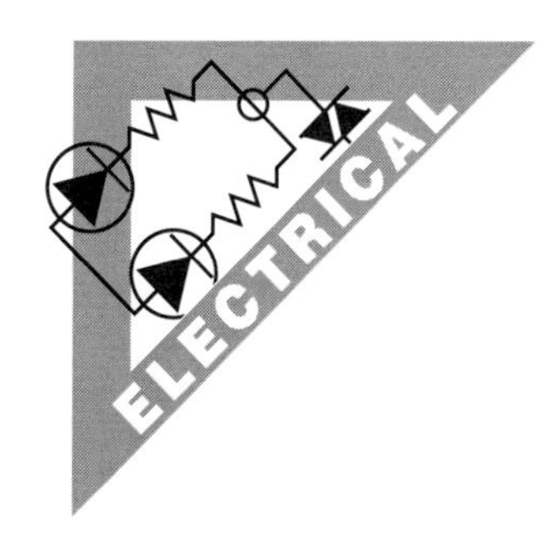

Exercise E18

PART A

STEP 1

In AutoCAD, generate a file that has 2 layers, 7 lines, a circle, and an arc. Change the limits of the file, plus the snap and the grid. Also add some text so you can view it in the .DXF alphanumeric file.

STEP 2

Use DXFOUT to make a .DXF file. (Turn on FILEDIA if you are in Release 11 with Advanced User Interface.) Start another file in AutoCAD and import the first file using .DXF. Once in, take a look at it.

STEP 3

Exit the new file and enter WordPerfect (or your favourite word processor). Retrieve the .DXF file. At the appropriate area in the file, enter some geometry: 2 lines, 1 circle. Edit the text string.

STEP 4

Exit WordPerfect and save the file as a DOS text format (use Ctrl F5.)

STEP 5

Retrieve the new file in AutoCAD to make sure that the changes are correct.

STEP 6

Using the original .DXF file, perform a graphics conversion on the model and insert it onto a WordPerfect file as a .WPG file.

PART B

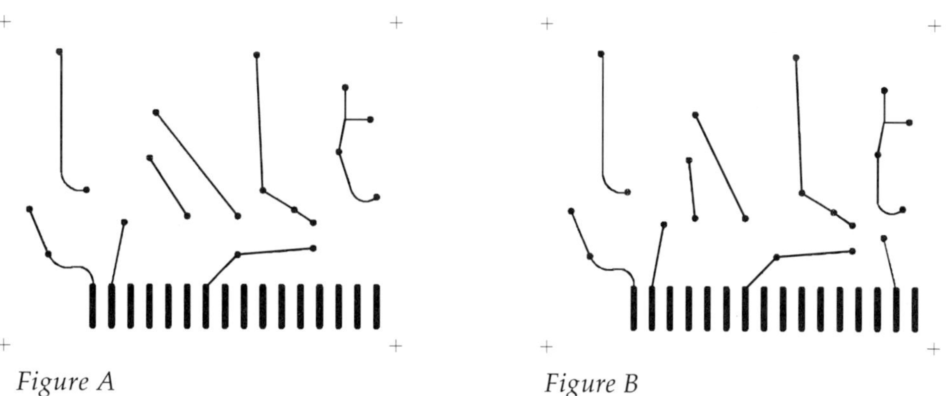

Figure A *Figure B*

STEP 7

Create the graphics and export using a .DXF format. Insert into a new file using DXFIN and check to see that your limits, etc. have changed as well. While in the graphics file, make note of the positions of the text, etc. for entry later in WordPerfect. Then retrieve the .DXF file in WordPerfect and make the necessary changes. Import it into an AutoCAD file to make sure that it is correct. Now import the .DXF file into WordPerfect as graphics.

Challenger 18

STEP 1

As you will not be expected to know all of the DXF formats, create a simple file with a pline in it. Use DXFOUT to create a graphic in WordPerfect.

STEP 2

In WordPerfect, using the first few lines of the PLINE command as a guide, develop an airfoil.

Note the points used to enter the pline data.

Once entered, figure out how to copy this pline and use PEDIT to create spline data.

You may have to enter and exit a few times to get it right.

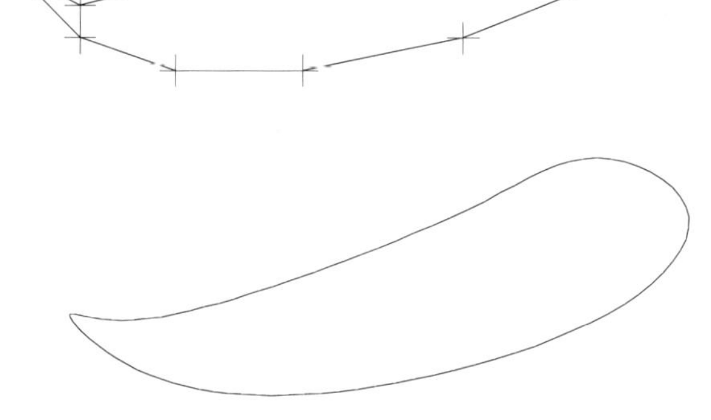

STEP 3

Now take the finished DXF file and generate a graphics file that will fit into a letter composed in WordPerfect explaining exactly how you did it.

MACROS

Upon completion of this chapter, the student should be able to:

1. Create a simple macro
2. Create a compound macro
3. Create a screen menu with the various custom macros

WHAT ARE MACROS

While working in AutoCAD, you may have noticed that there are a few commands you use frequently and would like to have automated. Generally speaking, most people use 20 percent of the commands 80 percent of the time. Thus, by creating macros and customized menus, design time should be much more efficient.

An example of a command that could be put into a macro is the MOVE command. It is possible you use the MOVE command three times per hour, and you always use it in conjunction with Window to select objects and END(*point*) to show the base point and displacement. If this is the case, then you can create a macro of this command that will automatically bring up Window and END(*point*).

Other possibilities for macros are INSERT with a specific wblock, ZOOM .5x, PAN, etc., and all those commands you use regularly. When designing with a set of wblocks that are always inserted at the same scale factor, a macro can save you three or four keystrokes per entry, and thus perhaps 100 or 200 keystrokes per day.

Macros can also save a lot of time for designers who do several repetitive processes to create objects. For example, when generating walls in a plan view using just AutoCAD, the designer must put in an outside wall, an inside of the same wall, a layer for insulation, and perhaps a finish to the same wall. With a macro, the designer can pick the WALL macro from a menu and three or four lines at a preset distance will be drawn. A wall macro, once devised, can be used on any file to generate a similar wall construction.

> ***Release 12 Notes***
>
> Release 12 has a full customization manual that covers areas of customization not found in this text. The format does not change from earlier releases.

If you have been using the AutoCAD pull-down menus, you will notice that many are automated. For example, from the Display menu, you have ZOOM Window, ZOOM Previous, etc. These are macros made up by AutoCAD to assist the user.

Once these automated commands are entered in a macro, you can generate your own custom menu where these custom macros can be waiting patiently and loyally for you to use.

There are also many third-party menus available, particulary in conjunction with third-party software you purchase. These will have the third-party macros on a specialized user menu. What we will be doing in this chapter is showing you how to create macros and menus. The reasons for this are two-fold: first, it will help you create your own customized macros and menus; and second, it will help you understand how macros and menus are created, so you can more intelligently assess the available third-party software and menus.

CREATING A MACRO

Macro means large. A macro command is just a series of commands that you are already familiar with that are stacked for ease of use; i.e., one large command as opposed to many small commands. Take, for example, the command ZOOM.

```
Command: ZOOM
All/Center/Dynamic/Extents/Left/Previous/Vmax/Win-
dow/<scale>(X/XP): W
First corner: (pick 1)
Other corner: (pick 2)
```

To make this command sequence into a macro that is acceptable for a menu, you would decide which option you wanted and take out all the non-essential data so that it looked like this:

```
[ZOOM W]^C^CZOOM W
```

Where:
[ZOOM W] is the name of the macro displayed on the screen

^C^C cancels or exits any previous command

ZOOM W is the actual command used

When creating macros, you are entering a different coding for the information you require. This coding is created on any word processor or text editor. Again, the most popular are:

- MS-DOS Editor (or the less useful DOS program, Edlin)
- WordPerfect's DOS text file option
- WordPerfect Library Program Editor
- WordStar in non-document mode
- PC Write
- Microsoft Word in text-only format
- Norton's Editor, Sidekick

If you want to create a menu and macro in AutoCAD, use Edlin Information on standard processes in Appendix F .

When you create macros, they must be added to a menu or .MNU to be accessible. Use .MNU as the file extension to make a menu file as opposed to a text (.TXT) file or a Drawing Interchange Format file (.DXF).

Once your macros are written, they must be put onto a menu to be read by AutoCAD in the Drawing Editor. The first step is to create the macros.

As stated earlier, macros and menus consist of specific codes or sets of characters that address the system for a specific purpose.

The various codes that will be used to create macros and menus are as follows:

Macro and Menu Characters

^B	Toggles SNAP	\	Pause for input
^C	Cancel	+	Continue to next line
^D	Toggles COORDs	;	Return
^E	Toggles ISOPLANE	[]	Encloses label
^G	Toggles GRID	*	autorepeat (causes command to be repeated until cancel is invoked), or page mark
^H	Backspace		
^M	Return	**<space>**	is seen as a Return character
^O	Toggles ORTHO	***icon**	to create icons
^P	Toggles MENUECHO	***screen**	screen menu
^Q	Toggles ECHO to printer	***buttons**	mouse or puck
^X	*Delete* in/out buffer	***tablet**	on digitizer board
		***pop1**	pop-ups on screen
^Z	*nothing* Inserted at the end of a line to suppress automatic space	***osnap**	for osnaps

Macros are built out of the AutoCAD commands you are already familiar with and the special macro codes above.

In this chapter we will create a set of simple macros for a screen menu, then create two complex menus for the same menu. Once you have decided on the macros you need, then decide where on the screen you want them to display. Do you want the menu to take over the screen menu on the right, or would you prefer to add some options onto the regular AutoCAD menu in a pop-up or pull-down form?

Figure 19-1, on the following page, gives a layout of the screen showing the addressable spaces, the pop-up menus, the side menu, and the mouse. The tablet, if you have one, would also be addressable.

Example: *Creating a Menu*

In order to access your macros, they must be selectable from a menu. Therefore, start by making some macros that will appear on the screen menu.

In any ASCII text editor, start a new file. Call it A:SAMPLE.MNU.

Where:
A: is the drive you are using

SAMPLE is the name of the menu

.MNU is the filename extension for a menu file

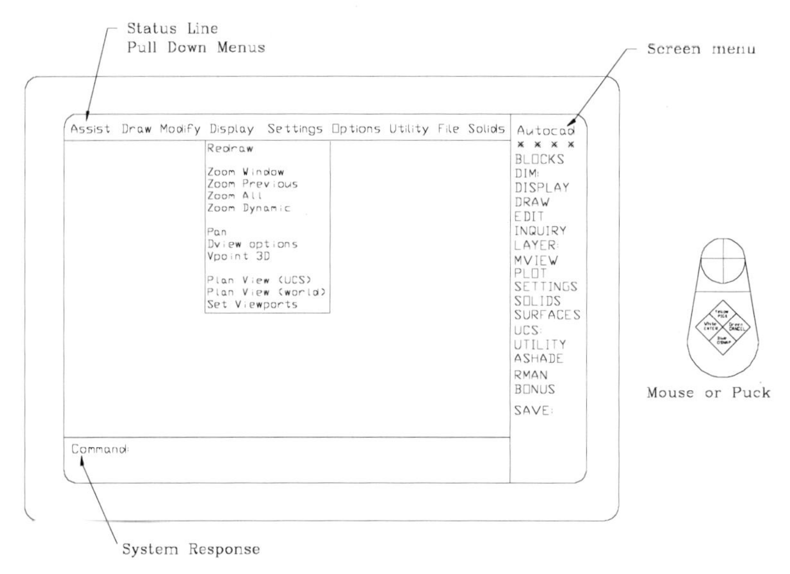

Figure 19-1. Screen layout

At the very top of the page, type in the following exactly as shown. A tilde character (~) indicates that a space is to be left after the last character in the line and before the **Enter** at the end of each line. There are also spaces to be left within each line.

```
***SCREEN
[ A ]
[ SAMPLE]
[ MENU]

[CIRCLE:]^C^CCIRCLE~
[ARC:]^C^CMULTIPLE ARC~
[LINE:]^C^CLINE~
[PLINE:]*^C^C^CPLINE \W .50 ;
[ERASE: L]^C^CERASE L ;
[ZOOM: W]^C^CZOOM W~
[ZOOM: P]'ZOOM P~
[TEXT]^C^CTEXT F~
[*CANCEL]^C^C
```

Do not enter the character, but insert a space instead.

Once you have entered this, save the file as DOS text.

Using the Special Characters

As you look at the above menu commands, dissect them for a full understanding of the special characters.

[] Everything inside the braces is a label for your screen. Remember that the menu macro label cannot exceed eight characters.

^C This is used frequently to ensure that each command starts from the Command: prompt. Either two or sometimes three ^Cs are needed to cancel all other commands (^ is SHIFT-6).

; The semicolon character signifies a Return, not to be confused with the space bar, which often does essentially the same thing. Notice that in the LINE command a semicolon (Return) is not needed because the space at the end of LINE will exit the command; but in the PLINE command a semicolon is needed because the command continues to prompt for options until Return is pressed. If you use the LINE command, you can end the command by using the space bar. In PLINE, however, using the space bar will only keep listing the options of PLINE.

* This causes the macro to repeat indefinitely until a ^C cancels it, use * (asterisk or star) at the beginning. It must be followed directly by ^C to be accepted; if not, it will not be read.

MULTIPLE This is much the same as * in that it repeats the command, but it does not repeat the options of the command. Use it for simple menu items and it can be quite useful.

\ The backslash character allows the user to input data. At this point you are prompted for a response, then the system will take over and complete the series of commands as programmed. This is used to advantage in an INSERT command where the blocks are all to be entered at a scale of 2 and at a 90-degree rotation angle. The only variable is the name of the file.

```
[INSERT 2]^C^CINSERT \ 2  90
```

' The apostrophe character can be used to indicate a transparent command. For example, the ZOOM Previous command can be used within another command string. If you want to use ZOOM P transparently, use ' rather than ^C^C.

`[PAN]'PAN` will allow a PAN within another command

Taking a look at the screen menu created, put the various elements together as follows:

Macro	Explanation
***SCREEN	*Indicates a screen menu.*
[A SAMPLE MENU]	*The words "A SAMPLE MENU" will display at the top of the menu area.*
[CIRCLE:]^C^CCIRCLE	*Creates a simple circle.* *^C^C cancels the command you were in.*
[ARC:]^C^CMULTIPLE ARC	*Creates multiple arcs.* *The same could be done by using* *Command: Multiple ARC* *^C^C cancels the command you were last in.*
[LINE:]^C^CLINE	*Creates a line.* *^C^C cancels the command you were last in.*
[PLINE:]*^C^CPLINE \W .50;	*This creates a pline at a width of .50. The \W picks the width from the PLINE menu, the .50 is the start width, and the space and semicolon ensure that the end width is entered as well.* repeats the command indefinitely, allowing you to add many plines. ^C^C cancels the command you were in.*
[ERASE: L]^C^CERASE L	*Erases the last item entered. ^C^C cancels the command you were in.*

[ZOOM: W]^C^CZOOM W	*Activates ZOOM with Window and prompts the user for the first corner.^C^C cancels the command you were in.*
[ZOOM: P]'ZOOM P	*Activates ZOOM with Previous and allows for a transparent zoom.*
[TEXT]^C^CTEXT F	*Starts the TEXT command and then chooses the Fit option. ^C^C cancels the command you were in.*
[*CANCEL]^C^C	*Cancel is always useful, particularly on a puck or mouse. It is required to get out of the Multiple ARC command as well.*

Once the text is entered, save it as a sample .MNU file. Save it as a DOS file and give it the extension .MNU.

Now, in an empty file in AutoCAD, try it out.

```
Command:MENU
Menu file name or . for none <acad>:a:sample
```

The extension is not needed when entering. Enter a period (.) if you want no menu loaded.

This should display your macro menu on the screen. To return to the AutoCAD Main menu, use the following:

```
Command:MENU
Menu file name or . for none <a:sample>:acad
```

Once you have used the .MNU file, it will be copied onto a .MNX file. AutoCAD compiles the menu when it is first loaded.

Problems You May Encounter

Once you are in the new menu, try all the options you have just created. While doing so, here are some of the problems you may encounter:

- The pointing device may not work for anything except picking points. This is because the address for your menu has not been determined. We will deal with this in the next chapter.
- Pull-down (or pop-up) menus do not work.
- If you have left more than one space after any particular entry, the last command line will be reloaded.

  `[LINE:]^C^CLINE ` *(one space only)*

  An extra space asks for a repeat of the previous command in the same way that pressing the space bar after each command will bring up the next command.
- If a command will not work, chances are you have a spelling error, or have not left a space after the entry of the command.

Many students are intimidated by macros at first and avoid them, thinking that they want to be designers and draftsmen, not programmers. Creating macros and menus is not that difficult. Making an intelligent and useful menu is quite a different story. If your macros get too complicated, consider learning LISP.

Example: *Complex Macros*

Now that you understand how simple macros work, how much harder can it be to write a complex macro?

In the next example, we are going to create a section detail marker. We will generate attributes for the marker and the pline for the section area, and then insert it at a scale factor for a ¼" = 1'0" layout.

STEP 1
Draw a circle at ½" or .50 with a line going horizontally through it.

STEP 2
Add the attributes for detail and sheet at 3/16" or .30 as shown.

On the left is the attributed block with the attributes DETAIL and SHEET, on the right is the wblock once it has been inserted with detail 1 on sheet A1.

STEP 3
Define the attributes as follows:

```
Command:ATTDEF
Attribute modes — Invisible-N, Constant-N, Verify-N, Preset-N
Enter (ICV) to change, RETURN when done:↵
Attribute tag:DETAIL
Attribute prompt:↵
Default attribute value:1
Justify/Style/<start point>:J (as in the TEXT command)
Align/Center/Fit/Middle/Right/TL/TC/TR/ML/MC/MR/BL/BC/BR::M
Middle point: (pick a point)
Height <0'0 3/16">:↵
Rotation angle <0>:↵

Command:ATTDEF
Attribute modes — Invisible-N, Constant-N, Verify-N, Preset -N
Enter (ICVP) to change, RETURN when done:↵
Attribute tag:SHEET
Attribute prompt:↵
Default attribute value:A1
Justify/Style/<start point>:J (as in the TEXT command)
Align/Center/Fit/Middle/Right/TL/TC/TR/ML/MC/MR/BL/BC/BR:M
Middle point: (pick a point)
Height <0'0 3/16">:↵
Rotation angle <0>:↵
```

STEP 4
WBLOCK the attributes and name the block A:DETMAR.

Now, so far you have the beginnings of an automated routine with the attributes defined. In addition to this attributed block, however, you still have to enter the pline, define its width for the arrowhead and linear section, place it, and add the two section detail attributes. The advantage in making a macro to do this is that, if you were to use this detail marker 20 times a day, you would avoid much of the following lengthy process.

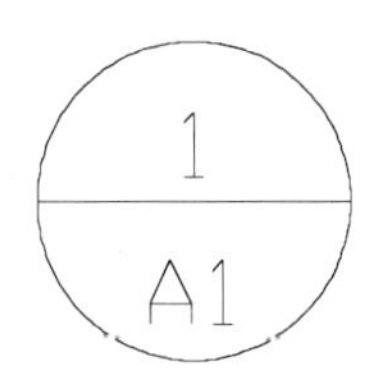

Figure 19-2. Attributed detail block

```
Command:INSERT
Block name or (?):a:detmar
Insertion point: (pick 1)
X scale factor <1>/Corner/XYZ:↵
Y scale factor (default x):↵
Rotation angle <0>:↵
Detail <1>:↵
Sheet <A1>:↵
Command:PLINE
From point: (pick 1)
Current line width is 0.0000.
Arc/Close/Halfwidth/Length/undo/Width/<Endpoint of line>:W
Starting width:0.0000
Ending width:0.2000
Arc/Close/Halfwidth/Length/undo/Width/<Endpoint of line>:@-.25,0
Arc/Close/Halfwidth/Length/undo/Width/<Endpoint of line>:W
Starting width:0.0250
Ending width:0.0250
Arc/Close/Halfwidth/Length/undo/Width/<Endpoint of line>: (pick 2)
Arc/Close/Halfwidth/Length/undo/Width/<Endpoint of line>: (pick 3)
Arc/Close/Halfwidth/Length/undo/Width/<Endpoint of line>: (pick 4)
Arc/Close/Halfwidth/Length/undo/Width/<Endpoint of line>:W
Starting width:0.2000
Ending width:0.0000
Arc/Close/Halfwidth/Length/undo/Width/<Endpoint of line>:@.25,0
Arc/Close/Halfwidth/Length/undo/Width/<Endpoint of line>:↵
Command:INSERT
Block name or (?):a:detmar
Insertion point: (pick 6)
X scale factor <1>/Corner/XYZ:↵
Y scale factor (default x):↵
Rotation angle <0>:↵
Detail <1>:↵
Sheet <A1>:↵
```

You will end up with a detail section marker that looks like Figure 19-3.

The command sequence above requires 34 keystrokes. If you create a macro for the same purpose, the user is required to enter only 6 responses. This is a considerable saving in time and energy, particularly if you use this type of symbol frequently.

Here is the macro for the above command sequence.

```
[]
[INSERT:D]^C^C^CINSERT;A:DETMAR;\;;;\\^C^CPLINE;END;\W;+ ↵
0;.20;@-.250,0;W;.025;;^O\\\W;.20;0;@.250,0;^C^CINSERT;+ ↵
A:DETMAR;\;;;\\ ↵
```

Use a hard return after the + sign at the end of each line.

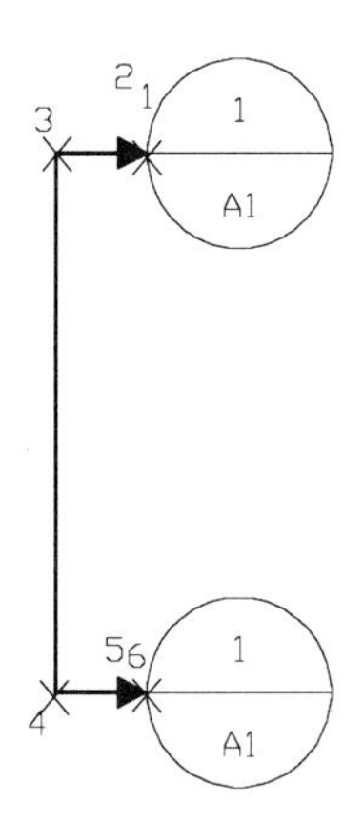

Figure 19-3. The macro detail

Detail Marker Macro Explanation

Use this explanation as a guide in creating your own macros.

[] leaves a space between macros on the menu.

[INSERT:D] is the macro label displayed on the menu.

^C^C^C cancels all previous commands.

INSERT A:DETMAR; invokes the command INSERT and the block a:detmar.

\;;; responses to the INSERT command.

\ Insertion point: *(pick 1)*

; X scale factor <1>/Corner/XYZ: *(accepts default)*

; Y scale factor /<1>Corner/XYZ: *(accepts default)*

; Rotation angle<0> : *(accepts default)*

\ Detail <1>: *(accept or change)*

\ Sheet<A1> :accept or change

^C^C cancels the end of INSERT command.

PLINE; invokes PLINE command.

END; asks for END(*point*) OSNAP for user response pick 2.

W; is the width of pline.

+ signals the end of the line. Hard return, no space.

0; response to Starting width:

.20; response to Ending width: semicolon ends the entry.

@-.250,0; allows for a .250-length arrow. Semicolon ends the entry.

W;; asks to change the width. Semicolon ends the entry, semicolon accepts end width.

.025; response to Starting width: semicolon ends the entry.

^O toggles ORTHO so the lines will be straight.

\\\ is the three user responses for the three points on the pline.

W; asks to change the width for the final arrow.

.20; response for Starting width: semicolon ends the entry.

0; response to Ending width: semicolon ends the entry.

@.250,0; gives relative distance of pline and arrow length.

^C^C makes sure all entries are completed.

INSERT; invokes the INSERT command. Semicolon ends the entry.

+ signals the end of the line, macro to be continued.

A:DETMAR; retrieves block a:detmar.

\;;;\\ responses to the INSERT command as above.

For practice, add this macro to the end of your sample menu and try it out. Certain codes or symbols such as the negative sign (@-.125) do not translate transparently. If your macro is not working, try saving it as an ASCII text file. (Save using Ctrl F5 if in WordPerfect.)

Tips and Tricks

- Create the desired geometry in AutoCAD first, and take note of *every* keystroke, including spaces.
- If the macro is not working, try saving it as DOS text.
- No space but hard return after +.
- Use a semicolon rather than spaces.

The best way to approach a complex macro is systematically. Figure out which commands you want to use, then note the number of keystokes, then type them in.

Exercise A19

STEP 1
Create the sample macros on page 334 and place them in a menu called A:SAMPLE.MNU. Create macros for the following commands and add them to the same menu:

```
LINE from an END(point) to a MID(dle point)
ARC Start END Radius
PLINE at .5
ELLIPSE
PAN
```

STEP 2
Add the detail marker macro to the menu.

STEP 3
Create a complex macro to create one of the following:

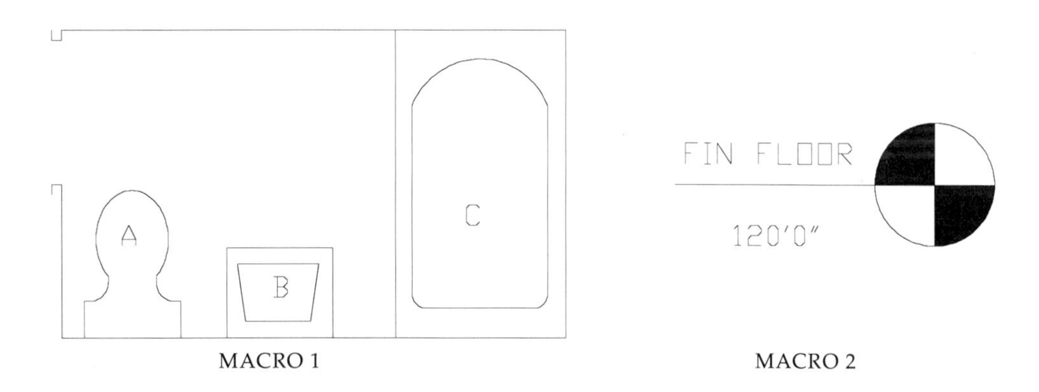

MACRO 1 MACRO 2

Macro 1
Create wblocks for a standard toilet, sink, and bath. Generate one single macro to select these blocks and place them as the user determines at a 1 = 1 scale with optional rotation.

Macro 2
Create an attributed block for the elevation datum marker. Create a macro to draw this block with an extendable pline of .1 width.

Exercise M19

STEP 1

Create the sample macros on page 334 and place them in a menu called A:SAMPLE.MNU. Create macros for the following commands and add them to the same menu:

```
LINE from an END(point) to a MID(dle point)
ARC Start END Radius
PLINE at .5
ELLIPSE
PAN
```

STEP 2

Add the detail marker macro to the menu.

STEP 3

Create a complex macro to create one of the following:

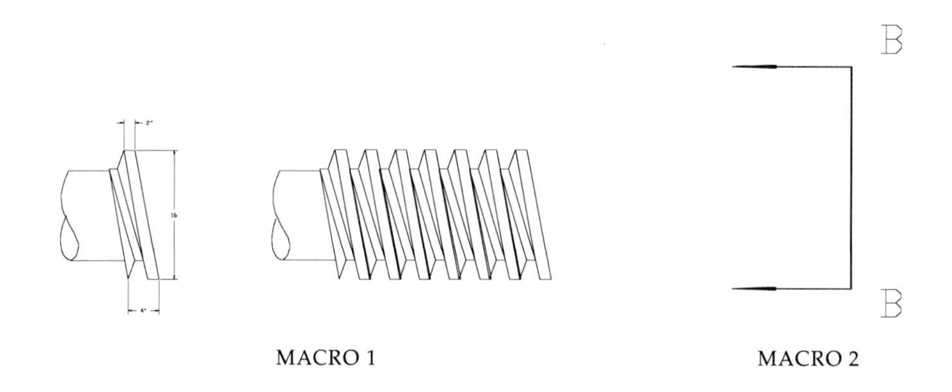

MACRO 1 MACRO 2

Macro 1

Create a macro to draw an external threading with variable sizing and repeatability.

Macro 2

Create an attributed block for the section indicator with an extendable pline at a width of .05.

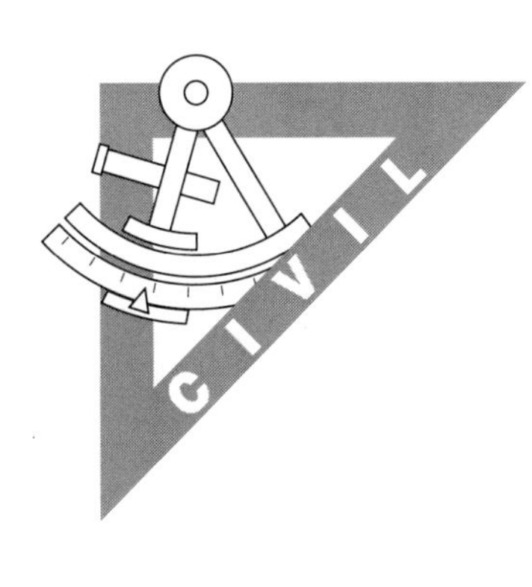

Exercise C19

STEP 1
Create the sample macros on page 334 and place them in a menu called A:SAMPLE.MNU. Create macros for the following commands and add them to the same menu:

```
LINE from an END(point) to a MID(dle point)
ARC Start END Radius
PLINE at .5
ELLIPSE
PAN
```

STEP 2
Add the detail marker macro to the above menu.

STEP 3
Create a complex macro to create one of the following:

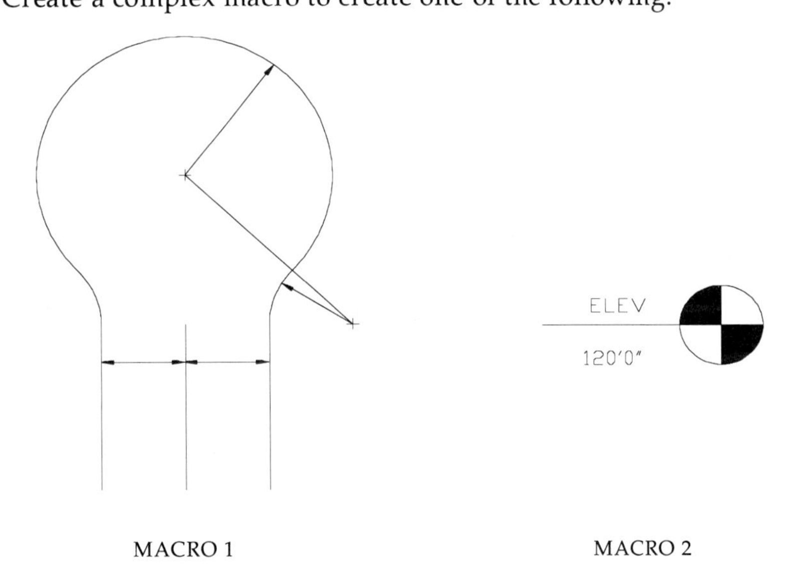

MACRO 1 MACRO 2

Macro 1
Create a macro to generate a cul-de-sac.

Macro 2
Create an attributed block for the elevation datum marker. Create a macro to insert this block with an extendable pline of .1 width.

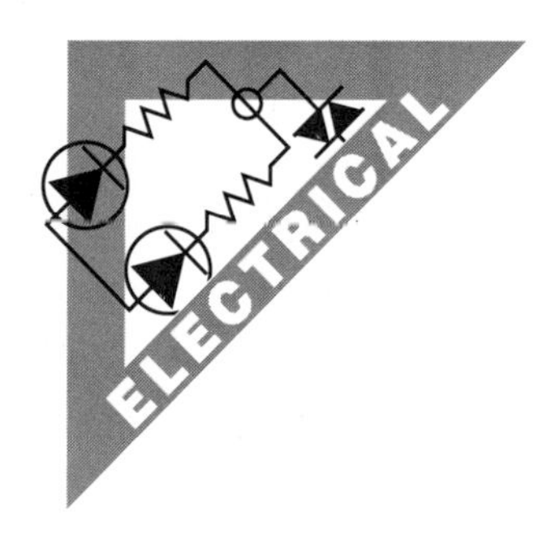

Exercise E19

STEP 1
Create the sample macros on page 334 and place them in a menu called A:SAMPLE.MNU. Create macros for the following commands and add them to the same menu:

```
LINE from an END(point) to a MID(dle point)
ARC Start END Radius
PLINE at .5
ELLIPSE
PAN
```

STEP 2
Add the detail marker macro to the above menu.

STEP 3
Create a complex macro for one of the following:

MACRO
Create a separate macro for each of these symbols using PLINE and DONUT.

Challenger 19

STEP 1
Create a macro for a circular staircase with user input for tread size, rise, and run.

STEP 2
Using quadrants, create a macro for the detail marker shown.

CUSTOMIZING MENUS

Upon completion of this chapter, the student should be able to:

1. Add commands to the existing ACAD.MNU screen menu
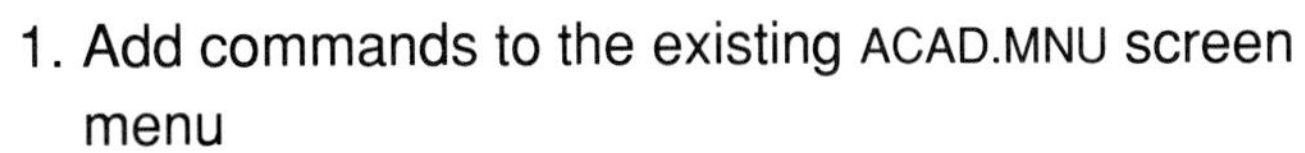
2. Create pop-up menus
3. Change the button addresses on a pointing device
4. Readdress the screen configuration
5. Address buttons on the tablet with macros
6. Reconfigure the tablet menu

THE AUTOCAD BASE MENU

You may have noticed that, after creating the A:SAMPLE menu in the previous chapter, the pull-down menus and 99 percent of the AutoCAD commands were not listed when the new menu was invoked. With a custom menu, all of the commands are available, but you have to type them in to be able to use them if they are not included on your new menu.

If you are creating your own menu, you will need not only the commands you entered in the last exercise, but all the submenus that lead to those commands. Basic AutoCAD now offers hundreds of different commands and options; so if you intend to simply sort out the ones you need and create a menu, you could be spending a lot of time at the keyboard.

A better approach, perhaps, is to simply add on your own menu macros to the available menus. In the last chapter you used the MENU command to read in a new menu; now you will learn how to integrate your menu macros into an existing menu.

While it is possible to add macros to the standard ACAD.MNU, you should avoid it. Instead, copy ACAD.MNU and give it a new name.

```
C:\acad>COPY ACAD.MNU a:TESTACAD.MNU
```

Release 12 Notes

Release 12 has a full customization manual that covers areas of customization not found in this text. The format does not change from earlier releases.

Depending on the configuration of your system, the .MNU file could be hidden in the source or support directory; in this case, use the following:

```
C:\acad\source>COPY ACAD.MNU a:TESTACAD.MNU
```

This DOS command will copy the menu from the ACAD directory or the ACAD Source subdirectory. A list of directories in the C drive or wherever AutoCAD resides should lead you to the directory where the AutoCAD menu resides. If your system is networked, you may have difficulty obtaining the file. If so, speak to your instructor, user assistant, or system manager to find out where it is and if it can be copied.

Once copied, you will be able to experiment with the base ACAD menu and the original will remain intact. Make sure it remains intact.

Before adding your own menus and macros, you should understand how AutoCAD's main menu is compiled. This will help you add macros that let you use AutoCAD more efficiently.

MENU DEVICES

The menus available in AutoCAD are the screen menu (one area), the pull-down or pop-up menus (ten areas), the icon section (one area), the tablet (four areas), and the mouse or puck (one or more areas, buttons and auxiliary).

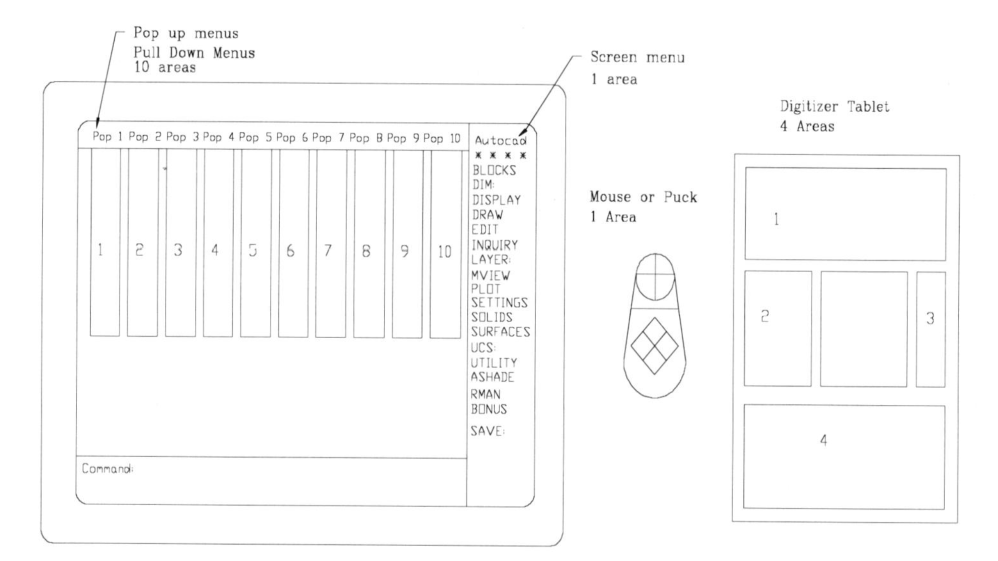

Figure 20-1. Available menus in AutoCAD

All of the above menus or devices are available in AutoCAD. Icon menus can be addressed as well. In addition, there is the Auxiliary menu — if there is a system mouse. Dialogue boxes are not part of this layout.

If you want to assign macros to any one area, simply state in the .MNU file the device you want to address.

***SCREEN *will address the screen area*

***BUTTONS *will address the button area*

***TABLET *will address the tablet area*

***POP1 *will address the first pop-up area*

***POP7 *will address the seventh pop-up area*

***ICON *will create a new icon menu*

In order to use the ACAD.MNU, you must learn a bit more of the code used to write it. Menus are made up of base menus and submenus. The information contained in a menu can be presented as a menu tree.

A typical menu tree would be as follows:

DRAW MENU

ARC	CIRCLE	DONUT	ELLIPSE	LINE
3	2P	Inside	Center	continue
SCA	3P	Outside	Radius	close
SCL	TTR	Center	Isoplane	undo
SER	D		Rotation	
SEA				
SED				

All geometry options stem from a geometry command which stems from the Draw menu. The Draw menu is found under the ACAD.MNU file as **DR.

Take a look at the Line submenu under the Draw menu. First, enter your text editor WordPerfect, WordStar, MS-DOS Editor, etc. and retrieve your new menu TESTACAD.

Look down the list of options and you will find:

```
[HATCH:]$S=X $S=HATCH ^C^CHATCH
[INSERT:]$S=X $S=INSERT ^C^CINSERT
[LINE:]$S=X $S=LINE ^C^CLINE
[MINSERT:]$S=X $S=MINSERT ^C^CMINSERT
```

This menu text could be many pages down your file. As with the DXF files, the tablet menu has many pages of set-up instructions.

The LINE command is between INSERT and MINSERT on the main Draw screen menu. The string itself is as follows:

```
[LINE:]$S=X $S=LINE ^C^CLINE
```

Where:
[LINE:] = the label that will be displayed on the menu

$ = the character that causes the display of a submenu. The characters that follow will be sent to the menu control centre, not the command line.

S=X = the system directive to go to submenu

$S=LINE = the screen submenu name, LINE

^C^CLINE will add LINE to the command string

This one string of text within the .MNU file means that LINE: is offered as a choice from the Draw menu, and, once picked, AutoCAD will automatically access the Line submenu for further screen menu choices and will add LINE to the command string.

When a menu item is followed with a $ character, a section name, an equals sign, and a submenu name, that submenu will be displayed. Each type of menu has a different submenu name.

$A *an auxiliary submenu*

$B *a button submenu*

$I *an icon submenu*

$Pn *a pop-up submenu, n being the submenu number ($P7)*

$S *a screen submenu*

$T *a tablet submenu*

This prefix tells AutoCAD where to look for the menu. Let us look at the submenu for LINE. It looks like this:

```
**LINE 1
[LINE:]^CLINE
[continue]^CLINE;
close
undo
```

Where:
****LINE 1** = a submenu called Line, which starts on the first line of the screen menu (1).

[LINE:]^CLINE = the word LINE: will show up on the menu, the last command will be cancelled, and the LINE command will be invoked.

[continue]^CLINE; = the default is to start a line continuing from the last point. The LINE command, followed by a Return signalled by the semicolon will connect the first point of the new line with the last point of the last line, as if you had entered another Return.

close = the listed option

undo = the listed option

The options listed under the submenus are not enclosed in brackets, but they will display on the screen.

You have seen how the .MNU file contains different menu areas, and you have seen how each menu has different submenus. The examples above were taken from a screen menu.

Let us take this one step further and add a few commands to the existing screen menu.

Modifying the Screen Menu

Example: *Screen Menu*

STEP 1
The section label for the screen menus is ***SCREEN. Retrieve your menu file TESTACAD.MNU. Use the search function of your word processor to find this area.

Using WordPerfect, go to the beginning of the document and search for the text string ***SCREEN. Press F2, type in ***SCREEN, and press F2 again for the search to begin.

The beginning of the screen menu will look like this:

```
***SCREEN
**S
[AutoCAD]^C^C^P$S=X $S=S (setq T_MENU 0)(princ) ^P$P1=POP1
$P2=P2DRAW $P4=P4DISP $P6=P6OPT $P8=POP8
[* * * *]$S=OSNAPB
[BLOCKS]$S=X $S=BL
[DIM:]$S=X $S=DIM ^C^CDIM
```

```
[DISPLAY]$S=X $S=DS
[DRAW]$S=X $S=DR
[EDIT]$S=X $S=ED
[INQUIRY]$S=X $S=INQ
[LAYER:]$S=X $S=LAYER ^C^CLAYER
[MVIEW]$S=X $S=MV
[PLOT]$S=X $S=PLOT
[SETTINGS]$S=X $S=SET
```

As you can see, all the choices are there. The words you are accustomed to are in braces, and the rest of the string usually initiates the command.

Add the detail marker macro from the previous chapter to the end of the Draw menu. If you have created a datum macro (from the last exercises) or another macro you think will work, use it.

Make sure you have created and tested your macro before adding it to the main menu because it is a very long menu.

STEP 2
Now search for the Draw menu. It should begin like this:

```
**DR 3
[ARC]$S=X $S=ARC
[ATTDEF:]$S=X $S=ATTDEF ^C^CATTDEF
```

Scroll down this menu until you come to the end of 3DFACE.

```
[TRACE:]$S=X $S=TRACE ^C^CTRACE
[3DFACE:]$S=X $S=3DFACE ^C^C3DFACE
```

Now add the macro. You can type it in again, or, if you are using WordPerfect, you can use SHIFT-F10 to retrieve the macro file into the current document.

```
[TRACE:]$S=X $S=TRACE ^C^CTRACE
[3DFACE:]$S=X $S=3DFACE ^C^C3DFACE
[]
[INSERT:D]^C^C^CINSERT;A:DETMAR;\;;;\\^C^CPLINE;END;\W;+
0;.20;@-.250,0;W;.025;;^O\\W;.20;0;@.250,0;^C^CINSERT;+
A:DETMAR;\;;;\\
```

Now exit the file and be sure to save it as ASCII text (Ctrl F5).

STEP 3
Start AutoCAD and ask for the new menu.

```
Command:MENU
New menu name:TESTMENU
```

Under the Draw menu, the new macro should be listed as INSERT: D or whatever name you called it. The [] at the beginning of the file should give you a space between this macro and the preceding one.

If you have entered everything correctly, it should work.

Compiling Your Own Screen Menus

As stated earlier, most people use 20 percent of the available commands 80 percent of the time. If you take the commands you regularly use and compile them into screen menus, these could save you a lot of time.

For example, take a look at the DRAW commands you generally use. There are two pages of DRAW commands, and the listing is arranged alphabetically rather than by frequency of use. You can easily compile a list of the DRAW commands you regularly use for the first page, then compile a list of DRAW commands you rarely use for the second page. If you use SOLID and TEXT quite regularly, but never use CHAMFER or DTEXT, this will save you from always having to access the second page of the DRAW menu just because the letters that begin the commands are further along the alphabet.

Further Notes On Screen Menu Creation

The amount of space available for the macros on the screen is limited. If you enter more words or macros than the space allows, you will have text running all over your menu area. Try to limit the number of on-screen macro offerings for each screen menu to a total of 15.

CREATING A PULL-DOWN OR POP-UP MENU

Creating pop-up menus is much the same as creating a screen menu. The pull-down (or pop-up) structure was created by Autodesk so that the menus would temporarily overlay a portion of the screen. This way, you can add a long string of commands that will be grouped together.

The pull-down or pop-up menus are separate items on the menu file. The screen menu is located only on the right of the screen, but the pop-ups are in 10 different sections. You can use all 10 of the pop-ups if you like. To specify which area you want to work with, use ***POP and then the number of the pop-up menu you want. For example, if you want to add something to the Display pop-up menu, use ***POP4. ***POP1 is the Assist menu and OSNAPS, etc. By going to the beginning of the TESTACAD.MNU file, then searching for ***POP1, you can find the pop-ups and scroll through them to see how they are constructed.

Notice in ***POP2 the length of the draw macro entries. These are obviously complex macros, not simple draw commands as you may have thought.

***POP3 contains the modify or edit commands, and you can see that these also are complex macros. The ERASE command, for example, looks like this:

```
[ERASE:]*^C^C$S=X $S=erase erase si auto
```

Where:
[ERASE:] is the command option as displayed on the menu

* is the symbol to repeat the command once completed

^C^C cancels the last command

$S=X is the system directive to go to submenu

$S=erase is the submenu name, Erase

erase is the AutoCAD command

si executes the command after one entity is selected

auto displays a Window or Crossing if no object is picked

The header on the pop-up menu, displayed on the status line, can have a maximum of 14 characters. The menu item labels can be any length. The menu is as wide as its longest point.

Pull-down menus look the same as screen menus and also use the same codes to describe the commands. They serve a slightly different purpose, however, as the menu will disappear as soon as you pick a selection. It is a good idea to keep all additions to this area simple. If you are doing a lot of work that calls for specific zooming or views, it is a good idea to add some custom display parameters to the current display menu.

Let us try an easy example of this with your sample menu from the last chapter. The ***POP8 is a very short menu. Add part or all of your sample menu to the bottom of this menu.

Once completed, you can exit the file and test the pop-up menu.

Example: *Pop-up Menus*

STEP 1
As with the screen menu, make sure that the file is the TESTACAD.MNU and not the ACAD.MNU file. Retrieve it into your word processor and search for ***POP8.

STEP 2
When you have located ***POP8, add some commands to the bottom of the list.

```
***POP8
[File]
[Save         ]^C^Csave
[End          ]^C^Cend
[Quit         ]^C^C$S=X $S=quit quit
[~--]
[Files        ]^C^Cfiles
[Plot         ]^C^Cplot
[Print        ]^C^Cprplot
[~--]
[EXCHANGE   >]$p8=p8xchg $p8=*
[]
[PDMODE:]^C^CPDMODE
[PDSIZE:]^C^CPDSIZE
[PICK BOX:]^C^CPICKBOX
```

Since you know how to enter commands now, what you are actually entering at this point is not as important as making sure that you can make the process work. Practise on simple lines and arcs, then create your own commands to fit your needs.

STEP 3
Now that the information has been entered, save the file as ASCII text, keeping the extension .MNU, and try it out.

Further Notes On Pop-Up Menus

If your hardware does not support AutoCAD's Advanced User Interface, you will not be able to see your macros.

When you are creating macros for this section, think about what you want the command to do before you write it. Consider whether you want it to:

*	*repeat*
si	*execute after one object is picked*
auto	*invoke an automatic Window*

Also note that you can add lines between sections.

[--]	*will create a line along the width of the menu*
[~--]	*will place two grey dashes only*
[~]	*greys out anything that follows*

ADDRESSING BUTTONS

Whether you are using a tablet or not, the buttons on the mouse, pick, digitizer, or whatever you are using can be re-addressed.

This is done under the ***BUTTONS section label.

When the driver for the pointing device is programmed, the buttons are mapped in a specific numeric order. The numbers on the driver do not necessarily follow the numbers on the buttons, if there are any. The appearance of the commands in the TESTACAD.MNU file, therefore, may not seem to have any logical relation to your own device. With a smaller three- or four-button device, this relationship takes only a few minutes to figure out. With the complex pointing devices, however, determining the button mapping can be quite disconcerting.

The buttons are easy to change once identified. In a standard three-button mouse, the first button is reserved as the pick function. It cannot be changed. The other buttons can be assigned to perform specific functions.

Like screen menus, you can have multiple pages of button items, but because it is such a dynamic device, this usually just creates problems. You can certainly change the order of the codes shown, however, and experiment to determine the one you prefer. If you use macros more than the cancel button, the cancel button can be easily reprogrammed. Let us assign an OSNAP END(*point*) macro to the cancel button just for practice.

Example: *Buttons*

STEP 1
Find the ***BUTTONS area on your .MNU file.

`***BUTTONS`	*Buttons menu*
`;`	*Return*
`$p1=*`	*Displays Assist pop-up menu 1 or Osnap*
`^C^C`	*Cancel*
`^B`	*SNAP On/Off toggle*
`^O`	*ORTHO On/Off toggle*
`^G`	*GRID On/Off toggle*
`^D`	*Coordinate display toggle*
`^E`	*Isoplane cross-hairs display*
`^T`	*Tablet On/Off toggle*

On a four-button mouse, the buttons are addressed in a counter-clockwise rotation around the pick button. The pick button can never be re-addressed. Thus the buttons are as follows:

`$S=osnapb` may also be used for the Osnap submenu

STEP 2
Just after the main prompt, add the macro for OSNAP END(*point*) and address it as [B3], or put it in the third position.

```
***BUTTONS
;
$p1=*
[B3 ]END \
```

STEP 3
Now save the file as ASCII text and test the button menu. Be careful with this macro; if you have not entered a DRAW or EDIT command before you use it, you could END your file.

The buttons can be re-addressed quite easily. It is possible to get a pointing device or mouse with as many as 16 buttons. I personally would never remember all the button functions, but even complex macros can be added to a button if necessary.

If you want many layers of commands on the buttons or many pages of options, be sure to have a button that will return you to the original layout.

TABLET BUTTONS

If your lab does not use a digitizer tablet, simply ignore this part of the chapter and proceed to the exercises.

In a classroom environment, teaching students how to recalibrate and re-address tablets is dangerous, mostly because some students are not considerate of other students using the labs and have a tendency to recalibrate the tablet and then forget to return the tablet to normal for other classes. If you are the kind of person who is likely to do this, remember how difficult your first few weeks of AutoCAD were and make an effort to remember. In technology, the learning curve is quite pronounced during the first few years, so some students may think it is clever to change things like menus that will mess up another student. Keep in mind, there will always be someone who knows more than you do and who may have a worse sense of humour than yours.

Addressing Tablet Buttons

Because the tablet, if you have one, is right in front of you with many empty buttons, this is the obvious choice for customization.

The tablet menu is divided into four distinct areas. These are usually active at the same time. To view the tablet settings menu file, simply search for ***TABLETn, n being the number of the tablet menu.

***TABLET1 is mostly empty, so it is the most obvious place to start filling with macros.

The A row has been reserved for user macros.

Like the button section described above, each box on the tablet menu is mapped according to the tablet coordinates. Here are the first few lines of the ***TABLET1 area of the .MNU file.

```
***TABLET1
[A-1]
[A-2]
[A-3]
[A-4]
```

There are 200 boxes that can be re-addressed or filled on the first section of the tablet. The TABLET.CFG file is used to break the tablet up into a specific number of columns (1–25) and rows (A–H). See Tablet Configuration in Figure 20-2 for more details.

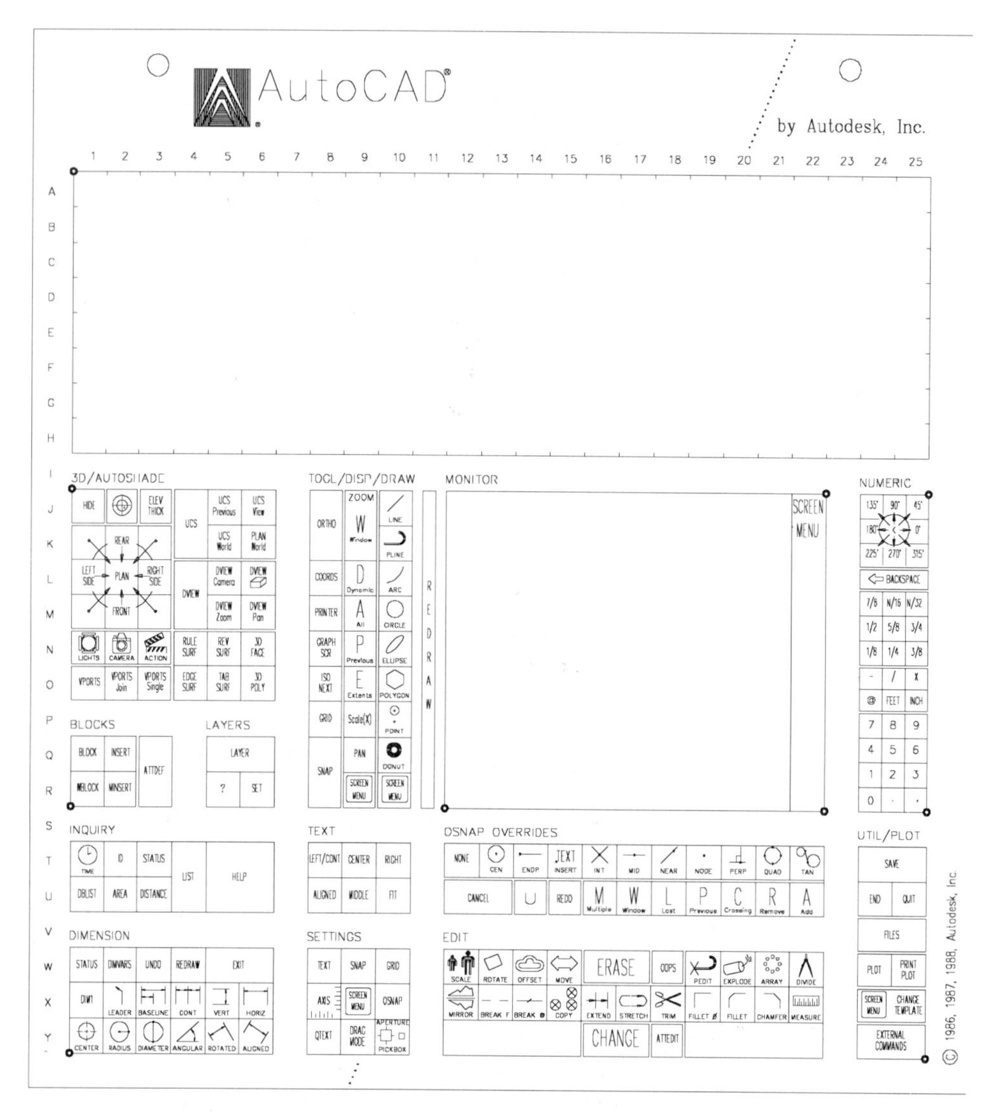

Figure 20-2. AutoCAD's main tablet menu

Addressing boxes in Releases 9 and 10 is a bit less complicated than Release 11 because the latter tablet incorporates the most recent developments. The first 10 columns are used for commands in Advanced Modeling Extension, AutoShade, and RenderMan. If you have no intention of using any of these packages, simply re-address these boxes with your own programs. By picking the tablet Area-1 icon, these boxes will be swapped for blank ones. This replaces the whole tablet with a ***TABLET1ALT menu, which changes other boxes as well and may not be what you want.

To address any of the boxes on the tablet, basically it is the same process as with the screen menu, except you must be aware of the box number. In the ***TABLET1 menu, this is easy because they are all listed. Note the address of B-5 on the following SOLCONE command.

```
[B-5]^C^C^P(progn(setq m:err *error*)(princ))+
(defun *error* (msg)(princ msg)(setq *error* m:err m:err nil f
```

```
nil)(princ))+
(if (null c:SOLCONE)(defun c:SOLCONE () (menucmd
"S=X")(menucmd "S=SOLLOAD");+
(terpri)(princ "ERROR:  Command not found. ")+
(princ "  Load AME or AMElite from the screen menu. ")+
(setq c:SOLCONE nil)(princ))+
(progn (menucmd "S=X")(menucmd "S=SCONE")))(princ);^PSOLCONE
```

If you want to assign a macro to a box in ***TABLET1, just find the address you want and type in the macro.

The other tablet areas can be re-addressed as well; but ***TABLET1 is already empty, so you might as well use it. Many companies have re-organized their menus to suit their own needs, but this takes a long time.

Once you have totally customized the tablet, you can create an overlay or template to fit on the tablet when you are using it. AutoCAD comes with a file named TABLET.DWG. This is a full drawing file with all the boxes filled as in the original template. Retrieve this file, copy it to your own disk with your own name XXXTABLET.dwg, fill in the areas where you have entered macros, plot it, and place it over the current tablet when you are on the system.

CONFIGURING THE TABLET MENU

As noted, the tablet menu consists of four distinct areas. The columns and rows are listed from 1 to 25 across the top and from A to Y down the side. The F10 key will turn the tablet on if it is off. You may need to reconfigure the tablet to set up your own custom menu because another student may have changed the configuration. The command for this is quite straightforward.

The TABLET command is used from within the Drawing Editor and allows you to pick a series of points to line up the tablet. While picking, make sure you have the right point, and you should have no trouble.

The first pick is at position A1 as shown on page 356. You will configure first Area 1, then areas 2, 3, and 4. You pick three points per area and then enter the number of rows and columns. There are two basic sizes for tablets, 11"x 11" and 8" x 8". The configuration below will suit both applications.

```
Command:Tablet
Option (ON/OFF/CAL/CFG):CFG

Digitize the upper left corner of menu area 1: (pick 1)
Digitize the lower left corner of menu area 1: (pick 2)
Digitize the lower right corner of menu area 1: (pick 3)
Enter the number of columns for menu area 1:25
Enter the number of rows for menu area 1:9

Digitize the upper left corner of menu area 2: (pick 4)
Digitize the lower left corner of menu area 2: (pick 5)
Digitize the lower right corner of menu area 2: (pick 6)
Enter the number of columns for menu area 1:11
Enter the number of rows for menu area 1:9

Digitize the upper left corner of menu area 3: (pick 7)
Digitize the lower left corner of menu area 3: (pick 8)
Digitize the lower right corner of menu area 3: (pick 9)
Enter the number of columns for menu area 1:9
```

```
Enter the number of rows for menu area 1:13
Digitize the upper left corner of menu area 4: (pick 10)
Digitize the lower left corner of menu area 4: (pick 11)
Digitize the lower right corner of menu area 4: (pick 12)
Enter the number of columns for menu area 1:25
Enter the number of rows for menu area 1:7
Do you want to respecify the screen pointing area (Y) ⏎
Digitize the lower-left corner of the screen pointing area:
(pick 13)
Digitize the upper-right corner of the screen pointing area:
(pick 14)
```

Follow the pick points below and you should have no trouble configuring the tablet. Be sure the tablet is turned on, then test it out.

CREATING TOTALLY NEW MENUS

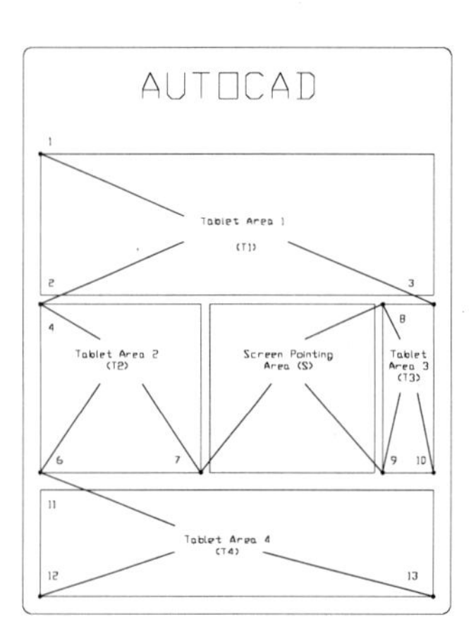

Figure 20-3. Using the Configure option

There are many people who always simply type in the commands they need. For these people, there is no need to have a screen menu at all. To get rid of the screen menu area, you could simply create a menu file that permits only pull-down menus, tablet, and buttons menus alone.

From the previous discussions of the possible menus and how to create them, you should now be equipped to generate your own custom menus with the information that only you need. With a few extra pointers, you should be able to fully customize your screen.

ERASING THE SCREEN MENU

When creating a new menu file that excludes the screen menu, the first line of the file should be blank, otherwise the contents appear in the screen area.

Once taken out, you can now use the configure AutoCAD area of the main menu, option 5, and have the screen menu area removed from the screen.

The new screen layout is enlarged and allows for bigger drawings as a result.

In Figure 20-3, the screen menu has been erased from the menu file by using the Configure option of the AutoCAD main menu.

The option to change in the Configuration menu is the Video display area option. You will be prompted to indicate which screen display areas you want to remove. If you remove the response area, you can still use F1 to see what command you are in.

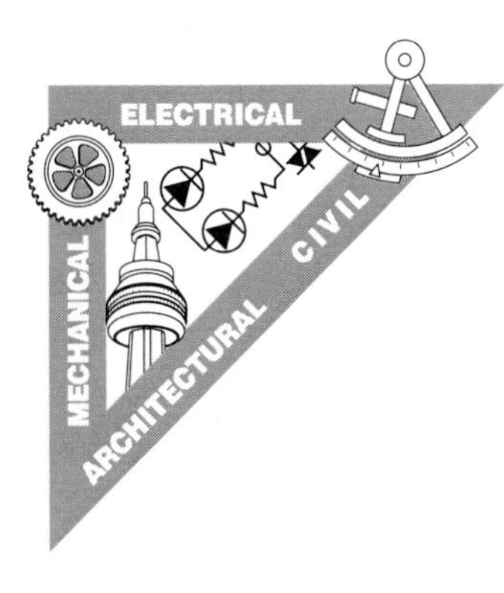

Exercises All

STEP 1
Copy the ACAD.MNU file to your own disk under your own name, e.g., SRKACAD.MNU.

Retrieve your menu file in WordPerfect or a similar word processing package that will create an ASCII-format file.

Add a complex macro to the ***SCREEN menu. Save it and test it.

STEP 2
Add a macro to the ***POP8 menu. Exit and try it out.

STEP 3
Reconfigure the buttons on the mouse and add an OSNAP END(*point*) macro. Test the buttons, then reconfigure the buttons to the original setting.

STEP 4
Add three macros to tablet Area 1 (***TABLET1). Reconfigure the tablet.

STEP 5
Exit your custom menu file and return to ACAD.MNU. Make sure the mouse has the same button configuration as when you started. Make sure the tablet is properly configured.

Challenger 20

Generate 25 custom macros and assign them to boxes on the tablet. Retrieve the TABLET.DWG file. Enter template symbols to indicate the location of your macros. Plot the drawing. (See below).

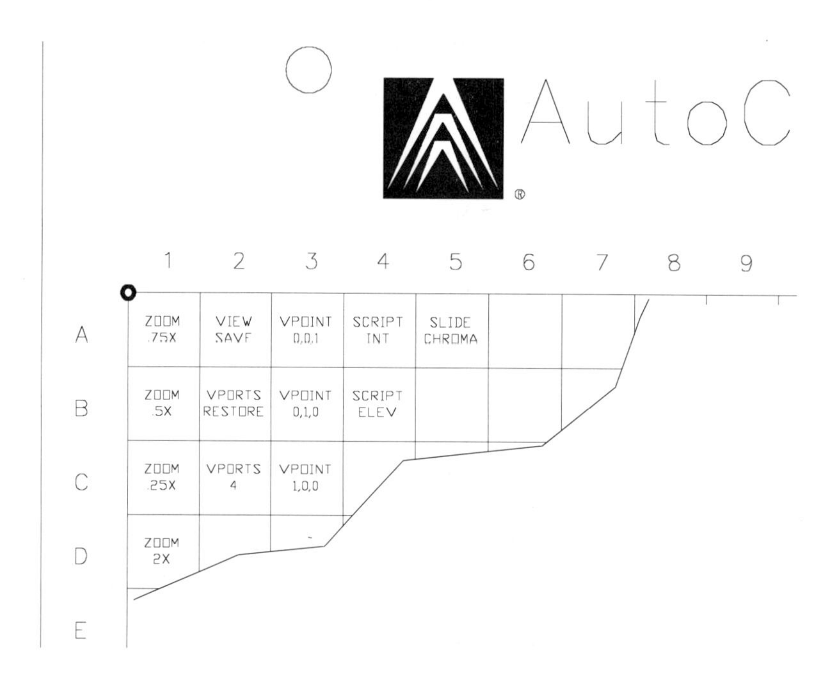

Now change the screen menu so that there is no menu, no status line, and no command line.

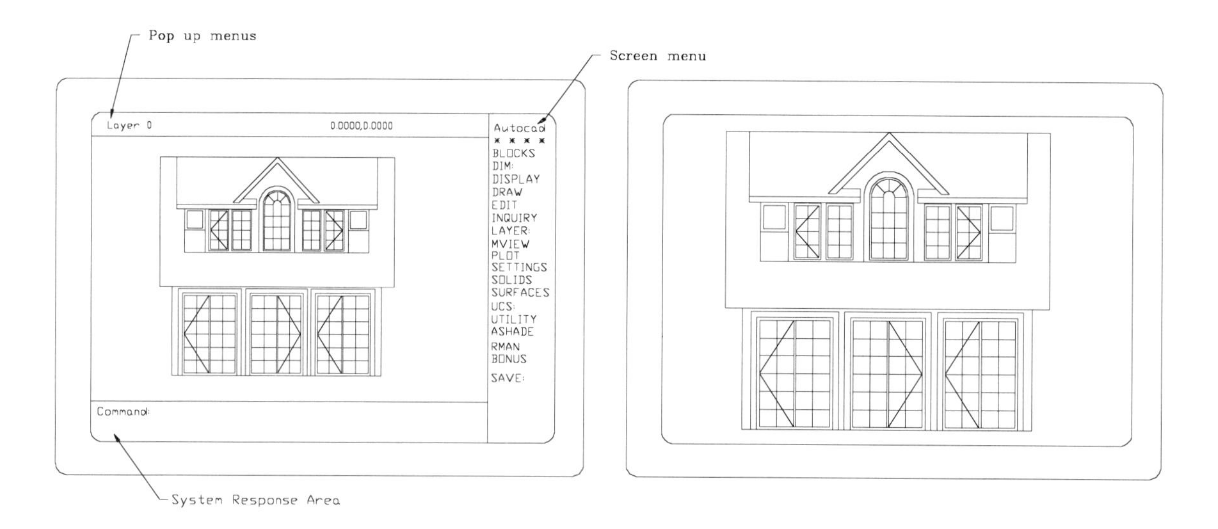

Be sure to change it back before you leave the lab.

CREATING ICON MENUS

Upon completion of this chapter, the student should be able to:

1. Create an icon menu and
2. Insert it into a custom menu

USING ICON MENUS

Release 12 Notes

Release 12 has a full customization manual that covers areas of customization not found in this text. The format does change from earlier releases.

When using the HATCH command, you can either type in the name of the hatch pattern within the HATCH command, or, if you do not know the name of the pattern you want to access, you can access the Hatch icon menu to view the icons and then pick the one you want. Similarly, there are icon menus for the VPOINT command, the DVIEW command, the TEXT STYLE command, etc. These help you to choose the option or style you want without having to know the name or rotation data.

Icon menus are useful for viewing user-defined patterns or blocks to ensure that the icon selected is appropriate for a particular application. They are also useful to double check the insertion base points and sizes of scales and symbols before inserting them. For those who need vertical fractions, the fractions can be stored as blocks and then entered through an icon menu.

For example, a residential designer should know the standard electrical symbols and how to use them. An AutoCAD user should have them on file as attributed blocks so that they can be inserted directly onto drawings, and have the list of necessary electrical outlets available immediately with ATTEXT. If you need a particular symbol and cannot remember the block name, an icon menu such as the one below may help you.

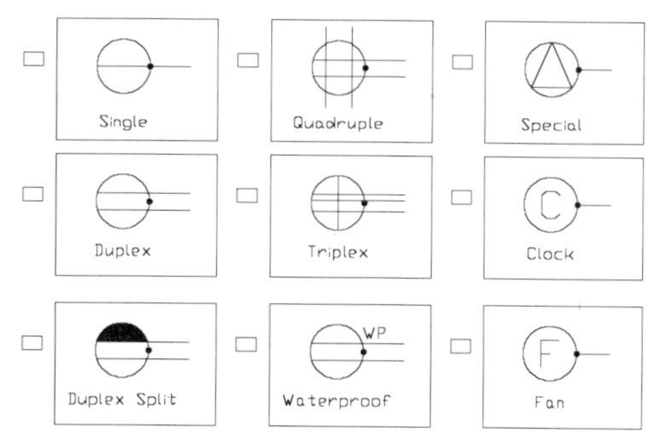

Figure 21-1. An icon box

To create a really useful icon box, first make the blocks. Then add attributes to the blocks so that they can be downloaded with the information you need, such as the name and the supplier and maybe the order number. The block is now ready to use and can be used as is or added to an icon menu.

Like pull-down menus, icon menus can be used only with display devices that support the AutoCAD Advanced User Interface. If the display driver on your system lacks this support, all the icon menus will be ignored. If you have not been able to use the Hatch pull-down menu, you have several options. First, check with your AutoCAD dealer to see that your installation has been done correctly. Then, if you have a hardware problem instead of an installation problem, consider buying a new graphics card.

THE ICON MENU

In a screen menu program file, braces [] are used to enclose information that will show up on the screen. In the icon menu format, the slide library file and slide name are shown in the braces and parentheses as shown below [slide library(slide name)]. Each icon menu is actually a submenu of the icon menu group. We will use as an example the icon menu for the TEXT STYLE command.

```
**fonts1
[Select Text Font]
[acad(romans)]^c^cstyle romans romans
[acad(romanc)]^c^cstyle romanc romanc
[acad(italicc)]^c^cstyle italicc italicc
[acad(romand)]^c^cstyle romand romand
[acad(romant)]^c^cstyle romant romant
[acad(italict)]^c^cstyle italict italict
[acad(monotxt)]^c^cstyle monotxt monotxt
[ Next]$i=fonts2 $i=*
[ Exit]^c^c
```

The first line of the file, [Select Text Font], is the title of the icon submenu. A typical line can be broken down as follows:

```
[acad(romans)]^c^cstyle romans romans
```

Where:
[acad = the slide library file

(romans)] = the slide name

^c^c cancels any previous command

style = the command to change the style

romans = the first response, i.e., style name

romans = the second response, i.e., font name

```
Command:STYLE
Text style name (or ?) <current>:Romans
Font file <default>:Romans
Height etc.
```

The name of the slide is shown in parentheses (). If you were to use a slide library other than ACAD to bring up a slide, you would also use the braces [].

```
Command:VSLIDE
Slide file name <default>:d:\myslides(single)
```

The above slide filename will be displayed in the icon menu as:

```
[d:\myslides(single)]
```

At the end of this submenu are two options which will access the next icon box in the submenu or exit from the icon menu. The first character after the left brace is empty indicating that the balance of the string will be displayed as text characters and no slide will be shown.

```
[ Next]$i=fonts2 $i=*
[ Exit]^c^c
```

Where:
[Next] = the word Next as an option on the menu

$i=fonts2 = the next page or page 2 of the menu

$i=* calls the next menu screen

[Exit] = the word Exit as an option on the menu

^c^c cancels

All keyboard keys other than the arrow keys and the Escape and Cancel functions are ignored.

The $i=* string allows you to construct a hierarchical menu structure by offering a selection that can take you to another icon menu. Any icon menu that has more than one page will have this option.

CREATING AN ICON MENU

There are four steps in creating an icon menu, these are:

1. Create the blocks, fonts, styles, or whatever you want the subject of your menu to be,
2. Make slides of the blocks or graphic,
3. Write the SLIDELIB file, and
4. Write the icon menu.

Creating the Blocks

In the electrical symbols of Figure 21-1, the blocks are quite simple.

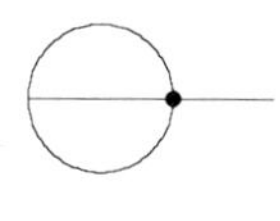

The slide contains the block itself, plus the name of the block reference for future reference. The insertion base point is shown with a donut. The size of the block could also be noted if this is of use later.

Creating the Slides

Any series of slides can be used to create an icon menu, but some care is needed in preparing slides that will be easy to identify and provide all the information you need.

If you are creating an icon box out of a complex block, it is a good idea to simplify it before creating a slide, because it may be difficult to see in the limited space provided and may slow the system down considerably. Insert the block, then explode it and delete unnecessary objects before taking your slide. Keep your slide file simple.

Use the MSLIDE command to "take a picture" of the entire screen; you cannot Window a slide. Therefore, the whole screen should be used to display the data for the slide. Remember that it will be shown at 1/4 to 1/16 the size that you are viewing it at; so keep it simple, but large. Centre it well on the screen using PAN or ZOOM Dynamic.

Many users do not add text to the slide. In many cases the text is not necessary, but occasionally it can be useful. In a block application, for example, you could find yourself inserting a large block onto the screen and then deleting it just to find out what the name of it is. There is no question that adding text will slow down the system, so do not add it unless it is useful.

When creating icon menus, keep in mind the purpose of the graphics. These menus are used largely for bringing up symbols or patterns that will be useful to use and are more easily accessed through visuals than through words. Try to avoid too many cryptic symbols, particularly if they are illustrating abstract concepts. If you want the end user to access a block or style that has two or three different steps to it, consider making a script file instead and load a one-word title for the script. The meaning of the slide will be lost if it is not obvious.

Example: *Creating the Slide Library*

The slide library facility places slides together in a particular file. This slide library can be used in a script file for a slide show or can be used to create an icon menu.

To create the slide library, follow these steps:

STEP 1

First create the geometry for the electrical symbols shown in Figure 21-1. Make each symbol into a separate wblock, then make a slide of each symbol. Use MSLIDE to create the slides; see Chapter 16 for more information on slides if you need it.

Once the blocks and slides are complete, exit to DOS. Find the SLIDELIB.EXE file. This should be under the ACAD\SAMPLE directory or the ACAD\SUPPORT directory.

Once you have located it, copy it to the directory where you want to create your icon file. On the hard drive create a directory called ICONS. Now copy the SLIDELIB.EXE file to this directory.

```
c:\acad>MD\ICONS
c:\acad>CD\ACAD\SAMPLE
c:\acad\sample>COPY SLIDELIB.EXE C:\ACAD\ICONS
```

If you are working with the A drive, use the following:

```
c:\acad>CD\ACAD\SAMPLE
c:\acad\sample>COPY SLIDELIB.EXE A:
```

A subdirectory such as ICONS can be used if desired.

```
a:\>MD\ICONS
a:\>c:
c:\acad>CD\ACAD\SAMPLE
c:\acad\sample>COPY SLIDELIB.EXE A:ICONS
```

STEP 2

Once SLIDELIB.EXE is loaded, you can create a slide library. Copy your slides into this directory. Your directory should contain the following:

```
c:\acad>dir a:

SLIDELIB    EXE    24112   07-06-90   12:49a
Single      SLD      547   01-01-92   08:05a
Duplex      SLD      457   01-01-92   08:06a
Triplex     SLD     1138   01-01-92   08:12a
etc.
```

STEP 3

The file SLIDELIB.EXE is used to execute a slide library within the directory that it is copied to.

At the DOS prompt, create the slide library using the command SLIDELIB as follows:

```
c:\acad>a:
a:\>SLIDELIB ELEC
```

The library file will be called ELEC. After pressing the Enter key you should see the following:

```
SLIDELIB  1.2  (3/8/89)
(c) Copyright  1987-89 Autodesk, Inc.
All rights reserved.
```

Now you must enter the name of the each slide; the extension is not required.

Single ↵
Duplex ↵
Dupspl ↵
Triplex ↵
Special ↵
Weather ↵
Quad ↵
Clock ↵
Fan ↵
^Z ↵ *(use F6 to end the sequence)*

Your slide library is now complete and ready to access. It should be on the drive that you copied the .EXE file to.

Example: *Creating an Icon Menu*

An icon menu can be called from any other menu by using the special code $i=. This code can be placed in pull-down menus as well as screen and tablet menus. The icons should be part of the icon section of your menu. The icon menu can be called from the POP7 menu by placing the code in the POP7 menu.

```
***POP7
[Utility]
[U              ]U
[Redo           ]^C^CRedo
[~--]
[Undo Mark      ]^C^CUndo M
```

```
[Undo Back      ]^C^CUndo B
[~--]
[Area           ]^C^C$S=X $S=area area
[Distance       ]^C^C$S-X $S=dist dist
[a:(elec)       ]^c^c $i=elec $i=*
[ID Point       ]^P(if(not m:xid)(defun m:xid(/ m:err m:id1)+
```

Then, under the icon section of your menu, add the following:

```
***icon
**elec
[Select Symbol]
[elec(single)]^c^cinsert single
[elec(duplex)]^c^cinsert duplex
[elec(dupspl)]^c^cinsert dupspl
[elec(triplex)]^c^cinsert triplex
[elec(special)]^c^cinsert special
[elec(weather)]^c^cinsert weather
[elec(quad)]^c^cinsert quad
[elec(clock)^c^cinsert clock
[elec(fan)]^c^cinsert fan
[ Exit]^c^c
[~--]
```

This will place the icon menu within the pull-down utility menu. From it you will be able to select any of the blocks that you stored in the ELEC directory of the floppy in drive A.

If you want to automate this program, you can add a few extra symbols to your menu file. For example, with an icon menu of electrical symbols, it is quite likely you will be entering many different symbols at the same time.

The following text string will allow you to insert a block, then redisplay the icon menu so you can choose another block.

```
[elec(single)]^c^cinsert single \\\\$i=elec $i=*
[elec(duplex)]^c^cinsert duplex \\\\$i=elec $i=*
```

Where:
\\\\ are the responses to the INSERT command

$i=elec $i=* will redisplay the icon menu called ELEC

$i=* as a menu command displays an icon menu and allows you to make a selection from it. This can be placed in any menu selection.

If you are adding attributes to the blocks, you may need to add more backslash (\) characters to account for the responses needed within that command.

An icon menu may contain a maximum of 16 selections. The title is not considered a section. If a menu has 16 selections, you should have 17 lines in your icon menu definition. If there are more than 17 lines, the extra lines will be ignored. If you have 17 items for a menu, split the number in two and create two menus. On the first menu, offer

```
[ Next]$i=fonts2 $i=*
[ Exit]^c^c
```

at the end of the first menu so that the second menu will be invoked by using the Next option.

The icons will be displayed in icon menus containing 4, 9, 12, or 16 spaces. Not all of the spaces need to be used.

A blank or null line terminates the icon menu.

It is considered good practice to always allow for an EXIT icon when designing icon menus, just in case you invoke the icon menu by accident. A ^C (Ctrl-C) or ESC (Escape) will work. When you are in an icon menu, all keyboard input is ignored.

AUTOMATING ICON MENU CREATION

An AutoLISP program can be written to make icon menu creation simpler. This program essentially takes care of creating the slide files and writing the icon file. You only need to have drawing files in a specific directory. There is documentation on this LISP routine called MAKEICON.LSP in *Cadence*, April 1991.

Release 12 Notes

Icon menus are displayed in groups of 20. In addition, there is a scrolling list box that contains the associated slide names or other text. The slide file names are listed in the scrolling bar. The slide name should be the same as it would be if entered in the VSLIDE command.

The menu command $I=* indicates the icon menu.

The icons are indicated by picking the actual slide as opposed to picking a box to the left of the slide. When you select an icon, the text label is highlighted. Similarly, if you select the text label from the scroll bar, a confirming box is drawn around the respective icon. A double click on the icon will act the same as clicking the icon then clicking OK.

The syntax of the icon menu labelling is as follows:

[sldname] = The slide *sldname* is displayed as an icon and the slide name *sldname* is displayed in the list box.

[sldname,labeltext] = The text *labeltext* is displayed in the list box, and the slide *sldname* is displayed as an icon.

[sldlib(sldname)] = The slide *sldname* from the slide library *sldlib* is displayed as an icon and the slide name *sldname* is displayed in the list box.

[[sldlib(sldname,labeltext)] = The slide *sldname* from the slide library *sldlib* is displayed as an icon and the text *labeltext* is displayed in the list box.

[blank] - will supply a blank line in the list box and a blank icon box.

[labeltext] = When the first character of the item label is left blank, the text supplied as *labeltext* displays in the list box and no icon is displayed.

Exercise A21

Create eight simple files for different bathroom designs. Make the bathrooms a standard size with standard fixtures.

Create wblocks of the bathrooms with names you will be able to recognize, then create a slide of each bathroom.

Copy the SLIDELIB.EXE file and generate a slide library of these slides.

Now generate an icon menu of the eight different bathroom designs.

Be sure to add a title and an EXIT option as shown in the example.

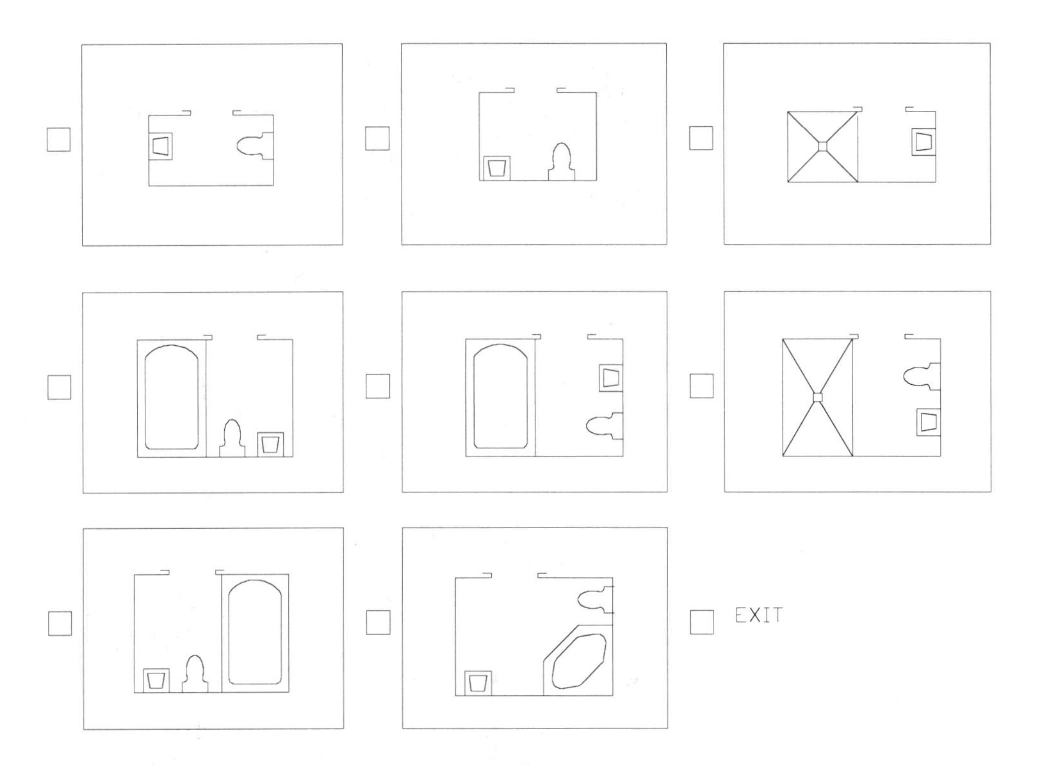

Exercise M21

Create eight simple files for different thread designs using three threads per unit. This will be a 2D thread design that can be inserted and then arrayed, etc. for any thread application. Make the threads a standard size. WBLOCK the thread design.

For ease in choosing the correct thread, offer a detail of the thread on screen before creating the slide file.

Copy the SLIDELIB.EXE file and generate a slide library of these slides.

Now generate an icon menu of the eight different thread designs.

Be sure to add a title and an EXIT option as shown in the example.

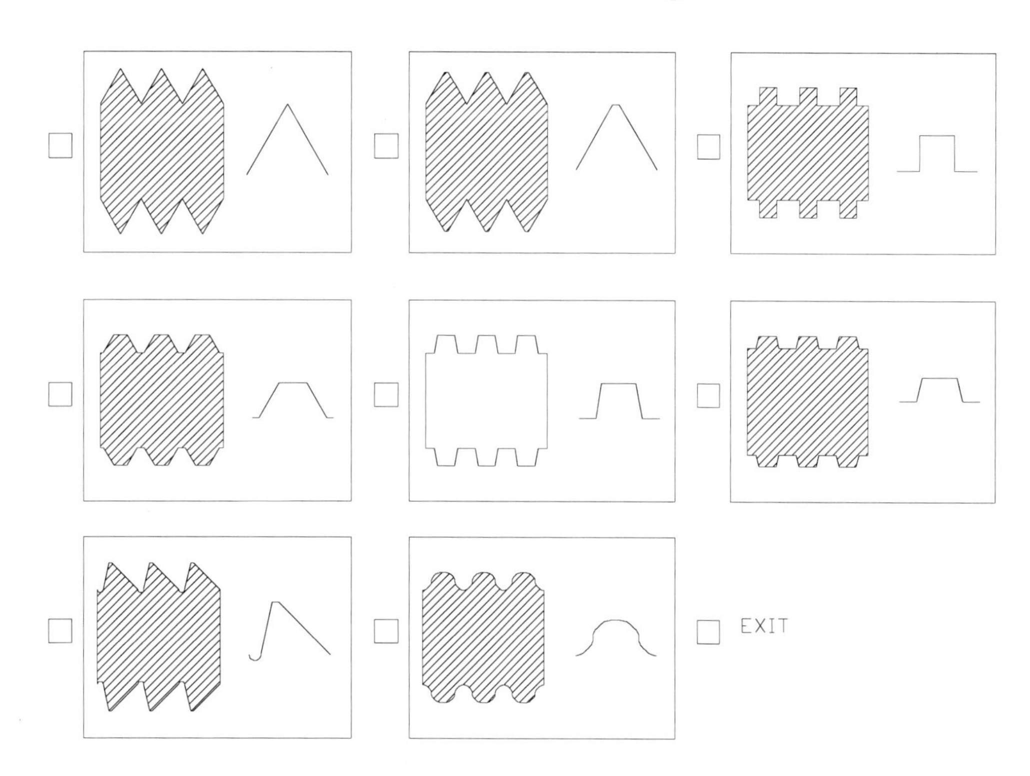

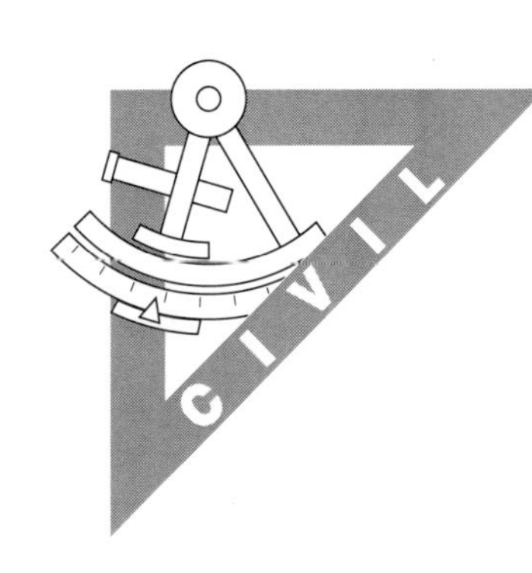

Exercise C21

Create eight simple files for different pool designs. Make the pools a standard size with standard springboard sizes.

Create a wblock for each pool and be sure to give it a recognizable name. Create a slide of each pool.

Copy the SLIDELIB.EXE file and generate a slide library of these slides.

Now generate an icon menu of the eight different pool designs.

Be sure to add a title and an EXIT option as shown in the example.

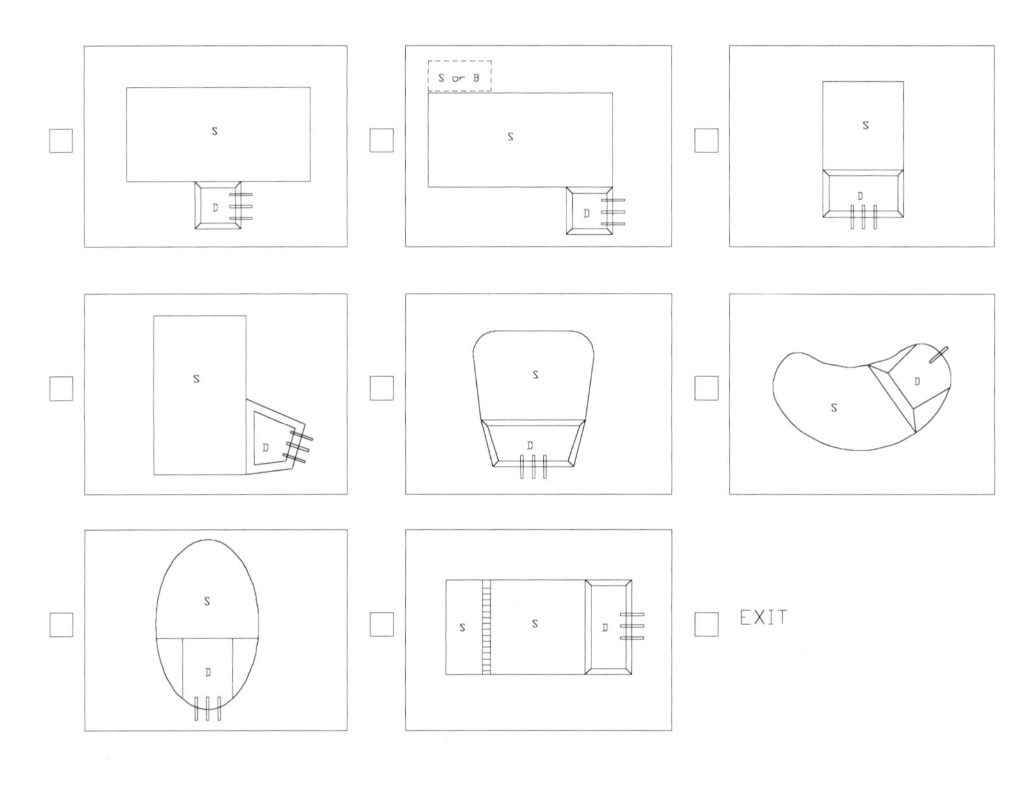

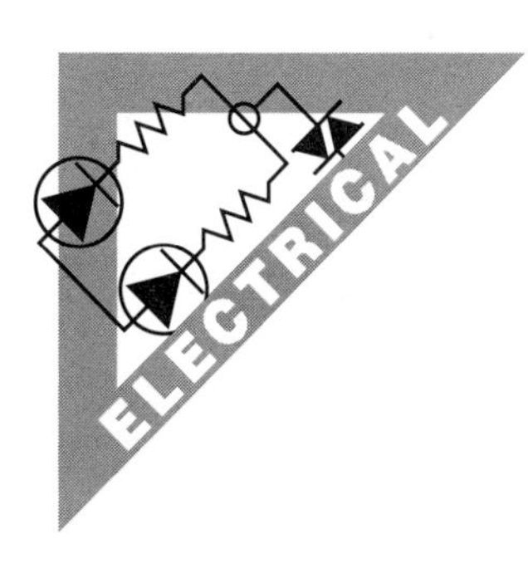

Exercise E21

Create eight simple files for different circuit components. Make sure that they are a standard size and will easily interconnect.

Create wblocks of the components with names that you will be able to recognise, then create a slide of each.

Copy the SLIDELIB.EXE file and generate a slide library of these slides.

Now generate an icon menu of the eight different circuit component designs.

Be sure to add a title and an EXIT option as shown in the example.

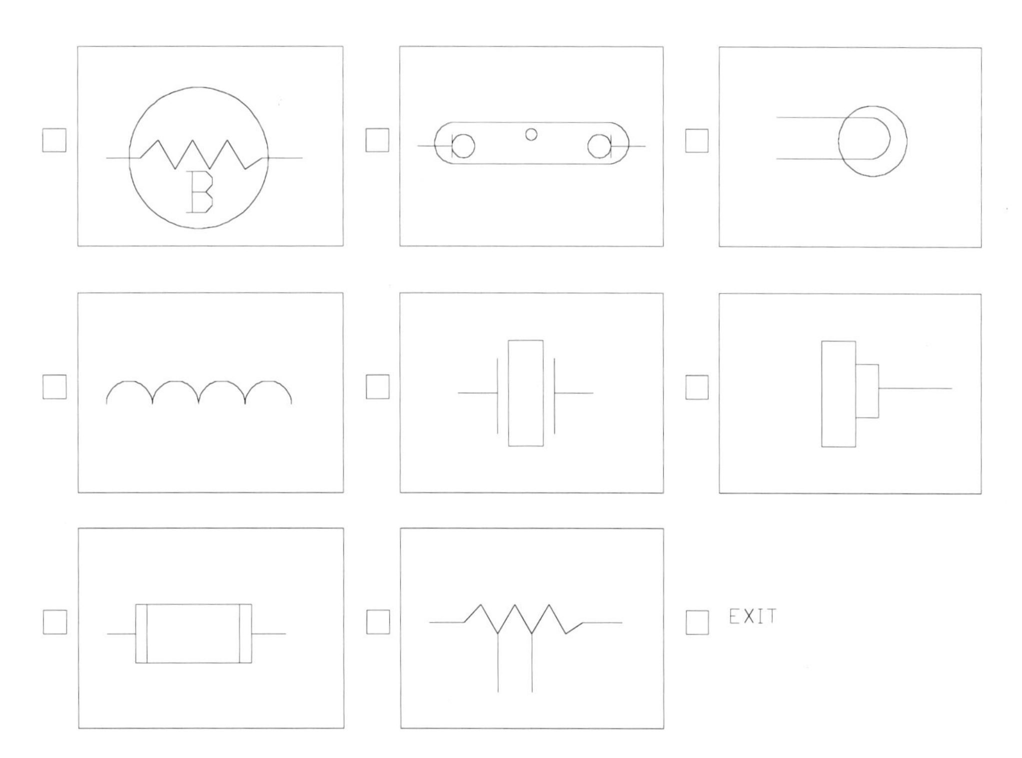

Challenger 21

Create eight simple files for standard plumbing fixtures. Make the fixtures a standard size: take them from a popular catalogue.

Create attributes for each fixture containing all of the relevant questions such as:

- product code
- supplier
- colour
- attachments needed

Create a wblock for each fixture and be sure to give it a recognizable name. Create a slide of each fixture.

Now generate an icon menu of the eight different fixtures. When inserting the block, allow user response for the aspect ratio, the rotation, and the colour, but no user response for the product code, supplier, or necessary attachments.

Be sure to add a title and an EXIT option as shown in the example.

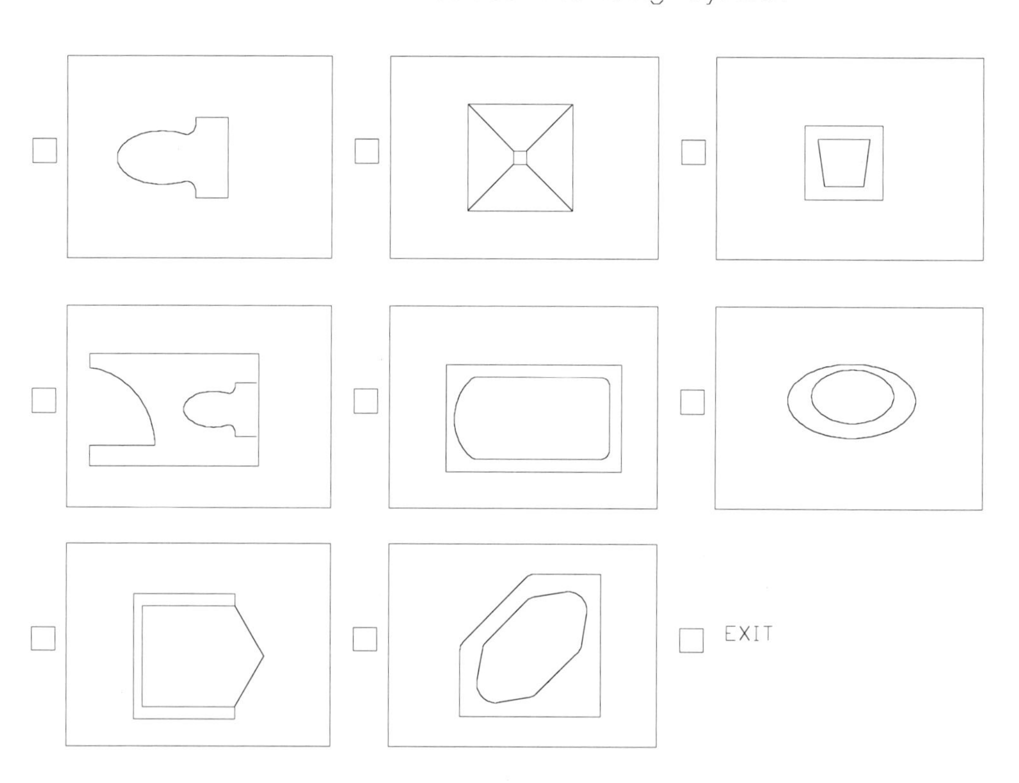

CUSTOMIZING PROTOTYPE DRAWINGS AND SYSTEM VARIABLES

Upon completion of this chapter, the student should be able to:

1. Create custom linetypes
2. Create custom hatch patterns
3. Understand custom text
4. Change setting variables when needed
5. Fine tune prototype drawings

LINETYPES

In Chapter 6 we looked at AutoCAD's various linetypes and how to load, set, and use them. AutoCAD has 24 different linetypes in the linetype library file, ACAD.LIN.

Many disciplines have their own specific library of linetypes to differentiate between different grades of metal, different types of property lines, or different materials in use. You can create your own custom library and file it under your own name for further use. We will start by looking at the basic patterns available in AutoCAD's linetype library.

```
border    — — . — — . — — . — — .
center    ___ _ ___ _ ___ _ ___ _ ___ _ ___
dashdot   — . — . — . — .
divide    - . . - . . - . . - . . - . . - . .
dot       . . . . . . . . . . . . . . . . . . .
hidden    - - - - - - - - - - - - - - - - - - -
phantom   ____ _ _ ____ _ _ ____ _ _ ____ _ _
```

As you can see, they are made up of a series of dots or periods (.), dashes (-), or underscores (_). To create your own linetypes, you can very simply change the spacing between the dots and the dashes.

Creating Linetypes

To create a linetype, you can use the C option under the LINETYPE command or generate a linetype library in a text editor. In the LINETYPE command, use the following:

```
Command:LINETYPE
?/Create/Load/Set:C
Name of linetype to create:TEST
File for Storage of linetype <ACAD>:A:MINE
```

The linetype you create will be found in the A:MINE.LIN library. The default library is ACAD.LIN. When you create your own library, the extension .LIN is not needed, AutoCAD will assume this is the type of file you are accessing.

AutoCAD will then prompt for descriptive text and linetype pattern. Let us assume that you are entering a pattern for a customer's material so it can be easily distinguished from your own.

```
Command:LINETYPE
?/Create/Load/Set:C
Name of linetype to create:Customer
File for Storage of linetype <ACAD>:A:MINE
Descriptive text:ministry203 ___....___....___....
Enter pattern: (on next line)
A,.3,-.1,0,-.1,0,-.1,0,-.1,0
New definition written to a file.
?/Create/Load/Set:↵
```

When entering the pattern, you are simply describing a series of pen-up and pen-down sequences. An *A* starts off each sequence indicating an alignment field. The dot pattern is written as follows:

```
*DOT . . . . . . . . . . . . . . . . . . . . . . . . .
A,0,-.25
```

Where:
A, = the alignment field

0, = a dot

- = the pen-up indicator

.25, = the distance between dots

The dashdot pattern would be written as follows:

```
*DASHDOT __ . __ . __ . __ . __ . __ . __ . __ . __
A,.5,-.25,0,-.25
```

Where:
A, = the alignment field

.5, = a pen-down for .5 units

-.25, = a pen-up for .25 units

0, = a dot

-.25, = a pen-up for .25 units

The line definitions in the library are always preceded by an asterisk. Positive numbers mean the pen is down for the specified distance and negative numbers indicate that the pen is up for the specified distance.

We could define a customer's material linetype as follows:

```
Command:LINETYPE
?/Create/Load/Set:C
Name of linetype to create:Customer
File for Storage of linetype <ACAD>:A:MINE
Descriptive text: (extended description optional)
Enter pattern: (on next line)
```

```
A,1,-.25,0
```

This will create the pattern: ____ .____ .____ .____ .____ .____

The new line is now ready to be set and used. It does not appear to be a great deal different from the other available linetypes, but it is certainly different enough to distinguish it on a large drawing. A different colour on this linetype's layer would, of course, make it show up on a screen more readily.

If you redefine the linetype within the ACAD library file, make sure you have a backup of the original.

If file locking has been enabled on your system, the library will be locked if you define, load, and set a new linetype. A file with the extension .LIK will be created as a backup to the original file.

CUSTOM HATCH PATTERNS

Creating custom hatch patterns is just as simple as creating custom linetypes. Usually, you would create a file under the main menu of hatch programs, ACAD.PAT (PAT for pattern). Regardless of where you store the pattern, the format is the same.

Under AutoCAD's ACAD.PAT file, you will get a listing of the hatch patterns and how they are created. You can easily copy this file to your own disk or directory and make changes or additions to it. The files are very similar to the linetype files in that they are described as a sequence of segments. The difference is that the segments have a different meaning.

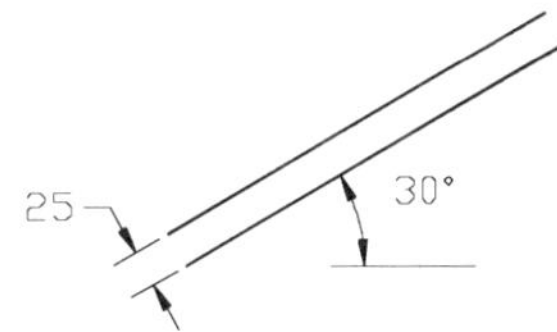

Figure 22-1. Sequence of lines for a hatch pattern

With hatch patterns, the description sequence is as follows:

```
angle, X-origin, Y-origin, delta-X, delta-Y [, dash-1, dash-2]
```

For example, a sequence of lines at 30 degrees spaced at .25 of a unit would be as follows:

```
*L30,30 degree lines
30,0,0,0,0.25
```

Where:

L30, = the name of the line

,30 degree lines = the extended description

30, = the angle of the lines

0, = the X-origin

0, = the Y-origin

0, = the delta-X

0.25 = the delta-Y

With hatches, all blank spaces are ignored. The lines are drawn at a 30-degree angle; starting at 0,0 the next line is drawn at .25 units in Y — or delta-Y — from the first point. The direction could be described by either the delta-X or the delta-Y entry; both mean that the spacing between the hatch lines will be .25 units. With this in mind, what pattern does ANSI32 describe?

```
*ansi32,ANSI Steel
45, 0,0, 0,.375
45, .176776695,0, 0,.375
```

DESCRIPTION: The first line will be at a 45-degree angle separated from the second line at a distance of .375. The second line will also be drawn at a 45-degree angle, starting from .176776695,0 or .176776695 units in X from the first line. The resulting pattern would be a repeated bar pattern extended to the hatch boundary.

In Canada, some companies want a concrete hatch pattern with 45-degree lines plus dots and triangles representing aggregate.

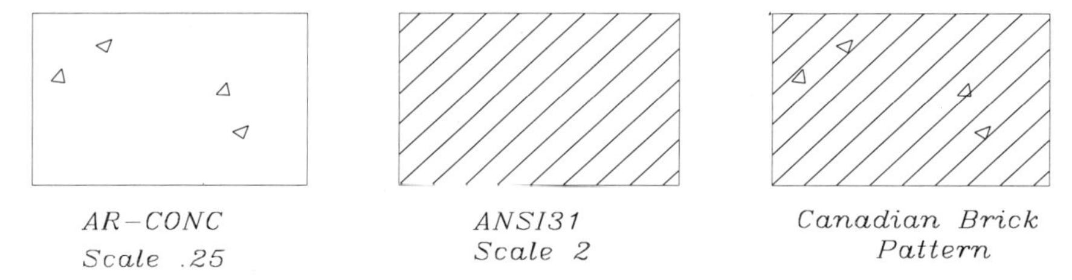

Figure 22-2. Creating the hatch pattern

In Figure 22-2, the Canadian brick pattern is a combination of the ACAD.PAT patterns AR-CONC and ANSI31. To create the hatch pattern on the right, the scales for each pattern must be changed before they are merged. The patterns are written as follows:

```
*ansi31,ANSI Iron, Brick, Stone masonry
45, 0,0, 0,.125

*AR-CONC, random dot and stone pattern
50,       0,0,       4.12975034,-5.89789472,        0.75,-8.25
355,      0,0,      -2.03781207,7.37236840,         0.60,-6.6
100.4514, 0.5977168,-0.0522934, 5.7305871,-6.9397673,
0.6374019,-7.01142112
46.1842, 0,2,        6.19462551,-8.84684208,        1.125,-12.375
96.6356, 0.88936745,1.86206693, 8.59588071,-10.40965104,
0.95610288,-10.51713
351.1842, 0,2,       7.74328189,11.0585526,         0.9,-9.9
21,       1,1.5,     4.12975034,-5.89789472,        0.75,-8.25
326,      1,1.5,    -2.03781207,7.37236840,         0.60,-6.6
71.4514, 1.49742233,1.16448394, 5.7305871,-6.9397673,
0.6374019,-7.01142112
37.5,     0,0,       2.123,2.567,                   0,-6.52,0,-
6.7,0,-6.625
7.5,      0,0,       3.123,3.567,                   0,-3.82,0,-
6.37,0,-2.525
-32.5,   -2.23,0,    4.6234,2.678,                  0,-2.5,0,-
7.8,0,-10.35
-42.5,   -3.23,0,    3.6234,4.678,                  0,-3.25,0,-
5.18,0,-7.35
```

As you can see, the ANSI31 pattern is more simple that the AR-CONC pattern, so the easiest way to create a hatch pattern with both of these would be to divide the ANSI31 delta values by eight (because the ANSI31 pattern is eight times larger) and join the two patterns together. This pattern could be added to the ACAD.PAT file and used with very little difficulty.

A study of the available hatch patterns will help you understand them better and thereby help you create your own.

The delta offsets offset the lines in both the negative and positive directions. Thus, if you want a hatch pattern to fit a boundary with equal spacing on both sides, change the UCS before calculating the offset value. (See Chapter 26.)

CUSTOM TEXT

AutoCAD's text fonts are files of shape definitions. Each of these definitions is filed under a corresponding ASCII-code number so it can be transferred to other ASCII-based systems. The ASCII codes allow the transfer of text from WordPerfect and other text editors to AutoCAD.

Defining a text font is very similar to defining a hatch pattern, but the process is more involved. First, the text font shape must be described using the SHAPE command, and then the font must be compiled according to its ASCII designation so it can be accepted as an ASCII character.

Release 12 Notes

With the inclusion of PostScript Adobe Type 1 direct importing, the insertion of .EPS files for text is made simpler. You can either use the text as blocks, or compile the .EPS files as .SHP or shape files.

The ASCII designations for each character have a standard numerical equivalent. For example, the letters A–E have the following numerical equivalents:

65 = A   66 = B   67 = C   68 = D   69 = E

Once the text font has been created, option 7 of the AutoCAD main menu compiles the shape description file, which can be accessed by the LOAD and STYLE commands. The file, once compiled, will have an extension of .SHX and will be accessible within the TEXT Style listings. Main menu option 7 prompts:

```
7. Compile Shape/Font description file:

Enter NAME of shape file:TEST
Compilation successful
Output file TEST.SHX contains nnn bytes.
```

The file is now compiled and added to the list of .SHX files. This is not model dependent and can be used on any file.

SHAPES AND TEXT

Shapes are special entities compiled from lines, arcs, and circles and stored as one entity in AutoCAD. They are similar to blocks by being a combination of entities representing only one entity; the difference is that the shape cannot be exploded but can be compiled for uses such as in the creation of text fonts. Using shapes is quite simple, but compiling them is not. For instructions on defining shapes, see Appendix B of the *AutoCAD Reference Manual*. Allow yourself four or five hours if you plan to create some.

Blocks and shapes can be used for many of the same purposes. Blocks take up much more room on a disk, but shapes are significantly more difficult to describe. A block is made by drawing the entities on the screen, then using Window or Crossing to block it. A shape is created parametrically, with each line of the shape being described by delta position and direction.

Release 12 Notes

Chapter 5 of the AutoCAD Customization Manual is dedicated to Shapes and Fonts.

The following is the description of the capital D taken from Appendix B of the *AutoCAD Reference Manual*:

```
*68,22,ucd
2,14,8,(-2-6),1,030,012,044,016,038,2,010,1,06C,2,050,
14,8,(-4,-3),0
```

The files must have complete descriptions to enable the STYLE command to apply variables such as:

height
width (aspect ratio)
vertical
obliquing angle
backwards
upside down

In order to create an entire symbol set you must describe all 26 letters, 10 numbers, and 30 or 40 symbols such as $, #,@, etc.

If you want to create just a small bit of text for a specific purpose, for example, vertical fractions, an umlaut (u), a cedilla (c), or any other special character font for different languages or cultures, it is probably a good idea to make these items as blocks and create a menu so they can be added to your drawings or files as a symbol. Third-party text-font suppliers are also an option, and will, possibly, be much more cost effective than spending the time to create your own alphabet.

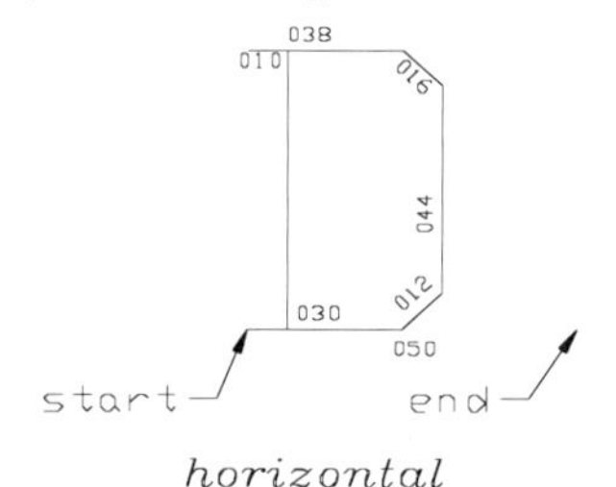

Figure 22-3. The capital D

SETTING VARIABLES OR SETVAR

You have probably found while working in AutoCAD that there are many things you would like to change. For example, the size of the aperture or the resolution of the screen. Many of these can be changed with the SETVAR command.

There are three different types of variables that can be set:

1. On/off toggle-switch variables:

BLIPMODE	*sets BLIP (+) on or off*
FILLMODE	*sets FILL on or off*
REGENMODE	*sets automatic REGEN on or off*

2. Scale and prompt default variables:

PDMODE	*sets the point display type and size*
CHAMFERA	*sets first chamfer size*
FILLETRAD	*sets the fillet default radius value*

3. Read-only variables:

TDCREATE	*displays the time that a file was created*
DATE	*displays the current date*
CECOLOR	*displays an entity colour*

You can use the SETVAR command transparently, within another command, or on its own. The PICKBOX or APERTURE setting is often used within another command to help isolate an entity that is overlapping another entity.

If you are uncertain of the name of the variable you want to change or the spelling of the system variable, use ? to obtain a full listing. The SETVAR command is as follows:

```
Command:SETVAR
Variable name or ?:BLIPMODE
New value for Blipmode <0>:1
```

To change the value of a system variable, simply type in the variable name you want to change and then enter the new value. To change variables such as PDMODE, you must know what the point display that you want to use looks like and the correct option number to enter. Often this information can be found in the Options pull-down menu.

In Release 11 you can change any variable without entering the SETVAR command, but you get only a listing of the variable with SETVAR ?. You must use SETVAR to change the variable transparently.

When creating a prototype drawing, you may want to change some of the system variables so they pertain to your specific application. A full listing of the system variables is found in Appendix B of this manual.

PROTOTYPE DRAWINGS

Hopefully, over the past few chapters, you have been making files that can be used in your prototype drawings, such as macros and menus. Only by using AutoCAD over a period of time will you become familiar with the areas that need customizing, and you may also discover you need two or three different prototype drawings for different drawing or model sizes and applications.

We looked at introductory prototype drawings in Chapter 11. Now we will look at how to incorporate your customized menus, macros, linetypes, etc. to create prototype drawings.

Using Prototype Drawings

When you begin a new file, you can access your prototype drawing in one of three ways:

Release 12 Notes

The new file utilities section od Release 12 will make opening and saving of files much simpler. It is located under File in the pull-down menus.

- Instead of using option 1, Begin a new Drawing, on the main menu, use option 2, Edit an existing File, and retrieve your prototype drawing. Then save the model or file under a new name.
- Start a new drawing with the prototype parameters by using the following:

```
Enter selection:1 (Begin a new drawing)
Enter name of drawing:NAME=PROTO
```

- Start a new file, then use DXFIN to import your prototype drawing.

You already know how to set up the file's limits, grid, snap, dimension variables, setting variables, text fonts and size, and hatch size and style. Now, if you have some customized macros, menus, linetypes, or hatches, plus regularly used attributed blocks and xrefs, these can be loaded as well. A fully customized file will make you much more efficient.

What Should Be Included In a Prototype File

The following list identifies the major items to be considered when setting up a prototype drawing. Once set up, the file can be edited at any time in case something important was missed the first time through. You will need to consider:

UNITS
LIMITS - SNAP - GRID
LAYER
LINETYPE and LTSCALE
BLOCK and XREF
HATCH
DIMVAR and SETVAR
MENU
MACRO
DISPLAY - VPORTs and VPOINT

All those highlighted may not have been included in your prototype drawing in the first section.

If your file is to be used exclusively to create drawings, the prototype file can be set up so all scales for dimensions, hatch, and linetypes are already set. If your file is to be used for many different purposes, you can create a macro or a script file that will load all the drawing-related data when you are ready for it. There are many items — title blocks, customized lines, text, hatches, section blocks, etc. — that will take up room on your disk, but will not necessarily be used with every file. Other items such as dimension and system variables will take up no room on the file.

There are many ways to set up prototype files, none of which can be considered the best way. Now that you can create menus, macros, and script files, consider which method will be the most efficient for setting up the following.

UNITS

Set the units to the type of display you generally use. Do not forget also to change your smallest denominator and angle description; for example, the default will be 1/16" in architectural units. If you are making floor plans, you will probably find a setting of 1 inch more useful.

Question: Do you need only one type of unit, or could you use a set of script files to create the five or six possible units settings you may need?

LIMITS

If your products are often of a similar size, change your limits to the size you generally use. Again, this is just a default and can be adjusted at any time. If limits are not required, turn them off.

GRID AND SNAP

These can be set relative to the limits setting. If you are not using limits, these can be set relative to your product size.

LAYERS

Use the standard layers of your discipline. Make sure to use the standard colours and linetypes so others can access your files easily. Keep in mind that xrefs and wblocks will affect your layer listing.

LINETYPES AND LTSCALE

If you have any custom linetypes, load them from your customized library. Also load the linetypes you usually use. Be careful not to load all the linetypes if you will not use them. This action would defeat the purpose of the prototype drawing by storing unnecessary information and taking up valuable storage space for no reason. The linetypes are always available when you need them.

With regard to LTSCALE, decide if this is to be a drawing-oriented prototype or a model-oriented prototype. If your final product is always a drawing at a particular scale, check the sizes listed in Chapter 11 and set the LTSCALE to the size that is appropriate for final drawings. If your office or class produces three sizes of drawings on a regular basis, consider generating three prototype drawings and set the LTSCALE for each one.

Question: Would you use a script file or a macro to set up the LTSCALE and drawing sizes?

BLOCKS

Again you must decide if the file is to be used for drawing purposes only, or if it is for manufacturing, marketing, or analysis as well.

If you are always creating drawings, you may want an attributed title block as part of the file. You may want a north arrow, a section marker, or any other frequently used blocks. These are particulary handy to have as part of a prototype file if you are in a classroom situation and frequently using floppy disks. There are few things more frustrating than having to redraw information knowing that you already have it at home on a floppy disk. If your prototype drawing contains this information as blocks, you do not need to add them as wblocks. Blocks do take up room, however; so if you are working on a network, xrefs may be more appropriate. Having the xrefs on file will save you time in looking up the names and paths of files.

HATCHES

The most important factor to consider when dealing with hatches on prototype drawings is the scale of the hatch. If you are using a hatch, you are probably concerned with a final drawing as opposed to an analysed, rendered, or manufactured model. This being the case, your hatch scale must be an appropriate size on the final drawing. You should have either one prototype drawing for each drawing size or one macro to set the appropriate scales for each drawing size. Again, see Chapter 11 for hatch scales. If you have any customized hatch patterns, these can be loaded onto your file.

DIMENSION AND SYSTEM VARIABLES

The variables you change in these commands will not take up any extra room on a disk and will be a great help in standardizing drawings within your company or discipline. The areas to change are notably those that pertain to your particular field. When setting the dimension variables, make sure *all* of the relative variables are set and do not change the text and arrowhead size without changing the extension and gap distance.

When changing system variables read through the variables, and make note of the variables you have changed. If someone less familiar with the system tries to use your prototype and has some recurring difficulty, a list of the changed system variables may help to correct the situation more quickly.

People have a tendency to assume their personal learning and comprehension curve is similar to those around them. Of course, the system variables are perfectly obvious to everyone in retrospect, but a less experienced user may have great difficulty selecting objects if the pickbox has been set to the lowest setting and they are not even aware that it can be set.

MENUS

Again, menus are an easy and useful addition to any file, but to those who are unaware that menus can be changed, the prompt

```
Can't find menu srkmenu
New menu filename or . for none:
```

can put an end to their editing session. If you have loaded a custom menu into a prototype file, be sure the ACAD basic menu is explained to users who may have a working knowledge of the commands but no experience with menus.

If a person who is familiar with AutoCAD drawings but unfamiliar with customizing is sent out to demonstrate the contents of a drawing file at another site, any customized menu file *must be loaded onto the floppy disk* to be accessed when the user retrieves the drawing file. If the user fails to access the file because he or she cannot display the menu, it is not the demonstrator, but the person sending him or her out unprepared, who is at fault.

In addition, if you have erased AutoCAD commands from a menu, make sure users realize that they can type in the AutoCAD commands even though they are not on the menu. Just because you never use a certain command does not mean that someone else will not want to.

MACROS

Macros can be a real benefit to a prototype drawing. If they are loaded correctly onto a menu, they can certainly speed up the editing session.

Instead of having different prototype files for each drawing size, consider using a macro or a script file to load blocks and scales for the final drawing. This may save space on the hard drive or network and be more practical in the long run.

DISPLAY — VIEWPORTS AND VIEWPOINT

This pertains to the third section of this book, which deals with the various viewports and views for creating 3D models. Even if you are only creating 2D views of objects, the paper space 2D drawing layout facility may be of real use. Viewports and viewpoints can be named and stored to save you entering five commands every time you setup a 3D screen.

In addition, certain size parameters can be set for check plots or printer plots to be sure objects are always a standard size. If you save a popular or useful viewport with a specific size ratio, all the scaled check plots from this display should be the same size. For further 3D information, see Chapters 26 and 27.

LISP

Now that you have been introduced to interfacing and customizing, you may want to learn AutoLISP programming. In many ways, AutoLISP is quicker and easier than using scripts and macros. The AutoLISP programs must be added to the AutoCAD program in order to be accessed on site.

Final Word On Customizing and Interfacing

AutoCAD controls the major portion of the CAD market for one reason only: its open architecture. Since the beginning of its upward climb, Autodesk has encouraged others to experiment with the software, to develop add-ons and customized software packages, "take the ball and run with it."

AutoCAD's approach has been tremendously successful as can be seen by the high profile of the company. When you are customizing AutoCAD for yourself or for others, assume that many of the people using the system do not know as much as you do at the moment. If you create macro, menu, or script files that are clearly esoteric and obscure, nobody will use them.

Recently I did some consulting for a company who had paid a significant amount of money to customize their system for the creation of drawings. Management wanted to make AutoCAD more "efficient." They did not want the users to waste time "playing around" on the system and had all the commands that the users would not need removed from the system. In addition, the manuals were taken away and the Help files erased. After two years of dwindling productivity, I was called in as a last resort before they went back to paper. It turns out that the "un-needed" commands were all the EDIT commands except ERASE, COPY, MOVE, and ROTATE plus all the DISPLAY commands except ZOOM and PAN. Only four commands were left in the Draw menu as well. The users were not allowed to ask questions or see the manuals and were getting frustrated with trying to produce drawings. After I had stopped laughing, I simply returned to the AutoCAD menu and taught the employees how to use the other commands, and now the company is fine.

Having taught CAD for 10 years, I can say that many of the students I introduced to the subject of CAD are much more well informed and knowledgeable than I currently am, and that in all likelihood, they will get even better. Most of these individuals are successful in their field and are kind enough to fill me in on what is happening in areas not directly connected with mine. AutoCAD is advancing at such a rate that no one could be expected to understand every command structure or application. A spirit of cooperation is probably the best bet and will serve you well with your customizing and interfacing efforts.

Exercises All

STEP 1
Create a linetype that is not found in ACAD.LIN and place it on a drawing at the appropriate LTSCALE.

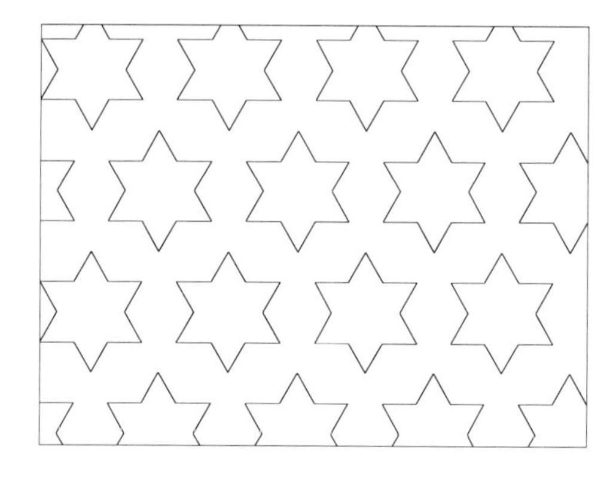

STEP 2
Find and study the hatch pattern of a six-point star.

Make a hatch pattern for a five-point star.

Create a 2-unit by 3-unit square and put the hatch pattern in it.

STEP 3
Create a prototype drawing for your discipline that will be capable of producing a drawing in the largest standard drawing size. Be sure to change your units, limits, grid, and snap.

Also be sure to set up the:

Layers
Linetypes and LTSCALE
Blocks and xrefs
Hatches
Dimensioning and system setting variables
Menus
Macros

STEP 4
Switch prototype files with another person in the class. Then insert one of your drawings onto your partner's prototype file and, without any verbal communication concerning the details of the files, see if your file is created at the correct size and scale. This will help you determine if your prototype is accessible.

STEP 5
Make sure your partner's prototype menu macros work and that all of the buttons, pull-down menus, and tablet options work properly.

ADVANCED BLOCKING AND XREFS

Upon completion of this chapter, the student should be able to:

1. Create nested blocks
2. Redefine blocks
3. Substitute blocks
4. Use xrefs to place blocks
5. Use XBIND

ADVANCED BLOCKING

In the first section of this book we learned how to create and utilize blocks and wblocks. Earlier in this session we used blocks to create attributes. In addition to being used as an assembly tool and as a format for generating attributes, blocks can be compiled for further efficiency of design. One block can contain any number of other blocks so that it can be edited as a group of blocks instead of just a single block entity.

Nesting Blocks

Nested blocks are blocks within blocks, or several overlapping uses of blocks. We can take as an example a car. If we were to design just the "wheel" component of the car, we may start with the axle, then we would add the rim, then we might add the tire, the bolts, and, finally, a hubcap. Even without adding any of the instrumentation, we would have five separate areas of the wheel that could each be stored as an individual block. To place the "wheels" we could either insert each block separately or store the whole assembly of the five blocks and insert it as one large block.

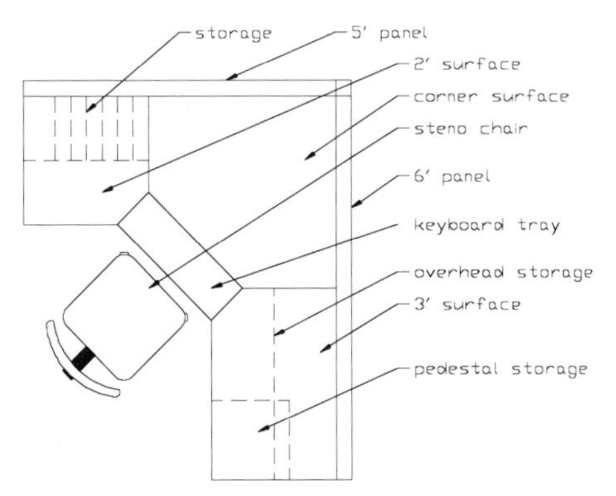

Figure 23-1. An office workstation

Release 12 Notes

XREFS can be accessed through the File pull-down menu. The command structure and uses are the same as in Release 11.

Another example would be a workstation in an office layout. In a large company there would certainly be some standards of what desk, storage, and chair arrangements could be used for each position. If each component of the workstation were stored as a separate block, the whole workstation could also be stored as a block and inserted separately as well.

In Figure 23-1, on the the previous page, each individual item could be blocked with the attribute information necessary to order it, and the whole unit could be blocked for easy insertion into the office layout. Inserting one workstation is, obviously, easier than inserting all of the individual blocks.

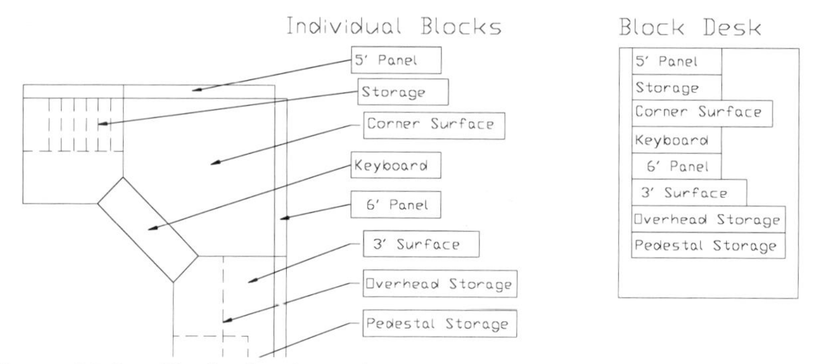

Figure 23-2. Blocks for the unit

All of the blocks are created individually, then they are blocked as a unit to be part of a single large block. The large block is then inserted as one unit.

Layering, Colour, and Linetype with Blocks

When you insert a block into a file, you will notice that all of the layers associated with the block are inserted as well. If the current layer listing does not contain all of the layers of the inserted block, the new layers will be created.

Each entity of the block is stored on the layer that it was assigned. If you have planned correctly, you should have control of the entities that are inserted, and the colour and linetype of each entity should be the same as when it was created. Usually, the color and linetype will be set using BYLAYER, but a COLOR or LINETYPE setting will override these.

All entities in layer 0 will take on the current colour and linetype, unless they are entered using *BLOCKNAME or exploded. If this happens, they will revert to the original layer colour and linetype.

When inserting blocks, it is often difficult to determine how best to set up and view the objects. In the example above, two or three manufacturers could be supplying the furnishings for the workstation. You may have the layers set up so that each manufacturer has its own layer. When inserting the workstations, however, you may wish to assign them a colour to represent a department. On one floor, there could be 12 secretaries representing four different departments, and you may wish to have the colours coordinate so that the departments, not the furniture manufacturers, are easily distinguished. If this is the case, the colour of the nested block can be set to BYBLOCK, and the current layer can be changed while inserting the 12 workstations so that the blocks, when inserted, will take on the colour of the department. The layer for each department must be set up, and the block must be inserted while that layer is current. The block's colour and linetype can be changed after it has been inserted by using CHPROP, and the colour or linetype can be set to BYBLOCK.

If the colour and linetype entities are set to BYBLOCK, they will take on the settings of the insertion layer at the time of insertion. Remember, if you insert a block on a layer that is frozen, the block will not be visible.

Block Redefinition

Once the blocks are inserted, you may encounter design changes that will make you want to substitute one block for another. Figure 23-3 shows the symbol for a coniferous tree on the left and a deciduous tree on the right. If both trees are blocks, it is possible to substitute one type of tree with another on a lot layout.

Figure 23-3. Two types of trees

On the lot in Figure 23-4, the client has asked for 11 coniferous trees. They have been inserted according to his specifications. He is happy with the layout, but, once completed, he decides that he wants deciduous trees instead.

Figure 23-4. A typical lot layout

As the blocks already exist in the drawing above, the reference points for the blocks are also included. To each reference point you can assign a different point by using the = or equal sign classification for the new block.

```
Command:INSERT
BLOCK name (or ?) <LAST>:CONIF=DECID
BLOCK conif redefined
Regenerating drawing
Insertion point:^c (or cancel)
```

The previous command has assigned a different block name to each of the reference points on the blocks called CONIF. The graphic information of the file DECID.DWG will replace the graphic information of the file CONIF.DWG, as shown in Figure 23-5.

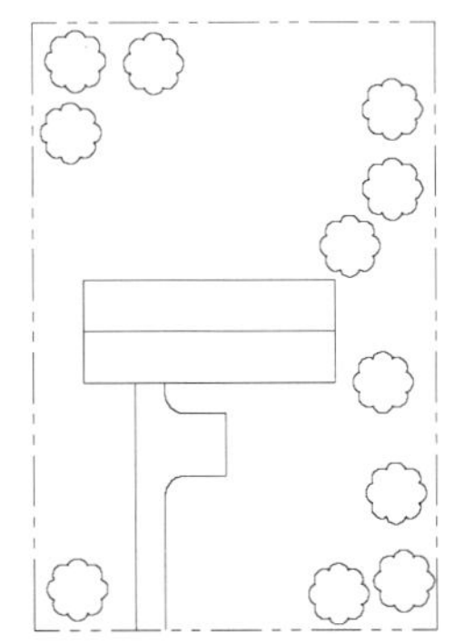

Figure 23-5. A lot with exchanged tree blocks

This function can be extremely useful when working on a large drawing or assembly where one of the components that has been entered as a block has been updated or replaced.

If you have created an office layout with 125 chairs, and management decides to change the manufacturer, simply redefine the blocks.

If you are working on an assembly with 150 components of the same type, simply redefine them if the component is upgraded.

Finally, if you are working on a large drawing that has a nested block or a large block with many entities, create a simple block, such as a rectangle, and substitute it for the large block to reduce visual clutter and improve redrawing speed. In this case you are redefining the block in order to substitute a simpler one temporarily. Use INSERT with the simple name equalling the complex block name.

```
Command:INSERT
BLOCK name (or ?) <CAR>:complex=simple
BLOCK conif redefined
Regenerating drawing
Insertion point:^c (or cancel)
```

XREFS

When you insert a block to a file, you are, in fact, adding all of the entities of the block to the current file. When you add an xref to a file, you are bringing the latest version of a current drawing into your drawing as an external reference. The entities are not actually added to the file. They are referenced for the duration of your editing time and then released. The xrefs are reloaded every time the drawing is loaded.

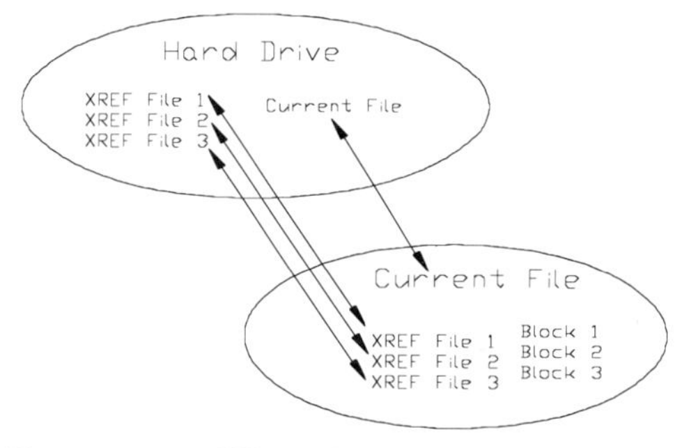

Figure 23-6. Where files reside

The great advantage of having xref files as opposed to blocks is that the xref files are separate drawing files and thus are subject to change. Every time a file containing an xref is retrieved, it will load the most current version of the referenced file. Any changes in the components of a drawing are automatically shown on the master drawing the next time it is retrieved. This feature is particularly useful when working on a networked system, because many people can access the same drawings for updating.

In addition, because the xref data is contained in another file, the file size is much smaller than it would be if data were inserted as the same amount of blocks.

Xrefs can be manipulated in exactly the same way as the blocks; the layers can be listed, the object can be edited as a single entity, the entities can be used as osnap positions, and the colours can be changed. As with blocks, individual items of geometry within the xref cannot be changed. The only difference between an xref and a block is that the xref is not added to the file.

The XREF Command

The XREF command offers you six options.

```
Command:XREF
?/Bind/Detach/Path/Reload/<Attach>:
```

Where :
? = a listing of current xrefs

Bind = an ability to add the xref to the current file, thus making a block.

Detach = a removal of xrefs from the current file.

Path = the path that AutoCAD uses when loading one or more xrefs.

Reload = an update of an xref without exiting the drawing editor.

Attach = an attachment of a new file or a copy of an xref that already exists in the file, much like INSERT.

If you are transporting a drawing to another machine or site, you must take along the xref files. If the file is not on the disk, it cannot be loaded. Similarly, when someone is backing up and erasing files from the hard drive, it is a good idea to provide him or her with a list of the files you will be needing to reference so that they are not backed up to an external hard drive and removed.

XREF Options

? will list all the xrefs in a file plus the path to the file. You can display a full listing of files, or just those from a specific path, or you can use * to obtain a wildcard listings with specific drawing names.

```
Command:XREF
?/Bind/Detach/Path/Reload/<Attach>:?

 Xref name                Path

Axle                   C:\ACAD386\1992
Tire                   C:\ACAD386\1991

Total Xref(s):2
```

Bind will change an xref into a block, making it a permanent part of a file. This option is most often used when sending files to a client or another user to ensure that all the files are contained in the drawing. It is also useful when archiving files to make sure that all the files are included in the one master file. The advantage of archiving is that all of the externally referenced files are incorporated into one file and you only need to file the one master model or drawing to get the most updated version of each file.

When using the Bind option, you can bind the xrefs individually, or you can bind them all by using the * wildcard.

```
Command:XREF
?/Bind/Detach/Path/Reload/<Attach>:B
Xref(s) to bind:STENO1
      Scanning. . .
```

Detach
When you erase an xref, the reference to the exterior file still exists, just as when you erase a block, the block reference still exists. To remove a reference

completely from a file use Detach. When you retrieve a drawing with an xref that has been erased but not detached it will bring the reference into the file but not display it, thus taking up valuable space in memory.

Detach will affect an xref whether it is displayed or not, and it will also remove any nested references it finds. Again, the * wildcard can be used to detach all xrefs.

```
Command:XREF
?/Bind/Detach/Path/Reload/<Attach>:D
Xref(s) to detach:Corner
      Scanning. . .
```

If the xref that you are detaching has multiple insertions, AutoCAD will not perform the function.

Path

If someone has updated or changed the directory of a referenced file, you will need to change the path to enable AutoCAD to locate and retrieve it. The Path option lets you change the path of loaded xrefs.

On a large model it is not unusual to have many or all of the xref source files in a separate directory. Path allows you to assign one or all of your source files to a separate directory. Use the * wildcard to list all of the files.

```
Command:XREF
?/Bind/Detach/Path/Reload/<Attach>:P
Edit path for which Xref(s):Corner
      Scanning. . .

XREF name:CORNER
Old path:C:\OFFICE\2NDFLR\CORNER
New path:C:\OFFICE\3RDFLR\CORNER

Reload Xref CORNER:C:\OFFICE\3RDFLR\CORNER
Corner loaded.
```

The Path option prompts you to enter the names of the xrefs that you want changed. Then you are given the old path name and prompted for the new path. You must enter the entire path name correctly. The problem most frequently encountered with this option is the spelling and nomenclature of the path. Pay careful attention to the use of backslashes (\) and colons (:).

Reload

There are two ways to reload your external files. The first way is simply by retrieving the file; the second is by using the Reload option.

Reload is used most frequently on a networked system where several people are working concurrently on the same project. If user 1 is updating a master file, and user 2 has made significant changes in one of the source files, user 1 may want to update the xref of user 2's file to see what effect the changes have on the master file.

If only one person is working on a project, Reload may be used when making significant changes to a portion of the drawing. If additions are made to a portion of a drawing that is an xref, it may be wblocked and then reloaded with the current changes. This function helps the file management process. Again, the * wildcard can be used to reload all of the xrefs.

```
Command:XREF
?/Bind/Detach/Path/Reload/<Attach>:R
Xref(s) to detach:Corner
      Scanning. . .
Reload Xref CORNER:C:\OFFICE\3RDFLR\CORNER
CORNER loaded.
```

The files are first detached to make sure that all references to the block are removed.

Attach

This is the default setting. It works much like the INSERT command in that it is used to place an existing xref somewhere on the current drawing. As with INSERT, the name of the last xref is used as the default.

```
Command:XREF
?/Bind/Detach/Path/Reload/<Attach>:A
Xref(s) to attach <CORNER>:A:24panel
Attach Xref 24panel:24panel
24panel loaded
Insertion point:6,5
X scale factor<1>:↵
Y scale factor<1>:↵
Rotation angle<0>:↵
```

If you are using AutoCAD's Advanced User Interface, you can also use the dialogue box by entering the tilde (~) character. This will display a list of all of the files already accessed.

USING XREFS

If you wanted to update a block, you would explode it, update it, and then, if the changes were significant and possibly useful on other files, you could wblock the revised data and reinsert it. (Before inserting, you would need to exit the file, re-enter and purge the existing block, end the file, and then return to the file.) If the block was entirely wrong, you could simply erase it.

You can erase an xref, but you can't explode it. Instead, you can access the external source file, update it, and reload it.

The reinserted wblock would reflect all of the changes that were made on the one update. With xrefs, the revised source file will affect every drawing in which the file is referenced.

Like blocks as well, only the entities created in model space will be loaded into the drawing. No paper-dependent or viewport-dependent entities will be read.

If one or more of the xrefs attached to a drawing is moved or erased, AutoCAD will display an error message when the file is retrieved.

```
"C:\OFFICE\2NDFLR\CORNER" Can't open file
** Error resolving Xref CORNER
```

A block with the name of the xref will be entered at the position the xref was to occupy. This error can be corrected by updating the path name or reloading the referenced file into the original directory.

Xrefs and Layers

All of the properties of the entities of the referenced files will be added to the current file in addition to the entities themselves. Layers, linetypes, colours, and text and dimension styles will be added to the master file.

When these properties are added, they are renamed in the current drawing using a temporary name to avoid confusion and duplication.

When new layers are added, the new name will have the xref filename followed by the layer name.

```
Command:LAYER
?/Make/Set/New/ON/OFF/Color/Ltype/Freeze/Thaw:?
Layer name(s) to list <*>:↵
 Layer Name          State      Color        Linetype
 0                    On        7 (white)    CONTINUOUS
 DIM                  On        1 (red)      CONTINUOUS
 3RDFLR|DIM           On        2 (yellow)   3RDFLR|HIDDEN
?/Make/Set/New/ON/OFF/Color/Ltype/Freeze/Thaw:↵
```

The colour and linetype of the referenced layers have the original file's properties.

Layer 0 is the exception to this layer renaming. Any entities on Layer 0 will be placed in Layer 0 of the current model, and all entities that are referenced will assume the settings associated with the current Layer 0.

MANAGING BLOCKS AND XREFS

As mentioned earlier, management is an important part of the file creation process. As you are creating files, make sure you are not using the same names for blocks and xrefs. If you try to attach an xref that has already been made into a block through the Bind option, you will have to either insert the block or rename the xref source file, or rename the block.

You can also use the = symbol to re-attach an xref that is a block on a current file.

```
Command:XREF
?/Bind/Detach/Path/Reload/<Attach>:A
Xref(s) to attach < CORNER>:A:36panel

**Error: A:36panel is already a standard block in the current
drawing.  *Invalid*

Command:XREF
?/Bind/Detach/Path/Reload/<Attach>:A
Xref(s) to attach < CORNER>: A:36panel2=a:36panel
```

This option is also useful if you are trying to load two different files that have the same name and are in different subdirectories.

When creating files, it is not a bad idea to record the file information on hardcopy, including such information as:

- layers plus creation date
- blocks plus first insertion date
- xrefs plus first insertion date

If you do not note this information, you can guarantee that you are going to need it.

Once you get to the stage where you have 3,000 entities on 48 layers with 24 blocks and 16 xrefs, you may find this extra documentation an advantage in remembering why and when certain objects were entered or changed. When working in a large office, this is particularly useful because people have methods of their own that work for them when they are on the job, but when they go on extended vacation or are transferred, it is often not completely obvious what they have done. Maintaining proper documentation will help.

As xrefs are inserted, AutoCAD creates an external log (.XLG) file of the inserted file. This ASCII text file records all relevant xref information concerning attached files and any subsequent xrefs added, and is located in the current drawing directory. It is updated every time an external reference file is attached. This file records a lot of the documentation explained above, but, because it can be deleted from the directory and often is if there is a lack of memory space, it is a good idea to keep a hard copy as well.

XBIND

With the XREF command, an external source file is added to a current or master file for the duration of the editing period, then the source file and all of its dependent "symbols" such as linetypes, text styles, layers, and dimension styles are returned to the original file. While part of the current file, the layers, linetypes, etc. are listed and referenced to the current file; they are not accessible and remain part of the external source file. If you wanted to use a custom linetype (see Chapter 22) that was part of an attached xref, you would not be able to do so, because, although you can see it on the attached file, you cannot use it in the drawing file.

The XBIND command allows certain of these "symbols" to be added to a current file so they will bind with the current file when it is saved and can therefore be accessed for use. This would allow you to use the customized xref linetype on your current file. At the end of the editing session, the xref would return to its original source file, and the linetype would remain with the current file.

The command offers 5 options.

```
Command:XBIND
Block/Dimstyle/LAyer/LType/Style:
```

Where:
Block = a block is to be added to the current file

Dimstyle = a customized dimension style is to be added to the current file

LAyer = a layer is to be added to the existing file

LType = a customized linetype is to be added to the current file

Style = a customized text style is to be added to the current file

```
Command:XBIND
Block/Dimstyle/LAyer/LType/Style:LA
Dependent LAYER name(s):STENO
    Scanning. . .
1 Layer bound
```

Once the layer is bound to the current drawing, the vertical bar is removed from the name and replaced with 0. If the above layer, for example, were on the externally referenced file called 3RDFLOOR, it would appear as 3RDFLOOR|STENO before it was bound and 3RDFLOOR0STENO after it was bound. This occurs so that a layer being bound to a current drawing will not take on the name of an existing layer and thus add all of its items to an existing layer. If the layer were called 3RDFLOOR|DIM for example, there is a good chance that there would already be a layer called DIM, so the new layer is 3RDFLOOR0DIM to distinguish the two. The new name can, of course, be renamed using the layer command.

The linetype and colour associated with the layer in the xref source drawing would remain with it when it is bound to the new drawing file.

The maximum number of characters that can be added or bound to a new drawing is 31; if any number greater than that is attempted, the command will not work.

Release 12 notes

AutoCAD can create an ordinary ASCII text file log of all of your XREF actions if your XREFCTL system variable is set to 1. This maintains a list of all of your actions during Attach, Detach, Reload operations as well as the time of loading for all XREFS.
The log file will have the current drawing name with the extension .xlg. When the drawing is loaded, AutoCAD will search for an associated .xlg file to load with it. If there is none available, AutoCAD creates a new one.
While working on a drawing, AutoCAD will continue to append to the .xlg file so that all entries will be logged. AutoCAD notes not only the title of the current drawing, the date and the time, but also any drawings or symbols that are dependent on the XREF being brought in to create a "reference tree." The tree will show which files were referenced and which files had their own external references.

```
- - - - - - - - - - - - - - - - - - - - - - - -
Drawing: Elevation
Date/Time: 10/01/93 14:45:36
Operation: Reload XREF
- - - - - - - - - - - - - - - - - - - - - - - -
Scan ENTRY_DR for nested references
ENTRY_DR     Xref
-FRAME       Xref
-HARDWARE    Xref
-DETAILS     Xref
```

Chapter 23 Exercises

While doing the following exercises, it is suggested that you note on paper the names of the blocks and xrefs you are using as files.

Exercise A23

STEP 1
Create the following files:

1. a plain steno chair **A:STENO1**
2. a steno chair with arms **A:STENO2**
3. a 5′ by 6′ workstation **A:5x6wst**
4. a 6′ by 7′ workstation **A:6x6wst**
5. an executive office **A:MGMT** *(use files from A4)*

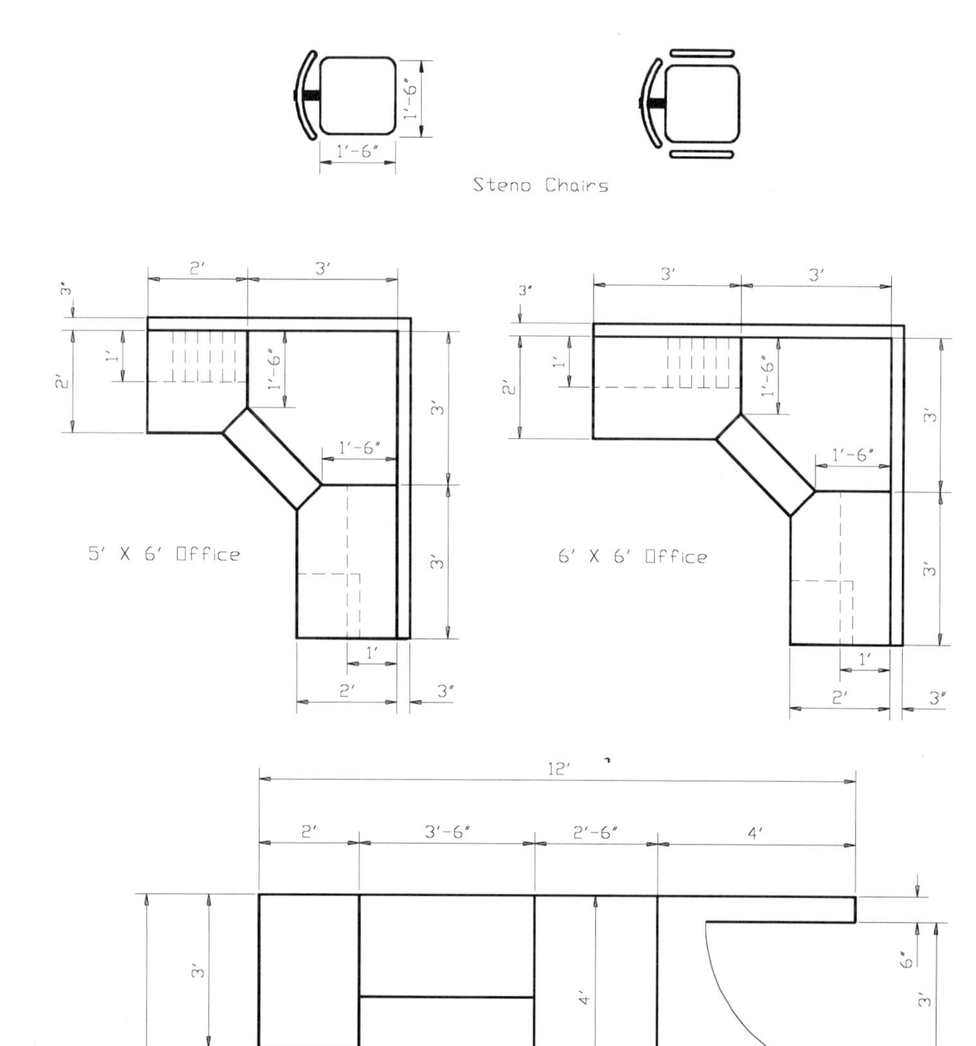

Exercise A23 (continued)

STEP 2
Create an office that is 48′ by 28′ with a 6′ double door.

STEP 3
Create a bank of eight 5 x 6 workstations **A:5x6wst** in the middle of the room by inserting them as blocks. Add an armless STENO chair **A:STENO1** to each workstation.

STEP 4
Using the XREF command, insert four management offices **A:MGMT**. Insert a STENO chair with arms **A:STENO2** into each management office.

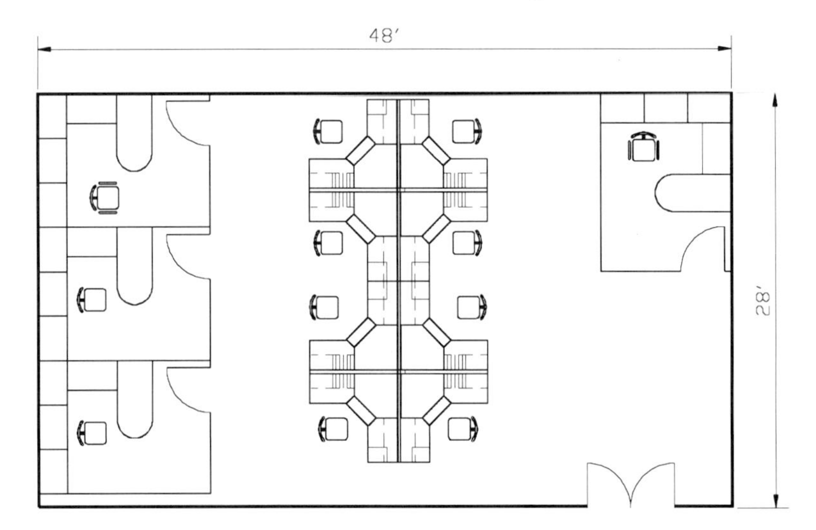

STEP 5
End the file and note the size of the file and the time.

File name ____________________ time______________ size ______

STEP 6
Enter the management source file and change the size of the curved desk. Add some filing cabinets and a plant. END the file.

STEP 7
Enter your office layout. Note the fact that the management offices have been automatically updated. Using the equal sign, change the 5 x 6 workstations **A:5x6wst** to 6 x 6 workstations **A:6x6wst**. Make all the chairs armchairs **A:STENO2** using =.

Bind your management offices to the office layout. END the file and note the size of the file.

File size ____________________.

Reenter the file, erase the management offices, detach them from your file and note the size of the file after you have ENDed.

File size ____________________.

Exercise M23

STEP 1

Create the following files:

1. an AutoCAD 11 station **A:ACAD11**
2. an AutoCAD 386 plus AME station **A:ACAD386+**
3. a machine tool as shown **A:TOOL1**
4. icons for Finite Element Analysis **A:FEA**

```
Materials A:MAT
Existing Parts A:EXPARTS
Standard Parts A:STPARTS
Machines A:MACH
Central Network or Data BASE A:DATA
```

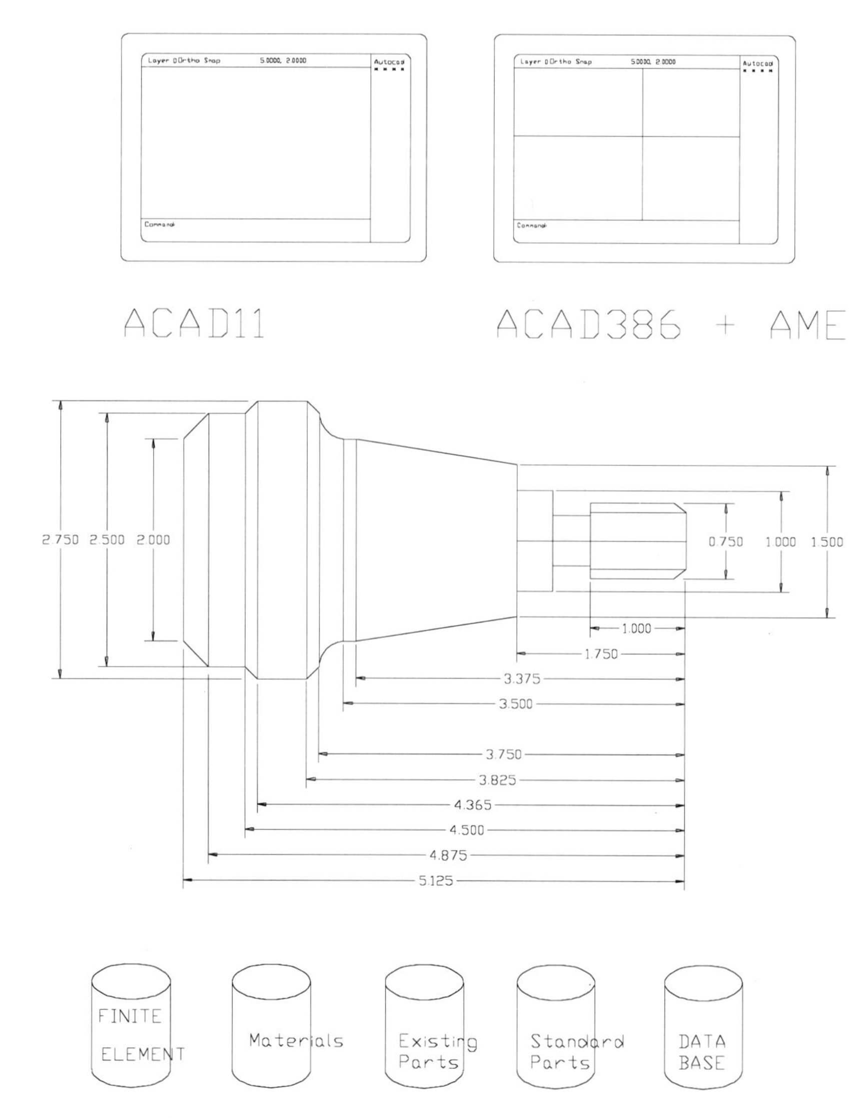

Exercise M23 (continued)

STEP 2
Create a data flow management chart as shown.

STEP 3
For the first chart use INSERT to place all of the icons. Use XREF and attach to place the ACAD11 stations at each section of the Data Flow Chart **A:ACAD11**. Use XREF also to place the machine tool **A:TOOL**.

STEP 4
End the file and note the file size and time.

```
File Size ____________
Time _________________
```

STEP 5
Enter the file again and Bind the **A:ACAD11** files to the Chart. Now, using the = sign, change the ACAD11 stations with ACAD386+ stations.

Once again note the size and time.

```
File Size ____________
Time _________________
```

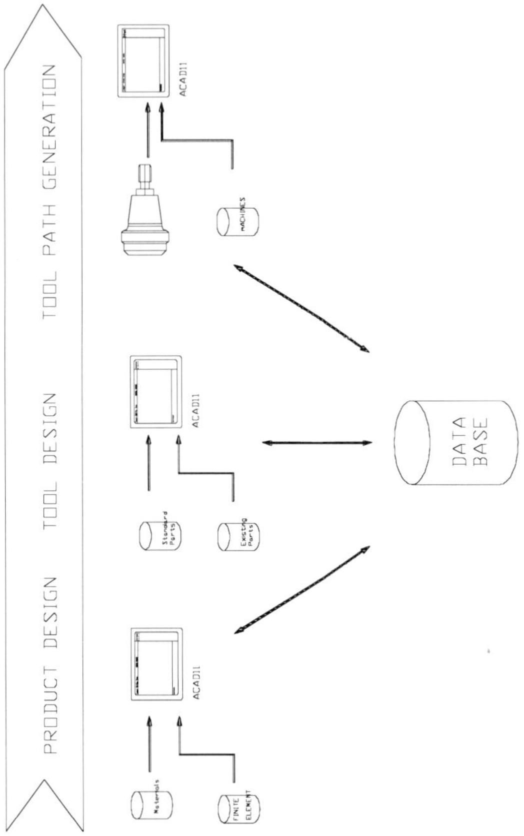

Step 6
Enter the Tool file **A:TOOL** and use STRETCH to change some of the parameters of the tool. Save the file.

STEP 7 Enter Flow Chart and note the fact that the tool has been automatically updated.

Bind your Tool file to the Flow Chart file.

END the file and note the size of the file.

```
File size ______________________.
```

Re-enter the file, erase the tools and ACAD stations and detach them from your file. Be sure that they are detached. Once more, note your file size.

```
File size ______________________.
```

Exercise C23

STEP 1

Create the following files:

1. a deciduous tree **A:DECID**
2. a coniferous tree **A:CONIF**
3. a 8-metre by 8-metre house (**A:house**)
4. a 10-metre by 12-metre house plus deck (**A:house2**)
5. a swimming pool (**A:Pool**)

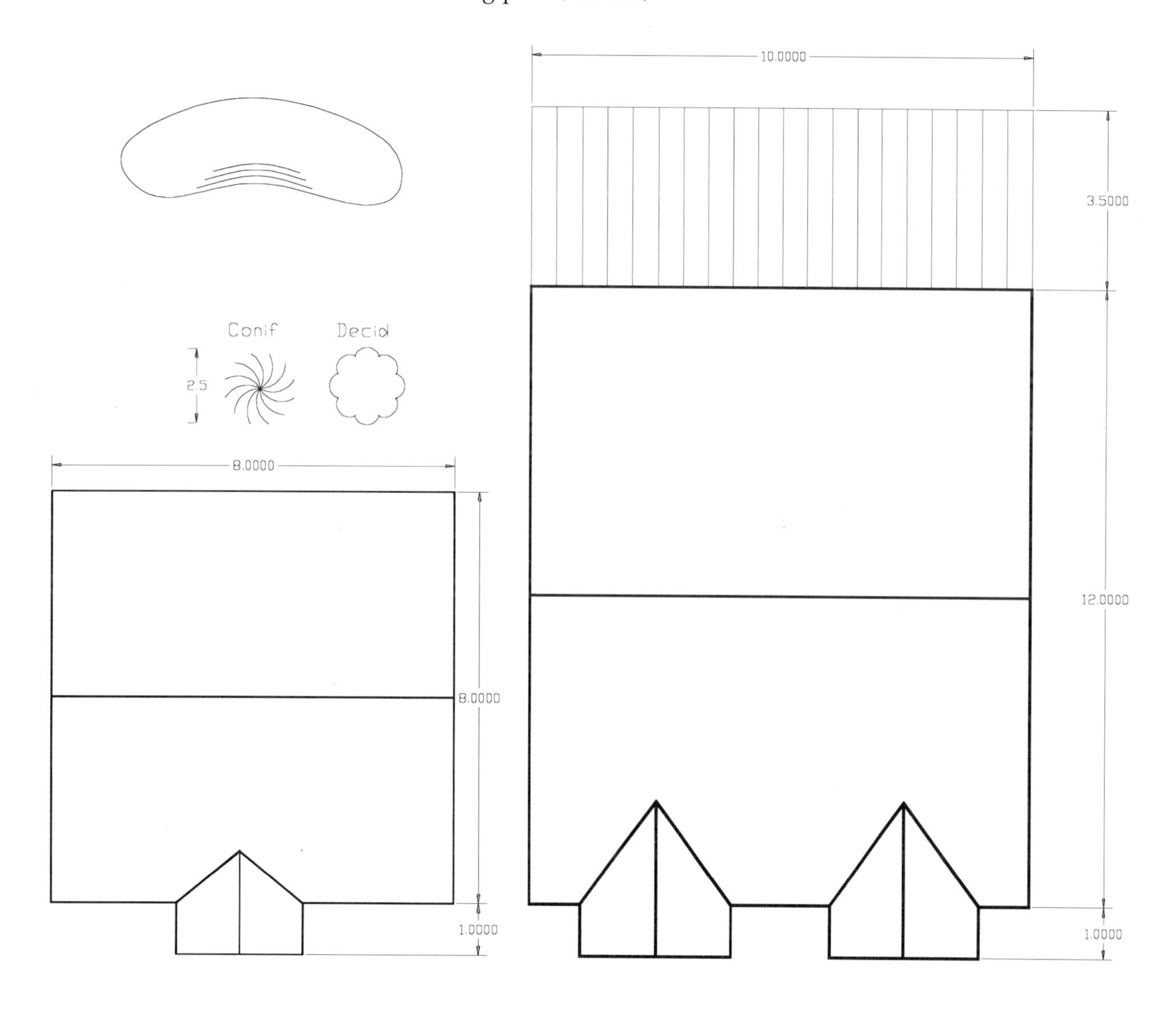

STEP 2

Create a plot plan for a single lot that is 20 metres by 30 metres. In this lot insert the first house (**A:HOUSE1**) and at least 12 coniferous trees (**A:CONIF**).

STEP 3

Using the XREF command, attach the pool in the back yard (**A:POOL**).

Exercise C23 (continued)

STEP 4
Using the = sign change the first house with the second house **A:HOUSE1=A:HOUSE2**. Now change the coniferous trees with the deciduous trees. **A:CONIF=A:DECID.** Now END the file and note the time and the size of your file.

Time ______________

Size ______________

STEP 5
While outside of the file, change the source file for the swimming pool **A:POOL**. Add a diving board and some "natural setting" vegetation.

STEP 6
Enter your site plan.

Note the fact that the pool has been automatically updated.

Bind your pool to the site plan master file.

END the file and note the size of the file.

File size ____________.

Re-enter the file, erase the pool. Detach it from your file and note the size of the file after you have ENDed.

File size ____________.

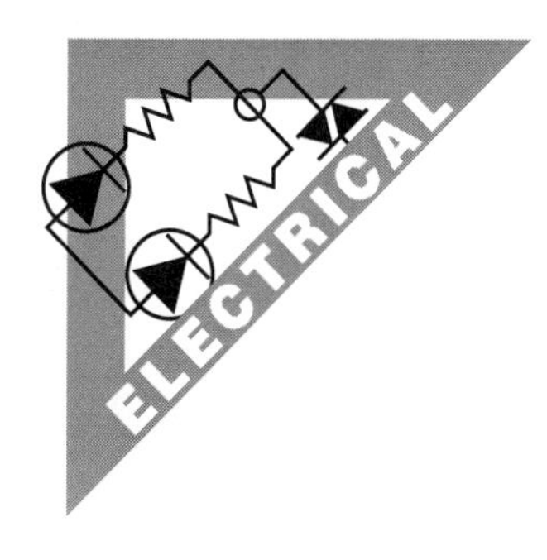

Exercise E23

STEP 1
Create blocks of the following:

1. a general resistor **A:RES1**
2. an adjustable resistor **A:RES2**
3. a bi-directional switch **A:SWITCH**
4. a magnetic core inductor **A:INDUCT**

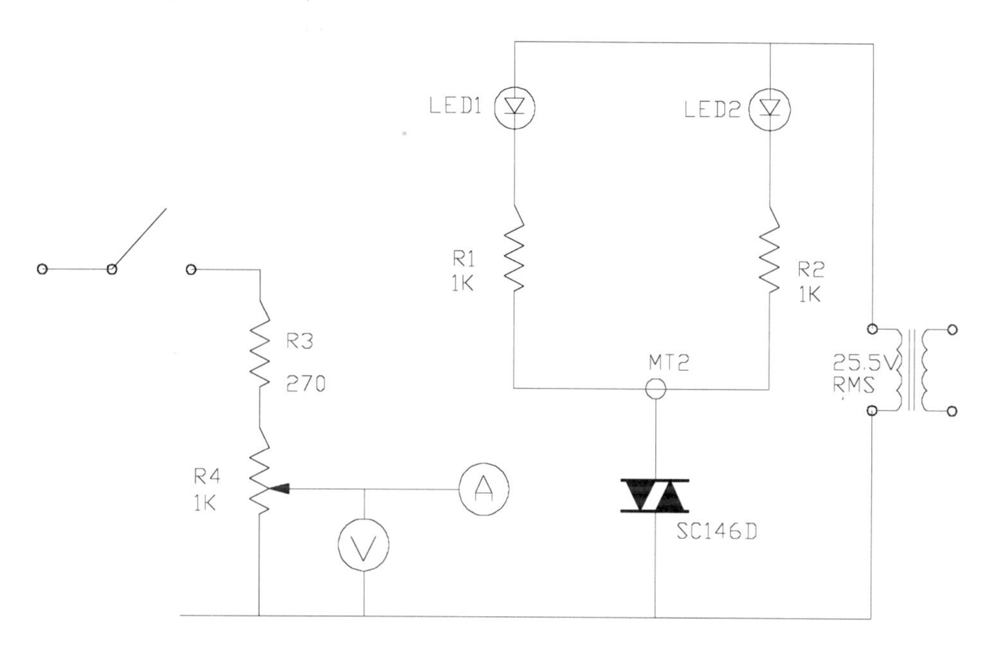

STEP 2
Create files of components that could fit into a similar schematic.

STEP 3
Create the schematic as shown.

STEP 4
Using the XREF command, revise the schematic and update the circuitry.

STEP 5
End the file and note the size of the file and the time.

File name time ________________ size ________

Challenger 23

Using the above exercises, create attributes for each block that is added. Also create new layers for each block.

Then create a data extract file to extract the files. When you exchange the first set of blocks with the second, generate another data extract file.

Finally, created a file of five nested xrefed drawings (5 lots, 5 office floors or 5 flow charts). Bind the drawings and save them, note the size. Then use INSERTing to create the same drawing and note any difference in the size of the files.

FINAL TESTS AND PROJECTS

FINAL TEST REVIEW

The next few pages will offer you 110 questions on the second 11 chapters of this book. Your instructor may offer you these or similar questions as a final exam. If you are not required to write a final test, these questions are nonetheless useful for you to do to have some idea of how much you understand.

FINAL TEST

CUSTOMIZING AND INTERFACING

Please circle the response that is the most correct. You will have 55 minutes for this test.

1. Before it can be inserted, an attribute must be:
a) blocked
b) edited
c) extracted

2. When using a Window to choose the series of attributes:
a) the last attribute defined is offered first
b) the attribute closest to the first Window position is chosen first,
c) the attribute in the highest position in Y is chosen first.

3. What happens if you don't define the prompt in the ATTDEF command?
a) the user will not be prompted
b) the tag is used as the prompt
c) the default is offered for the prompt

4. What are you "writing" when you define an attribute?
a) a program that will help the user define attributes
b) a script file
c) an attribute block

5. What happens when you accept the default by hitting ↵ when asked for the default ATTRIBUTE value?
a) the default value entered by the person writing the ATTDEF will be chosen
b) the system default will be chosen
c) the default will be .5

6. Is an ATTDEF filed with the model even if it hasn't been blocked or inserted?
a) yes
b) no

7. Within the ATTRIBUTE command, what does Invisible refer to?
   a) the lines around the block will be invisible
   b) the tags will be invisible
   c) the attributes when inserted will be invisible

8. Can you change the layer of an attributed block?
   a) yes
   b) no

9. What is the advantage of setting an ATTRIBUTE text height within a title block?
   a) the text will always be the same in all the title blocks
   b) the text will always have the same justification
   c) the height will not have to be changed in the STYLE command

10. Once the attribute is defined, how can you change the prompts?
    a) CHPROP
    b) ATTEDIT
    c) CHANGE

11. Must the attribute be exploded before it can be moved?
    a) yes
    b) no
    c) sometimes

12. How can you modify the color of an attribute?
    a) this is not possible because it has non-graphics data attached
    b) CHPROP
    c) ATTEDIT

13. If you would like to change the prompting sequence of the attribute instance, what must you do?
    a) CHPROP
    b) EXPLODE and reBLOCK
    c) change the default

14. What is a TAG?
    a) the title you give to the attribute definition
    b) the word used to define a prompt
    c) the word for non-graphics data

15. How can an attributed block be used in another file?
    a) ATTEXT
    b) save it as a WBLOCK
    c) insert it as an ATTDEF

16. What command do you use to define an attribute?
    a) ATTEXT
    b) ATTDEF
    c) ATTEDIT

17. When you want to attach an attributed block to a drawing, what command do you use?
    a) BLOCKS
    b) INSERT
    c) PURGE

18. What does the term GLOBAL mean when editing attributes?
a) a global edit affects just the graphics
b) a global edit edits all the attributes selected
c) a global edit affects just the TAGs

19. If you don't choose to select the attributes one by one, will all of the attributes on screen be selected?
a) yes, if you Window them all
b) yes, they are all inserted from the same block reference
c) no, only those selected one by one will be edited.

20. If you have inserted many attributed blocks, how do you change the default value and then keep inserting it?
a) it can't be done
b) ATTEDIT then CHANGE
c) EXPLODE, CHANGE and reBLOCK

21. What command do you use to modify the value of an attribute instance?
a) CHANGE and reBLOCK
b) EXPLODE and CHANGE
c) ATTEDIT

22. What command do you use to extract the values of all of the attribute instances to an ASCII-based format?
a) ATTEDIT
b) ATTEXT
c) ATTASCII

23. What command is used to change the position of an attribute instance?
a) ATTEDIT
b) MOVE
c) ATTEXT

24. Does QTEXT work on attributes?
a) yes
b) no

25. Why does your attribute extract have to be ASCII based?
a) ASCII is an Insertable code
b) ASCII is the accepted standard
c) ASCII has the alphabet that we use

26. Can you measure a solid?
a) yes
b) no

27. What is the quickest method to make five equal portions out of a stretch of geometry that contains two arcs and a circle?
a) block it and divide it
b) PEDIT and divide it
c) PEDIT and measure it

28. Can you use the MEASURE command on an ellipse?
a) yes
b) no

29. What can you do to see the division markers created with the DIVIDE command?
a) ZOOM Window
b) change PDMODE
c) change PDSIZE

30. What is the maximum size of the default point?
a) 10 x 10
b) no maximum
c) one pixel

31. If you wanted to have a donut shape as opposed to a point displayed as a division marker in the DIVIDE command, how would you do it?
a) change the PDMODE
b) make the donut a BLOCK
c) change the PDSIZE

32. Why will the Crossing option not work in the MEASURE command?
a) because the lines must be picked in a contiguous order
b) because the arcs must be selected first
c) because only one object can be selected at once

33. What is the key element when placing a block correctly within the MEASURE command?
a) the scale factor of the block
b) the insertion base point of the block
c) the attributes of the block

34. What does the ID command do?
a) allows the user to add an ID number to an object
b) gives the position of a point relative to the origin
c) lists the layer, position and block association of an object.

35. If you wanted to find the angle of a LINE relative to 0 what command would you use?
a) LIST
b) ANGLE
c) DBLIST

36. If you have the units set to two decimal points of accuracy (.00), will a LIST on the objects that you have created with this setting default to 2 decimal points of accuracy?
a) yes
b) no

37. Can you use OSNAP when you are calculating a distance?
a) yes
b) no

38. Does the AREA command calculate volume as well?
a) yes
b) no

39. How would you change the time setting on your computer?
a) TIME
b) DATE
c) TDCREATE

40. Where can you find the position of the last entered point?
a) ID
b) LIST
c) STATUS

41. What does the term "elapsed time" mean?
a) the time that has elapsed since the user signed onto a file
b) the time that has elapsed since the user signed onto the system
c) the time that has elapsed since the file was started

42. What is TDINDWIG?
a) the time and date indicator in ROM
b) the elapsed time setting value
c) the total editing time value

43. What is an EPS file?
a) Extract Printer Script
b) Encapsulated Post Script
c) Enhanced Printer Script

44. What is the difference between a raster file and a bit map?
a) a raster file only works on a VGA screen
b) a raster file accesses the pixels more rapidly
c) there is no difference

45. What is a pixel?
a) the smallest addressable portion of your screen
b) the center of your crosshairs
c) the aperture setting

46. What is a vector file?
a) a file that relates to the resolution of your screen
b) a file that records the number of lines on your file
c) a file that records the position of the objects in your file relative to a fixed origin

47. What three colors make up your screen display?
a) red, green, and blue
b) red, yellow, and blue
c) white, black, and green

48. What kind of information is used to make a slide file?
a) vector file
b) bit map
c) window file

49. What command would you use to get a list of slide files?
a) DIR *.SLD
b) DIR *.SCR
c) DIR *.SWR

50. Why does a REGEN take longer than a REDRAW?
a) because a REDRAW will only redraw the vector file
b) because a REDRAW will only redraw the bit map
c) because a REDRAW involves the GRID

51. What does the 1000 stand for in DELAY 1000?
a) one minute
b) one nano second
c) one second

52. What does RSCRIPT do?
    a) redraw the script
    b) regen the script
    c) repeat the script

53. What is a delimiter?
    a) the limit on the size of your file
    b) the code that indicates the end of an entry
    c) the code that indicates a change in direction

54. What code indicates a preloading of your slides in a script file?
    a) #
    b) *
    c) ^

55. What does the GL stand for in HPGL ?
    a) Graphics Language
    b) Gather Line
    c) Grab Line

56. What is a .PLT file?
    a) Perfect Line Type
    b) Pre Load Type
    c) PLOT

57. How can you make a PLT file into an HPGL file?
    a) rename it (as long as the driver is correct)
    b) copy it
    c) extract it

58. What is an image file?
    a) a non-graphics file
    b) a vector file
    c) a bit map file

59. What does ASCII have to do with DOS?
    a) DOS is written in ASCII
    b) DOS uses ASCII
    c) DOS owns ASCII

60. What is the difference between ASCII text and DOS text?
    a) ASCII text is more flexible than DOS text
    b) DOS text is more flexible than ASCII text
    c) there is no difference

61. How do you load an AutoLISP routine in AutoCAD, ASCTEXT for example?
    a) load ("ASCTEXT")
    b) [load "ASCTEXT"]
    c) (load "ASCTEXT")

62. Can you load an AutoLISP routine into any ASCII-based file ?
    a) yes
    b) no

63. What does DXF stand for?
    a) Drawing eXtract File
    b) Data eXtract File
    c) Data eXtract Format

64. What is parametric programming?
a) programming using only existing geometry
b) programming by entering the parameters of the geometry without the use of a graphics screen
c) programming in ASCII

65. When you DXFIN what are you doing?
a) taking a DXF file into ASCII
b) taking a DXF file into AutoCAD
c) taking a DXF file into WordPerfect

66. What is the purpose of a DXF file?
a) to perform parametric programming
b) to perform ASCII programming
c) to extract a graphics file in an ASCII format

67. When reading a DXF file, what does the term HEADER mean?
a) the beginning of a section
b) the top of a page
c) the beginning of a file

68. What does the term scroll mean?
a) to have the file printed onto scrolled paper
b) to have the text run continuously on your screen
c) to have a file that takes up more than the space provided for it on screen

69. Can you load a release 10 file into Release 11 without using a DXF?
a) yes
b) no

70. Can you load a release 11 file into Release 10 without using a DXF?
a) yes
b) no

71. What is file locking?
a) having to use a password to enter your file
b) having an automatic lock on your hard drive
c) having a locking facility within the files

72. What does the term third party mean?
a) developers and suppliers between AutoCAD and the end user
b) the party that uses the third version of software
c) the dealers of AutoCAD

73. What is the difference between a simple macro and a compound macro?
a) a compound macro has LISP programs; a simple one doesn't
b) a simple macro performs only one function
c) a compound macro actually produces geometry whereas a simple macro is only for display

74. When reading a macro, what does ^C stand for?
a) Crossing
b) Control
c) Cancel

75. What does the extension .MNU mean?
a) the AutoCAD menu file
b) a menu file that has not yet been used
c) any menu file

76. Explain the term "toggle"?
a) the way to get into a macro
b) an On/Off switch
c) a tablet switch

77. What is an icon?
a) a graphic that indicates a function or facility
b) a graphic that indicates a menu
c) a graphic on a pull-down menu

78. What is the difference between a pop-up and a pull-down menu?
a) pop-ups are in Release 11, pull-downs where in Release 10
b) pull-down menus are longer than pop-up menus
c) there is no difference

79. What does the Auxiliary menu do?
a) so far, nothing
b) addresses the tablet
c) addresses the buttons

80. What does $p1=* mean in a button menu?
a) the Osnap menu
b) the cancel button
c) pick

81. What does ***SCREEN mean?
a) the HEADER that addresses the screen
b) the screen menu in the .MNU file
c) the option for changing the screen size

82. What is the difference between a return and hitting the space bar?
a) there is no difference
b) the return key is always a delimiter, the space bar is a delimiter in certain commands only
c) the space bar is only used within DRAW menu commands

83. What is the purpose of a macro?
a) to fill up the tablet menus
b) to automate the design process
c) to make large commands out of small ones

84. How many macros can you fit on a pop-up menu?
a) only 12
b) no limit
c) limit of three pages

85. What does "Bad command or file name" mean?
a) the command, as you have typed it in, does not exist
b) the command as entered from the screen menu does not exist
c) the command as entered from the tablet does not exist; turn tablet on

86. What is a keystroke?
   a) every time you use a key on the keyboard it is a keystroke
   b) every entry made by the user, whether by the keyboard or by the cursor is a keystroke
   c) every entry used to create the model is a keystroke

87. How many ***SCREEN menus can you have?
   a) 16 only, due to the limited area on the screen
   b) no limit
   c) no more than three pages per submenu; therefore, 54

88. What does the ; stand for within a macro?
   a) cancel
   b) user response
   c) space

89. What does ^O stand for within a macro?
   a) LIMITS
   b) ORTHO
   c) UNDO

90. What is a transparent command?
   a) a command that can be entered within another command
   b) a display command
   c) a command from the pull-down menus

91. What command do you use to load the AutoCAD main menu?
   a) (load "ACAD.MNU")
   b) ******MENU
   c) MENU ACAD

92. Can you put an icon menu on the button menu?
   a) yes
   b) no

93. Which of the following is an example of a submenu?
   a) pop 3
   b) EDIT
   c) OSNAP

94. What do the square brackets [] mean in the menu file?
   a) whatever is within the brackets will be written on the menu on screen
   b) whatever is within the brackets will be included in the macro
   c) whatever is within the brackets will be loaded with the macro as a LISP routine

95. What kind of files are needed for icon menus?
   a) script files
   b) slide files
   c) screen files

96. What options can change on a button menu?
   a) everything can change
   b) everything but Enter can change
   c) everything but Pick can change

97. How do you turn your tablet function off?
a) ***TABLET then blank
b) F10
c) MENU TABLET OFF

98. How many tablet areas are there?
a) 4
b) 5
c) unlimited

99. What command do you use to recalibrate your tablet?
a) F10
b) TABLET CFG
c) F10 CFG

100. What command would you use to replace 24 blocks called one with 24 blocks called two?
a) insert one=two
b) insert two=one
c) explode one=two

101. Can a block contain XREFs?
a) yes
b) no

102. Can an XREF contain blocks?
a) yes
b) no

103. If an XREF contains user-defined hatch patterns, can these hatch patterns be used on the file in which the XREF appears?
a) yes
b) no

104. Can text be created from a user-defined linetype?
a) yes
b) no

105. Can a user-defined linetype be placed in a macro without the linetype being loaded?
a) yes
b) no

106. Can you access a user-defined text without loading it?
a) yes
b) no

107. What is the difference between ANSI and ASCII ?
a) ANSI is a drafting standard, ASCII is a computer standard
b) ANSI is an American standard, ASCII is an international standard
c) ANSI is an AutoCAD standard, ASCII is an IBM standard

108. What is a .SHP file?
a) a SHiPping file
b) a SHaPe file
c) a SHoP file

109. How can a menu be used to automate drawing creation?
a) a menu can be loaded with macros
b) a menu can be loaded with scripts
c) a menu can be loaded with LISP routines
d) all of the above

110. What type of files will you need to copy along with a prototype file to make sure that the prototype will work?
a) .MNU, .SHP, .PLT
b) .MNU, .SHP, .BAK
c) .MNU, .SHP, .SWR

FINAL PROJECT

This section is particularly difficult to combine into a Final Project because there is so little graphic information. Most of the information covered in this section pertains to aiding the creation of graphics data and exchanging this data with other types of computer documents. Final projects are offered after the review section to ensure that your understanding of the section is complete and to help you to combine all of the skills learned in this section. There is no final project for the Electrical discipline.

The projects can be marked on the following:

- **ACCESSIBILITY** can others understand your communications?
- **USEFULNESS** are your macros, attributes, etc. realistic?
- **"CLEAN-NESS"** are your data transfers and menus logical and free of repetition ? Are all statements properly qualified?
- **STYLE** - has the resulting data been presented in an agreeable and professional manner?

To complete the final projects, use a CAD file that you are currently working on or take the final project from the last term and add to it. The skills offered in this section should help you in an office atmosphere, and to fine-tune the skills learned in the introductory section. If you have already studied AutoCAD's 3D capabilities, your next step will be to take an AutoLISP course.

ARCHITECTURAL FINAL PROJECT

Create a floor plan for a commercial building.

On the floor plan, have at least two customized hatch patterns and two customized linetypes.

Create an attributed BLOCK with the following:

a) the area of each room
b) the final floor finish
c) the wall color
d) the trim colour
e) the length of trim (floor trim) needed

Download this data onto a spreadsheet so that final amount calculations can be made.

On the same document, add an illustration of how the trim should be applied using a graphic transfer.

Create a script file containing a SLIDE for the overall plan and the various innovative ideas that you feel make this the superior design.

Compile at least three complex macros and include them in a customized menu that you used to help you create this project. Include in your custom menu the following:

a) a macro that created a block for mullion and was used with the DIVIDE command either on windows or on double doors,
b) a macro that can be used to replace the existing bathroom fixtures with another blocked fixture, and
c) a macro that replaces a large portion of the drawing with a simple block.

When completed, you should submit the following:

- your plotted drawing.
- your quotation with interior finishes and details on paper.
- a floppy disk containing your menu and macros.

MECHANICAL FINAL PROJECT

Create an assembly drawing of a vehicle, either motorized or not.

On the drawing have at least two customized hatch patterns and two customized linetypes.

Create an attributed block with the following:

a) the part number of each component
b) the supplier of each component
c) the size of each component
d) the trim colour
e) the approximate market value of each component

Download this data onto a spreadsheet so that final amount calculations can be made.

On the same document, add an illustration of how the one component should be attached to another using a graphic transfer.

Create a script file containing a SLIDE for the overall design and the various innovative ideas that you feel make this the superior design.

Compile at least three complex macros and include them in a customized menu that you used to help you create this project. Include in your custom menu the following:

a) a macro that created a block that was used with the DIVIDE command either on one component or to place many components.
b) a macro that can be used to replace the existing wheels with other blocked wheels, and
c) a macro that replaces a large portion of the drawing with a simple block.

When completed, you should submit the following:

- your plotted drawing.
- your quotation with the bill of materials and details on paper.
- a floppy disk containing your menu and macros.

CIVIL FINAL PROJECT

Create a drawing of a waterfront development with many lots along the water's edge.

On the drawing have at least two customized hatch patterns and two customized linetypes.

Create an attributed block with the following:

a) the lot numbers of each site
b) the lot size
c) the legal description of the properties
d) the area of each lot
e) the approximate market value of each lot

Download this data onto a spreadsheet so that final amount calculations can be made.

On the same document, add an illustration of how one lot in particular is different than the others using a graphic transfer.

Create a script file containing a SLIDE for the overall design and the various lots and their particular design and location.

Compile at least three complex macros and include them in a customized menu that you used to help you create this project. Include in your custom menu the following:

a) a macro that created a block that was used with the DIVIDE command to place the lots at an equal distance along a road.
b) a macro that can be used to replace the existing property markers with other markers, and
c) a macro that replaces a large portion of the drawing with a simple block.

When completed, you should submit the following:

- your plotted drawing.
- your quotation of the price of the lots and details on paper.
- a floppy disk containing your menu and macros.

GENERATING 3D MODELS

Upon completion of this chapter, the student should be able to:

1. Use VIEWPORT to set up a multi-view screen
2. Use VIEWPOINT 3D to rotate the views
3. Use simple geometry to create 3D wireframe models

INTRODUCTION TO 3D

In AutoCAD, you can create 3D models using the commands described in Chapters 25 to 36. In addition, you can create images that appear to be 3D by using the ISOPLANE command.

A 3D model may be used to create three-dimensional drawings and to generate data concerning the design of a three-dimensional part. The model, once fully described, can be rotated to allow the viewer to examine the part more closely, and hidden lines can be automatically removed. The 3D data may also be used to generate analysis of the structure of the 3D part, or to generate data for cutting the part out of metal or foam, or reproducing the model using any of the 3D plotting technologies.

If you are only concerned with a 2D representation of a 3D model, similar to what you can get by drawing it with pencil on paper, the ISOPLANE command can be used to create an image much more quickly than you could create it using full 3D modelling techniques. The following three pages outline how to create images of 3D objects. The result will not be a 3D model, but will look 3D.

2D Illusions in 3D

This introduction is for the Release 9 version where working in 3D is very difficult, or for those who only need a "quick" 3D image, not a 3D database. If you are interested in full 3D, please advance to page 419.

You can generate a drawing that looks 3D but is 2D isometric. Set the SNAP to Isometric and the GRID will follow. The crosshairs will also be in isometric, and the ORTHO will be set to an isometric as well.

```
Command:SNAP
Snap spacing or ON/OFF/Aspect/Rotate/ Style:S
Standard or Isometric:I
Vertical Spacing:.5
```

Top
Left -30°
Right 30°

```
Command:GRID
Grid spacing or ON/OFF/Aspect:.5
```

Using GRID and SNAP as the set-up in the above, you can draw all lines as they would appear.

Text can be added as well, setting the obliquing angle to 30 or negative 30, then entering the text to fit. In order to enter arcs, however, you will want to use ISOPLANE.

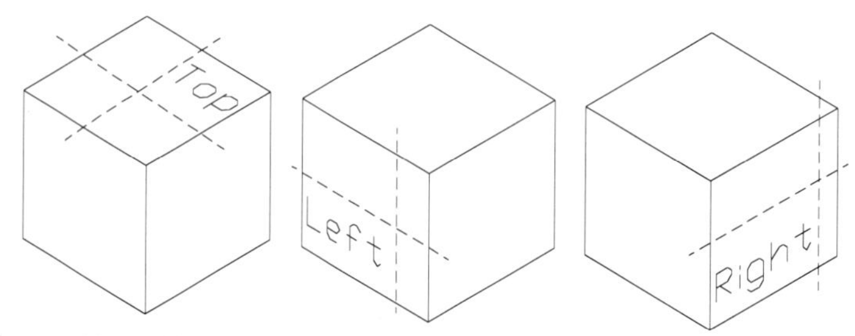

Figure 25-1. Using ISOPLANE

ISOPLANE allows you to work on any of the three planes of AutoCAD's isometric projection — left, right, and top. ISOPLANE sets the cross-hairs to correspond to the plane on which you are working.

```
Command:ISOPLANE
ISOPLANE Left/Top/Right/<toggle>:R
```

ISOPLANE will act as a toggle switch that toggles through the three planes and then off. ISOPLANE is also toggled by Ctrl-E.

ORTHO is useful when using ISOPLANE to make rectangular shapes.

Drawing Circles

To make a circle appear in the isometric, use the ELLIPSE command with the Isocircle option. This allows you to draw circles on any of the three planes. On the left a circle is drawn using the CIRCLE command.

```
Command:ELLIPSE
Axis endpoint 1/Center/Isocircle:I
Center of the circle: (pick 1)
radius/Diameter: (pick 2)
```

The current isoplane governs the plane in which the circle will be drawn; change the ISOPLANE to change the orientation of the circle. The second box has circles drawn relative to the Left isoplane, the third box has circles on the remaining two planes.

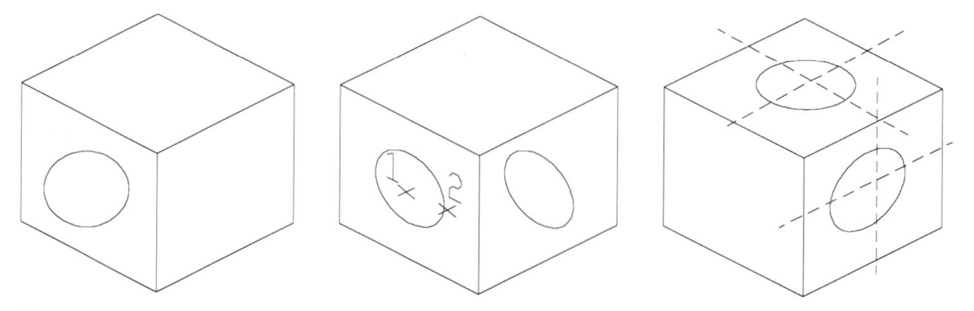

Figure 25-2. Aligning circles to planes

Drawing Lines at Angles

Because this is a 2D drawing, lines are drawn relative to the X-Y plane.

Thus, lines drawn at angles will not be rotated relative to the ISOPLANE. In this illustration, the lines are drawn as rotated normal to the X-Y plane.

```
Command:LINE
From point: (pick 1)
To point:@1<0
Command:LINE
From point: (pick 1)
To point:@1<30
```

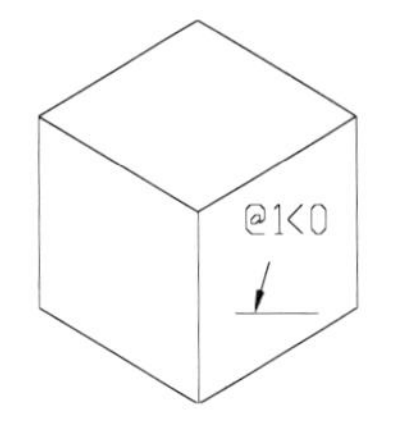

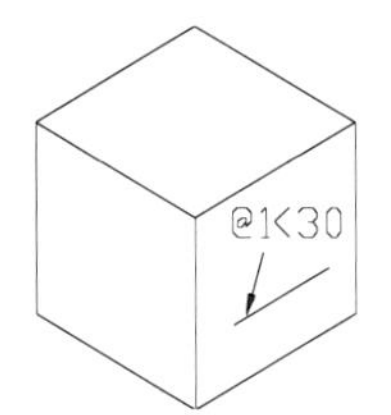

All the above are merely optical illusions that create the appearance of a 3D image. This data cannot be accessed for tooling, analysis, or rotation as 3D. It can be useful, however, if you want a quick image for display purposes.

For those who prefer to use the dialogue boxes, the Ddrmodes pull-down menu on the right is available under the Settings menu as Drawing Tools.

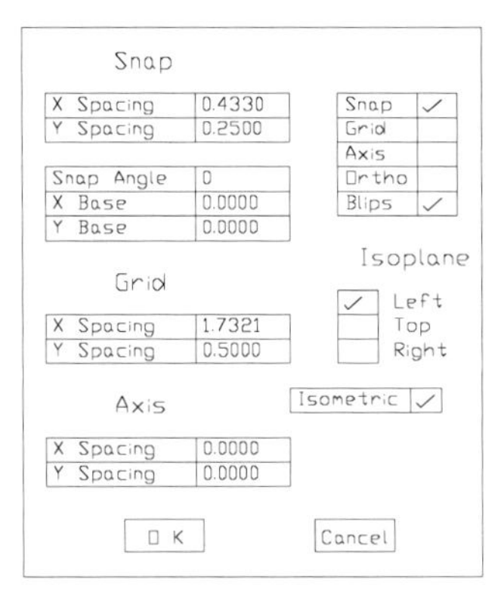

MOVING INTO 3D

AutoCAD Release 9 had the beginnings of 3D imagery. Release 10 took this one step further to the point where surfacing was possible. By Release 11, the 3D software was quite sophisticated and could be used to generate complex surfaces and shapes. Release 12 is much better yet.

In this chapter we will be concentrating on setting up the screen for maximum access to the model. Then we will learn how to enter the data in point format to gain control of the model.

Before getting started, let us consider for a moment who you are and how you are going to address this procedure. If you are an experienced draftsperson, you may have difficulty in grasping 3D at first because you are convinced of the logic of the paper-drawing format. Those who have not spent as much time drawing are not as fluent with drafting techniques, and therefore, sometimes take more easily to 3D. You are not drafting now, you are creating a 3D database.

Consider how people who are not accustomed to reading drawings become totally lost and try to bluff their way through a technical experience which includes drawings. The reason for this is that they are not aware of protocols. In drafting, these protocols allow a person to communicate to another person by means of an accepted set of symbols and views. It is exactly these accepted protocols that could hinder your understanding of 3D. If you forget about the drafting board entirely, 3D will be easier to learn.

You are not making a drawing: you are making a model.

Think of yourself as being in a model-making class as opposed to being in a drafting class. To be successful, put objects in only where they exist, not as a 3D illusion.

VIEWPORTS or VPORTS

In order to enter an object properly, you must be able to see it not just from one angle, but from many. If you see the object only in one view, it is easier to make mistakes and place objects on the wrong plane.

While performing 3D model construction, independently scaled and oriented views can be placed within the viewports of the screen layout. These views are non-overlapping. In Release 10, up to four views are possible, and on Release 11 or later, up to 16 views are possible.

For most applications, four viewports will be sufficient. In the illustration of Figure 25-3, the left screen shows two viewports, the right screen shows four. The current viewport contains the cross-hairs and its outline is also highlighted for clarity. To make a viewport current, simply pick it.

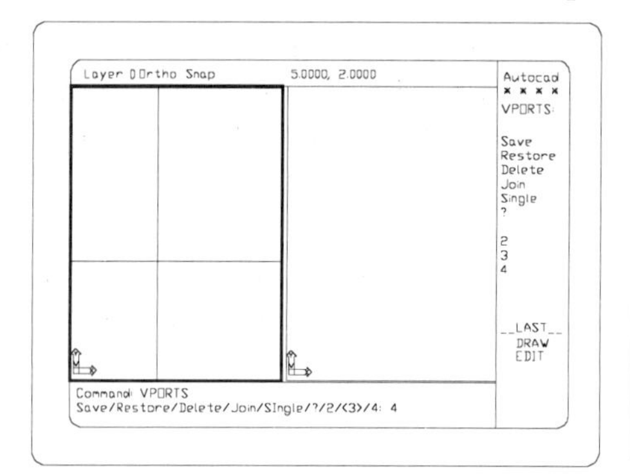

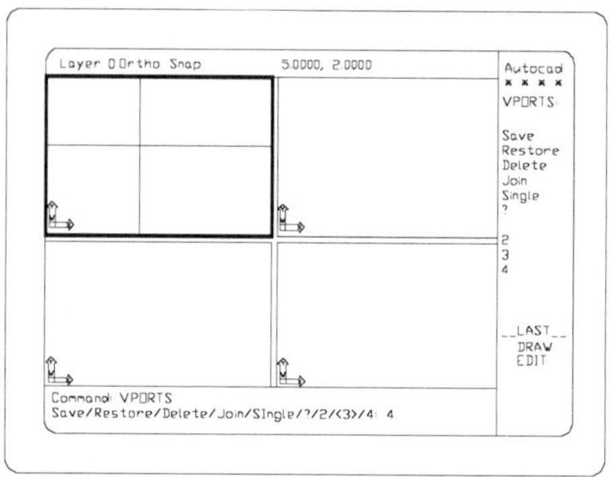

Figure 25-3. Using VPORTS to set multiple views

Before starting on any 3D model, it is important to set up at least two different views.

While you are creating a model, there is, in fact, only one database being made. If you have two viewports, then you will have two views of the same model. If you have four viewports, then you will have four views of the same model. You will not have four models, only four views.

This concept is the same as that of television. The actor conversing with the talk show host is, at different times during the show, viewed from different angles because there are cameras set up throughout the studio. There are not four actors.

Keep in mind that you are creating a model, not a drawing.

Finding VPORTS

In Release 11 the VPORTS command is found in the Settings menu, or you can type in the command. It will look like this:

```
Command:VPORTS
Save/Restore/Delete/Join/?/SI/2/<3>/4:
```

Where:

Save names and stores a viewport configuration

Restore brings back a saved configuration

Delete deletes unwanted viewports

Join joins two viewports

? displays a list of saved viewports

> ***Release 12 Notes***
>
> In Release 12, use the View pull-down menu, the Layout option, then the Tiled Viewports option to get an icon menu similar to Figure 25-5. This will offer the 12 layouts shown plus eight empty boxes for custom layouts.

SI returns to a single viewport

2,3,4 divides the current screen display into the selected number of viewports

Three viewports is the default value and will configure the screen into three areas. You must choose how you want your screen set up.

```
Command: VPORTS
Save/Restore/Delete/Join/?/SI/2/<3>/4: ↵
Horizontal/Vertical/Above/Below/Left/<Right>: ↵
```

The default setting will give you a screen with three viewports; the one on the right will be the largest.

This configuration is popular because it allows for an isometric view in the large screen and a top and front in the smaller screens on the left.

The current view of Figure 25-4 is the large viewport.

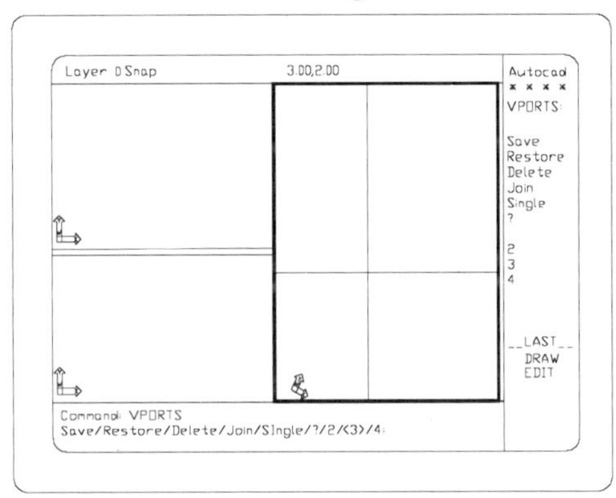

Figure 25-4. A three-view configuration

In Releases 9 and 10, the Vports pull-down menu is found under the Display menu. Pick Set Viewports and the dialogue box of Figure 25-5 will display. You can divide the screen into different viewports simply by choosing one of the configurations offered.

For those using Release 10, the icon menu of Figure 25-5 will give you an idea of the various viewport configurations available.

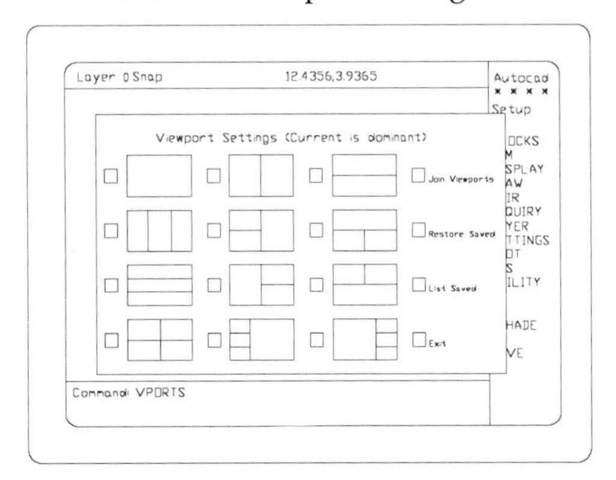

Figure 25-5. The Vports icon menu

If you have copies of both Releases 10 and 11 and find this icon menu useful, you can always add it to your menu (see Chapter 20).

Orienting Views within Vports

Now that you have changed the configuration of the screen, you can rotate your views within the viewports by using the command VPOINT. This command allows you to view the object from any angle.

In both Release 10 and Release 11, the VPOINT command is found under Display on the screen menu. Below is the icon menu for Vpoint under the Display pull-down menu.

> **Release 12 Notes**
>
> The VPOINT command is found under the View pull-down menu, under the Set View option. The icon menu in Figure 25-6 is not present.

Figure 25-6 shows the choices you can make for each viewport:

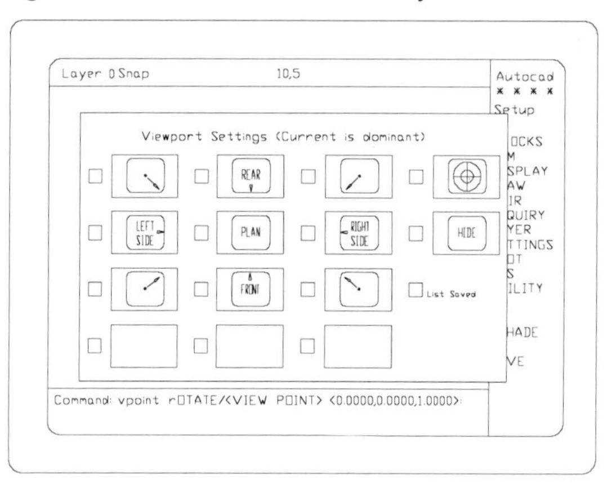

Figure 25-6. The Vpoint icon menu

The command is called VPOINT 3D. The direction from which you are viewing the model is called the viewpoint. The plan view will always be the X-Y plane.

MAKING A VIEWPORT CURRENT

Before orienting a view, you must ensure that the viewport you want to orient is the current viewport, i.e., the viewport that will be affected by the VPOINT command. Simply pick the viewport you want to have current. The cross-hairs will show up there and this will be the viewport affected by all display commands.

When you pick one of the above icons to rotate a view, the system response area will show you which view of the object you have chosen and will give you the current rotation from the X-Y plane.

```
Command:VPOINT
Rotate/<Viewpoint> <2.0000,-2.0000>:F (for Front)
Enter angle in X-Y plane from X axis <90>:
Enter angle from X-Y plane <33>:0
```

The angle given from the X-Y plane is the current angle you have in this view. If you have chosen Front, Back, or either side, this value should be 0. If not, the view will be slightly rotated and the image may not be the one you want.

The easiest way to set up the screen is to first pick the viewport you want to set and then to bring up the icon box above and choose the view you want to see.

The default viewing point is 0,0,1 or 0 in X, 0 in Y and 1 unit in Z, looking back at the origin. The line of sight is along the Z axis. This is referred to as the Plan view as you are looking at the X-Y view.

To look at the object in 3D or isometrically, you rotate the object so that you can access each part of it.

In the diagram of Figure 25-7, you can see that all axes go through 0,0. The centre point is the origin.

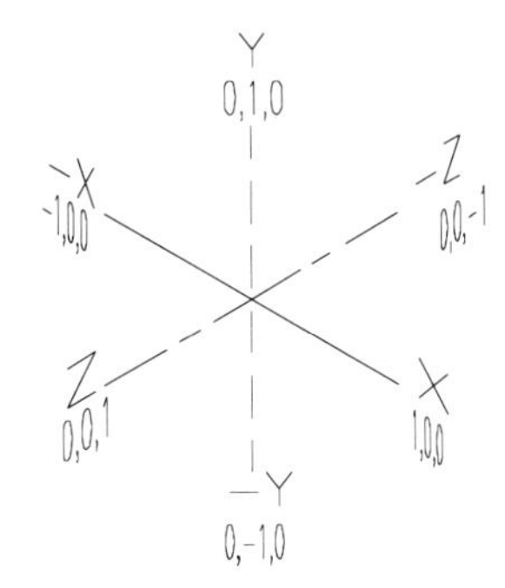

Figure 25-7. Cartesian Coordinate System

To get an isometric view, you must pick a point that is looking back from a point in X, Y, and Z. Your viewpoint must be a non-zero for all reference points.

If your viewpoint reference point contains a zero, you will be positioned directly on one of the axes, so your view will be of one of the planes and not isometric.

To get an isometric view, you can either pick the globe icon from the Display Vpoint 3D pull-down icon menu (top right) or type in the numbers that correspond to the view you want to take. The globe icon is handy, but the numbers are more exact.

THE GLOBE ICON

If you want to use the globe icon from the Viewpoint 3D menu, there are four ways of doing this:

1. Go to the Display Vpoint 3D pull-down menu and pick the icon that looks like cross-hairs on a bull's eye;

2. Choose Globe icon from the tablet menu;

3. Choose the Axes option from the Vpoint screen menu; or

4. Hit the Return key in the VPOINT command. It will default to the globe icon.

The globe icon shows the drawing as a flattened globe. The centre point is the North Pole, the inner ring is the equator, and the outer ring is the South Pole. Below the inner ring is the southern hemisphere, and above it is the northern hemisphere. The cross-hairs represent the X and Y axes, dividing the globe into four quadrants. When you pick a spot on the globe, you are choosing a position from which to view the part.

When the globe icon is picked, you are given a reference point on the globe which you move around the globe in order to get the orientation you require on the part.

As you move the cursor, the XYZ axis is shown by a tripod which moves dynamically with your cursor to give you an idea of what orientation you will finally have.

As you can see in the illustration on the right, the axes rotate according to the position of the cursor point on the globe.

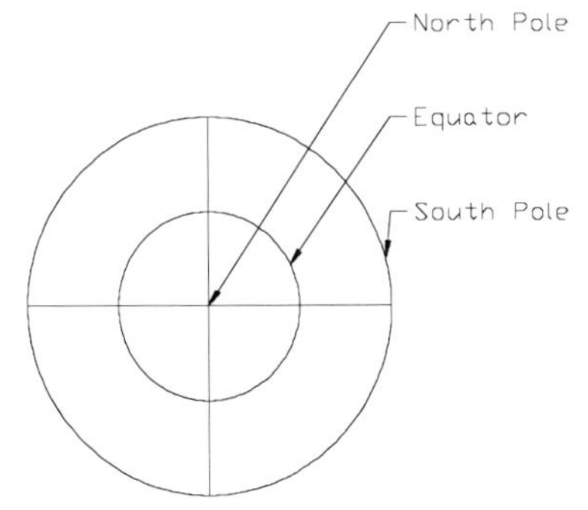

If you want to see the top of the part, indicate a point between the Equator and the North Pole.

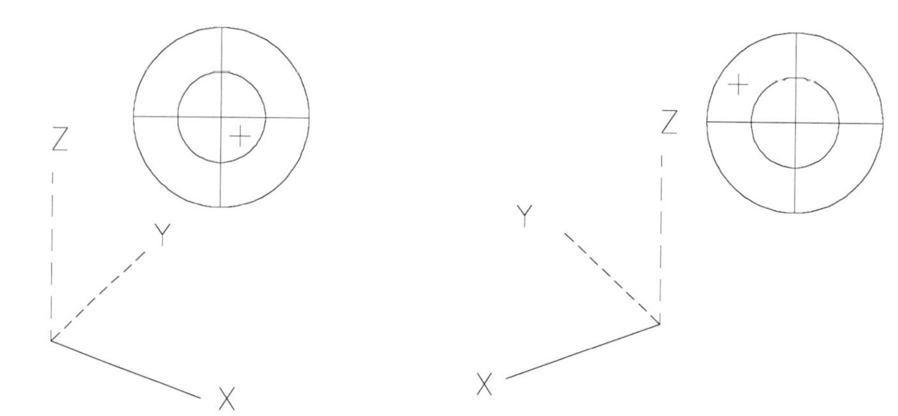

Figure 25-8. The globe icon

Be careful you do not pick a point of view from under the object by picking in the outer circle. This could be very confusing.

With the globe icon, you will not get a position that is as exact as when you type in the view coordinates.

If you want to use coordinates to set the orientation view, use the following:

```
Command:VPOINT
Enter vpoint <0.0000,0,0000,1.0000>:
```

In Figure 25-9 the VPOINT coordinates are 2,-2,2:

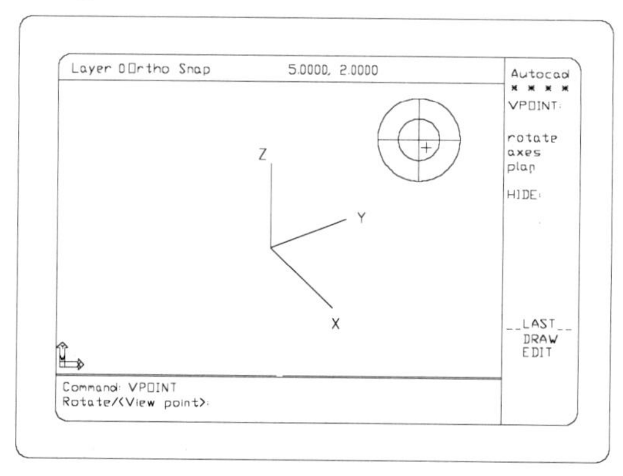

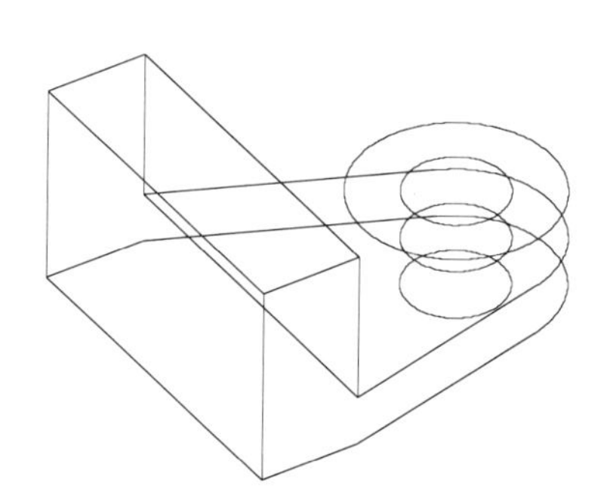

Figure 25-9. An isometric view

In Figure 25-10 the VPOINT coordinates are -2,-2,2:

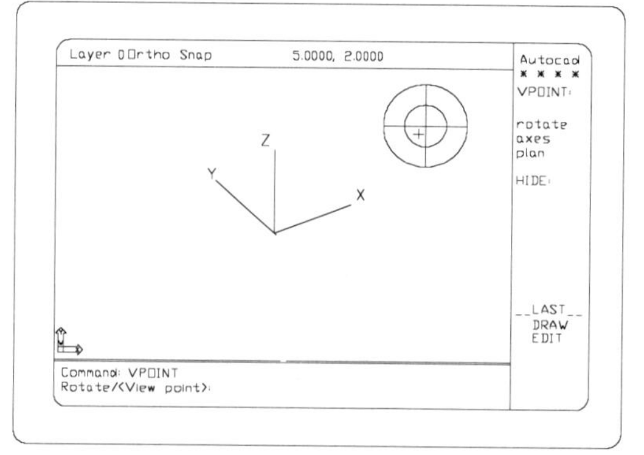

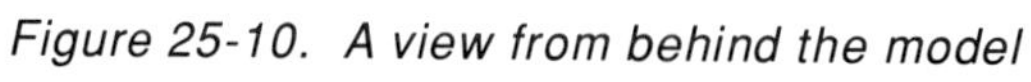

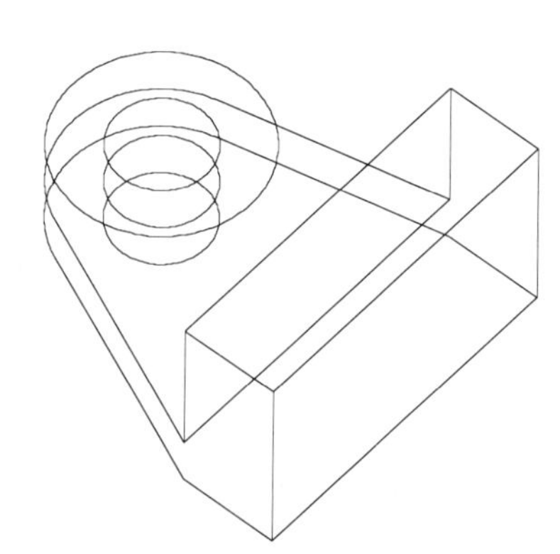

Figure 25-10. A view from behind the model

In Figure 25-11 the VPOINT coordinates are -2,2,2:

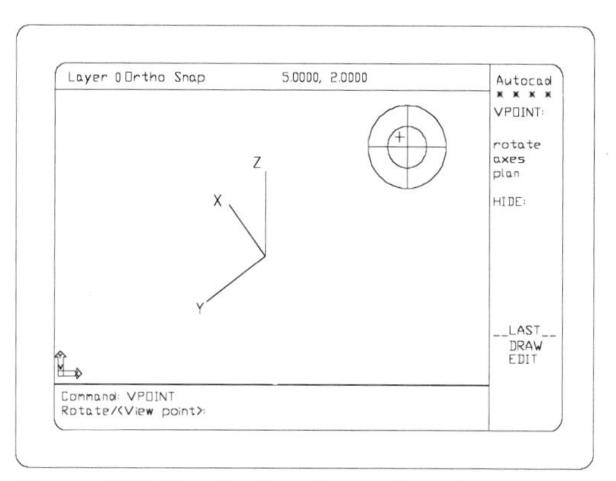

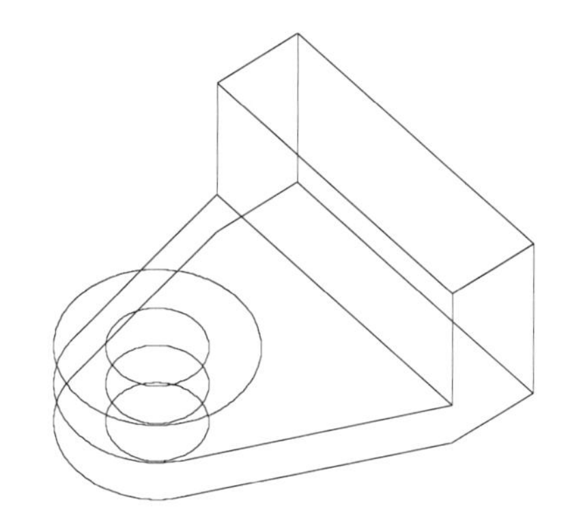

Figure 25-11. A view from the left side

In Figure 25-12 the VPOINT coordinates are 2,2,2:

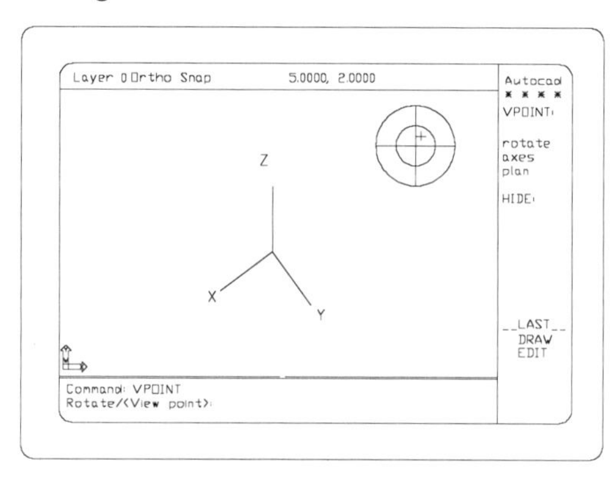

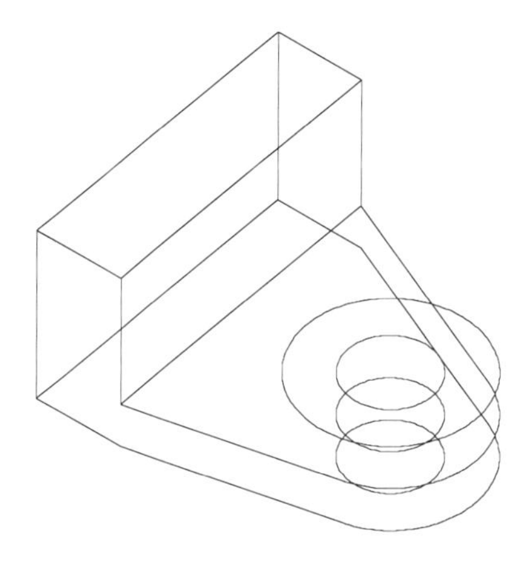

Figure 25-12. An isometric view

When you get into the habit, coordinate entry will offer a useful standardized view.

Whatever view you take, you will always be looking back at the image towards the origin or 0,0.

GETTING STARTED

We will now set up a couple of views of a part in order to access and develop the geometry.

Let us try an example with two viewports, one being the plan view and another being an isometric view, and then we will create some simple 3D geometry.

Example: *VPOINT*

Using the VPORTs command, create a view with two viewports.

Then with the VPOINT command, make one a plan view and the other a 3D view.

```
Command:VPORTS
Save/Restore/Delete/Join/?/SI/2/<3>/4:2
Horizontal/<vertical>:
```

Pick the right view to make it current.

```
Command:VPOINT
Enter vpoint <0.0000,0,0000,1.0000>:2,-2,2
```

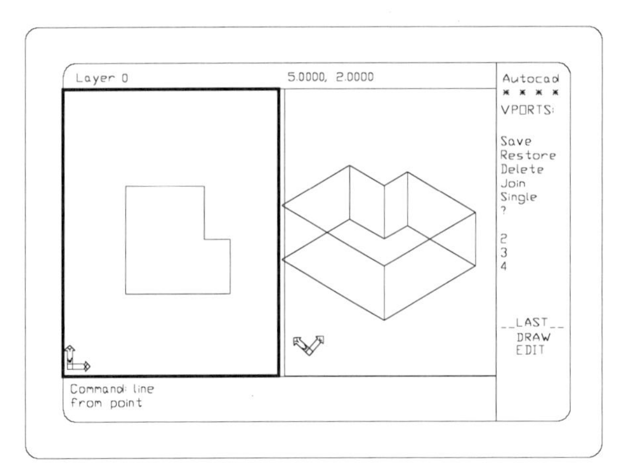

Figure 25-13. A two-view configuration

You have now oriented the views, you are ready to enter the geometry. Note that with the 2,-2,2 orientation in the isometric view, the Z-axis is pointing up.

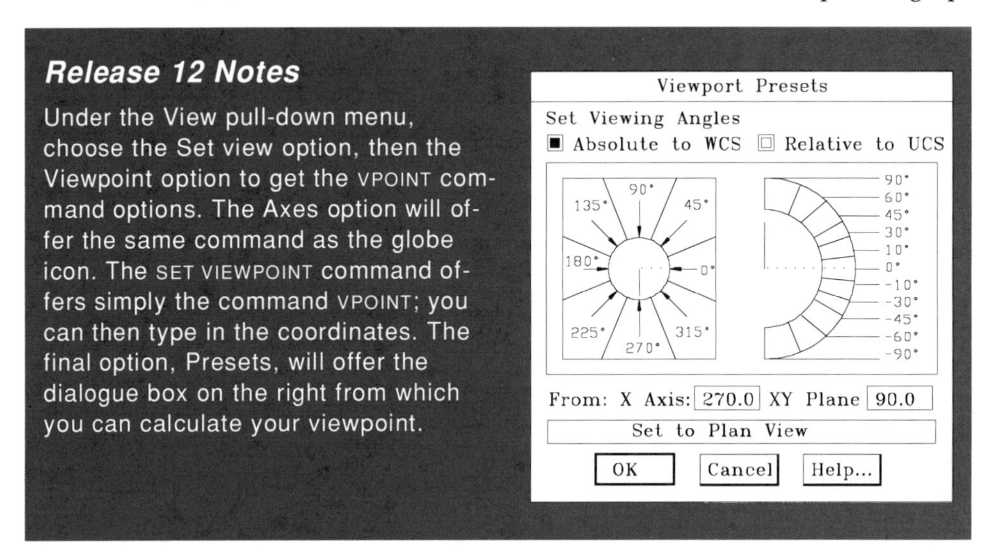

Release 12 Notes

Under the View pull-down menu, choose the Set view option, then the Viewpoint option to get the VPOINT command options. The Axes option will offer the same command as the globe icon. The SET VIEWPOINT command offers simply the command VPOINT; you can then type in the coordinates. The final option, Presets, will offer the dialogue box on the right from which you can calculate your viewpoint.

3D GEOMETRY

Keep in mind that you are creating a model, not a drawing.

What we are going to be doing is using the geometry and editing commands we already know to develop parts in 3D. This will start you thinking in 3D and you will be well on the way to creating parts that can be cut out of metal or analysed.

While working in 2D, you were able to enter points in three distinct fashions:

1. coordinate entry — absolute, incremental, and polar,

2. selecting a portion of an existing item, and

3. picking a point in space.

While in 3D, these concepts remain the same, but you are much more dependent upon points since the object is more complicated and is viewed from a variety of angles. Now that you have your screen set up, let us create the object in Figure 25-13. First we will enter the lines on the Z = 0 plane.

```
Command:LINE
From point:0,0
To point:5,0
To point:5,2
To point:4,2
To point:4,4
To point:0,4
To point:c
```

```
Command:LINE
From point:0,0
To point:@5,0
To point:@0,2
To point:@-1,0
To point:@0,2
To point:@-4,0
To point:c
```

You could also set your grid and snap and enter the above points by picking the appropriate points on the screen.

Now that the first plane is in, you can enter the second plane in a variety of ways. The first way is to simply incorporate the Z-depth in the LINE command. With incremental entries, if the Z axis does not change, you do not need to include it.

```
Command:LINE
From point:0,0,3
To point:5,0,3
To point:5,2,3
To point:4,2,3
To point:4,4,3
To point:0,4,3
To point:c
```

```
Command:LINE
From point:0,0,3
To point:@5,0
To point:@0,2
To point:@-1,0
To point:@0,2
To point:@-4,0
To point:c
```

This would draw the geometry on the Z = 3 plane. An easier way would be to use the COPY command.

```
Command:COPY
Select objects:W (pick 1, pick 2, pick everything)
Select objects:↵
<Base point or displacement>/Multiple: (pick 3)
Second point of displacement:@0,0,3
```

This will copy everything to the Z = 3 plane.

To complete the part, set your OSNAP to END and enter lines from the ends of the lines on one plane to the ends of the lines on the next plane.

You may notice that if you do not set your OSNAP to END(*point*), your plan view will be a mess. This occurs because when you are working in a rotated 3D or isometric view, the points you pick on the screen will be created on the Z = 0 plane. While lines may look as if they are properly placed from the isometric view, even a slight turn of the part or a view of it from a different angle will show that it does not work.

In order to access items on a different plane, you must use OSNAP or type in the full coordinates, including Z.

Now we have completed a fairly simple exercise, let us work on a more complex one.

Example: *Entering Wireframe Geometry*

It is a very good idea to set up the viewports and viewpoint again. Start a new drawing, set two viewports and rotate the 3D view at 2,-2,2. The Z axis will again be pointing up. We will start from Z = 0.

```
Command:LINE
From point:0,0
To point:4,0
To point:4,2
To point:6,2
To point:6,4
To point:0,4
To point:0,0
```

Now that the Z = 0 plane is in, extend the next lines vertically from the endpoints, and you can see the distance in positive Z.

```
Command:LINE
From point: (pick point A)
To point:@0,0,2
```

Points A and B are on Z = 0, you can pick them on the screen if your snap is on. You can also use END or INT to pick them up or simply type in the coordinates.

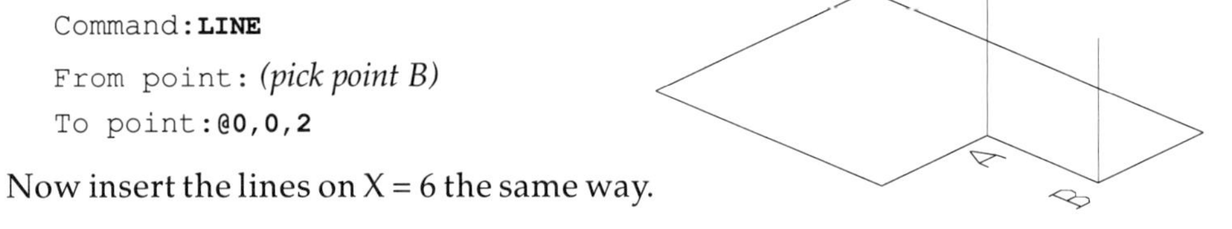


```
Command:LINE
From point: (pick point B)
To point:@0,0,2
```

Now insert the lines on X = 6 the same way.

```
Command:LINE
From point:6,4,0
To point:@0,0,3
To point:@-6,0,0
To point:@0,0,-3

Command:LINE
From point:6,4,3
To point:@0,-1,0
Command:LINE
From point:0,4,3
To point:@0,-1,0
```

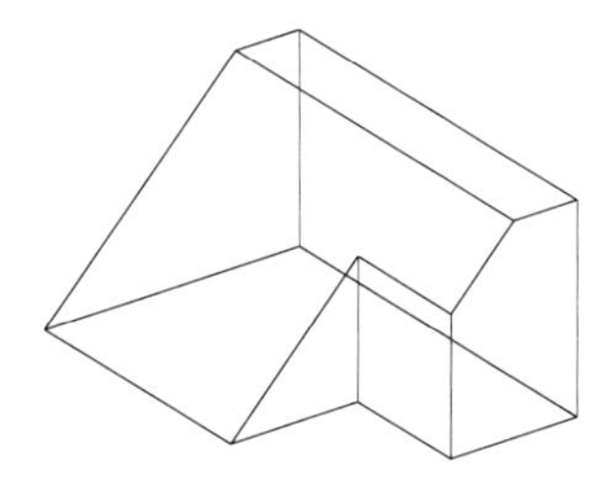

Now just join the points together to make a finished part.

If the point you are accessing is not on Z = 0, make sure you access points with an OSNAP or type in the coordinates. If not, you will not be accessing the correct Z-depth.

When entering information by means of the accepted coordinate systems, type in the values as before; the third entry will be the Z-depth. Using incremental entries is no problem in either geometry or editing commands.

While working on a part, keep in mind that the display commands work only in the current viewport. ZOOM and PAN work very well, as do the others. If you want to redraw the viewports, you can use REDRAWALL.

If you lose the geometry in any one view, use ZOOM All to retrieve it. If you are completely lost, U will undo the past commands.

EXERCISES

On the following two pages are 20 simple shapes. You will find that your success in AutoCAD, particularly in the 3D area, is directly related to the amount of time you spend practising. Think of each line in terms of where it is. What are the coordinates? Should OSNAP be used? Do not forget LIST.

STEP 1
For each part, set your viewports to either 2, 3, or 4.

STEP 2
Use VPOINT to orient your views. You may want to use 2, -1.5, 1.5 if your lines are overlapping.

STEP 3
Use DRAW and EDIT commands to enter the geometry.

Release 12 Notes

The icon menus have been updated to allow for greater space for the image on screen, and to allow for further customizing by the user.

In the VPORTS icon menu there are the 12 layouts offered in earlier versions, plus there are eight spaces left for the user specified viewport configurations. Once the viewports have been configured, left-top-iso-right, the viewport can be saved and put into this menu. For further information see Chapter 20.

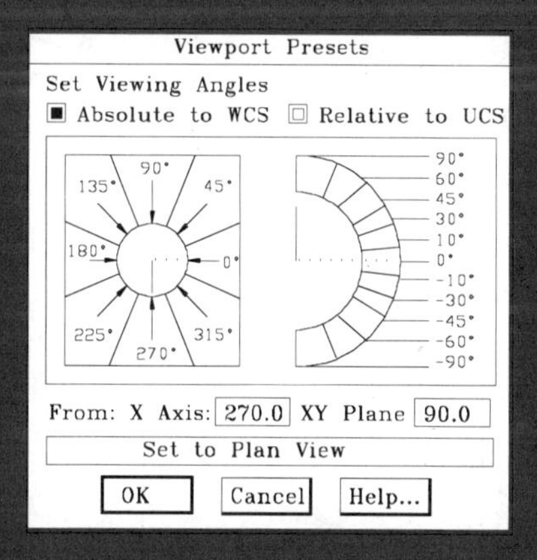

As with other Release 12 icon menus, the user can either pick the icon itself or the name for the vport configuration from the listing on the left.

Exercises All

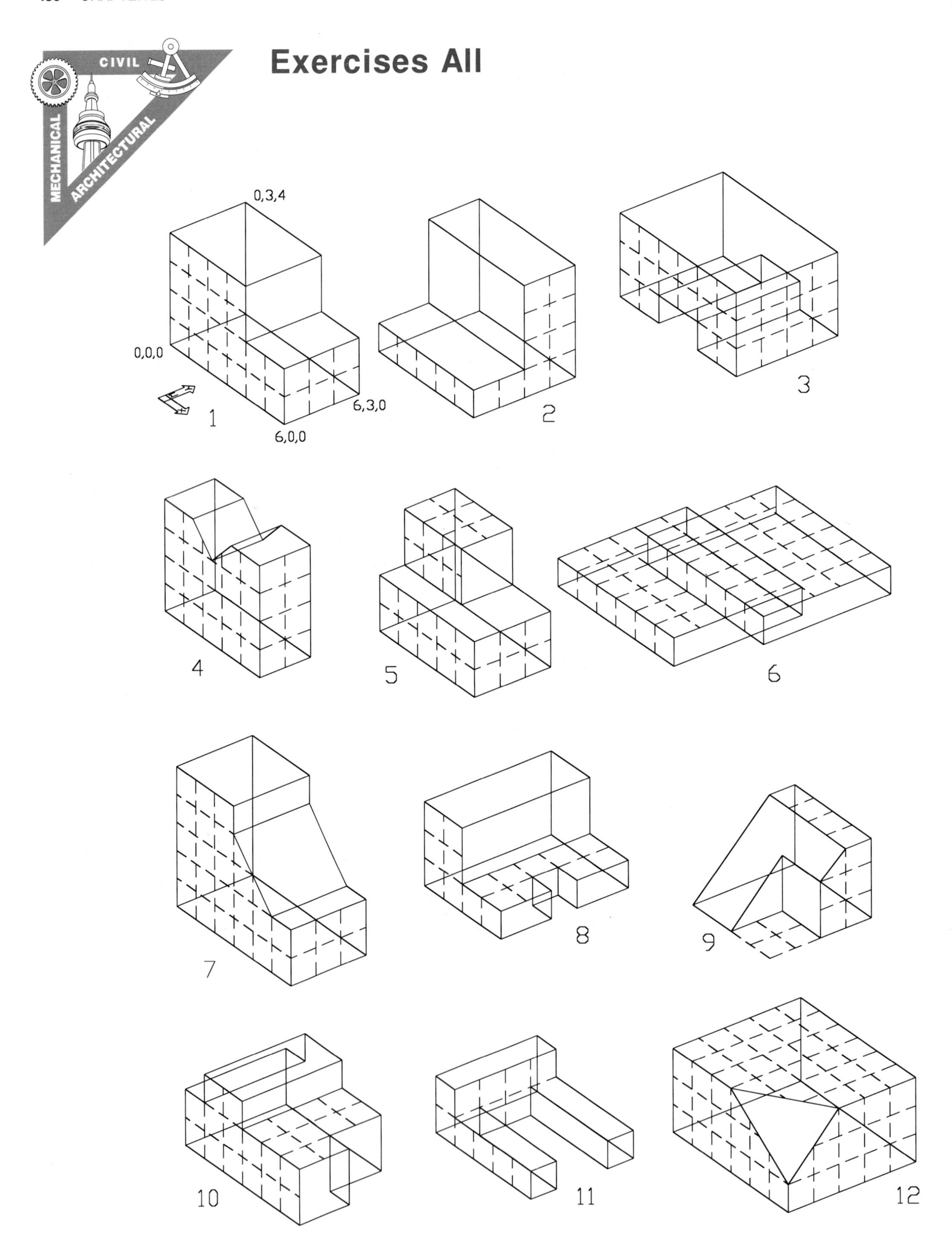

Exercises All (continued)

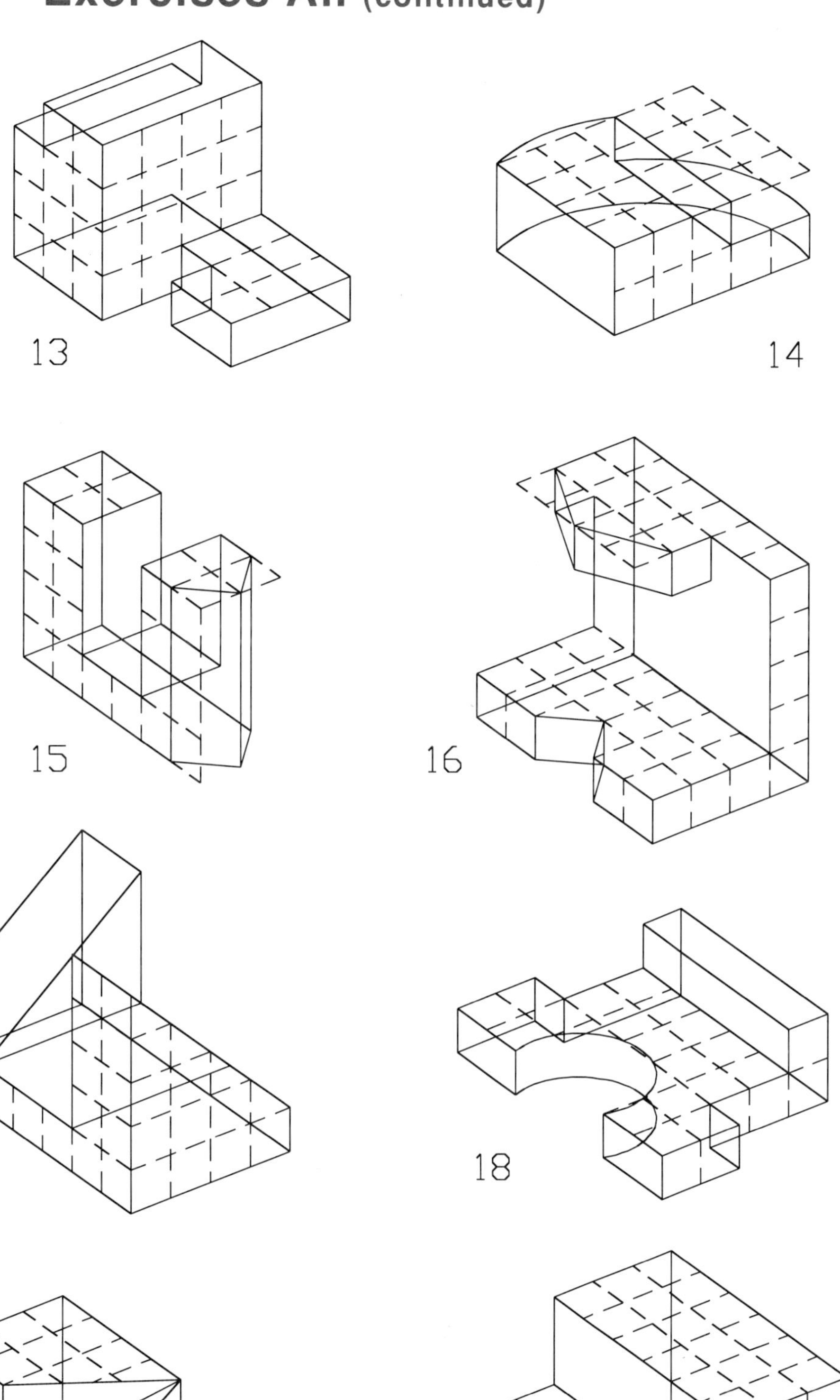

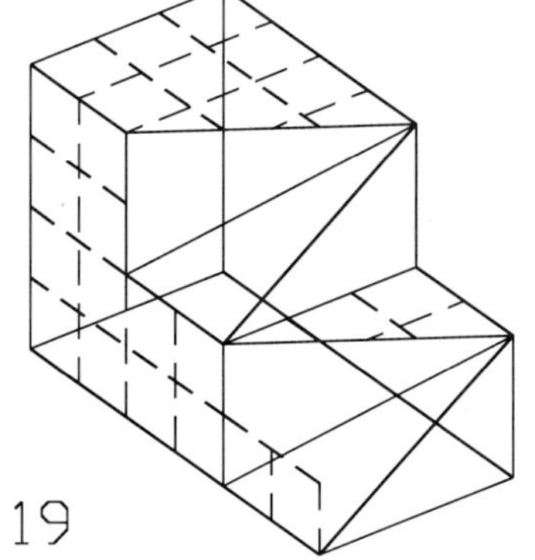

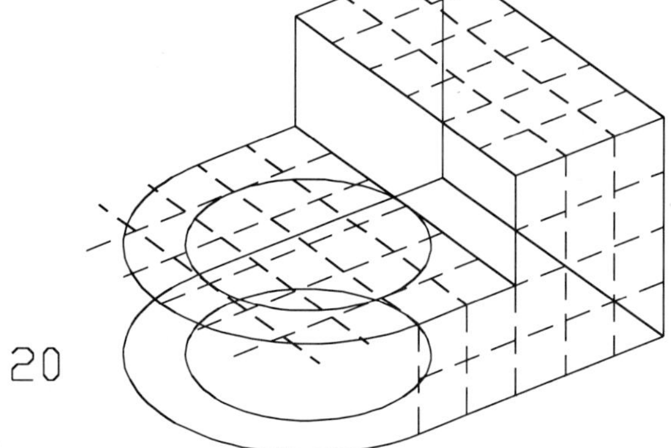

Challenger 25

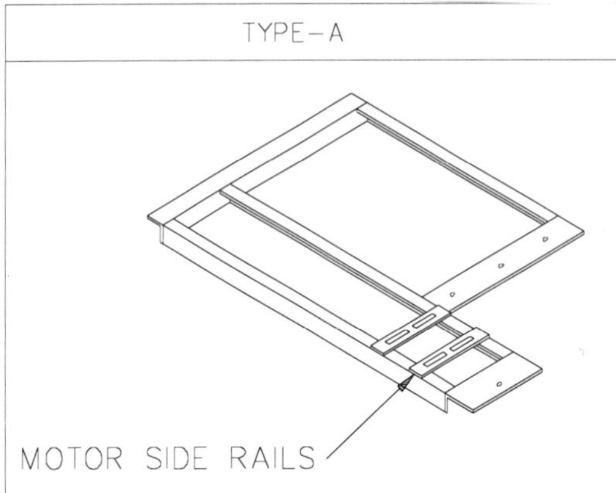

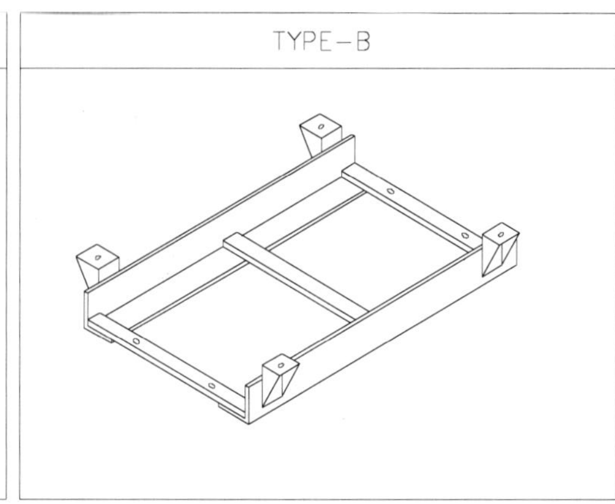

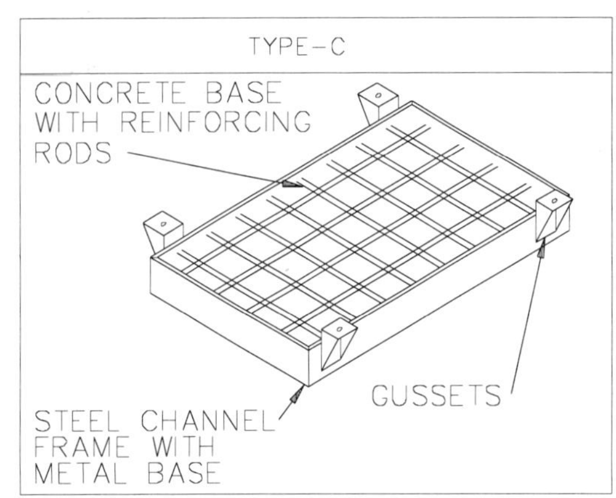

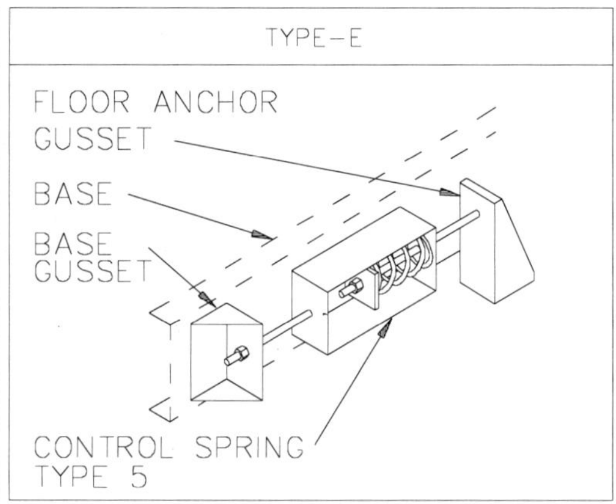

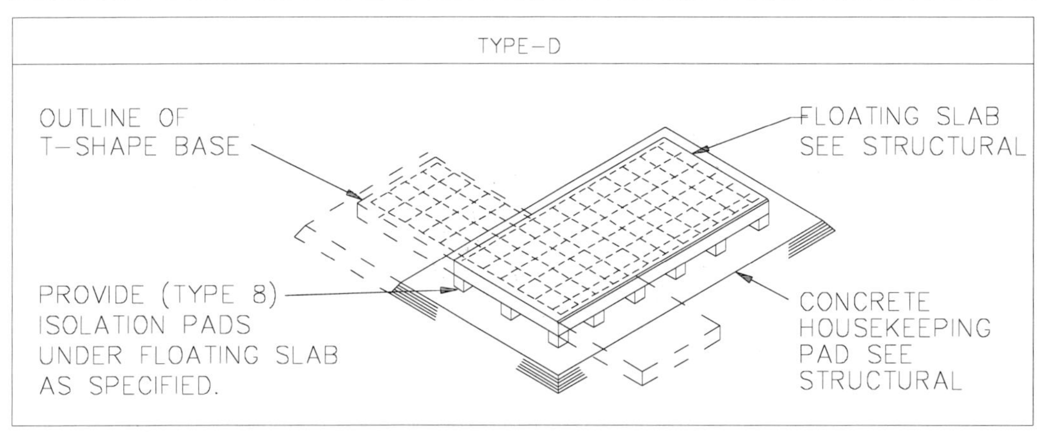

Create these roof sections with the proper annotation in the view. These should be created in wireframe.

(Many thanks to UMA for this drawing.)

EXTRUDING 2D SHAPES INTO 3D SHAPES

Upon completion of this chapter, the student should be able to:

1. Extrude a 2D image using THICKNESS
2. Change elevation to make objects 3D
3. Use HIDE to create an image with hidden lines
4. Save and restore viewports

GENERATING 3D IMAGES

The previous chapter was developed as a basis for all 3D, but also to give an indication of the correct way to develop items if your intention is to add surfacing, solids, and anything else leading to production. For a part to be produced through CAM, stereolithography, or other 3D part production tools, the part must be completely described in 3D space.

If your application is not mechanical, and you have no intention of producing a 3D model in the near future, you still need to consider the data as being "fully described" for analysis and area programs to work.

Not far down the road we will be seeing a lot of model production for architecture, site planning, and development downloaded from AutoCAD data. The production of a model is entirely dependent on the integrity of the design, be it an automotive, a development, or an architectural model.

If you are interested at this point in developing images in 3D for primarily display purposes, there are several tools that will generate a very agreeable and useful image. The easiest process is an extrusion of the data, developed on the X-Y plane to a specified Z depth.

Any 2D image can be extruded along the Z axis using the ELEV and THICKNESS commands. The 3D image will be similar to that produced with a specified amount of dough and a cookie cutter. The effects of the extrusions can be viewed using the VPORTS and VPOINT commands.

The command you would use is ELEV. The two options are:

ELEVATION sets or changes the Z depth

THICKNESS actually extrudes or expands the data along the Z axis

> ***Release 12 Notes***
> The ELEV command has not changed in Release 12.

ELEV lets you set a current elevation to your drawing. If you were making a house, the bottom ledge of the windows would be elevated to 24 inches or 36 inches or whatever the starting height would be; the thickness of the window would be the actual height of the window itself.

THICKNESS adds an extrusion thickness to objects.

Elevation is measured from the X-Y plane, thickness is measured from the elevation.

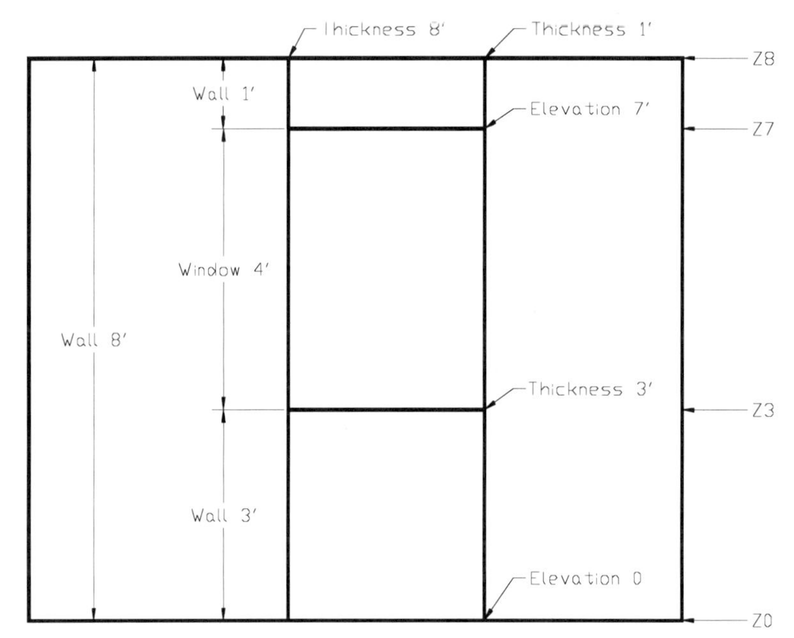

Figure 26-1. Using ELEVATION and THICKNESS

In the wall in Figure 26-1, you can see that the first panel is put in at an elevation of 0′ with a thickness of 8′.

In the middle section, the wall supporting the window is at an elevation of 0′ with a thickness of 3′.

The upper portion of the wall is put in at an elevation of 7′ and a thickness of 1′, taking the height of the wall to 8′.

The upper and lower sections of the wall containing the window are separate objects; either two lines or two plines.

USING ELEVATION AND THICKNESS

There are two ways of using ELEV and THICKNESS. The first is to draw everything onto the Z = 0 plane, then use CHANGE or CHPROP to change the thickness, and MOVE to get the object to the correct elevation. The second is to set the ELEVATION and THICKNESS, then draw the information in.

Changing Existing Geometry

If you have a plan view of an object and wish to create a 3D model, simply pick the objects and use CHANGE or CHPROP to alter the thickness, and you will be prompted to choose what you want to change.

To change the pline for the upper wall section of Figure 26-1, use:

Release 12 Notes

The Elev option has been reinstated into the CHANGE command.

```
Command: CHANGE
Select objects: (pick the items to change)
Properties/<change point>: P
Change What property (Color/LAyer/LType/Thickness): T
New Thickness <0.0000>: 1
Change What property (Color/LAyer/LType/Thickness): ↵
```

If the objects are *not* showing up where expected, look at your plan view. A common error is to pick points in the isometric view. These will be "line-of-sight" on the Z = 0 plane and may not be in the correct position.

Once you have changed the thickness of the items, move them to the correct elevation.

```
Command:MOVE
Select objects: (pick the objects to move)
Base point: (pick anywhere on Z = 0)
Displacement:@0,0,7
```

This will move the objects to an elevation or Z depth of 7.

Setting Up Elevation and Thickness for New Geometry

The second way to use ELEV and THICKNESS is to preset the values. You can simply type in ELEV to get a prompt that will change both the elevation and thick values.

ELEV

ELEV will set or change the Z depth of an item. It refers to the base Z coordinate or the Z value under LIST. The elevation is relative to the current X-Y plane and thus changes with the UCS (see Chapter 27). After you set the elevation, all objects constructed will have the elevation or Z value chosen. To date, all of the geometry you have constructed has been at an elevation of 0.

```
Command:ELEV
New Current Elevation <0.000>:↵ (accepts 0 as a base)
New current Thickness <0.000>:3 (makes 3 the thickness)
```

To change only the thickness, use THICKNESS.

THICKNESS

To set the thickness of items prior to creating them, use ELEV or THICKNESS. This is used when every item you create is to be the same thickness.

As with ELEV, resetting THICKNESS does not affect items already drawn; it just sets the variable for objects being entered.

```
Command:THICKNESS
New current Thickness <0.000>:5 (makes 5 the thickness)
```

In Release 9 or 10, you can find Thickness only under SETVARS.

```
Command:SETVAR
Variable name or ?:Thickness
New value for THICKNESS <0.0000>:1
```

SETVAR changes the system variables of a drawing. For more information on SETVARs, see page 378.

EXAMPLE: *Elevation and Thickness*

Let us try setting up a screen and then try some elevations.

Set VPORTS to two viewports.

Set VPOINT to PLAN and 2,-2,2.

Now change the elevation as above to 1 and the thickness to 5.

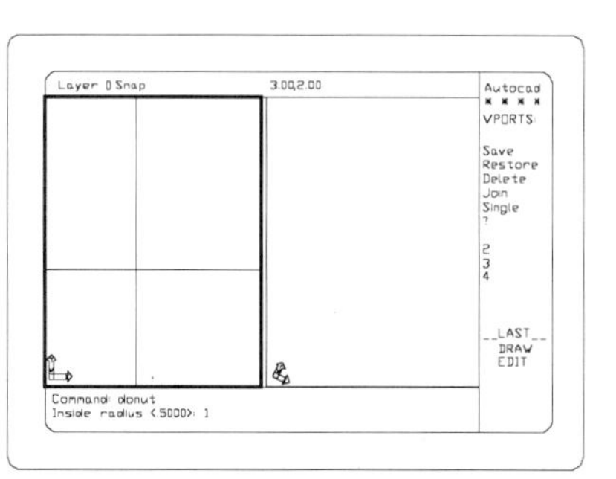

Draw in a single line, four lines in a square, a circle, a donut, and a pline.

Notice how the items show up in the isometric view. Note that it may be easier to place them if you keep your snap on.

The objects should look like Figure 26-2.

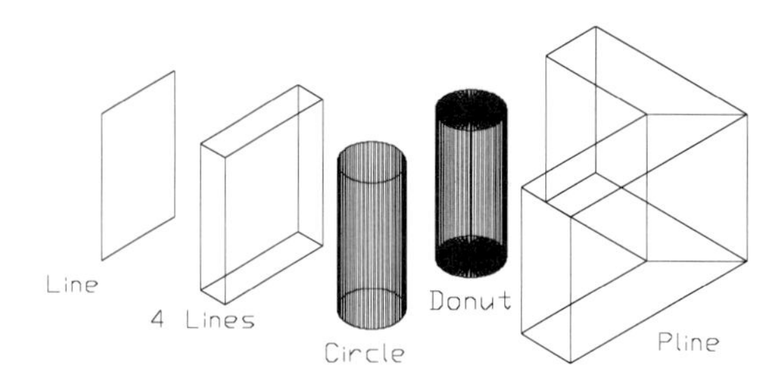

Figure 26-2. Objects drawn with a Thickness

They will have a Z depth of 5 and should start with a Z value of 1.

A negative value will extrude down from the elevation value, which in this case is 0.

To check that the items are entered correctly, use LIST.

Now let us observe what happens to these objects when the HIDE command is used. Pick the isometric viewport and make it current. Then pick the HIDE command under the Display menu or just type it in.

HIDE

HIDE allows a part to be viewed with all the hidden lines removed. In 3D construction, a wireframe of the model is created. This allows the designer to create the part from its base geometry. If the user also wants the part to be viewed as a traditional isometric view, then all lines that would be hidden in the "Iso" must be removed. These can be removed from a complex model using 3DFACE and then HIDE, or, if the designer has planned the part for this kind of view and not for production, THICKNESS and HIDE can be used.

```
Command:HIDE
Removing hidden lines:
```

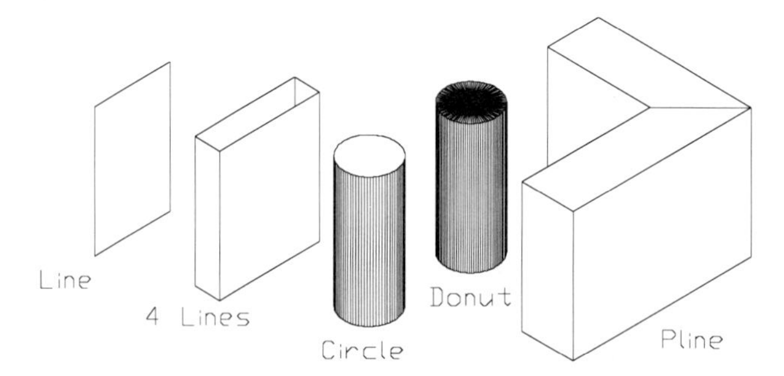

Figure 26-3. Objects after the HIDE command

HIDE is a very simple command to use — the trick is in using it at the correct time. You will note that the number of lines hidden is displayed by HIDE. The drawing is being mathematically reconstructed with regard to the number of hidden lines. If HIDE is selected when the part is not properly rotated or all the required objects are not displayed, this command is a real time-waster.

Once objects are hidden, they will remain hidden only until the view is regenerated by using either REGEN or any of the Display commands that regenerate the screen, such as PAN and ZOOM.

HIDE and LAYERS

HIDE affects objects on layers that are turned off. You may have lines obscured by objects that are not on-screen; the objects are on layers that have been turned off. HIDE will not affect objects on layers that are frozen, however; so freeze layers instead of turning them off to avoid complications.

If you want to identify the hidden lines with a different colour and control their display, create a layer called HIDDENXXXXX, XXXXX being the name of the layer for hidden lines (for example, Layer ROOF and Layer HIDDENROOF). Then, any hidden objects will display on the identified HIDDENLAYER in the specified colour. This will not work on the PLOT command.

HIDE and PLOT

You may have noticed a "Remove hidden lines" option in the PLOT command. If you use this option, it will take a long time to calculate the hidden lines. If you are using Release 10, this is your only choice. If you are using Release 11 or higher, use the HIDEPLOT option under DVIEW.

EXAMPLE: *Hide and Plot*

Let us try a real part and see the effect. We will use the example from M7.

The object in Figure 26-4 was created using FILLET and CIRCLE.

Retrieve the file and Freeze the dimensions layer. If you have not got a different layer for dimensions, make one and change them to it.

Use at least two viewports to view the object from plan and iso.

Now use CHANGE to change the thickness and MOVE to change the elevation of the objects.

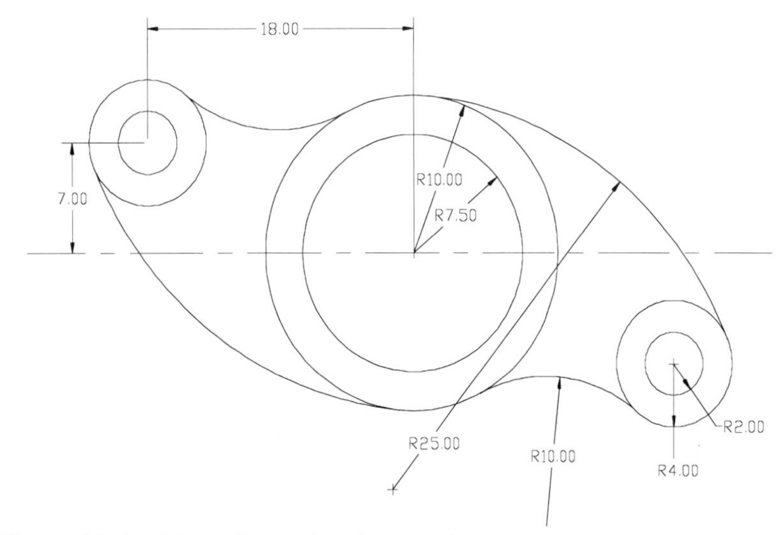

Figure 26-4. A two-dimensional example

Release 12 Notes

Use the CHANGE or CHPROP command to alter both the thickness and the elevation. MOVE is not necessary.

```
Command:CHANGE
Select objects: (pick the two outer circles on each end)
Select objects:↵
Properties <change point>:P
Change What property (Color/LAyer/LType/Thickness):T
New Thickness <0.0000>:10
Change What property (Color/LAyer/LType/Thickness):↵
Command:MOVE
Select objects: (pick the same objects)
Select objects:↵
Base Point: (pick anywhere)
Displacement:@0,0,4
```

Finish off the part using CHANGE or CHPROP and MOVE in the same way to extrude all the cylinders.

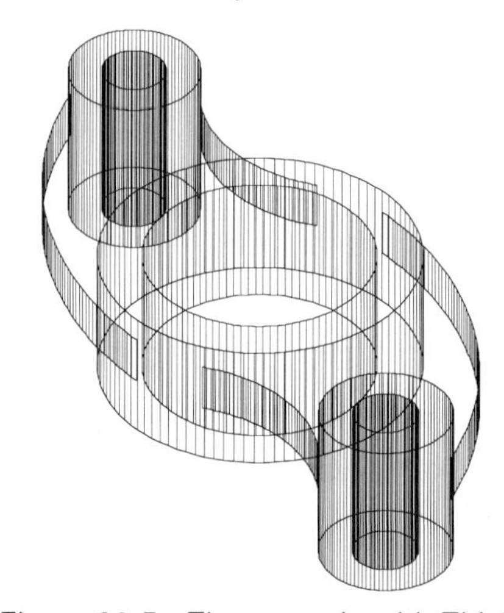

Figure 26-5. The example with Thickness

This will change the thickness of the objects as you see them and give you a view of what the part may look like in 3D. The cylinders are complete, but the surface between the cylinders is not fully described. The illustration in Figure 26-4 should now look like Figure 26-5.

To generate a 3D from a 2D, create the plan view of the item in the X-Y view. Then set the elevation and thickness for each object. The elevation is the absolute Z value and the thickness is the incremental distance or the value of the Z depth of the item from the smallest Z value to the largest.

You can either set these factors as you are designing or change certain items once they are entered.

To gain a better understanding of how completely an object needs to be described, let us hide the part.

Note that the two objects are rendered differently using circles or donuts (see Figure 26-6). The donut will surface the top section of the three cylinders but the circles will not.

The extruded end is also only in one direction, or open-ended.

CIRCLE and DONUT can both be used for circular or cylindrical shapes; the circle will have a closed top, and the donut will have a thick wall, or a top with a midpoint.

It is still only a partially described model, however, as not all the shapes are defined by surfaces. The THICKNESS command is useful to give us an idea of what the object may look like, but, without using surfaces, you can't cut it. If you finish early, you may want to create mesh surfaces using REVSURF and EDGESURF to complete the object.

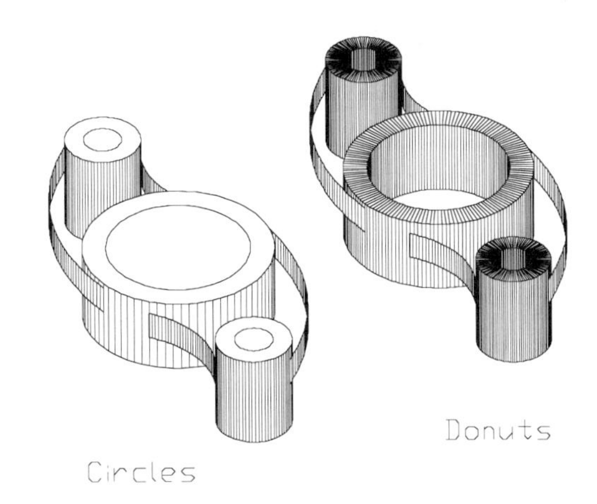

Figure 26-6. Circles and donuts with HIDE

LINE and PLINE build objects in 3D as planes. We will see in later chapters that they are less flexible than other methods, but, for display purposes, they are very useful commands.

After these exercises, you should have a much better understanding of 3D and how it works.

VPOINT

VPOINT, as seen in the previous chapter, allows an object to be viewed from any angle. You used the default in the last exercise to set the VPOINT relative to the origin. You should be aware that you can also rotate the view around the various axes.

```
Command:VPOINT
Rotate/<view point>:R
Enter angle in X-Y plane from X axis <current angle>:
Enter angle from X-Y plane <current angle>:
```

Enter a number for the angle or by entering points on the screen.

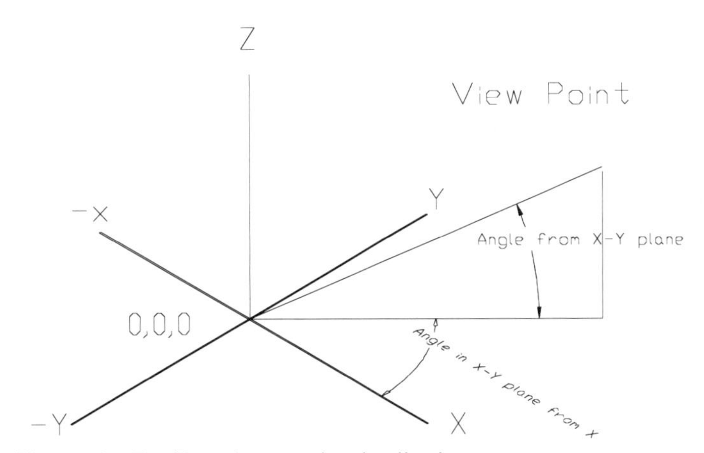

Figure 26-7. Rotation angles in display

Remember that the VPOINT command does not control the distance from the object, only the angle at which you will view it.

If you have defined a viewpoint that could be useful to you later, you can save the viewpoint by naming it.

```
Command:VIEW
?/Delete/Restore/Save/Window:SAVE
View name to save:ISO
```

The other options of the VIEW command are:

?	*lists the views stored with this model.*
DELETE	*deletes identified views.*
RESTORE	*restores a named view.*
SAVE	*names and saves a view.*
WINDOW	*names and saves a window from the view.*

When you save and restore a view, updates to the model will be shown on the updated view.

SAVING VPORTS AND A VPORT CONFIGURATION

The VPORTS command allows an object to be viewed from many different angles at the same time. The data seen in one view is the same as the data seen in the next view from a different angle.

If you have your views set up in a manner useful to you, you can save them and give them a name. Then, when you want to bring the viewport configuration back, you simply use Restore and enter the name of the configuration.

The VIEW command is used to name and save one view of the model. The VPORTS command can name and save a configuration of views. To save a viewport configuration, use the following.

```
Command:VPORTS
Save/Restore/Delete/Join/SIngle/?/2/3/4:S
?/Name for new viewport configuration:4QUAD
```

This will store the current configuration of four viewports under the name 4QUAD.

```
Command:VPORTS
Save/Restore/Delete/Join/SIngle/?/2/3/4:SI
```

This will create a single viewport containing the view of the model that is in the active viewport.

```
Command:VPORTS
Save/Restore/Delete/Join/SIngle/?/2/3/4:R
?/Name of viewport configuration to restore:4QUAD
```

This will restore the screen to four viewports containing the orientation of the views that were originally set up. The model will be updated in all views to contain all changes made while in the single view.

PICKING VIEWPORTS

During most draw commands you can pick the viewport within the command string. Within the display commands, however, you cannot. Be sure to pick the viewport before you activate the display commands.

PICKING OR DIGITIZING

When you are picking the screen, try to keep in mind the type of pick you are doing. Basically, there are three types of picks or digitizes.

1. Picking a point in space
When using this type of pick, you are entering a point "line-of-sight" onto the X-Y plane. If your snap is on, you can pick a point accurately to the snap integer. Without the snap on, your pick could be anywhere in the general area. If you are picking a point to describe an item (line, circle, ellipse), then you will probably want the snap on. If you are picking a point to describe a Window or Crossing, it will not matter if your snap is on.

2. Picking a portion of an existing object
When picking using osnap or Object Snap to describe an item, your pick will be very accurate. If your pick is not selecting the item you want, it could be because the aperture is too large. If so, change the size using the SETVAR command. If you are set to an osnap, you may find it will override a coordinate entry in a 3D isometric view. Turn the Osnap mode off if you are having difficulty entering coordinates and simply use OSNAP within the command.

3. Picking a Viewport
You need to pick a viewport in order to activate it. This pick can take place before the display commands or within the draw or edit commands. This pick will not pick up an item if used properly.

EXERCISES

Unless you have done 3D modelling in another system or are one of the 10 percent of people who truly thinks in 3D, you may find it takes some time to get used to the concepts and to be able to work around a model with any degree of confidence.

A good way to check that you are creating the geometry properly is to have at least two viewports going at all times and change the rotation of your isometric view every now and again just to make sure that all the ends meet where they are supposed to meet.

There are some people who find the concepts in Chapter 25 absolutely brutal. If this is the case for you, keep going. Your eyes will bring you to understand the concepts much more quickly than any reading on theory can. Do all of the exercises on the next few pages if you have time.

Practice 26

If you have time, try these practice exercises.

Create a caster like the one illustrated. Take the dimensions from Chapter 6.

Try using both CIRCLE and DONUT to enter the wheel itself. Use HIDE to make it look acceptable.

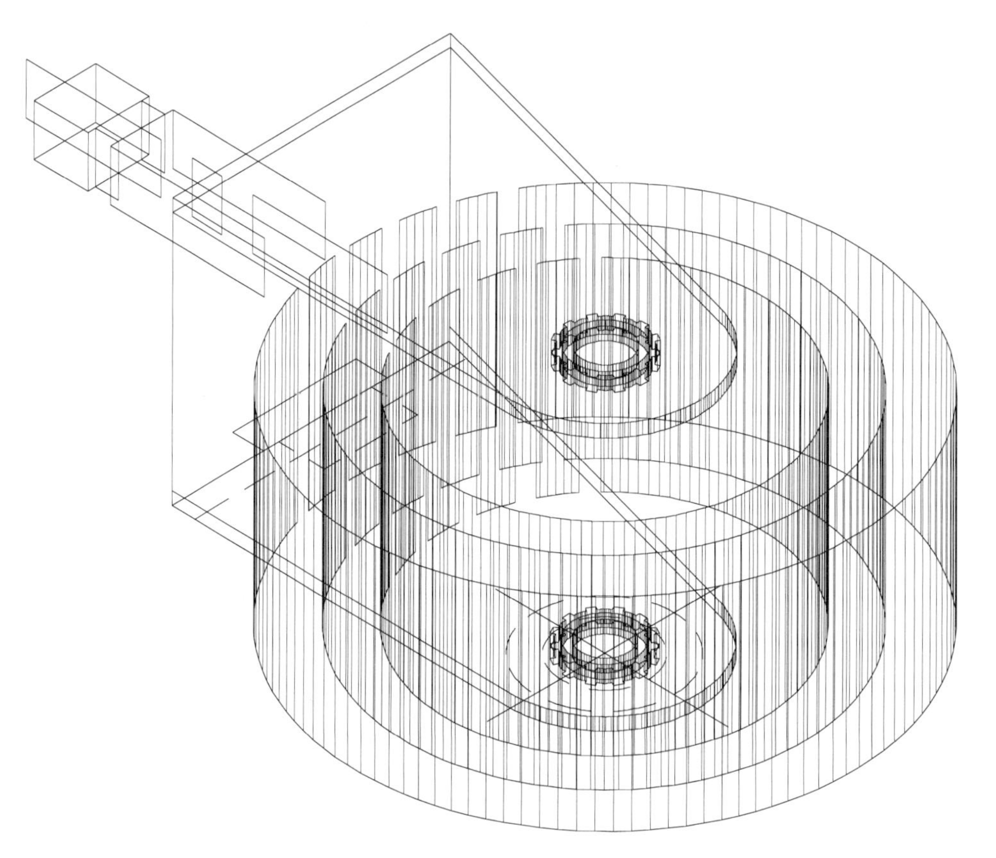

Practise on some smaller parts to see the difference between entering information with coordinates and then changing the thickness.

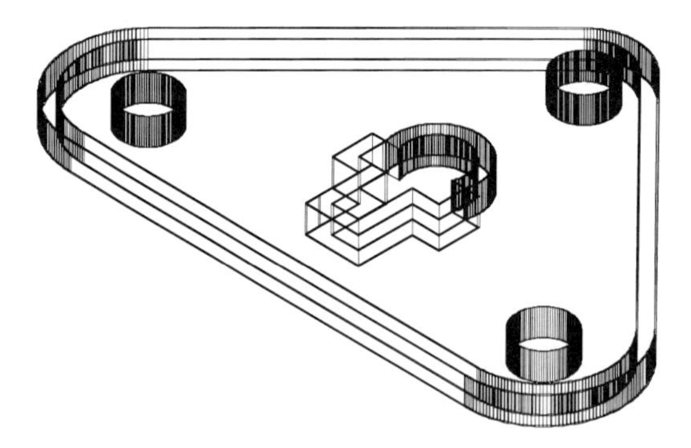

Try entering this information by setting THICKNESS before it is entered.

Practice 26 (continued)

Create the 3D pentagon as seen below using 3DFACE and a circle.

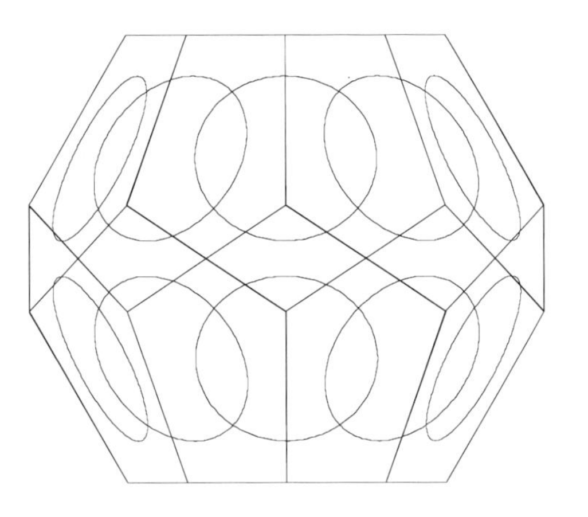

Plan View

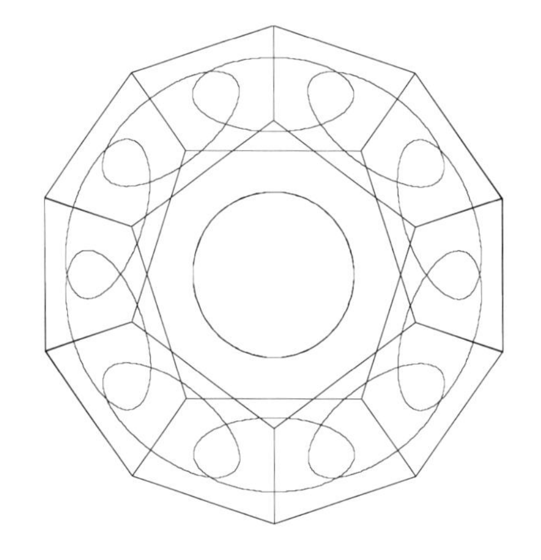

Front View

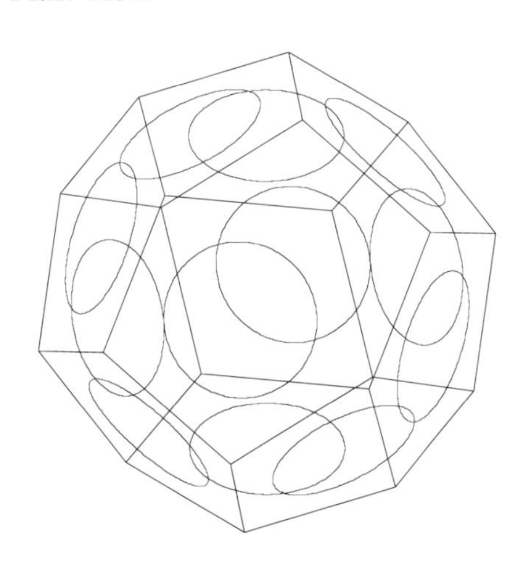

Iso View

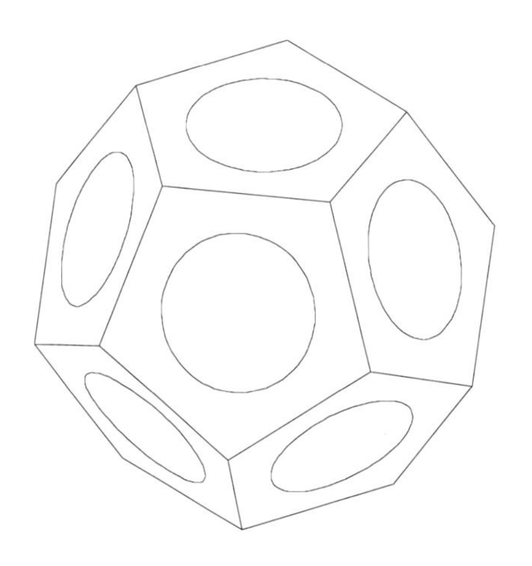

Iso View with HIDE

Exercise A26

Using PLINE, make a layout for the walls of a house. The walls should be 6 inches to 8 inches thick (.5 or .6 at 1 unit = 1 foot). Leave spaces for the windows.

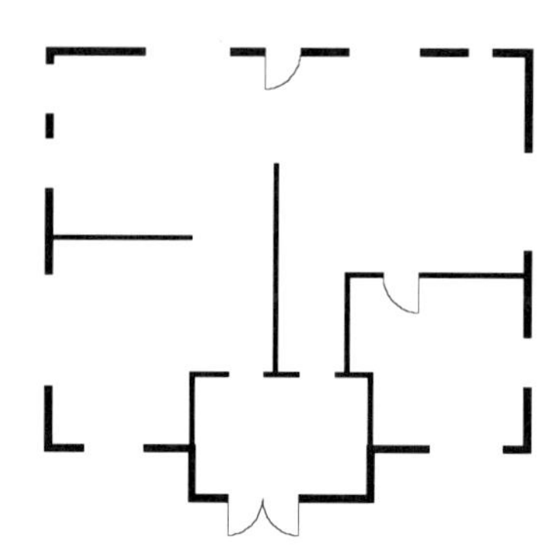

Change your viewports so that you have at least two. Orient one to plan and the other to 2,-2,2.

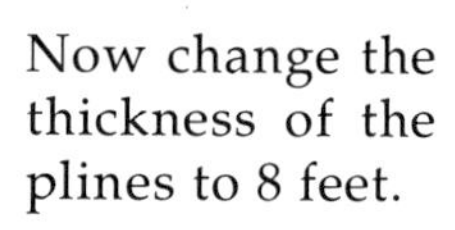

Now change the thickness of the plines to 8 feet.

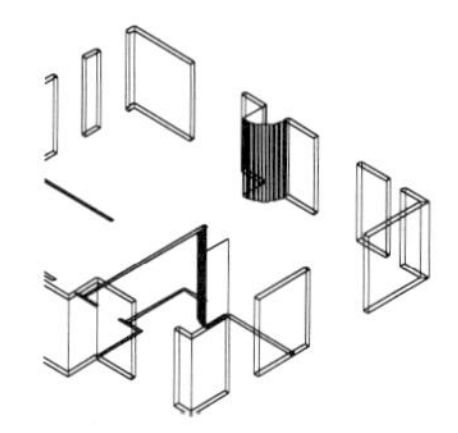

Using PLINE again, create the bottom of the walls underneath the windows.

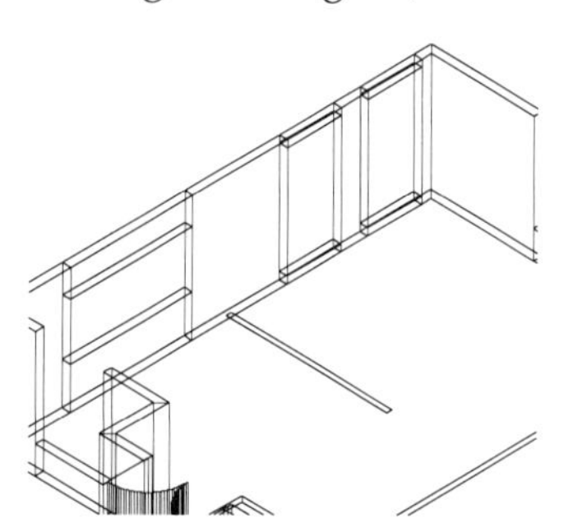

As the windows will all be different heights, set the thickness and elevation to different heights as you enter them.

Now copy those plines to a positive Z depth that will leave a space for the windows but line up with the top of the existing walls at 8 feet.

Note that you must add two different walls at different elevations or Z depths to get the wall spaces where the windows will be.

Use HIDE to view the image.

If you have time, advance to the challenger, or simply add a staircase or some kitchen or bathroom counters.

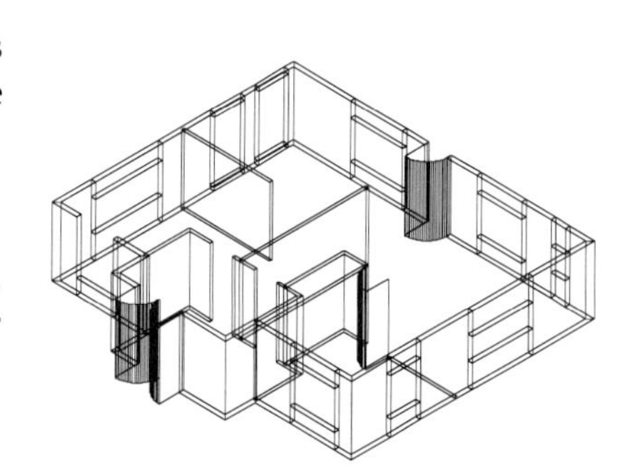

Exercise M26

Using the model from Exercise 7, change the thickness of the various components of the part.

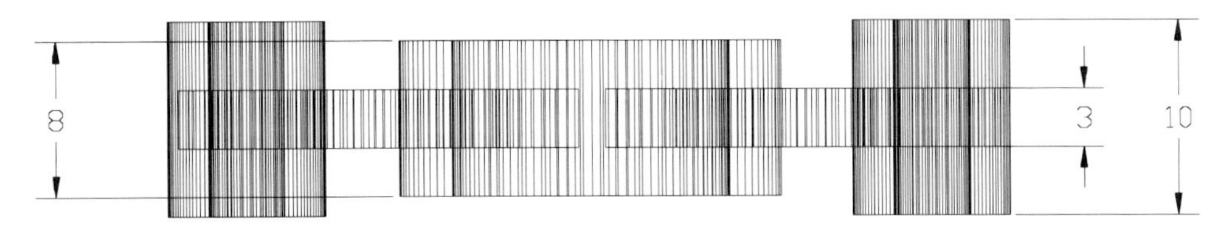

Once you have changed all the circles and arcs, try creating the same part using DONUT.

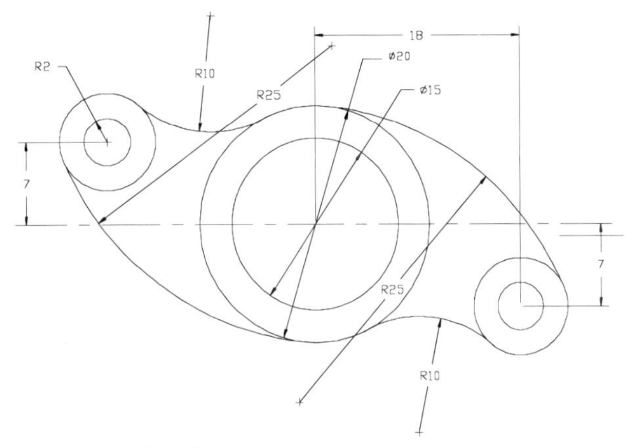

Note the differences in the data entered.

Try using HIDE on both parts to see the differences in the views, then try using both LINE and PLINE to create these two objects.

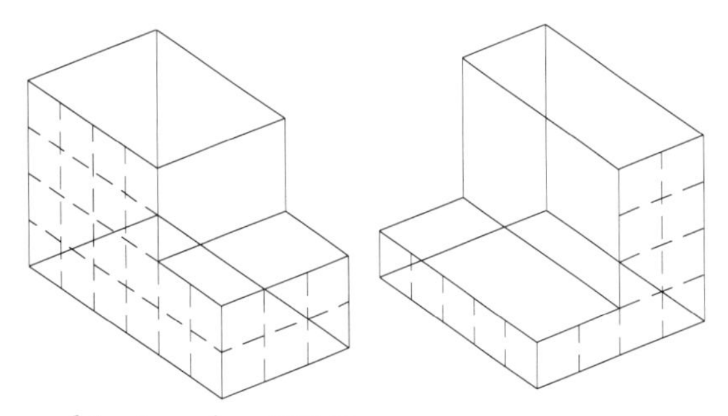

Now try the same objects using SOLID.

After the HIDE command, is there a difference in the final display of the objects?

Which method is the easiest to use?

Which method is the most practical?

Try the practice exercise if you are ready.

Exercise C26

Create a survey using PLINE and PEDIT for the contour lines. Then place the houses at the accepted setbacks as in the example. Add roads and services if you have time.

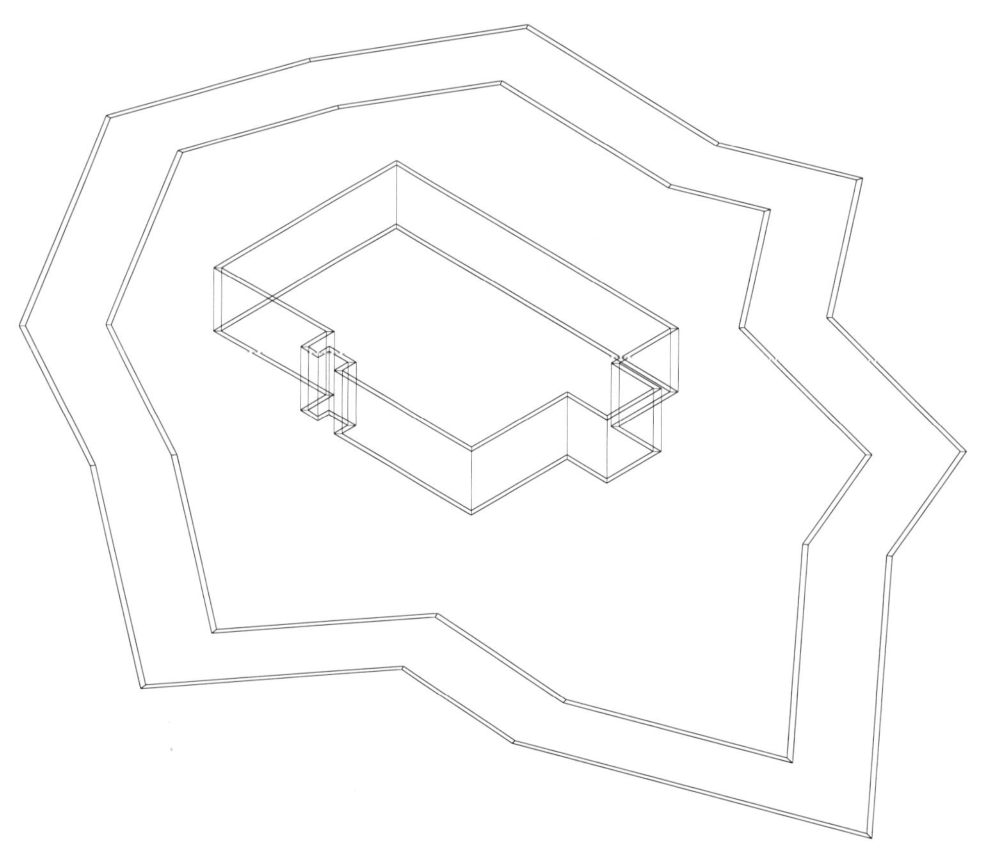

Keep changing the view to get your eyes used to working in 3D.

You can use the same house on each lot in this exercise, but if you do this in real life, people will know you have no creativity.

Challenger 26

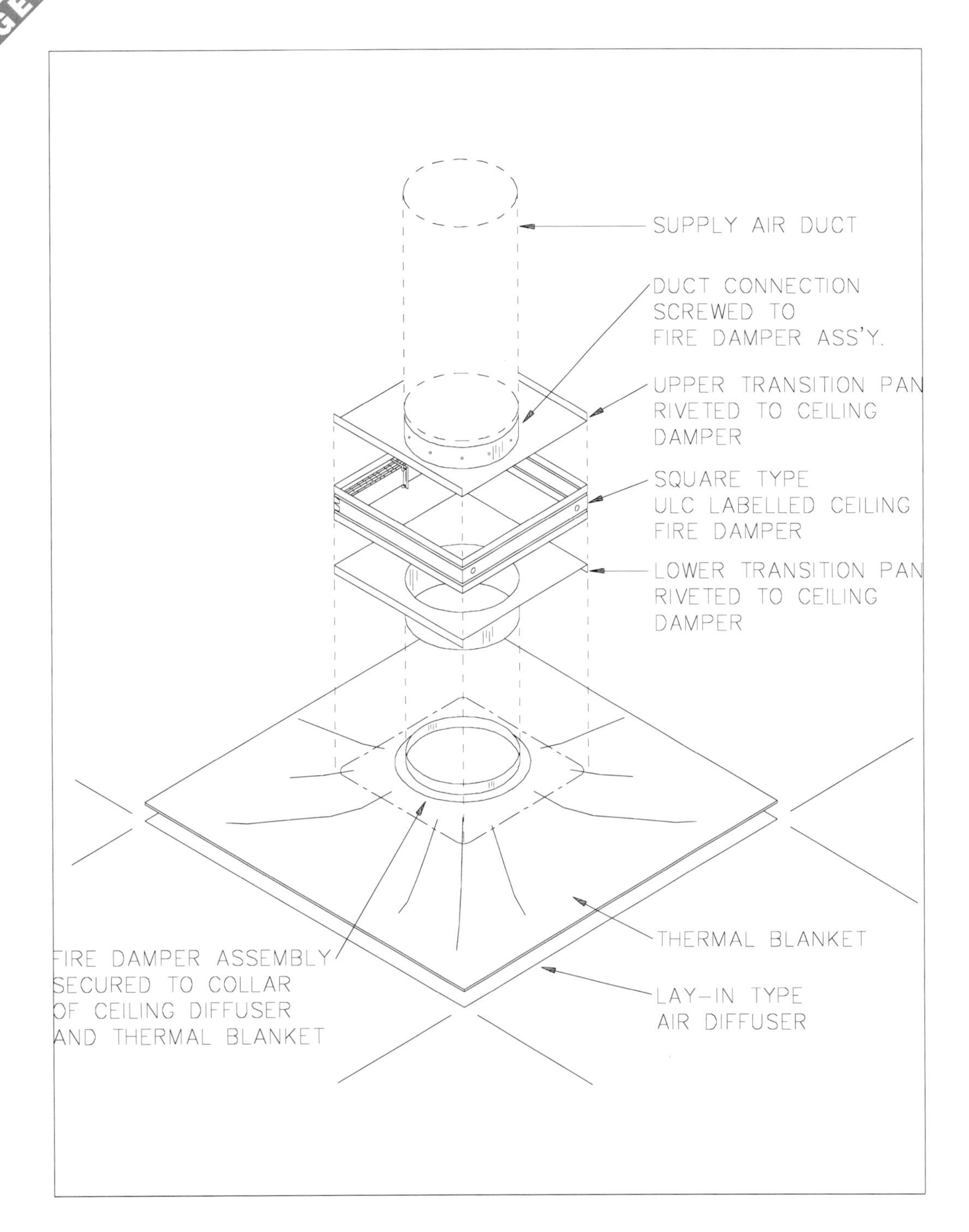

Use your own dimensions to create this object, and then add the notations normal to the viewing plane.

(Many thanks to UMA for this drawing.)

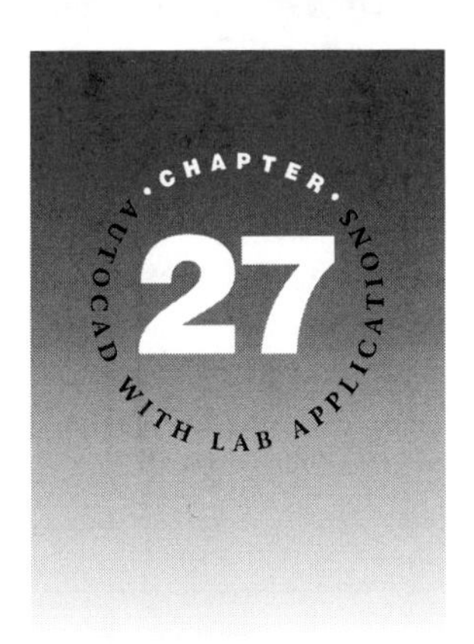

USER COORDINATE SYSTEM

Upon completion of this chapter, the student should be able to:

1. Set the User Coordinate System (UCS) wherever it is needed
2. Use the UCS dialogue box
3. Save a UCS
4. Create geometry on any given plane

You may have noticed while working with 3D models and images that any item with a defined radius such as an arc, an ellipse, or a circle could only be produced on the *X-Y* plane. This is because such items are planar by definition and may only be made relative to the *X-Y* plane.

Also, many of the editing commands such as ARRAY, ROTATE, OFFSET, FILLET are limited to the *X-Y* plane. They are calculated normal to or perpendicular to the *X-Y* plane.

ROTATE	*rotates around Z.*
ARRAY	*creates multiple copies along an X or a Y axis, never along Z because the calculation is normal to Z.*
OFFSET	*offsets along X or Y.*

Obviously you will want to access these commands in other planes, so AutoCAD developed the UCS so you can do this.

The User Coordinate System allows the user to reorient the X-Y plane and work relative to any identifiable portion of the part. The user identifies not only the plane, but the new temporary origin. The axes will always be identified from the origin according to positive X, Y, and Z.

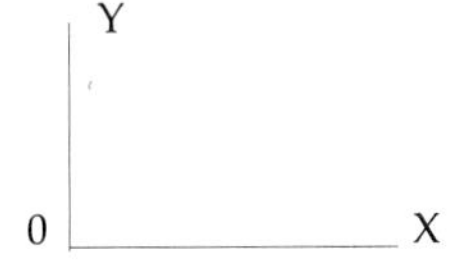

Figure 27-1. The X-Y plane and origin

Given this, positive Z will always be towards the user from the origin.

As most development in CAD is driven by the Numerical Control or manufacturing people, it makes sense that many CAD concepts are taken from this technology. A case in point is the concept of the Right-hand Rule which is derived from mechanical practices. The Right-hand Rule indicates that if positive X is heading from the origin to the right, and positive Y is heading from the origin straight up, then positive Z is heading towards the viewer.

This is referred to as the Right-hand Rule because you can use your right hand to illustrate the position of the axes on any given object.

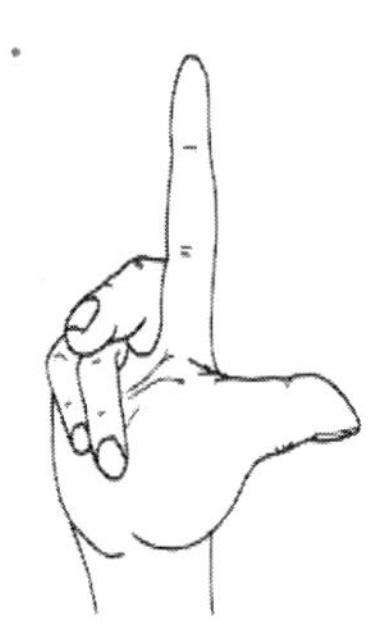

Figure 27-2. Fingers illustrating the right-hand rule

As you can see in Figure 27-2, the extended right thumb represents X, the-pointing index finger represents Y, and the middle finger when pointing out represents the proper position of Z every time.

You can rotate your hand around any way you want and it will still give you the correct position of Z.

If you are trying to find the position of positive Z, this is the quickest way to do it.

THE UCS ICON

When working in 3D, you are well advised to change the viewports and to use multiple viewports as specified in Chapter 25. In each oriented viewport, the UCS is specified by a UCS icon. This icon helps you visualize where the origin of the current UCS is. So far, it has always been the X-Y plane of the World view.

The current UCS refers to the current orientation of the X, Y, and Z axes. The UCS icon will echo this orientation, the cursor rotates as well to the plane of the UCS. The W on the icon stands for World. The other viewports will have a representation of either this same icon twisted to show the position of X and Y or another icon which represents a broken pencil. The icons show whether or not you can access the commands in that viewport.

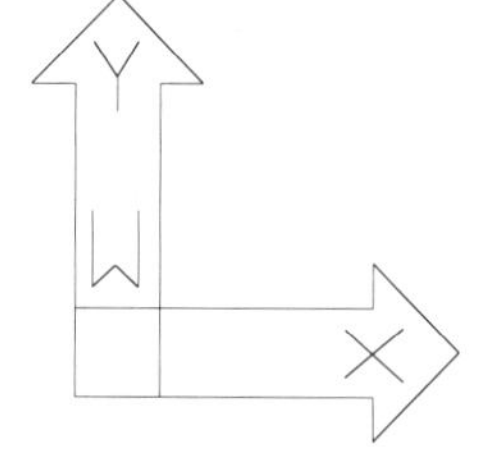

Figure 27-3. The UCS icon

If you have a viewport that contains a broken-pencil icon, you can indicate items within that viewport using the available osnaps, but you cannot pick a point in space because the X-Y plane is perpendicular to the screen and thus difficult to pick.

Remember that the point picked or digitized will always be placed line-of-sight onto the X-Y plane of whatever plane you are working in. If you pick a point in a plane where the X-Y icon is slanted, you will be indicating a point line-of-site from the screen onto the plane behind it. It is always a good idea to use OSNAP for anything but on your current X-Y plane.

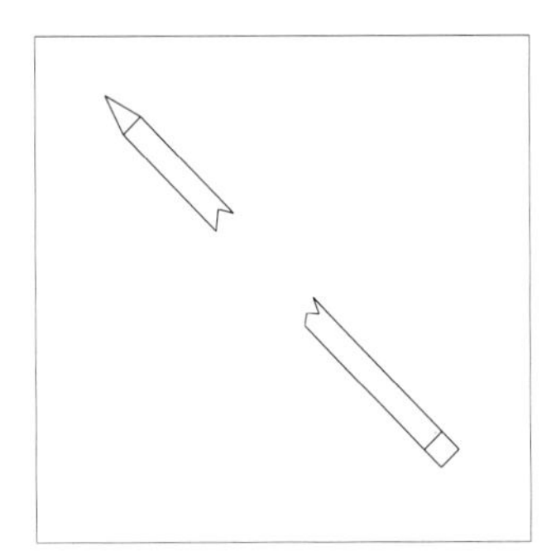

Figure 27-4. The broken pencil icon

While working with multiple viewports, you can see how, if all views are rotated, there is only one viewport with an X-Y icon perpendicular to your view.

The isometric view will have an icon at an angle, and, if two views are different from the X-Y plane (top or front), there will be two broken pencils.

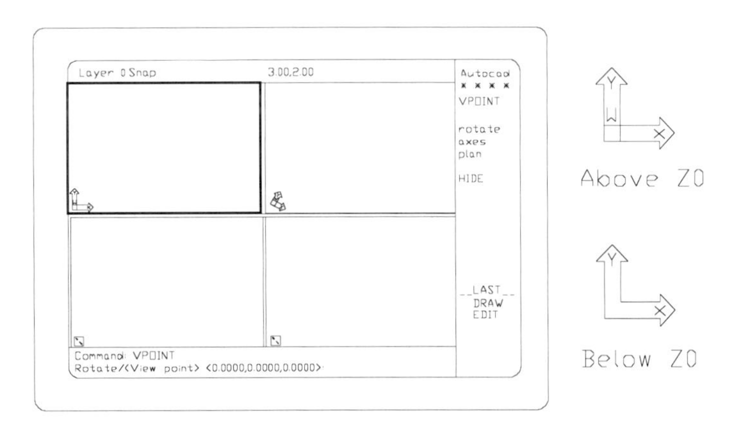

Figure 27-5. Icons within the viewports

When you change the UCS, the icon will change in every viewport to show the current UCS.

When we get to paper space in Chapter 30, you will notice another icon which is the paper space world coordinate icon.

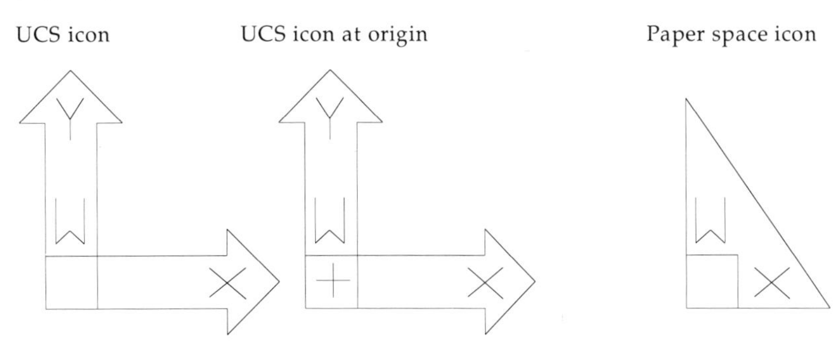

Figure 27-6. Icons illustrating different positions

In both the paper space icon and the model space icon, if there is a square in the bottom-left corner, as in Figure 27-5, it means you are looking down the positive-Z axis. If the box is missing, you are looking at the model from below or up the negative-Z axis.

Usually, the icon is placed on the bottom-left of the screen, but you can have it positioned on the current origin. The command for the icon is as follows:

```
Command:UCSICON
ON/OFF/All/Noorigin/Origin <ON>:OR
```

Where:
On toggles the icon on.

Off toggles the icon off.

All updates all visible viewports.

Noorigin displays the icon in the lower-icon left corner of the screen.

OR displays the icon on the origin of the UCS.

CHANGING THE UCS

So far we have been working in the X-Y plane of all our models. When the UCS is not rotated, AutoCAD refers to the orientation as the World Coordinate System. If you want to reorient your UCS, use the UCS command. You can also save, restore, and delete UCSs from your current file with this command.

```
Command:UCS
Origin/ZAxis/3point/Entity/View/X/Y/Z/Prev/Restore/Save/Del/?/
<World>:
```

Where:
Origin shifts the origin of the UCS without changing the rotation of the axes.

ZA*(xis)* defines the UCS origin and the rotation of the axes by placement of the positive Z.

3point allows placement by three points — the origin, the X, and then the Y in that order only.

Entity sets UCS according to a planar entity and sets the extrusion relative to that entity.

View sets a new UCS with the Z axis parallel to the viewing direction.

X rotates the current UCS around the X axis, keeping the same origin.

Y rotates the current UCS around the Y axis, keeping the same origin.

Z rotates the current UCS around the Z axis, keeping the same origin.

Previous restores the previous UCS.

Restore restores a UCS previously stored and named.

Save saves the current UCS with a given name.

Del deletes a UCS that has been previously stored and named.

? lists the stored UCSs.

World sets the UCS to the World Coordinate System.

As with most other commands, only the capitalized letters of the option are required to call up an option. Once you have made your choice, the UCS icon will change direction to reflect your new position. Also as with other commands, when a point is required, any kind of point entry is acceptable. You can enter the coordinates of that point or use OSNAP with an existing entity or pick a point on the screen.

Be careful to be specific with the 3point entry, or you will get the response **points are collinear**. This means that when entering the points for the origin and X and Y, two points were the same. This happens frequently when indicating an endpoint of an item and not picking far enough along the item to have the endpoint calculated at the end required.

REORIENTING THE UCS

The illustration on the right has been drawn in a 3D view using the orientation 2,-2,2. The sides are 4 units in X and 3 units in Y.

The UCS icon is set to OR *(origin)* to show the origin of the part.

When the orientation of the UCS is changed and a circle is added, the circle and the icon will illustrate the new X-Y plane.

Command:**UCS**

Origin/ZAxis/3point/Entity/View/X/Y/Z/
Prev/Restore/Save/Del/?/<World>:**O**

Origin Point<0.00,0.00,0.00>:**END** *(pick 1)*

This keeps the same axes and moves the origin to a new location. This is very useful in orienting parts from the new origin point if those coordinates are clear rather than having to use points relative to the origin.

Command:**UCS**

Origin/ZAxis/3point/Entity/View/X/Y/Z/
Prev/Restore/Save/Del/?/<World>:**ZA**

Origin Point <0.00,0.00,0.00>:**END** *(pick 1)*

Point on positive portion of Z-axis
<0,0,0>:**END** *(pick 2)*

This orients the origin at point 1 and the Z axis at point 2. The X and Y will relocate relative to the right hand rule.

Command:**UCS**

Origin/ZAxis/3point/Entity/View/X/Y/Z/
Prev/Restore/Save/Del/?/<World>:**3**

Origin Point <0,0,0>:**END** *(pick 1)*

Point on positive portion of X-axis
<0,0,0>:**END** *(pick 2)*

Point on positive Y portion of the UCS X-
Y plane <0,0,0>:**END** *(pick 3)*

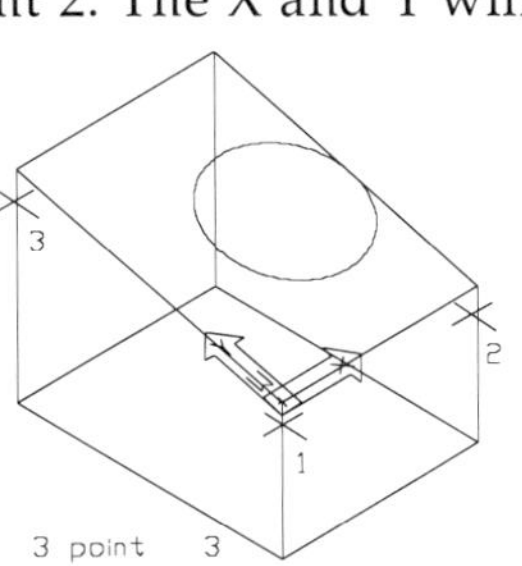

Be sure to use OSNAP.

Command:**UCS**

Origin/ZAxis/3point/Entity/View/X/Y/Z/
Prev/Restore/Save/Del/?/<World>:**E**

Select object to align UCS: *(pick 1)*

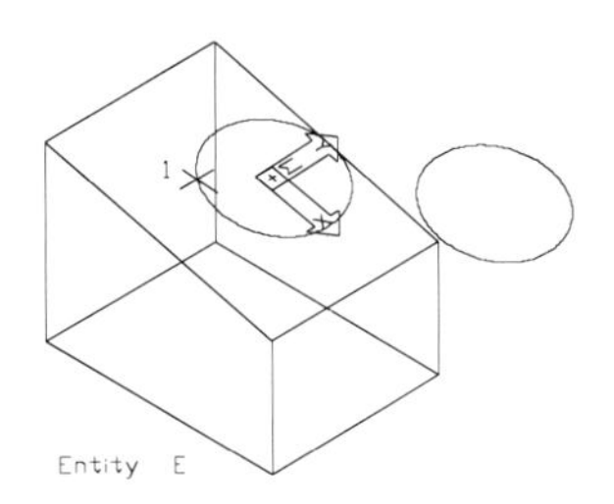

This object should be planar in nature, i.e., it must be an arc, circle, ellipse, or pline with defined radii. The origin takes the centre point of the radius and the endpoint of the item will be positive X.

A line, dimension, 3D face or solid can also be used; the X axis will be calculated relative to the origin.

```
Command:UCS
Origin/ZAxis/3point/Entity/View/X/Y/Z/
Prev/Restore/Save/Del/?/<World>:V
```

This will give you a UCS perpendicular to your point of view. It is extremely useful for labelling data that is on a 3D plane. Once the part or data are entered, change the UCS to View and do your notations line-of-site for maximum reading value.

```
Command:UCS
Origin/ZAxis/3point/En-
tity/View/X/Y/Z/Prev/Restore/Save/Del/
?/<World>:X
Rotation angle about X axis:45
```

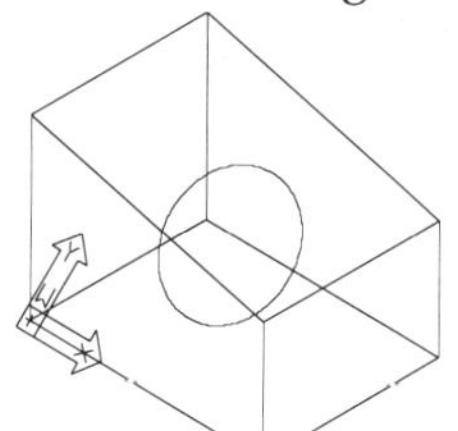

This will rotate the UCS around the *current* UCS. You will usually want to have it rotated around the World UCS, so make sure you return to World before rotating.

```
Command:UCS
Origin/ZAxis/3point/Entity/View/X/Y/Z/
Prev/Restore/Save/Del/?/ <World>:Y
Rotation angle about Y axis:45
```

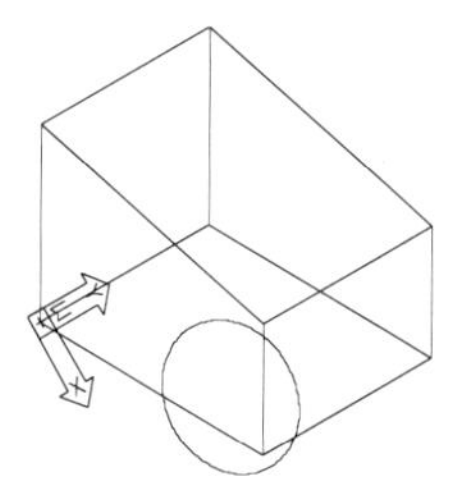

Again, the UCS is rotated around the current UCS. This is useful for putting in cylinders through existing shapes. Once the UCS is rotated, just enter a circle in to make sure the UCS is the one you want.

The rotation angle is calculated counter-clockwise looking down the axis to the origin.

```
Command:UCS
Origin/ZAxis/3point/Entity/View/X/Y/Z/
Prev/Restore/Save/Del/?/<World>:Z
Rotation angle about Z axis:45
```

AutoCAD uses the Right-hand Rule to calculate the positive rotation around the selected axis.

If an object is the required distance around the axis, for example, a line that you want to align your UCS to, this can be used as a reference point. Of course, any orientation of the UCS to an object without the aid of OSNAP would be totally useless.

If you want to orient your view in both X an Y, use the following:

```
Command:UCS
Origin/ZAxis/3point/Entity/View/X/Y/Z/Prev/Restore/Save/Del/
?/<World>:X
Rotation angle about Z axis:45
Command:UCS
Origin/ZAxis/3point/Entity/View/X/Y/ Z/Prev/Re-
store/Save/Del/?/<World>:Z
```

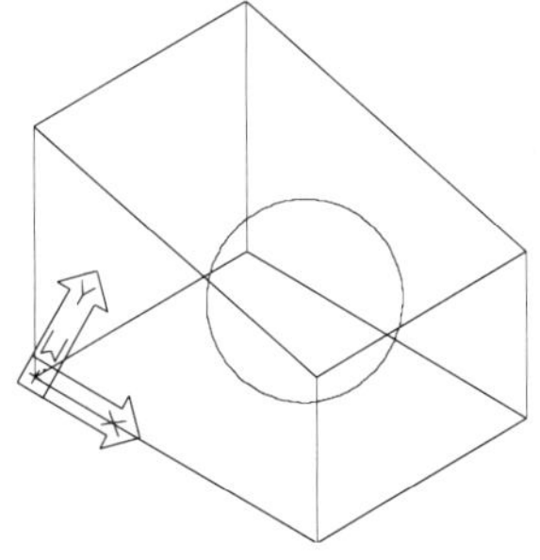

```
Rotation angle about Z axis:45
```

This will give you a rotation in two directions. Remember that this will rotate around the last UCS. You can rotate around the World Coordinate System or around any other current UCS.

While orienting your UCS, you can also use Previous to return to the UCS just used.

```
Command:UCS
Origin/ZAxis/3point/Entity/View/X/Y/Z/Prev/Restore/Save/Del/?/
<World>:P
```

Using the Previous option will simply take you back to where you were in the last UCS.

NOTE: If your UCS icon is not being repositioned as you reorient the UCS, and you have set UCSICON to OR *(origin)*, try changing it back to the World Coordinate System. Your next UCS orientation should have the icon at the origin.

The most flexible of the commands listed above is the 3point option. As long as you remember the order being Origin, X, and then Y, you will have no problem with orientation.

If you ever find yourself totally lost, reset to the World Coordinate System and start again.

SAVING AND RESTORING UCS

Once you have oriented a UCS to work on a particular section of your model, you may want to save this orientation for later use. There are several dialogue boxes that make saving and restoring the UCS quite simple. These are found under the pull-down menus under Settings.

Figure 27-7 illustrates the UCS dialogue box; it displays a listing of the UCSs you have already created. This is found under the Settings pull-down menus under UCS control.

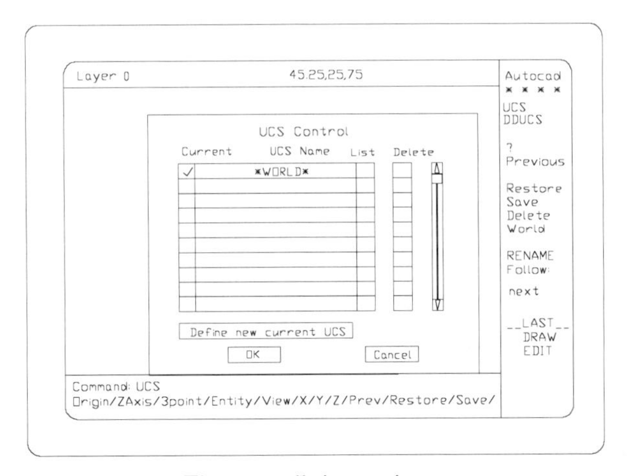

Figure 27-7. The UCS dialogue box

Notice that you can be prompted to create a new one, or, unlike LAYER, delete one from the current list as well. This is quite handy if you have forgotten the name of a UCS.

You can also save your UCS by using:

```
Command:UCS
Origin/ZAxis/3point/Entity/View/X/Y/Z/Prev/Restore/Save/Del/?/
<World>:Save
?/Desired UCS name:TOPFACE
```

If you are entering a new UCS, the dialogue box will automatically change to the entry dialogue box. This offers you a more automated way of entering information, and will name and save this information for future use.

Again, when naming a UCS, try to get all the information you need in the title of the UCS and refrain from using names or titles that have no connection to the work on hand.

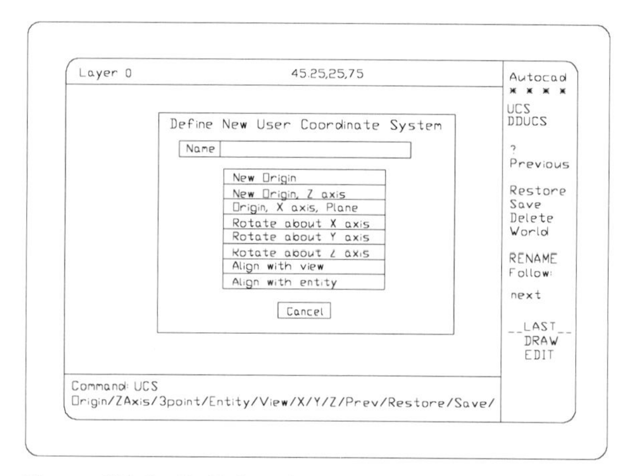

Figure 27-8. Defining the UCS within a dialogue box

By picking Define new Current UCS, the entry dialogue box of Figure 27-8 will give you all the information you need to enter the new UCS.

Once entered, you can retrieve a UCS either through the original dialogue box or through the screen menu by using Restore. The only trick to retrieving a UCS is remembering what you named it.

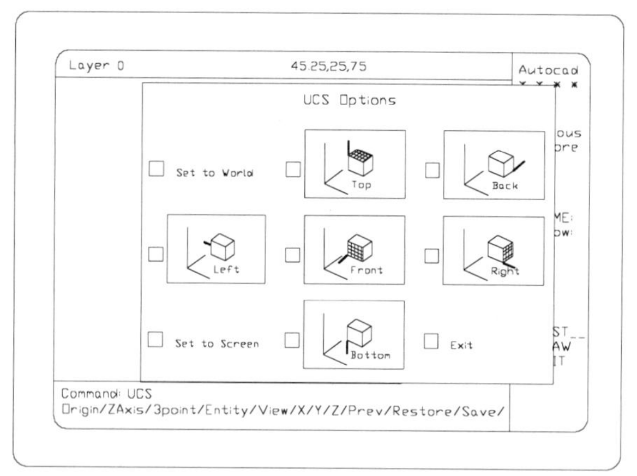

Figure 27-9. The UCS rotation icon menu

This icon menu in Figure 27-9 is also available by using DDUCS. By using this box you can choose any of the sides available on a rectangle. Make a note of the position of the origin in each case.

The Set to screen option in this box is similar to the VIEW command in the display menu.

UCS PROTOTYPES

If you are creating a number of parts that will be merged or are the same basic shape, it would be a good idea to create a prototype file containing all of the UCSs you intend to use in addition to the layers, linetypes, viewports, etc. Prototypes will save you time in setting up the UCS, and will ensure that object design and the spelling of text is the same in each case.

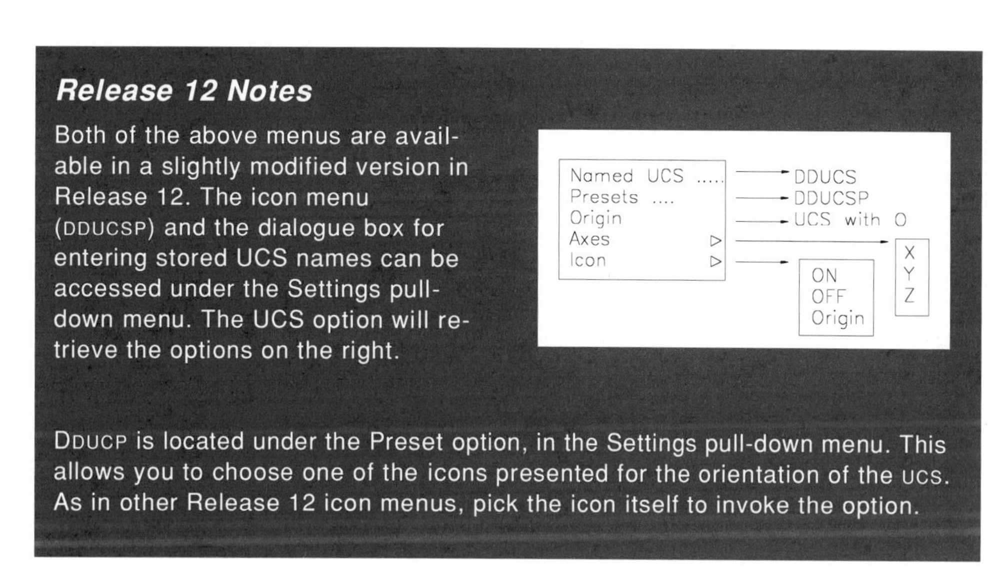

Release 12 Notes

Both of the above menus are available in a slightly modified version in Release 12. The icon menu (DDUCSP) and the dialogue box for entering stored UCS names can be accessed under the Settings pull-down menu. The UCS option will retrieve the options on the right.

DDUCP is located under the Preset option, in the Settings pull-down menu. This allows you to choose one of the icons presented for the orientation of the UCS. As in other Release 12 icon menus, pick the icon itself to invoke the option.

Practice 27

You may want to practise orienting your UCS on this object before you start the next exercise.

STEP 1
Set up four viewports.

STEP 2
In your four viewports set up the following views:

```
Front
Plan
Rside
Iso
2,-2,2
```

Now create the object below; 4 units in X, 3 units in Y, and 3 units in Z at X = 0, plus 2 units in Z at X = 4.

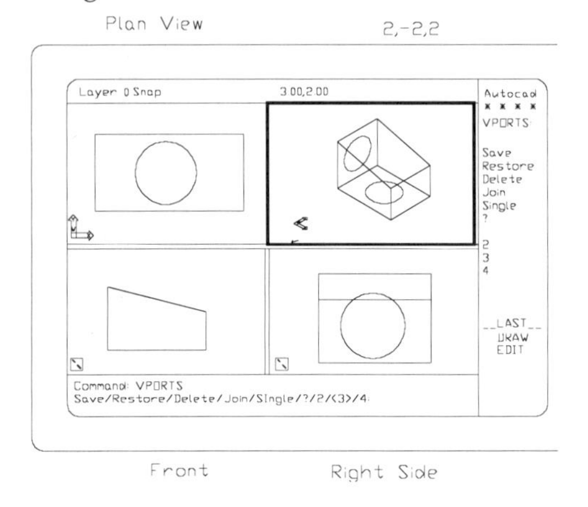

Use the UCS command to orient your UCS, then place a circle on each plane.

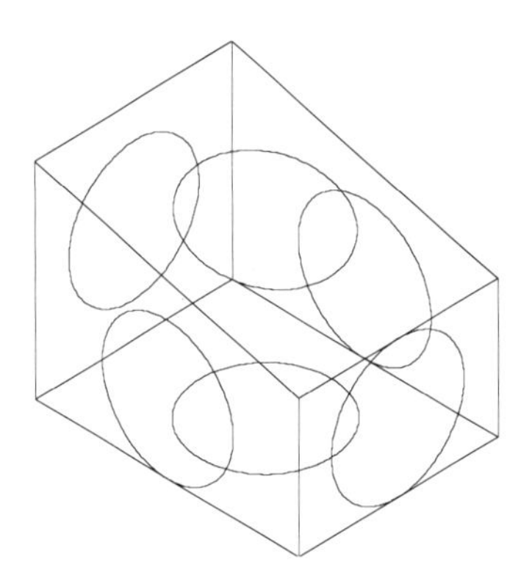

Try to get the circle precisely in the centre of the plane.

Use ZOOM All and ZOOM .7x to display the model in each view. When zoomed, the model will expand to fit the viewport provided.

Exercise A27

Construct a food preparation area of the appropriate standard sizes.

Minimum 4-inch kick space.

Minimum 36-inch counter height.

Minimum 18-inch space between counter and upper cabinets.

Minimum 36-inch for overhead cabinet height.

Change your UCS to position the counter top elements and sinks. Change it again to fit on the stove fan and other details.

A refrigeration centre may be added if you have the time.

Use the correct sizes and shapes so these objects can be used as prototypes or base drawings for further design in this area.

Save the file; we will be using it in the file merge chapter later on.

If you are having difficulty entering objects using your coordinates, try turning your Osnap mode off.

In Release 11, there are slight problems with Osnap endpoint on rotated 3D views. Try using Intersect instead.

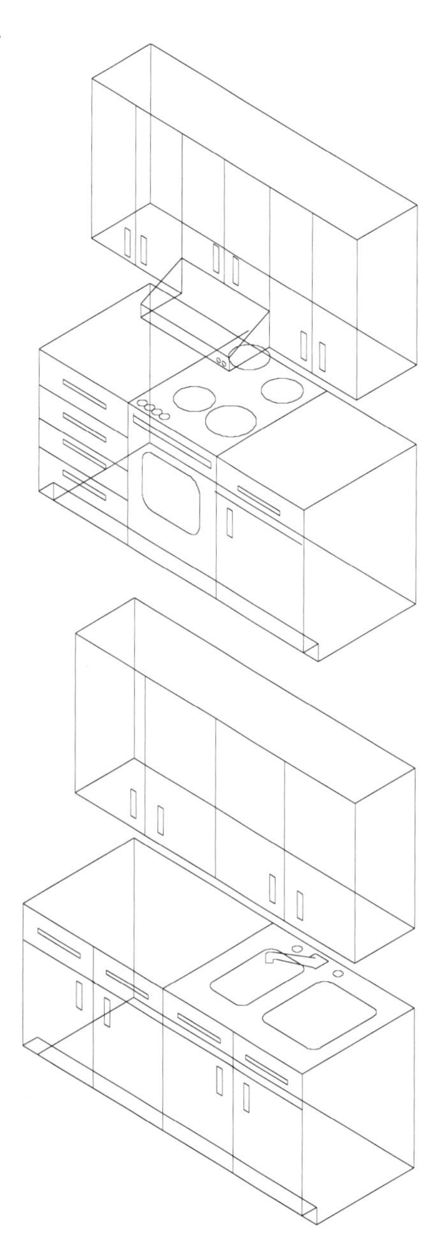

MECHANICAL

Exercise M27

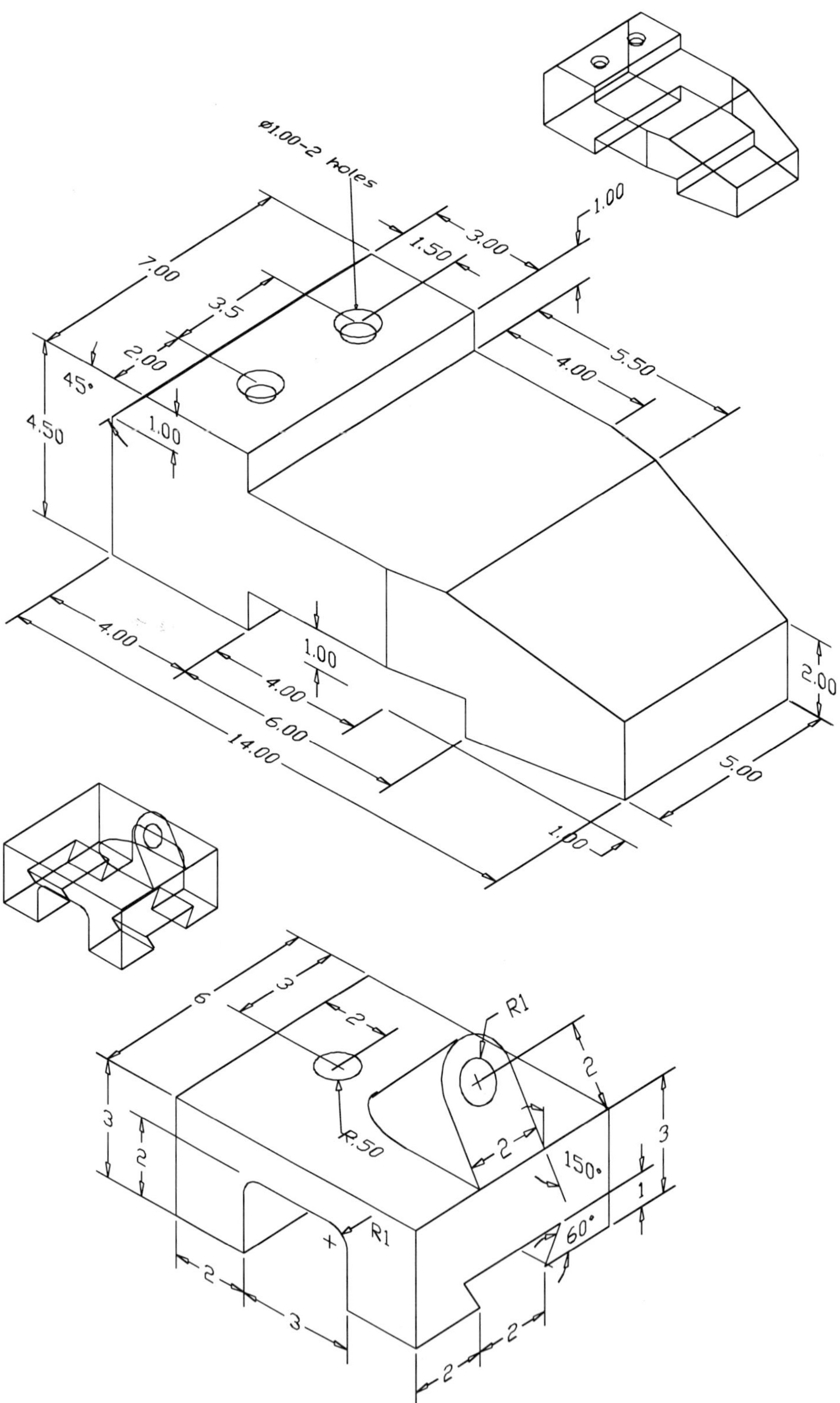

Create both of these parts if you have the time. Create full wireframe models as in the smaller detail. Change the UCS as needed.

Exercise C27

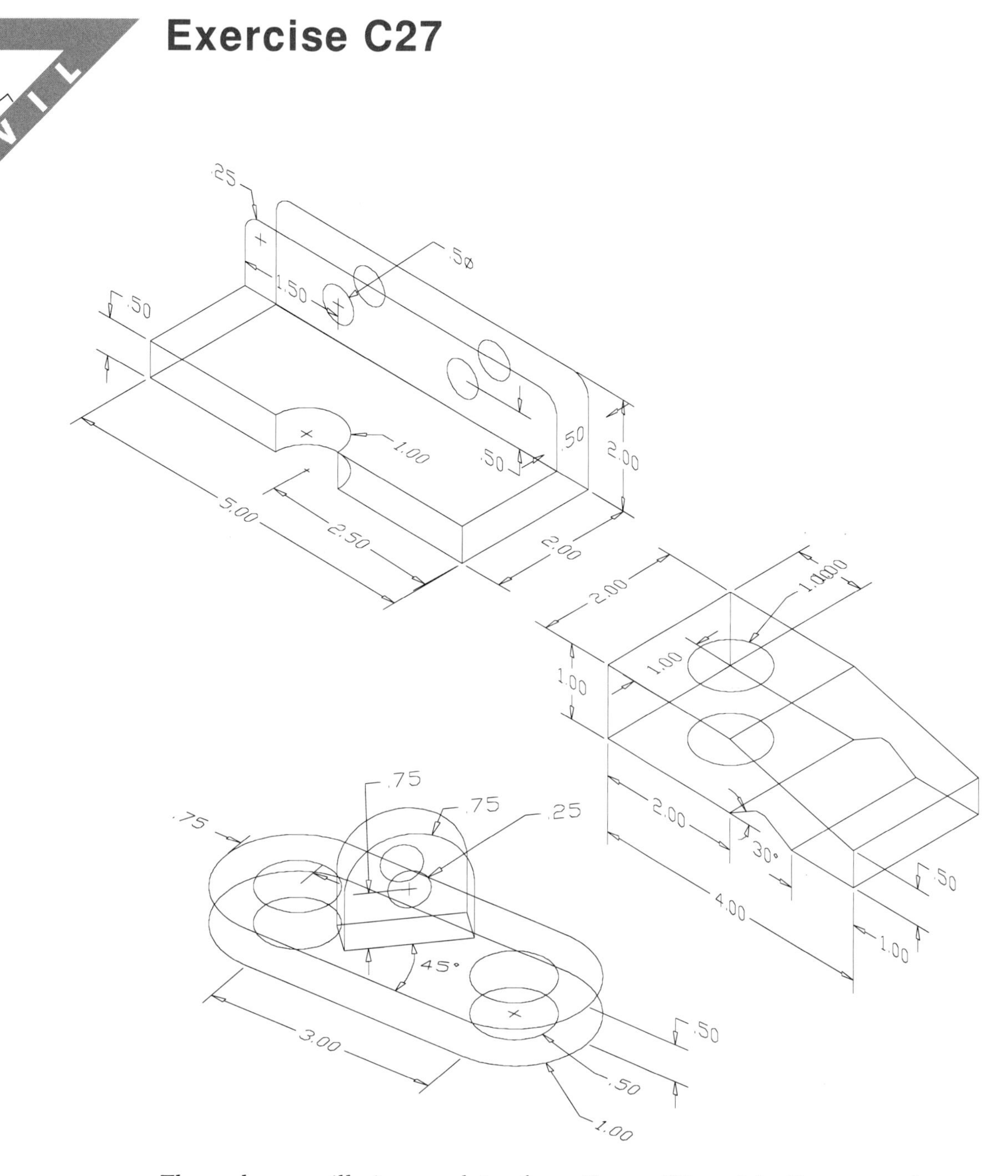

These shapes will give you lots of practice on 3D models. Be sure to change the UCS when needed.

If using UCS with the Entity option, be sure to note the position of the origin. Often it is not where you expect it the first few times.

When you finish these, try Exercise M27.

Challenger 27

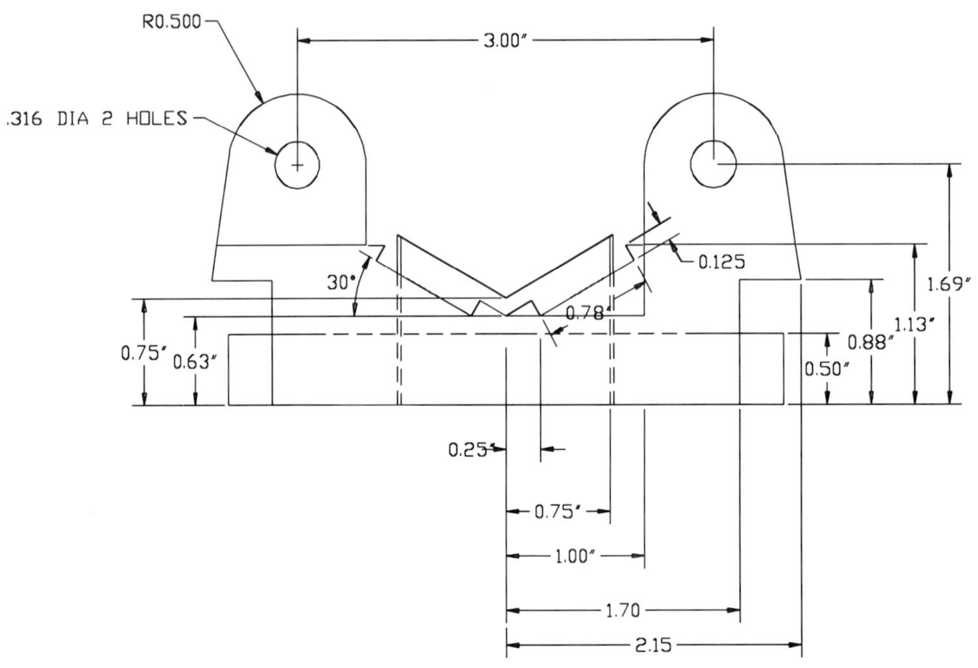

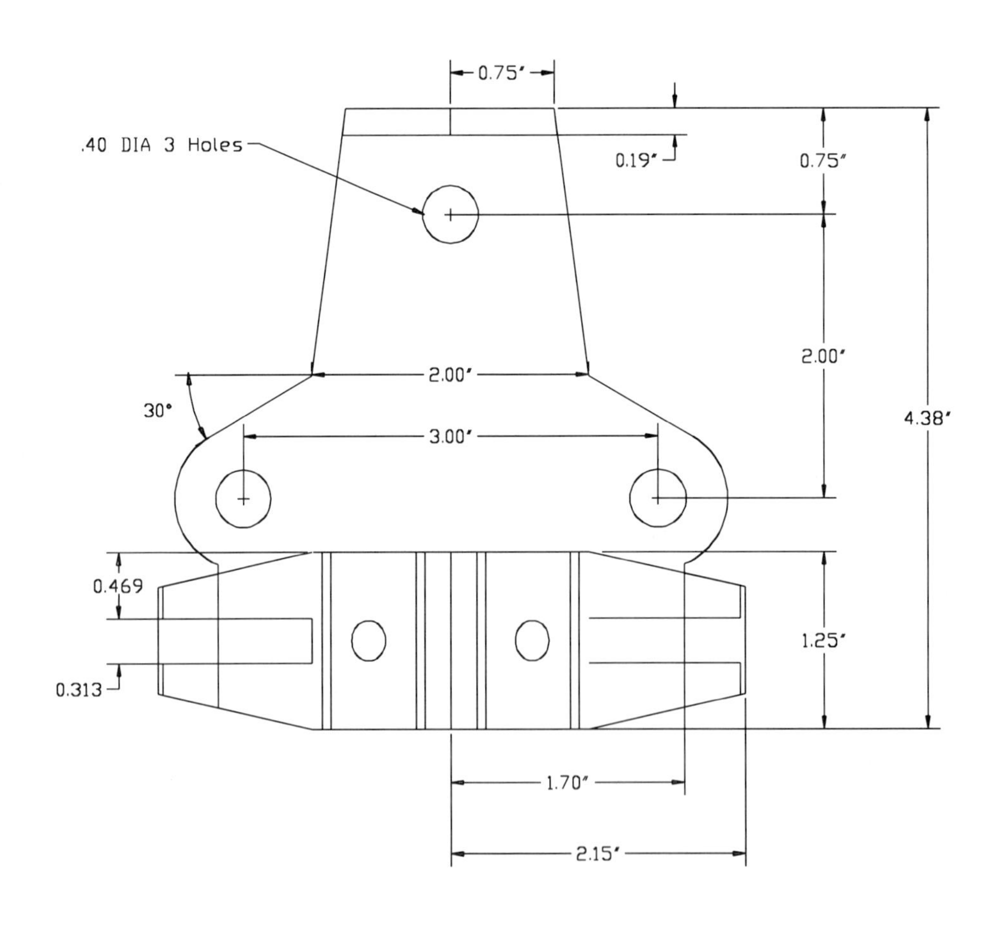

Challenger 27 (continued)

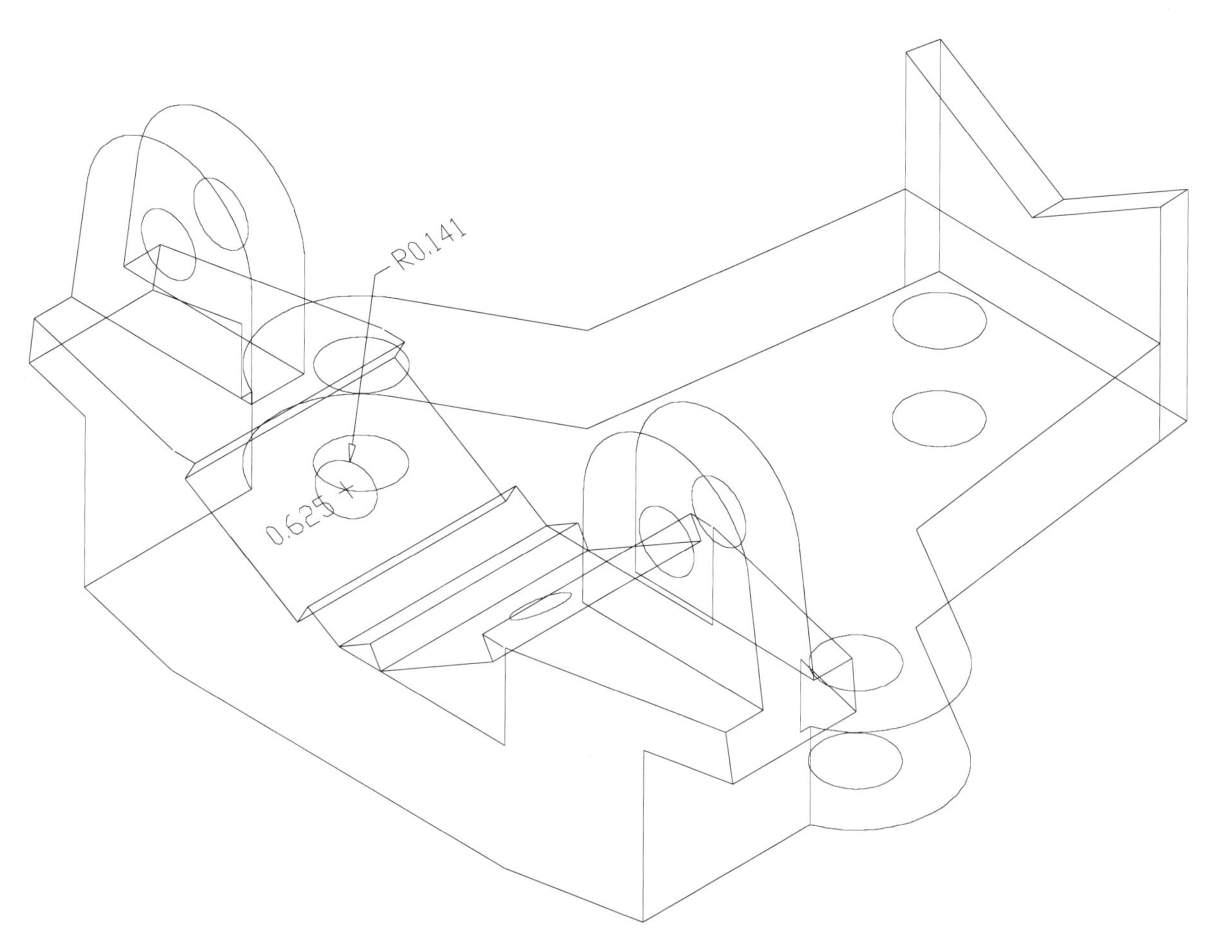

Generate a wireframe of this pipe vise base. If you finish early, the rib and wall thickness is 1/8", so you can turn it over and add some depth to it.

When finished, save the model so you can practise isometric dimensioning.

While working on this model, you may want to save a three-view viewport layout so you can access the front and plan views in more detail.

3DFACE AND POINT FILTERS

Upon completion of this chapter, the student should be able to:

1. Generate a 3DFACE on any surface
2. Use HIDE to create an isometric view from a wire frame model
3. Use X,Y,Z filters
4. Use SHADE

3DFACE

The 3DFACE command creates an entity that is a planar surface a section of a plane. The purpose of this command is to have a continuous, coherent plane for viewing of an object. The 3DFACE looks like wireframe in that there is no surface display, but it acts as a surface.

For example, instead of having six or seven different extruded plines describing a wall, the 3DFACE can be seen as the final finish, covering the wall so that the construction is not visible. Any or all edges of the surface can be "invisible" to allow a more visually pleasing surface. This command is used primarily for creating images for viewing as opposed to creating images for manufacturing, but can be used to create a quick, simple flat "surface" with straight lines between the points describing it.

The 3DFACE is entered in much the same way as SOLID, by pairs of points, but whereas the SOLID is confined to one plane, the 3DFACE is defined by X, Y, and Z, and can exist anywhere in space. The 3DFACE can be used to create a hidden or opaque effect. The pick point order in 3DFACE is also a little more natural than that of SOLID; you can choose your points in either a clockwise or a counter-clockwise rotation. The 3DFACE creates a planar effect for creating opaque views, and can't be extruded like other purely geometric entities.

Creating 3DFACEs

The 3DFACE command prompts you for a series of points — first, second, third, and fourth — in the same manner that the SOLID command does, as stated earlier. These points can be described by coordinate entry, by osnaping to existing items or by placing points in space.

```
Command: 3DFACE
First point: 0,0
Second point: 4,0
Third point: 4,4
Fourth point: 0,4
Third point: ↵
```

0,4 4,4

0,0 4,0

Release 12 Notes

The 3DFACE command is located under the Draw pull-down menu under the 3D Surface option as well as on the screen menu under Draw.

The command on the previous page describes a four-unit square plane starting at 0,0. If the user wanted to continue with the plane, entries could be made in successive pairs of points. If a final single point is needed, instead of a pair, just press enter instead of a point.

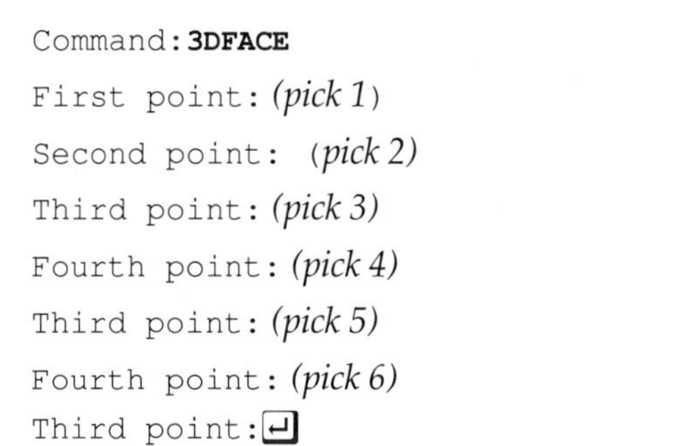

```
Command: 3DFACE
First point: (pick 1)
Second point: (pick 2)
Third point: (pick 3)
Fourth point: (pick 4)
Third point: (pick 5)
Fourth point: (pick 6)
Third point: ↵
```

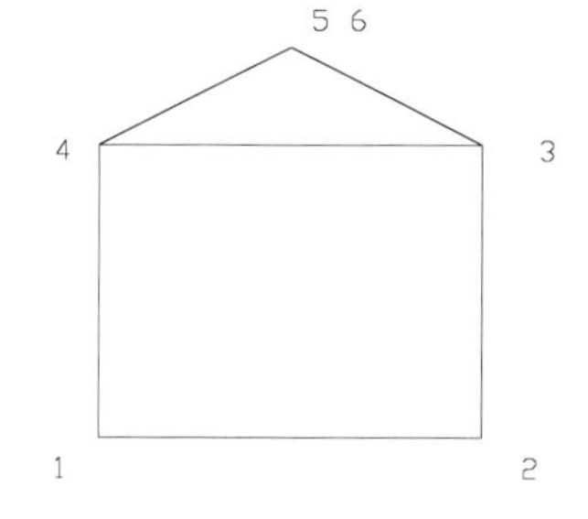

If you would like to make the line between pick 3 and pick 4 invisible, you can instruct AutoCAD to do so by picking the **I** or Invisible option before the pick *that precedes the first point of the line*. In the above illustration you would use an **I** (plus space) before the first prompt for the Third point:

In the following example, the line between 3 and 4 is invisible to create the view on the left of Figure 28-3, on the following page. Without using I (for invisible) before the third point, you would get the view on the right.

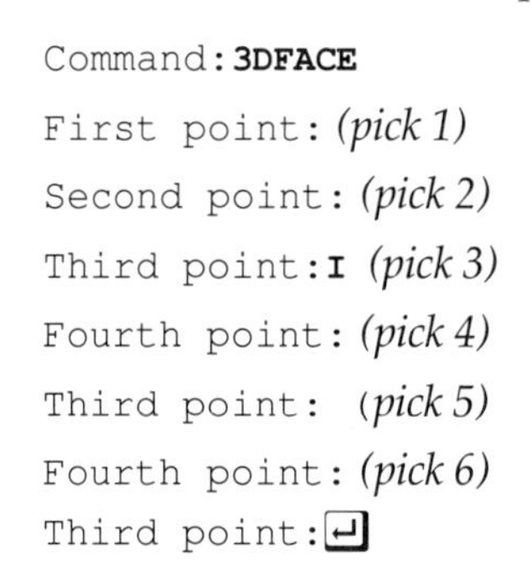

```
Command: 3DFACE
First point: (pick 1)
Second point: (pick 2)
Third point: I (pick 3)
Fourth point: (pick 4)
Third point: (pick 5)
Fourth point: (pick 6)
Third point: ↵
```

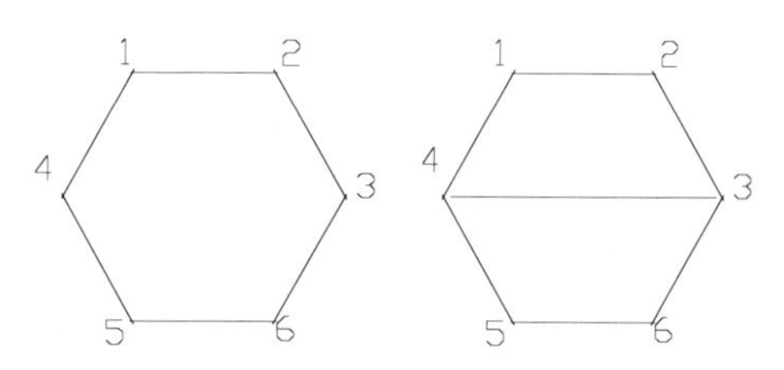

3DFACE can be used to create an opaquing plane to help visualize objects that are already created in wireframe, or it can be used to draw planar shapes on its own. In the following exercise the object is created by a series of 3DFACES and nothing else.

Example *3DFACE*

You can see how the object is constructed. Change your VPOINT to 2,-2,2 then start with the bottom 3DFACE to create a plane.

```
Command: 3DFACE
First point: 0,0
Second point: 4,0
Third point: 4,3
Fourth point: 0,3
Third point: ↵
```

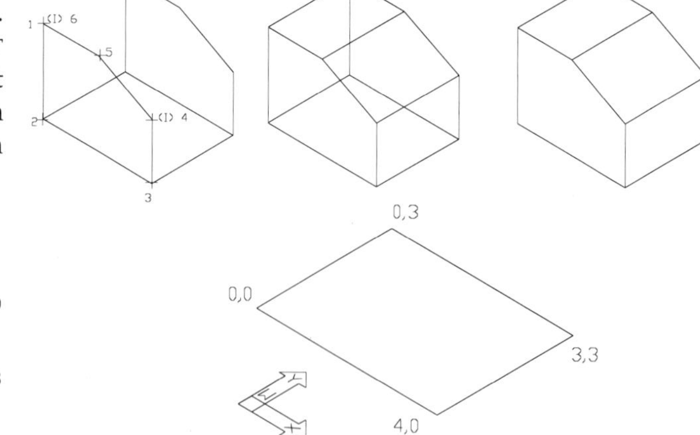

To construct the front plane you can either change your UCS and pick the points from the screen, or you can use coordinates.

If you are using coordinates, try the following:

NOTE: A space must be entered after the I for invisible.

```
Command:3DFACE
First point:0,0,3
Second point:0,0,0
Third point:4,0,0
Fourth point:I 4,0,2
Third point:2,0,3
Fourth point:I 0,0,3
Third point:↵
```

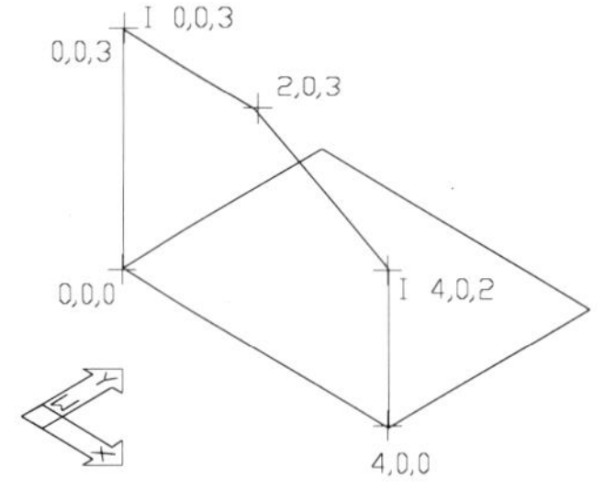

The X and Z change but the Y remains constant.

Now you can create the same 3DFACE on Y3.

```
Command:3DFACE
First point:0,3,3
Second point:0,3,0
Third point:4,3,0
Fourth point:I 4,3,2
Third point:2,3,3
Fourth point:I 0,3,3
Third point:↵
```

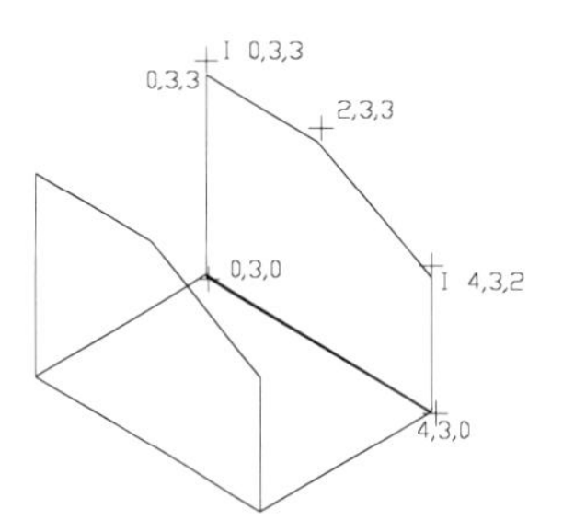

You could also copy the front plane onto the back.

Activate your Osnap mode to END*(point)* and generate the other three planes using 3DFACE and picking up the appropriate endpoints.

Command:**3DFACE**
First point:(END) *(pick 1)*
Second point:(END) *(pick 2)*
Third point:(END) *(pick 3)*
Fourth point:(END) *(pick 4)*
(etc.)

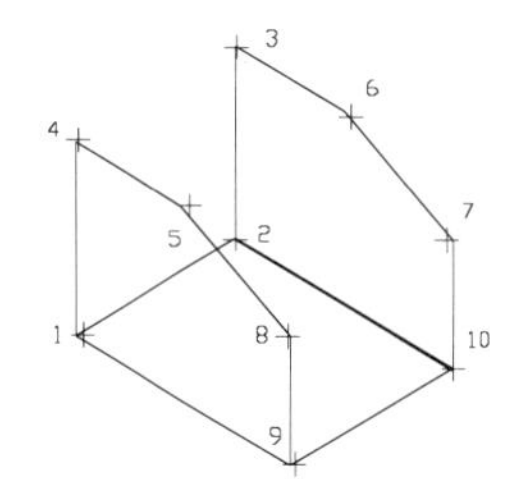

Finally, use HIDE and the object will have only those parts visible from your line of sight.

If you rotate the VPOINT to 2,2,2 you will have a completely different view of the object and you can try HIDE again to see if it really works.

Example: 3DFACE

3DFACE can be used on existing wireframe models to add planes for creating hidden lines. Let's take an example from the previous chapter to see how this might work. We are using the mechanical example number 1 from Chapter 27. In the illustration on the right, the data has been created in wireframe and properly dimensioned.

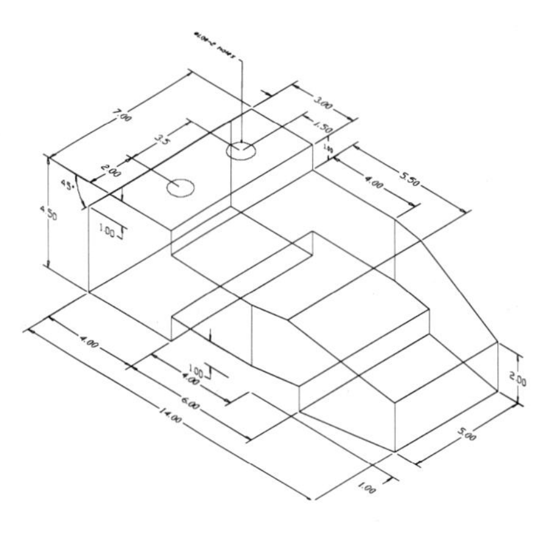

What we would like is an isometric view with the appropriate lines hidden. To do this we can place 3DFaces over the existing geometry. Turn the DIM *(dimension)* layer off, and create a layer to contain your 3DFaces.As the lines already exist, we will use OSNAP to access them quickly.

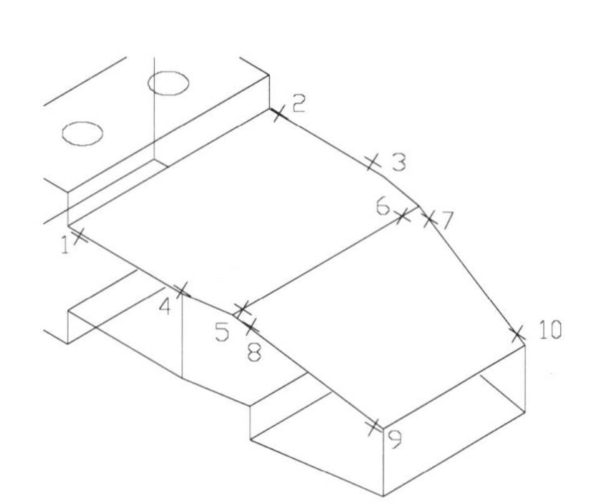

Command:**OSNAP**

Object snap modes:**END** *(endpoint)*

Command:**3DFACE**

First point: *(pick 1)*

Second point: *(pick 2)*

Third point:**I** *(pick 3)*

Fourth point: *(pick 4)*

Third point: *(pick 5)*

Fourth point: *(pick 6)*

Third point:↵

Command:**3DFACE**

First point: *(pick 7)*

Second point: *(pick 8)*

Third point: *(pick 8)*

Fourth point: *(pick 10)*

Third point:↵

Command:**HIDE**

Other Uses of 3DFACE

If there is a database that contains a lot of items that you would like temporarily blocked out, you can use 3DFACE to create an entirely invisible plane, i.e., none of the outline will appear, it will act only as a screen. An example of when this might be handy is perhaps when showing a portion of a drawing to a client, but not wanting to show how the rest is progressing. Another example would be in a house design when you want all the interior walls, fixtures, etc., to disappear and only the outline remains. This is similar to turning LAYERs off, but will block out all layers in one specific area.

X, Y, AND Z FILTERS

X,Y, and Z Filters are used to make the entry of geometry easier.

In the illustration on the following page, assume that you have the vertical and diagonal lines and are trying to construct the pline starting at the same X value as the middle of the diagonal line, and the same Y value as the top of the vertical line.

As the numbers in illustration **a** of Figure 28-2 are quite simple, you could probably figure out what the coordinates are, and simply type them in.

In illustration **b** however, this could be a difficult process and possibly involve the use of calculators or other archaic tools.

Release 12 Notes

There is no change in the use of filters in Release 12.

If we use filters to access points, we can enter this PLINE quite simply.

Command:**PLINE**

From point:**.X** of **MID** *(pick 1)*

(Need YZ) **.y** of **END** *(pick 2)*

(Need Z) **0**

(Current line-width is etc.)

The starting point was taken from the existing geometry. For MID and END, the OSNAPs were used.

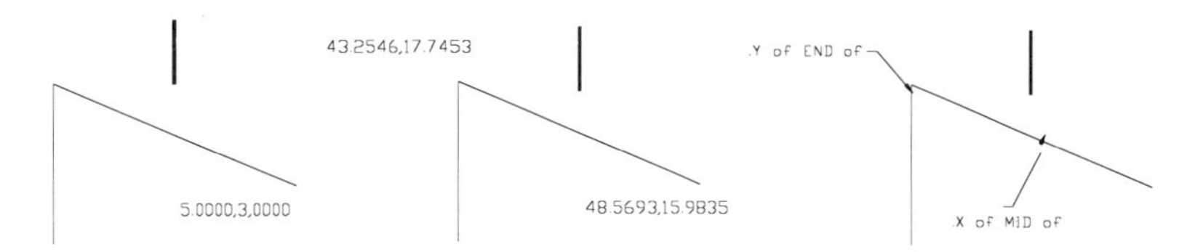

Figure 28-1. Using point filters in 2D

In the above example, you could create a horizontal line from the top of the vertical line and a vertical line from the middle of the diagonal line. Then once these were created, you could start the pline from the INT*(ersection)* of the two construction lines, but filters are much easier, and you don't need to either create or erase construction lines.

Using X, Y, and Z Filters

Filters "copy" coordinates of existing geometry.

With the construction lines, the draftsperson lines up one view with another using his or her ruler.

In English, you might say, "Let's draw a horizontal line here taking this other line and lining the straight edge up with it."

With the CAD drawing, the user picks points on the other views to have the computer calculate the perfect spot on the new view.

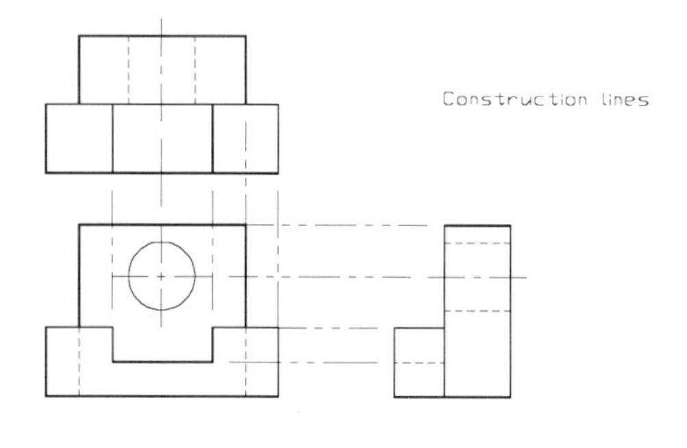

An English translation might be "Let's enter a line taking the X value of the end of this object and adding a Y of 1." Or even better, "Let's enter a line here taking the X value of this line and the Y value of that."

Now you have determined the first point of the line and you simply need to put in the second point (see illustration on the right).

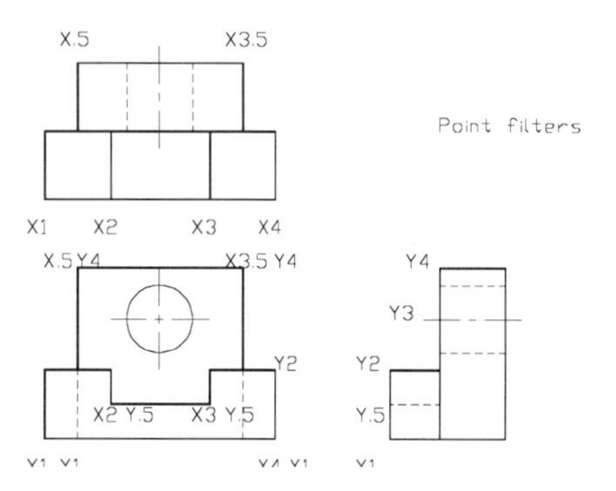

On a part where the views are all on regular increments, the SNAP might be just as easy to use. But on a part where there are areas not on snap points, this offers two great advantages:

- the drawing will be much quicker because you don't have to go to LIST to pick up the point needed
- the accuracy will be far greater as you will trust the system to enter the correct number instead of figuring it out, writing it down so you won't forget, and then typing it in. In the three steps needed to determine and enter a coordinate, there is a high rate of errors.

The following is an easy exercise to see how two-dimensional point filters work. Then we will go on to Z.

Example: *X, Y Filters*

Looking at the drawing on the right, you can see that the side view would be easy to create once the front view is done, simply by lining up the horizontal lines with existing lines on the front view.

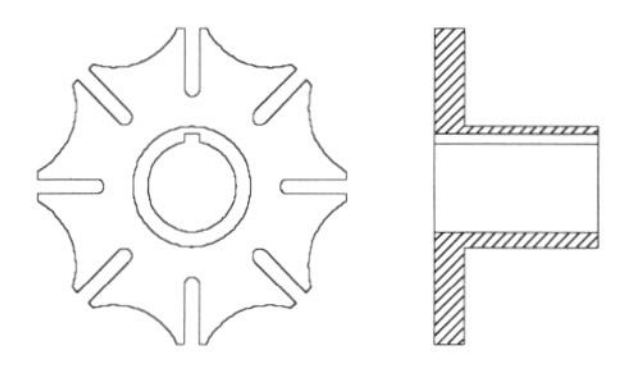

For a really accurate model X , Y filters are the easiest method.

Generate the geometry below using LINEs, ARCs, EXTEND, CIRCLE, and ARRAY.

The easiest way to approach it would be to draw the two inner circles plus the keyway, then draw one of the exterior scallops completely and array it.

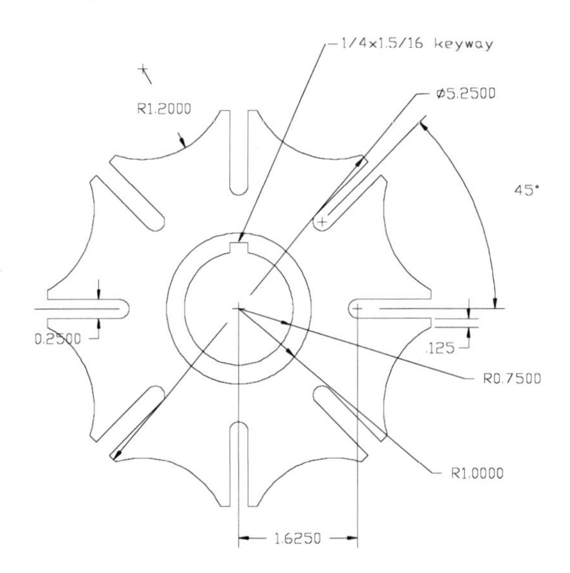

Once completed, you can start entering the cross section using the existing geometry as a guide.

USING POINT FILTERS

Point filters work much the same way as OSNAP in that you are asking for a property or parameter on something that already exists. The difference is that you are asking for only the X or the Y or the Z value instead of all of the coordinates attached to a particular object.

When used with OSNAP, Filters filter out only the coordinate that you need.

Filters Without OSNAPs

If you are using a point in space to reference your filter, the value requested — .X or .Y — is taken from the point that you actually pick. If your SNAP is on, you will pick the coordinate with a preset integer, if not, you will pick exactly the point that you hit on the Z0 plane of the UCS.

If you are referencing an object with the use of one of the OSNAPs — CEN*(ter)*, END*(point)*, MID*(dle)*, etc., — you must request first the filter .X, or .Y.

As with the Invisible option in 3DFACE, a space must be entered after your filter option. When you hit the space bar after this entry your screen will show *.X of* or *.Y of*. Then you can pick the OSNAP that suits your purpose.

```
Command:LINE
From point:.X of END (pick 1) (this gets the X value)
```

Instead of the endpoint or middle of an object, you are asking for only the X value or the Y value of the specific portion of the object that you have chosen.

To call up the filter, pick .X or .Y from the Line menu, or type in .X or .Y. (Don't forget the .) AutoCAD will then pick up only the X or Y value of the point indicated. Once you have picked up the value that you require, you are prompted to fill in the other coordinates needed to complete the point.

Example: *Continuing with Filters*

```
Command:LINE
From point:.Y of END (pick 1) (this gets the Y value)
(need XZ):12,0 (positions the first point of the line)
To point:@2,0,0 (gives the length of the line at 2 in X)
To point:↵
Command:LINE
From point:.Y of END (pick 2) (this gets the Y value)
(need XZ):12,0 (positions the first point of the line)
To point:@2,0,0 (gives the length of the line at 2 in X)
To point:↵
```

Remember that your default for a filter is to pick up the point in space that you have picked. The filter won't pick up a portion of an existing object without the help of an osnap.

Your object should look like this:

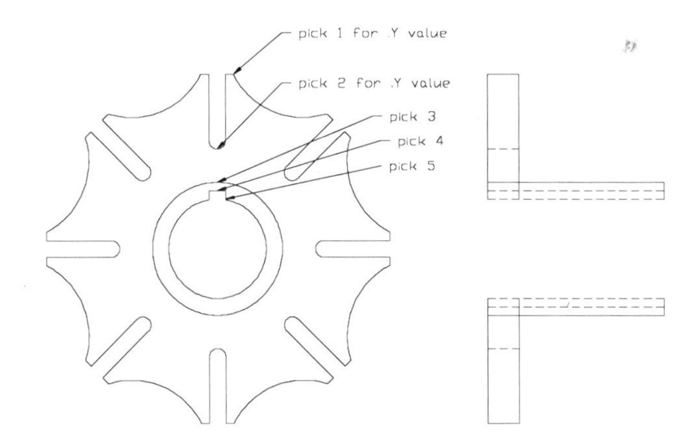

Once the horizontal lines are in, complete with LINE and MIRROR.

Z FILTERS

The Z filter is exactly the same as the X and Y filters in that it picks up that value of the point indicated. The Z filter is only a little more difficult to use because it is, for some, more difficult to visualize. In the following, see how the Z filter saves a lot of time placing a circle at the bottom of the object.

First bring up the 3D shape from the 3DFACE exercise. Then set the UCS to the top slanted plane using UCS 3point and END*(endpoints)*.

Now we want to position a circle as a cylinder going through the part.

```
Command:CIRCLE
From point:.X of MID (pick 1) (this gets the X value)
(need YZ):.Y of MID (pick 2) (this gets the Y value)
(need Z):0 (positions the circle in the middle of the Z0 plane)
```

To get the circle on the bottom plane use:

```
Command:CIRCLE
From point:.X of MID (pick 1) (this gets the X value)
(need XZ):.Y of MID (pick 2) (this gets the Y value)
(need Z):.Z of MID (pick 3) (this gets the Z value and positions the circle at the bottom of the part in line with the one above)
```

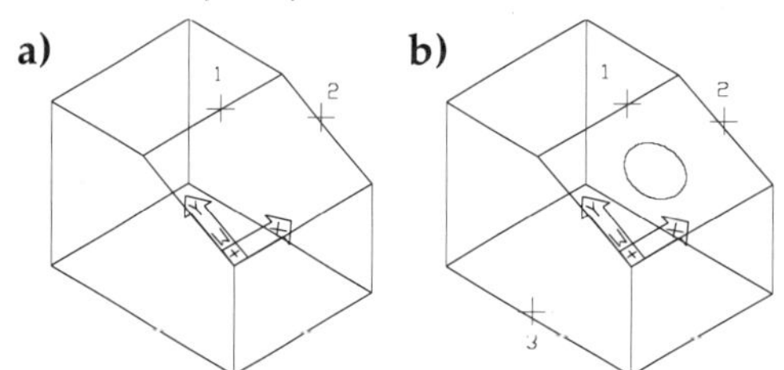

Figure 28-2. Orienting a circle on a plane

As shown in Figure 28-2, the second circle takes the X of pick 1, the Y of pick 2 and the Z of pick 3.

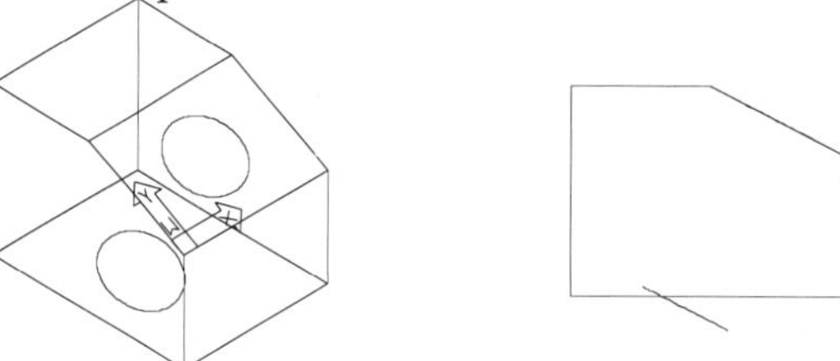
Figure 28-3. Using point filters in 3D

Figure 28-3 shows a view with both circles in. The illustration on the right shows both circles in the front view.

XYZ filters can be used in any combination. You can choose a filter for an X value and a Y value from a two-dimensional view and then enter the Z coordinate from the keyboard. Filter values are taken from the current UCS.

SHADE

This command is as easy to use as HIDE. You simply type in the word SHADE at the command prompt and you will quickly produce a shaded image in the current viewport. The light source in this command is always directly behind the user.

There are no options needed to complete the command. The shaded image will remain in the viewport until the next regeneration occurs.

If you have a graphics card that offers 15 colours, there is usually a light and dark version of the same hue. Check the CHROMA slide to see if this is the case. These altering shades can be used to create a very pleasing image with SHADE. With 3DFACE, the outline of the face will be the colour used for that shaded plane. The SHADEDGE setting can be used to alter the image.

Exercise A28

Rotate your view to 2,-2,2 using VPOINT. Using LINE, make a floor plan for an 8′ x 10′ "Bunky" or toolshed.

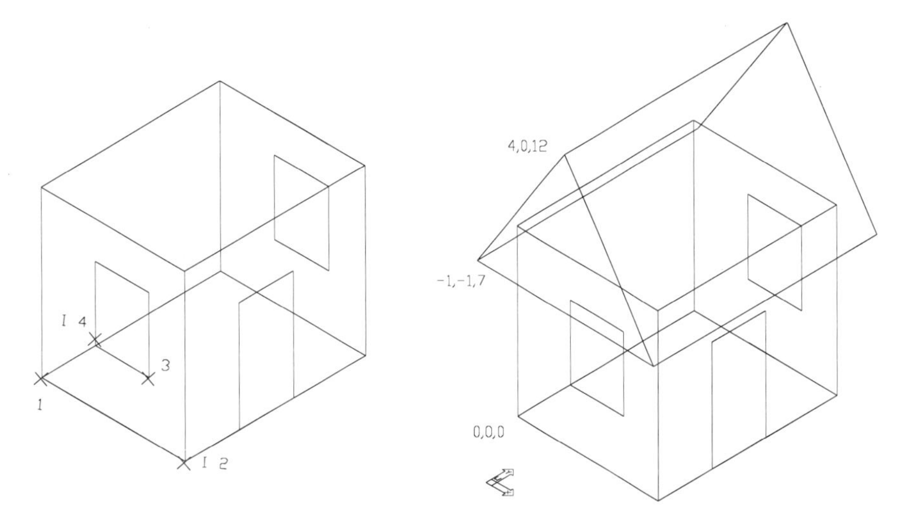

Generate 3DFACE walls on all four sides, leaving two 3-foot window openings on the 8-foot walls and a 3-foot door on the front. You will need more than 1 3DFACE per side. One way of entering the 3DFACEs is as in the example above. Create 4 3DFACES with invisible lines between points 2 and 3 and points 4 and 1.

Using 3DFACE, put on a roof. Make sure that the 3DFACE of the roof is *above* the top line of your wall. If it is not, the wall will come through the roof.

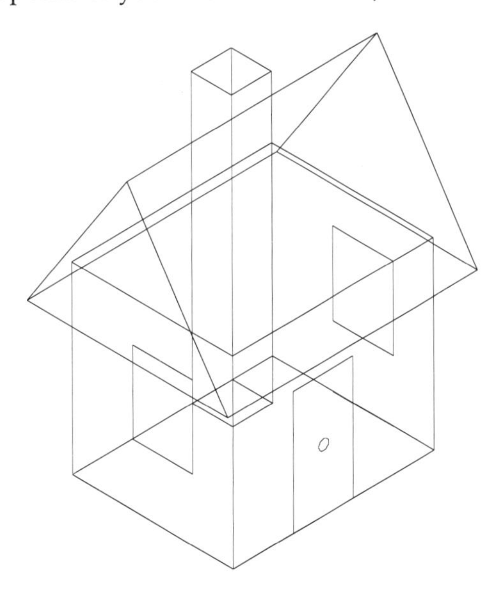

Use HIDE to create a "solid" building.

Using X, Y, Z filters place a circular doorknob in the center of the front door.

Add a chimney and other details.

Use SHADE for a shaded image.

Save the file.

Exercise M28

Use 3DFACE to create the Camera Flash at right.

Use X, Y, Z filters to add details to the shape.

Use HIDE to view it properly.

Use SHADE for a shaded image.

Save the file.

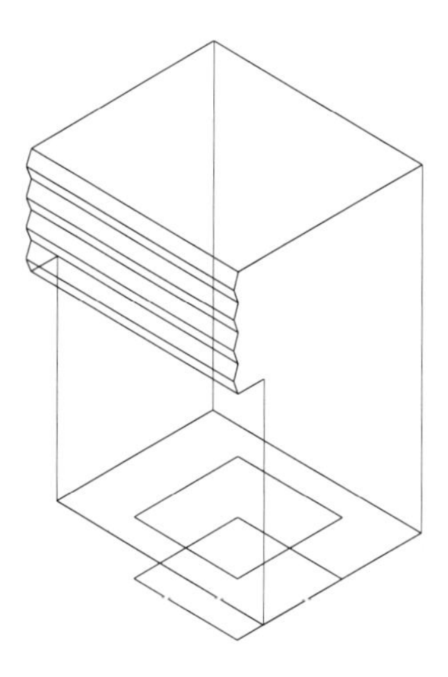

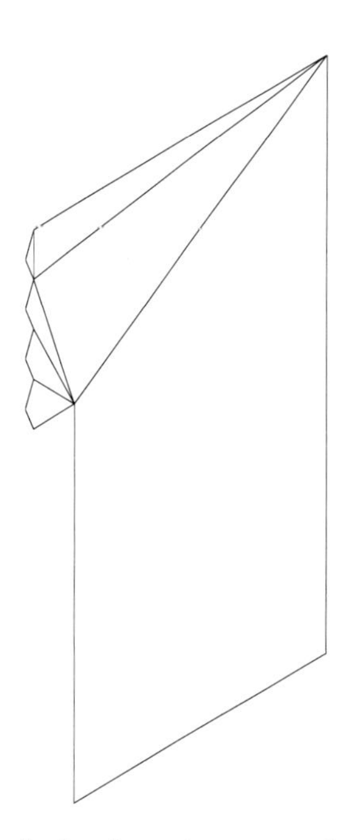

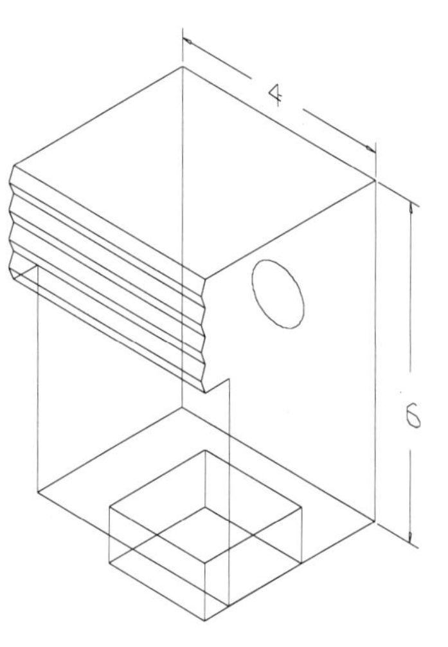

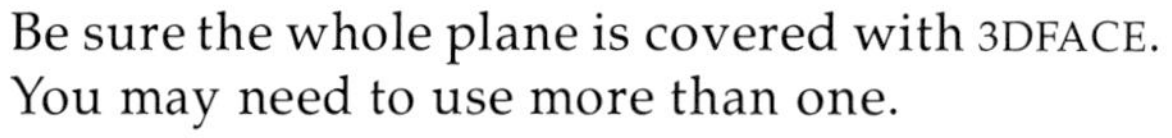

Be sure the whole plane is covered with 3DFACE. You may need to use more than one.

Exercise C28

Use 3DFACE to create the Box Slide at right.

Use X, Y, Z filters when placing the interior shape.

Use HIDE to view it properly.

Use SHADE for a shaded image.

Save the file.

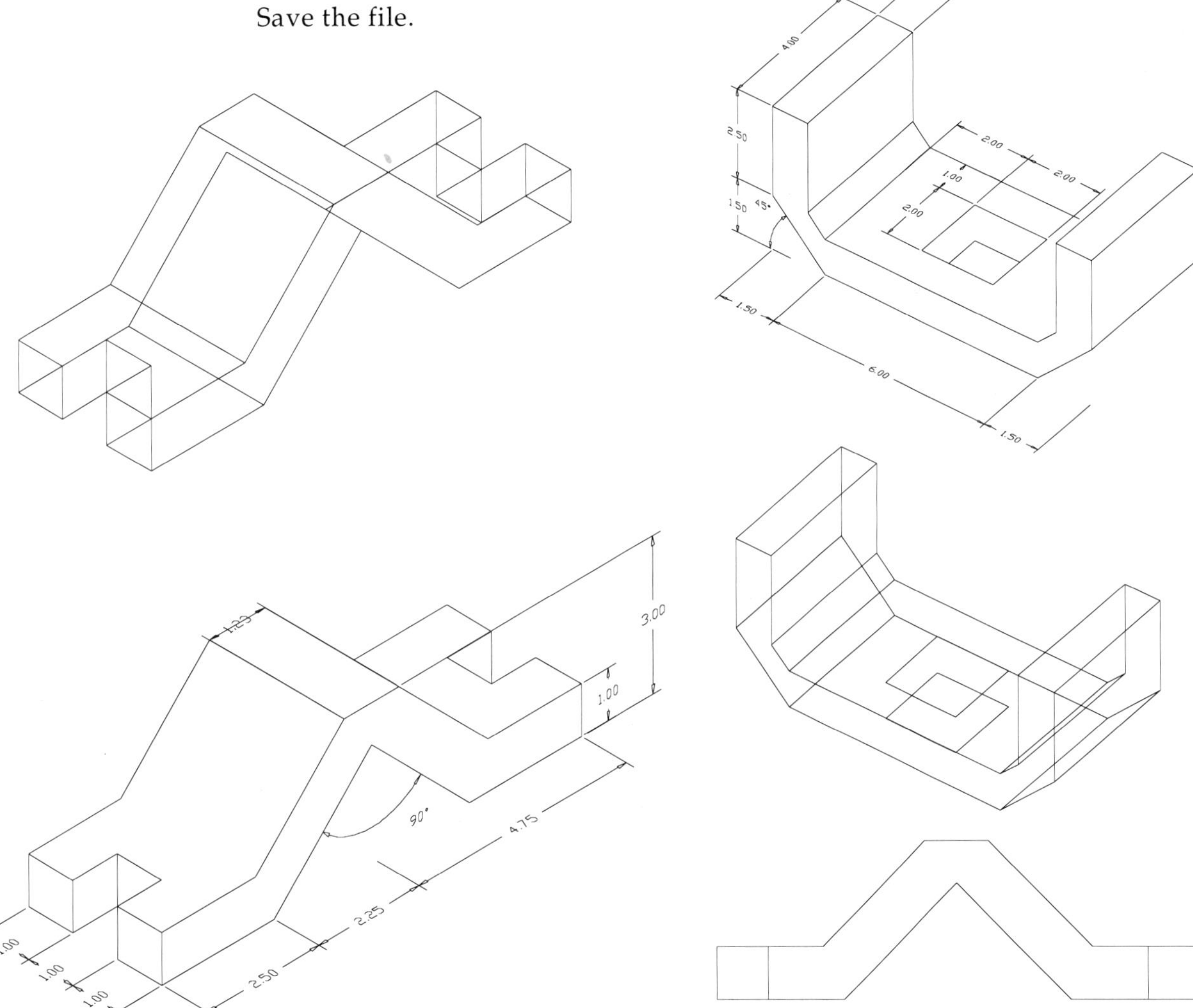

1. Use 3DFACE to create the shape at left.
2. Use HIDE to view it properly.
3. Use SHADE for a shaded image.
4. Save the file.

Challenger 28

Taking the actual dimensions of a fireplace from the following chart, create an interior fireplace.

Fireplace Opening Width	Fireplace Opening Height	Depth	Backwall Width	Vertical Backwall Height	Inclined Backwall Height	Flue lining Out Side	Flue lining In Side
24	24	16-18	14	14	16	8 1/2 x 13	10
28	24	16-18	14	14	16	8 1/2 x 13	10
36	28	16-18	22	14	18	8 1/2 x 13	12
48	32	18-20	32	14	24	13 x 13	15
60	40	20-22	44	17	30	18 x 18	18
72	40	22-28	51	17	30	18 x 18	18

Create the surfaces using 3DFACE.

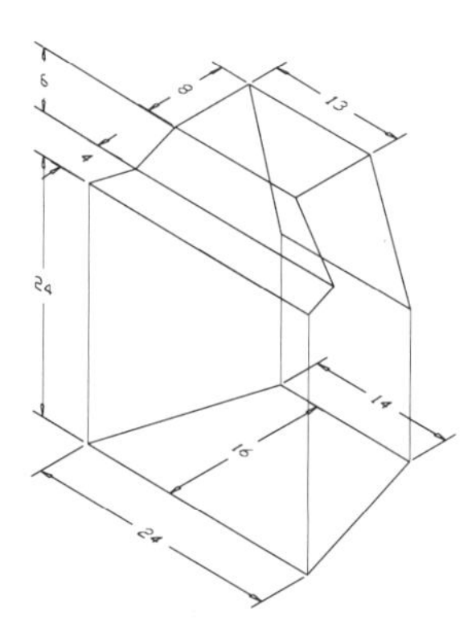

By creating this in a planar or surface mode, you can later take this data with the exterior surface and load it onto AME or analysis software and calculate such things as weight, strength, etc. If you do it strictly with line data, this can't be transferred into a solid or shading mode as quickly.

The intent of this model is to have it accessible for experimentation with other facilities when completed, and to create a model for sectioning.

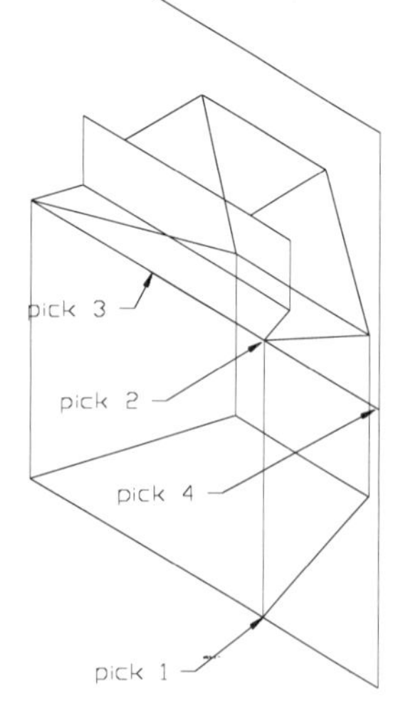

Once the interior is completed, use 3DFACE to create the exterior walls and mantel, etc. for the fireplace. Remember that using I will make unwanted lines invisible. In this case use the following.

Command: **3DFACE**

First point: *(pick 1)*

Second point: **@12,0,0** *(taking the smallest above)*

Third point: **i @0,0,24**

Fourth point: **i end** *(of pick 2)*

Third point: **i mid** *(of pick 3)*

Fourth point: **i** @0,0,24

Third point: **@0,0,24**

Fourth point: **end** *(of pick 4)*

Third point: ↵

Challenger 28 (continued)

Now that the front is finished, create flues, cold air vents, etc., where they would be on a cold air fed fireplace.

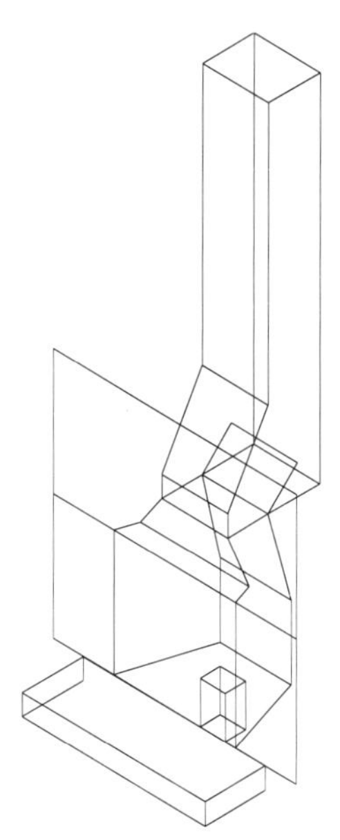

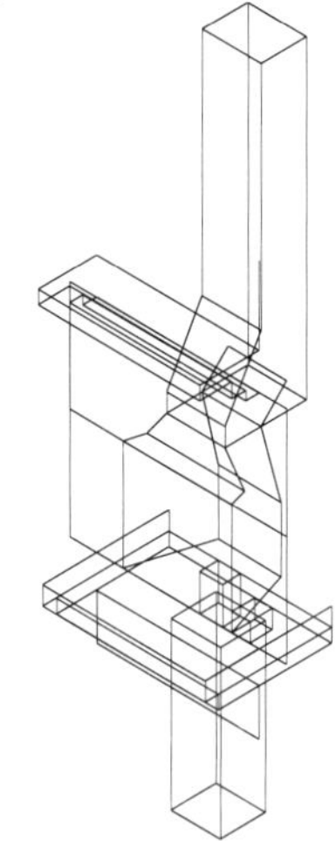

Add a ledge by the fireplace opening slightly cantilevered (12 inches) over the floor, and the mantel details at whatever height you feel is appropriate.

While entering all these details, keep in mind that you will want to have only certain items visible on the final drawing, so keep the parts in various different layers for future flexibility.

Having completed the fireplace, file the model for use on solids, analysis, and AME applications.

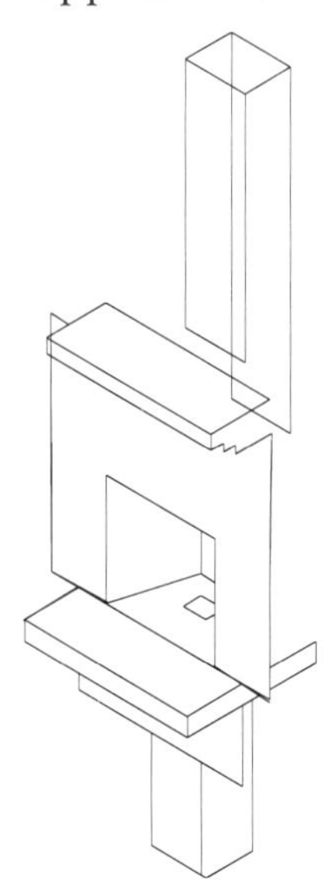

Now offset the 3DFACEs to create the firebrick and other masonry details. Use DVIEW with Clip to get a cross section. Make all appropriate dimensions and notations, and create a full drawing.

Having used 3DFACE to create many of your surfaces, you will also be able to generate a nice, fairly comprehensive cut-away view of the finished fireplace with the HIDEPLOT command in MVIEW.

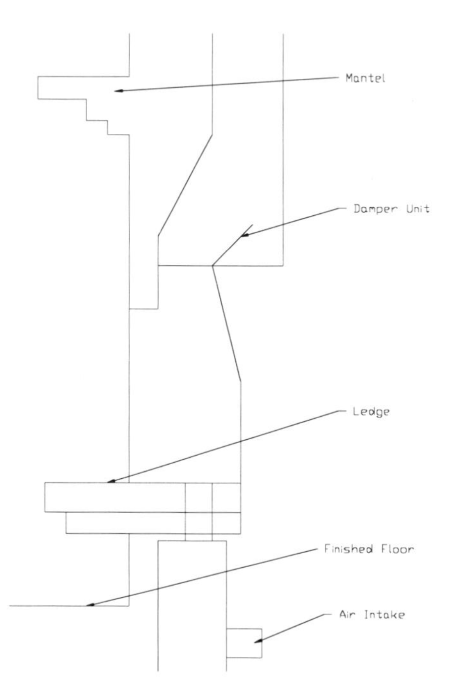

Once your final drawing is assembled, plot it, or use SHADE to get a shaded image.

DYNAMIC VIEWING

Upon completion of this chapter, the student should be able to:

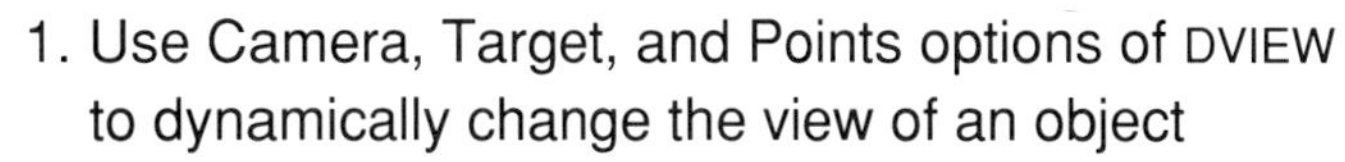

1. Use Camera, Target, and Points options of DVIEW to dynamically change the view of an object
2. Generate a perspective view of an object using the Distance option of DVIEW
3. Use other Dynamic View options to create an ideal view of an object

AUTOCAD'S MODEL SPACE

In order to fully understand AutoCAD's advanced viewing commands, it is necessary to have a complete understanding of how the model space works. In model space, the object exists as a 3D entity. The views can be seen as different cameras focusing on the object or model itself. The user uses the VPORTs to view the model.

Let's take a look at how AutoCAD's model space is arranged in order to let you view objects in 3D space. Then we will look at AutoCAD's options for making views both more accessible and more useful for presentation purposes.

In Figure 29-1 you will see the two viewing angles through which you can rotate using the VPOINT command.

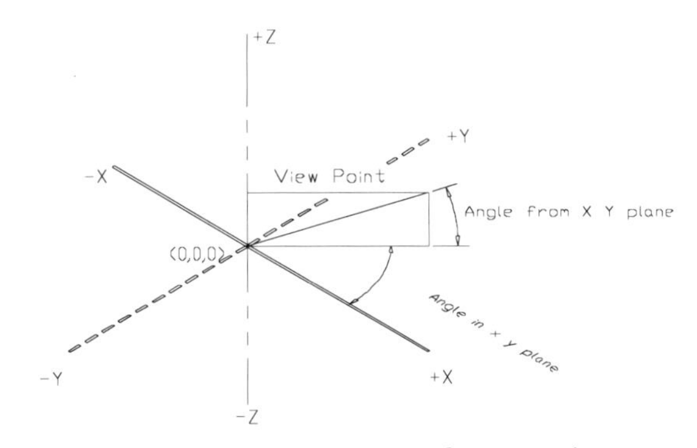

Figure 29-1. Using the VPOINT Command

Release 12 Notes

There is no difference in the DVIEW command. It is found under the View pull-down menu.

The angle in X-Y plane is essentially a rotation around Z.

The angle from X-Y plane is essentially a rotation above or below the X-Y plane.

If the angle in X-Y plane is 0, then you are rotating around Y with the angle from X-Y plane. You will be looking at the model origin from the 3 o'clock position of a 12-hour clock.

If the angle in X-Y plane is 90, then you are rotating around X with the angle from X-Y plane. You will be looking at the model origin from the 12 o'clock position.

You can rotate your viewpoint anywhere on the screen with the Rotate option of the VPOINT command. As in everything else in AutoCAD, all angles will be counter-clockwise. In rotations, this is counter-clockwise from the viewpoint looking back towards the origin or 0,0,0.

Where many people, particularly those in mechanical areas, like to start when drawing an item is with a regular orthographic view.

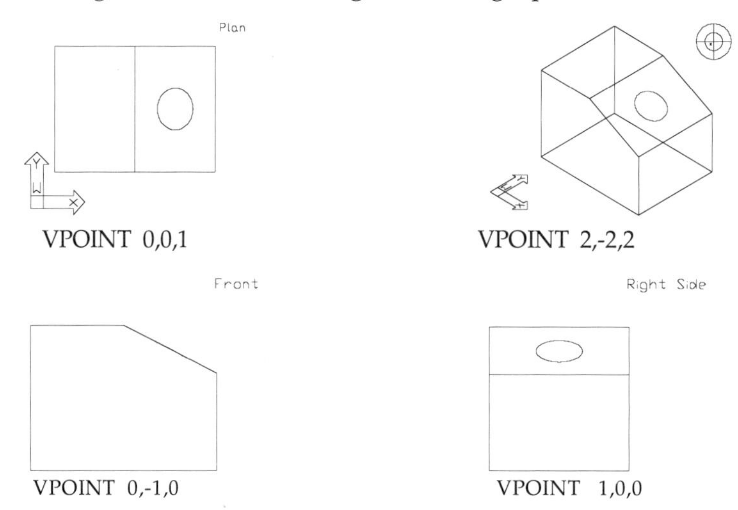

The four views can also be taken directly from the pull-down menu Vpoint 3D. Use PLAN for the top view, FRONT for the front view, RIGHT SIDE for the side view and 2,-2,2 for the isometric view.

With UCS unchanged, the Z axis will be extended vertically from the PLAN view. The UCS in this case is set to World, as can be seen in the icons. The top view or PLAN view has the X-Y plane, the front view has the X-Z plane and the side view has the Y-Z plane.

This layout will give you access to all views and all planes for modification. This is possibly the most practical viewport layout, particularly for mechanical applications, because it allows you to see all necessary views.

This layout is also practical if you are creating drawings from your 3D models as it offers you the traditional views needed for communication of information concerning the part being designed.

You can store this layout as a prototype drawing if you are planning to use it often. If not, you can simply save it as a vport and add it to your menu system. Use Chapter 19 and 20 of this book to learn how.

DVIEW OPTIONS

For many reasons, you may wish to rotate views while you are designing the part. This is one of the great advantages of the CAD environment. AutoCAD has developed the Dview options (Dynamic view) for this purpose. This command is used most frequently when preparing presentations either on screen or on paper.

In essence, what is happening is that you are making a dynamic use of the rotation capabilities outlined on page 479. The DVIEW commands perform in the same way as a user holding a camera which is focused on a particular point or target on the object.The DVIEW command is as follows:

```
Command:DVIEW
CAmera/TArget/Distance/POints/PAn/Zoom/TWist/Clip/Hide/Off/
Undo/<eXit>:
```

Where:

CA = the "camera" angle relative to the part.

CL = the clip of the object, or sets the front and back clipping planes.

D = the distance between the "camera" and the target or object.

H = a removal of hidden lines within the dynamic view.

O = perspective off.

PA = pan within the DVIEW command.

PO = points for the "camera" and object or target.

TA = a rotation of the object.

TW = twist. It twists the dynamic view relative to the line of sight.

U = undo.

X = exit from the DVIEW command.

Z = zoom within the DVIEW command. It sets the lens length.

The line between the Camera (user) and the Target (object) forms the line of sight the same as a user and the object.

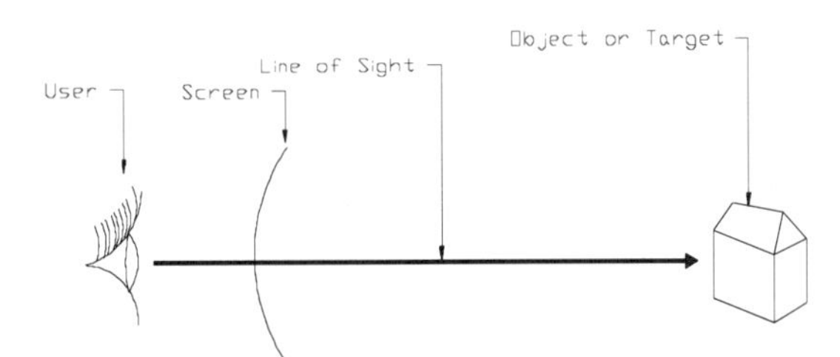

Figure 29-2. How DVIEW works

You can move the camera or the object or target separately or together to view 3D objects from any angle. Then you can change the distance between the two, zoom the object in, pan it, or twist it. Once positioned, you can clip and hide it as well.

Using DVIEW Options

The DVIEW command affects only the active or current viewport. Once you have entered the command, AutoCAD will prompt you for the objects that you would like to have displayed while you are rotating. The object select option allows you to minimize the objects to be dynamically viewed. If you have a small (less than 50,000K) file, there is no problem with dynamically viewing it. A large file, however, will take a very long time to drag. With this in mind, AutoCAD developed the default model which is an image of a small house with a chimney. This is the image that you will get if you don't select any objects to rotate.

AutoCAD searches for a user-defined file or block called DVIEWBLOCK which can be an image appropriate for the application or firm. If this block is not defined, AutoCAD will bring up this house:

Having selected the objects to drag, AutoCAD now offers you a choice of options. As in most AutoCAD commands, you need only choose the capitalized letters of the option to bring it up. The image will then be manipulated according to your choice of option.

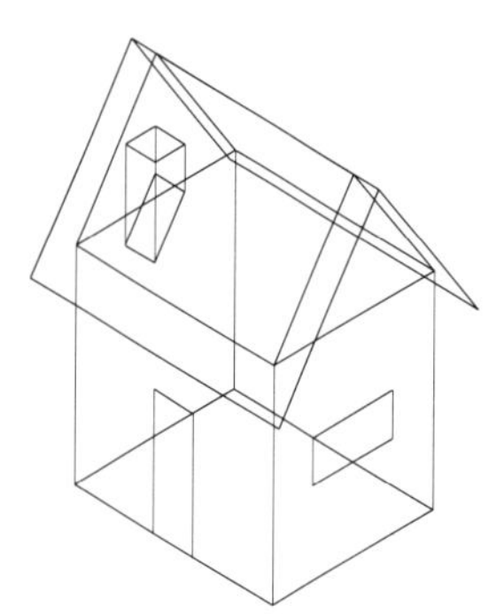

Figure 29-3. The DVIEW default image

The easiest way to get to some of the Dview options is through the icon menu. This is under the Display pull-down menu. DVIEW is also found under the Display screen menu.

Camera

Let's start by establishing the viewing direction, or how you are looking at the object.

One of the most important options in DVIEW is the Camera facility. With this, you get to play the keygrip on the movie set. The image is where it is supposed to be, and you are slowly moving the camera around it until you get to the precise position that you want.

The Camera option rotates the object in the same way that the Rotate option of VPOINT rotates. The differences are that the camera rotates around the target point, not around 0,0, and the order of the angle prompts is reversed.

Once the Camera option has been invoked, you are requested to choose the rotation as specified before; the angle from the X-Y plane and the angle in the X-Y plane. The current angle is provided on a slide bar within the current viewport.

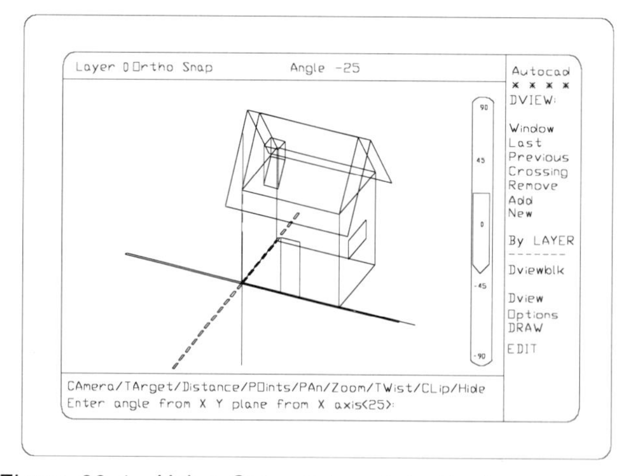

Figure 29-4. Using Camera to rotate the image

In the first rotation, the angles are from 90 to -90, with 0 being parallel to the ground plane, 90 being a bird's eye view, and -90 being a worm's.

You can see from the sliding bar how the bar changes the position by degrees from 0. The image moves along with the bar as you slide it. Again, the more items you are dragging, the longer it takes. All of this is dependent on the size of your computer's RAM as well.

```
Command:DVIEW
CAmera/TArget/Distance/POints/PAn/Zoom/TWist/Clip/Hide/Off/
Undo/<eXit>:CA
```

`Enter angle from X-Y plane:` *(above) (0 – 90 degrees will be above the house)*

`Enter angle in X-Y plane from X axis:` *(next page)*

Once you have picked the angle you would like *from* the X-Y plane, you are prompted for the angle *in* the X-Y plane.

This rotation has the sliding bar across the top, and the numbers for a full 360 degrees, from -180 on the left to 180 on the right.

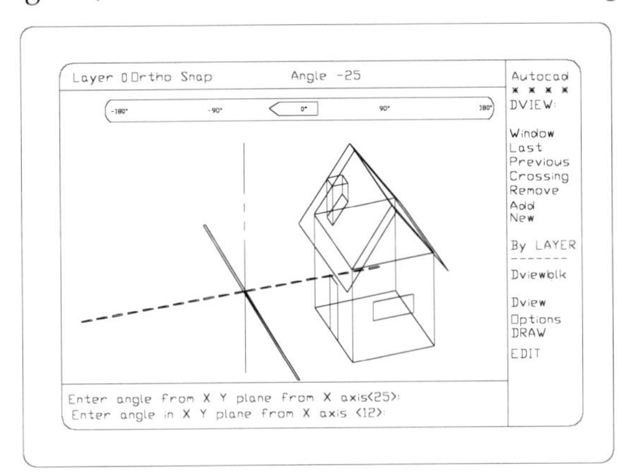

Figure 29-5. Rotating into the X-Y plane

The image rotates virtually all around the Z axis from the positive X looking at the origin 0, 180 degrees in both directions: negative left and positive right. This is the same as the first rotation on page 479.

With the Camera option, you are moving the camera around the target or object, thus you will always see the object on the screen if you are not moving the cursor too quickly. Figure 29-6 maps the movement from above.

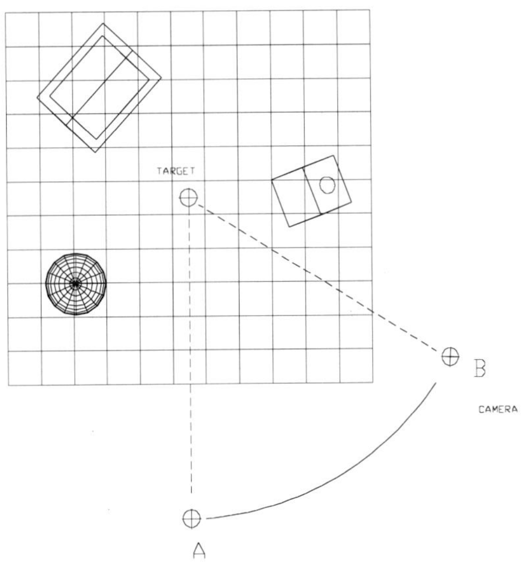

Figure 29-6. Orientation of objects in plane

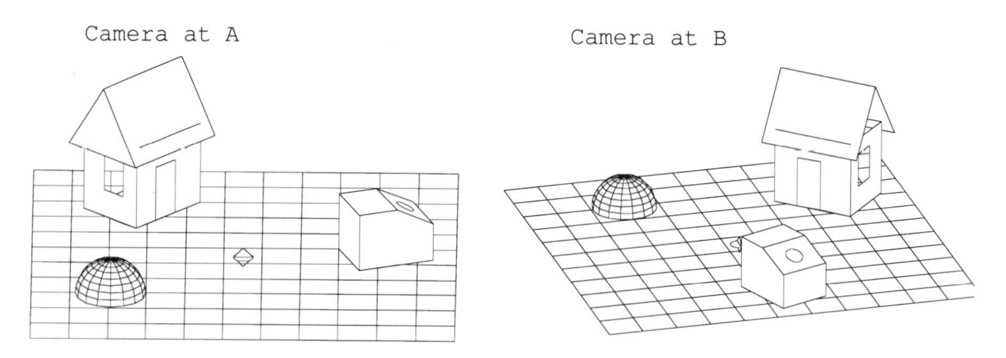

The camera is moving around the set and the set remains the same.

To create this view, the camera spot B is 60 degrees away from the camera spot A. Camera spot A, from the target, is -90 degrees, and camera spot B is thus -30.

An angle of 90 would be looking at the back of the house. The other objects are, obviously a rock and a very trendy compost bin.

Note that the angle used in this and other Dview options is the angle of the UCS, not the angle in the WCS.

While moving the bar across the screen in the camera option, you will see an angle written at the top of the screen. The slider bars are very useful for getting a view of the rotation of the object. If you want to have a standardized view, once you have picked the approximate view with the slider bar, you can type in an exact number for the angle and use this as a standard. This is a good technique if you are rotating several rooms or several parts that you would like for presentation purposes.

Note that the Dview option automatically turns SNAP off. You can toggle it back on again, but this varies with the orientation of your view. If you set your SNAP to .005556, the right slider bar will move in 1 degree increments and if you set it to .0044562 it will move the top slider in 1 degree increments.

The Camera option is also a very good way to check your 3D images for integrity of design. By picking the Camera option and turning the part a bit, you can see if it will hold up or if it falls apart at the first rotation. If your parts crumble in camera, you are not using OSNAP and UCS properly. The most common error in 3D for beginning students is picking points line-of-sight onto the X-Y plane. With Camera, the objects created this way are immediately apparent.

Target

The Target option is similar to Camera in that it positions the object relative to the camera. Target is extremely useful for doing walk-throughs of houses and other types of activities where you are in the centre of the part and want to turn the focus on different areas of it.

In the VPOINT command, the rotation always takes place around the origin point. In Target, you can change the position at which the view is focused.

If we take the analogy of a movie set once more, instead of the camera moving around the set with the actors stationary as in Camera, the actor is moving around the set and the camera is following.

The camera stays in the same place, but the target moves. Other than that, the option is the same as that for Camera.

Command:**DVIEW**

CAmera/TArget/Distance/POints/PAn/Zoom/TWist/Clip/Hide/Off/
Undo/<eXit>:**TA**

Enter angle from X-Y plane<14>:**20**

(0 – 90 degrees will be above the house)

Enter angle in X-Y plane from X axis:**64**

To illustrate the TARGET command, we will take the same set. In Figure 29-7 the camera is now at point 0 and the objects move according to it.

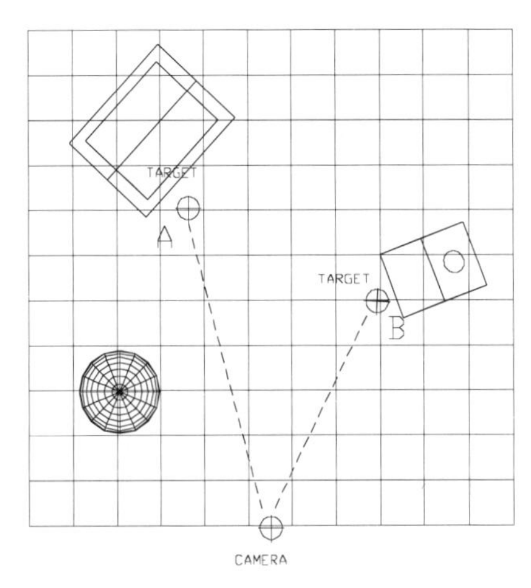

Figure 29-7. Orientation of objects in plan view

At point B the target is rotated 65 degrees away from 0. At point A the target is rotated 105 degrees away from 0. Using any angle over 180 degrees will obviously not work as there is nothing behind the camera.

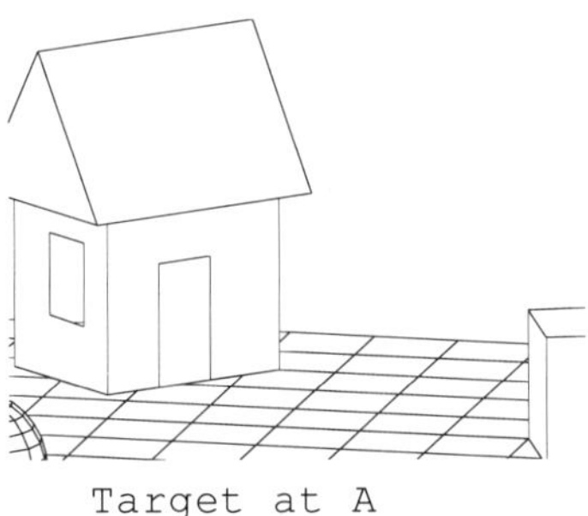

Target at A

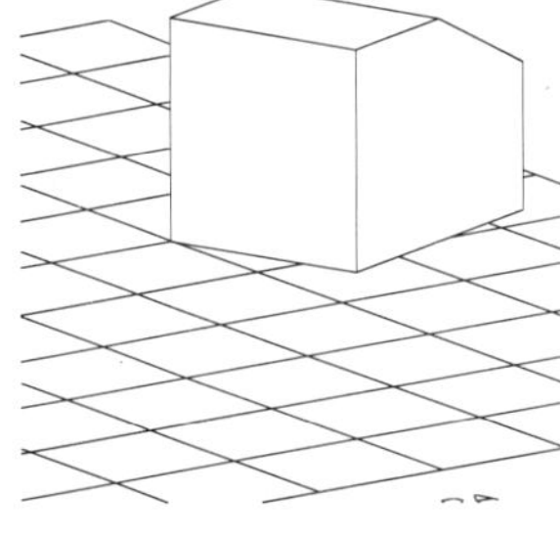

Target at B

Your default position for target is always 0,0.

Points

Another way to set up the screen is to set the line of sight with the Points option. This option combines a movement of the Camera with a movement of the Target.

Command:**DVIEW**

CAmera/TArget/Distance/POints/PAn/Zoom/TWist/Clip/Hide/Off/
Undo/<eXit>:**PO**

Enter target point <25,30,0>:**4,4,4**

Enter camera point <0,0,5>:**30,30,30**

Once you have picked the spot for your target, you have a rubber band effect with a line from the target to the camera until you have chosen the camera's position.

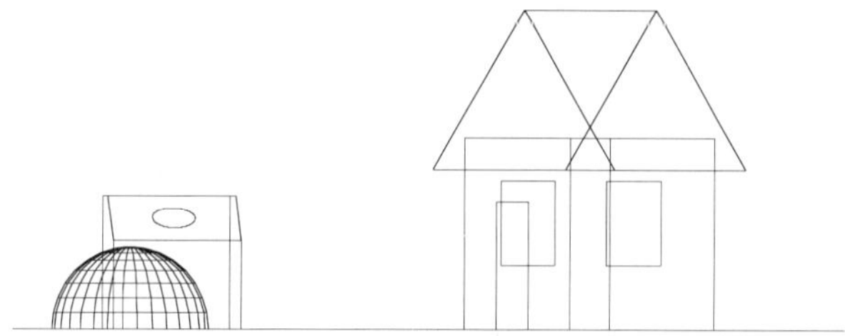

Figure 29-8. Images to be rotated

In Figure 29-8 we have the same layout as in the previous illustrations. From the front the objects look like this. The house is higher than the hedge and compost bin.

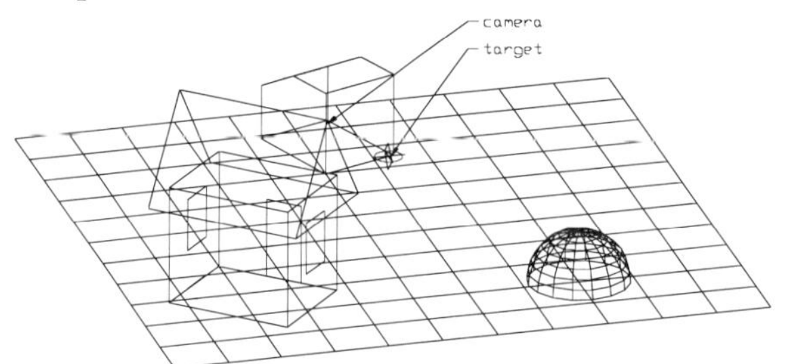

Figure 29-9. Changing the target and camera points

In Figure 29-9 the target point is the bottom corner of the compost bin and the camera is the top peak of the roof of the house. The two points are lined up exactly.

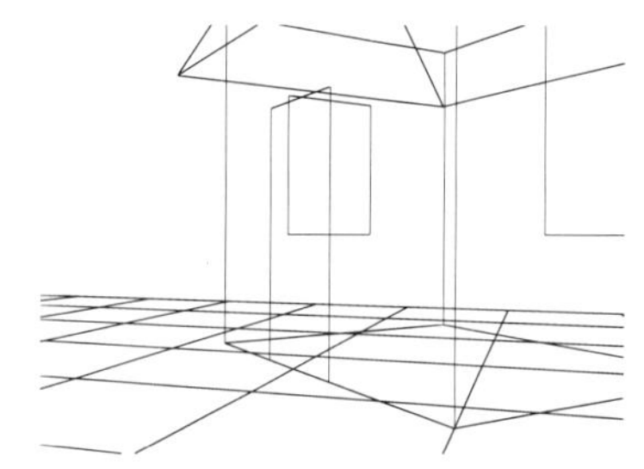

Figure 29-10. Altering the viewpoint with Points

In Figure 29-10 the target is the bottom ledge of the window within the house and the camera is the middle point on the right side of the door. You can see by this that it will often be useful to place a point or line at the exact position that you would like your camera to be. Otherwise you will be looking throught the objects as we are looking through the side of the door.

The Points option gives you the possibility of having exactly the view you are after from the angle that you want.

Distance

Many applications call for a perspective view of a house or object. The perspective command in DVIEW is invoked with the Distance option.

The camera is moved along a constant line of sight toward or away from the target. The scale this time is from 0X (on the left) to 16X (on the far right).

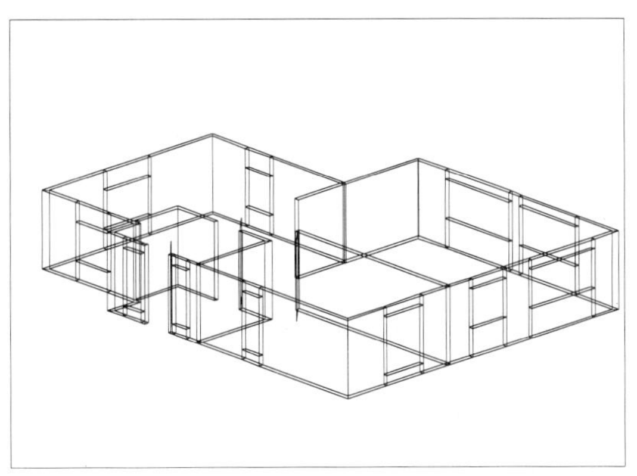

Figure 29-11. Before using the Distance option

Above is a parallel view of the object before the Distance option has been employed.

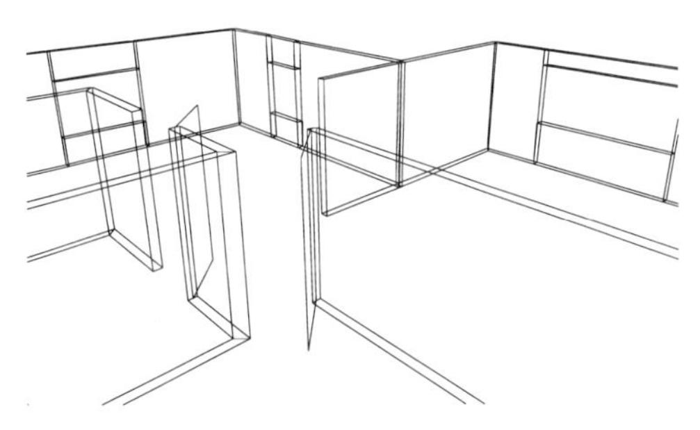

Figure 29-12. Using the Distance option

This second view, Figure 29-12, has the Distance set at 4X, and the third view, Figure 29-13, has the Distance set at 12X.

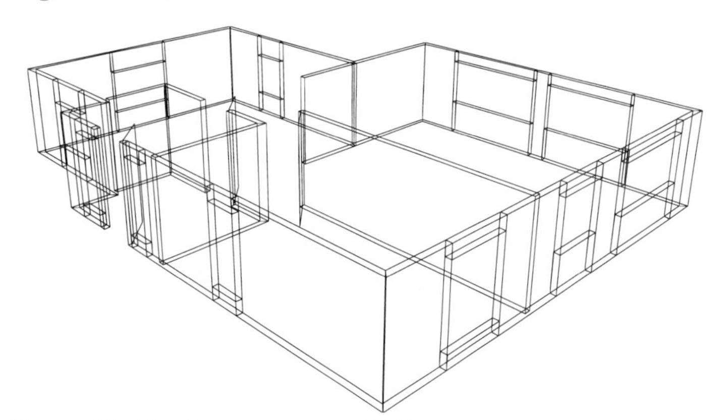

Figure 29-13. Distance set at 12X

Note that the X in this case has nothing to do with the coordinate X.

The sliding bar in this option wil invoke a continuous updating of your screen until you get the view that you want. Again take note of the exact distance for standardized views.

Once you have perspective on, you will notice that there are many commands that are disabled. The icon in the corner of your screen will change as well to the one on the next page.

To get back to a view where you can work with the geometry and display commands that you need turn DVIEW off.

```
Command:DVIEW
CAmera/TArget/Distance/POints/PAn/
Zoom/TWist/Clip/Hide/Off/Undo/<eXit>:OFF
```

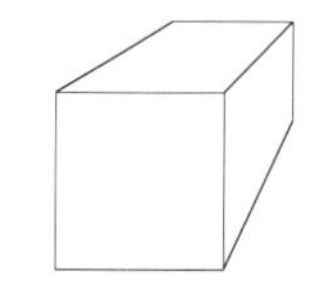

Clip

One of the most useful options for creating drawings is Clip. With Clip you can identify a section of the part and extract it for viewing. For many models this is useful for viewing areas that are obscured by foreground objects. In addition, this offers a relatively easy way to get section views. LAYERS can be used effectively for viewing, but in many cases, the LAYERS are created for ease of viewing and manipulating the whole part, not just one plane. The more complex the wireframe model, the more readily you will turn to this command.

The clipping planes are perpendicular to the line of sight, between the camera and the target. In essence, it's like a huge knife or cheese cutter slicing through the part. You can place both a foreground and a background plane at a specific distance from the target. By specifying a positive value, you are cutting from between the target and the viewer; a negative number will cut behind the target.

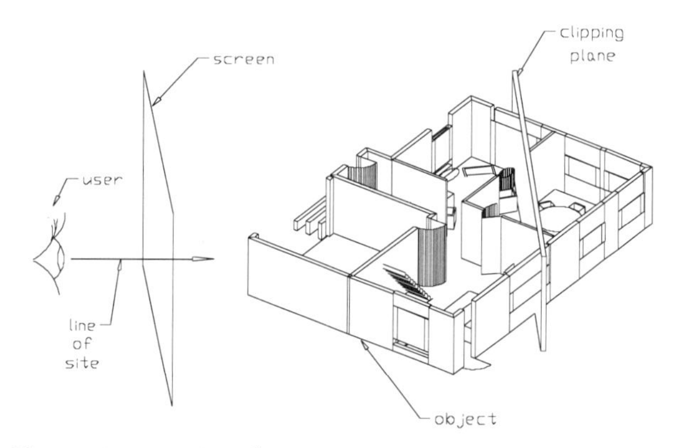

Figure 29-14. Viewing the clipping plane

In the above illustration, the user is looking line-of-sight at the 3D floor plan. The cutting plane is perpendicular to the user. A Front clip would take out all objects in front of the clipping plane leaving only the dining room. A Back clip would take out everything behind the cutting plane.

```
Command:DVIEW
CAmera/TArget/Distance/POints/PAn/Zoom/TWist/Clip/Hide/Off/
Undo/<eXit>:CL
Back/Front/:B
ON/OFF/distance from target:
```

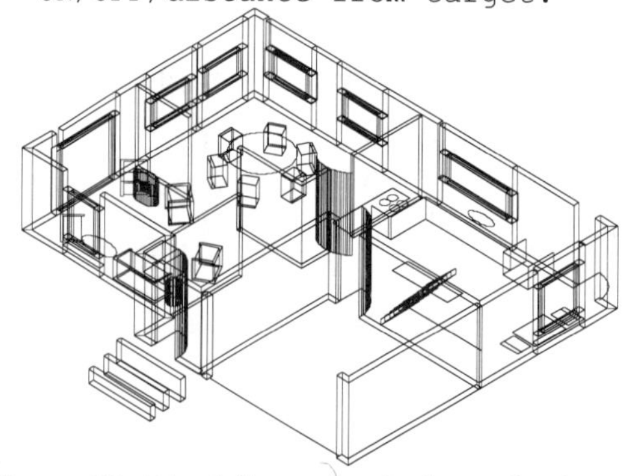

Figure 29-15. A floor plan before clipping

Figure 29-15 is a view of Exercise A26. It is a simple 3D layout of a house. The UCS is set to World, but the VPOINT is set to 2,-2,2.

You can see how you are getting an isometric view of this house.

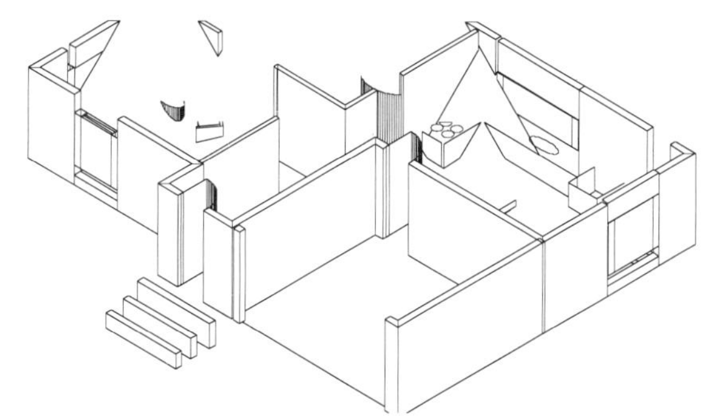

Figure 29-16. Clipping off the back of the house

In figure 29-16, the room has been clipped from the back. The clipping has been done perpendicular to the line of sight, 19 feet from the target.

The clipping, as you can see, has taken out part of the back wall. The clip has gone straight through the house.

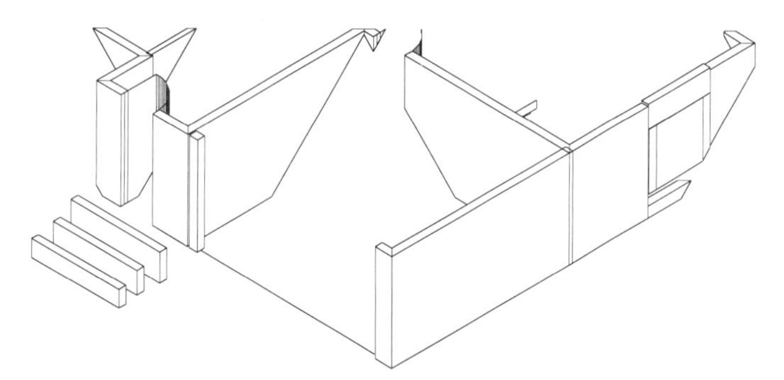

Figure 29-17. Clipping off more of the back

This second clip, shown in Figure 29-17, has taken off almost all of the back portions of the house.

HIDE (Hideplot in MVIEW) has been used in both of these clips to show the wall cuts. In this view the garage has a section of the back wall taken out.

This type of view could be used on a house for structural presentations. Once the clip has taken place, the UCS can be changed to View and notations can be added.

The clipping can also be useful for the front sections of houses, particularly for showing sizes of rooms, etc. The Front clipping plane obscures all objects between the selected plane and the camera. Again negative and positive numbers can be used as well.

Figure 29-18 shows the first 15 feet of the house cut off to show us the inside of the dining room. Again the slider bar, cut into quarters, drags the front clipping plane and updates the screen as the cursor is moved. The distance from the clipping plane is shown on the status line above. Positive values indicate a plane between the target and the camera, negative values indicate a plane behind the target or on the back of the target, thus defeating the purpose of using Front.

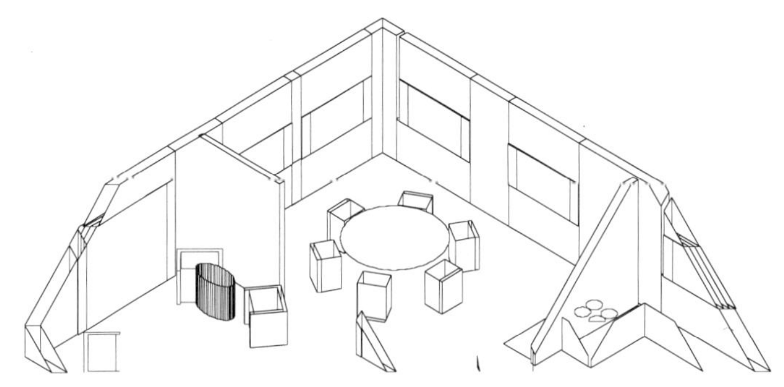

Figure 29-18. Clipping off the front

With the Eye option, the front clipping plane moves to the position of the camera.

CLIPPING AND DISTANCE

If perspective (Distance) is off, you can change the front clipping plane at any time. If perspective is on, however, the front clipping plane remains on always, until perspective is turned off. If you turn the clipping plane off while perspective is on, the clipping plane will move to the camera position, i.e., nothing is clipped.

Clipping to Create Sections

Clipping can be done for presentation or display purposes as seen in the example above, or it can be used to create sections of 3D objects. The most obvious reason for doing this is to make a view for drawing purposes. Another reason is to remove duplicate lines on a view to minimize objects on screen and objects that need to be plotted. When you plot a 3D object with a pen plotter, the pen will draw every object that is on the screen. If there are many objects overlapping, each one of these objects will be drawn. By the time the pen has drawn the 10th line in the same place, the paper will be ripped and you will risk damaging the plotter itself. Try to eliminate overlapping items with the Clip option of the DVIEW command.

In the example on the right, we will take the mechanical part from Chapter 26 and clip it. To make the part easier to see we have taken the countersinks to the bottom of the part and covered them with ruled surfaces. If you would like to try this, simple use RULESURF and pick the two circles to be surfaced.

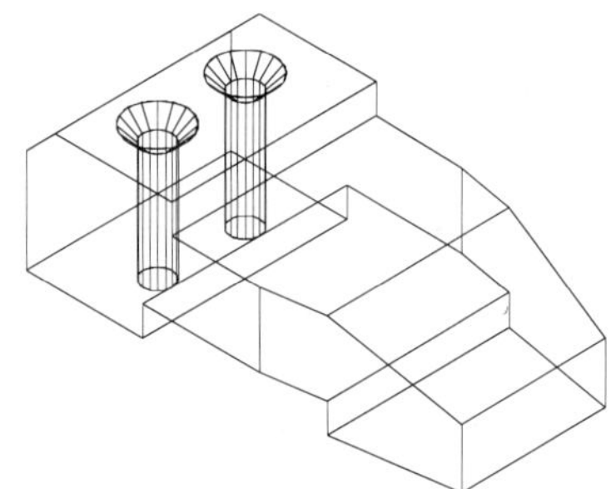

Example: *DVIEW Clip*

When we look at the part from the right side (VPOINT 5,0,0), we see the object in its entirety.

STEP 1
Bring up the part and use VPOINT to view it from the right side (5,0,0).

Many of the lines are overlapping, and we have a difficult time seeing the part that we would like to section because there are so many horizontal lines.

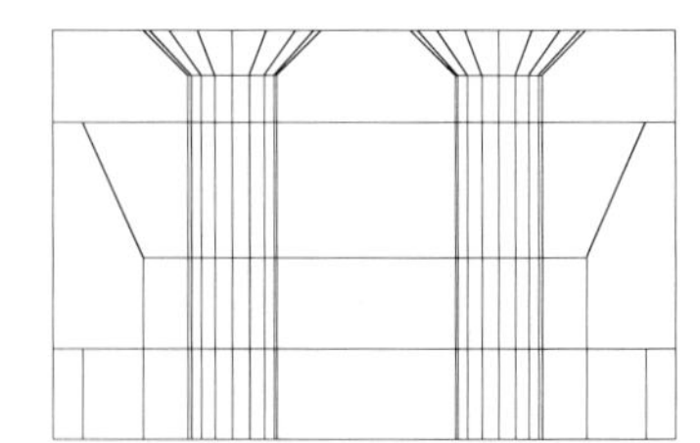

We would like to section just the area where the countersinks are.

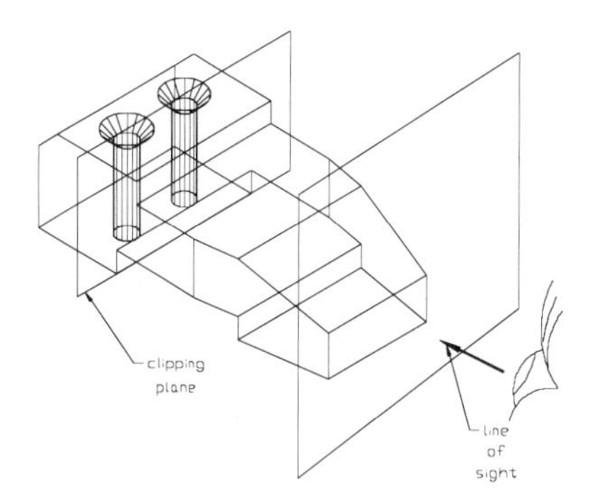

As you can see from the illustration on the right, the user is looking line-of-sight through the part. The desired clipping plane is positioned just before the countersinks.

Using the Clip option, we can clip off the front section of the part.

STEP 2

Use DVIEW with Clip to clip off the front section of the part.

```
Command:DVIEW
CAmera/TArget/Distance/POints/PAn/Zoom/TWist/Clip/Hide/Off/
Undo/<eXit>:CL
Back/Front/:F
ON/OFF/ance from target:
```
(move the cursor until you have an appropriate view)

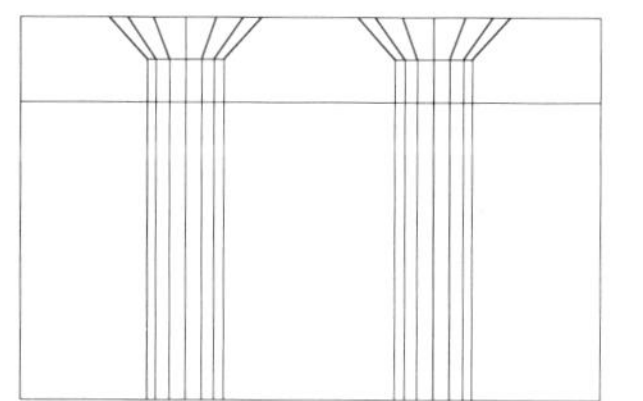

This is the view that you will have once the clip has been performed. You can now change the UCS to the front of the plane and hatch the section and dimension it for final drawing purposes. This technique can be used on all types of parts.

Using HiddenXXXX, you can create a hidden line at the top for plotting. See page 437.

TWIST

While we're exploring line-of-sight, another option for viewing is Twist. This rotates the image line-of-sight from the viewer.

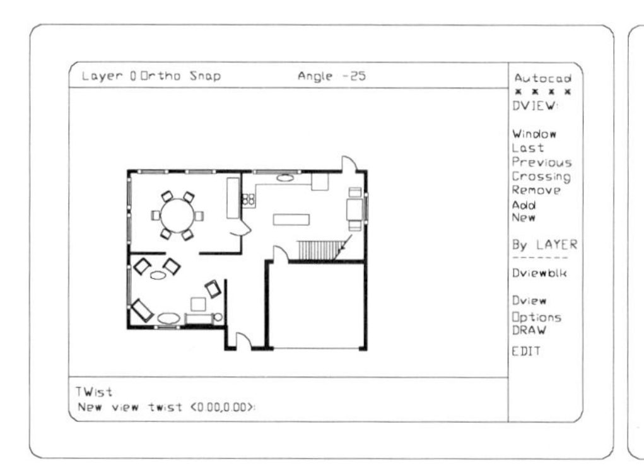

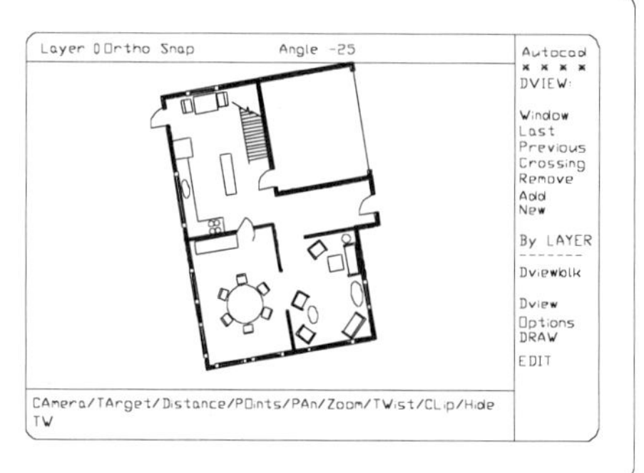

Figure 29-19. Using the DVIEW Twist option

```
Command:DVIEW
CAmera/TArget/Distance/POints/PAn/Zoom/TWist/Clip/Hide/Off/
Undo/<eXit>:TW
New view twist:85
```

This looks the same as the editing command ROTATE; the difference is that the geometry has the same coordinates after a twist, but the geometry has totally different coordinates after a rotate.

ZOOM AND PAN

These commands are the same within the DVIEW command as they have been throughout your AutoCAD experience. The reason that they are contained within the DVIEW command is that they cannot be invoked from outside the command if the perspective has been changed. There are also slight differences in the commands.

ZOOM

ZOOM will change the magnification of the view of the object, but you are prompted for the lens length or focal distance instead of the scale factor.

```
Command:DVIEW
CAmera/TArget/Distance/POints/PAn/Zoom/TWist/Clip/Hide/Off/
Undo/<eXit>:Z
Adjust lenslength<2mm>:25
```

If you have used the Distance option, you won't be able to use the command ZOOM; you must zoom with this command. To get a good perspective view you may need to use Distance and Zoom many times before you have the view you want.

PAN

With PAN, you are asked for a displacement as in the DISPLAY command. Again, this takes some practice before you are adept at using Distance without the PAN option.

```
Command:DVIEW
CAmera/TArget/Distance/POints/PAn/Zoom/TWist/Clip/Hide/Off/
Undo/<eXit>:PA
Displacement Base point: (pick 1)
Second point: (pick 2)
```

HIDE, UNDO, AND EXIT

These options are also very similar to the commands with the same name that you are already familiar with. Hide will give you a view of the objects with all the hidden lines removed. This is included within the command simply for convenience. Note, however, that only the objects selected for viewing within the DVIEW command will have hidden lines removed, and that the full wire-frame will return once the DVIEW command has been exited. Use Hide to remove all hidden lines after DVIEW has been done.

Undo will undo the previous option allowing the user to retain all of the options changed within the command already. This is an advantage if there is only one portion of the options that is unsuccessful, and several operations are just what you want.

Exit (X) ends the DVIEW command and gets you back to AutoCAD. Keep in mind that if you used Distance to change your perspective, the perspective icon will still be in the bottom left of your viewport, and you will not be able to use certain commands.

You are meant to generate all the parameters of your image within the DVIEW command and have it ready to print when the command is finished. Similar to the CHANGE command, while working in DVIEW you can use one or all options before exiting from the command.

In order to have a view with hidden lines, use the Hide option in the PLOT or PRPLOT command, or use the Hideplot option in MVIEW. Also note that you can't change viewports or go to paper space within the DVIEW command.

As children, most people learn basic theories of physics by watching their parents' prized possessions as they plummet time after time to the floor and shatter. Similarly, you will have a much more complete and all-encompassing understanding of the DVIEW options from playing with them a bit and seeing how they work than by reading miles of text on the theory.

If you are creating a prototype for drawings, note that many of these options are saved under system variables. LENSLENGTH for Zoom, BACKZ and FRONTZ for clipping planes, TARGET, VIEWTWIST, and VIEWDIR for the camera position. These will be stored with the model.

Release 12 Notes

The DVIEW command in Release 12 has become more sophisticated.
With the camera option, the status line offers the readout on your angle, and you can move transparently between the two angle input modes. By moving the cursor horizontally, you change the angle in the X-Y plane. You can create a full 360-degree rotation.
By moving the cursor vertically, you create a rotation from the X-Y plane. A setting of -90 has the camera looking straight up at the model from below. A positive 90 will give a bird's eye or plan view.

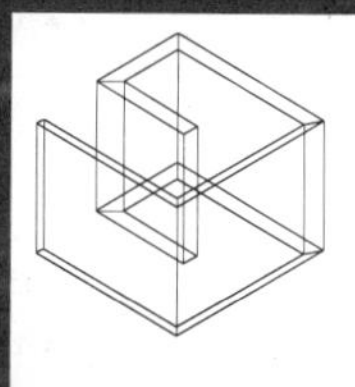
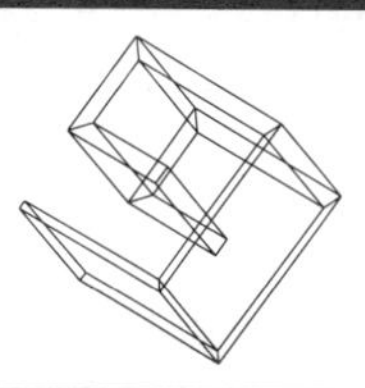
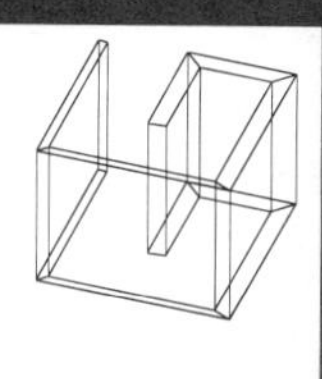

You can enter angles from the keyboard as well as rotating the view by moving the cursor. Enter a T to toggle from one angle to the next.
The other options are similarly streamlined, while in principle maintaining the same theory as in previous releases.

Exercise A29

STEP 1
Insert Exercise A26 into a new drawing, and with the superior knowledge of your retrospective vision, spend 15 minutes, no more, making it more presentable and adding a roof, more fixtures, etc.

STEP 2
Using the DVIEW command, create a walk-through of your house, looking at each room independent of the others. Remember that there are big bucks in selling real estate. The following are expected views. At least six views will be needed.

> **A.** Change the Target and Camera distance, using Points if it is easier.
> **B.** Use Distance to create a perspective of each room and of the house with a roof on.
> **C.** Use Clipping to get rid of all the rooms that you don't need to see if they are obstructing your view.
> **D.** Use Zoom and Pan within the DVIEW command to get a perfect view of the object.

STEP 3
If you have completed Chapter 17, create slides of each room using MSLIDE and generate a short slide show. If you haven't taken slides and slide shows, but have lots of room on your disk, you can save each room as a separate file. If you can't do either of the above, make sure you instructor takes note of each one that you have finished before going on to the next because it is not easy to get back, except with Undo.

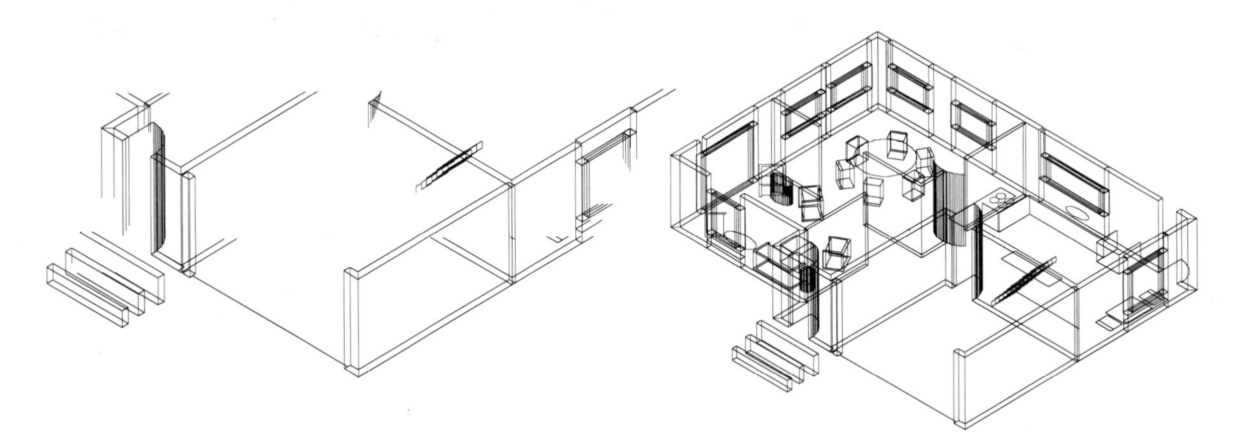

Be careful not to erase objects as they will be needed in other views. Just change your Points and clip all areas not needed. It is OK to have a few portions of another room present as long as there is no mistaking which room you are actually looking at.

Exercise M29

STEP 1
Create a grid the size of Exercise M26.

STEP 2
Insert Exercise M26 onto the grid, and create 3DFACE on all sides. If you haven't completed M26, M27 or M28 will do just as well.

STEP 3
You are trying to convince the client who has commissioned you to do this part that it is perfect in every detail. You will thus create views of the part from all four sides plus the bottom and top, making use of perspective and Hide to make it look really impressive.

A. Change the Target and Camera distance, using Points if it is easier.
B. Use Distance to create a perspective of each view.
C. Use Clipping to create at least one section of the object.
D. Use Zoom and Pan within the DVIEW command to get perfect views of the object.

STEP 4
If you have completed Chapter 17, create slides of each view using MSLIDE and generate a short slide show. If you haven't taken slides and slide shows, but have lots of room on your disk, you can save each room as a separate file. If you can't do either of the above, make sure your instructor takes note of each one that you have finished before going on to the next because it is not easy to get back, except with Undo.

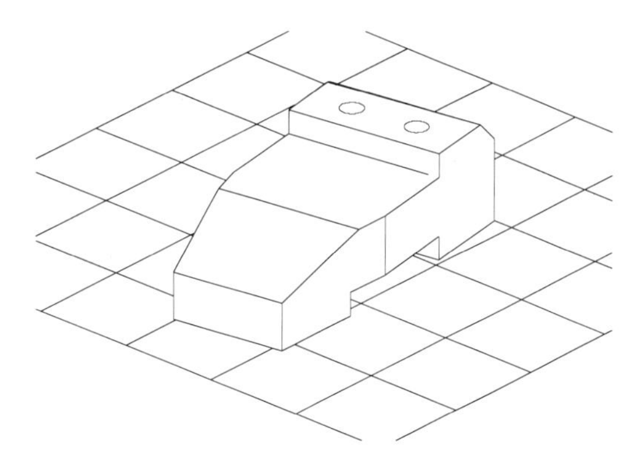

The part should be enhanced by the DVIEW command. You can create a junk layer and add lines from the corners, etc., to aid you in placing the camera or the targets. Once placed, these can be turned off.

Try a section through the centre of the part.

Exercise C29

STEP 1
Create a grid the size of your Exercise C26.

STEP 2
Insert Exercise C26 onto the grid, and create 3DFACE on all sides.

STEP 3
You are trying to convince the developer who has bought the land that this layout is perfect in every detail. You will thus create views of the survey from all four sides plus the end of the street, making use of perspective and Hide to make it look really impressive.

A. Change the Target and Camera distance, using Points if it is easier.
B. Use Distance to create a perspective of each view.
C. Use Clipping to get create at least one section of the land.
D. Use Zoom and Pan within the DVIEW command to get perfect views of the object.

STEP 4
If you have completed Chapter 17, create slides of each view using MSLIDE and generate a short slide show. If you haven't taken slides and slide shows, but have lots of room on your disk, you can save each room as a separate file. If you can't do either of the above, make sure your instructor takes note of each one that you have finished before going on to the next because it is not easy to get back, except with Undo.

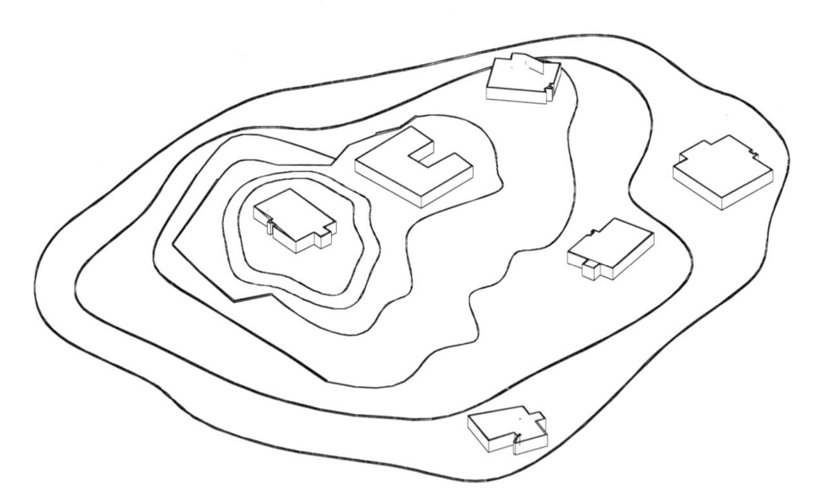

Since you have so much data, make sure you have lots of room on your disk before starting.

Challenger 29

Create a floor plan that has a few indentations and a moderately difficult roof plan. Use this example if you choose.

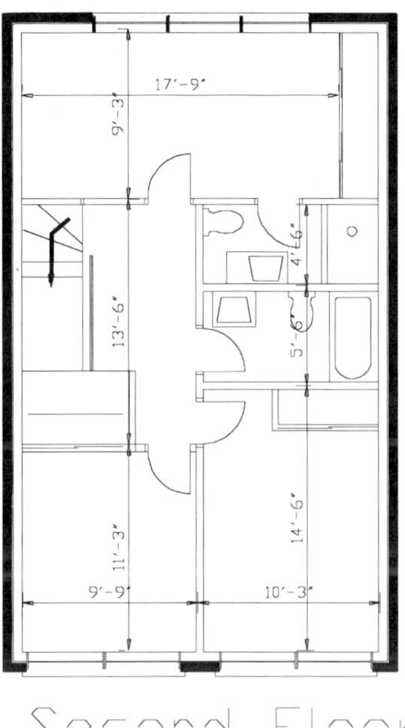

Second Floor

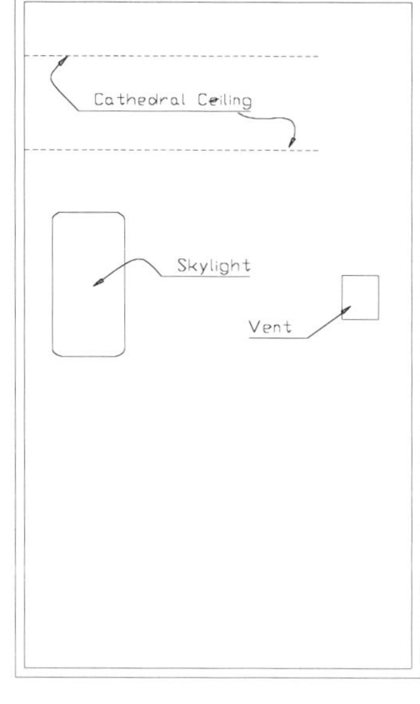

Roof Plan

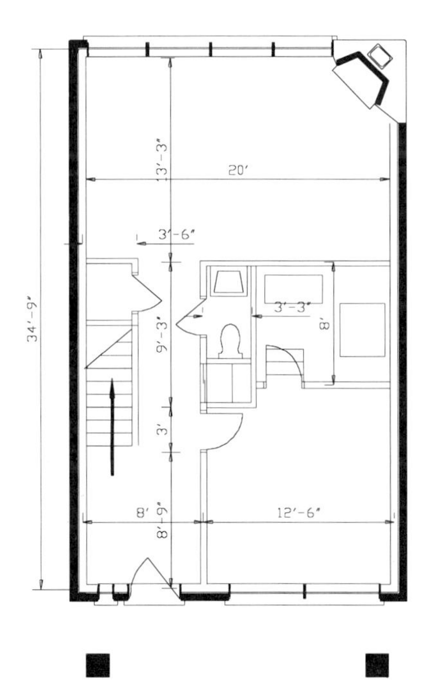

Ground Floor

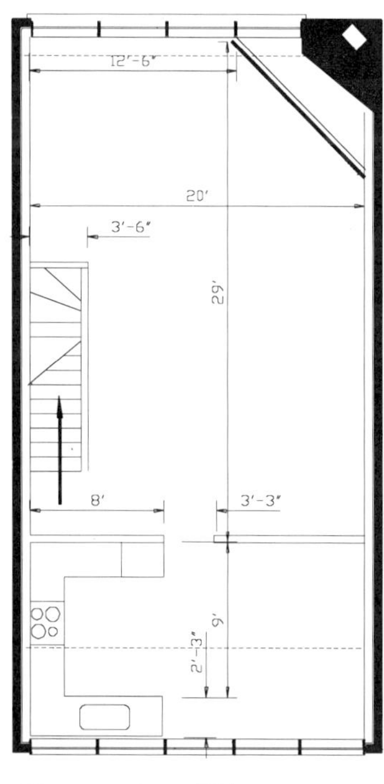

First Floor

CREATING 3D DRAWINGS

Upon completion of this chapter, the student should be able to:

1. Change the model space to paper space
2. Use MVIEW to place multiple views on the drawing
3. Use ZOOM XP to scale the views
4. Use VPLAYER, to control the layer display
5. Use MVSETUP to automate the plotting process
6. Complete a paper space drawing

3D VIEW DRAWINGS

For the past five chapters we have been learning how to create 3D wireframe models and orient them for viewing. In this chapter we will learn how to create a drawing from these various parts by placing them onto a "page" for plotting.

While creating the model, we have been working in model space. This means that we have been working in a three-dimensional mode, accessing the part from any view at any time for means of construction. Once we have the model completed we can create a drawing of the 3D part using the standard views — Front, Top, Side, and Iso — or any others that will properly communicate the model data to the viewer.

Remember that a drawing is, after all, a way of communicating data from one person to another. We read drawings according to the particular communication protocols that we are used to. Each discipline will have a different way of presenting ideas and technical information; different symbols, accepted views, necessary sections, etc. are needed for the reader to understand the various drawings.

In order to make a drawing out of a model or part, we need to be able to rotate the part to be viewed from the most appropriate or accessible vantage points. Then we extract each view that we need to use to describe the part. Once we have decided on the views, we make two-dimensional representations of our model and add dimensioning, hatching, annotation, and details to complete the drawing.

Let's use as an example a simple 3D mechanical part in a typical layout. Planning of the drawing is an important first step. For this part we will choose four standard views — Front, Top, Side, and Iso — plus a detail. We will then decide on the scale of each view, use ZOOM XP to scale each view for paper space, then enter paper space to compile the drawing. We will enter the title block that we need, then add the views to the paper space layout. Finally we will add any notations needed for the drawing, then we will plot it.

A short discussion of the various commands needed to create the drawings will be followed by some in depth-examples.

PAPER SPACE

If you are using Release 10, 9, or 2, paper space is not available, so you will have to compile the drawing using blocks. If this is the case, please continue on to the heading "Multi-View Drawings Using Blocks" on page 512.

Essentially, paper space is a 2D document layout facility. Once the views are completed with all the dimensioning required, the paper space takes these views and translates them to a "paper" much like a cut and paste routine so that they can be compiled as a drawing.

In 3D, paper space extends the multiple viewport facility; the multiple viewports that you used to create the model can be automatically translated to a paper space layout.

- With model space — you have been working in model space so far — you have been describing part geometry. Whether you are creating a house, a survey, an airplane, or a mould for a contact lens, you have been relating to the system the physical properties of real world objects.
- With paper space you are adding to the part geometry all of those things that relate to paper.

In a traditional engineering shop or architectural office, you would have a minimum of two areas where information concerning the final product is created. You would have draftspeople creating drawings and you would have model builders. In AutoCAD, as in any other CAD, the process of design takes place on the system in the model stage, then once the designer is pleased with the results of the design process, the drawings are generated so that the object can be constructed or cut.

While working in model space, you have been working in an environment that is referred to as multi-tiled. This means that your viewports have been like tiles placed together edge to edge. While working with the multi-tiled screen, each viewport contains the same information:

- the same model,
- the same layers,

but in different views and possibly with different zoom factors.

With paper space, you will be opening up the viewports, or getting rid of the viewport edges so that you will have the views of the object set up as you like, but there will be no viewport border lines in between. Paper space acts like a sheet of paper through which the object is seen; you can then annotate as if you were drawing on paper.

With paper space, it is as if you have taken photographs of the model and now you are compiling them on a board or paper for use in communicating the information to someone else.

In the illustration on the following page, the screen on the left is in model space and the screen on the right is in paper space. Both are filled with four views of a simple camera body.

Notice that on the screen on the left the cross-hairs are in one view only. On the right the cross-hairs cover the screen. In the view on the left you have a UCS icon in every viewport, on the right there is only one UCS paper space icon. In the screen on the left there are four separate "tiles," four areas totally enclosed and separate from each other, on the right you have one screen cut into four sections. The borders for the views will not be plotted on the final drawing if they are made on a different layer.

Model Space

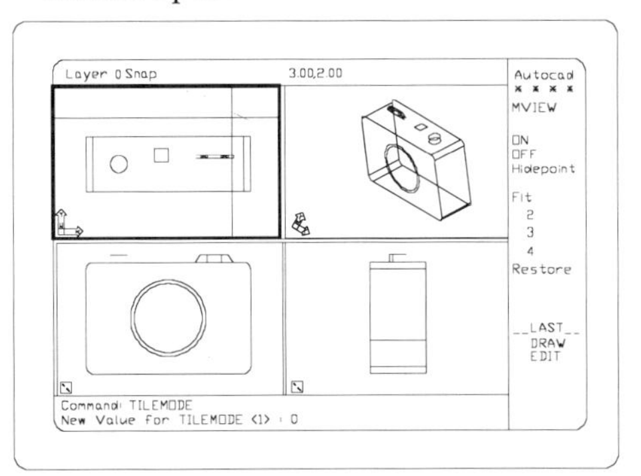

Paper Space

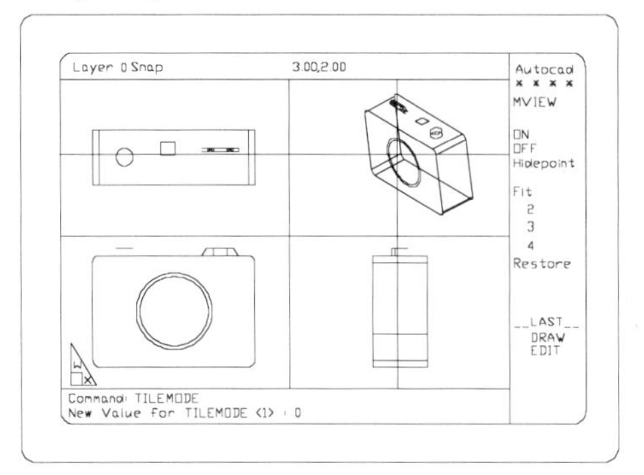

Figure 30-1. Using Tilemode 1 and 0, respectively

To create this type of drawing before paper space, you would have used blocks. Paper space is not only much easier to use than blocks, but also saves a lot of space both on your disk and on the drawing because there are many fewer overlapping lines. When using blocks to compile a drawing, there are four sets of lines in a four-view drawing. With paper space, the data within the file is only one model, thus the storage is much smaller. To get into paper space use TILEMODE.

TILEMODE

Getting from model space to paper space is quite simple. All you need to do is toggle the TILEMODE option to 0 rather than 1.

```
Command:TILEMODE
New value for TILEMODE <1>:0
Entering paper space. Use MVIEW to insert model space view-
ports.
Regenerating drawing.
```

> **Release 12 Notes**
>
> Paper space and model space are both located under the View pull-down menu. The only difference from Release 11 is that these can be added transparently (within a command string).

Once this command is completed, you won't be able to see your drawing until you make some "holes in the paper" using MVIEW. If you have saved the four viewports in VIEWPORTS command, you can bring up the views as they were. If you want to set up four different views you can do this as well, but the first way is simpler. For both methods use MVIEW.

Once you have created your views, you can use either TILEMODE or the commands MSPACE and PSPACE to toggle between the two modes.

```
TILEMODE 1 = Model Space for modelling  =  MSPACE
TILEMODE 0 = Paper Space for drawing    =  PSPACE
```

MVIEW

The MVIEW or Make VIEWs command is used to identify views that will be used in paper space. The screen before MVIEWS is the same as a blank piece of paper. The MVIEW command allows you to add views of the model to this paper format.

Once paper space has been accessed and the views are made, you can toggle between model space and paper space quite readily. When you turn TILEMODE back on, returning to model space, AutoCAD restores the viewport configuration that was active before paper space was entered.

Release 12 Notes

The MVIEW command is located under the View pull-down menu and has options for setting up two, three or four viewports, turning them on or off and changing VPLAYER and hideplot.

When using the MVIEW command, you can create various configurations of viewports, select viewports for hidden line removal, and have different layers active in different viewports.

The default setting is for the user to specify the parameters of a single new viewport.

```
Command:MVIEW
ON/OFF/Hideplot/Fit/2/3/4/Restore/<First Point>: (pick 1)
Other corner: (pick 2)
```

You can use this single viewport to create a single view of the model for plotting and drawing purposes. This will give you a single view on screen containing the view of the model that was current in model space. If you want more than one view, choose another option.

Restore

If your configuration of viewports was stored using the VPORTS command under the name 4QUAD, then you simply restore this screen layout in paper space by using Restore and the name, 4QUAD.

```
Command:VPORTS
Save/Restore/Delete/Join/SIngle/?/2/<3>/4:S
?/Name for new viewport configuration:4QUAD

Command:TILEMODE
New value for TILEMODE <1>:0
Entering paper space. Use MVIEW to insert model space view-
ports.
Regenerating drawing.

Command:MVIEW
ON/OFF/Hideplot/Fit/2/3/4/Restore/<First Point>:R
Name of window configuration to insert <ACTIVE>:4QUAD
Fit/ <first point>:F
```

The Restore option will translate any configuration stored under VPORTS and scale the restored viewport to fit the graphics area. The scaling of each individual viewport will be discussed shortly. Each view becomes an individual viewport entity.

If you have no stored Vport, AutoCAD will take the current viewport configuration labelled as ACTIVE. You can also display a list of stored viewports with a ? (question mark).

On/Off

The default is to have the drawing show up in the viewports as soon as they are configured. If you would like to have one or more vports turned off, usually to save regen and redraw time, just turn the viewport off. You can always turn it back on again later.

When turning viewports on and off, you are prompted to Select objects:, the viewports are considered entities and can be turned off and on much like a block, with one pick. Pick the border of the viewport.

2/3/4

If you haven't saved the layout, use the following to get a regular four-quadrant space.

```
Command:MVIEW
ON/OFF/Hideplot/Fit/2/3/4/Restore/<First Point>:4
Fit/<first point>:F
```

This will create a layout of four quadrants, as shown in Figure 30-2. The view in each quadrant will be the view in your active viewport when you had model space active.

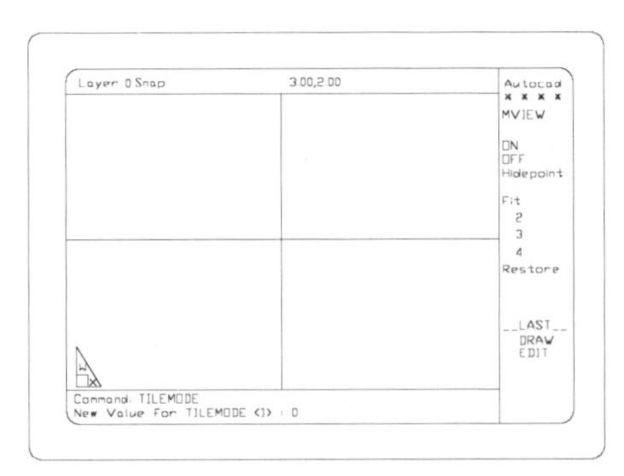

Figure 30-2. A layout of four quadrants

If you want to add three viewports in model space, just ask for the 3 option.

```
Command:MVIEW
ON/OFF/Hideplot/Fit/2/3/4/Restore/<First Point>:3
Horizontal/Vertical/Above/Below/Left/<right>:
```

Figure 30-3 shows configurations of the three-view MVIEW option. Use Horizontal/Vertical, etc. to place them where you want them.

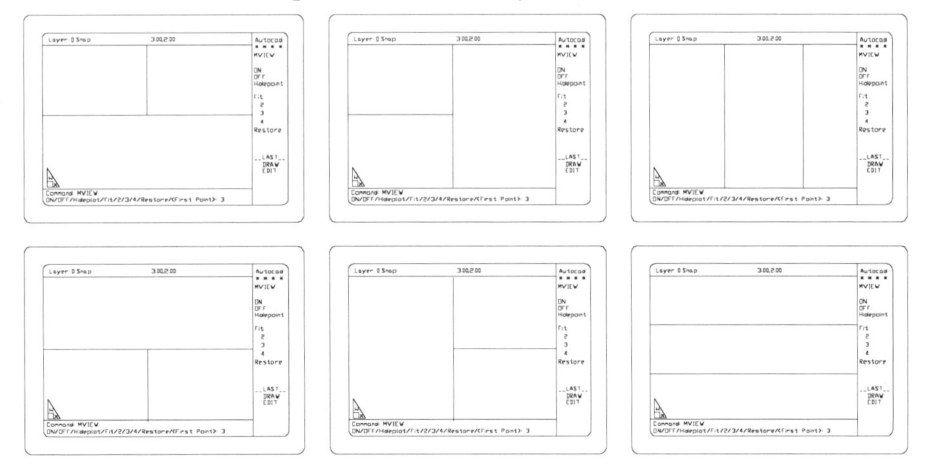

Figure 30-3. Using the MVIEW option

With the 2 option, you can have the screen in horizontal or vertical sections.

First Point

When creating an outline for a drawing, you may also wish to have overlapping views. Viewports created using VPORTS are always non-overlapping or "tiled" views. With MVIEW the viewports can overlap. So far AutoCAD only offers rectilinear viewports in MVIEW with a horizontal-vertical justification.

```
Command:MVIEW
ON/OFF/Hideplot/Fit/2/3/4/Restore/<First Point>: (pick 1)
Other point: (pick 2)
```

With this command, you can place multiple viewports overlapping each other. The rectangle used to make the view will not show up on the drawing; only the geometry contained within it will show up. Make sure that your geometry does not overlap. If it does, simply move the viewport over. Each viewport in paper space is considered an entity; it can be picked up on the "frame," not on the enclosed object.

Hideplot

While in model space, you can use the HIDE command to see your objects with hidden lines in the active viewport. As soon as the viewport is regenerated, however, the items are restored. Using HIDE before the PLOT command in model space will not hide the entities in the plot. While there may be no entities shown on the screen, the entities will show up on the paper.

With the Hideplot option, the entities hidden in any particular viewport will appear hidden when you finally plot.

```
Command:MVIEW
ON/OFF/Hideplot/Fit/2/3/4/Restore/ <First Point>:H
ON/OFF:ON
Select objects: (pick one or more viewports)
```

While selecting the objects, remember that the viewport is considered an object. The geometry is not.

Use the Off option to turn the hidden lines back on.

AutoCAD will switch immediately to paper space if you ask for the MVIEW command in model space, then it will return to model space once the command is finished.

ENTERING THE TITLE BLOCK

Before you start trying to determine the size of your views, it is a good idea to determine the size of your title block. The MVIEW command allows you to set the size of the paper. Make the size of your paper through MVIEW the same size as the paper that you wish to plot on. Your title block should then be inserted onto the "paper" so that there is enough room on the outer edges to permit the plotter's rollers to grasp the paper. Now you can move and scale the views so that they fit onto the paper.

SCALING VIEWS WITHIN A DRAWING

In model space, as soon as you have used the command ZOOM All, you have lost any relation to the actual scale of the part being designed; the image expands to fit the space provided.

In paper space, you will want the views to be scaled to a relative size. The Zoom option XP allows you to scale the object relative to the paper scale units.

The Zoom option X scales the object relative to its current size within the viewport. In paper space, the scale factor of XP gives you a zoom factor "times the paper scale" or relative to the paper and also relative to the actual part. To draw the part at full scale or 1 = 1 use a zoom of 1XP. A setting of .5XP will result in the scaled view being exactly one-half of the size of the original. A zoom of 2XP will result in a view twice the size of the original.

You can use the scales from Chapter 11 to determine the size of zoom that you require. For a final drawing at a scale of 1/4" = 1'0" you would use 0.020833XP or 1/48 (4 X 12) of the original size.

The easiest way to perform these scale factors is once all of the views have been added to the paper. Here is an example of how scaling works.

Figure 30-4 is an illustration of a screen with four viewports showing a simple part in the standard views.

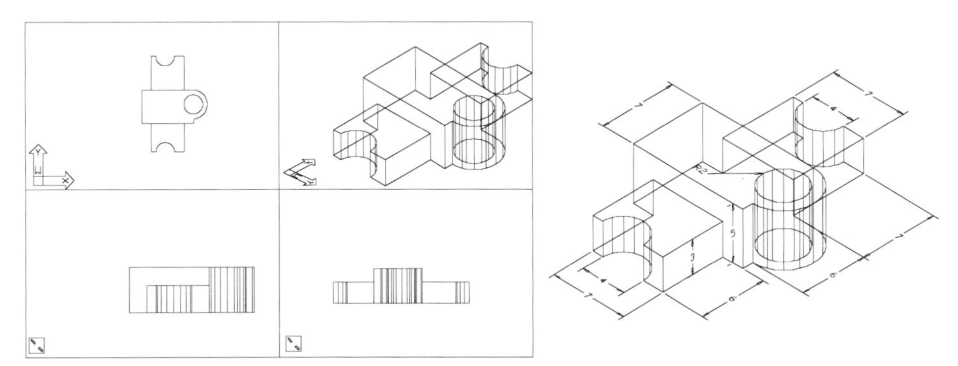

Figure 30-4. A screen with four viewports

What we would like to do is have these four views lined up and scaled on a 17 x 11 sheet of paper.

1. Because border lines will show up in the layer created, it is suggested that you create a new layer at this point and set to it before entering paper space.

2. Use the VPORTS command to save the screen configuration so that you can easily bring it up in paper space. We will use 4QUAD as the stored name for the viewport.

3. Enter paper space through TILEMODE. Use MVIEW to restore the four views at the correct paper size.

```
Command:MVIEW
ON/OFF/Hideplot/Fit/2/3/4/Restore/<First Point>:R
Name of window configuration to insert <ACTIVE>:4QUAD
Fit/<first point>:0,0
Other corner:17,11
```

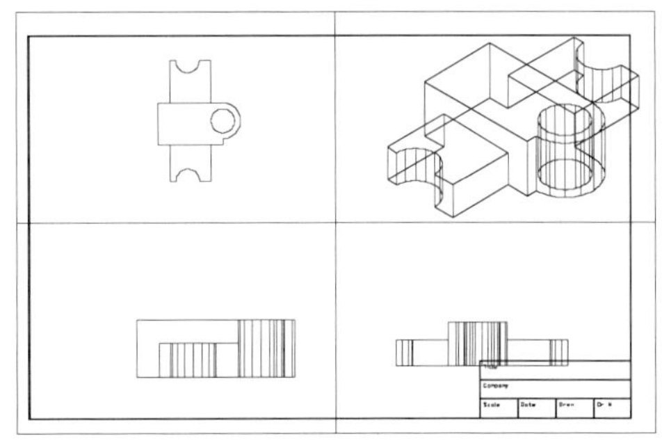

Figure 30-5. The same views in paper space

In MVIEW, you have determined the paper size at 17 x 11. The configuration of views that you saved from model space will be placed in paper space. Notice, in Figure 30-5, that the icons associated with each viewport are gone as this is now simply one "paper." The information within the views is no longer accessible.

4. Insert a title block at a size that will suit the paper while leaving room for the plotter's rollers. Coordinates of .5,.5 x 16.5,10.5 should work in this case.

5. Now that the views are on the paper, you can scale them and then move them around so that they line up. Use the following command sequence to scale the views.

```
Command:MSPACE (toggles back to model space for zooming)
```

After setting up the views in paper space, toggle back to model space to use ZOOM XP. ZOOM XP has the same effect as ZOOM X in paper space.

Once back in model space, each viewport will be an independent unit, and you can zoom each one independently. In this case, the part is approximately 10" x 14". At a scale of 1 = 1, the part would not fit on the paper, so we will reduce the size by half.

```
Command:ZOOM
All/Center/Dynamic/Extents/Left/Previous/Vmax/Window/<Scale
(X/XP)>:.5XP
```

Use a scale of .5XP for Top, Front, and Side views.

```
Command:ZOOM
All/Center/Dynamic/Extents/Left/Previous/Vmax/Window/<Scale
(X/XP)>:1XP
```

Use a scale of 1XP for the rotated view.

Then toggle back to paper space and use the MOVE command to line the views up on the paper.

```
Command:PSPACE
```

When picking the views to move them across the drawing, pick the border of the view, not the information contained within the view.

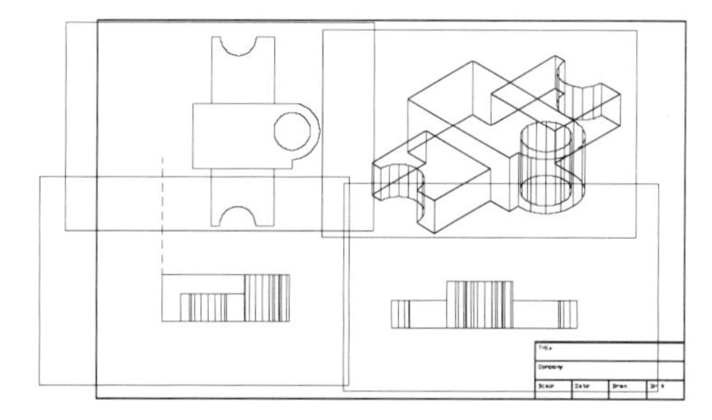

Figure 30-6. MOVE used to orient paper space viewports

Use either construction lines (see hidden line) or point filters to move the information across the screen to line it up. The data contained within the views is accessible for reference either for filters or for osnaps, but is not accessible for editing purposes.

When you use the ZOOM command in paper space, it affects the entire page or paper. A ZOOM .5X will result in the paper with the views intact at half the size that it was before.

In model space you can pan the objects within the viewports; in paper space the MOVE command will move the views relative to the other views. Be careful not to zoom the views in model space after scaling them with ZOOM XP.

6. Once the views are lined up and scaled to your requirements, freeze the layer that contains the view borders.

Add your notations and any additional logos or symbols in paper space. These will be plotted relative to the paper size.

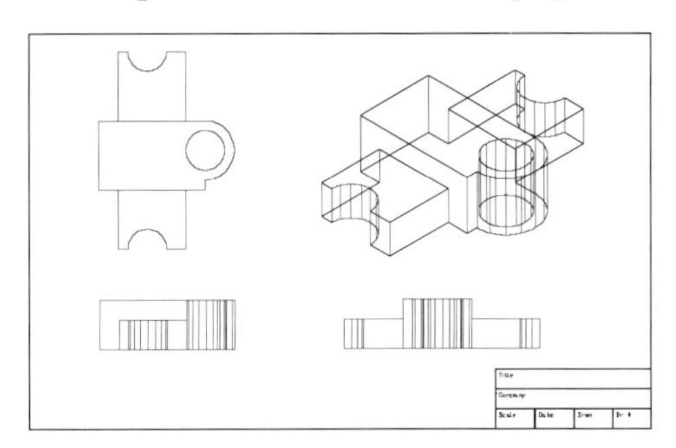

Figure 30-7. The paper space layout with borders off

The drawing is now ready to plot. As you have scaled the views to the paper size, and you have accounted for the paper used by the plotter to run the plot, you can plot at a scale of 1 = 1.

VPLAYER

Because you are using one model to create the drawing, and because each view of the drawing will contain dimensions and other information relative to that specific view and no others, you will need to have the facility of having certain layers displayed in only one view of the drawing at the same time. VPLAYER allows you to do this.

The VPLAYER command allows you to perform layer freezing in selected viewports rather than as a global command.

As with the MVIEW command, this command only shows up in paper space, when the TILEMODE is off (or set to 0). You can use VPLAYER in either model space or paper space TILEMODE 0, but the system will automatically switch to paper space if you try to use it in model space. The command options are explained below.

```
Command:VPLAYER
?/Freeze/Thaw/Reset/Newfrz/Vpvisdflt:
```

Where:

? will give you a listing of the layers that are frozen in any selected viewport.

Freeze will freeze a layer or layers in selected viewports.

```
Command:VPLAYER
?/Freeze/Thaw/Reset/Newfrz/Vpvisdflt:F  (freeze)
Layer(s) to Freeze:DIM1  (name of the layer)
All/Select/<current>:S  (allows you to select the viewport)
```

If you are still in model space you will also get a prompt:

```
Switching to Paper space.
```

The prompts allow you to choose the layer to be modified, and the objects to be selected for freezing. You can enter multiple layers by putting commas between the layer names.

Thaw *performs the reverse of Freeze. It turns on selected layers in selected viewports.*

Newfrz *creates a layer that is new in the VPLAYER command. This layer is created frozen in all viewports, and is primarily used for creating a layer that is to be viewed only in one viewport ever. You first create the layer, then you Thaw it in the desired viewport.*

```
Command:VPLAYER
?/Freeze/Thaw/Reset/Newfrz/Vpvisdflt:N (Newfrz)
New viewport frozen letter names:Title (name of the LAYER)
```

Reset *the default display for layers created in the LAYER command is thawed. In the VPLAYER command, the display defaults to Frozen. Using the Reset option, the layers are returned to their original default setting.*

```
Command:VPLAYER
?/Freeze/Thaw/Reset/Newfrz/Vpvisdflt:R (Reset)
Layer (s) to Reset:0,DIM1,DIM2 (no space between names)
All/Selected/<current>:
```

Vpvisdflt *lets you set a default visibility for any layer in any viewport. This could be useful for resetting the layers. The command determines the default visibility of all layers in existing viewports.*

For most of the above options, none of the changes will take place until you complete the command.

CREATING DRAWINGS

In the following example we have taken a simple camera body from the modelling stage right through to the plotting stage.

The dimensioning of the part has been created on different layers. Very simply, set your UCS to the plane on which you would like your dimensions to appear. For more details on dimensioning in 3D turn to Chapter 37. Decide on the scale of each view relative to the paper before you set your DIMSCALE. You can change the DIMSCALE once the drawing has been compiled by switching back to MSPACE, then using DIMSCALE and UPD*(ate)*.

It is a good idea to try this example on a simple camera body or similar part before starting on a large project.

Example: *Creating a Drawing from a 3D Model*

STEP 1
Once the part is completed, decide on the size of paper that you would like to plot the drawing on, and the scale of each separate view. It may be a good idea to make a simple sketch of the final drawing noting the view scales and the dimscales. Use Chapter 11 for dimscales and text/hatch and linetype scales.

Then create new layers for the dimensions and for the paper space borders called:

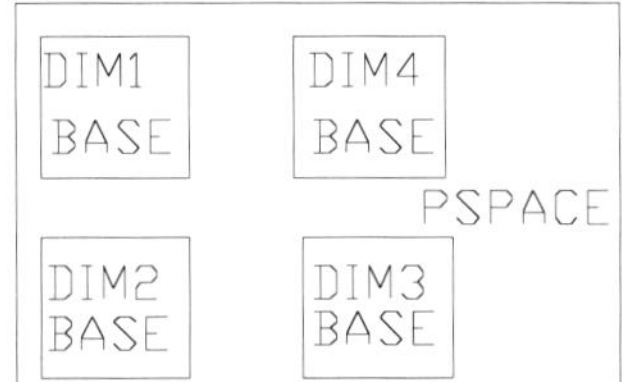


```
DIM1
DIM2
DIM3
DIM4
PSPACE
```

In the top view, generate dimensions on layer DIM1. On the front view generate dimensions on DIM2. Use DIM3 and DIM4 for the other views. Compose each view as it will be plotted, adding notations, view titles and scales or any symbols that you feel necessary at this point.

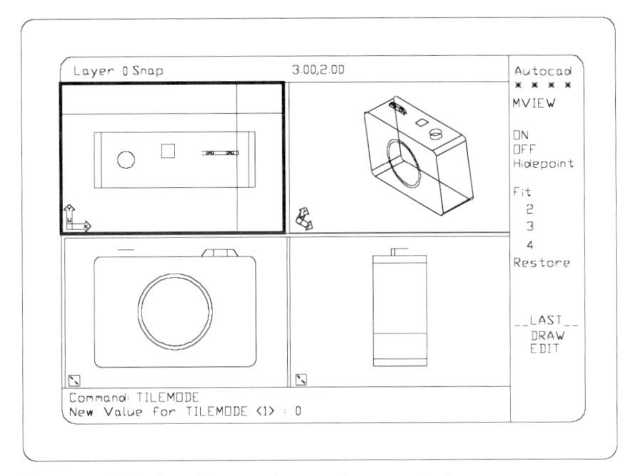

Figure 30-8. Four views in model space

Note that any detail views will require different dimscales.

STEP 2

Once the dimensions are complete, save the view and name it 4QUAD.

```
Command:VPORTS
Save/Restore/Delete/Join/SIn-
gle/ ?/2/<3>/4:S
?/Name for new viewport config-
uration:4QUAD
```

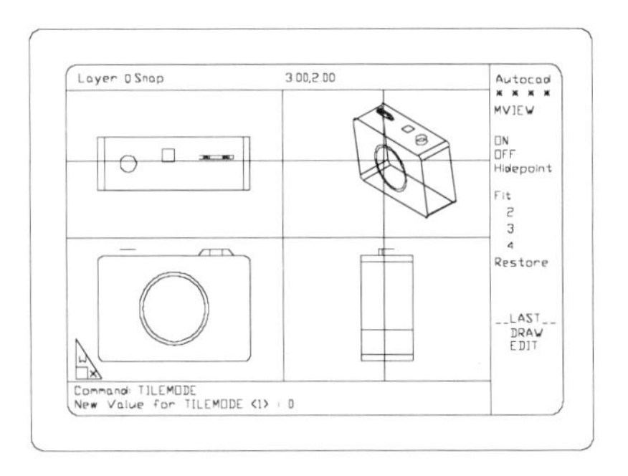

Now zoom into a detail of the shutter release and save it as a view.

```
Command:VIEW
?/Delete/Restore/Save/Window:S
View name to save:Detail1
```

STEP 3

Change TILEMODE to Off or 0. You will now be changing from model space to paper space.

STEP 4

Now that you have paper space on, use MVIEW to restore the view 4QUAD that you have already saved. Change your layer to Pspace layer before doing this so that you can freeze it before plotting. This layer will contain your view borders.

```
Command:MVIEW
```

ON/OFF/Hideplot/Fit/2/3/4/Restore/<First Point>:**R**

Name of window configuration to insert <ACTIVE>:**4QUAD**

Fit/<first point>:**0,0**

Other corner:**17,11**

This will restore the saved view that you had for the camera body. The paper size is the exact paper size that you will be using.

Now use MVIEW to add a detail of the shutter release.

Command:**MVIEW**

ON/OFF/Hideplot/Fit/2/3/4/Restore/<First Point>: *(pick 1)*

Other point: *(pick 2)*

You have a spot for the detail of the part. This view will contain the view of the part that was current when you switched to paper space. If this is not the detail view, use the following command to place the detail view in the viewport created for it:

Command:**VIEW**

?/Delete/Restore/Save/Window:**R**

View name(s) to restore:**Detail1**

Restoring Model space view.

Select Viewport for view: *(pick the border of the view created for the detail)*

STEP 5

Now that your views are all restored, use VPLAYER to make sure that only the layers needed are displayed in each particular viewport. With all layers displayed you will not be able to properly view the object.

Do the same with all the views until you have each one with the dimensions associated with it displayed.

Command:**VPLAYER**

?/Freeze/Thaw/Reset/Newfrz/

Vpvisdflt:**F** *(Reset)*

Layer(s) to Freeze:**DIM1,DIM2,**

DIM3 *(in detail view)*

All/Selected/<current>: *(pick 1)*

(pick the detail layer)

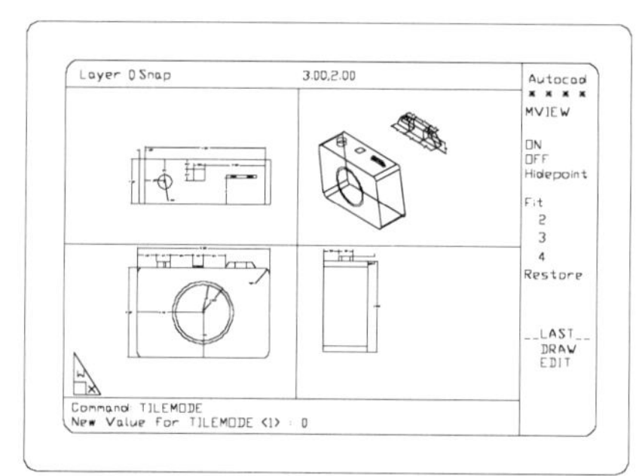

STEP 6

In order to see the space that you have to work with, add the title block so that all views can be scaled and moved to create a balanced drawing. Be sure to change your layer to one other than Pspace as Pspace will be frozen during plotting.

Command:**Insert**

Block name (or ?):**TB17X11**

Insertion point:**0,0**

X scale factor <1>/Corner/XYZ:↵

Y scale factor (default=X):↵

Rotation angle <0>:↵

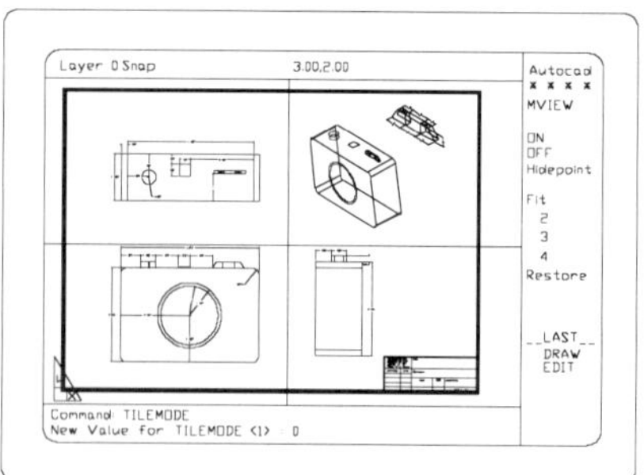

Be sure that the title block allows for the plotter's rollers. If you don't have a title block, use PLINE to draw in a border.

STEP 7

Using the MVIEW command, hide the information not needed in the isometric views. If you have used 3DFACE, thickness or surfacing on the camera, you should have no trouble with this. If you are using a pen plotter, also hide the other views to stop the plotter from drawing all duplicate lines in the views.

```
Command:MVIEW
ON/OFF/Hideplot/Fit/2/3/4/Restore/<First Point>:H
ON/OFF:ON
Select objects: (pick one or more viewports)
```

This will provide you with a good isometric view of the object with hidden lines removed in plotting, plus views that will be plotted with no extra lines.

STEP 8

Enter model space to scale your views relative to the final drawing.

```
Command:MSPACE
Command:ZOOM
All/Center/Dynamic/Extents/Left/Previous/Vmax/Window/<Scale
(X/XP)>:2XP
```

This will make the selected view twice its actual size on the drawing. This factor would be used on the detail in this drawing; the others may be drawn at a scale of 1XP. Be sure to use ZOOM XP on all views, as they may appear correct on the screen if the scale is close to 1 = 1, but without the ZOOM command, you can't be sure that it will show up perfectly on the drawing.

STEP 9

Return to paper space and use MOVE to line up the views.

Then turn off the PSPACE layer so that the view borders will be removed and add any final notations, symbols or title block information that you may need on the final drawing.

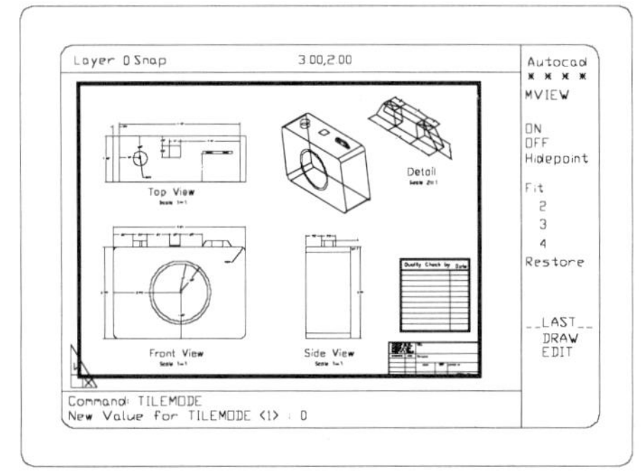

When creating geometry in paper space, the geometry exists on the paper itself, not within the view of the part. It is as if the views of the part have been photographed, then placed on transparent decals or slides and arranged on the paper. Any lines, circles, blocks, or related data added at this point will enhance the drawing but in no way affect the views. Objects drawn in paper space should be on a separate layer so that they can be frozen when you return to the model. Items drawn in paper space are not accepted as part of the 3D database.

Note that the plines etc. are superimposed on the views themselves. The title block is brought in and positioned using INSERT. The text for filling in the details on the title block is put in simply by using the TEXT command.

While you are in paper space, you may erase geometry, dimensions, and text that have been entered in the paper mode. But you can't erase data that was created in model space and therefore is contained within a view.

If the data is entered in model space, then it is part of your 3D data. To erase it, you must toggle to model space.

```
Command: MSPACE
Command: ERASE
Select objects: (pick 1)
Select objects: ↵
Command: PSPACE
```

All data created in paper space plus the viewports created in paper space are created on the current layer.

Other commands such as CHANGE and CHPROP will affect the view as a whole in paper space mode. Again the entire viewport is accepted as a single entity much the same way that a block is considered a single entity.

Dimensioning can also be done entirely in paper space by creating new layers in VPLAYER, having them thawed in the appropriate viewport and then being displayed. One problem with doing this is that while dimensioning an isometric in paper space, you will not get the correct dimension text. The isometric view will have been translated to a 2D format within paper space and thus the actual vectored distance of the items being dimensioned will have changed. It's just as easy to do it outside of paper space.

The above exercises are described using the Release 11 software. If you are not yet using Release 11, you can still produce a multi-view drawing using blocks, but it will take up more room on your disk.

MULTI-VIEW DRAWINGS USING BLOCKS

RELEASE 9 AND 10

In the drawing on page 510, there are five views of an item, four of which contain dimensions relative to a specific view. It would be quite simple to create a block of an item and insert it five times at different scale factors and rotations, but it would not be possible in one drawing to insert the same block five times with different layers being displayed in each insertion. Thus the dimensions must be entered after the part is inserted, or must be on four different layers in the original model, with five different insertions of the same wblock being done. The first method takes up less space. That is what we will use.

Example: *Creating a 3D Drawing with Blocks*

STEP 1
Create the geometry for the part or model.

STEP 2
Once complete, block the model.

STEP 3
Insert the model on your screen. Use a scale of 1 = 1 if you like. If this is the World Coordinate System, this will give you a plan or top view.

STEP 4
Change the UCS to rotate around X at 90 degrees. Insert the same block. Pick a point directly above the first insertion. This will give you the front view.

STEP 5

Change the UCS back to World. Then change it to Y 90. Insert your right view.

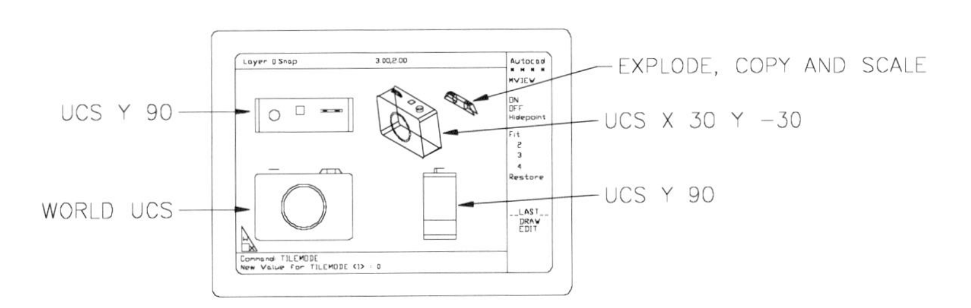

STEP 6

Change the UCS back to World. Then change the UCS to first X 30, then Y -30. Now insert the ISO view.

STEP 7

Explode the isometric block. Copy the shutter release over to the right and then scale it to three times original size.

STEP 8

Generate your dimensions, add the title block, and add other notations as in a single view. Keep in mind that the hidden view will not be hidden in the PLOT command unless specified within the PLOT command. To "fake it," erase the lines that would not be showing in an ISO view.

MVSETUP

This is an AutoLISP routine that should be located on the (BONUS) screen menu. If it is not part of the bonus menu, this means that the lisp programs contained on your disks from AutoDESK have not been entered.

This program effectively replaces the SETUP program of earlier releases, allowing the user to quickly set up views for drawing creation. If the program has not been used before at your site, it will take longer to start a multi-view setup program as the system offers you the option of having the title blocks placed on your disk as wblocks. Subsequent uses of the program will take much less time.

MVSETUP can be used instead of MVIEW to set up you drawing layout. It is an automated way to create, align, and scale you viewports, and enter your title block.

`Command:`**`MVSETUP`** *(can be typed in as MVS or taken from the [BONUS] menu)*

`Paperspace/Modelspace is disabled. The old setup will be invoked unless it is enabled. Enable Paper/Modelspace? y:`↵

`Entering Paper space. Use MVIEW to insert Model space viewports.`

`Regenerating drawing.` *(existing viewports will appear)*

`Align viewports/Create viewports/Title block/Undo:`**`C`** *(Create)*

`Delete objects/Undo/<create viewports>:`**`D`** *(Delete)*

`Select objects to delete:` *(pick all existing viewports)*

`Delete objects/Undo/<create viewports>:`↵

`Add/Delete/Redispaly/ <number of entry to load>:`↵

`Align viewports/Create viewports/Scale viewports/Title block/Undo:`**`T`** *(title block)*

```
Delete objects/Origin/Undo/<Insert title block>:↵ (Insert title)

Available title block options:

0:      None
1:      ANSI-V Size
2:      ANSI-A Size
3:      ANSI-B Size
4:      ANSI-C Size
5:      ANSI-D Size
6:      ANSI-E Size
7:      Arch/Engineering  (24 x 36)

Add/Delete/Redisplay/<Number of entry to Load>:3
Create a drawing named ansi-b.dwg? <Y>:↵
Align viewports/Create viewports/Scale viewports/Title
block/Undo:C
Delete objects/Undo/<Create viewports>:↵

Available Mview viewport layout options:

0:       None
1:       Single
2:       Std.Engineering - Top, Front, Right, and 3D isometric
3:       Array of Viewports

Add/Delete/Redisplay/ <Number of entry to Load>:2
Align viewports/Create viewports/ Scale viewports/ Title
block/Undo:S
Select the viewport to scale:
Select objects: (pick the viewport to scale)
Select objects:↵
Enter the ratio of paper space units to model space units . .
Number of paper space units.<1.0> 4

Align viewports/Create viewports/ Scale viewports/ Title
```

You have now set up a B scale title block containing the four standard views with one view having a scale of 4 = 1.

You can also use MVSETUP to automatically align views in two different viewports by choosing the Align viewports option. You will be prompted to choose a vertical or horizontal alignment, and then to choose the points that you will use for reference.

MVSETUP can also be customized to allow you to enter your own title blocks and your own customized screen layouts.

In an environment where you would be generating a large number of drawings, it would be a good idea to write some LISP routines to control layer visibilty and entering of standard views as well.

Exercise A30

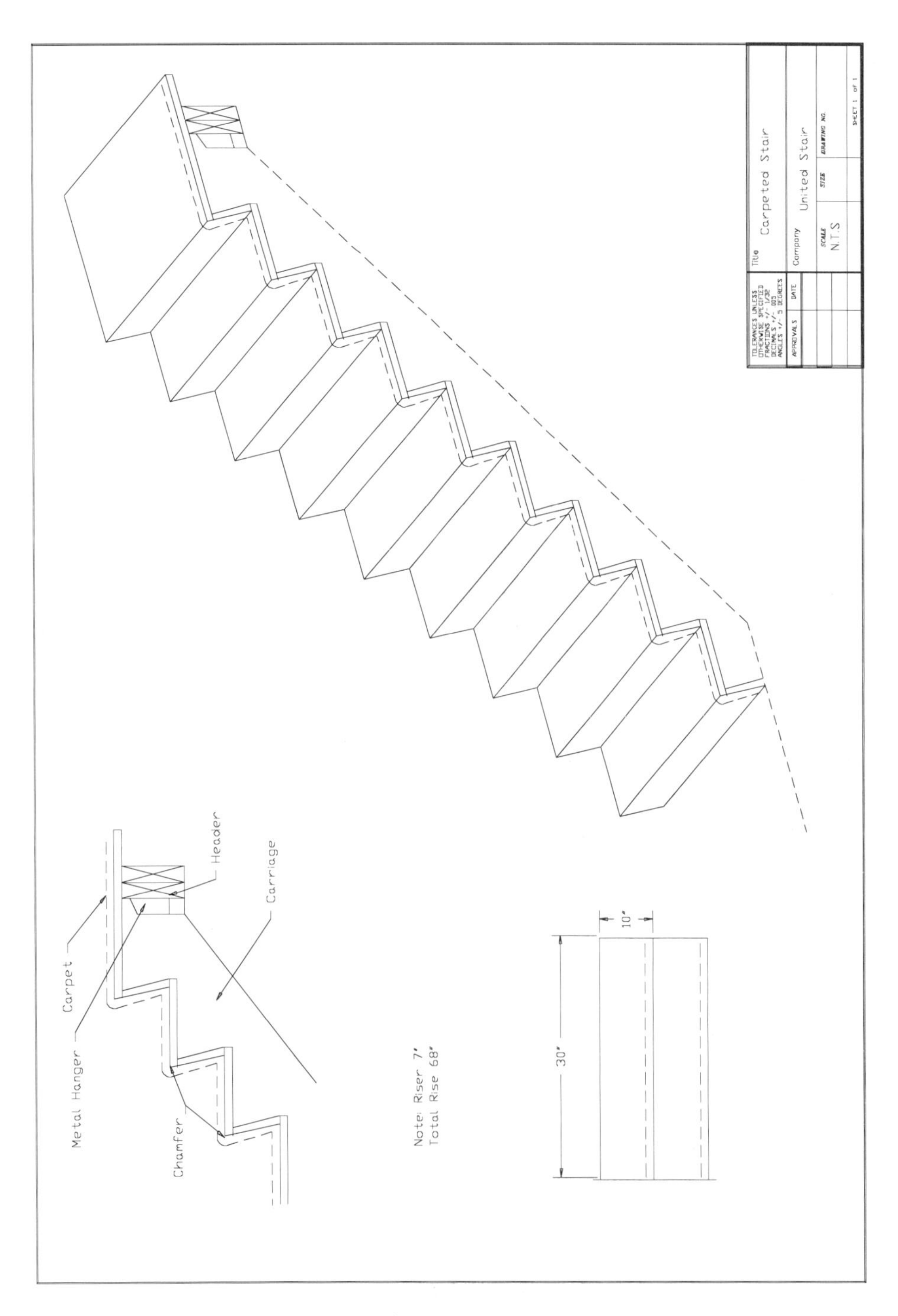

Releases 11 and 12 — Create the carpeted staircase as in the example, and use paper space and model space to generate a drawing as shown.

Releases 9 and 10 — Create the carpeted staircase in 3D, block it, change the UCS, insert the model three times, explode, complete the necessary views, and annotate to get the image above.

Hints on A30

STEP 1

Create a new file and set up five layers as follows:

Layer Name	Colour	Linetype
Stairs	White	Continuous
Hidden	White	Hidden
FRDIM	Red	Continuous
SDDIM	Cyan	Continuous
Borders	Green	Continuous

STEP 2

Set your screen to four viewports with Plan, Front, Side, and Iso set at 2,-2,2.

STEP 3

Draw the staircase by creating one tread and riser then copy it using Multiple until you have 14 treads. Add dimensions on the Front view in LAYER FRDIM. Turn this layer off and add dimensions on the Side view in LAYER SDDIM.

STEP 4

In DVIEW, zoom in to each view, clip back planes so that extra data is not entered in the views. Save your views by naming them RIGHT, PLAN, FRONT, and ISO. Use the VIEW command to do this.

STEP 5

Change TILEMODE to 0, switching to paper space.

STEP 6

Use MVIEW to set up three viewports, and add the appropriate view into the three viewports by using VIEW and RESTORE. Use MVIEW to Hideplot in the ISO view.

STEP 7

Use VPLAYER to freeze the layers not needed for viewing in each viewport.

STEP 8

Use CHPROP to change the viewport borders to LAYER Border. Turn LAYER Border off. Insert a title block, add a pline to create a full drawing border. Make a checkplot.

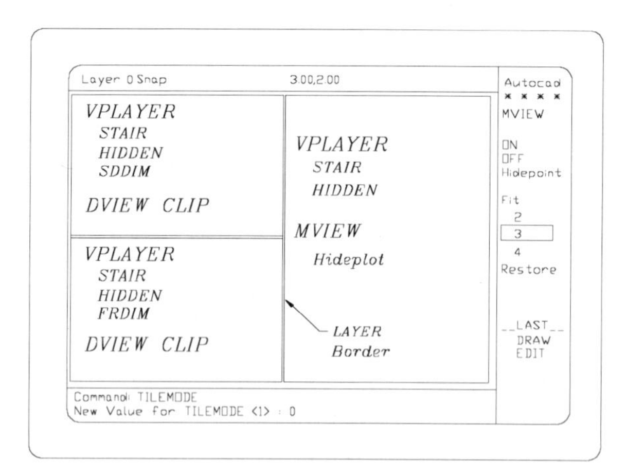

Remember that you can't change your geometry in PSPACE.

MECHANICAL

Exercise M30

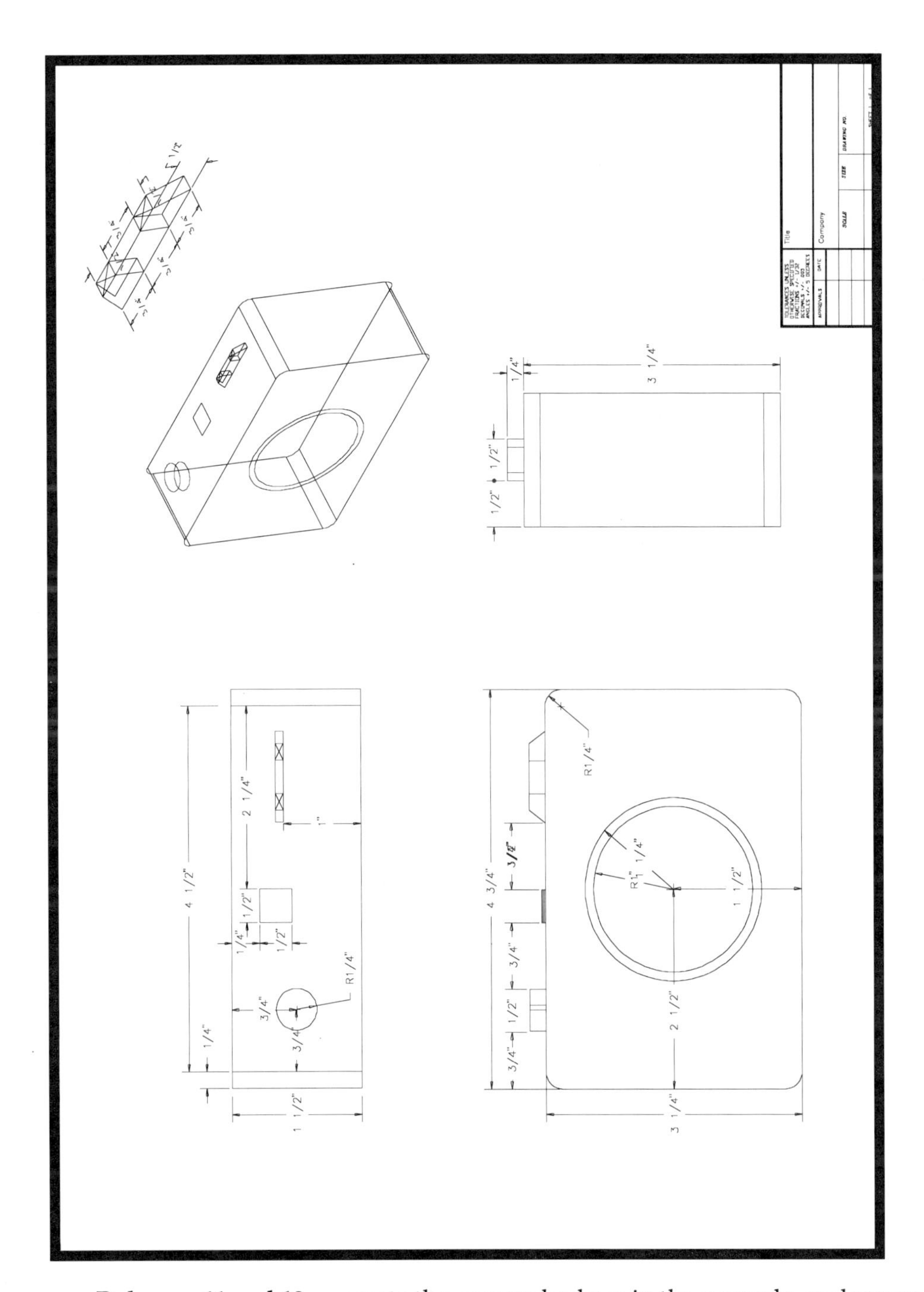

Releases 11 and 12 — create the camera body as in the example, and use paper space and model space to generate a drawing as in the above.

Releases 9 and 10 — create the camera body in 3D, block it, change the UCS, insert the model three times, explode, complete the necessary views, and annotate to get the image above.

Hints on M30

STEP 1

Create a new file and set up six layers as follows:

Layer Name	Colour	Linetype
Geometry	White	Continuous
ISODIM	Cyan	Continuous
FRDIM	Red	Continuous
SDDIM	Yellow	Continuous
TPDIM	Blue	Continuous
Borders	Green	Continuous

STEP 2

Set your screen to four viewports with Plan, Front, Side, and Iso set at 2,-2,2.

STEP 3

Draw the camera base as shown. Add dimensions on the Front view in LAYER FRDIM. Turn this LAYER off and add dimensions on the Side view in LAYER SDDIM. Do the same for the Top and Iso detail.

STEP 4

In DVIEW, zoom in to each view, clip back planes so that extra data is not entered in the views. Use the VIEW command to save your views by naming them RIGHT, TOP, FRONT, and ISO. Then zoom into the ISO view and create another view called ISOD for the film advance detail.

STEP 5

Change TILEMODE to 0, switching to paper space.

STEP 6

Use MVIEW to set up four viewports, and add the appropriate view into the three viewports by using VIEW and RESTORE. Use MVIEW to Hideplot in the ISO view. Use MVIEW to add another view for the detail.

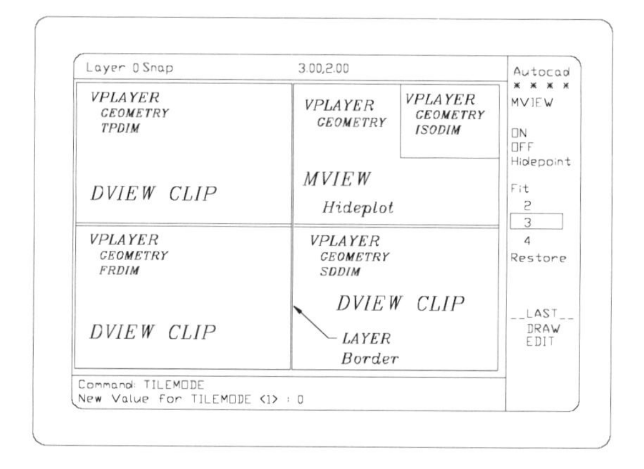

STEP 7

Use VPLAYER to freeze the layers not needed for viewing in each viewport.

STEP 8

Use CHPROP to change the viewport borders to LAYER Border. Turn LAYER Border off. Insert a title block, add a pline to create a full drawing border. Make a checkplot.

Exercise C30

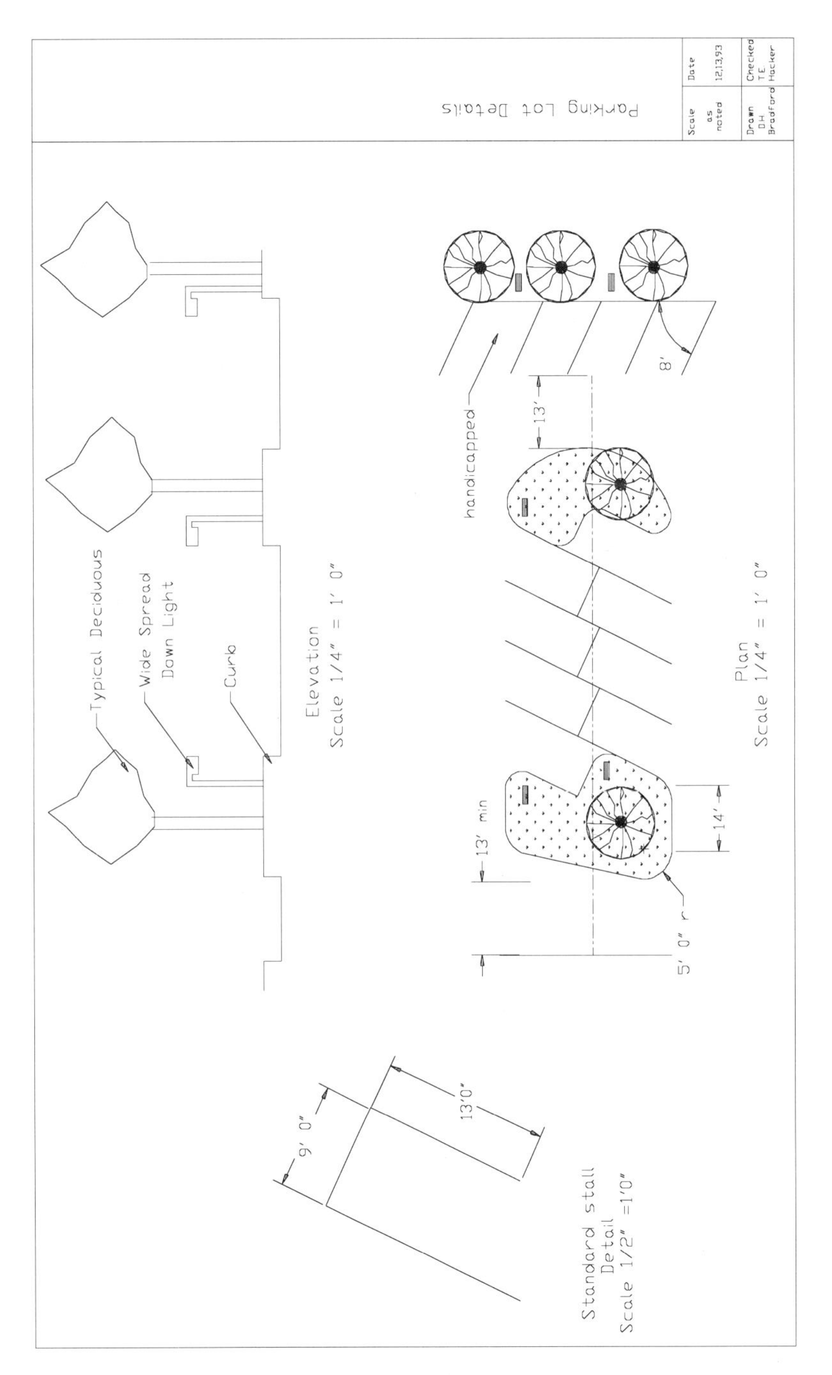

Releases 11 and 12 — Create the parking lot as in the example, and use paper space and model space to generate a drawing as in the above.

Releases 9 and 10 — Create the parking lot in 3D, block it, change the UCS, insert the model three times, explode, complete the necessary views, and annotate to get the image above.

Hints on C30

STEP 1

Create a new file and set up six layers as follows:

Layer Name	Colour	Linetype
Geometry	White	Continuous
Detail	Blue	Continuous
FRDIM	Cyan	Continuous
TPDIM	Red	Continuous
DETDIM	Yellow	Continuous
Borders	Green	Continuous

STEP 2

Set your screen to two viewports with Plan and Front.

STEP 3

Draw the parking area as shown. Add dimensions on the Front view in LAYER FRDIM. Turn this layer off and add dimensions and hatching to the Top view in LAYER TPDIM. Change the layer of one stall to Detail and dimension this in LAYER DETDIM.

STEP 4

In DVIEW, zoom in to each view, clip back planes so that extra data is not entered in the views. Use the VIEW command to save your views by naming them TOP and FRONT. Then zoom into the ISO view and create another view called DETAIL for the stall detail.

STEP 5

Change TILEMODE to 0, switching to paper space.

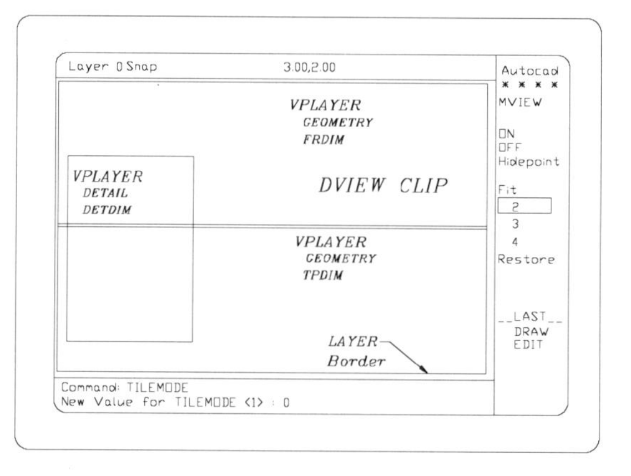

STEP 6

Use MVIEW to set up two viewports, and add the appropriate view into each viewport by using VIEW and RESTORE. Use MVIEW to create another view overlapping on the left for the detail.

STEP 7

Use VPLAYER to freeze the layers not needed for viewing in each viewport.

STEP 8

Use CHPROP to change the viewport borders to LAYER Border. Turn LAYER Border off. Insert a title block, add a pline to create a full drawing border. Make a checkplot.

Challenger 30

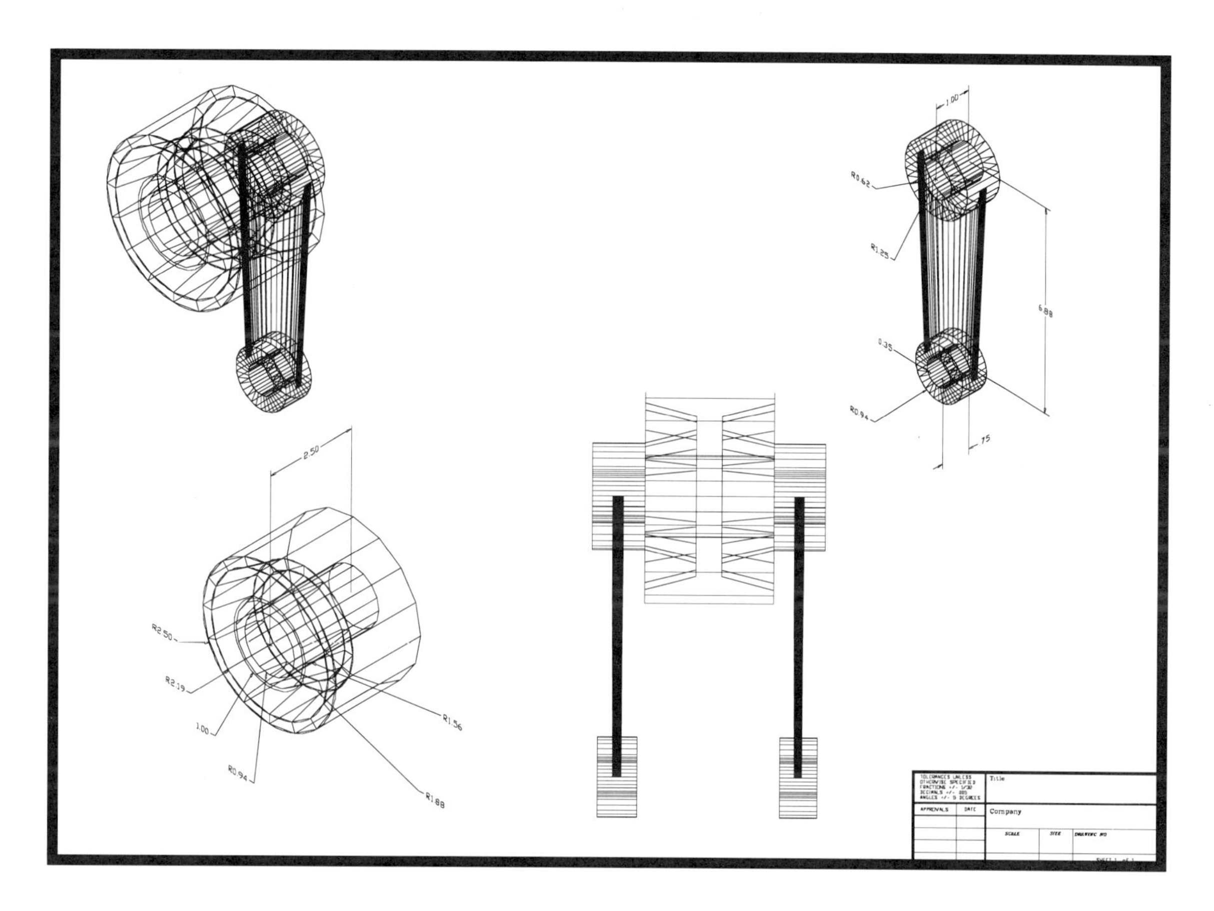

Two-step drawing.

This is the first step on a Belt Pulley Tensioner. Be very careful to name your layers in a logical manner as there are six more objects to add to this model in the next chapter.

When completed, you should be able to compile the entire model on a page.

Keep both dimesions and surfaces on separate layers. Make sure that your title block is on a separate drawing file so that it can be inserted again on the next stage of the drawing.

SURFACING

Upon completion of this chapter, the student should be able to:

1. Create a simple ruled surface (RULESURF) and define the difference between this and a 3DFACE
2. Create a surface of revolution (REVSURF)
3. Create a tabulated surface (TABSURF)
4. Create an edge-defined surface patch (EDGESURF)
5. Create 3D polylines (3DPOLY)

CAD SURFACES

With the exception of 3DFACE, you have been working in 3D so far with linear elements. This means that the information you have entered has a defined start and a defined end, but is not surfaced. If you had your materialized model in your hand, you could touch the edges, but your hand would go right through the wireframe mesh.

With surfacing, you are covering the wireframe with a surface that will let both you, the user, and the system or software determine where the planes actually are, and more importantly, where the inside is relative to the outside.

Release 12 Notes

Surfaces are listed under the Draw pull-down menu under 3D Surfaces. There is no difference in how they are used.

Most applications in 3D CAD are headed for a fully surfaced model, because only with a fully surfaced model can you do such things as cut the part out of metal, download the part to a stereolithography machine, and perform Finite Element Analysis and other analysis routines. The reason for this is fairly clear and easy to understand: if the system can only see lines or wireframe, then it is guessing at where the surface of the part actually is.

In this chapter we will look at the surfaces used to define simple shapes, and in the next chapter we will look at the 3D shapes that are available for constructing objects.

AUTOCAD'S SURFACES

What you are after in a surfacing environment is a software package that can fully describe any three-dimensional shape. This software was available in the early 1980s for approximately $300,000 per seat or over a million dollars for a three or four-user computer station.

The surfacing capabilities of AutoCAD are truly astounding when you look at the cost for the same capabilities only 10 years ago.

AutoCAD cannot do everything needed to describe every surface yet, but for a system at a reasonable cost, it is very good.

More sophisticated surfacing and 3D model-making capabilities will be available very shortly in Releases 13 and 14.

3D POLYLINE MESHES

The following surfaces are made up of 3D Faces meshed together according to the tabulation factors determined by the variables SURFTAB1 and SURFTAB2. These surfaces are described as meshes because they are compiled of a series of planar surfaces or edges. The 3DMESH command will be explained in Chapter 33.

RULESURF *creates a surface between two lines or curves. The defining linear element for a ruled surface can be either a line, a polyline, an arc, or a circle. The ruled surface can be stretched between any combination of these elements or any one of these elements and a point.*

REVSURF *creates a surface by taking a linear element and revolving it around an axis; the defining profile sweeps around the axis creating a surface. The linear element used to define the surface can be either a line, a polyline, an arc, or a circle. The surface can be a complete 360-degree surface or any portion thereof.*

TABSURF *creates a surface by taking a defined line and projecting it along a defined line. It approximates a tabulated surface by moving a curve along a vector.*

EDGESURF *creates a polygon mesh by merging sets of four edges whose endpoints are coincident, approximating a Coon's surface patch.*

3DFACE VS. RULESURF

3DFACE

When creating 3D Faces you are in fact creating planar surfaces using points to define a boundary. With a 3D Face the points can be anywhere in space. An extruded 2D solid may look the same as a 3D Face, but the edges will have a different definition, and the transparency properties will also be different.

For creating rectilinear surfaces, 3DFACE is probably the easiest method since it allows the greatest flexibility, i.e., you can place the points anywhere in space. The major problems with 3DFACE are that it will not support curves and it does not create a mesh. It is strictly a 3D planar surface.

To create a surface between two lines you can easily create a 3D Face using the endpoints of the lines for boundary definition (see page 548). To create a surface between two arcs, you need to be able to identify the arc or radius. An extruded arc will give you a surface relative to an existing arc, but the UCS must be perpendicular to the arc. In addition, the resulting surface is difficult to see and select as an item once it is created. This is where RULESURF comes in.

Ruled Surfaces (RULESURF)

By far the easiest type of surface to create is the ruled surface. Again this is simply a surface that is generated between two rails, calculated from the nearest endpoint of each rail.

The two entities can be any kind of linear element: line, arc, circle, pline, ellipse, etc.

A linear element is something you could draw with a pencil without taking your pencil from the paper or overlapping any edges. The linear elements are used extensively to describe items of geometry. In the first half of this book, we used linear elements almost exclusively.

In Figure 31-1, there are two circles and two lines. The surface is generated between these two items simply by picking them.

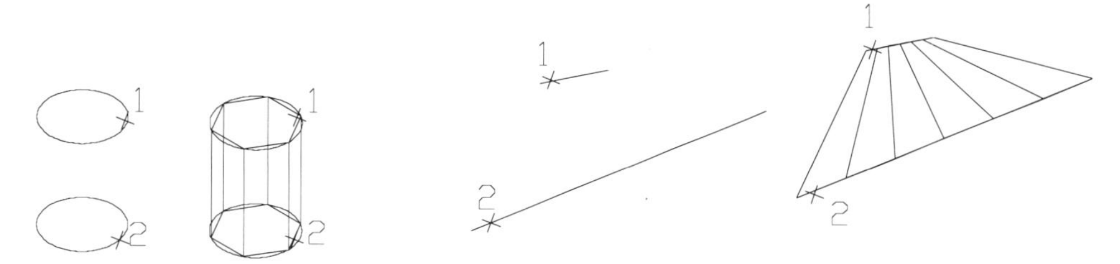

Figure 31-1. Using RULESURF

```
Command: RULESURF
Select first defining curve: (pick 1)
Select second defining curve: (pick 2)
```

In both cases, the surface that is drawn is much like a surface you would draw by using a ruler to join the items with straight lines, starting from one end and working your way to the other end.

In the examples in Figure 31-2, the ruled surfaces are created in the same way using either two arcs, two lines, an arc and a point, or two plines.

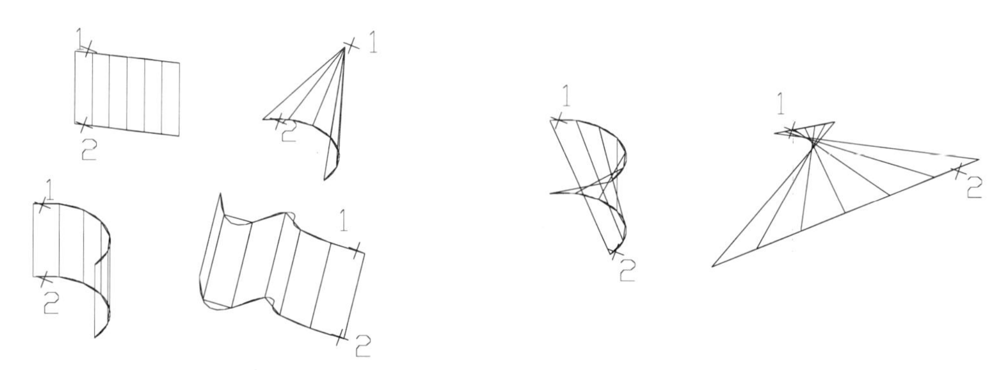

Figure 31-2. RULESURF using arcs, points, and plines

The only major difficulty with RULESURF is that the system generates the surface between the closest endpoints of the items selected. You can see that in the two last examples of Figure 31-2 the two endpoints selected are at different ends of the object, thus the surface is reversed. This is reminiscent of the solid command, giving a bow-tie effect, but in 3D. Try picking the "other" end of the entity to generate the surface without the bow tie.

It is a very good idea to have an isometric view while generating surfaces so that you can easily pick the end of the item you need to surface.

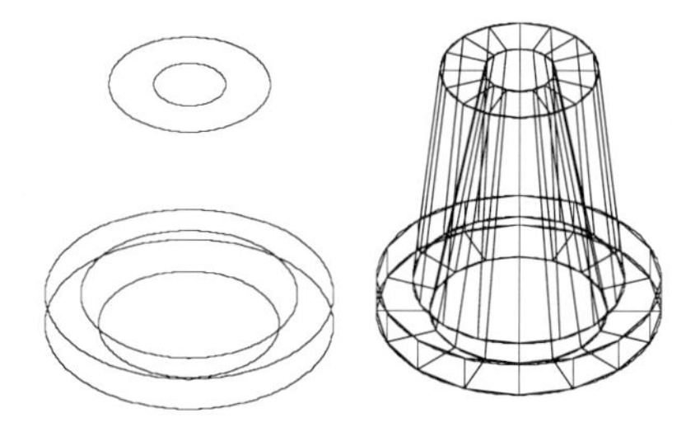

Figure 31-3. Ruled surfaces

The RULESURF command is used extensively to generate surfaces through arcs: a series of arcs, for example, can be created by using the RULESURF command or the REVSURF command.

In Figure 31-3, on the previous page, ruled surfaces cover the entire surface. This can now be transferred to a solid modelling package or shading package, or NC information can be generated.

Ruled surfaces are always done in pairs of rails.

Problems with RULESURF

In addition to picking the correct end of items, you may encounter problems with closed surfaces. If you are generating a ruled surface with a circle, the second object must be a circle, a point, or another type of closed entity: not a line.

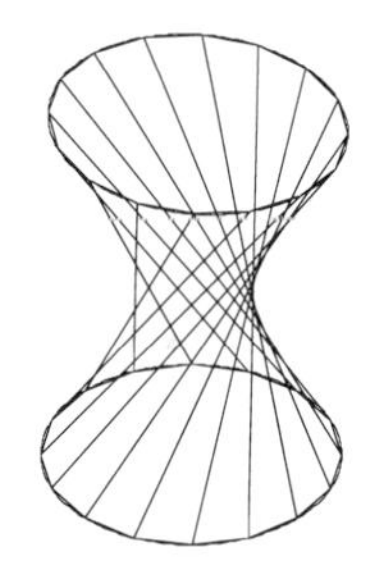

Another problem encountered is the direction of the closed entity. While the endpoint of the entity is not considered when generating a ruled surface, the direction from the endpoint is; thus, you can produce a cylinder that resembles an hourglass with very little effort (see illustration on the right). This problem usually occurs when you have been changing the UCS and you have drawn two circles, one from the bottom of the part and the other from the top. If this occurs, simply mirror the curve through its centre and delete the original object.

SURFACE DISPLAY

While your surface is fully described, you may find it difficult to see the surface if the display lines are too far apart. Also, the part may take on the appearance of a solid if the lines are too close together. The lines are actually edges; if you explode the surface, you will get a series of 3D Faces.

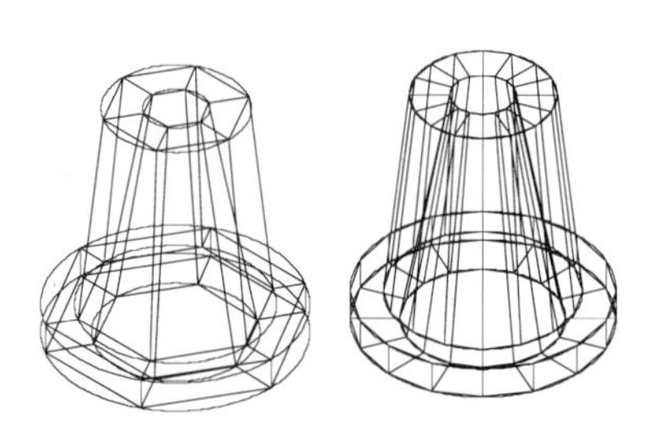

The mesh density is controlled by the SURFTAB1 setting (under SETVAR in Release 10). Change the setting and your surfaces will have a different mesh density. In the illustration on the right, the left object has a mesh density of 6, while that on the right has a mesh density of 16. The value represents the number of individual, equal-sized meshes along a defining curve.

In Figure 31-4, let us look at an irregularly shaped object and see how to put a surface on it.

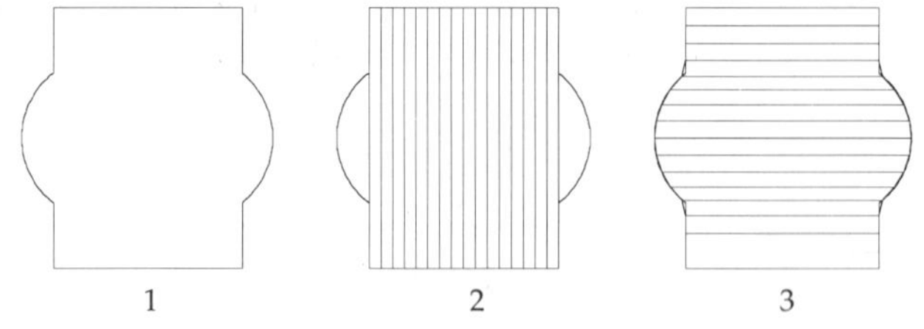

Figure 31-4. Putting a surface on an irregular shape

On the left (1), we have a front face of an object that we want to surface. If we added a 3D Face or extruded the bottom line, we would get part of the surface of the face covered (2), but we would still be missing the arced areas. By using

RULESURF we can create a surface between the arcs and the lines (3) or we can make the lines and arcs on each side into single pline entities. If you have an item that is not symmetrical, you will have to do this.

If the items on the right side of the face are an arc and two lines, you can change these into a pline or single entity for surfacing by using PEDIT.

```
Command:PEDIT
Select polyline: (pick a line)
Select objects:↵
Object is not a polyline. Do you want to
make it into one? <y>:↵
Close/Join/Width/Edit vertex/Fit
curve/Spline curve/Decurve/Undo/eXit <X>:J
Select objects: (pick the arc)
Select objects: (pick the second line)
Select objects:↵
2 segments added.
```

4

If the sides are not symmetrical, you will notice that the lines or segments describing the item are not always straight. Depending on your application, you may want to change the number of segments. To do this, use SURFTAB1. For most applications, this will be close enough.

CREATING SURFACES WITH HOLES

There are many instances where you will be required to create surfaces that have holes in them. In these cases, the ruled surface is the best surface to choose because you cannot cut a "hole" in either a 3D Face or an extruded surface. In order to create a surface hole you must define the two "curves" as plines; either complex polylines or polyline circles. When defining the plines, you must be sure to line up the two ends of the polylines, and make sure that they are constructed in the same direction.

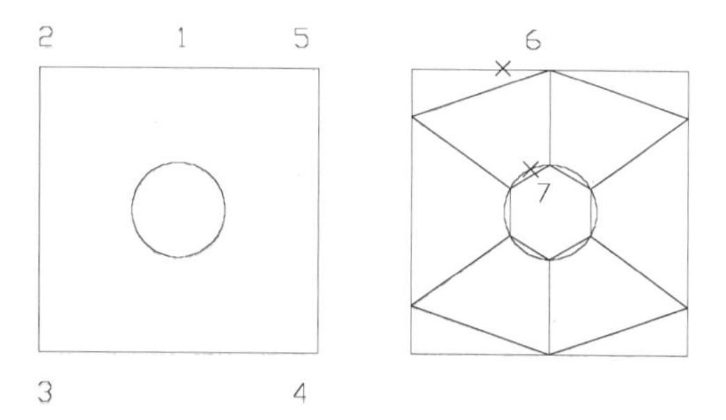

Figure 31-5. Using plines to create a ruled surface

In Figure 31-5, a pline has been created with four sides, but using five line segments so that the start- and endpoint are in the centre at the top of the surface. Then the pline circle is also started at the top and continues counter-clockwise as in the line segments.When the RULESURF command is invoked (picks 6 & 7), it will result in the surface shown.

If the endpoints do not line up, as in Figure 31-6, the surface will not line up; it will be generated from the endpoint of the first pline to the endpoint of the second pline counter-clockwise to the ends of both plines. The result is even more bizarre if your plines were created going in opposite directions, which often happens if you are using two different UCSs to define a plane.

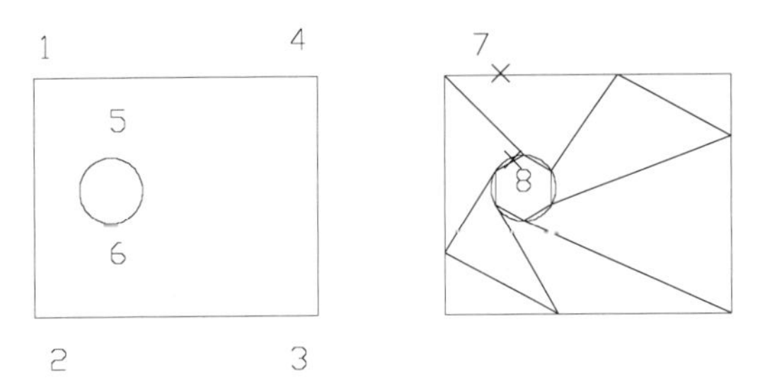

Figure 31-6. When endpoints are not lined up

In the example of Figure 31-7, the linear pline was constructed in a counterclockwise direction, while the pline circle, either through a change in the UCS or the MIRROR command, was constructed in a clockwise direction. In either case, the result is less than desirable.

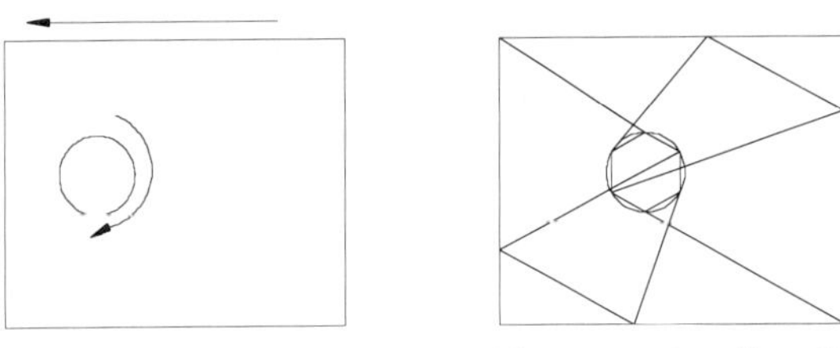

Figure 31-7. Plines created in opposite directions

In addition to the same endpoints and the same direction, if one pline is finished using Close, the other must be finished using Close as well. If not, the surface will not be generated correctly, if it is generated at all.

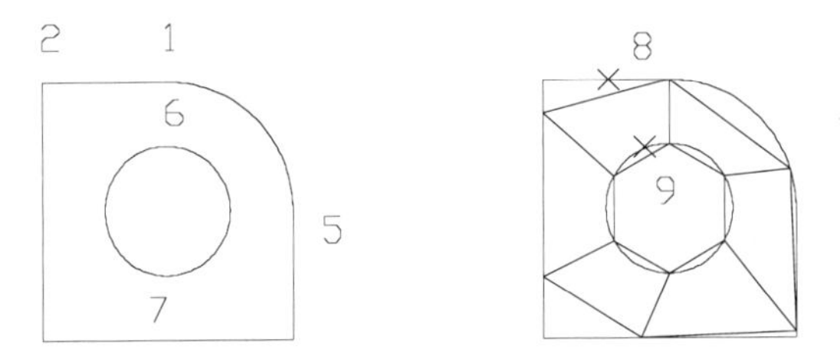

Figure 31-8. Using pline effectively

As long as you maintain consistency in the method you employ to enter plines, you can use any number of line or arc segments to define the final curve. You can also use PEDIT to spline the curve or fit it through a circle before surfacing.

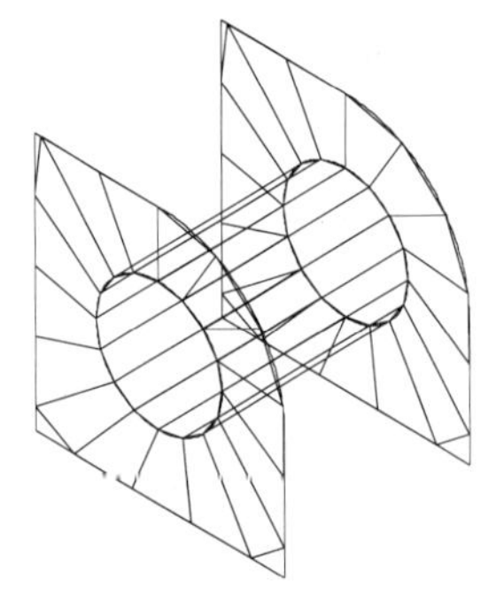

Figure 31-9. Plines used to create RULESURFS

The result is well worth the effort, however, as can be seen in the illustration of Figure 31-9.

When constructing surfaces, keep in mind that the item selection indicator will pick up a surface if it lies on "top" of a linear element such as a line, circle, or pline. Keep the surfaces on a different layer so you can turn them off if you need to.

REVOLVED SURFACE OR REVSURF

Another extremely easy surface to generate is the revolved surface. Very simply, the REVSURF command takes any linear element and rotates it around a defined axis. The linear elements are described as a path curve or profile whether they are curved or not. The obvious choice for a REVSURF demonstration is a glass; clearly a champagne flute is the most desirable.

In the example below, the profiles for the glass are entered using PLINE and then PEDIT with Spline.

The next step is to generate a line that will act as the axis. (Do not forget ORTHO.)

The REVSURF command is then invoked and you pick the entities as prompted.

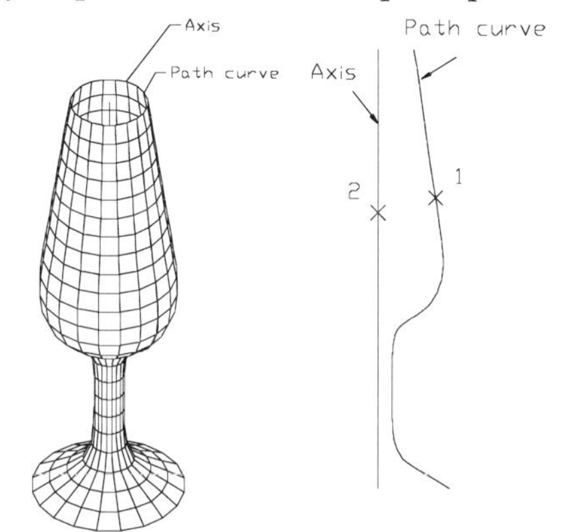


```
Command:REVSURF
Select path curve: (pick 1)
Select axis of revolution:(pick 2)
Start angle <0>:↵
Included angle (+=ccw,-=cw)<full
circle>:↵
```

Where:
Select path curve = one item only; a pline is easier than a set of lines.

Select axis of revolution = a line or a 2D or 3D pline. If a pline is chosen, the axis is assumed to be from the first vertex to the last vertex ignoring all vertices in the centre of the pline.

Start angle = if 0 is chosen, this indicates that the generated surface will start where the path curve is. A non-zero value will cause the surface to commence at the measured distance from the path curve.

Included angle = the number of degrees that the surface will be wrapped around the axis; a positive number is counter-clockwise, a negative number is clockwise, the default is 360 degrees or a full circle.

If the axis is neither a line nor a pline, AutoCAD will prompt:

```
Entity not usable as rotation axis
```

This often happens when you are trying to pick up a linear element that has been used to describe another surface. By picking the general area, you can pick either the linear element you want or the surface that you do not want. You can be sure that, given the choice, a CAD pick will always pick the item or entity that you do not want. Put your surfaces on a series of different layers and freeze them while you are completing the surfacing. This will also help you to visualize the surface better.

Also, your axis of revolution must be parallel to the UCS to attain the curve you require. It is quite simple to generate a surface yet not know that it was generated with your UCS on the wrong plane.

If the surface does not show up and there is no error prompt, try LIST on the area to see if it was generated on a different rotation than expected. The problem is the UCS.

Try using REVSURF to create a revolved surface for a beverage container. It takes only a minute and will help you get a feel for surfacing. If your taste is more towards the beer end of the beverage scale, a profile of a beer bottle will give you the same effect as the champagne glass. A pop bottle will work as well.

In industry, you will probably never have to create a wine glass, except maybe for demonstration purposes. A more practical example would be a curved corner of an item using a revolved surface for the 90-degree angle.

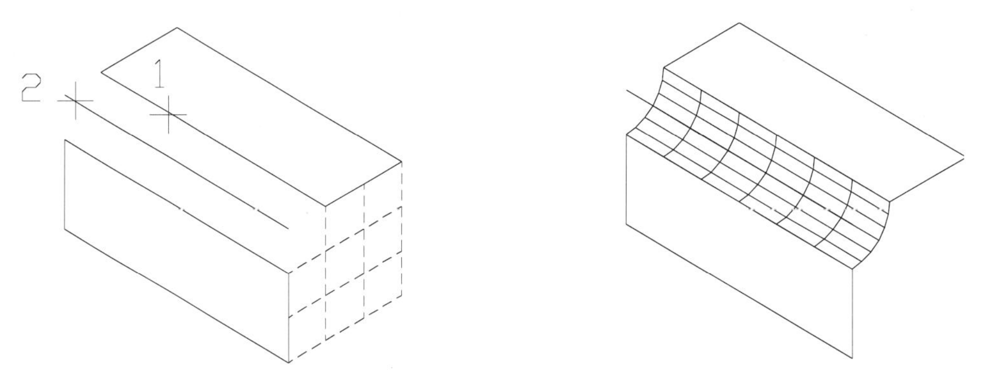

Figure 31-10. Creating a curved surface with REVSURF

In Figure 31-10, we have two planes described by four lines each at 90 degrees from each other. We have drawn a line for the axis of revolution at 1 unit in from the first or horizontal plane and 1 unit up from the second or vertical plane.

The command to create a curved corner is:

```
Command:REVSURF
Select path curve: (pick 1)
Select axis of revolution: (pick 2)
Start angle <0>:↵
Included angle(+=ccw,-=cw)<full circle>:-90
```

The line describing one corner of the horizontal plane is taken as the path curve for the curved corner. The start angle remains 0 since this is where we want it to start, and the included angle is -90 degrees because we want to have the curve sweeping in a clockwise manner looking down the axis.

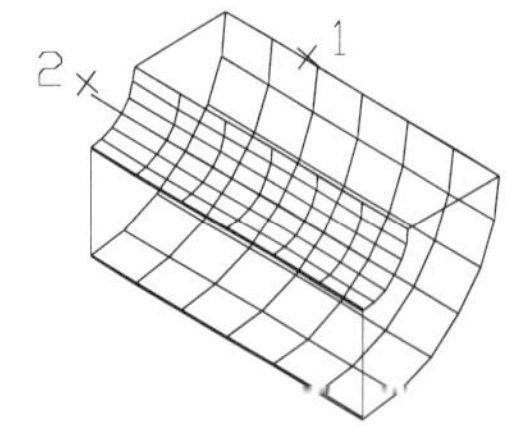

Figure 31-11. Creating an elbow with REVSURF

We will use the same axis of revolution and the line on the back to create the outside corner of this part.

The angles will remain the same. Notice that the outside curve is much larger than the first because of the distance away from the axis of revolution. This is similar to the size of a circle relative to the radius.

Now we can copy the four lines on the vertical and horizontal planes away from the object and generate surfaces between these lines using RULESURF or 3DFACE.

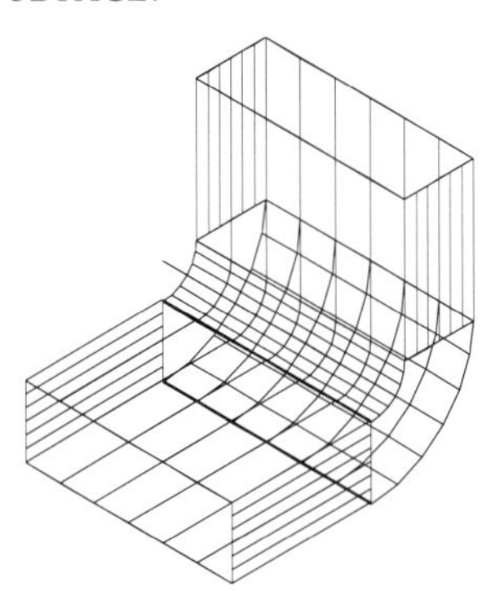

Figure 31-12. Using RULESURF and REVSURF

Notice that the lines on the mesh displaying the longer edge of the surfaces are further apart than the lines on the shorter edges (see Figure 31-12). This again is because the display, set through SURFTAB1, generates a similar number of lines on each surface relative to the length of the defining line or arc.

Since the surface is described by lines going in a number of different directions, you can change both SURFTAB1 and SURFTAB2 to get the image you want.

The SURFTAB1 variable changes the mesh display in one direction, while the SURFTAB2 variable changes the display in the other direction.

From the side view we can see that the surfaces are in fact placed around the defining axis. At least two viewports are necessary to enter the information in where you want it.

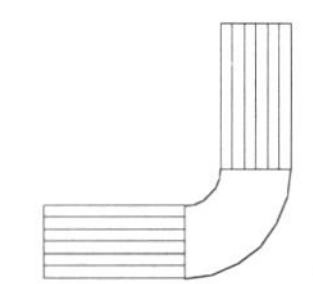

TABULATED SURFACE OR TABSURF

The TABSURF command creates a tabulated or tabular surface. It is similar to RULESURF and REVSURF in that two objects are needed to define the surface. Like REVSURF, it uses a straight line, not to revolve around, but to stretch along. The surface, of course, will always have the same shape.

The path curve in this case is called a directrix, and the axis is a direction vector describing the magnitude and direction of the required surface. This direction is referred to as a generatrix.

The two objects you need are:

- a linear element for the path curve or directrix; this can be either a line, an arc, a pline, a circle, or any other linear element
- a line or pline along which the outline or directrix will be stretched

Command: **TABSURF**

Select path curve: *(pick 1)*

Select direction vector: *(pick 2)*

The surface maintains the shape of the original curve (see Figure 31-13).

This is a useful surface for predetermined area or profiles. The same effect can be achieved with two outlines spaced at the correct distance and using RULESURF, but TABSURF will often be easier, particularly if a number of items are being tabulated relative to a standard vector.

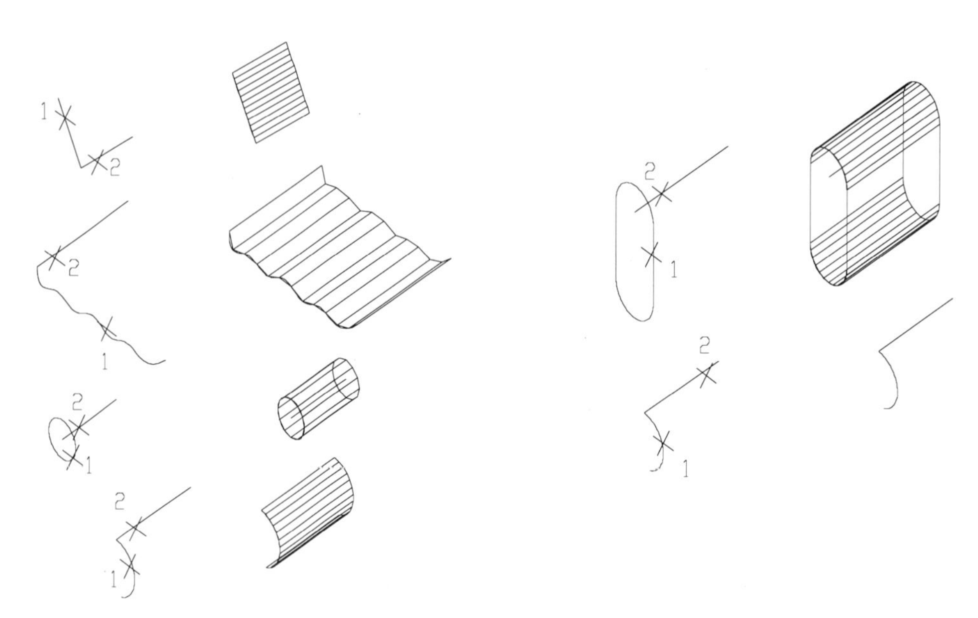

Figure 31-13. Using TABSURF

The display is again dependent on the TABSURF1 setting.

The only trick with this surface is to make sure your line or generatrix is in fact a line and can be easily picked. If surfaces or other data are overlapping it, you may get the "Entity not usable as a direction vector" prompt.

EDGE SURFACES OR EDGESURF

This surface is generated by curves which, like the ruled-surface curves, can be either curved or straight. It is quite simple to use as long as all four curves are bounded, or touch at the corners. The surface tabulation is in two directions like REVSURF. EDGESURF offers much greater flexibility in geometric construction than either RULESURF or TABSURF, which essentially create surfaces that are constructed with straight edges either between two defining curves or along a specific vector.

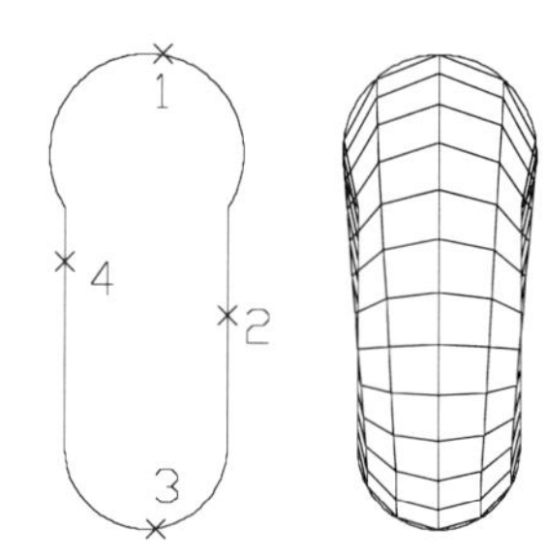

Because the surface is tabulated in two different directions, you will need both SURFTAB1 and SURFTAB2 to define the display of the surface.

The surface is generated as a 3D polygon mesh which approximates a Coon's patch. Stephen Coon was an American mathematician who developed mathematical programs to describe surfaces for automotive companies.

In this case, the surface is described by four arcs (see illustration above).

The screen was divided into a minimum of three viewports containing a plan view, a right-side view, and an isometric view. The two arcs picked as 1 and 3 were entered while the UCS was in World.

The UCS was then changed to the right-side view using the View option. Then the second two arcs were entered using END to make sure that the ends of all arcs met.

The next step is the command itself.

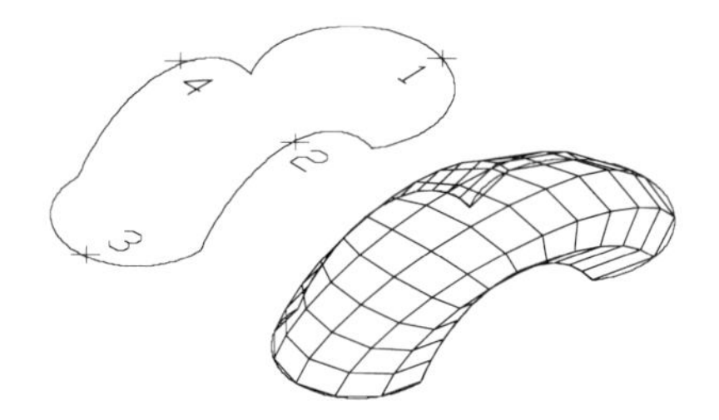

```
Command:EDGESURF
Select edge 1: (pick 1)
Select edge 2: (pick 2)
Select edge 3: (pick 3)
Select edge 4: (pick 4)
```

As long as all the endpoints meet, the surface will work.

As demonstrated in the illustration above, students have the most difficulty when the screen is not set up properly. Be sure you have at least three views of the object, otherwise you will not be able to visualize it.

This surface can be very useful for describing handles on kettles and that sort of thing. Again, a 15-week course on EDGESURF alone is not out of the question.

3DPOLY OR THREE-DIMENSIONAL PLINES

You may notice that plines are only two-dimensional entities. For use on surfaces, particularly EDGESURF and 3DMESH, you need to have a three dimensional facility for making plines or polylines.

```
Command:3DPOLY
From point:0,0,0
Close/Undo/ <Endpoint>:1,1,1
Close/Undo/<Endpoint>:1,2,2
Close/Undo/ <Endpoint>:2,3,3
Close/Undo/ <Endpoint>:c
```

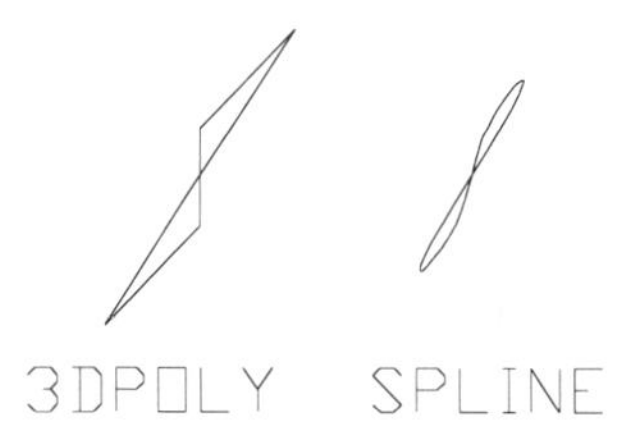

This will give you a 3D loop. The Close option works the same in this command as in the PLINE command, as does Undo.

As with the EDGESURF and 3DMESH commands, this is the basis for some very tricky mathematical manoeuvres. Your use of 3DPOLY is essentially as good as your use of polynomials. In a manufacturing environment, it is an extremely useful command for those in industrial, automotive, and aerospace design, but not totally necessary for those in other fields. It is primarily used for fitting three-dimensional b-spline curves to vertices. There are some very good books available on the mathematics of surfaces if this is where you want to head.

In mapping and architecture, 3D polylines are used to provide contour lines in plot plans in 3D.

The illustration on the right demonstrates 3DPOLY in a top, front, side, and iso view. In the Practice exercise on the following page, 3DPOLY is used to define a linear element along the surface of a curved surface that will act as one of the edges on EDGESURF.

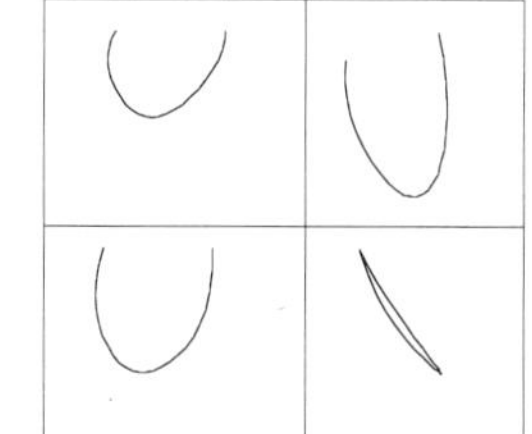

The 3D polyline consists of straight-line segments that are edited into splines by PEDIT.

The PEDIT command with 3DPOLY has fewer options than with PLINE because it is used for different purposes.

Practice 31

What we are doing here is creating a handle for the tripod in M31. We will use 3DPOLY and EDGESURF to create the necessary geometry.

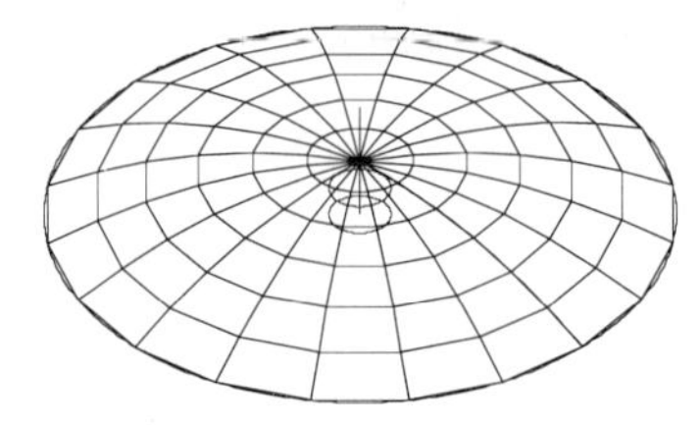

The bottom section that screws onto the top of the tripod is created with RULESURF and REVSURF.

Note the location of your origin.

Now enter an arc where the end of the handle should be. It will show up on the Z = 0 plane. Create lines from this arc through the surface above it so you can access the points of intersection to create a 3D polyline. The accuracy of your 3D polyline and ultimately of your surface is completely dependent on the number and quality of points used to describe it.

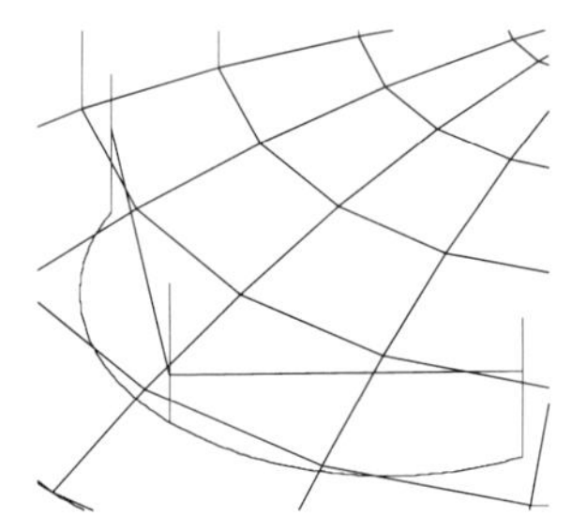

With the 3D polyline created along the edge of the defined surface, mirror this over to the other side of the surface and connect these two 3D polylines with either an arc or, preferably, another 3D polyline defined in space. Make sure the endpoints are connected. Generate an EDGESURF with these four linear elements.

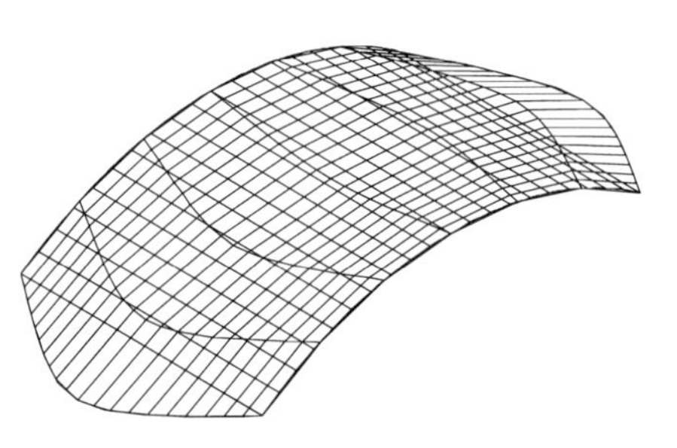

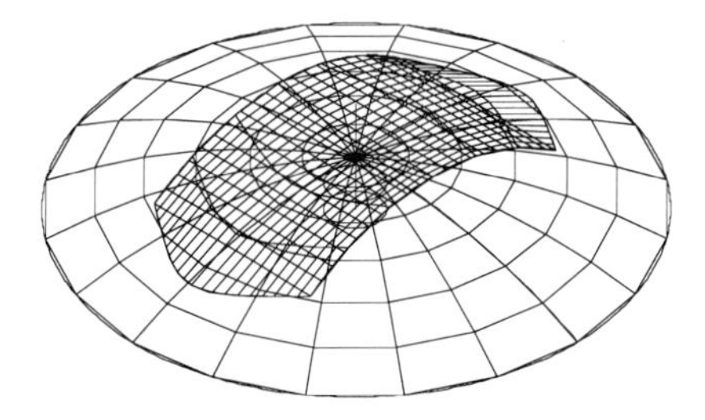

Your final part should be fully surfaced.

Exercise A31

Many people think that an architectural student you will not need to know surfacing. Any of the periodicals written about CAD — *CADENCE, CADALYST*, or *IEEE* — will feature a good example almost monthly.

There are possibilities for architectural models, however, using the various methods of 3D plotting. In essence, this technology is very similar to manufacturing in that the final product is something you hold in your hand as opposed to something you look at on paper. It is possible to do 3D plotting with stereolithography as well as with low-cost foam or wax models on NC 3D plotting equipment. In the past, few architects have been interested in this idea, but if the astounding deflation of cost in CAD technology over the past decade is followed by an equally severe drop in the cost of stereolithography and 3D plotting equipment, more architects will begin to see this as a reasonable method of presentation.

We are going to try something very simple to start with — a gazebo in the classical style.

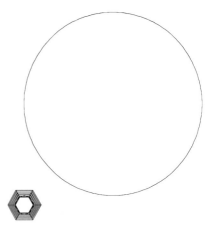

First set up your screen with at least three viewports. Then draw in a circle that will be the centre area of the gazebo and place a pillar at a reasonable distance from the centre to make a room. In the tropics, such facilities are commonly used for dining and recreation and can easily have a diameter of 20 feet.

Once the outline for the building is entered, change your UCS to the top of the pillar and enter some interesting profiles for the detailing on the top of the pillar.

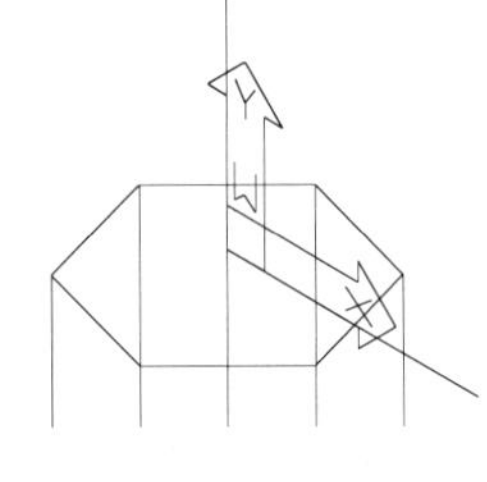

Draw a line for the axis of revolution through the pillar, then add another line to act as the X value and orient your UCS relative to it.

You will need a central axis of revolution for the path curve to revolve around.

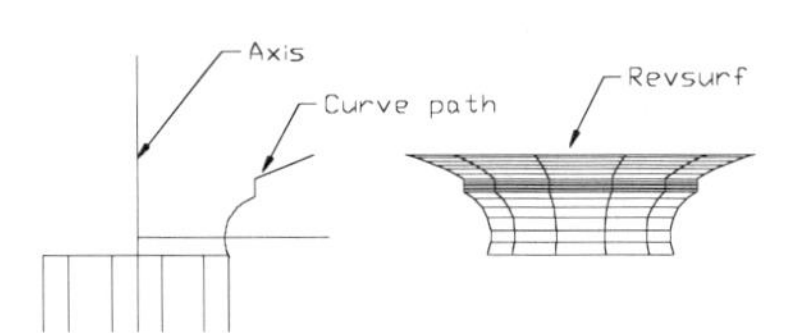

You may notice as well that the path curve must be at the same Z depth as the interior of your building, or the revolved surface will be much too big.

Be sure to change your UCS so that the Z = 0 plane is contained within the model. Use 3point with OSNAP for the best results. Lines may have to be added to access the origin, X, and Y.

Exercise A31 (continued)

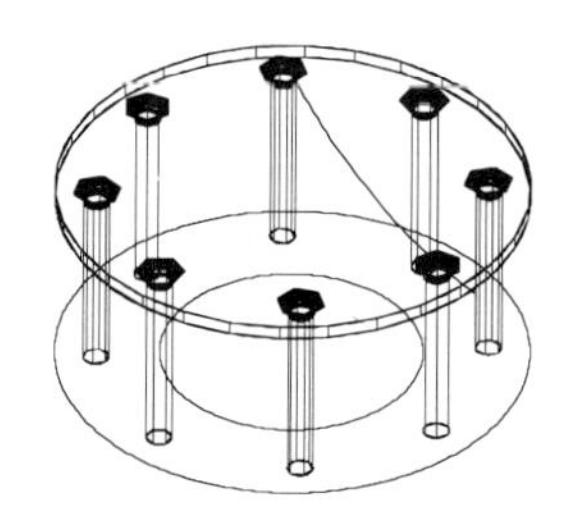

Now back in the UCS World and the plan view, array the completed pillars around the centre of the gazebo.

Add a ceiling on the gazebo and give it some depth using RULESURF so that the roof can be supported.

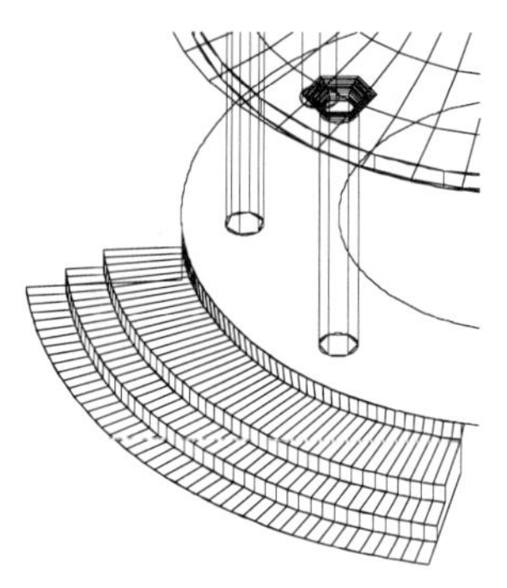

Now add some front steps by placing arcs at a reasonable distance from the main floor. Use RULESURF to surface the steps.

You will notice that it is difficult to pick the arcs through which you are generating the surfaces with the surfaces present. Just turn your surface layer off while picking the new surface rails.

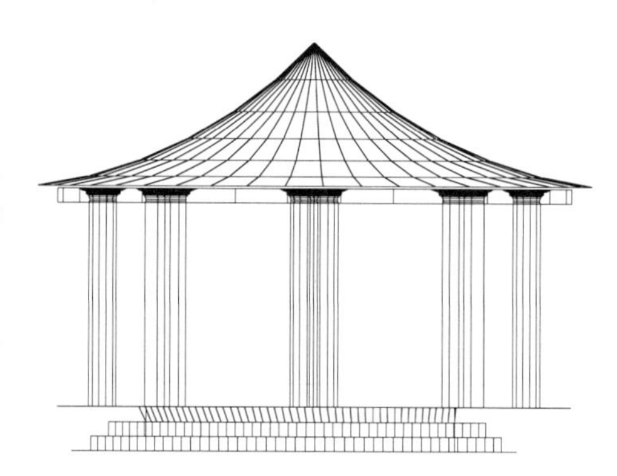

Once the steps are completed, you can change the UCS once more and generate a sloping roof over the gazebo.

This is a very simple design and may take less than two hours to complete. If so, do some variations on the columns to make them more interesting, and maybe add a platform on the inside of the gazebo.

If the floor is to be poured concrete, you may also need to slope it.

Once finished, use HIDE in the isometric view to see what the final design might look like.

Save the model.

Exercise M31

Using the PLINE command, create ruled surfaces on the camera body created in Chapter 30.

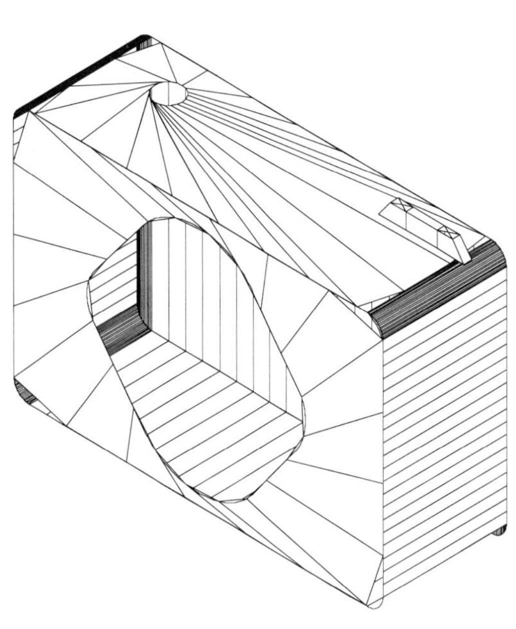

You will need to use at least two layers to create these surfaces because the curves that will define the surfaces will not be accessible once the surfaces are created.

If you have one layer for created surfaces and one layer for curves, you can turn off the surfaces for one plane or set of planes while you create the others.

If the plines and pline curves are not centred and regular, the surface will not display as an even pattern. Simply make sure that the entire surface is defined and covered and no overlapping occurs at the necessary openings.

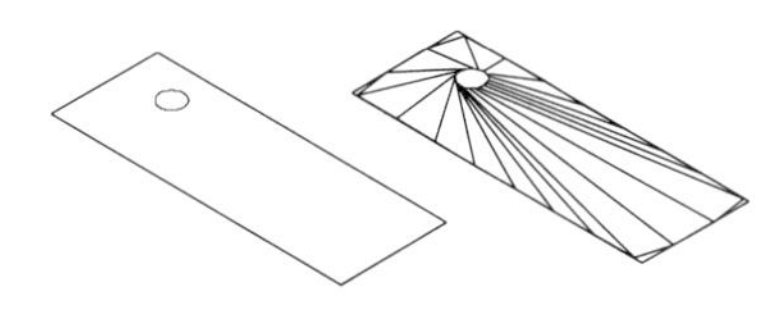

Use the commands illustrated on page 328 to create the plines and pline circles to create the complex surfaces.

When you complete this part, you may want to add some detailing for other features of the camera or continue with the tripod illustrated over the next few pages.

Exercise M31 (continued)

Create the tripod shown using RULESURF, REVSURF, and TABSURF. Once completed, you can use EDGESURF to generate a handle for it as described in the Practice exercise.

Before starting, set up at least three viewports — top, front, and iso. You will not be able to visualize your data without these viewports.

Also make sure you have several layers so that you can turn off your surfaces when you need to. You will find it almost impossible to pick the defining arcs and circles with surfaces attached to them.

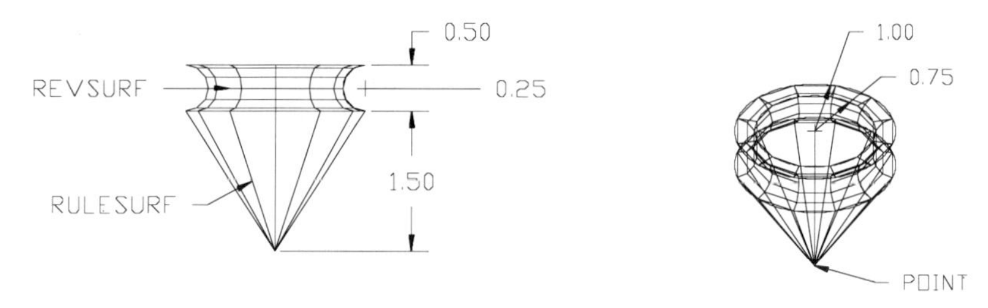

Create the leg end using RULESURF and REVSURF. You will need to move your UCS, so it is a good idea to start the part on 0,0,0 so that you can locate your Z depths later.

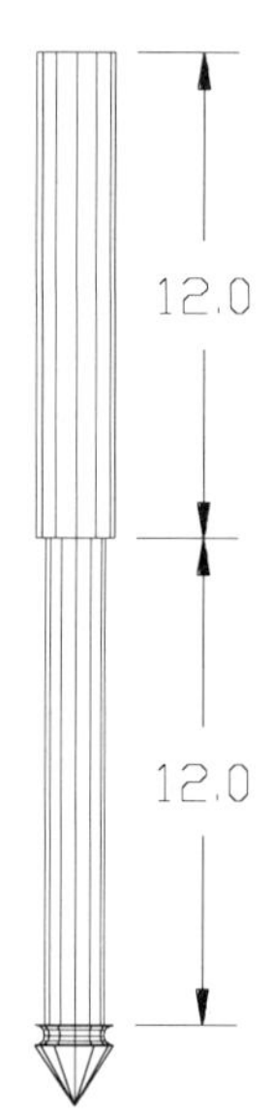

Now place a central axis through the .75-radius circle at 12 inches in positive Z. Use this to create a tabular surface.

Using the end of the axis, generate another circle at the end with a radius of 1 unit. Create another axis from the centre of this circle going up in positive Z at least 12 inches. Then create another tabular surface on this circle for the collapsible tripod legs.

At the top of this leg, create a circle in the same orientation as the others for a base for the three tripod legs. Place a circle on the top of the leg just created, and generate another circle concentric with the last one at a radius of .85.

This last circle will be used to generate a half sphere, the ballbearing that the tripod legs move on. Through the circle, create a line through which the circle will be revolved. Now use REVSURF to surface the sphere. Remember, only 180 degrees is necessary for your angle.

Exercise M31 (continued)

The top or base for your camera tripod is now ready to complete.

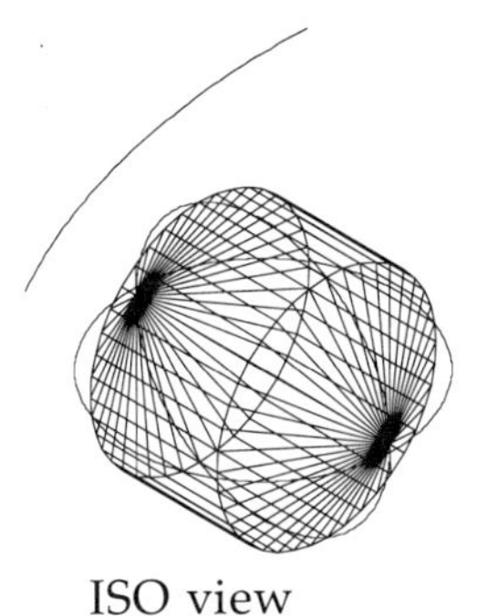

ISO view

Copy the 5-inch circle to 1 inch in positive Z. In the centre of these circles place two smaller circles at a radius of .5".

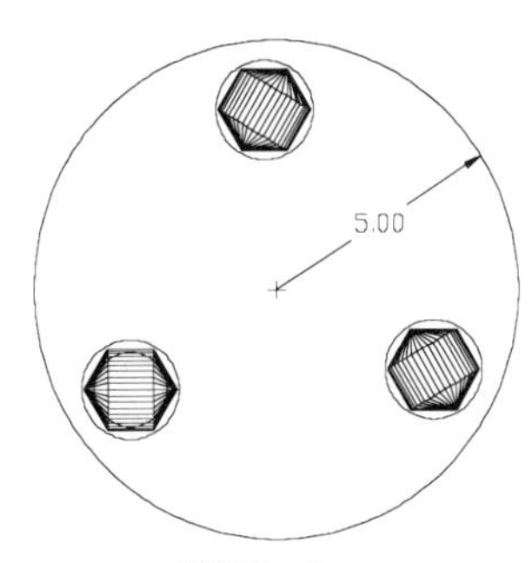

TOP view

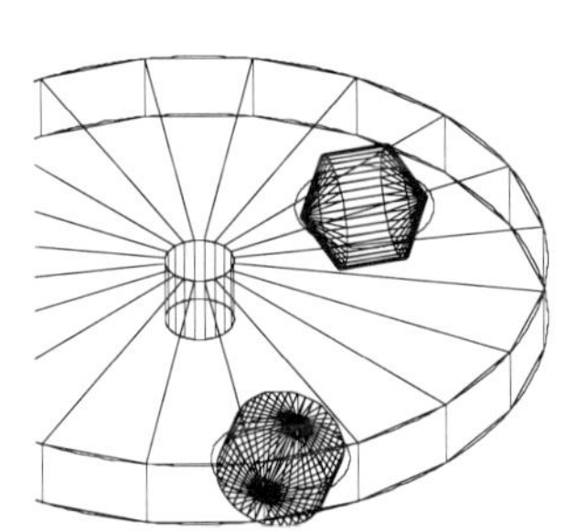

Now use RULESURF to surface the top, inside, and outside edge of the tripod base.

The spheres should fit nicely within the tripod base.

We will leave the underside of the base for the moment. The surfaces, presented as they are, will give you adequate HIDE possibilities.

If you have difficulty selecting items with surfaces on them, turn off your surface layer.

On the bottom of the tripod base, create the end of a bolt. You will first create a 180-degree arc either by using ARC or by using CIRCLE and breaking it. Then put in an axis through which you will revolve the arc.

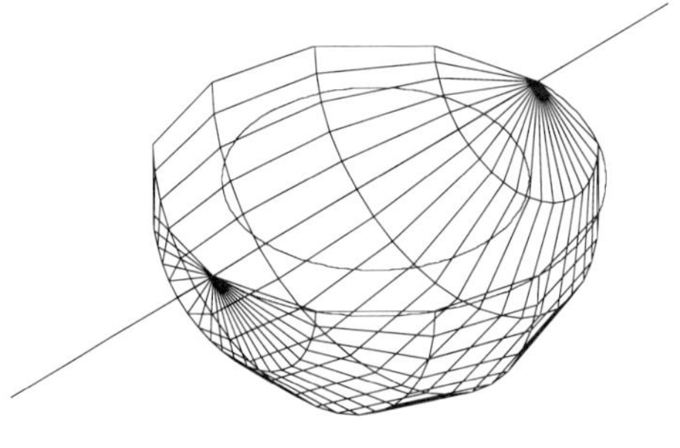

Bonus marks are given to those who can put in the half-sphere correctly the first time.

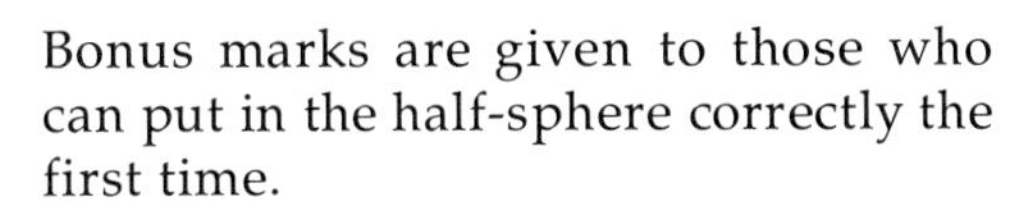

Now we just need to put in the remainder of the bolt and the tripod is finished.

Exercise M31 (continued)

This tripod should take about two hours to complete.

For those who finish early, try putting threads on the bolt.

You can use RULESURF with a 3D polyline to generate threads or use REVSURF and PLINE to simulate threading.

You will have probably noticed how many times you changed viewports while designing this piece. This is not unusual.

When finished, save the model to use later.

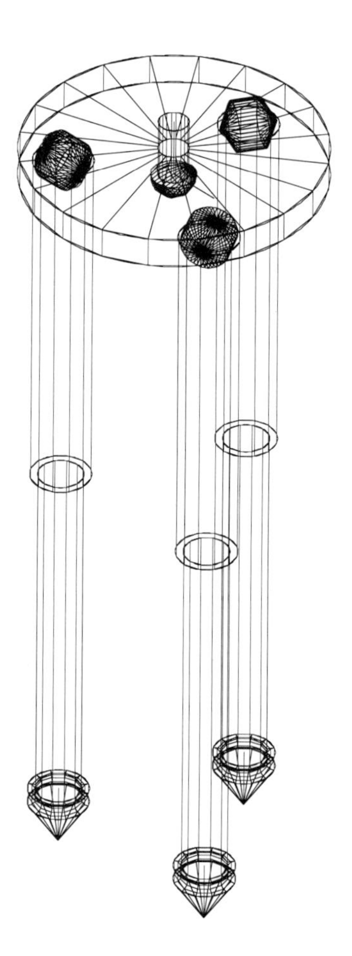

Exercise C31

Before starting, look at page 545 to see what you are going to create; it might help you to visualize the various components.

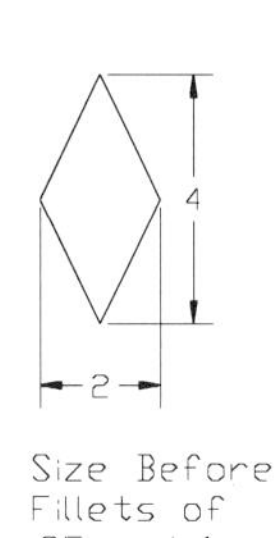

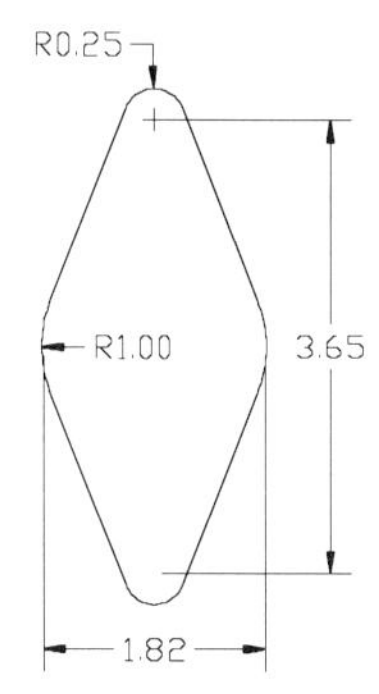

STEP 1

Set the screen into three views — front, plan, and 2,-2,2. Then draw in the column base as in the illustration on the right. Use a snap of 1 and this should take you very little time.

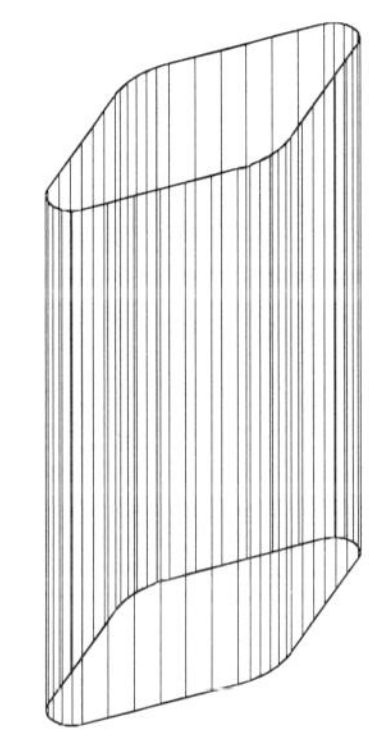

STEP 2

Use the COPY command to copy your base from the Z = 0 to the Z = 6 plane.

Create a layer for surfaces and create the surfaces on the columns as in the illustration.

If you encounter the prompt "cannot surface the item selected," it means that your surfaces are overlapping your lines and arcs. If so, turn off your surfacing layer, create the surfaces in layer 0, and use CHPROP to change them to the undisplayed layer.

STEP 3

With the column base created, change your UCS so that the origin is in the centre of the column, the X will remain the same, and the Y will replace the World coordinate Z.

The easiest way to do this is to place a line from the centre of the arc at the major axis on the top face to the centre of the arc directly opposite it. Change the UCS to the midpoint of this line. Then rotate the UCS 90 degrees around the X axis.

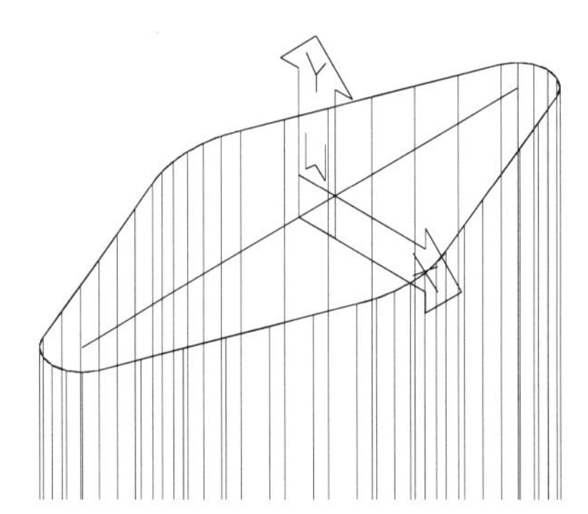

The new UCS should be placed as in the illustration above.

Exercise C31 (continued)

STEP 4
Copy the existing column base 8 units in the X direction.

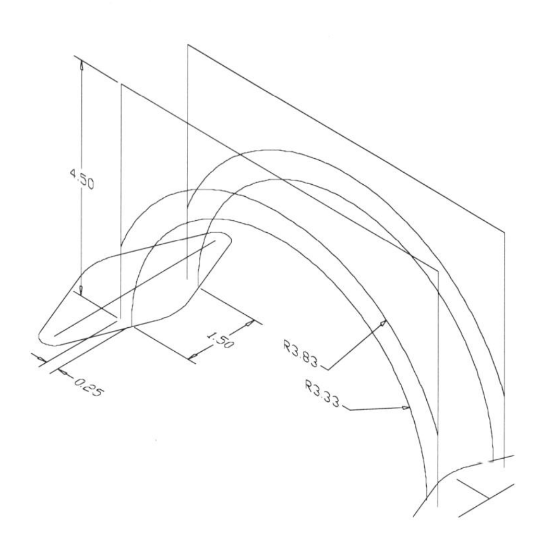

Now using the new UCS, create the four arcs and six lines in the example.

First create a .75 unit line on the second base from the middle of the long line in the negative X direction. Create the first arc using SER from the end of this line to the end of the corresponding line on the other column. Now offset this arc at a distance of .5.

Move both arcs .75 unit in positive Z, then copy them 1.5 units in negative Z.

Finally, create 4.5-unit lines from the endpoints of the interior lines in the Y direction and trim the arcs to the lines as shown.

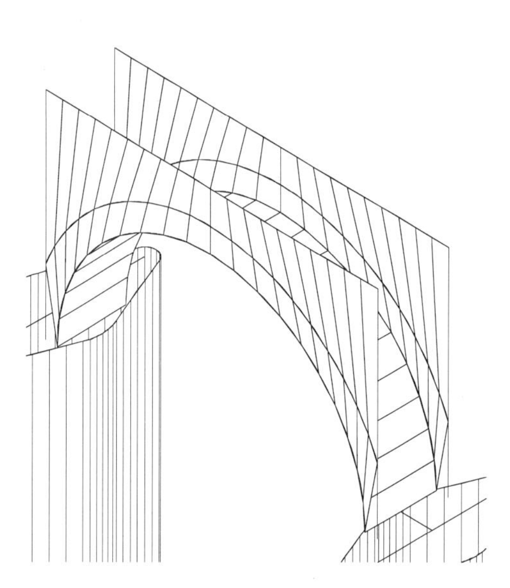

STEP 5
On your surfacing layer, add the surfaces as shown.

You may need to change the SURFTAB1 option to get the surfaces at the same distance as in the illustration. In the column base, the SURFTAB1 is set to 6. In the arches, the SURFTAB1 is set to 20.

The display lines are relative to the length of the objects determining the surface. Since these objects are longer than the in the first set, the SURFTAB1 needs to be a higher number.

Exercise C31 (continued)

STEP 6

On the top face of the column base, create the four lines and two arcs (FILLET is the easiest command to use) as in the diagram. You will of course need to rotate your UCS to do this.

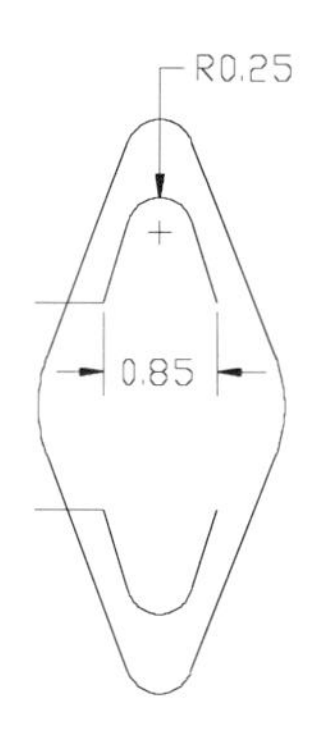

The 3point option may be an easy way to create these, and the existing objects can again be used as references.

You may want to create another few layers at this point as well so that you can view some of the new surfaces being entered without viewing the existing surfaces as well.

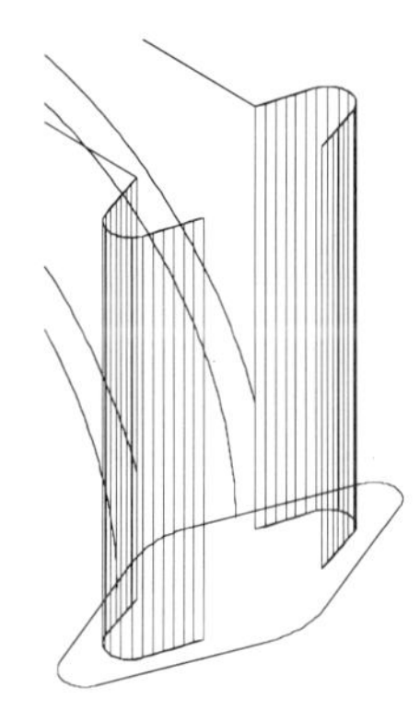

STEP 7

Now copy the new data 4.5 units in the Z direction.

Change your SURFTAB1 back to 6 because these objects are quite small and a smaller display factor is required.

Turn off any layers you will not need to create these surfaces and then use RULESURF to create the bridge support shown on the left.

STEP 8

The bridge now needs some finishing.

Take the lines and arcs that define the very top edge of the bridge and offset these by .25 unit. If your UCS is still parallel to World, this should be easy.

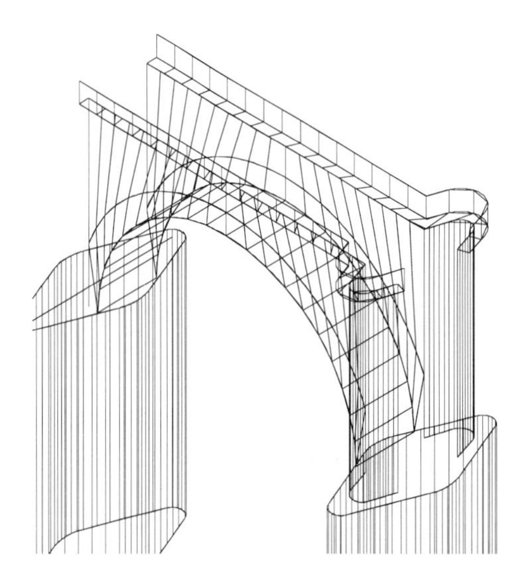

Now copy these new objects .5 unit in the Z direction. You now have the outline for the top edge of the bridge. Use RULESURF to create the surface between the outlines.

Will you need to change the SURFTAB variables? Would it be easiest to use PEDIT to make these line and arc segments one entity into a single entity before offsetting and copying?

Exercise C31 (continued)

STEP 9
Finally, you will need to enter the interior surface of the bridge itself.

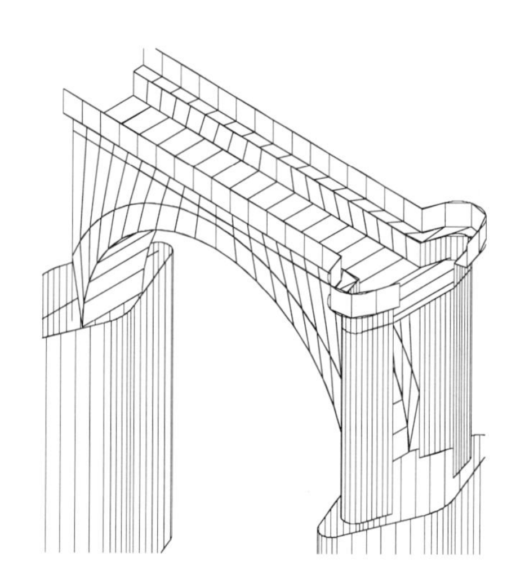

If you have changed the lines and arcs in Step 8 to plines, you can copy these plines down 1 unit in the negative Z direction.

Turn off any obstructing layers and add a surface for traffic.

You can also finish the interior of the bridge to your satisfaction.

STEP 10
Now that you have one complete bridge section, use CHPROP to change one of the column bases to an undisplayed layer.

If you have created the surfaces on layers separate from the linear elements that define them, turn off the linear elements — lines, arcs, and plines — before arraying. Since you already have the surface data, these objects are not necessary and will just take up unnecessary room on the disk.

Save your file, just in case you are running out of room on the disk.

Now use the ARRAY command to create the full bridge as in the example on the next page.

With ARRAY, make eight columns at a spacing of 8 units each as shown in the illustration on the right.

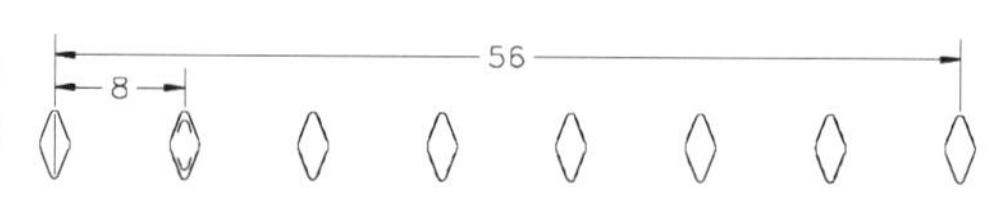

Many people think that surfacing and 3D are not applicable for civil and surveying applications. This example may help you see how this technology can help to figure out how the Romans built a bridge that has lasted 2,000 years.

Exercise C31 (continued)

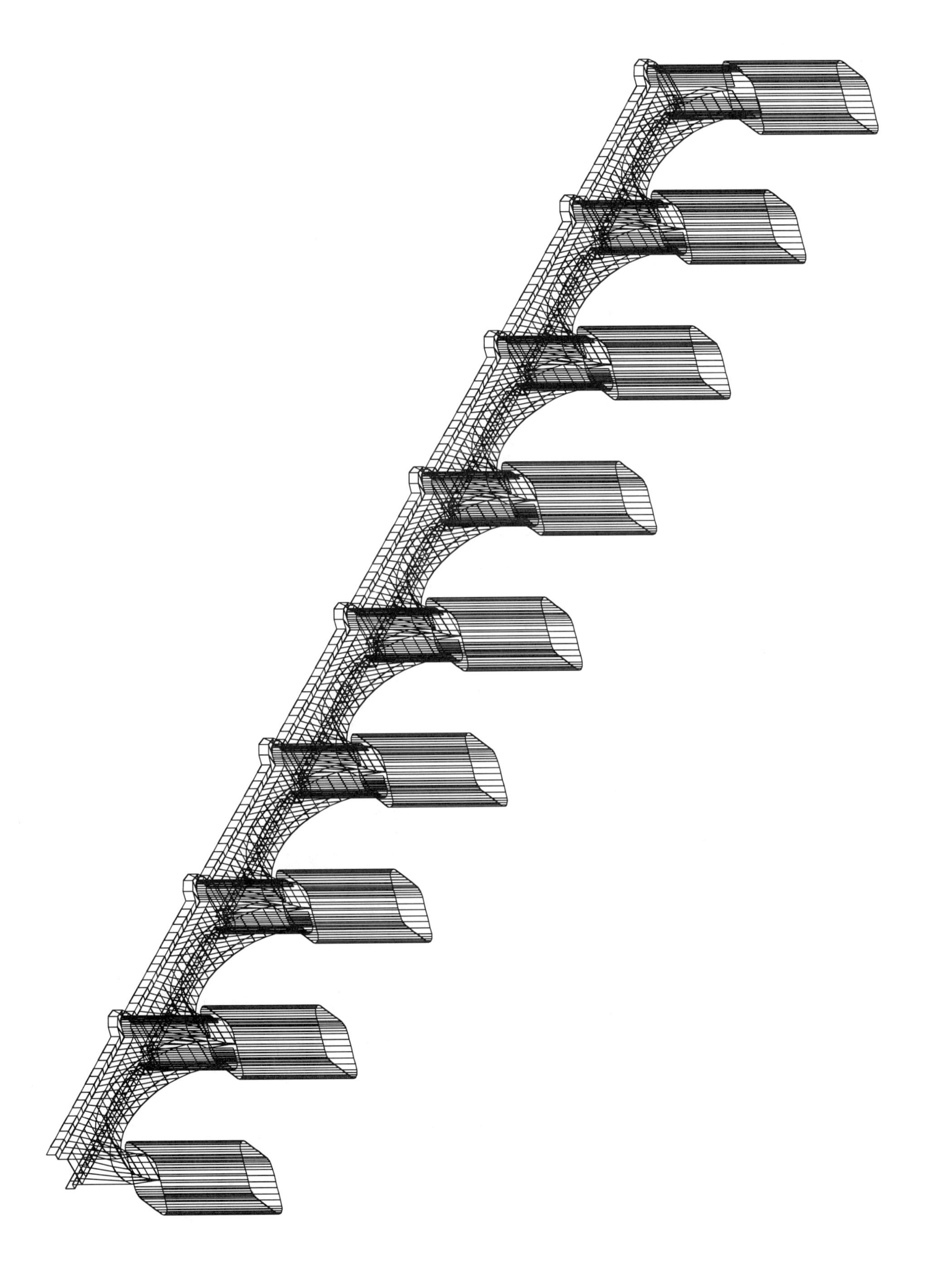

Challenger 31

Using the coordinates from the model of Chapter 30, use RULESURF and REVSURF to generate this section of the Belt Pulley Tensioner Assembly.

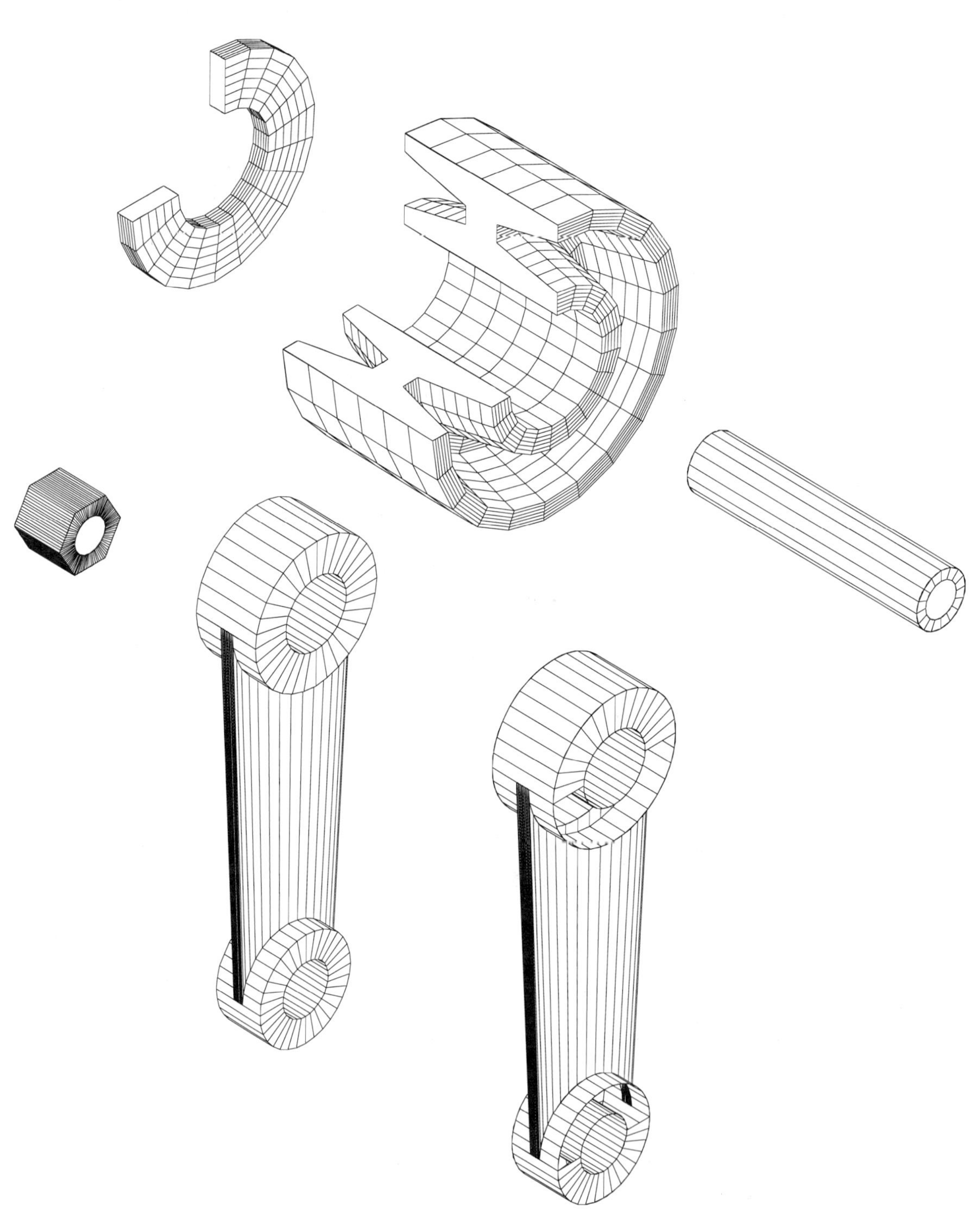

3D SHAPES

Upon completion of this chapter, the student should be able to:

1. Generate any kind of 3D shape on the AutoCAD 3D icon menu
2. Manipulate 3D shapes in space
3. Generate a mesh with PFACE

3D ENTITIES IN AUTOCAD

So far we have been using AutoCAD to construct objects in space starting from the origin by working with extrusions, the UCS, and basic items of geometry to create objects.

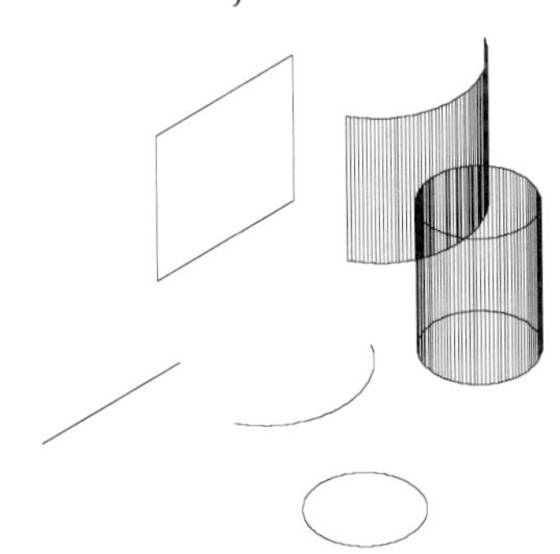

Figure 32-1. Basic items of geometry

We have used lines, arcs, circles, etc. that are extruded in 3D, 3D faces, and the various surfaces used in 3D. All of the objects in Figure 32-2 exist in 3D space.

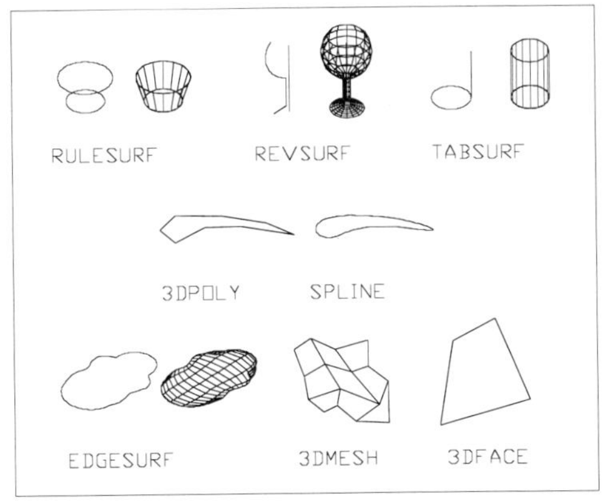

Figure 32-2. Examples of surface types

Creating surfaces in 3D space is essential for generating real 3D objects for manufacturing and analysis purposes. By combining, for example, such things as 3D polylines and ruled surfaces, you can generate some very sophisticated geometry.

The airfoil shapes on the right are examples of how the computing power of a CAD system makes a rather complicated shape easy to produce.

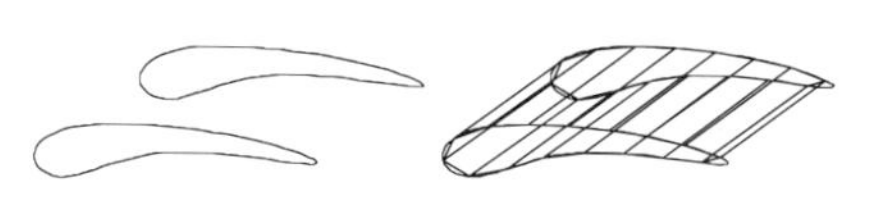

In creating 3D geometry with AutoCAD, there is another set of commands that can be quite useful; these are the 3D objects. The 3D Objects icon menu is located in the Draw pull-down menu under the Object option. It offers a series of shapes that can be constructed directly from the menu.

Release 12 Notes

3DSHAPES are located under the Draw pull-down menu, under the #D Surface option, under the name 3D Objects. The menu is in the new icon format and has 11 open spots for user-defined shapes or objects.

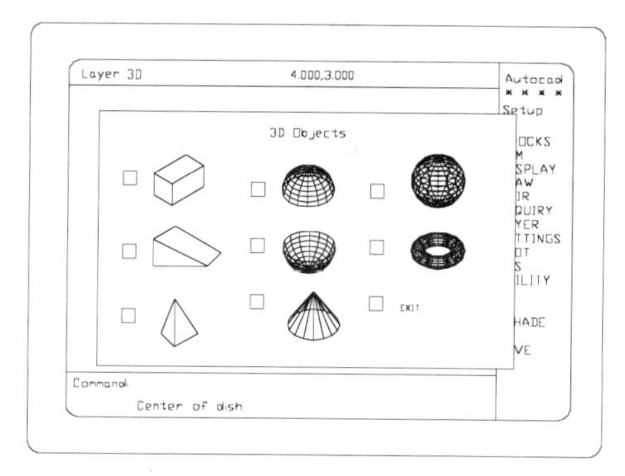

Figure 32-3. The 3-D Objects icon box

These AutoLISP routines create CAD-primitive shapes made up of 3D meshes. You do not have to be a programmer to use them; if you are interested in learning more, refer to the *AutoLISP Programmer's Reference.*

The shapes are selected in the same way as almost all other items in icon boxes — with a single pick.

Once the shapes are picked, you are prompted for the pertinent information: diameter, length, etc. needed for completion.

Once the objects are in your drawing, they behave in the same way as a block. All parts are affected by editing commands, and a single pick identifies the whole shape. Like blocks as well, the item can be exploded into its various component 3D Faces.

3D Objects icon menu is used to create objects more quickly than other methods.

3D OBJECTS

The 3D objects available are:

BOX CONE DOME DISH PYRAMID SPHERE TORUS WEDGE

We will look at each shape offered in the order they appear on the menu and then see how we can use them.

The objects are shown in the World Coordinate System with the Viewpoint at 2,-2,2.

BOX

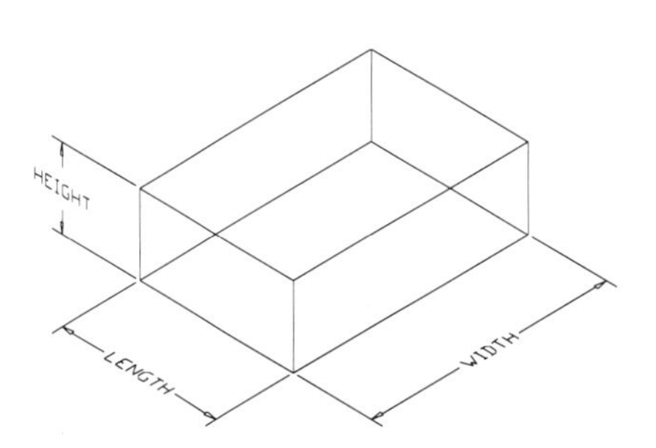

Command:**BOX**

Starting point of box: *(pick 1)*

Length:**3**

Cube <Width>:**5**

Height:**1**

Rotation angle about Z axis:**0**

If you specify the Cube option, the width, length, and height will all be the length input.

WEDGE

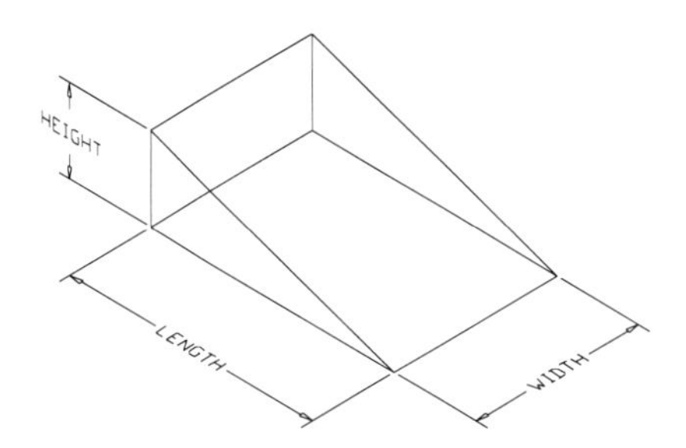

Command:**WEDGE**

Corner of wedge: *(pick 1)*

Length:**5**

Width:**3**

Height:**1**

Rotation angle about the Z axis:**0**

The BOX and the WEDGE commands are quite similar in that you specify first the point where the item will start, then the length, width, and height. Finally, in both, you specify the rotation around the Z axis. The height is in the Z direction.

PYRAMID

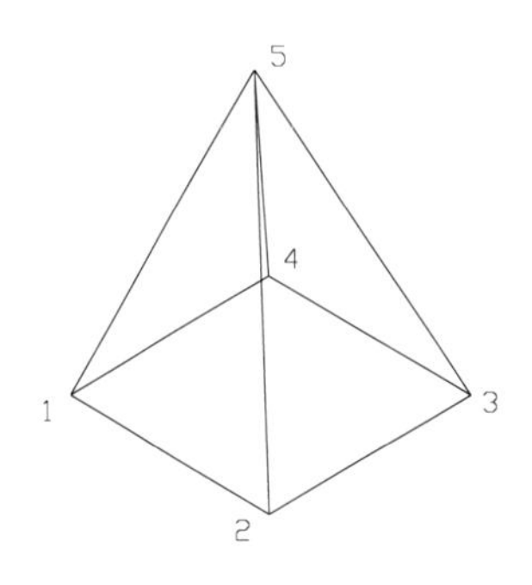

Command:**PYRAMID**

First base point:**0,0**

Second base point:**3,0**

Third base point:**3,3**

Tetrahedron/<Fourth base point>:**0,3**

Ridge/Top/<apex point>:**1.5,1.5,3**

This illustrates the default, a quadrilateral base. With the default, you can choose an apex point or two points to define a ridge.

Command:**PYRAMID**

First base point:**0,0**

Second base point:**3,0**

Third base point:**3,2**

Tetrahedron/<Fourth base point>:**0,2**

Ridge/Top/<apex point>:**R**

First ridge point:**1,1,2**

Second ridge point:**2,1,2**

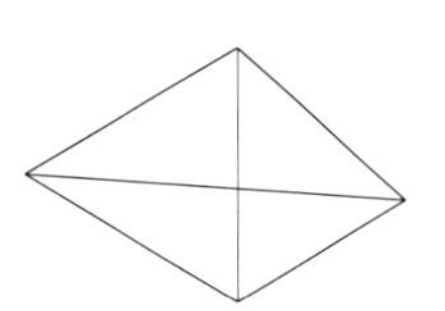

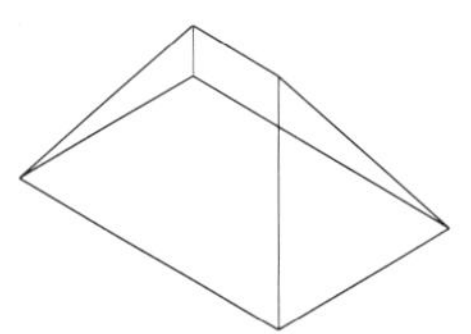

If you wanted a tetrahedron, you would specify only the first three points. You would then get a pyramid option for the apex.

DOME

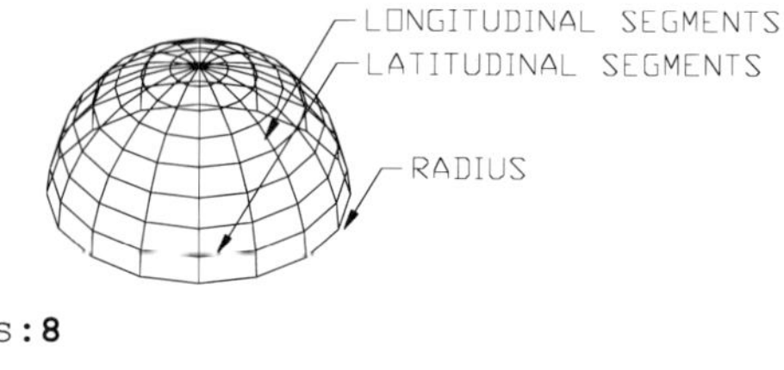

Command:**DOME**
Center of dome: *(pick 1)*
Diameter/<Radius>:**.5**
Number of longitudinal segments:**8**
Number of latitudinal segments:**9**

DISH

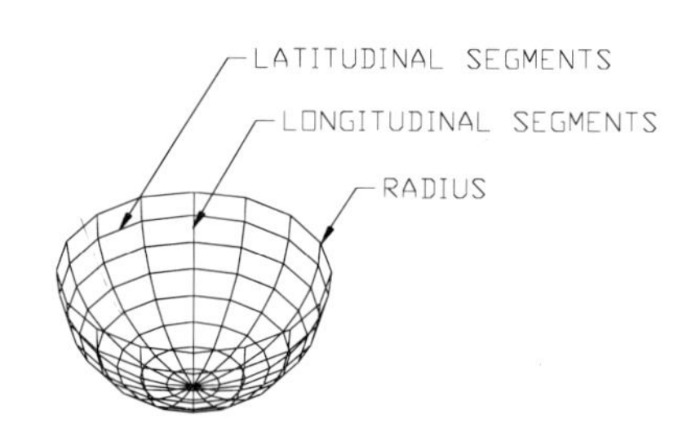

Command:**DISH**
Center of dome: *(pick 1)*
Diameter/<Radius>:**.5**
Number of longitudinal segments:**8**
Number of latitudinal segments:**10**

The ability to select the number of longitudinal and latitudinal segments gives you more control over the display quality. You will change these options relative to the size of the part.

CONE

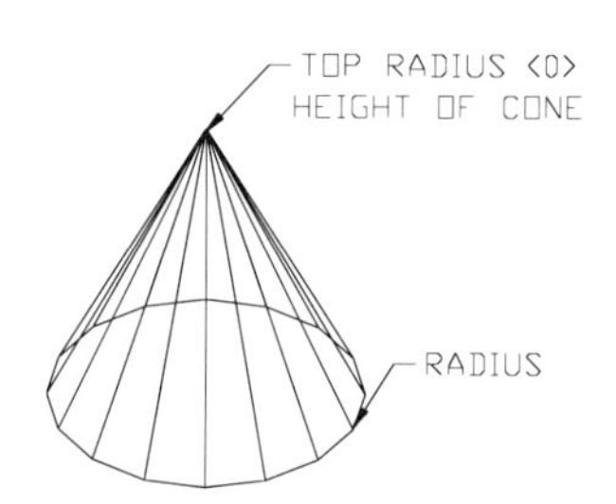

Command:**CONE**
Base center point: *(pick 1)*
Diameter/<Radius of base>:**1**
Diameter/<Radius> of top<0>:↵
Height:**2**
Number of segments:**16**

Again the number of segments selected will provide a different display.

SPHERE

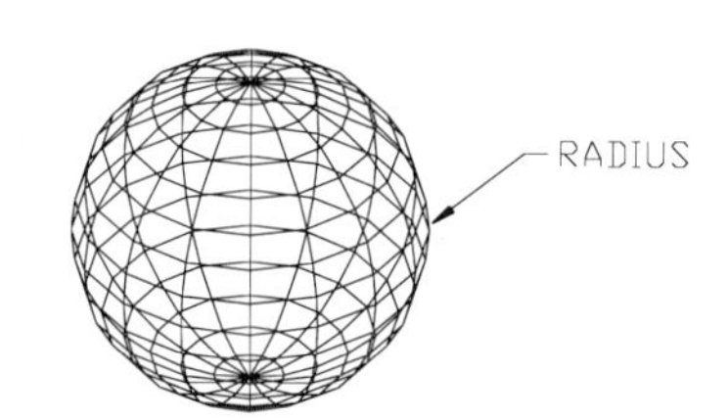

Command:**SPHERE**
Center of sphere:**3,3,3**
Number of longitudinal segments<16>:**16**
Diameter/<Radius>:**1**
Number of latitudinal segments<16>:**16**

TORUS

Command:**TORUS**
Center of torus:**4,4,4**
Diameter/<Radius> of torus:**4**
Diameter/<Radius> of tube:**.5**
Segments around the tube circumference:**10**
Segments around the torus circumference:**12**

The 3D Objects commands are quite simple and straightforward to use. It is a good idea to practise with these shapes to get ready for AME or the Advanced Modelling Enhancements. In many books, these objects have been left out because there is such a vast improvement in the AME software, but it is worth the effort to learn how to use them to better visualize objects in 3D.

USING 3D OBJECTS

The main purpose for using CAD is to have a more efficient way of producing drawings and data for manufacturing and analysis purposes. This being the case, it makes sense to try to use the software in the most efficient way possible.

Let us look at these automated programs and see how they can be used to speed up surface generation.

BOX versus 3DFACE

If you were to draw a rectangular shape with 3DFACE, with all six sides of the object covered in a 3D face surface, it would take six 3DFACE commands to do it; one for each face. Even if you were to wrap the faces around the rectangle, you would still need three commands to do it.

```
Command:3DFACE
First point:1
Second point:2
Third point:3
Fourth point:4
Third point:5
Fourth point:6
Third point:7
Fourth point:8
Third point:↵
```

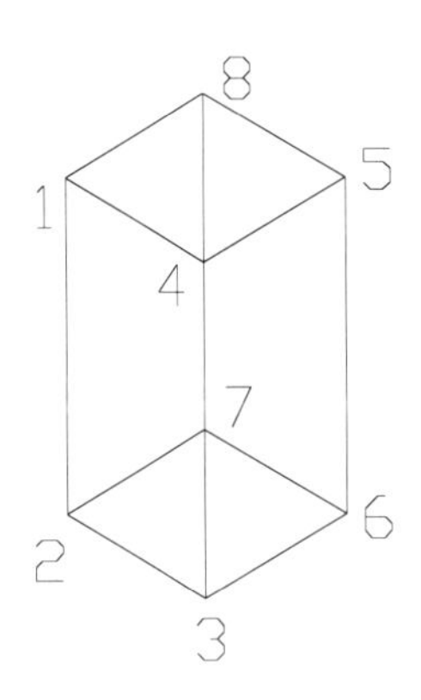


```
Command:3DFACE
First point:1
Second point:4
Third point:5
Fourth point:8
```

```
Command:3DFACE
First point:2
Second point:3
Third point:6
Fourth point:7
```

The points in the 3D faces can be entered using coordinates or existing geometry, or

```
Command:BOX
Starting point of box: (pick 1)
Length:2
Cube <Width>:2
Height:5
Rotation angle about Z axis:0
```

Clearly the BOX command takes less time.

Similarly, with the CONE command, there is much less work than in either the RULESURF or TABSURF commands.

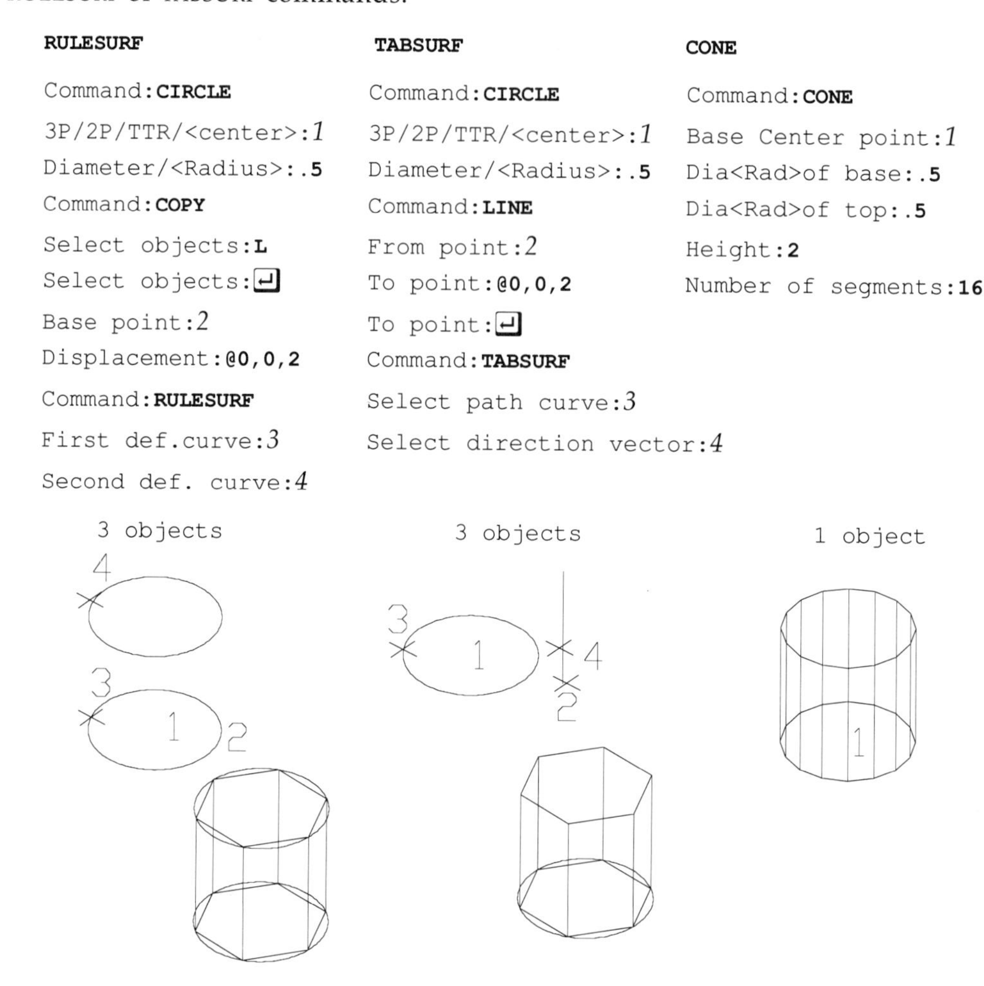

RULESURF
Command:CIRCLE
3P/2P/TTR/<center>:1
Diameter/<Radius>:.5
Command:COPY
Select objects:L
Select objects:↵
Base point:2
Displacement:@0,0,2
Command:RULESURF
First def.curve:3
Second def. curve:4
TABSURF
Command:CIRCLE
3P/2P/TTR/<center>:1
Diameter/<Radius>:.5
Command:LINE
From point:2
To point:@0,0,2
To point:↵
Command:TABSURF
Select path curve:3
Select direction vector:4
CONE
Command:CONE
Base Center point:1
Dia<Rad>of base:.5
Dia<Rad>of top:.5
Height:2
Number of segments:16
3 objects
3 objects
1 object

Figure 32-4. Surfacing versus 3D Objects

You can see from Figure 32-4 that CONE is by far the easiest way to create the cylinder in this case, assuming that the geometry does not already exist. If it does exist, the completion time would be about the same. There is another point to be considered, however, and that is the number of items or objects in the file. In the first two cases, you have two extra items that should be put on a different and non-displayed layer. In the third example, there is only one object.

If there is a chance that you could accidentally erase the cone, you may have trouble remembering where it is; so the first two examples could save time and trouble. But if the cone is easily located, clearly the third example makes for a neater file.

The examples above illustrate the difference between using the 3D Objects commands and the surfacing methods provided by AutoCAD. Again, the 3D Objects are simply AutoLISP programs designed to speed up the process.

If you are creating a box shape, but you want to have one face with a difference series of surfaces, you can explode the box and erase the 3D Face that is in your way.

USING PFACE

The last type of surface we will look at is the PFACE mesh. This was developed in Release 11 to lead into the AME software (see Chapter 34). In essence it is a polygon mesh defined by vertices and faces composed of those vertices. Like 3DMESH, this is often used in conjunction with AutoLISP.

This command is much like the 3DFACE command, but whereas 3DFACE creates a series of faces with overlapping edges, this gives you a single face generated from multiple points. The command asks you to identify the three-dimensional coordinates of each point along the edge of the object you want to describe. The points are, in fact, vertices.

```
Command:PFACE
Vertex 1:0,0,0
Vertex 2:1,1,1
Vertex 3:etc...
Vertex 10:↵
```

Press E to indicate that you are finished entering vertices. You will then be prompted to identify which vertices are on which faces, starting with Face 1 and continuing until you indicate with a ↵ that no more faces are required.

Next the PFACE command will prompt you for the vertices for each face.

```
Face 1, vertex 1:1
Face 1, vertex 2:2
Face 1, vertex 3:3
```

You can enter as many points as you like, and you will be prompted for as many faces as you like. You enter the vertex numbers in succession that define the face you are describing. When you have completed the vertices of one face, press the Enter key to advance to the next. When you have completed all the faces, a second Enter will exit the command.

You can also enter either the letter C for COLOR or the letter *L* for LAYER to have the next face shown in a different colour or on a different layer. Once you specify the new value, the face and vertex will be requested.

In the following example, there are two faces in a simple object described.

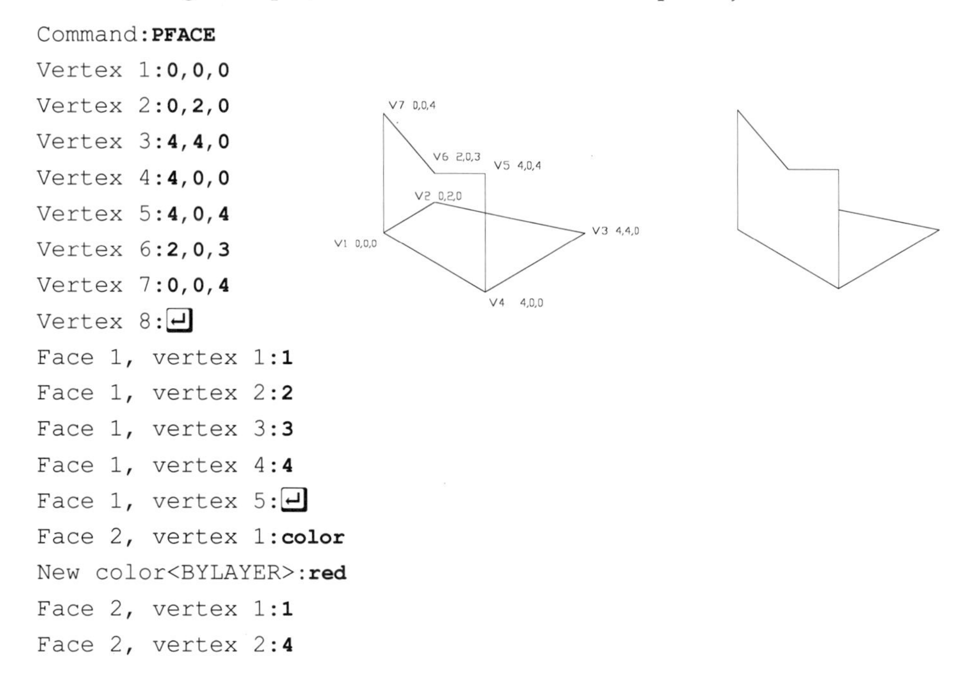


```
Command:PFACE
Vertex 1:0,0,0
Vertex 2:0,2,0
Vertex 3:4,4,0
Vertex 4:4,0,0
Vertex 5:4,0,4
Vertex 6:2,0,3
Vertex 7:0,0,4
Vertex 8:↵
Face 1, vertex 1:1
Face 1, vertex 2:2
Face 1, vertex 3:3
Face 1, vertex 4:4
Face 1, vertex 5:↵
Face 2, vertex 1:color
New color<BYLAYER>:red
Face 2, vertex 1:1
Face 2, vertex 2:4
```

```
Face 2, vertex 3:5
Face 2, vertex 4:6
Face 2, vertex 5:7
Face 2, vertex 6:↵
Face 3, vertex 1:↵
Command:HIDE
```

The result is the mesh shown in the illustration.

If you want any edge invisible, enter a negative number for the beginning vertex of the edge.

You cannot edit this mesh with PEDIT, but the other editing commands such as ARRAY, MOVE, COPY, ROTATE, etc. can be used.

The visible entities can be snapped.

As you can see from the example, creating a PFACE mesh can be a tedious job, and you may be better off with another type of surface; but if the geometry already exists, you may want to try it.

Release 12 Notes

While the surface and mesh generation in PFACE and 3DMESH are essentially the same as in previous releases, the display is much easier to work with as a result of Release 12's faster response times.

In addition, the Release 12 selection filters are greatly improved. The new filters allow the user to filter the selection with such filters as, for example, only the lines on the 0 layer or only the circles with a radius larger than 2.0. These advanced features are found under the SSGET "X" option.

Exercise A32

Use the 3D Objects menu to create an outdoor activity area which includes a pool (using BOX and WEDGE for a deep end), a wading pool (using DISH), a sidewalk surround (using 3DFACE), a barbecue (using BOX and PYRAMID with the Ridge option), a change room (using CONE), and some pool recreational items (using SPHERE and TORUS).

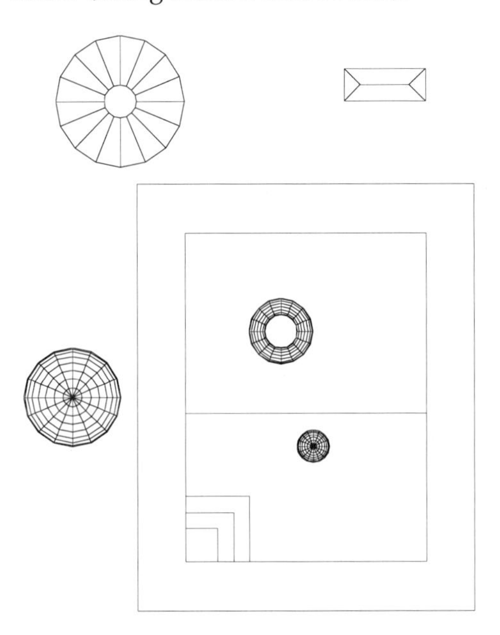

Be sure the plan view works,

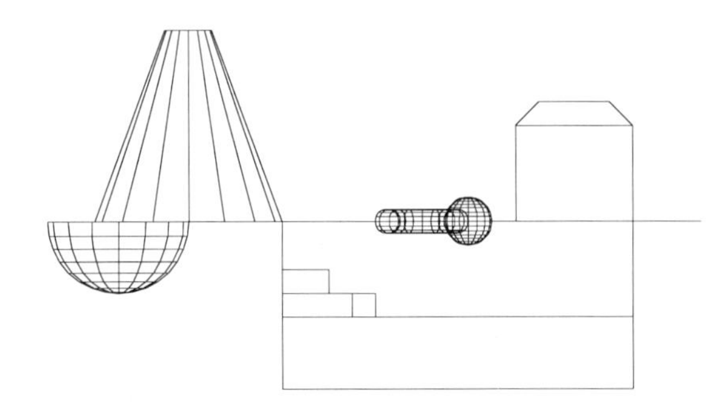

and you have a good elevation.

If you have time, you can also create some landscaping on the lot.

While this may seem like an easy exercise, you will have to change your UCS more than once to get the shapes to fit in exactly where you want them.

If you finish early, use PSPACE to create a new drawing.

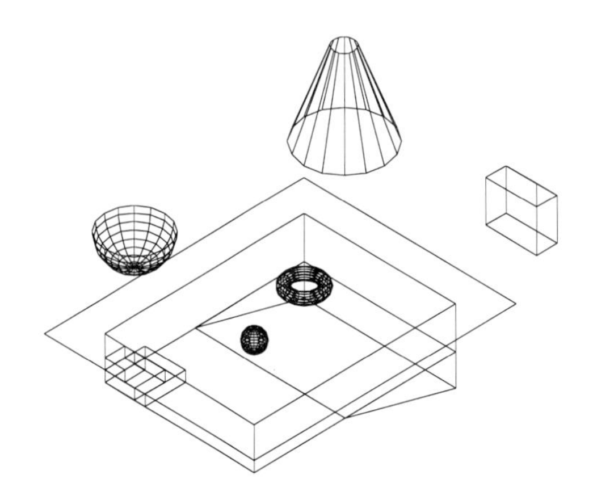

Exercise M32

Using 3D Objects commands plus the other surfacing commands you know, generate a lens, a lens base, and a viewfinder for the camera. Make sure the sizes you choose are the same as those for the lens area on your camera base, but do not use the same model. Make a note of your origin and axes, and save the models when they are completed.

You can make the lens and the lens base with:

DOME
CONE
PLINE

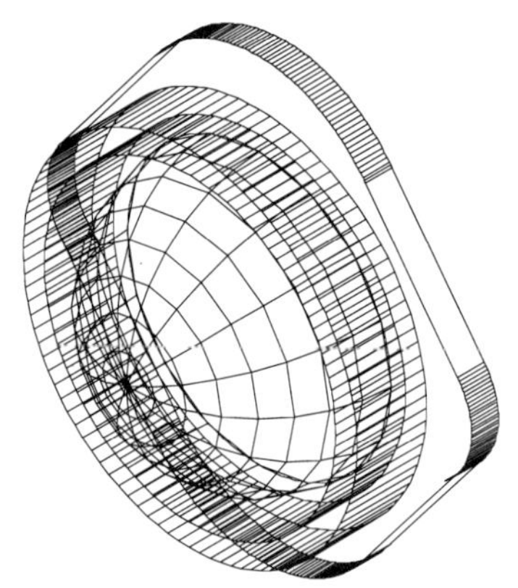

Make a note of your origin and axes.

You can make your viewfinder using:

BOX
WEDGE
PYRAMID

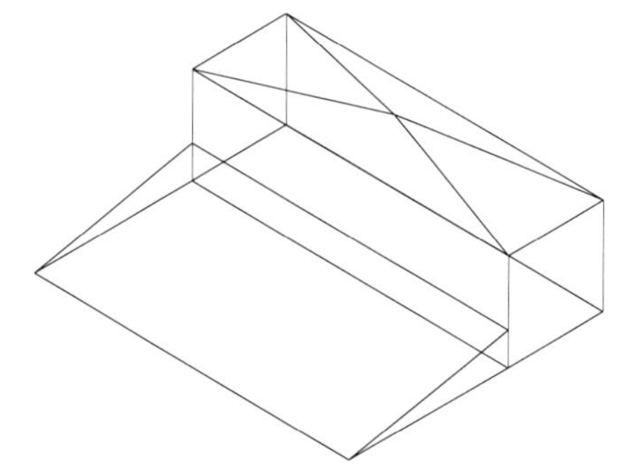

Be sure these are not too large to fit on your camera base.

Exercise C32

Use BOX, WEDGE, and CONE to construct the lookout tower on the bridge from Exercise C31 as in the illustration. You may need to change the UCS to place the wedges.

Use ARRAY to add the cones for the detailing on the top.

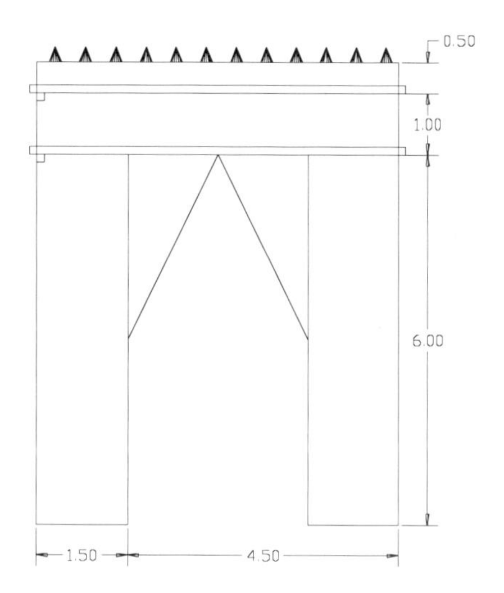

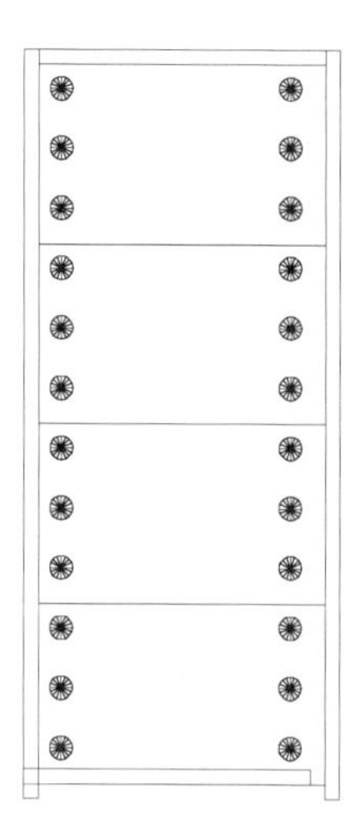

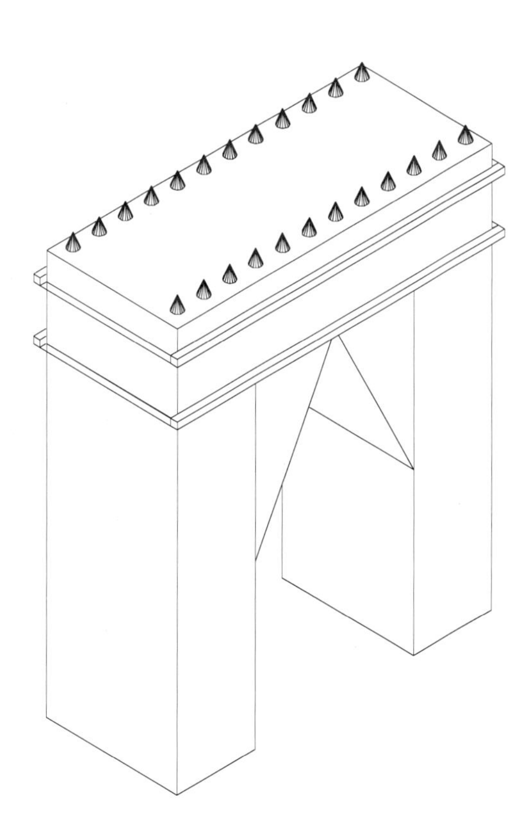

This exercise will give you good practice in constructing shapes in 3D.

Challenger 32

Using 3DSHAPES, create this staircase. Make sure thatthe treads are not more than 10 inches in depth and that there is a 7-inch rise between stairs.

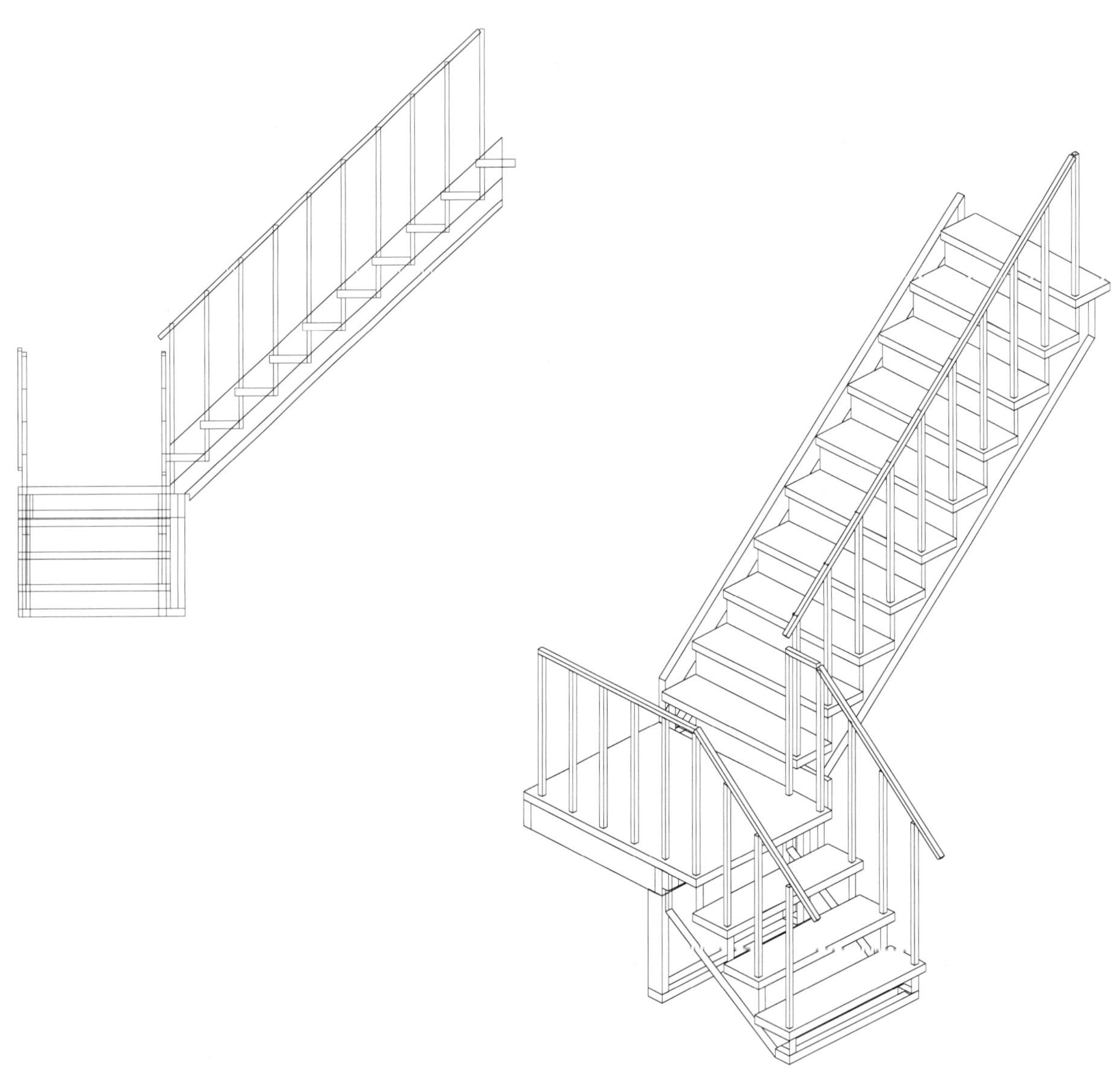

MERGING 3D MODELS

Upon completion of this chapter, the student should be able to:

1. Recognize the type of surface needed on a model
2. Create and edit a 3DMESH surface
3. Edit surfaces within a model
4. Merge 3D models into the same model
5. Create a drawing of a merged model
6. Know when to use the SHADE command instead of the HIDE command

FINAL NOTES ON 3D

While you are constructing geometry, the wireframe method is generally the most practical place to start. If the geometry is simple, you can use 3D Objects to construct it, but anything that has complicated polygonal surfaces or undulating shapes is going to need some definition in order to be surfaced.

Now that you have an understanding of how the wireframe and surfacing commands work on a small model, we will look at what happens to these commands on a larger model. In addition, we will look at the factors to consider when choosing the surface to use for a model. The first consideration is, What will the model be used for? Some of the possibilities are:

1. Manufacturing
2. AutoShade
3. Analysis
4. Marketing — creating isometric views with hidden lines
5. Marketing — creating images that can be used dynamically in slide shows or AutoFLICKs

If you are planning to do any manufacturing and/or analysis with AutoCAD, you will need to consider both the integrity of the final design data and the accuracy of the surface intersections. A model that is being cut out of metal needs a lot more consideration to surface integration than a model that is being used simply for promotion. The AME Advanced Modelling Extension package offers distinct advantages, but there are many cases where "traditional" 3D modelling is still better.

Before we discuss AME, we will summarize the first eight chapters of this section to help clarify the advantages of each different surface type and to give you some final information on model management with 3D models. This discussion should prove useful when preparing your final project.

USING SURFACES FOR DISPLAY

There are three ways of creating objects that will allow the HIDE command to create an obstructing object to remove hidden lines:

1. extrusions (THICKNESS)
2. 3DFACE
3. 3D mesh surfaces (RULESURF, TABSURF, REVSURF, 3DMESH, and EDGESURF)

AutoLISP 3D Objects as explained in the previous chapter are simply automated methods of using either 3DFACE or meshes; the surfaces created are compiled of the three basic types of surfaces.

Each type of surface offers advantages and disadvantages. It is important to recognize the pros and cons of the three ways of putting in surface information in order to decide which method would offer the best results for each different application.

Extrusions

Extrusions are the easiest way to create complex geometry; but, there are disadvantages.

You can set the thickness and elevation of objects just by typing in THICKNESS or ELEV. Once the thickness is changed, you can use the extruded lines, arcs, etc. to define any objects you like. The advantages to this are:

1. They are easy to use
2. The item becomes a full 3D item and you can snap to any portion of it

The major disadvantage of extrusions is that while the item looks as if it is made up of a top, a bottom, and the area in between, it is still only one object. The item cannot be exploded into the visual entities that appear before you, and thus it cannot be easily edited. If you use an extruded line to create a wall, you cannot put a door on it. If you use an extruded circle to make a cylinder, you cannot intersect it with any other object.

Extruding is a good way to draw an item initially to get a view of what it looks like in 3D, but you may have to change it to a surfaced wireframe later if the part becomes complicated.

3D Faces

The 3DFACE and PFACE commands are good commands to use, particularly for hiding objects, because they are also easy to use and do not produce a lot of lines on the screen. In the display area, it does not take up much room.

The disadvantage of using this method of construction is that 3DFACE does not work on any surface that has curved lines. If you encounter curved area, you must use a mesh.

In addition, when compiling a complex object, because the 3D face has no surface display, you may forget that there is a surface and cover it with a ruled or tabular surface and create unneccessary geometry. This can lead to serious problems in manufacturing.

The 3DFACE command is very useful for display purposes or when used as PFACE to make large objects which have regularly spaced integers that are easily calculated and entered as an AutoLISP routine.

Editing Surfaces

Meshes are, in general, more useful than the other types of surfacing techniques because they curve and give true shape to an object. The 3DFACE and PFACE commands put a flat surface on an object, and an extruded line or arc provides a type of surface for hidden lines, etc., but a mesh goes further in describing an item fully.

In addition, mesh surfaces can be edited. You can use the standard edit commands such as SCALE, COPY, MOVE, ROTATE, etc. on each model, and you can also use STRETCH to place the parts of each model where needed.

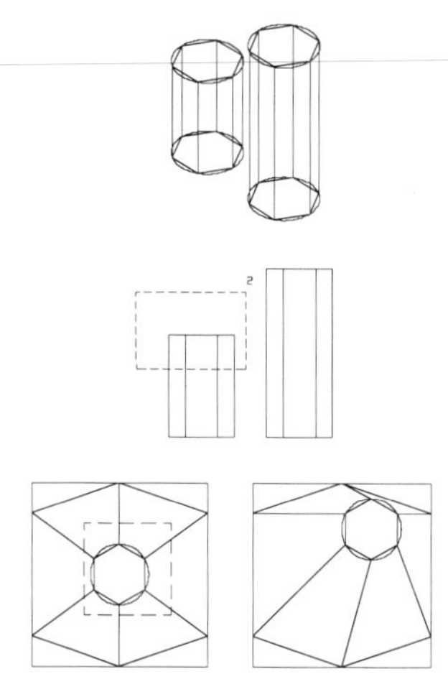

In the illustration on the right, the STRETCH command is used to make a cylinder longer. By picking Crossing, the top portion of the cylinder can be accessed.

In this next illustration, the STRETCH command is used to change the position of a hole in a ruled surface that was made between two polylines.

In both cases, the STRETCH command edits the surface itself, not just the geometry used to create the surface.

In this example, the surface has been scaled by 2, resulting in a curved or filleted surface that is twice the original size.

You can see from these examples that the exact specification of the points can be even more crucial in 3D than it is in 2D design.

For all these surfaces, the edit commands will perform edits that change the size of the surface but do not change the basic shape. If you need a surface that is a little more flexible than these, use 3DMESH.

3DMESH

The 3DMESH command creates a three-dimensional wireframe mesh according to defined points which create vertices. The surface is made up of rows and columns which pass through a matrix of points in space creating a rectilinear surface pattern.

This surface, like EDGESURF, is a polynomial surface, a surface defined in both directions by many numbers or points. The points on mesh surfaces are entered at a specific integer and are generally calculated by LISP programs to automatically generate the mesh points.

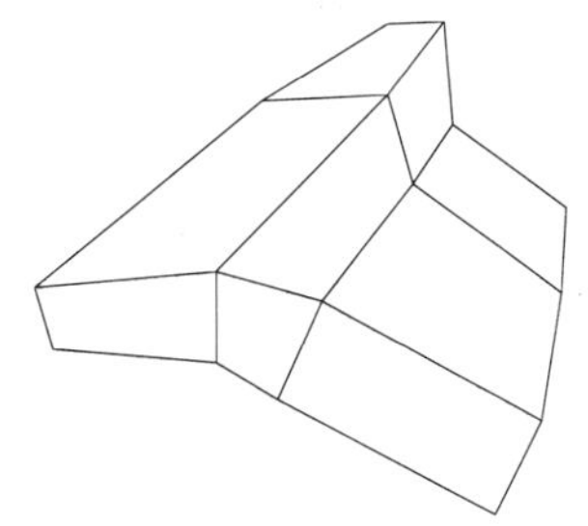

Figure 33-1. Surface generated by 3DMESH

If you look at the majority of manufactured goods, everything from car dashboards to contact lenses, razors, kettles, airplanes, etc., all these objects were designed with surface programs much like these.

The surface of Figure 33-1 was generated by simply picking 16 points; 4 points in the *n* direction and 4 points in the *m* direction. *M* and *n* are indices specifying the number of rows and columns that make up a mesh.

In the next mesh, we have entered specific points.

```
Command:3DMESH
Mesh M size:4   (four rows in one direction)
Mesh N size:4   (four rows in the other direction)
Vertex <0,0>:0, 0,0
Vertex <0,1>:10,0,0
Vertex <0,2>:20,0,0
Vertex <0,3>:30,0,0
Vertex <1,0>:0,10,10
Vertex <1,1>:10,10,10
Vertex <1,2>:20,10,10
Vertex <1,3>:30,10,10
Vertex <2,0>:0,15,15
Vertex <2,1>:10,15,15
Vertex <2,2>:20,15,15
Vertex <2,3>:30,15,15
Vertex <3,0>:10,20,20
Vertex <3,1>:20,20,20
Vertex <3,2>:30,20,20
Vertex <3,3>:40,20,20
```

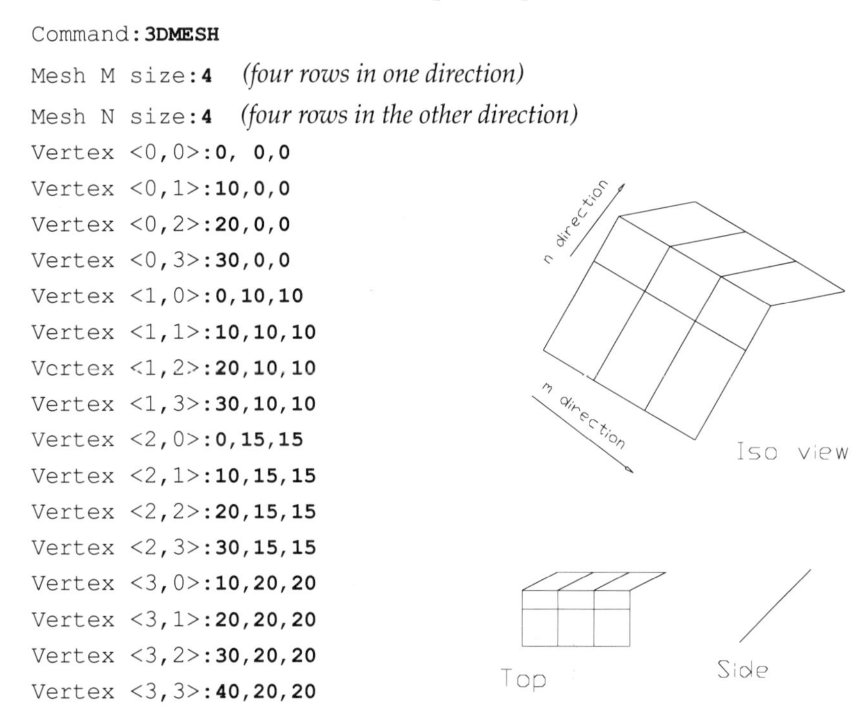

The default of course is to have a mesh of one-unit squares. To visualize how this surface is put into use, imagine that you have created a model out of chicken wire, like the base of papier-mâché figures. The 3D mesh is like the paper that will cover the chicken wire to create the final product. The points are where the wire mesh meets.

It is important that you know that this surface exists, as this is the major sales feature of any CAD system to a manufacturing firm. The points must be entered row by row and column by column, so the command lends itself well to AutoLISP. The PFACE command creates a similar surface. It uses a smaller and less rigid formula. The major advantage of 3DMESH is that it can be used to make extensive undulating surfaces which can later be edited.

USING PEDIT TO EDIT 3D MESHES

Three-dimensional meshes are constructed through a series of points defined in two directions. The PEDIT command can be used with PLINE to create either a spline or a fit-curve polyline. It is used with 3DMESH in the same way, along two different axes. In addition, PEDIT can be used to edit one or more vertices of the surface to have the surface fit through a different series of points.

In order to understand how PEDIT works, let us first look at PEDIT with PLINE.

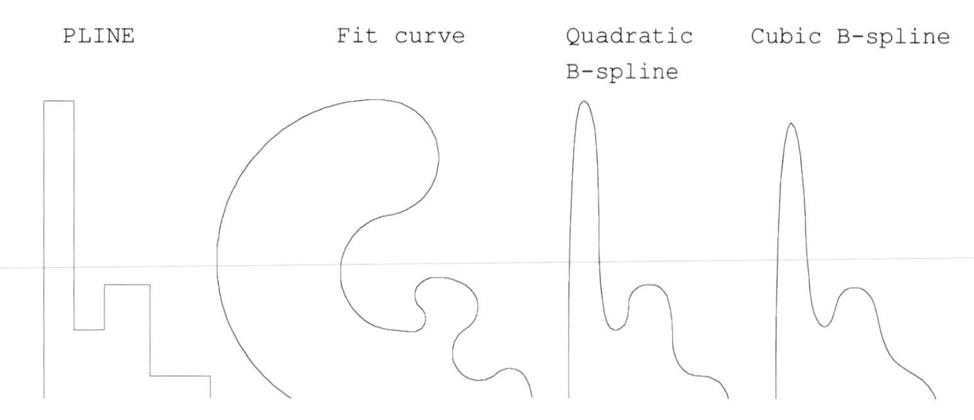

As noted in Chapter 3, the PEDIT command creates either a curve segment or a spline using the vertices of the selected plines as the control points for the curves. With the Fit curve option, the curve is constructed by pairs of arcs passing directly through the control points. With the Spline option, the curve fits through the two endpoints of the pline and is then pulled towards the other points on the pline, but does not necessarily pass through the other control points.

The SPLINETYPE system variable controls the type of spline curve to generate; option 5 creates a quadratic B-spline, and option 6 creates a cubic B-spline.

The SPLINESEGS system variable controls the number of line segments between each pair of control points. The greater the number, the more line segments, thus a smoother representation of the spline curve.

With 3D meshes, the PEDIT command performs the same way, except in two different directions and into the Z depth.

In this example, we have created a 3D mesh through a series of regularly space points.

```
Command:3DMESH
Mesh M size:4
Mesh N size:6
Vertex (0,0):0,0
Vertex (0,1):0,0,4
Vertex (0,2): etc.
```

Once completed, the PEDIT command can be used to smooth the surface either with a quadratic B-spline or a cubic B-spline equation. In addition, AutoCAD offers the Bézier surface.

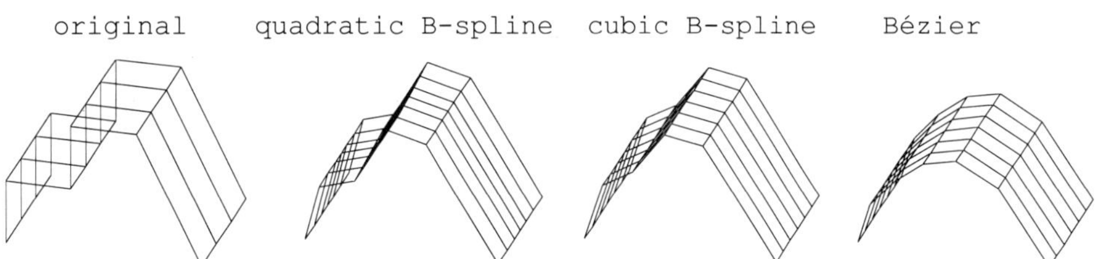


```
Command:PEDIT
Select polyline: (pick the surface)
Edit vertex/Smooth surface/Desmooth/Mclose/Nclose/Undo/eXit
<n>:S
```

```
Generating segment 2...
Edit vertex/Smooth surface/Desmooth/Mclose/Nclose/Undo/eXit
<n>:
```

The surface type is determined by the system variable SURFTYPE. The available surface types are as follows:

Surftype	Description
5	Quadratic B-spline
6	Cubic B-spline
8	Bézier

The minimum mesh size to create a quadratic B-spline surface is 3 by 3 units. The minimum mesh size for cubic is 4 by 4 units. PEDIT will not be able to calculate any surface with more than 11 vertices in either direction.

The system variable SPLFRAME controls the display of the polygon meshes to which surfaces have been fit. The Decurve option will take the curve out of the surface.

In editing a pline, you can used PEDIT to move the position of any of the vertices in order to create a more pleasing spline. With a 3D mesh, this is even more important as the Edit vertex option can be used to edit the entire surface.

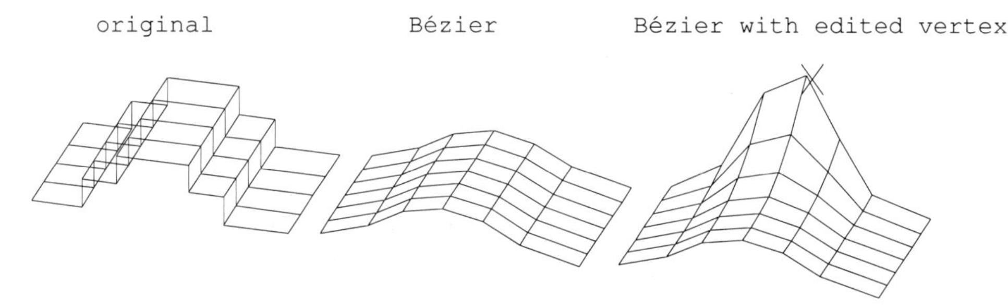


```
Command:PEDIT
Select polyline: (pick the surface)
Edit vertex/Smooth surface/Desmooth/Mclose/Nclose/Undo/eXit
<n>:E
 Vertex(0,0).Next/Previous/Left/Right/Up/Down/Move/REgen/eXit
<N>:M
Enter new location:
```

You can respond with either a 3D point location or by selecting the point on the screen.

The command will toggle through each control point in the order they are entered. A large *X* will be shown to highlight your position. The Left and Right options allow you to move in the *N* direction, Up and Down allow you to move in the *M* direction. The Move option, as illustrated above, moves the vertex to a new location.

MERGING 3D FILES

While working on large projects, it is often desirable to have two or more separate files of different parts of the final object or assembly. These can be either inserted as blocks or referenced as xrefs when the part is ready to be merged and to be drawn. Having several files saves time and space in RAM and on backup disks.

Once completed, the various parts of the assemblies can be loaded onto the same file and compiled in paper space for drawing purposes. This also allows you to use component parts not just on one drawing or project, but on many.

Over the past few chapters we have been compiling a group of parts that can now be merged into a single model. If you have been working with the mechanical examples, you should have a group of parts of a camera. If you have been working in the architectural examples, you will have a group of parts that can be used in a residence. In the surveying example, you have many components of a municipality.

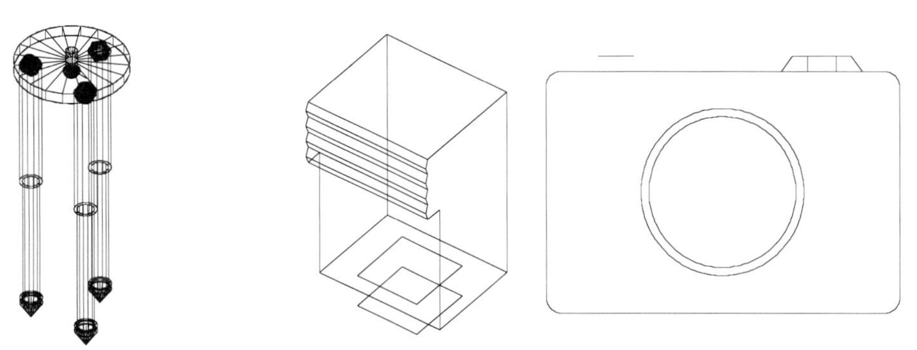

The camera parts below are in different files and can now be merged as a whole.

Before merging, make sure you know the origin and axes of all your files. If you have not noted these, go into each of your files, return to the World Coordinate System, and make a note of them.

Your insertion point on all these files will be 0,0,0 unless you used WBLOCK. The direction of positive Z must also be noted so that the files will be fit in the correct direction. If the origin is not in a logical spot on the model, either move your model so that it is, or wblock the model changing the insertion point.

Once everything is ready, insert your models onto a blank base model. Create a full assembled part from the various separate files.

If the model is entering at an incorrect angle, change the UCS to accommodate the base model's origin.

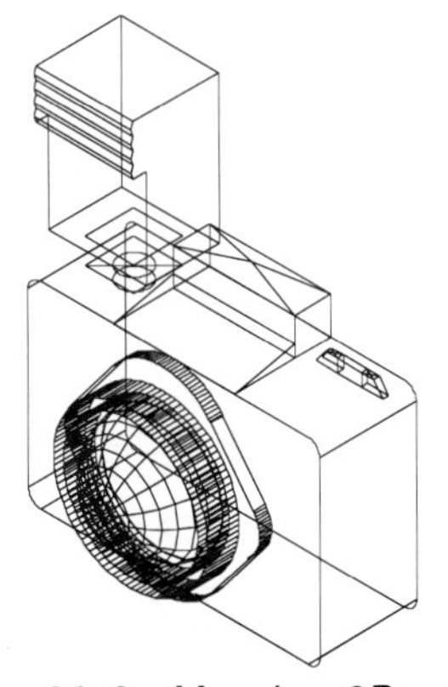

Figure 33-2. Merging 3D parts

There are really only three things to consider when inserting: the model scale, origin, and axes.

The 3point UCS is often the easiest to use when lining something up because you can be exact, even on slanting surfaces.

MODEL MANAGING

There are many tricks and tips that can be used to make assembling large drawings easier. In short these tricks involve three main concerns.

1. Your origin should be well placed
2. Your scale should be 1 = 1
3. Your layers should be well organized

Origin

If your origin is not well placed on the model you are trying to insert, you could spend a long time moving it, zooming in on it, and generally messing about with it.

If you are using blocks of 3D models extensively, you should create either an icon menu or a slide that will show the exact size of the part and the location of the origin.

Scale

If the objects are entered at a 1 = 1 scale, there will be no problem inserting them. Again, make sure your data is well documented on-line to make the process easier.

Layers

You may have noticed that the models inserted into your file come complete with all of their respective layers. Xref files will also have layers that are added to your list.

You will probably want to create a drawing of the finished part, and thus you will probably want to use paper space to view certain areas with the layers turned off. If you have used a different series of layers for each view, this will not be a problem. If, on the other hand, you have used all the same layer names, you will spend a lot of unnecessary time changing information to different layers and experimenting with items so that they show up clearly in the view you want.

It is not unusual to have a layer designation sheet available for consultation during the design of a part. In fact, with large projects, this is absolutely necessary to maintain continuity. Most companies have standard formats for layer designation, and the layers used are generally standard throughout their industry.

A layer designation sheet may be set up as in the following example:

```
                          PART NAME

Start Date:                                        Back-up dates:

Company:
Part no:
Designer:

Directories:
```

LAYER	Date created	Comments
FFPLAN	July 1 1992	first floor
FFWIN	July 1 1992	Pella windows - cat. 445

```
FFDOOR                    July 1 1992          Pella doors
- cat. 478

FFDIM                     Sept 12 1992         - all
```

The same sheet should document what models were used, when they were inserted (in case of updates and changes), and in which directories they are located.

Even with the use of layers and icon menus, the management of a very large model can be a difficult task. In small, 2D models, it is often difficult to remember what a layer name means or what directory something was taken out of; in a large file, this is almost impossible without some form of documentation.

It is a good idea to back up your documentation at the same time you back up your model.

AUTOCAD AND WINDOWS OR UNIX

Once you have been working with CAD for a while, you will become accustomed to the hardware you are using, and you will notice, in your travels, that a lot of people have better systems than you do. This being the case, definitely make an effort to go to local trade shows to keep abreast of developments in the trade.

You may also notice that you are more interested in documenting information on screen than in writing by hand. Your automatic impulse will be to transfer from a graphics screen to a word processing environment quickly and easily.

If you are using a UNIX system, you can transfer almost immediately to a word-processor or spreadsheet format with the system's built in multitasking capabilities. For DOS users, the process will take a bit longer.

If you are working on AutoCAD Release 11 and your hardware is adequate, you will be happy to have the WINDOWS capabilities. Again, for most people, this will simply allow you to access the information on your documentation sheet and switch from drawings to alphanumeric information much more readily.

In Release 12, AutoCAD has addressed external databases with the AutoCAD SQL Extension (ASE). This provides an interface to the various relational database management systems. SQL is a language described in ANSI and ISO standards, and is a widely accepted language syntax for database management. This can greatly enhance you design documentation and should be considered when purchasing a system.

The Release 11 386 and 12 operates in the WINDOWS environment. Although it is not meant to be true multitasking, it has some of the advantages of a UNIX environment. For those who are planning to go a long way with CAD, it is worthwhile to take a look at UNIX-based systems. The UNIX operating system is a much more mature product and is really much more useful. The DOS environment will not have UNIX capabilites for quite some time.

Regardless of your operating system, it is always advisable to document your project and to keep up a regular backup routine.

Exercise A33

Create a 3D mesh that will represent a lot or a property. Now retrieve the various 3D files you have been working on over the past few chapters that can be used as part of a residential layout.

If you have no difficulties, you will have proved that your model management skills are good.

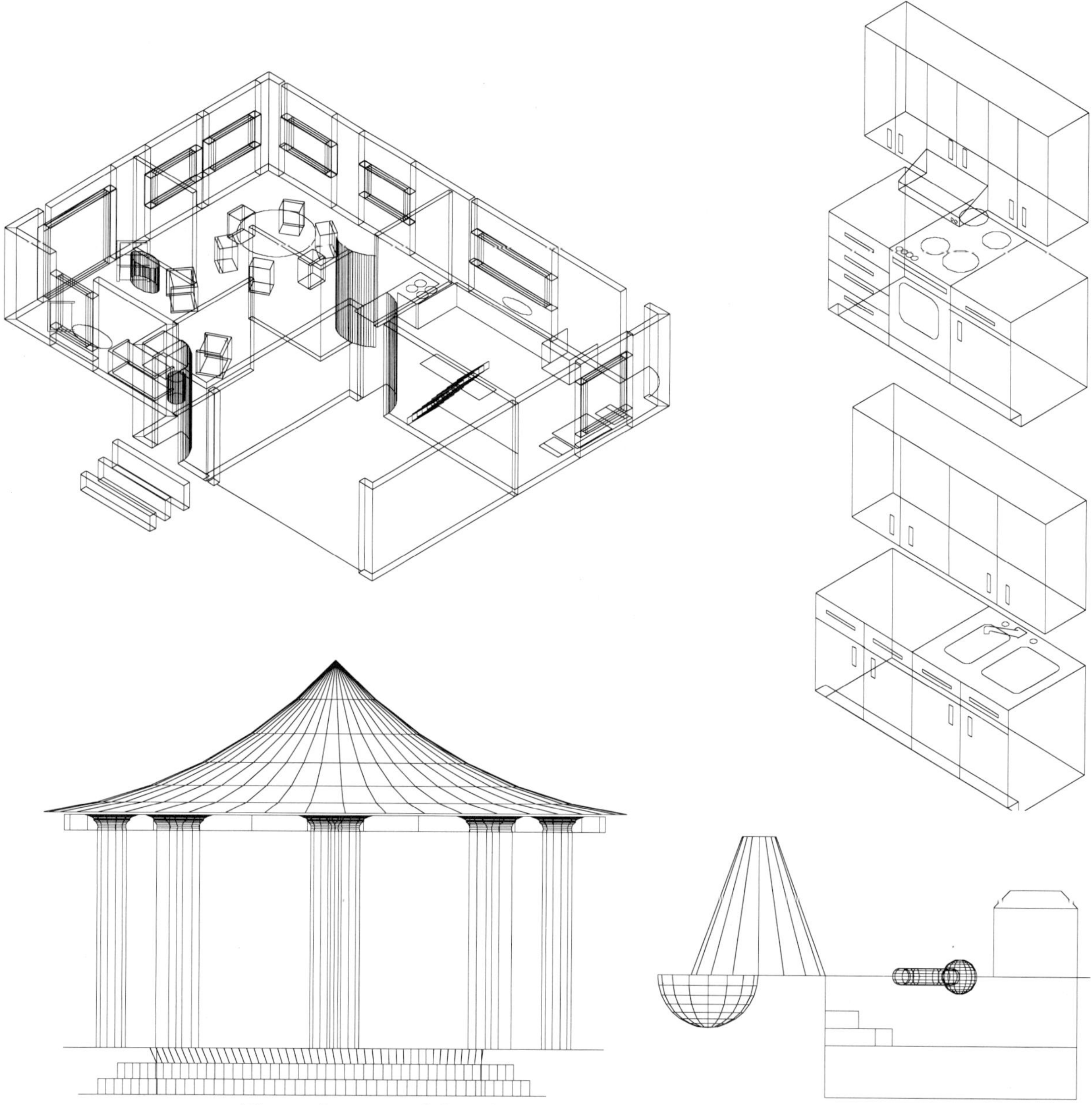

The staircase and fireplace can be added as well. Once fully inserted, create a drawing of the total model with the following:

1. A lot plan
2. An elevation
3. A section through the house showing the stairs and the fireplace

Exercise M33

Merge the various parts of the camera created in the preceeding exercises.

Going back to the original files and changing the layers, etc. so that you can create a good assembly drawing in paper space is much easier than changing all the layers once they are on-screen, particularly if you have less than 8MB of RAM.

Once merged, create a drawing file of the total part including the following:

1. Top, front, and side views properly clipped
2. An isometric view, fully surfaced with hidden lines removed
3. A cross-section view through the body of the camera and the flash.

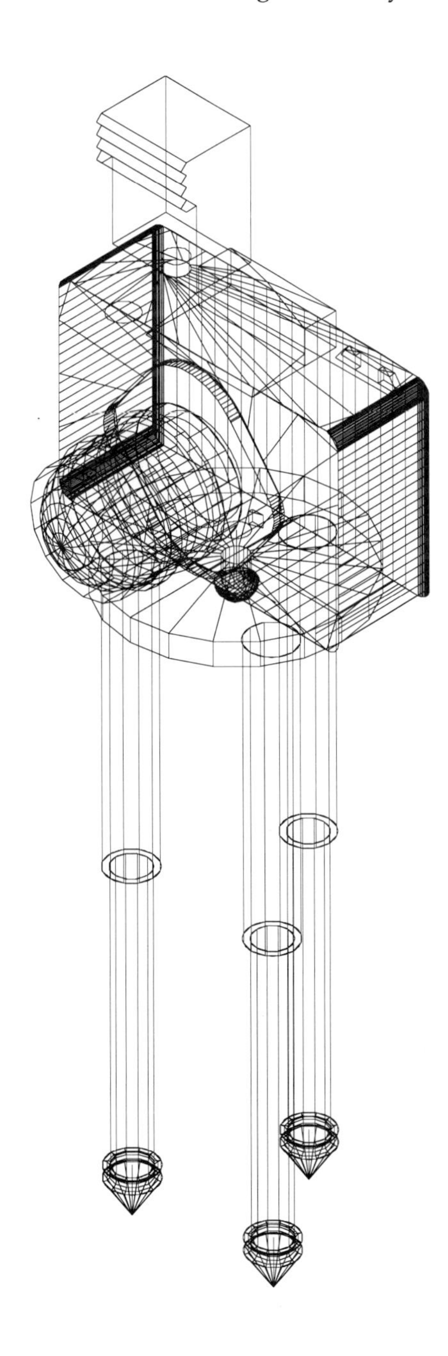

Exercise C33

Because of the size of the files, this exercise will take up a lot of room. Be sure to use at least a 1.2MB disk or a hard drive.

Retrieve the exercise from Chapter 29.

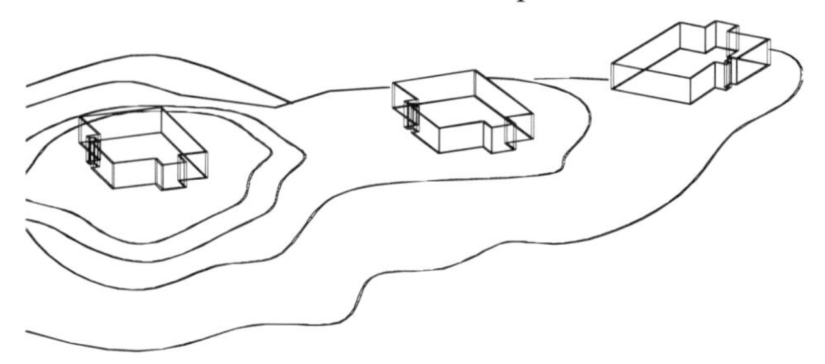

This is a survey adjacent to the old bridge. Insert the bridge.

Keep in mind that the bridge columns should extend into the earth. Thus, the plines in your survey should be surfaced so that part of the columns will be obscured with HIDE.

Create surfaces on either side of the bridge so that the bridge looks as if it is part of the surrounding countryside.

Now, because this bridge is so old, it is most likely a tourist attraction. This being the case, you can expect tourists to show up sooner or later, a parking lot will be needed for their cars. Insert a parking lot.

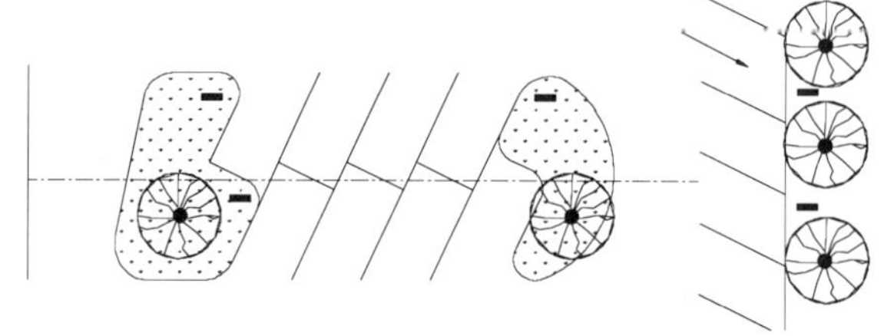

Once inserted at the proper size and position, create some views showing your client how the parking lot in no way interferes with the beautiful view of the bridge. Place these on a drawing layout using PSPACE and Hideplot to create a really impressive drawing.

Challenger 33

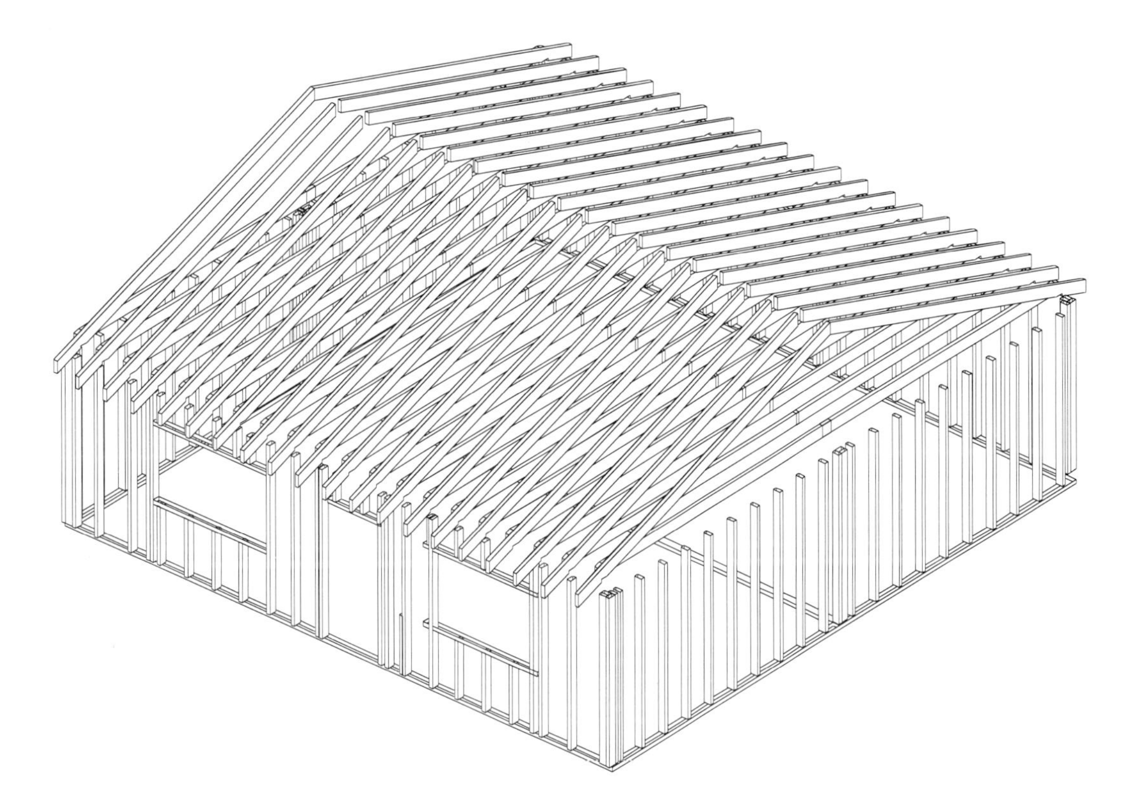

Taking a very plain house as the initial model, and attach an addition. Draw the house from a framer's point of view.

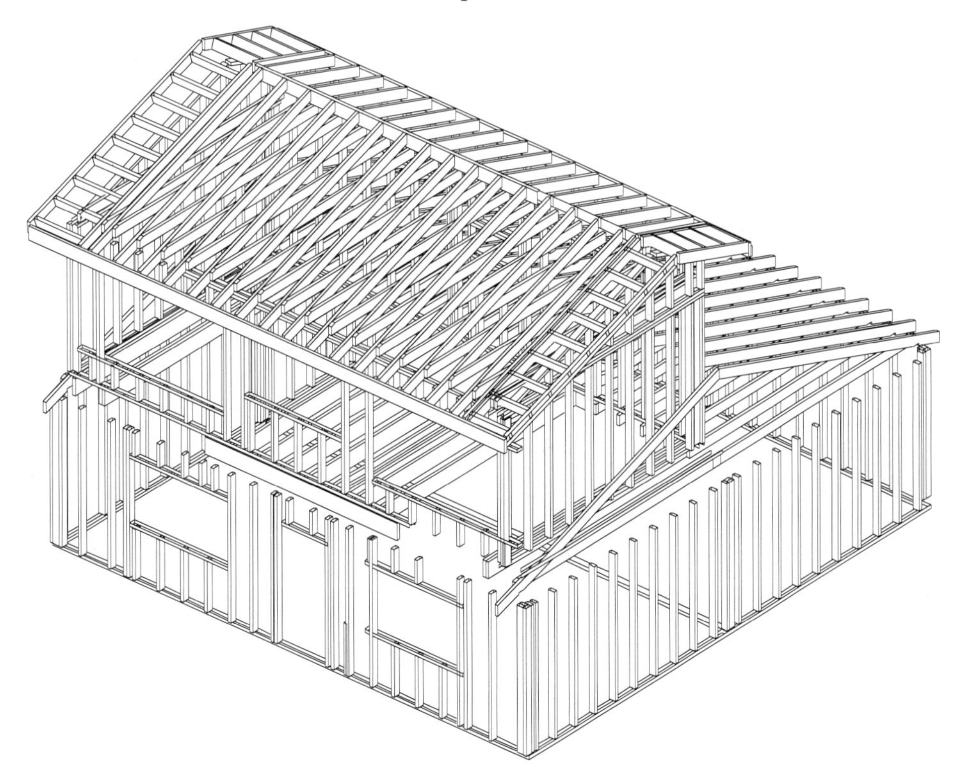

Challenger 33 (continued)

Include the structural details that you will need, then add 3D Faces where necessary to make the house attractive for your client.

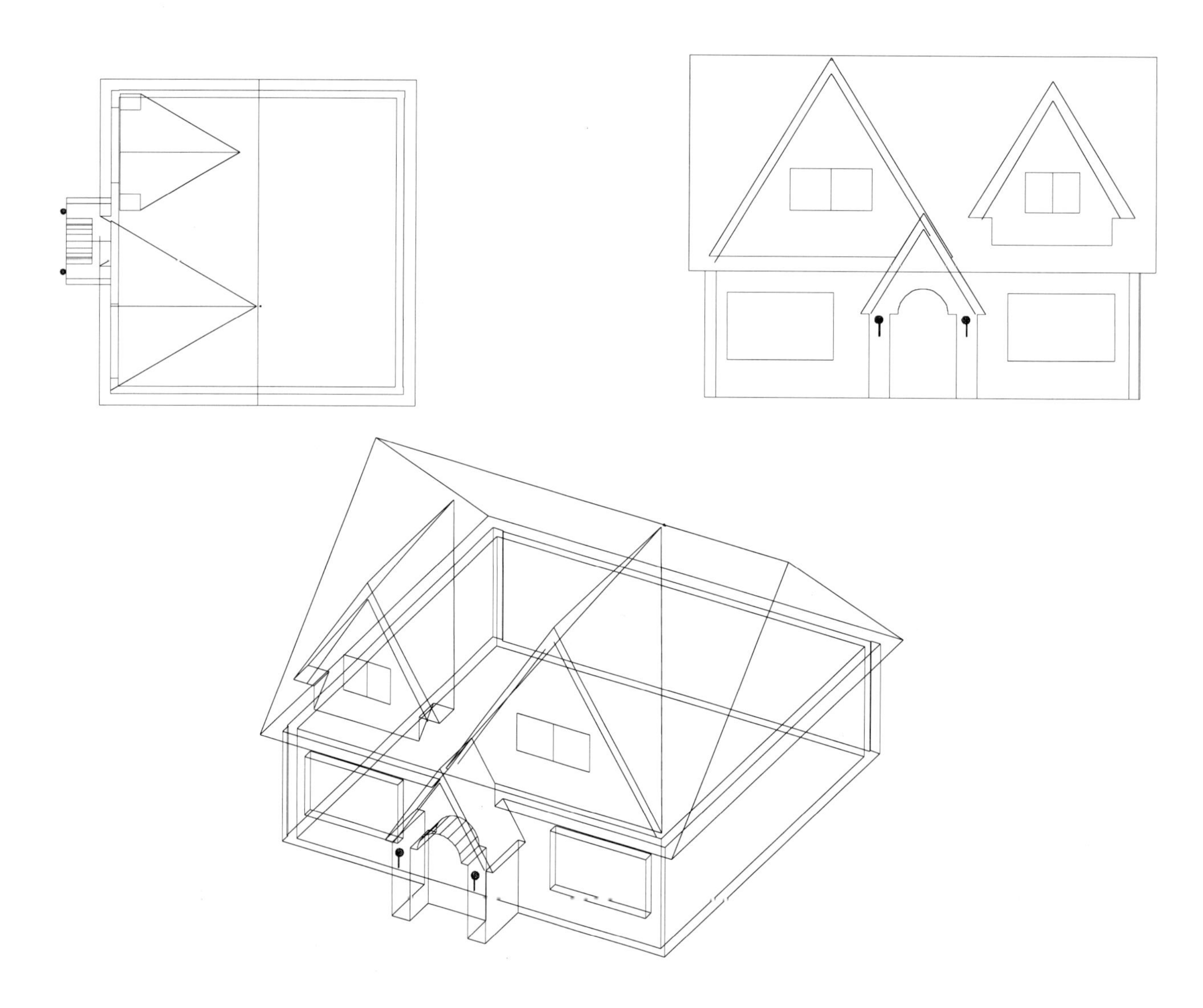

Use SHADE to make a really impressive presentation.

CREATING 3D MODELLING USING AME

Upon completion of this chapter, the student should be able to:

1. Use AME to create and merge solid 3D objects
2. Use AME to edit 3D objects
3. Use AME to create regions or 2D images with holes

WHAT IS AME ?

In the previous nine chapters, we learned how to use AutoCAD's three-dimensional capabilities to create fully surfaced 3D objects and images that can be downloaded onto a cutting tool or stereolithography system to produce a metal, foam, wax, or plastic part. The objects would be constructed out of two-dimensional objects placed together to create three-dimensional objects.

In the early years of CAD, there where basically two methods of describing 3D parts. The first was the wireframe method that allowed you to create an image using points, lines, and arcs to describe the structure; once described, it could be covered with a surface. The second approach was to create parts using a series of existing 3D shapes or primitive objects that could be merged into the desired final product.

In the first few chapters of this section we created 3D geometry and surfaced it; now we will create geometry using shapes or Boolean geometry. AutoCAD's Advanced Modelling Extension option provides this. Once you have been introduced to both the wireframe and the AME approach to 3D modelling, you will be able to see which is most applicable to your specific application.

Essentially, there are three reasons for using AME software:

1. You can create solid 3D objects. This provides a method of describing geometry that is often simpler than the wireframe method.
2. You can also create images containing holes using 2D regions or the region modeller. This simplifies the description of boundaries for hatches, area calculations, and analysis.
3. Finally, AME offers volume and mass analysis on the created data to calculate centroids, moments of inertia, and simple finite-element routines. The AME option allows you to determine many of the properties of an object.

Loading AME

If you are loading AME for the first time, you will need an authorization number. Your dealer should have supplied you with a number to call to obtain an authorization number. The AME AutoCAD package costs more than the regular Release 11 or 12 software. The basic software, AMELITE, boots immediately, while AME requires an access code.

AME is an integral part of the Release 11 software and should be loaded into the same directory as your basic AutoCAD software. It is not available and will not run on releases prior to 11.

Accessing AME

Once the AME package is loaded, you can access it through the Solids pull-down menu. This should be in the area of POP-10 unless your menus have been customized. Once you have picked Solids, you will be offered two choices:

```
Load AME
Load AMElite
```

The AME package takes up a lot of room in memory and takes a while to load. If you only want to construct objects (SOLBOX, SOLSPHERE, SOLCYL, etc.) and not process them (SOLUNION, SOLSUB, SOLINT, etc.), you can use AMElite. This takes up much less room because only a small selection of the AME software is loaded.

If you prefer to type in the commands, AME has an AutoCAD ADS function and can be loaded as any AutoLISP function is loaded, but you use XLOAD not LOAD.

```
Command:(xload "ame")
Command:
```

or

```
Command:(xload "amelite")
Command:
```

Either of the above methods may be used to access the AME package. If AME is not loaded, the commands are not accessible. You will get a response saying that the command is not recognized. This is not because the system has found an error, it is because you have not loaded the routines.

If you are working in an environment where AME is used everyday, AME can be loaded automatically by adding a statement in your ACAD.LSP or ACAD.ADS file. See the *AutoCAD Reference Manual* for details.

AME Version

The following examples show how to create 3D objects using the AME option. The AME 2.0 package was used to generate the images, but AME 1.0 is also capable of performing most of the operations specified.

CREATING 3D OBJECTS

In Chapter 32 we used the 3D objects offered through AutoCAD's basic 3D surface modelling. These predefined primitive shapes consisted of:

BOX CONE DOME DISH PYRAMID SPHERE TORUS WEDGE

These shapes were defined by parameters that you entered to determine the size and position. The resulting objects were composed of a series of 3D faces and other known geometry.

With AME, the process of entering the base geometry is similar, but the results are much more useful. Each of the 3D shapes has a specific spatial image, and thus a specific set of properties; in other words, a sphere is always going to be round in shape and a box will always have flat edges. In addition, the AME objects are accepted as solid objects and thus are composed of the properties associated with each shape such as centre of mass and volume.

For many applications, using AME objects for construction should make 3D modelling easier and more accurate, and the results should be more useful than with the wireframe surface method.

Constructive Solid Geometry

AutoCAD calls the construction of AME objects CSG or Constructive Solid Geometry. The process of creating the objects on-screen is similar to that of creating the 3D shapes; the difference is that once the objects are constructed, you can process them. There are three basic operations you can perform on objects:

Union — *one object can be merged with another, thus adding all or part of one object to another.*

Subtraction — *one object can be subtracted from another, thus removing all or part of one object from another.*

Intersection — *one object can be made to intersect another, thus preserving only those parts that the objects share.*

When creating 3D objects, always divide your screen into at least two viewports (four is often the best), and make sure you always have at least one isometric view.

Be sure the point entry is accurate. Once you start processing, there is no easy way of turning back.

The creation of objects in CSG is very similar to that of 3D objects as will be shown in the following examples.

If you do not remember the 3D shape commands, quickly scan Chapter 32.

Union of Objects

The following two examples show how the SOLUNION command is used to merge two 3D objects.

Example: *SOLUNION*

Start a new file and create at least two viewports, one with an X-Y plane, the other with an isometric using 2,-2,2 for the rotation factor. Now, under the Solids pull-down menu, choose Load AME.

It will take a few seconds to load AME the first time, but once loaded, you should have no problem accessing it. Now, from the menu choices pick BOX. If you are typing in the command, use SOLBOX.

```
Command:SOLBOX
Corner of box: (pick 1)
Cube/Length/<other corner>:Length
Length:2
Width:5
```

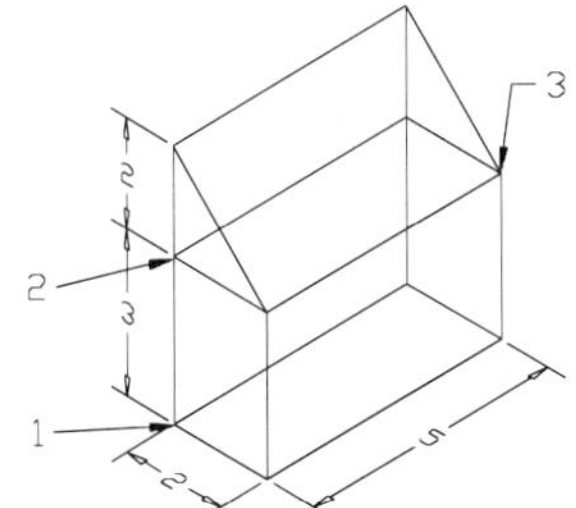

Height:**3**

Command:**SOLWEDGE**

Corner of Wedge:**END** *(pick 2)*

Length/<other corner>:**END** *(pick 3)*

Height:**2**

As in 3D Objects, the shapes are determined by length, width, and height.

Once the two objects are created, use SOLUNION to join them or make them into one object. From the Solids menu pick SOLPRIMs, then MODIFY, then UNION or type SOLUNION.

Command:**SOLUNION**

Select objects: *(pick the box)*

Select objects: *(pick the wedge)*

Select objects:↵

Phase I - Boundary evaluation begins

Phase II - Tessellation computation begins

Updating the Advanced Modeling Extension database

The two objects have now become one object and can be edited as one object.

The next example joins two spheres, a cone and a cylinder.

Example: *SOLUNION*

From the SOLMODIFY menu pick PRIMITIVE, then SPHERE, or type in SOLSPHERE.

Command:**SOLSPHERE**

Center of Sphere:**0,0,0**

Diameter/<Radius>:**5**

Command:SOLSPHERE

Center of Sphere:**5,0,0**

Diameter/<Radius>:**2**

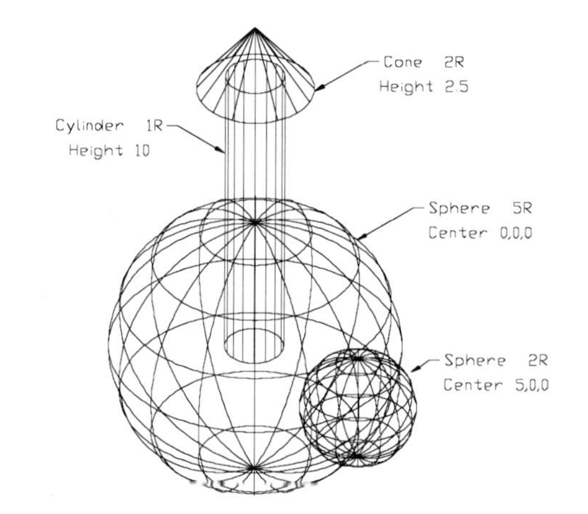

Command:**SOLCYL**

Center of Sphere:**0,0,0**

Diameter/<Radius>:**1**

Height of cylinder:**10**

Command:**SOLCONE**

Center of Sphere:**CEN** *(of cylinder top)*

Diameter/<Radius>:**2**

Height of cone:**2.5**

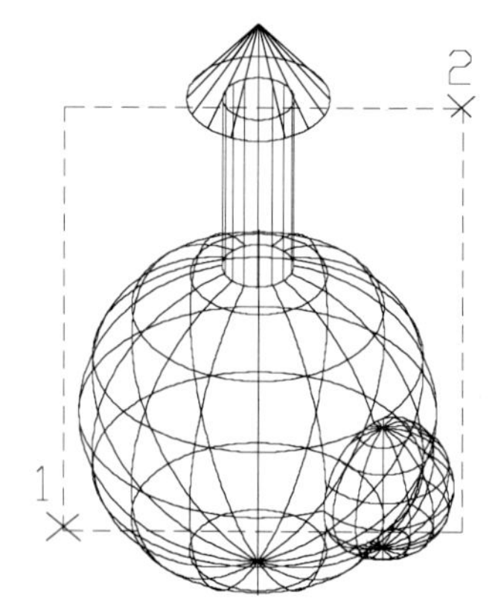

Command:**SOLUNION**

Select objects:**Crossing** *(pick 1 & 2)*

Select objects:↵

Phase I - Boundary evaluation begins

Phase II - Tessellation computation begins

Updating the Advanced Modelling Extension database

As in the previous example, the SOLUNION command has combined the solids into a composite. All four objects are now one object. This is referred to as a Boolean union operation.

Any object-selection method can be used to select the objects to join.

The objects must be intersecting to be joined with the SOLUNION command. If you try to join solids that do not intersect, you will get an error message:

`Null solid encountered. Automatically separating.`

Subtracting Objects

This operation is similar to SOLUNION in that it is a Boolean operation. It subtracts a specified object from another specified object.

Example: *SOLSUB*

Create another box.

Command:**SOLBOX**

Corner of box: *(pick 1)*

Cube/Length/<other corner>:**L**

Length:3

Width:**5**

Height:**3**

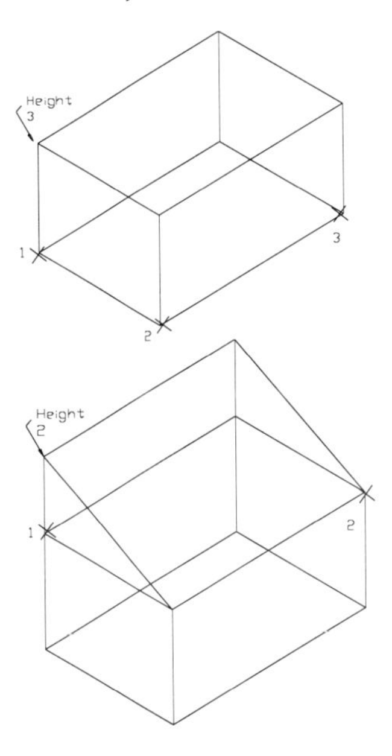

Now place a wedge on top of it.

Command:**SOLWEDGE**

Corner of Wedge:**END** *(of pick 4)*

Length/<other corner>:**END** *(of pick 5)*

Height:**2**

Once this is done, create another box inside the first box and wedge.

This box should extend out the top.

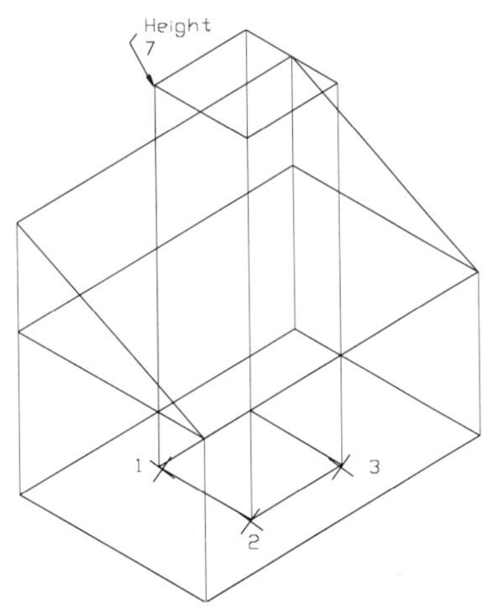

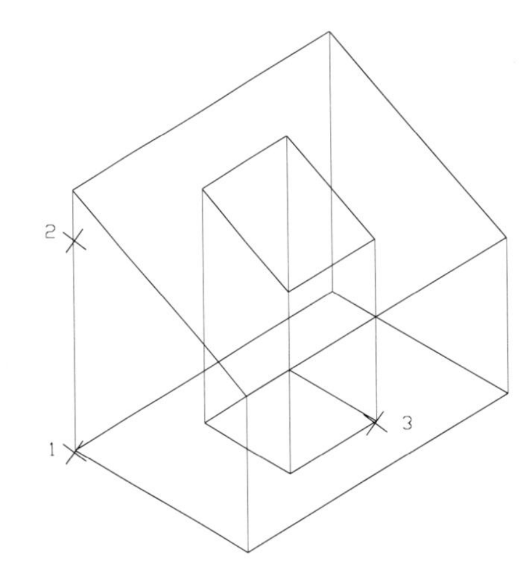

Command:**SOLSUB**

Source objects. . .

Select objects: *(pick the box)*

Select objects: *(pick the wedge)*

```
Select objects:↵
Adjusting current boundary
Objects to subtract from them
Select objects: (pick the tall box)
Sclcct objccto:↵
Phase I - Boundary evaluation begins
Phase II - Tessellation computation begins
Updating the Advanced Modelling Extension database
```

As you can see from the final image on page 577, the large box and wedge have been joined, and the tall, thinner box has been subtracted from them to create one object.

Using the same objects as in Example 2, we will now subtract the small sphere and the cylinder from the large sphere and the cone.

```
Command: SOLSUB
Source objects. . .
Select objects: (pick the large sphere)
Select objects: (pick the cone)
Select objects:↵
Objects to subtract from them...
Select objects: (pick the small sphere)
Select objects: (pick the cylinder)
Select objects:↵
Phase I - Boundary evaluation be-
gins
Phase II - Tessellation computation begins
Updating the Advanced Modelling Extension database
```

The new solid objects remain after the command has finished. Note that the source objects will remain and the subtracted objects will disappear entirely, leaving only the indentation that their shapes formed on the surfaces of the Source objects.

The SOLSUB command is located under the AME pull-down menu under MODIFY, or type SOLSUB, SUB, SUBTRACT, DIF, and DIFFERENCE to get the same command. These are command aliases, all of which are noted in Appendix C.

If you use SOLSUB to create more than one composite solid at one time, the resulting composite will be one solid, even if it is in two parts, and could thus lead to confusion.

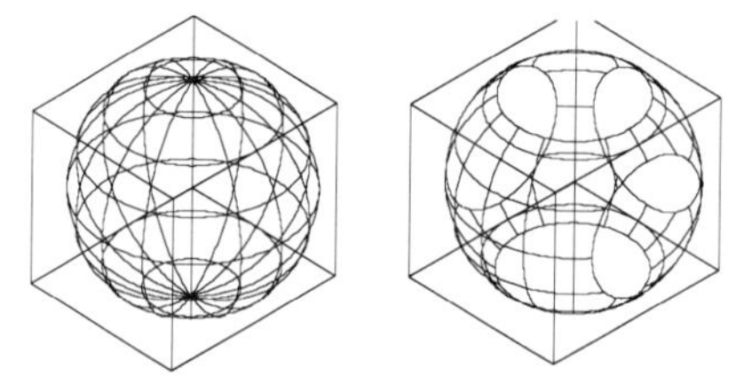

Figure 34-1. SOLSUB on two standard shapes

This command can be used to create many objects that are difficult to calculate using "traditional" wireframe modelling.

Intersecting Objects

Sometimes you need the intersection of two objects; just the common part that would remain if you were to subtract everything that does not overlap. In this case, use SOLINT.

Example 2: *SOLINT*

Using our previous examples as models, let's generate the intersections of the overlapping parts.

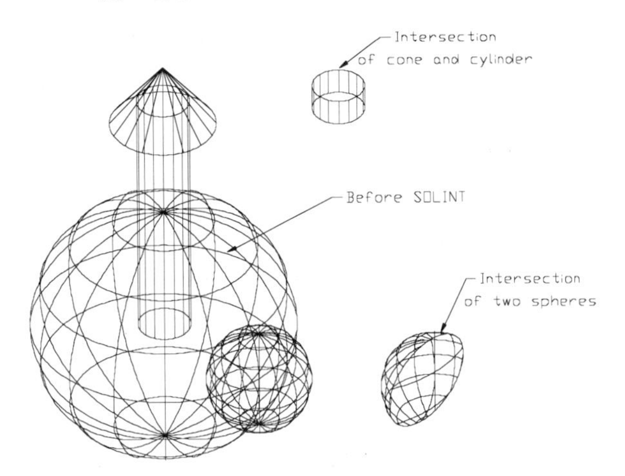

Figure 34-2. Extracting the intersection of two solids

Again, do not try to create more than one intersection at a time. If the part overlaps a number of other objects, this object will need to be copied to generate intersections with non-adjacent parts. Only one intersection can be created from each object.

In this example, another sphere must be created to calculate the portion of the cylinder that would be inserted into the centre of the large sphere. The surface of the sphere has already been cut to create the intersection with the smaller sphere.

The large sphere was copied or duplicated at its original position to create the final intersection.

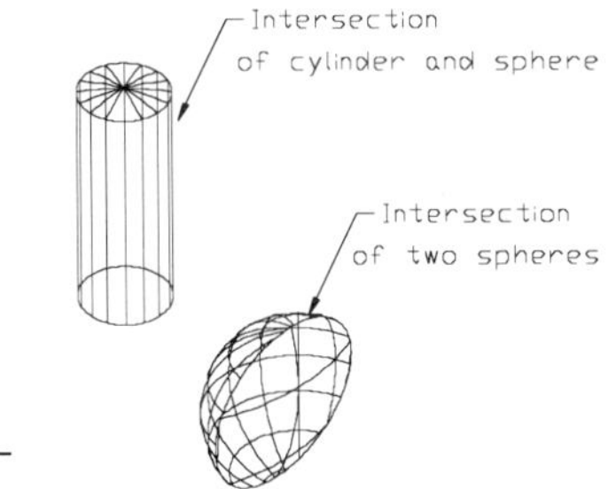

Command:**SOLINT**

Select objects: *(pick the large sphere)*

Select objects: *(pick the cylinder)*

Select objects:↵

Phase I - Boundary evaluation begins

Phase II - Tessellation computation begins

Updating the Advanced Modelling Extension database

The resulting shapes are a result of a Boolean operation that created a new composite solid object.

If you had tried to create both the intersection of the two spheres and the intersection of the sphere and the cylinder, you would have been unsuccessful. The system would have responded first with:

```
Updating solid
Null solid encountered. Automatically separating.
```

In the example on page 575, the same approach must be taken. While the wedge and the box were automatically joined to perform the SOLSUB, in the example on the next page, SOLUNION must be used before SOLINT will work.

Example: SOLINT

This command produces an object representing the common volume of two objects.

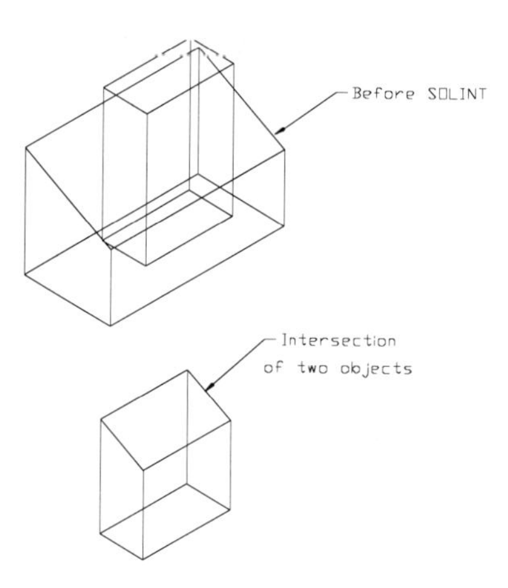

The SOLINT command can also be invoked with INT and INTERSECT as well as by the Solids and Modify pull-down menus.

If a 2D object is encountered within the command, SOLSOLIDIFY will attempt to make it into an intersection. If the 2D object has thickness, this may work. The variable SOLVAR setting will determine if the 2D object is always, sometimes, or never converted.

EDITING CSG SOLIDS

If you are creating complicated geometry with FILLET and CHAMFER, etc., AME makes the process much simpler. Once the object is accepted as one object, one solid with a mass and volume, the fillets and chamfers can be easily extracted from the objects.

The SOLCHAM Command

Example: SOLCHAM

Let us take an example with three boxes.

Create the boxes with SOLBOX and use SOLUNION to create one Boolean object.

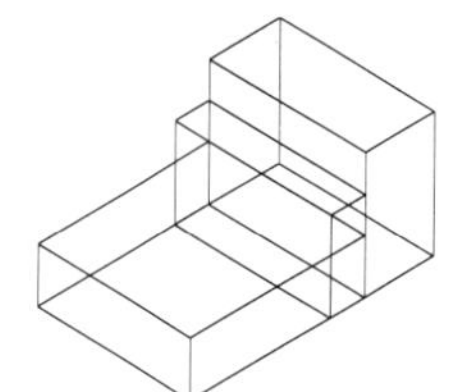

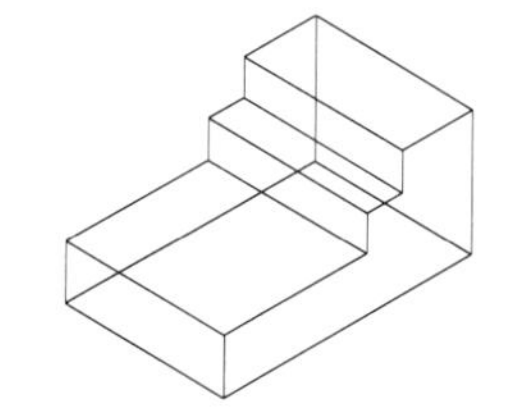

Figure 34-3. Union of solids

Now use the SOLCHAM command to chamfer the edges on both the front and back of the first surface. The SOLCHAM command can be accessed with SOLC and CHAM.

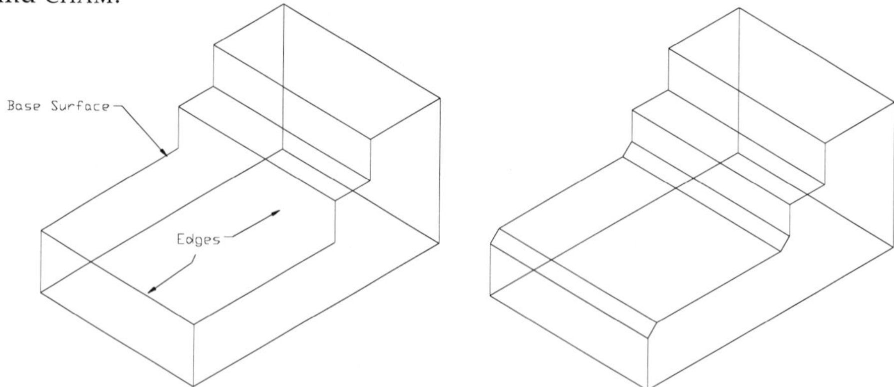

Figure 34-4. Chamfering of solids using SOLCHAM

You must indicate both the base surface and the edges to be chamfered within the command.

You can chamfer any edge on any flat, concave, or convex surface.

```
Command:SOLCHAM
Select base surface: (pick the surface)
<OK>/Next:↵
Select edges to be chamfered: (pick an edge)
Select edges to be chamfered: (pick an edge)
Select edges to be chamfered:↵
Enter distance along first surface<0.00>:.5
Enter distance along second surface<0.00>:.5
Phase I - Boundary evaluation begins.
Phase II - Tessellation begins.
Updating the Advanced Modelling Extension database.
```

The SOLCHAM command creates a bevelled edge on a specified surface and finishes the corners of the bevel on the unbevelled sides as well. Spheres and toruses cannot be chamfered because there is no edge; but wedges, cones, and cylinders can be chamfered.

Only straight and circular edges can be chamfered, so the Ellipse option of SOLCONE and SOLCYL cannot be used.

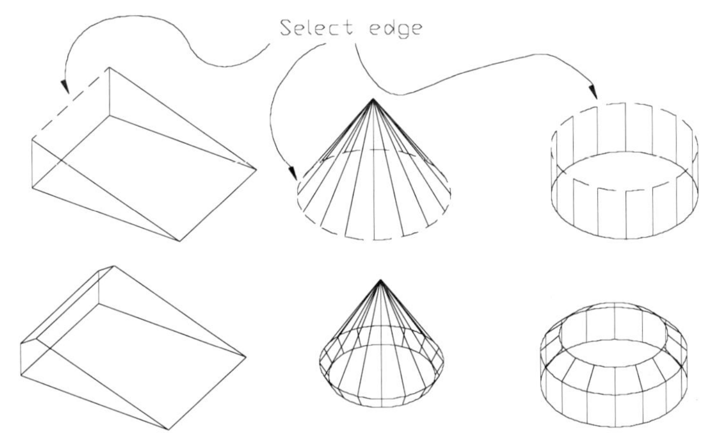

Figure 34-5. The SOLCHAM command

If you select an edge not adjacent to the highlighted surface, it will not be chamfered.

If you have moved, copied, rotated, or in any way edited the object, you may see the response:

```
Surface has been edited
Repeat selection
```

If so, simply choose the base surface again, and it should be picked up.

The SOLFILL Command

The SOLFILL command is similar to SOLCHAM in that it edits the edges of an existing object. Let us use the object of Figure 34-4 to show how some edges are filleted instead of chamfered.

Example 3: SOLFILL

Command: **SOLFILL**

Select edges to be filleted

(press enter when done): *(pick the edges)*

3 edges selected

Diameter/<Radius> of fillet

<0.00>: **.5**

Phase I - Boundary evaluation begins.

Phase II - Tessellation begins.

Updating the Advanced Modelling Extension database.

As with the SOLCHAM command, the edges are edited and finished. Either the radius or the diameter can be specified. Cones, wedges, and cylinders can also be filleted.

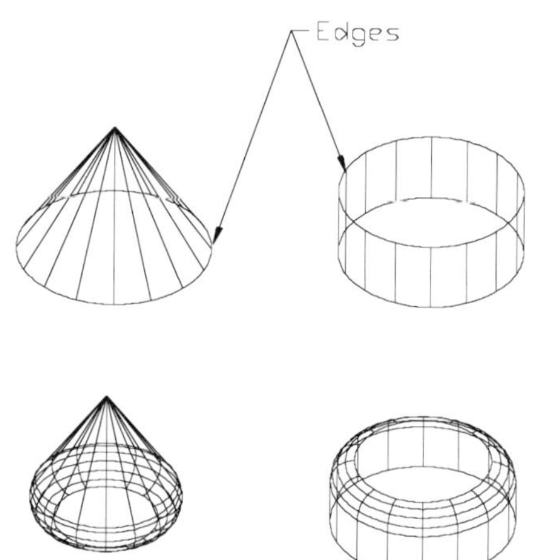

The fillets will always be shown in the same colour as the layer that the selected surface is on.

The SOLFILL command can also be accessed with SOLF and FIL once AME has been loaded.

The edges you choose can be concave or convex. The resulting geometry is a solid primitive that is added to or subtracted from the existing solids.

You must pick the edges individually; Window will not work.

Tips and Tricks

When selecting the base surface to perform a chamfer, the object selection pick must be on an edge. In a solid, there are always two surfaces that are attached to each edge. When picking the surface, the only thing you can be absolutely sure of is that the edge you pick will represent the surface that you do not want. In order to get the surface you want, use the Next option.

Command: **SOLCHAM**

Select base surface: *(pick the surface)*

<OK>/Next: **N**

<OK>/Next: ↵

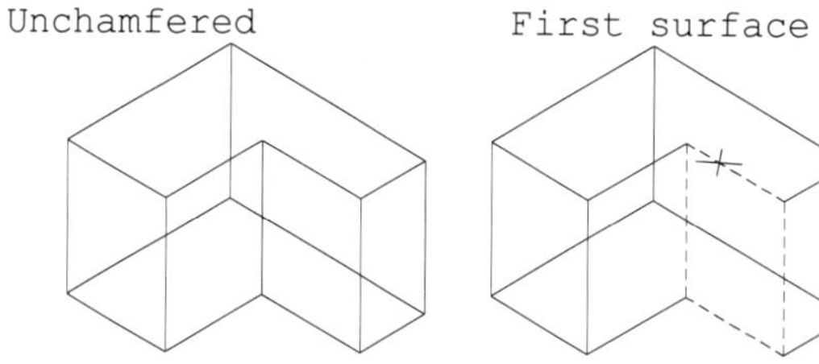

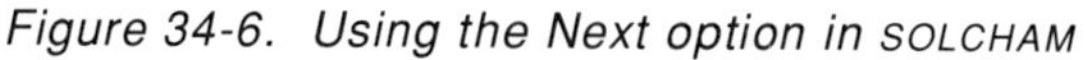
Figure 34-6. Using the Next option in SOLCHAM

The order in which you pick the corners is extremely important because it will determine the extents of your fillet or chamfer.

The edges for the chamfer were chosen first in two separate commands, then in one. You can see that with two commands there will be a continuous chamfer, but with one command there will not.

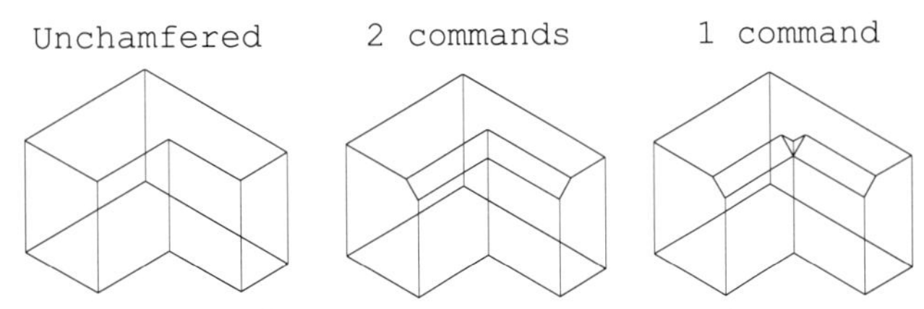

Figure 34-7. Effective use of SOLCHAM

The opposite is true of the FILLET command. The illustration below shows a continuous fillet with one command, but a non-continuous fillet with two separate commands.

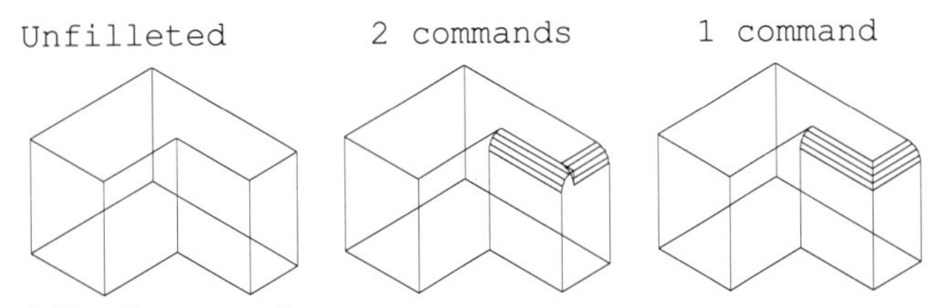

Figure 34-8. Effective use of SOLFILL

This final illustration shows the method for creating a curved interior fillet. The inside curve must be filleted to get a continuous upper fillet.

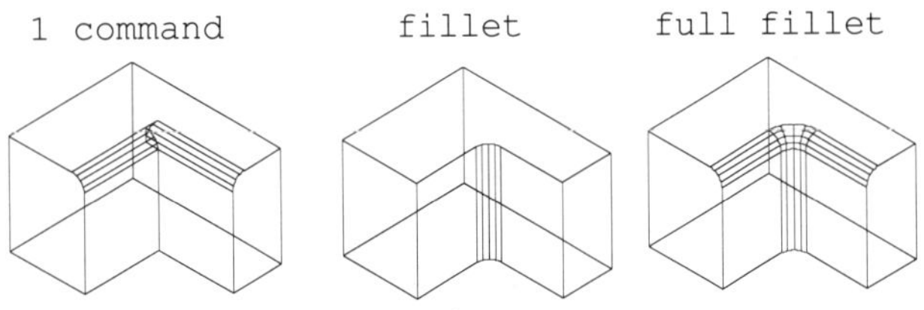

Figure 34-9. Using SOLFILL *on three surfaces*

ADDITIONAL COMMANDS

In order to create the models in the exercises, there are two further commands that you will find useful.

SOLREV

The SOLREV command is similar to the REVSURF command in that it utilizes a path curve around a specified axis. This command is useful for a revolved solid to make the complicated shapes that are possible with SOLBOX, SOLSPHERE, and SOLCYL.

```
Command:SOLREV
Select polyline or circle for revo-
lution:
Select objects: (pick the pline)
Select objects:↵
Axis of revolution - En-
tity/X/Y/<start point of axis>:E
Entity to revolve about: (pick axis)
Included angle <full circle>:↵
```

PLINE

AXIS

Only one pline or circle can be used for each solid: it will not automatically join a series of plines.

The most common problem with SOLREV is crossing or intersecting. You will get the response:

```
Lines intersect
Unable to create extrusion
```

If it is not a closed pline — a pline that is continuous with no end — the solid is created as if there were a straight line between the endpoints of the pline (shown in dot, on the right). You must add line segments (PEDIT and Join) to the pline so that the lines do not intersect.

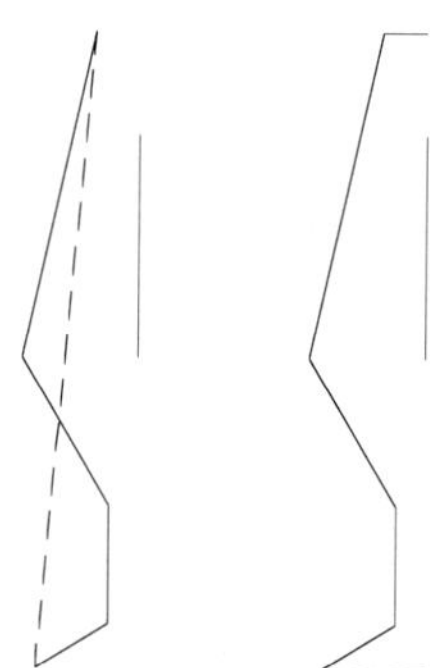

The SOLREV command can also be entered as REV and REVOLVE once the AME software has been entered.

SOLSEP

The SOLSEP command separates a composite model that has been created with SOLUNION, SOLSUB, or SOLINT. Like Undo, it undoes, in reverse order, the operations performed to create the composite model.

Each use of the command undoes a Boolean operation that created a composite solid. If you have joined a number of solids with one command, it will separate them all in one command.

Practice Exercise

This short exercise should prepare you for the day's exercise.

Use SOLBOX to create a box that is 8 units by 5 units, 1 unit high.

Use SOLFILL to fillet the corners by .5 unit.

Use SOLCYL to create cylinders 1 unit in from each corner with a .5 radius.

Use SOLBOX to create another box 1 unit by 5 units, extending 4 units above the original box.

Use SOLUNION to join these two boxes.

NOTE: You can create the second box on the Z plane with a height of 5 units, or create it on the plane of Z = 1 with a height of 4 units.

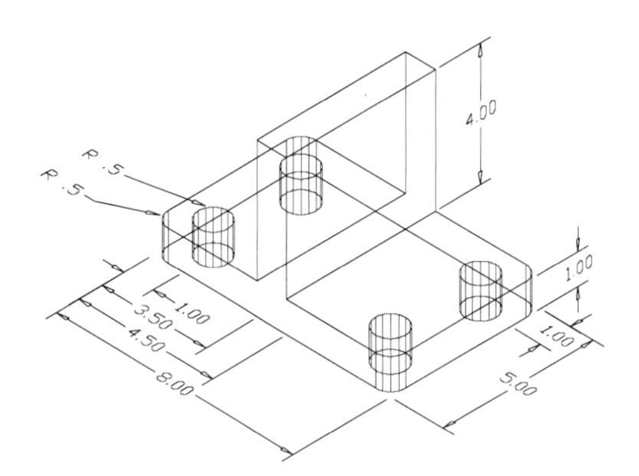

Change the UCS by using 3point so that it is placed as in the illustration on the left.

Now use SOLCYL to place a cylinder on top of the second box. The radius will be 2.5 and the height will be 1.

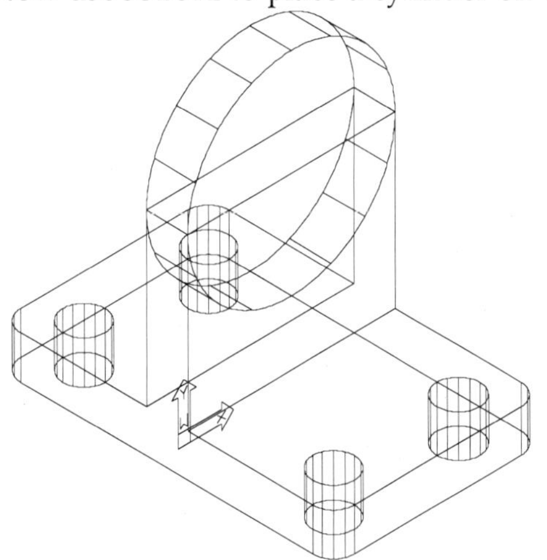

You can use MID to place it exactly on the midpoint of your top line.

You will find that at least two viewports are needed for this data to be entered correctly. If you are only using one, use DVIEW Camera to be sure the objects are being created as desired.

Use SOLCHAM to create chamfers on the edges connecting the two boxes. The distance in both directions should be .5 unit.

If you have not used SOLUNION to join the two boxes, the chamfer will be entered in the wrong direction. Both chamfers and fillets will subtract from the existing object instead of joining to an adjacent object if they are not joined with SOLUNION. This can be very frustrating if you do not know why it is happening.

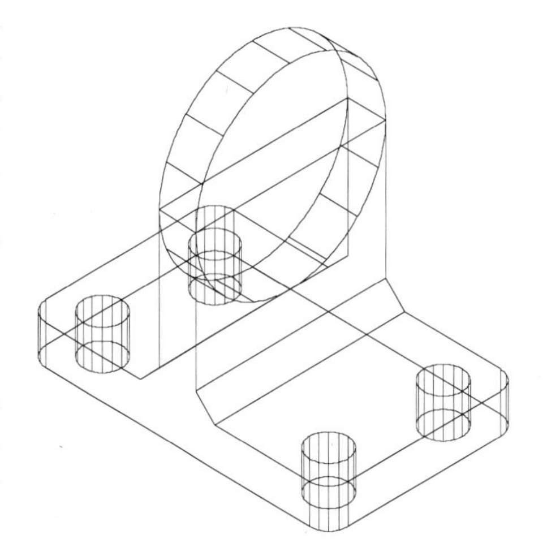

Use SOLCYL to enter the two cylinders. You can easily do this by creating the cylinder at Z = 0 and then moving it back 2 units in negative Z; see if you can remember how to use filters.

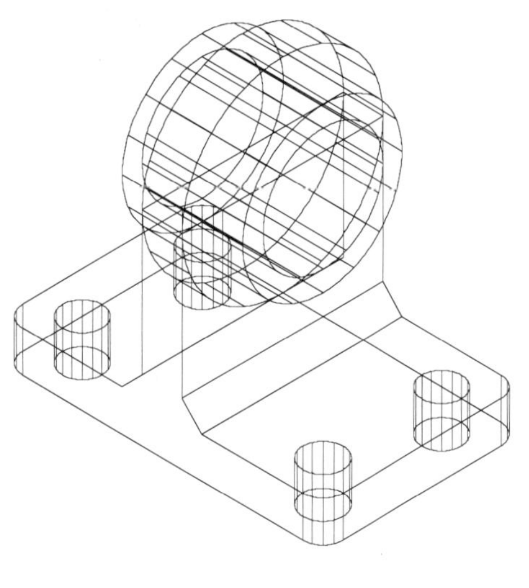

```
Command:SOLCYL
Elliptical/ <center point>:.x
of mid (pick the top line of the box at Z = 0)
(needs YZ):.y of mid (pick the same line)
(needs Z):-2
Diameter/<Radius>:2
Height of cylinder:3
```

Enter the second cylinder with a 1.5 radius.

Once all of the component objects are in, you can then process them using SOLUNION, SOLSUB, and, when needed, SOLINT. As noted above, it is often necessary to create a SOLUNION before the part is finished.

You will note that the time taken to calculate Phase I and Phase II of the processing will take an increasingly long time. If you have limited RAM or your part is extremely large, this can be frustrating. Even with adequate RAM it is a good idea to save a number of processing operations for one or two operations as opposed to five or six operations to save time.

What you are after is a composite object: one that contains all the objects you initially entered, subtracting those objects that will create holes or spaces in the final part.

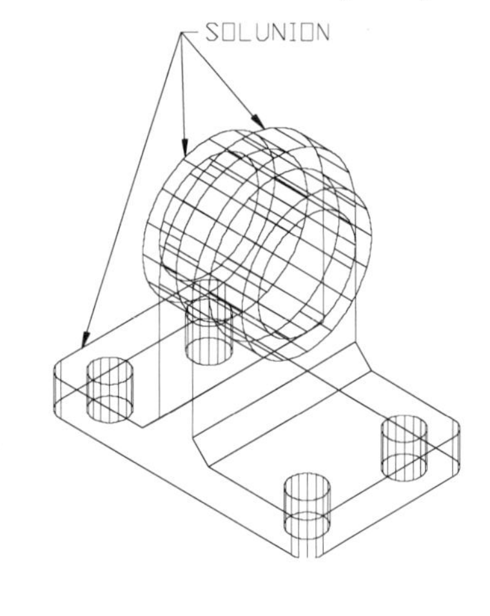

At this stage we must first join the various parts together using SOLUNION. The parts to be joined are the boxes (already joined), the 1-unit cylinders, and the exterior cylinder that is 2 units in radius.

Use LIST to find the objects if you are having difficulty picking them.

Use SOLSUB to subtract the four cylinders on the base and the cylinder that extends through the centre of the upper area.

Again, using one command rather than five for this will save a lot of time.

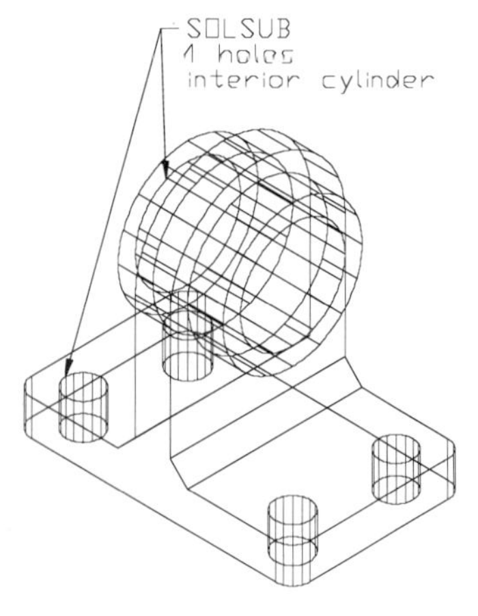

The part is now complete and you can save it to try some analysis on in the next chapter.

The objects you have created are solid objects. What you see are the boundary representations.

The boundaries are simply a set of lines derived directly from the equations used to describe the model. They are not 3D faces or meshes. Therefore, if you decide to remove the hidden lines, the model will look like the illustration on the next page.

To get a "real" hidden-line picture, use the MESH command on the AME Display pull-down menu to change the objects into meshes. Once changed, the object should hide quite well. Use MVIEW and Hideplot if plotting.

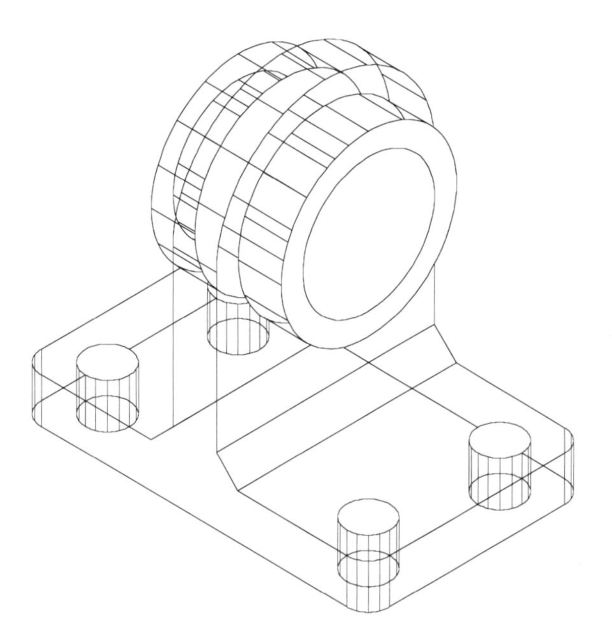

Exercise A34

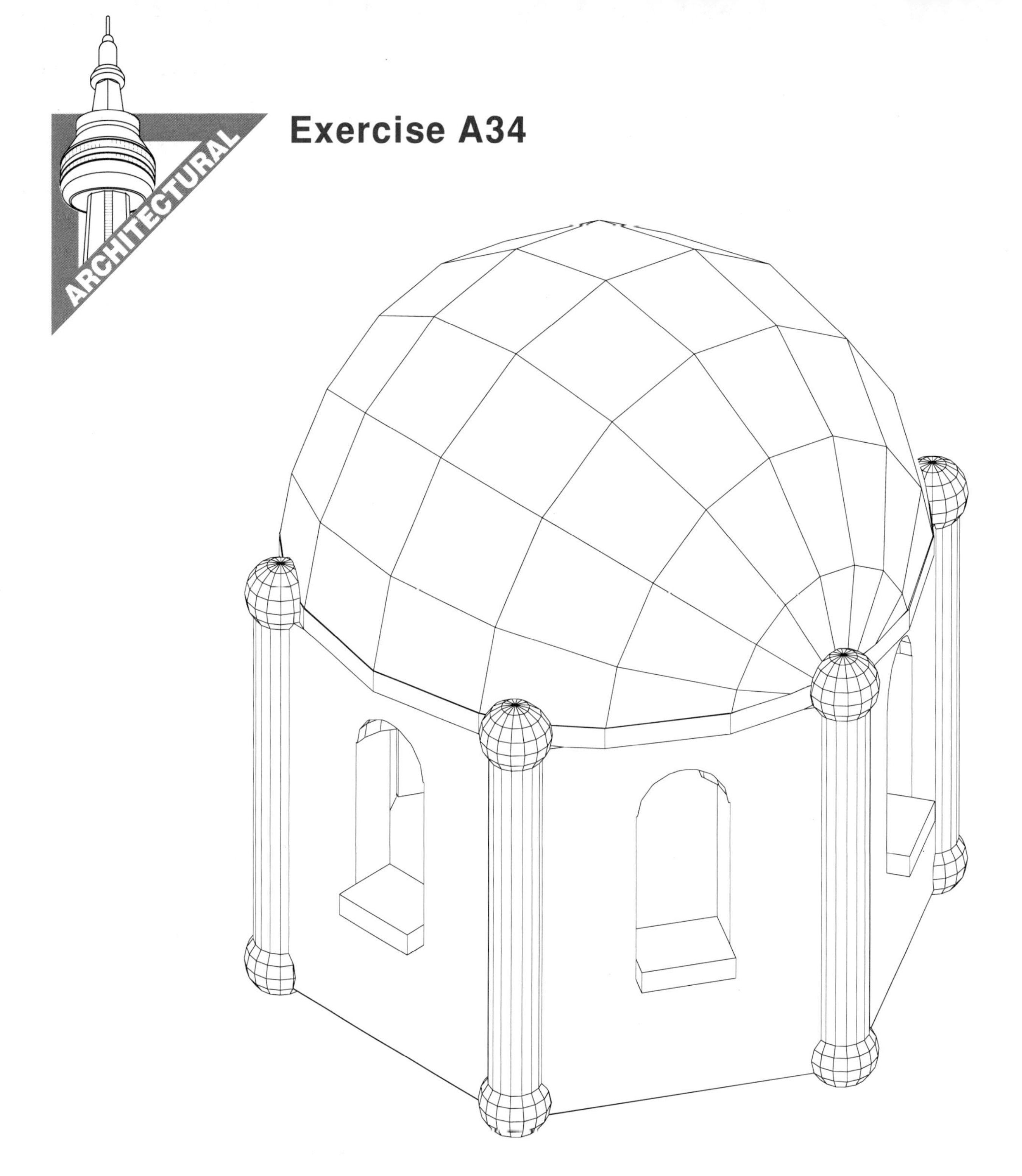

This small, domed, turret detail will give you an idea of how different solids can be attached to one another. Use this model or create one of your own with a similar use, but different detailing.

A34 Hints

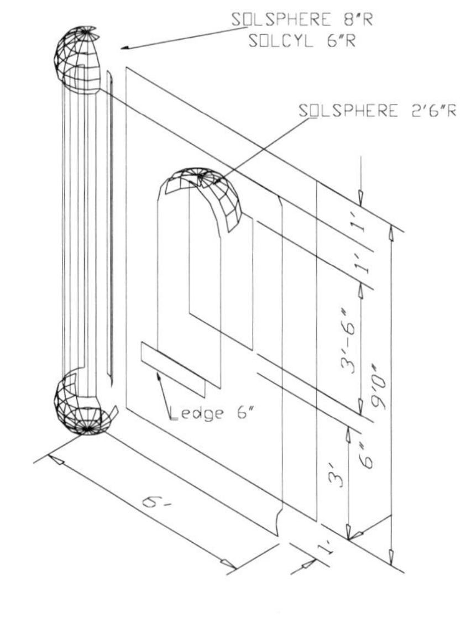

The turret will be constructed with six sides, all with a window and some detailing on the sides.

Create this geometry using SOLBOX, SOLSPHERE, and SOLCYL. You will not need to change the UCS just yet.

Use filters as well as point entry and osnaps to place the items.

Be sure to make your dome on the top of the window the correct size so that the window will curve gracefully in at the top.

You will probably need at least three viewports for this design — an isometric, a front, and a plan.

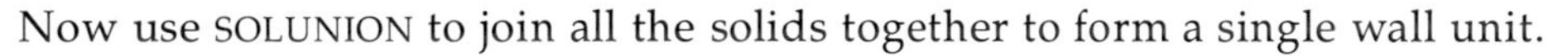
Now use SOLUNION to join all the solids together to form a single wall unit.

It may be quicker to join the solids into one unit now, then to array them and join them later.

Once unified, use ARRAY in the plan view to create the room layout. Be sure the boxes are overlapping, or the walls will not join later.

If the inside face of the wall is 6 feet, the centre of the polar array will be 5′2" from the middle of the wall.

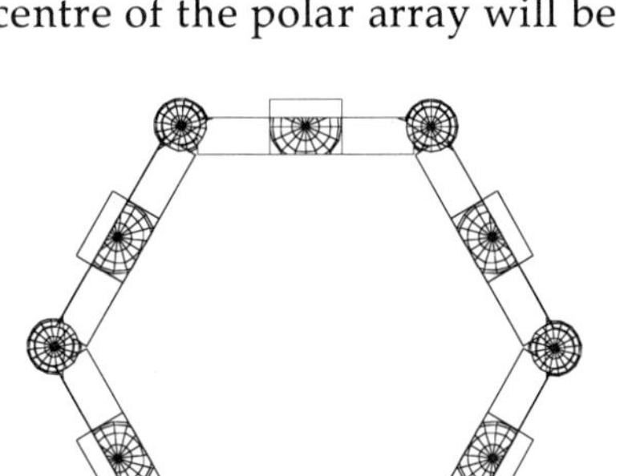

Now the dome must be created. The easiest way to create a dome is by using SOLREV. This is very similar to REVSURF in that the curve or pline is revolved around an axis. The difference is that here we are creating a solid, not just a surface.

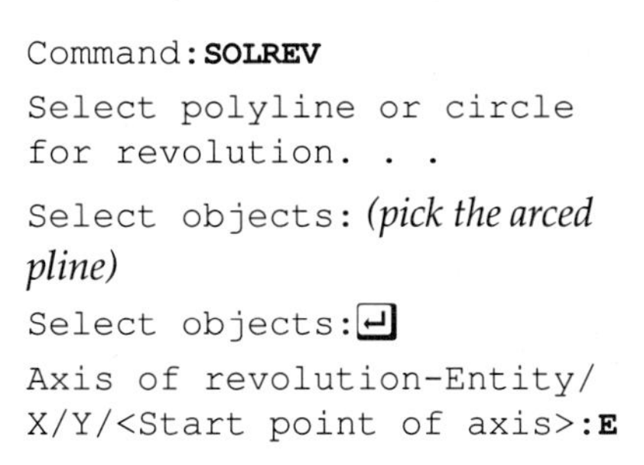
`Command:`**`SOLREV`**

`Select polyline or circle for revolution. . .`

`Select objects:` *(pick the arced pline)*

`Select objects:`↵

`Axis of revolution-Entity/X/Y/<Start point of axis>:`**`E`**

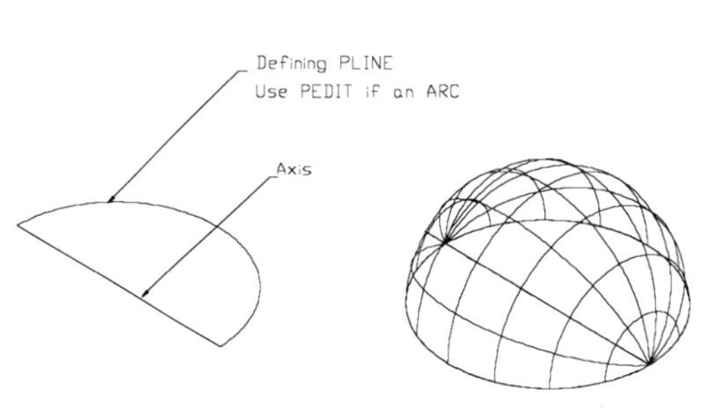

```
Select object: (pick the line)
Included angle<full circle>:180
```

This command will give you the inside of the dome. Make sure it fits all the interior corners of the top of the walls.

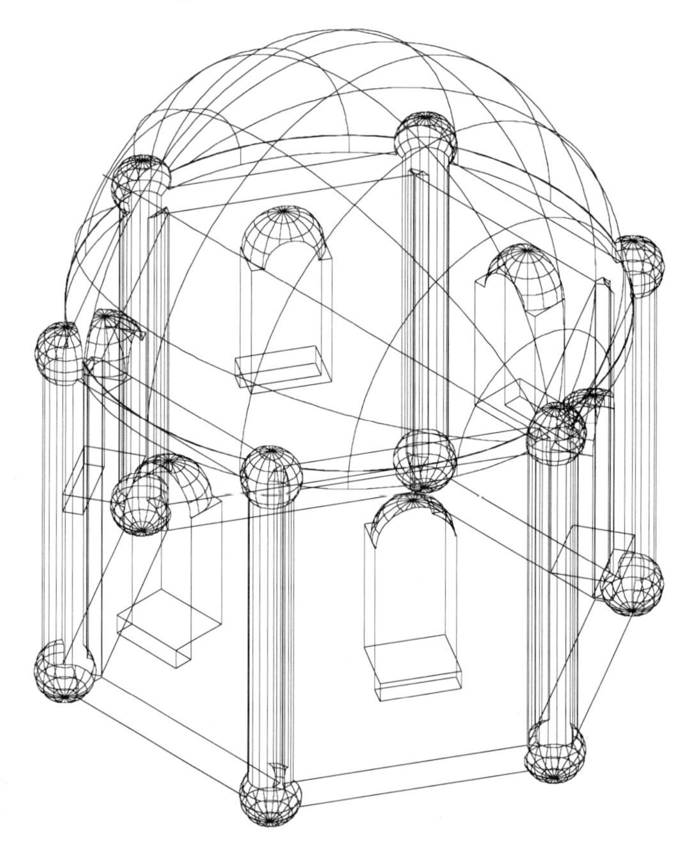

Again make sure that the inside surface of the dome is attached to the top of the wall. Solid cylinders can be used as a base for the revolved solids.

Revolved solids create solid entities from the centre of the pline path.

While SOLTORUS and SOLSPHERE can add lovely detailing, unless you have 20MB of RAM, these calculations will take a long time.

Once assembled, use SOLUNION to join six walls, the exterior dome, and the exterior cylinder if you have one.

Now use SOLSUB to subtract the inside of the dome and the interior cylinder from the dome at the top. If you do not subtract the interiors, the dome will be solid throughout.

If you want a hidden-line view of this turret, use SOLMESH under the AME Display menu to create a mesh out of the assembled solids. Then use HIDE or DVIEW and Hideplot.

Exercise M34

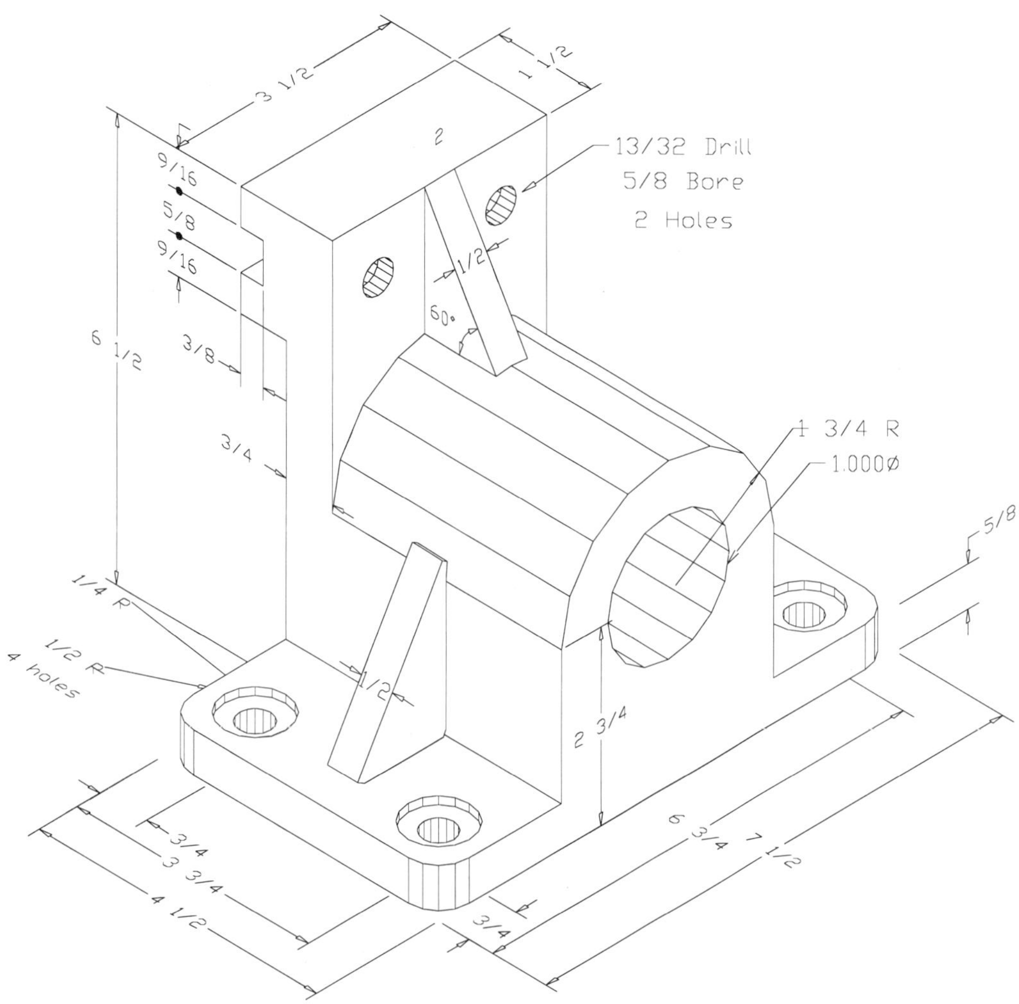

Rounds and Fillets 1/2
Interior Thickness 1/5

This Slide Support is composed of solid boxes and solid cylinders with four solid fillets. It is nonetheless a little tricky to create as there are many UCS changes.

We suggest that you enter all the solids first, then process them.

You will need at least three layers; one for base geometry, one for cylinders, and one for additional geometry. If you are planning to dimension the part, add a layer for dimensions as well.

Once it is completed, create a mesh of the part under the AME Display menu and use HIDE to get the final result.

M34 Hints

The base geometry is quite simple to enter. Start with a large base. Add the solid boxes for the upper surface either by calculating their coordinates or by using filters and osnaps.

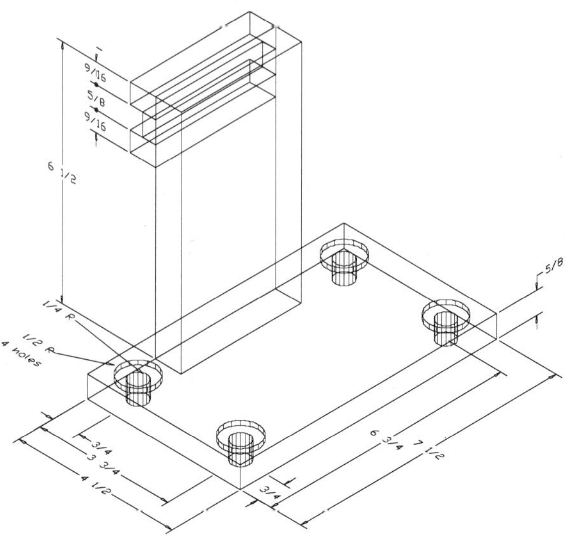

Once in, add the solid cylinders.

You will find that a plan, right side, and iso view will help you place the cylinders quickly, making sure that the top indentation is at the correct height.

Add the solid cylinders and the two diagonal solid boxes that will form the reinforcing veins. The two boxes can be added, then moved and rotated, or you can change your UCS. The UCS will need to be reoriented in order to add the cylinders, so you can easily rotate the UCS at a 30-degree angle to add the first box.

Be sure the box is the correct size and does not extend below the base. Also make sure there are no gaps between the diagonal box and the cylinder. Once in, the UCS can be changed to Previous, and the box can be mirrored through the centre of the part.

If you have oriented your model the same as in the examples, the bottom-right illustration will be your front view.

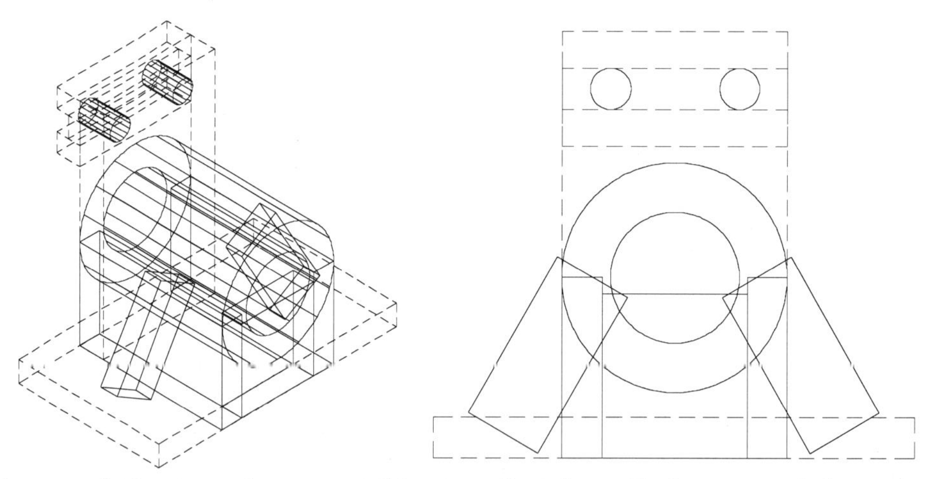

It is a good idea to make sure at this stage that the cylinders extend through the part.

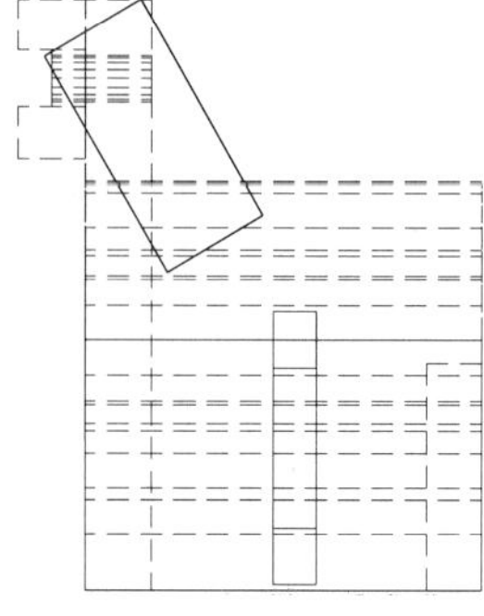

Check the model from all views before processing because the processing takes a bit of time, so any errors encountered and fixed at this stage will save time later.

Metal parts manufactured in this way are usually hollow on the underside. If not, the stock under the large cylinder would be over an inch thick, thus wasting stock and making an unnecessarily heavy part.

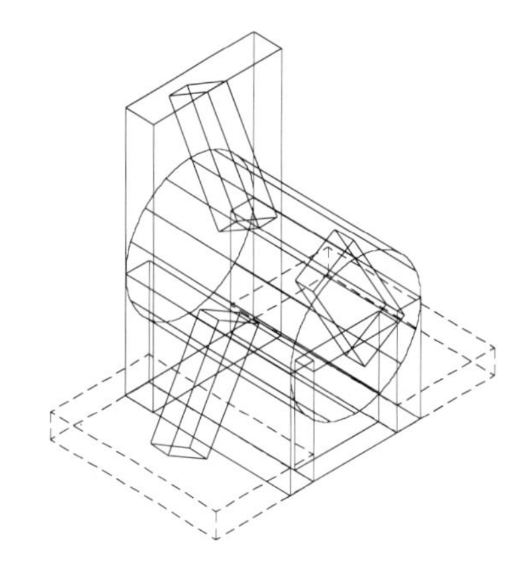

If you have created the base box in one piece as in the example, you will need to create two smaller base parts (shown in hidden lines) and erase the large 4 ½ x 7 ½ box.

Add boxes ½" in thickness along the front and up both sides as shown, leaving the bottom of the part hollow.

It is a good idea to save your file at this point if you have not already done so.

For ease in selection, turn off the interior cylinder layer.

Now use SOLUNION to join the boxes and the large cylinder.

Depending on the size of your RAM and processor, this could take a few minutes. Now is the time to start considering the value of a new computer.

Now add the cylinder layer and use SOLSUB to subtract all the interior cylinders from the base part.

Again this could take a bit of time.

In effect, your part is now complete except for the fillets.

Use DVIEW Camera to rotate the iso view to pick the fillet on the back corner if you cannot pick it as it is.

If you use HIDE at this point, you will be disappointed by the results because the only surfaces that will opaque objects are the cylinders.

If you want a view with all the hidden lines removed, you must use the MESH command under the AME Display menu.

The SOLMESH command changes the surface of the solids into pfaces, approximating the original shape.

```
Command:SOLMESH
Select solids to be meshed
Select objects: (pick the solid)
Select objects:↵
1 solid selected.
Solid meshing of current solid is complete.
Creating block of mesh representation. . .
Done.
```

Once this is completed, the solid object is a series of multi-edged pfaces and can be used with HIDE or DVIEW Hideplot to get a hidden-line image.

NOTE: If you are planning to do further work on the part, it is a good idea to copy the solid over and create one meshed part and one AME part as the object snaps, such as END*(point)*, CENt*(er)*, MID*(point)*, will not be accepted once the model is a meshed block.

If there are entities that are not part of the solid, you will get a response saying:

```
Try to solidify the highlighted entity? <N>
```

Simply press the Return key and the non-solid, whatever it is, will be ignored.

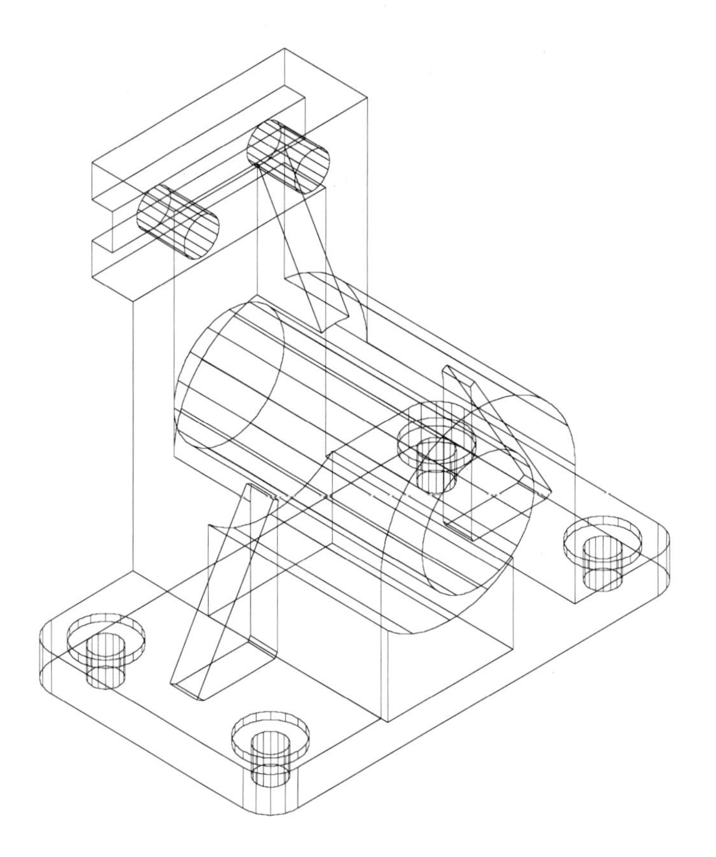

Exercise C34

Use the AME software to create a truss.

You can use one of the trusses or the example below.

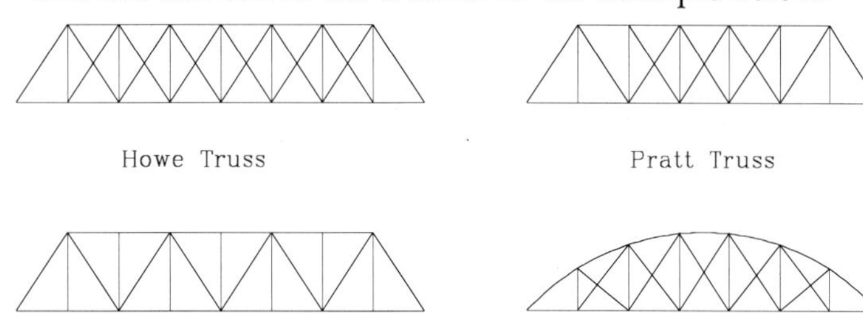

Warren Truss

Bowstring Truss

On the right is a simple beam truss design.

Use SOLBOX to create the upper panel. Then change your UCS and use SOLCYL to create the support bars.

Because they must be rounded at the corners and intersecting, you will need to use SOLREV with CIRCLE to create partial toruses on the ends of the beams as shown below.

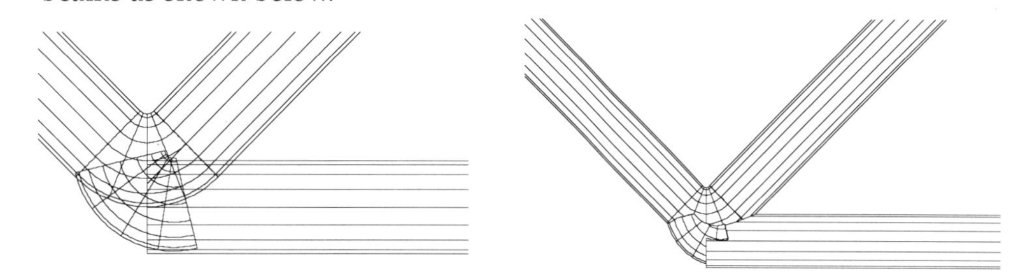

Use SOLUNION to create a composite solid of the part. The edges should be as even as these.

Challenger 34

Create an appliance such as the hair dryer illustrated with the Solid Primitives.

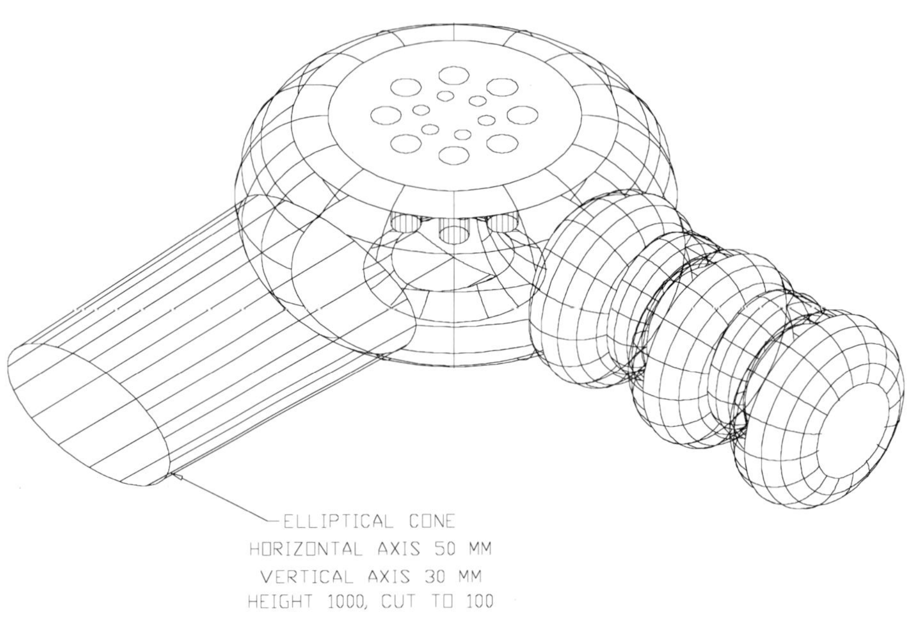

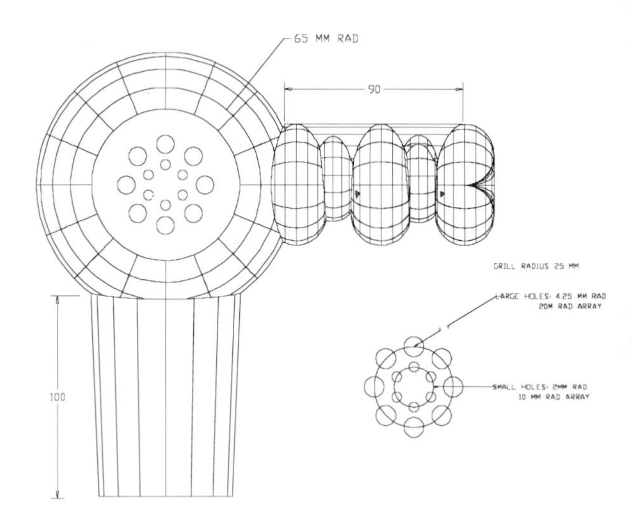

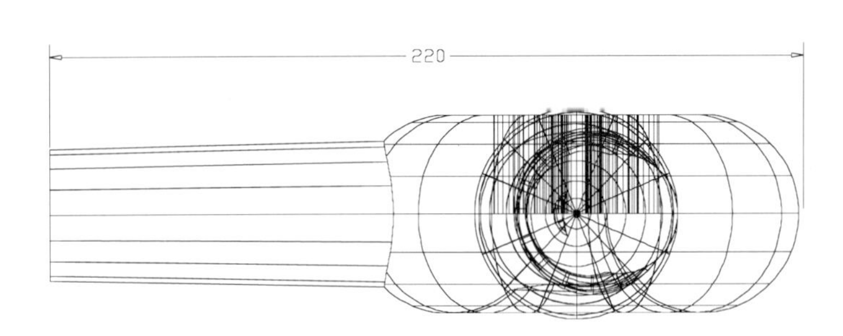

REGIONS AND CALCULATIONS ON AME MODELS

Upon completion of this chapter, the student should be able to:

1. Use Advanced Modelling Extension to create a 2D region
2. Change portions of a region or solid
3. Extrude 2D objects to make 3D objects
4. Use AME to calculate mass properties
5. Use AME to calculate volumes

This section of the textbook has been dedicated to 3D modelling. We will first take a step back to a 2D environment to start our analysis of composite models. Once you have mastered 2D models, you will be better prepared to master 3D solid models.

AME REGIONS

AutoCAD uses the term *region* to define a series of 2D objects (lines, circles, arcs, plines, etc.) that are picked up by the computer in AME operations as one solid object. The region can be a simple outline or it can contain holes. The outer edge of the region is called the "outer loop" and the holes are called "inner loops." Regions can exist anywhere in space, but they are 2D entities.

Creating a Region Primitive

To create a region from a series of 2D objects, use the regular 2D commands to generate the outline, then use the command SOLIDIFY to make it into a solid region.

We are going to use three different examples to show how this works because the applications and uses are very different.

1. We will use a simple template to calculate mass properties.

2. When designing turbine blades, propeller blades, etc., the method is to generate a series of cross sections, calculate the centroids, stack the sections, and rotate them according to the required blade angle. We will calculate the centroid of a closed spline.

3. The simple truss will be used to calculate moments of inertia, weight, and other relevant factors.

Simply draw in the objects as plines and then use SOLIDIFY. In order for the SOLIDIFY command to work, the objects must be 2D objects having a non-zero thickness. Circles, traces, donuts, plines, and ellipses can be used. You cannot solidify anything that has thickness or is a 3D object.

Once drawn in, load AME and use SOLIDIFY to create regions. If you get the response

```
Object cannot be solidified
Press space bar to continue
```

use LIST to see which object is not 3D (has zero thickness).

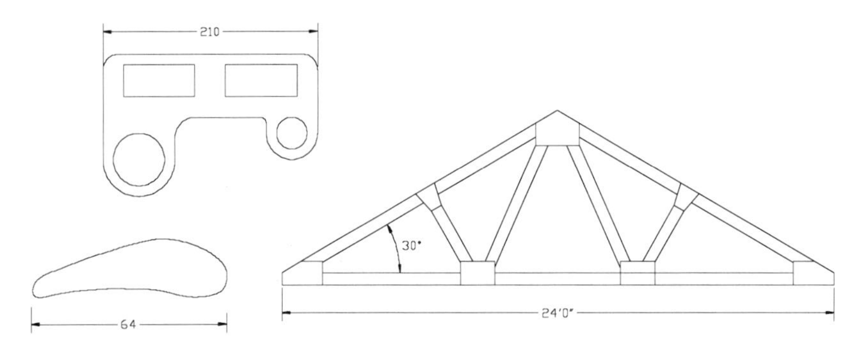

Figure 35-1. Three 2D objects: template, airfoil, truss

After selecting the objects to be solidified, the evaluation process begins and an outer loop is created. The outline must be solidified first.

When you have created the outer loop of the region, use SOLSUB to subtract the interior boundaries or inner loop. In the illustration of Figure 35-2, the airfoil shape has no interior boundaries, but the template and truss do.

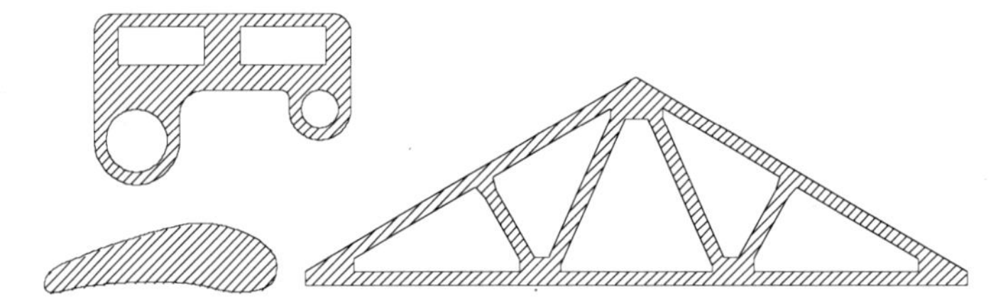

Figure 35-2. Regions

The SOLIDIFY command will automatically display a hatch pattern within the selected object. Use the SOLVAR submenu under the AME main menu to change the following variables *before* using SOLID.

The default may be a hatch of 1 unit. If your outer loop is large, this may crash the file if you do not change SOLHSIZE. Use the following commands to change the hatch defaults.

```
Command:SOLHPAT
Hatch pattern <none>:ansi31

Command:SOLHSIZE
Hatch size <1.0000>:12

Command:SOLHANGLE
Hatch angle <45.00>:0
```

When creating the airfoil, make it very small with very few defining points. Once you have used PEDIT Spline fit to create the shape, LIST the pline. If it has more than 500 vectors, you will not be able to solidify it in Release 2 of AME.

Processing Regions

If there are many regions adjacent to one another, they can be joined together using SOLUNION. If you want to see just the intersection of two regions, use SOLINT. Editing commands such as MIRROR, COPY, MOVE, etc. can be used to reposition the objects before processing.

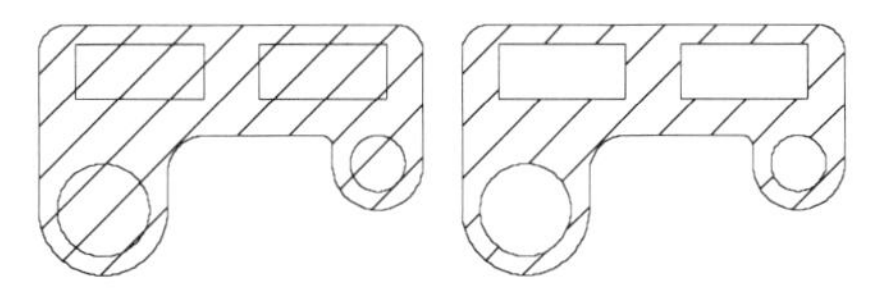

Figure 35-3. Single and interior boundary regions

Once you have processed these objects, they are ready for calculations. We will look at editing composite regions and solids first.

THE CSG TREE

Once you have used SOLUNION, SOLSUB, or SOLINT, the region becomes a composite region: composed of different regions. The AME system keeps track of the processing operations that make up the composite regions in a CSG or Constructive Solid Geometry tree. The tree keeps track of the order of the processing commands for purposes of editing.

Objects and operations are entered in a paired format so the tree is automatically balanced to produce the fewest number of levels.

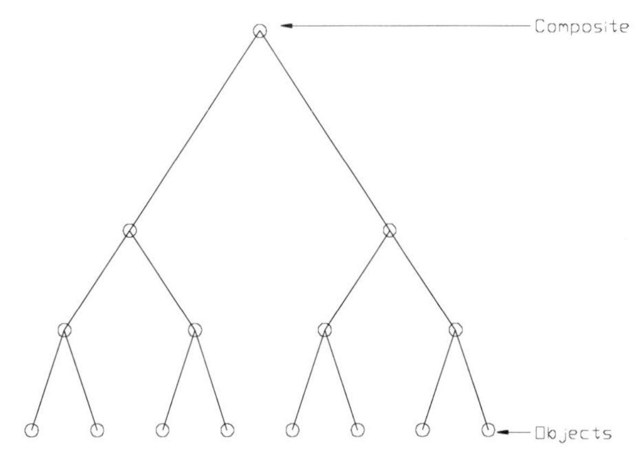

Figure 35-4. The CSG Tree Is in a Paired Format

For each operation performed, whether adding or processing geometry, a level is created on the tree. Even small parts can have large CSG tree structures.

In the following example of a wrench, the outline is made first using a pline made up of two line segments and two arc segments. Another pline made up of six line segments is then subtracted from the original solid.

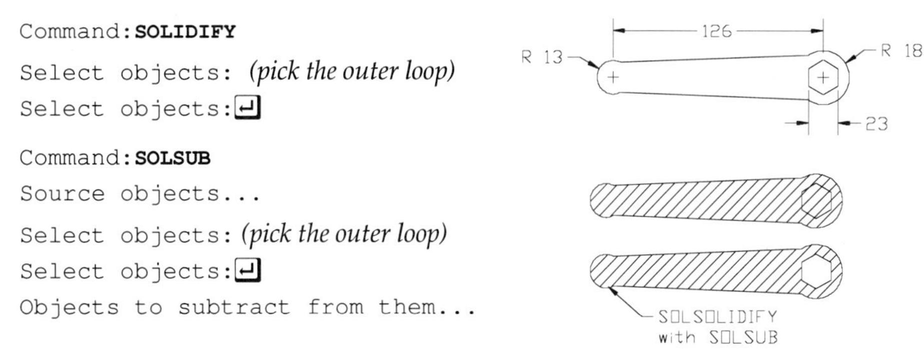

Command:**SOLIDIFY**

Select objects: *(pick the outer loop)*

Select objects:↵

Command:**SOLSUB**

Source objects...

Select objects: *(pick the outer loop)*

Select objects:↵

Objects to subtract from them...

```
Select objects: (pick the inner loop)
Select objects: ↵
```

With a simple part like this one, the CSG tree would have one level.

SOLLIST

Each level of the CSG tree, each circle on the diagram, is given a handle or name. These are referred to as the various nodes of the CSG tree. The objects that make up the tree can be listed by using SOLLIST. The list will begin with the composite and then list each object in reverse chronological order. Each object will be listed with its handle and node level. This listing is extremely useful when editing a complex solid or region. Be careful not to erase the handles in your drawing. The command SOLLIST will look like this.

```
Command: SOLLIST
Edge/Face/Tree/<Solid>: Tree
Select Objects: Last (the wrench)
Select objects: ↵
Object type = SUBTRACTION Handle 1CB8
 Component Handles: 1C71 and 1C87
 Area not computed  Material = MILD_STEEL
 Representation = WIREFRAME  Shade type = CSG

....Object type = REGION (6)   Handle 1C71
.... Area not computed  Material MILD_STEEL
.... Representation = WIREFRAME  Shade Type = CSG
.... Node level = 1

....Object type = REGION (6)  Handle 1C87
.... Area not computed  Material MILD_STEEL
.... Representation = WIREFRAME  Shade Type = CSG
.... Node level = 1
```

Let us look at the solid listing for the template.

```
Command: SOLLIST
Edge/Face/Tree/<Solid>: Tree
Select Objects: Last (the template)
Select objects: ↵
Object type = SUBTRACTION   Handle 54E
 Component Handles: 4BF and 4DC
 Area not computed  Material = MILD_STEEL
 Representation = WIREFRAME  Shade type = CSG

....Object type = REGION  Handle 4BF
.... Area not computed  Material MILD_STEEL
.... Representation = WIREFRAME  Shade Type = CSG
.... Node level = 1

....Object type = UNION  Handle 4DC
.... Component handles: 4DA and 4DB
.... Area not computed  Material MILD_STEEL
.... Representation = WIREFRAME  Shade Type = CSG
.... Node level = 1

....Object type = UNION  Handle 4DA
```

```
.... Component handles: 4C7 and 4CF
.... Area not computed  Material MILD_STEEL
.... Representation = WIREFRAME  Shade Type = CSG
.... Node level = 2

....Object type = REGION  Handle 4C7
.... Component handles: 4C8 and 4CE
.... Area not computed  Material MILD_STEEL
.... Representation = WIREFRAME  Shade Type = CSG
.... Node level = 3

....Object type = REGION(4)  Handle 4CF
.... Area not computed  Material MILD_STEEL
.... Representation = WIREFRAME  Shade Type = CSG
.... Node level = 3

....Object type = UNION  Handle 4DB
.... Component handles: 4D4 and 4D9
.... Area not computed  Material MILD_STEEL
.... Representation = WIREFRAME  Shade Type = CSG
.... Node level = 2

....Object type = CIRCULAR REGION (25.00000) Handle 4D4
.... Area not computed  Material MILD_STEEL
.... Representation = WIREFRAME  Shade Type = CSG
.... Node level = 3

....Object type = CIRCULAR REGION (15.00000) Handle 4D9
.... Area not computed  Material MILD_STEEL
.... Representation = WIREFRAME  Shade Type = CSG
.... Node level = 3
```

Each paragraph represents a different primitive or composite region. A composite will have five lines of text and a primitive will have four. It is important to understand this tree when you start editing solids and regions.

EDITING REGIONS AND SOLIDS

SOLCHP

The *CHP* of the SOLCHP command means CH*(ange)* P*(rimitive)*. This allows you to change or modify the primitives contained in a solid or region without having to undo or SOLSEP the composite. When you enter SOLCHP, you are first prompted to choose the object to change, then you are given a choice of options. Typing the capital letter will select the option. The options are straightforward.

```
Color/Delete/Evaluate/Instance/Move/Next/Pick/Replace/Size/
eXit:
```

Where:

Color changes the colour of a solid primitive.

Delete deletes a solid primitive from the composite.

Evaluate forces the system to re-evaluate the changes made during the SOLCHP command. Many of the changes will not be apparent until you exit from the command.

Instance makes a copy of the primitive on the spot it currently occupies.

Move moves portions of the primitive. Chamfers and fillets as well as inner loops can be moved within or from a solid.

Next selects another solid primitive within the solid primitive.

Pick allows you to pick another primitive.

Replace replaces one primitive with another.

Size acts like the SCALE command allowing you to change the relative size of the objects.

eXit exits the command.

The SOLCHP command is used to change the various primitives in a composite solid. The regular editing commands will not work on individual portions of the solid composite or region in the same way that the editing commands will not work on portions of a block once it has been created. The SOLCHP command saves you from having to explode the solid composite.

The SOLSEP command takes you backwards up the CSG tree, and allows you to modify the positions of the branches.

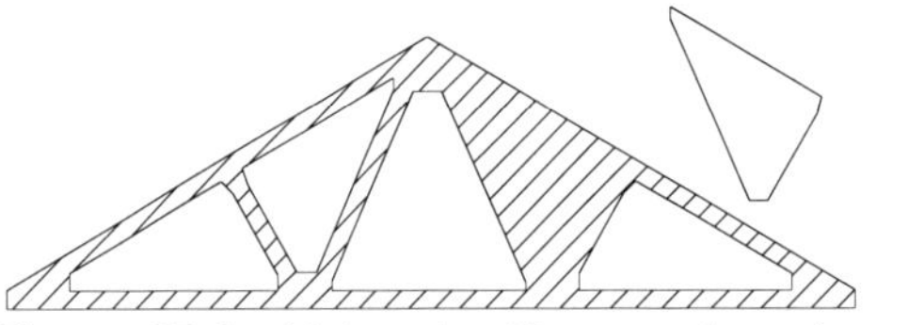

Figure 35-5. Using the Move option of SOLCHP

In the example of Figure 35-5, one portion of the truss structure is taken out using the Move option. When the part was constructed, the outer loop was generated as a region, then the five inner loops were subtracted.

With the SOLSEP command you would have to separate all the inner loops from the outer loop, take out the section that is not required, and use SOLSUB again. This could take a few minutes.

In complex parts where there are many steps involved in the compiling process, you would need to use SOLSEP many times to get back to the area you want to edit, and then repeat the construction steps.

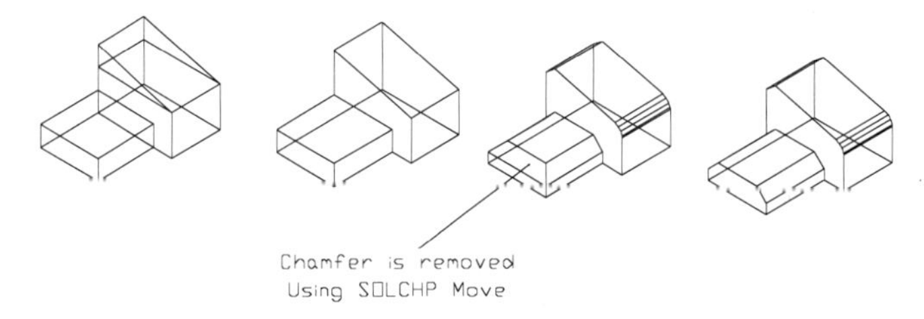

Figure 35-6. Using SOLCHP

In Figure 35-6, the composite model is composed of three primitives which were joined with UNION. The part was then chamfered on three edges with SOLCHAM, and chamfered with a different distance on the top edge. Finally it is filleted. At this point the designer decides to get rid of one of the chamfers. The SOLCHP command makes this a simple process.

```
Command: SOLCHP
Select solid: (pick the composite solid, anywhere)
Select Primitive: (pick the chamfer identified)
```

Color/Delete/Evaluate/Inst./Move/Next/Pick/Replace/Size/eXit:**M**

Base point of displacement: *(pick a point)*

Second point of displacement: *(pick another point well away from the model — this will remove the chamfer entirely)*

Color/Delete/Evaluate/Inst./Move/Next/Pick/Replace/Size/eXit:

Phase I - Boundary evaluation begins.

Phase II - Tessellation computation begins

Updating the Advanced Modelling Extension database.

The process takes a bit of time, but is much quicker than using SOLSEP.

SOLMOVE

The SOLMOVE command is very similar to the SOLCHP command in that only solids and regions can be edited. The SOLCHP command allows you to move a primitive from within a composite solid, while the SOLMOVE command allows you to move or rotate a solid or region as a whole. The SOLMOVE command allows you both to move and to rotate objects based on a motion description code. The options available are much more detailed than in the SOLCHP Move command.

Because the SOLMOVE command is dependent upon a description of the movement, a Motion Coordinate System or MCS icon is temporarily displayed to help you orient the objects. In this icon, *X* has one arrow, *Y* has two arrows, and *Z* has three arrows. The icon will display during every SOLMOVE command.

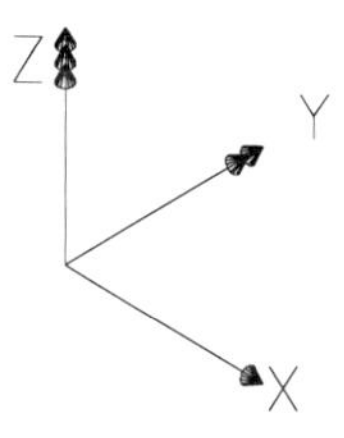

The SOLMOVE command options are as follows:

Command:**SOLMOVE**

Select objects: *(pick one or more objects)*

Select objects:↵

Redefining block XXXX

<Motion description>/?:**?**

The ? symbol displays the following list of available motions and descriptions.

```
align - with selected coordinate system
ae = aligns edge of objects with axes
af = aligns face of objects with axes
au = aligns objects and axes with current UCS
aw = aligns objects and axes with WCS
rotate - about a selected axis
rx = rotates objects around the X axis
ry = rotates objects around the Y axis
rz = rotates objects around the Z axis
move - or translate along a specific axis
tx = moves along the X axis
ty = moves along the Y axis
tz = moves along the Z axis
orient axes
e  = orients axes to align with the edge of a solid
f  = orients axes to align with the edge of a face
```

```
u  = orients axes to align with the current UCS
w  = orients axes to align with the current WCS
o  = returns the objects and axes to their original location
and orientation
```

Figure 35-7 illustrates several examples of the SOLMOVE command.

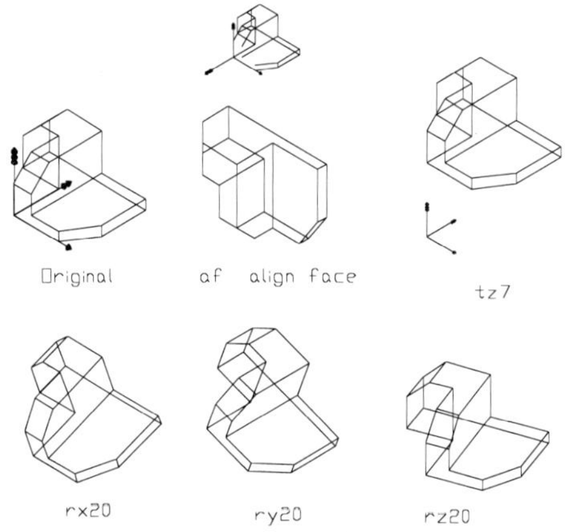

Figure 35-7. Examples of the SOLMOVE *command*

The *af* illustration resulted by choosing the top face of the existing solid and moving the solid relative to the axes.

The *r* options rotate the object without having to change the UCS.

The *t* option moves or translates the object the same way that the MOVE command does, assuming always that the base point is constant.

SOLEXT OR EXTRUSIONS

Often, objects are not as easy to create with solid primitives as they are with the use of PLINE. For complex profiles that have a uniform height, the SOLEXT command is perfect.

Using the SOLEXT command is much the same as changing a thickness, the difference is that the extruded shape is considered a solid.

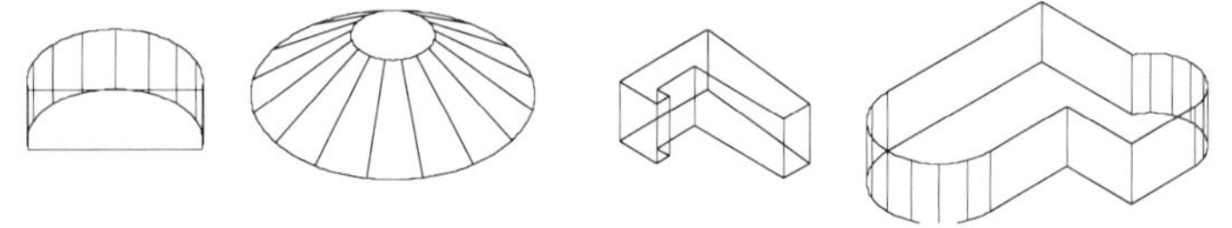

Figure 35-8 The SOLEXT *command*

You can extrude only pline, circle, ellipse, and region entities. If you want to extrude a line or an arc, use PEDIT to change it into a pline, then use SOLEXT. When extruding objects comprised of spline curves, you may exceed the maximum number of vertices, thus creating holes in the model. It is best to avoid this so far. The pline must contain at least three vertices, but not more than 500.

As in the SOLREV command, if the pline is not closed, the solid will be created as if there were a straight line between the endpoints of the pline. If any of the pline crosses or overlaps, the extrusion will not work.

The objects on the right cannot be extruded beacuse the lines overlap.

The command can also be used to taper the top end.

```
Command: SOLEXT
Select polylines and circles for extrusion: (pick object)
Select objects: ↵
Height of extrusion:1
Extrusion taper angle from Z<0>: ↵
Phase I - Boundary evaluation begins
Phase II - Tessellation computation begins
Updating the Advanced Modelling Extension database
```

AME CALCULATIONS

One of the main reasons for using AME is for ease of modelling in 3D. The other major advantage of this software is its ability to define and calculate the properties of solid models. The following commands are used to perform calculations on existing solids or regions.

SOLAREA *calculates the total surface area of one or more solids.*

SOLMASSP *calculates the mass properties of one or more objects.*

SOLMAT *allows the listing of mass properties using the actual material of an assigned solid.*

AME System Variables — SOLVAR

SOLAREAU *allows the user to change the current unit of measure for area calculations.*

SOLDECOMP *determines the direction in which the "rays" are fired in calculating mass.*

SOLMASS *determines the current unit of measure for calculating the mass of solid.*

SOLSUBDIV *controls the density of the "rays" or the subdivision level in a mass properties calculation.*

SOLMATCURR *stores the current material.*

SOLPAGELEN *SInce many of the calculation commands occupy several display pages, this allows the user to specify the length of page and the number of pages to be read at any one time.*

SOLVOLUME *determines unit of measure for volume calculations.*

SOLWDENS *determines the number of tessellation lines drawn on curved surfaces.*

USING VARIABLES

A common error when changing the variables is to change the wrong variable.

SOLAREAU *changes the current unit of measure for area.*

SOLMASS *changes the current unit of measure for mass.*

SOLVOLUME *changes the current unit of measure for volume.*

It is not necessary to change the SOLMASS variable just because you are using SOLMASSP.

SOLMASS

This AME system variable command allows you to change the current unit of measure for the SOLMASSP command. Like SOLAREAU, you simply enter the desired unit of measure. This will set the measurement unit to pounds as opposed to grams.

```
Command: SOLMASS
Mass units <gm>: lb
```

SOLMATCURR

This stores the name of the current default material. It is a read-only variable that simply informs you of the material. This default is given to all solids entered unless the SOLMAT has been changed.

SOLPAGELEN

The SOL*(id)* PAGE LEN*(gth)* variable will set the size of the page on which the SOLMASSP results are listed. The listing is in lines. This allows only 15 lines of text to be written on the screen at any one time.

```
Command: SOLPAGELEN
Length of text page <0 = continuous scroll>: 15
```

SOLVOLUME

This variable lets you set the current volume units.

```
Command: SOLVOLUME
Volume units<cu cm>: cu in
```

SOLAREA Command

The SOLAREA command calculates the enclosed area of a region by calculating the area of the outer loop and subtracting the area of the inner loop.

```
Command: SOLAREA
Select objects: (pick the object)
Select objects: ↵
Surface area of solids is 12183 sq cm
```

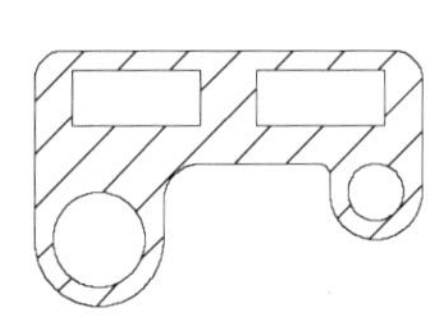

The area calculated is for the region illustrated above. The command first meshes the surface and then adds the area of the meshes. To obtain a more accurate area calculation, you can increase the wire density of the solid with the SOLWDENS variable.

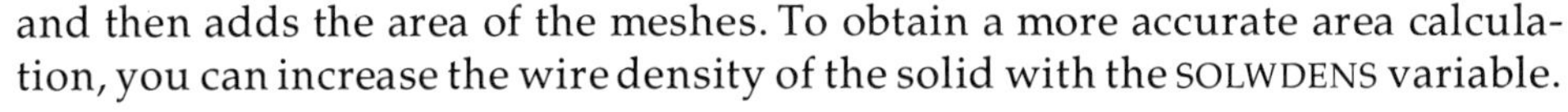

The calculation in this case is in square centimetres. To change the units of measurement we can use the SOLAREAU system variable.

```
Command: SOLAREAU
Area units<sq cm>: sq yd
```

This will change the unit of measurement to square yards rather than square centimetres.

The room on the right was created using PLINE. The SOLEXT command (see page 604) was used to extrude the pline.

The SOLAREA command may be used to calculate the surface area of the walls to calculate the number of coats of paint or finish material required.

SOLMAT Command

In order to calculate many of the mass properties of solid objects, the material must be specified. The SOLMAT command lets you set the default material. In addition, it maintains a list of materials already defined within the file. The command is as follows:

```
Command:SOLMAT
Change/Edit/<eXit>/LIst/LOad/New/Remove/SAve/SEt/?:
```

Where:

Change allows you to change the material of a solid.

Edit allows you to edit the current material.

eXit exits the SOLMAT command.

LIst displays the current definition of a material.

LOad lets you load a new material.

New allows you to define a new material.

Remove allows you to remove a material from the list.

SAve allows you to save the current material definition in an external file (so that it can be accessed in other drawings).

Set sets the current material.

? displays a listing of materials currently defined.

A default material file lists materials that may be used in any file (ACAD.MAT). Other materials can be added to this file or new .MAT files can be created to contain the materials that you use most often.

We will first look at the list of available materials, and then at the properties of bronze.

```
Command:SOLMAT
Change/Edit/<eXit>/LIst/LOad/New/Remove/SAve/SEt/?:LI

Material to list <MILD_STEEL>/?:
List materials from file acad:↵

Defined in drawing:
MILD_STEEL
Defined in file:

ALUMINUM
BRASS              –  Soft Yellow Brass
BRONZE             –  Soft Tin Bronze
COPPER
GLASS
HSLA_STL           – High Strength Low Alloy Steel
LEAD
MILD_STEEL
NICU               – Monel 400
STAINLES_STEEL     – Austenic Stainless Steel

Material to list <MILD_STEEL>?:BRONZE

Material: Bronze
```

```
Soft Tin Bronze
Density:                              8874 kg/cu_m
Young's module:                       109.6 GN/sq_m
Poisson's Ratio                      0.335
Yield strength:                        128 MN/sq_m
Ultimate strength:                     275 MN/sq_m
Thermal conductivity:                   62
Linear expansion coefficient:          18.3 alpha/1e6
Specific heat                        0.436 kJ/(kg deg_C)
```

This should give you an idea of how the SOLMAT command works. If you want to add your own new materials, use the New option. To make these accessible to other files, add them to the ACAD.MAT file. Consult the AME reference manual for assistance.

SOLMASSP Command

This is probably one of the biggest advantages of the AME package. The SOLMASSP command calculates the mass properties of an object and lets you write this data to a selected file.

We will take two examples; a region and a solid.

Using an airfoil as region example, we will use SOLMASSP.

Command: **SOLMASSP**

Select objects: *(pick the region)*

Select objects: ↵

```
----------Regions-----------

area:        3.542 sq cm
perimeter:   9.642 cm

Bounding box:          X: 13.2    -    17.51   cm
                       Y:  4.91   -    6.151   cm
Centroid:              X: 15.62   cm
                       Y:  5.467  cm
Moments of inertia:    X:  106.2 sq cm sq cm
                       Y:  868.4 sq cm sq cm
Products of inertia:  XY:   302.6 sq cm sq cm
Radii of gyration:     X:  5.475 cm
                       Y:  15.66 cm
Principal moments (sq cm sq cm) and X-Y directions around cen-
troid
                       I:  0.2903 about (0.9985 -0.05561)
                       J:  4.423  about (0.05561 -0.9985)

Write to a file <N>:
```

You will notice that the responses are in cm. Change the SOLAREAU to sq in and you will get the following:

Command: **SOLMASSP**

Select objects: *(pick the region)*

Select objects: ↵

```
————————-Regions———————-
area:        0.5489 sq in
perimeter:   1.494 in
```

A point will be created at the centroid.

The SOLMASSP command can be used on both regions and solids. In the following exercise we will take the mechanical exercise from the last chapter and calculate its mass properties.

Command: **SOLMASSP**

Select objects: *(pick the solid)*

Select objects: ↵

```
Ray projection along X axis, level of subdivision - 3

Mass:        435.7 gm
Volume:      55.44 cu cm (Err 7.018)

Bounding box:  X:-17.75  —  112.5 cm
               Y: 28.75  —  36.25 cm
               Z: 5.204e-16 — 6.5 cm

Centroid:      X: -14.95 cm (Err:1.8411)
               Y: -32.09 cm (Err:4.032)
               Z: 1.846 cm (Err:0.3365)

Moments of inertia:  X: 4.522e+05 gm sq cm (Err:56635)
                     Y: 1.006e+05 gm sq cm (Err:11890)
                     Z: 5.478e+05 gm sq cm (Err:68107)
Products of inertia: XY: -2.089e+05 gm sq cm (Err:25551)
                     YZ: 26007 gm sq cm (Err:4805)
                     ZX: -12288 gm sq cm (Err:2207
Radii of gyration:   X:  32.22 cm
                     Y:  15.2 cm
                     Z:  35.46 cm
Principal moments (gm sq cm) and X-Y-Z directions about cen-
troid
                     I:  1585 along [0.4125 -0.5022 -0.76011]
                     J:  2284 along [0.7508 -0.2852 0.5958]
                     K:  1939 along [-0.516 -0.8164 0.2594]
Write to a file <N>:
```

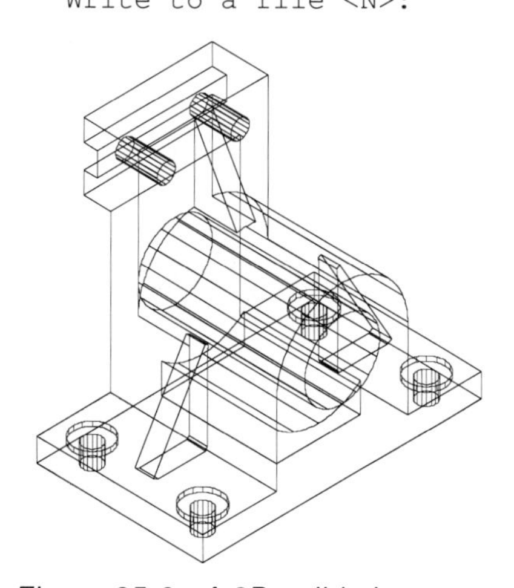

Figure 35-9. A 3D solid shape

AutoCAD's mass properties and calculation software are intended to assist those who need this information. If you have a limited knowledge of how mass properties are used, this program is not going to help you.

While this software makes the calculation process much simpler, it does not have the ability to tell you if your information is logical or not. The ease of calculation may give a false sense of security to those who do not know what is logical and what is not.

It is suggested that, the first few times you use this package in industry, you double check the results with someone who knows the applications of mass properties. The results you get will be accurate with regard to what you have entered, but you may have entered data that is not practical. The results could be costly, if not dangerous.

ACCURACY OF SOLID MODEL CALCULATIONS

The volume calculations of solids is an approximation. AutoCAD calculates the mass properties with a ray classification technique. Rays are fired at the solid model and then classified as to whether they intersect or not. The accuracy of SOLMASSP is dependent on the SOLDECOMP (SOL*(id)* DECOMP*(osition)* in ray firing) and SOLSUBDIV (SOL*(id)* SUBDIV*(ision)* ray level) variables.

The SOLDECOMP variable determines the direction in which the rays are fired. This direction is called the decomposition direction. The SOLSUBDIV variable determines the density of the rays and is known as the subdivision level. Both of these variables are extremely important with regard to the accuracy of the final calculations.

When calculating volumes, AutoCAD creates a box around the solid being analysed at the smallest possible distance away from the solid. The subdivision level determines the number of times the box enclosing the solid is subdivided. It is subdivided according to the following formula, where 1 is the subdivision level.

$$(2^{1})^{2}$$

The number of details on a model will determine the subdivision level needed to maintain accuracy. As the number of details increases, you will need to increase the subdivision level or SOLSUBDIV to maintain accuracy.

The decomposition direction is also important in determining the exact size of the model, in that it will determine the direction in which the rays are fired. You can optimize the subdivision by choosing a decomposition direction that fires rays perpendicular to curved surfaces. X, Y, and Z axes can be changed relative to the current UCS.

The rays are fired at the solid in a random fashion, thus some error is associated with the calculations. Choose a decomposition direction that is parallel to the UCS to achieve the highest degree of accuracy. Increasing the subdivision level will also improve accuracy.

Exercise A35

In this exercise we will design a balcony, make it solid, calculate the weight, mass, volume, etc., then calculate the size of the required supporting beams.

This is a layout of a basic 5′ x 8′ balcony. This design is quite simple; you are welcome to make it more complex.

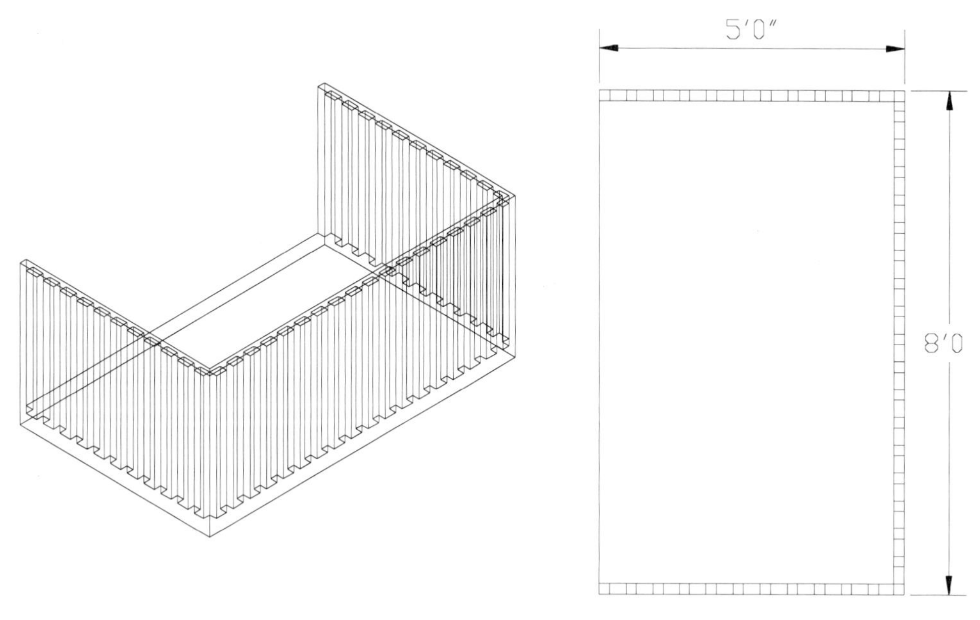

Be sure your railings comply with code requirements.

Once designed, use SOLUNION to create one solid balcony.

Now, change your SOLAREAU, SOLMASS, and SOLVOLUME variables to a unit of measure that is easy to work with and generate your SOLMASSP.

With the information provided, design the support for the balcony.

When complete, make a note of all the mass properties of your new balcony.

Now calculate the area of the balcony to see how much paint and sealer you will require.

This may not seem to be an important matter on one single balcony, but if there are 200 in an apartment complex, this could add up to a lot of paint.

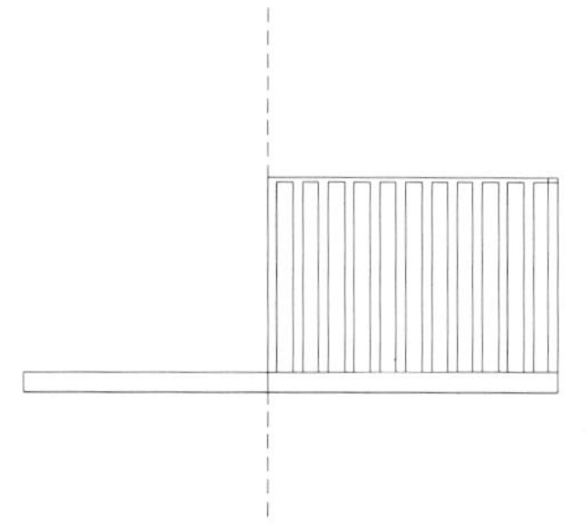

Exercise M35

This part will give you more practice on creating composite solids as well as using the SOLEXT function which will make some of the design a lot easier.

All fillets and rounds should be at two units.

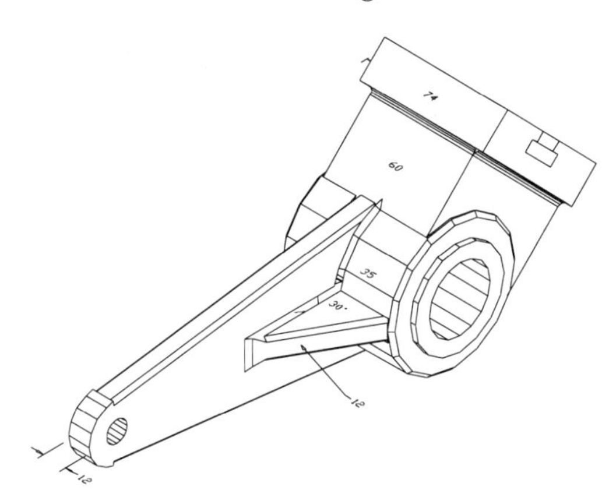

The first step is to draw the part as shown in these views.

Once complete, use SOLUNION and SOLSUB to create a composite of the part.

Then change the SOLMASS and SOLVOLUME to the units you prefer to work with.

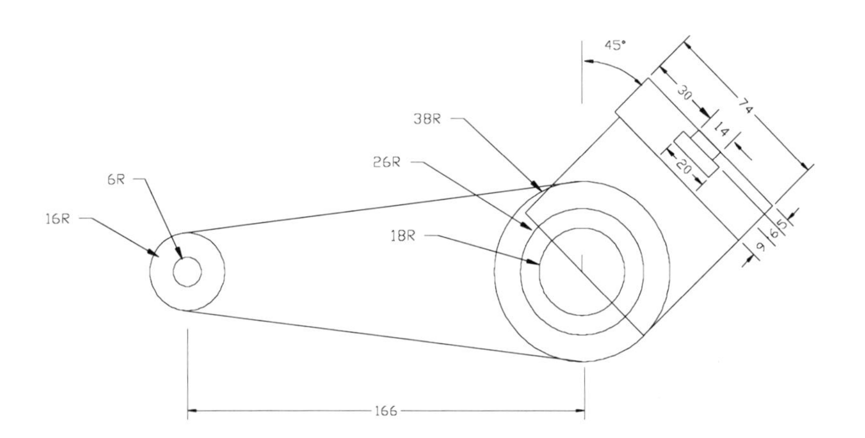

Once completed, use SOLMASSP to calculate the mass properties of the part. Is this an efficient design?

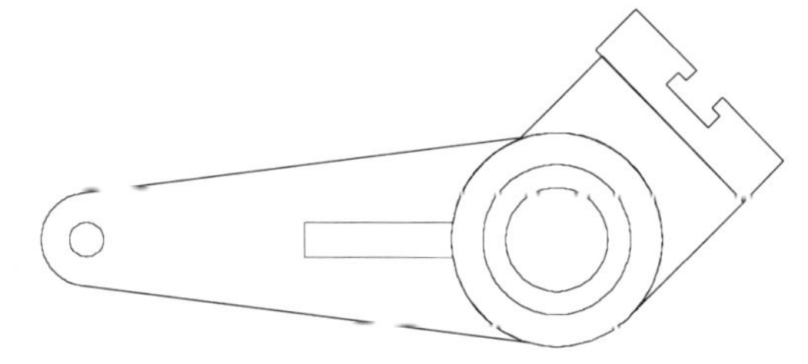

Exercise C35

This bridge will give you an idea of how to use SOLEXT and provide practice at using the commands you already know.

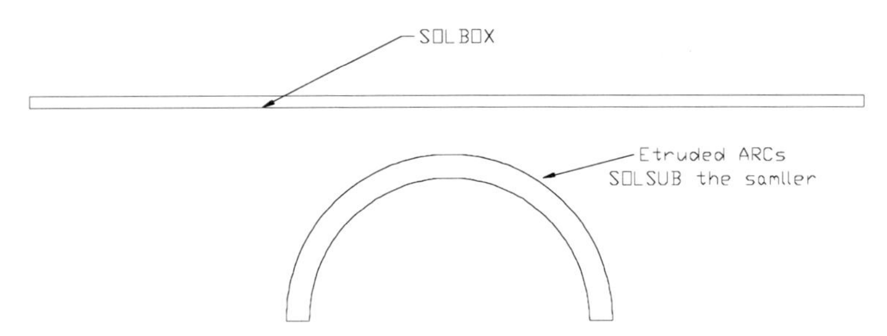

Determine the size of the bridge you want and the area you want to leave open with the arc. Use SOLEXT to create the arc.

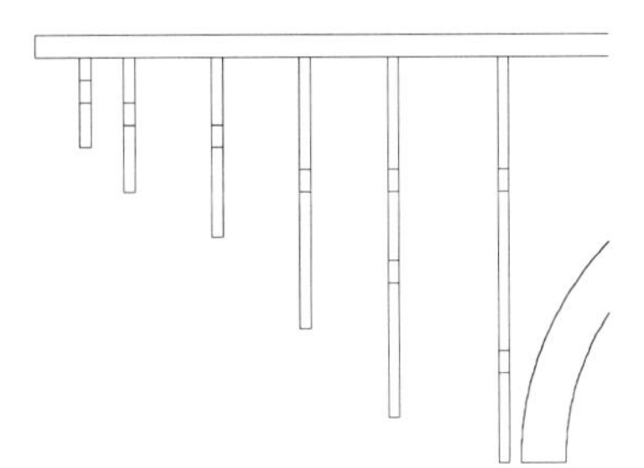

Now start putting in the structure of the bridge. Make sure the supports are evenly spaced and of sufficient height. You can enter one half of the support and then use MIRROR.

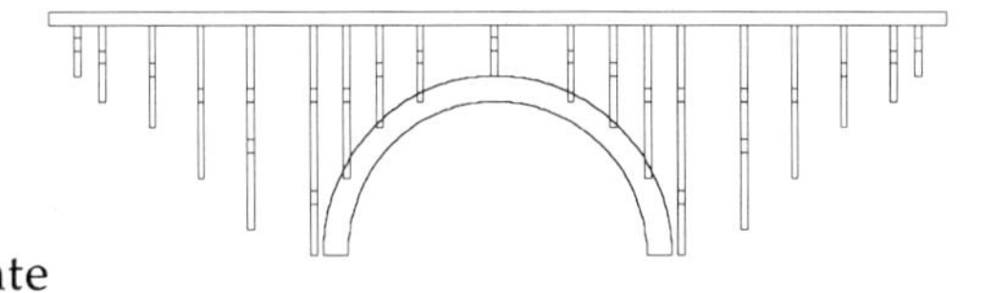

Once the bridge has been designed, change the SOLAREAU, SOLMASS, and SOLVOLUME variables to reasonable units. Now use SOLMASSP to calculate the volume, weight, and moments of inertia of the bridge.

You can also use the SOLAREA command to calculate the total area of the bridge. This can be important when calculating exposed surface for environmental impact, salt spray damage, or amount of paint required.

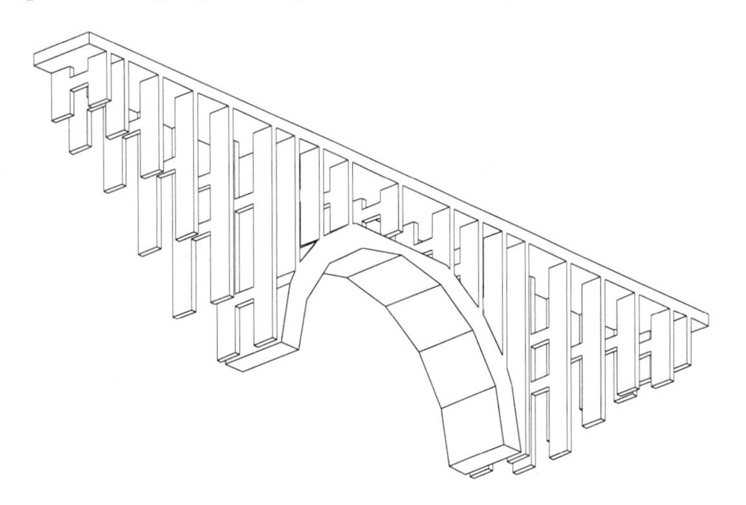

Use MESH, DVIEW Camera, and HIDE to display a view of the structure of the bridge from the bottom.

Challenger 35

The mass properties calculations are essential in calculating the centroid of objects suspended in air. In this example, we have a very simple chair lift used at skiing resorts. Other examples are in cable cars, helicopters, and even birdfeeders.

Design a ski-chair. Remember that the chair must be suspended at an angle from the support cable because the cable must be able to move.

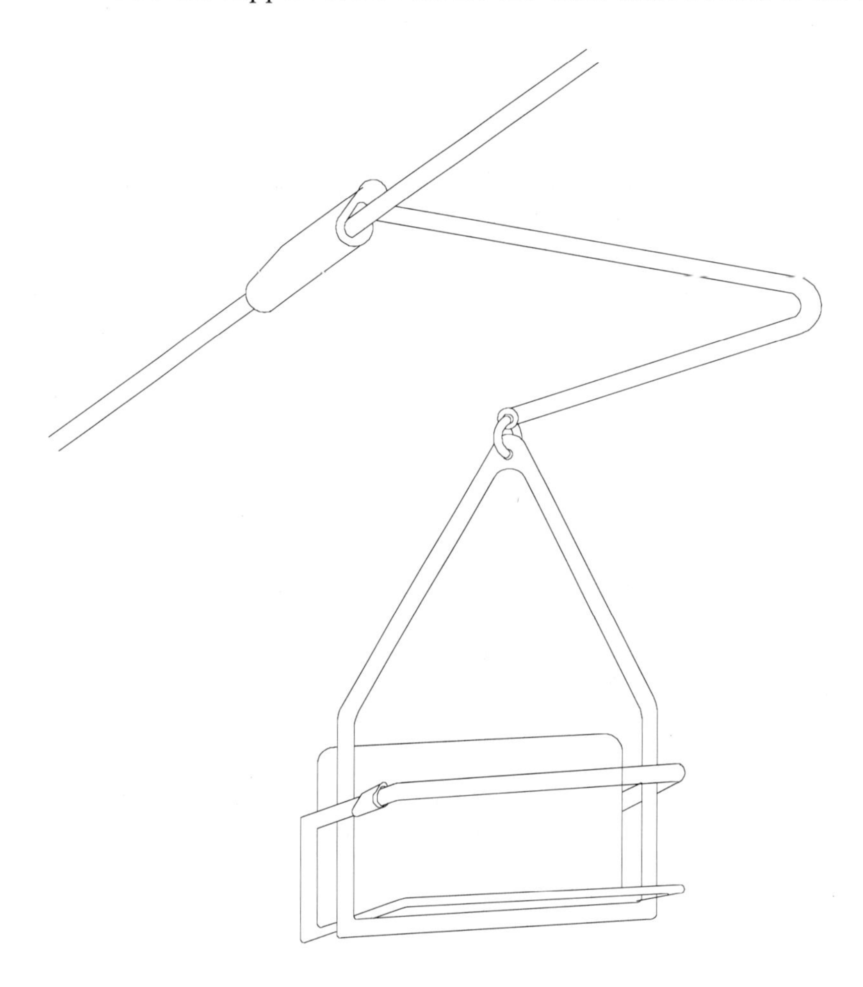

Once complete, change your variables so that the calculation units are logical.

Then use SOLMASSP to calculate the weight and volume of the chair. Remember, if these are not logical, i.e., the centroid is not under the cable, it will not work.

DIMENSIONING 3D PARTS

Upon completion of this chapter, the student should be able to:

1. Set the UCS for dimensioning a 3D part
2. Use the Oblique option for associative dimensions
3. Change the dimension variables and settings for 3D dimensioning.

3D DIMENSIONING

There are two ways of creating 3D dimensions: the first is simply to align the UCS to the plane on which you want your dimensions; the second is to use blocks for arrowheads at the correct degrees and create a text font that has the correct obliquing angle for an "isometric view" done in 2D, and then use the Oblique option under the Dimensions menu.

On a true 3D object, changing the UCS is often the simplest method.

Dimensioning by Aligning the UCS

There are several advantages for using this method of 3D dimensioning over the following method:

- it is available on all releases after 9, while oblique dimensions are only available on Release 11 and after
- the UPD*(ate)* command will not offer as many surprises if you need to update a text font
- for many people, it takes less time to set up a UCS than to create blocks and deal with the dreaded dimension variables.

This method for creating isometric dimensions is quite simple. In this simple camera box, the shutter release button is created using 3DFACE.

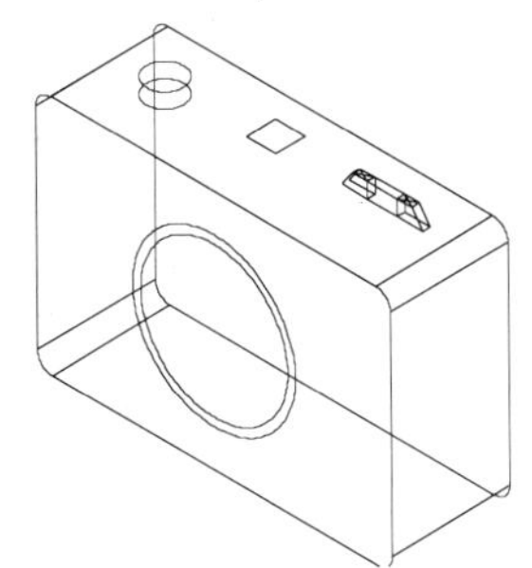

Figure 36-1. Use 3DFACE to create shutter release button

Then it is dimensioned in the isometric view by changing the UCS to the plane on which the dimensions are to appear.

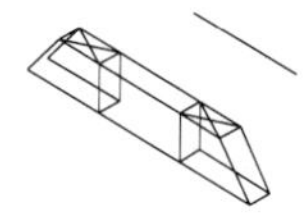

Change the UCS using 3POINT and use END as an osnap on the 3D faces to make sure that you have the correct plane.

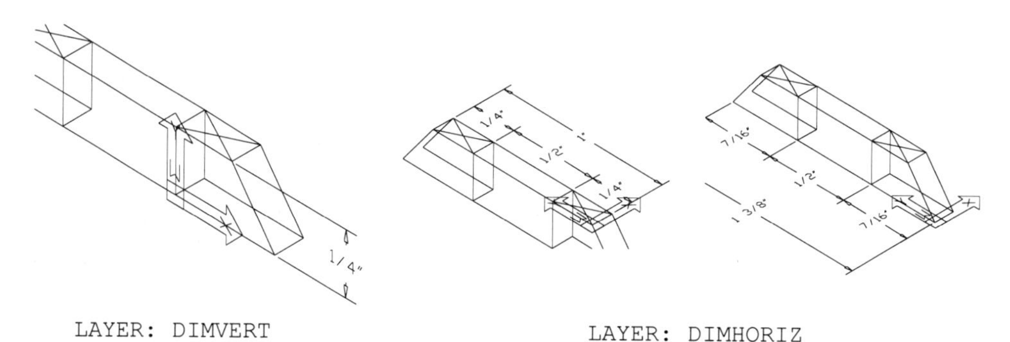

In each case, the UCS has been changed to the plane shown by the UCS icon. The dimension text, arrowhead, lines, and all related data will line up according to the UCS plane. This method is also useful when your view is not exactly 30 degrees. In the following method, you would have to adjust the blocks or the text to fit slightly off-centre views.

It is a good idea to create separate layers for each plane or orientation of dimensions.

Dimensioning by Changing the Dimension Variables

This method of isometric dimensioning is available in Release 11 and further releases that have the OBLIQUE associative dimension command.

The trick to this method of dimensioning is to change your SNAP to Style Isometric. The SNAP must be on in the view that you want to dimension; i.e., if you are dimensioning the top of a model, the SNAP must be aligned to this view.

The lines you draw will thus snap to a 30- or 150-degree angle.

```
Command:SNAP
Snap spacing or ON/OFF/Aspect/Rotate/Style<1.5>:S
<Standard>/Isometric:I
Vertical Spacing <1.5>:
```

Then change the obliquing angle of the dimension text that you use to fit this angle. Make sure that you have DIMBLK set and your text STYLE with the correct obliqued angle set, and just dimension as usual. You will, of course, need to change the STYLE and DIMBLK for each orientation.

While putting in the dimension, your text may have the wrong slant. You need to define and name two text styles with 30-degree and -30-degree obliquing angles. If you are using a prototype drawing, these can be defined and then left with the drawing. The first one will be used with an arrowhead that slants to the left. The second can be used with an arrowhead that slants to the right.

If your arrowheads, meant for orthographic view, do not have the sloped backs needed for isometric drawings, these are easy to create. To define your arrowheads, create a solid or use three lines that take up the area defined by 0,0, -0.9,0.15, and -1.0915,-0.182. Once you have created either the lines or the solid, make a block or even a wblock for it. Now mirror the first one over and use it for another block or wblock.

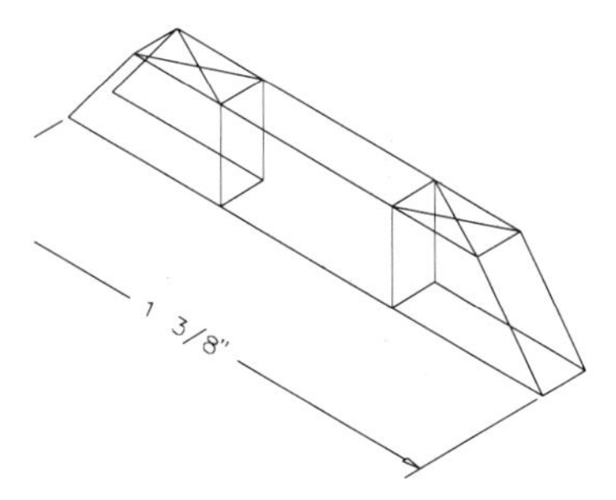

Figure 36-2. A dimension without aligned text

Once you have both the text and the arrowhead blocks created, you simply need to set your text to the desired font (using a 30- or -30-degree obliquing angle) and change the DIMBLK variable for the desired arrowhead block.

Now dimension the drawing using Rotate with the dimension line set to 30 degrees. Next use the OBLIQUE command to change the angle of the extension lines to 150 degrees, and it should look like the illustration of Figure 36-3.

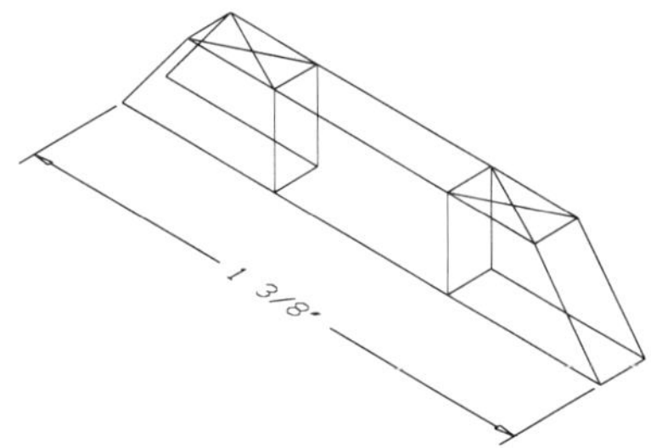

Figure 36-3. Aligning the text to the dimensions

There are many LISP routines that will make the dimensioning of such parts easier as well. If you find these options useful, consider using LISP to automate the process you have just completed because it takes time to exit DIM to change text fonts and also to change your DIMBLK. Also consider these for a prototype drawing.

In the following exercise, practise on a project that you completed earlier. Line up your UCS with the plane on which you want the dimensions and create the dimensions.

Now try a second exercise changing the dimension variables. Determine which method you prefer.

Exercises All

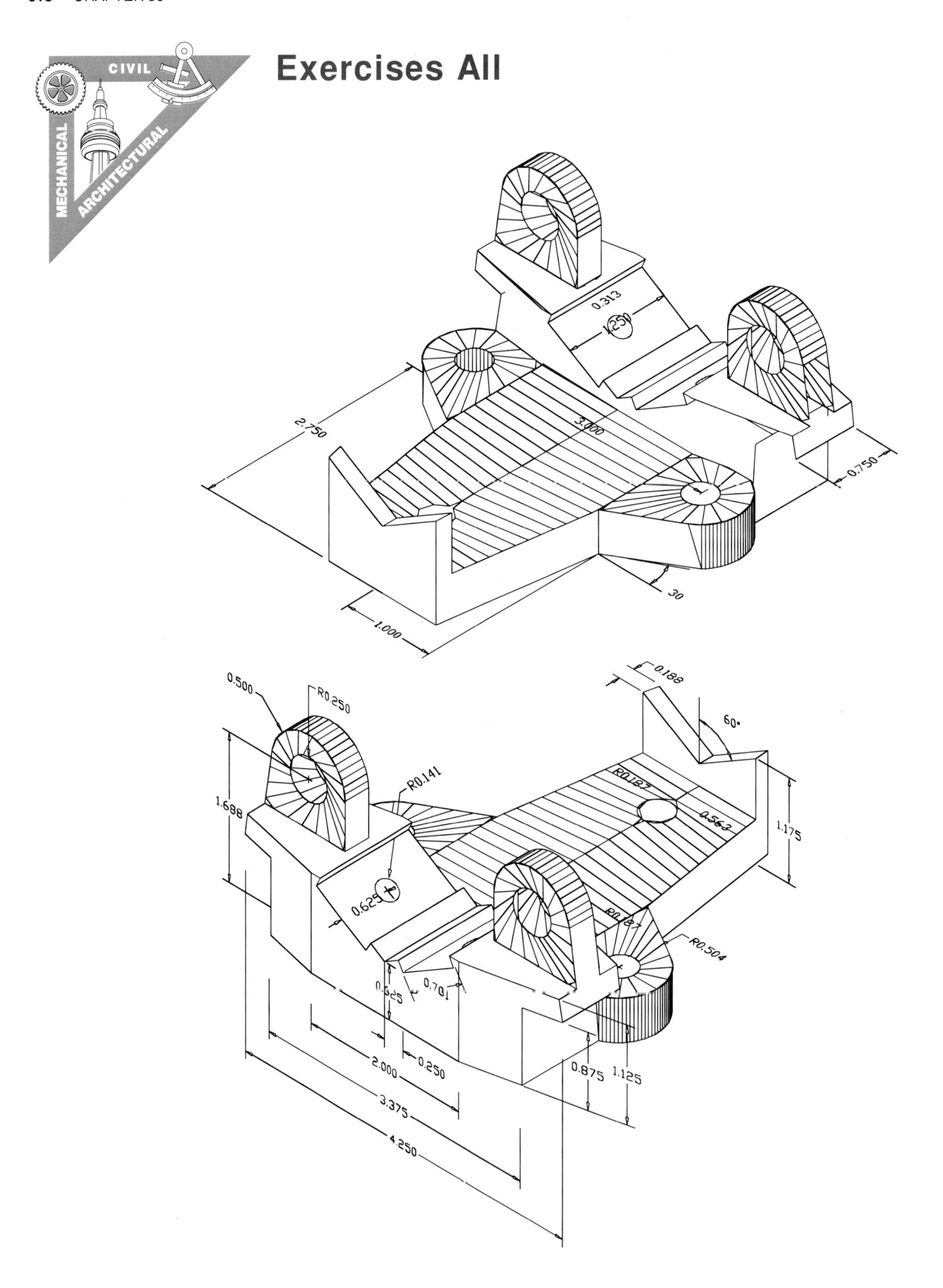

FINAL TEST AND PROJECTS

The second half of this book has basically presented two different AutoCAD-based subjects; 3D modelling and engineering analysis. The final projects presented in this chapter incorporate both these aspects with a 3D model accompanied by documentation on the project itself. If you are not using AME, simply create the 3D models.

If you have been working through the projects as outlined, you should have no trouble completing the final projects. It may be a good idea to start the final project six or seven weeks before the end of term so that you will have adequate time to finish, plot, and present it.

There are, again, three projects presented:

1. Mechanical
2. Architectural
3. Civil

As a college instructor, it is always interesting to follow graduating students through their various careers to see, first, if what you are trying to teach is of any value to the student upon graduation, and, secondly, where life picks up after schooling has been completed. I am always astounded to see students that were headed towards brilliant careers in residential house design doing work on piping layouts and exhaust fan moulds, and to see the opposite — mechanically trained students doing presentation drawings for architectural purposes.

Whether you are trained as a technologist, a technician, an engineer, or an architect, it is always a good idea to learn how to read drawings produced by other disciplines. The more proficient you are with AutoCAD or any other CAD package, the more marketable your skills will be upon graduation. If the building industry is in a slump, there is nothing wrong with taking a job in a different area until the market turns around.

The examples presented in this book should give you an introduction to how to present information through AutoCAD in three different disciplines. You are well advised to learn some design work in all the areas presented. When you have completed one of the projects illustrated, go on to another if you have the time. Any effort you put into using the AutoCAD software, regardless of the application, will increase your skill as a CAD designer. Do not forget to keep a backup.

The next few pages will offer you 100 questions on the third 12 chapters of this book. Your instructor may offer you these or similar questions as a final exam. If you are not required to write a final exam, these questions are nonetheless useful to do so that you have some idea of how much you understand.

FINAL TEST

Choose the answer that is most correct.

1. An ISOPLANE
   a) creates a plane in 3D for you to work on
   b) creates a 2D plane that looks like a 3D plane
   c) creates a UCS in 3D

2. Changing the ISOPLANE
   a) can be useful for making "circles" on oblique surfaces
   b) can be useful for placing text on an oblique surface
   c) can be useful for creating cylinders

3. How many areas can the screen be divided into?
   a) 4
   b) 12
   c) 16
   d) no limit

4. What command do you use to divide the screen into various tiled viewports?
   a) VPORTS
   b) VPOINT
   c) VIEWRES
   d) MAKEVIEW

5. What does Restore mean in the above command?
   a) restores a named view
   b) restores a named screen layout
   c) restores the previous screen

6. What is the Right-hand Rule?
   a) always use your right hand on the mouse
   b) if *X* is your index finger and *Y* is your middle finger, *Z* will be perpendicular to them
   c) if your thumb is *X* and your fully extended index finger is *Y*, then your middle finger pointed straight out will be positive *Z*

7. What does the middle circle stand for in the globe icon?
   a) the equator
   b) the centre of the screen
   c) Z 0

8. How do you find the globe icon?
   a) use the space bar after the VPOINT command
   b) use the pull-down menu for set viewports
   c) both of the above

9. Can you use polar coordinates in an isometric view?
   a) no
   b) yes
   c) sometimes

10. On what plane will a point show up if you pick it in the isometric view?
    a) on the Z 0 plane of the World Coordinate System
    b) on the Z 0 plane of the UCS
    c) line-of-sight onto the X plane

11. Why is OSNAP important in the isometric view?
a) because you cannot enter coordinates in 3D
b) because you cannot pick points in 3D space in iso views
c) because existing geometry is readily accessible

12. What command do you use to extrude an existing object?
a) THICKNESS
b) SETVAR
c) CHANGE

13. What command do you use to change the Z coordinate of an existing object?
a) MOVE
b) CLIP
c) CHPROP
d) a and b
e) a and c

14. If you have extruded a line to 4 units, can you break a section out of the bottom of the image (Z 0) but keep the top (Z 4) intact?
a) no
b) yes

15. What command do you use to make hidden lines a different colour in a plot?
a) LAYER HIDDENXXX
b) PLOT HIDDENNAME
c) HIDEPLOT

16. Will a REDRAW update your screen after HIDE?
a) yes
b) no

17. What can you do to make sure your next five items will be on the Z depth of Z 5?
a) set the THICKNESS
b) set the ELEVATION
c) change your UCS to X5

18. Why can a circle not be placed on an X-Z plane?
a) it must be normal to the UCS Z 0 plane
b) it must be placed on an ISOPLANE
c) it must be on a Y-Z plane

19. How do you change the UCS from the World Coordinate System orientation to the Y-Z plane?
a) rotate around X
b) rotate around Y
c) rotate around Z

20. What command do you use to get back to the World Coordinate System?
a) UCS U
b) UCS W
c) UCS P

21. What does the broken-pencil icon mean?
    a) the X-Y plane is not visible within that viewport
    b) the X-Z plane is active
    c) the UCS has been changed

22. If you change the X option of the UCS command to 90 degrees, what plane is it that you want to have the UCS on?
    a) X-Z
    b) X-Y
    c) Y-Z

23. How many times can you change the UCS before saving?
    a) only 8
    b) 16
    c) unlimited

24. What does the + symbol mean in the bottom of the UCS icon?
    a) you are looking at the top of the object
    b) you are looking at the bottom of the object
    c) you have the icon on the origin of the UCS

25. What does the UCS option 3point do?
    a) lets you orient the UCS relative to 3 points
    b) lets you orient the UCS relative to 1 point and an origin
    c) lets you orient the UCS using OSNAP

26. What does the term "toggle" mean?
    a) this turns an item off
    b) this turns a function on or off
    c) this turns the grid off

27. What does the *E* option stand for in the UCS command?
    a) Exit
    b) Enter
    c) Entity

28. What does the *P* option stand for in the UCS command?
    a) Pline
    b) Previous
    c) Partial

29. What does the response "lines are collinear" mean?
    a) you have chosen two points along the same line
    b) you have described a line that already exists
    c) you have entered a null code
    d) all of the above

30. Of what use is the UCS dialogue box?
    a) saves stored viewports
    b) saves stored orientations of the UCS
    c) helps access stored UCSs
    d) all of the above

31. If you are working in the isometric view and you use the STRETCH command, does it stretch relative to the UCS or line-of-sight in the view?
    a) relative to the line-of-sight
    b) relative to the World coordinates
    c) relative to the UCS
    d) all of the above

32. Can you use 3DFACE on a curved surface?
a) yes, if you have exploded it
b) yes, if you have stored it
c) no

33. Can you use 3DFACE on a pline?
a) yes, as long as there are no curves
b) yes, as long as you use PEDIT
c) no

34. What is 3DFACE used for?
a) creating planes for describing 3D objects
b) creating planes for viewing
c) creating obliquing planes
d) all of the above

35. How do you indicate that you want to enter an X filter?
a) .X
b) @.x
c) x of

36. Can you enter both an X and a Y filter?
a) yes
b) no

37. What happens to Z when you have entered filters for both X and Y?
a) Z needs to be specified
b) Z remains at 0
c) Z takes the current Z depth

38. What command do you use to make lines that were hidden with HIDE reappear?
a) REGEN
b) REDRAW
c) ZOOM A
d) all of the above may work

39. What happens if you plot a view in which lines have been hidden with the HIDE command?
a) the lines are hidden on the plot
b) the lines are shown in a different colour
c) the lines are not hidden on the plot

40. What happens if you print a view in which you have used HIDE?
a) the lines are hidden on the printout
b) the lines are shown in a different colour
c) the lines are not hidden on the printout

41. What is model space?
a) the default space in AutoCAD
b) the space used for modelling
c) the space many viewports have access to
d) all of the above

42. What command do you use to get to paper space?
a) TILESPACE
b) TILECHANGE
c) TILEMODE

43. What is paper space for?
a) it is a facility for hiding lines in plots
b) it is a 2D layout facility
c) it is for creating 3D parts
d) all of the above

44. Does a file using paper space take up much more room on the disk?
a) it depends on the file
b) always takes more room
c) never takes more room

45. What does the *D* stand for in DVIEW?
a) Drawing
b) Dynamic
c) Delta

46. What does a Target do?
a) positions the viewer relative to the object
b) positions the objects relative to the viewer
c) changes the size of the view file

47. How do you change the orientation of an object for viewing?
a) DVIEW Points
b) DVIEW Camera
c) PAN
d) all of the above

48. How do you get a perspective view?
a) DVIEW PE
b) DVIEW D
c) DVIEW I

49. Why can you not change the ZOOM if you have created a perspective view?
a) the objects have been modified so that the vector files are no longer accessible for magnification
b) the objects have been expanded to fit the screen
c) the objects are not accessible by a simple magnification process because they have been edited

50. What do the letters *PA* stand for in the DVIEW option?
a) Point Advance
b) PAn
c) Point Access

51. What effect does Twist have on the view?
a) rotates the view relative to the UCS Z
b) rotates the view relative to the screen
c) rotates the objects like a ROTATE command

52. If you have made a total mess of your view, how do you get back to where you were in the DVIEW command?
a) U
b) DVIEW Undo
c) DVIEW Erase
d) all of the above

53. How does the Points option in DVIEW work?
a) lets you set the Target and Camera positions
b) gives two points which will act as the *X* and *Y* of your screen
c) lets you rotate the view along the X-Y plane and from the X-Y plane

54. What is the difference between Twist and ROTATE?
a) Twist is a display function, whereas Rotate moves the objects relative to the origin
b) no difference
c) Rotate is counter-clockwise and Twist is clockwise

55. How do you place dimensions on a surface that is not perpendicular to the viewer in a 3D model?
a) change the view with DVIEW
b) change the UCS
c) use the dimensional variables

56. What is VPLAYER?
a) the layer control within a viewport in PSPACE
b) the layer accessed in the Hideplot option
c) the layer used for viewing objects
d) all of the above

57. What advantage does MVIEW provide?
a) it allows for multiple viewports to be viewed
b) it allows for overlapping of viewports
c) it allows for compiling of drawings
d) all of the above

58. What is the difference between Hideplot and HIDE?
a) HIDE is used within a view and Hideplot is used within a viewport
b) HIDE is used to show hidden lines on a view and Hideplot is used to show hidden lines on a drawing
c) HIDE is only for printouts where Hideplot is used for both plots and printouts

59. What does the term TILEMODE mean?
a) a mode that turns your screen off
b) the ability to plot hidden lines in a different colour
c) the partitioning of your screen for 2D layout or 2D and 3D design
d) enables paper space

60. What does the option Restore do in the MVIEW command?
a) restores a saved drawing
b) restores a saved configuration of viewports
c) restores a saved orientation of DVIEW commands

61. What does Vpvisdflt mean?
a) Viewport visible display fit
b) Viewport visibility default
c) View parity display default

62. How can you create a surface that curves?
a) REVSURF
b) RULESURF
c) THICKNESS
d) all of the above

63. Which surface is generated through two existing objects?
   a) REVSURF
   b) RULESURF
   c) THICKNESS
   d) all of the above

64. What command uses a central axis?
   a) REVSURF
   b) RULESURF
   c) THICKNESS
   d) all of the above

65. How do you change the number of segments on a surface?
   a) TABSURF1
   b) SURFTAB1
   c) VIEWRES
   d) all of the above

66. What do you need for a tabulated surface?
   a) a path curve and a direction vector
   b) a pline and a line
   c) an axis and a path curve

67. When will you get the response "Entity not usable as rotation axis" in the REVSURF command?
   a) when the object used as an axis is not on the same Z depth as the path curve
   b) when the axis is an arc
   c) when the axis is not a pline

68. If you have a line that you want to act as one rail of a surface, and an arc and a line as the other rail of a surface, how do you do it?
   a) make the arc a closed entity
   b) make the line and arc one object using PEDIT
   c) make the line a pline

69. How many edges can you have in an EDGESURF command?
   a) 4
   b) 8
   c) any multiple of 4
   d) no limit

70. How many vectors can you have in a 3D mesh?
   a) maximum 16
   b) maximum 32
   c) no limit

71. Which surface would you use to create a car dashboard?
   a) REVSURF
   b) RULESURF
   c) 3DMESH

72. What is the similarity between 3DFACE and the other surfaces?
   a) they all hide objects behind them in HIDE
   b) they all are composed of a minimum of two linear elements
   c) they all have a maximum of 16 edges
   d) all of the above

73. What happens if you give a negative number for the included angle in the REVSURF command?
a) the revolved surface will be clockwise instead of counter-clockwise
b) REVSURF will not work
c) the revolved surface will have a the negative Z value

74. Why do you need to surface an object to use AutoShade?
a) the object must be accepted as a solid
b) the system needs to determine the inside and outside of the objects
c) the object must have a volume
d) all of the above
e) none of the above

75. What is the advantage of using 3D Objects?
a) to simplify the design process
b) to cut down on the number of objects on the screen
c) to create polynomial surfaces

76. How can you define your own 3D objects and have them available?
a) make them into blocks
b) create LISP routines for the shapes you need
c) create script files
d) any of the above

77. How many objects are there in a completed sphere using the 3D Objects routine?
a) 1
b) 2
c) 3

78. How does SURFTAB1 affect the 3D Object CONE command?
a) it tabulates the surface along the cone's height
b) it changes the display of the cone
c) there is no effect

79. How many faces can you have in a PFACE command?
a) any multiple of 2
b) any number
c) any multiple of 4

80. What is the quickest way to create a surfaced item that is 4 inches long, 3 inches high, and 2 inches wide, all with straight lines?
a) BOX
b) SOLBOX
c) PFACE

81. What is the secret to inserting 3D models?
a) know your axes and origin
b) change your UCS
c) record the scale of the object
d) all of the above

82. How many models can you merge?
a) as many as your RAM can take
b) as many as your drive or directory can take
c) as many as the .$a file can hold
d) as many as the Xrefs can support

83. Which of the following are affected by the size of your RAM?
  a) AME
  b) SURFTAB
  c) PSPACE
  d) all of the above

84. What do you need from Autodesk or your vendor in order to access AME?
  a) 4MB of RAM
  b) an authorization code
  c) a reference manual

85. Is the DISH command available as a primitive in AME?
  a) yes
  b) no

86. Which command can you use to change a pline into a solid?
  a) SOLEXT
  b) SOLIDIFY
  c) both of the above

87. If you were trying to add half of a sphere to a solid, how would you do it?
  a) SOLSPHERE plus UNION
  b) SOLREV plus UNION
  c) SOLEXT plus UNION

88. Which of the following calculates a centroid in a solid or region?
  a) SOLAREA
  b) SOLMASS
  c) SOLMASSP

89. Why should you avoid extruding spline curves in SOLEXT?
  a) there is a limit to the number of vertices the command can accept
  b) you cannot extrude a curved shape
  c) you cannot extrude a pline

90. What command would you use to remove the volume of a solid cylinder from a solid box?
  a) SOLSEP
  b) SOLSUB
  c) SOLCHP
  d) all of the above

91. What command will let you reposition a solid?
  a) MOVE
  b) SOLMOVE
  c) ROTATE
  d) all of the above

92. Can you break a solid?
  a) no
  b) yes

93. Can you change the colour of a solid?
  a) no
  b) yes

94. Can a region be considered a composite?
  a) no
  b) yes

95. How can you create a hidden solid in a plot?
a) make it a mesh and use HIDE
b) make it a mesh and use Hideplot
c) use PSPACE and Hideplot

96. How can you create a 3D donut shape?
a) use SOLTORUS
b) use SOLDONUT
c) use SOLSPHERE

97. What is the default setting for Z on a region?
a) non-specified
b) current UCS
c) WCS Z 0

98. What operation can you not perform with a pline that has a thickness?
a) you cannot use SOLEXT
b) SOLHPAT will not work
c) you lose the thickness

99. When will you get the response "Lines Intersect" when you try SOLREV on a pline?
a) when the axis is not as long as the path curve
b) when the pline is closed
c) when the direct line from the open ends of the pline intersects the axis of rotation

100. What does the SOLSEP command do?
a) separates the solid into primitives
b) retraces the steps of the CSG tree
c) changes the solid to a mesh

Architecture Final Project

Use the 3D commands and the AME commands to design the foyer of a large public building. The foundations for the building should be adequate to support the building, and the interior of the foyer should be a minimum of two storeys in height.

When designing, make maximum use of layers so that final calculations can be made for volumes of different materials and mass properties calculations can be made on all structural elements.

Once created, analyse the building with regard to strength and weight. Use mass properties to determine the total volume of concrete required and the total volume of structural steel or wood frame required.

To be submitted along with your presentation quality drawings are the mass properties of the foyer, the interior area of the foyer for calculations concerning cost for finish, the volume of concrete used in the foundations for estimating calculations, and a list of materials for estimating purposes.

Mechanical Final Project

Use the 3D commands and AME to create a new design for an appliance or health care item (such as the heart pacer provided).

Make maximum use of layers so that you can submit with your drawings a full mass properties analysis and bill of materials.

Civil Final Project

Using a typical residential survey, provide two 3D layouts of 22 houses on varying sizes of lots. On the first drawing indicate the new developer's access route. On the second survey, illustrate the alternate access route preferred by the residents.

Include with your drawings a report on how much cut and fill needs to be done with both designs. Use AME to help you calculate these.

Architectural Final Project

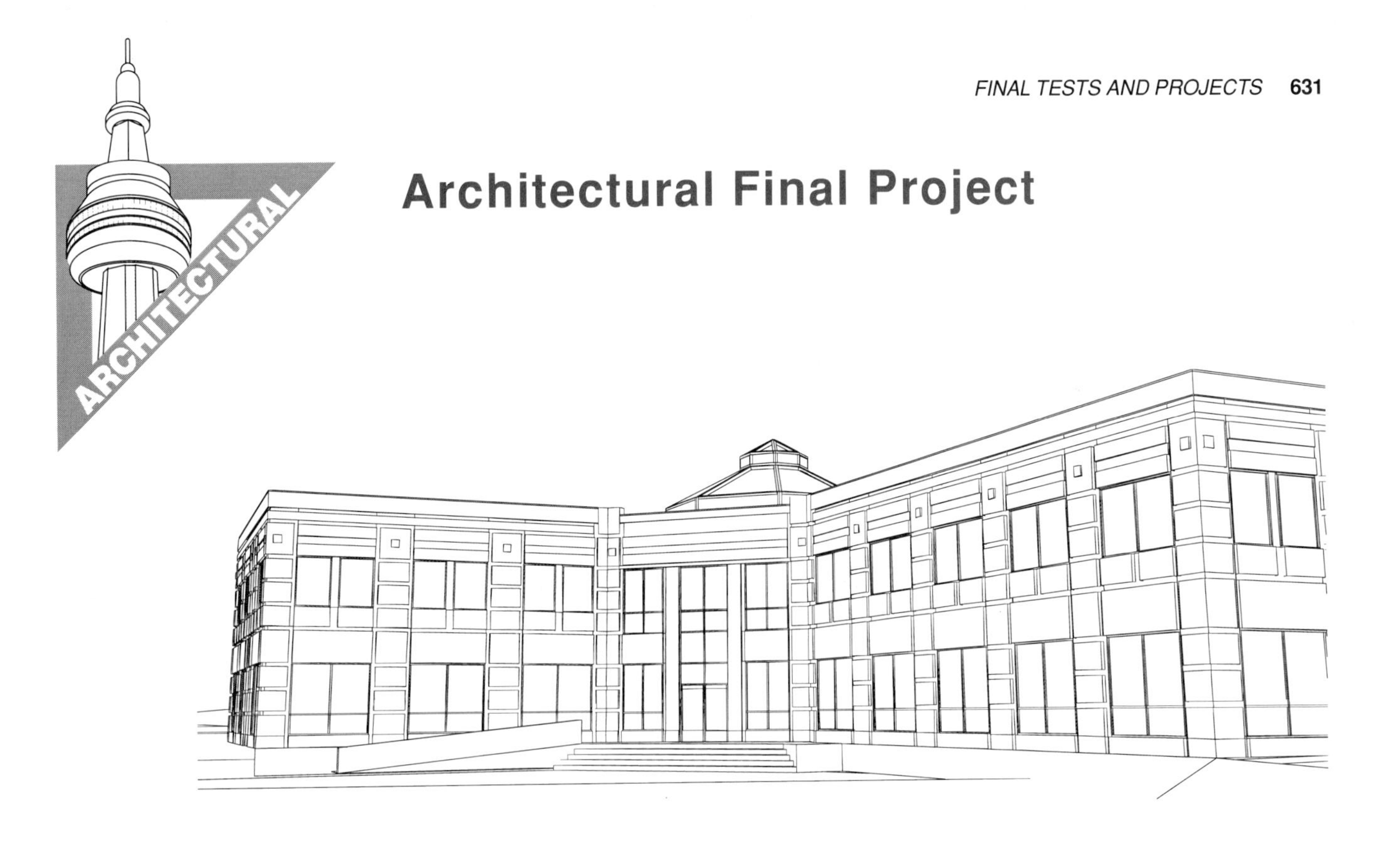

Use the 3D commands and the AME commands to design the foyer of a large public building. The foundations for the building should be adequate to support the building, and the interior of the foyer should be a minimum of two storeys in height.

When designing, be sure to make maximum use of layers to make your final calculations easier.

Once created, analyse the building with regard to strength and weight. Submit these calculations with your drawings.

To be submitted along with your presentation quality drawings are the mass properties of the foyer, the interior area of the foyer for calculations concerning cost for finish, the volume of concrete used in the foundations for estimating calculations, and a list of materials for estimating purposes.

The graphics presented are offered courtesy of Dave Umbach of Parsons, Brinckerhoff, Gore and Storrie. This project would possibly take more time than one person has for a final project. It will also be very difficult to create without the use of a hard drive.

This size of project would not be impossible for a group of three or four students. It would offer much in the way of CAD project development as opposed to traditional methods as well as experience with networking on a large project and system management.

A large project is highly recommended. It will not be easy, but you will learn a lot.

Architectural Final (continued)

Niagara Falls New York
Water Treatment Plant

BODY2 = **Client**

City of Niagara Falls
NEW YORK

BODY2 = **Consultant**

Parsons, Brinckerhoff, Gore and Storrie Inc.

BODY2 = **Drawn By**

Dave Umbach

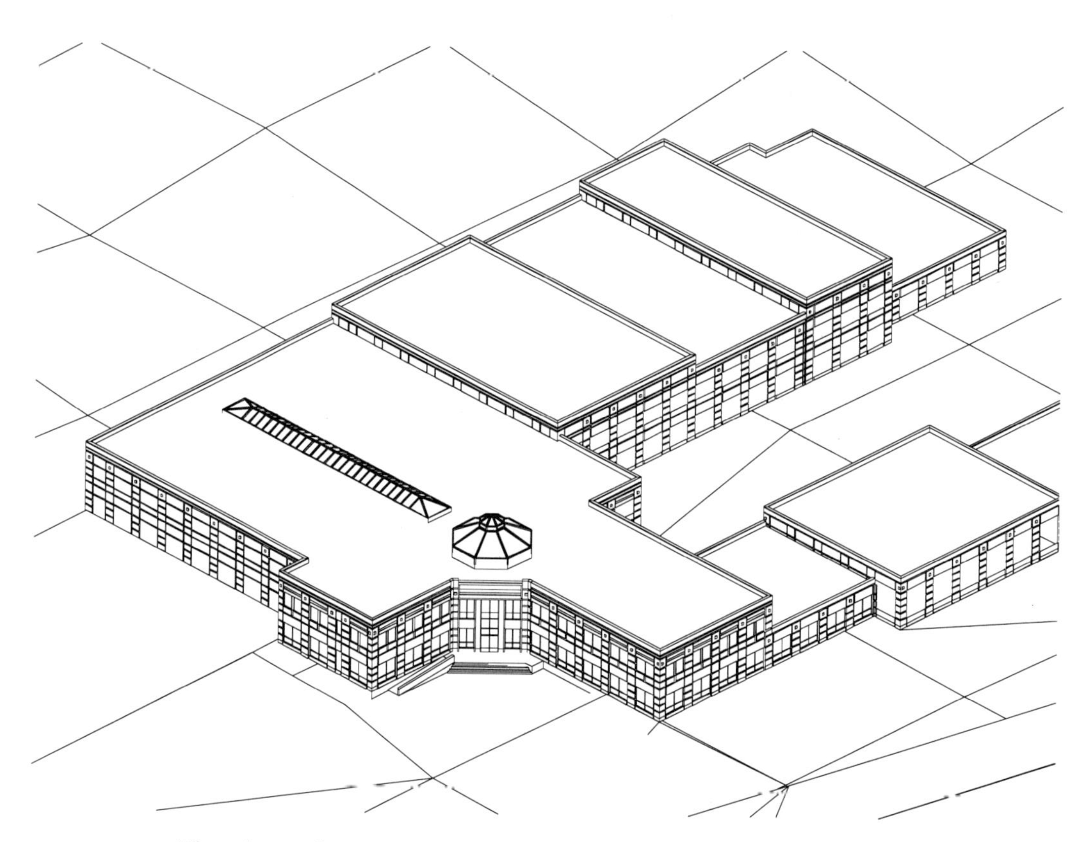

The above drawing was created using a variety of 3D commands and finally surfaced.

The presentation drawing was then put into paper space with Hideplot.

To import the file, it was generated as a plot file using an HP configuration, then imported directly as an HPGL file.

Architectural Final (continued)

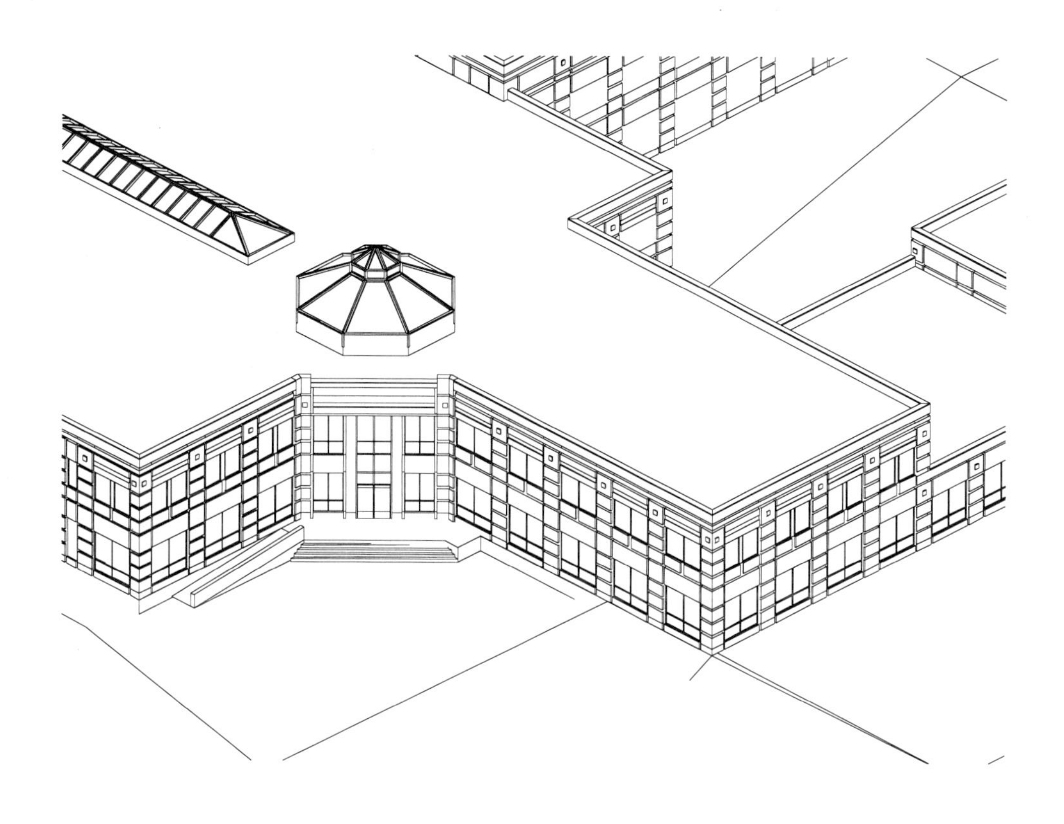

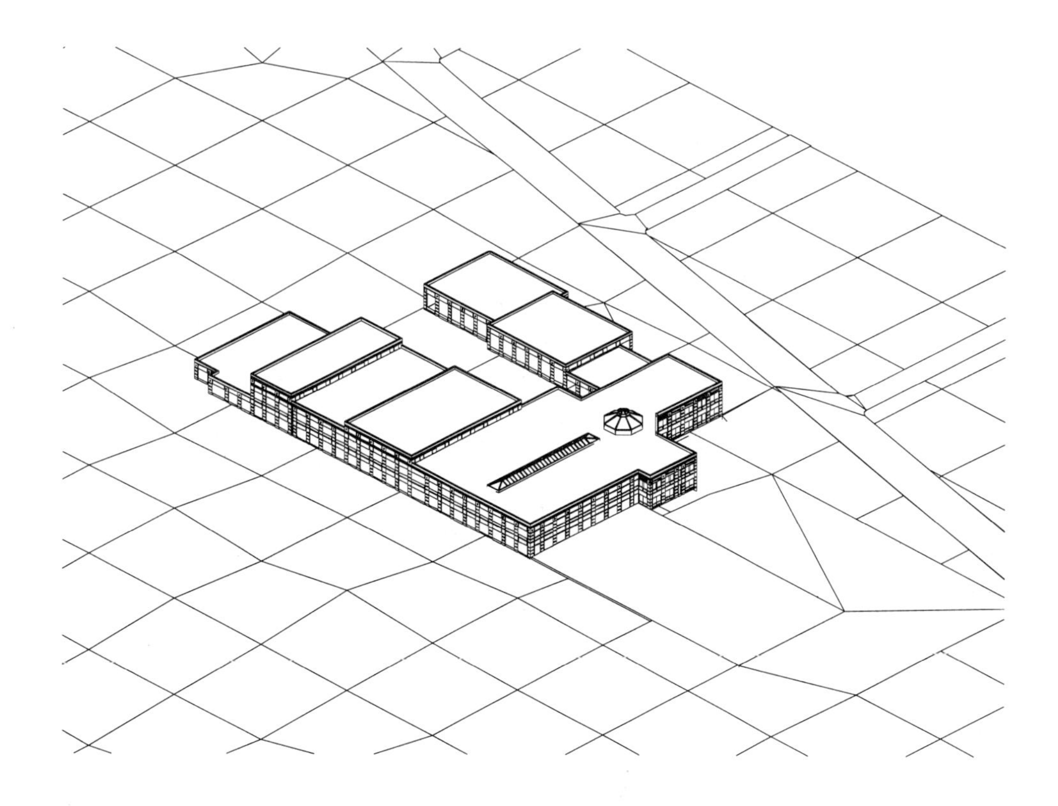

Mechanical Final Project

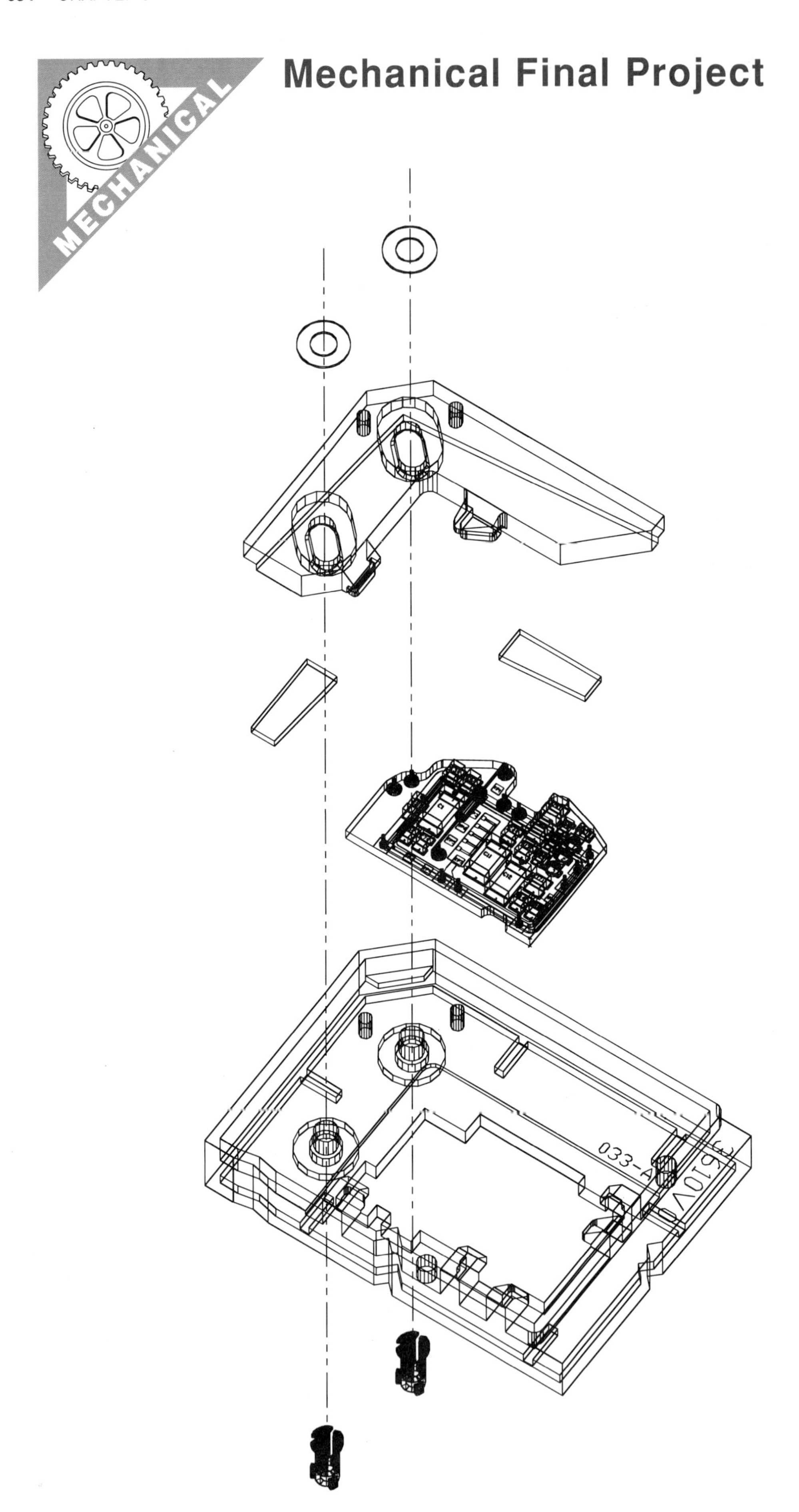

Mechanical Final (continued)

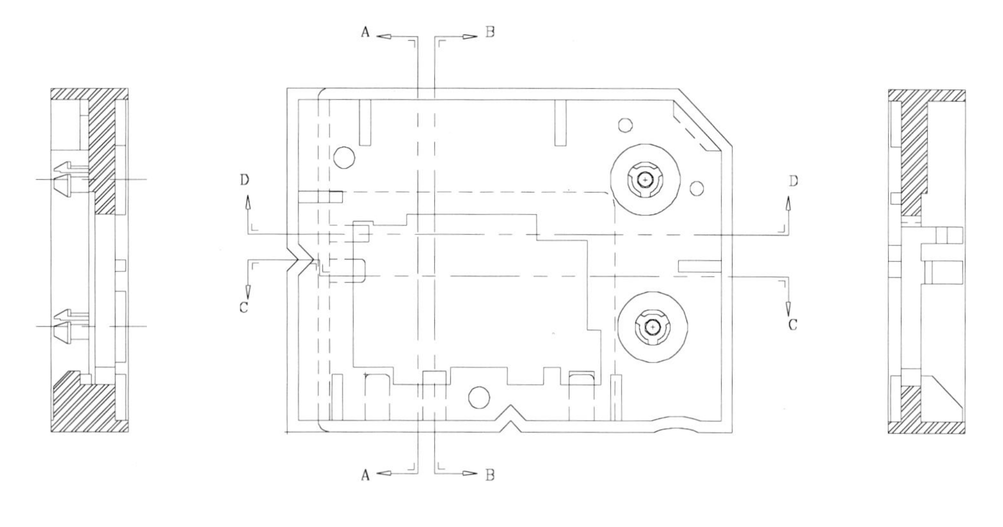

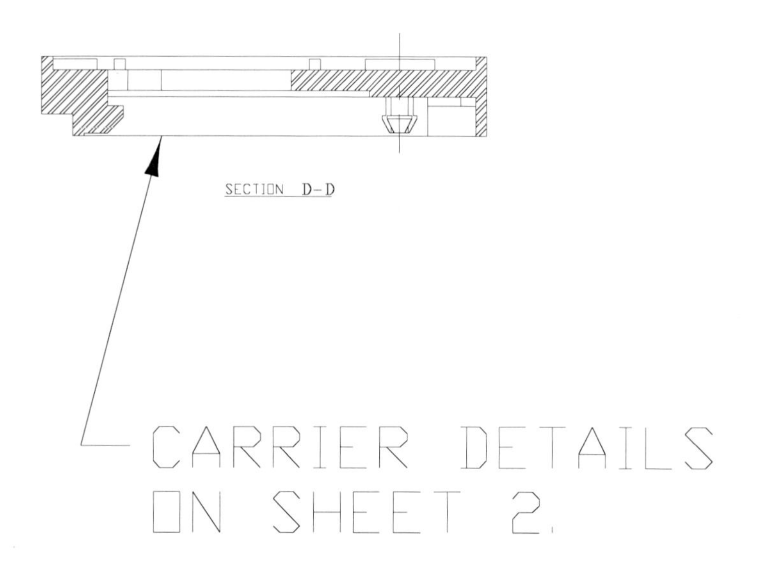

Mechanical Final (continued)

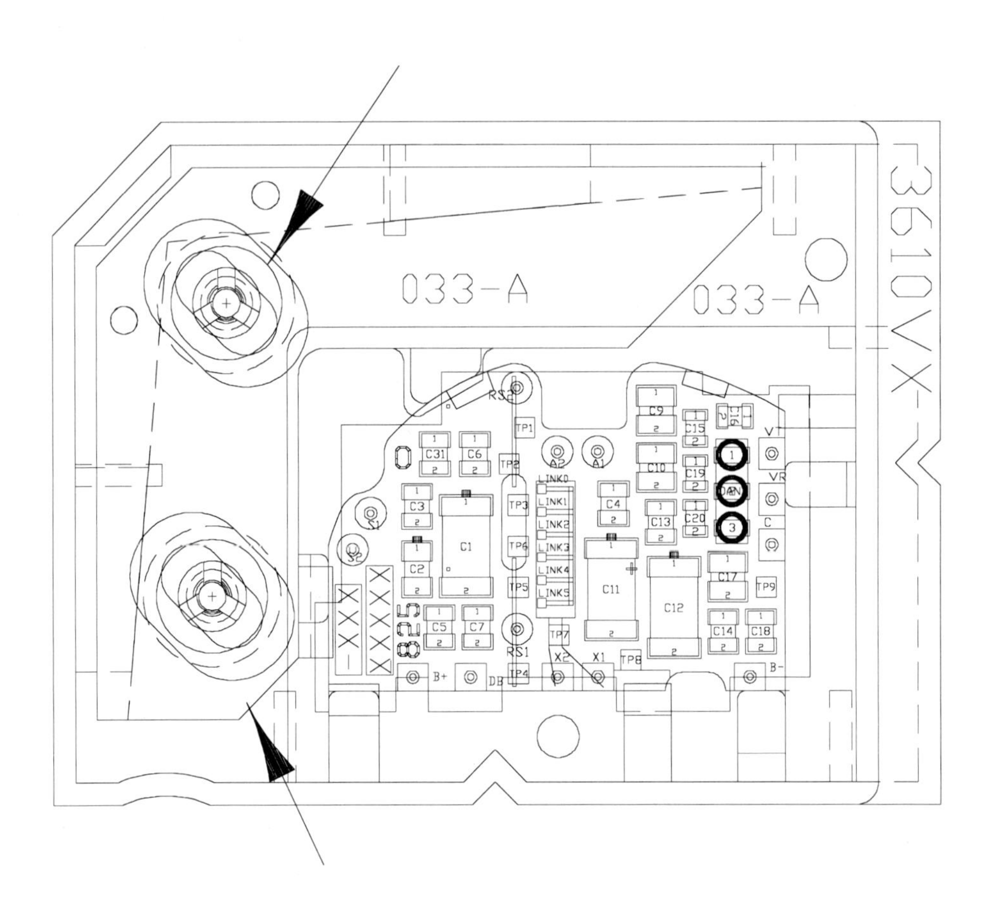

NOTES UNLESS OTHERWISE SPECIFIED.

1. MATERIAL: VECTRA A-700
   WEDGE: VECTRA A-130
2. STANDARD WALL THICKNESS: .050″
3. FILLETS & RADII: .032 MAX (VENDOR OPTION)

△4 MOLDER: GATE ON THIS SURFACE.

△5 FOR GATE PURPOSES ONLY. GATE MUST BREAK OFF BELOW SURFACE -A-.

△6 MOLD TO BE MARKED (.06 HIGH CHARACTERS) WITH PART NO., DASH NO., AND MOLD REV. LETTER AS SHOWN.

△7 NO DRAFT ON INDICATED SURFACES. ALL OTHER SURFACES MAY HAVE 2° MAX DRAFT AT VENDOR OPTION.

△8 NO PARTING LINE ALLOWED ON THIS FEATURE.

Mechanical Final (continued)

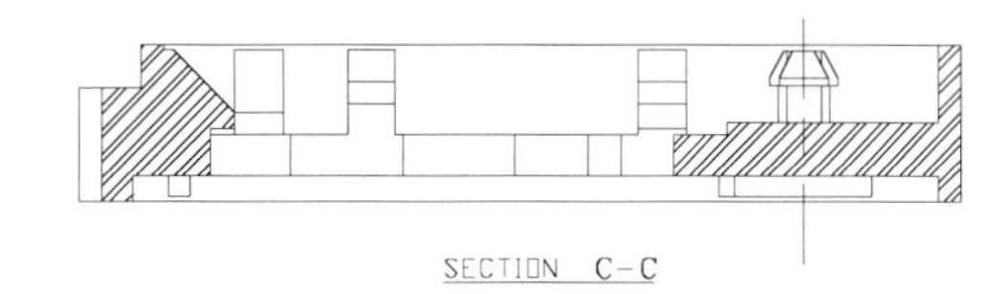

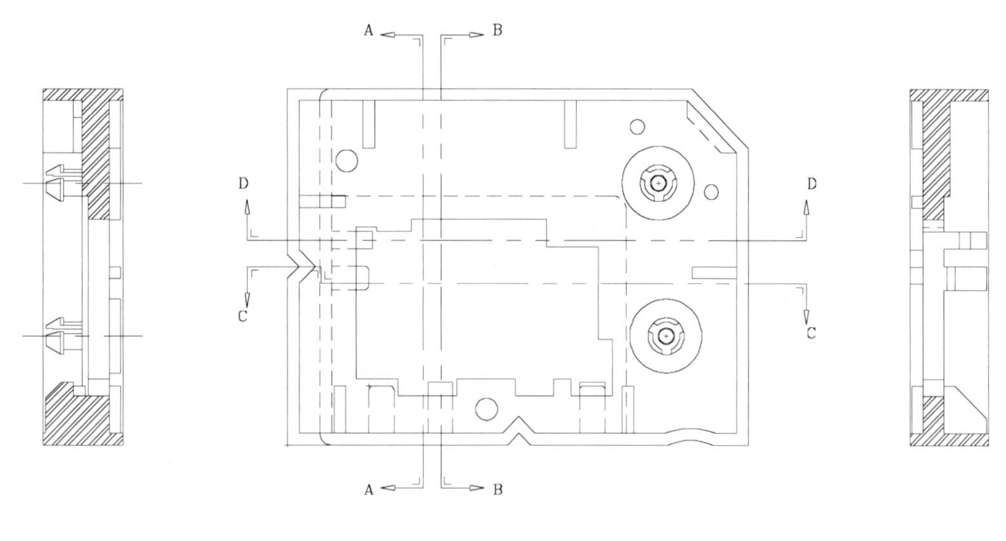

SECTION B-B

SECTION A-A

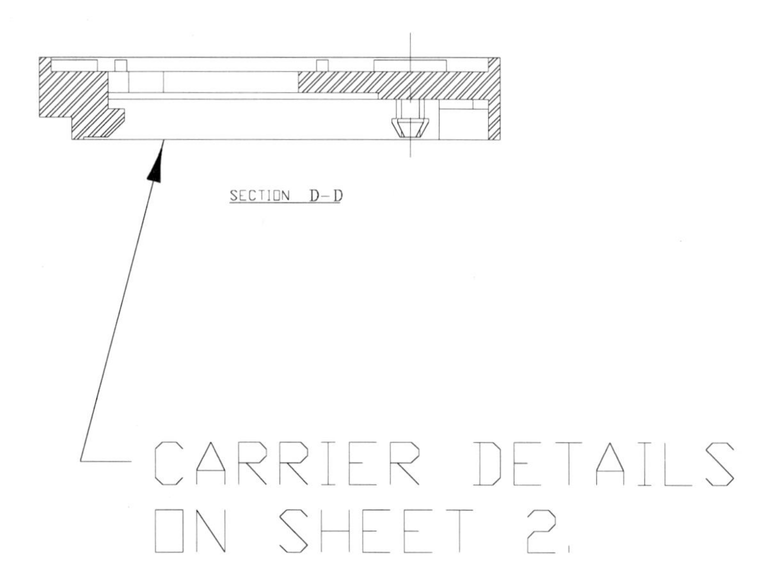

Civil Final Project

This example is offered courtesy of Andy Slupecki.

Using a typical residential survey, provide two 3D layouts of 22 houses on varying sizes of lots. On the first drawing, indicate the new developer's access route. On the second survey, illustrate the alternate access route preferred by the residents.

Include with your drawings a report on how much cut and fill needs to be done with both designs. Use AME to help you calculate these.

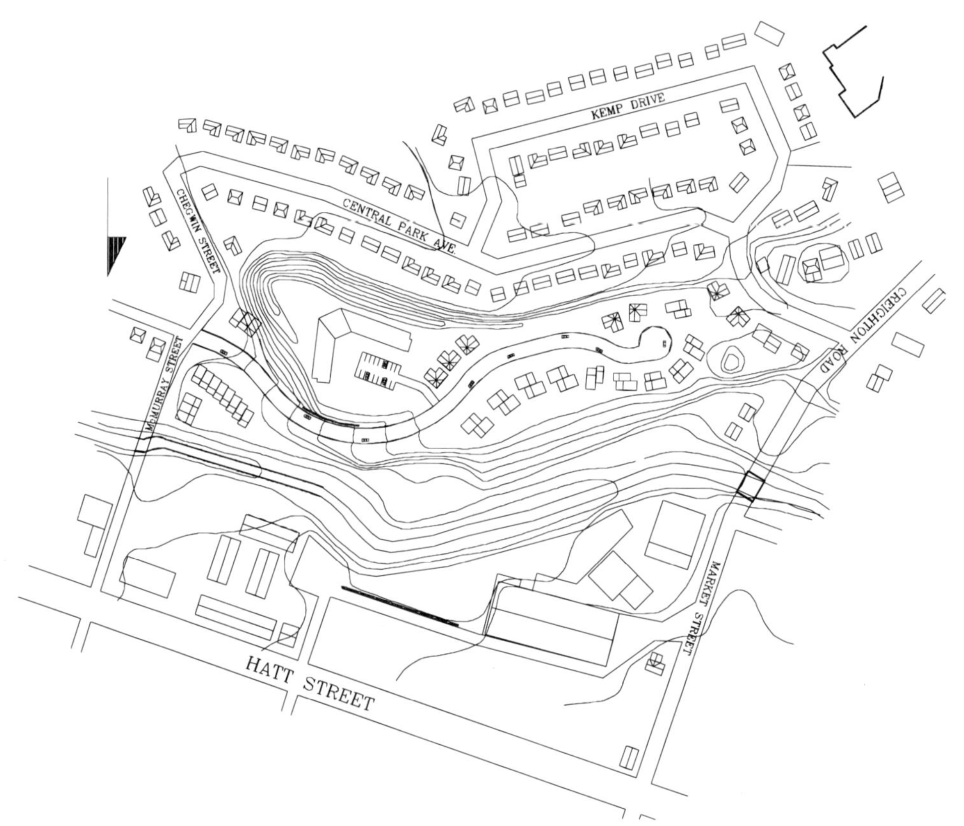

The drawing above shows the contour lines plus the main arteries. These would remain the same on both designs.

Be sure to use the layers effectively so you can freeze the first route when the second is being shown.

Civil Final (continued)

Trees and cars can be added to give the design a realistic look.

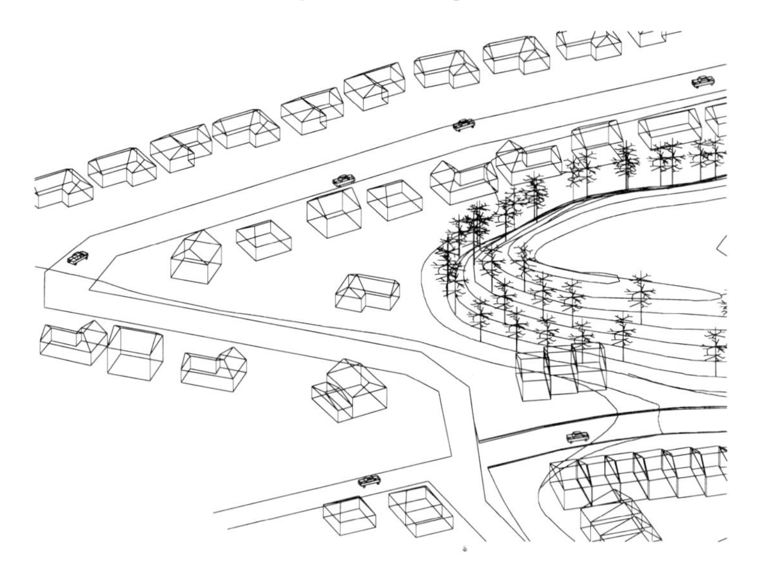

For the final presentation, rotate the image so it is viewed from an isometric view, and then add a title block and notations with the UCS at View.

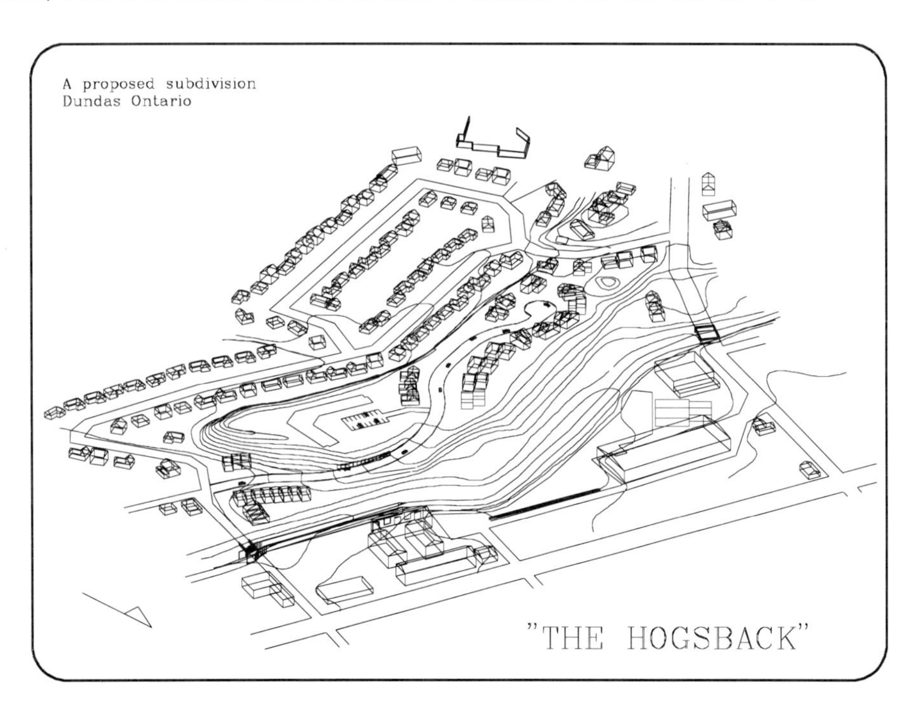

Glossary of Terms

absolute coordinates	Points located in space relative to the file's fixed origin.
addressable point	Any position specifiable in device coordinates.
ADE	Advanced Drafting Extension. There are three program extensions available to the basic AutoCAD package. When you enter AutoCAD, the ADE level is printed on the top of the main menu on releases prior to Release 9. AutoCAD Copyright (c) 1982-90 Autodesk Inc Version 2.6 (4/3/87) IBM PC Advanced Drafting Extension 3 Serial number: 117 02345 This book assumes that all ADE packages are included.
ADI	Autodesk Device Interface.This device driver standard allows third-party developers to write their own driver software for peripherals such as graphic cards, digitizers, and plotters.
ADS	AutoCAD Development System. This programming interface allows third party developers to include applications written in high-level languages such as C.
aliasing	Visual effects that occur when the detail of an image exceeds the resolution of the device space, i.e., a stair-step line on a raster display.
alpha character	Any letter from A to Z.
alphanumeric	Any letter or number. Alphanumeric screens are show only alphanumeric characters and no graphics.
AME	Advanced Modelling Extension. See Chapters 34 and 35 for description.
anti-aliasing	A process which removes the effects of pixel addressing on a raster display.
API	Application Programming Interface
ASCII	American Standard Code for Information Interchange

ASCII code The code which describes each alpha, numeric, or special character in computer language. This code translates characters into a series of 0s and 1s which is recognized by a large percentage of computer languages.

aspect ratio The image height-to-width ratio on a CAD display screen.

AUI Advanced User Interface. Allows the use of pull-down menus, icon menus, pop-up dialogue boxes, and other interfaces that overlap the graphics editor.

Autodesk The company that produces AutoCAD software.

AutoLISP A programming language built into the AutoCAD program. It is an open program and users are encouraged to learn AutoLISP in order to create their own programs. To enter an AutoLISP program use the following: Command:**(load "d;/path/filename")**

Autoshade Autodesk's shading package.

.BAK The filename extension of a backup file.

baseplane An AME option that lets you define a temporary UCS on which the solid primitive is created. Used in relation to the solid primitive creation commands.

batch processing A type of computer processing in which input is followed—often minutes or hours later—by output. The user does not interact with the computer while processing is taking place.

bit A binary digit, 0 or 1; a digit in a base 2 number system.

bit map A digital representation of a display image as a pattern of bits, where each bit maps one or more pixels. Multiple bit maps may be used in colour graphics to assign values to each pixel, which may be used as indices for a colour look-up table.

Boolean An algebraic system used in AME commands that defines the relationship between entities of a set. Named after the nineteenth century mathematician George Boole, this method allows you to add two sets of solids together, subtract two solids and find the intersection of two solids.

branch In AME, a branch is any portion of a solid model's Constructive Solid Geometry (CSG) tree. It extends from some point in the tree and the leaves represent the objects in a composite region.

B-spline A mathematical representation of a smooth curve.

B-spline surface A mathematical description of a 3D surface which passes through a set of B-splines, i.e., Bézier, Coons.

buffer	A storage area which receives, stores, and subsequently releases transient data.
byte	A unit of measure, a binary element string of eight bits.
CAD	Computer Aided Design
CAE	Computer Aided Engineering
CAM	Computer Aided Manufacturing
character	An instance of a numeral, letter, linguistic, mathematical, or logical symbol.
character font	The style of the character set.
circular array	Multiple copies of drawing objects around an arc or circle.
CL File	Cutter Location File
color	American spelling for colour.
composite model	A general term used in AME to describe both composite solids and regions.
composite video	A single video signal encoding RGB data.
computer animation	The use of computer graphics to generate motion pictures.
Computer Graphics	Using computers to generate pictures.
Construction Plane (CP)	An option used in AME to define a plane for the purpose of locating a single point.
Constructive Solid Geometry (CSG)	The method of using intersection, union, and subtraction operations to construct composite solids.
coordinates	Cartesian coordinates overlayed on the number space of the display screen. A pair of numbers (XY) or a triplet of numbers (XYZ) that corresponds to a point on a plane (X-Y) or in space (XYZ).
CP	Construction Plane
cross-hair	Crossed horizontal/vertical lines representing a cursor, with the intersect being used to indicate desired device coordinates.
CSG	Constructive Solid Geometry
CSG tree	Keeps track of the order in which Boolean operations are performed in AME. See Chapter 35 for details.
cursor	A symbol or a pair of intersecting lines on the screen that indicates the position for the entry of the next item or character. In graphics, used in conjunction with the digitizer or mouse to indicate points or items on the screen.

database Comprehensive collection of information having predetermined structure and organization suitable for communication, interpretation, or processing.

default A pre-defined value used for a program input or parameter.

dialog American spelling for dialogue.

digitizer A device that tracks the relative position of the cursor for the purpose of recording the relative location of an item.

disk A magnetic data storage device.

Distributed Intelligence A computer system with several processors.

dithering Increasing the variations of colour or intensity on raster displays by trading picture resolution for patterns of pixel arrays.

DOS Disk Operating System. The Microsoft program that controls the CPU, output peripherals, etc.

.DWG The filename extension of a drawing file.

edge In AME, a feature that bounds a surface.

electrostatic printer\ plotter A computer output peripheral that prints and plots by placing electrostatic charges on treated paper in the desired patterns, upon which toner is spread and baked.

endpoints Either of the points that mark the end of a line, arc, circle, or other primitive.

entity Fundamental building blocks which the designer uses to represent a product—lines, arcs, ellipses, text, splines. Also known as an item or object.

face A finite, planar, cylindrical, conical, spherical, or toroidal surface on a solid model.

FEM Finite Element Modelling

Fill To fill an area of the display surface bounded by vectors with a solid colour or pattern.

flatbed plotter A plotter in which the drawing medium is placed on a flat surface and the pen carriage moves on a gantry that spans the table.

font The style of a letter or character.

function keys A keyboard key designated as F*n*, where *n* is a number from 1 to 12. A function key may initiate a specific function or act as a toggle switch.

graphics processor A controller which accesses the display list, interprets the display instructions, and passes coordinates to the vector generator.

gray scale An ordered description of the tonal levels of an input image.

grid Uniformly spaced points on a computer screen which create a visual drawing aid to determine distance.

group technology Facilitation of processing through a combination of similar parts into production "families."

hardcopy Any printed or plotted printout.

hatching A drawing function for filling polygons with standard patterns.

hidden lines The line segments which should not be visible to a viewer of a three-dimensional display item because they are "behind" other parts of the same or other display items.

hue Characteristic of a colour that allows it to be named, i.e., green, red, blue, yellow, and that is often defined by an angle representing its gradation.

icon A graphic image of a function or facility to help either choose or recognize your position and options. The UCS icon in the bottom-left corner of a screen is an example.

IGES Initial Graphic Exchange Format

impact printer\ plotter An output device that uses an impact mechanism to strike a dot image or character die through a carbon ribbon onto the paper.

incremental vector A relative vector or points located at a distance from the last current point.

ink jet plotter A plotter which uses electrostatic technology to first atomize a liquid ink and then control the number of droplets that are deposited on the plotting medium.

instance When used in conjunction with blocks, the block is created and thus stored apart from the actual drawing or model. Every time the block is inserted, it is one instance or copy of the block, but the block remains intact in memory. This is like a rubber stamp, the impression of the stamp being an instance.

integer value Many commands have options available by choosing a number such as 0, 1, 2, etc. These are integer values for the command.

Interactive Graphics The use of a computer terminal to generate graphics command by command; opposite to Batch processing.

K Kilo, usually kilobyte; 1,000 bytes of computer-coded information.

Laser Plotter A plotter which produces images through the use of a laser (Light Amplification through Stimulated Emission of Radiation).

loop A closed programming statement that repeats. In AME, any closed multi-segment line that makes up a region. A loop can be the outside boundary or a hole in a region.

mass properties Calculation of physical engineering information of a part, e.g., perimeter, centroid, volume, weight, and moments of inertia. See Chapter 35 for details.

menu A list of options or functions displayed on the CRT (Cathode Ray Tube).

mesh A representation of three-dimensional object fully described. In AME, the representation of a solid object that displays edges and tessellation lines within the object.

model A geometrically accurate representation of an object. In AutoCAD, graphic data is often referred to as a model as opposed to a drawing because the data is not always used to create drawings, particularly in 3D applications.

model space The original position of the origin and axes with regard to the model. The World Coordinate System uses model space.

mouse A data entry device that echoes the position of the cursor on the screen and helps the user to define a point or item.

NC Numerical Control. Prerecorded information providing instructions for the automatic computer control of machine tools.

NBS National Bureau of Standards

nesting Imbedding data in levels of other data so that certain routines or data can be executed or accessed continuously or in a loop.

null solid A composite solid that contains no volume.

on-line documentation Information about the commands within the database.

origin The fixed 0,0,0 point of the model. The point on the coordinate system where all values are zero.

Operating System The microcomputer software program which controls the CPU (Central Processing Unit) and the input/output peripherals.

PAN To move from one zoom view to another without changing size; a horizontal translation.

patch Any enclosed area of a region.

pixel The smallest section of a screen; dot resolution of image. The discrete display element of a raster display represented as a single point with a specified colour or intensity.

platform The level of capability of a computer system; i.e., XT, 386, 486.

pline Polynumeral line. A line composed of many different vertices.

post-processor Software program or procedure which interprets graphical data and formats it into data readable by an NC machine or other program.

primitive The simplest and most basic geometry you can create—lines, circles, arcs, etc. are all primitives.

prompt Any message or symbol from the computer system informing the user of possible actions or operations. A guide to the operator indicating possible actions or options.

raster A uniform pattern of lines produced by the beam in the CRT. These lines form the point addressable matrix that is the number space.

raster scan Line-by-line sweep across the entire display surface to generate elements of a display image.

read-only Data which can be read but not edited.

refresh To redraw the lines of images on the screen.

region A closed 2D area created by solidifying 2D AutoCAD entities such as plines, arcs, and circles.

relative coordinates Incremental coordinates

rendering A shaded and hidden-line image of solid objects.

RenderMan Autodesk's advanced image processing software.

resolution The smallest points on a graphic device at which the points can be detected as distinct. The number of pixels on your screen, measured horizontally and vertically.

Right-hand Rule A method of determining which is the positive direction of rotation around an axis by using the right-hand to grasp the axis with the thumb pointing away from the origin; the fingers then point in the positive rotation direction.

RGB colour A colour described in terms of its red, green, blue intensity levels.

ROM Read-Only Memory. A memory chip that contains the commands to start the computer and address the various peripherals. The contents of a read-only chip cannot be changed.

rubber band — A line that stretches dynamically in conjunction with the cursor during many editing and drawing commands.

scale factor — A number which multiplies the vector endpoint coordinates to produce scaling.

shading — Image processing; a technique which indicates light sources in a three-dimensional image. Autoshade is Autodesk's shading software.

SNAP — A drawing aid function which allows you to place entities at a preset spacing.

solid — In AME, any object that is composed of solid primitives.

solid assembly — A solid model that has been stored on the disk as a separate file from the AutoCAD drawing.

solid primitive — The simplest and most basic solid objects you can create, such as solid boxes and cones.

string — A sequence of characters.

stylus — A device analogous to a pencil which is used in conjunction with a data tablet to input coordinate information.

swap files — Files needed by AutoCAD to create a temporary file, typically with hexidecimal numbers and the extension .SWR. Normally, these files are erased when you exit the program, but if the system locks up for any reason, you can erase these files from your directory.

tablet — An input device which digitizes coordinate data indicated by stylus position.

tessellation lines — Lines displayed on a curved surface to help you visualize a curved surface.

third-party developers — Companies offering software enhancements to AutoCAD users that are based on AutoCAD software. AutoCAD has maintained an open policy to developers, offering a great deal of support to those who want to customize their software for specific purposes.

toolpath — Centre line of an NC cutting or drilling tool in motion of a specific cutting operation.

UCS — User Coordinate System. The three-axis coordinate system that can be rotated and placed at any location in order to help create a model.

vector — A straight line which has both magnitude and direction and is always defined by two endpoints.

virtual screen A pixel map of the current regenerated view. This is stored in memory and determines the speed of redraws with regard to the percentage of the drawing that is regenerated in addition to the actual on-screen image.

window A selected rectangle for image display or processing.

wireframe A representation of a solid object that displays edges and tessellation lines.

wraparound The phenomenon whereby a vector which overflows the number space is continued on the opposite edge of the drawing.

World Coordinate System WCS. The original position of the origin and axes on the model.

File Extensions

ADT	Audit report file
BAK	Drawing file backup
BAS	Basic program file
BAT	Batch file
BIN	Binary image file
BKN	Emergency backup file
CFG	Configuration File
COM	Machine language command file
DWG	Drawing file
DXB	Binary drawing interchange file
DXF	Drawing interchange file
DFX	Attribute extract file in DFX format
EPS	Encapsulated PostScript
ERR	Error file
EXE	DOS executable file
FLM	Filmroll file for use in AutoShade
GIF	Graphic image file
HPG	Hewlett Packard graphics file
HLP	Help file
IGS	IGES interchange file
LIN	Linetype library file
LSP	AutoLISP format file
LST	Printer plot output file
MAT	Materials file
MNU	Menu source code file
MNX	Compiled menu source file
MSG	Message file
OLD	Original version of converted drawing file
PAT	Hatch pattern library file
PGP	Program parameters file
PLT	Plot file
PRP	ADI printer plotter output file
PWD	Logon file
SCR	Script file
SHP	Shape file
SHX	Shape/font-definition source file
SLB	Slide library file
SLD	Slide file
TIF	Tagged image file
TXT	Attribute extract or template file
UNT	Units file
WPG	WordPerfect graphics file
XLG	External references log file
$AC	AutoCAD temporary file
$A	AutoCAD temporary file

Commands not Explained Elsewhere

In an attempt to make this text a reasonable size, a few commands that have not been fully explained. These are presented here. Those commands that are part of the SETVAR or variables section will be explained there.

ACADPREFIX A system variable (read-only); stores the directory name.

ACADVER A system variable (read-only); stores the AutoCAD version number.

AFLAGS A system variable; determines the settings for Invisible, Constant, and Verify in the ATTDEF command.

ANGBASE A system variable; stores the angle for the 0 direction.

ANGDIR A system variable; controls clockwise or counterclockwise angle direction.

APERTURE A system variable; controls size of target box on Object Snap mode.

ATTDISP This allows you to change the visibility of attributes:

```
Command:ATTDISP
Normal/On/Off:
```

Where:

Normal *displays attributes relative to the ATTDEF command*
On *turns all attributes on regardless of ATTDEF*
Off *turns all attributes off regardless of ATTDEF*

ATTMODE A system variable; three-way toggle switch controlling the display of attributes:
0 - never displayed
1 - displayed according to command definition
2 - always displayed

ATTREQ A system variable; toggle switch that determines whether or not the user will be prompted for entry in attribute insertion. In the case of no prompting, the default values are always used.

AUDIT

Examines the AutoCAD file to determine its validity with relation to damaged or corrupted files. The command will attempt to correct these errors. This command was not available before Release 11 and will therefore not be able to recover damaged files in releases earlier than 11.

```
Command:AUDIT
Fix any errors detected?:↵
2  Blocks edited
Pass 1  19  entities audited
Pass 2  19  entities audited
total errors found 2
```

AUNITS

A system variable; sets method and mode of angle representation.

AUPREC

A system variable (Angle Unit Places ReCord); determines the number of decimal places displayed during an angle measure.

AXIS

Allows you to display ruler lines and change the tick marks along the X and Y axes of your screen. You can vary the spacing along the X and Y axes:

```
Command:AXIS
Tick spacing (X) or On/Off/Snap/Aspect'
-1.00":A
Horizontal spacing(X) '-1.00":5X
Vertical spacing(Y) '-1.00":2.5X
```

Where:

On *turns on the ruler lines as in the default*
Off *turns off the ruler lines*
Snap *locks the tick marks to the current SNAP*
Aspect *allows you to change the relative X and Y values*
'-1.00" *is the default; a numeric entry will change the value of X and Y*
X *sets the value to a multiple of the snap value, the tick size changes when the snap is changed.*

AXISMODE

A system variable; toggle switch for axis ruler line.

AXISUNIT

A system variable; controls the spacing of tick marks along the axis ruler line.

BACKZ

A system variable; sets the distance from the target point to the back clipping plane.

BASE

This will set a different base point on a drawing. It is used to modify the base point before creating a block or on an Xref file:

```
Command:BASE
Base point: (pick the point)
```

BLIPMODE A system variable; toggle switch controlling the display or repression of the temporary marker blips.

BYBLOCK An option for setting the colour and linetype of blocks so they can be changed later. Also, hatch patterns and dimensions can be exploded; the linetype and colour settings will always be set to BYBLOCK. (The layer of an exploded dimension or hatch will always be set to 0.)

CDATE A system variable (read-only); displays the current date and time.

CECOLOR A read-only system variable (Current Entity Color); displays current colour setting.

CELTYPE A system variable (Current Entity Linetype); displays current linetype setting.

CHAMFER This creates chamfers on corners. Like the Fillet command, this trims two intersecting lines a specific distance on both sides:

`Command:`**`CHAMFER`**

`Polyline/Distance/first line:` *(pick line)*

`Select second line:` *(pick second line)*

CHAMFERA A system variable; sets first chamfer distance.

CHAMFERB A system variable; sets second chamfer distance.

CLAYER A system variable (read-only); displays current layer setting.

CMDECHO A system variable; toggle switch determines display or non-display of commands executed by AutoLISP.

CVPORT A system variable; used in macros and AutoLISP to determine the active viewport.

DATE A system variable (read-only); displays date in Julian calendar format; actual days, not years, days, months.

DDATTE This allows the Edit Attributes dialogue box to be displayed on-screen. This allows for interactive editing of existing attributes. The ATTDIA dialogue box offers information on the attributes before they are inserted. This dialogue box allows you to edit attributes after they have been inserted:

`Command:`**`DDATTE`**

`Select block:` *(pick the attributed block)*

This will display all the attributes associated with this block and allow you to dynamically edit them.

DDEDIT

This allows you to edit text and attributes inside a dialog box. Text characters can be added or changed in the text strings created by the TEXT or DTEXT commands and in the tag, prompt, and default values in the ATTDEF command. The DDATTE command allows you to edit the attribute instance; this allows you to edit the attribute definition.

'DDEMODES

Dynamic Dialog Entity Modes; displays the Entity Creation Modes dialogue box which allows you to control the current colour, linetype, layer, elevation, and thickness used for subsequent entities. This can also be accessed through the Entity Creation option of the Options pull-down menu.

'DDLMODES

Dynamic Dialog Layer Modes; displays the Modify Layer dialog box and allows you to edit current layer names, colours and linetypes as well as create new layers. See Chapter 6 for details.

'DDRMODES

Dynamic Drawing Modes; displays a dialogue box that permits interactive control over most of the on-screen drawing aids such as GRID, SNAP, ORTHO, AXIS, and ISOPLANE. It gives you a listing of current settings and the ability to dynamically change them. The dialogue box is also available by choosing the Drawing Tools option under the Settings menu.

DDUCS

Dynamic Dialog User Coordinate System; allows you to choose a saved UCS, change the current User Coordinate System, delete a coordinate system, define a new coordinate system, or rename an existing coordinate system. It can also be accessed by choosing the UCS Control option under the Settings pull-down menu.

DELAY

This is usually used in conjunction with script files (see Chapter 16) but can be used to cause AutoCAD to pause for a specified period of time before continuing with the next command.

DIASTAT

A system variable (read-only); tells you whether you used Cancel or OK to exit the last dialogue box that you entered.

DIM-NEWTEXT

This allows you to edit an existing associative dimensioning text string:

```
Command:DIM
Dim:NEWTEXT
Enter new dimension text:5
Select objects: (pick the object)
Select objects:↵
```

DIM-OBLIQUE

This allows you to change the orientation of the associative linear dimension lines. The resulting lines will tilt at an oblique angle relative to the dimension lines.

DIM-ORDINATE

This allows you to add ordinate or datum dimensions to a drawing. It measures, draws, and annotates selected features within a drawing at an orthogonal angle relative to the current origin. If you want the dimensions relative to a specific point on the object, move the origin with the UCS command.

DIM-OVERRIDE

This allows you to change an existing associative dimension relative to identified dimension variables without changing the settings of the dimension variables:

```
Dim:OVERRIDE
Dimension variable to override:DIMTAD
Current value /87 New Value:Off
Dimension variable to override:↵
Select objects: (pick an object)
Select objects:↵
```

This will change the DIMTAD for the dimension selected without changing the DIMTAD setting.

DIM-RESTORE

This allows you to use a previously saved dimensioning style. Once you have saved a set of dimensioning variables, this will change the current dimensioning variable settings to those of the saved settings, thus providing a set of dimensioning variables that can be accessed for any drawing.

DIM-SAVE

This saves the current dimensioning variable values for future reference. To restore this set of variables, use DIM-RESTORE.

DIM-TEDIT

This allows you to change the position of existing text in an associative dimension. This is like the STRETCH command in that it allows you to move the text, and the lines and arrowheads will automatically realign with the new position. The angle of the text can also be changed.

DIM-TROTATE

This allows you to rotate the text in an existing associative dimension.

DIMALT

A system variable; toggle switch offers alternate unit dimensions.

DIMALTD

A system variable; controls number of decimal places of accuracy in alternate unit dimensions.

DIMALTF

A system variable; controls alternate unit factor.

DIMAPOST	A system variable; controls insertion of text suffix to follow alternate unit dimensions.
DIMASO	A system variable; toggles Associative Dimension mode on and off.
DIMASZ	A system variable; controls arrowhead size.
DIMBLK	A system variable; allows insertion of a user-defined block instead of the AutoCAD arrowhead.
DIMBLK1	A system variable; allows insertion of a user-defined block instead of the first arrowhead only.
DIMBLK2	A system variable; allows insertion of a user-defined block instead of the second arrowhead only.
DIMCEN	A system variable; controls size of centreline cross.
DIMCLRD	A system variable; controls dimension line colour.
DIMCLRE	A system variable; controls extension line colour.
DIMCLRT	A system variable; controls dimension text colour.
DIMDLE	A system variable; controls amount of extension of the dimension line past the intersection of the extension line.
DIMDLI	A system variable; controls the distance between dimension lines in baseline and ordinate dimensions.
DIMEXE	A system variable; controls amount of extension of the extension line past the intersection with the dimension line.
DIMEXO	A system variable; controls gap distance between the object line and the extension line.
DIMGAP	A system variable; controls the minimum distance between extension lines and text in a dimension.
DIMLFAC	A system variable; can be used to apply a scale factor to a length measured in a dimension command; e.g., if a length is actually 4, a DIMLFAC of 2 will make the dimension text display 8.
DIMLIM	A system variable; toggles the dimension limits on or off.
DIMPOST	A system variable; can be used to add a dimension text suffix.
DIMRND	A system variable; sets a rounding-off value for dimensions.

DIMSAH	A system variable; toggle switch controls whether DIMBLK1, DIMBLK2, or only DIMBLK can be used.
DIMSCALE	A system variable; controls the scale of the display of the dimensions.
DIMSE1	A system variable; toggles for suppression of first extension line.
DIMSE2	A system variable; toggles for suppression of second extension line.
DIMSHO	A system variable; toggles for display or repression of new dimensions while they are being updated.
DIMSOXD	A system variable; toggle to suppress dimension lines outside of extension lines.
DIMSTYLE	A system variable; controls the style of the dimension text.
DIMTAD	A system variable; toggles for the dimension text to be above or within the dimension line.
DIMTFAC	A system variable; controls scale factor for tolerancing.
DIMTIH	A system variable; toggles text within the extension lines to be horizontal or parallel to the dimension line in dimensions.
DIMTIX	A system variable; can be used to force dimension text within the extension lines.
DIMTM	A system variable; controls minus tolerance value.
DIMTOFL	A system variable; toggles to force dimension line within extension lines even if it would default to the outside.
DIMTOH	A system variable; toggles text to be horizontal or parallel to the dimension line in dimensions where the text defaults to the outside of the extension lines.
DIMTOL	A system variable; toggles tolerancing in dimensions on or off.
DIMTP	A system variable; controls plus tolerance value.
DIMTSZ	A system variable; controls the dimension tick size.
DIMTVP	A system variable; controls the position of the text relative to the dimension line.
DIMTXT	A system variable; controls dimension text size.
DIMZIN	A system variable; controls the way that 0 inches is

displayed in a feet-and-inches dimension.

DISTANCE A system variable (read-only); stores the last distance shown in the DIST command.

DRAGMODE This allows you to see an image of the results of many of the editing commands before the command is completed. When objects are copied, moved or inserted, a ghost image of the object will allow you to see the size and placement of it before the base point for the intended object has been chosen:

```
Command:DRAGMODE
ON/OFF/Auto <current>:
```

DRAGP1 A system variable; controls the number of times an object is redrawn as it is dragged across the screen.

DRAGP2 A system variable; controls how frequently the cursor position is checked as the cursor is dragged across the screen.

DVIEWBLOCK This allows you to add your own image for the block used for display in the DVIEW command:

```
Command:BLOCK
Block name (or ?):DVIEWBLOCK
Block DVIEWBLOCK already exists.
Redefine it?:Y
Insertion base point:0,0,0
Select objects: (pick the objects)
Select objects:↵
Block DVIEWBLOCK redefined
Regenerating drawing
```

DWGNAME A system variable (read-only); displays the current drawing name.

DWGPREFIX A system variable (read-only); displays the drive, directory, and path in the drawing name.

DXBIN This allows you to load a binary DXB file such as that produced by a scanner.

EXTMAX A system variable (read-only); displays the current maximum extents of the drawing file.

EXTMIN A system variable (read-only); displays the current minimum extents of the drawing file.

FILLETRAD A system variable; controls the size of the fillet radius.

FILMROLL This produces files for the RenderMan software.

FRONTZ A system variable; controls the distance of the target point from the front clipping plane.

'GRAPHSCR This causes AutoCAD to flip from the text screen to the graphics screen when you are running AutoCAD on a single-screen system. This is offered as a command so that it can be incorporated in script files.

GRIDMODE A system variable; toggles the grid on or off.

GRIDUNIT A system variable; determines the size of the grid.

HANDLES This determines whether AutoCAD assigns a unique identifier or handle to every entity in a drawing. It is also used to delete handles:

```
Command:HANDLES
Handles are disabled
ON/DESTROY:
```

With HANDLES on, every item will have a specific identifier.

HIGHLIGHT A system variable; toggles the highlighting of selected objects on or off.

IGESIN IGES is the Initial Graphics Exchange file format. Like the Drawing Interchange Format (DXF), this allows you to import graphics from otherwise incompatible CAD systems. This command converts an IGES file into an AutoCAD drawing file.

IGESOUT This converts an AutoCAD file to an IGES file, thereby making it compatible with systems that do not recognize AutoCAD file format.

INSBASE A system variable; allows you to change the 0,0,0 insertion base point of a drawing file.

LASTANGLE A system variable (read-only); displays the ending angle of the last arc entered.

LASTPOINT A system variable; stores the coordinates of the last point entered and allows you to change these coordinates.

LASTPT3D A system variable; stores the XY values of the last point entered plus the current elevation.

LIMMAX A system variable; stores the maximum value of the LIMITS.

LIMMIN A system variable; stores the minimum value of the LIMITS.

LUNITS A system variable; stores the current UNIT setting.

LUPREC A system variable (Linear Units Places Record);

stores the number of decimal places in UNITS.

MAXACTVP Maximum Active Viewports. This determines the maximum allowable number of active viewports in paper space. This may be any integer value from 2 to 16. This simply determines how many viewports will be regenerated, limiting the maximum number to 16 to save time and memory. The PLOT command will pick up all viewports regardless of the MAXACTVP setting.

MAXSORT This determines the maximum number of file or symbol names that will be sorted to alphabetical order by commands that display lists. Commands such as INSERT, LAYER, LINETYPE, XREF, etc. will sort the input from the user relative to the number specified. The default is 200.

MENUECHO A system variable; three-way toggle to control the echoing of menu items in the command line:

```
0 - commands are echoed on the screen
    and on the printer
1 - suppresses echo
2 - commands are echoed on the screen
    but not on the printer
```

MENUNAME A system variable (read-only); displays the name of the current menu.

MIRRTEXT A system variable; toggle switch determines whether the text will be mirrored along with other objects in the MIRROR command.

PDMODE A system variable; controls display style of points.

PDSIZE A system variable; controls the size of displayed points.

PERIMETER A system variable (read-only); displays the last value calculated by AREA, LIST, or DBLIST.

PFACEVMAX A system variable (read-only); displays the maximum number of vertices per face entity.

PICKBOX A system variable; controls the size of the pick box used to select objects.

PLATFORM A system variable (read-only); displays the type of system your computer system was designed to run on (system = platform).

POINT This draws a point at the position specified. The display of the point is determined by PDMODE and PDSIZE. An Object snap will pick up a point. The point coordinates can be entered with filters or by coordinate entry:

```
Command:POINT
Point:3,4,5
```

POLYGON

This draws an equal-sided polygon having from 3 to 1024 sides at the position specified. This is a closed polygon that can be edited with PEDIT. The polygon is specified either by giving the length of an edge or the radius of a circle:

```
Command:POLYLINE
Number of sides:9
Edge/Center of polygon: (pick point A)
Inscribed in circle/Circumscribed about
circle (I/C):C or I
Radius of circle:2
```

```
Command:POLYLINE
Number of sides:9
Edge/Center of polygon:↵
First endpoint of edge: (point A)
Second point on edge: (point B)
```

PRPLOT

This will immediately print what is on the graphics screen. Either type in this command or choose PRINTER under the PLOT command options. Depending on the type of printer you have, you may want to keep the options the same or rotate the image 90 degrees.

Also, depending on the type of printer you have, this command will give you at least one and up to five sheets of paper along with the plot you require.

REDRAWALL

This will refresh the entire screen regardless of the number of viewports.

REGENALL

This will regenerate the entire screen regardless of the number of viewports.

REGENAUTO

This controls whether the drawing will be regenerated by the actions of commands such as LTSCALE, LAYER, and PAN. This can be a timesaver when you have a large model. The REGENAUTO is a toggle. Once turned off, you simply use the command REGEN to regenerate the model or drawing.

REGENMODE

A system variable; toggle switch to determine whether certain AutoCAD commands will automatically cause the drawing to be regenerated.

RENAME

This allows you to change the name of blocks, layers, etc.:

```
Command:RENAME
Block/Dimstyle/LAyer/LType/Style/Ucs/
VIew/VPort:LA
Old Layer name:FROMT
New Layer name:FRONT
```

'RESUME

This reactivates a script file after a ^C (Ctrl-C) or Backspace. Chapter 16 has information on script files.

Use RESUME if the command prompt is shown and 'RESUME (apostrophe RESUME) if the script was cut in the middle of a command to enter a transparent resume.

SCREENSIZE

A system variable (read-only); displays the resolution of your screen in pixel dimensions.

SELECT

This creates a set of selected objects that can be used by another command. Once selected, the objects can be used with the Previous option in any editing command. This option is often used in macros to help automate a program that uses the same set of objects.

SH

The same as SHELL; allows you to leave AutoCAD temporarily to access the internal operating system.

SHADE

This lets you quickly provide a shaded image in the current viewport. It is a very quick version of the type of shading available in AutoShade.

SHADEDGE

A system variable; a three-way toggle that controls the quality of a shaded image.

SHADEDIF

A system variable; calculates the shading of faces, percentage of diffused reflection, and ambient light.

SKETCHINC

A system variable; controls the record increment in the SKETCH command.

SKPOLY

A system variable; toggle switch determines whether the object(s) created in the SKETCH command are individual lines or a polyline.

SNAPANG

A system variable; controls the SNAP angle.

SNAPBASE

A system variable; controls the base point of the SNAP.

SNAPISOPAIR

A system variable; three-way toggle to determine the active plane in a drawing using an isometric snap; almost the same function as ISOPLANE.

SNAPMODE A system variable; toggles SNAP on or off.

SNAPSTYL A system variable; toggles SNAP from Standard to Isometric.

SNAPUNIT A system variable; controls the value of the SNAP integer.

SOLAMEVER A read-only variable that displays the version of AME currently in use.

SOLAXCOL This determines the colour of the AME motion coordinate icon.

SOLDELENT A toggle switch that lets you determine whether an original 2D entity is automatically deleted after the object has been made solid in the AME package.

SOLDISPLAY A toggle switch that lets you determine whether a solid is displayed as a wireframe or a mesh.

SOLFEAT This lets you copy an edge or face from a solid object so it can be placed on a 2D drawing. The new entity will be created in the same position as the original.

SOLIN This lets you import solid assemblies created either in Autodesk's AutoSOLID package or through SOLOUT in the AME package.

SOLLENGTH This determines the unit of measure for the length of solid objects.

SOLOUT SOLOUT is similar to IGESOUT and DXFOUT. It allows you to export solid objects created in AME to the Autodesk AutoSOLID program.

SOLPROF This allows you to make a copy of a solid in lines, arcs, and plines. The command creates a profile of selected solid objects. Only the edges and silhouettes are generated.

SOLPURGE This allows you to purge information about solid objects from a file and thereby reduce the size of a file.

SOLRENDER This allows you to change the colours of the solids making up a solid assembly.

SOLSECT This creates a cross-section through selected solid objects but not regions. The user can specify the plane for the section; the hatch pattern will be determined by the SOLHPAT, SOLHSIZE, and SOLHANGLE commands. The result is a block made up of arcs, circles, lines, and plines with the hatch.

`Command:` **`SOLSECT`**

`Select objects:` *(pick the solid)*

```
Sectioning plane by Entity/Last/Zaxis/
View/XY/YZ/ZX/points:XY
Point on XY plane:0,0,0
```

SOLSERVMSG — Solid Server Message display; determines the display of messages after a solid command. The default is:

```
Phase I - Boundary evaluation begins
Phase II - Tessellation computation begins
Updating the Advanced Modeling Extension
database
```

SOLSUBD — This determines the number of rays shot at a solid for mass property calculations.

SOLUCS — This allows you to align the UCS with the face or edge of an existing solid or the edge of an existing region.

SOLWIRE — This displays selected solids as wireframe.

SPLFRAME — A system variable; toggles on or off the display of the frame of a spline curve.

SPLINESEGS — A system variable; controls the number of lines used to display a spline between two control points.

SPLINETYPE — A system variable; controls the type of spline curve generated in the PEDIT command: Quadratic or Cubic.

SURFTYPE — A system variable; controls the type of surface fitting used in determining the smoothness of a surface in the PEDIT command; Quadratic, Cubic, Bézier.

SURFU — A system variable; controls the density of a 3D mesh in the *M* direction.

SURFV — A system variable; controls the density of a 3D mesh in the *N* direction.

TDCREATE — A system variable (read-only); displays the time and date of a drawing creation in Julian calendar format.

TDUPDATE — A system variable (read-only); displays the time and date that a file was last updated in Julian calendar format.

TDUSRTIMER — A system variable (read-only); displays the elapsed time set by the TIME command.

TEMPREFIX — A system variable (read-only); displays the directory used to store the temporary files.

TEXTEVAL	A system variable; toggle switch controls the responses to prompts either in literal text or AutoLISP expressions.
'TEXTSCR	Text Screen. This is usually used within script files to flip the screen from the graphics screen to the text screen; the opposite of, GRAPHSCR.
TEXTSIZE	A system variables; controls the size of text as set in the STYLE command.
TRACEWID	A system variable; controls the trace width of the TRACE command.
UCSFOLLOW	A system variable; toggle switch allows you to display the plan view or XY plane of the current UCS every time you change the UCS.
UCSNAME	A system variable (read-only); displays the current UCS name.
UCSORG	A system variable (read-only); displays the current origin point.
UCSXDIR	A system variable (read-only); displays the direction of X in the current UCS relative to the World Coordinate System origin.
UCSYDIR	A system variable; displays the direction of Y in the current UCS relative to the World Coordinate System.
UNDEFINE	This allows you to enter an AutoLISP command instead of a regular AutoCAD command by deleting a command and replacing it with the LISP program.
UNITMODE	A system variable; toggle switch allows user to control the display of dashes in the feet and inches display.
USERI1-5	A system variable; stores 1–5 integer values for AutoLISP purposes.
USERR1-5	A system variable; stores 1–5 real number values for AutoLISP purposes.
VIEWCTR	A system variable (read-only); stores the centre point in the screen display.
VIEWDIR	A system variable (read-only); stores the viewing direction of the current viewport.
VIEWMODE	A system variable (read-only); stores the view of the current viewport as one of six integer values: 0 = perspective off, front and back clipping off 1 = perspective viewing is on 2 = the front clipping plane is on 4 = the back clipping plane is on

8 = the UCS follow mode is on
16 = the front clipping plane isn't at the camera point

VIEWRES

This offers control of the degree of accuracy in displaying arcs or circles on the graphics screen. It offers fast zooms, by attempting to perform all PAN, ZOOM and VIEW commands at redraw speed rather than regenerating the drawing:

```
Command:VIEWRES
Do you want fast zooms? Y:↵
Enter circle zoom percent (1-20000)d:
```

VIEWSIZE

A system variable (read-only); displays the current view height.

VIEWTWIST

A system variable (read-only); displays the current twist angle.

VISRETAIN

A system variable; toggle switch determines whether or not the On, Off, Freeze settings of imported Xref drawings will assume current drawing format.

VPOINTX

A system variable (read-only); displays the current *X* viewpoint value.

VPOINTY

A system variable; displays the current *Y* viewpoint value.

VPOINTZ

A system variable; displays the current *Z* viewpoint value.

VSMAX

A system variable (read-only); displays the drawing coordinate point of the upper-right corner of the current virtual screen.

VSMIN

A system variable (read-only); displays the drawing coordinate point of the lower-left corner of the current virtual screen.

WORLDUCS

A system variable (read-only); displays whether or not the current UCS is the same as the World Coordinate System.

WORLDVIEW

A system variable; toggle switch determines whether or not the points and angles entered in the DVIEW and VPOINT commands will be relative to the WCS or the UCS:
0 = UCS
1 = WCS

Abbreviations and Aliases

AutoCAD's .PGP file is an ASCII-based text file containing AutoCAD program parameters. Within this file you can abbreviate frequently used AutoCAD commands by defining aliases for them.

Any ASCII editor can be used to edit the ACAD.PGP file. Any AutoCAD, AutoLISP, ADS, AME, operating system or graphics display driver command can be abbreviated.

To write the aliases, separate the abbreviation from the command with a comma, and prefix the command with an asterisk.

The following is a partial list of AutoCAD and AME commands as they would be written to create the abbreviations or aliases:

```
A,       *ARC
C,       *CIRCLE
CP,      *COPY
DV,      *DVIEW
E,       *ERASE
L,       *LINE
LA,      *LAYER
M,       *MOVE
MS,      *MSPACE
P,       *PAN
PS,      *PSPACE
PL,      *PLINE
R,       *REDRAW
Z,       *ZOOM
SUB,     *SOLSUB
CONE,    *SOLCONE
SOL,     *SOLIDIFY
UN,      *SOLUNION
```

Problems, Fixes, and Work-arounds

The following are a series of typical hardware and software problems and AutoCAD and DOS responses that you may not immediately have a workable solution for. The usual causes of the problems and their solutions are outlined here.

Do you want to try to save your changes? Y
You have used a command or a series of commands that the system cannot interpret, or you have used up all the space on your floppy disk.

Solution: There is really nothing you can do but save your changes, clean up your floppy disk by erasing unnecessary files, etc., and re-enter AutoCAD. Be careful when you save a file on the floppy disk that has been disabled because of a HATCH command. If there is no accessible hard drive and if the file in question is more than half of the memory capacity of your floppy, you will *not* be able to get your file back. In this case, do not save it.

Bad command or file name
You are typing in a command or filename and have misspelt it, or you are trying to access a command (like an AME or LISP command) that is not loaded on the system.

Solution: Check your spelling and check to see if the command is on the system.

Bad numeric value for field RS12, record 1
In your template file, you have entered an *N* instead of a *C*.

Solution: Use a C.

Block WHEEL already exists. Redefine it?
You have already created a block with this name. If you redefine it, the first file will be replaced with the current block.

Solution: If you want to replace the old block with the new block use *Yes* to redefine it. If you want both blocks, use *No* to exit the BLOCK command, then start again and select a different name for the new block.

Cannot set MAXACTVP to that value. *Invalid*
You have tried to enter a value that is less than 2 or more than 16 in the MAXACTVP command.

Solution: Choose a number between 2 and 16.

**** Command not allowed in Paper Space ****
Many commands such as DVIEW, DIM, etc. cannot be used while in paper space.

Solution: Change back to model space either with the MSPACE command or Tilemode system variable.

**** Command not allowed with this display configuration ****
The graphics display (hardware) does not support the AutoCAD Advanced User Interface.

Solution: Buy a more upgraded system.

****Command not allowed unless TILEMODE is set to 0 ****
You have tried to enter a command that does not accept TILEMODE 1.

Solution: Change TILEMODE to 0.

Almost Full. You have used up most of the room on your disk drive

Solution: Exit AutoCAD, use END, not SAVE, and erase unnecessary files from your disk.

Edge x does not touch another edge
In the EDGESURF command, all edges must be touching.

Solution: Either use FILLET Radius 0 or MOVE, etc. to get the edges to touch.

Entity not parallel with current UCS
You have tried to edit or generate an area from an entity that is not parallel to the current UCS.

Solution: Change the UCS to be parallel to the entity selected and try again.

Entity not usable as rotation axis
You have tried to pick an object other than a line or pline or 3D polyline as the axis of rotation in a REVSURF command.

Solution: Use a line, pline or 3D polyline to create the axis. It is possible that you have an arc or circle in front of and obliquing the line you are trying to access for the axis. Use DVIEW to rotate your view so that you can pick the line or pline.

EREAD 23
Your floppy disk is shot.

Solution: Try to copy the files to a new formatted disk, and then reformat the bad disk. If you get a BAD SECTORS message, throw the disk out.

****Error: Cannot INSERT and X_REF. Use XREF Attach, instead. *Invalid***
You have tried to insert a file that is already part of the existing file using the XREF command.

Solution: Use the Attach option in the XREF command to access the file in question.

Fatal Error
You have encountered a command that AutoCAD cannot complete, or, more likely, you are in a lab where access to AutoCAD is only possible if there is a floppy disk in the A or B drive and you have not addressed that drive.

Solution: Do not forget to enter A: when signing on.

File I/O Error Retry, Fail?
During the PLOT command, either while trying to enter a plot or trying to generate an .HPG or .PLT file, you have used an unacceptable name, for example A:COM1. Save the file before plotting to avoid losing the file as a result of this type of error.

Solution: Use a different filename.

**** Insufficient node space ****
You have tried to load a LISP routine and your system does not have enough space for it.

Solution: Change the LISPHEAP value.

Internal Error
You have encountered a command that AutoCAD cannot compute. This is usually not your fault.

Solution: AutoCAD will try to save the file before exiting. Once you are out of AutoCAD, use CHKDSK to check your disk. If there are any serious problems, use the Recover Damaged File option in the Main menu.

Invalid point
You have entered a point that is not acceptable to the system because it is not on the correct UCS or is outside the limits or for some other reason.

Solution: Enter a new point. If you are trying to get a point on a certain plane, use coordinate entry or, if you can, access objects already on the desired plane with the aid of OSNAP.

Last command did not undo anything
You have tried to redo an UNDO command. The command must be used directly after the UNDO command has taken place; there can be no other commands between UNDO and REDO.

Solution: There is nothing you can do to bring back the undone commands at this point. If you saved the file before using the UNDO command, you can quit the current file and bring back the file as it was before you started the UNDO sequence. If not, simply start drawing it again.

Lines intersect
The highlighted object cannot be solidified. Press space bar to continue in the SOLIDIFY command. If you create a pline that is not closed, the system will assume a straight line between the two endpoints of the pline. If this intersects or overlaps the pline, the SOLIDIFY command cannot be completed.

Solution: Edit the pline and try again.

Mouse
You have signed on to AutoCAD, possibly set your SNAP and GRID, then noticed that your mouse does not respond and there are no cross-hairs on your screen.

Solutions: If you have set the SNAP much larger than your screen size (i.e., your SNAP is set to 20 and your limits are the default limits), your mouse will not respond because there is no point accessible on the screen. Turn your SNAP off and see if it shows up. If it still is not moving, try entering a line by typing the coordinates that should be visible on the screen. Move your mouse to see if it now responds. If not, quit the file and try entering another file. If the cross-hairs still do not show up, exit AutoCAD and type the word MOUSE followed by the Enter key; this should load it.

If you have entered AutoCAD and the first prompt on the screen is similar to *Logitek mouse disabled* or something saying that the mouse is not connected, exit AutoCAD and type MOUSE. This should load it. If nothing happens or if you get a prompt that says the mouse cannot be found, check to see that the mouse has been plugged in properly; check the cable, and try again.

If none of the above solutions work, call the technician.

n selected, n found (n not parallel with UCS)
The extrusion direction of the entity you have chosen is not parallel with the current UCS and thus will not be affected by the CHANGE command.

Solution: Change your UCS to be parallel with the object selected before using the CHANGE command.

No Endpoint selected for specified point
You have set your OSNAP to ENDpoint and then either missed the object with the object selection digitizer or chosen an object like a circle or ellipse that has no specified endpoint.

Solution: If you have simply missed the object while trying to pick it up, try again. Changing the PICKBOX variable in the SETVAR command will change the size of your pick box. If it is too small, you can make it larger by making the PICKBOX variable a larger number.

Primitive does not belong to the selected solid
You have tried to use SOLCHP to edit a primitive that is not part of the composite solid you originally identified for editing.

Solution: Exit SOLCHP and use SOLUNION to join the primitive to the composite solid or use SOLCHP on only the primitive.

Point or option keyword required
You are trying to complete a command without providing the information required.

Solution: Read the system response area and respond to the prompts.

Requires numeric distance or two points
You have tried to exit a command without completing the required information.

Requires an integer value
The command you are trying to invoke requires a number such as 0 or 1.

Solution: Enter the appropriate number.

SHELL error; insufficient memory for command
You have tried to temporarily access the DOS environment with the SHELL command, but more memory is available required.

Solution: Save your file and exit AutoCAD to access the DOS environment.

Tablet not responding
Your digitizer tablet is not responding, or you get a message saying that the tablet is not responding.

Solution: Check to see that it has been properly plugged in. If it is connected properly, turn the computer off by using the power bar if there is one, and turn it back on again. On many of the older tablets, the system "cannot find the tablet" if the digitizer tablet power source is not turned on.

Unknown command. Type ? for a list of commands
You have typed an AME command before AME has been loaded, or you have typed a LISP program that has not been loaded; or your spelling is incorrect.

Solutions: Check your spelling, load AME or the LISP program, and try it again. To load a LISP program, use the following:

```
Command: (load "programname")
Command:programname
```

Value must be positive
You have entered a single number when an XY coordinate is needed.

Solution: Think about where the point is and type it in.

View is not plan to UCS. Command results may not be obvious
The current viewport you are using is not plan, and the XY plane of the current UCS cannot be accessed from it. Commands such as CHAMFER, TEXT, BREAK, and many more may not work as you expect them to.

Solution: Change either your UCS or your current viewport.

```
Waiting for file, C:\GEAR1.DWG
locked by S.R.Kyles
at 3:30 on 06/29/92
```

access denied
You have been forced to abandon a file before you had a chance to save it, and you cannot re-access the file because it is locked.

Solution: Copy the file and give it a new name, then try to access it again under the new name.

Text Editing

EDLIN

GETTING INTO EDLIN

You can access EDLIN in AutoCAD by using EDIT if you have sufficient memory. If EDIT doesn't work, try SH or SHELL to access DOS. You will only enter EDLIN with these commands if you are running DOS prior to Release 5.

Once in, you will then be prompted to enter the File to edit: to which you respond

```
A:NAME.SCR
```

Where:
a: *is the directory or drive*
name *is the name of the drive*
.SCR *is the extension indicating a SCRIPT file*

To get into EDLIN in DOS use;

```
C:EDLIN A:NAME.SCR
```

This is all you need; there are no user prompts as it assumes you don't need them.

ONCE IN

The prompt is *. This means you are requested to enter your command.

*I = *INSERT*. This allows you to insert your command or program and will offer you the first line of text.

*I ↵

```
1:*
```

At this point you add the command, e.g. VSLIDE A:BUBBLE1.

*5 = *line 5 of your text program*. If you have made an error, this will offer you the line of text to change.

*5 ↵

```
5:*DERAY 1000
5:*
```

At this point you can change the typing error, e.g. DELAY 1000.

*LIST = *a list of your program starting at the point indicated*. If you are entering the text for the second time, the EDLIN editor assumes that you want to add information. Use *LIST to get a readout of what entries you have.

GETTING OUT

^Z = *the delimiter*. This tells the editor that you would like to exit the text. This is used within the text to return to EDLIN.

```
    12:*^Z
*
```

At this point you can enter LIST to see what you have done, or a number of a line which you would like to see or edit.

*E = *exit*. This will exit you from EDLIN. You will return to the AutoCAD drawing editor.

When editing an EDLIN file on an A: drive, you may come across this prompt that will prevent you from saving the file.

```
Sharing violation reading drive A:
Abort Retry Failure
```

This is an attempt to save you from overriding existing files, etc.

Example: *EDLIN*

Command:**EDIT** *(screen turns black)*

File to edit:**A:NAME**.**SCR** *(you must add the directory, name, and extension)*

When entering SCRIPT files (.SCR) or slide files (.SLD), there may be no warning prompt given if you are using the name of a file that has already been used. If you do use the same file name twice, the first file will be erased and there is no automatic back-up.

***I** ↵

```
1:*VSLIDE A:BUBBLE 1
2:*DELAY 1000
3:*VSLIDE A:BUBBLE 2
4:*DELAY 1000
5:*RSCRIPT
6:*^Z ↵
```

***E** ↵

Other options

?	*displays a list of commands*
a	*loads a portion of a file*
c	*copies a block*
d	*deletes a block*
m	*moves a block*
p	*displays a file one page at a time*
q	*quits without saving*
r	*searches for string and replaces*
t	*merges contents from to existing file*
^c	*stops insert*
^v	*controls characters* (tone ^G)

WORDPERFECT

GETTING INTO WORD PERFECT

While in DOS, enter the sign on code for WordPerfect, usually WP, WP51, etc.

Once you are in WordPerfect, you will automatically be in a file ready to use. Your default settings will be for an 8½ x 11 sheet with a margin at the top and bottom of the page, as well as a 1 inch indent on the left.

Simply type in the information that you need.

```
VSLIDE A:BUBBLE1
DELAY 1000
VSLIDE *A:BUBBLE2
DELAY 2000
VSLIDE
```

End each line with a hard return, but be careful not to add hard returns at the end of the file.

If you make a mistake, the Backspace key over the Return key will erase the last letter or string.

The arrows either up or down will help you move around the screen.

Delete is also a very useful key to hit when needed.

Note that when exiting from WordPerfect, you need only enter the character or the choice; there is no return needed to enter the numbers as in AutoCAD number or menu choice selections.

GETTING OUT

To file your WordPerfect file as an ASCII file (a DOS file) use the following:

Ctrl-F5 for exiting

1 for DOS Text

1 for save

Name the file **A:BUBBLES.SCR**

To file your WordPerfect file in the regular WordPerfect format, use F7. You will then be prompted for:

```
save the file     Yes or No
exit WordPerfect Yes or No
```

While entering the text, each sentence will automatically wrap around any graphics that you add. If you are entering a full paragraph of information, don't hard return at the end of each line.

The following is a list of functions available through the WordPerfect function keys:

Backspace	*backs up over characters thereby erasing them*
F1	*cancel*
F2	*search; enter word , use F2 again*
F3	*help files; lists functions*
F5	*lists files on disk or in directory. Add A: when needed*
F6	*bold*
F7	*save file and exit*
F8	*underline*
F9	*field specification for merging*
F10	*save file while working*

Shift F1	*setup*
F2	*search*
F3	*flip screen to alternate document*
F4	*indent*
F5	*date formats*
F6	*centre*
F7	*print*
F8	*document format*
F9	*field specification for merging*
F10	*retrieve document*

Control F1	*DOS functions*
F2	*spell check*
F3	*windows and lines*

F4	*move commands*
F5	*text in and out*
F6	*align*
F7	*footnotes*
F8	*fonts; colour and size*
F9	*merge*
F10	*macro definition*

Alt F1	*thesaurus*
F2	*multiple replace*
F3	*reveal codes*
F4	*block*
F5	*mark text*
F6	*flush right*
F7	*columns, Tables and Math*
F8	*document style*
F9	*graphics*
F10	*macros*
Home Home up	*will take you to the top of your sheet*
Home Home Down	*will take you to the bottom of your sheet*
0 Ins	*will toggle you into and out of the Typeover option*

When exiting from WordPerfect, you need only enter the character — either the number — 1 or the choice; there is no hard return needed to enter the numbers as in AutoCAD number or menu-choice selections.

LOTUS 1-2-3

GETTING INTO LOTUS

While in DOS (C:) enter the sign-on code for Lotus 1-2-3, usually LOTUS or 123. You will be placed in a file or worksheet that has a number of different columns or cells created by the intersection of a numbered row and a lettered column. The highlight bar inside the worksheet is called the cell pointer. The cells are used to perform mathematical functions on columns of numbers.

MOVING AROUND AND SETTING UP THE WORKSHEET

The LOTUS 1-2-3 command structure is quite straightforward. All the commands can be accessed through the menus. You can access the commands either by typing or by highlighting.

When you press the slash (/) or less than symbol, to display the main menu, a rectangular highlight, called the menu pointer, will appear on the second line of the control panel.

The main menu contains the sections Worksheet, Range, Copy, Move, File, Print, Graph, Data, System, Add-in, and Quit. Each of these menus has a series of submenus to take you to the various sections of the program.

Using the arrow keys you can easily move around the columns. To access the command options, use a slash (/), then choose the option you require. If you are inserting a set of attributes, move the cell pointer to the top row of the column that you would like to adjust, then change the column size by using:

/ = *slash*

W = *worksheet*

C = *column*

Then indicate the number of characters in that column. Once you use enter ⏎, the column will be changed, and you will be returned to the prompt area of the screen.

Using Lotus 1-2-3 with Attributes
When entering tags, insert the tags at the top of each of the columns. This will set up a field to accept the attributes.

FORMULAS FOR ADDING FIELDS
Each field will accept a set of information. This information can simply be added, or it can be multiplied by a certain percentage or number. For example:

A	B	C	D	E	F
Product Code	Colour	List	Discount	+ Profit	Profit Only
PE6660	Blue	586	301.79	362.148	60.35

To calculate the discount price, use the following formula:

discount
+(C12x51.5%)

Where:
+ = *the entry of an equation*

(= *the start of the equation*

C12 = *the list price*

x48.5% = *the discount price*

) = *the end of the equation*

+profit
+(D12x20%)+D12

Where:
+ = *the entry of an equation*

(= *the start of the equation*

D12 = *the discounted price*

x20% = *the profit margin*

) = *the end of the equation*

+D12 = *added to the profit to equal price*

Your sheet should include these equations before the attributes are entered:

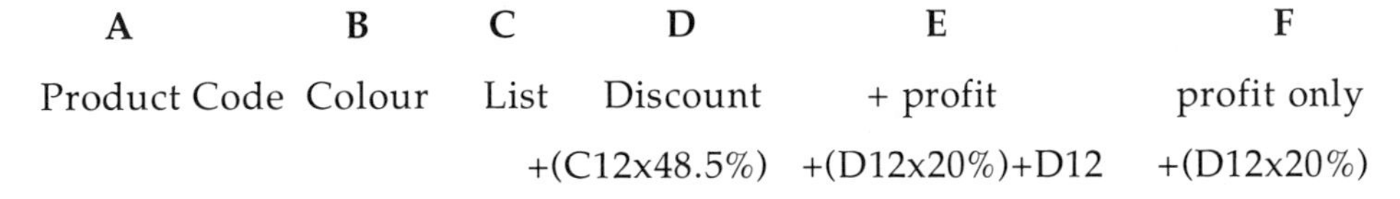

A	B	C	D	E	F
Product Code	Colour	List	Discount	+ profit	profit only
			+(C12x48.5%)	+(D12x20%)+D12	+(D12x20%)

Use the / Copy command to take the information from column C to the columns for discount, discount plus profit and pure profit columns. Go to the column where you would like to start your copy. Use / Copy then grab the column that you want by moving your arrow keys. Use Enter to indicate that this is what you want. Now move the cursor to the column where you want the copy to take place and anchor it with a period (.). Indicate the total space for your copy with the arrow keys, then use Enter to finish the copy.

GETTING A SUM TOTAL

Once the information is in the proper column, you can get a sum total for the column by using the following:

s will give you a listing of the prices with totals at the bottom.

When entering prices in AutoCAD for a LOTUS 1-2-3 download, avoid using a dollar sign ($) because this code is used for another purpose in LOTUS 1-2-3.

PRINTING LARGE COLUMNS OF TEXT

When creating spreadsheets to list many objects and descriptions, you may run out of room on a regular 8 1/2 x 11 sheet. To create a sheet printed horizontally instead of vertically use the following:

NORTON EDITOR

Depending on the size of the computer's memory, you may be able to access Norton Editor directly from AutoCAD. It is a menu-driven editor that is quite powerful and very useful.

GETTING INTO NORTON EDITOR

While in DOS (C:>), enter the sign-on code for Norton Editor. It is usually NE or NU. You can also try using the SHELL command to access Norton directly.

```
Command:SHELL
DOS command:NE SLIDES.SCR
```

Once you have accessed Norton, you will automatically be in a file ready to use. Simply type in the information you need.

VSLIDE A:BUBBLE1
DELAY 1000
VSLIDE *A:BUBBLE2

DELAY 2000

VSLIDE ETC.

End each line with a hard return (↵) but have no hard return at the end.

If you make a mistake, the backspace key will erase the last letter or string.

The delete key erases the letter directly after the cursor.

The arrows either up or down will help you move around the screen.

GETTING OUT OF NORTON EDITOR

Depending on the editor, there are different ways to exit. Be sure to save as an ASCII (DOS) file by using the following:

DOS 5.0 EDIT

This is the industry standard, and is possibly the easiest editor to use. It is far superior to EDLIN and more user-friendly.

GETTING INTO DOS 5.0 EDIT

If the computer has enough memory, you will be able to access DOS 5.0 directly from AutoCAD. Type EDIT, SH or SHELL and you will be prompted for the name of the file. Don't forget the extension .SCR.

ONCE IN

This editor reacts much the same as the regular word processing software.

VSLIDE A:BUBBLE1
DELAY 1000
VSLIDE *A:BUBBLE2

DELAY 2000
VSLIDE

End each line with a hard return (↵) but have no hard return at the end.

If you make a mistake, the backspace key will erase the last letter or string.

The delete key erases the letter directly after the cursor.

The arrows either up or down will help you move around the screen.

The DOS 5.0 text file will automatically be in an ASCII format and will be ready to use as soon as you exit.

Wildcards

With any function in AutoCAD in which a list is used the following characters can be used to make your list more efficient. Blocks, layers, linetypes, views, custom hatches, etc., can all be listed using the wild cards.

* (asterix) **matches any string**		
*	anything	
n*	anything starting with an N	*next,nines,n12*
***mn**	anything ending in mn	*column, 098mn*
mn	anything with mn in the string	*smnstr,armnh,mn1*
~*mn*	anything not having mn in the string	*wheel, gear*
‘*mn	anything with mn in the string	*omni, mn345*

@ (at) **matches any alpha character**		
@	anything with only one alpha character or letter	*a,t,n*
@n	anything that has two letters ending in n	*wn,rn,jn*

# (pound) **matches any numeric value**		
#	any number	*2,7,6*
#nm	anything starting with a number and ending with	*nm 5nm, 7nm*
nm#	anything starting with nm and ending with a number	*nm5, nm2*

. (period) **matches any non-alphanumeric character**		
.	any non-alphanumeric character	*#,&,*,$*
.ac	anything stating with a non-alphanumeric and ending with ac	*$ac,#ac*
m.	any m plus a non-alphanumeric	*m%,M@*

? (question) **matches any single character**		
?	any single character	*0,*,T,2*
pi?	any 3 character string starting with pi	*pit, pi6, pi#*
?pi	any 3 character string ending with pi	*spi, 4pi, $pi*

~ (tilde) **matches anything but the pattern**		
~#	anything not ending in a number	*wall, fireplc*
~*fat*	anything without fat	*celry, grpfrt, 12*
~.	anything that is alphanumeric	*wall2, floor, 324*

-[] (hyphen) **uses inside brackets to specify a range for a single character**		
[m-z] x	anything starting with letters between m and z ending in x	*tx, wx, px*
[~m-z] x	anything except strings starting with letters between m and z ending x	*ax, dx, lx*

[. . .] matches any one of the characters enclosed
[lm] n ln or mn

[~. . .] matches any character not enclosed
[~aeiou] any string without a vowel

‘ (reverse quote) **reads the character that follows as a literal character**
‘*wall **wall*
‘*wall* **walls, *wall2, *wall$*

Release 12's CAL Command

Geomcal is a Release 12 ADS application that allows the user to calculate complex geometry using command-line expressions. There are over 40 functions, six numeric operations and seven vector operators available. The expressions can access the existing geometry using osnap functions such as INT or END, or can be used independently. You can use CAL in the following ways:

- enter CAL at the command prompt to perform a calculation
- enter 'CAL within a command line to calculate something relevant to that command
- select CAL from the Assist pull-down menu
- use 'CAL within an AutoLISP routine

USING CAL AT THE COMMAND PROMPT

Enter calculations just as you would with a calculator.

```
Command:CAL
>Expression:486/14 ↵
34.7143

Command:CAL
>Expression:A=2+3*4^5 ↵
3074.0
```

The second expression stores the calculated value as the AutoLISP variable A:

USING CAL WITHIN A COMMAND

Enter CAL within a command line to calculate a value for the command.

```
Command:CIRCLE
3P/2P/TTR/???point: (pick 1)
Diameter/???radius:'CAL
???>Expression:1.25*5
```

This will result in a circle with a radius of 6.25.

```
Command:CIRCLE
3P/2P/TTR/???point:'CAL
???>Expression:(mid+cen)/2
???>Select entity for mid snap: (pick line)
???>Select entity for cen snap: (pick arc)
Diameter/???adius:'CAL
???>Expression:1/3*rad
>Select circle, arc or polyline segment for RAD function: (pick arc)
```

The first expression calculates the centre of the new circle as the midpoint between the midpoint of the line chosen and the centre of the arc. The second calculates the radius at one-third of an existing circle.

Remember that to use CAL within a command string you must pick it up transparently from the pull-down menu under Assist or remember to add ' before the command when typing ('CAL).

USING CAL FROM THE ASSIST MENU

Like many of the display commands from the Display pull-down menu, 'CAL can be accessed transparently within relevant commands.

Syntax of Expressions

OPERATOR	OPERATION
+	*adds numbers*
-	*subtracts numbers*
*	*multiplies numbers*
/	*divides numbers*
^	*exponentiation of numbers*
()	*parentheses used to group expressions*

INDEX

Release 11's Primary Screen Menus

****	BLOCKS	DIM:	DISPLAY	DRAW	EDIT	INQUIRY	LAYER:	MVIEW	PLOT	SETTINGS	SOLIDS	SURFACES	UCS:	UTILITY	ASHADE	RMAN	BONUS	SAVE
HELP	ATTDEF:	DIM:	ATTDISP:	ARC	ARRAY:	AREA:	DDLMODES:	MVIEW:	PLOTTER	DDEMODES	SOLBOX:	EDGSURF:	UCS:	ATTEXT:	LIGHT:	RMSETUP:	Sample	
CENter	BASE:	DIM1:	DVIEW:	ATTDEF:	ATTEDIT:	DBLIST:	LAYER:	ON	PRINTER	DDRMODES	SOLCONE:	REVSURF:	DDUCS:	AUDIT:	VLIGHT:	RMPROP:	AutoLISP	
ENDpoint	BLOCK:	angular	MVIEW:	CIRCLE	BREAK:	DIST:		OFF		APERTUR:	SOLCYL:	RULSURF:	RENAME:	DXF/DXB	CAMERA:	RMATTAC:	Routines	
INSert	INSERT:	Dim Vars	PAN:	DONUT:	CHAMFER:	HELP:		Hideplot		AXIS:	SOLSPH:	TABSURF:		FILES:	VCAMERA:	RMEDIT:		
INTersec	MINSERT:	leader	PLAN:	DTEXT:	CHANGE:	ID:		Fit		BLIPS:	SOLTORS:	Surftb1:		IGES	FINISH:	RMCOPY:		
MIDpoint	WBLOCK:	oblique	REDRALL:	ELLIPSE:	CHPROP:	LIST:		2		COLOR:	SOLWEGE:	surftb2:		MENU:	SCENE:	RMLIST:		
NEArest	XBIND:	ORDINAT:	REDRAW:	HATCH:	COPY:	STATUS:		3		DRAGMOD:	SOLEXT:	3DFACE:		PURGE:	CAMVIEW:	FILMROL:		
NODe	XREF:	radial	REGEN:	INSERT:	DDATTE:	TIME:		4		ELEV:	SOLREV:	3DMESH:		RENAME:	FILMROL:	DEFAULT:		
PERpend		status	REGNALL:	LINE:	DDEDIT:			MSPACE:		GRID:	SOLIDIFY	PFACE:		SCRIPT:	DEFAULT:	RMSCAN:		
QUAdrant		style	RGNAUTO:	MINSERT:	DIVIDE:			PSPACE:		HANDLES:	MODIFY	3DPOLY:		SLIDES	RMSCAN:			
QUICK		trotate	VIEW:	OFFSET:	ERASE:			TILEMODE:		LINETYP:	INQUIRY	3d		External				
TANgent		undo	VIEWRES:	PLINE:	EXPLODE:			VPLAYER:		LIMITS:	DISPLAY	objects		Commands				
NONE		TEdit	VPOINT:		EXTEND:						UTILITY			END:				
CANCEL:		EXIT	ZOOM:	POINT:						LTSCALE:				QUIT				
U:				POLYGON:	FILLET:					OSNAP:								
REDO:		HOMETEXT		SHAPE:	MEASURE:					QTEXT:								
REDRAW:		UPDATE		SKETCH:	MIRROR:					SETVAR:								
SETVAR:		NEWTEXT		SOLID:	MOVE:					SNAP:								
		Dimstyle		TEXT:	OFFSET:					STYLE:								
		Save		TRACE:	PEDIT:					TABLET:								
		Restore		3DFACE:	ROTATE:					UCS:								
		Override		3D Surfs	SCALE:					UCSICON:								
		Variabls		SOLIDS	SELECT:					UNITS:								
		?			STRETCH:					VPORTS:								
					TRIM:													
					UNDO:													

Release 12's Primary Screen Menus

****	ASE	BLOCKS	DIM:	DISPLAY	DRAW	EDIT	INQUIRY	LAYER:	MODEL	MVIEW:	PLOT	RENDER	SETTINGS	SURFACES	UCS:	UTILITY	SAVE
HELP	SET ROW:	ATTDEF:	Aligned	ATTDISP:	ARC	ARRAY:	AREA:	?	SOLEXT:	MVIEW:	PLOT	RENDER:	DDEMODES	EDGSURF:	UCS:	ATTEXT:	
CENter	MK CINK:	BASE:	Angular	DVIEW:	ATTDEF:	ATTEDIT:	DBLIST:	Make	SOLREV:			HIDE:	DDRMODES	REVSURF:	DDUCS:	AUDIT:	
ENDpoint	Q-LINK:	BLOCK:	Diameter	MVIEW:	BHATCH:	BREAK:	DIST:	Set	SOLIDIFY	ON	PSOUT	DDVIEW...	APERTUR:	RULSURF:		DXF/DXB	
INSert	Q-VIEW:	INSERT:	Horizntl	PAN:	CIRCLE	CHAMFER:	HELP:	New	DDSOLPRM	OFF		LIGHT...	BLIPS:	TABSURF:	?	FILES:	
INTersec	Q-EDIT:	MINSERT:	Leader	PLAN:	DONUT:	CHANGE:	ID:	ON		Hideplot		SCENE...	COLOR:		Previous	IGES	
MIDpoint	MAKE DA:	WBLOCK:	Ordinate	REDRALL:	DTEXT:	CHPROP:	LIST:	OFF	SOLUNION	Fit		FINISH...	DRAGMOD:	Surftb1:	Restore	MENU:	
NEArest	RELD DA:	XBIND:	Radius	REDRAW:	ELLIPSE:	COPY:	STATUS:	Color	SOLSUB:	2		RPREF...	ELEV:	surftb2:	Save	PURGE:	
NODe	SQLEDIT	XREF:	Rotated	REGEN:	HATCH:	DDATTE:	TIME:	Ltype	SOLINT:	3		STATS...	GRID:		Delete	PSOUT:	
PERpend	SELECT:		Vertical	REGNALL:	INSERT:	DDEDIT:		Freeze		4		REPLAY..	HANDLES:	3DFACE:	World	RENAME:	
QUAdrant	SET		Dim Styl	RGNAUTO:	LINE:	DDMODIFY		Thaw	SETUP	MSPACE:		SAVEIMG	LINETYP:	3DMESH:		SCRIPT:	
QUICK	LINK		Dim Vars	SHADE	MINSERT:	DIVIDE:		Lock	PRIMS	PSPACE:			LIMITS:	PFACE:	RENAME:	SLIDES	
TANgent	ROW			VIEW:	OFFSET:	ERASE:		Unlock	MODIFY	TILEMODE:		Unload:	LTSCALE:	3DPOLY:	Follow:	External	
NONE	UTILITY		Baseline	VIEWRES:	PLINE:	EXPLODE:			INQUIRY	VPLAYER:			ORTHO	3d		Commands	
CANCEL:	TERMINATE		Continue	VPOINT:	POINT:	EXTEND:			DISPLAY	PSLTSCL:		RMAN	OSNAP:	objects	Origin		
U:			Center	ZOOM:	POLYGON:				UTILITY				QTEXT:		Zaxis	NEW...	
REDO:			Status		SHAPE:	FILLET:							SETVAR:		3 point	OPEN,,,	
REDRAW:			Exit		SKETCH:	MEASURE:							SNAP:			SAVE AS:	
SETVAR:					SOLID:	MIRROR:							STYLE:		X	QSAVE...	
					TEXT:	MOVE:							TABLET:		Y		
					TRACE:	OFFSET:							UCS:		Z	END:	
					3DFACE:	PEDIT:							UCSICON:			QUIT	
						ROTATE:							UNITS:		View		
					3D Surfs	SCALE:							VPORTS:		Entity	ABOUT:	
					MODELER	SELECT:										CONFIG:	
						STRETCH:										COMPILE:	
						TRIM:										RECOVER:	
						UNDO:										REIN IT	